The 1982 Dow Jones-Irwin Business and Investment Almanac

The 1982 DOW JONES-IRWIN
Business and Investment Almanac

Edited by

Sumner N. Levine
State University of New York
at Stony Brook
and Editor
Financial Analyst's Handbook
and
The Investment Manager's Handbook

Executive Editor
Caroline Levine

DOW JONES-IRWIN
Homewood, Illinois 60430

ISBN 0-87094-273-5 (paperbound)
ISBN 0-87094-275-1 (casebound)

Printed in the United States of America

1 2 3 4 5 6 7 8 9 0 K 8 7 6 5 4 3 2 1

Contents

Ref
330904
0752
1982

v

Preface

The current sixth edition of *The Dow Jones-Irwin Business Almanac* (as it was formerly titled) contains a number of changes which will enhance its usefulness to those seeking investment information and data.

In order to emphasize these additions, the title has been expanded to *The Business and Investment Almanac*. New material includes increased coverage of real estate, mutual funds, stock options, futures, gold, diamonds, and fixed income securities. Sections have been added on how to read newspaper quotations pertaining to stocks, bonds, options, and futures. Explanations of various stock market strategies and terms have also been included.

A new section containing data on various industries and representative companies within the industries has been added. A detailed summary of the new (1981) tax law is also included.

As with previous editions, the editor welcomes comments and suggestions from the readers. These should be sent to: *Dow Jones-Irwin Business and Investment Almanac*, PO Box 2116, Setauket, New York 11733.

Sumner N. Levine
Editor

Business in Review

2 Key indicators of the economy rose 1.2% in November, but the ratio of the index of coincident indicators and the index of lagging indicators dropped for the second consecutive month. These mixed signals added to the debate on whether the business recovery can survive the current high interest rates.

Auto makers plan to build 1,795,100 cars in the first quarter, barely more than last year's depressed level and one of the lowest rates for the period in the past 15 years. The plans may be cut further if stalled sales don't improve soon.

Algeria increased oil prices $3 a barrel, the same as Nigeria's first quarter boost, but $1 a barrel less than the rise in Libya's prices. The move suggests that the average price rise in OPEC will be slightly less than the 10%, or $3.20 a barrel, that had been predicted.

Braniff's airline unit received lower ratings by Standard & Poor's on certain notes, certificates and debentures. S&P cited Braniff's substantial losses over the past two years.

Farm prices fell 1.1% in December on continued weakness in livestock prices and lower-than-expected activity in grain markets, the Agriculture Department said.

5 Factory orders rose 1% in November to an adjusted $159.63 billion after increasing a revised 1.8% in October. Construction spending climbed 2.5% in November to an adjusted $231.8 billion annual rate after rising a revised 1.1% in October. But many analysts believe business activity slowed in December because of record interest rates.

Purchasing agents said in a survey that the U.S. economy slumped last month because of high interest rates. A sharply increased number of companies reported lower production and new orders compared with November, the National Association of Purchasing Management survey showed.

Short-term interest rates probably will continue tumbling in the near future, many forecasters believe. This view was bolstered Friday as most major banks cut their prime rate to 20½% from a record 21½%, following the lead of four other banks. But the economists differ on 1981 predictions for the prime rate, with a range of as high as 30% and as low as 9%.

GM'S latest price boost on 1981 model cars is causing speculation as to whether Ford and Chrysler will follow suit. There has been increasing sentiment among some dealers for at least a temporary freeze on car prices to stimulate demand. GM's cars will be an average of $149 a unit. or 1.5%, more expensive, starting today.

Money supply numbers have created a schism among economists over whether the Fed ought to issue the figures every week or wait for more meaningful monthly numbers. Many economists believe the financial markets overreact to the weekly statistics.

6 Interest rates plummeted, sending bond prices up sharply, after the Fed reported an unexpectedly steep decline in the nation's money supply. M1-A fell $2.5 billion in the week ended Dec. 24, while M1-B dropped $2.8 billion. Morgan Guaranty Trust cut its prime rate to 20% from 21½%, leapfrogging other banks that lowered their fee last week to 20½%.

The dollar plunged more than 1.5% against major currencies and gold's price rose $7.30 an ounce to $593.60 as U.S. interest rates continued to drop.

Stock prices, prompted by easing interest rates, rose sharply and broadly in trading of more than 58 million shares. The Dow Jones industrial averaged closed at 992.66, up 19.88 points.

Auto output rose 3.6% last month to 465,427 cars, but remained at about the lowest level in 20 years. The figure was 7.5% short of the 503,400-unit December estimate as sales continued soft.

Toyota raised its U.S. passenger car prices an average 2.8%, or $172. The step puts prices on Toyota's smallest and most fuel-efficient imports in much closer competition with those on GM's smallest models.

7 Stock prices surged, pushing the Dow Jones industrial average to 1004.69, its highest level in more than four years. Volume soared to nearly 68 million shares, the ninth largest on record. IBM and other blue-chip stocks led the 12.03-point advance. Brokers attributed the strong gain to the recent decline in interest rates.

The prime rate was lowered to 19½% from 20½% by Chemical Bank, undercutting a few banks that cut the fee to 20%. But other major banks, in an apparent attempt to bolster their profit margins, held fast to the 20½% rate instituted last week.

Ford, following GM, raised its car prices an average of $85 a unit, or 1%. The move includes lower prices on some models, higher prices on some and no change on others. But Chrysler isn't going along with the increase. It said its efforts to stimulate sales by offering credit buyers 7% cash rebates "is working well."

Chrysler may receive "conditional" approval of a restructuring plan before the Carter administration leaves office, Chrysler Loan Guarantee Board officials said The board is studying the auto maker's latest proposal to wring $1 billion in concessions from its lenders, workers and suppliers over the next 29 months in a bid for an additional $40.4 million in federally backed loans.

The dollar was little changed in nervous foreign-exchange dealings as traders tried to assess the extent of the decline in U.S. interest rates. Gold's price rose $4.20 an ounce to $597.80.

8   The stock market retreated, with the Dow Jones industrial average plummeting 23.80 points to close at 980.89. Volume surged to a record 92,890,000 shares. Triggering the broad decline, analysts said, was an overnight sell recommendation issued to clients by Joseph Granville, an influential investment adviser in Holly Hill, Fla.

Gold's price plummeted $26.30 an ounce to $571.50 and the dollar surged in foreign-exchange trading on trader speculation that the U.S. and Iran are nearing agreement on release of the hostages. Higher short-term interest rates also propelled trading.

Mortgage rates appear to have peaked and housing economists expect them to begin a slow decline in the months ahead. But any improvement in housing starts won't show up until spring, they add.

Commodity prices fell broadly on news of higher interest rates. Unlike the stock market, many of the declines were modest and volume usually was described as moderate.

Bond prices plunged and interest rates surged as the Fed drained reserves from the banking network at a time when the key interest rate on federal funds was hovering at 18¾%. The move dashed investor hopes that the Fed would soon relax its grip on the nation's credit.

Auto makers were granted waivers by the EPA on some pollution standards that cover carbon-monoxide and nitrogen-oxide emissions.

Six U.S. oil companies raised wholesale prices for gasoline and home heating oil as much as five cents a gallon, following smilar boosts by four other concerns.

9   The current account will show a $10 billion surplus this year, a Treasury official predicted. He added that the U.S. balance of payments for 1980 could show a $5 billion surplus, which would be the first surplus since 1976. A sharp decline in U.S. purchases of foreign oil and a rapid growth of U.S. exports were cited.

The prime rate was reduced by several more banks to 20% from 20½%, but others continued to take a wait-and-see attitude toward the fee.

A tax cut shouldn't be delayed even though the federal deficit this fiscal year is approaching a record level of $60 billion, said David Stockman, Reagan's choice for director of the Office of Management and Budget.

Stock prices plunged broadly, with the Dow Jones industrial average falling 15.19 points to close at 965.70. The weakness was attributed to some carry-over of the selling ignited by the sell recommendation of investment adviser Joseph Granville.

12   The economy ended 1980 with continued inflation and unemployment and some economists say it may get worse before it improves. Producer prices for finished goods rose an adjusted 0.6% in December, matching November, and 11.7% above a year ago. Unemployment slipped to 7.4% from November's 7.5%, but the 7.1% average for the year was considerably higher than 1979's 5.8%.

U.S. aircraft makers could lose a large share of the foreign airliner market unless they concentrate on quieter, mid-size jets. A two-year study of noise standards abroad says increasing sensitivity to noise is forcing airlines to look for smaller, quieter planes.

Public pension funds will be channelled into residential mortgage markets under pilot plans of $20 million each started in Texas and Massachusetts. Oregon has begun a $100 million program to use pension money to buy commercial property for the state.

13   Consumer borrowing rose $839 million in November, or at a 3% annual rate. The latest report includes revisions back to 1975 and indicates the recovery in borrowing, following a steep slide early in 1980, will be slower than had been expected.

Synthetic-fuel projects costing up to $3 billion are being pushed by the Energy Department despite Republican opposition. The choices could narrow the Reagan administration's options by eliminating some applicants and types of technology.

U.S. Steel said it will raise prices of certain plates, structurals and pilings an average of 7.5% March 1. Buyers had expected smaller increases and some said the boosts might not be sustained by market conditions.

14 Retail sales fell 1.3% in December to an adjusted $80.83 billion after posting a 1.6% rise in November. Economists took the decline as evidence of the economic weakness they have expected since last fall.

Capital spending by businesses in 1981 will increase by an inflation-adjusted 1.5%, the Commerce Department said. The increase would be an improvement over the 0.5% "real" decline last year, the agency added.

Oil company profits for 1980's fourth quarter should about equal last year's record levels, analysts say. But they expect companies getting crude oil supplies from Saudi Arabia to report gains of 15% to 20%.

Mexican gas prices for export to the U.S. were raised 7.9% to $4.82 a thousand cubic feet, retroactive to Jan. 1. Mexico's state oil agency said the new prices will remain in effect at least through the first quarter of 1981.

15 Oil prices posted by OPEC members for the first quarter are settling at a weighted average just under $35 a barrel. That's up about $3, or slightly less than 10%, from rates prior to December's meeting. Iran, which is exporting small amounts of oil despite its war with Iraq, raised its prices to $37 a barrel for light crude and $36 for heavy.

An antitrust suit against AT&T goes to trial today, and some observers think it could be the longest in U.S. history. But the trial judge has imposed innovative techniques to shorten it that could become models for similar cases.

AT&T plans to raise $5.7 billion to $6.2 billion externally in 1981, compared with $6.8 billion last year. The reduction stems from FCC moves allowing accelerated depreciation for the company.

Chrysler reached a tentative agreement with lenders, suppliers and the UAW reducing its outstanding debt and curbing labor cost increases. The actions are expected to speed approval of an additional $400 million in federal loan guarantees.

16 Carter's budget for fiscal year 1982, beginning Oct. 1, sets a spending increase to $739.3 billion and a deficit of $27.5 billion. Fiscal 1981 spending is estimated at $662.7 billion with a deficit of $55.2 billion. The incoming Reagan administration is expected to ask Congress for quick personal tax cuts and accelerated depreciation for business. Reagan planners hope to balance the budget through deep cuts in spending, especially in the entitlement programs. Nonetheless, total federal debt is expected to exceed $1 trillion for the first time next November.

Defense spending is slated to rise 14.2% to $180 billion in the Carter budget. But after inflation adjustment, that represents a real gain of 4.4%, the Pentagon says. Reagan, who pledged higher military spending in his campaign, is almost certain to ask Congress for a larger increase.

General Motors will close six U.S. and Canadian assembly plants for one to two weeks beginning Jan. 26 and will extend the closing of two other facilities for a week.

Criminal penalties would be dropped from a law barring payoffs abroad under legislation recommended by Reagan advisers. Their report also recommends budget cuts for the SEC and greater reliance on states to combat securities fraud.

Bond prices fell across a broad front, pushing interest rates higher. Traders had expected Penn Central's investment of a $2.1 billion government settlement to buoy the market.

Industrial production in December rose an adjusted 1%, an unexpectedly strong showing, the Fed said. It was the fifth gain in a row, but most economists doubt the increases can be sustained.

17 American Telephone would be required to divest itself of part of Western Electric and at least one of its 23 local telephone companies to settle antitrust charges, sources close to the trial said. A federal judge termed a settlement "essentially complete," and recessed the two-day-old trial until Feb. 1.

Gross national product will increase 1.5% to 2%, after inflation, between the final quarters of 1980 and 1981, Carter's Council of Economic Advisers forecast. But the economy should grow at a 3.5% rate in the second half and in 1982, Charles Schultze, council chairman, said.

Factory operating rates rose to 79.8% of capacity in December, the fifth increase in a row, the Fed said. The recession low, reached last July, was 74.9%.

Wage-price guidelines were over-whelmed by events and appeared to be a dismal failure at damping inflation, the Council on Wage and Price Stability said.

20 The economy held up surprisingly well at the end of last year, two Commerce Department reports indicate. Personal income rose 0.9% in December after a 1.1% increase in November, and housing starts slipped a modest 1% to a 1,548,000-unit annual rate following a 0.4% gain the month before. Both measures were stronger than many economists had expected.

Ten oil companies agreed to settle charges of price-control violations. The settlements call for customer refunds totaling $180 million and a $2 billion reduction in price increases the companies are allowed. Two concerns also agreed to add $510 million to domestic capital-spending plans.

21 American Telephone and the government may both see a victory in the "tangible accord" reached to settle their antitrust case. In return for divesting itself of part of Western Electric and some operating units, AT&T may be allowed to enter the data processing field.

Stock prices had their sharpest Inaugural Day decline in decades, with the Dow Jones industrial average tumbling 20.31 to close at 950.68. Analysts attributed the weakness to disappointment over Reagan's inaugural speech. Volume expanded to 41,570,000 shares.

22 The economy expanded at a healthy clip in last year's fourth quarter, a Commerce Department report shows. Gross national product, after inflation adjustment, rose at a 5% annual rate in the period, following a 2.4% growth rate in the third quarter. Most analysts expect it to slow in the first part of 1981.

Federal regulation will be curbed as part of a broad plan to spur growth by reducing government spending and taxes, David Stockman, OMB director, said. He called the program a "full-throttle, four-year plan without equivocation." Separately, Murray Weidenbaum, a leading critic of government regulations, was picked to head the Council of Economic Advisers.

Bond prices tumbled and interest rates soared on a Commerce Department report that inflation surged in 1980's fourth quarter. Large Treasury securities sales by the Fed added to the upward pressure on rates.

General Motors is recalling about 80,000 midsize station wagons built in 1979 and equipped with electrical rear-window defoggers. There have been about 400 reports of windows shattering on the cars, so dealers will apply special coatings to parts of the windows' electrical grids to prevent the problem.

23 Car makers scheduled more temporary plant closings. Ford will idle a car assembly line for two weeks, Chrysler will close the two plants building its K-cars the week of Feb. 2, GM will have six U.S. and two Canadian plants closed next week, and AMC will idle an assembly line.

Financial markets face a crisis unless interest rates decline, Reagan adviser Alan Greenspan told the Joint Economic Committee. He repeated his support of extraordinary federal spending restraint to trim federal borrowing and help bring down interest rates.

26 Inflation pressures won't ease soon, the administration is warning, and most economists see little slowing in the pace of price increases this year. The Labor Department reported that consumer prices jumped an adjusted 1.1% in December, pushing the index up 12.4% for the year, only slightly less than 1979's 13.3% rise.

Mobil Corp. loaned its ailing Montgomery Ward retailing unit another $100 million, for a total of $300 million, and extended repayment to Jan. 31, 1985. Mobil said it is committed to further financing this year if conditions warrant.

Machine tool orders fell 25% in December from the year-earlier month. The drop partly reflects high interest rates and customers' reluctance to place orders until Congress indicates the effective dates of proposed tax-law changes.

Auto sales declined 9.4% in mid-January to an estimated 135,449 units. General Motors' sales fell 11%, Ford's 14% and AMC's an estimated 44%. VW of America said its sales rose 6.6% and Chrysler reported a 13% increase.

27 Gold's price tumbled $30.10 an ounce to $521.50 on the Comex, the lowest since May 28 and far below the record $875 of Jan. 21, 1980. Traders cited eased international tension, hopes for a slowing of inflation under Reagan, and Fed policies on interest rates that increase costs of commodity speculation. The dollar advanced against most major currencies.

Bache Group and its Bache Metal unit were named in a suit by Irving J. Louis, the unit's former president. Louis charges that Bache falsified silver-trading records during the silver market's collapse last March.

28 Price decontrol of domestic crude oil, expected today, would increase oil-industry revenue by $8 billion to $16 billion this year and bring the government as much as $6 billion to $10 billion in taxes, according to industry and government forecasts.

Broker-loan rates were cut to 20% from 20½% by several big lenders, including Citibank and Chemical Bank. The reduction could help pave the way for a drop in the prime rate, currently 20%.

29 The prime rate was cut to 19½% from 20% by Marine Midland, a move analysts expect to become widespread. Some economists expect an economic slowdown to push the fee as low as 13% by midyear.

Car makers pared first quarter production schedules to 1,558,800 units, an 11% cut from last month's forecast for the period and down 10% from year-ago output.

The U.S. trade deficit narrowed to $32.25 billion in 1980 from $37.21 billion in 1979. A surge in oil imports pushed December's gap to $2.98 billion, the largest since May.

30 Budget cuts "bigger than anyone has ever attempted" were vowed by Reagan to gain control of inflation. The President repeated his pledge to cut the size of government, announced a 60-day freeze on more than 100 pending federal health and safety regulations and ended Carter's wage-price monitoring system.

Surface-mining policy is expected to change quickly under Interior Secretary Watt. Industry and government officials say he intends to increase the number of federal coal-mine leases and to soften strip-mining controls.

February 1981

2 The economy is slowing from the effects of high interest rates, but the extent is uncertain, economists say. They cite inconclusive statistical data and lack of details about Reagan's economic strategy. The Commerce Department's index of leading economic indicators fell 0.8% in December after six consecutive increases, confirming the slowdown.

Business productivity fell at an adjusted 1.1% annual rate in the fourth quarter and was off 0.5% for all of 1980. It was the third consecutive year of decline.

Higher prices for industrial materials were reported in January by 64% of purchasing agents in a survey. In December, 54% reported higher prices.

3 Bond prices plunged as much as 1¾ points on traders' worries over the market's ability to absorb the Treasury's $8.5 billion refunding, starting today.

Increased oil drilling may not be in the national interest, a new study by two Cornell University scientists says. It predicts that industry soon may be using more energy drilling for oil than it is finding.

4 A federal debt limit increase to $985 billion from $935.1 billion was approved unanimously by the House Ways and Means Committee. Treasury Secretary Regan said the new ceiling should meet the government's borrowing needs through Sept. 30, the end of the current fiscal year.

A treasury offering of $8.6 billion set for Monday may have to be reduced if Congress delays further action on a debt-ceiling increase. The sale is intended to raise $650 million in new funds.

Fuel prices continued to surge as Exxon raised quotes on all oil products five cents a gallon, its second boost in less than a week. Every major oil company has increased wholesale prices since decontrol.

The dollar hit its highest level in more than nine months but ended mixed after profit taking and central bank intervention. Gold gained $12.70 an ounce closing at $494.70 on the Comex.

Criminal charges were brought against two former Morgan Stanley merger and acquisition specialists and three other individuals. The government charged them with conspiring to profit from takeovers by trading on confidential information.

The prime rate was cut to 19½% from 20% by most major banks, reflecting reduced loan demand and lower costs of obtaining funds for lending. But other rates rose under pressure from new Treasury securities issues.

5 Budget cuts totaling $35 billion to $40 billion are planned by Reagan for fiscal 1982, but the administration also hopes to trim $13 billion from this year's spending. Targets are likely to include synthetic fuels, urban development, Medicaid, education aid, extended unemployment compensation, food stamps, highways and some Social Security benefits.

Domestic car sales fell 20% in January to 465,876 units, but analysts considered that a good showing when compared with robust sales a year earlier. Sales of imports declined 17% to 172,210.

A debt limit rise to $985 billion from $935.1 billion was approved by the Senate Finance Committee by an eight-to-five vote. The House Ways and Means Committee previously passed the bill unanimously.

Bond prices rose sharply on signs the Fed

might tolerate eased credit conditions. Gains ranged to more than 1¼ points and came despite a heavy supply of new issues.

Mortgage rates averaged 15.37% in January, up from 14.95% in December, the Federal Home Loan Bank said. It was the fifth consecutive increase since August.

6 Retail sales in January showed mediocre gains, mostly on markdowns. Sears and Ward had 5% increases, Penney sales were even and Woolworth's fell 1.4%. Based on stores open at least a year, K mart sales rose 2% to 4% and Dayton-Hudson's 1.5%.

A drop in inflation is possible by year-end if the government slashes the budget and cuts business regulations, Fed Chairman Volcker said. But he warned that price increases this year are likely to match last year's and be only somewhat lower in 1982.

The U.S. dollar jumped against most major currencies as traders took remarks by Fed chief Volcker to indicate continued high interest rates. Gold rose $10 an ounce to close at $500.50 on the Comex.

A debt limit bill to raise the ceiling to $985 billion from $935.1 billion was passed by the House in a 305-to-104 vote. Republicans broke with past practice to support the measure, which was requested by the Reagan administration.

Car makers plan to close eight more plants next week, bringing the total of idle facilities to 16 in the U.S. and one in Canada.

Intermarket trading on a limited basis would be expanded beginning Sept. 30 under an SEC experiment. The test would link seven exchanges and the OTC market to allow brokers to select the best price for their customers.

9 The prime rate probably will fall soon, mainly on pressure from a drop in loan demand and a reduction in banks' costs of obtaining funds. Some economists see a decline to 19% from the current 19½% as early as this week. But they warn that other short-term rates, after sliding for almost three weeks, could stay near current levels for the rest of the month.

The unemployment rate held steady in January at an adjusted 7.4%, down from 7.5% in November and 7.6% in October. But the Labor Department warned that the statistics provide mixed signals because of seasonal adjustments.

A debt limit bill raising the ceiling to $985 billion from $935.1 billion was passed by the Senate on a 73-to-18 vote and sent to Reagan. Broad GOP support for the measure, considered by many Republicans to be politically distasteful, was seen as a victory for the President.

The Fed's Open Market Committee decided to set lower monetary growth targets for the first quarter. At its December meeting it also agreed to let the federal funds rate fluctuate between 15% and 20%, up from the fourth quarter's 13% to 18%.

10 The prime rate was lowered to 19% from 19½% by Morgan Guaranty, a move analysts expect to become industrywide soon. But other interest rates rose, reflecting heavy supplies of debt securities.

Iraq's oil exports are increasing, and some former customers have been invited to negotiate agreements for renewed shipments. Saudi Arabia and Libya reportedly are using the supply disruptions to raise prices.

Spot oil purchases for the Strategic Petroleum Reserve are being made in small quantities, the Energy Department said. If the move doesn't cause adverse reactions from producing nations, larger purchases may be resumed.

Gold's price rose $14.20 an ounce to $518.70 on the Comex, sparked by fears of a Soviet invasion of Poland. The U.S. dollar was up slightly in light trading.

11 Investment income would be taxed at a maximum 50%, rather than the current 70%, under a proposal being considered by the administration. Treasury Secretary Regan said that effective dates for tax cuts haven't been set, but that he advocates making reductions for business effective Jan. 1. Individual taxes may be cut May 1 or July 1.

Consumer borrowing rose an adjusted $1.62 billion in December, or at a 6% annual rate. The slight increase pushed outstanding consumer debt for 1980 to $313.44 billion, up 0.5% for the year. It was the smallest expansion since 1958, when credit declined 0.5%.

Profit margins for retail gasoline dealers are being squeezed by a surge in wholesale quotes. Dealers in many parts of the country are unable to pass along higher prices because of competitive pressures.

12 Retail sales rose 2% in January to an adjusted $84.01 billion. December sales were revised to show a 0.3% gain to an adjusted $82.36 billion. The latest figures suggest continuing strength in the consumer segment of the economy, but private analysts say that many retailers are pessimistic about the short-term outlook.

The Postal Rate Commission is expected to approve a boost in first-class postage to 18 cents from 15 cents. The increase is two cents less than the Postal Service had requested, and business mailers feared they might have to make up the cut.

Three big refiners, Phillips, Atlantic Richfield and Texaco, are cutting off gasoline supplies to several hundred retail outlets. Decontrol freed the companies of the obligation to find other suppliers for the outlets before taking the action.

Bowery Savings Bank, New York's biggest, posted a $60.8 million operating loss for 1980. Eight other of the city's 10 largest also had losses, stemming from low-yielding fixed-rate mortgages and restrictions of a state usury law.

13 Business inventories fell 0.2%, or $963 million, in December to an adjusted $457.02 billion. Spurred by high sales, it was the first drop in five years. But a Commerce Department analyst said the decline could be wiped out in revisions over the next two months.

"Real" GNP will edge up 1% this year and then climb 4% in 1982 and 5% in 1983 based on Reagan's economic plan, his economic advisers said. They also see inflation slowing from 11% this year to 8.25% next year, 6.25% in 1983 and about 5.5% in 1984.

General Motors will close four car plants and a truck plant next week to balance inventories with lagging sales. Two Ford facilities will remain closed.

Money-market funds assets rose about $2.9 billion in the week ended Wednesday. The 3.3% increase brought total assets of the funds to a record $89.9 billion, a 20% gain in the past six weeks alone.

17 Income-tax cuts for individuals will be phased in July 1, starting with 5% this year, 10% in each of the next two years and a final 5% Jan. 1, 1984, under Reagan's plans. Accelerated business depreciation would be phased in over five years, retroactive to Jan. 1.

Producer prices for finished goods rose an adjusted 0.9% in January, or at a 10.8% annual rate. The Labor Department attributed 40% of the rise to higher energy costs, and some economists warned of further escalation resulting from decontrol.

General Motors rebates of up to $700 on cars are expected in a major sales incentive program. Sources say the drive will begin tomorrow and include dealer contests and quotas and sharp price cuts.

Car sales fell 7.4% in early February to an estimated 134,554 units. GM's sales declined 19% and Chrysler's 7.6%. Ford's rose 26%, VW of America's 72%, and AMC's an estimated 25%.

A major synfuel plant was blasted in un-published government reports for poor management, technical problems and cost overruns. The $1.4 billion coal liquefaction project, sponsored by Gulf Oil and the Energy Department, may be scuttled by Reagan.

Morgan Stanley quietly reorganized into two operating groups bringing the mergers and acquisitions and corporate finance units together. Officials said the move was disclosed internally before an indictment charging two former employes with profiting from insider merger information.

"Trigger" prices for steel imports will be raised 4.4% in the second quarter to a minimum of $422.95 a net ton. The price for imports from Japan's more efficient mills will be increased 4.77%.

18 Cash rebates on new cars ranging from $500 to nearly $1,800 were announced by GM and Ford. But the costly programs are risky, analysts say, because of their short-lived effect in boosting sales. And actual reductions may be less if dealers reduce their contributions to the plans. The actions may force Chrysler to continue its own rebates, further draining badly needed cash.

Industrial production rose an adjusted 0.6% in January. It was the sixth gain in a row and brought the Fed's index to 151.8% of the 1967 average, about 0.6% below the year-earlier level.

Gasoline and heating oil prices were raised by more than half the nation's major refiners in the past week. A Gulf official said gasoline will rise a further 20 cents a gallon but won't top $2 a gallon this year.

19 Reagan's plan for economic recovery was outlined in his State of the Union address and a separate printed message. The program, as expected, calls for a 30% cut in individual taxes over three years, beginning with a 10% reduction July 1. The top rate on unearned income would be trimmed to 50% from 70%, and on capital gains to 20% from 28%. Faster depreciation for business investment would be retroactive to Jan. 1 and amount to $59.3 billion annually by fiscal 1986.

Federal spending would be pared sharply, beginning with a $4.8 billion cut in fiscal 1981. For fiscal 1982, $41.4 billion would be trimmed, $79.7 billion in fiscal 1983 and $123.8 billion in fiscal 1986.

Economic indicators continued to rise in January. Personal income increased 0.9%, or $21.3 billion, to an adjusted $2.298 trillion annual rate, the Commerce Department said, while housing starts rose 3.4% to an adjusted annual rate of 1,585,000 units. The Fed said the nation's factories ran at 80% of capacity last month, up from 79.8% in December. The broker-loan rate was cut to 18% from 18½% by several large banks. Changes in the fee often precede moves on the prime rate and could put pressure on more banks to lower that charge to 19% from 19½%.

20 Oil output cuts are expected soon by Saudi Arabia, Kuwait and Libya. Observers see the action resulting from a mounting world-wide glut and softening prices in the spot market. Cutbacks could amount to two million to three million barrels a day, they say.

Postal rate increases of three cents for letters, 1% to 27% for second class and 7% to 24% for third class were recommended by the Postal Rate Commission. The $2.7 billion total is $1.1 billion less than the Postal Service sought.

Ford Motor had a fourth quarter loss of $316 million, bringing its deficit for the year to $1.54 billion, believed a record for a U.S. company.

Economic growth figures for 1980's final quarter were revised to show an annual rise of 4% in real GNP rather than the 5% estimated earlier. But a Commerce Department economist said the revision signals continued growth in the first quarter.

Auto makers plan temporary closings at six assembly plants next week, primarily to balance inventories with sluggish sales.

23 Machine tool orders in January fell 40% from a year earlier to $279.6 million. But producers hope for a pickup resulting from Reagan's proposal to accelerate business depreciation.

24 The prime rate was cut to 19% from 19½% by most major banks while many smaller banks posted a cut to 18½%. Many economists expect declining loan demand and costs for lendable funds to push it down further to 17% in the next several weeks. And some specialists see the Fed lowering or removing its special three percentage point surcharge on the basic discount rate, currently 13%.

General Motors plans to recall 6.4 million cars, the second largest recall on record. The company will replace rear suspension bolts on 6.4 million mid-size cars built from 1978 through early 1981. The bolts could corrode and break, causing the rear axle to separate from the car.

Chrysler rebates of 7% in cash will be continued past Saturday, but will require dealers to participate by putting up the first $200. The new plan is similar to current programs of GM and Ford.

25 Durable goods orders fell an adjusted 2.2% in January to $80.85 billion. It was the first decline since August and tended to confirm that the economy is slowing a bit after a surprisingly strong fourth quarter performance.

Auto sales fell 23% in mid-February to an estimated 167,487 units. The decline was greater than expected, but industry officials see a stronger showing into March from new GM and Ford rebate programs.

Chrysler reached a compromise with a group of balking lenders providing for early repayment of $68 million. The agreement reportedly was approved by the government loan board, paving the way for federal loan guarantees of rescue funds.

Ginnie Mae options trading on the CBOE was approved by the SEC. The move may presage options trading for many other nonequity securities on several exchanges.

Record yields were posted by some new debt issues, with $275 million of triple-A rated New Jersey Bell debentures paying 14.8%. Louisiana rejected bids for its $145 million bonds because rates were too high.

26 Consumer prices rose an adjusted 0.7% in January, the smallest increase since last July, and equal to an 8.4% annual rate before compounding. But analysts cautioned that a temporary easing in food and housing increases accounted for most of the slowdown.

Monetary restraint will be exerted by the Fed to support Reagan's economic program, Volcker told the Senate Banking Committee. Slower money growth is an important element in administration plans to curb inflation.

Budget outlays for fiscal 1982 were underestimated by several billion dollars, the administration says. Reagan called on officials to find new cuts to offset the extra spending. The news caused a slump in bond prices over fears of projected government borrowing needs.

Chrysler tentatively set its $400 million sale of 10-year notes for tomorrow. The issue, which may yield more than 15%, will be priced tonight. The company won federal backing for the notes after the federal loan board waived some requirements. Separately, Chrysler wants permission to replace two corporate jets it agreed to sell with long-term leases on three others.

Air fare increases of 2% or more on domestic routes will be permitted Sunday, the CAB said. Boosts of 4.3% to 6% on international routes will be allowed April 1,

The agency cited sharply higher fuel costs.

Undiscovered natural-gas estimates were raised by the Interior Department to 594 trillion cubic feet from 484 trillion in 1975. But estimates of undiscovered oil were practically unchanged at 83 billion barrels.

An SEC standard to prove fraud in disciplinary actions is correct, the Supreme Court ruled. The court said the agency need show only a "preponderance" of evidence, rather than meet a more stringent standard of "clear and convincing" evidence.

27 Budget cuts will be pushed through the Senate rapidly by the Republican majority, which hopes for passage of a "reconciliation" resolution by the end of March. Lawmakers hope to capitalize on public support and put pressure on the House. But the House is resisting and plans to act under the normal timetable, possibly delaying final action until summer.

Budget Director Stockman countered criticism that the proposed cuts would unduly penalize Northeastern states. He told the House Appropriations Committee that plans to extend unemployment benefits on a state-by-state basis would tend to favor the Northeast.

Business productivity fell in the fourth quarter at an adjusted 1.9% annual rate after growing at a 3.8% pace in the third period. For the year, productivity fell at an adjusted 0.6% rate, its third consecutive decline.

Fuel prices were raised at wholesale by at least nine major refiners last week. But the increases for gasoline, heating oil and diesel fuel weren't as sharp as in the weeks immediately following decontrol.

Chrysler's note issue, with a 14.9% coupon, tentatively was priced at 98 to yield 15.31% to maturity in 1990. Approval of the $400 million issue's pricing by the federal loan board is expected today.

March 1981

2 Chrysler's loss for the fourth quarter was $235 million, bringing its deficit for the year to $1.71 billion. The company sold $400 million of federally guaranteed notes and set a new rebate program requiring dealer contributions. Auditors declined an opinion on Chrysler's financial statements because they couldn't determine whether to consider it a going concern.

Auto makers pared first quarter production plans to 1,530,905 units, 13% fewer than a year ago, to avoid an inventory surge after rebate programs end. They may cut more if the programs don't spur sales.

Leading economic indicators fell 0.4% in January after a decline of 0.9% in December. A Commerce Department economist called the latest figures inconclusive, while analysts increasingly are terming the current condition of the economy "stagflation."

The U.S. trade deficit on a merchandise basis widened to a near-record $5.44 billion in January from $3.11 billion in December. The figures include the U.S. Virgin Islands for the first time.

Wages and salaries in the private sector rose an average 2% in 1980's last quarter, slightly less than the third period's 2.2%, the Labor Department said. At year-end, they were 9% higher than a year earlier, but consumer prices rose 12.4% in the same period.

Farm prices slipped 0.4% in February, the same as in January, because of good harvest forecasts abroad and high U.S. interest rates. But the Agriculture Department expects prices to resume rising this month.

3 Major institutions in the savings and loan and insurance industries could face insolvency if interest rates spurt again, a high administration official asserted. Separately, Budget Director Stockman said recovery efforts will squeeze the economy for the next few months. He added that Reagan will propose $46 billion in budget cuts on March 10, about $4.6 billion more than envisioned two weeks ago.

The prime rate was lowered to 18½% from 19% by Chemical Bank, and analysts expect more banks to follow. But other rates rose on uncertainty over Fed policies and government financing needs.

Gold's price plunged $20 an ounce to close on the Comex at $461.50, its lowest level in nearly 15 months. The dollar, meanwhile, spurted to its highest level in almost 10 months.

Construction spending rose 5.4% in January to an adjusted $255.6 billion annual rate following a 4.7% increase in December. But the January level trailed the year-earlier rate by 1.5%.

Commodity markets tumbled on beliefs a stronger dollar will curtail exports and speculative money will flow into high-yield money market funds.

4 Oil production likely will be held at record levels by Saudi Arabia until OPEC's May meeting. The action, in the face of growing supplies, could achieve the Saudis'

pricing strategy of annual increases in quarterly increments. The rises would be geared to producers' inflation rates and currency changes. Thus they would be predictable and avoid sudden oil-price shocks.

Savings and loans are having "exceptional difficulties," Fed Chairman Volcker said, but government programs will help maintain their stability. He told the House Ways and Means committee that the main cure is to stop inflation.

The prime rate was cut to 18½% from 19% by most major banks, and analysts suggest further cuts may come soon. They cite sluggish loan demand, the lower cost of lendable funds and slower growth of the money supply.

An industrial process using a computer formula is patentable if the process is new, the Supreme Court ruled. Previously, the court had held that mathematical formulas aren't patentable and indicated that computer programs aren't, either.

5 Pentagon spending authority would more than double by 1986 to $368 billion a year under Reagan proposals. Initially, the bulk of the money would go for weapons procurement, including a new manned bomber and another nuclear aircraft carrier, as well as sharp rises in military pay. Increases would begin with an added $32.6 billion spending authority and $5.8 billion in new outlays by October 1982.

U.S.-make car sales spurted almost 21% in the last part of February, mostly due to extensive factory-dealer rebate programs. But analysts predict they will slump again when the rebates expire in the middle of this month.

Factory orders fell 0.3% in January to an adjusted $161.3 billion, the first decline since May. A Commerce Department economist said that, after a December surge in shipbuilding and military tank orders, the figures indicate a continued moderate expansion of the economy.

Construction contracts fell 4% in January to $10.5 billion, McGraw-Hill's F.W. Dodge unit said. The decline was attributed to public-construction cutbacks and high interest rates.

6 Oil exports from Iraq and Iran have risen to nearly two million barrels a day, sources say, but they caution the figure isn't firm. There is speculation that the rising output might prompt Saudi Arabia to end its "war relief" production of 500,000 barrels a day.

Retail sales in February rose 6% to 8% for most chains, above expectations but minimal when adjusted for a 7% general-merchandise inflation rate. Increases included 7.6% for Penney, 7.5% for Sears, 7.2% for Montgomery Ward and 6.9% for K mart.

Mortgage rates at S&Ls averaged 15.3% nationally last week, the Federal Home Loan Mortgage Corp. said. It was the third consecutive increase, and was up from 15% in the first week of February.

New York City bonds received a triple-B, or investment grade, rating from Standard & Poor's. Moody's, however, kept its single-B rating, and specialists say it's unlikely to change it despite prodding by city officials.

9 The inflation rate may be moderating under the effects of a sluggish economy despite sharp rises in energy and capital equipment prices, analysts say. They also observe that a slight drop in unemployment masks a growing labor force. Government data show producer prices for finished goods rose an adjusted 0.8% in January, or at a 9.6% annual rate before compounding. The jobless rate fell to an adjusted 7.3%, slightly trailing the 7.4% rate of the previous two months.

Prices in February were generally higher, purchasing agents indicated, but economic activity was little changed from January's sluggish pace. A trade group said a spurt in new orders may have been in anticipation of higher prices later this year due to oil decontrol.

Consumer borrowing rose $869 million in January, equal to a 3% annual rate. It was the sixth rise in a row, but its small size reflected what economists see as slowing economic growth.

10 Spending cuts of $48.6 billion will be asked from Congress by Reagan to hold fiscal 1982 spending to his $695.5 billion target. The reduction was expanded by $7.2 billion from his Feb. 18 request because of underestimates of next year's outlays.

11 First-class postage will rise to 18 cents from 15 cents March 22, with post cards going to 12 cents from 10 cents. The Postal Service also raised expedited second class 27%, other second class 1%, and fourth-class parcel post 13%. Postal governors called the increases, recommended by the Postal Rate Commission, inadequate.

12 Seagram offered to acquire St. Joe Minerals for $2.03 billion, or $45 each for the 45.1 million shares outstanding. The offer is conditioned on receipt of at least 23.4 million shares, or 52%. St. Joe executives, taken by surprise, called the bid "grossly inadequate."

Retail sales rose an adjusted 0.9% in February to $85.83 billion. The gain followed an upward-revised 2.9% increase in January, which analysts attributed to a spate of post-Christmas sales.

Broker loan rates were cut by several large banks, reflecting downward pressure on the prime rate. Continental Illinois lowered broker loan rates to 16¼% from 17¼% and Irving Trust lowered them to 16½% from 17%.

13 Sohio agreed to acquire Kennecott Corp. for $1.77 billion, or $62 a share. Sohio, 53%-owned by British Petroleum, said the transaction is subject to a Kennecott holders vote sometime in May. It was the third time in a week a company has used oil earnings to bid for a mineral concern. The mining companies are seen as vulnerable because of sagging profits and a potential turnaround.

Stock prices soared on a flurry of takeover bids and a falling prime rate. Mining stocks were especially active, reflecting recent offers for St. Joe Minerals and Amax. The Dow Jones industrial average jumped 22.15 to close at 989.82.

The prime rate was cut to 17½% from 18% by Chemical Bank. It was the second reduction this week, and came on reduced costs for lendable funds, sluggish loan demand and increased competition from foreign banks.

St. Joe Minerals rejected Seagram's $2.03 billion tender offer as "grossly inadequate." A source said defensive tactics could include "innovative" legal and investment banking moves.

16 Inventories were kept under tight control in January because of high interest rates and uncertainty over the economy. An increase of 1.1%, or $5.04 billion, brought inventories in the month to $461.81 billion. But that represented only 1.36 months' sales, down from 1.37 months' sales in December, and a record low.

Sales of U.S. cars rose 8.2% in early March to 202,569 units. The increase, due mainly to extensive rebate programs, was in line with analysts' expectations.

Tax cuts proposed by Reagan will win congressional acceptance more easily than spending cuts, Budget Director Stockman said. Separately, Richard Schweiker, Secretary of Health and Human Services, said he will recommend merging some Social Security trust funds to support the retirement fund.

Strategic stockpile purchases will be resumed after a 20-year lapse. The government will spend an estimated $100 million on strategic materials, beginning with 1.2 million pounds of cobalt.

17 Auto makers could save $5 billion in capital costs in the next five years under eased regulations being considered by the administration. And a Cabinet task force meets today to devise an aid package that could include import limits, tax assistance, tariff adjustments and health and safety rule changes.

Tax cuts of up to $51.4 billion in fiscal 1982 were endorsed by the Senate Finance Committee, as were budget cuts of $9.3 billion in programs under its jurisdiction. The panel still could alter the specifics of Reagan's requests.

The prime rate was cut to 17½% from 18% by more big banks, matching Chemical Bank's reduction last Thursday. Many economists expect the fee to fall to about 15% this spring.

18 The economy slowed in February on the effects of inflation and high interest rates, and new government figures support economists' predictions of sluggish performance this year. Housing starts plunged nearly 25% to an adjusted annual rate of 1,218,000 units, while industrial output fell an adjusted 0.5% after six consecutive gains. Personal income rose an adjusted 0.7%, its smallest gain since June, and the savings rate in January, at 4.4%, was the lowest in three decades.

Budget cuts proposed by Reagan were endorsed by the Senate Budget Committee, which added some cuts of its own. But the panel still must act on controversial proposals to trim spending for Medicare and various nutritional programs.

Stocks were unable to hold above the 1000 level, and the Dow Jones industrial average slumped 10.26 points to close at 992.53. Volume swelled to nearly 66 million shares.

Bond prices soared as traders reacted to government reports indicating a slowdown in the economy. Several economists predicted a decline in the prime rate to 17% within a week and a new wave of bond offerings soon.

19 The prime rate was cut to 17% from 17½% by Chemical Bank, its fourth reduction this month, and other banks are expected to follow. Other rates also fell, spurring hope the Fed may drop a special discount rate surcharge soon and perhaps reduce the discount rate itself to 12% from the current 13%.

Corporate profits after taxes totaled $163.1 billion last year, off 2.8% from 1979. Revised Commerce Department figures also show "real" GNP expanded at an adjusted 3.8% annual rate in the fourth quarter, rather than the 4% rate estimated last month.

U.S. factories operated at 79.3% of capacity

in February, the Fed reported, off from 80% in January and 79.9% in December. The drop had been expected because of a decline in industrial production.

Spending cuts to curb the growth of such social programs as Medicaid, welfare and unemployment were endorsed by the Senate Budget Committee. The panel is drafting instructions for other committees to achieve specified reduction levels.

Reagan's plans for tax and spending cuts won unanimous endorsement of the House Ways and Means Committee, which referred them to the Budget Committee. The approval signals a cooperative mood so far in the Democratic-controlled House.

Voluntary curbs on Japanese car exports to the U.S. will likely be sought at the suggestion of an administration auto-industry task force. A two-year restraint would be aimed at averting more stringent limits.

Gasoline stocks have reached record levels, prompting production cutbacks, price reductions and dealer rebates.

20 Japanese car imports should be voluntarily limited. Reagan and a cabinet task force reportedly agreed. But a final decision will be postponed until the President meets with congressional leaders and Japan's foreign minister next week.

Bache Group received a takeover bid from Prudential Insurance totaling $385 million, or $32 a share. The move is designed to avert an acquisition by the Belzberg family, which owns 22.6% of Bache's stock.

23 A synfuel plant in West Virginia was threatened further by the expected withdrawal of West Germany's 25% participatioh. The administration wants to end U.S. funding for the $2 billion coal liquefaction plant.

Bache Group likely will be bought by Prudential Insurance despite possible opposition by the Belzberg family. Bache talks continue with Baldwin-United Corp. on a joint life insurance venture.

Exxon said it halted work on an energy-saving device for electric motors, saying it wouldn't be competitive. Exxon bought Reliance Electric for $1.2 billion nearly two years ago to expedite the device's development and marketing.

24 The Hunt brothers retain most of their 63-million-ounce silver holding despite loan terms calling for its "orderly" disposal. But Fed officials said they haven't pressured banks to force a sale and loan terms don't set a deadline.

New York City offered $75 million of bonds, its first issue since 1975. The offer was oversubscribed at prices yielding from 8% in 1982 to 11½% in 2000.

25 Consumer prices rose an adjusted 1% in February, equal to a 12% annual rate before compounding. The Labor Department said about two-thirds of the rise was due to higher energy-products prices resulting from decontrol. Government and private economists don't expect such costs to rise as rapidly in coming months.

The money supply is growing faster and may be more inflationary than thought, some bankers and economists say. They question the Fed's method of compiling money statistics and the effect on credit rates.

Sales of U.S. cars jumped nearly 30% in mid-March to an estimated 323,445 units, primarily due to GM and Chrysler rebate programs. GM sales surged 52% and Chrysler's rose more than 18%. But Ford, despite its own rebates, posted an 8.1% decline and VW's sales of U.S.-built cars fell more than 17%.

26 Stock prices surged on a late wave of buy orders, sending the Dow Jones industrial average to its highest level since January 1973. The index rose 19.09 points to close at 1015.22 on volume of 56.3 million shares. More than 1,000 issues posted gains for the day.

Auto production will be boosted at two GM assembly plants, resulting in the recall of 3,900 workers. But an output cut at a light-truck unit will cause the layoff of 1,500.

Seagram sought to force St. Joe Minerals to obtain SEC clearance of a plan to repurchase 15.5% of its own stock at $60 a share. Meanwhile, St. Joe directors acted to improve management stock-option and pension benefits in the event of a change in control.

27 Auto regulations on a variety of emission and safety standards would be eased or scrapped under administration plans. Reagan aides say the package could save manufacturers $2 billion in the next five years, and save consumers as much as $5 billion.

GM and Ford will close a total of four light-truck plants next week to balance inventories. Separately, GM said it is recalling 105,000 of its 1981 cars to replace an engine electrical ground cable that could fail.

Gulf Oil sees sharply lower first quarter earnings due to rising crude-oil prices and sluggish markets. The company cited sizable losses in European and U.S. refining and marketing operations.

Mobil will close its Buffalo oil refinery because of falling demand and the unit's age. Mobil said its seven U.S. refineries are operating at about 70% of capacity.

30 St. Joe Minerals reportedly agreed to sell its 92% interest in CanDel Ltd. to Sulpetro Ltd., Calgary, for $545.9 million (Canadian), or $44.55 a share. St. Joe's ownership of CanDel has been regarded as an impediment to non-Canadian bids to thwart a takeover offer from Seagram.

The economy faces tough going, a government forecasting measure indicates. The composite index of leading indicators fell 0.3% in February following revised decreases of 0.6% in January and 0.1% in December.

Steel imports in February fell 26% from a year earlier to 1.2 million tons, or 15% of the domestic steel market.

Machine tool orders fell to $276.7 million in February, off 1.5% from January and down 45% from a year earlier. Officials blamed economic uncertainty, high interest rates and a buying pause by auto and aircraft customers, but they see orders increasing about midyear.

31 Market reaction to Reagan's shooting was forestalled, as stock exchanges in the U.S. and Canada closed at 3:17 P.M. to avoid a selling wave. The Dow Jones industrial average, up more than six points at 2:30 P.M., closed at 992.16, off 2.62, and exchange officials were unsure if their markets would open as usual this morning. Bond prices plunged on initial reports and volume slumped. Pricing of some corporate issues was delayed, and government-securities dealers halted operations at 4 P.M.

The dollar, already weak on easing tension in Poland, plunged further, spurring Fed efforts to stabilize it. Gold fell $17.20 an ounce on Polish events, and closed on the Comex at $512.10. Comex trading ended before the shooting.

The prime rate could return to 20% or higher if the U.S. doesn't gain control of the budget, Reagan told an AFL-CIO building-trades group. He stressed the need for his proposed 10% annual tax cut for the next three years.

New single-family home sales fell 5.3% in February to an adjusted annual rate of 487,000 units, the Commerce Department said. The decline followed a 0.2% rise in January.

April 1981

1 Fluor Corp. offered to acquire St. Joe Minerals in a two-step transaction valued at $2.73 billion. Fluor agreed to buy 20.4 million St. Joe shares, or 45%, at $60 each for a total of $1.22 billion. Each remaining share would be exchanged for 1.2 shares of Fluor, for a total of $1.51 billion at current market prices. The bid counters a competing $2.13 billion offer from Seagram, which St. Joe opposes. Seagram said its $45-a-share offer remains open.

Farm prices fell 1.9% in March following declines of 0.4% each in February and January, the Agriculture Department said. Most major commodities declined, leaving the agency's farm-price index 10% above the year-earlier level.

Kodak will introduce a system for enlarging color negatives and slides in home darkrooms. The process, based on instant-camera technology, is expected to be available this fall.

2 Auto production by U.S. makers is expected to rise 24% in the second quarter to 2,025,100 cars from an extremely low year-earlier level. Plans are still cautious, however, as producers expect sales to drop after rebates end. The schedule, which is 3.7% higher than planned a month ago, would be the second lowest second quarter output since the spring of 1975.

Construction spending in February fell 3.6% to an adjusted annual $252.5 billion rate, due to high interest levels. The drop, which followed a 5.9% rise in January, was the first decline since July.

Industrial revenue bond sales swelled to $8.4 billion last year, drawing concern from a House Ways and Means subcommittee, which plans hearings. A government report said sales may reach $35 billion by 1985 and could cost the Treasury $4.4 billion in lost revenue by 1986.

The prime rate was lowered to 17% from 17½% by Chase Manhattan, and most other large banks followed. Bankers see further declines on sluggish loan demand and increased competition.

St. Joe Minerals dropped most legal challenges to Seagram's takeover offer after accepting a $2.73 billion merger bid from Fluor. Separately, four St. Joe lead mines in Missouri were struck.

3 Money fund assets rose $3.2 billion in the week ended Wednesday to a record $112.26 billion. Fund assets have soared 50% since the beginning of the year. The average annual yield offered by the funds in the latest week was 15½%, well above the maximum 12.524% that banks and savings institutions could offer on six-month certificates during the period.

Xerox cut rental and lease prices on six copier models 18% to 37% for customers using 100 or more. The low-priced models have faced fierce Japanese competition.

The Fed is considering changing the way it releases money-supply figures. The method has been criticized because of sharp fluctuations in the data that have caused financial markets to overreact.

The U.S. dollar soared against major currencies on new nervousness over Poland and higher interest rates on dollar deposits. Gold rose to $517.50 an ounce on the Comex from $516.60.

6 A weak ecomony with only modest improvements in the inflation rate appeared more likely based on two U.S. reports. Producer prices for finished goods surged an adjusted 1.3% in March, and the unemployment rate stayed at an adjusted 7.3% of the work force for the second consecutive month. The price rise was enlarged by Reagan's decontrol of domestic oil prices in January.

U.S. credit markets may face sharp jolts leading to higher interest rates. Many economists believe the money supply will rise sharply. Also, data released by the Fed indicates that it is adopting a tougher credit policy and that it didn't want interest rates to fall as sharply as they did early last month.

GM will raise new-car prices 3.5%, or $351 a unit. The boost, which raises its average sticker price to more than $10,200, surprised analysts and irritated some dealers.

Corporate buying agents see the U.S. economy improving, a monthly survey indicated. New orders and output in March were found at the highest levels since November.

Directors of Fluor and St. Joe Minerals approved a $2.65 billion merger. Fluor would acquire 45% of St. Joe for $60 a share and the rest through a stock swap. A $45-a-share bid by Seagram is set to expire Friday.

Sohio will have to spend at least $1 billion to modernize Kennecott's facilities. The largest U.S. copper producer, which has accepted Sohio's $1.77 billion merger proposal, is said to have the highest production costs in the industry largely because of legal and financial troubles in the 1970s.

7 Interest rates soared and bond prices slumped on word that the Fed took a tougher credit stance than expected. The deteriorating market caused the delay of several issues, including $150 million of Pennsylvania Bell debentures and $50 million of Borg Warner Acceptance notes. Stock prices also retreated in slower trading, with the Dow Jones in-

dustrial average losing 12.87 to close at 994.24.

Auto makers would be aided by administration plans to ease, scrap or delay 34 environmental and safety regulations. Officials say the changes would save the industry $1.4 billion and consumers $9.3 billion over five years, equal to $150 for each car or truck.

8 Consumer credit posted its largest gain in a year, rising an adjusted $2 billion in February, or at an 8% annual rate. The expansion compares with a more modest increase of $869 million in January, and paralleled a jump in new car sales resulting from rebate and sales incentive programs.

Home mortgage rates rose in March to an average 15.7% from 15.34% in February. Economists were divided on how to interpret the rise.

9 Oil prices were cut by Ecuador and Mexico, the first decreases in posted rates during the current glut. Ecuador dropped its price $1.67 a barrel to $36.33 and Mexico $2.50 a barrel to $30. Experts say other countries may do the same, possibly led by Libya or Nigeria, followed by North Sea producers. Algeria and the United Arab Emirates could join the rollbacks.

10 Retail sales in March were surprisingly strong, and merchants and analysts expect April, bolstered by Easter, to be as good or better. Brisk sales of clothing were reported as weather in most of the country was warmer than anticipated. Sears had its first double-digit rise since June 1978 with a 12.9% gain. Montgomery Ward posted a 9.1% increase, K mart 8.6% and Penney 3.6%.

Gasoline prices have been trimmed by four companies, and five major refiners are offering dealer rebates. But demand remains soft and inventories high.

13 Oil prices paid by several U.S. refiners were reduced $1 a barrel. The cutbacks apply to heavy crudes produced in the Rocky Mountain area, generally the first affected by an oil glut. Some analysts see additional reductions in the next few weeks. There also were signs that more foreign producers are under pressure to trim prices, and some experts think Libya, Nigeria and Algeria may do so soon.

OPEC members apparently are worried that they have pushed oil prices too high and too fast. They believe that the increases have forced major consumers to accelerate their search for substitutes. As a result, demand for OPEC oil is dropping too fast, as could happen soon to revenue.

Synfuel plants slated for cutbacks or elimination by the White House apparently have little chance of surviving intact. The administration hopes the restructuring will save $1.4 billion through fiscal 1982 and several times that amount by 1985.

14 Chrysler said it hasn't any further interest in a merger with Ford, which last Friday rejected a proposal for a combination. Separately, Chrylser Defense, a unit, received a $216.8 million Army contract for 360 M1 tanks with an option for a further 209.

No tax compromise is seen by Reagan on his planned 30% three-year tax reduction. He said he remains "fully committed" to the cut and hadn't authorized anyone in the administration to offer a compromise.

The prime rate was raised to 17½% from 17% by several more banks. Higher costs of attracting funds were cited. But other rates fell and bond prices rebounded on reports of sluggish March retail sales, which indicated the economy may be slowing.

General Motors said it won't raise prices again on its 1981-model cars following last week's boosts of $351 a unit, or 3.5%. Ford and Chrysler didn't follow the increases.

A&P said its loss in the fiscal fourth quarter, ended Feb. 28, was slightly less than $4.2 million, compared with a $13.5 million loss a year earlier. Sales rose 12.6% to $1.89 billion. For the year, the loss totaled $43 million, widening sharply from $3.8 million.

15 New car sales by U.S. makers fell 12% in early April, slightly more than analysts had forecast. The industry sold 161,421 cars in the period, equal to an annual rate of about six million units. The companies expected only a short dip after the end of rebate programs last month, but some observers see the possibility of a longer slump. GM had a 23% decline in the period, and VW of America's sales fell 9.6%. Chrysler sales jumped 33% and Ford's rose 4.8%. AMC had an estimated 33% drop.

Business loans at foreign units of U.S. banks have increased $3.2 billion, or almost 75%, since Jan. 1. The heavy credit demand could push domestic short-term rates up and cushion a decline in the prime rate, bankers and economists say.

Municipal bond markets are being crimped in an investment strategy switch by property and casualty insurers. The insurers have slashed tax-exempt buying in favor of higher-yield taxable issues to offset mounting underwriting losses.

16 Industrial production rose an adjusted 0.4% in March following a 0.4% decline in February. Analysts said output would have been flat if auto rebates hadn't boosted sales. Business inventories in the month rose $4.88 billion, or $1.1%, to an adjusted $469.99 billion. The figures indicate the economy is stagnant but isn't declining.

Reagan's economic plan won't be compromised, Bush said, emphasizing White House intentions to get it through Congress intact. Treasury Secretary Regan reinterated the stance, saying the program of tax-and-spending-cut proposals is "an interlaced one."

Loan-loss reserves are rising at many major banks, and a sharp increase in write-offs has been reported by several. The defaults stem partly from high interest rates driving companies into bankruptcy court.

Savings and loans had a record $1.7 billion fund outflow in March, squeezing liquidity and darkening mortgage lending prospects. A trade association spokesman said the outflow appears to be continuing in April.

17 Housing starts rose a slight 5.8% in March to an adjusted annual rate of 1,284,000 units, but the gain hardly made up for the 26.9% slide in February. Factories operated at an adjusted 79.5% of capacity in the month, barely ahead of the 79.4% February rate. The figures confirmed a growing belief that the economy will experience a lackluster second quarter.

Retail gasoline prices fell 0.6 cent a gallon in the first two weeks of April, the first drop since September. Dan Lundberg, a marketing expert, said prices could fall a further 1.5 cents by June 30, but after that cuts would be difficult.

OPEC's strategy for the long term may be fading as demand slackens and disagreements grow. The major conflict centers on the forumla for future oil price rises, and disputes have arisen over aid to poorer nations and consideration of industrialized countries' economic problems.

Money-fund assets rose $1.63 billion, or 1.5%, in the week ended Wednesday to a record $117.29 billion. The funds have soared 57% since Jan. 1.

20 The oil glut was engineered by Saudi Arabia to stabilize and unify prices, the kingdom's oil minister said. Sheik Yamani said his nation will continue record production of 10.3 million barrels a day until prices fall close to the $32 a barrel the Saudis charge. He also hinted the kingdom may drop objections to the U.S. strategic petroleum reserve when a unified price is reached.

The SEC likley will postpone the scheduled Sept. 30 start of an experimental electronic link of the OTC market and seven exchanges. Exchanges oppose the link and the NASD, a major supporter, says the date is unrealistic because a design hasn't been agreed on.

Personal income rose 0.8% in March to an adjusted $2.335 trillion annual rate. It was the second month in a row of slower increases and provided further evidence of an economic slowdown.

Corporate profits after taxes fell 2.7% in 1980 to $163.2 billion, the Commerce Department said. In the fourth quarter, profits rose 3.3% to an adjusted $164.3 billion annual rate.

21 Economic growth in the first quarter reached an adjusted 6.5% annual rate after inflation, the Commerce Department said. The strength surprised administration officials, who cautioned that the performance is unlikely to be repeated soon. Commerce Secretary Baldrige attributed much of the gain to momentum from 1980's fourth quarter.

American Express and Shearson Loeb Rhoades said they are discussing a merger linking the financial services giant and the nation's second largest securities firm. Terms are being discussed and an announcement on developments is promised this morning.

22 American Express agreed to buy Shearson Loeb Rhoades, the nation's second largest securities firm, for stock valued at $864 million. The merger was triggered by Prudential's $385 million takeover of Bache, and may presage the formation of other huge financial conglomerates.

A national-market test was postponed by the SEC until March 1, 1982. The experiment, linking the OTC and seven exchanges, had been scheduled for Sept. 30, but the industry said the deadline couldn't be met.

Durable goods orders rose an adjusted 1.3% in March to $83.35 billion. The Commerce Department said much of the jump was caused by aircraft orders, while most major industry groups had declines.

Voluntary export cuts of Japanese cars appear likely to be agreed on. Officials in Tokyo reportedly are proposing that exports be held to about 1.7 million cars, a compromise between last year's shipments and a level suggested in Congress.

Satellite TV broadcasts directly to homes were approved by the FCC. The agency accepted the first application for the service, expected to start in about five years, from a Comsat subsidiary.

23 Nabisco and Standard Brands agreed to merge into a new company, Nabisco Brands Inc. In 1980, the two major food companies earned $232 million on sales of more than $5.5 billion. Terms call for each share of Nabisco stock to be converted into 1.4 shares of Nabisco Brands, while Standard Brands shares would be exchanged on a one-for-one basis.

Reagan's economic plan was criticized by Henry Kaufman, an influential financial analyst. Kaufman supported increased arms spending and eased regulation, but called the overall program "extremely expansionary" and said it may aggravate inflation.

24 Consumer prices rose an adjusted 0.6% in March, equal to a 7.2% annual rate before compounding. The increase compares with a 1% rise in February and reflects a slowdown in energy price rises, the Labor Department said. Analysts believe the March rate could be repeated in the next few months, but some think inflation could accelerate in 1981's second half.

Federal S&Ls and mutual savings banks will be able to peg mortgage rates to public indexes and vary terms to reflect market conditions. The new rule was adopted by the FHLB board yesterday, but it may be years before such loans become common.

Sales of U.S. cars in mid-April continued at depressed levels. Deliveries totaled 147,406 units, up 0.8% from a year earlier and equal to a 5.7 million annual rate.

Spot oil prices are poised for a sharp drop, traders say, with Libya, Algeria and Nigeria most likley to be affected. One observer thinks their oil could fall to $34 a barrel from $36.50, with heavier crude dropping to $32 from $34.50.

Strategic oil reserve funds, severely cut by the Senate, will be taken up by the Cabinet today. Proposals include a direct congressional appropriation, "borrowing" synfuel funds, and authorizing Treasury borrowing to pay for the program.

27 Savings withdrawals from the nation's S&Ls exceeded deposits by a record $2.26 billion in March, far wider than the $1.7 billion gap an industry group had forecast. The $786 million total outflow in the first quarter was the first since 1974's third period. The industry has been unable to compete with high yield money-market funds, which have gained an average $2.7 billion a week since Jan. 1.

Machine tool orders rose in March after five

consecutive declines. Orders totaled $350.8 million, up 26% from February but off 34% from the year earlier. Some executives doubt the pickup will be sustained until later this year.

Limits on brokers' providing banklike services are expected to be a major issue at the Securities Industry Association meeting. Some officials fear that the growth of such services makes it harder to argue against banks entering securities activities.

28 General motors first quarter earnings rose 23% to $190.3 million, or 63 cents a share, on flat sales of $15.72 billion. GM attributed the gain chiefly to extensive cost-cutting measures, which reduced expenses by $94.9 million from a year earlier. Analysts had expected a profit decline.

Car export curbs by Japanese auto makers may be agreed on soon. U.S. Trade Negotiator Brock begins high-level talks in Tokyo tomorrow, but the administration emphasized that the Japanese must work out their own restraint plan.

Business productivity rose at an adjusted 3.6% annual rate in the first quarter, following a revised 0.4% decline in 1980's fourth period. The increase was expected because of the strong 6.5% annual growth rate of the economy in the quarter.

Dairy price supports that could cost more then $4 billion over the next four years were approved by the Senate Agriculture Committee. Dairy interests successfully lobbied against White House proposals to limit spending to $2.3 billion.

29 President Reagan urged a joint session of Congress to clear his tax and budget cuts as soon as possible. The speech was timed to coincide with consideration of his economic plan by both the House and a Senate committee. He endorsed an alternate budget measure in the House differing from one approved earlier by the House Budget panel.

A budget resolution backed by the White House was passed by the Senate Budget Committee. The measure, which sets targets for fiscal 1981 through 1984, was assailed by some Democrats as based on "gimmicks" and "phony accounting."

Ford and Chrysler losses continued in the first quarter. Ford's deficit widened to $439.5 million from the year earlier $163.6 million. Sales declined 3.1%. Chrysler's loss narrowed to $298.4 million from $448.8 million, but was about $30 million greater than expected. Sales rose 3.4%.

U.S. Steel profit jumped 115% in the first quarter, buoyed by improved steelmaking performance and a gain on the sale of coal properties. But Bethlehem, citing cost increases, posted a 52% drop on a 3.7% sales decline.

The U.S. trade gap on a merchandise basis narrowed in March to an adjusted $451.4 million. The Commerce Department credited a surge in exports and a sharp drop in oil imports for the improvement.

30 Leading indicators of the economy rose 1.4% in March, following three consecutive declines. Economists, however, doubt the turnaround signals future economic vitality. They cite a statistical distortion caused by the rapid rise in crude oil prices following decontrol in late January.

The prime rate was raised to 18% from 17½% by many of the nation's largest banks, which cited jumps in their own borrowing costs. The increase set the Dow Jones industrial average plummeting 12.61 points to 1004.32. Bond prices also fell amid concerns about inflation.

Ford will boost car prices an average of 2.1%, or $178 a unit, effective tomorrow. It had vowed to freeze prices through today, and analysts said cost pressures forced the increase.

Building awards rose 27% in March to $13.9 billion from $10.94 billion a year earlier, McGraw-Hill's F. W. Dodge unit said.

New-home sales rose 0.6% in March to an adjusted annual rate of 511,000. The performance was 8.5% above a year earlier and followed a decline of 3.2% in February.

May 1981

1 Chrysler and Mitsubishi agreed in principle to allow the Japanese company to set up its own U.S. dealer network. Mitsubishi will provide Chrysler with a wider range of products and will consider investing in the U.S. car maker. Chrysler also said it is raising prices on domestic cars and options an average 2.6%, or $194 a unit.

Auto production in May is scheduled to increase 27% from the distressed year-earlier month. Car makers plan 666,220 assemblies to rebuild dealers' stocks and carry them through summer plant closings.

Factory orders rose 1.3% in March to an adjusted $164.87 billion. The total was buoyed by strength in aircraft and aircraft parts.

Large railroads are under a Justice Department criminal antitrust investigation. The agency seeks to determine if they conspired to reduce boxcar rentals from smaller railroads.

Farm prices fell 0.4% in April, the fourth drop in a row. Declines were recorded for such major products as soybeans, wheat, corn and chickens.

4 Japan's accord limiting its car exports to the U.S. has eased a trade rift and averted a clash between Reagan and Congress over quotas. The pact calls for Japan to limit exports for two years and possibly a third. Shipments in the first year will be held to 1.68 million, compared with 1.82 million in 1980. But sales could be increased if the domestic market improves.

The U.S. auto market may see higher import prices, but the Japan pact is likely to have a relatively modest effect on the U.S. industry. Economists say it probably won't help sell many more domestic cars or reduce industry unemployment soon.

Construction spending fell 2.4% in March to an adjusted $248 billion annual rate. It was the second decline in a row, following a revised 3% drop in February, but was still 4.6% above the depressed level of March 1980.

Higher interest rates are sure to follow last week's surprising $4.2 billion jump in the money supply, specialists say. Bankers warn of a swift rise to 19% for the prime rate.

5 The discount rate was raised to a record 14% from 13% by the Federal Reserve System and the penalty surcharge for frequent borrowers to four percentage points from three. The measures to curb the soaring money supply followed a boost in the prime rate to 19% from 18% by most major banks. Treasury bill yields surged at the latest auction, with the 13-week issue rising to 15.963% and 26-week bills to 15.104%. Both rates were the highest since Dec. 15.

GM is delaying parts of its $40 billion, five-year capital spending program because of a cash crunch caused by sluggish car sales. Despite the pinch, directors voted to pay a regular 60-cent quarterly dividend.

6 The prime rate could rise again soon to 19½% or 20% from the 19% level set Monday. Bankers say pressure for an increase is mounting because of continuing rises in their own borrowing costs. The Treasury auctioned $3 billion of three-year notes at a record yield of 15.81%, up sharply from a 13.37% rate for comparable notes last Feb. 17.

Sales of U.S. cars fell 17% in April from the depressed year-earlier levels. Deliveries totaled 529,271 units, the lowest level since last June. Import sales rose 7.4% in the month to 216,500 units.

The U.S. dollar hit its highest level in more than four years, then retreated on profit taking. On the Comex, gold rose 20 cents an ounce to $480.90.

7 Antitrust cases against AT&T and IBM show little hope of settlement, Assistant Attorney General Baxter said. He also advocated broad changes in antitrust laws and their application, but has decided against attempting to repeal the Robinson-Patman act.

Lower oil prices called for by Saudi Arabia apparently won't be pressed by the country's oil minister. Sheik Yamani, at a meeting of Arab oil producers, denied urging reductions, saying he advocated a long-term policy of gradual, predictable increases.

Gasoline price wars are reappearing in the Midwest. Several big refiners, including Arco, Mobil and Indiana Standard, have trimmed wholesale quotes as much as seven cents a gallon. They attribute the cuts to fierce competition resulting from sharply lower consumption.

Nonstock options trading could be broadened by the addition of Treasury securities. The SEC called for comment on the proposal, which would expand authority to trade Ginnie Maes that the agency granted in February. The Chicago Board of Trade has sued to overturn that action.

8 Budget cuts of $36.6 billion were approved in a House resolution, 253 to 176. The measure, similar in size and nature to a $36.9 billion Senate resolution, targets social programs, including school lunches, food stamps and health and environment outlays. House and Senate committees now must implement the cuts for congressional approval in a process expected to take until mid-June at the earliest.

Consumer credit rose an adjusted $3.11 billion in March, the biggest gain in 1½ years and equal to a 12% annual rate. More than half the increase came from auto loans.

Retail sales were strong for the second month in a row in April on rising consumer confidence, greater credit use and a continued low saving rate. Montgomery Ward posted a 22% gain, Penney 21.8%, Sears 20.4% and K mart 18.4%.

A second AT&T rise in rates was approved by the FCC. The action affects a long-distance service heavily used by government and big companies, and brings the total increase to 35%.

Mortgage rates on federally backed home loans were allowed to rise to a record 15½% by the government. The move, from the previous high of 14½%, stems from surging interest rates generally.

11 The U.S. Economy may worsen soon from April's showing, economists fear. Producer prices for finished goods rose an adjusted 0.8% last month, equal to a 9.6% annual rate before compounding, and unemployment held steady for the third month in a row at 7.3% of the work force. But economists say energy and food prices may accelerate soon, and a slowing economy could worsen the jobless rate.

Interest rates and prices will fall only gradually through 1982, economists for 20 major companies told the Business Council. They forecast long-term interest rates of 14% to 16% through next year, and inflation rates of 10.8% in 1981 and 9% in 1982.

Crude oil prices in the U.S. fell, reflecting a world-wide glut and sagging consumption. Cities Service and Phillips cut the price they'll pay for U.S. production $2 a barrel, and other major refiners also trimmed quotes.

AT&T long-distance rates for conventional and WATS service will increase 16% Thursday. Private-line charges will increase 35%, and former Telpak users will pay an additional 72.8%.

LIFO accounting can be used by subsidiaries while the parent company uses FIFO for consolidated results, a federal court said. The ruling, in a case involving Insilco Corp., may cause many concerns to switch accounting methods.

International air fares can be raised 3½% to 11% effective June 1, the CAB ruled. The size of the increases will depend on whether carriers take them for two months or four.

12 The prime rate was raised to 19½% from 19% by most major banks, the fourth rise in a month. Bankers cited increased costs of obtaining lendable funds and a surge in loan demand. Bond and commodity prices tumbled, while the Dow Jones industrial average lost 12.96 to close at 963.44. At the Treasury's latest auction, the average yield on 13-week bills soared to 16.433% and on the 26-week issue to 15.531%.

The French franc sank 3.2% against the U.S. dollar in the wake of Mitterrand's election. It was the lowest level in almost 10 years and helped pull other European currencies down. Prices on the Paris Bourse tumbled on a wave of sell orders by nervous investors. But in French foreign policy, analysts see little chance of abrupt changes.

U.S. Steel prices will be raised at least $10 a ton across the board to cover energy costs and some quotes will rise as much as $50 a ton.

Allied Corp. agreed to acquire Bunker Ramo in a transaction valued at $358 million. Terms call for Allied to offer $55 each for 1,175,000 Bunker Ramo common and convertible preferred shares, and accept a further 434,000 under certain conditions.

Social Security cuts intended to save $7.9 billion a year reportedly are expected to be proposed by Reagan today. A White House spokesman indicated the major effect of the program would be on future retirees.

The winter-wheat crop was forecast at a record 2.08 billion bushels this year, 10% greater than in 1980. The Agriculture Department also predicted an 11% increase in the Soviet grain harvest.

13 Social Security cuts of more than $46 billion over five years were added to Reagan's proposal, with lower tax rates a year or two after enactment of the bill. Total savings through 1986 are estimated at up to $111 billion. The plan would pare benefits for persons retiring between age 62 and 65, and change the date for computing cost-of-living adjustments to September from June. The adjustments also would be based on a 12-month period rather than the first quarter.

Retail sales fell 1% in April to an adjusted $86.31 billion, the first decrease since May 1980. The March total was revised upward to show a rise of 0.4% to $87.17 billion. A sharp drop in auto sales was blamed for April's decline.

Kuwait's oil output was cut 250,000 barrels a day to 1.2 million. The move, reflecting the current glut and a desire to conserve resources, may pressure Saudi Arabia to trim its production of over 10 million barrels a day.

Conrail's sale to other railroads was endorsed by the Senate Commerce Committee. The action enhanced prospects of full backing by Congress.

14 Sales of U.S. cars in early May rose 6.1% from the depressed year-earlier level. The increase, to an estimated 133,763 units, was far less than analysts had expected, perhaps due to price increases. Chrysler posted a 38.8% rise and Ford 22.5%. GM sales fell 2.3%, Volkswagen of America's 14.4%, and AMC had an estimated 16% drop.

Business inventories rose $1.04 billion, or 0.2%, in March to an adjusted $471.84

billion. February's increase was revised to $5.7 billion, or 1.2%.

Reagan's tax plan faces amendments to win Finance Committee support, several Senators suggested. But Treasury Secretary Regan reiterated the President's commitment to the measure until "we see something superior."

An antitrust probe of the auto industry was dropped by the FTC. The agency cited economic changes and increased competition among car makers for ending the five-year investigation.

15 A budget compromise was reached by House and Senate conferees. The $695.45 billion measure projects a fiscal 1982 deficit of $37.65 billion, very close to Reagan's program. The plan is likely to win easy approval by both houses next week.

Retail gasoline discounts for customers paying cash are being considered by Exxon. The refiner cited evidence that motorists would prefer the policy, which would cut administrative costs and could touch off a wave of price reductions.

The surging U.S. dollar reached its highest level in eight years before ending slightly lower on profit taking. Gold rose $5 an ounce on the Comex to $483.40.

Savings bank losses at 10 big New York City institutions exceeded $112 million in the first quarter. The results caused alarm for the nation's other, more troubled thrifts.

U.S. oil imports fell in April to 5.4 million barrels a day, their lowest level since 1973. The total was off 22.6% from 1980 and covered 35% of domestic consumption compared with 42% a year earlier.

18 Industrial output in April was "stronger than expected but weak compared with previous recoveries," one economist said. Production rose 0.4% last month after increasing 0.5% in March and declining 0.1% in February. The Fed said production would have climbed 0.7% if coal miners hadn't been on strike.

Bethlehem Steel undercut U.S. Steel's boosts for domestic steel prices after the Commerce Department said its trigger prices for most imported steel wouldn't be increased for the third quarter. Inland Steel price boosts also appeared to undercut U.S. Steel's.

19 The economy has slowed since the first quarter but hasn't lost all its steam, three government reports show. Personal income rose 0.6% in April, the smallest rise since June, and personal consumption spending increased a slight 0.2%. But housing starts rose an adjusted 4.2% last month, and the nation's factory operating rate climbed to an adjusted 80.3% of capacity.

The prime rate was raised to 20% from 19½% by most large banks because of increased loan demand and the banks' high borrowing costs. But bond prices rose on hopes that interest rates may be near their peak. The rate on 13-week Treasury bills fell to 16.034% from 16.433% and dropped on the 26-week issue to 15.025% from 15.531%.

Private pension plans may reduce a retired employee's benefits by the amount of a workers' compensation award, the Supreme Court ruled. States also can't bar pension plans that contain such offset provisions, the Justices said.

The Supreme Court ruled that businesses that prove they faced price discrimination also must prove they were injured before damages are awarded. The decision rejects an Alabama car dealership's suit against Chrysler Corp.

A federal agency will begin to pay about $60 million to insured depositors of Economy Savings & Loan of Chicago. It is the first time in nearly a decade that the Federal Savings & Loan Insurance Corp. has paid depositors of a defunct S&L.

20 Gross National Product expanded at an 8.4% annual rate after inflation during the first quarter, a revised Commerce Department report said. The new estimate is stronger than the 6.5% growth rate reported a month ago and is the most robust since the 9% rate in the second quarter of 1978. The department also said aftertax corporate profits rose 2.4% in the quarter to a $168.3 billion annual rate.

22 A prime rate boost to 20½% from 20% appears increasingly likely, bankers say, because of surges in their own borrowing costs. But they caution that today's reports on the money supply and consumer prices could ease pressures on short-term rates.

Xerox Corp. is prepared to reduce copier prices further to fight stiff Japanese competition and increase market share. The company, which operates 16 retail stores in the U.S. and the U.K., said it will double that number in the next few months.

The dollar surged against major currencies, buoyed by an increase in interest rates and the weakness of the French franc. Gold's price fell $14.30 an ounce to $467.

The Fed's Open Market Committee voted in late March to ease its short-term money and credit growth targets, but the Fed later was forced to increase its bank lending rate to stem a surge in money growth.

Currency controls to bolster the French franc were imposed by Pierre Mauroy, who was named prime minister after Socialist leader Francois Mitterrand was inaugurated as president. The controls resist foreign-currency purchases by French exporters and other businesses to finance operations and curb purchases of foreign exchange by French residents to buy foreign securities.

U.S. auto makers planned to build 156,928 cars this week, 6.9% less than last week but 34% more than a year earlier when 14 plants were closed.

26 Bond markets welcomed government reports that the nation's money supply fell and inflation slowed. But many traders and analysts say they expect inflation to speed up this summer, with interest rates hitting highs.

Savings and loan associations had a record $4.6 billion net savings outflow in April, according to preliminary government figures. Officials cited competition from money-market mutual funds and seasonal withdrawals by taxpayers waiting until the last moment to meet the April 15 filing deadline.

Consumer prices won't continue to grow at April's modest rate unless wages and interest rates ease, economists warn. Prices rose 0.4% in April, or at a 4.8% annual rate before compounding, and marked the smallest increase since July.

Machine tool orders fell 25% in April from a year earlier, and industry executives say they don't see any signs of an immediate upturn. Producers cite high interest rates and slack plant capacity.

27 U.S. Steel partially rolled back planned price increases to match more modest boosts posted by Bethlehem Steel. U.S. Steel said the rises will take effect June 21.

Chrysler and Peugeot, the French auto maker, plan to build a new subcompact car in the U.S. for the 1986 model year. Chrysler also agreed to buy 450,000 Peugeot four-cyclinder diesel engines over five years, beginning with 1984 models.

28 Oil product prices on the domestic spot market fell in the wake of OPEC's failure to agree on unified quotes. Gasoline and heating oil dropped a cent a gallon and experts say further cuts are likely. Crude oil was firm, but traders expect a decline of as much as $1 a barrel early next week. One trader said retail gasoline prices could fall as much as 10 to 15 cents a gallon in the next few months.

OPEC members set the stage for reaching a comprehensive price and production accord by year-end. Officials froze current prices but didn't mention Saudi Arabia's lower quotes, and the Saudis apparently left the door open for an increase in their $32-a-barrel price later this year.

Business productivity rose at an adjusted 4% annual rate in the first quarter, the Labor Department said. The increase had been put at 3.6%, but was revised to reflect in part an upward adjustment in overall economic growth.

29 Leading indicators of economic activity rose a modest 0.4% in April, protending slower business growth ahead. While most analysts acknowledge a substantial slowdown has occurred, few expect weakness to the point of a decline.

The prime rate fell slightly as Chase Manhattan shaved the fee to 20% from 20½% and some smaller banks posted similar cuts. The move follows recent sharp declines in banks' own borrowing costs.

Oil price cuts of up to $6 a barrel will be sought on foreign crude by several international oil companies. In a tough new bargaining stance, officials say they'll sharply cut or terminate supply contracts if producers refuse.

June 1981

2 Two failing S&Ls, in New York and Illinois, were merged into stronger institutions, one a savings bank. The cost to the Federal Savings and Loan Insurance Corp. of paying depositors wasn't disclosed, but is expected to be substantial.

Oil prices will be frozen at least through 1982 and may have reached a peak for the next several years, a top OPEC official said. A Western analyst said further price increases could threaten the organization's existence.

IBM and the government rested their cases in their 12-year-old antitrust battle. The company said it requested a meeting to discuss settling or dropping some issues, apparently due to a recent decision in an AT&T unit case.

3 Chrysler in on target with goals set last winter when it recieved its most recent federal loan guarantee. Sales are up from last year, and market share is stronger, but a second quarter profit isn't expected by analysts.

Commodity options trading on futures exchanges would be opened under regulatory proposals. Contracts based on gold, sugar and Ginnie Mae securities futures would be listed, but obstacles remain before trading can begin.

4 The British pound fell more than five cents to trade below $2 for the first time in more than two years. Traders expect U.K. oil revenue to head lower.

Spot oil prices tumbled, with a cargo of Arab light crude selling at $32.15 a barrel. Libya reportedly will cut its price $5 a barrel by allowing spot sales at $36, and there were indications that contract prices are poised to drop both in the U.S. and abroad.

5 A 25% tax cut over 33 months beginning Oct. 1 was endorsed by Reagan. The announcement followed a series of meetings with Republican and Democratic lawmakers to fashion a bipartisan coalition to enact the measure. The proposed bill also drops the top rate on investment income to 50% from 70%.

Retail sales rose at most big chains in May as consumer confidence continued a slow recovery. Sears had a 12.7% gain, K mart 9.9%, Dayton Hudson 26.8%, Federated 14% and Montgomery Ward 12.2%.

The U.S. dollar soared to its highest level in nearly 10 years as selling pressure mounted against European currencies. The British pound fell nearly three cents to $1.9615, after a drop of more than five cents Wednesday.

Common Market steelmakers will cut production and raise prices between 15% and 20% July 1. The voluntary agreement by members' economics ministers is intended to restore the industry's competitive stance internationally.

8 Nigeria cut its oil price $4 a barrel for some crude, the first major cut by an OPEC member. Observers think the world price soon will be $3 to $4 a barrel lower than at the start of the year, a drop of about 10%.

Coal miners ratified a new 40-month contract, ending a 72-day strike. But miners in some areas are expected to remain off the job pending a separate settlement by 11,000 UMW mine construction workers, which could come this week.

West Side Federal a New York City S&L and the East Coast's largest, may be a bellwether case in shaping government policy on troubled thrifts. Analysts fear its collapse could cost federal insurers as much as $700 million and shake public faith in savings institutions.

9 Exxon cut prices of heavy-fuel oil on the East Coast for the second time in less then three weeks. New prices for the fuel, used by large buildings, heavy industry and electrical utilities, range from $26 to $34 a barrel, and should put additional downward pressure on quotes for other petroleum products.

Spot-market oil purchases for the strategic petroleum reserve will be stepped up by the Energy Department with part of a $1.3 billion supplemental appropriation.

The money had been earmarked for contract purchases.

10 The prime rate is under growing pressure for a reduction to 19½% from 20%, bankers say. They cite continued sluggish business-loan demand and reduced costs for lendable funds. The broker-loan rate was trimmed to 19½% from 20½% by several big banks while others lowered it to 20% from 21%.

Soviet grain purchases from the U.S. could resume by Sept. 30, U.S. negotiators indicate, but the Soviets don't appear anxious to buy. An agreement, covering six million metric tons of corn and wheat valued at $856 million, doesn't commit Moscow to make the purchase.

11 The prime rate was cut to 19½% from 20% by Marine Midland Bank, reflecting declines in its own borrowing costs. Bankers expect the new rate to become widespread by early next week, and analysts say further declines are likely this month if the economy slows and business-loan demand remains sluggish.

Gasoline prices were cut as much as three cents a gallon at wholesale by five of the top 10 marketers in the past two days. The reductions primarily in the Midwest and South reflect excess supplies and a determination to avoid high storage costs.

The U.S. bought oil for the strategic petroleum reserve for $178 million on the spot market. The 5.5 million barrels purchased represent about 3.5% of the amount offered under its latest bid.

AT&T offered 16.5 million shares at $57 each, a total of $941 million. Despite the big sale, the price of the company's shares remained stable in Big Board trading.

12 Retail sales rose a slim 0.2% in May to an adjusted $85.89 billion, providing further evidence that the economy has reached a plateau. The gain failed to make up for a revised 2.1% decline in April. But the lack of growth also indicated that prices were relatively stable, a Commerce Department analyst said.

Mitsubishi won't invest in Chrysler until both concerns are financially healthier, the Japanese auto maker said. Mitsubishi blamed "at least half" of its 41% earnings drop last year on its partnership with Chrysler.

S&L's don't need a bailout but could use new lines of business, Federal Home Loan Bank Board Chairman Pratt said. He and other regulators are working on plans to let thrifts invest in commerical property and widen their depositors.

15 Interest rates seem ready for further siza-

ble declines this summer. Many brokers and economists say reduced inflation, a sluggish ecomony and deceleration in the growth of the nation's money supply will ease pressure on capital markets. And some economists contend that an expected surge in corporate bond offerings will allow repayment of bank borrowings, easing short-term demand.

16 The prime rate was reduced by Chemical Bank to 19% from 20% and other short-term interest rates fell. The declines helped spark rallies in bond and stock prices, pushing the Dow Jones industrial average up 5.71 points to 1011.99. The average return on 13-week Treasury bills auctioned yesterday plummeted to 13.451% from 14.982% and the return on 26-week bills fell to 13.356% from 14%.

U.S. car sales rose more than 10% in early June to about 174,170, up from last year's depressed level. But the sales were still at one of the lowest rates in the past two decades.

North Sea oil prices were slashed nearly 11% by Britain, to $35 a barrel. The government will link future changes more closely to Saudi Arabia's quotes rather than those of North African producers, who sell the most expensive oil on the market.

Federal curbs on strip mining were upheld by the Supreme Court. The ruling permits the Interior Department to enforce the law's stiff environmental controls even as Secretary Watt is moving to loosen them.

17 Housing starts fell 14% in May to an adjusted annual rate of 1,152,000 units, the lowest level in a year, as high interest rates discouraged buyers. Industrial output rose a modest 0.3%. Both figures showed the sluggishness in the economy that experts predicted for the second quarter.

18 A strict OSHA rule limiting workers' exposure to cotton dust was upheld by the Supreme Court. In a five-to-three vote, Justices said benefits of such federal safety rules shouldn't be measured against the costs, which are estimated at $656.5 million or more for the textile companies.

The decision will force many other industries to give workers more protection against disease-causing substances. It also is expected to spur a trend toward more efficient textile equipment.

Personal income rose 0.6% in May, the same as in April, to an adjusted $2.367 trillion annual rate. The operating rate of U.S. factories edged up to an adjusted

80.1% last month from 80% in April. The reports added to expectation of flat economic growth this summer.

19 Interest rates surged and bond prices plunged, causing IBM and General Foods to postpone major financings. Several major banks raised broker-loan rates. Soaring interest rates pushed the dollar up in foreign-exchange trading and helped drive stock prices down. The Dow Jones industrial average closed at 995.15, off 11.41 points.

The economy won't expand in the second quarter, preliminary government statistics indicate. Estimates also show inflation is slowing substantially from a 9.8% clip in the first quarter. Gross national product adjusted for inflation grew at an 8.6% annual pace in the first quarter, up from 8.4% estimated earlier.

A current account surplus of $3.09 billion was registered in the first quarter. But a government spokesman predicted foreign nations are likely to subsidize exports, making it harder for the U.S. to compete.

22 The oil glut will last as long as three years because of significant changes in oil consumption, OPEC members believe. Venezuela's oil minister is pushing for a freeze at $36 a barrel for two or three years on the organization's benchmark crude.

Durable goods orders fell an adjusted 0.4% in May to $83.94 billion, the first decline since January. The retreat followed a revised increase of 0.1% in April to $84.29 billion.

Lower interest rates could return after last week's turmoil in credit markets, bankers and economists contend. They predict further downward pressure for much of the summer.

23 A nationwide strike by air traffic controllers was narrowly averted as their union agreed to a $40 million-a-year pact with the government. But the 42-month accord, which must be approved by the union's 15,000 members, could meet resistance in a ratification vote expected to be completed within three weeks. The agreement provides average pay boosts of 6.6%, or about $2,000 a year, immediately and provides overtime after 36 hours.

Reagan stepped up personal lobbying for his tax-cut and budget-restraint measures. The budget issue could emerge on the House floor this week, and White House aides view it as the toughest fight yet on the administration's economic package.

Employers can close part of a business for

economic reasons without bargaining with employes, the high court ruled. The decision could push unions to include bargaining over partial closures in future labor pacts.

Oil-market turbulence is intensifying as refiners back away from contracts and spot-market prices continue to tumble. A price barrier was broken when Saudi light crude came on the market 50 cents below the official $32-a-barrel price.

24 Mexico proposed raising its average oil price $2 a barrel, trimming a recent $4 cut. Four African nations said they intend to keep crude prices at current official levels.

Consumer prices rose an adjusted 0.7% in May, or at an 8.4% annual rate before compounding, the Labor Department said. Mortgage costs helped accelerate the rise, though food prices fell and fuel increases were moderate. Commerce Secretary Baldrige reiterated a prediction that consumer prices will climb about 9% this year.

25 U.S. car sales fell 8.6% in mid-June, surprising analysts, who had predicted a slight gain and couldn't explain the decline. Sales were estimated at 170,870 units, down from 186,979 a year earlier.

Japan set quotas for its car makers' shipments to the U.S. in the first year of a three-year export restraint program, eliciting protests from the companies. Separately, Ford said talks about Toyota on a possible joint venture in the U.S. again are focusing on producing a passenger car rather than a van.

A synfuels plant agreement with the U.S. for a project in West Virginia was scrapped by West Germany and Japan. The plan, opposed by the Reagan administration, was shelved because of "unforeseen cost increases" and other problems, U.S. energy officials said.

26 The Senate cleared the way for approving a massive budget cutback bill that would trim scheduled spending in the next fiscal year about $39.4 billion. Over four fiscal years, the cuts would total over $140 billion, through more than 200 changes in existing laws. And by curbing domestic social programs, the Senate may reverse 50 years of federal government expansion.

Reagan's tax package passed the Senate Finance Committee with only minor changes. The measure calls for a 25% cut in individual tax rates, faster business depreciation write-offs and provisions to spur savings and investment. Over four fiscal years, the package's tax cuts total

about $3.4 billion less than proposed by Reagan.

29 Reagan's budget triumphs gave him new political momentum and a firmer grasp on economic policy. The last serious obstacle to White House budget policy collapsed Friday when the Democratic House voted to cut as much as $145 billion through fiscal 1984. Senate and House victories allow the President to reduce or kill more than 200 programs.

Economic gains slowed in June, as high interest rates hurt expansion and production, a monthly survey of industrial purchasing managers found.

The trade deficit narrowed in May to an adjusted $3.44 billion as oil imports fell to the lowest level in six years. That drop was largely offset by burgeoning nonoil imports, however, and Commerce Secretary Baldrige predicted the year's deficit will be "several billion dollars" wider than 1980's.

Machine-tool orders fell 47% in May to $229.8 million. High interest rates and uncertainty over tax policy concerning capital equipment continue to depress orders, industry officials say.

Foreign-steel sales and possible dumping of steel products are under investigation by the Commerce Department in a bid to head off independent action by domestic producers. May steel imports were high for the second consecutive month, the agency said.

30 American Telephone was found guilty of monopolization, predatory and anticompetitive conduct against Litton Industries' efforts to maintain an office switchboard and key telephone business. Litton tentatively was awarded $92.2 million, which under antitrust law could be tripled, in its $570 million four-year-old suit.

Home sales rose 15.6% in May to an adjusted annual rate of 504,000 units despite near-record interest rates. The median price of new homes increased to $72,600 from April's $69,000.

The Treasury issued rules allowing the sale of $15 billion in tax-exempt single-family mortgage subsidy bonds this year. Sales of the bonds, applicable only to low- to moderate-income housing, are expected to begin within two weeks.

Construction contracts fell an adjusted 7% in May to $13.4 billion, F. W. Dodge said. Attributing the continuing decline to high interest rates and budget curbs, McGraw-Hill's economic forecasting unit predicted a second half rebound.

Gold plummeted $14.40 to $426.80 an

ounce on the Comex, fueled by a strong dollar and expectations of easing U.S. inflation.

July 1981

1 Leading indicators of the economy fell 1.8% in May, after two monthly increases. The index's decline was the largest since May 1980's 2.5% drop. The Commerce Department also reported that new factory orders, bolstered by a 21% jump in aircraft orders, rose 0.6% in May to an adjusted $164.93 billion.

The New York Futures Exchange, over competitors' protests, won permission to trade futures in bank certificates of deposit. The CFTC decision gives the fledgling Big Board unit a head start against established Chicago exchanges in trading what's expected to be a hot item. Trading may begin in two or three weeks.

OPEC may hold an extraordinary meeting as soon as September, reportedly spurred by Algeria's concern about declining demand for its oil. Libya offered a $1.10-a-barrel cut in its third quarter quote, to about $40 a barrel.

2 Economic recovery will develop next year, led by stronger auto and housing sales and easing inflation and interest rates, Treasury Secretary Regan predicted. The second quarter economy was flat, following strong first quarter growth, and this quarter may be "negative," with increased unemployment, he said. But Regan forecast a fourth quarter turnaround.

Construction spending fell 4.7% in May, the Commerce Department said, supporting the widely held view that the economy is weakening. The decline, to an adjusted $237.3 billion annual rate, was the fourth consecutive montly drop and was the largest since a 5.1% decline in April 1980.

6 Job opportunities and the economy have stopped growing, analysts say. The Labor Department reported the unemployment rate fell to an adjusted 7.3% of the work force in June, but analysts cited statistical flaws.

Interest-rate futures markets are expected to gain substantial participation because of federal action allowing wider trading by savings and loans. New rules permit the nation's nearly 4,000 federally insured S&Ls to take positions hedging all their assets.

The Supreme Court upheld a state tax on coal mined in Montana. The ruling, a boon for mineral-rich states, rejected a challenge by Commonwealth Edison and 10 other utilities. Their suit argued that the tax's severity interfered with interstate commerce, violating the Constitution.

7 Dupont agreed to buy Conoco for $6.82 billion. The company resulting from the largest transaction in corporate history would have annual revenue of about $32 billion, placing it seventh on the Fortune 500 list. The plan includes $3 billion in bank loans and is considered an attempt to thwart Seagram's $2.55 billion unwanted bid for 41% of Conoco's common.

The dollar rose to its highest level against West German currency in nearly five years and hit a record against the French franc. The mark toppled on German economists' predictions of a merely sluggish 1981 economic recovery and low international confidence in the currency.

Gold fell below $400 before closing at $400.20 an ounce on the Comex, its lowest level in 20 months. Yesterday's $11.90 slide marked the ninth consecutive day of falling bullion prices and reflected European selling and a strong U.S. dollar.

Economists who predicted low mid-year interest rates in January are undeterred by their miscalculation: most foresee lower rates by year-end.

Home mortgage rates rose to record levels in early June. A Federal Home Loan Bank Board survey said lenders requested an average 16.75% effective interest rate for a standard 25-year mortgage, up from early May's 16.12%.

9 The prime rate was raised to 20½% from 20% by major banks, bringing the rate to within one percentage point of December's record 21½%. Citibank initiated the increases, matching boosts last Thursday by Chase and First National Bank of Chicago. Bankers said the move reflected continued high borrowing costs and businesses' increased use of short-term credit.

The Justice Department dropped two civil antitrust suits, reflecting the administration's antitrust policy. One suit charged Mack Trucks, a Signal Cos. unit, with conspiring to fix prices and the other challenged the merger of two large facing-brick makers.

10 Retail sales rose in June from a year earlier, when credit restraints choked consumer spending. Sears, the biggest retailer, posted a 17.8% gain; K mart, the No. 2 chain, a 17.1% boost. Analysts called the results, after adjustment for inflation, es-

sentially flat, but said an October tax cut could help sales.

13 Seagram will battle Du Pont for control of Conoco. The Canadian distiller increased and broadened its cash bid to $85 a share for 51% of the ninth-largest U.S. oil company. The value of Seagram's offer is $3.77 billion. Conoco said it's studying the amended bid.

The money supply fell $1.3 billion to an adjusted $427.3 billion for the week ended July 1, the Federal Reserve said. The decline in the measure, known as M1-B, fuels bankers' and economists' contentions that the Fed is easing credit reins.

14 SEC Chairman John Shad said the billions of dollars spent on corporate takeovers is healthy for the economy. Takeovers by Canadian firms add capital to the marketplace. But he expressed concern that foreign investors, exempt from U.S. credit requirements, have an unfair advantage.

15 Du Pont sweetened its purchase offer for Conoco to about $7.5 billion in cash and stock, escalating the bidding war for the nation's ninth-largest oil company. Conoco's board approved the revised bid of $95 a share for 40% of Conoco's stock and 1.7 Du Pont common shares for each remaining Conoco share. But Seagram said its bid remains competitive and observers expect a proposal from Mobil as early as today.

U.S. car sales fell 18% to an estimated 127,817 units in early July, continuing an unexpected dive that began in mid-June. Indicators favored an upturn, and analysts still can't explain the decline.

Pan American plans to trim flights and routes about 10% by this fall in an effort to stem mounting losses. In slashing certain vacation routes, major parts of the former National Air system, acquired in 1980, will be dismantled.

16 The 1981 budget deficit will be "in the range of $55 billion," said Budget Chief David Stockman, trying to refute Wall Street fears that the deficit, and Treasury borrowing, will exceed administration projections. His office also estimated a federal deficit of $42.5 billion for fiscal 1982. High interest rates raised spending, but an offsetting rise in tax receipts kept the projected deficits close to initial estimates.

U.S. industrial output fell an adjusted 0.1% in June, indicating economic stagnation. The production decline, the first since February, is "pervasive, though not sizable," a Fed analyst said. Overall eco-

nomic growth isn't expected to resume until the fourth quarter.

17 Fed Chairman Paul Volcker said monetary policies won't be relaxed, despite complaints that high interest rates here are hurting European economies. The U.S. shouldn't and can't assume responsibility "for all the economic difficulties" of other nations, he told a congressional panel in advance of next week's economic summit in Ottawa.

Factory operating rates slowed in June to an adjusted 79.6% of capacity from 80.1% in May as weakness pervaded the economy. The sluggish demand reflected in the low operating rate is expected to soften prices and help reduce inflation.

20 Mobil's decision to join the chase for Conoco provides new challenges for federal antitrust enforcers and for congressional opponents of "Big Oil" and big mergers. Immediately after Mobil offered $90 each for half of Conoco's shares and said it would seek the remaining stock, the Justice Department said it would closely examine the proposed $7.83 billion merger for potential antitrust infractions in national and regional markets.

Housing starts declined 11% in June to an adjusted annual rate of 1,032,000 units, its lowest level since May 1980. Economists believe the level will continue to fall, considering June's steep 16.4% plunge in building permits to an adjusted 976,000 annual rate.

22 Monetary expansion goals for the balance of this year and for 1982 have been lowered by the Federal Reserve Board. Fed Chairman Volcker told a House panel the program is necessary to stem inflation, but one committee member called for the board's resignation.

Personal income rose in June by a modest 0.6%, or $14.5 billion, to a seasonally adjusted $2.382 trillion annual rate. High interest rates stalled economic growth, and the income gain, after adjustment for inflation, was even less than indicated.

New factory orders for May were revised by the Commerce Department to show a 0.9% increase, rather than the 0.6% gain reported earlier. The revision was part of an overhaul of factory-order figures for the past several years.

Financing of takeovers may not be the most pressing money need of big oil companies, analysts say. Many refiners also are committed to huge capital outlays requiring vast new debt or equity financing.

23 The economy contracted at an adjusted 1.9% annual rate in the second quarter, and many analysts see continued weakness through the fall. They attributed the decline largely to high interest rates. Price increases in the period slowed to a 6% annual rate, down sharply from the 9.8% pace of the preceding quarter.

Durable-goods orders fell 0.8% in June to an adjusted $87.46 billion. It was the first decline since a 2.7% drop in January. May's performance was revised to show a 1.1% gain rather than the 0.4% drop reported earlier.

Mobil's bid for Conoco may be boosted from $90 a share amid rumors that Seagram will raise its $85-a-share offer for 51% of Conoco's stock. Conoco filed an antitrust suit to block Mobil's bid, but Mobil denied any anti-trust problems.

Chrysler earned $11.6 million in the second quarter, its first profit in more than two years. The company hopes to parlay the improved performance into increased car sales by reestablishing buyer confidence.

24 Consumer prices rose an adjusted 0.7% in June, or at an 8.4% annual rate before compounding, matching the May gain but exceeding April's 0.4% increase. Inflation slowed in the second quarter to a 7.4% compounded annual rate from the first period's 9.6% pace. But government and private economists worry that third quarter increases may hit double-digit levels.

Seagram raised its bid for Conoco to $92 a share from $85, for a new total of $4.08 billion, and extended the offer to Aug. 5. But observers believe the moves may make it harder for Seagram to complete its bid for 44,350,000 Conoco shares, or 51% of the total outstanding.

U.S. car sales rose 6% in mid-July to an estimated 159,779 units. The gain, the first since early June, was greater than analysts had expected.

27 Interest rates appear ready to decline. Bankers and economists say the $5.9 billion drop in the nation's money supply reported Friday, coupled with recent signs that the economy is weakening, could encourage the Fed to ease tight credit conditions. Some economists predict a drop in the 4% surcharge on the Fed's basic discount rate, currently 14%.

Machine-tool orders rose 35% to $307.2 million in June from May's level, but were 33% below the year-earlier level. The low order level was said to be due to high interest rates and uncertainty about taxes.

Soviets bought 450,000 metric tons of U.S. corn, valued at $58 million, for delivery after Sept. 30. Officials of the two nations will meet in Vienna next week to discuss their five-year-old grain-trading agreement.

28 Offers for Conoco were sweetened by Mobil and Du Pont. Mobil raised the cash price in the first step of its takeover plan to $105 a Conoco share from $90, while lowering the value of preferred stock and debentures to be issued in the transaction's second step to $85 from $95. Du Pont broadened its offer of $95 a share in cash to 45% of Conoco's shares from 40%.

General Motors posted second quarter profit of $514.6 million, its highest quarterly earnings in more than two years. Increased factory sales and cost-cutting were said to be responsible for the improvement.

OPEC's African members met secretly in Tripoli to form a "common front of resistance" to pressures for oil price cuts. Export revenues of the four producers have declined because buyers have walked away from their contracts, high-priced at $40 to $41 a barrel.

British Petroleum delayed its planned $1.25 billion production program in the North Sea's Andrew field, citing the burden of new British oil taxes. For the same reason, a Phillips Petroleum group is reconsidering a $3 billion project.

29 U.S. Steel profit more than doubled to $167.6 million, or $1.89 a share, from 1980 second quarter operating profit, on a 20% gain in sales to $3.79 billion. The nation's largest steelmaker said it had boosted its bank credit line to $3 billion but wouldn't say why.

Commercial paper is a security under a law that bars banks from underwriting securities, a federal judge ruled. Her decision overturns part of a 1980 Fed ruling allowing Bankers Trust to sell commercial paper and is likely to discourage other banks from underwriting the corporate IOUs.

Du Pont announced a lead over rivals Seagram and Mobil in the race to acquire Conoco. Du Pont said that at the close of business Monday it had been tendered 43.7 million Conoco shares, more than half the total outstanding. Meanwhile, Seagram launched a public relations campaign to improve its chances.

30 Congress embraced the President's call for massive tax cuts for individuals and business. Democrats' traditional economics of income redistribution and consumer-demand management through fiscal policy were rejected, as were Republicans' old prescriptions for fighting inflation through economic austerity. The Senate accepted the bill by a vote of 89-to-11; the House vote was 238-to-195.

Leading indicators of the economy fell 1.3% in June, their second consecutive monthly decline. The economy contracted in the second quarter after robust first quarter growth, with much of its sluggishness attributed to high interest rates. But economists agree it's premature to forecast a recession.

Du Pont said Conoco holders tendered more than 48 million shares, or 56%, under its offer. Over 38.7 million shares were tendered for cash, Du Pont said, more than it has said are eligible to receive cash. Seagram advisers said the Du Pont offer's tax-free feature mightn't be available for most Conoco holders.

31 The SEC issued the final segment of its proposals to overhaul filing rules for publicly traded companies. The eight changes would streamline registration filings and make it less expensive for firms to raise money.

Home sales plunged 17.2% to an adjusted annual 408,000 units in June from May, as high mortgage interest rates discouraged buyers.

Business productivity fell at an adjusted 0.9% rate in the second quarter, indicating economic weakness. The decline follows a revised 4.3% first quarter gain. Unless this quarter and next show declines, 1981 productivity should exceed last year's, a Labor Department economist predicts.

August 1981

3 Tax conferees assembled a final tax-cut package expected to be voted on by the Senate today and by the House tomorrow. The measure provides reductions estimated at $37.6 billion in fiscal 1982 and as much as $199.3 billion in fiscal 1985. The bill could go to Reagan by tomorrow.

A final budget bill was approved by the House and Senate providing cuts of $35.2 billion for fiscal 1982 and more than $130 billion for fiscal 1981 through 1984. Separately, the House voted to preserve a minimum Social Security payment but the measure is likely to die in the Senate.

The economy deteriorated in July as production, employment and new orders plummeted, according to a survey of purchasing agents. A trade group likened some production and new-order data to

those when the country was emerging from the 1980 recession.

Factory orders rose 0.9% in June to an adjusted $170.89 billion. It was the fifth increase in a row, but some economists warn that the appearance of continued strength could be misleading.

Long-term interest rates could soar, economists fear, unless foreign investors participate actively in this week's $22 billion Treasury offerings. Bond prices continued to slide despite a Fed report that the nation's basic money supply was unchanged in the week ended July 22.

4 Air travel was disrupted nationwide by a walkout of air traffic controllers. About 35% of the 14,000 normally scheduled commercial flights were grounded, as were 50% of general aviation flights. Reagan warned strikers they will be fired if they don't return to work by 11 A.M. EDT tomorrow, and federal officials said they'll seek civil and criminal penalties that could total millions of dollars. The government also won a court order freezing the controllers' strike fund.

The controllers are seeking a four-day workweek and a $10,000 across-the-board pay raise, arguing that their careers are often limited to 10 to 15 years and the strain causes medical disabilities. The union rejected a tentative accord calling for a $40 million-a-year wage and benefit package.

Salomon Brothers will merge into Phibro Corp., an international commodities trader. Salomon's 62 partners will receive $250 million of 9% convertible debentures and withdraw their $300 million of capital in the firm, which Phibro will then replenish.

Mobil raised its bid for Conoco to $115 a share, apparently edging into a narrow lead in three-way bidding for the company. Conoco shares closed at $1 above Du Pont's $95 cash offer and $4 over Seagram's $92 bid.

The U.S. dollar soared to its highest level in nearly 11 years on expectations of continued high interest rates and confidence in Reagan's economic program. Gold fell $15 an ounce on the Comex to close at $388.50, its lowest price in over a year and a half.

Long-term bond prices plunged to record lows on intensified worries over the Treasury's massive quarterly financing. Short-term rates soared, and the average yield on the Treasury's 13-week bills at the latest auction rose to 15.674% while the 26-week issue climbed to 15.571%.

Home mortgage rates hit a record 17.11% nationally last week because of a weak bond market and cash-strapped S&L industry.

5 Du Pont raised its Conoco bid by $3 a share to $98 for the cash portion of the offer and said it held tenders for an estimated 60% of Conoco's stock. Mobil boosted its competing offer by $5 a share to $120 and sought to temporarily restrain the Du Pont offer in federal court. Mobil also asked the SEC to extend the Du Pont offer's withdrawal deadline of midnight tonight.

U.S. car sales in July improved slightly from recent months but remained at the lowest level for the month in 20 years. Sales of 494,825 domestic cars were off 8.4% from a year earlier.

The House approved the final version of the tax-cut bill by a 282–95 vote and sent it to the White House. Reagan is expected to sign both it and the budget measure as early as tomorrow.

Bond markets rallied on renewed investor demand sparked by record interest rates at the Treasury's extensive note sale. The $4.25 billion of 39-month notes pay an average yeild of 15.96%.

6 Du Pont received about 47 million Conoco shares, or 55% of the total, making it the apparent winner in a three-way battle for control of the oil company. Mobil said it will tender about 735,000 Conoco shares it bought on the open market to Seagram Co., another bidder, but left its own offer open. Mobil added that it is still seeking a Justice Department ruling on whether it would be allowed to merge with a major oil company.

   The combination of Du Pont and Conoco would result in a company with annual sales exceeding $32 billion, and a vast source of petroleum-based raw materials for chemical, plastic and fiber products. But the two companies initially are expected to operate as they did before the merger.

Two synfuel projects will receive $3.1 billion in federal loan guarantees, the Energy Department said. A coal gasification project headed by American Natural Resources will receive $2 billion in guarantees and an oil shale project involving Tosco will get $1.1 billion.

7 Retail sales showed spotty gains in July, reflecting a pause or a downturn in the consumer spending recovery. Merchandisers said inflation and a sluggish economy crimped spending, and they see only modest gains for the rest of the year. K mart had a 22% gain, Dayton Hudson 27%, Sears 8.1% and Penney 3.7%. Woolworth fell 0.2% and Montgomery Ward was off 0.5%.

Speculation that Du Pont might spin off Conoco's coal unit was termed "utter nonsense" by Conoco Chairman Ralph E. Bailey. He called Consolidation Coal an essential part of the company's energy reserves, but said some other assets may be shed.

Auto makers will close 19 car and seven truck assembly plants next week, for model changeover and to reduce inventories.

10 Unemployment could rise in coming months because of economic weakness despite a recent drop in joblessness. The unemployment rate fell in July to an adjusted 7% of the work force, off from June's 7.3% and a 15-month low. The improvement was greater than expected, but a Labor Department spokeswoman said it may have occurred in part because companies anticipated a boost from tax cuts and higher defense spending.

Lower interest rates could result from growing pressure on the Federal Reserve System to relax its credit reins. Many economists and bankers say steps will be necessary soon to avoid a severe slump, and some observers say moves already taken may show up in interest-rate declines as early as this week.

11 Natural gas prices likely won't be decontrolled until Reagan resolves thorny political and economic questions. He must weigh his commitment to speedy decontrol against the political risk of sharp price increases just before 1982 congressional elections.

The dollar soared in foreign-exchange trading, fueled by tensions in Poland and confidence in the Reagan administration. Gold gained 80 cents an ounce to close on the Comex at $397.30.

Consumer debt rose in June an adjusted $1.93 billion, or a 7% annual rate. The increase was stronger than May's but trailed the preceding three months.

Antitrust policy under Reagan won't vary much from recent enforcement in matters of horizontal mergers, antitrust chief Baxter said. But he reiterated that he sees fewer problems than his predecessors with vertical mergers, and will put his views on paper next winter or spring.

12 Bond prices rallied on renewed hopes the Federal Reserve will loosen its credit reins. Investor optimism sparked declines in short-term rates, buoying chances of a reduction in the prime rate, currently 20½%. But economists remained divided over the interest rate outlook, and dealers continued to worry over heavy Treasury financing plans.

Hospitals are diversifying in an effort to

staunch the flow of red ink. Investments so far include such diverse enterprises as restaurants, a construction company, an insurance concern and a shopping center.

Auto safety recalls have been made by Ford and Chrysler without public announcements, to avoid hurting car sales. In recent months, Ford has made eight such recalls of its Escort and Lynx models and Chrysler has recalled its K models twice.

13 Retail sales rose 1.3% in July to an adjusted $88.03 billion, following an upward-revised 1.7% gain in June. The July increase was surprisingly strong in view of economists' assertions that the economy is buckling under continued high interest rates.

GM and Suzuki, Japan's leading "minicar" maker, said they will cooperate in developing and producing small cars. The venture will include Isuzu Motors, GM's 34%-owned Japanese affiliate.

Price increases on gasoline antiknock additives can't be publicized by their manufacturers until 30 days after they're effective, an FTC hearing officer ruled. The order stems from government charges of "price signaling" by the four makers of the compounds.

IBM's personal computers were introduced with prices ranging from $1,565 to $4,500. Analysts say the systems, designed for homes, schools and offices, are likely to pose a tough challenge for current makers and could lead the market within two years.

14 Car sales rose an unexpectedly strong 30% in early August, sparked by extensive promotions and rebates. U.S. makers delivered an estimated 153,472 units in the period, a sharp improvement over the sluggish pace of the past four months. GM posted a 34% gain, Ford 25%, Chrysler 25%, AMC 33% and VW 3.2%. Producers plan 93,716 assemblies this week, a 41% gain from last week.

Business inventories climbed 0.7% in June to an adjusted $493.51 billion after posting a similar gain in May to $490.25 billion. Some economists had feared a larger buildup because of the sluggish economy, but unexpected sales strength checked an increase.

Reagan signed into law both the tax-and budget-cut bills. The measures are called the most far-reaching domestic economic legislation since the New Deal.

Proposed bond options trading on the Big Board met resistance from member firms. Industry officials expressed concern over duplication of contracts also being sought by the Amex and the Chicago Board Options Exchange.

17 Inflation is slowing, but with an uncertain effect on the economy, a Labor Department report shows. The agency said producer prices for finished goods rose a moderate, adjusted 0.4% in July, or at a 4.8% annual rate before compounding. That followed June's 0.6% rise, or a 7.2% annual rate. The Federal Reserve said industrial production climbed 0.3% in July after a 0.1% drop in June. Analysts said the latest figure gave little evidence of much economic strength or of serious weakness.

Further budget cuts of $40 billion to $60 billion are necessary to keep Reagan's economic plans on track, his aides are expected to tell him. Few new cuts can be made in fiscal 1982, they say, and savings in fiscal 1983 and 1984 will have to focus on the Pentagon and Social Security and Medicare programs.

Mortgage-rate ceilings on single-family home loans backed by the government were raised to a record 16.5% from 15.5%. The move, effective today, reflects "current market conditions," the Department of Housing and Urban Development said.

18 Du Pont holders approved a proposed merger with Conco by an overwhelming margin. But some voiced concern over the future role of Seagram, which will have a 20% stake in Du Pont after converting its 28 million Conoco shares.

Factories operated at 79.6% of capacity in July, off from 79.7% in June. The July rate was the lowest this year, but economists are uncertain whether it signals a pause in business growth or an outright recession.

Stock prices fell sharply over a broad range on apprehension about high interest rates and the severity of a possible recession. The Dow Jones industrial average closed at 926.75, off 10.18 and at its lowest level since Dec. 16.

S&Ls can swap old, low-yielding loans for more marketable securities of the Federal Home Loan Mortgage Corp. under new rules. And the Federal National Mortgage Association said it will pay cash for old mortgages if regulatory changes are approved.

Short-term interest rates climbed in listless trading as many investors and dealers remained fearful of higher rates because of large federal borrowing needs. At the Treasury's latest auction, the average yield on 13-week bills rose to 15.705% and on the 26-week issue to 15.644%.

19 Personal income rose in July an adjusted 1.6%, aided by an 11.2% cost-of-living increase in Social Security and other federal payments. Housing starts in the month climbed 3.3% to a 1,055,000-unit annual rate, but permits for new houses fell 4%.

Municipal bond prices fell as two new state issues failed to spark investor enthusiasm. Some issues plunged 2½ points in the secondary market.

Moody's lowered Du Pont's rating on its senior unsecured long-term debt to double-A from triple-A. The investors service cited the increase in Du Pont's debt resulting from the Conoco merger.

U.S. Steel matched Bethlehem's 4% to 6% price increases on plate and structural sections, effective Sept. 27.

20 Corporate profits after taxes fell 11.3% in the second quarter, the Commerce Department said, indicating the economy was weaker than had been thought. Gross national product declined at an adjusted 2.4% annual rate after allowing for inflation. The department had estimated the decline at a 1.9% pace. Revised figures also showed that prices in the period, measured on a GMP-based gauge, rose at a 6.6% annual rate. That was significantly slower than the first period's 9.8% pace but higher than a preliminary estimate of 6% made last month.

21 Saudi Arabia blocked OPEC efforts to reach a unified oil price. The proposal called for a $35-a-barrel price, $3 more than the Saudis charge but $1 less than other members' base price. Stunned ministers adopted a recommendation that their heads of state communicate with Saudi King Khalid.

The Treasury sold $4.75 billion of two-year notes at a record 16.26% discount rate. The cost reflected growing investor worries about the government's ability to meet its budget forecasts.

Ailing S&Ls would be required to give the Federal Savings & Loan Insurance Corp. an equity interest in return for financial aid, under an agency proposal. But the FSLIC chief said he still preferred mergers with stronger institutions. Separately, the Federal Reserve Board activated a program to extend credit to banks and S&Ls with sustained cash-flow problems.

24 Consumer prices soared an adjusted 1.2% in July, or at a 14.4% annual rate. The jump, which was the biggest monthly increase in more than a year, was mainly due to rising food prices and continued high mortgage rates. But analysts believe the increase in the inflation rate will be short-lived and will return to single-digit levels by fall.

U.S. car sales rose in mid-August to about 203,375 units, up 18.5% from a year earlier. The improvement was attributed to the promotion programs that the auto makers began recently.

Sales of mutual funds invested chiefly in common stocks fell to $446 million in July, off 13% from a month earlier, according to the Investment Company Institute.

The budget deficit shrank to $10.34 billion in July from $14.99 billion a year earlier, the Treasury said.

The bond market rallied yesterday afternoon, with many issues winding up near Monday's closing level.

25 Mexican oil purchases by the U.S. to fill the strategic petroleum reserve could prompt criticism from other big producers. Saudi Arabia has tried to prevent such long-term agreements. Mexico hopes to establish a special relationship with the U.S. in case Mideast supplies are disrupted.

Durable-goods orders rose 0.9% in July to an adjusted $89.12 billion, after a revised June increase of 0.2% to $88.3 billion. The latest boost was the sixth in a row, with most of the gain in defense-related industries.

26 Stock and bond prices fell sharply on a surge in interest rates. The Dow Jones industrial average fell 20.46 points, its biggest drop since January, to close at 900.11, its lowest level in more than 13 months. Prices of some actively traded government bonds plummeted nearly three points.

The dollar soared in foreign-exchange trading and gold's price fell $18.30 an ounce to $414.30 because of the rising U.S. interest rates. Prices of nearly every commodity fell on the news. Coffee, grain and soybean prices were among the hardest hit.

Nigeria's weakened economy will force it to become the first OPEC member to lower its oil quote to $37 a barrel from the $39 to $40 currently charged, analysts say. But Nigeria still may be strong enough to obtain concessions from its customers at talks in Lagos this week, they add.

27 Nigeria cut the price of its crude $4, to $36 a barrel. The step could push Libya and Algeria to lower their quotes from $40. Further cuts could come from Iran, Iraq, Kuwait and Qatar, all of which charge $36 a barrel.

Business productivity rose at an adjusted 0.7% annual rate in the second quarter, rather than declining as the Labor Department predicted. The disparity between this slight gain and the 2.4% drop in GNP posted last week is partly due to a statistical discrepancy, a government economist said.

Foreign investment in the U.S. rose 20.2% in 1980 to $65.48 billion. Investment by members of OPEC increased almost 50% to $576 million.

Industrials slipped 2.57 points to finish at 899.26, a 13-month low, after an early stock-market rally attempt failed. Transportation and utility indexes closed higher.

The federal funds rate fell to 13% from Tuesday's average 17.21%, tugging the dollar lower against most major currencies in thin foreign-exchange trading.

28 The U.S. trade deficit on a merchandise basis narrowed to an adjusted $1.46 billion in July, as petroleum imports fell to the lowest level since the 1973–74 oil embargo. Exports fell 3% to an adjusted $19.26 billion after rising in June.

Algeria and Libya are offering to barter oil pegged at $40 a barrel. But the tactic to stave off cuts in the price of their crude isn't working. Tenneco and Honda refused Algerian proposals.

Canada set up a watchdog agency to assure significant Canadian participation in major Canadian projects, particulary energy ventures. The move reflects a growing split with the U.S. on the issue of free trade, a U.S. official said.

The Treasury sold $3.25 billion of five-year, two-month notes at a record average annual yield of 16.14%.

Fixed-rate mortgages accepted under the Federal Home Loan Mortgage Corp.'s weekly purchase program averaged a record 17.663% yield, up from 17.092% a week earlier.

31 The economy is likely to remain sluggish, based on the latest decline in the composite index of leading indicators. The index fell 0.1% in July, after a revised 1% decline in June and a 1.6% drop in May. But government and private experts don't see any signs of a recession.

September 1981

1 Two big banks lowered their prime rate to 20% from 20½%, the first reduction in the fee by major lenders since July 8. But bond prices plunged on worries about huge federal borrowing needs and Federal Reserve policies. The drop was fueled by Washington Public Power's $500 million tax-exempt issue, which was tentatively priced to yield as much as 15%. The triple-A bonds reportedly lured investors from other securities.

Stock prices rose early in the day but nosedived later. The Dow Jones industrial average fell 10.75 to close at 881.47, its lowest since July 2, 1980. The dollar gained in foreign exchange trading on the belief the Fed would continue its restrictive monetary policies.

New-home sales rose 2.4% in July to an adjusted annual rate of 420,000, up from June's revised 410,000 pace, but still at recession levels. The median selling price in July rose to $69,800, up only $100 from June. But mortgage rates rose to a record 17.48% average, up from 16.64% at the beginning of the month.

2 New factory orders rose 1.3% in July to an adjusted $173.1 billion. It was the sixth rise in a row, with most of the gain in transportation industries. Construction spending in the month fell 1.5% to an adjusted $235.1 billion annual rate, the sixth consecutive decline, following a revised drop of 0.4% in June.

Auto makers plan to build 1,614,600 cars in the fourth quarter, the lowest output for the period since 1970's strike-depressed level. The slow pace indicated they no longer expect a sales recovery this year.

Oil prices will fall as more OPEC countries cut their quotes on the face of weak demand, Saudi Arabia's oil minister predicted. But he said the Saudis won't let prices fall below their own $32-a-barrel rate.

Sears Roebuck will expand its real estate and financial service operations. The retailer will begin offering a money market investment service late this year and plans a major move in residential real estate brokerage.

Antitrust judgments are expected to be reduced sharply by the Justice Department, an official said. The agency will ask courts to amend or drop those that have anticompetitive effects.

Fannie Mae yields soared to records at its latest auction of four-month commitments to buy home loans. Average yields ranged from 18.366% on federally insured mortgages to 18.896% on graduated payment FHA loans.

3 OPEC oil output has fallen to a 13-year low of 20 million barrels a day because of sluggish economic activity and resistance to high prices. One source says produc-

tion could fall another million barrels a day by December.

Air traffic reductions in August caused by the controllers' strike were smaller than analysts had expected. TWA reported a 12% decline while United's traffic was off 15%, and both carriers filled a higher percentage of available seats. Regional airlines were affected even less because they operate mainly from less congested airports.

Aluminum producers are slashing output and delaying expansions to avoid the high costs of excess capacity and heavy inventories. High interest rates continue to depress demand for the metal in most consumer durable industries.

Semiconductor makers face bleak prospects of slumping prices, slow demand and marginal earnings for the rest of the year. Observers say shipments will about equal 1980's $5.46 billion, and a recovery isn't seen until 1982's first quarter.

4 All savers rules governing the new tax-free certificates were issued by federal regulators. Individuals may earn up to $1,000 and couples filing jointly $2,000 in tax-exempt income on a one-time basis. The certificates are expected to draw $250 billion in deposits, with 75% of the total required to be invested in the housing and agricultural industries.

The IRS decided that certificates linked to bonus programs can remain tax-free if issuers separate the two and eliminate penalties for failing to convert repurchase agreements to certificates. Financial institutions that had backed away from bonuses prepared to resume the program, though many planned more modest offers.

Retail sales rose modestly in August, most chains said, reflecting consumers' skittishness and the late Labor Day holiday. K mart had a 21% gain, Montgomery Ward 7.1%, Penney 6.8% and Sears 5%.

Car sales jumped 17% in August with domestic makers showing a 24% gain while import sales were nearly flat. Deliveries were spurred by incentives offering $150 to $1,000 off prices.

8 OPEC could collapse if its share of the world oil market continues to fall, Saudi Arabia's oil minister warned. Sheik Yamani, whose nation produces about half of the Organization of Petroleum Exporting Countries' total output, also voiced concern that the group's average price could fall below $32 a barrel. Prices currently average less than $33, off from $34 as recently as last month.

Producer prices and unemployment rose moderately in August, but analysts cautioned against undue optimism over the economy. Producer prices for finished goods rose an adjusted 0.3% or at a 3.6% annual rate. Joblessness increased to 7.2% of the workforce from July's 7%.

9 Two failing thrifts, West Side Federal of New York City and Washington Savings of Miami, were acquired by National Steel. The S&Ls will receive roughly $10 million a month in subsidies from federal insurers, which agreed to cover any losses from loan portfolios for 10 years. National will provide $75 million of new capital, beginning in September 1982. Two other S&Ls, Franklin Society of New York City and First Federal of Rochester, N.Y., also were merged with federal help.

Iran canceled contracts with international oil companies operating there before the revolution. The move will have little effect on world supplies because of a sharp drop in exports resulting from the revolution and the war with Iraq.

Bond prices tumbled to record lows on continued investor fears over the Treasury's financing needs. Stock prices also fell, with the Dow Jones industrials closing at 851.12, off 10.56.

10 Economic controls were threatened by some congressmen in the face of continued high interest rates. Senate Majority Leader Baker said angry and indignant lawmakers were talking of credit controls, reorganizing the Federal Reserve, a windfall profits tax on interest income, and wage and price controls. House Republican Leader Michel of Illinois suggested Congress might resort to tougher regulation of financial institutions.

Reagan is debating where and how to make an additional $15 billion in spending cuts to hold the projected fiscal 1982 budget deficit to $42.5 billion. Options under study include new presidential authority to impound, or refuse to spend, appropriated funds.

Bond prices surged on warnings from the House Republican leader that Congress might impose credit controls if interest rates don't fall soon. Prices on some long-term bonds rose about 1½ points. The federal funds rate plunged as low as 3% at one point.

Paris brokers halted trading in companies the French government plans to nationalize. The action was requested by the Finance Ministry while a nationalization bill is deliberated.

11 Federal reserve action to ease credit could be hastened by congressional unrest over high interest rates, analysts say. Moves could include a one or two percentage point reduction in the Fed's 4% sur-

charge on its basic 14% discount rate. But a change in the 3½% annual growth target for the money supply is thought unlikely. Economists also contend that pressure is building for a general decrease in the prime rate to 20% from 20½%.

OPEC's future is threatened by a continuing trend toward conservation and alternate energy sources, Indonesia warned. The comments echo remarks early this week by Saudi Arabia's oil minister.

The Soviet grain crop could be the poorest of three bad years in a row, U.S. grain and weather experts say, because of damage from drought and other problems. Analysts believe the crop will total 175 million metric tons, far below the Soviets' 240 million-ton target.

Business spending plans for 1981 will show little or no growth after adjustment for inflation, a Commerce Department report indicates. An agency analyst said the outlook reflects an increase in the inflation projection for the year.

14 Reagan risks criticism from Congress and Wall Street on his decision to pare the Pentagon's budget just $13 billion, or 2% in the next three fiscal years. Further big cuts are planned in politically sensitive social programs to trim $90 billion from spending to achieve a balanced budget by 1984. Pressure has been mounting to find much of the savings in military spending plans.

The U.S. payments deficit on a current-account basis will run between $10 billion and $20 billion in 1982, the administration predicts. The wider gap stems primarily from sharp appreciation of the dollar. The largest previous deficits were $14.1 billion in both 1977 and 1978.

A bond price rally depends largely on further spending cuts by the administration, according to bankers and economists. The Fed reported that the money supply fell $1.1 billion in the week ended Sept. 2. Analysts had expected an increase.

15 Military spending may be cut more sharply than the $13 billion over three years requested by Reagan. Moderate House Republicans insist the Pentagon absorb steeper cuts than the President wants. And a leading conservative Democrat, Phil Gramm of Texas, said a $5 billion cut in defense spending for fiscal 1982 isn't "unrealistic." Reagan is asking for only $2 billion. Both groups supported the President in cutting $35 billion from social spending earlier this year.

Short-term interest rates fell broadly in what some economists said were signs the Fed may be easing its credit reins. Yields

plunged more than a point at the latest Treasury auction, with 13-week bills averaging 14.412% and the 26-week issue 14.657%. The falling rates pulled the dollar sharply lower in foreign exchange trading.

Business inventories rose an adjusted 1.1% in July to $499.52 billion after a revised 0.8% gain in June. The latest figure reflects softness in consumer demand, presaging lackluster manufacturing activity, a Commerce Department aide said.

16 S&Ls must limit interest-bearing checking accounts to nonprofit groups with IRS tax exemptions or government educational bodies, a federal judge ruled. The decision strikes down a proposed rule that would have extended eligibility to all nonprofit agencies and governments.

U.S. car sales rose 8.3% in early September to an estimated 150,681 units, reflecting extended sales promotion programs.

Yields rose to a record average of 18.736% at the Federal National Mortgage Association's latest auction of four-month commitments to buy home loans.

Stock prices sank despite a reduction in short-term interest rates. The Dow Jones industrial average fell 7.80 to 858.35.

17 Industrial output fell an adjusted 0.4% in August following a 0.3% increase in July. It was the first decline since April, and resulted primarily from sharp drops in the interest-rate-sensitive auto and construction industries. Excluding the automotive sector, output was off 0.1%.

Volcker vowed to continue the Federal Reserve's tight credit policies. The Fed chairman said spending must be cut a further $16 billion in fiscal 1982 and $83 billion by 1984 to meet the administration's own targets.

18 Housing starts fell 10.7% in August to an adjusted 937,000-unit annual rate, the third lowest monthly level since World War II. Personal income in the month rose a surprisingly strong 1.1%, and economists were encouraged by a rise in consumption. The nation's factories operated at 79.3% of capacity, down from July's 79.8%. The three reports suggest the economy is stagnant and may be headed for a pronounced downturn.

Reagan plans to announce next week his plans for an added $16 billion in fiscal 1982 spending cuts. They include a three-month delay in cost-of-living increases for Social Security and other benefit programs.

Synfuels aid would end as early as 1984 under administration plans, even if early projects prove viable. The head of the government's Synthetic Fuels Corp. said the White House wants to limit spending to the $13 billion the corporation has on hand.

The balance of payments showed an adjusted $1.07 billion surplus on the current account in the second quarter, down sharply from a $3.26 billion surplus in the first period.

Minimum steel prices for imports will be maintained despite European producers' complaints that exchange rates are hurting them. The U.S. also plans to crack down on attempts to evade the trigger price system.

21 Inflation-adjusted GNP in the third quarter will be "flat to slightly down," said Assistant Commerce Secretary Robert Dederick. New figures indicate the economy contracted at an adjusted 1.6% rate in the second quarter compared with the 2.4% rate previously reported.

The Gold Commission agreed on little in its first public meeting, other than the U.S. must find a path to long-term price stability. The panel studying gold's role in monetary systems also agreed to extend its own existence.

22 The FED cut to three percentage points from four the interest rate surcharge it imposes on frequent bank borrowers but left the basic discount rate unchanged at 14%. Hours earlier, Chase Manhattan trimmed its prime rate to 19½% from 20%, and several banks followed.

After the Fed's announcement, bond prices gave up most of their gains, and one banker called the market "disappointed" that the central bank's reduction wasn't larger. Gold gained $16.60 to settle at $467.50 an ounce on the Comex, bolstered by the lower rates and a further decline by the dollar. The stock market rose 10.37 points on volume of 44,-570,000 shares.

Banks and S&Ls could offer 3½-year certificates free of interest rate controls under a proposal being considered today by federal regulators. Final action isn't likely today, but the proposal is expected to be offered for public comment; Treasury officials hope it can be approved in December.

Morgan Stanley agreed to exchange as much as $20 million of Wells Fargo debt it owns for as many as 600,000 of the bank's common shares. This is Morgan's second such swap in a week and may indicate a trend among banks and utilities for strengthening balance sheets.

23 Durable goods orders fell in August for the first time since January, with the sharpest drops registered in the metals industry. Orders fell 2.5% last month to an adjusted $87.22 billion after rising a revised 1.3% in July to an adjusted $89.44 billion.

The July estimate initially showed a 0.9% gain.

The prime rate was cut to 19½% by more banks. But most other interest fees surged and bond prices fell amid renewed worries over the White House's ability to push its budget-cutting program through Congress. In a surprise move that intensified market concerns, the Fed drained reserves from the banking network.

The Big Board may give up its year-long struggle to establish an independent financial futures market. The exchange doesn't plan to dissolve the NYFE, however; a merger with the Comex financial futures unit is being discussed.

The futures industry received federal authority to form a regulatory trade association. The Commodity Futures Trading Commission has complained that it can't police the industry as thoroughly as it would like.

24 OSHA plans to exempt almost three-fourths of all U.S. manufacturing companies from routine safety inspections after Oct. 15. Massachusetts Sen. Edward Kennedy expressed concern that weakened enforcement and standards have "emasculated" worker protection under federal law.

Treasury yields at a $3.25 billion sale of four-year notes set a record annual average of 15.91%. That was well above the previous high of 14.29%, set March 25, 1980.

OPEC members' U.S. investments totaled nearly $70 billion at midyear, a Treasury aide said, adding that the administration "welcomes" foreign investment. The accuracy of the Treasury's data was impugned by the chief of a House government operations panel, Rep. Benjamin Rosenthall (D., N.Y.).

25 Reagan's latest budget plan, announced in a televised address last night, includes $13 billion in further cuts for the fiscal year beginning Thursday. The package contains $3 billion in new tax measures for the year, and would help the President come within $600 million of his original $4.25 billion deficit for fiscal 1982.

Consumer prices rose an adjusted 0.8% in August, or at a 9.6% annual rate before compounding, with housing costs responsible for half the increase. The gain followed July's adjusted 1.2% rise, or 14.4% annual rate. Economists predict an inflation rate of about 10% for the year, compared with 1980's 13.5% pace.

Boston Edison plans to cancel a 1,150,000-kilowatt nuclear plant at Plymouth, Mass. It has spent about $291 million on such considerations as engineering and equipment. The project's estimated cost has risen tenfold, to $4 billion, since 1971. Washington Public Power's nuclear plant units No. 4 and No. 5 would be mothballed for two years under a plan approved by a panel representing its 88 member firms. The plan, however, faces several hurdles.

S&L Industry losses continued at near-record levels last month, as the net worth of federally insured S&Ls fell $482 million to $29.7 billion. August's decline is second only to July's revised record loss of $541 million. Withdrawals exceeded deposits by $3.7 billion.

28 Machine tool orders totaled $214 million in August, up 10% from July's depressed level but down 4.7% from the year earlier. Sluggish orders, attributed to high interest rates and economic uncertainty, are seen continuing through 1982's first quarter.

The aluminum industry slump is worsening, as auto, appliance, building and construction industries cut output. Aluminum workers will slash operating rates, currently below 80% of capacity, and 1981 earnings will fall as much as 50% below weak 1980 levels, analysts predict.

29 Prices closed higher on the New York Stock Exchange, as heavy institutional buying helped avert the predicted "Blue Monday." Prices plummeted on markets overseas, however, as analyst Joseph Granville's forecast of gloom compounded already pervasive doubts about the world economy. Tokyo stocks fell to a record level. London and Paris quotes plunged, too, but the Bourse, unlike most foreign markets, recovered from its slump.

Bond prices closed higher after plunging to record lows early yesterday. Short-term rates edged lower, and Continental Illinois National Bank & Trust cuts its prime rate to 19% from 19½%. Other bankers predicted a 19% prime would be prevalent within a week.

Citicorp lost its top credit rating. Citing declines in earnings and returns on investment, Standard & Poor's cut its rating on long-term debt securities to double-A-plus from triple-A and on preferred stock to double-A from double-A-plus.

Federally insured S&Ls incurred a $1.5 billion loss in this year's first half, their first loss for a six-month period in 40 years of record-keeping. An even greater loss is expected for the second half.

30 Chrysler is rolling back hefty 1982 model price increases announced a month ago, in a bid to bolster unit sales. The auto maker will raise prices on new cars an average of $306 each, or 3.7%, down

from the $622, or 7.7%, previously announced. The move leaves tags on the least expensive subcompacts and compacts unchanged from 1981 levels and undercuts GM and Ford. GM is boosting 1982 models an average of 5.8%, Ford, 4.7%.

Earnings forecasts by securities analysts for most industries are being depressed by pessimism about the U.S. economy. Companies realize an expected upturn in business isn't coming, an analyst said. Paine Webber trimmed 1981 earnings estimates for 96 companies last month and raised estimates for only 65.

Three OPEC members will run out of oil by the end of the decade, and three others will be reduced to minor exporters in the 1990s, a former top OPEC official predicted. By 2000, almost 90% of the oil from OPEC's remaining members will come from the Persian Gulf area, compounding the region's turbulence, he added.

October 1981

1 Economic indicators fell 0.5% in August. The decline in the Commerce Department's composite index of leading indicators followed a 0.4% increase in July, previously estimated to be a 0.1% decline. Some economists believe the indicators' weakness is signaling a recession.

Home sales sank 14% in August to an adjusted 362,000 annual rate, the lowest one-month level since the 1980 recession. Housing analysts don't expect a significant improvement until mortgage interest rates fall three or four percentage points.

Oil producers face intensified pressure to reduce prices during the current oil glut, as many contracts come up for renewal in the fourth quarter. Prices will continue to be cut slowly, on a contract-by-contract basis, oil company officials expect.

Treasury borrowing needs continue to pressure depressed credit markets, helping to push up interest rates. The agency sold $1.75 billion of 20-year, one-month bonds at a record average annual yield of 15.78%. It also sold $9 billion in short-term bills, with the return on 13-week bills averaging 14.669% and the return on 26-week bills averaging 14.932%.

Futures must limit the size of a speculator's holdings in all actively traded commodities, the Commodity Futures Trading Commission said. The new requirement is designed to prevent the turmoil that hit silver markets last year.

Industry Surveys*

The following provides information about a number of industries as well as financial data on companies in each industry. The meaning of the SIC (Standard Industrial Classification) numbers referred to in the Industrial Trends Tables is given at the end of this section. Financial Ratios are defined in the section *Financial and Investment Terms* (pp. 304).

EXPLANATIONS OF FINANCIAL AND STOCK MARKET INFORMATION

Most of the tabular content in the stock tables is self-explanatory, but the following notes will help to clarify some of them, as follows:

Earnings Per Share Earnings per share are on a fully diluted basis, where applicable, and extraordinary items have been excluded.

Earnings Yield This is the reciprocal of the price/earnings ratio, or, stated another way, the earnings per share dividend by the price. In effect, it is a useful way to measure the earnings power of the company in relation to the price you must pay for its shares. Investors considering stocks selling at high multiples in bull markets might do well to consider this concept: For example, a stock with earnings of $2 and a price

of 100, would have a P/E of 50, but its earnings yield would only be 2 percent. The late Benjamin Graham, regarded as the founder of modern security analysis, uses the ratio in his classic book, "The Intelligent Investor."

5-Year Earnings Growth Rate The compound annual growth rate over the last five years, computed by the least squares method. During interim periods, the latest 12 months E.P.S. are used for the sixth point in the equation on a time-weighted basis.

STANDARD FOOTNOTES

GENERAL FIELD FOOTNOTES

NA—Item not applicable to this type of stock.
NC—Data required for calculation currently incomplete in our files.
NE—Negative earnings invalidate calculations.

EARNINGS PER SHARE DATA

q—First quarter
s—First six months
n—First nine months
f—Fiscal year

MARKET AND INDEX

N—New York Stock Exchange
A—American Stock Exchange
O—Over-the-Counter
★—Denotes an S&P 500 Stock

---

* The financial data on companies in each industry come from *The Media General Financial Weekly*, Media General Financial Services, 301 E. Grace Street, Richmond, VA 23261; June 1, 1981.

NEW CONSTRUCTION PUT IN PLACE: TRENDS AND PROJECTIONS 1978–81 (in millions of current dollars)

Type of construction	1978	1979	1980 [1]	Percent change 1979–80	1981 [1]	Percent change 1980–81
Total new construction	205,457	228,950	228,300	0	270,330	18
Private construction	159,556	179,948	171,600	−5	206,700	20
Residential buildings	93,424	99,030	84,000	−15	109,800	31
New housing units	75,808	78,587	60,800	−23	83,000	37
Additions and alterations	16,349	18,236	20,000	11	23,000	15
Nonhousekeeping	1,267	2,206	3,200	45	3,800	20
Nonresidential buildings	36,293	47,298	53,100	12	60,700	14
Industrial	10,994	14,950	13,800	−8	15,200	10
Office	6,574	9,461	13,200	40	17,200	30
Other commercial	11,991	15,463	17,800	15	19,600	10
Religious	1,248	1,548	1,600	5	1,700	5
Educational	729	806	1,200	50	1,300	10
Hospital and institutional	3,347	3,530	3,500	0	3,500	0
Miscellaneous	1,410	1,540	2,000	30	2,200	10
Farm, nonresidential	5,253	5,700	5,700	0	5,700	0
Public utilities	23,302	26,467	27,300	3	28,900	6
Telephone	5,418	6,343	7,300	15	8,400	15
Electric light and power	14,384	16,009	15,200	−5	13,700	−10
Gas	1,929	2,266	2,700	20	4,300	60
Railroad	1,037	1,259	1,500	20	1,800	20
Petroleum pipelines	534	591	600	0	700	10
All other private	1,283	1,452	1,500	0	1,600	10
Public construction	45,902	49,003	56,700	16	63,600	12
Buildings	15,241	15,857	18,100	14	20,100	11
Housing and redevelopment	1,051	1,211	1,600	35	2,000	28
Industrial	1,184	1,411	1,800	30	2,300	30
Educational	6,264	6,903	7,700	12	8,500	10
Hospital	1,822	1,648	1,600	0	1,600	0
Other public	4,919	4,684	5,400	15	5,700	5
Highways and streets	10,712	11,915	15,500	30	17,800	15
Military facilities	1,512	1,640	1,700	5	2,000	20
Conservation and development	4,457	4,587	5,000	10	5,500	10
Other public construction	13,989	15,003	16,400	9	18,200	11
Sewer systems	6,765	7,298	7,700	5	8,500	10
Water supply facilities	2,661	2,490	3,500	40	4,200	20
Miscellaneous	4,563	5,215	5,200	0	5,500	5

[1] Estimated by Bureau of Industrial Economics.

Source: Bureau of the Census and Bureau of Industrial Economics.

Source: U.S. INDUSTRIAL OUTLOOK 1981, U.S. Department of Commerce.

Company and Market	Relative Price					Earnings Per Share				Other					
	Common Equity			P/E Ratio		Latest 12 Months			5-Year	Profit	Return	Return On Common	Debt	Dividend	Market
	Per Share	Price To Equity	Earnings Yield	Current	5-Year Average	Amount	Change	Date	Growth Rate	Margin	On Assets	Equity	Equity Ratio	Yield	Value
	$	%	%	-	-	$	%	-	%	%	%	%	%	%	$Mil
Residential Construction															
Anthony Ind .... N	12.81	80	13.5	7.4	4.5	1.38	-41	3-81q	6	1.6	10.0	18.5	38	4.3	27
Kaufman Broad .... *N	13.64	101	12.7	7.9	8.7	1.74	7	2-81q	30	4.4	2.2	12.3	122	1.7	163
Key Company .... A	11.30	66	16.4	6.1	5.4	1.23	-19	1-81q	297	5.3	7.5	13.6	50	5.3	4
Lennar Corp .... N	10.34	207	12.4	8.1	4.9	2.64	14	2-81q	21	11.5	10.3	26.5	96	.9	171
McKeon .... A	6.43	93	21.7	4.6	7.9	1.30	-1	11-80n	38	5.6	7.3	19.8	54	.0	21
Natl Homes .... N	4.84	72	-26.0	NC	26.0	-.91	NE	3-81q	NE	-7.9	NE	NE	97	.0	24
Nu-West Ariz .... O	2.48	176	-4.6	NC	NC	-.20	NC	9-80n	72	7.5	4.1	77.4	642	.0	16
Oriole Homes .... A	18.87	96	19.0	5.3	7.2	3.44	-15	3-81q	71	12.5	7.5	22.5	133	5.5	35
Presley Co .... N	14.52	92	20.5	4.9	4.9	2.74	-4	1-81f	73	8.4	6.4	19.9	51	3.0	53
Ryan Homes .... N	17.37	138	8.3	12.1	9.1	1.98	-37	3-81q	5	3.6	7.5	13.6	15	5.4	158
Ryland Group .... A	14.97	105	11.8	8.5	6.6	1.86	-27	3-81q	1	2.6	9.7	14.4	0	4.6	48
Shapell Ind .... N	49.95	87	13.9	7.2	4.2	6.01	-21	3-81q	11	4.7	5.5	20.4	149	.2	86
Std-Pacific .... N	12.55	107	14.0	7.2	4.0	1.87	-27	3-81q	10	7.0	5.4	17.6	63	5.2	51
Walter, Jim .... *N	43.63	58	11.5	8.7	7.2	2.91	-46	2-81s	-4	3.8	3.4	10.4	93	7.5	415
Wash Homes .... A	6.33	26	-37.5	NC	4.3	-.61	-100	1-81s	-36	-3.1	NE	NE	199	.0	2
Contractors - General															
Am Med Bldg .... A	3.11	193	1.2	NC	16.1	.07	-71	3-81q	-33	-.4	4.0	10.2	90	.0	21
Arundel Corp .... A	13.97	47	-12.2	NC	10.5	-.81	NE	3-81q	-32	-1.5	NE	NE	31	.0	12
Dravo Corp .... N	19.69	118	7.1	14.0	9.8	1.66	-19	3-81q	-5	1.9	3.2	8.8	36	4.1	290
Elcor Cp .... N	12.25	153	2.5	39.9	8.1	.47	-74	3-81n	0	3.3	5.5	15.4	85	1.6	66
Fluor Corp .... *N	11.57	323	7.7	13.0	10.7	2.87	35	1-81q	21	2.7	7.7	23.9	14	2.1	1,782
Grt Lakes Intl .... N	24.00	167	5.2	19.2	6.3	2.08	-48	3-81q	7	9.2	6.5	11.3	32	2.6	127
Jetero Corp .... A	6.76	148	14.1	7.1	8.8	1.41	107	3-81q	21	3.8	3.2	16.0	0	2.0	16
Morrison Knuds .... N	18.75	177	10.6	9.4	5.7	3.52	13	3-81q	22	1.8	4.1	16.3	42	3.3	317
Parsons Corp .... N	9.97	359	6.5	15.5	8.0	2.31	13	3-81q	15	3.5	9.3	22.1	18	2.8	435
Perini Corp .... A	24.27	118	9.7	10.3	7.5	2.79	52	3-81q	12	.9	3.4	8.8	14	2.1	97
Raymond Intl .... N	27.91	88	8.2	12.3	8.7	2.00	42	3-81q	-16	.9	1.9	4.6	27	4.1	143
Stone & Web .... N	21.99	173	13.2	7.6	8.0	5.02	47	3-81q	7	17.3	11.8	23.1	0	4.9	278
Turner Constr .... A	16.94	141	14.8	6.8	6.9	3.53	27	3-81q	22	16.4	2.2	20.2	0	5.4	49

Building Materials and Supplies

VALUE OF SHIPMENTS OF BUILDING MATERIALS, PROJECTIONS 1979–81 (in millions of current dollars except as noted)

SIC Code	Industry	1979	Percent change 1978–79	1980	Percent change 1979–80	1981	Percent change 1980–81
3211	Flat glass	1,850	4	1,810	−2	2,155	19
3241	Cement, hydraulic	3,960	10	3,950	0	4,620	17
3261	Vitreous plumbing fixtures	500	9	475	−5	575	21
3271	Concrete block and brick	1,550	13	1,520	−2	1,795	18
3272	Concrete products, n.e.c.	3,930	14	4,050	3	4,655	15
3273	Ready-mixed concrete	8,875	12	9,230	4	10,700	16
3431	Metal sanitary ware	590	6	540	−8	650	20
3432	Plumbing fittings and brass goods	1,370	12	1,460	7	1,740	19
3441	Fabricated structural metal	6,770	10	7,725	14	8,500	10

Source: U.S. INDUSTRIAL OUTLOOK 1981, U.S. Department of Commerce.

CEMENT, HYDRAULIC: TRENDS AND PROJECTIONS 1975–81 (in millions of current dollars except as noted)

Item	1975	1976	1977	1978	1979 [2]	1980 [2]	Percent change 1979–80 [2]	1981 [3]	Percent change 1980–81 [3]
Industry (SIC 3241)									
Value of shipments [1]	2,334	2,604	3,042	3,603	3,960	3,950	0	4,620	17
Value added	1,333	1,461	1,672	1,959	2,140	2,110	−1	—	—
Value added per production worker-hour ($)	29.55	33.06	37.64	41.72	—	—	—	—	—
Total employment (000)	29	28	28	29	29	28	−3	—	—
Production workers (000)	23	22	22	23	23	22	−4	—	—
Average hourly earnings (Dec.—$)	6.80	7.39	8.17	8.98	9.82	[4] 10.69	[4] —	—	—
Year-to-year percent change in average hourly earnings (Dec.–Dec.)	13.0	8.9	10.6	9.9	9.4	[5] 10.0	[5] —	—	—
Year-to-year percent change in industry price index (Dec.–Dec.) [6]	14.6	10.4	6.6	11.0	11.8	[5] 8.8	[5] —	—	—
Capital expenditures	355	201	297	306	—	—	—	—	—
Product (SIC 3241)									
Value of shipments [7]	2,295	2,556	2,971	3,522	3,870	3,850	−1	—	—
Year-to-year percent change in Producer Price Index (Dec.–Dec.) [6]	14.6	10.5	6.6	11.0	11.8	[5] 8.8	[5] —	—	—
Trade									
Value of exports [8]	28	27	24	21	30	27	−10	—	—
Value of imports [8]	71	67	96	191	302	220	−27	—	—

[1] Value of all products and services sold by the industry (SIC 3241).
[2] Estimated except for hourly earnings, price indexes, and 1979 trade data.
[3] Forecast.
[4] As of July 1980.
[5] July 1979 to July 1980. Note: Months may differ for the price and earnings indexes.
[6] 1967 is the base period for index.
[7] Value of shipments of hydraulic cement produced by all industries.
[8] Includes cement, clinker, wet and dry mixes.

Source: Bureau of the Census (industry and trade data), Bureau of Labor Statistics (hourly earnings and price indexes). Estimates and forecasts by the Bureau of Industrial Economics.

Source: U.S. INDUSTRIAL OUTLOOK 1981, U.S. Department of Commerce.

Company and Market	Per Share $	Price To Equity %	Earnings Yield %	Current	5-Year Average	Amount $	Change %	Date	5-Year Growth Rate %	Profit Margin %	Return On Assets %	Return On Common Equity %	Debt Equity Ratio %	Dividend Yield %	Market Value $Mil
Cements															
Alpha Portland .... *N	31.83	42	-50.4	NC	5.2	-6.74	-100	3-81q	-42	-4.4	NE	NE	39	.0	23
Calif Port Cmt .... A	42.35	119	11.1	9.0	6.7	5.62	-19	1-81n	31	13.7	10.4	15.8	24	4.0	213
Conrock Co .... A	34.60	100	14.0	7.1	6.2	4.85	0	3-81q	31	7.1	10.6	13.5	1	3.5	69
Fla Rock Ind .... A	13.83	104	18.8	5.3	6.9	2.70	22	3-81s	64	5.9	9.3	17.6	49	2.1	65
Gen Portland .... *N	26.15	101	12.8	7.8	12.0	3.40	-20	3-81q	85	8.1	7.9	14.0	36	3.8	184
Giant Portland .... N	13.67	49	-8.9	NC	35.0	-.60	-100	3-81q	-34	-3.3	NE	NE	0	.0	12
Gifford Hill .... N	23.14	100	15.0	6.7	5.0	3.49	12	3-81q	21	4.2	4.5	13.8	148	4.0	171
Ideal Basic Ind .... *N	27.50	115	13.0	7.7	6.6	4.12	-10	3-81q	15	11.5	6.3	14.1	89	5.4	425
Kaiser Cement .... N	27.44	106	8.5	11.7	7.1	2.47	-38	3-81q	21	8.0	10.2	19.8	54	4.8	203
Lone Star Ind .... *N	37.32	88	14.8	6.8	7.4	4.84	-5	3-81q	24	6.5	5.6	13.3	77	5.6	353
Louisville Cem .... A	46.30	62	10.1	9.9	7.2	2.90	-39	3-81q	0	7.7	6.4	8.1	2	5.7	45
NWn State Port .... O	45.47	53	10.9	9.2	5.1	2.65	-48	2-81q	-10	8.4	4.6	6.9	19	7.4	24
Oregon Port Cem .... O	43.37	126	11.8	8.4	5.8	6.45	-20	3-81q	10	10.5	7.6	14.2	58	2.6	51
Puerto Rican C .... N	13.98	38	32.7	3.1	3.9	1.76	66	3-81q	31	4.8	4.0	13.4	129	.0	11
Texas Ind .... N	18.75	212	11.3	8.8	7.0	4.51	-19	2-81n	63	14.9	13.2	33.0	103	1.9	273
Whitehall Cem .... O	41.60	161	5.1	19.4	6.4	3.45	60	3-81q	27	5.1	24	5.8	93	.9	17
Lumber and Wood Products															
Bohemia Inc .... O	27.58	80	14.8	6.7	6.5	3.26	-48	1-81n	56	11.0	10.9	20.7	21	3.0	82
Boise Cascade .... *N	47.94	93	11.5	8.7	6.7	5.16	-22	3-81q	12	4.5	5.1	10.6	63	4.2	1,191
Champion Intl .... *N	29.33	87	11.3	8.9	7.4	2.88	-28	3-81q	6	4.9	5.5	10.4	51	5.8	1,377
Etz Lavud Ltd .... A	2.11	314	5.7	17.4	10.7	.38	-42	12-80n	92	2.8	2.7	55.6	219	3.3	11
Georgia-Pacifc .... *N	19.32	152	7.8	12.9	11.9	2.28	-25	12-80f	11	4.9	5.4	11.7	64	7.6	2,902
La Pacific .... *N	21.11	136	6.4	15.5	8.2	1.85	-44	3-81q	8	5.0	9.7	16.5	25	2.8	882
MacMln Bldel .... N	36.83	97	9.5	10.5	7.9	3.39	-53	3-81q	33	4.6	5.5	12.3	70	NA	761
Medford Corp .... O	22.34	179	10.0	10.1	10.0	3.98	-3	3-81q	31	6.6	12.2	17.0	15	2.5	99
Pac Lumber .... N	7.72	382	6.4	15.5	13.4	1.90	-6	3-81q	12	14.5	16.0	22.6	9	4.1	713
Ply-Gem .... A	12.43	56	14.3	7.0	4.9	1.00	-49	3-81q	5	2.4	11.2	16.6	2	5.7	8
Pope & Talbot .... N	18.05	129	7.4	13.4	6.9	1.73	-45	3-81q	11	5.3	5.9	9.9	44	3.4	143
Potlatch Cp .... *N	33.88	120	7.2	13.9	8.8	2.94	-30	3-81q	-2	6.0	4.8	9.6	64	3.4	621
Redlaw Ind .... A	2.35	48	24.9	4.0	9.1	.28	NE	3-81s	-4	-2.0	NE	NE	67	.0	5
Tech Sym .... A	3.33	244	1.4	NC	16.1	.11	-70	3-81q	21	2.2	2.7	5.2	28	.0	37
Trus Joist Cp .... O	8.64	307	6.8	14.7	9.3	1.80	-10	3-81q	31	8.0	11.6	21.0	48	1.1	97
Weyerhauser .... *N	22.56	157	5.7	17.4	12.8	2.03	-48	3-81q	1	7.1	6.1	11.3	50	3.7	4,441
Willamette Ind .... O	28.78	155	8.2	12.1	7.9	3.68	-17	3-81q	7	6.3	7.3	13.8	53	3.4	661

Lumber and Wood Products

SAWMILLS AND PLANING MILLS: TRENDS AND PROJECTIONS 1975–81 (millions of current dollars except as noted)

Item	1975	1976	1977	1978	1979[2]	1980[2]	Percent change 1979–80[2]	1981[3]	Percent change 1980–81[3]
Industry (SIC 2421)									
Value of shipments[1]	6,635	8,744	10,867	12,522	11,890	9,500	−21.1	11,000	15.7
Value added	2,652	3,754	4,453	5,294	5,112	4,218	−17.5	4,685	11.1
Value added per production worker-hour ($)	9.43	12.44	14.10	15.73	15.85	14.39	−9.2	15.10	4.9
Total employment (000)	160	169	175	173	177	164	−7.3	175	6.7
Production workers (000)	142	141	156	153	156	144	−7.7	153	6.3
Average hourly earnings (Dec.—$)	4.49	5.00	5.81	6.36	6.74	[4]6.84	[4]1.5	—	—
Year-to-year percent change in average hourly earnings (Dec.–Dec.)	10.9	11.3	16.2	9.5	6.0	[5]1.5	[5]1.5	—	—
Year-to-year percent change in industry price index (Dec.–Dec.)[6]	14.9	27.3	15.3	18.1	−1.9	[5]−9.7	[5]−9.7	—	—
Capital expenditures									
Product (SIC 2421)									
Value of shipments[7]	6,333	8,477	10,466	12,290	11,415	9,125	20.0	10,550	15.6
Quantity shipped (unit of measure)[7]	31,679	35,612	37,899	37,712	36,520	32,200	−11.8	35,500	10.2
Year-to-year percent change in producers price index (Dec.–Dec.)[8]	13.0	25.9	15.5	16.6	−0.1	[5]−8.7	[5]−8.7	—	—
Trade									
Value of exports	487	568	563	659	1,015	1,115	9.8	1,200	7.6
Value of imports	787	1,333	1,989	2,554	2,735	2,200	−19.6	2,460	11.8

[1] Value of all products and services sold by the Sawmills and Planing Mills Industry (SIC 2421).
[2] Estimated except for hourly earnings price indexes, and 1979 trade data.
[3] Forecast.
[4] As of June 1980.
[5] July 1979 to August 1980. Note: Months may differ for the price and earnings indexes.
[6] December 1971 is the base period for index.
[7] Value of shipments of Lumber Products produced by all industries.
Source: Bureau of the Census (industry and trade data), Bureau of Labor Statistics (hourly earnings and price indexes). Estimates and forecasts by the Bureau of Industrial Economics.

Source: U.S. INDUSTRIAL OUTLOOK 1981, U.S. Department of Commerce.

Chemicals, Plastics and Rubber

CHEMICALS AND ALLIED PRODUCTS: TRENDS AND PROJECTIONS 1975–81 (in millions of current dollars except as noted)

Item	1975	1976	1977	1978	1979²	1980²	Percent change 1979–80²	1981³	Percent change 1980–81³
Industry (SIC 28)									
Value of shipments¹	89,721	104,140	117,532	134,000	159,000	185,000	16.5	212,000	14.6
Value added	44,976	51,407	56,523	64,300	75,000	85,000	13.3	95,000	11.8
Value added per production worker-hour ($)	—	—	—	—	—	—	—	—	—
Total employment (000)	842	851	878	900	925	920	–0.5	—	—
Production workers (000)	510	520	541	555	570	550	–3.5	—	—
Average hourly earnings (Dec.–$)	5.61	6.14	6.67	7.28	7.91	⁴8.35	⁴—	—	—
Year-to-year percent change in average hourly earnings (Dec.–Dec.)	10.0	9.4	8.6	9.1	8.7	⁵9.7	⁵—	—	—
Year-to-year percent change in industry price index (Dec.–Dec.)⁶	5.5	2.6	3.1	3.8	18.1	⁵17.1	⁵—	—	—
Capital expenditures	6,353	7,122	8,489	—	—	—	—	—	—
Trade									
Value of exports⁷	9,386	10,799	11,705	13,660	19,012	23,000	21.1	—	—
Value of imports⁸	4,191	5,032	6,273	6,711	7,762	9,000	15.9	—	—

¹ Value of all products and services sold by the chemicals and allied products industry (SIC 28).
² Estimated except for hourly earnings, price indexes, and 1979 trade data.
³ Forecast.
⁴ As of July 1980.
⁵ July 1979 to July 1980. Note: Months may differ for the price and earnings indexes.
⁶ December 19 is the base period for index.
⁷ Bureau of the Census—Schedule B. Section 5 plus 231.2, 266, 267, 651.4.
⁸ Bureau of the Census—Schedule A. Section 5 plus 233.1, 266, 651.02.

Source: Bureau of the Census (industry and trade data), Bureau of Labor Statistics (hourly earnings and price indexes). Estimates and forecasts by the Bureau of Industrial Economics.

Source: *U.S. INDUSTRIAL OUTLOOK 1981*, U.S. Department of Commerce.

PLASTIC MATERIALS AND RESINS: TRENDS AND PROJECTIONS 1975–81 (in millions of current dollars except as noted)

Item	1975	1976	1977	1978	1979[2]	1980[2]	Percent change 1979–80[2]	1981[3]	Percent change 1980–81[3]
Industry (SIC 2821)									
Value of shipments[1]	7,043	9,202	10,818	12,146	14,700	16,100	10	18,000	12
Value added	2,771	3,524	4,143	4,544	5,585	6,070	9	6,840	13
Value added per production worker-hour ($)	40.33	48.27	54.09	59.42	71.60	77.82	9	—	—
Total employment (000)	54.3	56.2	57.2	58.4	58.7	58.8	—	—	—
Production workers (000)	34.0	36.4	36.7	37.6	37.4	37.2	—	—	—
Average hourly earnings (Dec.—$)	5.70	6.24	7.13	7.78	8.43	[4]8.87	—	—	—
Year-to-year percent change in average hourly earnings (Dec.–Dec.)	9.6	9.5	14.3	9.1	8.4	[4]9.8	—	—	—
Industry Price Index (Dec.)[6]	N.A.	100.6	103.1	104.4	134.3	[5]146.3	—	—	—
Year-to-year percent change in industry price index (Dec.–Dec.)[6]	N.A.	N.A.	2.5	1.3	28.6	[5]17.1	—	—	—
Capital expenditures	637.8	746.4	862.1	1,011.4	—	—	—	—	—
Product (SIC 2821)									
Value of shipments[7]	7,748	10,455	12,181	13,710	16,500	18,000	9	20,000	11
Quantity produced, total (million pounds)	24,868	29,680	34,623	38,878	41,871	38,500	–8	42,000	9
Producers Price Index (Dec.)[6]	186.4	194.9	198.6	200.9	262.7	[5]286.2	—	—	—
Year-to-year percent change in producers price index (Dec.–Dec.)[6]	1.7	4.6	1.9	1.2	30.8	[5]18.4	—	—	—
Trade									
Value of exports	1,173	1,672	1,733	[8]2,088	3,241	4,150	28	5,500	32
Value of imports	230	321	401	[8]531	640	700	9	775	11

[1] Value of all products and services sold by the plastics materials, synthetic resins and nonvulcanizable elastomers industry (SIC 2821).

[2] Estimated except for hourly earnings, price indexes, 1979 trade data and production.

[3] Forecast.

[4] As of June 1980; percent change June 1979 to 1980.

[5] July 1979 to 1980.

[6] June 1976 is the base period for the industry price index; 1967 for the producers price index.

[7] Value of shipments of plastics materials, synthetic resins and nonvulcanizable elastomers produced by all industries.

[8] Due to changes in classification, data are not strictly comparable to previous years.

N.A. = Not available

Source: Bureau of the Census (industry and trade data), Bureau of Labor Statistics (hourly earnings and price indexes). Estimates and forecasts by the Bureau of Industrial Economics.

Source: U.S. INDUSTRIAL OUTLOOK 1981, U.S. Department of Commerce.

		Relative Price					Earnings Per Share				Other					
		Common Equity			P/E Ratio		Latest 12 Months			5-Year			Return On	Debt		
Company and Market		Per Share	Price To Equity	Earnings Yield	Current	5-Year Average	Amount	Change	Date	Growth Rate	Profit Margin	Return On Assets	Common Equity	Equity Ratio	Dividend Yield	Market Value
		$	%	%	-	-	$	%	-	%	%	%	%	%	%	$Mil
Chemicals, Synthetics																
Air Pd & Chem	N	23.39	188	9.5	10.5	11.4	4.20	2	3-81s	17	8.1	6.6	17.4	60	1.8	1,255
Akzona Inc	*N	26.07	53	.4	NC	26.1	.06	-96	3-81q	-27	.3	.4	1.0	78	5.8	168
Allied Corp	*N	49.69	109	15.5	6.4	7.5	8.42	25	3-81q	16	5.2	6.4	15.0	53	4.1	1,817
Am Cyanamid	*N	29.93	118	9.9	10.1	8.8	3.51	1	3-81q	5	4.6	5.5	11.1	38	4.5	1,696
Big Three Ind	N	11.18	300	6.5	15.3	13.8	2.19	35	3-81q	22	13.1	10.6	18.3	31	1.8	1,419
Cabot Corp	N	16.53	166	11.5	8.7	7.7	3.15	22	3-81s	42	6.7	8.1	18.1	44	3.3	867
Celanese Corp	*N	70.70	89	12.6	7.9	7.6	7.93	-17	3-81q	17	3.6	4.6	11.1	69	6.0	902
Diamond Shmrk	N	22.08	138	11.3	8.8	8.5	3.45	-11	3-81q	-1	6.4	7.2	16.2	68	5.5	1,715
Dow Chemical	*N	24.30	133	11.9	8.4	9.8	3.85	-17	3-81q	8	7.6	7.0	18.1	77	5.6	6,141
DuPont	*N	37.21	132	9.3	10.8	9.7	4.56	-28	3-81q	11	5.2	7.5	12.6	20	6.4	7,199
Essex Chemical	N	10.29	164	11.0	9.1	6.1	1.86	13	3-81q	6	3.2	6.0	18.1	120	4.7	44
Ethyl Corp	N	34.66	92	12.5	8.0	5.9	3.97	-23	3-81q	7	5.2	7.4	12.8	31	4.7	610
Grace W R	*N	37.98	117	14.2	7.1	8.3	6.27	27	3-81q	21	4.7	6.5	15.8	62	5.2	2,074
Hercules Inc	*N	23.79	100	11.7	8.6	9.8	2.77	-13	3-81q	10	4.6	6.0	11.3	33	5.1	1,008
Imperial Chem	A	10.63	56	24.5	4.1	6.7	1.47	25	6-80s	18	8.0	7.5	15.4	41	6.7	3,540
Koppers Co	N	22.73	109	7.3	13.7	9.1	1.82	NC	3-81q	-7	2.9	4.0	7.7	49	5.6	688
Liquid Air Cp	O	19.43	134	11.0	9.1	10.6	2.85	13	3-81q	0	7.2	6.6	13.2	50	6.2	265
Monsanto Co	*N	77.63	98	5.7	17.6	9.0	4.31	-53	3-81q	-17	2.3	2.6	5.3	49	5.0	2,749
Pacer Tech&Res	O	.65	654	1.2	NC	NC	.05	NC	9-80n	NE	-25.0	NE	NE	0	.0	22
Penmalt Corp	N	43.64	67	13.2	7.6	7.9	3.83	-25	3-81q	2	3.6	5.2	11.0	45	7.6	261
Publicker Ind	N	9.14	59	-6.1	NC	NC	-.33	NE	3-81q	NE	.5	7.5	11.3	6	.0	45
Reichold Chem	N	24.93	56	13.4	7.5	8.7	1.87	19	3-81q	-3	1.8	3.8	7.8	47	3.4	97
Rohm & Haas	N	54.49	115	12.2	8.2	9.9	7.62	0	3-81q	25	5.4	7.6	13.3	33	3.7	806
Stauffer Chem	*N	20.94	113	13.4	7.5	7.6	3.18	-3	3-81q	4	7.2	5.8	13.0	43	5.6	1,044
Stepan Chem	A	26.96	131	9.0	11.1	7.1	3.20	36	3-81q	2	3.4	3.9	10.7	52	2.8	66
Union Carbide	*N	61.06	93	16.5	6.1	6.6	9.40	-5	3-81q	11	6.7	6.3	13.8	44	5.6	3,840
Witco Chemical	N	26.70	106	13.3	7.5	6.4	3.75	-18	3-81q	13	3.5	7.6	18.1	49	5.7	254
Specialty Chemicals																
Betz Laboratories	O	13.94	371	6.1	16.3	17.0	3.17	20	3-81q	21	11.0	16.8	21.4	1	2.3	405
Bio Rad Lab B	A	5.03	415	3.3	30.7	14.5	.68	-13	3-81q	22	4.1	5.0	13.9	113	.0	59
Chemed Corp	O	16.86	251	7.0	14.2	12.7	2.97	2	3-81q	14	8.0	12.5	17.5	0	5.4	421
Chomerics	O	6.60	348	4.3	23.5	31.8	.98	-4	9-80n	21	8.1	7.8	15.3	63	.0	40
Church & Dwight	O	29.91	104	14.9	6.7	9.6	4.62	6	3-81q	16	7.2	9.0	17.2	48	5.8	43
Crompt & Knwl	N	28.85	86	13.6	7.3	6.1	3.37	3	3-81q	13	3.2	5.2	11.0	63	5.5	53
Dexter Corp	N	17.03	159	10.0	10.0	8.5	2.71	-1	3-81q	12	4.8	8.1	16.4	37	3.7	248
Diamond Crys Salt	O	42.86	50	6.7	14.8	7.6	1.45	-70	3-81f	-10	3.1	8.4	11.2	7	5.6	29
Ferro Corp	N	28.99	86	13.7	7.3	6.6	3.43	-16	3-81q	8	4.2	6.7	13.0	27	4.8	193
Fuller H B Co	O	14.40	163	10.5	9.6	6.3	2.46	36	2-81q	17	3.3	6.6	15.0	40	2.0	105
Grt Lks Chem	A	13.07	425	4.8	20.8	12.2	2.67	-5	3-81q	19	14.9	16.0	20.3	7	.8	395
Hunt Chem A	N	10.13	95	5.1	19.6	12.3	.49	-63	3-81q	-13	3.8	5.1	6.9	11	4.2	55
Intl Flav Frag	*N	8.61	250	8.0	12.4	16.3	1.73	3	12-80f	20	14.1	15.2	20.0	0	4.3	787
Kin-Ark Corp	A	3.45	105	.8	NC	36.5	.03	-91	3-81q	-42	.3	.3	.7	96	.0	16
Lawter Int	N	4.10	305	8.2	12.1	13.3	1.03	2	3-81q	13	14.7	19.9	24.0	2	5.3	143
LeaRonal Inc	A	6.42	364	7.1	14.1	6.3	1.66	34	2-81f	39	3.4	17.0	26.1	0	1.7	113
Loctite Cp	N	11.66	229	5.2	19.1	13.8	1.40	-48	3-81n	10	13.0	14.4	22.6	14	2.1	264
Lubrizol Corp	N	18.86	317	8.7	11.4	11.8	5.22	-1	3-81q	21	12.1	17.5	24.2	0	1.8	1,189
MacDermid	O	12.64	194	9.6	10.4	8.2	2.36	-6	12-80n	25	9.3	14.4	20.6	0	3.7	50
Mallinckrodt	O	16.23	209	7.4	13.5	12.5	2.51	10	3-81q	10	8.1	9.6	13.9	18	2.9	480
Nalco	N	15.33	369	6.6	15.1	11.2	3.75	16	3-81q	13	11.7	17.4	23.6	3	3.5	1,130
NCH Corp	N	12.91	175	11.7	8.6	12.0	2.64	7	1-81n	13	8.7	13.0	20.2	3	3.2	246
Nuclear Metals	O	5.88	374	4.0	25.3	15.6	.87	-6	3-81s	19	7.8	8.8	16.4	30	.0	59
Oakite Products	N	12.84	177	11.1	9.0	8.4	2.53	12	3-81q	9	6.5	13.0	17.4	0	6.2	40
Park Chemical	A	15.36	110	14.2	7.0	6.0	2.40	-21	3-81q	10	5.2	12.9	15.1	0	5.3	6
Petrolite Corp	O	9.43	445	5.4	18.7	15.8	2.25	56	1-81q	15	9.8	14.2	22.2	11	1.9	499
Prod Research	N	4.92	259	5.6	18.0	11.7	.71	-7	3-81s	19	7.8	10.9	16.4	23	2.5	58
Quaker Chemical	O	11.61	140	11.0	9.1	7.4	1.79	-9	3-81q	8	6.7	10.4	15.7	13	3.0	56
Robintech	A	13.78	48	-6.0	NC	NC	-.40	NC	3-81n	NE	-.4	NE	NE	48	.0	14
Sigma-Aldrich	O	16.12	406	4.8	21.0	13.7	3.12	16	3-81q	20	12.4	14.5	18.7	0	1.1	282
Sun Chem Cp	N	21.80	135	12.9	7.7	4.3	3.80	-2	3-81q	22	6.1	6.9	21.1	107	1.6	217
Univar Cp	N	13.26	122	14.3	7.0	6.3	2.30	7	11-80n	19	1.8	5.0	17.9	77	4.8	104

SYNTHETIC RUBBER: TRENDS AND PROJECTIONS 1975–81 (in millions of current dollars except as noted)

Item	1975	1976	1977	1978	1979[2]	1980[2]	Percent change 1979–80[2]	1981[3]	Percent change 1980–81[3]
Industry (SIC 28220)									
Value of shipments [1]	1,456	1,702	1,863	1,971	2,225	2,100	−5.6	2,500	19.0
Value added	469	511	569	574	675	630	−6.7	750	19.0
Value added per production worker-hour ($)	34.49	34.28	40.15	39.61	—	—	—	—	—
Total employment (000)	9.9	10.6	10.5	10.1	10.1	10.0	−1.0	—	—
Production workers (000)	7.0	7.6	7.2	7.3	7.3	7.0	−4.1	—	—
Average hourly earnings (Dec.—$)	5.70	6.24	6.76	7.78	7.92	[4]8.20	[4]9.6	—	—
Year-to-year percent change in average hourly earnings (Dec.–Dec.)	9.6	9.5	8.3	15.1	7.2	[5]—	[6]	—	—
Year-to-year percent change in industry price index (Dec.–Dec.) [6]	1.3	3.3	9.8	7.3	17.8	[5]20.8	[5]—	—	—
Capital expenditures	35	46	53	30	—	—	—	—	—
Product (SIC 28220)									
Value of shipments [7]	1,820	2,204	2,343	2,839	3,175	2,975	−6.3	3,580	20.3
Quantity shipped (unit of measure) [7]	4,500	5,450	5,650	5,850	5,900	4,800	−18.6	5,425	13.0
Year-to-year percent change in producers price index (Dec.–Dec.) [6]	−2.0	7.9	8.6	8.9	18.6	[5]20.3	[6]—	—	—
Trade									
Value of exports	267	334	325	369	601	750	24.8	—	—
Value of imports	73	97	139	158	177	177	0.0	—	—

[1] Value of all products and services sold by the synthetic rubber industry (SIC 2822).
[2] Estimated except for hourly earnings, price indexes, and 1979 trade data.
[3] Forecast.
[4] As of July 1980.

[5] July 1979 to July 1980. Note: Months may differ for the price and earnings indexes.
[6] December 1967 is the base period for index.
[7] Value of shipments of synthetic rubber produced by all industries.
Source: Bureau of the Census (industry and trade data), Bureau of Labor Statistics (hourly earnings and price indexes). Estimates and forecasts by the Bureau of Industrial Economics.

Source: *U.S. INDUSTRIAL OUTLOOK 1981*, U.S. Department of Commerce.

TIRES AND INNER TUBES: TRENDS AND PROJECTIONS 1975–81 (in millions of current dollars except as noted)

Item	1975	1976	1977	1978	1979[2]	1980[2]	Percent change 1979–80[2]	1981[3]	Percent change 1980–81[3]
Industry (SIC 3011)									
Value of shipments[1]	7,143	7,714	9,540	8,887	9,875	9,350	−5.3	11,000	17.6
Value added	3,463	3,534	4,538	4,107	4,545	4,400	−3.2	5,175	17.6
Value added per production worker-hour ($)	22.68	25.98	25.65	30.40	33.07	—	—	—	—
Total employment (000)	106	104	114	103	101	84	−16.8	88	4.8
Production workers (000)	80	79	88	81	79	62	−15.2	66	6.4
Average hourly earnings (Dec.—$)	5.70	7.15	7.33	7.82	9.04	[4]9.50	[4]12.3	—	—
Year-to-year percent change in average hourly earnings (Dec.–Dec.)	4.4	25.4	2.5	6.7	15.6	[5]—	[5]—	—	—
Year-to-year percent change in industry price index (Dec.–Dec.)[6]	5.8	13.4	−0.1	9.4	9.0	[5]15.0	[5]—	—	—
Capital expenditures	272	244	286	356	—	—	—	—	—
Product (SIC 3011)									
Value of shipments[7]	6,107	6,528	8,135	8,300	9,175	8,700	−5.2	10,235	17.6
Year-to-year percent change in producers price index (Dec.–Dec.)[6]	5.8	13.6	−1.4	5.5	24.3	[5]15.4	[5]—	—	—
Product classes									
Value of shipments[7]									
Passenger cars	3,392	3,631	4,540	4,496	5,000	4,950	−1.0	5,600	13.1
Truck and bus	1,709	1,754	2,308	2,529	2,800	2,450	−12.5	3,100	26.5
Quantity shipped (millions of tires)									
Passenger cars	167	177	195	200	184	165	−10.3	175	6.1
Truck and bus	27	31	37	44	41	32	−22.0	38	18.8
Trade									
Value of exports	306	219	309	280	353	525	48.7	—	—
Value of imports	566	889	962	1,056	1,373	1,425	3.8	—	—

[1] Value of all products and services sold by the tire and inner tube industry (SIC 3011).
[2] Estimated except for hourly earnings, price indexes, and 1979 trade data.
[3] Forecast.
[4] As of July 1980.
[5] July 1979 to July 1980. Note: Months may differ for the price and earnings indexes.
[6] December 1967 is the base period for index.
[7] Value of shipments of tires and inner tubes produced by all industries.

Source: Bureau of the Census (industry and trade data), Bureau of Labor Statistics (hourly earnings and price indexes). Estimates and forecasts by the Bureau of Industrial Economics.

Source: U.S. INDUSTRIAL OUTLOOK 1981, U.S. Department of Commerce.

Company and Market		Relative Price					Earnings Per Share				Other					
		Common Equity		Earnings Yield	P/E Ratio		Latest 12 Months			5-Year Growth Rate	Profit Margin	Return On Assets	Return On Common Equity	Debt Equity Ratio	Dividend Yield	Market Value
		Per Share	Price To Equity		Current	5-Year Average	Amount	Change	Date							
		$	%	%	-	-	$	%	-	%	%	%	%	%	%	$Mil
Tires and Inner Tubes																
Aegis Corp	A	2.79	108	7.7	13.0	7.6	.23	-15	3-81q	-5	1.3	2.6	6.3	63	.0	33
Alliance Tire	A	6.10	230	8.2	12.2	9.0	1.15	39	3-81q	10	6.1	.2	23.8	15	.0	38
Armstrong Rub	N	58.97	63	-20.5	NC	4.7	-7.63	-100	3-81s	-39	-4.1	NE	NE	82	3.8	64
Bandag Inc	N	13.04	174	10.2	9.8	10.0	2.31	12	3-81q	12	8.3	12.2	17.6	9	3.5	271
Cooper Tire	N	32.04	103	22.2	4.5	4.1	7.34	226	3-81q	12	4.0	7.0	19.5	85	2.7	65
Dunlop Holding	A	3.95	44	-4.6	NC	4.4	-.08	-100	6-80s	-21	NC	.0	NE	115	8.6	232
Firestone Tire	*N	23.27	56	-11.5	NC	10.8	-1.50	-100	1-81q	-47	-2.5	NE	NE	44	2.3	750
Gen Tire	N	40.06	69	8.0	12.5	6.6	2.21	-2	2-81q	-20	1.8	2.3	4.1	24	5.4	666
Goodyear Tire	*N	32.12	58	15.2	6.6	8.0	2.81	52	3-81q	7	2.4	3.9	9.0	54	7.0	1,328
Mohawk Rub	N	21.97	83	16.4	6.1	5.5	2.99	375	3-81q	-3	2.6	5.1	11.9	52	4.9	33
Uniroyal Inc	*N	16.30	58	4.1	24.4	NC	.39	NE	3-81q	-93	-.3	NE	NE	122	.0	252
Rubber and Plastic Products																
Amerace Corp	N	44.99	51	12.1	8.3	7.7	2.79	-22	3-81q	4	3.1	4.7	8.7	47	5.7	57
Am Biltrite	A	20.99	43	-49.5	NC	7.0	-4.52	-100	3-81q	NE	-6.2	2.8	6.0	52	3.3	24
Carlisle Corp	N	11.43	433	6.1	16.5	5.8	3.00	36	3-81q	43	6.8	13.1	24.7	40	1.5	465
Chemplast Inc	A	7.31	142	10.5	9.5	7.6	1.09	-9	2-81s	20	8.5	13.1	16.4	7	2.7	16
Crest-Foam	A	5.03	72	2.5	40.3	9.8	.09	-83	2-81q	3	1.3	7.0	10.6	17	.0	5
Dayco Corp	N	25.98	48	7.3	13.7	7.6	.91	-51	4-81s	-11	1.2	1.9	5.9	115	4.5	71
Fluorocarbon	O	5.88	238	6.1	16.5	8.7	.85	-21	4-81q	21	4.5	8.2	14.2	41	1.1	61
GIT Inds	A	-1.96	0782	9.3	10.8	7.0	.22	-33	3-81q	32	.5	1.3	NE	-787	.0	3
Grt Amer Ind	A	15.07	105	25.1	4.0	2.7	3.98	-1	3-81q	24	5.6	9.5	24.1	63	.0	23
Intercole	A	6.42	113	3.7	26.9	15.7	.27	NC	1-81s	27	4.7	6.3	11.1	22	.0	14
Kleer-Vu Ind	A	5.14	131	19.7	5.1	10.4	1.33	224	3-81q	33	3.7	8.1	22.7	86	.0	3
Kroy Ind	O	2.82	1738	2.8	35.5	45.2	1.38	1871	6-80q	42	17.9	23.6	41.5	6	.2	154
NVF Co	N	3.19	121	3.6	27.7	12.5	.14	-77	12-80f	23	1.6	4.7	25.2	260	2.1	311
OSullivan Cp	A	15.69	109	13.3	7.5	5.0	2.28	24	3-81q	8	6.7	14.6	19.1	0	3.5	32
Pantasote Inc	A	8.27	54	10.0	10.0	9.9	.45	29	3-81q	-18	.8	1.3	3.7	48	.0	18
Plymth Rub A	A	6.77	79	1.1	NC	NC	.06	NE	2-81q	NE	.2	.4	.9	0	.0	9
Richdson Co	N	24.68	82	5.3	18.9	11.5	1.07	-24	3-81q	-18	1.3	2.4	3.6	17	6.4	42
Rogers Corp	A	11.02	226	.1	NC	25.8	.03	-98	3-81q	-40	.8	1.0	2.2	64	.5	70
Rubbermaid	N	17.97	210	7.3	13.6	11.2	2.77	-6	3-81q	11	6.5	9.4	14.5	11	2.9	291
Schulman, A Inc	O	21.67	85	9.2	10.8	4.4	1.71	-54	2-81s	12	2.5	7.2	14.7	17	3.9	40
Sealed Air	N	12.58	274	7.0	14.3	9.4	2.41	24	3-81q	26	7.2	11.7	18.6	6	1.6	112
SGL Indus	A	13.20	107	14.9	6.7	6.4	2.10	23	1-81s	18	4.9	10.0	13.4	0	4.7	20
Velcro Industries	O	6.58	175	15.2	6.6	6.2	1.75	5	3-81s	6	13.4	13.1	24.7	10	6.1	35
Voplex Corp	A	13.00	88	5.2	19.3	8.3	.59	-57	3-81q	-26	1.6	2.9	4.8	32	4.6	13

BIOLOGICALS: TRENDS AND PROJECTIONS 1975–81 (in millions of current dollars except as noted)

Item	1975	1976	1977	1978[1]	1979[2]	1980[2]	Percent change 1979–80[2]	1981[3]	Percent change 1980–81[3]
Industry (SIC 2831)									
Value of shipments[1]	663	719	899	1,007	1,114	1,245	12	1,417	14
Value added	429	446	563	656	724	809	12	—	—
Value added per production worker-hour ($)	30.00	30.10	32.56	37.92	41.85	46.76	12	—	—
Total employment (000)	13.4	13.0	15.7	17.8	18.0	18.2	1	—	—
Production workers (000)	7.2	7.3	8.8	9.2	9.3	9.4	1	—	—
Average hourly earnings (production workers)	4.74	5.02	5.23	5.40	5.91	—	—	—	—
Year-to-year percent change in average hourly earnings	8.7	5.9	4.2	3.3	9.4	—	—	—	—
Capital expenditures	43	32	34	65	—	—	—	—	—
Product (SIC 2831)									
Value of shipments[4]	788	874	1,068	1,187	1,325	1,484	12	1,678	13
Selected product categories									
SIC 28311									
Blood and blood products	165	180	243	268	299	335	12	381	14
SIC 28312									
Vaccines and antigens	76	91	99	105	117	128	9	144	10
SIC 28314 and 28316									
Diagnostics and industrial biologics	427	478	496	565	631	704	12	795	13
SIC 28315									
Biologicals for veterinary use	73	92	121	138	154	173	12	194	12
Trade									
Value of exports (FT 610)	97	108	138	187	296	390	31.7	523	34.1
Value of imports (FT 210)	3.9	5.6	7.1	9.2	9.0	11.0	22.2	12.7	15.4

[1] Value of all products and services sold by the biologicals industry (SIC 2831).
[2] Estimated except for trade data.
[3] Forecast.

[4] Value of shipments of biologicals produced by all industries. Source: Bureau of the Census (industry and trade data), Bureau of Labor Statistics (price indexes). Estimates and forecasts by the Bureau of Industrial Economics.

Source: *U.S. INDUSTRIAL OUTLOOK 1981*, U.S. Department of Commerce.

PHARMACEUTICAL PREPARATIONS: TRENDS AND PROJECTIONS 1975–81 (in millions of current dollars except as noted)

Item	1975	1976	1977	1978	1979[2]	1980[2]	Percent change 1979–80[2]	1981[3]	Percent change 1980–81[3]
Industry (SIC 2834)									
Value of shipments[1]	9,388	10,765	11,459	13,291	15,480	18,158	17	21,210	17
Value added	6,923	7,975	8,214	9,037	9,941	10,935	10	12,029	10
Value added per production worker-hour ($)	59.94	66.12	66.74	68.91	71.40	74.00	4	76.80	4
Total employment (000)	122.8	124.0	126.4	136.8	143.6	149.3	4	—	—
Production workers (000)	60.2	62.1	63.1	66.1	68.7	70.8	3	—	—
Average hourly earnings (production workers)	5.49	5.90	6.33	6.77	7.40	[4]7.75	4.7	—	—
Year-to-year percent change in average hourly earnings	9.6	7.5	7.3	7.0	9.3	[5]9.8	[5]5.4	—	—
New capital expenditures	321	309	419	539	—	—	—	—	—
Product (SIC 2834)									
Value of shipments[7]	8,247	9,217	9,640	10,799	12,170	13,800	13	15,800	14
Producers price index (estimated composite)	122	129	135	140	157	176	12.1	—	—
Year-to-year percent change in producers price index[6]	7.0	5.7	4.7	3.7	12.1	[5]12.1	—	—	—
Product classes (selected) Value of shipments[7]									
SIC 28342 Central nervous system	2,086	2,228	2,254	2,429	2,782	3,171	14	3,647	15
SIC 28343 Cardiovascular system	642	755	748	800	916	1,173	15	1,360	16
SIC 28344 Respiratory system	765	878	871	1,055	1,055	1,140	8	1,230	8
SIC 28346 Skin preparations	499	562	613	684	765	857	12	960	12
SIC 28347 Vitamins, hematinics	999	1,115	1,315	1,726	2,009	2,330	16	2,703	16
Trade									
Value of exports (FT 610)	270	284	320	335	339	366	8	403	10
Value of imports (FT 210)	34	34	34	50	57	66	16	75	14

[1] Value of all products and services sold by the pharmaceutical preparations industry (SIC 2834).
[2] Estimated except for price indexes and trade data.
[3] Forecast.
[4] As of July 1980.
[5] July 1979 to July 1980. Note: Months may differ for the price and earnings indexes.
[6] December 1967 is the base period for index.
[7] Value of shipments of pharmaceutical preparations produced by industries.

Source: Bureau of the Census (industry and trade data), Bureau of Labor Statistics (price indexes). Estimates and forecasts by the Bureau of Industrial Economics.

Source: U.S. INDUSTRIAL OUTLOOK 1981, U.S. Department of Commerce.

COSMETICS: TRENDS AND PROJECTIONS 1975–81 (in millions of current dollars except as noted)

Item	1975	1976	1977	1978	1979²	1980²	Percent change 1979–80²	1981³	Percent change 1980–81³
Industry (SIC 2844)									
Value of shipments¹	5,155	5,896	6,557	7,179	8,184	9,494	16	11,100	17
Value added	3,443	4,025	4,527	4,924	5,706	6,503	14	—	—
Value added per production worker-hour ($)	59.37	64.50	71.97	79.31	91.30	104.05	14	—	—
Total employment (000)	48.3	49.2	50.9	53.5	57.0	57.2	—	—	—
Production workers (000)	30.3	32.1	32.8	33.4	34.1	34.4	1	—	—
Average hourly earnings (production workers)	4.59	4.70	5.07	5.69	5.92	6.10	3	—	—
Year-to-year percent change in average hourly earnings	8.8	2.4	7.9	12.2	4.0	3.0	−25	—	—
Capital expenditures	70.6	75.7	105.6	139.4	—	—	—	—	—
Product (SIC 2844)									
Value of shipments⁶	5,179	5,883	6,394	6,795	7,746	8,990	16	10,500	17
Producer price index	129	134	142	149	167	193	20	—	—
Year-to-year percent change in producers price index (Dec.–Dec.)⁵	4	4	6	5	12	♦20	♦67	—	—
Product classes									
Value of shipments⁶									
SIC 28441									
Shaving preparations	213	268	268	299	335	379	13	432	14
SIC 28442									
Fragrances	919	1,007	1,097	1,251	1,430	1,660	16	1,940	17
SIC 28443									
Hair preparations	1,306	1,408	1,475	1,468	1,645	1,875	14	2,155	15
SIC 28444									
Oral hygiene products	537	628	660	734	815	915	12	1,040	14
SIC 28445									
Cosmetics, NEC	2,145	2,446	2,597	2,782	3,160	3,666	16	4,290	17
Trade									
Value of exports (FT 610)	113	148	168	225	256	305	19	380	25
Value of imports (FT 210)	30	29	37	60	78	110	41	145	32

¹ Value of all products and services sold by the cosmetics industry (SIC 2844).
² Estimated except for price indexes and 1979 trade data.
³ Forecast.
⁴ July 1979 to July 1980. Months may differ for the price and earnings indexes.
⁵ December 1967 is the base period for index.
⁶ Value of shipments of cosmetics produced by all industries.

Source: Bureau of the Census (industry and trade data), Bureau of Labor Statistics (hourly earnings and price indexes). Estimates and forecasts by the Bureau of Industrial Economics.

Source: U.S. INDUSTRIAL OUTLOOK 1981, p. 173, U.S. Department of Commerce.

Company and Market	Relative Price					Earnings Per Share				Other					
	Common Equity		Earnings Yield	P/E Ratio		Latest 12 Months			5-Year Growth Rate	Profit Margin	Return On Assets	Return On Common Equity	Debt Equity Ratio	Dividend Yield	Market Value
	Per Share	Price To Equity		Current	5-Year Average	Amount	Change	Date							
	$	%	%	-	-	$	%	-	%	%	%	%	%	%	$Mil
Drug Manufacturers															
Abbott Labs *N	16.63	335	6.5	15.5	13.2	3.60	18	3-81q	21	10.5	10.4	20.9	18	2.6	3,443
Am Home Prod *N	9.47	359	8.6	11.6	13.4	2.93	13	3-81q	13	10.9	18.8	30.3	0	5.6	5,288
Block Drugs Co O	13.36	155	11.8	8.5	7.4	2.44	13	12-80n	13	9.9	12.3	16.7	7	4.8	154
Bolar Phar O	1.71	943	3.4	29.3	11.4	.55	10	3-81q	57	17.8	27.3	31.8	0	1.2	62
Bristol-Myers *N	20.90	257	7.9	12.7	11.7	4.21	15	3-81q	14	8.6	12.2	19.6	8	3.4	3,519
Carter-Wallace N	17.54	83	8.8	11.3	9.4	1.28	22	3-81f	59	4.2	3.9	6.0	14	2.8	113
Cooper Labs N	20.05	203	9.0	11.1	10.5	3.68	95	1-81q	44	12.0	9.8	22.3	53	2.0	191
Forest Labs A	2.89	826	3.0	33.2	31.6	.72	16	12-80n	20	9.6	10.3	20.0	26	.0	54
GNC Inc N	5.70	667	3.3	30.4	NC	1.25	NC	1-80f	72	5.2	NC	22.2	25	.2	306
ICN Pharm N	3.02	224	4.1	24.1	19.1	.28	NE	2-81q	NE	1.4	NE	NE	74	.0	44
Key Pharm A	1.61	2446	.9	NC	39.6	.36	80	3-81q	82	13.5	18.6	22.7	3	.2	343
Lilly Eli Co *N	22.92	282	7.3	13.8	13.6	4.70	4	3-81q	13	13.4	13.1	19.7	2	3.6	4,896
Marion Labs N	8.11	290	4.5	22.2	13.6	1.06	15	3-81n	-2	7.3	8.4	12.5	17	2.7	193
Merck & Co *N	24.93	403	5.7	17.7	15.7	5.69	9	3-81q	14	15.2	14.5	22.3	11	2.6	7,512
Morton Norwich N	25.81	120	11.5	8.7	12.8	3.56	3	3-81n	34	5.6	7.7	13.7	28	4.9	417
Newport Ph O	.04	5625	.5	NC	NC	.05	NC	1-81n	NE	-6.4	NE	NE	0	.0	77
Pfizer Inc *N	21.41	245	6.8	14.8	11.5	3.55	6	3-81q	11	8.4	7.6	16.2	37	3.0	3,857
Reid Prov Labs O	3.24	235	2.9	34.7	22.7	.22	38	12-80s	-5	5.2	5.0	7.1	5	.9	10
Robins, AH N	11.08	115	8.9	11.2	9.1	1.14	-34	3-81q	1	5.9	6.5	9.1	9	3.3	320
Rorer Group N	8.15	291	8.0	12.4	12.6	1.91	15	3-81q	15	10.3	12.5	20.5	3	3.9	420
Scherer RP Co O	9.35	213	5.6	17.9	11.6	1.11	102	3-81f	3	5.0	4.3	7.0	9	1.3	152
Scher Plough *N	22.03	174	11.7	8.5	10.8	4.48	6	3-81q	12	13.7	12.1	19.1	3	4.4	2,032
Searle, GD *N	9.28	348	5.6	17.8	12.0	1.81	5	3-81q	16	8.7	7.9	18.2	50	1.6	1,703
SmithKline Cp *N	14.85	566	5.9	16.9	13.8	4.97	26	3-81q	42	17.4	19.8	31.2	14	2.3	5,577
Squibb Corp N	20.85	176	7.1	14.1	12.3	2.60	3	3-81q	2	7.3	6.5	12.2	40	3.3	1,777
Sterling Drug *N	13.20	175	8.8	11.3	10.8	2.04	10	12-80f	9	7.2	9.8	15.5	6	4.3	1,396
Syntex Corp N	23.94	257	8.0	12.5	11.4	4.92	29	1-81s	25	13.0	10.6	17.7	27	2.6	1,043
Thompson Med N	6.05	298	14.2	7.0	8.0	2.56	64	2-81q	51	10.5	26.2	41.3	0	.0	72
Unimed Inc O	1.04	1394	1.9	NC	24.8	.27	NC	3-81s	40	28.0	23.3	26.9	0	.0	36
Upjohn Co *N	28.89	220	9.0	11.1	11.2	5.75	9	3-81q	21	9.7	10.2	19.7	35	3.1	1,904
Warner-Lambrt *N	18.67	125	1.8	NC	12.3	.43	-73	3-81q	-19	5.5	6.5	13.0	38	5.6	1,862
Cosmetics and Grooming Aids															
Alberto-Culver *N	15.80	89	9.4	10.6	12.0	1.33	37	3-81s	27	1.9	3.8	7.4	7	2.8	54
Avon Products *N	15.31	250	10.6	9.4	12.6	4.05	-3	3-81q	8	9.4	15.4	26.2	0	7.8	2,301
Chesbgh-Pnds *N	15.48	239	8.7	11.5	11.5	3.23	20	3-81q	17	7.3	10.9	19.9	26	4.1	1,201
Del Labs A	24.76	77	17.8	5.6	8.6	3.38	745	3-81q	8	6.5	7.8	13.7	37	3.2	20
Faberge Inc *N	21.85	117	1.6	NC	15.5	.40	-61	3-81q	-23	.8	1.0	1.7	22	1.9	143
Gillette Co *N	23.72	142	11.8	8.5	8.9	3.97	3	3-81q	12	5.4	7.3	17.3	39	5.6	1,019
GRI A	5.27	111	6.0	16.8	34.3	.35	NE	2-81q	NE	-.9	NE	NE	7	.0	15
Helene Curtis N	16.48	101	14.1	7.1	6.2	2.34	92	2-81f	12	2.8	3.8	7.8	29	.9	32
Jhirmack Entrprs O	5.89	183	5.7	17.6	11.9	.61	-45	1-81n	11	8.8	7.9	13.4	31	.0	26
Johnson Prod A	5.87	72	-13.4	NC	28.0	-.57	NE	2-81s	-35	-6.8	NE	NE	0	.0	17
La Maur Inc A	8.55	187	5.7	17.6	10.0	.91	65	3-81q	19	2.8	6.8	9.7	0	1.3	27
Mary Kay Cos N	5.48	1186	3.7	26.9	10.8	2.42	50	3-81q	40	9.0	20.3	39.1	8	.6	459
MEM Co A	21.29	69	14.4	6.9	6.4	2.13	5	3-81q	-1	5.9	8.5	10.2	3	7.3	25
Minnetonka O	1.91	818	5.3	18.8	8.4	.83	277	3-81q	107	7.5	18.7	41.4	11	.0	117
Nestle-Le Mur A	4.63	121	6.4	15.6	15.5	.36	57	3-81q	98	4.3	6.6	7.5	0	2.7	8
Noxell O	15.21	226	9.1	11.0	8.4	3.12	16	3-81q	17	7.2	15.5	19.8	0	2.8	168
Redken Labs O	12.34	144	10.0	10.0	8.7	1.77	-8	1-81s	3	5.9	8.4	14.1	31	2.0	40
Revlon Inc *N	26.54	156	11.1	9.0	12.6	4.61	5	3-81q	15	8.7	8.5	16.2	43	4.4	1,492

HEALTH AND MEDICAL SERVICES: TRENDS AND PROSPECTS 1976-81 (billions of dollars unless otherwise indicated)[1]
(billions of dollars unless otherwise indicated)[1]

	1976	1977	1978	1979[1]	1980[1]	Percent change 1979-80	1981[1]	Percent change 1980-81
Total Expenditures	148.9	170.0	192.4	216.9	244.6	13	276.1	13
Health services and supplies	140.1	161.2	183.0	207.0	234.1	13	264.7	13
Personal health care	132.1	149.1	167.9	190.2	215.5	13	244.1	13
Hospital care	59.8	67.9	76.0	86.0	97.3	13	111.0	14
Physicians' services	27.7	31.2	35.3	39.9	45.0	13	50.5	12
Dentists' services	10.1	11.7	13.3	15.4	17.9	16	20.6	15
Other professional services	3.2	3.7	4.3	5.0	5.7	14	6.5	14
Drugs and drug sundries[2]	12.8	13.8	15.1	16.5	18.1	10	19.7	9
Eyeglasses and appliances	3.2	3.5	3.9	4.3	4.7	9	5.1	9
Nursing home care	11.5	13.4	15.8	18.5	21.6	17	25.0	16
Other health services	3.9	4.0	4.3	4.7	5.2	11	5.7	10
Expenses for prepayment and administration[3]	4.2	7.8	10.0	10.8	11.6	7	12.4	7
Government public health activities	3.7	4.3	5.1	6.0	7.0	17	8.2	17
Research and medical facilities construction	8.8	8.7	9.4	9.9	10.5	6	11.4	9
Research[4]	3.6	3.7	4.3	4.7	5.2	11	5.8	12
Construction	5.3	5.0	5.2	5.2	5.3	2	5.6	6
Medical Care Services Consumer Price Index (1967=100)	197.1	216.7	235.4	258.3	—	—	—	—

[1] Estimated.
[2] Includes only expenditures for prescription drugs, over-the-counter drugs, and medical sundries dispensed through retail channels. Spending for drugs dispensed in hospitals and by physicians are reported within those cost categories.
[3] This category represents a) the difference between premiums received and benefit claims paid by private health insurance organizations and b) administrative expenses of Federally financed programs.

[4] Research expenditures of drug companies and other manufacturers and providers of medical equipment and supplies are included in the expenditure class in which the product falls and excluded from research expenditures.

Source: Office of Research, Demonstration and Statistics, Health Care Financing Administration, Department of Health and Human Services.

Source: *U.S. INDUSTRIAL OUTLOOK 1981*, U.S. Department of Commerce.

X-RAY AND ELECTROMEDICAL EQUIPMENT: TRENDS AND PROJECTIONS 1975–81 (in millions of current dollars except as noted)

Item	1975	1976	1977	1978[2]	1979[2]	1980[2]	Percent change 1979–80[2]	1981[3]	Percent change 1980–81[3]
Industry (SIC 3693)									
Value of shipments[1]	836	947	1,885	2,262	2,600	2,910	12	3,345	15
Value added	519	515	1,232	1,478	1,700	1,920	13	—	—
Value added per production worker-hour ($)	24.82	26.01	36.99	40.94	44.50	47.76	7	—	—
Total employment (000)	18	18	31	33	35	37	6	—	—
Production workers (000)	11	10	17	19	20	21	5	—	—
Average hourly earnings (Dec.—$)	5.18	5.60	6.02	6.44	6.89	7.23	5	—	—
Year-to-year percent change in average hourly earnings (Dec.-Dec.)	—	8	8	7	7	5	—	—	—
Capital expenditures	29	23	63	—	—	—	—	—	—
Product (SIC 3693)									
Value of shipments[4]	740	820	1,838	2,205	2,535	2,840	12	—	—
Trade									
Value of exports	196	223	338	539	717	820	14	985	20
Value of imports	173	199	235	238	275	290	5	320	10

[1] Value of all products and services sold by the X-ray and electromedical industry (SIC 3693). 1977 data are not comparable with prior years because of changes in product classifications.

[2] Estimated except for 1979 trade data.

[3] Forecast.

[4] Value of shipments of X-ray and electromedical equipment produced by all industries. 1977 data are not comparable with prior years because of changes in product classifications.

Source: Bureau of the Census (industry and trade data), Bureau of Labor Statistics (hourly earnings). Estimates and forecasts by the Bureau of Industrial Economics.

Source: U.S. INDUSTRIAL OUTLOOK 1981, U.S. Department of Commerce.

SURGICAL AND MEDICAL INSTRUMENTS: TRENDS AND PROJECTIONS 1975–81 (in millions of current dollars except as noted)

Item	1975	1976	1977	1978	1979[2]	1980[2]	Percent change 1979–80[2]	1981[3]	Percent change 1980–81[3]
Industry (SIC 3841)									
Value of shipments[1]	1,517	1,800	1,829	2,051	2,320	2,575	11	2,910	13
Value added	954	1,138	1,212	1,387	1,565	1,755	12	—	—
Value added per production worker-hour ($)	19.44	21.43	21.12	21.77	24.11	25.51	6	—	—
Total employment (000)	40	43	43	46	49	51	4	—	—
Production workers (000)	26	28	29	32	34	35	3	—	—
Average hourly earnings (Dec.—$)	4.01	4.20	4.44	4.71	4.99	[4]5.49	[4]10	—	—
Year-to-year percent change in average hourly earnings (Dec.–Dec.)	—	5	6	6	6	10	—	—	—
Capital expenditures	84	60	85	87	—	—	—	—	—
Product (SIC 3841)									
Value of shipments[5]	1,539	1,849	1,891	2,290	2,610	2,925	12	—	—
Trade									
Value of exports	299	360	401	365	410	470	15	525	12
Value of imports	70	80	92	126	146	170	16	195	15

[1] Value of all products and services sold by the surgical and medical instruments industry (SIC 3841).
[2] Estimated except for hourly earnings, and 1979 trade data.
[3] Forecast.
[4] As of June 1980.
[5] Value of shipments of surgical and medical instruments produced by all industries.

Source: Bureau of the Census (industry and trade data), Bureau of Labor Statistics (hourly earnings). Estimates and forecasts by the Bureau of Industrial Economics.

Source: U.S. INDUSTRIAL OUTLOOK 1981, U.S. Department of Commerce.

DENTAL EQUIPMENT AND SUPPLIES: TRENDS AND PROJECTIONS 1975–81 (in millions of current dollars except as noted)

Item	1975	1976	1977	1978	1979[2]	1980[2]	Percent change 1979–80[2]	1981[3]	Percent change 1980–81[3]
Industry (SIC 3843)									
Value of shipments[1]	672	729	787	895	1,000	1,100	10	1,230	12
Value added	380	435	459	481	540	600	11	—	—
Value added per production worker-hour ($)	19.00	20.15	21.63	22.17	23.68	25.21	6	—	—
Total employment (000)	15	15	16	17	18	19	6	—	—
Production workers (000)	10	11	11	11	12	12	0	—	—
Average hourly earnings (Dec.—$)	4.40	4.69	4.86	5.30	5.72	5.89	3	—	—
Year-to-year percent change in average hourly earnings (Dec.-Dec.)	—	7	4	9	8	3	—	—	—
Capital expenditures	13	17	16	22	—	—	—	—	—
Product (SIC 3843)									
Value of shipments[4]	549	600	661	779	870	950	9	—	—
Trade									
Value of exports	82	85	92	79	101	130	29	155	19
Value of imports	20	23	30	45	42	40	-5	45	13

[1] Value of all products and services sold by the dental equipment and supplies industry (SIC 3843).
[2] Estimated except for 1979 trade data.
[3] Forecast.
[4] Value of shipments of dental equipment and supplies produced by all industries.

Source: Bureau of the Census (industry and trade data), Bureau of Labor Statistics (hourly earnings and price indexes). Estimates and forecasts by the Bureau of Industrial Economics.

Source: *U.S. INDUSTRIAL OUTLOOK 1981*, U.S. Department of Commerce.

		Relative Price					Earnings Per Share				Other					
		Common Equity			P/E Ratio		Latest 12 Months			5-Year Growth	Profit	Return	Return On Common	Debt Equity	Dividend	Market
Company and Market		Per Share	Price To Equity	Earnings Yield	Current	5-Year Average	Amount	Change	Date	Rate	Margin	On Assets	Equity	Ratio	Yield	Value
		$	%	%	-	-	$	%	-	%	%	%	%	%	%	$Mil
Medical Instruments and Supplies																
ADAC Labs	O	2.76	697	NC	NC	29.4	.00	-100	3-81s	36	4.8	6.6	12.2	4	.0	65
Affil Hospit Pd	A	10.67	129	9.5	10.6	6.5	1.30	86	3-81q	-1	3.1	5.0	9.1	12	.0	22
Am Hosp Sply	*N	23.91	197	6.7	14.9	13.6	3.16	12	3-81q	15	5.2	8.4	13.6	19	2.3	1,914
Am Monitor	O	3.00	1350	.5	NC	23.5	.21	NE	3-81n	-9	4.7	4.2	12.6	101	.0	130
Am Sterilizer	N	9.61	121	9.8	10.2	11.4	1.14	14	3-81q	20	4.8	7.6	11.7	20	2.9	103
Bard C R	*N	12.85	230	6.3	15.8	11.7	1.87	29	3-81q	15	6.7	8.2	13.3	27	1.5	287
Bausch Lomb	N	20.70	258	6.2	16.0	9.3	3.33	-11	3-81q	20	9.0	12.7	21.2	14	2.9	633
Baxter Travenol	*N	24.46	222	6.4	15.7	16.8	3.46	12	3-81q	18	9.3	9.1	15.1	32	1.4	1,893
Becton, Dick	*N	25.09	191	7.0	14.2	13.4	3.36	8	3-81s	11	6.9	7.7	12.9	20	2.1	961
Bentley Labs	O	13.60	324	4.8	20.7	19.9	2.13	24	2-81q	28	8.6	9.9	14.6	2	.0	98
Cavitron Corp	A	8.81	411	5.6	17.8	14.7	2.04	30	3-81s	38	5.4	9.7	19.6	20	.6	44
Charles Riv Brdg	O	10.85	387	4.1	24.4	15.1	1.72	19	1-81q	22	11.1	11.0	15.4	15	.9	105
Cobe Labs	O	19.88	172	8.4	11.9	11.7	2.87	21	3-81q	16	6.0	8.0	13.7	34	.0	70
Coherent Inc	O	8.39	334	2.6	38.4	35.4	.73	-37	3-81s	54	2.3	3.4	8.1	5	.0	70
Cordis Cp	O	21.78	85	-13.1	NC	13.1	-2.42	-100	3-81n	-21	2.6	2.1	5.1	98	.0	47
Damon Corp	N	8.52	114	1.3	NC	NC	.13	-55	2-81s	6	1.7	2.1	4.2	47	2.1	63
Datascope Cp	O	4.52	581	3.8	26.5	17.5	.99	NC	3-81n	6	6.8	8.9	13.5	5	.0	61
Dentsply Intl	N	16.33	100	6.7	14.9	14.4	1.09	-42	3-81s	11	2.4	3.4	8.3	66	5.4	73
Dynatech Cp	O	5.45	624	4.1	24.3	10.9	1.40	18	3-81f	28	6.9	13.3	24.4	28	.0	87
Electro Nucleonic	O	2.44	702	3.8	26.3	NC	.65	27	3-81n	85	4.3	7.6	22.4	124	.0	52
Elscint	O	.58	3491	1.6	NC	27.7	.32	78	3-80f	28	5.7	4.3	54.5	173	.0	115
Everest & Jenn	A	8.71	149	8.5	11.8	5.4	1.10	-23	3-81q	36	5.3	7.8	11.4	9	.8	101
Frigitronics	N	8.25	195	8.6	11.7	15.8	1.38	24	2-81n	18	4.1	8.4	13.3	25	1.9	48
Gelman Sci	A	4.38	397	18.7	5.3	50.0	3.25	408	4-81n	101	.9	1.2	3.8	90	.0	41
Haemonetics	O	4.76	572	3.7	27.0	22.4	1.01	19	3-81f	30	9.2	11.3	16.5	0	.0	59
Health-Chem	A	2.10	851	1.8	NC	24.2	.32	3	3-81q	17	3.0	4.8	15.9	122	.0	181
Hillenbrand Ind	N	29.47	133	11.8	8.5	7.3	4.63	-8	2-81q	19	7.7	10.1	17.0	37	3.7	195
House of Vision	A	4.07	46	-71.2	NC	NC	-3.21	NE	3-81q	NE	-15.1	NE	NE	68	.0	3
Intermedics	O	4.78	753	3.8	26.7	15.4	1.35	41	1-81q	50	10.2	12.1	26.8	68	.0	343
IPCO Corp	N	7.94	68	-9.9	NC	42.7	-.53	-100	3-81n	-34	-1.9	NE	NE	45	2.2	28
Jensen Inds	A	7.78	67	1.5	NC	14.4	.08	-88	3-81q	-44	.8	9.9	11.8	4	.0	6
Johnsn & John	*N	12.23	313	5.6	17.7	16.3	2.16	8	3-81q	15	8.3	12.0	17.7	3	2.3	7,099
Kallestad	A	2.07	1039	3.3	30.7	18.9	.70	37	3-81n	45	11.6	17.6	25.5	22	.0	53
Lee Pharm	A	3.26	146	-8.8	NC	NC	-.42	-100	3-81s	-45	-5.5	NE	NE	2	.0	9
Medex	O	1.01	1287	3.5	28.9	NC	.45	NC	3-81n	71	13.0	25.0	37.5	6	.0	21
Medtronic Inc	N	11.18	369	6.8	14.7	10.5	2.80	28	1-81n	8	14.3	15.1	22.4	10	1.2	640
Millipore Corp	O	10.69	338	3.8	26.6	20.4	1.36	-20	3-81q	10	7.0	7.7	13.0	25	.8	479
Narco Scien	N	17.98	88	6.1	16.4	12.9	.97	20	8-80n	-13	2.2	2.1	4.0	47	4.3	29
Natl Patent	A	3.45	301	-4.5	NC	NC	-.47	NE	3-81q	-72	-8.4	NE	NE	75	.0	97
Newport Cp	O	3.99	652	6.2	16.0	12.3	1.62	NC	1-81s	57	14.3	23.2	33.3	2	.0	40
Nuclear Med	O	.23	3152	.6	NC	NC	.04	NC	2-81n	-8	6.3	8.3	11.1	0	.0	28
Omega Optical	O	3.86	172	10.6	9.5	15.9	.70	67	4-81s	0	5.4	8.4	16.5	57	3.0	24
Puritan Bennett	O	19.64	131	6.1	16.3	10.9	1.58	-8	3-81q	-1	4.8	6.2	8.5	13	1.6	74
St Jude Med	O	1.14	2500	1.1	NC	40.4	.30	-42	3-81q	29	12.4	24.2	35.6	0	.0	113
Sterndent	N	16.70	129	3.4	29.5	11.8	.73	-70	12-80f	42	.7	1.7	4.4	74	2.8	46
Stryker Cp	O	4.98	459	4.6	21.6	14.0	1.06	25	3-81q	33	8.9	14.8	20.0	1	.0	73
Survival Tech	O	1.65	591	.5	NC	19.8	.05	-91	1-81s	39	4.5	9.0	17.1	10	.0	25
Sybron Corp	N	25.84	69	12.5	8.0	8.3	2.21	8	3-81q	-1	3.0	4.2	9.3	46	5.1	169
Tampax Inc	O	13.87	215	10.1	9.9	10.3	3.01	-18	3-81q	2	17.9	19.7	23.2	0	8.5	337
Unit Industl	N	16.48	223	8.7	11.6	6.9	3.18	11	3-81q	16	5.0	8.4	18.0	5	2.6	103
US Surgical	O	5.86	610	2.5	39.7	19.7	.90	32	12-80f	43	9.3	6.7	14.7	88	.0	332
USR Ind	A	5.48	52	-6.6	NC	12.3	-.19	-100	3-81q	NE	-3.6	4.3	6.6	23	.0	3
Valleylab Inc	O	4.17	516	3.5	28.7	33.4	.75	317	3-81n	-6	1.5	1.9	3.8	28	.0	51
West Co	N	16.50	192	8.8	11.4	6.6	2.79	35	3-81q	16	6.7	9.4	15.5	20	1.9	123

Company and Market	Relative Price					Earnings Per Share				Other					
	Common Equity			P/E Ratio		Latest 12 Months			5-Year			Return On	Debt		
	Per Share	Price To Equity	Earnings Yield	Current	5-Year Average	Amount	Change	Date	Growth Rate	Profit Margin	Return On Assets	Common Equity	Equity Ratio	Dividend Yield	Market Value
	$	%	%	-	-	$	%	-	%	%	%	%	%	%	$Mil
Institutional Services															
Am Med Intl ★N	11.95	379	5.0	19.8	10.4	2.28	25	2-81s	30	6.0	6.0	18.2	131	1.4	683
Anta Corp O	14.64	135	11.3	8.9	6.4	2.23	69	3-81n	22	4.7	7.3	12.0	27	2.2	84
Auto Med Labs O	1.60	523	-.5	NC	NC	-.04	-100	3-81q	-18	.7	9.0	21.2	64	.0	21
Beverly Enterp A	7.17	345	5.0	20.0	10.3	1.24	32	3-81q	49	2.9	3.3	13.5	211	1.3	217
Biomed Ref Lab O	3.73	851	3.4	29.4	16.6	1.08	32	3-81q	42	10.2	17.1	26.5	20	.0	121
Brookwood Health O	8.05	637	1.2	NC	9.8	.59	-75	3-81q	-6	4.3	3.6	17.8	319	.8	151
Cenco Inc N	5.27	230	5.9	17.1	18.9	.71	27	1-81n	24	3.9	3.0	10.3	185	.0	122
Cetus Corp O	.92	1943	.1	NC	NC	.01	NC	6-80f	NE	1.1	.5	.6	3	.0	393
Charter Med A	7.90	619	4.3	23.3	7.1	2.10	44	3-81s	61	4.6	4.9	20.5	270	.0	174
Commun Psych N	5.49	551	4.4	22.6	9.6	1.34	24	2-81q	34	14.1	11.7	23.9	66	1.3	184
Comprhen Care O	2.44	1650	2.7	37.6	18.1	1.07	49	2-81n	61	6.7	12.9	32.9	85	.5	154
Diagnostic Data O	1.35	667	-1.2	NC	NC	-.11	NE	2-80f	NE	-17.2	NE	NE	0	.0	40
Genetech Inc O	6.12	592	.1	NC	NC	.03	NC	12-80f	NE	2.2	.4	.4	0	.0	283
Hazleton Labs O	8.01	290	3.9	25.8	16.6	.90	1	3-81n	12	4.6	4.9	10.3	47	1.0	78
Hosp Cp Am ★N	10.33	486	3.7	26.9	11.3	1.87	29	3-81q	25	6.6	5.0	17.3	165	.7	2,280
Humana Inc ★N	5.97	756	4.2	24.0	12.0	1.88	53	2-81s	57	5.8	4.9	22.9	334	1.3	1,646
Huntington Hlth A	8.37	148	4.8	20.6	8.0	.60	-29	2-81s	-4	2.6	3.9	8.7	78	1.6	25
Lifemark Corp N	11.34	423	4.3	23.4	9.4	2.05	38	3-81q	27	5.8	4.8	16.7	160	1.3	285
Manor Care Inc A	4.41	561	5.5	18.3	7.7	1.35	61	2-81n	33	6.6	5.1	21.9	246	1.6	134
Medcom O	3.61	305	3.9	25.6	12.5	.43	54	3-81q	27	4.6	5.1	10.5	5	.0	18
MetPath Inc A	7.75	287	4.9	20.6	24.5	1.08	209	3-81s	11	6.3	4.9	11.6	94	.9	142
Metrocare Inc A	6.40	154	7.5	13.3	8.1	.74	7	1-81f	48	5.8	6.2	12.1	40	.0	14
Natl Health Ent A	9.14	293	6.6	15.2	6.9	1.76	48	3-81f	46	3.5	3.8	15.5	243	.7	56
Natl Med Care N	5.37	438	6.2	16.2	9.9	1.45	27	3-81q	28	10.1	11.6	25.8	48	2.0	417
Natl Med Ent ★N	5.48	490	4.3	23.2	10.9	1.16	49	2-81n	39	4.8	4.9	14.4	129	1.3	1,124
Omnimedical Inc O	1.39	1583	3.4	29.7	26.9	.74	1133	3-81q	28	8.5	1.7	5.6	94	.0	51
Quality Care O	2.36	254	.5	NC	NC	.03	-90	8-80n	14	1.8	3.0	8.6	100	.0	19
Servicemaster O	4.70	931	3.5	28.8	17.5	1.52	24	3-81q	25	3.3	23.7	30.8	0	2.6	428

Metals: Steel, Copper and Aluminum

STEEL MILL PRODUCTS: TRENDS AND PROJECTIONS 1975–81 (in millions of net tons except as noted)

	1975	1976	1977	1978	1979	1980[5]	Percent change 1979–80	1981[7]	Percent change 1980–81
(SIC 3312, 3315, 3316, 3317)									
Raw steel production[1]	117	128	125	137	136	111	−18.4	126	13.5
Steel mill products:									
Industry shipments									
Quantity[1]	80	89	91	98	100	82	18.0	91	10.9
Value ($ millions)[2]	29,204	32,762	36,201	43,372	48,373	40,381	−16.5	49,358	22.2
Exports[2]									
Quantity	3.0	2.7	2.0	2.4	2.8	4.1	46.4	2.5	−39.0
Value ($ millions)	1,862	1,255	1,037	1,329	1,878	2,604	38.7	1,832	−29.6
Imports[2]									
Quantity	12	14	19	21	18	15.0	−16.7	15.5	3.3
Value ($ millions)	4,093	4,025	5,531	6,917	6,967	6,585	−5.5	7,444	13.0
Apparent domestic steel consumption ..	89.0	101.1	108.5	116.6	115.0	90.9	−20.9	104	14.4
Imports as percent of apparent consumption	13.5	14.1	17.8	18.1	15.2	16.6	—	14.9	—
Exports as percent of industry shipments	3.7	3.0	2.2	2.5	2.8	5.0	—	2.7	—
Total employment (000)[3]	469	469	470	472	477	429	−10.1	472	9.9
Production workers (000)[3]	368	369	369	374	379	333	−12.1	381	14.5
Average hourly earnings[4]	7.54	8.08	9.13	10.14	11.26	11.86[6]	—	—	—
Percent change (Dec.–Dec.)[4]	10.7	7.2	13.0	11.1	11.0	9.6[6]	—	—	—
Producers price index of steel mill products (1967 = 100)[3]	202.2	220.7	237.5	262.1	289.3	301.0[4]	—	—	—
Percent change (Dec.–Dec.)	5.4	9.1	7.6	10.4	10.4	5.9[6]	—	—	—

[1] American Iron and Steel Institute.
[2] Bureau of the Census.
[3] Bureau of Labor Statistics (annual average).
[4] Bureau of Labor Statistics (December value).
[5] Estimated except for hourly earnings and prices.
[6] Value is for July 1980; percent change is July 1980 over July 1979.
[7] July 1978 to July 1979.

Source: American Iron and Steel Institute; Bureau of the Census; estimates and forecasts by Bureau of Industrial Economics (OBI).

Source: *U.S. INDUSTRIAL OUTLOOK 1981*, U.S. Department of Commerce.

Company and Market	Relative Price					Earnings Per Share				Other					
	Common Equity Per Share $	Price To Equity %	Earnings Yield %	P/E Ratio Current	P/E Ratio 5-Year Average	Latest 12 Months Amount $	Change %	Date	5-Year Growth Rate %	Profit Margin %	Return On Assets %	Return On Common Equity %	Debt Equity Ratio %	Dividend Yield %	Market Value $Mil
Iron Mining															
Clevel-Cliffs Ir .... N	28.16	138	8.8	11.4	10.0	3.43	-7	3-81q	7	10.9	6.9	11.9	8	4.2	476
Grt N Iron Ore .... N	6.93	375	9.8	10.2	11.3	2.54	-35	12-80f	20	60.3	35.5	36.5	0	9.6	39
Hanna Mining .... N	46.76	69	16.5	6.0	8.8	5.31	-13	3-81q	-2	11.6	6.6	9.3	13	6.2	286
Hollinger Mines .... A	44.18	89	13.1	7.6	9.7	5.19	28	12-80f	12	35.0	3.9	11.7	143	NA	232
Mesabi Trust .... N	NA	NA	5.4	18.6	12.9	.86	-39	1-81f	-1	95.8	75.5	NA	NA	6.4	210
Iron and Steel Furnaces, Mills, Foundries															
Allegheny Int .... N	49.87	106	12.9	7.7	7.2	6.81	108	3-81q	24	7.2	5.7	13.8	97	4.2	379
Ampco-Pitts .... N	22.92	81	24.8	4.0	5.5	4.61	39	3-81q	31	3.5	7.2	17.1	47	3.2	71
Armco Inc .... ★N	36.93	92	12.3	8.2	6.7	4.15	-7	3-81q	15	4.7	7.0	12.9	27	4.8	1,874
Athlone Indus .... N	20.64	134	14.1	7.1	6.1	3.89	20	3-81q	16	3.7	5.7	18.9	124	5.4	74
Bethlehem Stl .... ★N	60.03	43	8.2	12.2	6.9	2.11	-66	3-81q	24	1.8	2.3	4.6	39	6.2	1,125
Bliss & Laughl .... N	14.53	139	12.0	8.3	6.4	2.43	-6	3-81q	17	7.2	9.7	16.9	28	5.7	135
Bundy Corp .... N	15.87	73	5.8	17.4	37.3	.67	-25	4-81n	-37	.1	.2	.3	46	5.2	46
Carpenter Tech .... N	29.10	173	9.5	10.5	6.8	4.78	-6	3-81n	18	7.7	12.2	17.3	2	4.0	433
Cascade Stl Rolling .... O	7.76	187	8.2	12.2	8.5	1.19	-39	3-81q	80	7.0	9.0	20.8	69	1.4	40
Chromalloy Am .... N	28.16	98	9.1	11.0	6.8	2.51	-8	3-81q	2	2.9	4.5	11.2	73	4.0	382
Copperweld Cp .... N	26.61	117	12.1	8.3	7.0	3.78	2	3-81q	5	4.1	7.4	15.2	36	5.1	178
Cyclops Corp .... N	54.64	67	16.2	6.2	7.4	5.93	293	3-81q	17	2.1	4.5	11.5	44	3.7	117
Dayton Mall Iron .... O	32.93	59	-12.2	NC	8.9	-2.38	-100	2-81s	-33	-4.1	NE	NE	2	5.1	29
Eastern Co .... A	20.02	77	8.6	11.6	8.9	1.32	-46	3-81q	-7	3.3	6.3	8.8	20	7.8	17
Fla Steel Cp .... N	14.79	243	9.9	10.1	8.6	3.57	37	3-81q	72	6.5	11.9	21.1	35	1.9	213
Foote Minl .... A	11.99	75	8.2	12.2	19.2	.74	-17	3-81q	17	3.8	4.0	7.3	39	3.3	65
Friedman Ind .... A	7.35	162	14.4	6.9	5.1	1.71	20	12-80n	31	4.6	14.4	21.9	19	2.0	33
Gen Steel .... N	12.87	115	7.7	12.9	6.2	1.14	-14	3-81q	8	4.4	5.6	8.9	32	3.0	46
Harsco Corp .... N	36.00	111	12.9	7.8	6.0	5.13	-7	3-81q	5	4.7	7.6	13.8	35	5.3	394
Hofmann Indus .... A	6.50	33	-79.5	NC	5.1	-1.69	-100	1-81n	-40	-4.9	NE	NE	58	.0	4
Inland Steel .... ★N	61.63	54	3.3	30.0	10.5	1.11	-82	3-81q	-28	.9	1.0	2.3	62	6.0	701
Interlake Inc .... ★N	55.30	64	5.8	17.1	9.3	2.08	-75	3-81q	-15	1.3	2.0	4.1	40	6.2	217
Kaiser Steel Cp .... N	97.11	48	-.4	NC	24.7	-.17	NE	12-80f	-28	NC	NE	NE	39	.0	326
Keystone Cons .... N	58.75	30	-24.6	NC	20.8	-4.36	NE	3-81n	-50	-.9	NE	NE	46	.0	33
Laclede Steel .... O	30.00	53	NC	NC	39.2	.00	-100	3-81q	-25	-.3	.1	.4	67	.0	35
Lindberg Corp .... O	7.32	273	6.5	15.5	7.3	1.29	-18	3-81q	17	7.2	11.3	18.0	23	3.3	70
Lukens Steel .... N	26.14	57	8.8	11.4	8.9	1.31	87	3-81q	-18	1.3	1.9	3.4	19	4.0	78
McLouth Steel .... N	22.35	36	-29.5	NC	7.6	-10.36	-100	3-81q	-82	-9.0	NE	NE	136	.0	44
Natl-Standard .... N	27.00	54	6.8	14.8	7.8	.99	-62	3-81s	-16	1.7	2.8	4.8	20	8.5	60
Natl Steel Cp .... ★N	74.36	38	-12.9	NC	11.2	-3.61	-100	3-81q	-21	2.1	4.0	8.9	47	7.1	531
N Amer Royal .... A	8.01	247	8.1	12.4	8.2	1.59	31	1-81n	14	11.9	9.1	15.3	13	.8	130
NWn Stl & Wr .... N	33.44	81	10.8	9.3	10.2	2.92	-27	4-81n	10	5.3	6.7	9.0	0	4.4	204
Ohio Ferro Alloys .... O	22.18	76	-1.4	NC	11.4	-.23	-100	3-81q	-52	-.1	NE	NE	24	.6	33
Phoenix Steel .... A	.24	1354	-10.8	NC	NC	-.35	-100	3-81q	75	.4	.5	30.4	4273	.0	30
Proler Intl .... N	43.78	74	13.6	7.3	12.1	4.40	-34	1-81f	1	6.8	10.7	15.2	17	4.3	53
Quanex Corp .... N	13.52	320	7.7	12.9	7.2	3.35	21	4-81s	23	6.7	9.4	20.9	52	1.8	306
Rep Steel .... ★N	93.18	34	12.4	8.1	6.9	3.88	-37	3-81q	2	1.4	1.7	3.4	43	6.4	508
Roblin Indus .... A	5.83	86	-45.2	NC	12.9	-2.26	NE	3-81q	-49	-5.3	NE	NE	359	.0	12
Sharon Steel .... A	3.13	168	2.5	40.4	43.0	.13	-75	3-81q	-15	.4	5.3	22.8	189	6.9	431
Sifco Indus .... A	11.29	107	8.0	12.5	7.3	.97	-5	3-81s	7	2.3	4.1	8.4	41	3.0	26
Signode Corp .... N	38.90	106	10.5	9.5	8.1	4.35	-26	3-81q	6	5.5	8.1	12.4	9	4.4	331
Std Alliance .... A	42.00	94	4.1	24.5	6.7	1.61	-63	3-81q	-11	1.1	5.4	12.4	51	2.5	17
Tubos Mexico .... A	4.41	193	9.4	10.6	8.0	.80	33	3-81q	26	11.6	.4	19.3	53	.0	34
Union El Steel .... O	24.17	87	12.1	8.2	6.4	2.55	-33	12-80f	6	9.1	8.2	10.6	16	8.6	33
US Steel Corp .... ★N	59.98	54	20.6	4.8	11.9	6.73	NE	3-81q	8	3.7	3.9	8.7	45	6.1	2,876
Vulcan Inc .... N	19.00	80	13.2	7.6	4.7	2.00	-27	3-81q	-5	2.9	4.9	9.7	41	6.0	29
Wehr Corp .... O	30.22	55	4.8	20.7	8.4	.81	-65	3-81q	-28	1.2	4.0	6.3	26	4.8	15
Weld Tube Am .... A	14.25	118	13.5	7.4	8.2	2.27	-5	1-81f	22	7.5	9.3	16.5	45	1.8	33
Wheel-Pitts St .... ★A	90.75	37	6.6	15.1	NC	2.24	-80	3-81q	26	1.4	1.5	3.5	79	.0	131

PRIMARY COPPER: TRENDS AND PROJECTIONS 1975–81 (in millions of current dollars except as noted)

Item	1975	1976	1977	1978[2]	1979[2]	1980[2]	Percent change 1979–80[5]	1981[3]	Percent change 1980–81[3]
Industry (SIC 3331)									
Value of shipments[1]	3,113	3,550	3,918	3,795	5,725	5,300	−7.5	5,730	8.1
Value added	357	746	864	882	1,010	NA	—	—	—
Value added per production worker-hour ($)	14.82	33.00	42.04	43.75	50.00	NA	—	—	—
Total employment (000)	15.5	14.3	13.1	12.5	12.5	12.3	−1.6	12.3	0
Production workers (000)	12.1	11.3	10.6	10.5	10.5	10.4	−1.0	10.4	0
Average hourly earnings (Dec.— $)	6.86	7.51	8.14	8.85	9.60	—	—	—	—
Year-to-year percent change in average hourly earnings (Dec.–Dec.)	14.5	9.5	8.4	8.7	8.5	—	—	—	—
Year-to-year percent change in industry price index (Dec.–Dec.)[5]	−16.8	7.2	−4.1	−1.5	NA	—	—	—	—
Capital expenditures[5]	164.6	52.4	D	D	NA	—	—	—	—
Product (SIC 3331)									
Value of shipments[6]	2,372	2,997	3,204	NA	NA	—	—	—	—
Year-to-year percent change in producers price index (Dec.–Dec.)[5]	−16.3	7.9	−4.2	−1.4	40.1	[4] 9.5	—	—	—
Trade									
Value of exports	220.9	156.4	70.0	130.2	128.7	35.0	−72.8	50.0	42.9
Value of imports	169.0	453.3	476.2	611.9	387.6	650.0	67.7	355.0	−45.4

[1] Value of all products and services sold by the primary copper industry (SIC 3331).
[2] Estimated except for hourly earnings, price indexes, and 1979 trade data.
[3] Forecast.
[4] July 1979 to July 1980. Note: Months may differ for the price and earnings indexes.
[5] December 1972 is the base period for index.
[6] Value of shipments of primary copper produced by all industries. D = withheld to avoid disclosing operations of individual companies.

Source: Bureau of the Census (industry and trade data), Bureau of Labor Statistics (hourly earnings and price indexes). Estimates and forecasts by the Bureau of Industrial Economics.

Source: *U.S. INDUSTRIAL OUTLOOK 1981*, U.S. Department of Commerce.

Company and Market	Relative Price					Earnings Per Share				Other					
	Common Equity			P/E Ratio		Latest 12 Months			5-Year Growth Rate	Profit Margin	Return On Assets	Return On Common Equity	Debt Equity Ratio	Dividend Yield	Market Value
	Per Share	Price To Equity	Earnings Yield	Current	5-Year Average	Amount	Change	Date							
	$	%	%	-	-	$	%	-	%	%	%	%	%	%	$Mil
Copper Mining															
Atlas Consol B .... A	2.24	162	8.0	12.5	14.8	.29	- 51	3-81q	20	12.0	11.0	23.0	54	5.5	303
Campbell Resc .... A	8.52	160	15.4	6.5	15.4	2.10	213	12-80s	29	36.0	19.4	24.9	2	.0	61
Hudson Bay .... ⋆N	33.33	75	8.5	11.7	29.8	2.14	- 53	3-81q	85	5.6	4.8	12.3	30	NA	254
Marindge Mine .... A	8.53	14	-49.7	NC	NC	- .59	-100	3-81q	NE	-12.5	1.7	2.8	33	.0	111
Newmont Mng .... ⋆N	30.79	198	12.2	8.2	46.5	7.47	11	12-80f	44	22.5	13.7	23.0	27	3.3	1,564
OOkiep Copp .... A	26.54	184	7.7	13.0	16.6	3.74	185	12-79f	- 35	8.8	8.9	14.0	0	2.4	50
Rancher Explor .... A	11.45	473	2.8	35.8	14.8	1.51	17	3-81n	38	15.8	10.1	13.9	3	.5	165
Copper Refining															
ASARCO Inc .... ⋆N	44.37	93	8.5	11.8	7.3	3.48	- 71	3-81q	137	11.9	10.6	16.5	21	3.8	1,060
Kennecott Cp .... ⋆N	48.60	121	3.6	28.0	NC	2.10	- 59	3-81q	169	4.1	2.9	5.7	46	2.4	1,674
Phelps Dodge .... ⋆N	50.34	83	7.7	13.0	20.0	3.23	- 51	3-81q	37	6.3	5.5	10.6	58	3.8	876
Reading Indus .... A	2.54	54	-50.5	NC	8.4	- 2.07	NE	12-80f	NE	- 1.5	NE	NE	470	.0	1
Revere Copper .... ⋆N	31.84	73	14.3	7.0	11.9	3.30	- 9	3-81q	63	2.9	5.1	12.1	78	.4	131
Aluminum Refining															
Alcan Alum .... ⋆N	30.45	106	18.2	5.5	7.3	5.88	4	3-81q	59	10.4	9.9	22.0	37	5.6	2,609
Alum Co Am .... ⋆N	39.25	83	17.4	5.7	7.3	5.70	- 19	3-81q	32	9.1	9.1	16.0	35	5.5	2,394
Kaiser Alum .... ⋆N	32.89	77	21.7	4.6	7.2	5.49	- 3	3-81q	44	7.7	7.7	17.5	49	5.5	1,072
Reynolds Metal .... ⋆N	68.16	52	21.0	4.8	6.4	7.46	- 15	3-81q	22	4.9	5.8	13.4	64	6.8	680

ALUMINUM: TRENDS AND PROJECTIONS 1975–81 (in millions of current dollars except as noted)

	1975	1976	1977	1978	1979 [2]	1980 [2]	Percent change 1979–80 [2]	1981 [3]	Percent change 1980–81 [3]
Value of product shipments [1]	8,440	10,934	13,093	15,781	18,898	19,182	1.5	21,815	13.7
Quantity shipped (million pounds) [1]									
Total	9,929	12,425	12,964	14,347	14,880	13,800	−7.3	14,352	4.0
Exports	818	836	725	747	1,023	2,000	95.5	1,300	−35.0
Domestic	9,111	11,589	12,239	13,600	13,857	11,800	−15.0	13,052	10.6
Value added [4]									
SIC 3334	1,220	1,466	1,939	1,963	2,835	2,877	—	—	—
SIC 3353, 3354, 3355, 3361	2,443	2,983	3,425	4,399	5,102	5,179	—	—	—
Value added per production worker-hour ($)									
SIC 3334	31.92	35.40	43.52	40.24	57.48	57.49	—	—	—
SIC 3353, 3354, 3355, 3361 [5]	16.49	16.97	18.30	20.84	22.92	26.15	—	—	—
Total employment (000) [5]	173	194	206	225	227	216	—	—	—
Production workers (000)									
SIC 3334	19	21	23	24	24	24	—	—	—
SIC 3353, 3354, 3355, 3361	78	89	94	106	106	99	—	—	—
Average hourly earnings (Dec.–$) [6]									
SIC 3334	6.71	7.66	8.91	9.55	10.53	[8] 11.55	—	—	—
SIC 3353	6.73	7.51	8.29	9.31	10.08	[8] 10.99	—	—	—
SIC 3361	5.32	5.61	6.24	6.91	7.09	[8] 7.30	—	—	—
Year-to-year perchant change in average hourly earnings (Dec.–Dec.) [6]									
SIC 3334	5.7	14.2	16.3	7.2	10.3	[9] 13.0	—	—	—
SIC 3353	13.7	11.6	10.4	12.3	8.3	[9] 14.7	—	—	—
SIC 3361	10.6	5.5	11.2	10.7	2.6	[9] 4.3	—	—	—

Producer price index (Dec.) [7]									
SIC 3334	163.9	192.3	213.7	220.3	266.6	[10] 310.7	—	—	—
SIC 3352	162.4	—	—	—	—	—	—	—	—
SIC 3353	—	115.8	128.1	143.2	151.7	[10] 157.6	—	—	—
SIC 3354	—	113.7	126.3	138.6	158.0	[10] 168.3	—	—	—
SIC 3355	—	108.8	115.2	122.8	140.5	[10] 147.6	—	—	—
Year-to-year percent change in producers price index (Dec.–Dec.)									
SIC 3334	0	17.3	11.1	3.1	21.0	[11] 25.6	—	—	—
SIC 3352	2.8	—	—	—	—	—	—	—	—
SIC 3353	—	15.8	10.6	11.8	5.9	[11] 5.2	—	—	—
SIC 3354	—	13.7	11.1	9.7	14.0	[11] 10.8	—	—	—
SIC 3355	—	8.8	5.9	6.6	14.4	[11] 10.9	—	—	—
Capital expenditures									
SIC 3334	227	189	153	174	—	—	—	—	—
SIC 3353, 3354, 3355, 3361	313	255	343	461	—	—	—	—	—
Trade									
Value of exports	460	493	515	575	926	1,890	103.4	1,400	−26.0
Value of imports	393	555	758	1,118	1,035	866	−16.3	1,100	27.0

[1] Value estimated by Bureau of Industrial Economics (BIE). Represents shipments to consuming industries and exports; includes shipments of aluminum products made by all industries. Covers SIC Codes 3334, 3353, 3354, 3355, 3361 and parts of 3341, 3357, 3399 and 3463.

[2] Estimated except for hourly earnings and price indexes.

[3] Forecast.

[4] Total for specified industries only; not comparable with value of shipments estimated in the first line of the table.

[5] Estimated.

[6] Average hourly earnings obtained from Bureau of Labor Statistics; SIC Code 3354 is not a published series; SIC Code 3355 is no longer available as a separate estimate—is merged with SIC Code 3356.

[7] Producers price index base periods: Sic 3334—year 1967; SIC 3352—December 1968, Code changed in December 1975; SIC 3353, 3354 and 3355—December 1975.

[8] As of June 1980.

[9] June 1979 to June 1980.

[10] As of August 1980.

[11] August 1979 to August 1980.

Note: Description of SIC Codes used: 3334—primary aluminum production; 3352—rolling, drawing and extruding aluminum; 3353—aluminum sheet, plate, and foil; 3354—aluminum extruded products; 3355—aluminum rolling and drawing, n.e.c.; 3361—aluminum foundries (castings).

Source: Bureau of the Census (industry and trade data), Bureau of Labor Statistics (hourly earnings and price indexes). Estimates and forecasts by Bureau of Industrial Economics (BIE).

Source: *U.S. INDUSTRIAL OUTLOOK 1981*, U.S. Department cf Commerce.

See p. 63 for Companies.

Energy (Oil, Coal, Gas)

CONSUMPTION TRENDS BY FUEL TYPE AND SECTOR: 1950–79

	Residential-commercial		Industrial		Transportation		Electric utilities		Total[1,3]
	Quantity[1]	Market share[2]	Quantity[1]	Market share[2]	Quantity[1]	Market share[2]	Quantity[1]	Market share[2]	
Oil									
1950	3.0	22.6	2.7	20.3	7.1	53.4	0.6	4.5	13.3
1960	5.3	26.6	4.0	20.1	10.7	50.3	0.6	3.0	19.9
1970	7.1	24.1	5.0	16.9	15.3	51.9	2.1	7.1	29.5
1975	6.4	19.6	5.5	16.8	17.6	53.8	3.2	9.8	32.7
1979	6.9	18.6	7.4	19.9	19.2	51.8	3.6	9.7	37.1
Natural gas									
1950	1.6	26.7	3.6	60.0	.1	1.7	.7	11.7	6.0
1960	4.3	34.7	6.0	48.4	.4	3.2	1.8	14.5	12.4
1970	7.5	34.4	9.5	43.6	.7	3.2	4.1	18.8	21.8
1975	7.6	38.0	8.5	42.5	.6	3.0	3.2	16.0	20.0
1979	7.6	37.1	8.6	42.0	.5	2.4	3.6	17.6	20.5
Coal									
1950	3.0	23.3	5.9	45.7	1.7	13.2	2.4	18.6	12.9
1960	1.1	10.9	4.7	46.5	.1	1.0	4.2	41.6	10.1
1970	.4	3.1	4.9	39.4	—	—	7.2	56.7	12.7
1975	.2	1.6	3.8	29.7	—	—	8.8	68.8	12.8
1979	.3	1.0	3.6	24.0	—	—	11.2	74.7	15.0

[1] Quadrillions of BTUs.
[2] Percentages.
[3] Sum of parts may not equal total due to independent rounding.

— Less than .1 quadrillion British Thermal Units (BTU); negligible.

Source: *U.S. INDUSTRIAL OUTLOOK 1981*, U.S. Department of Commerce.

Source: U.S. Department of Energy

PRODUCTION AND CONSUMPTION OF PETROLEUM
PRODUCTS

Year	Produc- tion[1]	Consump- tion[2]	Imports[3]	Imports as per- centage of con- sumption
1950	11.45	13.32	1.89	14.2
1960	14.93	19.92	4.00	20.1
1970	20.40	29.52	7.47	25.3
1971	20.03	30.56	8.54	27.9
1972	20.04	32.95	10.30	31.3
1973	19.49	34.84	13.47	38.7
1974	18.57	33.45	13.13	39.3
1975	17.73	32.73	12.95	39.6
1976	17.26	35.17	15.67	44.6
1977	17.45	37.18	18.76	50.5
1978	18.43	37.97	17.82	46.9
1979	18.06	37.15	17.64	47.5

[1] Crude oil and lease condensate in quadrillions of British Thermal Units (BTUs).
[2] Refined products, natural gas liquids, and crude oil in quadrillions of BTUs.
[3] Crude oil and refined products in quadrillions of BTUs.
Source: U.S. Department of Energy

Source: *U.S. INDUSTRIAL OUTLOOK 1981*, U.S. Department of Commerce.

Company and Market		Relative Price					Earnings Per Share				Other					
		Common Equity			P/E Ratio		Latest 12 Months			5-Year Growth Rate	Profit Margin	Return On Assets	Return On Common Equity	Debt Equity Ratio	Dividend Yield	Market Value
		Per Share	Price To Equity	Earnings Yield	Current	5-Year Average	Amount	Change	Date							
		$	%	%	-	-	$	%	-	%	%	%	%	%	%	$Mil

Oil and Natural Gas Producers

Company and Market		$	%	%	Cur	5Yr	$	%	Date	%	%	%	%	%	%	$Mil
Adobe Oil Gas	A	7.95	403	4.6	21.8	18.7	1.47	40	3-81q	34	13.9	7.7	18.9	69	.6	457
Alaska Intrste	N	17.72	146	19.9	5.0	9.4	5.16	269	12-80f	29	24.6	10.8	28.9	105	2.3	325
Am Res Mgmt	O	.22	0227	-.8	NC	NC	-.18	NE	12-80f	NE	-44.8	NE	NE	1506	.0	160
Argo Pet	A	1.94	715	2.8	35.6	NC	.39	129	3-81q	53	16.5	1.4	5.4	196	.0	106
Asamera Inc	A	8.53	167	10.9	9.1	35.0	1.56	-16	3-81f	26	3.0	8.5	21.7	54	2.4	105
Baruch-Foster	A	2.85	526	7.5	13.4	23.9	1.12	26	3-81q	27	29.3	23.7	35.5	15	.0	33
Belco Pete	N	18.11	159	12.5	8.0	5.7	3.60	4	3-81q	26	9.4	7.8	18.6	9	2.1	667
Buttes Gas Oil	N	11.53	159	12.6	8.0	NC	2.31	136	12-80f	7	8.3	4.0	23.2	364	.0	85
Cdn Occid Pet	A	4.96	292	9.0	11.2	10.0	1.30	69	12-80f	14	16.1	10.0	24.5	91	NA	298
Cdn Pac Enter	N	14.45	140	18.2	5.5	NC	3.68	NC	9-80n	34	7.9	6.0	22.0	85	5.5	2,846
Coastal Corp	N	27.03	152	9.5	10.5	4.8	3.91	-18	3-81q	12	2.1	2.7	18.7	129	1.2	881
Consol O & G	A	4.50	358	7.1	14.1	NC	1.14	338	2-81q	20	33.0	8.0	22.0	118	.0	173
Crystal Oil	A	2.22	1436	.8	NC	NC	.24	-61	3-81q	23	3.3	3.1	21.0	174	1.1	624
Damson Oil	A	5.03	268	3.8	26.5	NC	.51	NC	3-81s	54	11.3	NC	8.4	113	.0	99
Delhi Intl Oil	A	4.12	1942	.8	NC	33.3	.63	24	3-81q	29	17.7	5.5	11.6	81	.1	602
Dome Petrol	A	20.02	470	6.5	15.3	7.7	6.14	39	3-81q	44	23.6	5.7	20.7	298	NA	4,630
Dorchstr Gas	A	6.85	301	9.2	10.9	8.5	1.89	3	2-81s	32	5.7	10.4	28.2	66	.8	370
Dyco Petroleum	N	2.29	1354	4.4	22.8	12.4	1.36	66	3-81q	49	26.2	10.1	30.6	175	.2	222
Energy Minrls	A	2.78	351	3.6	27.9	12.9	.35	6	12-80n	4	24.7	9.9	25.3	73	.0	40
Equity Oil	O	2.40	573	3.3	30.6	23.6	.45	88	3-81q	8	31.0	11.8	17.3	0	1.5	162
Felmont Oil	A	7.23	467	4.3	23.4	16.3	1.44	41	3-81q	35	23.9	11.3	18.2	23	.3	350
Forest Oil Corp	O	15.06	212	1.0	NC	32.8	.33	-58	3-81q	-37	2.4	.5	2.1	237	4.1	215
Francana	A	9.72	242	10.7	9.3	NC	2.52	89	3-81q	24	25.1	NC	25.8	0	.0	306
Gen Amer Oil	*N	15.75	233	5.6	17.8	18.5	2.07	-4	3-81n	21	24.7	12.6	15.3	2	1.2	883
Gulf Energy Dev	O	5.33	371	6.1	16.5	12.9	1.20	-1	3-81q	31	13.3	7.9	21.5	133	.8	86
Gulf Interstate	O	12.58	167	4.6	21.6	8.2	.97	-49	3-81q	6	18.9	6.7	8.9	15	2.4	70
Hamilton Bros Pet	O	12.66	160	10.8	9.3	10.2	2.18	-66	3-81q	44	30.2	9.9	19.0	44	.5	282
Howell Pet	N	21.72	83	3.1	32.7	NC	.55	NC	3-81q	28	11.9	1.7	3.8	26	.0	68
Hudsons B Oil	A	8.90	333	5.7	17.4	9.3	1.70	183	3-81q	14	24.2	11.9	21.5	5	NA	2,250
Inexco Oil	N	8.46	291	3.9	25.7	18.1	.96	19	3-81q	21	15.4	4.1	11.1	102	.5	594
Juniper Pet	A	3.99	360	5.1	19.7	16.5	.73	-32	3-81q	88	15.7	8.7	21.3	98	.0	63
La Land Exp	*N	19.63	180	13.4	7.5	9.5	4.71	-4	3-81q	18	17.7	15.8	24.2	13	5.1	1,339
Mapco Inc	N	17.48	200	11.7	8.5	11.0	4.11	11	3-81q	8	6.9	8.2	21.9	84	5.1	967
Marion Corp	O	5.40	192	20.1	5.0	7.0	2.09	18	1-81f	37	5.1	10.1	33.0	99	1.9	113
May Petrol	O	9.76	343	2.4	41.9	20.1	.80	57	12-80f	24	20.2	5.2	7.1	2	.0	217
Maynard Oil	O	3.18	440	7.3	13.7	22.3	1.02	NC	3-81q	50	16.4	4.0	12.9	41	.0	89

		Relative Price					Earnings Per Share				Other					
		Common Equity			P/E Ratio		Latest 12 Months			5-Year Growth Rate	Profit Margin	Return On Assets	Return On Common Equity	Debt Equity Ratio	Dividend Yield	Market Value
Company and Market		Per Share	Price To Equity	Earnings Yield	Current	5-Year Average	Amount	Change	Date							
		$	%	%	-	-	$	%	-	%	%	%	%	%	%	$Mil
MCO Holding	A	5.18	290	5.8	17.2	16.4	.87	- 8	3-81q	54	9.2	3.9	16.9	199	.0	201
McRae Cons O&G	O	2.58	1105	2.2	44.5	38.5	.64	94	8-80f	14	6.5	8.4	24.6	26	.0	426
Mesa Petrol	★N	7.59	347	5.8	17.4	14.9	1.52	69	3-81q	30	30.0	6.7	18.7	93	.5	1,775
Mitchell Energy	A	4.06	742	7.0	14.3	8.8	2.10	65	1-81f	35	14.5	7.8	31.3	112	.8	1,441
Natomas Co	N	18.53	132	17.0	5.9	5.9	4.17	40	3-81q	28	15.9	11.6	21.7	47	4.9	1,268
N Cdn Oils	A	6.38	249	6.0	16.7	11.9	.95	- 1	12-80f	10	24.3	6.3	11.7	46	NA	71
Numac O & G	A	7.19	334	2.1	47.1	31.4	.51	- 20	3-81q	8	24.8	3.8	7.4	34	.8	226
Occidental Pet	N	24.50	118	27.6	3.6	8.4	7.99	- 12	3-81q	20	5.7	10.7	31.2	51	8.6	2,257
Pauley Petroleum	O	8.93	165	- 2.6	NC	25.8	- .39	-100	2-81s	- 21	1.0	1.8	7.0	174	.0	42
Petro-Lewis	A	3.25	612	7.1	14.1	11.5	1.41	58	3-81n	65	17.2	6.3	32.5	239	.0	404
Phoenix Res	O	14.62	291	2.2	44.7	24.6	.95	- 34	12-80f	23	19.0	4.6	6.4	0	.0	235
Prairie Oil Roy	A	11.67	142	9.9	10.1	14.8	1.64	34	3-81q	25	42.7	8.8	14.0	0	.0	33
Ranger Oil	A	1.34	858	4.2	24.0	35.9	.48	118	3-81q	23	18.2	8.5	31.6	147	.0	691
Sabine	N	11.06	420	4.1	24.6	17.5	1.89	39	3-81q	- 4	21.0	10.3	15.6	18	.8	676
Scurry Rainbow	A	28.53	179	4.5	22.3	13.3	2.29	NC	3-81s	31	29.9	8.6	17.0	33	.0	137
Southland Roy	N	3.62	715	4.4	22.7	NC	1.14	NC	3-81q	20	17.0	9.8	32.5	177	.2	1,201
Statex Pet	A	3.88	715	3.3	30.5	16.8	.91	168	1-81q	56	25.3	13.7	19.6	0	.0	80
Summit En	A	8.24	228	3.3	30.2	13.0	.62	77	1-81s	15	33.9	8.0	9.3	0	1.1	45
Sundance Oil	A	.20	3250	- 4.5	NC	35.2	- 1.20	NE	3-81q	- 75	-51.9	NE	NE	5857	.0	282
Sunlite Oil Ltd	O	3.05	414	.2	NC	NC	.02	NE	12-80s	NE	-20.0	NE	NE	6	.0	42
Superior Oil	★N	71.04	272	7.2	13.9	12.8	13.86	25	3-81q	51	22.3	9.7	18.5	42	.4	4,900
Tejon Ranch	A	9.00	889	1.5	NC	NC	1.20	14	3-81q	42	5.8	5.0	13.3	27	.0	100
Tesoro Petrol	N	26.15	72	20.2	4.9	6.2	3.79	- 28	3-81s	78	2.9	14.7	27.7	4	1.6	283
Texas Am Enrg	A	4.48	220	8.6	11.6	10.7	.85	21	3-81q	25	3.2	3.0	16.5	220	1.3	64
Texas Oil&Gas	★N	5.50	643	4.9	20.4	11.1	1.73	41	2-81s	32	11.9	9.2	27.0	89	.5	3,366
Texas Pacific	N	2.35	1723	5.6	17.9	17.3	2.26	81	3-81q	38	63.1	40.7	51.8	0	.6	191
Tipperary Cp	O	5.31	518	4.3	23.3	17.4	1.18	74	9-80f	- 18	7.3	6.4	22.3	190	.0	146
Tomlinson Oil	O	4.02	196	4.7	21.3	11.4	.37	- 71	11-80q	17	4.8	5.7	19.6	139	.0	31
Tosco Corp	N	10.89	220	- 2.9	NC	9.2	- .70	-100	3-81q	19	1.9	5.3	19.5	106	.0	520
Total Petro NA	A	14.12	130	4.8	20.9	10.7	.88	- 54	3-81q	18	3.0	4.1	13.3	115	2.6	315
Transcont Engy	A	7.06	212	8.2	12.2	10.8	1.23	NE	3-81q	4	3.2	2.7	7.5	105	.0	78
Triton Oil Gs	A	4.05	537	2.8	35.7	37.6	.61	30	2-81n	28	17.5	5.7	13.6	57	.0	125
Univ Rsourcs	A	7.22	383	4.1	24.7	12.8	1.12	75	1-81q	16	18.5	8.2	12.5	8	.6	221
Weatherford Inc	A	9.33	275	8.5	11.7	11.0	2.19	51	3-81q	37	10.1	11.6	21.8	37	1.2	207
Westcst Petro	O	15.34	126	5.7	17.6	12.1	1.10	- 17	3-81q	11	26.5	4.7	8.5	25	NA	127
Wichita Indus	A	3.39	549	4.1	24.2	19.3	.77	33	3-81q	41	18.1	14.5	24.1	25	.0	43
Wilshire Oil	N	5.63	226	10.0	10.0	34.0	1.27	1055	3-81q	4	18.9	2.0	4.1	67	.0	98
Wiser Oil	O	21.31	382	7.5	13.4	9.4	6.08	18	3-81q	20	29.9	19.7	23.2	0	2.9	247
Woods Petrol	N	5.41	545	2.5	39.3	12.2	.75	- 57	3-81q	- 3	22.9	13.0	19.6	12	1.4	343

Company and Market		Relative Price					Earnings Per Share				Other					
		Common Equity		Earnings Yield	P/E Ratio		Latest 12 Months			5-Year Growth Rate	Profit Margin	Return On Assets	Return On Common Equity	Debt Equity Ratio	Dividend Yield	Market Value
		Per Share	Price To Equity		Current	5-Year Average	Amount	Change	Date							
		$	%	%	-	-	$	%	-	%	%	%	%	%	%	$Mil
Oil Refineries and Marketing Companies																
Adams Res	A	4.62	703	-2.1	NC	19.0	-.68	NE	3-81q	-42	-1.1	NE	NE	122	.0	191
Amerada Hess	N	29.31	97	25.4	3.9	5.9	7.23	30	3-81q	41	6.9	9.2	22.9	46	3.9	2,278
Am Petrofina	A	39.98	129	16.7	6.0	7.3	8.65	-10	3-81q	31	5.0	7.7	19.3	64	12.4	558
Ashland Oil	N	34.66	91	11.2	8.9	6.9	3.53	-47	3-81s	12	2.4	5.9	16.9	69	7.6	833
Atlantic Rchfld	★N	26.26	167	14.4	7.0	8.7	6.31	15	3-81q	27	6.8	8.4	19.1	52	5.0	10,430
British Petrol	N	28.61	110	25.9	3.9	5.7	8.15	-12	12-80f	63	6.8	10.4	32.5	47	7.1	12,175
Charter Co	N	25.93	39	.4	NC	7.4	.04	-100	3-81q	-19	1.1	2.9	7.4	87	10.0	216
Cities Service	★N	30.96	135	10.2	9.8	7.9	4.26	-19	3-81q	21	6.1	8.9	18.5	46	3.8	3,487
Clark Oil Refin	N	13.64	202	6.4	15.7	7.0	1.75	-52	3-81q	38	2.6	9.2	21.3	21	3.6	396
Conoco	★N	42.51	121	17.0	5.9	7.1	8.80	-4	3-81q	26	5.6	9.3	22.4	35	5.0	5,566
Crown Cen Pet	A	28.41	71	-3.3	NC	5.5	-.67	-100	3-81q	4	1.5	3.5	9.9	58	4.0	118
Exxon	★N	58.81	110	19.0	5.3	7.3	12.31	3	3-81q	24	5.5	10.0	22.2	19	9.3	27,995
Getty Oil	★N	50.44	126	16.7	6.0	10.0	10.65	21	3-81q	34	8.6	10.5	20.9	15	3.8	5,237
Gulf Canada	A	8.47	270	7.3	13.7	9.5	1.67	22	3-81q	24	9.4	10.3	19.7	16	NA	5,204
Gulf Oil Cp	★N	49.36	65	19.6	5.1	6.2	6.26	-16	3-81q	15	5.3	7.5	14.6	15	7.8	6,223
Husky Oil Ltd	A	6.50	219	8.7	11.5	7.4	1.24	-4	3-81q	32	7.2	6.6	17.8	56	NA	1,119
Imperial Oil	A	24.14	122	13.3	7.5	9.0	3.92	-4	3-81q	20	10.2	9.6	15.9	16	NA	4,629
Kerr-McGee	N	51.81	135	9.8	10.2	11.4	6.87	2	3-81q	10	5.2	6.5	13.6	39	2.9	1,813
Marathon Oil	N	31.97	147	10.9	9.1	8.3	5.14	-12	3-81q	16	4.6	7.5	19.7	60	4.3	2,795
Mobil Corp	★N	61.47	93	21.6	4.6	5.8	12.30	9	3-81q	31	4.7	8.6	21.5	27	7.0	12,115
Murphy Oil	N	14.25	212	14.2	7.0	8.9	4.30	37	3-81q	38	7.5	5.5	19.5	70	2.5	1,128
Pacific Res	O	8.99	172	4.9	20.4	8.1	.76	-54	3-81q	6	2.5	5.9	22.2	124	3.2	160
Pennzoil Co	N	19.88	194	13.9	7.2	8.4	5.37	2	3-81q	30	12.4	11.9	28.6	79	5.7	1,982
Phibro Cp	★N	18.44	172	21.4	4.7	6.6	6.79	55	12-80f	114	2.0	8.6	37.3	34	3.7	2,162
Phillips Petrol	★N	27.57	132	19.1	5.2	8.1	6.94	7	3-81q	26	7.8	10.5	20.9	15	6.0	5,536
Quaker St Oil	N	10.57	143	7.9	12.7	11.8	1.19	-24	12-80f	1	3.1	5.2	11.2	42	5.3	329
Royal Dutch	★N	49.48	68	46.0	2.2	4.9	15.52	184	12-79f	17	100.0	28.8	29.8	0	4.9	9,725
Shell Oil Co	★N	22.68	185	11.8	8.5	6.8	4.95	20	3-81q	19	7.7	7.0	16.1	65	4.3	12,971
Shell Transport	N	30.78	105	28.0	3.6	5.7	9.07	-9	9-80n	32	99.5	27.6	29.7	0	7.1	8,942
Std Oil Cal	★N	32.38	117	18.9	5.3	6.4	7.14	18	3-81q	30	5.9	10.8	21.7	17	5.3	12,915
Std Oil Ind	★N	28.06	184	11.4	8.8	8.0	5.88	0	3-81q	20	6.9	8.8	18.0	31	5.0	15,055
Std Oil Ohio	N	19.04	241	16.7	6.0	12.7	7.65	26	3-81q	75	16.4	15.0	39.7	77	5.2	11,268
Sun Co Inc	★N	31.64	107	12.2	8.2	6.8	4.14	-37	3-81q	14	5.0	9.4	18.6	21	6.2	4,131
Texaco Canada	A	10.62	252	10.8	9.2	NC	2.90	NC	3-81q	41	10.5	14.3	29.2	8	NA	3,225
Texaco	★N	39.22	88	24.8	4.0	6.9	8.55	13	3-81q	32	4.3	7.7	16.5	32	8.1	9,266
Union Oil Cal	★N	20.04	153	12.2	8.2	7.7	3.74	20	3-81q	24	6.5	9.6	18.6	33	2.6	5,335
U.S. Industries	N	21.20	42	7.1	14.1	7.1	.64	-63	3-81q	-5	1.8	5.9	9.7	22	8.4	214
Other Mining Including Coal																
Barber Oil	N	35.40	26	40.3	2.5	17.8	3.73	-20	9-80n	31	8.2	5.7	10.9	60	17.3	24
Eastern Gas Fl	★N	19.93	122	10.5	9.6	13.7	2.55	8	3-81q	5	5.5	5.4	12.6	52	4.1	551
Gen Energy	O	5.86	627	.2	NC	NC	.08	-27	3-81q	-22	.4	.4	.7	47	.3	175
ND Resources	O	.89	618	-4.9	NC	NC	-.27	NE	12-80s	NE	-29.2	NE	NE	71	.0	25
N Amer Coal	★N	24.56	122	7.6	13.2	9.7	2.27	-46	3-81q	7	2.3	1.2	12.4	709	2.4	100
Northgate Exp	N	8.46	87	4.5	22.3	31.2	.33	-78	3-81q	22	21.7	12.6	16.6	0	NA	53
Penn Va	O	26.89	186	5.4	18.5	15.3	2.70	21	3-81q	-12	15.8	5.9	8.6	28	3.0	176
Pittston Co	★N	17.73	154	7.1	14.0	16.6	1.95	30	3-81q	-10	3.8	5.8	11.5	19	4.4	1,027
Placer Develop	A	11.02	184	9.1	11.0	9.7	1.84	-25	3-81q	47	26.3	11.4	20.7	39	NA	720
US Energy Cp	O	1.15	957	.6	NC	NC	.07	NC	6-80n	34	2.0	1.7	3.3	7	.0	30
Westmoreland Coal	★O	26.14	99	-.8	NC	NC	-.20	NE	3-81q	-28	.1	.1	.2	47	.0	177

METAL CUTTING MACHINE TOOLS: TRENDS AND PROJECTIONS 1975–81 (in millions of current dollars except as noted)

Item	1975	1976	1977	1978	1979[2]	1980[2]	Percent change 1979–80[2]	1981[3]	Percent change 1980–81[3]
Industry (SIC 3541)									
Value of shipments[1]	2,727	2,510	2,812	3,589	4,776	6,028	+26	7,594	+26
Value added	1,643	1,550	1,866	2,262	2,866	3,617	+26	4,556	+26
Value added per production worker-hour ($)	20.08	22.64	23.13	—	—	—	—	—	—
Total employment (000)	63	60	69	73	80	82	2.5	—	—
Production workers (000)	41	39	45	47	55	56.5	2.7	—	—
Average hourly earnings (Dec.—$)	5.96	6.45	6.99	7.67	8.26	[4]9.15	[4]10.7	—	—
Year-to-year percent change in average hourly earnings (Dec.–Dec.)	8.1	8.2	8.4	9.8	7.7	[5]10.7	[5]—	—	—
Year-to-year percent change in industry price index (Dec.–Dec.)	3.0	7.1	9.8	13.7	16.7	[5]16.6	[5]—	—	—
Capital expenditures	52.2	65.2	80.4	112.8	—	—	—	—	—
Product (SIC 3541)									
Value of shipments	1,790	1,558	1,790	2,206	2,930	3,721	+27	4,688	+26
Year-to-year percent change in producers price index (Dec.–Dec.)	3.0	7.1	9.8	13.7	16.2	[5]17.8	[5]—	—	—
Trade									
Value of exports	343	290	247	366	545	660	+22	800	+21
Value of imports	248	245	319	582	1,043	1,250	+20	1,600	+28

[1] Value of all products and services sold by the metal cutting machine tools industry (SIC 3541).
[2] Estimated except for hourly earnings, price indexes, and 1979 trade data.
[3] Forecast.
[4] As of October 1980.
[5] July 1979 to September 1980. Note: Months may differ for the price and earnings indexes.

Source: Bureau of the Census (industry and trade data), Bureau of Labor Statistics (hourly earnings and price indexes). Estimates and forecasts by the Bureau of Industrial Economics.

Source: *U.S. INDUSTRIAL OUTLOOK 1981*, U.S. Department of Commerce.

METAL FORMING MACHINE TOOLS: TRENDS AND PROJECTIONS 1975–81 (in millions of current dollars except as noted)

Item	1975	1976	1977	1978	1979[2]	1980[2]	Percent change 1979–80[2]	1981[3]	Percent change 1980–81[3]
Industry (SIC 3542)									
Value of shipments[1]	1,110	1,085	1,130	1,289	1,676	1,823	+8.7	2,240	+22.8
Value added	621	533	722	774	1,006	1,112	+10.5	1,366	+22.7
Value added per production worker-hour ($)	17.27	19.41	22.31	—	—	—	—	—	—
Total employment (000)	26	22.9	25	26	27.9	28.3	+1.4	—	—
Production workers (000)	17.7	15.9	17.5	17.9	18.4	18.6	+1.1	—	—
Average hourly earnings (Dec.—$)	5.51	5.94	6.44	7.55	8.15	[4]8.78	[4]—	—	—
Year-to-year percent change in average hourly earnings (Dec.–Dec.)	6.4	7.8	8.4	—	—	[5]—	[5]—	—	—
Year-to-year percent change in industry price index (Dec.–Dec.)	3.8	7.3	11.5	16.3	17.3	[5]15.9	[5]—	—	—
Capital expenditures	23.9	28.3	24.7	—	—	—	—	—	—
Product (SIC 3542)									
Value of shipments	616	562	651	799	1,028	1,125	9.4	1,383	+23
Year-to-year percent change in producers price index (Dec.–Dec.)	3.8	7.3	11.5	16.3	12.7	[5]15.9	[5]—	—	—
Trade									
Value of exports	225	257	221	194	220	275	+25	330	+20
Value of imports	69	73	90	133	211	265	+26	340	+28

[1] Value of all products and services sold by the metal forming machine tool industry (SIC 3542).
[2] Estimated except for hourly earnings, price indexes, and 1979 trade data.
[3] Forecast.
[4] As of October 1980.
[5] July 1979 to September 1980. Note: Months may differ for the price and earnings indexes.

Source: Bureau of the Census (industry and trade data), Bureau of Labor Statistics (hourly earnings and price indexes). Estimates and forecasts by the Bureau of Industrial Economics.

Source: *U.S. INDUSTRIAL OUTLOOK 1981,* U.S. Department of Commerce.

Company and Market	Relative Price					Earnings Per Share				Other					
	Common Equity			P/E Ratio		Latest 12 Months			5-Year Growth Rate	Profit Margin	Return On Assets	Return On Common Equity	Debt Equity Ratio	Dividend Yield	Market Value
	Per Share	Price To Equity	Earnings Yield	Current	5-Year Average	Amount	Change	Date							
	$	%	%	-	-	$	%	-	%	%	%	%	%	%	$Mil
Machine Tools and Accessories															
Acme-Clevelnd ....★N	26.73	110	11.3	8.9	8.6	3.31	-28	3-81s	48	4.2	6.5	14.6	62	4.8	126
Aro Corp .... N	24.37	74	10.9	9.2	6.9	1.96	-49	2-81q	1	5.8	6.6	9.2	20	5.6	39
Barden Corp .... O	19.45	186	10.6	9.4	5.9	3.84	13	4-81s	48	11.2	13.4	18.5	11	2.8	72
Brenco Inc .... O	5.80	211	10.0	10.0	11.8	1.23	-16	3-81q	18	17.0	22.4	26.2	0	2.9	121
Brown & Shrpe ....★N	27.98	94	14.8	6.8	7.5	3.90	-8	3-81q	67	6.4	8.2	16.7	50	5.0	82
Chi Pneu Tool ....★N	34.62	68	10.4	9.6	12.8	2.44	-27	3-81q	15	2.5	3.1	7.0	67	8.6	114
Cinn Milacron ....★N	13.75	305	5.5	18.3	8.2	2.29	-6	3-81q	45	6.4	8.4	16.6	32	1.7	948
Clausing Corp .... A	9.46	124	12.3	8.1	7.6	1.45	-14	3-81n	20	5.7	8.1	16.8	54	6.8	33
Cross Trecker .... O	12.52	300	7.9	12.7	8.2	2.95	11	3-81s	44	9.4	12.1	21.5	10	1.7	465
Ex-Cell-O ....★N	23.01	147	10.1	9.9	6.9	3.41	0	2-81q	12	4.9	8.8	15.4	18	4.4	521
Fedl-Mogul .... N	18.01	146	10.6	9.5	5.4	2.77	-11	3-81q	11	5.1	10.1	18.6	19	5.0	327
Giddings Lewis ....★N	20.26	201	12.2	8.2	5.8	4.96	5	3-81q	64	9.6	15.9	23.7	13	2.5	281
Gleason Works .... N	20.99	85	19.5	5.1	6.5	3.46	5	3-81q	27	6.7	8.8	15.5	24	4.5	90
Ill Tool Wk .... N	21.45	146	10.3	9.7	10.1	3.22	4	3-81q	16	11.0	12.9	16.9	1	3.4	384
Lodge & Ship .... A	4.63	127	8.0	12.5	10.1	.47	7	3-81q	11	4.1	5.5	11.2	32	2.4	20
LSB Ind Inc .... A	5.84	101	10.7	9.3	7.0	.63	34	3-81q	10	2.3	2.6	9.9	114	.0	16
Matrix Cp .... A	2.26	1366	2.3	44.1	22.7	.70	21	2-81s	23	9.7	12.2	16.0	0	.0	80
Mesta Machine .... N	46.70	31	-23.6	NC	17.0	-17.77	NE	3-81q	-65	-11.2	NE	NE	1	.0	14
Monarch Mach ....★N	15.70	150	15.2	6.6	5.1	3.58	30	3-81q	34	9.5	13.7	22.0	0	3.4	84
New Hamp Ball .... A	13.50	211	8.8	11.4	7.5	2.50	24	3-81n	28	6.8	8.6	16.1	58	2.9	47
Omark Ind .... N	17.01	131	15.1	6.6	6.7	3.36	-6	3-81n	40	10.0	11.0	21.7	47	4.0	155
Ransburg Corp .... A	9.21	383	5.0	19.8	8.3	1.78	18	2-81q	27	9.6	79.9	18.8	10	1.8	253
Raven Ind .... A	7.89	81	8.0	12.5	7.1	.51	-68	4-81q	-12	1.8	3.3	6.3	49	6.0	8
Regal-Beloit .... A	8.23	210	7.3	13.7	8.4	1.26	-31	3-81q	13	6.5	9.9	17.1	51	3.7	32
Spectra-Phys .... N	10.62	305	6.1	16.3	15.1	1.99	-3	12-80q	23	7.0	9.8	18.3	14	.0	136
Timken Co ....★N	68.00	107	11.2	8.9	7.0	8.19	-7	3-81q	10	6.9	9.0	12.1	4	5.0	818
Wadell Equip .... A	3.16	127	8.8	11.4	NC	.35	NE	3-81q	48	3.9	3.9	9.5	33	.0	3

Electronic Components and Equipment

ELECTRONIC COMPONENTS: TRENDS AND PROJECTIONS 1975–81 (in millions of current dollars except as noted)

Item	1975	1976	1977	1978	1979[2]	1980[2]	Percent change 1979–80[2]	1981[3]	Percent change 1980–81[3]
Industry (SIC 367)									
Value of shipments[1]	10,089	12,433	15,387	18,368	21,582	24,607	14	28,055	14
Value added	5,984	7,568	9,256	11,049	12,982	14,800	14	16,870	14
Value added per production worker-hour ($)	15.32	17.25	18.20	19.10	20.05	20.95	4	21.50	3
Total employment (000)	302	323	374	415	492	520	6	545	5
Production workers (000)	198	219	258	280	333	339	2	370	9
Average hourly earnings (Dec.—$)	4.00	4.32	4.69	5.14	5.73	[4]6.15	[4]7	—	—
Year-to-year percent change in average hourly earnings (Dec.-Dec.)	7	8	9	10	11	[5]15	—	—	—
Capital expenditures	536	650	782	940	—	—	—	—	—
Product (SIC 367)									
Value of shipments[7]	9,872	12,230	14,273	16,975	19,946	22,742	14	26,336	16
3671—Receiving tubes	130	113	1,257	1,431	1,645	1,925	17	2,120	10
3672—TV picture tubes	514	605	—	—	—	—	—	—	—
3673—Transmitting tubes	417	446	—	—	—	—	—	—	—
3674—Semiconductors	3,038	4,291	4,532	5,544	6,813	8,107	19	9,720	20
Discrete devices	1,320	1,693	1,835	2,154	2,542	2,982	17	3,520	18
Integrated circuits	1,718	2,598	2,697	3,390	4,271	5,125	20	6,200	21
3675—Capacitors	535	655	736	896	985	1,063	8	1,200	13
3676—Resistors	466	481	583	598	645	683	6	740	8
3677—Coils and transformers	488	539	605	618	667	707	6	765	8
3678—Connectors	839	838	986	1,305	1,555	1,705	10	1,905	12
3679—Other comp., N.E.C.	3,445	4,262	5,574	6,583	7,636	8,552	12	9,885	16
Producers price index (Dec.)	114.3	117.3	121.6	130.0	146.1	156.7	[5]7	—	—
Year-to-year percent change in producers price index (Dec.-Dec.)[6]	–2	3	4	7	12	[5]7	—	—	—
Trade									
Value of exports	1,987	2,532	2,683	3,006	3,946	5,290	34	7,190	36
Value of imports	1,160	1,645	2,018	2,678	3,562	4,660	31	6,151	32

[1] Value of all products and services sold by the electronic components industries (SIC 367).
[2] Estimated except for hourly earnings, price indexes, and 1979 trade data.
[3] Forecast.
[4] As of July 1980.
[5] July 1979 to July 1980. Note: Months may differ for the price and earnings indexes.
[6] December 1967 is the average base period for index.
[7] Value of shipments of electronic components produced by all industries.

Source: Bureau of the Census (industry and trade data), Bureau of Labor Statistics (hourly earnings and price indexes). Estimates and forecasts by the Bureau of Industrial Economics.

Source: *U.S. INDUSTRIAL OUTLOOK 1981*, U.S. Department of Commerce.

RADIO AND TELEVISION COMMUNICATION EQUIPMENT: TRENDS AND PROJECTIONS 1975–81 (in millions of current dollars except as noted)

Item	1975	1976	1977	1978	1979[2]	1980[2]	Percent change 1979–80[2]	1981[3]	Percent change 1980–81[3]
Industry (SIC 3662)									
Value of shipments[1]	11,911	13,248	14,900	16,876	19,240	22,100	14.9	25,100	13.6
Value added	7,558	8,500	9,950	11,413	13,100	15,000	14.5	—	—
Value added per production worker-hour ($)	24.34	27.04	29.61	30.68	32.27	36.14	12.0	—	—
Total employment (000)	316	316	335	372	406	415	2.2	—	—
Production workers (000)	160	159	173	192	215	219	1.9	—	—
Average hourly earnings (Dec.—$)	5.38	5.73	6.17	6.81	7.43	[4]7.66	[4]7.6	—	—
Year-to-year percent change in average hourly earnings (Dec.–Dec.)	14.7	6.5	7.7	10.4	9.1	[5]7.6	[5]—	—	—
Year-to-year percent change in industry price index (Dec.–Dec.)[6]	N.A.	—	—	—	—	—	—	—	—
Capital expenditures	256	356	472	654	—	—	—	—	—
Product (SIC 3662)									
Value of shipments[6]	10,755	12,078	13,906	15,897	18,120	20,800	14.8	23,700	13.9
Trade									
Value of exports	991	1,278	1,400	1,584	1,781	1,910	7.2	2,050	7.3
Value of imports	732	1,534	1,207	839	941	1,030	9.5	1,140	10.7

[1] Value of all products and services sold by the radio and television communication equipment industry (SIC 3662).
[2] Estimated except for hourly earnings, price indexes, and 1979 trade data.
[3] Forecast.
[4] As of June 1980.
[5] June 1979 to June 1980. Note: Months may differ for the price and earnings indexes.
[6] Value of shipments of radio and television communication equipment produced by all industries.

Source: Bureau of the Census (industry and trade data), Bureau of Labor Statistics (hourly earnings and price indexes). Estimates and forecasts by the Bureau of Industrial Economics.

Source: *U.S. INDUSTRIAL OUTLOOK 1981*, U.S. Department of Commerce.

Company and Market		Relative Price					Earnings Per Share				Other					
		Common Equity			P/E Ratio		Latest 12 Months			5-Year Growth Rate	Profit Margin	Return On Assets	Return On Common Equity	Debt Equity Ratio	Dividend Yield	Market Value
		Per Share	Price To Equity	Earnings Yield	Current	5-Year Average	Amount	Change	Date							
		$	%	%	-	-	$	%	-	%	%	%	%	%	%	$Mil
Electronic Equipment Manufacturers																
Adams-Russell	A	6.22	392	4.3	23.0	11.0	1.06	29	3-81s	37	7.5	7.3	13.5	51	.4	79
Adv Micro Dev	N	6.19	460	5.4	18.4	12.6	1.55	1	3-81f	66	8.0	14.1	26.6	17	.0	435
Alpha Indus	A	4.16	919	3.0	33.0	8.4	1.16	22	3-81f	55	9.5	12.6	22.9	25	.3	97
Altec Corp	A	- .72	0782	-34.1	NC	29.3	- .32	NC	3-81s	- 81	- .7	NE	NE	- 353	.0	5
Am Microsystems	O	13.46	179	5.1	19.5	23.0	1.24	36	3-81q	37	3.3	5.3	8.0	1	.0	97
Am Precision	A	10.30	195	11.3	8.9	5.9	2.27	46	3-81q	14	6.3	12.7	20.0	8	2.2	21
Analog	N	5.78	413	4.4	22.7	12.2	1.05	11	1-81q	35	6.9	7.5	19.1	106	.0	203
Anaren Micrwve	O	1.93	492	1.7	NC	23.6	.16	NC	3-81n	24	4.8	3.3	7.3	62	.0	31
Andrew Corp	O	11.09	361	4.3	23.3	NC	1.72	NC	3-81s	21	8.1	NC	13.6	8	.0	191
Anthem Electronics	O	4.01	455	6.3	15.9	NC	1.15	- 20	3-81f	24	6.1	20.5	32.5	0	.0	35
Applied Materials	O	5.49	592	3.8	26.4	10.0	1.23	- 2	4-81s	23	8.9	13.1	24.4	18	.0	153
Augat	N	9.30	513	4.2	23.8	12.9	2.01	2	3-81q	34	11.4	12.2	21.7	50	1.0	426
Avantek Inc	N	2.27	2115	1.9	NC	16.9	.92	44	3-81q	50	12.0	17.8	26.1	1	.0	392
Avnet Inc	N	24.11	246	7.6	13.1	7.2	4.52	- 1	3-81n	17	5.7	11.6	19.3	15	1.7	913
AVX Corp	N	14.47	239	4.2	24.0	9.6	1.44	- 34	3-81q	22	5.7	5.0	11.8	97	.9	162
Aydin Cp	N	8.08	452	5.9	16.8	9.4	2.17	58	3-81q	31	7.1	11.4	26.3	13	.0	126
Barnes Engin	A	5.08	140	4.4	23.0	21.9	.31	- 50	3-81n	40	2.3	3.8	13.9	100	.0	12
Buckbee-Mears	O	10.40	111	5.7	17.4	7.9	.66	- 55	3-81q	32	2.3	8.1	13.4	8	3.1	35
Bunker Ramo	N	27.94	191	7.4	13.5	6.6	3.97	1	3-81q	42	5.8	8.2	15.4	40	2.6	313
Calif Microwv	O	5.50	564	2.9	34.4	47.4	.90	275	3-81n	- 10	.5	.8	1.8	63	.0	78
Cetec Corp	A	5.74	122	9.6	10.4	10.5	.67	22	3-81q	29	2.5	5.3	11.3	54	1.7	15
Cohu Inc	A	5.50	168	9.0	11.1	10.8	.83	15	3-81q	43	5.3	8.8	14.0	10	1.7	16
Commun Ind	O	5.52	716	3.1	31.9	11.7	1.24	53	3-81q	21	10.9	15.4	19.7	3	.9	183
Comtech Telecom	O	.34	1912	-39.1	NC	17.1	- 2.54	NC	1-81s	- 63	-41.3	NE	NE	1008	.0	23
CTS Corp	N	24.27	118	8.6	11.6	8.0	2.47	6	3-81q	- 2	5.5	8.1	9.7	1	3.1	126
Cubic Corp	A	17.92	157	11.0	9.1	6.6	3.08	19	3-81s	13	4.2	7.4	15.5	52	2.1	83
Diodes Inc	A	1.03	255	- 3.8	NC	41.5	- .10	NE	1-81n	NE	-10.4	NE	NE	5	.0	5
Drexler Technlgy	O	3.60	778	3.4	29.5	13.1	.95	10	3-81f	145	11.0	16.7	24.5	0	.0	56
E Systems	N	20.33	271	3.8	26.6	10.5	2.07	- 25	3-81q	- 7	2.9	5.4	9.1	13	1.8	376
Edo Corp	A	14.68	140	5.6	17.8	9.2	1.16	- 23	3-81q	0	2.6	3.8	7.3	26	1.9	48
EECO Inc	A	8.08	203	4.7	21.3	10.6	.77	- 21	3-81q	12	12.9	16.8	27.8	20	1.5	40
EG & G Inc	N	6.18	676	4.6	21.9	13.2	1.91	17	3-81q	29	4.3	12.8	25.2	13	1.2	587
Espey Mfg El	A	14.21	198	5.6	17.9	12.9	1.57	89	3-81n	24	4.5	4.8	5.6	9	.9	11
Gen Instrument	N	32.72	381	5.5	18.0	8.0	6.92	28	2-81f	51	8.3	10.0	17.2	17	.8	1,199
GenRad	N	9.79	240	4.9	20.3	13.0	1.16	- 14	3-81q	51	6.1	6.9	13.8	52	.3	179
Granger Assc	A	- .79	0782	2.9	34.0	10.4	.92	NE	2-81s	- 67	-21.4	NE	NE	- 742	.0	28
GTI Corp	A	2.46	203	5.2	19.2	15.0	.26	- 46	3-81q	27	9.8	17.9	32.1	25	2.4	11
Gulton Ind	N	14.26	101	15.5	6.4	6.8	2.23	0	2-81f	40	4.2	6.6	14.2	44	4.2	40
Harris Cp	★N	14.89	341	5.8	17.4	13.1	2.92	14	3-81n	22	6.1	7.0	17.6	48	1.6	1,576
Hazeltine Corp	N	22.03	105	9.7	10.3	6.5	2.24	- 18	3-81q	- 1	3.6	5.3	10.6	8	3.5	47
Hi-G Inc	A	8.16	190	9.9	10.1	15.5	1.54	41	12-80n	71	3.3	3.8	16.5	122	.8	21
Intel Corp	★O	10.13	405	4.2	24.0	17.5	1.71	- 16	3-81q	33	11.3	12.6	22.3	35	.0	1,752
Intl Rectifier	N	15.71	110	11.4	8.8	12.4	1.97	- 31	3-81n	25	5.8	7.3	20.3	67	1.9	48
Jetronic Ind	A	5.32	47	-11.6	NC	8.4	- .29	-100	1-81f	- 20	- 1.3	4.1	8.9	22	.0	4
King Radio	A	14.53	194	9.0	11.1	6.5	2.55	- 25	3-81q	33	7.2	16.7	24.6	8	1.7	77
Koss Corporation	O	3.68	336	7.0	14.2	NC	.87	107	12-80s	63	7.3	10.1	19.3	51	1.9	30
KRATOS Inc	O	8.92	213	7.6	13.2	9.0	1.44	17	3-81q	50	6.1	8.7	13.7	4	.0	55
Kyoto Cer	N	10.88	414	3.6	28.0	21.4	1.61	58	3-80f	NC	12.7	11.3	17.8	3	.6	1,350
La Pointe Inds	A	4.33	55	-71.2	NC	9.5	- 1.69	NE	12-80s	- 82	-13.9	NE	NE	57	.0	2
Loral Corp	N	13.16	301	5.2	19.3	11.6	2.05	25	12-80n	20	8.1	7.1	11.4	19	1.8	398
Lynch Comm	N	7.59	171	-14.7	NC	10.6	- 1.91	-100	3-81q	- 38	- 6.6	NE	NE	155	.8	25
M/A - Com	★N	3.04	1123	2.7	37.1	16.1	.92	74	3-81s	41	7.7	8.9	16.4	29	.4	1,250
Marshall Ind	A	10.52	202	- 2.6	NC	9.5	- .55	-100	2-81n	- 29	2.2	5.5	14.0	7	.0	25
Matsushita El	N	29.15	267	6.1	16.4	7.3	4.75	82	2-81q	13	4.3	4.6	10.7	7	.8	10,528
MicroMask	O	4.70	277	8.6	11.6	7.4	1.12	- 3	3-81n	37	8.0	13.3	22.1	36	.0	22
Molex Inc	O	9.63	511	5.2	19.4	9.7	2.54	11	3-81n	33	12.2	15.7	23.6	7	.1	322
MSI Data	A	7.09	342	6.1	16.3	7.2	1.49	28	3-81f	18	6.3	10.3	16.3	3	1.6	56
Narda Micro	A	5.79	479	4.6	21.7	13.6	1.28	28	3-81n	60	5.8	9.2	18.5	40	.7	41
Natl Semicon	★N	11.21	308	7.7	12.9	19.0	2.67	19	2-81n	36	5.3	9.3	23.2	43	.0	757
Northn Telecom	★N	21.15	210	- 1.5	NC	10.1	- .67	-100	3-81q	- 22	- 1.0	NE	NE	44	NA	1,532

Company and Market		Common Equity Per Share ($)	Price To Equity (%)	Earnings Yield (%)	P/E Ratio Current (-)	5-Year Average (-)	Latest 12 Months Amount ($)	Change (%)	Date (-)	5-Year Growth Rate (%)	Profit Margin (%)	Return On Assets (%)	Return On Common Equity (%)	Debt Equity Ratio (%)	Dividend Yield (%)	Market Value ($Mil)
Oak Ind	N	12.68	296	5.0	19.8	13.7	1.89	20	3-81q	61	5.2	4.9	12.6	87	.6	458
Paradyne Cp	A	5.59	868	1.7	NC	22.1	.84	62	3-81q	80	10.8	9.6	12.8	9	.0	605
Penril Corp	A	7.16	213	8.5	11.7	8.0	1.30	3	1-81s	23	5.4	7.3	13.4	43	1.0	29
Plantronics	N	8.49	289	4.9	20.6	13.7	1.19	-13	2-81n	10	8.2	9.4	14.8	23	.7	156
Plessey Co Ltd	N	22.45	272	8.7	11.5	8.6	5.30	75	12-80n	20	5.3	6.8	16.0	13	2.7	1,390
Ragen Precision	O	4.38	288	2.9	35.1	14.8	.36	-54	12-80q	21	3.0	3.8	10.1	96	.0	28
Ramtek Corp	O	5.75	267	3.4	29.6	17.5	.52	-4	3-81n	21	4.8	5.1	8.0	10	.0	40
Redcor Cp	O	3.27	703	5.5	18.1	11.5	1.27	72	3-81n	40	10.9	17.2	29.5	2	.0	59
REDM Cp	A	6.14	183	10.0	10.0	6.0	1.12	19	3-81q	45	5.9	10.1	17.9	8	.0	16
Regency Electro	O	5.86	339	6.7	14.8	14.3	1.34	46	3-81n	15	8.9	11.1	16.2	8	2.0	107
RMS	A	2.41	659	4.9	20.6	NC	.77	NC	3-81q	65	6.2	10.5	27.6	14	.0	23
Robinson Nugent	O	5.65	336	4.8	20.9	14.5	.91	-31	3-81n	38	10.4	15.6	20.4	10	.4	49
Sanders Assoc	N	16.78	364	4.4	22.8	11.8	2.67	4	4-81n	21	6.6	7.9	14.2	20	1.0	475
Scientific- Atla	*N	4.15	789	2.5	39.9	15.8	.82	46	3-81n	31	6.6	9.1	14.7	15	.2	695
Scope Inc	O	19.74	89	11.5	8.7	8.1	2.01	26	3-81q	0	3.5	4.8	10.4	35	3.4	21
Sealectro Corp	A	10.51	291	8.6	11.7	8.2	2.62	45	3-81q	83	6.3	9.1	17.9	38	.0	45
Semtech Cp	A	6.38	114	1.2	NC	29.8	.09	-85	1-81f	-21	1.3	1.4	1.9	2	.0	12
Sensormatic Elec	O	5.25	805	2.9	34.9	17.2	1.21	39	2-81n	46	15.4	11.6	18.3	8	.2	265
Servo Cp Am	A	6.54	94	NC	NC	17.4	.00	-100	1-81q	5	3.9	5.5	9.8	24	.0	4
SFE Tech	O	2.73	650	6.3	16.0	9.2	1.11	217	10-80f	30	7.7	4.3	12.5	99	.0	62
Siliconix Inc	O	12.74	131	6.6	15.2	11.2	1.10	-39	12-80f	15	4.1	4.8	8.7	19	.0	41
Siltec Corp	O	6.92	293	5.3	18.8	NC	1.08	-5	3-81q	38	6.0	7.7	17.9	85	.0	55
Solid State Sci	A	6.84	177	5.4	18.4	13.1	.66	-8	3-81q	25	4.5	4.2	10.7	84	.0	25
Solitron Device	A	4.84	227	5.5	18.0	18.1	.61	42	2-81f	32	7.6	7.4	9.1	7	.0	52
Spectrum Control	O	.98	753	3.3	30.7	16.9	.24	14	2-81q	27	7.7	11.6	28.2	46	.5	36
Std Microsystems	O	2.48	423	4.9	20.6	20.0	.51	2	2-81f	64	12.9	16.5	24.5	7	.0	53
Sun Electric	N	15.17	135	7.6	13.2	10.6	1.55	-28	1-81q	10	5.7	6.1	12.1	39	3.5	129
Sunair Electron	A	6.12	253	5.5	18.2	8.4	.85	-11	3-81s	14	17.2	13.7	14.6	0	2.5	37
T-BAR Inc	A	4.90	372	2.7	36.5	13.7	.50	-35	3-81q	13	4.7	5.3	11.2	16	.0	47
Technitrol	A	9.25	77	9.5	10.5	5.1	.68	-45	3-81q	-12	3.3	7.4	10.7	5	4.5	8
Tektronix Inc	*N	26.31	231	7.4	13.5	13.7	4.51	0	2-81n	23	8.8	10.1	17.6	28	1.5	1,123
Telescience Inc	A	6.02	282	-4.0	NC	11.3	-.68	-100	3-81q	-26	-7.5	NE	NE	0	.0	54
Tellabs Inc	O	1.38	2101	3.6	27.6	NC	1.05	NC	3-81q	116	15.1	NC	55.3	19	.0	179
Texas Inst	*N	50.08	229	7.4	13.5	16.0	8.49	5	3-81q	19	5.2	8.8	18.2	18	1.7	2,663
Texscan Cp	A	1.89	1038	2.9	35.0	12.7	.56	NC	1-81n	89	5.0	7.7	18.6	2	.0	70
Timeplex	A	2.46	676	2.9	33.9	15.6	.49	-4	3-81n	23	7.8	10.0	23.0	43	.0	64
Torotel Inc	A	2.20	773	1.6	NC	26.2	.27	NC	6-80q	-7	3.0	4.5	13.2	63	.0	39
Unitrode Cp	N	16.03	353	5.9	17.0	8.6	3.34	23	1-81f	39	9.9	12.5	16.7	4	.9	156
Varian Assoc	N	25.00	103	8.1	12.4	10.1	2.08	-28	3-81s	13	3.4	4.1	10.9	59	2.0	202
Vicon	A	5.54	314	5.3	18.9	8.2	.92	11	3-81s	28	6.7	9.6	14.5	14	.0	26
Vishay Inter	A	6.33	209	6.4	15.6	8.3	.85	-29	3-81n	18	8.6	8.0	18.9	54	.0	35
Wavetek	O	5.49	328	3.3	30.5	10.8	.59	-44	3-81s	12	6.3	7.8	15.3	25	.0	54
Wstn Digital	O	.87	1293	NC	NC	NC	.00	-100	3-81n	77	3.4	4.1	7.3	26	.0	146
Wyle Labs	N	5.91	176	11.2	8.9	6.7	1.16	-23	1-81f	23	2.6	7.2	20.2	88	3.9	57

Radio, TV, Phonograph, Stereo

Company and Market		Common Equity Per Share ($)	Price To Equity (%)	Earnings Yield (%)	P/E Ratio Current (-)	5-Year Average (-)	Latest 12 Months Amount ($)	Change (%)	Date (-)	5-Year Growth Rate (%)	Profit Margin (%)	Return On Assets (%)	Return On Common Equity (%)	Debt Equity Ratio (%)	Dividend Yield (%)	Market Value ($Mil)
Andrea Radio	A	6.69	194	4.7	21.3	14.3	.61	5	3-81q	38	9.4	.4	8.8	0	4.3	7
Armatron Intl	A	3.84	78	15.3	6.5	6.3	.46	NE	3-81s	-26	4.6	8.7	13.8	20	.0	7
Comp Vid Svc	O	5.86	328	6.0	16.7	15.3	1.15	34	1-81n	33	6.5	6.1	18.8	139	.0	56
Craig Corp	N	12.88	49	-10.8	NC	7.6	-.69	NE	3-81n	-25	-.3	NE	NE	15	.0	19
Emerson Radio	N	5.73	262	2.7	36.6	10.4	.41	-44	12-80n	14	2.0	4.1	9.6	40	.0	44
Esquire Radio	N	25.88	85	18.3	5.5	4.9	4.04	63	3-81q	14	3.3	6.5	8.8	0	3.0	11
Johnson EF	N	6.60	527	1.6	NC	NC	.55	15	3-81q	65	4.2	5.7	10.5	43	.0	97
Microdyne	O	1.00	3150	2.6	38.0	17.5	.83	9	1-81q	65	13.5	18.4	80.0	25	.1	126
Motorola Inc	*N	36.74	234	7.0	14.4	12.2	5.98	16	3-81q	18	6.0	8.8	16.2	29	1.9	2,697
Outlet Co	N	8.74	449	-.8	NC	8.3	-.31	-100	1-81f	-19	-.6	NE	NE	507	1.5	100
Pioneer Elec	N	13.09	273	5.8	17.1	9.9	2.09	13	12-80q	4	6.6	9.4	16.3	1	1.4	1,683
Sony Corp	N	6.29	395	5.3	18.7	14.7	1.33	93	1-81q	18	7.6	7.8	21.1	3	.5	5,364
Soundesign	A	13.56	85	8.3	12.0	16.7	.96	NE	3-81q	-33	.6	.8	2.2	34	1.7	26
Superscope	N	10.01	42	-21.9	NC	NC	-5.18	NE	3-81q	NE	-8.5	NE	NE	82	.0	10
Zenith Radio	*N	15.43	129	6.5	15.3	20.2	1.30	12	3-81q	2	2.2	4.0	9.1	56	3.0	375

ELECTRONIC COMPUTING EQUIPMENT: TRENDS AND PROJECTIONS 1975–81 (in millions of current dollars except as noted)

Item	1975	1976	1977	1978	1979[2]	1980[2]	Percent change 1979-80[2]	1981[3]	Percent change 1980-81[3]
Industry (SIC 3573)									
Value of shipments[1]	8,560	10,388	12,922	16,353	21,000	26,000	23.8	32,800	26.2
Value added	4,690	6,100	7,623	9,534	12,100	13,750	13.6	—	—
Value added per production worker-hour ($)	32.14	42.41	44.23	47.29	51.00	54.00	5.9	—	—
Total employment (000)	163	166	193	231	267	306	14.8	—	—
Production workers (000)	74	71	86	102	119	128	7.8	—	—
Average hourly earnings (Dec.–$)	5.19	5.32	5.45	5.76	6.28	[4]6.61	—	—	—
Year-to-year percent change in average hourly earnings (Dec.–Dec.)	+9.5	+2.5	+2.4	+5.7	+9.0	[5]+9.6	—	—	—
Capital expenditures	292	373	651	1,152	—	—	—	—	—
Product (SIC 3573)									
Value of shipments[6]	8,443	10,136	12,673	15,602	20,500	25,500	24.4	31,875	25.0
Trade									
Value of exports	2,254	2,632	3,310	4,194	5,500	7,500	36.4	9,000	20.0
Value of imports									
Excluding parts	129	235	253	388	509	540	6.1	—	—
Including parts	—	—	—	755	969	1,090	12.5	1,300	19.3

[1] Value of all products and services sold by the Electronic Computing Equipment Industry (SIC 3573).
[2] Estimated except for hourly earnings, and 1979 trade data.
[3] Forecast.
[4] As of June 1980.
[5] June 1979 to June 1980.
[6] Value of shipments of electronic computing equipment produced by all industries.

Source: Bureau of the Census (industry and trade data), Bureau of Labor Statistics (hourly earnings and price indexes). Estimates and forecasts by the Bureau of Industrial Economics.

Source: U.S. INDUSTRIAL OUTLOOK 1981, U.S. Department of Commerce.

Company and Market	Relative Price					Earnings Per Share				Other					
	Common Equity		P/E Ratio			Latest 12 Months			5-Year Growth Rate	Profit Margin	Return On Assets	Return On Common Equity	Debt Equity Ratio	Dividend Yield	Market Value
	Per Share	Price To Equity	Earnings Yield	Current	5-Year Average	Amount	Change	Date							
	$	%	%	-	-	$	%	-	%	%	%	%	%	%	$Mil
Computers, Subsystems and Peripherals															
Accuray Cp .... O	5.71	230	5.4	18.5	37.8	.71	69	3-81q	31	2.3	2.4	11.9	203	.0	46
Amdahl Corp .... A	14.20	309	2.4	42.2	22.0	1.04	767	3-81q	-19	3.9	3.9	6.3	11	.9	734
Analogic Corp .... O	3.73	938	2.8	36.1	13.6	.97	29	1-81s	58	9.0	11.7	21.4	36	.0	286
Andersn Jacob .... A	6.33	336	4.7	21.5	12.4	.99	8	12-80n	26	5.3	6.7	16.1	66	.0	46
Apple Compt .... O	.54	6134	1.0	NC	NC	.32	NC	12-80q	28	10.0	NC	45.2	3	.0	1,796
Applicon Inc .... O	2.66	1288	2.5	40.8	NC	.84	NC	1-81n	24	6.1	10.8	29.5	137	.0	193
Applied Devices .... A	.17	3162	-4.1	NC	19.4	-.22	NE	1-81q	-66	-4.5	NE	NE	2663	.0	25
Barry Wright .... N	4.63	429	6.7	14.8	8.6	1.34	17	3-81q	37	8.0	14.8	22.0	3	1.6	151
Beehive Intl .... O	2.90	517	9.3	10.8	9.7	1.39	276	3-81s	22	5.7	10.5	25.7	64	.0	38
Burroughs Cp .... *N	51.19	83	3.2	30.9	17.9	1.37	-82	3-81q	-23	2.9	2.1	3.9	18	6.1	1,759
Centronics Data .... N	12.38	113	22.8	4.4	12.0	3.19	7	3-81n	15	14.1	10.7	24.4	77	.0	84
Compuscan Inc .... O	-.21	0782	-49.2	NC	41.3	-2.09	NE	2-81n	NE	-31.9	NE	NE	-1250	.0	12
Cmp & Com Tch .... O	7.13	715	2.7	36.7	10.8	1.39	34	3-81q	12	7.2	12.2	18.9	6	.0	164
Computer Auto .... O	13.28	122	8.6	11.7	9.0	1.39	NE	3-81n	-15	5.7	9.0	17.4	6	.0	33
Computer Comm .... O	2.44	110	-79.6	NC	34.6	-2.14	NE	3-81n	-68	-49.3	2.4	5.7	32	.0	10
Computer Consol .... O	4.90	740	2.6	37.8	12.2	.96	28	12-80f	24	10.9	12.7	18.7	0	.0	190
Computer Prod .... O	3.41	400	4.2	23.9	14.0	.57	21	3-81q	28	11.1	12.5	15.0	6	.0	56
Computervision .... N	8.10	1091	2.4	42.3	14.7	2.09	82	3-81q	97	10.4	13.9	21.5	18	.0	1,183
Control Data .... *N	76.72	107	10.4	9.6	7.3	8.49	15	3-81q	34	5.3	5.8	10.2	9	1.1	1,510
Cray Research .... N	5.58	800	.7	NC	29.7	.31	-67	3-81q	23	18.0	10.4	14.4	10	.0	606
C3 Inc .... O	2.11	2133	2.7	37.2	NC	1.21	NC	12-80n	82	17.1	18.2	32.9	3	.0	187
Data Access .... A	7.60	184	10.4	9.6	7.0	1.46	-16	2-81s	27	13.7	10.6	24.8	79	.7	42
Data General .... N	31.00	217	6.7	15.0	15.8	4.48	-7	3-81s	20	8.4	8.5	17.2	45	.0	693
Data Term Sys .... N	8.96	156	2.0	50.0	29.4	.28	-85	1-81f	15	-2.5	9.4	21.3	61	.0	71
Datapoint Cp .... N	19.91	329	6.4	15.6	7.9	4.20	29	4-81n	38	10.5	15.0	19.8	2	.0	1,269
Dataproducts .... A	12.77	258	6.7	14.9	10.4	2.21	123	3-81f	7	6.4	4.2	8.0	25	.9	291
Dataram Corp .... O	4.79	201	9.4	10.7	12.0	.90	-39	1-81n	122	14.5	19.2	29.4	12	.0	22
Decision Data .... O	3.15	135	.9	NC	34.7	.04	-69	2-81q	-13	.2	.3	.6	45	.0	21
Denelcor Inc .... O	.26	6827	-.6	NC	NC	-.10	NC	6-80s	-59	-14.8	NE	NE	67	.0	60
Digital Equip .... *N	36.25	307	5.6	17.7	17.1	6.27	23	3-81n	27	10.6	9.4	15.1	30	.0	5,684
Dysan Corp .... O	2.48	1190	1.8	NC	NC	.53	NC	4-81s	34	12.7	10.5	30.2	33	.0	358
Electron Assoc .... N	5.90	129	6.7	15.0	NC	.51	-28	3-81q	35	4.1	7.2	11.1	9	.0	21
Electron Mem .... N	6.78	77	2.3	43.8	7.7	.12	-71	3-81q	-34	3.0	4.4	8.0	26	.0	28
Electronic Modules .... O	4.30	628	3.1	31.0	8.7	.87	NC	3-81s	32	6.7	10.3	18.1	0	.0	52
Fabri-Tek .... O	.51	1127	10.1	9.9	31.5	.58	76	3-81f	35	6.0	6.0	63.2	516	.0	21

continued

		Relative Price					Earnings Per Share				Other					
		Common Equity			P/E Ratio		Latest 12 Months			5-Year Growth Rate	Profit Margin	Return On Assets	Return On Common Equity	Debt Equity Ratio	Dividend Yield	Market Value
Company and Market		Per Share	Price To Equity	Earnings Yield	Current	5-Year Average	Amount	Change	Date							
		$	%	%	-	-	$	%	-	%	%	%	%	%	%	$Mil

Computers, Subsystems and Peripherals

Company and Market		Per Share	Price To Equity	Earnings Yield	Current	5-Year Average	Amount	Change	Date	Growth Rate	Profit Margin	Return On Assets	Return On Common Equity	Debt Equity Ratio	Dividend Yield	Market Value
Floating Point	O	6.06	978	2.2	46.3	23.1	1.28	52	1-81q	43	9.9	10.8	18.7	17	.0	220
Four Phase	N	20.20	208	2.8	36.2	15.9	1.16	-58	3-81q	-5	2.8	3.1	5.3	46	.0	229
Gen Automation	O	9.05	169	-37.3	NC	21.7	-5.69	NE	1-81s	-76	-12.0	NE	NE	197	.0	39
General Data	N	4.17	384	3.4	29.1	15.9	.55	15	12-80q	41	8.2	8.1	17.8	18	.0	66
Information Intl	O	7.20	194	3.3	30.4	17.3	.46	-38	1-81n	-5	8.7	8.2	9.8	0	1.3	38
Interface Mech	O	1.79	1159	3.0	33.5	21.7	.62	NC	9-80s	4	8.8	12.5	26.5	0	.0	39
Intl Bus Mach	★N	28.18	208	10.5	9.5	13.5	6.18	19	3-81q	10	13.6	13.3	21.6	13	5.9	34,299
ISC Systems	O	.95	9263	.7	NC	NC	.65	NC	6-80f	60	12.6	23.0	65.4	15	.0	241
Magnuson Comp	O	-1.73	0782	1.3	NC	NC	.45	NC	3-81q	77	8.3	NE	NE	-108	.0	168
Mangmt Assist	N	10.22	141	7.4	13.6	7.8	1.06	-62	3-81s	6	4.6	7.5	17.1	37	.0	116
Memorex Corp	N	19.83	62	-45.7	NC	6.5	-5.65	-100	3-81q	-34	-3.8	NE	NE	127	.0	89
Modular Comp	N	15.22	104	4.2	24.1	13.1	.66	-42	3-81q	12	4.7	5.5	9.5	20	.0	80
Mohawk Data	N	8.76	315	6.2	16.1	15.7	1.72	32	1-81n	50	6.6	6.9	17.8	98	.0	366
Monolithic Mem	O	6.58	334	8.3	12.1	NC	1.82	NC	3-81s	22	12.5	NC	23.9	16	.0	135
NBI Inc	O	2.19	1781	1.8	NC	NC	.70	79	3-81n	33	9.9	13.1	18.9	4	.0	356
Prime Computer	N	3.38	1398	2.4	41.4	18.0	1.14	54	3-81q	99	11.7	13.4	31.5	61	.0	1,382
Printronix	O	4.27	831	3.3	30.6	23.7	1.16	27	12-80n	22	8.4	13.4	22.0	18	.0	136
Recog Equip	N	10.50	135	5.9	16.8	14.2	.84	163	1-81q	5	4.3	4.1	7.8	32	.0	83
Rolm Corp	★N	3.22	1479	2.9	34.8	21.5	1.37	38	3-81n	80	8.6	14.7	34.5	52	.0	807
SCI Systems	O	8.22	368	4.1	24.6	19.0	1.23	43	3-81n	36	4.5	5.8	11.6	41	.0	67
Sperry Corp	★N	51.01	102	14.5	6.9	8.1	7.50	9	3-81f	15	5.8	6.5	13.6	20	3.4	2,123
Storage Technl	N	9.07	383	5.0	19.9	9.5	1.75	7	3-81q	45	7.5	6.2	18.0	115	.0	963
Sykes Data	O	6.00	1117	1.3	NC	13.0	.90	84	2-81f	104	14.0	11.2	13.6	3	.0	279
Tab Products	A	10.70	235	7.1	14.0	7.4	1.79	-18	2-81n	25	4.9	9.3	20.0	51	.8	48
Tandem Computers	O	7.01	1469	1.5	NC	NC	1.53	91	3-81s	34	9.8	11.2	15.2	2	.0	1,203
TEC Inc	A	6.79	77	4.4	22.8	10.0	.23	-60	3-81n	-29	1.3	1.7	3.6	34	1.5	4
Telex Corp	N	3.31	249	7.8	12.9	20.9	.64	700	3-81f	1	4.3	.7	2.4	153	.0	104
Threshold Tech	O	1.07	1145	-7.9	NC	NC	-.97	NE	3-81n	NE	-76.2	NE	NE	71	.0	24
Topaz Inc	O	2.94	672	3.6	27.8	17.0	.71	13	3-81f	69	6.8	12.0	21.1	19	.2	60
TRW Inc	★N	40.01	151	9.7	10.3	8.1	5.86	9	3-81q	12	4.3	7.4	16.5	30	4.0	1,929
Verbatim Corp	O	6.65	395	-1.3	NC	20.9	-.33	-100	3-81n	-17	2.6	3.6	9.2	92	.0	57
Vermont Resch	A	3.40	699	6.9	14.5	8.2	1.64	33	3-81s	24	17.4	26.4	44.4	14	.6	49
Vernitron Corp	A	6.90	277	6.9	14.5	8.9	1.32	39	3-81q	30	5.9	9.3	18.8	50	.5	109
Wang Labs B	★A	3.76	1167	2.9	34.3	17.4	1.28	54	3-81n	60	10.4	9.0	27.2	112	.3	2,468

MEASURING AND CONTROLLING INSTRUMENTS: TRENDS AND PROJECTIONS 1975–81 (in millions of current dollars except as noted)

Item	1975	1976	1977	1978	1979[2]	1980[2]	Percent change 1979–80[2]	1981[3]	Percent change 1980–81[3]
Industry (SIC 3822, 3823, 3824, 3829)									
Value of shipments[1]	3,384	3,815	5,149	5,977	7,112	8,179	15	9,569	17
Value added	2,174	2,594	3,435	3,937	4,694	5,398	15	—	—
Value added per production worker-hour ($)	19.37	21.40	23.30	24.97	26.08	32.02	23	—	—
Total employment (000)	107	108	134	143	149	144	4	—	—
Production workers (000)	59	64	81	86	91	85	6	—	—
Average hourly earnings ($)	4.83	5.11	5.46	5.88	6.15	[4]6.55	—	—	—
Year-to-year percent change in average hourly earnings	—	6	7	8	[5]5	[5]7	—	—	—
Capital expenditures	76	89	169	196	237	—	—	—	—
Product (SIC 3822, 3823, 3824, 3829)									
Value of shipments[6]	3,364	3,904	4,875	5,436	6,283	6,912	10	7,810	13
Trade									
Value of exports	829	960	1,128	1,185	1,424	1,724	21	1,999	16
Value of imports	98	143	160	165	195	347	78	444	28

[1] Value of all products and services sold by the measuring and controlling instruments industry (SIC 3822, 3823, 3824, 3829).
[2] Estimated except for hourly earnings and 1979 trade data.
[3] Forecast.
[4] As of August 1980.
[5] August 1979 to August 1980.
[6] Value of shi ments of measuring and controlling instruments produced by all industries.

Source: Bureau of the Census (industry and trade data). Bureau of Labor Statistics (hourly earnings). Estimates and forecasts by the Bureau of Industrial Economics.

Source: U.S. INDUSTRIAL OUTLOOK 1981, U.S. Department of Commerce.

Electronic Controls and Instruments

Company and Market		Common Equity Per Share $	Common Equity Price To Equity %	Earnings Yield %	P/E Ratio Current -	P/E Ratio 5-Year Average -	Latest 12 Months Amount $	Latest 12 Months Change %	Latest 12 Months Date -	5-Year Growth Rate %	Profit Margin %	Return On Assets %	Return On Common Equity %	Debt Equity Ratio %	Dividend Yield %	Market Value $Mil
Ametek Inc	N	11.74	293	6.1	16.4	9.9	2.10	-2	3-81q	9	5.4	8.5	17.1	44	2.9	370
Autom Switch	A	12.37	282	6.5	15.3	10.4	2.28	20	3-81q	22	12.6	15.4	18.3	0	2.3	287
Beckman Instr	*N	13.56	268	4.9	20.3	16.0	1.79	-2	3-81n	22	6.7	6.9	13.3	34	1.0	741
Bowmar Instr	A	1.20	500	3.0	33.3	NC	.18	350	3-81s	-9	2.3	3.9	9.4	51	.0	48
Clarostat Mfg	A	14.80	106	5.9	17.0	8.3	.92	-5	3-81q	-5	2.5	4.8	6.1	5	.0	9
CompuDyne	A	6.69	155	12.1	8.2	12.0	1.26	45	3-81s	31	1.8	3.1	17.7	237	.0	10
Conrac Corp	N	18.97	136	5.1	19.8	9.3	1.31	-41	3-81q	-10	3.2	4.8	10.5	54	3.1	55
Daniel Inds	N	9.15	249	6.2	16.0	9.9	1.42	28	3-81s	12	6.0	7.9	13.3	33	.8	174
Dynascan Cp	O	7.97	122	7.2	13.9	13.9	.70	289	3-81q	-16	3.7	5.4	7.0	0	.0	33
EIP Microwave	O	2.00	575	6.3	15.8	37.6	.73	NE	3-81s	-4	NC	.0	NE	0	.9	12
Electron Cp A	A	13.36	284	8.9	11.2	6.1	3.40	27	12-80f	40	13.6	12.6	25.7	64	3.7	64
Energy Conversion	O	.53	3019	-1.3	NC	NC	-.20	NE	3-81n	NE	-47.1	NE	NE	43	.0	47
Frequency Elec	A	1.26	3998	1.8	NC	NC	.89	NC	1-81n	24	8.6	17.8	33.3	0	.0	129
Hach Company	O	9.66	163	3.7	26.7	29.5	.59	392	10-80s	-20	1.5	1.1	2.2	55	.6	22
Hewlett-Pack	*N	25.69	413	4.5	22.4	19.1	4.73	24	4-81s	27	8.7	11.5	17.4	2	.4	6,413
Honeywell Inc	*N	84.03	109	14.1	7.1	7.5	12.83	25	3-81q	25	5.7	7.2	14.8	25	3.3	2,068
Instron Corp	A	23.54	138	7.9	12.6	6.4	2.56	-40	3-81q	47	4.8	5.5	12.2	33	1.2	32
Johnson Contr	N	25.17	116	9.8	10.2	10.0	2.87	10	3-81s	20	3.5	5.0	10.4	33	4.4	380
Knogo Corp	A	5.10	328	4.5	22.0	10.8	.76	3	11-80n	15	18.1	11.3	14.8	0	.0	65
Kollmorgen Cp	N	6.62	512	3.7	27.3	9.9	1.24	11	3-81q	22	5.3	8.0	19.0	60	.9	274
Mangood Corp	A	9.89	131	10.0	10.0	17.4	1.30	11	3-81q	39	2.0	3.4	8.6	9	.0	5
Mark Products	A	4.10	1180	6.5	15.4	7.3	3.14	155	3-81q	37	13.7	5.8	13.6	63	.0	96
Measurex Corp	N	21.65	100	7.7	13.0	12.5	1.67	-40	2-81q	15	6.0	5.5	9.7	24	2.3	76
MTS Systems Cp	O	14.71	185	8.8	11.4	8.2	2.39	-16	12-80q	15	7.0	7.5	18.7	61	1.2	46
Nicolet Instr	O	5.82	376	4.6	21.9	11.6	1.00	0	3-81f	24	6.2	8.9	15.3	20	1.1	105
Nuclear Data	A	8.69	161	7.2	13.9	8.0	1.01	-26	2-81f	25	4.1	5.8	11.3	9	.0	24
Raymond Inds	A	8.87	265	5.2	19.3	16.0	1.22	45	3-81q	15	4.5	6.7	12.7	61	1.1	41
Robertshaw	N	30.86	91	7.9	12.7	7.9	2.21	-23	3-81q	0	2.9	4.7	9.4	40	5.0	99
Tenney Engr	A	2.63	356	6.5	15.4	12.0	.61	24	3-81q	65	5.3	9.6	21.2	52	.0	12
Teradyne Inc	N	20.58	217	5.0	20.1	14.4	2.22	-18	3-81q	29	6.9	7.8	13.7	36	.0	182
Tesdata Systems	O	7.92	123	-1.4	NC	23.9	-.14	-100	3-81q	-22	3.8	4.5	6.9	1	.0	13
Veeco Instrs	N	4.86	666	3.4	29.4	9.4	1.10	-3	3-81s	35	10.2	12.8	22.9	16	.6	311

Motor Vehicles

MOTOR VEHICLES: TRENDS AND PROJECTIONS 1975–81 (in millions of current dollars except as noted)

Item	1975	1976	1977	1978	1979[2]	1980[2]	Percent change 1979–80[2]	1981[3]	Percent change 1980–81[3]
Industry (SIC 3711)									
Value of shipments[1]	45,340	62,717	76,487	84,901	81,700	63,500	−22.3	82,800	30.4
Value added	10,441	15,844	18,672	20,490	18,700	13,100	−30	—	—
Value added per production worker-hour ($)	23.36	28.30	30.14	32.59	30.96	30.68	−0.9	—	—
Total employment (000)	283	324	343	359	370	296	−20.0	—	—
Production workers (000)	235	274	289	304	308	229	−25.7	—	—
Average hourly earnings (Dec.—$)	7.26	8.04	8.69	9.56	10.01	[4]10.65	—	—	—
Year-to-year percent change in average hourly earnings (Dec.–Dec.)	10.5	10.8	8.1	10.0	4.7	[5]8.2	—	—	—
Year-to-year percent change in industry price index (Dec.–Dec.)[6]	N.A.	6.4	6.7	5.9	8.1	[5]9.3	—	—	—
Capital expenditures	656	1,047	1,808	1,900	—	—	—	—	—
Product (SIC 3711)									
Value of shipments[7]	43,394	59,753	72,918	81,200	78,000	60,600	−22.3	79,000	30.4
Year-to-year percent change in producers price index (Dec.–Dec.)[6]	6.4	6.0	6.9	6.9	8.1	[5]8.8	—	—	—
Product classes									
Passenger cars									
Value of shipments[7]	28,833	39,746	46,813	50,819	49,900	42,000	−15.8	51,000	21.4
Quantity shipped (unit of measure)[7]	6,713	8,500	9,201	9,165	8,419	6,500	−22.8	7,300	12.3
Year-to-year percent change in producers price index (Dec.–Dec.)[6]	6.0	5.3	6.4	6.8	7.5	[5]8.2	—	—	—
Trucks & Buses									
Value of shipments[7]	12,166	16,968	21,996	26,422	24,200	15,600	−35.5	24,000	53.8
Quantity shipped (unit of measure)[7]	2,272	2,979	3,442	3,706	3,037	1,700	−44.0	2,400	41.2
Year-to-year percent change in producers price index (Dec.–Dec.)[6]	7.2	8.5	8.7	7.2	9.6	[5]10.4	—	—	—
Trade[8]									
Value of exports	2,247	2,227	2,153	2,501	2,972	2,700	−9.2	3,100	14.8
Value of imports	4,720	6,169	7,643	11,187	12,706	14,600	14.9	15,700	7.5

[1] Value of all products and services sold by the motor vehicle industry (SIC 3711).
[2] Estimated except for hourly earnings, price indexes, and 1979 trade data.
[3] Forecast.
[4] As of June 1980.
[5] July 1979 to July 1980. Note: Months may differ for the price and earnings indexes.
[6] December 1975 is the base period for index.
[7] Value of shipments of these products produced by all industries.
[8] Includes Canada.

Source: Bureau of the Census (industry and trade data), Bureau of Labor Statistics (hourly earnings and price indexes). Estimates and forecasts by the Bureau of Industrial Economics.

Source: *U.S. INDUSTRIAL OUTLOOK 1981*, U.S. Department of Commerce.

Company and Market	Common Equity Per Share $	Price To Equity %	Earnings Yield %	P/E Ratio Current -	P/E Ratio 5-Year Average -	Latest 12 Months Amount $	Latest 12 Months Change %	Latest 12 Months Date -	5-Year Growth Rate %	Profit Margin %	Return On Assets %	Return On Common Equity %	Debt Equity Ratio %	Dividend Yield %	Market Value $Mil
Auto Manufacturers															
Am Motors .... ★N	7.62	52	-74.0	NC	16.0	- 6.96	-100	3-81q	NE	- 7.7	NE	NE	25	.0	228
Chrysler Cp .... ★N	24.07	26	-63.1	NC	5.7	-23.15	NE	3-81q	- 96	-18.5	NE	NE	62	.0	427
Ford Motor Co .... ★N	71.06	32	-65.7	NC	4.2	-15.12	-100	3-81q	- 36	- 4.2	NE	NE	24	5.2	2,774
Ford of Can .... A	95.32	42	-38.1	NC	20.7	-15.42	-100	3-81q	- 40	- .8	NE	NE	4	NA	336
Gen Motors .... ★N	58.82	95	- 4.4	NC	5.9	- 2.47	-100	3-81q	- 23	- 1.3	NE	NE	12	4.3	16,579
Honda Motor .... N	14.61	339	11.3	8.8	23.2	5.60	118	11-80n	45	2.1	3.1	12.3	35	.9	3,602
White Motor .... O	24.68	10	-46.8	NC	NC	- 6.17	-100	6-80s	NE	.5	1.0	2.8	32	.0	23
Automotive Parts and Accessories															
Allen Group .... N	18.38	116	8.7	11.5	7.4	1.84	- 18	3-81q	5	2.5	4.6	10.8	57	4.7	94
Altamil Corp .... A	20.39	63	5.9	16.9	5.9	.76	- 66	2-81s	- 5	2.2	4.8	6.9	17	2.7	16
Arvin Indus .... N	23.08	68	7.3	13.7	6.9	1.14	- 38	3-81q	- 26	1.8	2.5	4.4	51	7.2	103
Barnes Group .... N	20.55	106	14.6	6.8	5.9	3.18	- 12	3-81q	20	5.6	9.7	17.1	13	4.6	151
Bendix Corp .... ★N	46.29	131	13.5	7.4	7.2	8.21	51	3-81s	13	5.0	7.0	15.7	38	4.9	1,154
Buell Indus .... A	17.26	56	3.2	31.5	10.7	.31	- 70	4-81s	- 42	.8	1.1	1.7	21	5.1	14
Champion Parts ..... O	9.63	67	12.6	7.9	7.4	.82	- 34	9-80s	20	2.5	4.3	12.1	138	3.1	11
Champion Sprk ...... ★N	10.60	104	7.8	12.8	9.1	.86	- 39	3-81q	- 7	4.6	5.8	9.1	10	7.3	421
Dana Corp .... ★N	27.65	112	6.8	14.8	7.0	2.09	- 58	11-80q	- 6	3.8	4.9	10.0	35	5.2	1,072
Donaldson .... N	15.64	203	5.8	17.3	9.1	1.83	- 21	4-81n	1	3.5	5.6	10.2	34	2.1	164
Dyneer Corp .... A	14.26	116	11.9	8.4	6.3	1.96	- 14	1-81s	13	4.5	7.8	15.4	46	3.8	53
Eaton Corp .... ★N	37.56	93	10.3	9.7	6.4	3.61	- 33	3-81q	4	3.6	5.0	11.5	52	4.9	935
Echlin Mfg .... ★N	9.00	151	3.2	31.7	15.0	.43	- 67	2-81s	- 16	2.9	3.7	6.1	36	3.8	218
Facet Entprs .... N	16.00	34	-17.7	NC	NC	- .95	NE	3-81s	- 79	- 2.9	NE	NE	57	2.8	15
Fruehauf Cp .... ★N	43.19	71	7.1	14.1	6.6	2.17	- 62	3-81q	- 12	1.5	2.1	6.1	75	7.9	374
Guardian Inds .... N	12.44	211	10.9	9.2	6.2	2.86	29	3-81q	23	9.5	8.9	22.4	86	1.5	267
Hayes Albion .... N	16.32	57	-15.0	NC	NC	- 1.41	NE	4-81n	- 29	- 1.6	NE	NE	38	.0	36
Hoover Univ .... N	17.22	129	8.9	11.2	6.5	1.99	- 38	10-80q	- 5	2.9	5.6	11.0	42	5.6	198
Kysor Ind .... N	13.82	83	8.9	11.3	6.2	1.02	- 59	3-81q	0	2.8	11.0	20.9	42	7.7	32
Premier Ind .... N	11.02	356	6.9	14.6	10.0	2.69	- 8	2-81n	26	9.1	19.0	24.8	0	1.7	408
Questor Corp .... ★N	13.21	62	- 9.9	NC	12.7	- .82	-100	3-81q	- 38	- 2.7	NE	NE	50	.0	80
Raybest-Man .... N	40.28	43	-17.6	NC	7.3	- 3.03	-100	3-81q	- 31	- 2.3	NE	NE	48	9.3	40
Rovac Corp .... O	.28	2768	- 3.2	NC	NC	- .25	NE	10-80q	NE	-00.0	NE	NE	17	.0	33
Seaport Cp .... A	2.56	54	- 2.2	NC	41.1	- .03	-100	3-81q	- 26	.4	.0	NE	11	.0	3
Sheller-Globe .... N	20.63	55	- .3	NC	5.4	- .03	-100	9-80f	- 17	.5	.7	1.6	89	2.7	70
Simpson Indust ...... O	8.01	190	6.6	15.1	7.6	1.01	- 13	3-81n	- 7	2.9	5.6	10.6	37	5.2	52
Smith, AO Cp .... N	43.25	38	- 1.0	NC	3.9	- .17	-100	3-81q	- 30	- .2	NE	NE	30	8.6	79
Sparton Corp .... N	9.36	211	6.4	15.6	9.6	1.27	4	3-81n	6	2.3	4.0	7.2	0	2.5	67
Std Motor Prd .... N	15.48	158	7.4	13.5	7.5	1.81	41	3-81q	- 5	2.6	3.5	7.3	52	2.6	72
Std Products .... A	31.26	52	4.6	22.0	6.2	.74	NE	3-81n	- 22	- 1.3	NE	NE	82	3.7	20
Superior Ind Int ..... A	5.77	87	36.2	2.8	10.1	1.81	NE	3-81q	12	-10.4	NE	NE	78	.0	18
Teleflex Inc .... A	7.93	460	4.8	21.0	9.2	1.74	30	3-81q	39	6.1	8.9	20.2	63	.8	109
Trico Prods .... O	57.01	53	19.1	5.2	7.3	5.72	- 44	12-79f	33	9.0	9.3	10.1	0	3.3	55
Wynns Intl .... N	18.35	93	13.2	7.6	6.1	2.24	3	3-81q	11	4.4	5.9	11.4	31	3.5	62

TEXTILE MILL PRODUCTS: TRENDS AND PROJECTIONS 1975–80 (in millions of current dollars except as noted)

Item	1975	1976	1977	1978[2]	1979[2]	1980[2]	Percent change 1979–80[2]
Industry (SIC 22)							
Value of shipments[1]	31,064	36,389	40,694	43,830	46,850	51,160	9.2
Value added	12,045	14,495	15,851	17,547	18,220	19,677	8.0
Value added per production worker-hour ($)	8.29	8.72	10.46	11.12	11.71	12.56	7.3
Total employment (000)	931.5	835.1	876.5	866.9	858.2	849.6	—1.0
Production workers (000)	724.9	765.3	760.0	750.9	742.6	731.5	—1.5
Average hourly earnings (Dec.—$)	3.57	3.85	4.14	4.48	4.87	[3]4.99	[3]7.3
Year-to-year percent change in average hourly earnings (Dec.–Dec.)	8.5	7.8	7.5	8.2	8.7	[4]7.3	[4]7.3
Capital expenditures	997	1,088	1,235	1,396	1,423	1,544	8.5
Product (SIC 22)							
Year-to-year percent change in producers price index (Dec.–Dec.)[5]	N.A.	3.7	3.9	3.0	5.7	[5]10.0	[5]10.0
Trade							
Value of exports	1,532.7	1,855.2	1,857.3	2,073.4	3,028.9	3,480.0	14.9
Value of imports	1,211.9	1,626.3	1,764.8	2,212.0	2,213.8	2,460.0	11.1

[1] Value of all products and services sold by the textile mill industry (SIC 22).
[2] Estimated except for hourly earnings, price indexes, and 1979 trade data.
[3] As of July 1980.
[4] July 1979 to July 1980.
[5] December 1975 is the base period for index.

Source: Bureau of the Census (industry and trade data); Bureau of Labor Statistics (hourly earnings and price indexes). Estimates by the International Trade Administration (OTEXA).

Source: *U.S. INDUSTRIAL OUTLOOK 1981*, U.S. Department of Commerce.

MAN-MADE FIBER WEAVING MILLS: TRENDS AND PROJECTIONS 1975–80 (in millions of current dollars except as noted)

Item	1975	1976	1977	1978[2]	1979[2]	1980[2]	Percent change 1979–80[2]
Industry (SIC 2221)							
Value of shipments[1]	4,632	5,869	6,326	7,148	7,977	8,846	10.9
Value added	1,965	2,600	2,791	3,149	3,509	3,783	7.8
Value added per production worker-hour ($)	7.51	8.78	10.13	11.09	12.62	13.84	9.7
Total employment (000)	151.7	161.1	151.0	147.7	145.3	142.1	−2.2
Production workers (000)	135.2	144.0	134.6	131.2	129.5	126.9	−2.0
Average hourly earnings (Dec.—$)	3.68	4.00	4.37	4.74	5.15	[3]5.13	[3]8.5
Year-to-year percent change in average hourly earnings (Dec.–Dec.)	9.8	8.7	9.2	8.5	8.6	[4]8.5	[4]8.5
Year-to-year percent change in industry price index (Dec.–Dec.)[5]	N.A.	N.A.	N.A.	15.5	1.6	[4]5.5	[4]5.5
Capital expenditures	192.2	245.6	260.2	—	—	—	—
Product (SIC 2221)							
Value of shipments[6]	5,202	6,675	7,285	8,231	8,845	9,676	9.4
Year-to-year percent change in producers price index (Dec.–Dec.)[7]	N.A.	6.4	−2.4	22.8	−1.3	[5]4.4	[5]4.4
Trade							
Value of exports	333.8	357.7	321.9	390.4	601.8	716.0	19.0
Value of imports	222.2	291.0	328.0	474.4	455.1	673.5	48.0

[1] Value of all products and services sold by the Man-Made Fiber Weaving industry (SIC 2221).
[2] Estimated except for hourly earnings, price indexes, and 1979 trade data.
[3] As of June 1980.
[4] June 1979 to June 1980.
[5] December 1977 is the base period for index.
[6] Value of shipments of man-made fiber broadwoven fabrics produced by all industries.
[7] December 1975 is the base period for index.

Source: Bureau of the Census (industry and trade data); Bureau of Labor Statistics (hourly earnings and price indexes). Estimates by the International Trade Administration (OTEXA).

Source: *U.S. INDUSTRIAL OUTLOOK 1981*, U.S. Department of Commerce.

COTTON WEAVING MILLS: TRENDS AND PROJECTIONS 1975–80 (in millions of current dollars except as noted)

Item	1975	1976	1977	1978 [2]	1979 [2]	1980 [2]	Percent change 1979–80 [2]
Industry (SIC 2211)							
Value of shipments [1]	2,957	3,718	4,431	5,579	6,000	6,510	8.5
Value added	1,337	1,687	1,944	2,454	2,699	2,961	9.7
Value added per production worker-hour ($)	7.24	8.26	9.07	11.52	12.32	13.40	8.8
Total employment (000)	106.8	109.8	117.2	109.7	119.6	121.4	1.5
Production workers (000)	97.8	100.5	107.2	100.1	100.1	102.4	1.3
Average hourly earnings (Dec.—$)	3.63	3.95	4.30	4.66	5.07	[3] 5.01	[3] 7.3
Year-to-year percent change in average hourly earnings (Dec.–Dec.)	11.7	8.8	8.9	8.4	8.8	[4] 7.3	[4] 7.3
Year-to-year percent change in industry price index (Dec.–Dec.) [5]	13.3	12.4	3.4	6.9	6.9	[4] 9.1	[4] 9.1
Capital expenditures	133.4	124.3	187.2	—	—	—	—
Product (SIC 2211)							
Value of shipments [6]	3,590	4,625	5,645	7,107	8,181	8,754	7.0
Year-to-year percent change in producers price index (Dec.–Dec.) [7]	N.A.	13.3	1.3	11.0	6.4	[5] 6.7	[5] 6.7
Trade							
Value of exports	375.7	498.7	438.5	425.9	623.4	686.0	10.0
Value of imports	219.6	383.6	344.9	420.3	375.0	356.4	−5.0

[1] Value of all products and services sold by the Cotton Weaving industry (SIC 2211).
[2] Estimated except for hourly earnings, price indexes, and 1979 trade data.
[3] As of June 1980.
[4] June 1979 to June 1980.
[5] December 1972 is the base period for index.
[6] Value of shipments of Cotton broadwoven fabrics produced by all industries.
[7] December 1975 is the base period for index.

Source: Bureau of the Census (industry and trade data); Bureau of Labor Statistics (hourly earnings and price indexes). Estimates by the International Trade Administration (OTEXA).

Source: *U.S. INDUSTRIAL OUTLOOK 1981*, U.S. Department of Commerce.

WOOL WEAVING AND FINISHING MILLS: TRENDS AND PROJECTIONS 1975–80 (in millions of current dollars except as noted)

Item	1975	1976	1977	1978 [2]	1979 [2]	1980 [2]	Percent change 1979–80 [2]
Industry (SIC 2231)							
Value of shipments[1]	454	572	583	681	723	774	7.1
Value added	198	265	313	365	398	433	8.8
Value added per production worker-hour ($)	8.92	9.83	12.06	13.71	14.40	15.11	4.9
Total employment (000)	14.3	15.5	14.6	14.3	13.9	13.5	−2.9
Production workers (000)	11.8	13.1	12.6	12.4	12.0	11.6	−3.3
Average hourly earnings (Dec.—$)	3.66	3.95	4.31	4.54	4.98	[3]5.22	[3]10.4
Year-to-year percent change in average hourly earnings (Dec.–Dec.)	5.2	7.9	9.1	5.3	9.7	[4]10.4	[4]10.4
Capital expenditures	10.9	41.7	14.9	—	—	—	—
Product (SIC 2231)							
Value of shipments[5]	436	555	581	679	719	768	6.8
Year-to-year percent change in producers price index (Dec.–Dec.)[6]	9.0	13.9	9.7	5.7	8.2	[6]6.1	[6]6.1
Trade							
Value of exports	3.6	3.1	3.1	2.7	3.2	3.9	21.9
Value of imports	31.6	46.8	66.8	81.6	79.0	80.0	1.3

[1] Value of all products and services sold by the Wool Weaving and Finishing industry (SIC 2231).
[2] Estimated except for hourly earnings, price indexes, and 1979 trade data.
[3] As of June 1980.
[4] June 1979 to June 1980. Note: Months may differ for the price and earnings indexes.
[5] Value of shipments of wool fabrics produced by all industries.
[6] April 1967 is the base period for index.

Source: Bureau of the Census (industry and trade data); Bureau of Labor Statistics (hourly earnings and price indexes). Estimates by the International Trade Administration (OTEXA).

Source: *U.S. INDUSTRIAL OUTLOOK 1981*, U.S. Department of Commerce.

KNIT FABRIC MILLS: TRENDS AND PROJECTIONS 1975–80 (in millions of current dollars except as noted)

Item	1975	1976	1977	1978 [2]	1979 [3]	1980 [2]	Percent change 1979–80 [2]
Industry (SIC 2257–58)							
Value of shipments[1]	4,056	4,201	4,577	4,870	5,390	5,886	9.2
Value added	1,328	1,398	1,478	1,629	1,743	1,877	7.7
Value added per production worker-hour ($)	10.52	10.77	11.36	12.63	14.29	15.00	5.0
Total employment (000)	75.7	75.2	75.5	72.8	70.5	68.8	−2.4
Production workers (000)	63.5	63.7	64.0	60.9	58.0	57.0	−1.7
Average hourly earnings (Dec.—$)	3.38	3.61	3.80	4.12	4.52	[3]4.71	[3]10.1
Year-to-year percent change in average hourly earnings (Dec.–Dec.)	6.0	6.8	5.3	8.4	9.7	[4]10.1	[4]10.1
Capital expenditures	127.8	129.1	147.9	—	—	—	—
Product (SIC 2257–2258)							
Value of shipments[5]	4,115	4,285	4,680	4,992	5,536	6,062	9.5
Year-to-year percent change in producers price index (Dec.–Dec.)[6]	—	−6.9	1.1	2.6	14.7	[6]11.3	[6]11.3
Trade							
Value of exports	46.7	57.5	42.7	28.8	55.2	67.9	23.0
Value of imports	49.1	39.9	32.6	35.0	22.7	20.2	−11.0

[1] Value of all products and services sold by the knit fabric industry (SIC 2257-58).
[2] Estimated except for hourly earnings, price indexes, and 1979 trade data.
[3] As of June 1980.
[4] June 1979 to June 1980.
[5] Value of shipments of knit fabric produced by all industries.
[6] December 1975 is the base period for index.

Source: Bureau of the Census (industry and trade data); Bureau of Labor Statistics (hourly earnings and price indexes). Estimates by the International Trade Administration (OTEXA).

Source: *U.S. INDUSTRIAL OUTLOOK 1981*, U.S. Department of Commerce.

	Relative Price					Earnings Per Share				Other					
	Common Equity			P/E Ratio		Latest 12 Months			5-Year Growth Rate	Profit Margin	Return On Assets	Return On Common Equity	Debt Equity Ratio	Dividend Yield	Market Value
Company and Market	Per Share	Price To Equity	Earnings Yield	Current	5-Year Average	Amount	Change	Date							
	$	%	%	-	-	$	%	-	%	%	%	%	%	%	$Mil
Weaving Mills															
Avondale Mills .... A	41.45	46	13.5	7.4	9.0	2.57	25	2-81s	0	2.3	5.2	7.6	2	6.3	42
Belding Hemin .... N	11.38	66	8.5	11.7	8.3	.64	-38	3-81q	-2	1.8	3.5	5.4	23	4.8	27
Bibb Co .... O	44.16	25	-33.1	NC	6.9	-3.72	-100	12-80n	-25	.7	1.2	2.6	51	5.3	18
Burlington Inds .... *N	39.52	59	12.0	8.3	7.5	2.83	-2	3-81s	-5	2.8	3.8	7.3	48	6.5	660
Cannon Mills .... N	34.78	77	8.4	11.9	7.7	2.25	-47	3-81q	9	3.1	4.7	6.3	0	4.5	251
Chatham Mfg .... O	25.72	50	11.0	9.1	6.4	1.41	22	3-81q	-11	2.3	4.0	5.3	16	6.2	23
Chelsea Indus .... N	18.87	46	16.1	6.2	4.7	1.39	-33	3-81s	-13	1.0	2.3	5.6	84	7.0	19
Collins & Aikm .... N	15.34	71	10.7	9.4	6.7	1.16	-12	2-81f	-6	2.4	4.8	8.6	29	6.6	136
Concord Fab .... A	9.09	47	-17.4	NC	12.8	-.74	NE	2-81s	-48	-3.1	NE	NE	43	.0	8
Cone Mills .... *N	56.37	62	22.6	4.4	4.2	7.90	-4	3-81q	10	7.0	12.3	15.8	6	6.3	202
Courtaulds Ltd .... A	3.54	44	19.8	5.0	8.5	.31	11	3-80f	-10	2.1	3.0	8.6	67	14.7	427
Crompton Co .... A	47.89	38	.8	NC	5.7	.14	-98	3-81s	-23	4.3	6.3	11.2	41	4.4	24
Crown Crafts .... A	10.07	36	-5.2	NC	8.7	-.19	-100	12-80n	-74	.4	.6	1.4	51	.0	3
Dan River Inc .... N	34.64	60	14.0	7.1	5.0	2.89	-30	3-81q	15	3.2	5.1	9.9	48	5.4	117
Edmos Corp .... A	3.15	44	-13.8	NC	NC	-.19	NE	3-81q	NE	.3	NE	NE	90	.0	3
Fab Indus .... A	14.43	98	22.4	4.5	3.4	3.16	-17	2-81q	34	6.5	14.2	25.3	4	3.5	33
Fieldcrest Mill .... N	42.96	73	12.1	8.2	5.6	3.82	-32	3-81q	5	3.3	5.5	11.0	49	6.3	120
Graniteville .... N	24.16	52	14.7	6.8	NC	1.84	17	3-81q	1	3.3	6.5	10.6	20	8.0	54
Liberty Fabrics .... A	17.55	63	19.5	5.1	4.3	2.14	78	3-81q	9	3.6	6.1	10.8	40	.0	8
Lowenstn Sons .... *N	44.56	64	7.5	13.4	6.8	2.12	NE	3-81q	7	.8	1.5	3.3	57	3.5	94
Mount Vern Mls .... A	62.45	59	16.7	6.0	17.1	6.15	-12	3-81q	97	3.9	13.8	10.3	11	4.6	30
Opelika Mfg .... N	21.94	50	-1.5	NC	9.2	-.16	-100	3-81s	-24	1.3	1.5	4.0	57	1.8	11
Reeves Bros .... *N	51.71	78	17.6	5.7	5.1	7.09	5	3-81n	17	5.1	9.0	13.9	22	5.5	94
Riegel Textile .... N	34.27	73	16.7	6.0	5.3	4.15	0	3-81s	4	4.2	7.2	13.8	33	7.2	94
Roselon Indust .... O	8.04	37	-82.3	NC	10.0	-2.47	-100	6-80f	-41	-13.1	NE	NE	14	.0	5
Ruddick Corp .... A	21.06	63	15.1	6.6	4.6	2.00	10	3-81s	13	1.7	5.4	13.9	104	4.2	31
Springs Mills .... *N	38.49	68	13.7	7.3	5.8	3.57	-14	3-81q	21	4.1	6.3	9.6	16	5.2	227
Std-Coosa .... A	63.14	63	10.7	9.3	5.7	4.28	27	3-81s	-2	1.7	3.4	6.2	35	4.0	21
Stevens JP .... *N	36.47	46	6.6	15.2	6.7	1.10	-64	1-81q	-16	1.1	1.9	3.9	59	7.2	241
Ti-Caro .... N	18.35	92	18.1	5.5	3.8	3.05	12	3-81s	7	6.3	10.8	15.4	19	6.9	92
Unit Mer Mfrs .... N	9.62	55	-99.0	NC	8.4	-5.20	-100	3-81n	NE	-4.0	NE	NE	457	.0	31
Vertipile Inc .... A	5.03	84	20.2	4.9	8.8	.86	-40	2-81f	104	4.8	17.5	28.1	16	3.5	5
West Point-P .... *N	69.71	70	17.2	5.8	6.3	8.43	25	2-81s	12	3.4	7.3	13.1	37	6.5	236
Wright Wm Co .... O	9.48	65	9.6	10.4	8.6	.59	31	9-80q	-6	3.0	4.2	5.8	4	4.6	15
Knitting Mills															
Adams-Millis .... N	11.47	53	14.5	6.9	5.8	.89	-21	3-81q	7	2.8	5.4	8.3	27	3.3	14
Aileen Inc .... N	6.90	53	8.8	11.3	NC	.32	-20	1-81q	NE	2.9	.6	.9	21	.0	18
Alba-Waldens .... A	9.53	43	6.5	15.3	9.1	.27	-40	3-81q	-1	1.0	1.9	3.1	28	1.2	6
Damon Creatn .... A	10.41	30	15.4	6.5	7.6	.48	71	3-81q	-17	1.5	2.4	4.4	49	.0	4
Fair-Tex Mills .... A	8.34	36	10.0	10.0	6.5	.30	-75	1-81q	21	2.7	5.6	9.6	37	.0	5
Guilford Mills .... A	14.14	181	16.5	6.0	3.5	4.24	0	3-81n	55	9.2	19.7	32.7	27	2.3	123
Lehigh Valley .... N	-.12	0782	13.6	7.4	9.4	.17	143	3-81q	-11	1.0	2.1	29.7	-3812	.0	9
Russell Corp .... A	17.82	165	13.1	7.6	5.1	3.85	32	3-81q	30	8.7	12.4	20.2	30	2.3	170
Stanwood Cp .... A	11.92	61	18.2	5.5	4.5	1.32	13	1-81s	159	3.4	6.2	12.4	50	.0	16
Stevcoknit Inc .... A	6.20	36	1.8	NC	28.8	.04	NE	1-81f	-39	.1	NE	NE	60	0	5
Texfi Ind .... N	4.53	108	-78.2	NC	NC	-3.81	NE	4-81s	NE	-14.9	NE	NE	349	.0	17
Unifi Inc .... O	4.69	314	11.8	8.5	7.4	1.74	211	3-81n	28	1.1	3.0	9.5	98	.0	55
V.F. Corp .... *N	23.68	150	14.7	6.8	6.6	5.24	25	3-81q	22	7.2	11.9	17.6	12	5.6	287

Apparel

APPAREL AND OTHER TEXTILE PRODUCTS: TRENDS AND PROJECTIONS 1975–80 (in millions of current dollars except as noted)

Item	1975	1976	1977	1978[2]	1979[2]	1980[2]	Percent change 1979–80[2]
Industry (SIC 23)							
Value of shipments[1]	31,430	34,759	40,263	43,540	47,276	51,540	9.0
Value added	14,749	16,860	19,677	21,241	23,106	25,234	9.2
Value added per production worker-hour ($)	7.80	8.41	9.65	9.78	10.97	12.11	10.4
Total employment (000)	1,214.2	1,270.5	1,334.8	1,351.1	1,331.0	1,313.6	−1.3
Production workers (000)	1,058.4	1,109.3	1,157.1	1,172.7	1,151.1	1,131.9	−1.7
Average hourly earnings (Dec.—$)	3.25	3.52	3.76	4.07	4.38	[3]4.51	[4]7.1
Year-to-year percent change in average hourly earnings (Dec.–Dec.)	5.2	8.3	6.8	8.2	7.6	[4]7.1	—
Capital expenditures	380.6	422.7	457.4	—	—	—	—
Product (SIC 23)							
Year-to-year percent change in producers price index (Dec.–Dec.)[5]	N.A.	N.A.	N.A.	4.2	5.5	[4]7.6	—
Trade[6]							
Value of exports	340.6	434.2	524.1	551.0	772.1	976.5	26.5
Value of imports	2,318.1	3,256.5	3,649.7	4,833.3	5,015.0	5,550.2	10.7

[1] Value of all products and services sold by the apparel industry (SIC 23).
[2] Estimated except for hourly earnings, price indexes, and 1978 and 1979 trade data.
[3] As of June 1980
[4] June 1979 to June 1980.
[5] December 1977 is the base period for index.
[6] Includes only apparel.

Source: Bureau of the Census (industry and trade data); Bureau of Labor Statistics (hourly earnings and price indexes). Estimates by the International Trade Administration (OTEXA).

Source: *U.S. INDUSTRIAL OUTLOOK 1981*, U.S. Department of Commerce.

MEN'S AND BOYS' OUTERWEAR: TRENDS AND PROJECTIONS 1975–80 (in millions of current dollars except as noted)

Item	1975	1976	1977	1978[3]	1979[2]	1980[2]	Percent change 1979–80[2]
Industry (SIC 2311, 2321, 2327, 2328)							
Value of shipments[1]	8,934	10,085	11,062	11,927	12,932	14,137	9.3
Value added	4,251	5,035	5,631	5,988	6,492	7,094	9.3
Value added per production worker-hour ($)	7.38	8.00	8.90	9.01	9.78	10.49	7.3
Total employment (000)	370.0	391.5	398.0	389.6	380.4	383.8	0.9
Production workers (000)	328.4	349.2	352.7	346.6	337.1	339.9	0.8
Average hourly earnings (Dec.—$)	3.16	3.44	3.65	3.98	4.34	[3]4.43	[4]7.5
Year-to-year percent change in average hourly earnings (Dec.-Dec.)	3.9	8.9	6.1	9.0	9.0	[4]7.5	—
Capital expenditures	79.3	110.9	118.6	—	—	—	—
Trade							
Value of exports	88.6	106.4	143.6	133.7	217.0	260.1	19.9
Value of imports	579.7	1,059.6	1,138.5	1,411.6	1,567.3	1,842.2	17.5

[1] Value of all products and services sold by the men's and boys' outerwear industry (SIC 2311, 2321, 2327 and 2328).
[2] Estimated except for hourly earnings, and 1978 and 1979 trade data.
[3] As of May 1980.
[4] May 1979 to May 1980.
Source: Bureau of the Census (industry and trade data); Bureau of Labor Statistics (hourly earnings). Estimates by the International Trade Administration (OTEXA).

Source: *U.S. INDUSTRIAL OUTLOOK 1981*, U.S. Department of Commerce.

WOMEN'S AND MISSES' OUTERWEAR: TRENDS AND PROJECTIONS 1975–80 (in millions of current dollars except as noted)

Item	1975	1976	1977	1978[2]	1979[2]	1980[2]	Percent change 1979–80[2]
Industry (SIC 233)							
Value of shipments[1]	9,988	10,749	12,720	13,916	15,402	17,176	11.5
Value added	4,786	5,274	6,430	7,031	7,862	8,853	12.6
Value added per production worker-hour ($)	7.61	7.82	9.73	10.04	11.46	12.96	13.1
Total employment (000)	401.9	426.7	447.4	459.9	460.0	454.8	−1.1
Production workers (000)	349.0	372.2	387.4	397.3	397.2	393.5	−0.9
Average hourly earnings (Dec.—$)	3.28	3.54	3.72	3.99	4.35	[3]4.50	[4]8.2
Year-to-year percent change in average hourly earnings (Dec.–Dec.)	4.8	7.9	5.1	7.3	9.0	[4]8.2	—
Capital expenditures	127.0	128.2	133.6	—	—	—	—
Trade[5]							
Value of exports	47.4	58.3	71.7	89.5	105.0	120.2	14.5
Value of imports	676.7	882.2	1,000.6	1,230.4	1,384.9	1,447.2	4.5

[1] Value of all products and services sold by the women's and misses' outerwear industry (SIC 233).
[2] Estimated except for hourly earnings, and 1978 and 1979 trade data.
[3] As of May 1980.
[4] May 1979 to May 1980.
[5] Includes only SIC 2331, 2335, and 2337.

Source: Bureau of the Census (industry and trade data); Bureau of Labor Statistics (hourly earnings). Estimates by the International Trade Administration (OTEXA).

Source: *U.S. INDUSTRIAL OUTLOOK 1981*, U.S. Department of Commerce.

Company and Market	Relative Price					Earnings Per Share				Other					
	Common Equity			P/E Ratio		Latest 12 Months			5-Year Growth Rate	Profit Margin	Return On Assets	Return On Common Equity	Debt Equity Ratio	Dividend Yield	Market Value
	Per Share	Price To Equity	Earnings Yield	Current	5-Year Average	Amount	Change	Date							
	$	%	%	-	-	$	%	-	%	%	%	%	%	%	$Mil
Textile Manufacturers															
After Six Inc A	16.78	38	3.6	27.7	11.2	.23	-41	3-81n	-35	.4	.4	1.1	66	.0	10
Angelica N	10.42	163	8.5	11.7	7.2	1.45	27	1-81f	17	5.0	8.1	14.0	39	2.8	105
Barco of Cal A	4.88	72	6.3	15.9	17.7	.22	-19	3-81n	-9	2.3	3.8	4.4	2	3.4	8
Billy The Kid A	7.57	.101	10.6	9.4	7.1	.81	-15	3-81s	8	1.9	3.4	11.9	143	.0	15
Blue Bell Inc *N	31.98	83	16.2	6.2	5.2	4.30	-29	3-81s	0	4.9	7.8	16.9	15	6.8	334
Bobbie Brooks N	7.00	54	-22.4	NC	19.1	-.84	NE	1-81n	-33	-2.6	NE	NE	74	.0	17
Champ Prods A	20.37	97	13.9	7.2	6.3	2.74	15	3-81q	14	3.6	6.1	11.3	35	3.6	34
Cluett Peabody *N	23.38	57	15.1	6.6	5.5	2.02	10	3-81q	1	2.6	4.5	9.2	51	5.1	119
CS Group A	2.99	67	-38.5	NC	11.5	-.77	-100	1-81f	-25	-3.5	8.8	20.0	53	9.0	3
Farah Mfg N	2.39	565	5.3	19.0	14.6	.71	109	1-81q	56	3.0	2.0	8.4	187	.0	81
Garan Inc A	16.75	101	16.8	5.9	4.9	2.86	42	3-81s	5	5.3	8.8	15.0	26	5.9	46
Genesco Inc *N	-.24	0782	5.8	17.2	NC	.58	NE	4-81n	NE	.4	1.1	3.8	-3703	.0	126
Hampton Ind A	12.61	56	21.7	4.6	3.7	1.52	12	3-81q	8	3.2	7.2	12.5	45	.0	14
Jon Logan *N	26.62	42	7.9	12.6	8.5	.88	-35	3-81q	-17	1.5	2.2	4.2	26	5.4	58
Kellwood Co N	22.32	51	10.1	9.9	37.1	1.15	NE	1-81n	-39	NC	.1	.3	87	3.5	40
Kennington Ltd O	9.73	92	26.1	3.8	4.1	2.35	-9	12-80f	32	12.9	20.7	24.1	1	.0	51
Leslie Fay Inc N	12.10	90	17.9	5.6	6.0	1.95	5	1-81n	13	3.2	7.8	14.5	22	4.4	39
Levi Strauss *N	20.34	180	13.9	7.2	5.6	5.10	4	2-81q	21	7.9	15.4	26.9	17	4.1	1,496
Manh Indus N	14.83	83	12.5	8.0	4.0	1.53	NE	1-81f	-25	1.7	NE	NE	124	2.4	35
Movie Star Inc A	20.24	59	10.2	9.8	5.5	1.22	-43	2-81n	0	3.0	6.0	8.1	7	5.0	10
Munsingwear N	25.79	81	-7.4	NC	8.7	-1.17	-100	3-81q	-25	-.4	NE	NE	58	.0	30
Noel Industries A	5.41	92	11.8	8.5	8.0	.59	97	1-81q	-1	1.7	3.1	8.3	13	.0	6
Olga Co O	13.03	111	11.9	8.4	6.5	1.73	30	3-81q	4	3.8	7.6	12.9	15	4.1	15
Oxford Inds N	23.23	85	13.8	7.3	7.3	2.72	46	2-81n	4	2.2	4.4	8.1	26	4.3	57
Palm Beach N	19.35	147	14.1	7.1	4.2	4.02	31	3-81q	16	3.5	6.6	17.0	43	4.2	104
Phil-Van Heu N	30.40	43	13.0	7.7	6.5	1.69	-27	1-81f	27	1.3	3.5	8.5	67	4.6	39
Puritan Fash N	4.58	423	-3.3	NC	NC	-.63	-100	3-81q	NE	-2.1	NE	NE	52	.0	69
Russ Togs N	15.80	100	15.9	6.3	6.6	2.53	19	1-81f	10	4.8	8.7	14.3	18	6.3	54
Salant Corp N	15.97	50	.3	NC	11.7	.02	-98	2-81q	-57	.2	.3	1.2	66	5.0	26
Schrader, Abe A	6.66	120	16.8	6.0	22.6	1.34	306	1-81s	-5	3.2	8.5	10.5	0	1.0	14
Stardust Inc A	2.79	85	-26.9	NC	NC	-.64	NE	9-80q	NE	-6.2	NE	NE	3	.0	3
Superior Surg A	18.01	75	15.3	6.6	5.3	2.06	30	3-81q	17	3.3	5.6	11.2	53	3.3	16
Tultex Corp A	9.53	138	14.6	6.9	3.4	1.91	19	2-81q	12	4.1	6.6	17.2	74	3.7	58
Warnaco Inc N	22.54	100	15.6	6.4	5.3	3.52	16	3-81q	31	3.6	6.3	14.8	48	4.4	89
Wayne Goss N	19.87	49	15.3	6.5	9.2	1.49	NE	3-81q	17	3.3	4.1	7.7	59	1.5	12
Wilson Bros A	4.57	27	-15.2	NC	7.9	-1.44	NE	3-81q	-71	-7.6	NE	NE	140	.0	3
Winter, Jack N	9.90	71	-4.4	NC	NC	-.31	NE	2-81q	-29	-4.8	NE	NE	2	7.1	26
Wolf, Howard A	5.18	46	-5.1	NC	19.8	-.12	-100	2-81n	40	4.8	5.9	7.1	0	4.2	3
Work Wear Inc A	15.51	67	7.9	12.7	6.5	.82	-50	3-81q	0	1.9	2.9	6.6	69	4.6	31

Household Appliances and Furniture

HOUSEHOLD APPLIANCES: TRENDS AND PROJECTIONS, 1975–81 (in millions of dollars except as noted)

	1975	1976	1977	1978	1979 [a]	1980 [2]	Percent change 1979–80 [2]	1981 [3]	Percent change 1980–81 [3]
Industry (SIC 363) [1]									
Value of shipments	7,940	9,161	10,742	11,660	12,637	12,370	−2	14,196	15
Cooking equipment (3631)	1,088	1,457	1,707	1,945	2,065	1,900	−8	2,242	18
Refrigerators-freezers (3632)	2,042	2,106	2,577	2,773	3,025	2,935	−3	3,345	14
Laundry equipment (3633)	1,340	1,559	1,793	1,946	2,015	2,015	—	2,297	14
Electric housewares (3634)	1,904	2,152	2,531	2,650	2,982	3,100	4	3,534	14
Vacuum cleaners (3635)	509	618	644	683	745	730	−2	818	12
Sewing machines (3636)	212	269	306	330	360	345	−4	386	12
Household appliances, n.e.c. (3639)..	845	999	1,184	1,333	1,445	1,345	−7	1,574	17
Value added by manufacture	3,601	4,454	5,278	5,708	6,210	6,078	−2	6,975	15
Value added per production worker-hour ($)	17.25	19.41	21.70	22.76	25.73	27.32	6	30.08	10
Total employment (000)	145	157	162	167	161	150	−7	156	4
Production workers (000)	111	122	129	133	128	118	−8	123	4
Average hourly earnings (Dec.—$) ...	4.70	5.14	5.50	6.07	6.66	6.94 [4]	—	—	—
Year-to-year percent change in average hourly earnings (Dec.–Dec.).	6.8	9.4	7.0	10.4	9.7	9.6 [5]	—	—	—
Capital expenditures	176	210	207	—	—	—	—	—	—
Product (SIC 363) [6]									
Value of shipments	7,321	8,531	10,108	11,065	11,975	11,692	−2	13,434	15
Cooking equipment (3631)	1,101	1,514	1,819	2,049	2,175	2,000	−8	2,360	18
Refrigerators-freezers (3632)	1,611	1,578	2,006	2,158	2,355	2,285	−3	2,605	14
Laundry equipment (3633)	1,254	1,445	1,697	1,842	1,905	1,905	—	2,172	14
Electric housewares (3634)	1,687	1,979	2,304	2,412	2,715	2,825	4	3,220	14
Vacuum cleaners (3635)	544	645	710	753	820	804	−2	900	12
Sewing machines (3636)	204	258	260	280	305	292	−4	327	12
Household appliances, n.e.c. (3639) [6].	920	1,103	1,383	1,571	1,700	1,581	−7	1,850	17
Quantity shipped, selected appliances (000 units):									
Ranges/surface cook tops	4,122	5,203	5,760	5,845	5,637	4,622	−18	—	—
Portable microwave ovens	785	1,252	1,284	1,475	1,590	2,100	32	—	—
Refrigerators	4,552	4,911	5,674	5,586	4,988	4,490	−10	—	—
Freezers	2,644	1,482	1,548	1,419	1,912	1,816	−5	—	—
Washing machines	4,123	4,510	4,972	5,024	4,940	4,495	−9	—	—
Dryers (including combination)	2,753	3,197	3,588	3,638	3,511	3,055	−13	—	—
Dishwashers	2,463	3,075	3,200	3,370	3,350	2,515	−25	—	—
Trash compactors	224	253	260	296	270	216	−20	—	—
Fans	9,994	13,530	15,270	19,032	22,709	24,000	6	—	—
Coffee makers	8,480	8,449	9,787	13,329	16,188	15,400	−5	—	—
Disposers	2,002	2,455	2,823	3,212	3,177	2,732	−14	—	—
Year-to-year percent change in producers price index (Dec.–Dec.) ..	5.4	3.9	4.7	5.5	6.2	8.1 [7]	—	—	—
Trade									
Value of exports	424	542	601	670	745	855	15	965	13
Value of imports	495	671	795	954	928	970	4	1,150	18

n.e.c.=Not elsewhere classified.
—=Not available or insignificant.
[1] Value of all products and services sold by the household appliance industry (SIC 363).
[2] Estimated except for hourly earnings, price indexes, and 1979 trade data.
[3] Forecast.
[4] As of July 1980.

[5] July 1979 to July 1980.
[6] Value of shipments of household appliances produced by all industries.
[7] August 1979 to August 1980.
Source: Bureau of the Census (industry and trade data), Bureau of Labor Statistics (hourly earnings and price indexes). Estimates and forecasts by the Bureau of Industrial Economics.

Source: *U.S. INDUSTRIAL OUTLOOK 1981*, U.S. Department of Commerce.

HOUSEHOLD FURNITURE: TRENDS AND PROJECTIONS, 1975–81 (in millions of current dollars except as noted)

	1975	1976	1977	1978	1979 [2]	1980 [2]	Percent change 1979–80 [2]	1981 [3]	Percent change 1980–81 [3]
Industry (SIC 251) [1]									
Value of shipments [1]	7,770	9,041	10,383	11,962	13,020	12,515	−4	14,150	13
Wood (2511)	3,095	3,780	4,140	4,820	5,400	5,150	−5	5,870	14
Upholstered (2512)	2,186	2,446	2,931	3,472	3,700	3,590	−3	4,020	12
Metal (2514)	939	1,080	1,307	1,408	1,450	1,400	−3	1,570	12
Bedding (2515)	1,110	1,231	1,398	1,560	1,715	1,665	−3	1,880	13
Wood-TV-radio cabinets (2517)	241	291	305	366	390	365	−6	415	14
Household furniture, n.e.c. (2519)	198	214	302	336	365	345	−5	395	14
Value added by manufacture	3,801	4,544	5,208	6,055	6,450	6,275	−3	7,100	13
Value added per production worker-hour ($)	9.08	9.74	10.31	11.38	12.83	12.96	1	14.10	9
Total employment (000)	266	290	310	326	325	299	−8	311	4
Production workers (000)	226	247	265	279	276	254	−8	264	4
Average hourly earnings (Dec.-$)	3.66	3.91	4.24	4.58	4.95	5.14 [4]	—	—	—
Year-to-year percent change in average hourly earnings (Dec.–Dec.)	7.0	6.8	8.4	8.0	8.1	8.7 [5]	—	—	—
Capital expenditures	149	180	211	218	—	—	—	—	—
Product (SIC 251)									
Value of shipments [6]	7,362	8,541	9,935	11,356	12,365	11,860	−4	13,411	13
Wood (2511)	2,746	3,270	3,891	4,517	5,060	4,800	−5	5,475	14
Upholstered (2512)	2,126	2,473	2,736	3,230	3,440	3,335	−3	3,735	12
Metal (2514)	895	992	1,231	1,275	1,315	1,275	−3	1,428	12
Bedding (2515)	1,121	1,255	1,482	1,641	1,805	1,750	−3	1,977	13
Wood-TV-radio cabinets (2517)	261	315	313	378	400	375	−6	428	14
Household furniture, n.e.c. (2519)	213	236	282	315	345	325	−6	368	13
Year-to-year percent change in producers price index (Dec.–Dec.)	3.4	6.0	4.9	7.8	8.6	10.8 [7]	—	—	—
Trade									
Value of exports	84	126	136	156	176	220	25	255	16
Value of imports	260	364	464	638	783	910	16	1,090	20

—=Not available.
n.e.c.=Not elsewhere classified.
[1] Value of all products and services sold by the household furniture industry (SIC 251).
[2] Estimated except for hourly earnings, price indexes, and 1979 data.
[3] Forecast.
[4] As of July 1980.
[5] July 1979 to July 1980.
[6] Value of shipments of household furniture produced by all industries.
[7] August 1979 to August 1980.

Source: Bureau of the Census (industry and trade data), Bureau of Labor Statistics (hourly earnings and price indexes). Estimates and forecasts by the Bureau of Industrial Economics.

Source: U.S. INDUSTRIAL OUTLOOK 1981, U.S. Department of Commerce.

Company and Market		Relative Price					Earnings Per Share				Other					
		Common Equity		P/E Ratio			Latest 12 Months			5-Year Growth Rate	Profit Margin	Return On Assets	Return On Common Equity	Debt Equity Ratio	Dividend Yield	Market Value
		Per Share	Price To Equity	Earnings Yield	Current	5-Year Average	Amount	Change	Date							
		$	%	%	-	-	$	%	-	%	%	%	%	%	%	$Mil
Appliances																
Health-Mor	A	9.11	97	16.3	6.1	4.4	1.45	- 16	3-81q	11	10.0	13.4	15.8	0	4.5	15
Hoover Co	O	18.79	68	12.9	7.7	9.5	1.65	- 50	3-81q	30	3.6	8.0	17.3	7	7.8	157
Magic Chef	N	14.55	99	7.2	13.8	10.6	1.04	- 5	3-81n	- 11	.8	1.4	3.4	78	3.3	112
Maytag Co	★N	12.33	219	10.0	10.0	10.6	2.69	- 22	3-81q	3	10.2	22.3	27.6	0	7.8	386
Mor-Flo Inds	O	7.24	157	6.2	16.3	13.0	.70	3	3-81q	- 7	1.2	2.2	9.5	175	.1	23
Natl Presto	N	29.31	122	11.8	8.5	8.0	4.24	96	9-80n	4	10.0	8.8	11.0	1	5.0	125
Preway Inc	O	8.37	149	11.6	8.6	6.0	1.45	- 39	3-81q	14	8.8	10.4	16.9	48	7.2	33
Rangaire	O	7.89	79	7.8	12.8	10.3	.49	- 38	1-81s	- 13	2.5	3.9	8.7	40	3.8	21
Roper Corp	★N	22.57	56	10.2	9.8	6.2	1.29	- 27	4-81n	- 12	1.5	3.8	8.0	69	7.1	47
Scott & Fetzer	N	25.04	116	10.6	9.5	7.1	3.08	- 29	2-81q	1	3.7	5.9	12.5	43	6.2	215
Scovill Mfg Co	N	22.24	88	12.6	7.9	6.7	2.48	- 31	3-81q	1	2.8	5.7	15.8	80	7.7	183
Singer Co	★N	24.23	87	10.3	9.7	5.7	2.16	NE	3-81q	- 23	1.4	2.5	8.9	69	.5	348
Sunbeam Corp	★N	26.71	73	16.1	6.2	7.2	3.15	- 5	3-81f	9	3.1	5.5	12.4	34	7.6	296
Whirlpool Cp	★N	19.97	140	10.9	9.2	8.2	3.06	4	3-81q	3	4.5	9.5	14.1	8	5.7	1,015
Furniture and Home Furnishings																
Am Furniture	O	9.34	60	10.8	9.2	35.6	.61	- 41	11-80f	28	2.4	4.2	6.5	14	3.6	16
Bassett Furniture	O	22.99	104	12.9	7.7	7.1	3.10	- 3	11-80f	18	8.3	11.8	13.7	1	4.8	170
Berkline Corp	O	13.54	62	15.2	6.6	4.9	1.27	- 4	3-81n	11	3.0	6.6	9.8	9	6.0	13
Flexsteel Ind	O	14.99	97	13.6	7.4	5.6	1.97	5	3-81n	1	3.9	8.5	11.9	26	4.7	28
Henredon Furn	O	23.77	109	10.5	9.6	6.4	2.72	17	3-81f	19	12.5	16.6	19.5	2	2.7	135
Hickory Furniture	O	15.83	63	21.9	4.6	5.6	2.19	30	1-81s	27	5.5	7.4	12.6	28	2.5	11
Kroehler Mfg	★N	15.66	34	-23.7	NC	NC	- 6.65	NE	3-81q	NE	-19.4	NE	NE	61	.0	7
La-Z-Boy Chair	O	16.81	76	16.2	6.2	6.9	2.07	16	1-81n	0	6.2	8.8	12.7	20	5.6	59
Lane Co Inc	O	41.82	91	14.8	6.7	5.8	5.68	16	3-81q	20	7.7	12.1	13.9	0	3.9	86
Leggett Platt	N	14.59	127	12.6	7.9	6.2	2.34	36	3-81q	10	3.7	7.5	14.2	37	3.0	72
Levitz Furn	N	30.94	107	9.4	10.6	9.3	3.10	- 36	1-81f	56	2.6	4.2	10.0	97	3.0	141
Newell Cos	N	12.65	136	14.8	6.8	5.5	2.55	5	3-81q	14	5.6	9.8	18.3	41	5.2	53
Ohio-Sealy	A	11.00	144	12.0	8.4	7.3	1.90	19	2-81q	24	8.2	11.6	17.2	16	5.0	36
Rowe Furniture	O	7.06	46	- 9.5	NC	13.5	- .31	-100	11-80f	- 48	- 2.0	NE	NE	61	2.5	8
Weiman Co	A	5.88	62	- 3.3	NC	NC	- .12	-100	3-81q	- 44	NC	5.2	10.5	44	2.2	3

RETAIL TRADE: TRENDS AND PROJECTIONS 1975–81 (millions of current dollars except as noted)

Item	1975	1976	1977	1978	1979	Percent change 1979–80	1980[1]	Percent change 1980–81	1981[1]
Retail trade total (SIC 52–59)									
Sales	587,141	654,002	722,608	799,054	886,047	7.0	948,070	9.5	1,038,137
Total employment (000)	12,824	13,431	13,903	14,496	14,966	1.5	15,190	2.0	15,494
Non-supervisory workers (000)	11,552	12,113	12,508	13,060	13,452	1.1	13,627	2.0	13,900
Average hourly earnings (Dec.—$)	3.40	3.65	3.92	4.31	4.61	—	—	—	—
Year-to-year percent change in average hourly earnings (Dec.-Dec.)	6.9	7.4	7.4	9.9	7.0	—	—	—	—

[1] Estimates by Bureau of Industrial Economics.
Source: Bureau of the Census (sales data), Bureau of Labor Statistics (employment and earnings), and Bureau of Industrial Economics estimate.

Source: *U.S. INDUSTRIAL OUTLOOK 1981*, U.S. Department of Commerce.

DEPARTMENT STORES: TRENDS AND PROJECTIONS 1975–81 (millions of current dollars except as noted)

Item	1975	1976	1977	1879	1979	Percent change 1979–80	1980[1]	Percent change 1980–81	1981[1]
Department stores (SIC 5311)									
Sales	58,914	64,853	72,607	81,276	89,127	8.0	96,257	9.0	104,920
Total employment (000)	1,658	1,702	1,747	1,891	1,834	—	1,834	1.0	1,852
Non-supervisory workers (000)	1,522	1,575	1,623	1,774	1,721	—	1,721	1.0	1,738
Average hourly earnings (Dec.—$)	3.31	3.52	3.85	4.17	4.52	—	—	—	—
Year-to-year percent change in average hourly earnings (Dec.-Dec.)	7.1	6.3	9.4	8.3	8.4	—	—	—	—

[1] Estimates by Bureau of Industrial Economics.
Source: Bureau of the Census (sales data), Bureau of Labor Statistics (employment and earnings), and Bureau of Industrial Economics estimate.

Source: *U.S. INDUSTRIAL OUTLOOK 1981*, U.S. Department of Commerce.

FOOD RETAILING TRENDS AND PROJECTIONS: 1975–80 (millions of current dollars except as noted)

	1975	1976	1977	1978	1979	1980[1]	Percent change 1979–80[1]	1981[2]	Percent change 1980–81[2]
Industry (SIC 54)									
Sales	138,006	145,939	158,519	171,997	191,326	215,000	12.4	245,000	14
Total employment (000)	2,007.2	2,038.6	2,106.3	2,198.9	2,298.1	[3]2,391.0	4.1	2475.0	3
Non-supervisory workers (000)	1,854.3	1,880.4	1,942.1	2,028.4	2,120.9	[3]2209.0	4.2	2287.0	3
Average hourly earnings (Dec.—$)	4.08	4.41	4.77	5.23	5.67	[3]6.13	8.1	—	—
Year-to-year percent change in average hourly earnings (Dec.–Dec.)	8.5	8.1	8.2	9.6	8.4	—	—	—	—

—Not available.
[1] Estimated sales.
[2] Forecast.
[3] As of June 1980.

Source: U.S. Bureau of Census; Bureau of Labor Statistics. Estimates by Bureau of Industrial Economics.

Source: U.S. INDUSTRIAL OUTLOOK 1981, U.S. Department of Commerce.

Company and Market		Common Equity Per Share $	Price To Equity %	Earnings Yield %	P/E Ratio Current ·	P/E Ratio 5-Year Average ·	Latest 12 Months Amount $	Latest 12 Months Change %	Latest 12 Months Date ·	5-Year Growth Rate %	Profit Margin %	Return On Assets %	Return On Common Equity %	Debt Equity Ratio %	Dividend Yield %	Market Value $Mil
Department Stores																
Alexanders Inc	N	14.63	97	-4.9	NC	8.1	-.69	-100	1-81s	-26	NC	NE	NE	126	.0	64
Allied Stores	★N	34.70	82	14.5	6.9	6.2	4.11	-7	1-81f	8	3.7	6.1	12.6	54	6.0	578
Almy Stores Inc	A	23.69	30	12.6	8.0	6.2	.88	-15	12-80f	-3	1.0	1.9	3.8	48	2.9	7
Ames Dept St	N	15.90	204	10.7	9.3	4.2	3.48	10	1-81f	22	2.6	6.9	19.0	75	1.9	75
Assoc Dry Gds	★N	38.09	75	13.5	7.4	8.0	3.86	19	1-81f	3	2.7	4.5	8.5	32	5.6	386
Caldor	A	10.39	351	6.9	14.4	7.6	2.53	5	4-81q	23	3.2	7.1	22.9	113	1.6	307
Carson Pir Sc	N	32.75	63	10.9	9.2	5.7	2.26	-34	4-81q	-5	2.1	3.0	10.5	166	5.8	72
Carter Hawley	★N	23.24	76	11.3	8.9	9.3	2.00	-19	1-81f	6	2.2	3.5	9.3	96	6.9	467
Crowley Milner	A	27.70	42	26.3	3.8	8.1	3.06	-28	4-81q	23	2.4	6.7	14.9	21	4.3	6
Dayton Hudson	★N	44.65	136	9.6	10.5	8.9	5.80	9	1-81f	17	3.4	6.4	13.0	30	3.3	1,444
Dillard Dept A	A	31.69	62	17.0	5.9	5.7	3.36	11	4-81q	6	1.8	3.2	8.8	118	2.0	58
Elder Beerman Str	O	14.86	44	17.2	5.8	4.4	1.12	4	1-81f	1	1.2	2.1	7.4	87	3.1	14
Fedrtd Dep Str	★N	37.74	108	11.2	8.9	9.5	4.54	8	1-81f	6	4.4	7.8	15.2	30	4.7	1,967
Garfinckel Brks	N	24.78	111	12.1	8.3	6.4	3.33	3	1-81f	11	3.1	5.9	13.5	68	5.1	120
Goldblatt Bros	A	11.01	20	-44.0	NC	43.4	-7.74	NE	1-81f	-71	-8.9	NE	NE	85	.0	7
Grand Centl	A	12.04	80	8.0	12.5	7.2	.77	24	4-81n	-12	.6	1.4	5.7	207	2.6	21
Hecks Inc	N	8.19	154	12.6	7.9	6.6	1.59	0	3-81q	22	3.6	6.6	18.7	100	1.9	123
Higbee Co	O	36.38	40	5.4	18.6	14.7	.78	117	1-81f	-21	.5	.8	2.2	110	.0	20
Holmes, D.H.	O	31.41	72	15.9	6.3	6.8	3.61	-11	1-81f	15	2.5	4.5	12.4	100	7.0	29
Jacobson Stores	O	21.52	64	9.1	11.0	7.1	1.26	-39	1-81s	-15	.5	.9	3.8	221	3.2	13
Jamesway Corp	N	13.65	65	15.8	6.3	4.5	1.40	-39	1-81f	17	1.4	7.1	17.1	74	1.4	24
Kings Dept St	N	12.65	63	6.6	15.1	8.9	.53	-75	1-81f	-15	.5	7.3	16.6	83	.0	59
Macy, R.H.	★N	36.25	169	11.5	8.7	7.0	7.06	9	4-81n	24	4.3	7.8	17.3	42	2.9	992
Marshall Field	★N	26.73	65	11.2	8.9	11.3	1.93	4	1-81f	-1	2.0	3.3	6.9	42	7.2	177
May Dept Strs	★N	28.12	106	13.9	7.2	8.0	4.15	7	4-81q	11	3.7	5.4	14.0	73	5.7	867
Mays, J.W.	N	13.36	37	2.0	50.0	35.7	.10	-76	1-81s	14	.2	.6	1.4	69	.0	11
Mercantile Strs	N	42.26	113	16.7	6.0	6.8	7.99	15	4-81q	11	3.8	9.4	17.1	37	3.7	282
Penney, JC	★N	36.15	95	12.4	8.1	9.7	4.28	21	4-81q	2	2.4	4.8	9.7	33	5.3	2,417
Sears, Roebuck	★N	23.53	80	10.2	9.8	10.6	1.92	-24	1-81f	4	2.4	4.9	10.8	33	7.2	5,952
Strawbrd & Cloth	O	59.86	46	11.8	8.5	5.9	3.25	21	1-81f	-6	3.3	4.8	10.3	61	4.8	108
Wieboldt	N	13.49	48	9.4	10.7	10.9	.61	11	1-81f	-9	1.0	1.5	4.0	80	6.8	18
Woodwd & Lothrop	O	41.06	69	14.0	7.2	5.7	3.95	-4	1-81f	-2	3.1	3.9	9.5	70	6.0	69
Food Chain Stores																
Albertsons Inc	N	14.08	170	11.3	8.9	8.0	2.70	8	1-81f	22	1.4	6.6	19.9	98	3.7	356
Arden Group Inc	O	8.40	45	27.7	3.6	17.7	1.04	131	12-80f	40	.8	1.9	6.6	133	.0	14
Bayless Mkts	O	23.16	46	20.1	5.0	5.5	2.16	16	12-80f	7	.7	4.4	9.8	43	5.6	12
Big V Supmkt	A	10.16	98	18.1	5.5	4.0	1.81	17	3-81q	28	1.3	9.0	19.5	55	3.4	26
Bormans Inc	N	10.97	36	.3	NC	NC	.01	-94	1-81f	-47	NC	.0	NE	109	5.0	12

Company and Market		Relative Price					Earnings Per Share				Other					
		Common Equity		Earnings Yield	P/E Ratio		Latest 12 Months			5-Year Growth Rate	Profit Margin	Return On Assets	Return On Common Equity	Debt Equity Ratio	Dividend Yield	Market Value
		Per Share	Price To Equity		Current	5-Year Average	Amount	Change	Date							
		$	%	%	-	-	$	%	-	%	%	%	%	%	%	$Mil
Brunos Inc	O	8.01	243	6.4	15.6	7.0	1.25	29	3-81n	32	1.9	9.7	25.3	53	1.5	166
Circle K Corp	A	6.36	267	8.6	11.6	7.3	1.46	-16	4-81f	28	2.2	11.1	27.0	86	4.0	170
Cullum Companies	O	16.76	197	11.9	8.4	5.8	3.92	24	3-81n	33	1.3	6.9	20.1	101	3.0	111
Dillon Cos	N	9.61	239	9.0	11.1	11.4	2.08	21	3-81n	8	1.3	6.3	16.8	62	4.7	390
Fst Nat Supermkts	O	9.84	89	21.7	4.6	10.1	1.90	109	12-80n	4	.4	2.5	14.1	236	.2	31
Fisher Foods	N	12.94	86	10.6	9.4	9.0	1.18	NE	3-81q	-21	.5	2.0	8.0	135	4.5	70
Food Town	O	6.95	486	5.7	17.6	10.3	1.92	18	3-81q	34	2.8	14.4	25.6	20	.6	290
Foodarama	A	15.04	32	-11.5	NC	5.6	-.56	NE	1-81q	-29	-.3	NE	NE	41	.0	7
Giant Food A	A	22.23	88	19.2	5.2	4.4	3.74	3	2-81f	14	1.2	5.8	16.6	84	6.2	96
Grt A & P Tea	*N	15.83	36	-20.4	NC	NC	-1.15	NE	2-81f	NE	-.6	NE	NE	84	.0	210
Hannaford Bros	A	22.26	100	18.6	5.4	4.9	4.14	64	3-81q	14	1.0	4.5	17.0	169	5.4	29
Jewel Co	*N	33.67	120	13.1	7.6	6.8	5.31	22	1-81f	16	1.5	5.0	13.4	75	5.5	460
King Kullen Groc	O	34.78	41	14.3	7.0	5.3	2.04	-24	9-80f	-1	.4	3.1	5.8	0	3.5	10
Kroger	*N	22.14	112	15.6	6.4	5.8	3.85	28	3-81q	19	1.0	4.8	14.0	56	6.1	687
Laneco Inc	A	12.32	96	16.4	6.1	4.1	1.95	9	3-81s	18	1.0	4.0	13.0	108	2.4	13'
Lucky Stores	*N	9.02	168	11.8	8.5	10.2	1.78	-9	4-81q	13	1.4	6.5	19.3	92	7.4	754
Marsh Supmkts	O	8.32	126	13.2	7.6	4.5	1.39	12	3-81f	16	.9	4.1	14.9	145	3.4	34
Meyer Fred	O	22.43	171	6.7	15.0	9.7	2.56	-14	9-80n	11	2.1	5.5	14.3	74	2.1	273
Motts Super	A	12.61	132	14.2	7.0	4.6	2.36	45	3-81q	42	1.4	9.4	16.9	4	1.2	30
Munford Inc	N	12.26	59	5.1	19.6	31.1	.37	-61	3-81q	20	.3	.6	2.3	183	.0	16
Natl Conv Str	N	5.89	261	10.3	9.7	7.5	1.58	10	3-81n	31	1.9	7.0	25.8	154	3.9	96
Natl Tea Co	N	8.98	68	13.9	7.2	6.1	.85	5	3-81q	39	.7	3.2	9.7	103	.0	61
Niag Fron Svc	A	23.93	113	15.3	6.6	5.6	4.14	-2	3-81n	8	1.8	7.5	18.0	85	3.7	57
Penn Traffic	A	22.43	75	17.9	5.6	5.5	3.00	-1	1-81f	9	1.5	6.7	13.4	52	7.2	36
Pneumo Corp	N	19.11	167	9.7	10.4	8.0	3.09	34	2-81q	10	1.4	3.9	15.2	100	2.5	146
Pueblo Intl	N	7.51	68	14.4	6.9	5.8	.74	-17	1-81f	49	.9	3.7	11.7	104	.0	20
Safeway Stores	*N	40.75	80	15.0	6.7	8.8	4.88	-4	3-81q	5	.8	3.6	11.2	99	8.0	849
Seaway Food Town	O	17.87	69	24.7	4.0	3.9	3.03	10	3-81s	20	1.3	5.3	15.7	98	5.9	20
Shop & Go	O	5.91	178	15.8	6.3	5.3	1.66	11	3-81f	32	4.0	14.5	25.6	22	2.7	31
Shopwell Inc	A	14.69	40	13.8	7.3	10.2	.81	11	3-81q	46	.3	1.5	6.3	164	1.7	8
Southland Corp	N	21.07	123	12.6	8.0	9.8	3.27	13	3-81q	16	1.6	4.9	13.6	111	4.2	615
Star Supermkts	A	21.61	53	20.5	4.9	4.8	2.33	-32	3-81q	10	.7	4.0	10.6	94	7.0	10
Stop & Shop	N	31.59	75	17.0	5.9	4.8	4.02	9	1-81f	5	.8	3.3	11.7	135	5.6	96
Sunshine-Jr	A	8.64	72	13.4	7.4	6.4	.84	-39	3-81q	2	1.0	6.5	10.2	3	6.4	11
Supermkts Gen	N	13.84	130	16.7	6.0	5.7	3.01	17	1-81f	30	1.0	4.5	19.7	156	3.0	148
Thorofare Mkts	A	11.43	35	9.0	11.1	12.6	.36	-38	1-81s	30	.2	1.9	4.1	26	1.0	5
Thriftimart A	A	49.83	75	19.7	5.1	3.4	7.33	18	3-81f	24	1.4	9.1	16.2	20	4.3	33
Victory Markets	O	7.93	57	13.3	7.5	9.8	.60	62	3-81q	9	.3	1.6	5.3	87	4.4	7
Waldbaum Inc	O	23.38	71	25.4	3.9	3.8	4.19	36	3-81q	16	.8	4.3	12.1	85	.0	42
Weis Markets	N	20.06	170	11.1	9.0	7.8	3.80	19	3-81q	17	4.8	15.1	18.1	0	2.9	311
Winn-Dixie A	*N	20.46	167	10.7	9.4	11.1	3.64	8	3-81n	13	1.7	10.2	19.4	21	5.6	868

TELEPHONE AND TELEGRAPH (4811 & 4821): TRENDS AND PROJECTIONS 1975–81 (in millions of dollars except as noted)

Item	1975	1976	1977	1978	1979	1980[1]	Percent change 1979–80	1981	Percent change 1980–81
Operating Revenues:									
Domestic telephone & telegraph	35,900	40,400	44,100	49,500	54,754	59,534	8.7	65,850	10.6
International telephone & telegraph	1,008	1,176	1,339	1,607	1,906	2,250	18.0	2,650	17.8
No. of telephone (000) (Dec.)	148,623	155,172	162,027	169,027	175,162	181,800	3.8	188,900	3.9
Total employment[2] (00)	985	971	975	1,013	1,070	1,106	3.4	1,140	3.1
Production workers[2] (000)	755	743	738	756	789	805	2.0	820	1.9
Average hourly earnings (Dec.–$)	5.65	6.35	6.91	7.53	8.09	[5]8.52	5.3	9.29	9
Year-to-year percent change in average hourly earnings (Dec.–Dec.)	15	12	9	9	7	5	—	—	—
Year-to-year percent change in productivity output per employee hour	9.0	10.8	6.1	6.6	3.9	—	—	—	—
Industry price index[4]	108.4	112.0	113.0	113.6	114.6	—	—	—	—
Year-to-year percent change in industry price index (Dec.–Dec.)[3]	3.0	3.3	.8	.5	.9	—	—	—	—
Capital expenditures	12,000	12,900	14,700	17,600	20,180	21,900	8.5	—	—
Gross cumulative plant investment	112,600	121,600	131,200	143,300	155,408	163,292	5.1	—	—

[1] Estimated by Bureau of Industrial Economics (BIE).
[2] Includes both telephone and telegraph workers.
[3] Implicit price deflator for gross revenues originating in telephone and telegraph services.
[4] 1972 = 100.
[5] As of July 1980.

Source: Bureau of the Census; Bureau of Labor Statistics. Bureau of Industrial Economics estimates, Federal Communications Commission, AT&T, U.S. Independent Telephone Association, Industry Publications and Annual Reports.

Source: *U.S. INDUSTRIAL OUTLOOK 1981*, U.S. Department of Commerce.

Company and Market		Relative Price					Earnings Per Share				Other					
		Common Equity		Earnings Yield	P/E Ratio		Latest 12 Months			5-Year Growth Rate	Profit Margin	Return On Assets	Return On Common Equity	Debt Equity Ratio	Dividend Yield	Market Value
		Per Share	Price To Equity		Current	5-Year Average	Amount	Change	Date							
		$	%	%	-	-	$	%	-	%	%	%	%	%	%	$Mil
Communications																
Allied Telephone	O	15.57	123	11.3	8.9	7.6	2.16	10	3-81q	16	6.4	3.3	13.8	242	4.8	63
Am Tel & Tel	✱N	65.51	88	14.2	7.0	8.1	8.23	2	3-81q	7	12.0	4.8	11.8	83	9.3	44,202
Bell Canada	N	21.09	75	13.1	7.6	7.9	2.07	-16	3-81q	1	6.0	4.2	11.8	110	NA	2,635
Cent Tel Utils	✱N	21.13	148	11.3	8.9	8.7	3.53	7	3-81q	11	10.4	4.9	15.4	136	6.7	823
Century Tel	N	9.87	77	13.0	7.7	7.6	.99	-16	3-81q	9	7.0	2.6	10.4	323	9.2	35
Cinn Bell	N	36.39	72	15.6	6.4	6.3	4.07	-15	3-81q	7	11.5	5.0	11.2	57	9.6	217
Comwlth Tel Ent	O	17.07	94	13.7	7.3	8.7	2.19	11	3-81q	7	8.2	3.3	11.5	156	8.1	40
COMSAT	N	51.95	115	7.7	13.0	9.0	4.59	-4	3-81q	9	12.8	6.6	9.2	1	3.8	479
Contl Tel	✱N	15.51	116	11.8	8.5	8.7	2.12	4	3-81q	10	9.9	3.8	12.2	166	8.0	981
Electrospace Sys	O	2.44	1035	4.2	23.8	11.7	1.06	34	3-81f	44	6.1	12.8	32.8	39	.5	66
Gen Tel Elec	✱N	28.89	102	12.6	7.9	8.1	3.72	-8	3-81q	5	6.2	3.5	14.6	149	9.2	4,569
Heritage Commun	O	2.40	719	7.4	13.5	NC	1.28	NC	6-80s	43	30.0	16.3	42.1	116	.0	86
Lincoln Telecom	O	21.11	111	13.9	7.2	7.1	3.27	19	12-80f	17	13.8	5.7	14.4	97	1.7	92
Magnetics Cont	O	10.92	224	6.2	16.2	9.8	1.51	-19	1-81q	42	6.4	8.7	13.0	21	.0	62
MCI Communicatn	O	2.42	1028	.7	NC	47.5	.17	NE	3-81f	62	8.0	2.3	9.0	221	.0	910
Mid-Cont Tel	N	18.12	97	13.1	7.6	7.9	2.30	-11	3-81q	6	13.0	3.7	11.7	194	9.8	203
Pac Tel Tel	N	21.69	59	14.7	6.8	8.3	1.89	3	12-80f	3	6.5	2.7	8.4	135	10.9	2,310
Philipp LD Tel	A	14.15	38	26.6	3.8	4.2	1.43	3	3-81q	5	24.6	.1	17.1	141	11.7	74
Rochester Tele	N	19.19	116	13.0	7.7	7.5	2.89	11	3-81q	12	14.3	6.3	12.9	88	8.3	220
So N Eng Tel	N	50.21	74	17.5	5.7	7.1	6.51	25	3-81q	8	9.4	4.4	10.6	87	11.0	486
Telecom Equip	O	1.33	1372	3.0	33.2	27.3	.55	34	12-80f	36	4.6	5.8	30.3	79	.0	46
Telephone Utils	O	14.70	92	15.7	6.4	6.2	2.12	9	12-80f	21	15.2	5.4	14.1	96	6.8	64
TIE Comm	A	.96	3190	2.0	49.4	17.2	.62	107	3-81q	79	5.7	3.5	22.2	0	.0	234
Unit Telecom	✱N	16.75	122	11.8	8.5	8.6	2.42	1	3-81q	7	9.2	4.2	14.2	140	7.8	1,457
Wstn Union Cp	N	35.74	66	8.0	12.6	9.0	1.88	NE	9-80n	-12	1.0	.4	1.2	126	5.9	370

COMMERCIAL BANKING: TRENDS AND PROJECTIONS 1975–81 (in billions of current dollars except as noted)

	1975	1976	1977	1978	Percent change 1978–79	1979	1980[1]	Percent change 1979–80	1981[1]	Percent change 1980–81
Assets	965	1,031	1,166	1,269	7	1,351	1,459	8	1,590	9
Loans	546	595	680	762	13	860	903	5	984	9
Investments	230	251	259	269	5	283	317	12	342	8
Demand deposits	324	337	383	399	−5	378	370	−2	363	−2
Time deposits	463	501	556	612	7	653	712	9	762	7
Employment (000) ...	1,226	1,255	1,321	[2]1,320	3	1,358	1,417	4	1,474	4

[1] Estimated by Bureau of Industrial Economics.
[2] New definition.

Source: Board of Governors of the Federal Reserve System, Bureau of Labor Statistics, Bureau of Industrial Economics.

Source: *U.S. INDUSTRIAL OUTLOOK 1981*, U.S. Department of Commerce.

Company and Market		Relative Price					Earnings Per Share				Other					
		Common Equity			P/E Ratio		Latest 12 Months			5-Year Growth Rate	Profit Margin	Return On Assets	Return On Common Equity	Debt Equity Ratio	Dividend Yield	Market Value
		Per Share	Price To Equity	Earnings Yield	Current	5-Year Average	Amount	Change	Date							
		$	%	%	-	-	$	%	-	%	%	%	%	%	%	$Mil
Middle Atlantic Banks																
Am Bk & Tr Pa	O	17.21	70	21.3	4.7	6.5	2.55	9	3-81q	13	9.7	1.0	14.9	11	8.3	93
Bank of NY Co	N	59.04	65	17.7	5.7	6.6	6.73	14	12-80f	9	4.6	.5	12.8	9	7.9	255
Bankers Tr NY	*N	35.94	86	26.7	3.7	5.6	8.29	52	3-81q	40	5.8	.4	12.3	43	6.0	764
Chase Manhttn	*N	70.25	73	17.8	5.6	6.9	9.10	4	3-81q	36	4.6	.5	13.6	43	6.1	1,657
Chem NY Corp	*N	80.50	71	16.9	5.9	5.6	9.72	22	12-80f	9	4.1	.4	12.9	49	6.7	861
Citicorp	*N	31.73	87	14.3	7.0	7.6	3.98	4	3-81q	8	3.6	.4	12.9	152	5.6	3,411
Citzn Fst NB	A	34.42	58	20.6	4.9	5.5	4.11	-40	3-81q	2	8.6	.8	13.0	4	10.0	23
Contl Bk Norrstwn	O	27.96	86	20.2	4.9	5.9	4.85	15	3-81q	14	10.6	1.1	16.8	20	8.0	107
Equimark Corp	N	28.49	34	18.7	5.3	6.1	1.80	13	12-80f	-2	3.3	.3	7.7	31	10.0	41
Fidelcor Inc	O	31.77	64	14.1	7.1	7.2	2.86	92	12-80f	-17	4.2	.4	8.9	46	3.2	101
Fidelity Un Bcp	N	53.91	48	23.5	4.2	5.9	6.15	5	12-80f	8	8.8	.7	11.5	18	10.7	99
Fst Natl State	N	38.47	61	21.5	4.7	6.2	5.07	13	12-80f	11	7.0	.5	10.9	22	9.3	98
Fst Penn Cp	*N	13.66	32	-98.7	NC	12.3	-4.32	-100	3-81q	-52	-9.7	NE	NE	302	.0	69
Girard Co	O	45.39	61	22.7	4.4	5.8	6.29	11	3-81q	27	7.7	.8	14.1	45	8.1	152
Guarantee Bk	A	5.45	89	5.5	18.1	11.2	.27	-69	3-81q	37	6.0	.6	10.8	13	4.1	21
Horiz Bncp	N	21.83	71	21.0	4.8	5.6	3.25	17	3-81q	23	9.9	1.0	14.9	37	8.3	58
Indus Val Bk Phil	O	29.01	60	21.5	4.6	5.5	3.77	-13	12-80f	3	4.9	.6	12.9	36	12.6	46
Irving Bk Cp	N	65.60	79	18.8	5.3	4.9	9.75	24	12-80f	15	4.9	.5	15.1	44	5.8	449
Key Banks	O	23.69	56	23.6	4.2	4.7	3.16	3	3-81q	7	8.4	.7	9.7	30	9.6	99
Lincoln First Bks	O	53.15	48	19.5	5.1	5.8	4.98	-6	3-81q	14	6.0	.6	11.5	50	7.8	83
LITCO Bancorp	N	23.22	121	7.0	14.3	7.0	1.96	-15	3-81q	-4	4.8	.5	7.9	26	3.6	75
Mfrs Hanover	*N	50.89	71	19.2	5.2	6.1	6.91	8	12-80f	9	4.4	.4	13.5	54	7.6	1,209
Marine Midland	N	39.66	55	18.0	5.5	8.7	3.92	10	3-81q	50	3.1	.3	7.7	46	4.8	416
Mellon Natl	*O	45.94	81	16.1	6.2	6.4	6.01	14	3-81q	16	7.2	.7	12.7	45	5.5	733
Midlantic Banks	O	65.58	49	21.1	4.7	5.9	6.75	8	12-80f	28	9.3	.8	14.7	26	7.9	89
Morgan, J.P.	*N	56.37	103	15.8	6.3	7.9	9.16	29	3-81q	16	7.1	.7	16.9	26	5.3	2,243
Natl Cent Finl Cp	O	27.26	57	25.1	4.0	5.6	3.89	7	3-81q	13	8.5	.9	13.7	21	10.1	70
Natl Cm Bk NJ	O	36.34	67	17.5	5.7	6.2	4.29	-6	3-81q	1	11.6	1.0	12.6	0	9.8	56
No Natl Cp	O	21.26	54	-49.7	NC	7.8	-5.72	-100	3-81q	-43	-16.3	NE	NE	4	.0	31
Phila Natl Cp	O	57.21	54	22.5	4.4	5.4	7.00	-10	12-80f	11	6.2	.7	12.2	35	9.4	181
Pitt Nat Corp	O	56.83	88	18.7	5.4	5.9	9.33	16	3-81q	16	8.8	.9	15.8	69	6.0	310
Provident Natl Cp	O	49.75	78	17.7	5.6	7.9	6.91	28	12-80f	26	10.5	1.1	14.6	19	6.7	166
Republic NY	N	21.62	163	19.1	5.2	4.4	6.74	125	12-80f	31	9.6	1.1	24.2	76	3.4	383
Union Natl Pitts	O	41.60	55	23.9	4.2	5.7	5.49	1	3-81q	20	13.9	1.3	12.7	0	9.0	69
Unit Bank Corp	O	30.50	78	17.3	5.8	6.4	4.12	17	3-81q	8	14.7	1.2	13.3	14	8.4	157
Unit Jer Bank	N	21.65	61	20.3	4.9	5.9	2.69	12	12-80f	14	6.3	.6	12.3	40	8.6	74
US Trust Cp	O	32.21	88	12.8	7.8	8.1	3.62	11	9-80n	4	4.3	.4	8.8	26	6.7	85
Pacific States Banks																
Bancal TriState	N	39.47	69	12.8	7.8	9.5	3.51	-9	3-81q	28	4.5	.5	9.8	35	4.4	126
Bancp Hawaii Inc	O	19.10	99	17.3	5.8	6.0	3.28	8	3-81q	22	10.6	1.1	18.0	27	5.6	141
BankAmerica	*N	26.55	98	16.9	5.9	8.0	4.39	7	12-80f	17	5.3	.6	16.5	31	5.8	3,823
Calif Fst Bk	O	25.10	56	21.9	4.6	5.5	3.09	-13	12-80f	16	4.7	.5	12.3	43	7.6	81
City Natl Corp	O	12.43	290	8.2	12.2	5.3	2.94	15	3-81q	39	10.7	1.1	21.2	4	1.7	247
Crocker Natl	N	49.58	75	15.6	6.4	5.8	5.80	-15	3-81q	15	6.5	.4	10.2	38	6.4	511
Fst Hawaiian	O	33.30	83	20.1	5.0	5.7	5.59	13	12-80f	13	8.8	.9	16.8	58	8.6	84
Orbanco Fincl Svcs	O	24.18	123	15.1	6.6	4.8	4.48	18	12-80f	19	7.8	1.0	14.6	229	3.0	86
Rainier Bncp	O	31.90	94	14.2	7.1	6.3	4.23	2	3-81q	11	6.9	.8	13.2	21	4.6	280
Seafirst Cp	N	31.78	88	16.5	6.0	6.8	4.63	5	3-81q	14	6.7	.7	14.4	23	4.6	433
Security Pac	N	42.26	95	16.3	6.1	5.5	6.57	10	12-80f	22	5.8	.7	15.5	31	5.5	1,115
US Bancorp	O	25.49	132	12.7	7.9	7.0	4.27	11	3-81q	17	11.0	1.2	16.0	61	3.6	481
Wells Fargo	N	39.93	78	17.2	5.8	5.8	5.32	-7	12-80f	17	4.8	.5	13.3	87	6.2	709
Wstn Bancorp	*N	37.24	107	15.1	6.6	5.7	6.01	5	3-81q	23	7.1	.7	16.7	49	4.6	1,512

LIFE INSURANCE: TRENDS AND PROJECTIONS 1975–81 (in billions of current dollars except as noted)

	1975	1976	1977	1978	1979	1980[1]	Percent change 1979–80	1981[1]	Percent change 1980–81
Premium receipts	58.6	66.4	72.3	78.8	84.9	91.7	8	100.0	9
New life insurance purchases ...	288.2	324.8	369.8	414.2	488.8	567.0	16	663.0	17
Life insurance in force in the U.S. ...	2,139.6	2,343.1	2,582.8	2,870.3	3,222.3	3,641.0	13	4,151.0	14
Total benefits payable in the U.S. ...	22.5	24.6	26.5	28.6	32.4	—	—	—	—
Life insurance assets	289.3	321.6	351.7	389.9	432.3	477.0	10	529.0	11
Total employment (000)	524.1	516.0	519.7	523.0	524.0	540.0	3	—	—

[1] Estimates by Bureau of Industrial Economics.

Source: American Council of Life Insurance, Bureau of Labor Statistics, and Bureau of Industrial Economics.

Source: U.S. INDUSTRIAL OUTLOOK 1981, U.S. Department of Commerce.

| | | Relative Price | | | | | Earnings Per Share | | | | Other | | | | | |
Company and Market		Common Equity Per Share $	Price To Equity %	Earnings Yield %	P/E Ratio Current -	5-Year Average -	Latest 12 Months Amount $	Change %	Date -	5-Year Growth Rate %	Profit Margin %	Return On Assets %	Return On Common Equity %	Debt Equity Ratio %	Dividend Yield %	Market Value $Mil
Life, Accident and Health																
Aetna Life Cas	*N	40.79	91	17.0	5.9	5.2	6.30	-9	12-80f	38	3.8	1.4	15.5	8	6.2	2,986
Am Family Cp	N	11.77	76	15.1	6.6	5.6	1.36	-44	12-80f	7	4.0	2.2	9.4	18	6.7	121
Am Heritage Lf	N	16.96	100	12.4	8.1	8.3	2.10	19	9-80n	16	5.0	3.0	12.2	5	4.2	54
Am Natl Ins	O	21.57	63	16.5	6.1	6.8	2.23	-14	3-81q	17	10.3	2.3	10.3	0	5.0	416
AVEMCO Cp	A	7.67	135	11.5	8.7	6.4	1.19	-21	3-81q	13	12.0	6.2	15.2	15	4.8	26
Benef Std A	A	21.09	108	10.4	9.7	4.7	2.37	-20	3-81q	32	6.6	2.5	11.5	27	1.7	132
Busn Mens Assur	O	35.60	95	16.3	6.1	5.9	5.53	16	3-81q	28	10.8	3.5	14.2	3	4.7	202
Capital Holdg	*N	24.68	93	14.0	7.1	8.2	3.20	8	12-80f	12	16.3	3.4	13.0	0	5.2	638
Colonial Penn	N	22.19	99	15.0	6.7	6.9	3.29	-26	12-80f	7	6.6	5.1	14.8	0	6.4	355
Comb Intl	N	19.25	109	16.8	5.9	5.7	3.53	3	3-81q	12	12.6	7.4	19.2	0	7.6	569
Conn Gen Ins	*N	54.06	101	14.0	7.1	6.2	7.66	17	12-80f	19	6.0	1.9	14.2	0	3.2	2,263
Equitable of Iowa	O	31.35	55	18.0	5.5	6.3	3.11	-18	3-81q	10	4.7	1.1	9.8	3	7.0	108
Fst Colony Life	O	22.65	201	6.7	14.9	9.2	3.05	29	3-81q	27	7.6	3.4	12.8	0	1.8	181
Govt Employ Life	O	15.24	112	11.1	9.0	7.5	1.88	3	12-80f	4	17.2	3.4	12.4	0	5.9	76
Gulf United Cp	N	18.75	125	11.1	9.0	6.8	2.59	7	12-80f	12	11.6	3.6	13.5	52	5.5	591
Home Beneficial	O	33.47	65	18.5	5.4	5.7	4.03	10	12-80f	12	18.7	3.5	12.0	0	5.3	139
ICH Corp	A	7.40	135	13.6	7.4	6.0	1.36	-11	9-80n	29	5.2	1.2	17.2	0	2.0	29
Jefferson-Pilot	*N	35.81	75	15.4	6.5	8.3	4.14	-9	3-81q	10	11.3	3.1	11.7	0	5.7	588
Kansas City Life	O	66.79	91	15.2	6.6	6.4	9.26	16	3-81q	12	13.9	2.2	12.8	3	3.6	175
Liberty Corp	N	19.41	80	15.0	6.7	6.2	2.33	-8	3-81q	12	9.9	2.6	12.0	10	4.6	198
Liberty Natl	N	27.23	93	13.8	7.3	8.4	3.48	9	12-80f	18	13.8	3.2	11.7	0	5.5	474
Life Inv Inc	O	20.70	114	8.5	11.8	7.0	2.01	-17	12-80f	33	5.8	2.3	9.4	7	1.0	204
Lincoln Nat	*N	57.11	77	16.4	6.1	6.2	7.22	5	12-80f	23	5.8	2.1	13.3	12	6.8	913
Manhattan Life	N	12.26	68	10.1	9.9	9.3	.85	15	12-80f	9	3.0	.6	6.6	0	3.8	40
Monarch Capital	O	28.07	78	15.2	6.6	6.5	3.33	-2	12-80f	16	12.8	3.1	11.8	7	6.0	191
Monumental Cp	O	26.96	68	12.7	7.9	7.7	2.32	-20	12-80f	5	9.3	1.6	8.6	17	5.5	122
Nationwide Corp	O	37.04	65	14.7	6.8	4.7	3.55	5	3-81q	12	5.5	1.3	9.5	0	2.9	248
NLT Corp	*N	32.61	99	11.9	8.4	6.8	3.84	0	12-80f	8	17.8	3.0	10.7	17	4.1	1,122
NWn Natl Life	O	48.66	57	16.4	6.1	5.6	4.53	-18	12-80f	11	11.8	2.6	9.3	8	4.5	97
Old Rep Intl	O	20.52	80	22.4	4.5	3.9	3.67	-7	12-80f	12	9.0	3.9	18.3	0	5.6	154
Orion Cap Cp	N	14.92	118	9.9	10.1	7.3	1.75	1	12-80f	26	5.7	2.2	11.9	39	2.7	130
PennCorp Fincl	N	13.69	43	18.9	5.3	5.2	1.11	-32	12-80f	36	4.5	1.0	8.4	143	2.7	110
Provident Lf Acc	O	54.51	84	14.7	6.8	6.3	6.76	-12	3-81q	8	6.9	2.8	12.4	0	4.8	453
Southland Fincl	O	11.80	169	6.9	14.6	8.8	1.37	8	12-80f	17	8.6	2.0	11.3	66	2.6	356
Travelers Corp	*N	62.42	78	17.6	5.7	5.6	8.58	-3	3-81q	21	4.2	1.7	13.8	3	5.9	2,069
Unit Cos Fincl	A	18.86	105	12.7	7.9	6.2	2.51	11	12-80f	10	4.9	2.1	11.6	124	4.1	32
Unit Republic	A	11.06	111	3.8	26.6	11.1	.46	-6	3-81q	-9	2.9	.4	3.3	33	2.0	19
USLIFE Corp	N	27.08	106	13.8	7.2	6.0	3.96	5	12-80f	13	12.3	2.7	13.9	45	2.7	637
Wash Natl Cp	N	27.37	110	11.3	8.9	6.3	3.38	6	3-81q	17	4.3	1.2	12.2	4	3.6	307

STANDARD INDUSTRIAL CLASSIFICATION CODES (SIC)

1972 Code	SIC Title
2011	MEAT PACKING PLANTS
2013	SAUSAGE & OTHER PREPARED MEATS
2016	POULTRY DRESSING PLANTS
2017	POULTRY & EGG PROCESSING
2021	CREAMERY BUTTER
2022	CHEESE, NATURAL & PROCESSED
2023	CONDENSED & EVAPORATED MILK
2024	ICE CREAM & FROZEN DESSERTS
2026	FLUID MILK
2032	CANNED SPECIALTIES [1]
2033	CANNED FRUITS & VEGETABLES [1]
2034	DEHYDRATED FRUITS, VEGETABLES, SOUPS
2035	PICKLES, SAUCES, SALAD DRESSINGS [1]
2037	FROZEN FRUITS & VEGETABLES [1]
2038	FROZEN SPECIALTIES [1]
2041	FLOUR & OTHER GRAIN MILL PRODUCTS
2043	CEREAL BREAKFAST FOODS
2044	RICE MILLING
2045	BLENDED & PREPARED FLOUR
2046	WET CORN MILLING
2047	DOG, CAT, & OTHER PET FOOD
2048	PREPARED FEEDS NEC
2051	BREAD, CAKE & RELATED PRODUCTS
2052	COOKIES & CRACKERS
2061	RAW CANE SUGAR
2062	CANE SUGAR REFINING
2063	BEET SUGAR
2065	CONFECTIONERY PRODUCTS
2066	CHOCOLATE & COCOA PRODUCTS
2067	CHEWING GUM
2074	COTTONSEED OIL MILLS
2075	SOYBEAN OIL MILLS
2076	VEGETABLE OIL MILLS NEC
2077	ANIMAL & MARINE FATS & OILS
2079	SHORTENING & COOKING OILS
2082	MALT BEVERAGES
2083	MALT
2084	WINES, BRANDY, & BRANDY SPIRITS
2085	DISTILLED LIQUOR EXC BRANDY [1]
2086	BOTTLED & CANNED SOFT DRINKS
2087	FLAVORING EXTRACTS & SIRUPS NEC
2091	CANNED & CURED SEAFOODS
2092	FRESH OR FROZEN PKGD FISH
2095	ROASTED COFFEE
2097	MANUFACTURED ICE
2098	MACARONI & SPHAGHETTI
2099	FOOD PREPARATIONS NEC
2211	WEAVING MILLS, COTTON
2221	WEAVING MILLS, SYNTHETICS
2231	WEAVING & FINISHING MILLS, WOOL
2257	CIRCULAR KNIT FABRIC MILLS
2258	WARP KNIT FABRIC MILLS
2281	YARN MILLS, EXC WOOL
2283	WOOL YARN MILLS
2284	THREAD MILLS
2311	MEN'S & BOY'S SUITS & COATS
2321	MEN'S & BOYS' SHIRTS & NIGHTWEAR
2327	MEN'S & BOYS' SEPARATE TROUSERS
2328	MEN'S & BOYS' WORK CLOTHING
2331	WOMEN'S & MISSES' BLOUSES & WAISTS
2335	WOMEN'S & MISSES' DRESSES
2337	WOMEN'S & MISSES' SUITS & COATS
2361	CHILDREN'S DRESSES & BLOUSES
2421	SAWMILLS & PLANING MILLS, GENERAL
2426	HARDWOOD DIMENSION & FLOORING
2435	HARDWOOD VENEER & PLYWOOD
2436	SOFTWOOD VENEER & PLYWOOD
2451	MOBILE HOMES
2511	WOOD HOUSEHOLD FURNITURE
2512	UPHOLSTERED HOUSEHOLD FURNITURE
2514	METAL HOUSEHOLD FURNITURE
2515	MATTRESSES & BEDSPRINGS
2517	WOOD TV & RADIO CABINETS
2519	HOUSEHOLD FURNITURE NEC
2541	WOOD PARTITIONS & FIXTURES
2611	PULPMILLS
2621	PAPERMILLS, EXC BUILDING PAPER
2631	PAPERBOARD MILLS
2641	PAPER COATING & GLAZING
2642	ENVELOPES
2643	BAGS, EXC TEXTILE BAGS
2645	DIE CUT PAPER & BOARD
2646	PRESSED & MOLDED PULP GOODS
2647	SANITARY PAPER PRODUCTS
2648	STATIONERY PRODUCTS
2649	CONVERTED PAPER PRODUCTS NEC
2651	FOLDING PAPERBOARD BOXES
2652	SET-UP PAPERBOARD BOXES
2653	CORRUGATED & SOLID FIBER BOXES
2654	SANITARY FOOD CONTAINERS
2655	FIBER CANS, DRUMS, & SIMILAR PRODUCTS
2661	BUILDING PAPER & BUILDING BOARD MILLS
2711	NEWSPAPERS
2721	PERIODICALS
2731	BOOK PUBLISHING
2732	BOOK PRINTING
2741	MISCELLANEOUS PUBLISHING
2751	COMMERCIAL PRINTING, LETTERPRESS
2752	COMMERCIAL PRINTING, LITHOGRAPHIC
2753	ENGRAVING & PLATE PRINTING
2754	COMMERCIAL PRINTING, GRAVURE
2761	MANIFOLD BUSINESS FORMS
2771	GREETING CARD PUBLISHING
2782	BLANKBOOKS & LOOSELEAF BINDERS
2789	BOOKBINDING & RELATED WORK
2791	TYPESETTING
2793	PHOTOENGRAVING
2794	ELECTROTYPING & STEREOTYPING
2795	LITHOGRAPHIC PLATEMAKING SERVICES
2812	ALKALIES & CHLORINE
2816	INORGANIC PIGMENTS
2819	INDUSTRIAL INORGANIC CHEMICALS NEC
2821	PLASTICS MATERIALS & RESINS
2822	SYNTHETIC RUBBER
2823	CELLULOSIC MAN-MADE FIBERS
2824	ORGANIC FIBERS, NONCELLULOSIC
2831	BIOLOGICAL PRODUCTS
2841	SOAP & OTHER DETERGENTS
2843	SURFACE ACTIVE AGENTS
2844	TOILET PREPARATIONS
2851	PAINTS & ALLIED PRODUCTS
2865	CYCLIC CRUDES & INTERMEDIATES
2869	INDUSTRIAL ORGANIC CHEMICALS NEC

1972 Code	SIC Title	1972 Code	SIC Title
2873	NITROGENOUS FERTILIZERS	3523	FARM MACHINERY & EQUIPMENT
2879	AGRICULTURAL CHEMICALS NEC	3524	LAWN & GARDEN EQUIPMENT
2895	CARBON BLACK	3531	CONSTRUCTION MACHINERY
2911	PETROLEUM REFINING	3532	MINING MACHINERY
3011	TIRES & INNER TUBES	3533	OILFIELD MACHINERY
3041	RUBBER & PLASTICS HOSE & BELTING	3534	ELEVATORS & MOVING STAIRWAYS
3069	FABRICATED RUBBER PRODUCTS NEC	3541	MACHINE TOOLS, METAL-CUTTING TYPES
3079	MISCELLANEOUS PLASTICS PRODUCTS	3542	MACHINE TOOLS, METAL-FORMING TYPES
3131	BOOT & SHOE CUT STOCK & FINDINGS	3544	SPECIAL DIES, TOOLS, JIGS, & FIXTURES
3142	HOUSE SLIPPERS	3545	MACHINE TOOL ACCESSORIES
3144	WOMEN'S FOOTWEAR EXC ATHLETIC	3551	FOOD PRODUCTS MACHINERY
3149	FOOTWEAR, EXC RUBBER, NEC	3552	TEXTILE MACHINERY
3151	LEATHER GLOVES & MITTENS	3555	PRINTING TRADES MACHINERY
3161	LUGGAGE	3561	PUMPS & PUMPING EQUIPMENT
3171	WOMEN'S HANDBAGS & PURSES	3563	AIR & GAS COMPRESSORS
3172	PERSONAL LEATHER GOODS NEC	3564	BLOWERS & FANS
3199	LEATHER GOODS NEC	3567	INDUSTRIAL FURNACES & OVENS
3211	FLAT GLASS	3573	ELECTRONIC COMPUTING EQUIPMENT
3221	GLASS CONTAINERS	3574	CALCULATING & ACCOUNTING MACHINES
3241	CEMENT, HYDRAULIC	3585	REFRIGERATION & HEATING EQUIPMENT
3261	VITREOUS PLUMBING FIXTURES	3612	TRANSFORMERS
3262	VITREOUS CHINA FOOD UTENSILS	3613	SWITCHGEAR & SWITCHBOARD APPARATUS
3263	FINE EARTHENWARE FOOD UTENSILS	3623	WELDING APPARATUS, ELECTRIC
3271	CONCRETE BLOCK & BRICK	3631	HOUSEHOLD COOKING EQUIPMENT
3272	CONCRETE PRODUCTS NEC	3632	HOUSEHOLD REFRIGERATORS & FREEZERS
3273	READY-MIXED CONCRETE	3633	HOUSEHOLD LAUNDRY EQUIPMENT
3312	BLAST FURNACES & STEEL MILLS	3634	ELECTRICAL HOUSEWARES & FANS
3313	ELECTROMETALLURGICAL PRODUCTS	3635	HOUSEHOLD VACUUM CLEANERS
3315	STEEL WIRE & RELATED PRODUCTS	3636	SEWING MACHINES
3316	COLD FINISHING OF STEEL SHAPES	3639	HOUSEHOLD APPLIANCES NEC
3317	STEEL PIPE & TUBES	3643	CURRENT CARRYING WIRING DEVICES
3321	GRAY IRON FOUNDRIES	3644	NONCURRENT CARRYING WIRING DEVICES
3322	MALLEABLE IRON FOUNDRIES	3645	RESIDENTIAL LIGHTING FIXTURES
3324	STEEL INVESTMENT FOUNDRIES	3646	COMMERCIAL LIGHTING FIXTURES
3325	STEEL FOUNDRIES NEC	3648	LIGHTING EQUIPMENT NEC
3331	PRIMARY COPPER	3651	RADIO & TV RECEIVING SETS
3332	PRIMARY LEAD	3652	PHONOGRAPH RECORDS
3333	PRIMARY ZINC	3661	TELEPHONE & TELEGRAPH APPARATUS
3334	PRIMARY ALUMINUM	3662	RADIO & TV COMMUNICATION EQUIPMENT
3339	PRIMARY NONFERROUS METALS NEC	3671	ELECTRON TUBES, RECEIVING TYPE [3]
3341	SECONDARY NONFERROUS METALS	3672	CATHODE RAY TELEVISION TUBES [3]
3351	COPPER ROLLING & DRAWING	3673	ELECTRON TUBES, TRANSMITTING [3]
3353	ALUMINUM SHEET, PLATE, & FOIL	3674	SEMICONDUCTORS & RELATED DEVICES
3354	ALUMINUM EXTRUDED PRODUCTS	3675	ELECTRONIC CAPACITORS
3355	ALUMINUM ROLLING & DRAWING NEC	3676	ELECTRONIC RESISTORS
3357	NONFERROUS WIREDRAWING & INSULATING	3677	ELECTRONIC COILS & TRANSFORMERS
3361	ALUMINUM FOUNDRIES (CASTINGS)	3678	ELECTRONIC CONNECTORS
3362	BRASS, BRONZE, & COPPER FOUNDRIES	3679	ELECTRONIC COMPONENTS NEC
3369	NONFERROUS FOUNDRIES NEC	3693	X-RAY APPARATUS & TUBES
3398	METAL HEAT TREATING	3711	MOTOR VEHICLES & CAR BODIES
3399	PRIMARY METAL PRODUCTS NEC	3713	TRUCK & BUS BODIES (INCL MOTOR HOMES) [4]
3411	METAL CANS	3715	TRUCK TRAILERS
3431	METAL SANITARY WARE	3721	AIRCRAFT
3432	PLUMBING FITTINGS & BRASS GOODS	3724	AIRCRAFT ENGINES & ENGINE PARTS
3433	HEATING EQUIPMENT EXC ELECTRIC	3728	AIRCRAFT EQUIPMENT NEC
3441	FABRICATED STRUCTURAL METAL	3731	SHIP BUILDING AND REPAIR [1]
3443	FABRICATED PLATEWORK (BOILER SHOPS)	3743	RAILROAD EQUIPMENT
3462	IRON & STEEL FORGINGS	3751	MOTORCYCLES, BICYCLES & PARTS
3463	NONFERROUS FORGINGS	3761	GUIDED MISSILES & SPACE VEHICLES
3465	AUTOMOTIVE STAMPINGS	3764	SPACE PROPULSION UNITS & PARTS
3482	SMALL ARMS AMMUNITION	3769	SPACE VEHICLE EQUIPMENT NEC
3483	AMMUNITION, EXC FOR SMALL ARMS NEC	3811	ENGINEERING & SCIENTIFIC INSTRUMENTS
3484	SMALL ARMS	3822	ENVIRONMENTAL CONTROLS
3511	TURBINES & TURBINE GENERATOR SETS	3823	PROCESS CONTROL INSTRUMENTS

1972 Code	SIC Title
3824	FLUID METERS & COUNTING DEVICES
3825	INSTRUMENTS TO MEASURE ELECTRICITY
3829	MEASURING & CONTROLLING DEVICES NEC
3832	OPTICAL INSTRUMENTS & LENSES
3841	SURGICAL & MEDICAL INSTRUMENTS
3843	DENTAL EQUIPMENT & SUPPLIES
3911	JEWELRY, PRECIOUS METAL
3914	SILVERWARE & PLATED WARE
3942	DOLLS
3944	GAMES, TOYS, & CHILDREN'S VEHICLES
3949	SPORTING & ATHLETIC GOODS NEC
3961	COSTUME JEWELRY

[1] Represents value of production or value of work done.
[2] Combination of SICs 3572 and 3579.
[3] Beginning in 1977, value of shipments data are combined for SICs 3671, 3672 and 3673.
[4] Combination of SICs 3713 and 3716.
Definitions: Constant dollar industry shipments data are derived by applying 4-digit industry deflators calculated by the Bureau of Economic Analysis to 4-digit current dollar industry shipments data published by the Bureau of the Census.
Source: Bureau of Economic Analysis and Bureau of the Census.
Source: *U.S. Industrial Outlook,* 1981.

PRESENT VALUE OF $1

Periods until Payment	1%	2%	4%	6%	8%	10%	12%	14%	15%	16%	18%	20%	22%	24%	25%	26%	28%	30%	35%	40%	45%	50%
1	0.990	0.980	0.962	0.943	0.926	0.909	0.893	0.877	0.870	0.862	0.847	0.833	0.820	0.806	0.800	0.794	0.781	0.769	0.741	0.714	0.690	0.667
2	0.980	0.961	0.925	0.890	0.857	0.826	0.797	0.769	0.756	0.743	0.718	0.694	0.672	0.650	0.640	0.630	0.610	0.592	0.549	0.510	0.476	0.444
3	0.971	0.942	0.889	0.840	0.794	0.751	0.712	0.675	0.658	0.641	0.609	0.579	0.551	0.524	0.512	0.500	0.477	0.455	0.406	0.364	0.328	0.296
4	0.961	0.924	0.855	0.792	0.735	0.683	0.636	0.592	0.572	0.552	0.516	0.482	0.451	0.423	0.410	0.397	0.373	0.350	0.301	0.260	0.226	0.198
5	0.951	0.906	0.822	0.747	0.681	0.621	0.567	0.519	0.497	0.476	0.437	0.402	0.370	0.341	0.328	0.315	0.291	0.269	0.223	0.186	0.156	0.132
6	0.942	0.888	0.790	0.705	0.630	0.564	0.507	0.456	0.432	0.410	0.370	0.335	0.303	0.275	0.262	0.250	0.227	0.207	0.165	0.133	0.108	0.088
7	0.933	0.871	0.760	0.665	0.583	0.513	0.452	0.400	0.376	0.354	0.314	0.279	0.249	0.222	0.210	0.198	0.178	0.159	0.122	0.095	0.074	0.059
8	0.923	0.853	0.731	0.627	0.540	0.467	0.404	0.351	0.327	0.305	0.266	0.233	0.204	0.179	0.168	0.157	0.139	0.123	0.091	0.068	0.051	0.039
9	0.914	0.837	0.703	0.592	0.500	0.424	0.361	0.308	0.284	0.263	0.225	0.194	0.167	0.144	0.134	0.125	0.108	0.094	0.067	0.048	0.035	0.026
10	0.905	0.820	0.676	0.558	0.463	0.386	0.322	0.270	0.247	0.227	0.191	0.162	0.137	0.116	0.107	0.099	0.085	0.073	0.050	0.035	0.024	0.017
11	0.896	0.804	0.650	0.527	0.429	0.350	0.287	0.237	0.215	0.195	0.162	0.135	0.112	0.094	0.086	0.079	0.066	0.056	0.037	0.025	0.017	0.012
12	0.887	0.788	0.625	0.497	0.397	0.319	0.257	0.208	0.187	0.168	0.137	0.112	0.092	0.076	0.069	0.062	0.052	0.043	0.027	0.018	0.012	0.008
13	0.879	0.773	0.601	0.469	0.368	0.290	0.229	0.182	0.163	0.145	0.116	0.093	0.075	0.061	0.055	0.050	0.040	0.033	0.020	0.013	0.008	0.005
14	0.870	0.758	0.577	0.442	0.340	0.263	0.205	0.160	0.141	0.125	0.099	0.078	0.062	0.049	0.044	0.039	0.032	0.025	0.015	0.009	0.006	0.003
15	0.861	0.743	0.555	0.417	0.315	0.239	0.183	0.140	0.123	0.108	0.084	0.065	0.051	0.040	0.035	0.031	0.025	0.020	0.011	0.006	0.004	0.002
16	0.853	0.728	0.534	0.394	0.292	0.218	0.163	0.123	0.107	0.093	0.071	0.054	0.042	0.032	0.028	0.025	0.019	0.015	0.008	0.005	0.003	0.002
17	0.844	0.714	0.513	0.371	0.270	0.198	0.146	0.108	0.093	0.080	0.060	0.045	0.034	0.026	0.023	0.020	0.015	0.012	0.006	0.003	0.002	0.001
18	0.836	0.700	0.494	0.350	0.250	0.180	0.130	0.095	0.081	0.069	0.051	0.038	0.028	0.021	0.018	0.016	0.012	0.009	0.005	0.002	0.001	0.001
19	0.828	0.686	0.475	0.331	0.232	0.164	0.116	0.083	0.070	0.060	0.043	0.031	0.023	0.017	0.014	0.012	0.009	0.007	0.003	0.002	0.001	
20	0.820	0.673	0.456	0.312	0.215	0.149	0.104	0.073	0.061	0.051	0.037	0.026	0.019	0.014	0.012	0.010	0.007	0.005	0.002	0.001	0.001	
21	0.811	0.660	0.439	0.294	0.199	0.135	0.093	0.064	0.053	0.044	0.031	0.022	0.015	0.011	0.009	0.008	0.006	0.004	0.002	0.001		
22	0.803	0.647	0.422	0.278	0.184	0.123	0.083	0.056	0.046	0.038	0.026	0.018	0.013	0.009	0.007	0.006	0.004	0.003	0.002	0.001		
23	0.795	0.634	0.406	0.262	0.170	0.112	0.074	0.049	0.040	0.033	0.022	0.015	0.010	0.007	0.006	0.005	0.003	0.002	0.001			
24	0.788	0.622	0.390	0.247	0.158	0.102	0.066	0.043	0.035	0.028	0.019	0.013	0.008	0.006	0.005	0.004	0.003	0.002	0.001			
25	0.780	0.610	0.375	0.233	0.146	0.092	0.059	0.038	0.030	0.024	0.016	0.010	0.007	0.005	0.004	0.003	0.002	0.001	0.001			
26	0.772	0.598	0.361	0.220	0.135	0.084	0.053	0.033	0.026	0.021	0.014	0.009	0.006	0.004	0.003	0.002	0.002	0.001				
27	0.764	0.586	0.347	0.207	0.125	0.076	0.047	0.029	0.023	0.018	0.011	0.007	0.005	0.003	0.002	0.002	0.001	0.001				
28	0.757	0.574	0.333	0.196	0.116	0.069	0.042	0.026	0.020	0.016	0.010	0.006	0.004	0.002	0.002	0.001	0.001	0.001				
29	0.749	0.563	0.321	0.185	0.107	0.063	0.037	0.022	0.017	0.014	0.008	0.005	0.003	0.002	0.001	0.001	0.001	0.001				
30	0.742	0.552	0.308	0.174	0.099	0.057	0.033	0.020	0.015	0.012	0.007	0.004	0.003	0.002	0.001	0.001						
40	0.672	0.453	0.208	0.097	0.046	0.022	0.011	0.005	0.004	0.003	0.001	0.001										
50	0.608	0.372	0.141	0.054	0.021	0.009	0.003	0.001	0.001	0.001												

SOURCE. By permission, from Robert N. Anthony, Management Accounting: Text and Cases, rev. ed. (Homewood, Ill.: Richard D. Irwin, Inc., 1960), p. 656.

Financial Statement Ratios by Industry

Many quantitative indicators are used to assess the financial strength of an enterprise and the success of its operations. The simplest is to assemble related financial items, such as sales and profits, and express the relationship in the form of a ratio. Using these ratios, various aspects of company operations may be compared with the performance of other companies or groups of companies of similar size or in a similar line of business.

The Quarterly Financial Report's (QFR) ratio formatted income statement and balance sheet tables are expressed as a percent of net sales and total assets, respectively. The operating and financial characteristics of the respective industries and asset size groups are thus reduced to a common denominator to facilitate analysis.

The ratio tables include the following additional basic operating ratios:

1. *Annual rate of profit on stockholders' equity at end of the period* is a ratio obtained by dividing income for the quarter before or after domestic taxes [including branch income (loss) and equity in the earnings of nonconsolidated subsidiaries net of foreign taxes] by stockholders' equity at the end of the quarter; all multiplied by four to put the ratio on annual basis.

2. *Current assets to current liabilities* is a ratio obtained by dividing total current assets by total current liabilities. It is expressed as the number of times total current assets cover total current liabilities.

3. *Total cash, U.S. government and other securities to total current liabilities* is a ratio obtained by dividing total cash, U.S. government and other securities by total current liabilities. It is expressed as the number of times (usually less than one) that such assets cover total current liabilities.

4. *Total stockholders' equity to debt* is a ratio obtained by dividing total stockholders' equity by the total of short-term loans, current installments on long-term debt, and long-term debt due in more than one year. It is expressed as the number of times total stockholders' equity covers the total debt as defined above.

5. *Annual rate of profit on total assets* is a ratio obtained by dividing income, as defined in deriving the rate of profit on stockholders'

equity, both before and after taxes, by total assets at the end of the quarter. The result is multiplied by four to put the ratio on an annual basis.

DESCRIPTION OF THE SAMPLE

The sample on which the QFR estimates for mining and wholesale and retail trade are based is a composite sample selected from two mutually exclusive sampling frames. Prior to the third quarter 1977, the sample drawn for manufacturing estimates was similarly based. The frame from which the major portion of the sample continues to be selected consists of the Internal Revenue Service file of those corporate entities which are required to file Form 1120 or 1120-S and which also have as their principal industrial activity manufacturing, mining, or wholesale or retail trade. The IRS file is sampled once each year. At the time the sample is selected, the file does not contain those corporate entities whose first income tax return has not been processed. In addition, several months elapse between the selection of this sample and its inroduction into the QFR program. To keep the mining and wholesale and retail trade QFR sample as up to date as possible, a separate sample is drawn each calendar quarter from a frame comprising applications for a Federal Social Security Employer's Identification Number filed with the Social Security Administration (SSA) during the previous quarter by new corporations. In processing the composite list of sample companies, a screening technique is used to insure that corporations drawn from the SSA frame could not have been drawn from the IRS frame.

In sampling from the IRS frame, stratification by industry and size is employed, but in sampling from the SSA frame, stratification is by size alone. The measure of size used in the IRS frame is total assets, while the measure of size used in the SSA frame is number of employees. Beginning with the third quarter 1977, the stratum comprised of manufacturing firms with assets of less than $250,000 is estimated by multivariant techniques. The sampling fractions applied to the other various industry-size strata vary according to both industry and size. They range from approximately one out of 350 to one out of one. Nearly all corporations with assets greater than $10 million that fall into the industries covered are included in the sample. Thus, "large" corporations are permanent sam-

Source: Quarterly Financial Report, Federal Trade Commission. The exhibits in this section are from the same FTC publication.

ple members, with a one out of one sampling fraction.

In those industry-size strata for which the sampling fraction is less than one out of one, a replacement scheme is utilized which provides that one eighth of the sample is replaced each quarter. Corporations removed are those that have been in the reporting group longest (usually eight quarters). Therefore, samples of small companies for adjacent quarters are seven-eighths identical; for quarters ending six months apart they are six-eighths identical; for quarters ending nine months apart they are five-eighths identical; etc.

PRECISION OF THE ESTIMATES

More than 3,000 aggregates or ratios are estimated each quarter. Each estimate has its own standard deviation, which indicates the difference that can be expected due to sampling between the estimate and a comparable total based on a complete canvass. An estimate will differ from a comparable total based on a complete canvass by less than one standard deviation approximately 68 times out of 100, by less than two standard deviations approximately 95 times out of 100, and by less than two and one-half standard deviations approximately 99 times out of 100. The sample is designed so that one standard deviation of the estimate for the item, "Income before income taxes and extraordinary items," for all manufacturing corporations amounts to approximately one half of 1 percent of that estimated aggregate. For most of the manufacturing industry groups, one standard deviation of the estimate for the same item amounts to less than 5 percent of the estimated aggregate, while the comparable figure for mining is approximately 5 percent and for retail trade and wholesale trade approximately 9 percent each.

Each report form received is reviewed by FTC accountants for adherence to generally accepted accounting principles and QFR guidelines. Should QFR requirements dictate a classification of data different from the reporting corporation's accounting, the accountant is responsible for reclassifying or adjusting the data item. If complex problems arise, reporting company officials are contacted to discuss proposed adjustments. In the review, the retained earnings reported in a company's balance sheet must be the same as the end-of-quarter retained earnings reported in the income statement, the retained earnings at the quarter's end must reconcile with those at the beginning of the quarter, and the retained earnings at the beginning of the quarter must be the same as at the end of the preceding quarter. Since corporations are added to and deleted from the sample each quarter, and since corporations are reclassified periodically by industry and size, *aggregated* estimates of retained earnings at the beginning of a quarter are seldom identical to the estimates of retained earnings at the end of the preceding quarter.

EXHIBIT 1:   INCOME STATEMENT FOR CORPORATIONS IN ALL MANUFACTURING, FOOD, TOBACCO, TEXTILE MILL PRODUCTS (ESIC industries 20, 21, 22)

	All Manufacturing*				
	1Q 1980	2Q 1980	3Q 1980	4Q 1980	1Q 1981
Income statement in ratio format	(percent of net sales)				
Net sales, receipts & operating revenues	100.0	100.0	100.0	100.0	100.0
Deduct: Depreciation, depletion, and amortization of property, plant and equipment	3.0	3.1	3.1	3.1	3.1
Deduct: All other operating costs and expenses (net of purchase discounts).......................................	89.7	90.1	90.4	90.5	90.3
Income (or loss) from operations	7.4	6.8	6.5	6.5	6.6
Non-operating income (expense)	−0.4	−0.3	−0.6	−0.4	−0.2
Income (or loss) before income taxes	7.0	6.4	6.0	6.1	6.4
Net income (loss) of foreign branches and equity in earnings (losses) of non-consolidated subsidiaries (net of foreign taxes)......................................	1.5	1.3	1.2	1.3	1.1
Deduct: Current and deferred domestic income taxes	3.2	2.9	2.7	2.5	2.8
Income (or loss) after income taxes	5.3	4.8	4.5	4.8	4.7
Operating ratios	(percent)				
Annual rate of profit on stockholders' equity at end of period:					
Before taxes	24.54	21.83	19.79	21.42	21.52
After taxes..	15.39	13.63	12.52	14.12	13.44
Annual rate of profit on total assets:					
Before income taxes	12.24	10.95	9.82	10.63	10.56
After taxes...	7.68	6.84	6.21	7.01	6.59

* During the first quarter of 1981 a considerable number of companies were reclassified by industry. To provide comparability, the four quarters of 1980 have been restated to reflect these reclassifications.

Food and Kindred Products*					Tobacco Manufactures*					Textile Mill Products*				
1Q 1980	2Q 1980	3Q 1980	4Q 1980	1Q 1981	1Q 1980	2Q 1980	3Q 1980	4Q 1980	1Q 1981	1Q 1980	2Q 1980	3Q 1980	4Q 1980	1Q 1981
(percent of net sales)					(percent of net sales)					(percent of net sales)				
100.0	100.0	100.0	100.0	100.0	100.0	100.0	100.0	100.0	100.0	100.0	100.0	100.0	100.0	100.0
1.8	1.8	1.8	1.8	1.9	2.2	3.3	2.7	2.4	2.9	2.5	2.5	2.6	2.5	2.6
93.3	92.9	92.7	92.7	93.2	79.9	79.2	78.5	83.0	80.7	91.7	92.3	92.6	92.4	92.4
4.9	5.3	5.5	5.5	4.9	17.8	17.6	18.8	14.5	16.4	5.9	5.2	4.8	5.1	4.9
−0.5	−0.6	−0.5	0.0	−0.5	−4.1	−2.3	−3.0	−3.4	−3.2	−0.8	−1.1	−1.1	−1.3	−1.1
4.3	4.7	5.0	5.5	4.4	13.8	15.2	15.8	11.1	13.3	5.0	4.1	3.7	3.8	3.9
0.5	0.5	0.5	0.6	0.5	6.0	3.6	4.7	3.1	5.2	0.1	0.0	−0.1	0.0	0.1
1.8	2.1	2.1	2.1	1.9	6.8	6.9	7.6	5.4	6.0	2.2	2.1	1.8	1.7	1.7
3.0	3.1	3.5	4.0	3.0	13.0	12.0	13.0	8.8	12.5	2.8	2.1	1.8	2.2	2.3
(percent)					(percent					(percent)				
20.45	22.30	24.23	26.10	20.36	32.26	32.01	35.19	24.68	31.29	19.69	15.97	13.30	15.26	15.63
12.84	13.47	15.15	17.39	12.57	21.25	20.32	22.25	15.27	21.17	10.96	7.92	6.63	8.60	8.83
9.95	11.06	11.90	12.65	9.83	16.28	16.59	17.71	12.30	15.12	10.10	8.20	6.71	7.66	7.73
6.25	6.68	7.44	8.43	6.07	10.69	10.53	11.20	7.61	10.23	5.62	4.07	3.35	4.31	4.36

EXHIBIT 2:   BALANCE SHEET IN RATIO FORMAT FOR CORPORATIONS
IN ALL MANUFACTURING, FOOD, TOBACCO, TEXTILE MILL PRODUCTS
(ESIC industries 20, 21, 22)

ITEMS STATED AS A PERCENT OF TOTAL ASSETS

	All Manufacturing*				
	1Q 1980	2Q 1980	3Q 1980	4Q 1980	1Q 1981
Assets					
Cash on hand and in banks	3.2	3.1	3.1	3.2	3.3
U.S. Government and other securities	2.0	1.9	1.9	2.1	1.9
Receivables	17.5	17.2	17.3	16.8	17.1
Inventories	20.9	20.9	20.1	19.6	19.8
Current assets not elsewhere specified	2.7	2.7	2.8	2.8	2.8
Total current assets	46.3	45.7	45.2	44.5	44.9
Land and depreciable fixed assets	62.6	63.2	63.5	63.7	63.4
Deduct: Accumulated depreciation, depletion					
& amortization	27.3	27.5	27.4	27.1	27.0
Net property, plant & equipment	35.3	35.7	36.0	36.6	36.4
Non-current assets not elsewhere specified, including investment in non-consolidated entities, other long term investments,					
intangibles, etc.	18.4	18.6	18.8	18.9	18.6
Total assets	100.0	100.0	100.0	100.0	100.0
Liabilities and stockholders' equity					
Short-term loans & current installments	5.4	5.3	5.4	4.9	5.1
Trade accounts and trade notes payable	9.8	9.4	9.3	9.8	9.7
Income taxes accrued, prior and current years, net of payments					
a. Federal	2.3	1.9	2.0	1.9	2.1
b. Other	0.4	0.4	0.4	0.4	0.4
Other current liabilities	9.7	9.7	9.8	9.7	10.0
Total current liabilities	27.5	26.7	26.9	26.7	27.2
Long-term debt due in more than 1 year					
a. Loans from banks	4.0	4.0	4.0	4.0	4.1
b. Other long-term debt	12.3	12.7	12.9	12.7	12.6
Non-current liabilities not elsewhere specified, including					
deferred income taxes	6.1	6.2	6.4	6.7	6.9
Minority stockholders' interest in consolidated					
domestic corporations	0.2	0.2	0.2	0.2	0.2
Total liabilities	50.1	49.8	50.4	50.4	50.9
Capital stock and other capital	13.0	13.0	12.8	12.7	12.7
Retained earnings	37.9	38.2	37.8	37.9	37.4
Deduct: Treasury stock, at cost	1.0	1.0	1.0	1.0	1.0
Stockholders' equity	49.9	50.2	49.6	49.6	49.1
Total liabilities and stockholders' equity	100.0	100.0	100.0	100.0	100.0
Balance sheet ratios			(times)		
Current assets to current liabilities	1.68	1.71	1.68	1.66	1.65
Total cash, U.S. Government and other securities to total					
current liabilities	.19	.19	.19	.20	.19
Total stockholders' equity to debt	2.30	2.28	2.23	2.30	2.26

* During the first quarter of 1981 a considerable number od companies were reclassified by industry. To provide comparability, the four quarters of 1980 have been restated to reflect these reclassifications.

Food and Kindred Products*					Tobacco Manufactures*					Textile Mill Products*				
1Q 1980	2Q 1980	3Q 1980	4Q 1980	1Q 1981	1Q 1980	2Q 1980	3Q 1980	4Q 1980	1Q 1981	1Q 1980	2Q 1980	3Q 1980	4Q 1980	1Q 1981
2.8	3.1	2.9	3.0	4.7	0.9	1.1	1.2	0.3	0.6	3.3	3.2	4.1	4.0	3.4
1.6	2.0	2.0	2.4	2.4	0.4	0.9	0.8	0.8	1.1	2.1	1.7	2.2	2.1	1.8
16.2	16.1	16.3	16.0	15.7	8.9	10.8	11.3	12.3	12.3	26.4	26.2	26.4	25.7	25.2
24.1	23.0	22.5	23.3	22.6	27.9	25.3	26.1	26.1	25.7	28.2	28.9	26.6	26.7	29.3
2.6	2.4	2.9	2.6	2.6	1.6	1.3	1.3	1.4	1.3	2.1	2.2	2.4	2.6	2.5
47.3	46.6	46.6	47.4	48.0	39.8	39.3	40.6	40.9	41.0	62.1	62.2	61.7	61.2	62.2
59.7	60.7	59.5	57.4	58.0	32.0	33.1	32.5	32.9	32.9	74.5	74.6	74.8	76.8	75.0
24.5	24.9	24.2	23.3	23.5	9.6	10.0	9.9	9.8	9.4	42.0	42.1	41.8	43.0	42.4
35.2	35.9	35.2	34.1	34.6	22.4	23.1	22.5	23.0	23.5	32.5	32.4	33.0	33.7	32.7
17.5	17.5	18.2	18.6	17.4	37.8	37.6	36.9	36.1	35.6	5.4	5.4	5.3	5.1	5.1
100.0	100.0	100.0	100.0	100.0	100.0	100.0	100.0	100.0	100.0	100.0	100.0	100.0	100.0	100.0
9.2	8.0	8.3	8.4	8.3	5.2	3.8	4.4	4.1	4.9	6.6	7.2	7.1	5.7	6.5
10.5	10.6	10.9	11.4	10.5	3.3	3.2	4.0	4.1	3.5	13.4	12.4	12.7	13.9	13.7
1.5	1.5	1.6	1.7	1.6	2.2	1.3	1.4	1.7	2.1	1.3	1.1	1.1	1.1	1.0
0.4	0.4	0.5	0.4	0.4	0.7	0.7	0.8	0.7	0.9	0.2	0.2	0.2	0.3	0.2
6.8	6.9	6.9	6.6	6.9	9.8	10.9	12.6	11.7	12.0	6.4	6.4	6.5	6.4	6.5
28.4	27.3	28.2	28.6	27.8	21.3	20.0	23.1	22.2	23.3	27.8	27.4	27.5	27.3	27.9
4.3	4.6	4.4	4.6	4.9	13.0	12.8	12.1	12.5	12.4	5.0	5.6	6.6	6.6	7.1
13.5	13.5	13.3	1.31	13.2	11.1	11.9	11.0	12.0	12.3	12.6	12.5	12.2	12.4	12.2
4.8	4.7	4.8	4.9	5.6	4.2	3.4	3.4	3.5	3.5	3.2	3.0	3.1	3.3	3.2
0.2	0.2	0.2	0.2	0.3	0.1	0.1	0.1	0.1	0.1	0.2	0.2	0.2	0.2	0.2
51.4	50.4	50.9	51.5	51.7	49.7	48.2	49.7	50.2	51.7	48.7	48.6	49.5	49.8	50.6
13.0	13.1	12.7	12.3	12.4	11.2	11.1	10.1	9.8	10.4	13.4	13.1	13.3	12.7	12.0
36.5	37.4	37.3	37.1	36.9	40.7	42.2	41.6	41.6	39.6	39.9	40.2	39.1	39.6	39.4
0.9	0.9	0.9	1.0	0.9	1.6	1.5	1.4	1.5	1.6	2.0	2.0	1.9	2.1	2.0
48.6	49.6	49.1	48.5	48.3	50.3	51.8	50.3	49.8	48.3	51.3	51.4	50.5	50.2	49.4
100.0	100.0	100.0	100.0	100.0	100.0	100.0	100.0	100.0	100.0	100.0	100.0	100.0	100.0	100.0
		(times)					(times)					(times)		
1.66	1.70	1.66	1.66	1.73	1.87	1.96	1.75	1.84	1.75	2.23	2.27	2.24	2.24	2.23
.16	.19	.17	.19	.26	.06	.10	.08	.05	.07	.19	.18	.23	.22	.19
1.80	1.90	1.89	1.85	1.83	1.71	1.81	1.83	1.75	1.64	2.13	2.03	1.96	2.03	1.92

EXHIBIT 3: INCOME STATEMENT FOR CORPORATIONS IN PRINTING AND PUBLISHING, CHEMICALS, DRUGS (ESIC industries 27, 28, 28.1, 28.3)

	Printing and Publishing*				
	1Q 1980	2Q 1980	3Q 1980	4Q 1980	1Q 1981
Income statement in ratio format	(percent of net sales)				
Net sales, receipts & operating revenues	100.0	100.0	100.0	100.0	100.0
Deduct: Depreciation, depletion, and amortization of property, plant and equipment	2.7	2.7	2.7	2.7	2.9
Deduct: All other operating costs and expenses (net of purchase discounts).....................................	88.4	87.7	87.5	88.0	88.9
Income (or loss) from operations	8.9	9.6	9.8	9.3	8.2
Non-operating income (expense)	−0.1	−0.1	−0.4	−0.1	−0.1
Income (or loss) before income taxes	8.8	9.5	9.4	9.3	8.3
Net income (loss) of foreign branches and equity in earnings (losses) of non-consolidated subsidiaries (net of foreign taxes)	0.3	0.4	0.6	0.2	0.2
Deduct: Current and deferred domestic income taxes	3.9	4.4	4.2	4.1	3.7
Income (or loss) after income taxes	5.1	5.6	5.8	5.5	4.8
Operating ratios	(percent)				
Annual rate of profit on stockholders' equity at end of period:					
Before income taxes	26.52	29.31	29.82	29.06	24.04
After taxes	14.97	14.77	14.66	14.38	13.64
Annual rate of profit on total assets:					
Before income taxes	13.32	14.77	14.66	14.38	12.01
After taxes	7.52	8.29	8.47	8.28	6.82

* During the first quarter of 1981 a considerable number of companies were reclassified by industry. To provide comparability, the four quarters of 1980 have been restated to reflect these reclassifications.
† Included in Chemicals and Allied Products.

	Chemicals and Allied Products*					Industrial Chemicals and Synthetics*†					Drugs†				
	1Q 1980	2Q 1980	3Q 1980	4Q 1980	1Q 1981	1Q 1980	2Q 1980	3Q 1980	4Q 1980	1Q 1981	1Q 1980	2Q 1980	3Q 1980	4Q 1980	1Q 1981
	(percent of net sales)					(percent of net sales)					(percent of net sales)				
	100.0	100.0	100.0	100.0	100.0	100.0	100.0	100.0	100.0	100.0	100.0	100.0	100.0	100.0	100.0
	3.5	3.6	3.8	4.0	3.7	4.6	5.0	5.3	5.6	4.9	2.4	2.5	2.3	2.4	2.4
	86.1	88.1	88.2	88.2	86.3	85.4	88.1	89.3	87.1	85.6	85.0	88.6	87.0	88.4	86.0
	10.5	8.3	8.0	7.9	10.0	10.0	6.9	5.4	7.3	9.4	12.6	8.9	10.7	9.2	11.7
	−0.4	0.2	0.0	−0.8	−0.7	−1.0	0.2	−0.6	−1.5	−0.8	1.5	1.3	2.5	0.2	−2.6
	10.1	8.5	8.0	7.1	9.3	9.0	7.1	4.8	5.7	8.7	14.2	10.2	13.2	9.4	9.1
	2.2	2.0	2.0	1.9	1.6	1.6	1.1	0.9	0.7	0.8	6.4	7.3	7.5	6.2	5.9
	4.3	3.4	2.9	2.7	3.6	3.8	2.5	1.0	2.0	3.0	6.5	5.1	5.6	4.2	4.6
	8.0	7.1	7.1	6.3	7.3	6.8	5.7	4.7	4.5	6.5	14.0	12.4	15.1	11.3	10.4
	(percent)					(percent)					(percent)				
	27.59	22.53	21.08	19.07	24.41	24.88	17.71	11.75	14.04	21.83	31.67	25.71	31.01	23.28	23.73
	17.95	15.25	14.95	13.31	16.25	15.99	12.26	9.61	9.74	14.91	21.64	18.28	22.62	16.94	16.42
	14.68	12.10	11.27	10.17	12.91	12.36	8.91	5.85	7.00	10.84	19.27	15.57	18.72	13.98	14.08
	9.55	8.19	7.99	7.10	8.60	7.94	6.17	4.79	4.86	7.40	13.17	11.07	13.65	10.17	9.74

EXHIBIT 4: BALANCE SHEET IN RATIO FORMAT FOR CORPORATIONS IN PRINTING AND PUBLISHING, CHEMICALS, DRUGS (ESIC industries, 27, 28, 28.1, 28.3)

ITEMS STATED AS A PERCENT OF TOTAL ASSETS

	Printing and Publishing*				
	1Q 1980	2Q 1980	3Q 1980	4Q 1980	1Q 1981
Assets					
Cash on hand and in banks	5.3	5.1	5.1	5.5	5.4
U.S. Government and other securities	3.2	2.5	2.5	2.9	3.2
Receivables	19.6	19.7	20.7	20.4	19.7
Inventories	12.4	12.5	12.1	11.3	11.6
Current assets not elsewhere specified	4.6	4.8	4.6	4.7	4.7
Total current assets	45.2	44.5	45.1	44.8	44.5
Land and depreciable fixed assets	54.5	55.1	55.0	54.8	55.8
Deduct: Accumulated depreciation, depletion & amortization	22.6	22.9	22.8	22.5	22.9
Net property, plant & equipment	31.8	32.3	32.3	32.3	32.8
Non-current assets not elsewhere specified, including investment in non-consolidated entities, other long term investments, intangibles, etc.	23.0	23.2	22.7	22.9	22.7
Total assets	100.00	100.0	100.0	100.0	100.0
Liabilities and stockholders' equity					
Short-term loans & current installments	4.5	4.9	5.3	4.4	4.1
Trade accounts and trade notes payable	8.7	8.4	8.5	8.7	8.5
Income taxes accrued, prior and current years, net of payments					
a. Federal	2.4	1.8	1.9	1.8	2.0
b. Other	0.4	0.3	0.4	0.5	0.5
Other current liabilities	7.5	7.8	7.8	8.1	8.2
Total current liabilities	23.6	23.1	23.8	23.6	23.2
Long-term debt due in more than 1 year					
a. Loans from banks	7.0	6.7	7.1	7.0	6.9
b. Other long-term debt	10.9	12.0	11.6	11.5	11.3
Non-current liabilities not elsewhere specified, including deferred incomes taxes	7.9	7.6	7.9	8.1	8.3
Minority stockholders' interest in consolidated domestic corporations	0.4	0.4	0.4	0.4	0.4
Total liabilities	49.8	49.6	50.8	50.5	50.0
Capital stock and other capital	11.2	11.4	10.4	10.8	11.2
Retained earnings	41.1	41.2	40.8	40.7	40.8
Deduct: Treasury stock, at cost	2.1	2.2	2.1	2.0	2.0
Stockholders' equity	50.2	50.4	49.2	49.5	50.0
Total liabilities and stockholders' equity	100.0	100.0	100.0	100.0	100.0
Balance sheet ratios			(times)		
Current assets to current liabilities	1.92	1.93	1.89	1.90	1.92
Total cash, U.S. Government and other securities to total current liabilities	.36	.33	.32	.36	.37
Total stockholders' equity to debt	2.23	2.15	2.04	2.16	2.24

* During the first quarter of 1981 a considerable number of companies were reclassified by industry. To provide comparability, the four quarters of 1980 have been restated to reflect these reclassifications.

† Included in Chemicals and Allied Products.

	Chemicals and Allied Products*					Industrial Chemicals and Synthetics*†					Drugs†				
	1Q 1980	2Q 1980	3Q 1980	4Q 1980	1Q 1981	1Q 1980	2Q 1980	3Q 1980	4Q 1980	1Q 1981	1Q 1980	2Q 1980	3Q 1980	4Q 1980	1Q 1981
	2.4	2.4	2.6	2.4	2.5	1.5	1.6	1.8	1.2	1.5	3.9	3.0	3.3	3.5	4.0
	1.2	1.2	1.3	1.4	1.4	1.0	0.9	1.2	1.2	1.3	0.3	0.8	0.3	0.1	0.2
	17.3	16.4	16.6	16.1	17.3	18.3	17.1	16.9	16.8	18.0	14.2	13.4	14.5	14.4	15.2
	17.5	17.9	16.7	16.6	16.6	14.9	15.5	14.5	14.4	14.3	18.0	18.7	17.8	17.5	17.2
	3.0	2.8	3.0	2.9	2.7	3.0	2.6	2.8	2.6	2.3	3.5	3.4	3.8	3.9	3.8
	41.4	40.6	40.3	30.4	40.5	38.6	37.7	37.1	36.1	37.3	40.0	39.2	39.8	39.4	40.4
	69.0	69.6	69.9	70.1	69.3	87.1	88.4	88.6	89.1	87.5	39.7	39.6	39.4	39.6	39.5
	30.8	31.0	31.0	30.7	30.4	42.3	42.8	42.7	42.5	41.8	15.2	15.1	14.8	14.7	14.7
	38.2	38.7	38.9	39.4	38.9	44.8	45.6	46.0	46.6	45.7	24.6	24.5	24.5	24.9	24.8
	20.4	20.7	20.8	21.2	20.6	16.6	16.7	16.9	17.2	17.0	35.5	36.3	35.7	35.7	34.8
	100.0	100.0	100.0	100.0	100.0	100.0	100.0	100.0	100.0	100.0	100.0	100.0	100.0	100.0	100.0
	4.9	5.2	4.7	4.5	4.2	4.8	5.0	4.9	4.2	3.9	6.0	6.0	5.5	5.7	5.5
	7.6	7.3	7.1	7.9	7.9	7.9	7.2	7.2	8.1	8.0	3.9	4.1	4.0	5.0	4.7
	2.2	1.6	1.7	1.6	2.0	1.9	1.2	1.0	1.0	1.3	2.8	1.8	2.2	2.2	2.7
	0.4	0.3	0.3	0.3	0.3	0.3	0.2	0.2	0.2	0.2	0.4	0.3	0.3	0.3	0.4
	7.0	6.9	6.9	6.8	7.0	7.2	7.0	6.7	6.7	7.1	8.1	8.8	8.9	8.2	8.0
	22.1	21.1	20.7	21.0	21.4	21.8	20.6	20.0	20.2	20.6	21.2	21.0	20.8	21.4	21.0
	2.5	2.5	2.5	2.5	2.5	2.2	2.3	2.7	2.3	2.2	1.2	1.3	1.3	1.2	1.6
	16.5	16.9	17.5	17.0	17.1	19.2	19.5	20.2	20.0	20.0	12.6	13.1	13.3	12.8	13.4
	5.4	5.5	5.6	5.9	5.9	6.6	6.9	6.8	7.1	7.2	4.2	4.1	4.2	4.5	4.6
	0.3	0.3	0.3	0.3	0.3	0.5	0.4	0.4	0.4	0.4	0.0	0.0	0.0	0.0	0.0
	46.8	46.3	46.6	46.7	47.1	50.3	49.7	50.2	50.1	50.4	39.2	39.4	39.6	40.0	40.7
	14.0	14.2	14.0	14.2	14.1	15.2	15.6	15.5	15.7	15.6	13.5	13.1	12.5	12.6	12.6
	40.1	40.4	40.4	40.1	39.6	35.5	35.8	35.3	35.1	34.7	48.1	48.2	48.8	48.4	47.7
	0.9	0.9	0.9	0.9	0.7	1.0	1.0	1.0	1.0	0.6	0.8	0.8	0.9	1.0	0.9
	53.2	53.7	53.4	53.3	52.9	49.7	50.3	49.8	49.9	49.6	60.8	60.6	60.4	60.0	59.3
	100.0	100.0	100.0	100.0	100.0	100.0	100.0	100.0	100.0	100.0	100.0	100.0	100.0	100.0	100.0
	(times)					(times)					(times)				
	1.88	1.92	1.95	1.88	1.89	1.77	1.83	1.85	1.79	1.81	1.89	1.87	1.91	1.84	1.92
	.16	.17	.19	.18	.18	.11	.12	.15	.12	.14	.20	.18	.17	.17	.20
	2.21	2.19	2.16	2.23	2.23	1.90	1.88	1.80	1.88	1.90	3.06	2.98	3.01	3.05	2.92

EXHIBIT 5:   INCOME STATEMENT FOR CORPORATIONS IN PAPER, PETROLEUM,
COAL, RUBBER, PLASTICS (ESIC industries, 26, 29, 30 and other nondurable
manufacturing products)

	Paper and Allied Products*				
	1Q 1980	2Q 1980	3Q 1980	4Q 1980	1Q 1981
Income statement in ratio format	(percent of net sales)				
New sales, receipts & operating revenues	100.0	100.0	100.0	100.0	100.0
Deduct: Depreciation, depletion, and amortization of property,					
plant and equipment	3.6	3.6	3.7	3.7	3.7
Deduct: All other operating costs and expenses (net of					
purchase discounts)......................................	88.9	88.5	89.7	89.9	89.3
Income (or loss) from operations	7.6	7.9	6.6	6.5	7.0
Non-operating income (expense)	−0.1	−0.6	−0.7	−0.9	0.2
Income (or loss) before income taxes	7.4	7.3	6.0	5.6	7.2
Net income (loss) of foreign branches and equity in earnings					
(losses) of non-consolidated subsidiaries					
(net of foreign taxes)	0.7	1.1	0.6	0.8	0.6
Deduct: Current and deferred domestic income taxes	2.8	2.8	2.0	1.5	2.6
Income (or loss) after income taxes	5.4	5.5	4.5	4.9	5.3
Operating ratios	(percent)				
Annual rate of profit on stockholders' equity at end of period:					
Before income taxes	19.60	19.52	15.25	15.14	18.65
After taxes...	13.05	12.96	10.56	11.55	12.46
Annual rate of profit on total assets:					
Before income taxes	10.42	10.48	8.24	8.05	9.79
After taxes...	6.93	6.96	5.70	6.15	6.54

* During the first quarter of 1981 a considerable number of companies were reclassified by industry. To provide comparability,
the four quarters of 1980 have been restated to reflect these reclassifications.

Petroleum and Coal Products*					Rubber and Miscellaneous Plastic Products*					Other Nondurable Manufacturing Products*				
1Q 1980	2Q 1980	3Q 1980	4Q 1980	1Q 1981	1Q 1980	2Q 1980	3Q 1980	4Q 1980	1Q 1981	1Q 1980	2Q 1980	3Q 1980	4Q 1980	1Q 1981
Percent of net sales					(percent of net sales)					(percent of net sales)				
100.0	100.0	100.0	100.0	100.0	100.0	100.0	100.0	100.0	100.0	100.0	100.0	100.0	100.0	100.0
3.3	3.5	3.6	3.5	3.4	2.8	3.0	3.0	2.9	3.0	1.1	1.1	1.0	1.1	1.2
86.5	87.2	87.7	90.0	90.3	92.9	93.2	93.5	91.8	91.3	93.9	94.0	93.2	93.1	93.5
10.3	9.3	8.7	6.5	6.4	4.2	3.8	3.5	5.2	5.7	5.0	4.9	5.8	5.9	5.3
0.4	1.1	0.2	0.4	0.3	−1.5	−2.4	−1.6	−1.2	−0.4	−1.1	−0.9	−0.5	−0.9	−0.9
10.7	10.5	8.9	6.9	6.6	2.7	1.5	1.9	4.0	5.3	4.0	4.0	5.2	4.9	4.4
3.3	2.6	2.2	2.2	2.4	0.7	0.7	0.8	0.4	0.6	0.5	0.4	0.4	0.4	0.5
5.0	4.7	3.9	2.8	3.2	1.3	0.7	1.0	1.7	2.3	2.0	1.9	2.4	2.1	2.2
9.0	8.3	7.2	6.3	5.7	2.2	1.5	1.6	2.7	3.6	2.5	2.5	3.3	3.2	2.7
(percent)					(percent)					(percent)				
36.78	32.89	27.57	25.47	25.87	11.49	7.39	8.76	14.92	19.37	20.51	20.30	27.66	24.60	20.95
23.72	21.05	17.84	17.45	16.52	7.27	4.85	5.35	9.18	11.97	11.44	11.39	16.26	14.62	11.54
19.65	17.70	14.45	13.15	13.21	5.22	3.38	4.01	6.99	9.03	9.01	8.78	11.93	11.50	9.56
12.67	11.33	9.35	9.02	8.44	3.31	2.22	2.45	4.30	5.58	5.02	4.93	7.01	6.84	5.26

EXHIBIT 6:   BALANCE SHEET IN RATIO FORMAT FOR CORPORATIONS IN PAPER,
PETROLEUM, COAL, RUBBER, PLASTICS (ESIC industries 26, 29, 30, and other
nondurable manufacturing products)

ITEMS STATED AS A PERCENT OF TOTAL ASSETS

	Paper and Allied Products*				
	1Q 1980	2Q 1980	3Q 1980	4Q 1980	1Q 1981
Assets					
Cash on hand and in banks	3.6	3.3	3.3	3.1	2.7
U.S. Government and other securities	1.5	1.8	1.9	1.7	1.3
Receivables	13.6	13.5	13.7	13.2	14.0
Inventories	13.8	13.6	13.0	13.1	13.5
Current assets not elsewhere specified	2.0	1.7	1.8	1.8	1.8
Total current assets	34.5	34.0	33.7	33.0	33.4
Land and depreciable fixed assets	86.4	88.1	88.5	88.1	88.0
Deduct: Accumulated depreciation, depletion					
& amortization	34.5	35.0	35.1	33.8	33.6
Net property, plant & equipment	51.9	53.0	53.4	54.4	54.4
Non-current assets not elsewhere specified, including investment in non-consolidated entities, other long term investment,					
intangibles, etc.	13.6	13.0	12.9	12.7	12.3
Total assets	100.0	100.0	100.0	100.0	100.0
Liabilities and stockholders' equity					
Short-term loans & current installments	3.4	3.3	3.6	3.3	3.3
Trade accounts and trade notes payable	7.2	7.0	7.0	7.6	8.1
Income taxes accrued, prior and current years, net of payments					
a. Federal	1.5	0.9	0.9	0.8	0.9
b. Other	0.5	0.4	0.4	0.3	0.3
Other current liabilities	5.4	5.5	5.5	5.4	5.7
Total current liabilities	18.0	17.1	17.3	17.5	18.3
Long-term debt due in more than 1 year					
a. Loans from banks	3.5	3.1	3.3	3.5	3.8
b. Other long-term debt	19.6	20.0	19.2	19.6	19.0
Non-current liabilities not elsewhere specified, including					
deferred income taxes	5.6	5.9	5.9	6.0	6.3
Minority stockholders' interest in consolidated					
domestic corporations	0.2	0.2	0.2	0.2	0.2
Total liabilities	46.9	46.3	46.0	46.8	47.5
Capital stock and other capital	14.9	15.2	15.2	15.0	14.9
Retained earnings	39.0	39.5	39.8	39.1	38.6
Deduct: Treasury stock, at cost	0.8	1.0	1.0	1.0	1.0
Stockholders' equity	53.1	53.7	54.0	53.2	52.5
Total liabilities and stockholders' equity	100.0	100.0	100.0	100.0	100.0
Balance sheet ratios			(times)		
Current assets to current liabilities	1.92	1.99	1.94	1.88	1.83
Total cash, U.S. Government and other securities to total					
current liabilities	.28	.30	.30	.27	.22
Total stockholders' equity to debt	2.01	2.04	2.07	2.00	2.01

* During the first quarter of 1981 a considerable number of companies were reclassified by industry. To provide comparability, the four quarters of 1980 have been restated to reflect these reclassifications.

	Petroleum and Coal Products*					Rubber and Miscellaneous Plastics Products*					Other Nondurable Manufacturing Products*				
	1Q 1980	2Q 1980	3Q 1980	4Q 1980	1Q 1981	1Q 1980	2Q 1980	3Q 1980	4Q 1980	1Q 1981	1Q 1980	2Q 1980	3Q 1980	4Q 1980	1Q 1981
	3.2	2.9	2.6	2.4	2.7	2.4	2.3	2.5	3.3	3.5	4.5	3.9	3.8	4.9	4.4
	2.8	2.6	2.1	1.7	1.8	0.7	0.9	1.1	1.4	1.3	1.5	1.0	1.5	1.8	2.1
	12.5	12.0	11.9	12.8	12.4	23.0	21.8	22.5	21.7	22.8	26.3	25.1	28.9	27.1	25.6
	7.7	8.7	8.6	7.6	7.7	23.2	22.7	20.6	20.6	20.5	34.0	36.6	33.5	32.3	33.7
	1.5	1.6	1.7	1.5	2.1	2.4	2.8	3.0	2.9	2.5	4.9	4.9	4.5	4.4	4.4
	27.8	27.8	26.9	26.1	26.7	51.7	50.6	49.7	49.8	50.5	71.2	71.5	72.2	70.5	70.1
	77.0	77.0	77.2	78.7	78.6	65.8	67.3	68.0	68.2	67.2	30.5	30.5	30.6	31.5	30.6
	30.9	30.9	30.3	30.3	30.2	31.9	32.4	33.1	33.2	32.9	13.3	13.4	13.2	13.6	12.9
	46.1	46.1	46.9	48.5	48.5	34.0	34.9	34.9	35.0	34.3	17.2	17.1	17.3	17.9	17.6
	26.1	26.1	26.2	25.4	24.8	14.3	14.5	15.4	15.1	15.2	11.6	11.3	10.4	11.6	12.2
	100.0	100.0	100.0	100.0	100.0	100.0	100.0	100.0	100.0	100.0	100.0	100.0	100.0	100.0	100.0
	1.9	2.1	2.3	1.8	2.1	8.5	8.4	8.2	7.0	7.6	10.6	11.7	13.1	10.8	10.7
	11.7	11.8	11.4	12.4	12.4	10.8	9.7	9.7	10.5	10.2	15.3	15.3	14.0	13.4	13.6
	3.4	2.9	3.1	2.9	3.0	1.6	1.4	1.4	1.4	1.6	1.6	1.3	1.4	1.4	1.5
	0.5	0.6	0.6	0.6	0.6	0.2	0.2	0.2	0.2	0.2	0.3	0.2	0.2	0.3	0.2
	4.1	3.9	3.8	3.9	4.4	8.4	8.4	8.4	8.8	8.8	8.4	8.5	8.8	8.5	8.9
	21.7	21.2	21.2	21.7	22.4	29.5	28.2	27.8	27.9	28.3	36.1	37.1	37.3	34.4	34.9
	2.7	2.1	2.1	2.2	2.2	5.9	6.4	6.5	5.8	6.0	5.9	5.9	5.8	5.9	6.7
	10.6	10.8	11.6	11.4	11.4	13.9	14.2	14.4	14.0	13.6	10.8	10.6	10.3	9.6	9.4
	11.3	11.9	12.5	12.9	12.8	5.1	5.3	5.3	5.3	5.3	2.6	2.5	2.8	2.8	2.9
	0.2	0.2	0.2	0.2	0.2	0.2	0.2	0.2	0.2	0.2	0.7	0.7	0.6	0.6	0.5
	46.6	46.2	47.6	48.3	48.9	54.5	54.3	54.2	53.1	53.4	56.1	56.8	56.9	53.2	54.4
	11.7	11.3	10.7	9.8	9.6	11.0	11.0	10.8	11.8	11.6	11.7	11.4	11.5	12.9	12.8
	42.4	43.1	42.3	42.5	42.2	36.3	36.5	36.9	37.2	37.0	33.9	33.7	33.6	36.0	35.1
	0.6	0.7	0.7	0.7	0.7	1.8	1.8	1.9	2.1	2.0	1.8	1.9	1.9	2.2	2.3
	53.4	53.8	52.4	51.7	51.1	45.5	45.7	45.8	46.9	46.6	43.9	43.2	43.1	46.8	45.6
	100.0	100.0	100.0	100.0	100.0	100.0	100.0	100.0	100.0	100.0	100.0	100.0	100.0	100.0	100.0
		(times)					(times)					(times)			
	1.28	1.31	1.27	1.20	1.20	1.75	1.80	1.79	1.79	1.79	1.97	1.93	1.93	2.05	2.01
	.28	.26	.22	.19	.20	.10	.11	.13	.17	.17	.17	.13	.14	.19	.19
	3.52	3.58	3.28	3.35	3.27	1.61	1.58	1.58	1.75	1.72	1.61	1.53	1.48	1.78	1.71

EXHIBIT 7: INCOME STATEMENT FOR CORPORATIONS IN STONE, CLAY, GLASS, PRIMARY METAL, IRON, STEEL, NONFERROUS METALS (ESIC industries 32, 33, 33.1–2, 33.5–6

	Stone, Clay and Glass Products				
	1Q 1980	2Q 1980	3Q 1980	4Q 1980	1Q 1981
Income statement in ratio format	(percent of net sales)				
Net sales, receipts & operating revenues	100.0	100.0	100.0	100.0	100.0
Deduct: Depreciation, depletion, and amortization of property,					
plant and equipment	4.3	4.0	3.7	4.1	4.4
Deduct: All other operating costs and expenses (net of					
purchase discounts)......................................	91.2	88.9	88.1	88.9	91.8
Income (or loss) from operations	4.5	7.1	8.2	7.0	3.7
Non-operating income (expense)	−0.4	−0.7	−0.7	−1.0	0.1
Income (or loss) before income taxes	4.1	6.4	7.5	6.0	3.7
Net income (loss) of foreign branches and equity in earnings					
(losses) of non-consolidated subsidiaries					
(net of foreign taxes)......................................	0.6	0.6	0.6	0.7	0.4
Deduct: Current and deferred domestic income taxes	2.2	2.3	2.6	2.3	1.9
Income (or loss) after income taxes......................	2.5	4.6	5.4	4.4	2.3
Operating ratios	(percent)				
Annual rate of profit on stockholders' equity at end of period:					
Before income taxes	11.18	17.35	21.42	17.29	9.55
After taxes...	5.85	11.49	14.42	11.46	5.32
Annual rate of profit on total assets:					
Before income taxes	5.77	8.95	11.00	9.00	4.90
After taxes...	3.02	5.93	7.40	5.96	2.73

* During the first quarter of 1981 a considerable number of companies were reclassified by industry. To provide comparability, the four quarters of 1980 have been restated to reflect these reclassifications.
† Included in Primary Metal Industries
‡ Revised.

	Primary Metal Industries*					Iron and Steel†					Nonferrous Metals*†				
	1Q 1980	2Q 1980	3Q 1980	4Q 1980	1Q 1981	1Q 1980	2Q 1980	3Q 1980	4Q 1980	1Q 1981	1Q 1980	2Q 1980	3Q 1980	4Q 1980	1Q 1981
	(percent of net sales)					(percent of net sales)					(percent of net sales)				
	100.0	100.0	100.0	100.0	100.0	100.0	100.0	100.0	100.0	100.0	100.0	100.0	100.0	100.0	100.0
	2.9	3.1	3.4	3.1	3.2	3.1	3.3	3.6	3.2	3.2	2.6	2.8	3.1	2.9	3.1
	89.9	91.0	94.3	91.8	90.8	91.8	92.6	95.8	92.0	91.5	86.8	88.3	92.0	91.4	89.4
	7.1	5.9	2.3	5.1	6.1	5.1	4.1	0.7	4.8	5.3	10.6	8.9	4.9	5.7	7.5
	−0.4	−0.9	−0.4	0.1	−0.1	0.0	−0.7	0.0	−0.2	0.3	−1.2	−1.0	−0.8	0.4	−1.0
	6.7	5.1	1.9	5.2	5.9	5.1	3.3	0.6	4.6	5.5	9.4	7.9	4.1	6.1	6.5
	1.2	1.0	1.0	0.9	0.6	0.7	0.7	0.5	0.6	0.4	2.0	1.4	1.6	1.5	0.9
	2.5	1.9	0.7	1.6	2.1	1.9	1.3	−0.2	1.5	2.1	3.5	2.8	2.1	2.0	1.9
	5.4	4.2	2.2	4.4	4.4	3.9	2.7	1.2	3.8	3.9	7.9	6.6	3.6	5.6	5.4
	(percent)					(percent)					(pecent)				
	24.46	17.03	7.48	17.14	18.69	18.87	12.04	3.02	16.20	18.81	32.91	24.19	13.78	18.48	18.51
	16.75	11.81	5.60	12.50	12.76	12.76	8.16	3.36	11.71	12.21	22.80	17.06	8.77	13.63	13.56
	11.01	7.94	3.47	7.89	8.49	8.33	5.43	1.37	7.24	8.41	15.25	11.87	6.64	8.87	8.61
	7.54	5.51	2.60	5.75	5.80	5.64	3.68	1.52	5.24	5.46	10.56	8.37	4.23	6.54	6.31

EXHIBIT 8: BALANCE SHEET IN RATIO FORMAT FOR CORPORATIONS IN STONE, CLAY, GLASS, PRIMARY METALS, IRON, STEEL, NONFERROUS METALS (ESIC industries 32, 33, 33.1–2, 33.5–6)

ITEMS STATED AS A PERCENT OF TOTAL ASSETS

	Stone, Clay and Glass Products				
	1Q 1980	2Q 1980	3Q 1980	4Q 1980	1Q 1981
Assets					
Cash on hand and in banks	3.6	3.4	3.6	3.8	3.4
U.S. Government and other securities	1.5	1.5	1.2	1.7	1.4
Receivables	17.2	17.8	18.8	17.0	17.2
Inventories	16.5	16.1	14.7	14.7	15.4
Current assets not elsewhere specified	2.5	2.2	1.9	2.3	2.1
Total current assets	41.3	41.0	40.3	39.6	39.6
Land and depreciable fixed assets	82.6	83.3	84.1	85.1	84.9
Deduct: Accumulated depreciation, depletion & amortization	34.8	35.2	35.5	25.9	35.9
Net property, plant & equipment	47.8	48.0	48.6	49.2	49.0
Non-current assets not elsewhere specified, including investment in non-consolidated entities, other long term investments, intangibles, etc.	11.0	11.0	11.1	11.3	11.4
Total assets	100.0	100.0	100.0	100.0	100.0
Liabilities and stockholders' equity					
Short-term loans & current installments	5.1	4.8	4.6	4.0	4.4
Trade accounts and trade notes payable	7.4	6.9	7.2	7.7	7.4
Income taxes accrued, prior and current years, net of payments					
a. Federal	1.4	1.1	1.3	1.3	1.2
b. Other	0.3	0.2	0.2	0.2	0.2
Other current liabilities	6.4	6.2	6.5	6.1	6.6
Total current liabilities	20.7	19.3	19.9	19.4	19.9
Long-term debt due in more than 1 year					
a. Loans from banks	6.6	6.9	6.2	6.3	5.9
b. Other long-term debt	15.6	16.8	16.9	16.5	16.8
Non-current liabilities not elsewhere specified, including deferred income taxes	5.4	5.3	5.6	5.7	5.9
Minority stockholders' interest in consolidated domestic corporations	0.1	0.1	0.1	0.1	0.1
Total liabilities	48.4	48.4	48.7	48.0	48.6
Capital stock and other capital	14.4	14.6	14.1	14.0	13.9
Retained earnings	38.6	38.2	38.5	39.2	38.7
Deduct: Treasury stock, at cost	1.3	1.2	1.2	1.2	1.2
Stockholders' equity	51.6	51.6	51.3	52.0	51.4
Total liabilities and stockholders' equity	100.0	100.0	100.0	100.0	100.0
Balance sheet ratios			(times)		
Current assets to current liabilities	1.99	2.12	2.03	2.04	1.99
Total cash, U.S. Government and other securities to total current liabilities	.25	.25	.24	.29	.24
Total stockholders' equity to debt	1.88	1.81	1.85	1.94	1.89

* During the first quarter of 1981 considerable number of companies were reclassified by industry. To provide comparability, the four quarters of 1980 have been restated to reflect these reclassifications.
 † Included in Primary Metal Industries.
 ‡ Revised.

Primary Metal Industries*					Iron and Steel†					Nonferrous Metals*†				
1Q 1980	2Q 1980	3Q 1980	4Q 1980	1Q 1981	1Q 1980	2Q 1980	3Q 1980	4Q 1980	1Q 1981	1Q 1980	2Q 1980	3Q 1980	4Q 1980	1Q 1981
2.5	2.8	2.6	3.1	2.7	2.5	3.2	2.9	3.4	3.2	2.6	2.2	2.2	2.7	1.9
1.8	1.5	2.1	2.1	2.1	1.8	1.5	2.3	2.5	2.9	1.5	1.3	1.6	1.4	0.9
18.7	16.9	16.8	16.8	17.8	19.2	17.0	17.2	17.6	18.8	18.0	16.6	16.1	15.5	16.2
18.6	18.9	17.8	17.7	17.7	18.4	19.0	17.6	17.3	16.9	18.8	18.8	18.0	18.3	19.0
1.6	1.7	1.8	1.9	1.9	1.4	1.6	1.6	1.8	1.9	1.9	1.9	2.1	2.1	2.1
43.2	41.8	41.0	41.6	42.2	43.4	42.4	41.6	42.6	43.6	42.8	40.9	40.1	40.0	40.1
83.6	85.3	86.2	84.8	83.6	93.7	95.5	96.9	94.5	92.7	67.7	69.2	70.1	70.1	69.6
39.6	40.4	40.7	39.7	39.2	47.5	48.5	49.2	47.7	47.0	27.1	27.7	27.8	27.6	27.3
44.1	44.9	45.5	45.2	44.4	46.3	47.1	47.7	46.9	45.7	40.6	41.5	42.2	42.5	42.3
12.8	13.3	13.5	13.2	13.4	10.4	10.6	10.7	10.5	10.7	16.6	17.6	17.7	17.5	17.7
100.0	100.0	100.0	100.0	100.0	100.0	100.0	100.0	100.0	100.0	100.0	100.0	100.0	100.0	100.0
4.2	3.8	3.8	3.4	3.7	3.7	3.6	3.4	2.6	2.9	5.0	4.4	4.9	4.7	4.7
9.2	8.3	8.3	9.0	9.1	9.3	8.4	8.3	9.6	9.4	9.2	8.2	8.5	8.2	8.6
2.3	1.7	1.7	1.7	1.7	1.9	1.3	1.4	1.4	1.4	2.9	2.3	2.2	2.1	2.0
0.4	0.4	0.3	0.4	0.3	0.4	0.4	0.4	0.4	0.4	0.4	0.3	0.3	0.3	0.3
8.4	8.4	8.2	8.3	8.7	9.8	10.0	9.7	9.7	10.3	6.4	6.0	6.0	6.2	6.2
24.5	22.6	22.5	22.8	23.4	25.0	23.6	22.9	23.7	24.5	23.8	21.2	21.9	21.5	21.8
3.6	3.5	3.9	3.8	3.8	3.1	2.8	2.9	2.7	2.4	4.5	4.6	5.3	5.5	5.8
19.4	19.5	19.5	19.4	19.2	20.2	20.7	21.0	20.8	20.0	18.1	17.7	17.2	17.3	18.1
7.0	7.3	7.2	7.5	7.8	7.3	7.6	7.7	7.8	8.1	6.6	6.7	6.6	7.1	7.3
0.4	0.4	0.5	0.4	0.4	0.2	0.3	0.3	0.2	0.2	0.7	0.7	0.8	0.6	0.5
55.0	53.4	53.6	54.0	54.6	55.8	54.9	54.8	55.3	55.3	53.7	50.9	51.8	52.0	53.5
12.8	13.3	13.3	13.1	12.9	12.6	12.8	13.0	12.7	12.7	13.0	14.0	13.7	13.6	13.2
33.1	34.3	34.0	33.9	33.8	32.6	33.4	33.4	33.2	33.1	33.9	35.7	35.0	34.9	34.7
0.9	0.9	0.9	0.9	1.2	1.1	1.1	1.1	1.2	1.1	0.6	0.6	0.5	0.5	1.5
45.0	46.6	46.4	46.0	45.4	44.2	45.1	45.2	44.7	44.7	46.3	49.1	48.2	48.0	46.5
100.0	100.0	100.0	100.0	100.0	100.0	100.0	100.0	100.0	100.0	100.0	100.0	100.0	100.0	100.0
(times)					(times)					(times)				
1.76	1.85	1.82	1.82	1.80	1.73	1.80	1.82	1.80	1.78	1.80	1.93	1.83	1.86	1.84
.17	.19	.21	.23	.20	.17	.20	.23	.25	.25	.17	.17	.17	.19	.13
1.66	1.73	1.70	1.72	1.71	1.64	1.67	1.67	1.71	1.76	1.68	1.84	1.76	1.75	1.63

EXHIBIT 9: INCOME STATEMENT FOR CORPORATIONS IN FABRICATED METAL, MACHINERY, ELECTRICAL AND ELECTRONIC EQUIPMENT, INSTRUMENTS (ESIC industries 34, 35, 36, and 38)

	Fabricated Metal Products*				
	1Q 1980	2Q 1980	3Q 1980	4Q 1980	1Q 1981
Income statement in ratio format	(percent of net sales)				
Net sales, receipts & operating revenues	100.0	100.0	100.0	100.0	100.0
Deduct: Depreciation, depletion, and amortization of property, plant and equipment	2.3	2.4	2.4	2.3	2.4
Deduct: All other operating costs and expenses (net of purchase discounts)......................................	90.3	91.0	91.4	91.4	90.4
Income (or loss) from operations	7.4	6.6	6.2	6.4	7.2
Non-operating income (expense)	−0.3	−0.9	−0.7	−0.4	−0.7
Income (or loss) before income taxes	7.1	5.7	5.5	5.9	6.5
Net income (loss) of foreign branches and equity in earnings (losses) of non-consolidated subsidiaries (net of foreign taxes)	0.6	0.7	0.8	0.7	0.6
Deduct: Current and deferred domestic income taxes	2.8	2.5	2.5	2.5	2.9
Income (or loss) after income taxes	5.0	4.0	3.8	4.1	4.2
Operating ratios	(percent)				
Annual rate of profit on stockholders' equity at end of period:					
Before income taxes	26.04	21.30	20.08	21.80	22.96
After taxes...	16.63	13.27	12.30	13.52	13.62
Annual rate of profit on total assets:					
Before income taxes	12.69	10.42	9.89	10.70	11.22
After taxes...	8.11	6.49	6.05	6.64	6.66

* During the first quarter of 1981 a considerable number of companies were reclassified by industry. To provide comparability, the four quarters of 1980 have been restated to reflect these reclassifications.

Machinery, Except Electrical*					Electrical and Electronic Equipment*					Instruments and Related Products*				
1Q 1980	2Q 1980	3Q 1980	4Q 1980	1Q 1981	1Q 1980	2Q 1980	3Q 1980	4Q 1980	1Q 1981	1Q 1980	2Q 1980	3Q 1980	4Q 1980	1Q 1981
(percent of net sales)					(percent of net sales)					(percent of net sales)				
100.0	100.0	100.0	100.0	100.0	100.0	100.0	100.0	100.0	100.0	100.0	100.0	100.0	100.0	100.0
3.4	3.5	3.7	3.5	3.8	2.5	2.6	2.7	2.6	2.8	3.6	3.5	3.7	3.5	3.8
87.1	86.7	87.0	87.4	86.8	89.6	90.2	89.9	90.3	89.4	86.1	85.0	84.0	85.4	85.2
9.4	9.8	9.3	9.1	9.4	7.9	7.2	7.3	7.1	7.8	10.3	11.6	12.3	11.1	11.0
−1.1	−1.3	−1.7	−1.3	−1.1	−0.2	−0.4	−0.6	0.1	0.4	1.4	1.4	0.4	0.9	2.2
8.3	8.5	7.6	7.8	8.3	7.7	6.8	6.7	7.2	8.3	11.7	12.9	12.7	11.9	13.3
1.4	1.6	2.0	2.7	1.5	1.0	1.3	1.2	1.2	0.9	2.1	2.3	2.6	2.2	2.0
3.6	3.6	3.4	3.3	3.6	3.6	3.3	3.1	3.2	3.5	5.0	5.8	5.7	4.8	5.3
6.0	6.5	6.2	7.3	6.1	5.2	4.8	4.8	5.2	5.7	8.8	9.4	9.5	9.4	10.0
(percent)					(percent)					(percent)				
22.69	23.8	21.20	24.02	21.96	27.01	25.00	23.34	25.22	26.06	25.67	28.76	28.54	27.01	27.42
14.11	15.39	13.67	16.63	13.79	15.99	14.76	14.14	15.58	16.23	16.34	17.75	17.83	17.86	17.87
11.68	12.22	10.86	12.44	11.15	12.48	11.58	10.83	12.02	12.46	16.27	18.38	18.20	17.26	17.44
7.26	7.88	7.00	8.62	7.00	7.39	6.84	6.56	7.43	7.76	10.35	11.34	11.38	11.41	11.36

EXHIBIT 10: BALANCE SHEET IN RATIO FORMAT FOR CORPORATIONS IN FABRI-
CATED METAL, MACHINERY, ELECTRICAL AND ELECTRONIC EQUIPMENT, INSTRU-
MENTS (ESIC industries 34, 35, 36, and 38)

ITEMS STATED AS A PERCENT OF TOTAL ASSETS

	Fabricated Metal Products*				
	1Q 1980	2Q 1980	3Q 1980	4Q 1980	1Q 1981
Assets					
Cash on hand and in banks	4.3	4.0	4.4	5.0	4.8
U.S. Government and other securities	2.2	2.3	2.9	3.0	2.4
Receivables	23.7	23.0	23.3	22.3	23.3
Inventories	27.5	27.0	25.3	24.5	24.3
Current assets not elsewhere specified	2.3	2.3	2.2	2.2	2.4
Total current assets	60.1	58.6	58.1	57.0	57.2
Land and depreciable fixes assets	51.8	53.0	53.8	54.6	55.1
Deduct: Accumulated depreciation, depletion, & amortization	24.0	24.5	25.0	25.0	25.1
Net property, plant & equipment	27.7	28.5	28.8	29.5	30.0
Non-current assets not elsewhere specified, including investment in non-consolidated entities, other long term investments, intangibles, etc.	12.2	12.9	13.1	13.5	12.8
Total assets	100.0	100.0	100.0	100.0	100.0
Liabilities and stockholders' equity					
Short-term loans & current installments	6.7	6.6	6.0	5.2	5.6
Trade accounts and trade notes payable	10.8	9.9	9.9	10.6	10.5
Income taxes accrued, prior and current years, net of payments					
a. Federal	2.1	1.7	1.9	1.8	2.0
b. Other	0.3	0.3	0.3	0.3	0.3
Other current liabilities	11.8	12.3	12.3	12.1	12.5
Total current liabilities	31.7	30.9	30.3	30.1	30.8
Long-term debt due in more than 1 year					
a. Loans from banks	5.3	5.5	5.7	5.8	5.8
b. Other long-term debt	10.6	11.4	11.6	11.3	10.9
Non-current liabilities not elsewhere specified, including deferred income taxes	3.6	3.2	3.2	3.7	3.5
Minority stockholders' interest in consolidated domestic corporations	0.1	0.1	0.1	0.1	0.1
Total liabilities	51.3	51.1	50.8	50.9	51.1
Capital stock and other capital	12.3	12.4	12.6	12.6	12.4
Retained earnings	37.8	38.1	38.2	38.1	38.3
Deduct: Treasury stock, at cost	1.4	1.5	1.5	1.6	1.8
Stockholders' equity	48.7	48.9	49.2	49.1	48.9
Total liabilities and stockholders' equity	100.0	100.0	100.0	100.0	100.0
Balance sheet ratios			(times)		
Current assets to current liabilities	1.90	1.90	1.92	1.89	1.85
Total cash, U.S. Government and other securities to total current liabilities	.21	.20	.24	.27	.23
Total stockholders' equity to debt	2.15	2.08	2.12	2.20	2.18

* During the first quarter of 1981 a considerable number of companies were reclassified by industry. To provide comparability, the four quarters of 1980 have been restated to reflect these reclassifications.

	Machinery, Except Electrical*				Electrical and Electronic Equipment*				Instruments and Related Products*				
1Q 1980	2Q 1980	3Q 1980	4Q 1980	1Q 1981	1Q 1980	2Q 1980	3Q 1980	4Q 1980	1Q 1981	1Q 1980	2Q 1980	3Q 1980	4Q 1980	1Q 1981
2.8	3.0	2.9	3.1	3.3	3.5	3.1	3.3	4.1	3.5	2.6	2.3	3.3	4.4	3.6
1.9	1.6	1.6	1.7	1.4	2.4	2.2	2.4	2.6	2.6	3.7	3.3	3.0	2.9	3.2
20.4	20.2	19.7	19.1	19.7	21.8	21.8	22.1	21.3	21.6	19.1	19.3	19.7	18.9	18.3
24.9	24.8	24.2	23.3	23.1	29.2	29.5	28.3	27.3	27.6	23.4	23.5	22.9	22.6	22.7
3.0	3.0	2.9	3.0	3.0	4.5	4.3	4.6	4.5	4.2	4.5	4.4	4.2	4.7	5.0
53.0	52.6	51.3	50.2	50.5	61.4	60.9	60.7	59.8	59.4	53.3	52.9	53.0	53.6	52.8
50.3	50.3	50.6	50.5	50.0	42.0	42.8	43.0	43.5	43.0	54.4	54.7	54.7	54.6	54.8
21.3	21.2	21.1	20.6	20.3	19.0	19.3	19.2	19.0	18.8	26.2	26.3	26.1	25.9	25.7
29.0	29.0	29.5	29.9	29.6	23.0	23.4	23.7	24.5	24.2	28.3	28.5	28.6	28.7	29.1
18.0	18.4	19.2	19.9	19.8	15.6	15.7	15.6	15.7	16.4	18.4	18.6	18.3	17.7	18.1
100.0	100.0	100.0	100.0	100.0	100.0	100.0	100.0	100.0	100.0	100.0	100.0	100.0	100.0	100.0
7.7	8.3	8.1	7.7	8.3	5.6	5.8	5.8	5.2	5.2	3.8	4.5	3.9	3.1	3.5
8.8	8.6	8.5	8.6	8.4	9.4	9.1	8.4	8.7	8.5	6.0	6.1	5.8	6.3	5.8
2.5	2.0	1.9	1.9	2.1	2.2	1.6	1.7	1.7	2.1	2.3	2.0	2.2	2.1	2.3
0.5	0.4	0.4	0.4	0.4	0.4	0.3	0.3	0.3	0.3	0.4	0.3	0.4	0.4	0.4
9.8	9.8	9.7	9.6	10.3	18.9	18.9	19.3	18.5	18.6	9.1	9.0	9.5	9.6	9.5
29.3	28.9	28.7	28.3	29.5	36.3	35.7	35.5	34.5	34.7	21.7	22.0	21.7	21.6	21.6
4.9	5.0	4.9	5.1	5.0	2.6	2.5	2.4	2.4	2.4	3.0	2.6	2.9	3.0	3.0
10.2	10.8	11.2	10.6	10.5	9.7	10.5	10.3	10.0	9.7	8.3	7.8	8.0	7.7	7.9
4.0	3.9	3.9	4.1	4.1	5.0	4.8	5.1	5.1	5.0	3.6	3.6	3.5	3.6	3.7
0.1	0.1	0.1	0.1	0.1	0.2	0.2	0.2	0.3	0.4	0.1	0.1	0.1	0.1	0.1
48.5	48.8	48.8	48.2	49.2	53.8	53.7	53.6	52.3	52.2	36.6	36.1	36.2	36.1	36.4
16.0	15.9	15.8	16.2	16.0	15.5	15.9	16.0	16.6	16.9	14.3	13.8	14.0	13.8	13.8
36.1	36.0	36.0	36.2	35.5	31.9	32.0	32.0	32.6	32.2	49.4	50.4	50.1	50.4	50.2
0.6	0.6	0.6	0.6	0.7	1.2	1.6	1.6	1.5	1.2	0.3	0.3	0.3	0.3	0.3
51.5	51.2	51.2	51.8	50.8	46.2	46.3	46.4	47.7	47.8	63.4	63.9	63.8	63.9	63.6
100.0	100.0	100.0	100.0	100.0	100.0	100.0	100.0	100.0	100.0	100.0	100.0	100.0	100.0	100.0
(times)					(times)					(times)				
1.81	1.82	1.79	1.77	1.71	1.69	1.71	1.71	1.73	1.71	2.46	2.41	2.45	2.48	2.44
.16	.16	.16	.17	.16	.16	.15	.16	.19	.18	.29	.26	.29	.34	.31
2.26	2.13	2.12	2.22	2.14	2.59	2.46	2.50	2.71	2.77	4.17	4.26	4.32	4.58	4.39

EXHIBIT 11: INCOME STATEMENT FOR CORPORATIONS IN TRANSPORTATION AND MOTOR VEHICLE EQUIPMENT, AIRCRAFT, GUIDED MISSILES (ESIC industries 37, 37.1, 37.7, other durable manufacturing products)

	Transportation Equipment*				
	1Q 1980	2Q 1980	3Q 1980	4Q 1980	1Q 1981
Income statement format	(percent of net sales)				
Net sales, receipts & operating revenues	100.0	100.0	100.0	100.0	100.0
Deduct: Depreciation, depletion, and amortization of property, plant and equipment	3.9	4.1	4.0	3.8	4.0
Deduct: All other operating costs and expenses (net of purchase discounts).....................................	94.9	97.0	97.0	93.5	93.7
Income (or loss) from operations	1.2	−1.1	−1.0	2.6	2.3
Non-operating income (expense)	−0.3	−0.4	0.9	−1.1	0.1
Income (or loss) before income taxes	0.9	−1.6	−2.0	1.6	2.4
Net income (loss) of foreign branches and equity in earnings (losses) of non-consolidated subsidiaries (net of foreign taxes)......................................	1.6	0.5	−0.2	0.6	0.5
Deduct: Current and deferred domestic income taxes	1.3	0.1	0.0	1.2	1.6
Income (or loss) after income taxes	1.2	−1.2	−2.1	1.0	1.3
Operating ratios	(percent)				
Annual rate of profit on stockholders' equity at end of period:					
Before income taxes	7.88	−3.38	−6.43	7.52	9.65
After taxes...	3.83	−3.64	−6.22	3.39	4.31
Annual rate of profit on total assets:					
Before income taxes	3.48	−1.45	−2.65	3.09	3.85
After taxes...	1.69	−1.57	−2.57	1.39	1.72

* During the first quarter of 1981 a considerable number of companies were reclassified by industry. To provide comparability, the four quarters of 1980 have been restated to reflect these reclassifications.
† Included in Transportation Equipment.

	Motor Vehicles and Equipment*†					Aircraft, Guided Missiles and Parts*†					Other Durable Manufacturing Products*				
	1Q 1980	2Q 1980	3Q 1980	4Q 1980	1Q 1981	1Q 1980	2Q 1980	3Q 1980	4Q 1980	1Q 1981	1Q 1980	2Q 1980	3Q 1980	4Q 1980	1Q 1981
	(percent of net sales)					(percent of net sales)					(percent of net sales)				
	100.0	100.0	100.0	100.0	100.0	100.0	100.0	100.0	100.0	100.0	100.0	100.0	100.0	100.0	100.0
	5.1	5.7	5.5	5.0	5.3	2.0	1.9	2.0	2.0	2.2	2.9	3.1	3.2	3.1	3.1
	96.9	100.9	101.0	94.5	95.3	91.9	92.1	91.9	92.1	91.0	90.2	91.1	90.3	90.5	92.2
	−2.0	−6.7	−6.6	0.5	−0.6	6.1	6.0	6.1	5.9	6.8	6.9	5.9	6.5	6.3	4.7
	−0.4	−0.5	−1.1	−1.0	−0.4	0.2	0.2	−0.4	−0.9	1.4	−0.8	−1.0	−0.9	−1.0	−0.5
	-2.3	−7.2	−7.7	−0.5	−0.9	6.3	6.2	5.7	5.0	8.2	6.1	4.8	5.6	5.3	4.2
	2.0	0.3	−1.2	0.4	0.4	1.0	0.8	1.1	0.8	0.5	0.1	0.3	0.3	0.1	0.2
	0.4	−1.8	−1.9	0.8	0.8	2.8	2.6	2.4	1.9	3.1	2.5	2.4	2.3	2.3	2.1
	−0.7	−5.2	−6.9	−0.9	−1.4	4.5	4.3	4.3	4.0	5.7	3.6	2.7	3.6	3.2	2.3
	(percent)					(percent)					(percent)				
	−0.99	−18.74	−23.03	−0.38	−1.82	26.72	26.83	24.18	22.88	31.39	21.18	16.88	19.68	18.80	14.08
	−2.12	−13.99	−17.98	−2.99	−4.31	16.57	16.59	15.41	15.45	20.36	12.34	8.84	11.96	11.17	7.41
	−0.54	−9.87	−11.40	−0.19	−0.87	8.75	8.69	7.83	7.40	10.08	10.06	8.09	9.41	9.04	6.70
	−1.14	−7.37	−8.90	−1.48	−2.07	5.42	5.38	4.99	5.00	6.54	5.86	4.23	5.72	5.37	3.52

EXHIBIT 12:   BALANCE SHEET IN RATIO FORMAT FOR CORPORATIONS IN TRANS-
PORTATION AND MOTOR VEHICLE EQUIPMENT, AIRCRAFT, GUIDED MISSILES (ESIC
industries 37, 37.1, 37.7, other durable manufacturing products)

ITEMS STATED AS A PERCENT OF TOTAL ASSETS

	Transportation Equipment*				
	1Q 1980	2Q 1980	3Q 1980	4Q 1980	1Q 1981
Assets					
Cash on hand and in banks..	3.4	3.2	3.0	3.1	2.5
U.S. Government and other securities	1.9	1.7	2.1	2.5	2.2
Receivables...	14.3	14.5	13.7	12.1	13.2
Inventories...	31.1	30.6	30.9	30.5	31.3
Current assets not elsewhere specified	2.9	2.5	2.8	3.0	2.9
Total current assets.....................................	53.6	52.5	52.5	51.2	52.1
Land and depreciable fixed assets	52.2	53.5	54.1	54.7	54.0
Deduct: Accumulated depreciation, depletion					
& amortization	25.8	26.2	26.4	26.4	26.1
Net property, plant & equipment	26.5	27.3	27.8	28.3	27.9
Non-current assets not elsewhere specified, including investment					
in non-consolidated entities, other long term investments,					
intangibles, etc..	19.9	20.2	19.7	20.5	20.0
Total assets...	100.0	100.0	100.0	100.0	100.0
Liabilities and stockholders' equity					
Short-term loans & current installments	4.2	3.8	4.5	3.6	4.1
Trade accounts and trade notes payable	10.9	10.0	10.0	10.3	10.1
Income taxes accrued, prior and current years, net of payments					
a. Federal	2.6	2.5	2.5	2.4	2.2
b. Other	0.3	0.3	0.3	0.3	0.2
Other current liabilities	22.3	22.8	23.6	23.8	24.0
Total current liabilities	40.4	39.6	40.9	40.3	40.6
Long-term debt due in more than 1 year					
a. Loans from banks......................................	2.4	2.9	2.9	2.9	3.1
b. Other long-term debt	7.9	9.1	9.4	9.4	9.5
Non-current liabilities not elsewhere specified, including					
deferred income taxes	5.1	5.2	5.4	6.2	6.8
Minority stockholders' interest in consolidated					
domestic corporations.....................................	0.1	0.1	0.1	0.1	0.1
Total liabilities...	55.8	57.0	58.8	59.0	60.1
Capital stock and other capital	9.6	9.6	9.5	9.8	10.0
Retained earnings	35.0	33.8	32.1	31.6	30.2
Deduct: Treasury stock, at cost	0.4	0.4	0.4	0.3	0.3
Stockholders' equity	44.2	43.0	41.2	41.0	39.9
Total liabilities and stockholders' equity................	100.0	100.0	100.0	100.0	100.0
Balance sheet ratios			(times)		
Current assets to current liabilities	1.33	1.33	1.28	1.27	1.28
Total cash, U.S. Government and other securities to total					
current liabilities	.13	.12	.12	.14	.12
Total stockholders' equity to debt............................	3.05	2.67	2.46	2.59	2.39

*During the first quarter of 1981 a considerable number of companies were reclassified by industry. To provide comparability, the four quarters of 1980 have been restated to reflect these reclassifications.
† Included in Transportation Equipment.

Motor Vehicles and Equipment*†					Aircraft, Guided Missiles and Parts*†					Other Durable Manufacturing Products*				
1Q 1980	2Q 1980	3Q 1980	4Q 1980	1Q 1981	1Q 1980	2Q 1980	3Q 1980	4Q 1980	1Q 1981	1Q 1980	2Q 1980	3Q 1980	4Q 1980	1Q 1981
2.6	2.3	2.3	2.5	2.1	4.9	4.5	3.8	3.7	2.8	4.9	4.8	4.8	4.5	4.1
1.9	1.9	2.4	3.4	2.0	2.1	1.6	2.1	1.7	3.0	1.6	1.8	1.7	1.6	1.4
14.8	15.3	14.0	11.4	13.5	11.9	12.3	12.0	11.4	11.1	19.3	19.4	20.2	19.1	19.2
20.7	18.8	18.6	17.2	18.1	48.7	49.4	50.4	50.5	51.0	23.5	22.9	22.6	22.2	22.3
3.7	3.4	4.0	4.2	3.8	1.9	1.5	1.4	1.6	1.8	3.8	3.8	3.7	4.3	4.2
43.6	41.6	41.3	38.8	39.5	69.5	69.3	69.6	68.9	69.7	53.0	52.8	53.0	51.7	51.2
63.4	66.3	67.4	69.0	69.0	33.8	34.1	34.4	34.5	33.7	63.2	63.7	62.6	63.6	64.0
32.3	33.7	34.1	34.7	34.9	17.2	17.1	16.9	16.7	16.2	25.2	25.6	25.0	25.3	25.4
31.2	32.6	33.3	34.3	34.1	16.7	17.1	17.5	17.9	17.5	38.0	38.1	37.6	38.3	38.7
25.2	25.7	25.4	26.9	26.3	13.8	13.6	12.9	13.2	12.8	9.0	9.2	9.4	10.0	10.1
100.0	100.0	100.0	100.0	100.0	100.0	100.0	100.0	100.0	100.0	100.0	100.0	100.0	100.0	100.0
4.5	4.2	4.9	3.9	4.7	3.1	3.3	3.4	2.7	3.0	9.2	9.3	9.5	9.0	8.6
12.4	10.6	11.2	11.2	11.3	9.2	9.5	8.8	9.7	9.1	9.7	9.5	9.8	9.2	9.5
0.9	0.8	0.8	0.7	0.3	5.6	5.3	5.3	4.9	5.1	1.8	1.3	1.1	1.1	1.3
0.2	0.2	0.2	0.2	0.1	0.5	0.5	0.5	0.4	0.4	0.3	0.2	0.2	0.2	0.2
13.5	13.7	14.6	14.9	14.9	36.8	37.3	37.9	37.4	37.1	6.0	6.0	6.0	6.0	6.1
31.5	29.5	31.6	30.8	31.2	55.3	55.8	55.8	55.0	54.6	26.9	26.1	26.7	25.6	25.6
1.6	2.9	2.8	2.4	2.2	2.4	1.9	2.1	2.5	2.8	7.7	7.7	7.6	7.5	7.7
6.8	8.7	9.4	9.6	9.9	6.4	6.6	6.3	6.1	6.4	13.5	13.4	13.4	13.6	14.0
5.8	6.1	6.5	7.5	8.6	3.1	3.3	3.3	4.0	4.1	4.1	4.6	4.3	4.9	5.0
0.2	0.2	0.2	0.2	0.2	0.0	0.0	0.0	0.0	0.0	0.3	0.3	0.3	0.3	0.1
46.0	47.3	50.5	50.5	52.1	67.3	67.6	67.6	67.7	67.9	52.5	52.1	52.2	51.9	52.4
8.7	8.9	8.9	9.8	9.9	10.9	10.5	10.3	10.0	10.4	13.2	13.3	13.1	13.2	13.1
45.7	44.1	40.9	40.0	38.2	22.2	22.2	22.4	22.7	22.0	36.3	36.5	36.7	36.8	36.2
0.4	0.4	0.3	0.3	0.2	0.3	0.3	0.3	0.3	0.3	1.9	1.9	1.9	1.9	1.7
54.0	52.7	49.5	49.5	47.9	32.7	32.4	32.4	32.3	32.1	47.5	47.9	47.8	48.1	47.6
100.0	100.0	100.0	100.0	100.0	100.0	100.0	100.0	100.0	100.0	100.0	100.0	100.0	100.0	100.0
(times)					(times)					(times)				
1.39	1.41	1.31	1.26	1.27	1.26	1.24	1.25	1.25	1.28	1.97	2.02	1.99	2.02	2.00
.14	.14	.15	.19	.13	.13	.11	.11	.10	.11	.24	.25	.24	.24	.22
4.19	3.35	2.90	3.13	2.86	2.74	2.76	2.75	2.88	2.67	1.57	1.58	1.57	1.60	1.57

EXHIBIT 13:   INCOME STATEMENT FOR CORPORATIONS IN MINING, RETAIL, WHOLESALE

	All Mining*				
	1Q 1980	2Q 1980	3Q 1980	4Q 1980	1Q 1981
Income statement in ratio format	(percent of net sales)				
Net sales, receipts & operating revenues	100.0	100.0	100.0	100.0	100.0
Deduct: Depreciation, depletion, and amortization of property, plant and equipment	9.5	9.7	9.5	9.7	10.2
Deduct: All other operating costs and expenses (net of purchase discounts)......................................	77.4	75.3	73.5	73.9	73.7
Income (or loss) from operations	13.1	15.0	16.9	16.4	16.1
Non-operating income (expense)	−1.2	−1.3	−0.5	0.6	0.9
Income (or loss) before income taxes	11.9	13.7	16.4	17.1	17.0
Net income (loss) of foreign branches and equity in earnings (losses) of non-consolidated subsidiaries (net of foreign taxes)......................................	2.1	1.7	2.7	1.1	1.5
Deduct: Current and deferred domestic income taxes	5.7	5.1	5.6	5.0	6.4
Income (or loss) after income taxes......................	8.3	10.3	13.4	13.1	12.0
Operating ratios	(percent)				
Annual rate of profit on stockholders' equity at end of period:					
Before income taxes	24.24	26.97	30.75	31.71	31.11
After taxes...	14.31	18.00	21.66	22.88	20.26
Annual rate of profit on total assets:					
Before income taxes	10.48	11.52	13.85	13.73	13.67
After taxes...	6.19	7.69	9.75	9.91	8.90

* During the first quarter of 1981 a considerable number of companies were reclassified by industry. To provide comparability, the four quarters of 1980 have been restated to reflect these reclassifications.

† See Publication Schedule, page 4. First quarter estimates for Retail Trade will be published in the form of a press release during July 1981.

	All Retail Trade*					All Wholesale Trade*				
	1Q 1980	2Q 1980	3Q 1980	4Q 1980	1Q† 1981	1Q 1980	2Q 1980	3Q 1980	4Q 1980	1Q 1981
	(percent of net sales)					(percent of net sales)				
	100.0	100.0	100.0	100.0		100.0	100.0	100.0	100.0	100.0
	1.2	1.2	1.1	1.1		0.7	0.7	0.7	0.7	0.7
	96.6	96.0	95.8	94.7		96.3	96.3	96.2	96.5	96.6
	2.2	2.8	3.0	4.2		3.0	3.0	3.1	2.8	2.7
	−0.5	−0.5	0.5	−0.6		−0.4	−0.4	−0.3	−0.4	−0.5
	1.7	2.3	2.4	3.6		2.6	2.6	2.8	2.4	2.3
	0.1	0.1	0.1	0.1		0.3	0.2	0.2	0.2	0.2
	0.7	0.9	0.9	1.3		1.1	1.0	1.1	1.0	0.9
	1.1	1.6	1.6	2.4		1.7	1.8	1.9	1.6	1.5
	(percent)					(percent)				
	13.88	18.37	19.93	31.73		27.87	27.34	29.49	26.73	24.60
	8.47	11.70	12.60	20.16		16.38	17.63	18.82	16.46	15.14
	5.44	7.30	7.77	12.54		9.95	9.89	10.75	9.42	8.65
	3.32	4.65	4.92	7.97		5.85	6.38	6.86	5.80	5.33

EXHIBIT 14:   BALANCE SHEET IN RATIO FORMAT FOR CORPORATIONS IN MINING, RETAIL, WHOLESALE

ITEMS STATED AS A PERCENT OF TOTAL ASSETS

	All Mining*				
	1Q 1980	2Q 1980	3Q 1980	4Q 1980	1Q 1981
Assets					
Cash on hand and in banks....................................	5.0	4.6	4.9	5.8	5.4
U.S. Government and other securities	2.4	2.7	2.8	2.5	2.1
Receivables...	13.3	13.3	13.3	13.5	13.6
Inventories...	5.0	5.1	5.2	4.9	4.6
Current assets not elsewhere specified........................	3.2	3.1	3.3	3.1	3.2
Total current assets.......................................	28.8	28.9	29.5	29.9	28.9
Land and depreciable fixed assets............................	87.2	86.7	85.3	84.5	85.7
Deduct: Accumulated depreciation, depletion					
& amortization	29.9	29.6	29.3	28.8	28.0
Net property, plant & equipment..........................	57.3	57.0	56.0	55.7	57.7
Non-current assets not elsewhere specified, including investment in non-consolidated entities, other long term investments,					
intangibles, etc..	13.8	14.1	14.4	14.4	13.4
Total assets.......................................	100.0	100.0	100.0	100.0	100.0
Liabilities and stockholders' equity					
Short-term loans & current installments	5.7	5.2	5.1	5.4	5.5
Trade accounts and trade notes payable	7.6	8.3	8.4	8.4	8.2
Income taxes accrued, prior and current years, net of payments					
a. Federal	1.1	0.7	0.5	1.2	1.3
b. Other	0.1	0.2	0.2	0.1	0.1
Other current liabilities	5.0	4.9	4.9	5.0	4.9
Total current liabilities	19.5	19.3	19.3	20.4	20.1
Long-term debt due in more than 1 year					
a. Loans from banks.....................................	14.8	14.6	12.5	12.7	12.0
b. Other long-term debt	14.3	15.1	14.4	15.1	15.5
Non-current liabilities not elsewhere specified, including					
deferred income taxes	7.8	8.0	8.4	8.2	8.2
Minority stockholders' interest in consolidated					
domestic corporations....................................	0.3	0.3	0.4	0.3	0.3
Total liabilities	56.8	57.3	55.0	56.7	56.1
Capital stock and other capital	19.2	19.1	21.0	18.7	18.9
Retained earnings	25.1	24.3	24.9	25.4	25.8
Deduct: Treasury stock, at cost	1.0	0.7	0.8	0.8	0.8
Stockholders' equity	43.2	42.7	45.0	43.3	43.9
Total liabilities and stockholders' equity...............	100.0	100.0	100.0	100.0	100.0
Balance sheet ratios			(times)		
Current assets to current liabilities	1.48	1.50	1.53	1.47	1.44
Total cash, U.S. Government and other securities to total					
current liabilities	.38	.38	.40	.41	.37
Total stockholders' equity to debt...........................	1.24	1.22	1.40	1.30	1.33

* During the first quarter of 1981 a considerable number of companies were reclassified by industry. To provide comparability, the four quarters of 1980 have been restated to reflect these reclassifications.

† See Publication Schedule, page 4. First quarter estimates for Retail Trade will be published in the form of a press release during July 1981.

	All Retail Trade*					All Wholesale Trade*			
1Q 1980	2Q 1980	3Q 1980	4Q 1980	1Q† 1981	1Q 1980	2Q 1980	3Q 1980	4Q 1980	1Q 1981
6.1	6.4	6.1	6.7		5.8	5.8	6.0	5.8	5.4
0.9	0.9	1.0	1.1		1.6	1.6	1.8	1.6	1.7
13.9	13.7	13.9	14.9		31.2	30.6	30.7	30.6	30.5
39.3	38.8	38.9	37.4		34.2	34.0	33.2	33.4	33.4
3.2	3.1	3.3	3.2		3.5	3.4	3.4	3.7	3.8
63.3	62.9	63.2	63.3		76.3	75.4	75.1	75.1	74.8
46.8	47.4	46.8	47.2		28.1	29.2	29.7	29.3	29.4
17.8	18.1	17.8	18.1		11.3	11.8	12.2	11.9	11.8
29.1	29.3	29.0	29.0		16.8	17.4	17.5	17.5	17.6
7.6	7.7	7.8	7.7		6.9	7.2	7.4	7.4	7.6
100.0	100.0	100.0	100.0		100.0	100.0	100.0	100.0	100.0
13.8	13.9	13.1	12.7		16.9	16.6	16.7	17.3	17.4
15.4	14.9	16.3	15.5		24.8	24.8	24.8	25.2	24.6
1.5	1.3	1.2	1.5		1.7	1.4	1.4	1.3	1.2
0.2	0.2	0.2	0.2		0.2	0.2	0.2	0.2	0.2
6.6	6.5	6.5	6.9		5.6	5.4	5.6	5.6	5.9
37.5	36.7	37.4	36.8		49.2	48.4	48.6	49.6	49.4
6.7	6.5	6.3	5.9		5.2	5.3	5.0	5.2	5.2
11.6	12.1	12.3	12.4		7.4	7.7	7.5	7.6	7.7
4.9	4.9	4.9	5.2		2.3	2.3	2.3	2.2	2.4
0.1	0.1	0.1	0.1		0.1	0.1	0.1	0.1	0.1
60.8	60.3	61.0	60.5		64.3	63.8	63.5	64.8	64.8
11.0	11.5	11.1	10.9		10.4	10.3	10.3	9.9	9.9
29.5	29.6	29.3	29.9		26.4	27.1	27.4	26.5	26.3
1.3	1.3	1.4	1.3		1.1	1.2	1.2	1.2	1.1
39.2	39.7	39.0	39.5		35.7	36.2	36.5	35.2	35.2
100.0	100.0	100.0	100.0		100.0	100.0	100.0	100.0	100.0
		(times)					(times)		
1.69	1.72	1.69	1.72		1.55	1.56	1.55	1.51	1.52
.19	.20	.19	.21		.15	.15	.16	.15	.14
1.22	1.22	1.23	1.27		1.21	1.22	1.25	1.17	1.16

General Business and Economic Indicators

SELECTED BUSINESS STATISTICS

SEASONALLY ADJUSTED WHERE APPLICABLE—SHADED AREA DENOTES RECESSIONS/ DEPRESSIONS

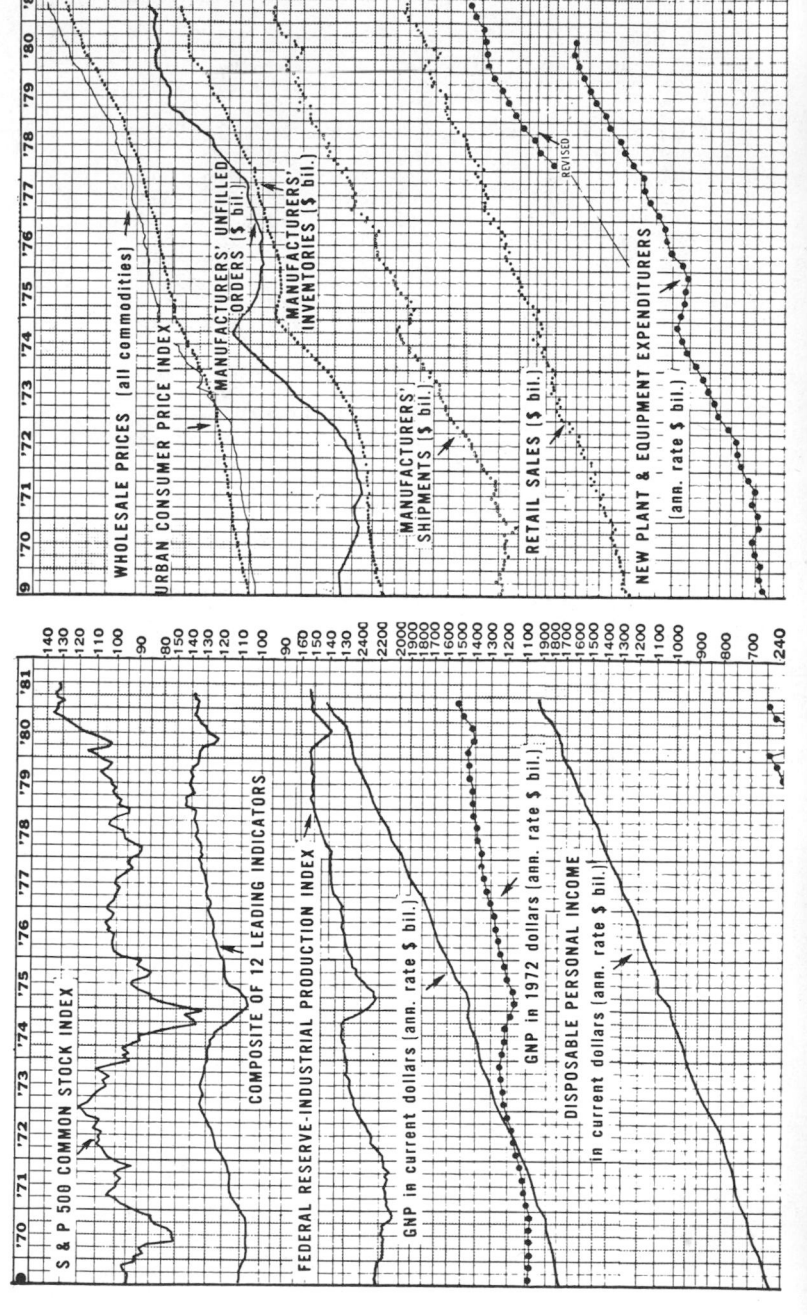

S & P 500 COMMON STOCK INDEX

COMPOSITE OF 12 LEADING INDICATORS

FEDERAL RESERVE-INDUSTRIAL PRODUCTION INDEX

GNP in current dollars (ann. rate $ bil.)

GNP in 1972 dollars (ann. rate $ bil.)

DISPOSABLE PERSONAL INCOME in current dollars (ann. rate $ bil.)

WHOLESALE PRICES (all commodities)

URBAN CONSUMER PRICE INDEX

MANUFACTURERS' UNFILLED ORDERS ($ bil.)

MANUFACTURERS' INVENTORIES ($ bil.)

MANUFACTURERS' SHIPMENTS ($ bil.)

RETAIL SALES ($ bil.)

REVISED

NEW PLANT & EQUIPMENT EXPENDITURES (ann. rate $ bil.)

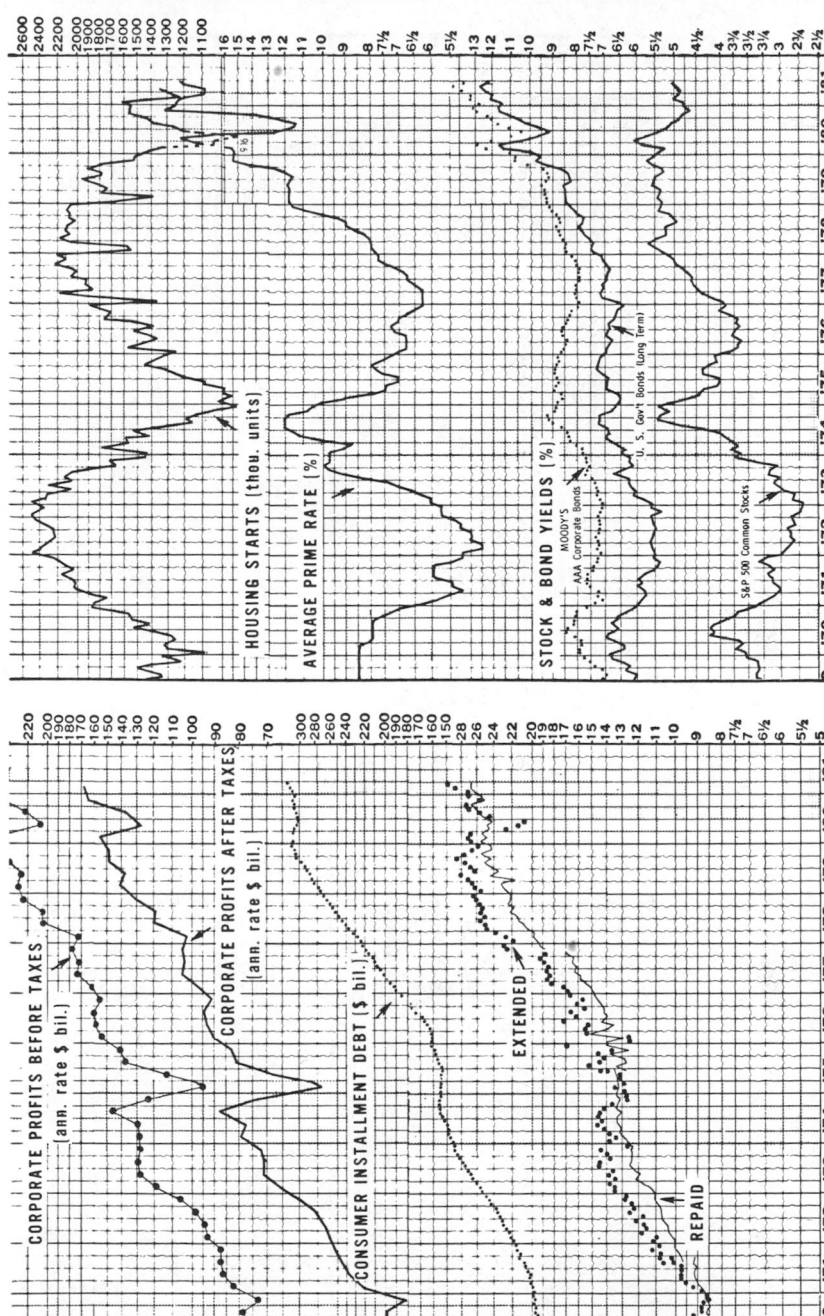

HOUSING STARTS (thou. units)

AVERAGE PRIME RATE (%)

STOCK & BOND YIELDS (%)

MOODY'S
AAA Corporate Bonds

U. S. Gov't Bonds (Long Term)

S&P 500 Common Stocks

CORPORATE PROFITS BEFORE TAXES
(ann. rate $ bil.)

CORPORATE PROFITS AFTER TAXES
(ann. rate $ bil.)

CONSUMER INSTALLMENT DEBT ($ bil.)

EXTENDED

REPAID

Source: 3-Trend CYCLI-GRAPHS. The charts are courtesy of Securities Research Company, 208 Newbury Street, Boston, Mass. 02116, July, quarterly edition, 1981.

COMPOSITE INDEXES AND THEIR COMPONENTS

COMPOSITE INDEXES

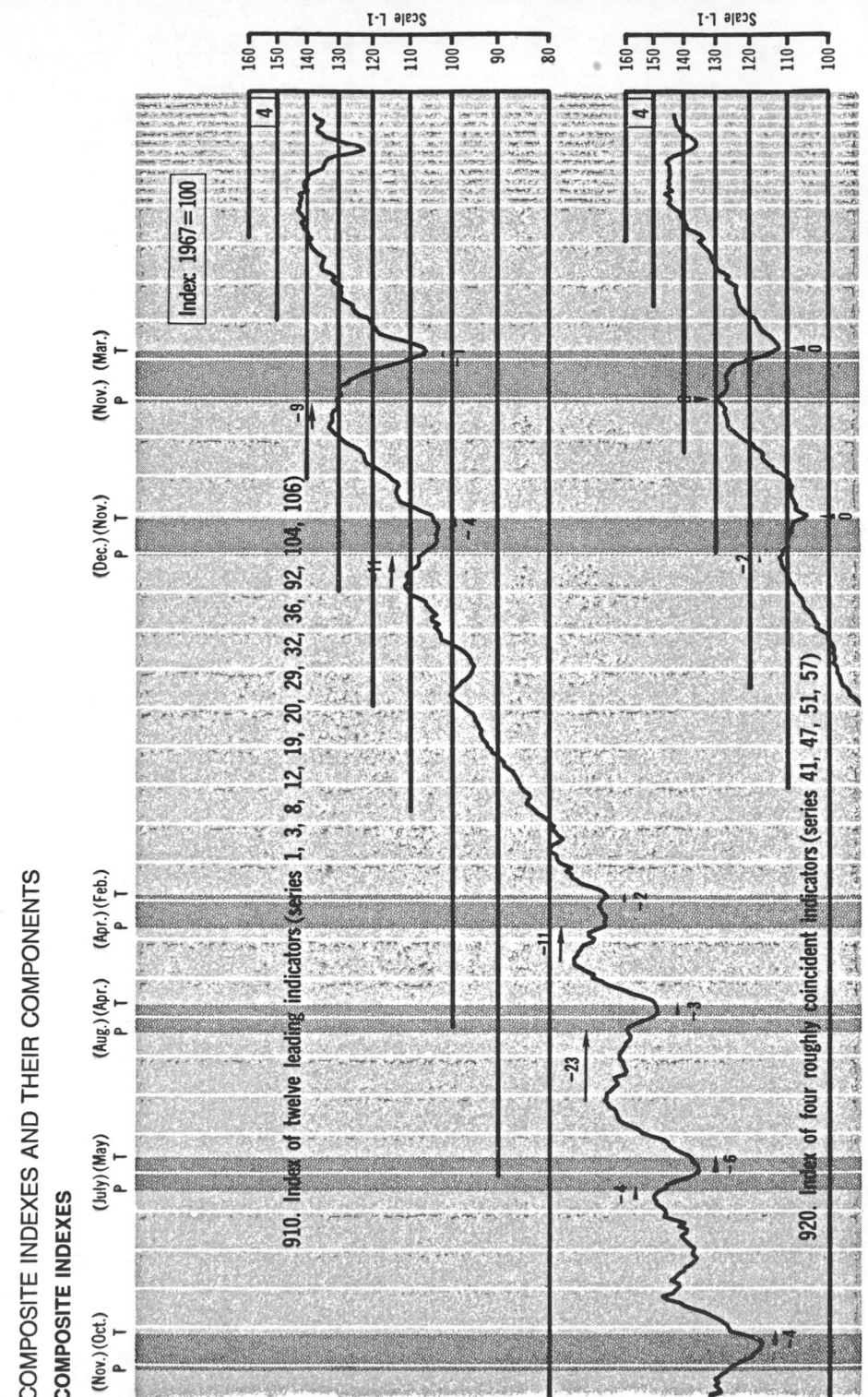

Index: 1967 = 100

910. Index of twelve leading indicators (series 1, 3, 8, 12, 19, 20, 29, 32, 36, 92, 104, 106)

920. Index of four roughly coincident indicators (series 41, 47, 51, 57)

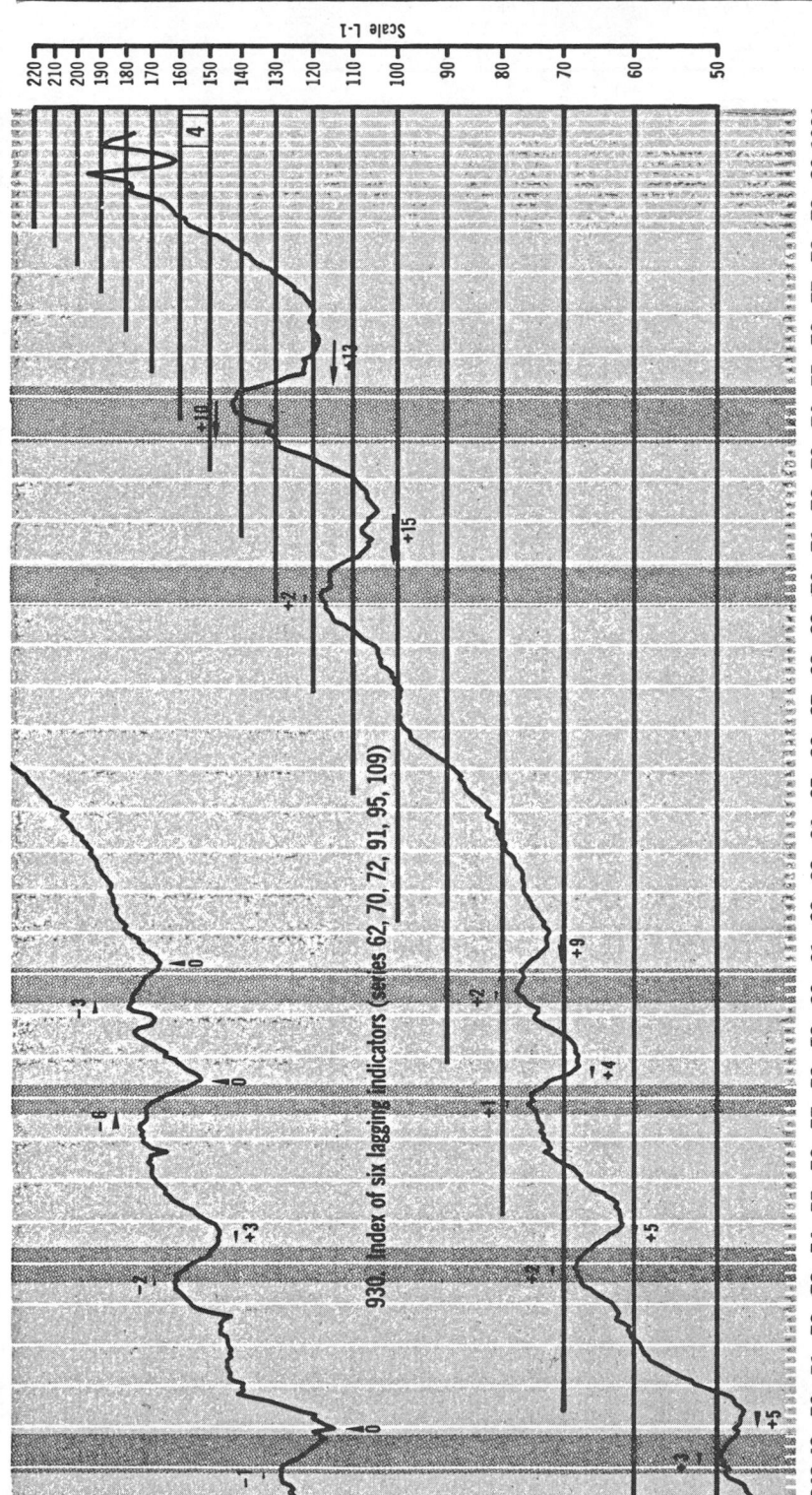

Scale L-1

220 210 200 190 180 170 160 150 140 130 120 110 100 90 80 70 60 50

1948 49 50 51 52 53 54 55 56 57 58 59 60 61 62 63 64 65 66 67 68 69 70 71 72 73 74 75 76 77 78 79 80 1981

930. Index of six lagging indicators (series 62, 70, 72, 91, 95, 109)

NOTE: Numbers entered on the chart indicate length of leads (−) and lags (+) in months from reference turning dates.

Source: *Business Conditions Digest*, U.S. Department of Commerce, Bureau of Economic Analysis.

SUMMARY OF RECENT DATA AND CURRENT CHANGES FOR PRINCIPAL INDICATORS

Series title	Timing classification[3]	Unit of measure	Basic data[1]								Percent change				Series number
			Average 1979	Average 1980	3d Q 1980	4th Q 1980	1st Q 1981	Feb. 1981	Mar. 1981	Apr. 1981	Feb. to Mar. 1981	Mar. to Apr. 1981	3d Q to 4th Q 1980	4th Q to 1st Q 1981	
I. CYCLICAL INDICATORS															
A. Composite Indexes															
910. Twelve leading indicators	L,L,L	1967=100	140.1	131.5	131.5	136.4	136.4	135.4	137.8	138.3	1.8	0.4	4.0	-0.3	910
920. Four coincident indicators	C,C,C	...do...	145.1	140.4	137.2	141.2	143.1	143.0	143.5	143.5	0.3	0.	2.9	1.3	920
930. Six lagging indicators	Lg,Lg,Lg	...do...	166.4	176.8	163.2	178.1	185.0	186.0	180.1	177.2	-3.2	-1.6	9.1	3.9	930
Leading Indicator Subgroups:															
913. Marginal employment adjustments	L,L,L	...do...	96.8	93.4	92.9	95.5	95.2	95.0	94.9	94.9	-0.1	0.	2.8	-0.3	913
914. Capital investment commitments	L,L,L	...do...	113.5	107.2	107.3	107.9	106.3	105.5	106.6	106.1	1.0	-0.5	0.6	-1.5	914
915. Inventory investment and purchasing	L,L,L	...do...	105.9	101.1	99.9	103.4	103.0	102.9	104.3	105.2	1.4	0.9	3.5	-0.4	915
916. Profitability	L,L,L	...do...	91.7	90.7	91.2	92.1	NA	92.9	NA	NA	NA	NA	1.0	NA	916
917. Money and financial flows	L,L,L	...do...	145.5	135.6	136.8	139.2	141.1	141.2	141.5	141.0	0.2	-0.4	1.8	1.4	917
B. Cyclical Indicators by Economic Process															
B1. Employment and Unemployment															
Marginal Employment Adjustments:															
*1. Average workweek, prod. workers, mfg.[3]	L,L,L	Hours	40.2	39.7	39.3	39.9	40.1	39.8	40.0	40.1	0.5	0.2	1.5	0.5	1
21. Avg. weekly overtime, prod. workers, mfg.[2]	L,C,L	...do...	3.3	2.8	2.6	2.9	2.9	2.9	2.8	2.9	-0.1	0.1	0.3	0.	21
2. Accession rate, per 100 employees, mfg.[2]	L,L,L	Percent	4.0	3.5	3.6	3.7	3.5	3.6	3.3	3.3	-0.1	-0.2	0.1	-0.2	2
5. Avg. weekly initial claims (inverted[4])	L,C,L	Thousands	381	484	513	411	413	402	421	408	-4.7	3.1	19.9	-0.5	5
*3. Layoff rate, per 100 employ., mfg. (inv.[4])[2]	L,L,U	Percent	1.1	1.7	1.7	1.2	1.4	1.4	1.4	1.4	0.	0.	0.5	-0.2	3
4. Quit rate, per 100 employees, mfg.[2]	L,Lg,U	...do...	2.0	1.5	1.3	1.4	1.5	1.5	1.4	1.3	-0.1	-0.1	0.1	0.1	4
Job Vacancies:															
60. Ratio, help-wanted advertising to persons unemployed[2]	L,Lg,U	Ratio	0.786	0.520	0.448	0.491	0.488	0.495	0.483	NA	-0.012	NA	0.043	-0.003	60
46. Help-wanted advertising[2]	L,Lg,U	1967=100	158	129	119	130	128	129	126	NA	-2.3	NA	9.2	-1.5	46
Comprehensive Employment:															
48. Employee hours in nonagri. establishments	U,C,C	A.r. bil. hrs.	169.72	169.96	168.17	170.41	172.34	171.80	172.19	170.48	0.2	-1.0	1.3	1.1	48
42. Persons engaged in nonagri. activities	U,C,C	Thousands	93,648	93,960	93,769	93,925	94,692	94,646	95,136	95,513	0.5	0.4	0.2	0.8	42
*41. Employees on nonagri. payrolls	C,C,C	...do...	89,886	90,657	90,131	90,932	91,616	91,652	91,714	91,494	0.1	-0.2	0.9	0.8	41
40. Employees in mfg., mining, construction	L,C,U	...do...	26,504	25,855	25,317	25,780	26,013	25,987	26,010	25,831	0.1	-0.7	1.8	0.9	40
90. Ratio, civilian employment to total population of working age[2]	U,Lg,U	Percent	59.25	58.51	58.27	58.18	58.43	58.38	58.61	58.89	0.23	0.28	-0.09	0.25	90

Comprehensive Unemployment:															
37. Total unemployed (inverted[4])	L,Lg,U	Thousands	5,963	7,448	7,921	7,897	7,788	7,754	7,764	7,746	-0.1	0.2	0.3	1.4	37
43. Unemployment rate, total (inverted[4])[2]	L,Lg,U	Percent	5.8	7.1	7.5	7.5	7.3	7.3	7.3	7.3	0.	0.	0.	0.2	43
45. Avg. weekly insured unemploy. rate (inv.[4])[2]	L,Lg,U	....do.	2.9	3.9	4.3	3.8	3.3	3.2	3.3	3.3	-0.1	0.	0.5	0.5	45
*91. Avg. duration of unemployment (inverted[4])	Lg,Lg,Lg	Weeks	10.8	11.9	12.4	13.5	14.3	14.4	14.0	13.7	2.8	2.1	-8.9	-5.9	91
44. Unemploy. rate, 15 weeks and over (inv.[4])[2]	Lg,Lg,Lg	Percent	1.2	1.7	2.0	2.2	2.1	2.1	2.1	2.0	0.	0.1	-0.2	0.1	44
B2. Production and Income															
Comprehensive Output and Income:															
50. GNP in 1972 dollars	C,C,C	A.r., bil. dol.	1483.0	1480.7	1471.9	1485.6	1516.0	...	...	...	...	...	0.9	2.0	50
52. Personal income in 1972 dollars	C,C,C	....do.	1197.4	1207.5	1207.6	1220.0	1230.5	1231.5	1232.4	1237.4	0.1	0.4	1.0	0.9	52
*51. Pers. income less transfer pay., 1972 dollars	C,C,C	....do.	1043.8	1043.2	1035.6	1050.3	1060.9	1062.3	1062.6	1066.5	0.	0.4	1.4	1.0	51
53. Wages and salaries in mining, mfg., and construction, 1972 dollars	C,C,C	....do.	247.2	231.0	226.0	231.0	233.3	232.6	232.3	231.3	-0.1	-0.4	2.2	1.0	53
Industrial Production:															
*47. Industrial production, total	C,C,C	1967=100	152.5	147.1	142.1	149.1	151.8	151.5	152.2	152.8	0.5	0.4	4.9	1.8	47
73. Industrial production, durable mfrs.	C,C,C	....do.	146.4	136.6	129.8	138.6	141.5	140.6	142.4	143.6	1.3	0.8	6.8	2.1	73
74. Industrial production, nondurable mfrs.	C,L,L	....do.	164.0	161.1	157.3	163.4	165.7	166.3	165.6	166.2	-0.4	0.4	3.9	1.4	74
49. Value of goods output, 1972 dollars	C,C,C	A.r., bil. dol.	674.5	665.2	657.5	662.9	689.6	...	...	...	...	...	0.8	4.0	49
Capacity Utilization:															
82. Capacity utilization rate, mfg., FRB[2]	L,C,U	Percent	85.6	79.0	75.7	79.2	79.9	...	...	...	...	...	3.5	0.7	82
83. Capacity utilization rate, mfg., BEA[2]	.....	....do.	82	78	76	78	NA	...	...	...	...	...	2	NA	83
84. Capacity utilization rate, materials, FRB[2]	L,C,U	....do.	87.4	79.8	74.9	80.0	81.6	...	...	...	...	...	5.1	1.6	84
B3. Consumption, Trade, Orders, and Deliveries															
Orders and Deliveries:															
6. New orders, durable goods	L,L,L	Bil. dol.	77.20	76.34	75.14	81.46	82.59	82.21	84.21	83.85	2.4	-0.4	8.4	1.4	6
7. New orders, durable goods, 1972 dollars	L,L,L	....do.	41.40	36.86	35.98	38.09	38.17	38.01	38.75	38.23	1.9	-1.3	5.9	0.2	7
*8. New orders, cons. goods and mtls., 1972 dol.	L,L,L	....do.	36.46	32.80	32.13	34.29	33.69	34.38	34.07	34.41	-0.9	1.0	6.7	-1.7	8
25. Chg. in unfilled orders, durable goods[2]	L,L,L	....do.	3.26	0.99	1.41	1.71	1.46	1.13	2.16	1.29	1.03	-0.87	0.30	-0.25	25
96. Mfrs.' unfilled orders, durable goods[5]	L,Lg,U	Bil. dol., EOP	267.88	279.75	274.62	279.75	284.11	281.95	284.11	285.40	0.8	0.5	1.9	1.6	96
*32. Vendor performance[2] (u)	L,L,L	Percent	63	40	35	45	49	50	52	56	2	4	10	4	32
Consumption and Trade:															
56. Manufacturing and trade sales	C,C,C	Bil. dol.	288.22	312.04	310.16	331.39	345.97	346.45	345.88	NA	-0.2	NA	6.8	4.4	56
*57. Manufacturing and trade sales, 1972 dollars	C,C,C	....do.	159.46	153.35	151.21	155.77	157.84	156.97	159.15	NA	1.4	NA	3.0	1.3	57
75. Industrial production, consumer goods	C,L,C	1967=100	150.8	145.5	143.0	147.4	147.6	147.0	148.5	149.7	1.0	0.8	3.1	0.1	75
54. Sales of retail stores	C,L,U	Mil. dol.	74,529	79,721	79,980	82,586	86,482	86,810	87,174	86,309	0.4	-1.0	3.3	4.7	54
59. Sales of retail stores, 1972 dollars	U,L,U	....do.	45,172	43,656	43,461	43,781	44,980	45,166	45,005	44,558	-0.4	-1.0	0.7	2.7	59
55. Personal consumption expend., autos	L,C,C	A.r., bil. dol.	65.3	61.8	58.7	66.1	74.8	...	...	...	...	...	12.6	13.2	55
58. Index of consumer sentiment (u)	L,L,L	I Q 1966=100	66.0	64.4	67.8	72.1	68.3	66.9	66.5	72.4	-0.6	8.9	6.3	-5.3	58
B4. Fixed Capital Investment															
Formation of Business Enterprises:															
*12. Net business formation	L,L,L	1967=100	131.7	121.1	117.9	120.0	NA	116.9	NA	NA	NA	NA	1.8	NA	12
13. New business incorporations	L,L,L	Number	43,714	44,337	44,604	47,470	NA	NA	NA	NA	NA	NA	6.4	NA	13

SUMMARY OF RECENT DATA AND CURRENT CHANGES FOR PRINCIPAL INDICATORS (continued)

Series title	Timing classification[3]	Unit of measure	Basic data[1] — Average 1979	1980	3d Q 1980	4th Q 1980	1st Q 1981	Feb. 1981	Mar. 1981	Apr. 1981	Percent change Feb. to Mar. 1981	Mar. to Apr. 1981	3d Q to 4th Q 1980	4th Q 1980 to 1st Q 1981	Series number
I. CYCLICAL INDICATORS—Con.															
B4. Fixed Capital Investment—Con.															
Business Investment Commitments:															
10. Contracts and orders, plant and equipment ...	L,L,L	Bil. dol. ...	25.47	24.66	24.23	25.96	26.39	23.74	28.04	25.72	18.1	-8.3	7.1	1.7	10
*20. Contr. and orders, plant and equip., 1972 dol. ...	L,L,L	....do. ...	14.65	13.25	13.06	13.58	13.58	12.34	14.24	12.96	15.4	-9.0	4.0	0.	20
24. New orders, cap. goods indus., nondefense ...	L,L,L	....do. ...	21.64	21.30	20.61	21.38	22.96	20.59	23.79	22.61	15.5	-5.0	3.7	7.4	24
27. New orders, capital goods industries, nondefense, 1972 dollars ...	L,L,L	....do. ...	12.68	11.72	11.42	11.51	12.07	10.95	12.37	11.59	13.0	-6.3	0.8	4.9	27
9. Construction contracts, commercial and industrial buildings, floor space ...	L,C,U	Mil. sq. ft. ...	90.52	77.96	69.50	85.24	84.37	84.41	90.00	77.53	6.6	-13.9	22.6	-1.0	9
11. New capital appropriations, mfg.[5] ...	U,Lg,U	Bil. dol. ...	22.20	26.36	24.29	25.81	29.88	...	...	...	...	...	6.3	15.8	11
97. Backlog of capital appropriations, mfg.[5] ...	C,Lg,Lg	Bil. dol., EOP	76.66	91.87	89.72	91.87	96.48	...	...	...	...	...	2.4	5.0	97
Business Investment Expenditures:															
61. Business expend., new plant and equipment ...	C,Lg,Lg	A.r., bil. dol.	270.46	295.63	296.23	299.58	310.10	...	...	...	...	...	1.1	3.5	61
69. Machinery and equipment sales and business construction expenditures ...	C,Lg,Lg	....do. ...	271.93	298.01	294.14	304.95	317.61	311.55	323.23	NA	3.7	NA	3.7	4.2	69
76. Industrial production, business equip. ...	C,Lg,U	1967=100. ...	171.3	173.3	170.3	174.9	179.2	178.2	180.4	182.6	1.2	1.2	2.7	2.5	76
86. Nonresid. fixed investment, total, 1972 dol. ...	C,Lg,C	A.r., bil. dol.	163.3	158.4	155.5	157.0	162.0	...	...	...	...	...	1.0	3.2	86
Residential Construction Commitments and Investment:															
28. New private housing units started, total ...	L,L,L	A.r., thous. ...	1,745	1,292	1,390	1,535	1,388	1,215	1,289	1,343	6.1	4.2	10.4	-9.6	28
*29. New building permits, private housing ...	L,L,L	1967=100. ...	123.6	96.6	110.5	106.8	95.1	94.1	93.1	95.4	-1.1	2.5	-3.3	-11.0	29
89. Fixed investment, residential, 1972 dol. ...	L,L,L	A.r., bil. dol.	59.1	48.1	44.7	50.6	50.8	...	...	...	...	...	13.2	0.4	89
B5. Inventories and Inventory Investment															
Inventory Investment:															
30. Chg. in business inventories, 1972 dol.[2] ...	L,L,L	....do. ...	10.2	-2.9	-5.0	-7.2	-2.3	...	...	...	...	...	-2.2	4.9	30
*36. Change in inventories on hand and on order, 1972 dollars (smoothed[6])[2] ...	L,L,L	....do. ...	10.49	-9.60	-13.69	-0.92	-6.26	-7.81	-4.76	NA	3.05	NA	12.77	-5.34	36
31. Chg. in book value, mfg. and trade invent.[2] ...	L,L,L	....do. ...	46.2	30.0	30.1	8.8	40.5	68.4	12.5	NA	-55.9	NA	-21.3	31.7	31
38. Chg. in mtl. stocks on hand and on order[2] ...	L,L,L	Bil. dol. ...	2.56	0.42	0.25	1.21	0.38	0.89	0.14	NA	-0.75	NA	0.96	-0.83	38
Inventories on Hand and on Order:															
71. Mfg. and trade inventories, total[5] ...	Lg,Lg,Lg	Bil. dol., EOP	426.80	461.72	454.57	461.72	471.84	470.80	471.84	NA	0.2	NA	1.6	2.2	71
*70. Mfg. and trade invent., total, 1972 dol.[5] ...	Lg,Lg,Lg	....do. ...	265.44	262.97	264.24	262.97	262.51	262.98	262.51	NA	-0.2	NA	-0.5	-0.2	70

Series	Unit	Code													Series No.
B6. Prices, Costs, and Profits															
65. Mfrs.' inventories of finished goods³	...do. ...	Lg,Lg,Lg	70.53	75.58	76.76	75.58	78.57	76.62	78.57	NA	2.5	NA	-1.5	4.0	65
77. Ratio, inventories to sales, mfg. and trade, constant dollars²	Ratio.	Lg,Lg,Lg	1.66	1.73	1.75	1.69	1.67	1.68	1.65	NA	-0.03	NA	-0.06	-0.02	77
78. Materials and supplies, stocks on hand and on order⁵	Bil. dol., EOP	L,Lg,Lg	199.20	204.27	200.63	204.27	205.41	205.26	205.41	NA	0.1	NA	1.8	0.6	78
Sensitive Commodity Prices:															
*92. Chg. in sensitive prices (smoothed⁶)² ⑬	Percent.....	L,L,L	1.98	1.49	1.14	2.28	2.33	2.15	3.54	3.89	1.39	0.35	1.14	0.05	92
23. Spot market prices, raw industrials ⑪	1967=100...	U,L,L	293.0	298.0	289.3	301.3	288.5	284.2	289.8	293.0	2.0	1.1	4.1	-4.2	23
Stock Prices:															
*19. Stock prices, 500 common stocks ⑪	1941-43=10..	L,L,L	103.01	118.78	123.28	133.12	131.52	128.40	133.19	134.43	3.7	0.9	8.0	-1.2	19
Profits and Profit Margins:															
16. Corporate profits after taxes	A.r., bil. dol.	L,L,L	167.8	163.2	159.1	164.3	168.3	...	...	...	...	...	3.3	2.4	16
18. Corp. profits after taxes, 1972 dollars	...do. ...	L,L,L	99.6	88.8	85.5	86.6	87.4	...	...	...	...	...	1.3	0.9	18
79. Corp. profits after taxes with IVA and CCAdj	...do. ...	L,C,L	109.2	100.3	99.4	98.1	112.2	...	...	...	...	...	-1.3	14.4	79
80. ...do. ...in 1972 dol.	...do. ...	L,C,L	65.5	55.1	54.0	52.2	58.6	...	...	...	...	...	-3.3	12.3	80
15. Profits (after taxes) per dol. of sales, mfg.²	Cents.....	L,L,L	5.7	4.9	4.6	4.9	NA	...	...	...	...	...	-0.3	NA	15
26. Ratio, price to unit labor cost, nonfarm bus. ...	1977=100...	L,L,L	96.8	96.3	96.5	96.4	96.6	...	...	...	...	...	-0.1	0.2	26
Cash Flows:															
34. Net cash flow, corporate	A.r., bil. dol.	L,L,L	257.1	265.4	262.9	272.0	279.3	...	...	...	...	...	3.5	2.7	34
35. Net cash flow, corporate, 1972 dollars	...do. ...	L,L,L	149.1	141.8	138.6	141.1	143.1	...	...	...	...	...	1.8	1.4	35
Unit Labor Costs and Labor Share:															
63. Unit labor cost, private business sector	1977=100..	Lg,Lg,Lg	119.9	132.4	133.9	137.0	139.5	...	...	...	...	...	2.3	1.8	63
68. Labor cost (cur. dol.) per unit of gross domestic product (1972), nonfin. corp.	Dollars.....	Lg,Lg,Lg	1.092	1.196	1.203	1.230	1.246	...	...	...	...	...	2.2	1.3	68
*62. Labor cost per unit of output, mfg.	1967=100...	Lg,Lg,Lg	175.8	195.1	200.9	200.1	203.8	204.2	204.3	204.8	0.	0.2	-0.4	1.8	62
64. Compensation of employees as percent of national income²	Percent.	Lg,Lg,Lg	74.4	75.3	75.3	75.4	75.2	...	...	...	...	...	0.1	-0.2	64
B7. Money and Credit															
Money:															
85. Change in money supply (M1-B)²	Percent. ...	L,L,L	0.60	0.52	1.35	0.35	0.93	0.72	0.93	1.56	0.21	0.63	-1.00	0.58	85
102. Change in money supply (M2)²	...do. ...	L,C,U	0.71	0.75	1.18	0.50	0.95	0.81	1.26	0.98	0.45	-0.28	-0.58	0.45	102
*104. Chg. in total liquid assets (smoothed⁶)²	...do. ...	L,L,L	0.97	0.73	0.76	0.88	1.06	1.10	1.04	0.94	-0.06	-0.10	0.12	0.18	104
105. Money supply (M1-B), 1972 dollars	Bil. dol. ...	L,L,L	215.8	202.1	201.9	201.2	199.3	199.0	199.6	201.8	0.3	1.1	-0.3	-0.9	105
*106. Money supply (M2), 1972 dollars	...do. ...	L,L,L	846.5	812.9	819.5	811.2	807.1	805.0	810.2	814.8	0.6	0.6	-1.0	-0.5	106
Velocity of Money:															
107. Ratio, GNP to money supply (M1-B)²	Ratio.	C,C,C	6.446	6.594	6.567	6.620	6.806	...	...	...	...	-0.006	0.053	0.186	107
108. Ratio, pers. income to money supply (M2)²	...do. ...	C,Lg,C	1.323	1.348	1.339	1.356	1.366	1.367	1.362	1.356	-0.005	...	0.017	0.010	108
Credit Flows:															
33. Change in mortgage debt²	A.r., bil. dol.	L,L,L	86.08	60.83	61.72	81.90	53.29	62.82	43.74	NA	-19.08	NA	20.18	-28.61	33
112. Change in business loans²	...do. ...	L,L,L	22.88	19.60	24.38	35.54	-19.64	-13.10	-46.48	53.46	-33.38	99.94	11.16	-55.18	112
113. Change in consumer installment credit²	...do. ...	L,L,L	38.69	2.90	1.38	12.64	23.89	23.95	37.30	NA	13.35	NA	11.26	11.25	113
110. Total private borrowing	...do. ...	L,L,L	356.98	284.12	282.74	340.72	NA	...	...	...	...	...	20.5	NA	110

SUMMARY OF RECENT DATA AND CURRENT CHANGES FOR PRINCIPAL INDICATORS (continued)

Series title	Timing classification[3]	Unit of measure	Average 1979	Average 1980	3d 1980	4th Q 1980	1st Q 1981	Feb. 1981	Mar. 1981	Apr. 1981	Feb. to Mar. 1981	Mar. to Apr. 1981	3d Q to 4th Q 1980	4th Q to 1st Q 1981	Series number
I. CYCLICAL INDICATORS—Con.															
B7. Money and Credit—Con.															
Credit Difficulties:															
14. Liabilities of business failures (inv.[4])	L,L,L	Mil. dol.	222.28	386.26	598.01	295.63	NA	NA	NA	NA	NA	NA	50.6	NA	14
39. Delinquency rate, instal. loans (inv.[4])[2][5]	L,L,L	Percent, EOP	2.64	2.57	2.70	2.57	2.53	2.51	2.53	NA	-0.02	NA	0.13	0.04	39
Bank Reserves:															
93. Free reserves (inverted[4])[2]	L,U,U	Mil. dol.	-1,131	-1,141	-508	-1,269	-872	-1,076	-624	-1,317	-452	693	761	-397	93
94. Borrowing from the Federal Reserve[2]	L,Lg,U	...do.	1,338	1,420	788	1,703	1,229	1,278	1,004	1,343	-274	339	915	-474	94
Interest Rates:															
119. Federal funds rate[2]	L,Lg,Lg	Percent	11.19	13.36	9.84	15.85	16.57	15.93	14.70	15.72	-1.23	1.02	6.01	0.72	119
114. Treasury bill rate[2]	C,Lg,Lg	...do.	10.04	11.61	9.24	13.71	14.37	14.90	13.48	13.63	-1.42	0.15	4.47	0.66	114
115. Treasury bond yields[2]	C,Lg,Lg	...do.	8.74	10.81	10.43	11.64	12.01	12.23	12.15	12.62	-0.08	0.47	1.21	0.37	115
116. Corporate bond yields[2]	Lg,Lg,Lg	...do.	10.05	12.77	12.18	13.88	14.37	14.60	14.49	15.00	-0.11	0.51	1.70	0.49	116
117. Municipal bond yields[2]	U,Lg,Lg	...do.	6.52	8.60	8.58	9.62	9.98	10.10	10.16	10.62	-0.06	0.46	1.04	0.36	117
118. Mortgage yields, residential[2]	Lg,Lg,Lg	...do.	10.89	13.42	13.40	14.31	14.69	14.79	15.04	15.91	0.25	0.87	0.91	0.38	118
67. Bank rates on short-term bus. loans[2]	Lg,Lg,Lg	...do.	13.18	15.27	11.56	15.71	19.91						4.15	4.20	67
*109. Average prime rate charged by banks[2]	Lg,Lg,Lg	...do.	12.67	15.27	11.61	16.73	19.21	19.43	18.05	17.15	-1.38	-0.90	5.12	2.48	109
Outstanding Debt:															
*66. Consumer installment credit[5]	Lg,Lg,Lg	Bil. dol., EOP	303.58	306.47	303.31	306.47	312.45	309.34	312.45	NA	1.0	NA	1.0	2.0	66
*72. Commercial and industrial loans outstanding, weekly reporting large comm. banks	Lg,Lg,Lg	Bil. dol.	147.06	163.76	162.81	170.91	172.23	173.15	169.28	173.74	-2.2	2.6	5.0	0.8	72
*95. Ratio, consumer install. credit to pers. income[2]	Lg,Lg,Lg	Percent	14.79	14.14	13.86	13.52	13.36	13.35	13.36	NA	0.01	NA	-0.34	-0.16	95
II. OTHER IMPORTANT ECONOMIC MEASURES															
B. Prices, Wages, and Productivity															
B1. Price Movements															
310. Implicit price deflator, GNP		1972=100	162.8	177.4	179.2	183.8	188.2						2.6	2.4	310
320. Consumer prices (CPI), all items		1967=100	217.4	246.8	249.6	256.2	262.9	263.2	265.1	266.8	0.7	0.6	2.6	2.6	320
320c. Change in CPI, all items, S/A[2]		Percent	1.0	1.0	0.6	1.0	0.8	1.0	0.6	0.4	-0.4	-0.2	0.4	-0.2	320
322. CPI, food		1967=100	234.5	254.6	257.5	267.4	270.7	270.6	271.6	271.6	0.4	0.	3.8	1.2	322
330. Producer prices (PPI), all commodities		...do.	235.6	268.8	272.9	279.2	286.7	286.9	289.6	292.8	0.9	1.1	2.3	2.7	330
331. PPI, crude materials		...do.	282.2	304.6	314.3	328.8	326.8	331.4	327.0	331.8	-1.3	1.5	4.6	-0.6	331
332. PPI, intermediate materials		...do.	242.8	280.3	283.3	290.4	298.6	297.9	301.1	304.3	1.1	1.1	2.5	2.8	332
333. PPI, capital equipment		...do.	216.7	239.8	242.9	249.5	255.5	255.8	257.7	260.1	0.7	0.9	2.7	2.4	333
334. PPI, finished consumer goods		...do.	215.7	248.9	253.5	258.6	264.1	263.6	267.2	269.3	1.4	0.8	2.0	2.1	334

B2. Wages and Productivity

No.	Series	Units												
340	Average hourly earnings, production workers, private nonfarm economy	do.	229.8	250.6	253.8	260.2	266.5	266.6	268.5	269.2	0.7	0.3	2.5	2.4
341	Real average hourly earnings, production workers, private nonfarm economy	1977=100	105.6	101.7	101.9	101.2	101.0	100.9	101.0	100.9	0.1	-0.1	-0.7	-0.2
345	Average hourly compensation, nonfarm bus.	do.	118.6	130.1	131.6	134.7	138.3	...	...	...	...	...	-2.4	2.7
346	Real avg. hourly comp., nonfarm business	do.	99.1	95.7	95.9	95.1	95.1	...	...	...	...	...	-0.8	0.2
370	Output per hour, private business sector	do.	99.4	99.0	99.2	98.9	99.8	...	...	...	...	...	-0.3	0.9

C. Labor Force, Employment, and Unemployment

No.	Series	Units												
441	Total civilian labor force	Millions	102.91	104.72	104.98	105.17	105.80	105.68	106.18	106.72	0.5	0.5	0.2	0.6
442	Total civilian employment	do.	96.94	97.27	97.06	97.28	98.01	97.93	98.41	98.98	0.5	0.6	0.2	0.8
37	Number of persons unemployed	Thousands	5,963	7,448	7,921	7,897	7,788	7,754	7,764	7,746	0.1	-0.2	-0.3	-1.4
444	Unemployed males, 20 years and over	do.	2,223	3,261	3,631	3,496	3,323	3,312	3,305	3,262	-0.2	-1.3	-3.7	-4.9
445	Unemployed females, 20 years and over	do.	2,213	2,547	2,600	2,734	2,718	2,680	2,725	2,721	1.7	-0.1	5.2	-0.6
446	Unemployed persons, 16-19 years of age	do.	1,528	1,640	1,689	1,667	1,747	1,762	1,734	1,763	-1.6	1.7	-1.3	4.8

Labor Force Participation Rates:

No.	Series	Units												
451	Males, 20 years and over[2]	Percent	79.8	79.4	79.4	79.2	78.9	78.7	79.2	79.4	0.5	0.2	-0.2	-0.3
452	Females, 20 years and over[2]	do.	50.6	51.4	51.5	51.4	51.9	51.9	52.1	52.3	0.2	0.2	-0.1	0.5
453	Both sexes, 16-19 years of age[2]	do.	58.1	56.9	56.4	56.4	56.9	57.0	56.6	57.7	-0.4	1.1	0.	0.5

D. Government Activities
D1. Receipts and Expenditures

No.	Series	Units												
501	Federal Government receipts	A.r., bil. dol.	494.4	540.8	540.8	573.2	619.9	...	...	...	...	...	6.0	8.1
502	Federal Government expenditures	do.	509.6	602.0	615.0	641.1	664.3	...	...	...	...	...	4.2	3.6
500	Federal Government surplus or deficit[3]	do.	-14.8	-61.2	-74.2	-67.9	-44.4	...	...	...	...	...	6.3	23.5
511	State and local government receipts	do.	351.2	384.0	386.8	403.4	411.9	...	...	...	...	...	4.3	2.1
512	State and local government expenditures	do.	324.4	355.0	358.2	366.3	373.9	...	...	...	...	...	2.3	1.0
510	State and local govt. surplus or deficit[2]	do.	26.7	29.1	28.6	37.1	37.9	...	...	...	...	...	8.5	0.8

D2. Defense Indicators

No.	Series	Units												
517	Defense Department obligations	Mil. dol.	11,141	13,392	13,319	13,905	NA	15,741	NA	NA	NA	NA	4.4	NA
525	Military prime contract awards	do.	5,356	6,961	7,270	7,010	NA	NA	NA	NA	NA	NA	-3.6	NA
548	New orders, defense products	do.	3,284	4,577	5,113	4,729	4,895	5,657	4,835	4,744	-14.5	-1.9	-7.5	3.5
564	National defense purchases	A.r., bil. dol.	111.2	131.7	131.4	141.6	145.0	...	...	...	...	...	7.8	2.4

E. U.S. International Transactions
E1. Merchandise Trade

No.	Series	Units												
602	Exports, total except military aid	Mil. dol.	15,137	18,390	18,727	19,060	20,008	19,764	21,434	NA	8.4	NA	1.8	5.0
604	Exports of agricultural products	do.	2,886	3,435	3,480	3,596	4,158	3,977	4,201	NA	5.6	NA	3.3	15.6
606	Exports of nonelectrical machinery	do.	3,009	3,788	4,081	3,968	4,188	4,155	4,352	NA	4.7	NA	-2.8	5.5
612	General imports, total	do.	17,160	20,417	19,597	20,548	22,022	21,922	20,949	NA	-4.4	NA	12.9	7.2
614	Imports of petroleum and products	do.	4,676	6,139	5,384	6,060	7,123	8,018	5,992	NA	-25.3	NA	12.6	17.5
616	Imports of automobiles and parts	do.	1,853	2,030	2,171	2,133	2,044	1,742	2,125	NA	22.0	NA	-1.8	-4.2

SUMMARY OF RECENT DATA AND CURRENT CHANGES FOR PRINCIPAL INDICATORS (concluded)

Series number	Series title	Unit of measure	Average 1978	Average 1979	Average 1980	4th Q 1979	1st Q 1980	2d Q 1980	3d Q 1980	4th Q 1980	1st Q 1981	Percent change 2d Q to 3d Q 1980	3d Q to 4th Q 1980	4th Q 1980 to 1st Q 1981
	II. OTHER IMPORTANT ECONOMIC MEASURES—Con.													
	E2. Goods and Services Movements Except Transfers Under Military Grants													
618	Merchandise exports	Mil. dol.	35,514	45,517	55,445	50,239	54,302	55,029	55,766	56,684	61,932	1.3	1.6	9.3
620	Merchandise imports	do.	43,953	52,864	62,284	59,397	65,006	62,282	59,155	62,692	65,622	-5.0	6.0	4.7
622	Merchandise trade balance³	do.	-8,440	-7,346	-6,838	-9,158	-10,704	-7,253	-3,389	-6,008	-3,690	3,864	-2,619	2,318
651	Income on U.S. investments abroad	do.	10,743	16,492	19,008	18,407	20,824	16,620	18,756	19,830	NA	12.9	5.7	NA
652	Income on foreign investment in the U.S.	do.	5,518	8,365	10,874	9,524	10,762	10,518	10,700	11,514	NA	1.7	7.6	NA
668	Exports of goods and services	do.	55,260	71,630	85,222	78,307	85,521	81,767	86,015	87,586	NA	5.2	1.8	NA
669	Imports of goods and services	do.	57,560	70,390	83,452	78,490	86,330	82,882	79,995	84,603	NA	-3.5	5.8	NA
667	Balance on goods and services²	do.	-2,301	1,240	1,770	-183	-809	-1,115	6,020	2,983	NA	7,135	-3,037	NA
	A. National Income and Product													
	A1. GNP and Personal Income													
50	GNP in 1972 dollars	A.r, bil. dol.	1436.9	1483.0	1480.7	1490.6	1501.9	1463.3	1471.9	1485.6	1516.0	0.6	0.9	2.0
200	GNP in current dollars	do.	2156.1	2413.9	2626.1	2496.3	2571.7	2564.8	2637.3	2730.6	2853.8	2.8	3.5	4.5
213	Final sales, 1972 dollars	do.	1422.9	1472.9	1483.6	1491.3	1502.8	1462.0	1476.9	1492.7	1518.3	1.0	1.1	1.7
224	Disposable personal income, current dollars	do.	1462.9	1641.7	1821.7	1710.4	1765.1	1784.1	1840.6	1897.0	1946.9	3.2	3.1	2.6
225	Disposable personal income, 1972 dollars	do.	981.5	1011.5	1018.4	1017.7	1021.0	1008.2	1018.5	1025.8	1033.2	1.0	0.7	0.7
217	Per capita GNP in 1972 dollars	A.r, dollars	6,568	6,721	6,646	6,731	6,767	6,578	6,597	6,640	6,762	0.3	0.7	1.8
227	Per capita disposable pers. income, 1972 dol.	do.	4,487	4,584	4,571	4,596	4,600	4,532	4,565	4,585	4,609	0.7	0.4	0.5
	A2. Personal Consumption Expenditures													
231	Total, 1972 dollars	A.r, bil. dol.	904.8	930.9	935.1	941.6	943.4	919.3	930.8	946.8	958.3	1.3	1.7	1.2
233	Durable goods, 1972 dollars	do.	146.3	146.6	135.8	146.0	145.4	126.2	132.6	139.1	146.4	5.1	4.9	5.2
238	Nondurable goods, 1972 dollars	do.	345.7	354.6	358.4	361.3	361.5	356.6	354.9	360.4	364.2	-0.5	1.5	1.1
239	Services, 1972 dollars	do.	412.8	429.6	440.9	434.3	436.5	436.5	443.3	447.3	447.7	1.6	0.9	0.1
230	Total, current dollars	do.	1348.7	1510.9	1672.8	1582.3	1631.0	1626.8	1682.2	1751.0	1805.8	3.4	4.1	3.1
232	Durable goods, current dollars	do.	199.3	212.3	211.9	216.1	220.9	194.4	208.8	223.3	237.3	7.4	6.9	6.3
236	Nondurable goods, current dollars	do.	529.8	602.2	675.7	639.2	661.1	664.0	674.2	703.5	725.2	1.5	4.3	3.1
237	Services, current dollars	do.	619.6	696.3	785.2	727.0	749.0	768.4	799.2	824.2	843.4	4.0	3.1	2.3
	A3. Gross Private Domestic Investment													
241	Total, 1972 dollars	do.	229.7	232.6	203.6	221.5	218.3	200.5	195.3	200.5	210.6	-2.6	2.7	5.0
243	Total fixed investment, 1972 dollars	do.	215.8	222.5	206.6	222.2	219.2	199.2	200.2	207.6	212.9	0.5	3.7	2.6
30	Change in business inventories, 1972 dol.²	do.	14.0	10.2	-2.9	-0.7	-0.9	1.3	-5.0	-7.2	-2.3	-6.3	-2.2	4.9
240	Total, current dollars	do.	375.3	415.8	395.3	410.0	415.6	390.9	377.1	397.7	435.4	-3.5	5.5	9.5

Series	(1)	(2)	(3)	(4)	(5)	(6)	(7)	(8)	(9)	(10)	(11)	(12)	No.
242. Total fixed investment, current dollars ......do......	353.2	398.3	401.2	410.8	413.1	383.5	393.2	415.1	432.8	2.5	5.6	4.3	242
245. Chg. in bus. inventories, current dol.[2] ......do......	22.2	17.5	-5.9	-0.8	2.5	7.4	-16.0	-17.4	2.6	-23.4	-1.4	20.0	245

A4. Government Purchases of Goods and Services

Series	(1)	(2)	(3)	(4)	(5)	(6)	(7)	(8)	(9)	(10)	(11)	(12)	No.
261. Total, 1972 dollars ......do......	277.8	281.8	290.0	285.3	290.1	291.9	288.2	289.8	293.2	-1.3	0.6	1.2	261
263. Federal Government, 1972 dollars ......do......	99.8	101.7	108.1	103.1	107.6	110.7	106.9	107.4	111.0	-3.4	0.5	3.4	263
267. State and local governments, 1972 dollars ......do......	178.0	180.1	181.9	182.2	182.5	181.3	181.3	182.4	182.2	0.1	0.6	-0.1	267
260. Total, current dollars ......do......	432.6	473.8	534.7	496.4	516.8	530.0	533.5	558.6	575.5	0.7	4.7	3.0	260
262. Federal Government, current dollars ......do......	153.4	167.9	198.9	178.1	190.0	198.7	194.9	212.0	221.5	-1.9	8.8	4.5	262
266. State and local governments, current dollars ......do......	279.2	305.9	335.8	318.3	326.8	331.3	338.6	346.6	354.1	2.2	2.4	2.2	266

A5. Foreign Trade

Series	(1)	(2)	(3)	(4)	(5)	(6)	(7)	(8)	(9)	(10)	(11)	(12)	No.
256. Exports of goods and services, 1972 dollars ......do......	127.5	146.9	161.1	154.8	165.9	160.5	160.5	157.4	166.8	0.	-1.9	6.0	256
257. Imports of goods and services, 1972 dollars ......do......	103.0	109.2	109.1	112.6	115.9	108.9	102.8	108.9	112.9	-5.6	5.9	3.7	257
255. Net exports of goods and serv., 1972 dol.[2] ......do......	24.6	37.7	52.0	42.2	50.1	51.7	57.6	48.5	53.9	5.9	-9.1	5.4	255
252. Exports of goods and services, current dol. ......do......	219.8	281.3	339.8	306.3	337.3	333.3	342.4	346.1	376.8	2.7	1.1	8.9	252
253. Imports of goods and services, current dol. ......do......	220.4	267.9	316.5	298.7	316.2	316.2	297.9	322.7	339.8	-5.8	8.3	5.3	253
250. Net exports of goods and serv., current dol.[2] ......do......	-0.6	13.4	23.3	7.6	8.2	17.1	44.5	23.3	37.0	27.4	-21.2	13.7	250

A6. National Income and Its Components

Series	(1)	(2)	(3)	(4)	(5)	(6)	(7)	(8)	(9)	(10)	(11)	(12)	No.
220. National income ......do......	1745.4	1963.3	2121.4	2031.3	2088.5	2070.0	2122.4	2204.8	2289.3	2.5	3.9	3.8	220
280. Compensation of employees ......do......	1299.7	1460.9	1596.5	1518.1	1558.0	1569.0	1597.4	1661.8	1721.9	1.8	4.0	3.6	280
282. Proprietors' income with IVA and CCAdj ......do......	117.1	131.6	130.6	136.3	133.7	124.9	129.7	134.0	131.8	3.8	3.3	-1.6	282
286. Corporate profits with IVA and CCAdj ......do......	185.5	196.8	182.7	189.4	200.2	177.9	177.0	183.3	202.6	5.1	1.2	10.5	286
284. Rental income of persons with CCAdj ......do......	27.4	30.5	31.8	31.0	31.2	31.5	32.0	32.4	32.7	1.6	1.2	0.9	284
288. Net interest ......do......	115.8	143.4	179.8	156.5	165.4	175.3	185.3	193.3	200.3	5.7	4.3	3.6	288

A7. Saving

Series	(1)	(2)	(3)	(4)	(5)	(6)	(7)	(8)	(9)	(10)	(11)	(12)	No.
290. Gross saving (private and govt.) ......do......	355.2	411.9	401.9	402.0	404.5	394.5	402.0	406.7	446.0	1.9	1.2	9.7	290
295. Business saving ......do......	279.1	312.7	331.6	315.7	326.7	325.8	334.6	339.3	359.1	2.7	1.4	5.8	295
292. Personal saving ......do......	76.3	86.2	101.3	80.7	86.4	110.0	111.4	97.6	92.2	1.3	-12.4	-5.5	292
298. Government surplus or deficit[2] ......do......	-0.2	11.9	-32.1	4.4	-9.6	-45.6	-45.6	-30.8	-6.4	-3.1	14.8	24.4	298
293. Personal saving rate[2] ......Percent	5.2	5.2	5.6	4.7	4.9	6.2	6.1	5.1	4.7	-0.1	-1.0	-0.4	293

NOTE: Series are seasonally adjusted except for those indicated by Ⓤ, which appear to contain no seasonal movement. Series indicated by an asterisk (*) are included in the major composite indexes. Dollar values are in current dollars unless otherwise specified. For complete series titles (including composition of the composite indexes) and sources, see "Titles and Sources of Series" at the back of BCD. NA = not available. a = anticipated. EOP = end of period. A.r. = annual rate. S/A = seasonally adjusted (used for special emphasis). IVA = inventory valuation adjustment. CCA = capital consumption adjustment. NIA = national income accounts.

[1] For a few series, data shown here have been rounded to fewer digits than those shown elsewhere in BCD. Annual figures published by the source agencies are used if available.

[2] Differences rather than percent changes are shown for this series.

[3] The three-part timing code indicates the timing classification of the series at peaks, at troughs, and at all turns: L = leading; C = roughly coincident; Lg = lagging; U = unclassified.

[4] Inverted series. Since this series tends to move counter to movements in general business activity, signs of the changes are reversed.

[5] End-of-period series. The annual figures (and quarterly figures for monthly series) are the last figures for the period.

[6] This series is a weighted 4-term moving average (with weights 1, 2, 2, 1) placed at the terminal month of the span.

Source: Business Conditions Digest, U.S. Department of Commerce, Bureau of Economic Analysis.

GROSS NATIONAL PRODUCT
BILLIONS OF DOLLARS (RATIO SCALE)

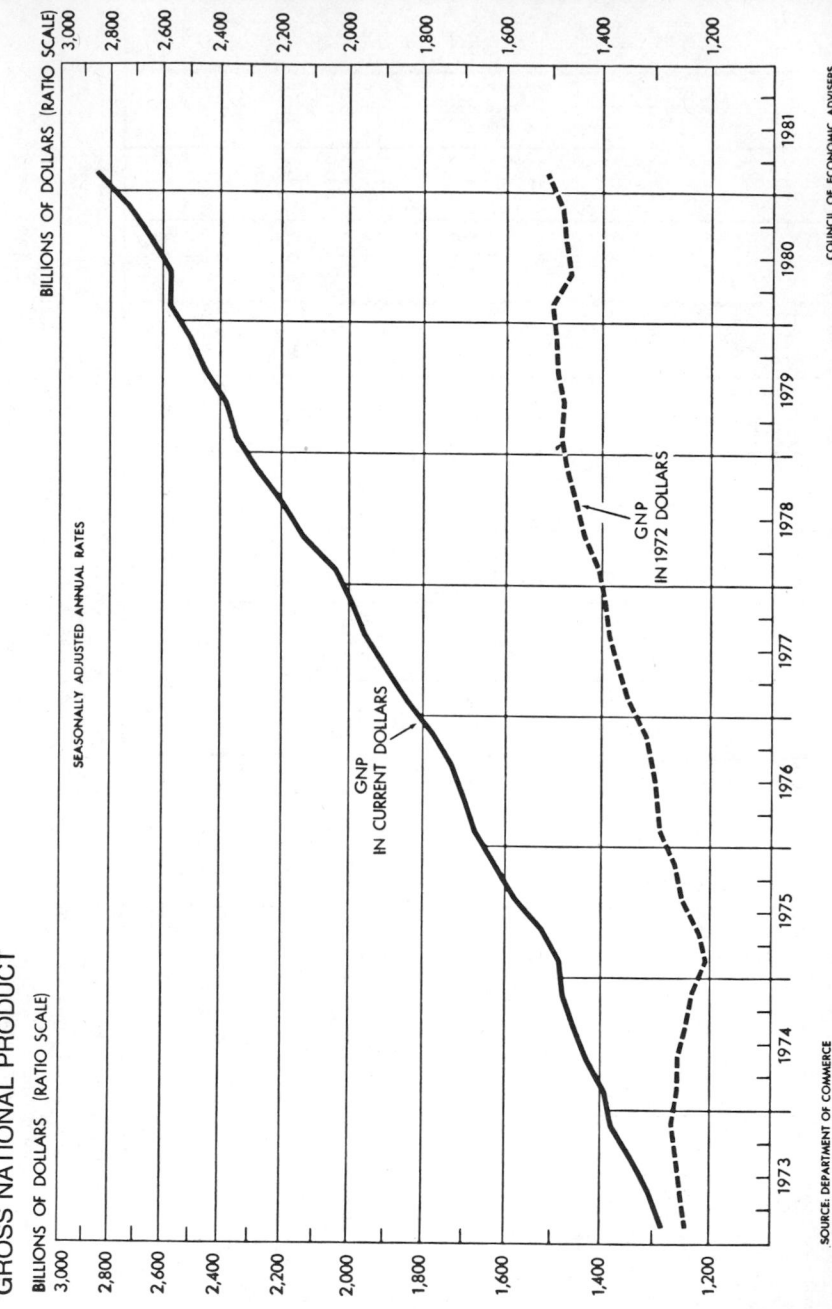

SEASONALLY ADJUSTED ANNUAL RATES

GNP
IN CURRENT DOLLARS

GNP
IN 1972 DOLLARS

BILLIONS OF DOLLARS (RATIO SCALE)

COUNCIL OF ECONOMIC ADVISERS

SOURCE: DEPARTMENT OF COMMERCE

[Billions of current dollars; quarterly data at seasonally adjusted annual rates]

Period	Gross national product	Personal consumption expenditures	Gross private domestic investment	Exports and imports of goods and services			Government purchases of goods and services					Final sales
				Net exports	Exports	Imports	Total	Total	Federal		State and local	
									Total	National defense	Non-defense	

Period	Gross national product	Personal consumption expenditures	Gross private domestic investment	Net exports	Exports	Imports	Gov Total	Federal Total	National defense	Non-defense	State and local	Final sales
1970	992.7	621.7	144.2	6.7	65.7	59.0	220.1	95.7	73.6	22.2	124.4	989.5
1971	1,077.6	672.2	166.4	4.1	68.8	64.7	234.9	96.2	70.2	26.0	138.7	1,070.0
1972	1,185.9	737.1	195.0	.7	77.5	76.7	253.1	101.7	73.1	28.5	151.4	1,175.7
1973	1,326.4	812.0	229.8	14.2	109.6	95.4	270.4	102.0	72.8	29.1	168.5	1,307.9
1974	1,434.2	888.1	228.7	13.4	146.2	132.8	304.1	111.0	77.0	33.9	193.1	1,420.1
1975	1,549.2	976.4	206.1	26.8	154.9	128.1	339.9	122.7	83.0	39.7	217.2	1,556.1
1976	1,718.0	1,084.3	257.9	13.8	170.9	157.1	362.1	129.2	86.0	43.2	232.9	1,706.2
1977	1,918.0	1,205.5	322.3	-4.2	183.3	187.5	394.5	143.9	93.3	50.6	250.6	1,897.0
1978	2,156.1	1,348.7	375.3	-.6	219.8	220.4	432.6	153.4	100.0	53.4	279.2	2,133.9
1979	2,413.9	1,510.9	415.8	13.4	281.3	267.9	473.8	167.9	111.2	56.7	305.9	2,396.4
1980	2,626.1	1,672.8	395.3	23.3	339.8	316.5	534.7	198.9	131.7	67.2	335.8	2,632.0
1979: III	2,444.1	1,529.1	421.7	17.9	293.1	275.2	475.4	165.1	112.0	53.1	310.4	2,430.8
IV	2,496.3	1,582.3	410.0	7.6	306.3	298.7	496.4	178.1	118.7	59.4	318.3	2,497.1
1980: I	2,571.7	1,631.0	415.6	8.2	337.3	329.1	516.8	190.0	125.0	64.9	326.8	2,569.1
II	2,564.8	1,626.8	390.9	17.1	333.3	316.2	530.0	198.7	128.7	70.0	331.3	2,557.4
III	2,637.3	1,682.2	377.1	44.5	342.4	297.9	533.5	194.9	131.4	63.5	338.6	2,653.4
IV	2,730.6	1,751.0	397.7	23.3	346.1	322.7	558.6	212.0	141.6	70.4	346.6	2,748.0
1981: I	2,853.0	1,810.1	437.1	29.2	367.4	338.2	576.5	221.6	145.2	76.4	354.9	2,848.5

Source: Department of Commerce, Bureau of Economic Analysis.

Source: *Economic Indicators*, Council of Economic Advisers.

GROSS NATIONAL PRODUCT IN 1972 DOLLARS (billions of 1972 dollars; quarterly data at seasonally adjusted annual rates)

Period	Gross national product	Personal consumption expenditures	Gross private domestic investment			Net exports	Exports of goods and services		Government purchases of goods and services			Final sales
			Non-residential fixed	Residential fixed	Change in business inventories		Exports	Imports	Total	Federal	State and local	
1970	1,085.6	672.1	113.8	41.0	3.8	3.9	70.5	66.6	251.1	110.6	140.5	1,081.8
1971	1,122.4	696.8	112.2	53.7	8.1	1.6	71.0	69.3	250.1	103.7	146.4	1,114.3
1972	1,185.9	737.1	121.0	63.8	10.2	.7	77.5	76.7	253.5	101.7	151.4	1,175.7
1973	1,255.0	768.5	138.1	62.3	17.2	15.5	97.3	81.8	253.6	95.9	157.6	1,237.8
1974	1,248.0	763.6	135.7	48.2	11.6	27.8	108.5	80.7	261.2	96.6	164.5	1,236.4
1975	1,233.9	780.2	119.3	42.2	-6.7	32.2	103.6	71.4	266.7	97.4	169.3	1,240.6
1976	1,300.4	823.7	125.6	51.2	7.8	25.4	110.1	84.7	266.8	96.8	170.0	1,292.7
1977	1,371.7	863.9	140.6	60.6	12.3	21.9	113.2	91.3	272.3	100.7	171.6	1,359.3
1978	1,436.9	904.8	153.4	62.4	14.0	24.6	127.5	103.0	277.8	99.8	178.0	1,423.0
1979	1,483.0	930.9	163.3	59.1	10.2	37.7	146.9	109.2	281.8	101.7	180.1	1,472.9
1980	1,480.7	935.1	158.4	48.1	-2.9	52.0	161.1	109.1	290.0	108.1	181.9	1,483.6
1979: III	1,488.2	933.4	166.4	58.6	7.6	41.1	151.3	110.2	281.1	99.9	181.2	1,480.6
IV	1,490.6	941.6	164.1	58.1	-.7	42.2	154.8	112.6	285.3	103.1	182.2	1,491.3
1980: I	1,501.9	943.4	165.0	54.2	-.9	50.1	165.9	115.8	290.1	107.6	182.5	1,502.8
II	1,463.3	919.3	156.1	43.1	1.3	51.7	160.5	108.9	291.9	110.7	181.2	1,462.0
III	1,471.9	930.8	155.5	44.7	-5.0	57.6	160.5	102.8	288.2	106.9	181.3	1,476.9
IV	1,485.6	946.8	157.0	50.6	-7.2	48.5	157.4	108.9	289.8	107.4	182.4	1,492.7
1981: I	1,516.4	960.2	162.0	51.0	-1.4	50.9	162.5	111.6	293.6	111.2	182.5	1,517.8

Source: *Economic Indicators*, Council of Economic Advisers.

SELECTED COMPONENTS OF GNP
SEASONALLY ADJUSTED ANNUAL RATES, QUARTERLY

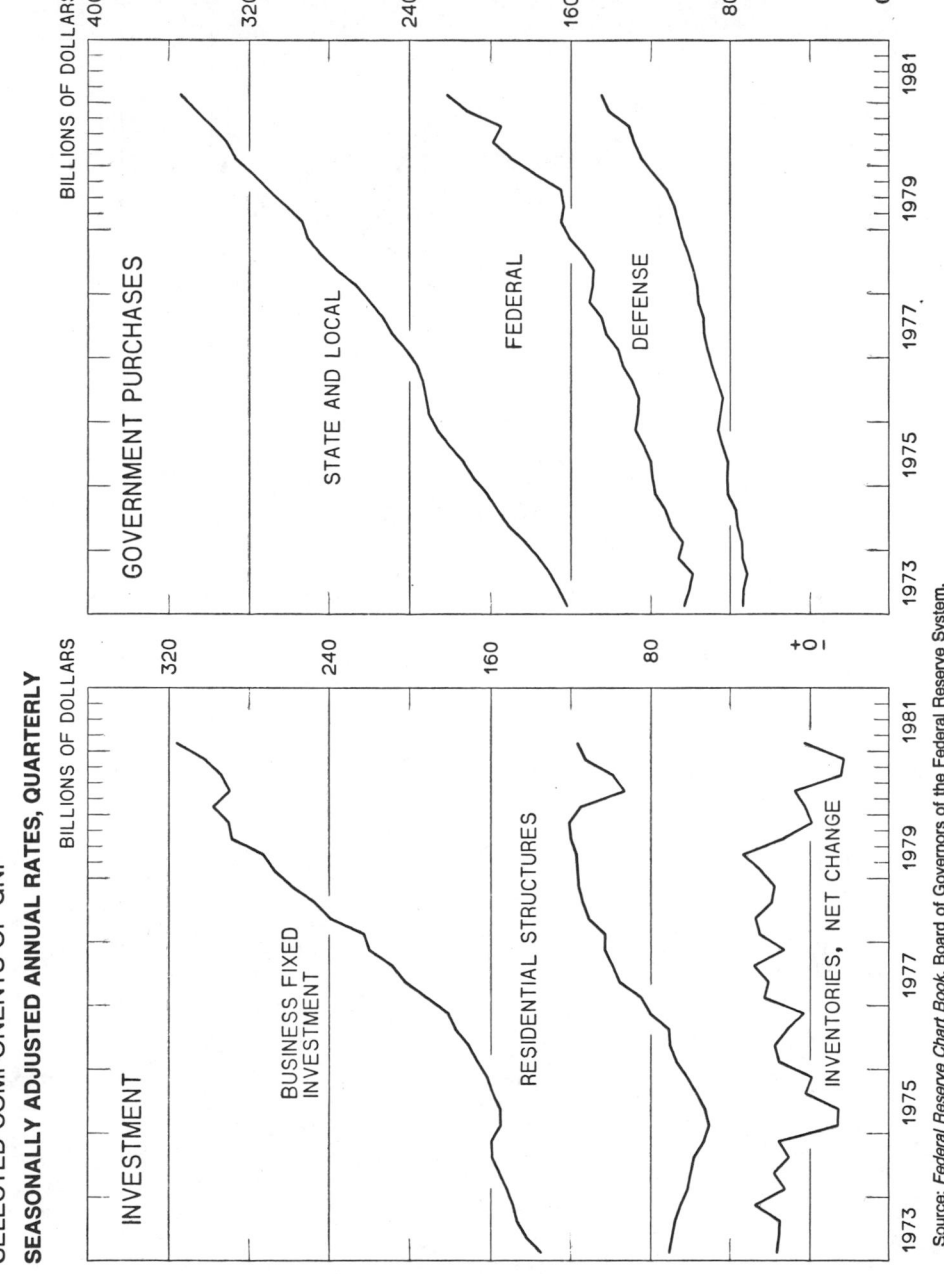

Source: *Federal Reserve Chart Book*, Board of Governors of the Federal Reserve System.

CORPORATE PROFITS

BILLIONS OF DOLLARS

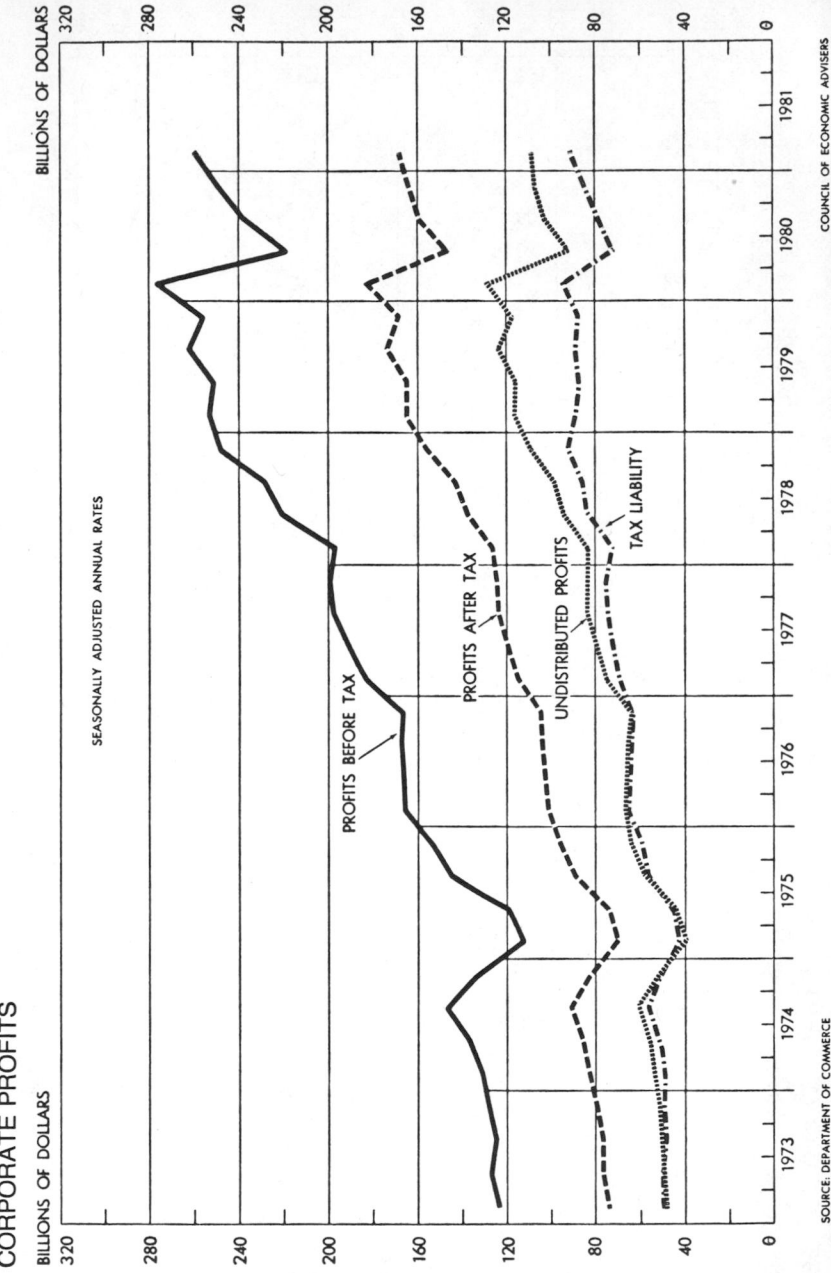

SOURCE: DEPARTMENT OF COMMERCE

[Billions of dollars; quarterly data at seasonally adjusted annual rates]

Period	Profits (before tax) with inventory valuation adjustment [1]						Profits before tax	Tax liability	Profits after tax			Inventory valuation adjustment
	Total [2]	Domestic industries							Total	Dividends	Undistributed profits	
		Total	Financial	Nonfinancial								
				Total [3]	Manufacturing	Wholesale and retail trade						
1970	68.9	62.4	12.1	50.2	26.6	9.5	75.4	34.2	41.3	22.5	18.8	−6.6
1971	82.0	74.9	14.1	60.8	34.1	11.7	86.6	37.5	49.0	22.9	26.1	−4.6
1972	94.0	85.3	15.3	70.0	40.7	13.4	100.6	41.6	58.9	24.4	34.5	−6.6
1973	105.6	92.0	15.9	76.0	45.5	13.9	125.6	49.0	76.6	27.0	49.6	−20.0
1974	96.7	80.4	15.0	65.4	39.0	12.5	136.7	51.6	85.1	29.9	55.2	−40.0
1975	120.6	107.6	11.8	95.8	52.6	21.3	132.1	50.6	81.5	30.8	50.7	−11.6
1976	151.6	137.4	17.1	120.3	69.2	22.4	166.3	63.8	102.5	37.4	65.1	−14.7
1977	176.7	161.2	23.5	137.7	76.2	27.0	192.6	72.6	120.0	39.9	80.1	−15.8
1978	199.0	179.3	29.3	150.0	85.3	24.5	223.3	83.0	140.3	44.6	95.7	−24.3
1979	212.7	182.4	31.6	150.8	88.9	23.0	255.4	87.6	167.8	50.2	117.6	−42.6
1980	199.8	168.7	30.6	138.1	74.5	20.9	245.5	82.3	163.2	56.0	107.2	−45.7
1979: III	215.6	180.5	31.5	149.0	84.4	25.6	262.0	88.4	173.6	50.2	123.5	−46.5
IV	204.5	172.9	32.6	140.3	80.2	22.6	255.4	87.2	168.2	51.6	116.6	−50.8
1980: I	215.6	179.0	33.3	145.7	92.1	14.8	277.1	94.2	182.9	53.9	128.9	−61.4
II	186.9	157.5	30.1	127.5	61.3	25.9	217.9	71.5	146.5	55.7	90.7	−31.1
III	195.9	165.0	28.7	136.2	68.5	20.4	237.6	78.5	159.1	56.7	102.4	−41.7
IV	201.0	173.4	30.5	142.9	76.2	22.6	249.5	85.2	164.3	57.7	106.6	−48.4
1981: I	219.9	194.4	28.7	165.7	91.4	27.5	259.1	91.1	168.0	59.6	108.4	−39.2

[1] See p. 175 for profits with inventory valuation and capital consumption adjustments.
[2] Includes rest of the world, not shown separately.
[3] Includes industries not shown separately.

Source: Department of Commerce, Bureau of Economic Analysis.

Source: Economic Indicators, Council of Economic Advisers.

PRICE DATA

Definitions are applicable to the exhibits on pages 161–171 and 174.

Price data are gathered by the Bureau of Labor Statistics from retail and primary markets in the United States. Price indexes are given in relation to a base period (1967 = 100, unless otherwise noted).

DEFINITIONS

The **Consumer Price Index** is a monthly statistical measure of the average change in prices in a fixed market basket of goods and services. Effective with the January 1978 index, the Bureau of Labor Statistics began publishing CPI's for two groups of the population. One index, a new CPI for All Urban Consumers, covers 80 percent of the total noninstitutional population; and the other index, a revised CPI for Urban Wage Earners and Clerical Workers, covers about half the new index population. The All Urban Consumers index includes, in addition to wage earners and clerical workers, professional, managerial, and technical workers, the self-employed, short-term workers, the unemployed, retirees, and others not in the labor force.

The CPI is based on prices of food, clothing, shelter, fuel, drugs, transportation fares, doctor's and dentist's fees, and other goods and services that people buy for day-to-day living. The quantity and quality of these items are kept essentially unchanged between major revisions so that only price changes will be measured. Prices are collected from over 18,000 tenants, 24,000 retail establishments, and 18,000 housing units for property taxes in 85 urban areas across the country. All taxes directly associated with the purchase and use of items are included in the index. Because the CPI's are based on the expenditures of two population groups in 1972–73, they may not accurately reflect the experience of individual families and single persons with different buying habits.

Though the CPI is often called the "Cost-of-Living Index," it measures only price change, which is just one of several important factors

Source: *Monthly Labor Review*, U.S. Department of Labor, Bureau of Labor Statistics.

affecting living costs. Area indexes do not measure differences in the level of prices among cities. They only measure the average change in prices for each area since the base period.

NOTES ON THE DATA

Beginning with the May 1978 issue of the *Review*, regional CPI's cross classified by population size, were introduced. These indexes will enable users in local areas for which an index is not published to get a better approximation of the CPI for their area by using the appropriate population size class measure for their region. The cross-classified indexes will be published bimonthly.

For further details about the new and the revised indexes and a comparison of various aspects of these indexes with the old unrevised CPI, see *Facts About the Revised Consumer Price Index*, a pamphlet in the Consumer Price Index Revision 1978 series. See also *The Consumer Price Index: Concepts and Content Over the Years*, Report 517, revised edition (Bureau of Labor Statistics, May 1978).

For interarea comparisons of living costs at three hypothetical standards of living, see the family budget data published in the *Handbook of Labor Statistics, 1977*, Bulletin 1966 (Bureau of Labor Statistics, 1977), tables 122–133. Additional data and analysis on prices changes are provided in the *CPI Detailed Report* and *Producer Prices and Price Indexes*, both monthly publications of the Bureau.

As of January 1976, the Wholesale Price Index (as it was then called) incorporated a revised weighting structure reflecting 1972 values of shipments. From January 1967 through December 1975, 1963 values of shipments were used as weights.

For a discussion of the general method of computing consumer, producer, and industry price indexes, see *BLS Handbook of Methods for Surveys and Studies*, Bulletin 1910 (Bureau of Labor Statistics, 1976), chapters 13–15. See also John F. Early, "Improving the Measurement of Producer Price Change," *Monthly Labor Review*, April 1978, pp. 7–15. For industry prices, see also Bennett R. Moss, "Industry and Sector Price Indexes," *Monthly Labor Review*, August 1965, pp. 974–82.

CONSUMER PRICE INDEX FOR ALL URBAN CONSUMERS AND REVISED CPI FOR URBAN WAGE EARNERS AND CLERICAL WORKERS, U.S. CITY AVERAGE (general summary and groups, subgroups, and selected items)

[1967 = 100 unless otherwise specified]

General summary	All Urban Consumers							Urban Wage Earners and Clerical Workers (revised)						
	1980 Mar.	1980 Oct.	1980 Nov.	1980 Dec.	1981 Jan.	1981 Feb.	1981 Mar.	1980 Mar.	1980 Oct.	1980 Nov.	1980 Dec.	1981 Jan.	1981 Feb.	1981 Mar.
All items	239.8	253.9	256.2	258.4	260.5	263.2	265.1	239.9	254.1	256.4	258.7	260.7	263.5	265.2
Food and beverages	241.0	255.5	257.4	259.3	261.4	263.7	265.0	241.2	256.6	258.7	260.5	262.1	264.3	265.5
Housing	254.5	271.1	273.8	279.9	279.1	280.9	282.6	254.4	271.0	273.7	277.1	279.1	280.7	282.2
Apparel and upkeep	176.0	183.9	184.8	183.9	181.1	182.0	185.1	175.1	182.8	183.3	182.9	180.8	181.8	184.3
Transportation	243.7	256.1	259.0	261.1	264.7	270.9	273.5	244.3	256.6	259.7	261.9	265.7	272.1	274.4
Medical care	260.2	272.8	274.5	275.8	279.5	282.6	284.7	260.9	274.3	276.3	277.6	281.4	284.4	287.0
Entertainment	200.6	210.9	211.2	212.0	214.4	216.7	218.2	199.5	209.2	209.9	210.1	212.2	215.0	216.1
Other goods and services	208.9	221.5	222.8	224.6	226.2	227.4	228.7	208.3	219.9	221.0	223.0	224.4	225.6	226.8
Commodities	228.0	240.7	242.5	243.8	245.4	248.3	249.8	228.1	240.8	242.9	244.3	245.8	248.8	250.2
Commodities less food and beverages	218.4	230.2	232.0	232.9	234.3	237.4	239.0	218.7	230.0	232.0	231.1	234.7	237.9	239.4
Nondurables less food and beverages	237.5	244.4	245.3	246.8	250.2	258.6	263.1	239.8	246.1	247.1	248.8	252.6	261.4	265.7
Durables	203.0	218.1	220.6	221.1	221.0	220.3	219.8	201.2	216.3	218.9	219.7	219.5	218.6	217.8
Services	261.3	277.9	280.9	284.7	287.7	290.1	292.5	261.7	278.6	281.5	285.5	288.4	290.8	293.1
Rent, residential	186.6	197.1	198.3	199.6	200.9	201.9	203.0	186.4	196.8	198.0	199.4	200.6	201.6	202.7
Household services less rent	307.3	327.4	331.9	338.4	342.3	345.4	348.8	309.6	330.3	334.8	341.9	345.5	348.5	351.8
Transportation services	233.4	250.8	253.3	255.8	258.7	260.5	262.5	232.7	249.6	252.2	254.7	257.7	259.7	261.3
Medical care services	281.5	294.8	296.6	297.9	302.1	305.2	307.5	282.2	296.6	298.7	300.0	304.3	307.4	310.2
Other services	212.9	226.7	227.2	228.1	230.4	232.3	233.2	213.5	227.4	227.9	228.4	230.2	232.1	233.0
Special indexes:														
All items less food	237.1	250.9	253.2	255.5	257.6	260.4	262.3	237.3	251.0	253.4	255.7	257.9	260.8	262.6
All items less mortgage interest costs	229.8	243.0	244.5	245.9	247.8	250.6	252.3	230.2	243.5	245.1	246.7	248.5	251.4	252.9
Commodities less food	216.7	228.3	230.0	231.0	232.4	235.4	237.0	216.9	228.2	230.1	231.2	232.7	236.0	237.4
Nondurables less food	232.6	239.6	240.5	242.0	245.3	253.2	257.5	234.8	241.3	242.2	243.9	247.5	255.9	259.9
Nondurables less food and apparel	264.1	271.1	272.1	274.7	281.1	294.4	297.3	266.3	272.8	273.9	276.6	283.0	294.7	299.5
Nondurables	240.3	251.0	252.4	254.1	256.9	262.3	265.2	241.4	252.3	253.8	255.6	258.3	263.8	266.6
Services less rent	275.4	293.2	296.4	300.7	304.2	306.9	309.5	275.9	294.2	297.4	302.0	305.2	307.9	310.4
Services less medical care	257.4	274.2	277.2	281.2	284.2	286.5	288.9	257.7	274.7	277.7	281.9	284.7	287.0	289.2
Domestically produced farm foods	231.2	247.3	249.2	251.1	252.4	254.0	255.4	231.0	247.0	249.1	251.1	252.1	253.9	254.9
Selected beef cuts	270.2	276.8	278.9	276.2	276.2	273.0	270.9	272.3	279.0	280.7	278.4	277.9	275.1	273.9
Energy	355.0	368.0	366.1	370.4	381.7	401.1	409.3	359.6	371.1	369.5	373.7	385.2	405.4	413.7
All items less energy	230.8	245.1	247.7	249.7	251.2	252.5	253.8	230.0	244.5	247.2	249.3	250.6	251.8	252.9
All items less food and energy	225.7	239.7	242.4	244.5	245.7	246.8	248.1	224.6	238.7	241.5	243.6	244.8	245.8	246.9
Commodities less food and energy	196.5	209.4	211.2	211.7	211.5	211.7	212.2	195.1	207.8	209.9	210.6	210.4	210.5	210.7
Energy commodities	398.5	399.1	400.2	404.9	c420.4	449.0	460.0	398.5	400.3	401.3	405.9	421.3	450.1	460.9
Services less energy	259.6	274.9	278.6	282.4	285.4	287.6	289.9	259.6	275.6	279.3	283.4	286.2	288.4	290.6
Purchasing power of the consumer dollar, 1967 = $1	$0.417	$0.394	$0.390	$0.387	$0.384	$0.380	$0.377	$0.417	$0.394	$0.390	$0.387	$0.384	$0.380	$0.377

CONSUMER PRICE INDEX (U.S. CITY AVERAGE, continued)

[1967=100 unless otherwise specified]

General summary	All Urban Consumers							Urban Wage Earners and Clerical Workers (revised)						
	1980				1981			1980				1981		
	Mar.	Oct.	Nov.	Dec.	Jan.	Feb.	Mar.	Mar.	Oct.	Nov.	Dec.	Jan.	Feb.	Mar.
FOOD AND BEVERAGES	241.0	255.5	257.4	259.3	261.4	263.7	265.0	241.2	256.6	258.7	260.5	262.1	264.3	265.5
Food	247.3	262.4	264.5	266.4	268.6	270.8	272.2	247.5	263.4	265.7	267.6	269.2	271.4	272.6
Food at home	243.6	260.0	262.1	263.9	265.6	267.3	268.6	243.1	259.7	262.0	263.9	265.1	267.0	268.1
Cereals and bakery products	238.6	253.7	255.8	258.5	262.9	265.3	266.7	239.3	254.3	256.8	259.5	263.0	265.0	266.5
Cereals and cereal products (12/77 = 100)	126.6	137.5	138.7	140.8	143.2	144.5	145.2	127.7	138.5	139.7	142.3	144.5	145.5	146.5
Flour and prepared flour mixes (12/77 = 100)	126.6	133.2	132.9	133.5	135.9	137.5	138.5	127.5	133.8	133.6	134.4	136.8	137.9	139.4
Cereal (12/77 = 100)	126.0	139.3	141.1	143.8	145.8	146.5	146.9	126.6	139.3	141.5	145.0	147.2	148.0	148.5
Rice, pasta, and cornmeal (12/77 = 100)	127.6	138.9	140.5	143.1	146.0	147.9	148.9	129.4	141.6	141.5	145.8	147.8	149.3	150.5
Bakery products (12/77 = 100)	126.1	133.1	134.3	135.4	137.7	139.0	139.7	126.2	133.3	134.7	135.7	137.5	138.5	139.2
White bread	212.0	222.7	224.9	226.3	229.5	231.4	232.9	212.1	222.6	225.2	226.6	229.4	230.9	231.2
Other breads (12/77 = 100)	125.6	132.5	133.1	134.1	137.1	137.3	137.9	129.3	135.8	137.0	137.9	139.4	140.1	140.3
Fresh biscuits, rolls, and muffins (12/77 = 100)	127.0	133.4	134.6	135.4	137.6	138.9	140.1	124.9	132.1	134.1	135.1	136.4	136.9	138.4
Fresh cakes and cupcakes (12/77 = 100)	124.4	132.5	133.4	135.3	138.5	139.5	140.0	123.2	132.6	133.1	134.2	136.8	138.1	139.5
Cookies (12/77 = 100)	124.4	131.0	133.1	134.9	138.0	139.0	139.7	125.6	132.5	133.5	136.1	139.0	139.8	140.6
Crackers and bread and cracker products (12/77 = 100)	120.2	126.4	126.9	127.0	127.0	128.6	129.1	121.8	126.5	125.7	126.5	126.8	128.6	129.6
Fresh sweetrolls, coffeecake, and donuts (12/77 = 100)	125.0	133.4	135.3	135.9	138.0	140.4	141.1	126.2	134.1	136.1	136.4	138.5	140.0	140.7
Frozen and refrigerated bakery products and fresh pies, tarts, and turnovers (12/77 = 100)	127.9	135.3	136.2	137.5	139.7	141.4	141.9	124.0	130.9	132.4	134.0	135.2	136.3	137.6
Meats, poultry, fish, and eggs	237.8	252.6	254.9	255.7	255.1	252.5	250.5	237.1	251.8	254.2	255.0	254.1	251.6	249.9
Meats, poultry, and fish	243.8	259.0	260.7	259.9	260.6	257.9	256.2	243.0	258.1	259.9	259.3	259.4	257.0	255.7
Meats	245.7	258.7	261.1	260.0	259.7	256.4	254.4	245.0	258.1	260.3	259.3	259.2	256.0	254.2
Beef and veal	269.1	275.8	277.9	275.3	275.3	272.3	270.3	270.8	277.4	279.1	276.8	276.4	273.8	272.6
Ground beef other than canned	275.3	275.8	277.1	276.1	276.3	272.8	269.7	278.7	278.9	280.4	281.0	279.3	275.7	272.9
Chuck roast	286.2	284.4	291.7	288.5	285.3	288.1	284.1	293.4	290.0	301.9	296.0	295.2	298.6	295.6
Round roast	244.2	250.6	251.2	245.7	250.0	248.0	243.9	244.5	251.1	249.9	246.6	249.6	247.5	248.8
Round steak	254.2	258.9	263.8	260.2	262.4	259.0	256.1	251.1	257.9	261.8	257.6	255.5	254.7	253.3
Sirloin steak	254.3	270.7	271.8	276.6	264.9	262.0	259.8	256.0	272.8	274.9	269.7	266.3	263.5	264.5
Other beef and veal (12/77 = 100)	153.8	161.0	161.8	160.4	160.3	157.7	157.8	153.7	160.3	160.3	159.2	159.5	156.9	156.7
Pork	202.6	225.8	228.6	229.1	228.1	223.6	221.6	203.0	226.0	228.5	228.8	228.1	223.6	221.3
Bacon	187.6	224.7	229.5	231.9	228.1	221.7	218.5	189.4	226.0	232.3	234.1	232.5	225.7	221.6
Chops	190.7	207.8	208.5	208.7	211.6	210.3	209.3	190.5	207.3	204.8	206.8	210.2	207.6	206.9
Ham other than canned (12/77 = 100)	95.8	105.5	107.9	107.8	104.1	100.0	98.7	94.7	106.0	106.0	105.7	102.2	98.2	96.3
Sausage	257.6	282.4	283.5	285.6	287.8	282.3	281.0	259.8	283.2	285.9	287.2	288.5	282.0	282.7
Canned ham	219.3	232.5	237.7	238.4	241.1	238.0	236.6	217.4	235.2	242.2	242.6	243.3	240.6	237.9
Other pork (12/77 = 100)	113.6	127.6	128.4	127.6	127.4	125.4	124.2	113.7	127.9	128.8	127.4	127.9	125.0	124.3

Other meats	256.0	259.1	260.4	259.4	259.0	255.8	241.5	258.5	260.8	262.9	262.8	261.8	259.4	245.8
Frankfurters	257.2	261.0	262.6	263.4	262.6	260.3	242.8	257.8	259.4	262.5	264.0	262.6	260.9	244.6
Bologna, liverwurst, and salami (12/77 = 100)	144.7	146.0	148.0	145.2	145.7	143.6	132.2	147.0	149.4	151.2	149.1	148.4	146.5	135.5
Other lunchmeats (12/77 = 100)	126.4	128.6	128.1	127.7	127.5	125.5	118.8	128.1	129.8	130.3	129.9	129.7	127.8	121.8
Lamb and organ meats (12/77 = 100)	146.0	147.8	147.8	148.5	147.7	146.5	144.3	144.7	144.1	145.0	146.1	146.1	146.1	142.3
Poultry	200.6	201.3	199.2	201.1	201.4	205.4	177.4	201.6	203.7	202.4	202.7	204.1	209.1	180.7
Fresh whole chicken	200.9	201.7	197.2	202.2	203.5	210.5	172.5	203.1	207.0	202.5	206.9	208.7	216.7	179.5
Fresh and frozen chicken parts (12/77 = 100)	130.1	131.9	131.3	132.3	131.6	133.5	116.3	131.6	131.9	132.7	131.8	131.8	134.7	116.8
Other poultry (12/77 = 100)	128.9	127.8	127.9	126.2	126.5	127.1	117.7	127.6	128.5	128.7	126.6	128.0	128.7	118.2
Fish and seafood	351.5	349.5	350.0	343.1	340.0	333.8	320.2	358.8	355.0	358.0	346.9	343.0	336.6	322.6
Canned fish and seafood (12/77 = 100)	136.2	135.9	135.3	133.7	135.5	131.2	119.5	138.9	138.0	137.4	136.4	136.0	133.9	120.4
Fresh and frozen fish and seafood (12/77 = 100)	132.5	131.4	132.0	128.8	127.0	124.6	123.5	135.3	133.5	135.7	129.6	127.5	124.8	124.3
Eggs	180.5	187.0	190.1	206.6	185.7	174.4	164.3	180.5	188.2	190.2	206.6	185.2	175.3	164.5
Dairy products	242.7	242.5	240.7	238.8	235.9	233.1	221.1	242.6	242.1	240.1	238.0	235.4	232.7	220.3
Fresh milk and cream (12/77 = 100)	134.1	134.1	133.4	132.2	130.4	129.1	124.2	134.3	134.0	133.0	131.9	130.4	129.1	124.1
Fresh whole milk	219.4	219.3	218.5	216.5	213.0	211.0	203.8	219.9	219.3	218.2	216.2	213.3	213.3	204.0
Other fresh milk and cream (12/77 = 100)	134.5	134.4	132.9	131.9	131.0	129.5	123.1	134.4	134.2	132.1	131.4	130.5	129.1	122.7
Processed dairy products (12/77 = 100)	141.8	141.6	140.1	139.2	137.9	135.8	126.2	141.1	140.8	139.6	138.2	136.9	134.9	125.1
Butter	146.0	146.0	146.5	144.1	144.4	142.5	140.9	143.0	142.2	142.7	141.0	141.5	138.0	138.3
Cheese (12/77 = 100)	140.0	139.6	138.3	137.4	136.2	133.8	125.5	139.8	139.2	138.2	137.0	135.9	133.4	124.9
Ice cream and related products (12/77 = 100)	146.1	146.8	144.3	143.2	140.9	139.1	127.2	145.3	145.9	143.6	141.4	139.1	138.0	125.1
Other dairy products (12/77 = 100)	136.1	135.0	132.9	133.1	131.9	129.4	121.9	135.1	134.5	133.3	132.4	130.6	129.0	121.6
Fruits and vegetables	275.0	266.5	255.1	253.9	251.4	252.3	230.1	278.2	267.3	257.6	255.6	253.3	254.2	232.4
Fresh fruits and vegetables	289.4	277.6	260.3	260.2	255.7	259.6	227.4	293.9	278.1	263.9	262.0	258.3	262.3	229.9
Fresh fruits	259.0	254.4	241.1	248.6	255.5	270.4	245.4	265.2	256.8	245.6	251.8	258.6	272.9	245.4
Apples	225.7	218.2	216.8	216.9	213.0	243.7	249.0	227.9	217.1	208.8	218.8	213.5	242.2	250.2
Bananas	258.8	249.4	258.9	239.2	232.0	230.2	240.8	287.4	256.9	237.8	237.8	237.5	234.4	249.9
Oranges	268.4	269.4	258.9	287.0	300.4	301.5	240.9	264.1	284.9	272.9	299.3	316.6	312.9	238.1
Other fresh fruits (12/77 = 100)	139.9	137.9	128.4	129.2	136.4	145.6	126.9	141.1	135.9	127.8	128.6	134.9	145.4	127.4
Fresh vegetables	316.9	337.1	277.8	270.9	256.0	249.9	211.3	320.8	298.0	281.1	271.5	258.0	254.2	215.5
Potatoes	359.6	347.1	322.9	298.0	289.9	292.0	200.3	363.9	350.2	326.1	297.7	293.0	295.6	203.3
Lettuce	219.3	225.6	229.9	253.8	267.2	241.3	203.8	225.2	220.4	234.2	253.3	273.5	249.1	208.3
Tomatoes	354.0	308.6	239.8	204.5	189.9	235.6	197.2	367.8	312.8	247.2	206.1	192.2	237.3	201.4
Other fresh vegetables (12/77 = 100)	177.1	164.8	156.9	156.2	140.0	129.6	123.0	177.0	163.5	157.8	156.3	139.6	129.7	125.4
Processed fruits and vegetables	261.3	256.4	251.3	249.0	248.8	246.4	235.0	263.3	257.8	253.0	250.9	250.1	247.5	237.2
Processed fruits (12/77 = 100)	137.5	133.8	129.9	129.1	129.4	128.5	123.9	137.6	133.5	129.9	129.0	129.1	127.8	123.9
Frozen fruit and fruit juices (12/77 = 100)	134.6	127.1	119.6	119.9	120.7	118.8	116.5	135.3	127.1	120.7	120.6	120.5	118.8	117.7
Fruit juices and other than frozen (12/77 = 100)	140.7	137.1	133.2	132.0	132.3	131.9	127.4	141.2	137.2	133.2	133.1	131.9	131.0	127.2
Canned and dried fruits (12/77 = 100)	136.3	135.8	134.7	133.3	135.5	132.7	125.9	135.7	134.9	134.1	133.1	133.3	132.0	125.5
Processed vegetables (12/77 = 100)	125.8	124.4	123.0	121.5	121.0	119.6	113.0	127.0	125.5	124.2	123.1	122.2	120.8	114.6
Frozen vegetables (12/77 = 100)	126.4	124.0	123.3	121.2	121.7	120.3	111.9	126.9	124.4	124.1	122.1	121.8	120.3	112.6

CONSUMER PRICE INDEX (U.S. CITY AVERAGE, *continued*)

[1967 = 100 unless otherwise specified]

General summary	All Urban Consumers							Urban Wage Earners and Clerical Workers (revised)						
		1980			1981				1980			1981		
	Mar.	Oct.	Nov.	Dec.	Jan.	Feb.	Mar.	Mar.	Oct.	Nov.	Dec.	Jan.	Feb.	Mar.
FOOD AND BEVERAGES Continued														
Food Continued														
Food at home Continued														
Fruits and vegetables Continued														
Cut corn and canned beans except lima (12/77 = 100)	116.0	122.5	124.1	124.5	126.0	128.2	128.4	115.4	120.9	121.8	122.8	124.5	126.5	126.3
Other canned and dried vegetables (12/77 = 100)	114.8	120.3	121.5	122.9	123.4	124.7	126.4	112.3	118.5	120.3	121.0	122.1	123.5	125.3
Other foods at home	292.0	311.5	314.8	317.1	320.5	323.0	324.1	290.9	311.7	315.7	317.8	320.8	323.6	325.2
Sugar and sweets	313.5	369.0	381.3	386.3	385.4	385.4	383.2	314.1	369.8	383.9	388.9	387.3	387.7	384.6
Candy and chewing gum (12/77 = 100)	123.8	134.7	135.7	136.9	138.6	141.1	142.8	123.9	135.4	136.8	137.4	139.4	142.0	143.6
Sugar and artificial sweeteners (12/77 = 100)	153.0	209.4	225.9	230.3	222.8	217.7	209.7	153.8	209.5	225.9	231.4	223.4	217.9	209.6
Other sweets (12/77 = 100)	120.4	131.5	132.5	133.7	137.1	137.7	139.3	119.3	129.2	131.9	133.1	135.5	137.3	138.2
Fats and oils (12/77 = 100)	236.8	246.0	247.4	251.9	260.4	267.3	268.9	236.8	247.0	248.2	252.6	261.8	268.9	270.5
Margarine	248.8	254.2	254.9	253.6	256.9	256.8	255.7	248.3	256.6	256.9	254.6	257.4	258.3	257.7
Nondairy substitutes and peanut butter (12/77 = 100)	117.9	125.6	127.4	139.6	156.0	171.8	179.3	118.5	125.5	128.0	139.9	156.4	172.7	180.0
Other fats, oils, and salad dressings (12/77 = 100)	123.7	128.5	129.0	129.1	130.3	131.0	129.9	123.4	128.7	128.8	129.1	131.0	131.4	130.3
Nonalcoholic beverages	387.1	404.9	405.5	405.2	409.7	411.9	412.2	384.4	405.8	407.8	407.4	410.7	413.6	415.4
Cola drinks, excluding diet cola	259.3	280.4	284.0	285.2	290.8	295.3	295.9	255.4	279.6	283.6	284.0	288.2	293.4	295.4
Carbonated drinks, including diet cola (12/77 = 100)	123.5	133.9	133.8	134.8	137.5	140.1	140.5	121.1	131.8	132.2	133.5	135.0	137.8	138.7
Roasted coffee	437.6	411.8	399.2	389.7	380.7	364.9	359.4	432.3	409.3	395.5	386.2	376.4	360.3	355.0
Freeze dried and instant coffee	381.7	368.1	364.9	356.5	354.6	345.3	340.8	380.3	366.3	364.0	358.1	355.8	347.0	343.9
Other noncarbonated drinks (12/77 = 100)	118.6	125.8	126.7	127.5	129.1	130.8	132.4	118.1	125.3	126.2	127.7	129.6	130.9	132.7
Other prepared foods	224.1	236.6	239.9	242.4	244.9	246.9	249.4	224.0	236.9	240.4	242.8	245.1	247.1	250.0
Canned and packaged soup (12/77 = 100)	118.0	124.1	125.1	127.2	128.1	128.7	128.4	117.6	124.9	125.6	128.0	127.9	129.3	127.1
Frozen prepared foods (12/77 = 100)	128.2	133.9	136.6	137.6	138.6	140.0	142.3	127.1	133.9	133.5	134.8	136.9	137.8	139.6
Snacks (12/77 = 100)	124.1	130.6	135.2	138.6	141.1	142.3	143.9	124.1	131.0	133.5	134.8	141.7	143.5	145.5
Seasonings, olives, pickles, and relish (12/77 = 100)	124.9	131.9	133.5	134.2	135.2	137.2	139.1	124.9	132.2	132.8	133.4	136.3	136.3	137.9
Other condiments (12/77 = 100)	126.0	133.4	133.3	133.5	134.4	135.8	138.1	126.6	135.3	136.5	136.3	136.3	137.3	140.0
Miscellaneous prepared foods (12/77 = 100)	122.2	132.0	133.5	133.8	135.4	135.8	135.9	122.2	131.7	133.8	133.5	135.2	136.0	136.2
Other canned and packaged prepared foods (12/77 = 100)	122.2	127.9	128.6	130.3	131.6	132.4	134.1	122.0	128.2	128.9	130.2	132.1	132.4	134.4
Food away from home	260.9	273.1	275.3	277.7	280.9	284.7	286.1	262.7	277.4	279.5	281.8	284.2	287.3	288.6
Lunch (12/77 = 100)	127.0	132.9	134.3	135.7	137.2	138.6	139.2	127.6	134.4	135.7	137.3	138.5	139.8	140.3
Dinner (12/77 = 100)	127.0	132.4	133.4	134.4	136.2	138.2	138.8	128.1	135.1	136.1	136.7	138.2	139.4	140.1
Other meals and snacks (12/77 = 100)	124.9	131.8	132.5	133.7	134.7	137.0	137.9	126.2	133.9	134.5	135.6	136.4	138.5	139.3

Item														
Alcoholic beverages	198.7	197.6	195.5	193.7	192.8	192.5	182.8	197.1	195.9	193.7	191.6	190.9	190.4	181.7
Alcoholic beverages at home (12/77 = 100)	129.6	128.8	127.6	126.5	125.9	125.6	119.3	128.1	127.4	126.1	124.9	124.4	124.0	118.2
Beer and ale	198.5	197.2	194.5	192.9	192.2	192.0	181.7	198.2	197.6	194.5	192.9	192.0	191.7	182.0
Whiskey	143.2	142.0	141.5	140.2	139.9	139.0	134.4	141.6	140.0	140.0	140.0	138.9	137.7	132.8
Wine	233.6	231.6	229.4	227.2	224.0	224.2	208.4	224.3	224.0	221.7	217.6	215.2	215.4	204.1
Other alcoholic beverages (12/77 = 100)	114.0	113.3	113.2	112.1	112.0	111.6	107.2	115.0	113.9	113.7	112.7	112.9	112.5	107.4
Alcoholic beverages away from home (12/77 = 100)	129.9	129.4	127.4	126.2	125.5	125.3	119.1	131.1	129.7	127.6	125.8	125.3	125.1	120.0
HOUSING	282.2	280.7	279.1	277.1	273.7	271.0	254.4	282.6	280.9	279.1	276.9	273.8	271.1	254.5
Shelter	302.6	301.7	301.7	300.4	296.4	292.0	272.7	301.6	300.5	300.1	298.5	294.7	290.4	271.6
Rent, residential	202.7	201.6	200.6	199.4	198.0	196.8	186.4	203.0	201.9	200.9	199.6	198.3	197.1	186.6
Other rental costs	283.5	278.3	273.6	267.3	268.4	268.8	258.6	283.6	278.5	273.9	267.7	268.3	268.8	258.6
Lodging while out of town	303.2	296.0	289.9	281.0	283.3	284.9	275.7	304.8	297.4	291.5	282.6	284.2	286.0	276.8
Tenants' insurance (12/77 = 100)	130.8	129.9	128.0	127.2	126.8	126.0	119.3	130.1	129.3	127.6	126.9	126.5	125.4	118.6
Homeownership	338.3	338.2	338.6	337.5	332.3	326.7	304.0	336.8	335.8	335.8	334.2	329.4	323.8	302.0
Home purchase	260.2	262.7	266.4	268.0	268.2	266.4	243.8	261.1	263.0	266.2	267.2	267.3	265.5	244.0
Financing, taxes, and insurance	446.4	442.6	441.3	436.0	423.1	410.8	384.1	441.1	437.1	435.2	429.4	416.9	407.4	379.9
Property insurance	379.9	376.6	373.2	369.0	367.8	365.3	337.4	375.6	373.1	369.8	365.8	364.5	362.0	335.7
Property taxes	201.0	206.6	197.9	196.4	194.7	193.8	189.9	199.0	198.5	196.0	194.5	192.8	192.0	188.2
Contracted mortgage interest cost	572.0	565.5	565.9	558.7	539.7	521.2	484.1	570.9	565.0	563.5	555.5	536.7	518.1	483.0
Mortgage interest rates	216.7	213.2	209.4	205.5	198.4	193.0	194.8	216.0	211.9	209.0	205.1	198.0	192.6	194.4
Maintenance and repairs	302.7	299.9	294.1	294.2	291.1	290.4	278.2	306.1	302.8	296.8	296.8	294.2	292.8	278.8
Maintenance and repair services	331.3	327.7	319.8	320.3	315.9	315.1	303.5	332.6	328.7	321.3	321.5	318.6	317.0	303.2
Maintenance and repair commodities	239.9	236.6	236.7	236.2	235.6	235.0	223.3	243.9	242.4	239.7	239.1	237.1	236.3	221.4
Paint and wallpaper, supplies, tools, and equipment (12/77 = 100)	138.5	136.9	135.1	139.4	134.7	133.1	123.6	143.7	141.6	139.5	139.2	137.4	136.9	125.0
Lumber, awnings, glass, and masonry (12/77 = 100)	122.4	122.3	122.7	122.9	122.0	122.5	119.9	123.3	124.0	123.4	123.2	122.3	122.4	117.6
Plumbing, electrical, heating, and cooling supplies (12/77 = 100)	127.8	127.0	124.5	124.9	124.6	126.6	119.3	127.6	127.3	125.2	124.8	124.2	123.8	116.4
Miscellaneous supplies and equipment (12/77 = 100)	128.8	127.8	127.9	126.3	126.4	125.9	118.2	125.9	125.2	124.7	124.2	123.7	123.3	117.0
Fuel and other utilities	309.4	305.6	297.5	290.7	286.3	288.0	268.7	308.4	304.5	296.7	289.9	285.7	287.6	268.0
Fuels	393.4	387.3	375.0	364.5	358.2	362.1	333.9	393.7	387.4	375.4	364.7	358.7	362.8	333.9
Fuel oil, coal, and bottled gas	696.3	678.5	627.9	587.0	568.3	559.9	554.1	693.4	675.6	625.9	585.3	567.0	558.7	553.4
Fuel oil	733.2	714.2	657.1	610.9	590.3	581.8	577.9	730.9	712.0	656.0	610.0	589.8	581.5	577.9
Other fuels (6/78 = 100)	162.9	159.4	154.1	150.1	147.3	144.8	139.5	161.5	157.5	152.3	148.4	145.7	143.1	138.3
Gas (piped) and electricity	325.9	322.1	317.7	313.4	309.8	316.0	283.9	326.7	322.9	318.5	313.9	310.5	317.1	284.0
Electricity	273.5	271.1	266.5	262.1	258.4	265.3	238.1	273.9	271.3	266.9	262.3	258.7	265.3	237.9
Utility (piped) gas	392.8	386.8	383.3	379.7	376.7	380.9	342.6	395.2	389.0	385.3	381.5	379.0	384.6	343.9

CONSUMER PRICE INDEX (U.S. CITY AVERAGE, continued)

[1967 = 100 unless otherwise specified]

General summary	All Urban Consumers							Urban Wage Earners and Clerical Workers (revised)						
	Mar.	1980			1981			Mar.	1980			1981		
		Oct.	Nov.	Dec.	Jan.	Feb.	Mar.		Oct.	Nov.	Dec.	Jan.	Feb.	Mar.
HOUSING – Continued														
Fuel and other utilities – Continued														
Other utilities and public services	161.9	167.8	169.0	170.6	171.9	173.6	174.2	161.9	167.8	169.1	170.7	172.0	173.9	174.4
Telephone services	133.2	137.5	138.7	140.3	141.1	142.4	142.5	133.1	137.4	138.7	140.3	141.1	142.5	142.6
Local charges (12/77 = 100)	103.3	106.6	108.3	110.5	111.6	113.5	113.6	103.2	106.5	108.3	110.6	111.7	113.6	113.7
Interstate toll calls (12/77 = 100)	97.4	102.1	101.7	101.8	101.8	101.8	101.8	97.5	102.1	101.8	101.8	101.9	101.9	101.9
Intrastate toll calls (12/77 = 100)	98.7	100.1	100.6	100.9	101.0	101.2	101.2	98.6	99.9	100.5	100.7	100.8	101.0	101.0
Water and sewerage maintenance	253.9	266.2	267.0	267.8	271.4	274.7	277.1	254.7	267.3	268.0	268.7	272.5	276.3	279.0
Household furnishings and operations	201.3	210.1	211.0	211.6	212.6	214.9	216.9	199.2	206.8	208.1	209.0	209.7	211.7	213.7
Housefurnishings	171.5	177.9	178.1	178.3	178.7	180.8	182.6	170.4	175.6	176.4	176.9	176.9	178.5	180.2
Textile housefurnishings	187.2	195.9	192.4	193.2	191.9	195.1	199.8	185.3	195.1	195.7	196.6	193.4	196.9	201.4
Household linens (12/77 = 100)	113.9	119.5	117.3	117.2	114.6	118.6	123.1	113.2	119.5	122.6	122.7	117.0	121.4	124.1
Curtains, drapes, slipcovers, and sewing materials (12/77 = 100)	119.7	124.9	122.7	123.8	124.9	124.8	126.1	118.2	124.1	121.2	122.4	126.6	124.4	127.2
Furniture and bedding	189.2	195.2	196.5	197.0	196.6	199.3	201.6	187.9	192.5	193.9	194.4	196.6	195.6	198.0
Bedroom furniture (12/77 = 100)	122.5	127.4	128.6	129.2	128.3	131.3	133.2	119.2	124.6	125.5	125.7	125.1	127.7	129.4
Sofas (12/77 = 100)	110.9	113.8	114.2	115.3	114.2	114.5	115.8	112.7	113.0	113.6	114.7	113.2	113.2	114.1
Living room chairs and tables (12/77 = 100)	110.8	113.0	113.3	113.1	113.1	115.9	116.5	111.9	114.4	115.6	115.2	114.3	115.2	116.7
Other furniture (12/77 = 100)	112.6	127.0	127.9	127.8	128.7	129.1	130.8	121.3	123.6	124.6	124.7	125.6	126.6	128.3
Appliances including TV and sound equipment	138.8	142.3	142.6	142.4	143.1	143.9	144.2	139.0	141.2	141.4	142.0	142.7	142.9	143.4
Television and sound equipment (12/77 = 100)	105.7	107.1	107.4	107.2	107.4	107.9	108.0	105.5	105.6	106.1	106.1	106.5	106.6	106.4
Television	104.0	104.7	105.1	105.2	105.6	105.7	105.6	102.9	103.2	103.8	103.7	104.2	104.2	104.3
Sound equipment (12/77 = 100)	108.3	110.3	110.6	110.1	110.2	111.0	111.2	108.7	108.7	109.1	109.2	109.4	109.6	109.3
Household appliances	160.2	166.0	166.2	165.9	167.2	168.2	168.9	160.7	165.3	165.2	166.3	167.6	167.8	169.0
Refrigerators and home freezers	157.9	165.8	166.1	166.5	168.0	168.4	168.5	161.4	169.4	169.2	170.9	171.7	172.3	172.7
Laundry equipment (12/77 = 100)	116.8	121.5	122.0	123.4	123.6	123.7	124.5	116.6	120.2	120.2	121.4	121.9	122.8	124.3
Other household appliances (12/77 = 100)	111.2	114.2	114.2	113.1	114.2	115.4	115.9	110.7	112.5	112.4	112.8	114.0	113.7	114.5
Stoves, dishwashers, vacuums, and sewing machines (12/77 = 100)	110.9	112.4	113.0	112.0	114.8	115.1	115.1	111.1	112.1	112.6	113.9	115.7	114.2	115.2
Office machines, small electric appliances, and air conditioners (12/77 = 100)	111.6	116.2	115.5	114.3	113.6	115.7	116.9	110.2	113.0	112.1	111.5	112.0	113.1	113.7

Item														
Other household equipment (12/77 = 100)	126.9	125.6	123.8	123.1	123.2	122.2	116.0	129.1	127.9	125.6	124.8	124.6	124.1	117.3
Floor and window coverings, infants', laundry, cleaning, and outdoor equipment (12/77 = 100)	116.4	120.8	118.9	118.4	119.0	118.2	110.8	130.7	128.7	125.7	124.6	124.3	123.3	116.4
Clocks, lamps, and decor items (12/77 = 100)	114.9	121.7	119.2	118.8	119.2	119.4	112.3	125.7	124.1	122.3	121.7	121.4	121.6	114.9
Tableware, serving pieces, and nonelectric kitchenware (12/77 = 100)	122.6	131.0	128.0	127.6	127.4	126.3	120.8	135.6	134.8	131.9	130.8	130.6	130.0	122.6
Lawn equipment, power tools, and other hardware (12/77 = 100)	112.2	123.8	123.8	122.3	122.3	120.9	115.0	120.8	119.9	118.7	118.7	118.4	117.9	112.2
Housekeeping supplies	261.2	260.1	257.5	256.0	253.5	251.2	235.5	264.2	262.8	259.5	257.7	256.0	253.6	238.0
Soaps and detergents	253.8	254.3	253.4	252.3	248.2	245.6	230.0	255.3	256.2	255.6	254.0	252.4	248.7	232.1
Other laundry and cleaning products (12/77 = 100)	130.3	129.6	129.0	127.6	126.2	125.1	116.9	129.7	129.3	128.8	126.7	126.7	117.0	117.0
Cleansing and toilet tissue, paper towels and napkins (12/77 = 100)	138.1	139.2	139.2	137.6	136.6	136.2	125.8	137.9	138.4	137.3	136.1	135.6	134.2	123.9
Stationery, stationery supplies, and gift wrap (12/77 = 100)	123.7	122.4	120.7	120.0	118.8	118.2	113.6	122.3	121.4	119.9	119.5	118.3	118.6	113.8
Miscellaneous household products (12/77 = 100)	128.9	132.2	129.3	129.5	128.4	126.7	118.3	137.3	135.9	132.6	132.5	131.1	129.5	120.9
Lawn and garden supplies (12/77 = 100)	128.5	126.1	122.7	122.5	122.5	121.0	114.0	136.6	134.0	130.0	128.4	128.0	126.9	121.4
Housekeeping services	283.3	279.4	276.4	273.8	272.5	271.0	262.7	284.8	281.6	279.6	277.1	276.1	274.5	263.6
Postage	274.2	257.3	257.3	257.3	257.3	257.3	257.2	274.3	257.3	257.3	257.3	257.3	257.3	257.3
Moving, storage, freight, household laundry, and drycleaning services (12/77 = 100)	139.0	137.8	134.3	131.8	131.4	130.2	126.1	139.0	138.2	137.0	134.4	134.6	133.3	125.4
Appliance and furniture repair (12/77 = 100)	123.8	122.4	121.5	120.6	119.7	119.2	116.0	124.5	123.6	122.4	121.4	120.7	120.3	115.8
APPAREL AND UPKEEP	184.3	181.8	180.8	182.9	183.3	182.8	175.1	185.1	182.0	181.1	183.9	184.8	183.9	176.0
Apparel commodities	175.8	173.3	172.6	175.3	176.0	175.6	168.7	176.3	173.2	172.6	176.0	177.2	176.4	169.2
Apparel commodities less footwear	172.3	169.6	168.7	171.6	172.5	172.2	165.7	172.7	169.6	168.9	172.5	173.9	173.1	166.2
Men's and boys'	174.9	172.2	171.7	174.4	174.8	173.8	166.0	175.0	171.6	171.1	174.3	174.8	173.9	165.6
Men's (12/77 = 100)	110.1	108.2	107.9	109.9	110.2	109.5	104.4	110.2	107.8	107.9	109.8	110.1	109.5	104.3
Suits, sport coats, and jackets (12/77 = 100)	98.5	96.1	95.1	98.2	99.4	99.7	96.4	103.2	100.5	99.9	103.5	104.7	104.3	99.9
Coats and jackets (12/77 = 100)	98.9	96.0	97.4	101.9	101.9	101.3	96.9	97.9	95.6	95.2	99.7	100.5	100.4	96.9
Furnishings and special clothing (12/77 = 100)	121.5	120.2	119.9	120.0	119.7	118.8	113.2	127.2	125.3	123.9	123.9	123.3	122.9	115.0
Shirts (12/77 = 100)	119.2	116.8	116.7	120.7	120.4	118.5	112.0	118.0	114.8	115.4	119.7	119.6	118.3	111.9
Dungarees, jeans, and trousers (12/77 = 100)	110.0	108.7	108.2	108.1	108.7	108.3	102.7	104.7	102.7	103.4	103.4	103.5	102.6	98.7
Boys' (12/77 = 100)	112.9	119.9	119.0	112.6	112.7	112.0	107.5	113.7	112.6	112.0	113.1	113.3	113.0	107.5
Coats, jackets, sweaters, and shirts (12/77 = 100)	109.5	107.0	107.9	111.8	112.5	112.0	105.0	106.5	104.3	104.8	108.6	109.4	109.2	102.5
Furnishings (12/77 = 100)	117.4	116.1	115.8	116.2	115.2	115.1	107.1	121.2	119.1	119.1	118.7	118.4	118.1	112.0
Suits, trousers, sport coats, and jackets (12/77 = 100)	113.9	114.2	113.9	112.0	111.9	111.5	108.2	116.5	116.6	114.8	114.3	114.3	113.9	109.8
Women's and girls'	158.9	155.4	153.9	158.2	159.9	160.3	154.9	157.5	153.4	152.1	157.4	159.9	159.7	155.5
Women's (12/77 = 100)	105.5	103.5	102.3	105.3	106.6	107.0	103.7	104.4	101.9	100.8	104.4	106.3	106.1	103.8
Coats and jackets	156.9	159.1	172.2	171.6	175.5	176.5	167.0	157.9	160.7	150.4	161.4	164.7	167.0	167.6
Dresses	154.3	150.5	147.3	154.3	157.7	157.5	157.5	166.4	156.9	155.5	163.8	168.1	170.0	169.3
Separates and sportswear (12/77 = 100)	101.6	99.7	100.1	102.4	102.8	103.6	101.0	99.3	97.1	98.2	101.4	102.9	101.6	99.8
Underwear, nightwear, and hosiery (12/77 = 100)	117.7	116.0	115.6	116.6	116.4	115.3	111.5	117.8	116.4	116.0	116.8	116.7	114.9	110.0
Suits (12/77 = 100)	109.5	159.1	95.5	102.5	99.0	99.0	95.7	93.0	90.0	87.8	91.9	97.4	98.2	91.6
Girls' (12/77 = 100)	106.4	102.7	102.5	106.1	106.8	105.1	100.1	106.4	102.8	103.6	102.9	102.9	107.0	101.8
Coats, jackets, dresses, and suits (12/77 = 100)	98.4	93.5	94.4	104.9	99.1	99.0	95.7	101.2	94.4	96.0	106.1	106.5	103.2	98.9
Separates and sportswear (12/77 = 100)	109.1	105.8	104.4	109.6	106.8	106.3	100.2	106.2	104.2	103.6	106.1	106.5	107.2	100.8
Underwear, nightwear, hosiery, and accessories (12/77 = 100)	114.6	112.5	112.2	112.2	112.6	112.8	107.8	115.6	113.9	113.1	113.8	114.0	113.8	108.4

CONSUMER PRICE INDEX (U.S. CITY AVERAGE, *continued*)

[1967 = 100 unless otherwise specified]

General summary	All Urban Consumers							Urban Wage Earners and Clerical Workers (revised)						
	Mar.	1980 Oct.	Nov.	Dec.	1981 Jan.	Feb.	Mar.	Mar.	1980 Oct.	Nov.	Dec.	1981 Jan.	Feb.	Mar.
APPAREL AND UPKEEP – Continued														
Apparel commodities – Continued														
Apparel commodities less footwear – Continued														
Infants' and toddlers'	231.4	244.1	248.9	250.1	249.7	254.3	255.3	237.3	249.2	254.0	255.4	256.9	264.0	266.4
Other apparel commodities	199.9	211.8	213.7	213.3	214.2	212.3	212.2	197.8	204.1	204.0	204.4	205.3	204.4	204.5
Sewing materials and notions (12/77 = 100)	107.1	111.9	110.3	110.6	111.9	112.2	113.3	107.2	112.0	110.2	110.0	110.8	112.2	113.3
Jewelry and luggage (12/77 = 100)	138.6	147.5	149.9	149.5	149.7	147.9	147.3	137.3	141.1	141.8	142.3	142.8	141.3	140.9
Footwear	187.0	196.1	196.5	196.6	194.9	194.9	197.4	186.3	195.6	196.4	196.7	195.5	194.9	195.9
Men's (12/77 = 100)	119.0	124.7	125.4	124.6	124.4	125.0	125.2	120.9	125.8	126.7	126.0	126.1	125.7	125.4
Boys' and girls' (12/77 = 100)	119.5	125.8	126.2	126.6	125.7	125.3	127.6	119.5	126.9	127.4	127.8	127.0	126.2	127.3
Women's (12/77 = 100)	114.2	119.6	119.4	120.0	118.1	117.9	120.0	110.9	116.3	116.5	117.5	115.9	115.9	117.0
Apparel services	225.9	240.0	241.9	243.4	246.3	249.9	254.2	223.5	238.1	239.9	242.2	245.5	248.7	251.5
Laundry and drycleaning other than coin operated (12/77 = 100)	132.5	141.1	142.4	143.5	145.3	147.6	149.6	132.3	140.9	141.6	143.2	145.5	147.3	149.3
Other apparel services (12/77 = 100)	122.1	129.2	130.0	130.5	131.7	133.3	133.7	119.6	127.4	129.1	129.9	131.1	132.9	133.9
TRANSPORTATION	243.7	256.1	259.0	261.1	264.7	270.9	273.5	244.3	256.6	259.7	261.9	265.7	272.1	274.4
Private	244.0	254.5	257.4	259.4	262.9	269.4	271.7	244.6	255.5	258.6	260.8	264.4	271.0	273.2
New cars	175.0	181.9	184.3	184.5	185.3	184.8	182.9	175.4	182.0	184.5	184.6	185.7	185.0	182.7
Used cars	195.2	222.7	230.8	234.4	234.0	234.3	235.4	195.2	222.7	230.8	234.4	234.0	234.4	235.4
Gasoline	370.9	370.5	370.5	373.3	385.2	410.8	420.7	372.7	371.7	371.7	374.4	366.6	412.5	422.3
Automobile maintenance and repair	260.9	276.0	278.4	280.1	282.7	285.4	287.7	261.7	276.6	278.9	280.6	263.2	285.4	288.2
Body work (12/77 = 100)	127.3	135.0	136.1	136.8	137.3	139.2	140.3	127.2	134.6	135.9	136.7	137.3	139.2	140.2
Automobile drive train, brake, and miscellaneous mechanical repair (12/77 = 100)	124.1	132.7	133.6	134.0	135.8	136.8	137.7	126.1	133.9	135.0	135.6	137.5	138.3	140.2
Maintenance and servicing (12/77 = 100)	123.1	130.0	131.0	131.6	132.5	133.7	134.8	122.8	130.2	131.1	131.7	132.7	133.5	134.7
Power plant repair (12/77 = 100)	123.5	129.8	131.3	132.7	134.4	135.5	137.0	124.0	129.6	130.8	132.2	133.5	134.7	135.9
Other private transportation	216.5	226.5	228.8	231.0	232.4	234.2	234.7	217.1	228.0	230.6	233.2	235.0	236.9	237.3
Other private transportation commodities	192.7	200.9	203.1	203.6	203.7	205.8	206.2	193.2	201.4	203.4	203.7	205.0	205.7	206.2
Motor oil, coolant, and other products (12/77 = 100)	126.4	136.5	137.8	138.8	139.1	141.6	141.6	126.1	135.4	137.3	139.0	139.2	139.0	139.8
Automobile parts and equipment (12/77 = 100)	124.3	128.9	130.3	130.6	130.6	131.8	132.1	124.7	129.4	130.6	132.0	132.4	133.4	133.7
Tires	170.1	179.2	181.7	182.1	181.5	183.5	184.1	172.5	180.8	182.5	184.7	184.8	186.6	186.9
Other parts and equipment (12/77 = 100)	127.2	126.9	127.3	127.6	128.6	129.3	129.2	124.4	125.7	126.9	127.8	128.9	129.3	129.5

Other private transportation services	225.0	235.6	237.9	240.6	242.4	244.0	244.6	225.7	237.3	240.1	242.9	244.9	247.0	247.4
Automobile insurance	244.0	251.5	251.9	252.5	252.3	253.7	254.4	243.8	251.2	251.5	252.0	251.8	253.2	253.9
Automobile finance charges (12/77 = 100)	137.4	149.9	154.4	159.4	163.4	165.1	164.3	135.2	148.3	153.2	157.9	161.7	163.9	163.4
Automobile rental, registration, and other fees (12/77 = 100)	110.8	114.6	115.0	115.8	116.2	116.7	118.2	116.6	116.3	116.7	117.5	118.2	119.3	119.9
State registration	145.3	146.5	146.6	146.9	146.9	146.9	146.9	145.5	146.5	146.6	147.0	146.9	147.0	147.0
Drivers licenses (12/77 = 100)	104.7	104.9	105.0	105.3	105.3	105.4	105.4	104.4	104.7	104.7	105.1	105.1	105.1	105.1
Vehicle inspection (12/77 = 100)	119.7	122.9	122.9	124.3	124.8	125.8	126.1	120.2	123.6	123.9	125.1	125.6	126.6	126.7
Other vehicle related fees (12/77 = 100)	122.0	130.0	130.7	132.7	133.7	134.7	138.4	127.6	139.1	140.0	142.0	144.1	147.2	148.9
Public	232.1	273.6	277.0	280.1	286.4	288.1	293.9	226.1	266.5	269.2	271.8	279.0	280.6	285.1
Airline fare	259.9	315.0	321.8	327.4	331.9	334.1	343.7	259.3	313.0	319.8	325.7	330.2	332.7	342.3
Intercity bus fare	290.7	307.1	308.0	310.1	310.7	312.8	323.2	290.2	306.9	308.0	309.8	310.6	312.2	323.9
Intracity mass transit	200.8	235.6	236.1	237.1	247.1	248.4	250.8	198.6	235.2	235.6	236.5	246.5	247.8	249.1
Taxi fare	245.6	267.9	269.2	269.7	271.0	271.4	273.8	251.2	274.7	275.6	275.9	275.5	277.7	280.5
Intercity train fare	237.2	255.6	255.6	270.1	276.4	276.5	276.7	237.1	255.7	255.7	270.3	276.8	276.9	277.1
MEDICAL CARE	260.2	272.8	274.5	275.8	279.5	282.6	284.7	260.9	274.3	276.3	277.6	281.4	284.4	287.0
Medical care commodities	163.5	172.5	173.8	175.1	176.7	179.2	180.7	164.4	173.0	174.1	175.6	177.5	179.6	181.2
Prescription drugs	150.9	158.5	159.6	160.7	162.7	165.0	166.5	152.0	159.5	160.2	161.5	163.4	165.3	166.8
Anti-infective drugs (12/77 = 100)	117.9	124.1	124.6	124.7	127.7	129.2	130.5	120.1	125.1	125.6	126.4	128.6	129.5	131.0
Tranquilizers and sedatives (12/77 = 100)	122.2	127.1	128.9	130.2	130.7	131.9	132.8	122.2	126.2	127.7	128.6	129.4	130.7	131.5
Circulatories and diuretics (12/77 = 100)	113.3	117.3	118.3	119.1	120.6	121.9	122.2	114.7	119.3	119.9	120.2	121.3	122.9	123.7
Hormones, diabetic drugs, biologicals, and prescription and supplies (12/77 = 100)	130.0	139.6	140.4	142.3	143.9	147.4	148.2	129.6	138.8	139.6	141.7	143.8	146.5	147.8
Pain and symptom control drugs (12/77 = 100)	120.5	126.3	126.7	126.9	128.7	130.9	132.7	121.3	128.7	128.3	129.6	131.4	133.3	134.1
Supplements, cough and cold preparations, and respiratory agents (12/77 = 100)	115.5	120.4	121.2	122.4	123.2	124.5	126.3	116.5	122.1	122.3	123.1	123.8	125.2	126.5
Nonprescription drugs and medical supplies (12/77 = 100)	117.3	124.4	125.3	126.2	127.1	128.9	129.9	118.0	124.4	125.5	126.5	127.9	129.4	130.5
Eyeglasses (12/77 = 100)	114.1	121.0	121.2	120.8	121.5	123.1	124.6	114.5	119.6	120.2	120.4	121.1	122.3	122.6
Internal and respiratory over-the-counter drugs	182.2	193.5	195.8	198.1	199.3	202.7	204.2	183.0	194.0	195.8	198.0	200.4	203.0	205.5
Nonprescription medical equipment and supplies (12/77 = 100)	115.1	121.3	121.5	122.5	123.6	124.5	125.0	116.1	121.8	123.0	123.7	125.1	126.5	127.1
Medical care services	281.5	294.8	296.6	297.9	302.1	305.2	307.5	282.2	296.6	298.7	300.0	304.3	307.4	310.2
Professional services	245.3	259.0	260.4	261.7	264.7	267.2	269.6	247.8	261.9	263.8	265.0	268.7	271.6	274.2
Physicians services	262.3	276.0	278.0	280.3	283.9	287.7	290.3	266.2	281.8	283.8	285.7	290.0	293.9	296.3
Dental services	234.1	247.5	248.0	248.6	251.4	252.8	254.9	235.7	249.0	250.4	251.3	254.9	257.0	259.8
Other professional services (12/77 = 100)	119.5	127.6	128.5	128.5	129.3	130.0	131.5	119.3	125.1	126.7	126.6	127.6	128.5	129.9
Other medical care services	325.3	338.0	340.5	341.6	347.3	351.1	353.4	324.4	339.2	341.6	342.9	347.8	351.3	354.4
Hospital and other medical services (12/77 = 100)	128.8	139.3	141.1	141.7	144.5	146.1	147.1	127.7	138.9	140.5	141.3	143.7	145.2	146.7
Hospital room	405.8	435.8	441.0	443.7	453.8	458.2	460.9	401.2	435.3	439.8	443.1	451.9	455.9	459.2
Other hospital and medical care services (12/77 = 100)	127.8	139.0	140.9	141.4	143.7	145.5	146.7	126.9	138.4	140.2	140.6	142.7	144.4	146.3

CONSUMER PRICE INDEX (U.S. CITY AVERAGE, *concluded*)

[1967 = 100 unless otherwise specified]

General summary	All Urban Consumers							Urban Wage Earners and Clerical Workers (revised)						
	1980				1981			1980				1981		
	Mar.	Oct.	Nov.	Dec.	Jan.	Feb.	Mar.	Mar.	Oct.	Nov.	Dec.	Jan.	Feb.	Mar.
ENTERTAINMENT	200.6	210.9	211.2	212.0	214.4	216.7	218.2	199.5	209.2	209.9	210.1	212.2	215.0	216.1
Entertainment commodities	203.4	213.7	214.5	215.3	217.1	219.7	221.1	200.3	209.0	210.2	210.9	213.0	216.2	218.0
Reading materials (12/77 = 100)	119.4	127.0	127.6	128.2	130.0	130.9	133.2	119.1	126.6	127.1	127.6	129.6	130.7	133.0
Newspapers	232.4	245.3	245.6	246.2	249.7	253.8	256.6	232.0	244.6	244.9	245.5	249.4	254.0	256.7
Magazines, periodicals, and books (12/77 = 100)	120.8	129.6	130.7	131.5	133.4	132.9	136.2	120.7	129.6	130.8	131.5	133.5	132.9	136.3
Sporting goods and equipment (12/77 = 100)	117.2	121.8	122.8	122.9	123.5	124.7	126.1	112.4	116.3	117.0	117.8	118.5	119.3	120.3
Sport vehicles (12/77 = 100)	118.7	(¹)	(¹)	(¹)	(¹)	126.5	128.5	110.8	(¹)	(¹)	(¹)	(¹)	118.1	119.5
Indoor and warm weather sport equipment (12/77 = 100)	109.5	114.5	114.7	116.2	115.7	115.9	116.2	109.3	112.5	112.2	113.4	114.5	115.3	115.2
Bicycles	177.2	185.3	185.7	184.7	185.9	187.2	188.4	177.8	185.4	185.8	184.9	186.7	188.3	189.4
Other sporting goods and equipment (12/77 = 100)	112.9	118.2	119.9	120.4	120.9	120.6	121.2	113.4	117.8	119.1	119.3	119.2	119.2	119.3
Toys, hobbies, and other entertainment (12/77 = 100)	116.9	122.8	122.8	123.5	124.4	126.3	127.2	116.4	120.9	121.6	121.8	122.9	125.8	126.3
Toys, hobbies, and music equipment (12/77 = 100)	115.7	120.9	120.7	121.3	122.4	124.7	125.6	114.9	117.4	118.4	118.5	119.4	123.0	123.1
Photographic supplies and equipment (12/77 = 100)	118.2	123.1	121.8	122.0	121.5	122.6	124.0	116.9	122.3	122.7	122.4	122.3	124.4	123.5
Pet supplies and expense (12/77 = 100)	118.2	125.8	127.3	128.4	130.1	132.0	132.3	119.0	126.4	126.8	127.6	129.7	131.9	132.8
Entertainment services	197.0	207.2	206.9	207.8	210.9	213.0	213.0	199.1	210.6	210.5	209.7	212.0	213.9	213.8
Fees for participant sports (12/77 = 100)	117.5	125.5	125.2	125.7	128.1	129.4	129.8	118.8	127.0	126.7	125.9	127.8	129.0	129.6
Admissions (12/77 = 100)	119.1	122.7	122.6	123.1	124.7	125.3	125.3	120.0	124.2	124.3	124.0	125.2	126.2	125.9
Other entertainment services (12/77 = 100)	113.2	119.0	118.7	119.4	120.1	122.0	121.0	113.9	121.6	121.6	121.8	122.0	123.0	121.7

OTHER GOODS AND SERVICES	208.9	221.5	222.8	224.6	226.2	227.4	228.7	208.3	219.9	221.0	223.0	224.4	225.6	226.8
Tobacco products	198.4	204.5	207.3	210.8	211.9	212.3	212.5	198.6	204.3	206.8	210.4	211.7	211.9	212.4
Cigarettes	201.2	206.8	209.6	213.5	214.6	214.8	214.8	201.6	206.7	209.3	213.2	214.5	214.5	214.9
Other tobacco products and smoking accessories (12/77 = 100)	116.3	123.2	124.3	124.9	125.4	126.5	128.0	115.7	123.1	123.9	124.5	125.4	126.4	128.1
Personal care	208.1	217.8	219.0	220.9	222.5	224.6	226.9	207.7	218.0	218.5	220.0	221.1	223.2	225.1
Toilet goods and personal care appliances	200.2	211.8	212.4	215.2	216.9	219.5	222.4	199.6	212.1	212.7	214.3	216.1	218.5	220.9
Products for the hair, hairpieces, and wigs (12/77 = 100)	116.6	124.5	124.5	125.2	126.3	128.3	131.4	114.9	123.6	123.2	125.3	126.2	126.7	128.4
Dental and shaving products (12/77 = 100)	119.2	126.0	127.2	128.4	130.8	132.9	135.3	118.4	125.3	125.9	125.4	128.3	131.2	133.3
Cosmetics, bath and nail preparations, manicure and eye makeup implements (12/77 = 100)	115.1	121.3	120.8	122.6	122.9	123.2	123.9	114.8	121.1	121.0	121.4	122.2	122.8	123.4
Other toilet goods and small personal care appliances (12/77 = 100)	114.7	120.8	122.2	124.8	125.5	127.5	128.3	116.6	123.6	125.3	126.8	126.6	129.0	130.7
Personal care services	215.7	223.8	225.5	226.8	228.3	230.0	231.7	215.8	224.0	224.4	225.8	226.3	228.1	229.4
Beauty parlor services for women	217.9	225.2	227.5	228.7	230.1	231.7	233.6	217.8	225.6	226.1	227.5	227.6	229.4	230.8
Haircuts and other barber shop services for men (12/77 = 100)	119.7	125.3	125.6	126.4	127.3	128.5	129.2	120.1	125.0	125.2	126.0	126.7	127.6	128.4
Personal and educational expenses	228.3	251.1	251.3	251.5	253.6	254.4	255.2	228.2	251.2	251.4	251.7	254.0	255.0	256.0
Schoolbooks and supplies	206.9	221.9	221.9	222.1	228.6	229.8	230.5	210.7	225.6	225.6	225.8	232.4	233.6	234.4
Personal and educational services	233.6	257.8	258.1	258.2	259.7	260.4	261.2	232.9	257.5	257.8	258.1	259.6	260.6	261.6
Tuition and other school fees	118.6	132.2	132.2	132.2	132.6	132.7	132.8	118.7	132.4	132.4	132.4	132.8	132.9	133.0
College tuition (12/77 = 100)	117.9	131.5	131.5	131.5	132.0	132.1	132.3	117.9	131.5	131.5	131.5	132.0	132.1	132.3
Elementary and high school tuition (12/77 = 100)	120.9	134.4	134.4	134.4	134.4	134.4	134.4	120.7	134.3	134.3	134.3	134.3	134.3	134.4
Personal expenses (12/77 = 100)	125.0	132.4	133.0	133.4	135.7	137.1	138.7	122.1	131.0	131.6	132.2	134.4	136.3	138.1
Special indexes:														
Gasoline, motor oil, coolant, and other products	365.5	365.5	365.5	368.3	379.9	404.8	414.5	367.2	366.6	366.7	369.4	381.2	406.3	415.9
Insurance and finance	326.3	346.4	355.3	364.5	368.9	370.7	373.6	325.6	346.7	355.6	364.7	368.8	370.4	373.0
Utilities and public transportation	230.9	254.9	253.1	255.8	259.4	262.3	265.2	230.2	253.5	251.6	254.4	258.0	261.0	263.6
Housekeeping and home maintenance services	292.0	304.7	306.4	308.4	309.5	314.6	318.3	292.0	302.4	303.5	306.6	307.4	313.4	317.2

¹ Not available.

Source: *Monthly Labor Review*, U.S. Department of Labor, Bureau of Labor Statistics.

CONSUMER PRICES

INDEX, 1967=100 (RATIO SCALE)

INDEX, 1967=100 (RATIO SCALE)

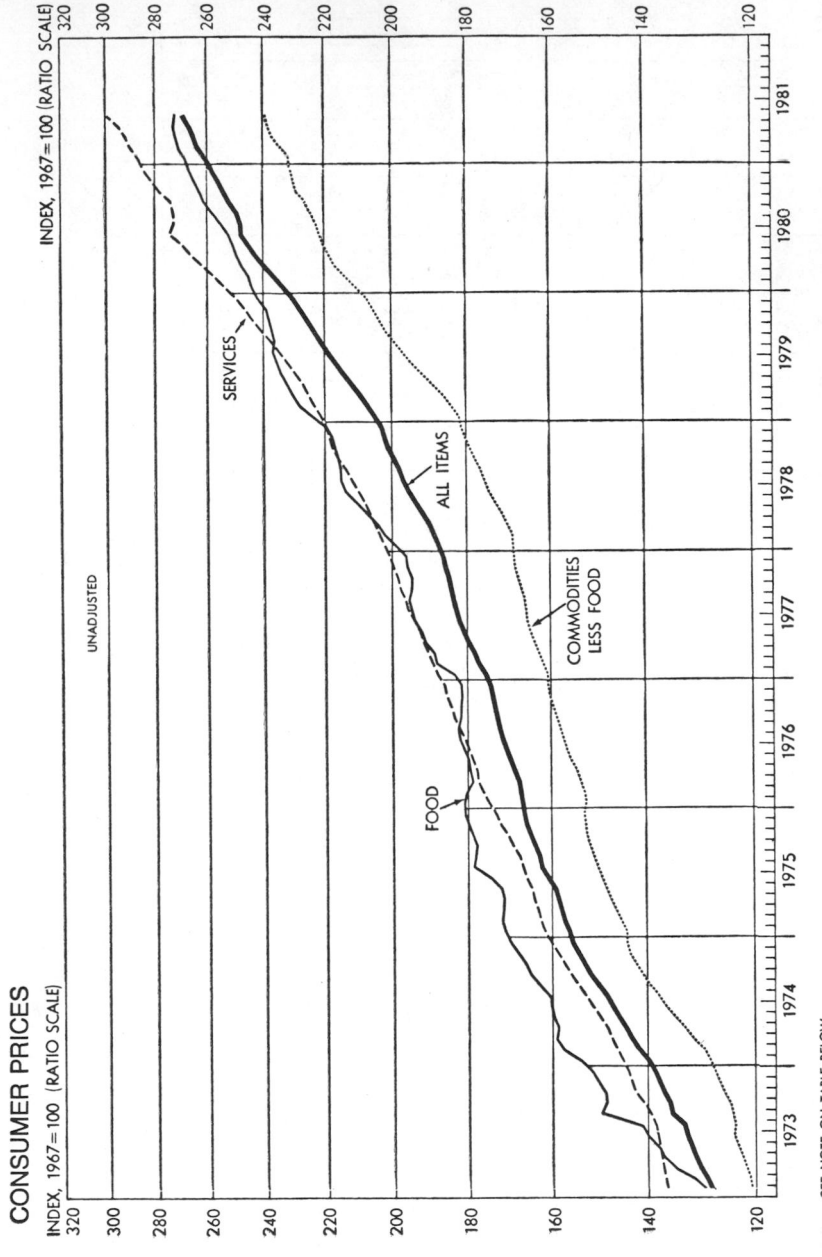

UNADJUSTED

SERVICES

ALL ITEMS

COMMODITIES LESS FOOD

FOOD

SEE NOTE ON TABLE BELOW
SOURCE: DEPARTMENT OF LABOR

[1967=100]

Note: In the following table, the first group of columns (All items, Food, Commodities less food, Services) is **Unadjusted**; the second group (All commodities through the final Services) is **Seasonally adjusted**.

Period	All items	Food	Commodities less food	Services	All commodities	Food — All	Food at home	Food away from home	Commodities less food — All	Durable	Non-durable	Services
1973	133.1	141.4	123.5	139.1	129.9	141.4	141.4	141.4	123.5	121.9	124.8	139.1
1974	147.7	161.7	136.6	152.1	145.5	161.7	162.4	159.4	136.6	130.6	140.9	152.1
1975	161.2	175.4	149.1	166.6	158.4	175.4	175.8	174.3	149.1	145.5	151.7	166.6
1976	170.5	180.8	156.6	180.4	165.2	180.8	179.5	186.1	156.6	154.3	158.3	180.4
1977	181.5	192.2	165.1	194.3	174.7	192.2	190.2	200.3	165.1	163.2	166.5	194.3
1978	195.4	211.4	174.7	210.9	187.1	211.4	210.2	218.4	174.7	173.9	174.3	210.9
1979	217.4	234.5	195.1	234.2	208.4	234.5	232.9	242.9	195.1	191.1	198.7	234.2
1980	246.8	254.6	222.0	270.3	233.9	254.6	251.5	267.0	222.0	210.4	235.2	270.3
			Unadjusted						Seasonally adjusted			
1980: May	244.9	250.4	220.2	269.2	230.7	249.3	244.9	263.7	219.5	206.7	234.9	269.4
June	247.6	252.0	221.4	274.2	231.6	250.5	245.8	265.6	220.3	207.7	235.5	274.1
July	247.8	254.8	222.2	272.4	233.0	252.9	248.7	266.9	221.3	208.8	236.4	272.4
Aug	249.4	258.7	224.2	272.5	235.9	257.6	254.6	268.9	223.4	212.1	237.4	272.7
Sept	251.7	261.1	226.6	274.8	238.9	262.0	259.8	271.4	225.9	215.2	238.4	274.6
Oct	253.9	262.4	228.3	277.9	241.1	264.4	262.2	273.6	228.0	217.6	239.2	277.9
Nov	256.2	264.5	230.0	280.9	243.5	267.6	265.6	276.5	230.0	220.4	240.3	281.5
Dec	258.4	266.4	231.0	284.7	245.2	270.2	268.0	279.4	231.3	221.3	242.0	285.5
1981: Jan	260.5	268.6	232.4	287.7	246.6	269.8	266.9	282.0	233.6	221.9	247.0	288.0
Feb	263.2	270.8	235.4	290.1	249.2	270.6	266.8	285.0	236.8	221.2	255.0	290.3
Mar	265.1	272.2	237.0	292.5	250.5	271.6	267.3	285.8	238.1	220.9	258.3	292.6
Apr	266.8	272.9	238.0	295.4	250.5	271.6	267.3	287.3	238.1	221.5	257.8	295.4
May	269.0	272.5	239.6	299.6	250.9	271.0	266.0	288.1	239.0	223.5	257.4	299.6

Note.—Data beginning January 1978 relate to all urban consumers. Earlier data relate to urban wage earners and clerical workers.

Source: Department of Labor, Bureau of Labor Statistics.

Source: *Economic Indicators*, Council of Economic Advisers.

CONSUMER PRICE INDEX (U.S. city average, and selected areas)

[1967=100 unless otherwise specified]

Area[1]	All Urban Consumers							Urban Wage Earners and Clerical Workers (revised)						
	Mar. 1980	Oct. 1980	Nov. 1980	Dec. 1980	Jan. 1981	Feb. 1981	Mar. 1981	Mar. 1980	Oct. 1980	Nov. 1980	Dec. 1980	Jan. 1981	Feb. 1981	Mar. 1981
U.S. city average[2]	239.8	253.9	256.2	258.4	260.5	263.2	265.1	239.9	254.1	256.4	258.7	260.7	263.5	265.2
Anchorage, Alaska (10/67=100)	223.5	...	...	...	240.1	...	241.1	220.2	...	...	...	235.0	...	236.2
Atlanta, Ga.	...	250.2	...	258.3	...	263.0	...	...	252.4	...	260.3	...	266.4	...
Baltimore, Md.	245.0	...	258.4	...	264.3	...	270.3	243.9	...	257.4	...	262.6	...	269.3
Boston, Mass.	234.2	...	248.8	...	256.4	...	262.3	234.2	...	249.2	...	255.7	...	261.8
Buffalo, N.Y.	...	239.6	...	246.5	...	251.4	...	...	238.2	...	245.2	...	249.7	...
Chicago, Ill.-Northwestern Ind.	235.5	253.7	259.9	260.3	258.9	259.6	259.7	235.2	252.8	258.9	258.9	258.1	258.8	258.9
Cincinnati, Ohio-Ky.-Ind.	247.8	...	262.1	...	264.5	...	266.1	249.7	...	236.5	...	249.7	...	267.7
Cleveland, Ohio	...	264.6	...	266.5	...	273.5	...	...	264.2	...	266.7	...	273.9	...
Dallas-Ft. Worth, Tex.	...	264.9	...	269.5	...	274.4	...	...	262.9	...	268.2	...	272.9	...
Denver-Boulder, Colo.	255.2	...	271.9	...	277.3	...	281.4	259.4	...	276.7	...	282.2	...	285.8
Detroit, Mich.	242.9	264.3	266.4	269.7	268.5	270.2	268.2	242.4	261.4	263.6	265.5	264.4	265.5	263.6
Honolulu, Hawaii	...	234.6	...	236.1	...	243.3	...	...	233.5	...	237.0	...	243.5	...
Houston, Tex.	...	272.3	...	274.8	...	281.5	...	...	269.4	...	272.1	...	277.7	...
Kansas City, Mo.-Kansas	...	254.8	...	259.1	...	261.9	...	...	253.0	...	257.2	...	260.1	...
Los Angeles-Long Beach, Anaheim, Calif.	241.3	252.6	255.5	258.7	259.4	261.6	263.3	243.9	254.9	258.4	262.2	262.7	265.0	266.5
Miami, Fla. (11/77=100)	127.7	...	133.9	...	137.3	...	140.0	128.8	...	135.6	...	138.8	...	141.7
Milwaukee, Wis.	242.7	...	262.1	...	266.2	...	269.9	247.8	...	267.5	...	271.9	...	274.6
Minneapolis-St. Paul, Minn.-Wis.	231.2	...	244.7	...	249.4	...	253.9	230.8	...	244.2	...	249.1	...	253.7
New York, N.Y.-Northeastern N.J.	229.0	247.0	247.0	247.3	252.4	252.7	257.6	231.3	242.6	249.5	247.2	255.1	252.7	260.6
Northeast, Pa. (Scranton)	...	247.0	...	247.3	...	252.7	...	...	242.6	...	247.2	...	252.7	...
Philadelphia, Pa.-N.J.	234.6	247.9	249.2	250.5	253.2	255.9	258.3	235.1	249.5	251.1	252.3	255.5	258.1	259.5
Pittsburgh, Pa.	...	256.3	...	262.0	...	265.5	...	...	257.6	...	262.9	...	266.4	...
Portland, Oreg.-Wash.	253.6	...	261.9	...	266.4	...	268.1	253.6	...	260.7	...	265.0	...	267.0
St. Louis, Mo.-Ill.	238.1	...	253.8	...	255.7	...	259.3	238.5	...	254.2	...	255.9	...	259.4
San Diego, Calif.	258.3	...	279.1	...	287.7	...	293.1	255.6	...	275.1	...	282.9	...	288.0
San Francisco-Oakland, Calif.	243.8	...	262.6	...	264.9	...	271.1	241.3	...	259.4	...	262.3	...	267.9
Seattle-Everett, Wash.	...	251.9	...	254.9	...	260.5	...	...	252.6	...	255.7	...	261.6	...
Washington, D.C.-Md.-Va.	238.8	...	253.6	...	257.2	...	262.3	239.2	...	255.7	...	259.4	...	264.2

[1]The areas listed include not only the central city but the entire portion of the Standard Metropolitan Statistical Area, as defined for the 1970 Census of Population, except that the Standard Consolidated Area is used for New York and Chicago. [2]Average of 85 cities.

Source: *Monthly Labor Review*, U.S. Department of Labor, Bureau of Labor Statistics.

NATIONAL INCOME (billions of dollars; quarterly data at seasonally adjusted annual rates)

Period	National income	Compensation of employees[1]	Proprietors' income with inventory valuation and capital consumption adjustments		Rental income of persons with capital consumption adjustment	Corporate profits with inventory valuation and capital consumption adjustments					Net interest
			Farm	Non-farm		Total	Profits with inventory valuation adjustment and without capital consumption adjustment			Capital consumption adjustment	
							Total	Profits before tax	Inventory valuation adjustment		
1970	810.7	612.0	14.3	51.9	19.7	71.4	68.9	75.4	−6.6	2.5	41.4
1971	871.5	652.2	15.0	54.4	20.2	83.2	82.0	86.6	−4.6	1.3	46.5
1972	963.6	718.0	18.7	58.1	21.0	96.6	94.0	100.6	−6.6	2.7	51.2
1973	1,086.2	801.3	32.8	61.0	22.6	108.3	105.6	125.6	−20.0	2.7	60.2
1974	1,160.7	877.5	26.5	62.2	23.5	94.9	96.7	136.7	−40.0	−1.8	76.1
1975	1,239.4	931.4	24.6	65.4	23.0	110.5	120.6	132.1	−11.6	−10.1	84.5
1976	1,379.2	1,036.3	19.1	75.0	23.5	138.1	151.6	166.3	−14.7	−13.5	87.2
1977	1,546.5	1,152.3	18.4	85.1	25.1	164.7	176.7	192.6	−15.8	−12.0	100.9
1978	1,745.4	1,299.7	26.1	91.0	27.4	185.5	199.0	223.3	−24.3	−13.5	115.8
1979	1,963.3	1,460.9	30.8	100.7	30.5	196.8	212.7	255.4	−42.6	−15.9	143.4
1980	2,121.4	1,596.5	23.4	107.2	31.8	182.7	199.8	245.5	−45.7	−17.2	179.8
1979: III	1,986.2	1,476.7	30.2	102.7	30.3	199.5	215.6	262.0	−46.5	−16.1	146.8
IV	2,031.3	1,518.1	29.5	106.8	31.0	189.4	204.5	255.4	−50.8	−15.1	156.5
1980: I	2,088.5	1,558.0	25.7	107.9	31.1	200.2	215.6	277.1	−61.4	−15.4	165.4
II	2,070.0	1,569.0	23.3	101.6	31.5	169.3	186.9	217.9	−31.1	−17.6	175.3
III	2,122.4	1,597.4	22.1	107.6	32.0	177.9	195.9	237.6	−41.7	−17.9	185.3
IV	2,204.8	1,661.8	22.5	111.6	32.4	183.3	201.0	249.5	−48.4	−17.8	193.3
1981: I	2,291.1	1,722.4	18.9	113.2	32.7	203.0	219.9	259.1	−39.1	−16.9	200.8

[1] Includes employer contributions for social insurance.

Source: Economic Indicators, Council of Economic Advisers.

Source: Department of Commerce, Bureau of Economic Analysis.

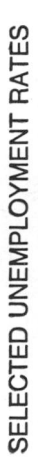

SELECTED UNEMPLOYMENT RATES

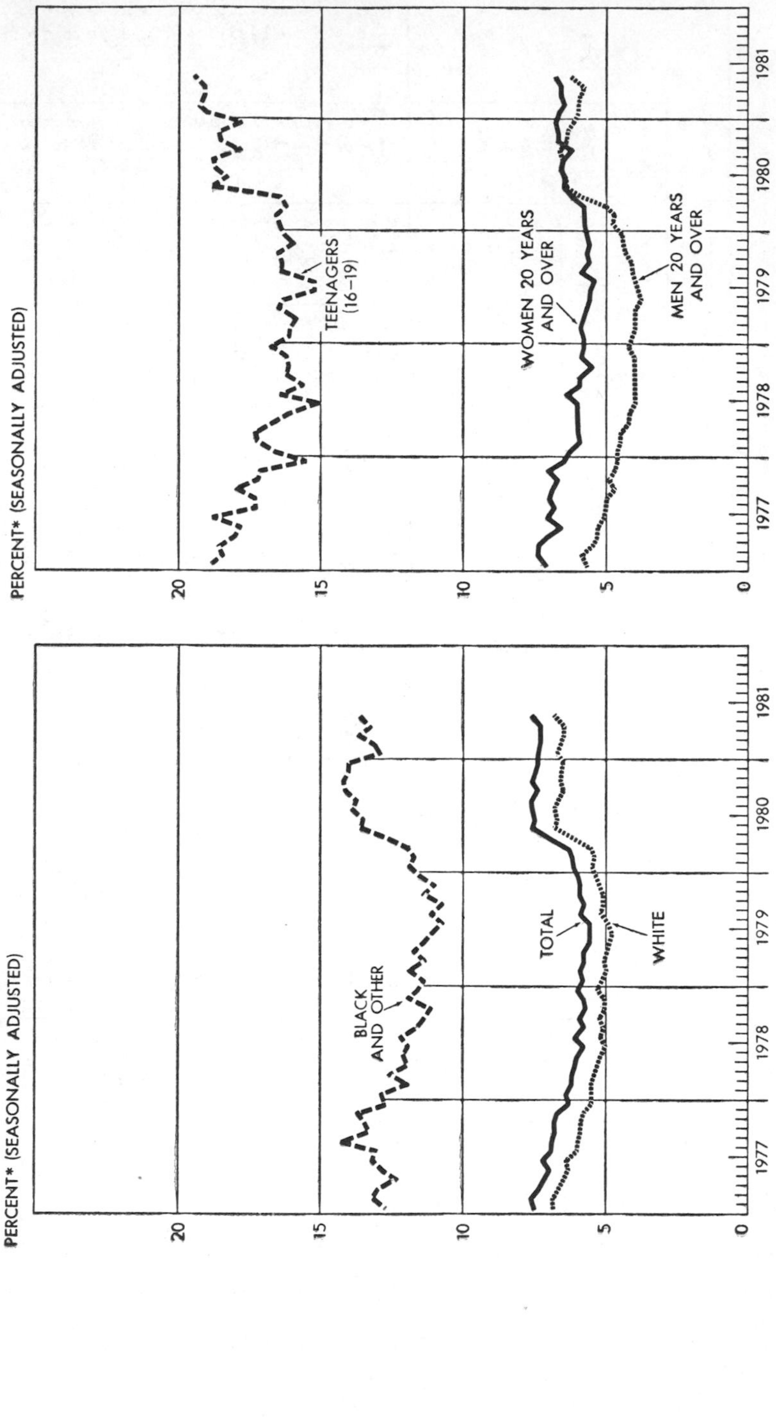
PERCENT* (SEASONALLY ADJUSTED)
20
15
10
5
0
BLACK AND OTHER
TOTAL
WHITE
1977
1978
1979
1980
1981
PERCENT* (SEASONALLY ADJUSTED)
TEENAGERS (16–19)
WOMEN 20 YEARS AND OVER
MEN 20 YEARS AND OVER

*UNEMPLOYMENT AS PERCENT OF CIVILIAN LABOR FORCE IN GROUP SPECIFIED.
SOURCE: DEPARTMENT OF LABOR

COUNCIL OF ECONOMIC ADVISERS

Unemployment Rates

[Monthly data seasonally adjusted]

Period	Total (all civilian workers)	By sex and age			By race		By selected groups					Labor force time lost (percent) [1]
		Men 20 years and over	Women 20 years and over	Both sexes 16–19 years	White	Black and other	Experienced wage and salary workers	Married men, spouse present	Women who maintain families	Full-time workers	Part-time workers	
1975	8.5	6.7	8.0	19.9	7.8	13.9	8.2	5.1	10.0	8.1	10.3	9.1
1976	7.7	5.9	7.4	19.0	7.0	13.1	7.3	4.2	10.0	7.3	10.1	8.3
1977	7.0	5.2	7.0	17.7	6.2	13.1	6.6	3.6	9.3	6.5	9.8	7.6
1978	6.0	4.2	6.0	16.3	5.2	11.9	5.6	2.8	8.5	5.5	9.0	6.5
1979	5.8	4.1	5.7	16.1	5.1	11.3	5.4	2.7	8.3	5.3	8.7	6.3
1980	7.1	5.9	6.3	17.7	6.3	13.2	6.8	4.2	9.1	6.8	8.7	7.9
1980: May	7.6	6.4	6.5	18.9	6.8	13.6	7.4	4.6	8.3	7.3	9.0	8.6
June	7.5	6.4	6.4	18.3	6.7	13.5	7.3	4.6	8.5	7.2	8.8	8.1
July	7.6	6.6	6.6	18.7	6.8	13.9	7.4	4.9	8.8	7.4	8.8	8.4
Aug	7.6	6.5	6.5	18.8	6.7	13.7	7.4	4.8	9.0	7.3	8.7	8.3
Sept	7.6	6.4	6.2	17.8	6.6	14.1	7.2	4.7	9.0	7.3	8.7	8.2
Oct	7.5	6.4	6.7	18.5	6.6	14.2	7.3	4.6	10.2	7.4	9.1	8.4
Nov	7.4	6.2	6.7	18.6	6.6	14.0	7.2	4.4	9.9	7.3	8.6	8.3
Dec	7.4	6.2	6.8	17.8	6.5	14.0	7.1	4.3	10.4	7.3	8.2	8.2
1981: Jan	7.4	6.0	6.7	19.0	6.7	12.9	7.1	4.2	10.5	7.1	9.2	8.2
Feb	7.3	6.0	6.5	19.3	6.6	13.1	7.0	4.1	9.6	7.1	9.1	8.1
Mar	7.3	5.9	6.6	19.1	6.5	13.7	7.0	4.1	9.4	7.1	9.0	8.1
Apr	7.3	5.8	6.8	19.1	6.5	13.2	6.8	3.8	9.8	6.9	9.0	8.2
May	7.6	6.3	6.8	19.5	6.8	13.6	7.4	4.1	10.3	7.3	9.7	8.6

Source: Department of Labor, Bureau of Labor Statistics.

[1] Aggregate hours lost by the unemployed and persons on part-time for economic reasons as percent of potentially available labor force hours.

Source: *Economic Indicators*, Council of Economic Advisers.

MONEY STOCK MEASURES AND LIQUID ASSETS

BILLIONS OF DOLLARS¹ (RATIO SCALE)

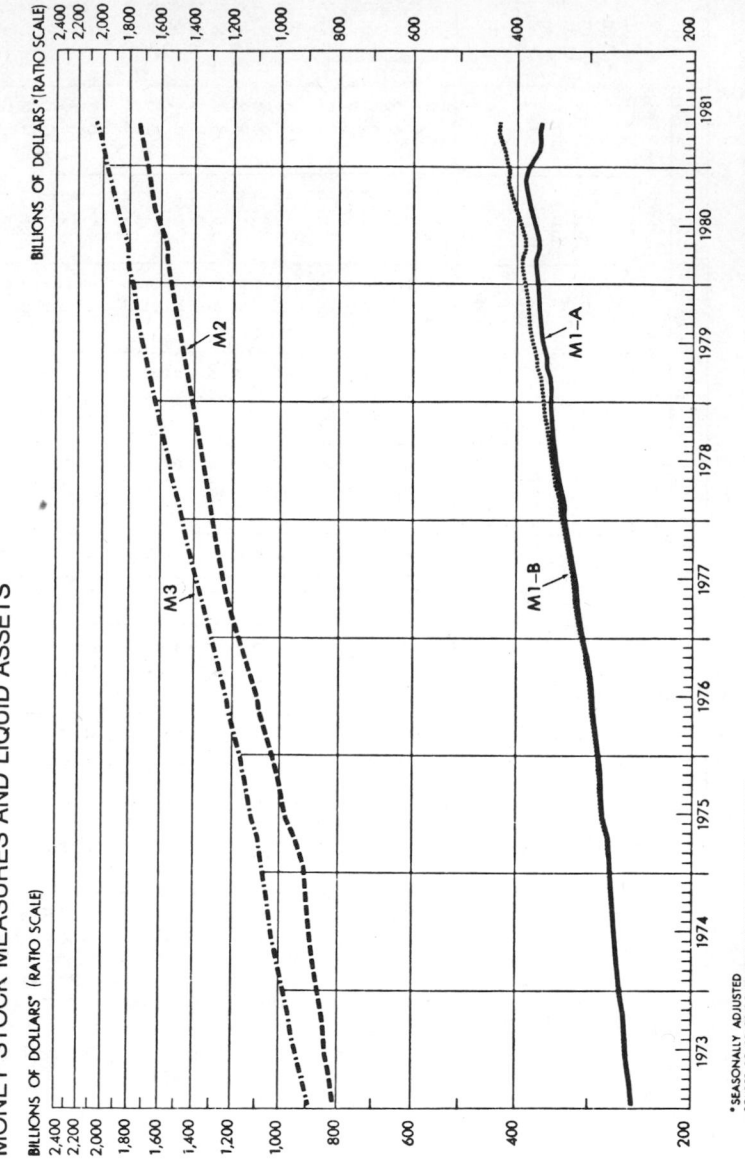

BILLIONS OF DOLLARS¹ (RATIO SCALE)

M2

M3

M1-A

M1-B

¹SEASONALLY ADJUSTED
SOURCE: BOARD OF GOVERNORS OF THE FEDERAL RESERVE SYSTEM

COUNCIL OF ECONOMIC ADVISERS

[Averages of daily figures; billions of dollars, seasonally adjusted]

Period	M1-A Currency plus demand deposits plus travelers' checks [1]	M1-B M1-A plus other checkable deposits (OCD) at banks and thrift institutions	M2 M1-B plus overnight RPs and Eurodollars, MMMF shares, and small time deposits at commercial banks and thrift institutions [2]	M3 M2 plus large time deposits and term RPs at commercial banks and thrift institutions	L M3 plus other liquid assets	Percent change from year or 6 months earlier [3] M1-A	M1-B	M2	M3
1977: Dec	331.4	336.4	1,296.4	1,462.5	1,722.7	--	--	--	--
1978: Dec	354.8	364.2	1,404.2	1,625.7	1,936.5	7.1	8.3	8.3	11.2
1979: Dec	372.7	390.5	1,525.2	1,775.1	2,151.1	5.0	7.2	8.6	9.2
1980: Dec	387.7	415.6	1,669.4	1,963.5	2,377.4	4.0	6.4	9.5	10.6
1980: May	370.4	391.3	1,568.2	1,832.8	2,231.5	-.4	1.3	6.8	7.8
June	373.6	394.9	1,589.3	1,851.9	2,246.0	.5	2.3	8.6	8.8
July	376.6	399.3	1,614.0	1,872.9	2,263.7	1.2	3.4	10.0	9.3
Aug	382.8	406.9	1,633.4	1,896.7	2,290.5	3.0	5.1	10.6	9.7
Sept	386.4	411.8	1,644.9	1,911.9	2,308.1	5.3	7.8	11.2	10.5
Oct	390.1	416.3	1,654.0	1,927.5	2,325.6	11.1	13.4	13.3	12.5
Nov	391.3	419.1	1,668.5	1,950.7	2,356.2	11.6	14.7	13.2	13.3
Dec	387.7	415.6	1,669.4	1,963.5	2,377.4	7.7	10.8	10.3	12.4
1981: Jan	375.1	419.2	1,680.8	1,988.3	2,408.1	-.8	10.2	8.4	12.7
Feb	367.2	421.2	1,695.7	2,007.9	2,431.2	-8.0	7.2	7.8	12.1
Mar	365.8	425.8	1,718.4	2,025.9	2,442.3	-10.4	6.9	9.1	12.3
Apr	366.6	433.7	1,737.8	2,044.3	--	-11.7	8.5	10.4	12.5
May p	364.9	431.5	1,743.7	2,059.8	--	-13.0	6.0	9.2	11.5

[1] Net of demand deposits due to foreign commercial banks and official institutions.
[2] Total M2 excludes demand deposits held by thrift institutions at commercial banks, not shown separately in components.
[3] Annual changes are from December to December and monthly changes are from 6 months earlier at a seasonally adjusted annual rate.

Source: Economic Indicators, Council of Economic Advisers.

Note.—Series revised after chart was prepared. Revised data not yet available prior to 1977.

Source: Board of Governors of the Federal Reserve System.

NEW MONETARY AGGREGATES

Money supply data has been revised and expanded to reflect the Federal Reserve's redefinition of the monetary aggregates. The redefinition was prompted by the emergence in recent years of new monetary assets—for example, negotiable order of withdrawal (NOW) accounts and money-market mutual fund shares—and alterations in the basic character of established monetary assets—for example, the growing similarity of and substitution between the deposits of thrift institutions and those of commercial banks.

Four newly redefined monetary aggregates replace the old M-1 through M-5 measures, and a very broad measure of liquid assets has been adopted. The principle underlying these new monetary aggregates is that similar assets should be combined at the same level of aggregation:

M1-A is one of two narrow transactions measures. It is basically the same as the old M-1 aggregate (currency plus demand deposits at commercial banks), which had been called total money supply, except that is excludes demand deposits held by foreign commercial banks and official institutions.

M1-B, the other narrow measure, adds to M1-A interest-earning checkable deposits at all depository institutions—namely NOW accounts, automatic transfer from savings (ATS) accounts, and credit-union-share draft balances—as well as a small amount of demand deposits at thrift institutions that cannot, using present data sources, be separated from interest-earning checkable deposits.

M-2 as redefined adds to M1-B overnight repurchase agreements (RPs) issued by commercial banks and certain overnight Eurodollars (those issued by Carribean branches of member banks) held by U.S. nonbank residents, money-market mutual fund shares, and savings and small-denomination time deposits (those issued in denominations of less than $100,000) at all depository institutions. Depository institutions are commercial banks (including U.S. agencies and branches of foreign banks, Edge Act Corporations, and foreign investment companies), mutual savings banks, savings and loan associations, and credit unions.

M-3 as redefined is equal to new M-2 plus large-denomination time deposits (those issued as in denominations of $100,000 or more) at all depository institutions (includ-

ing negotiable CDs) plus term RPs issued by commercial banks and savings and loan associations.

L, the very broad measure of liquid assets, equals new M-3 plus other liquid assets consisting of other Eurodollar holdings of U.S. nonbank residents, bankers acceptances, commercial paper, savings bonds, and marketable liquid Treasury obligations.

Consolidation adjustments have been made in the construction of each of the new measures, in order to avoid double counting of the public's monetary assets. A major consolidation adjustment involves the netting of deposits held by depository institutions with other depository institutions. In constructing M-1A, demand deposits held by commercial banks with other commercial banks have been removed. The procedure calls for the removal from M1-B of those demand deposit holdings of thrift institutions that are estimated to be used in servicing their checkable deposits, although at present the amount is negligible. Similarly, at the M-2 level all other demand deposit holdings of thrift institutions are deducted; currently that means all such demand deposits are netted from M-2. Savings and time deposits held by depository institutions are also appropriately netted at the M-2 and M-3 levels. The other major kind of consolidation adjustment involves removing the assets held by money-market mutual funds from several components appearing in the M-2, M-3, and L measures. These institutions issue shares to the public and use the proceeds to acquire a variety of liquid assets that are components of the new M-2, M-3, and L measures. In order to avoid first counting these amounts as money-market mutual fund shares and then counting them again as money market fund holdings of RPs, CDs, commercial paper, and so forth, holdings of each of these assets by money market funds are subtracted from the relevant components.

The procedure for constructing the new seasonally adjusted aggregates has been to seasonally adjust each component with a standard option of the Census X-11 program—wherever possible—and then to sum the components to derive the appropriate total. Some components have not been seasonally adjusted. In some cases sufficient historical data is not yet available. In other cases the components are dominated by such a strong trend that seasonal adjustment is not likely to be successful.

A detailed explanation of the new measures was published in the February 1980 issue of the *Federal Reserve Bulletin*. Monthly data from 1959 to date and weekly data from 1970 to date are available from the Banking Section of the Division of Research and Statistics at the Federal Reserve Board, Washington, D.C. 20551.

Source: Survey of Current Business.

FEDERAL BUDGET: PROCEDURE AND TIMETABLE

Congressional Budget Timetable

CONGRESSIONAL BUDGET ACT OF 1974: THE NEW BUDGET PROCESS IN TEN STEPS

1. To give Congress an earlier and better start in reviewing and reshaping the budget, the Executive Branch must submit a "current services budget" by November 10th for the new fiscal year that starts the following October 1st. The current services budget should project the spending required to maintain ongoing programs throughout the following fiscal year at existing commitment levels, or at commitment levels specified by existing legislation based on current economic assumptions. The Joint Economic Committee should review and assess the current services budget and report to Congress by December 31st.

2. The President will continue to submit his new budget to Congress in late January or early February. In addition to the traditional budget totals and breakdowns, the budget document must include a list of existing "tax expenditures"—i.e., estimates of revenues lost to the Treasury through preferential tax treatment— as well as any proposed changes in tax expenditures. The budget must also contain estimates of expenditures for programs for which funds are appropriated one year in advance and five-year budget projections of all federal spending under existing programs.

3. Reports of all standing committees to the House and Senate Budget Committees of the spending plans of those committees on all matters under their jurisdiction, including spending under new legislation, are required by March 15th for the upcoming fiscal year.

4. An annual report of the Congressional Budget Office to the Budget Committees on alternative budget levels and national budget priorities is required on or before April 1st.

5. By April 15th, the Budget Committees must report concurrent resolutions to the House and Senate floors, and Congress will have to clear the initial budget resolution by May 15th. This initial budget resolution sets target totals for appropriations, outlays, taxes, the budget surplus or deficit, and the federal debt. Within these overall targets, the resolution will break down appropriations and outlays by the functional categories used in the President's budget document, as well as by classifications used by the appropriations subcommittees for the 13 appropriations bills. The resolution will include any recommended changes in tax revenues and in the level of the federal debt ceiling.

6. Committees report bills or resolutions authorizing new budget authority by May 15th.

7. The basic appropriations process proceeds within the Appropriations Committees, but is subject to targets of the budget resolution.

8. Scorekeeping reports will be issued periodically by the Congressional Budget Office on the status of budget authority, revenue, outlays and debt legislation, comparing the amounts and changes in such legislation with the First Congressional Budget Resolution.

9. Subject to prior authorization, all appropriations bills have to be cleared by the middle of September—no later than the seventh day after Labor Day. By September 15th, after finishing action on all appropriations and other spending bills, Congress must adopt a second, and final, budget resolution that may either affirm or revise the budget targets set by the initial resolution. This resolution must provide for a final budget reconciliation by changing either one or more of the following: (1) appropriations (both for the upcoming fiscal year or carried over from previous fiscal years) and/or entitlements; (2) revenues; and (3) the public debt. The final resolution will direct the committees that have jurisdiction over these matters to report the necessary legislative changes. The Budget Committees will then combine these changes and report them to the floor in the form of a reconciliation bill.

If Congress has withheld all appropriations and entitlement bills from the President until passage of the final reconciliation bill, then this bill becomes the final budget legislation, subject to Presidential signature (or veto). If, on the other hand, each individual appropriations bill has been signed by the President upon passage by the Congress, the final reconciliation bill— upon signature by the President—supersedes all the previously passed individual bills.

10. The new fiscal year begins on October 1st.

FEDERAL BUDGET: PROCEDURE AND TIMETABLE
Congressional Budget Timetable

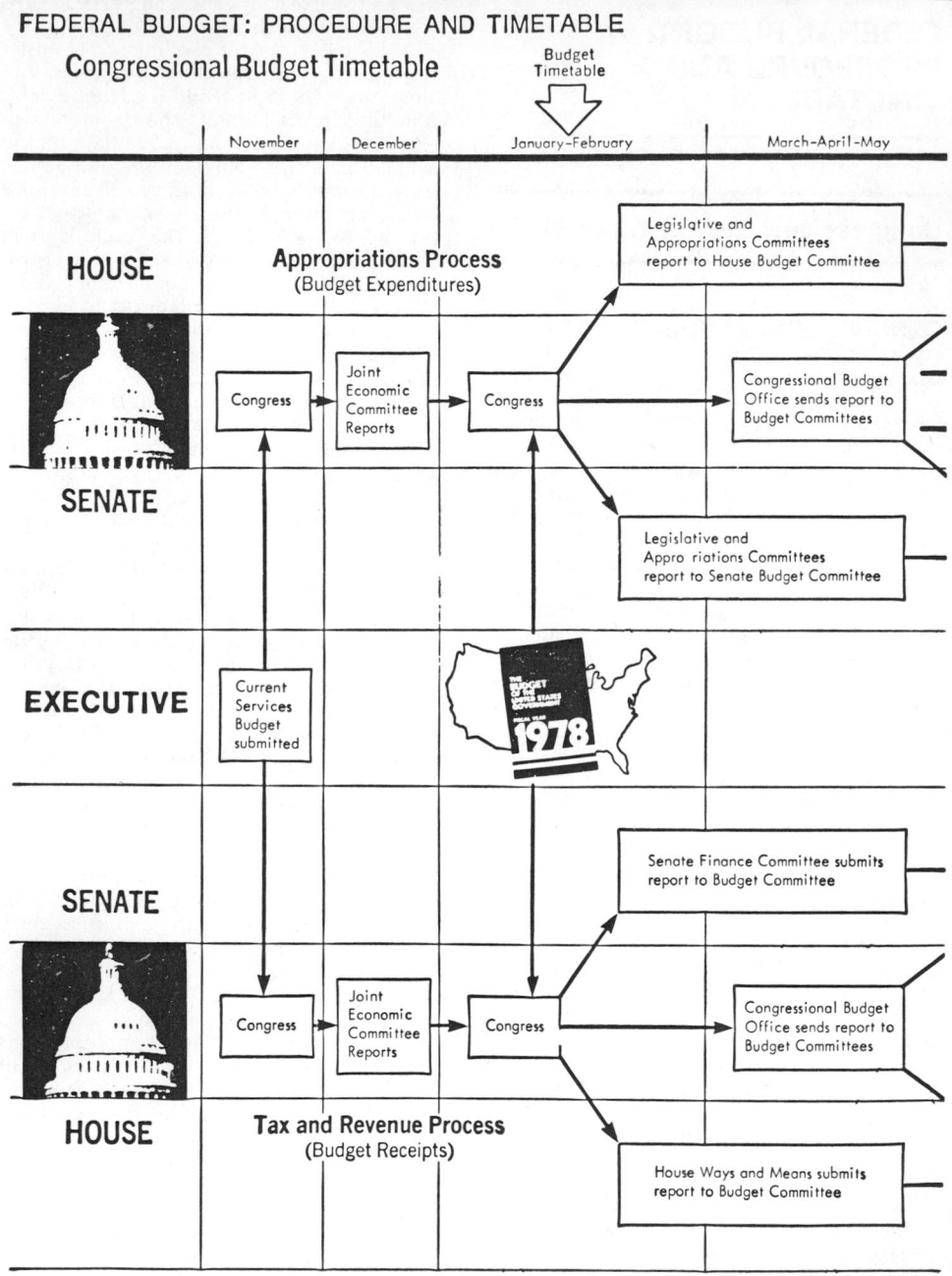

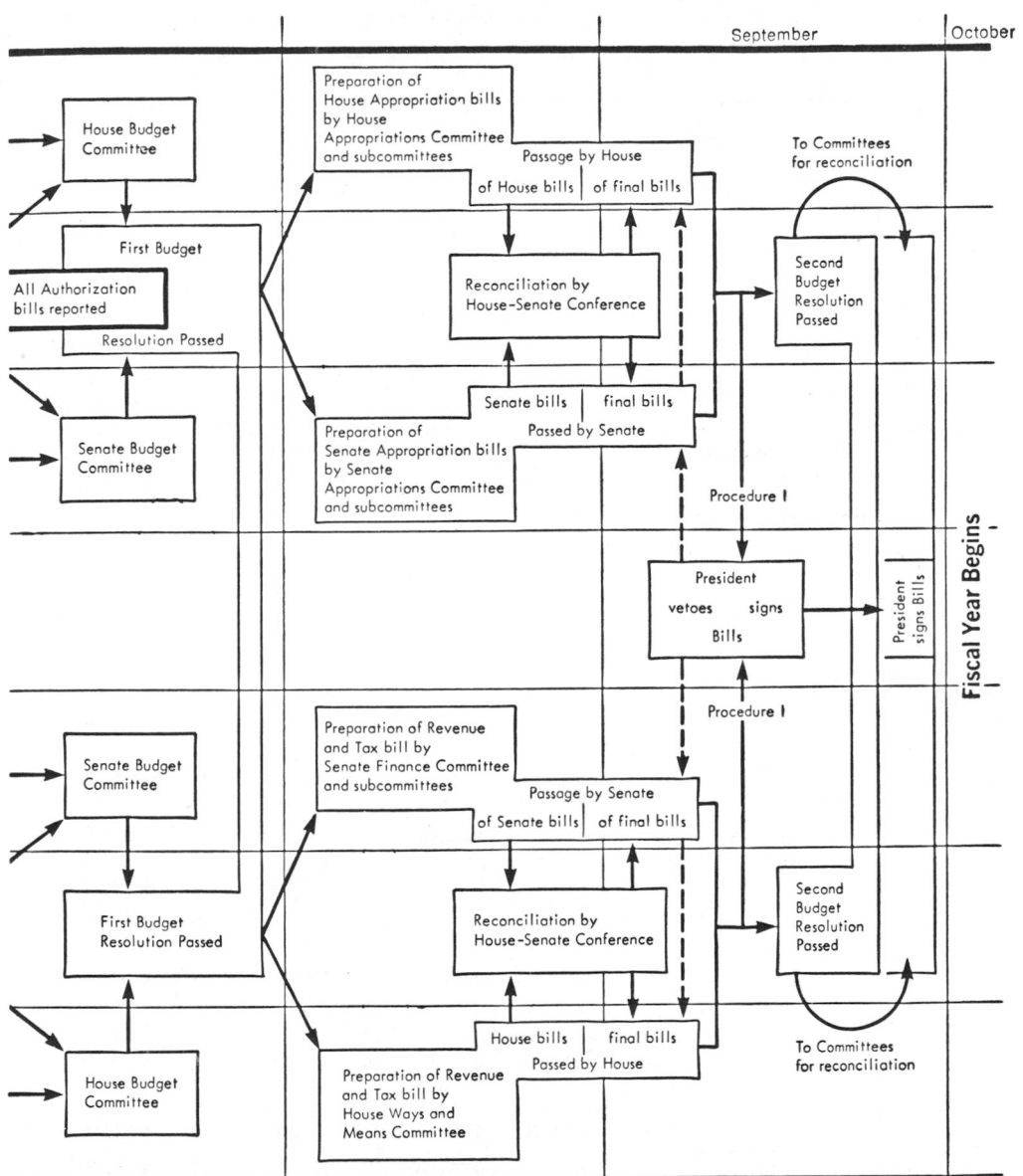

Source: The Conference Board, "The Federal Budget: Its Impact on the Economy," Michael E. Levy, assisted by Delos R. Smith.

Largest Companies

THE 100 LARGEST INDUSTRIAL CORPORATIONS
(ranked by sales)

Rank 1980	Rank 1979	Company	Sales ($000)	Assets ($000)	Assets Rank	Net Income ($000)	Net Income Rank	Stockholders' Equity ($000)	Stockholders' Equity Rank
1	1	Exxon (New York)[1]	103,142,834	56,576,558	1	5,650,090	1	25,412,637	1
2	3	Mobil (New York)	59,510,000*	32,705,000	3	3,272,000**	3	13,069,000	4
3	2	General Motors (Detroit)	57,728,500	34,581,000	2	(762,500)	490	17,814,600	2
4	5	Texaco (Harrison, N.Y.)	51,195,830	26,430,355	5	2,642,542**	4	12,526,100	5
5	6	Standard Oil of California (San Francisco)	40,479,000	22,162,000	7	2,401,000	5	11,077,000	6
6	4	Ford Motor (Dearborn, Mich.)	37,085,500	24,347,600	6	(1,543,300)	491	8,567,500	9
7	7	Gulf Oil (Pittsburgh)	26,483,000*	18,638,000	9	1,407,000	11	9,637,000	7
8	8	International Business Machines (Armonk, N.Y.)	26,213,000	26,703,000	4	3,562,000	2	16,453,000	3
9	10	Standard Oil (Ind.) (Chicago)	26,133,080	20,167,474	8	1,915,314	6	9,384,673	8
10	9	General Electric (Fairfield, Conn.)	24,959,000	18,511,000	10	1,514,000	10	8,200,000	10
11	12	Atlantic Richfield (Los Angeles)	23,744,302	16,604,844	12	1,651,423	8	7,438,628	12
12	13	Shell Oil (Houston)	19,830,000	17,615,000	11	1,542,000	9	8,100,000	11
13	11	International Telephone & Telegraph (New York)	18,529,655	15,417,183	13	894,326	15	6,273,515	13
14	15	Conoco (Stamford, Conn.)	18,325,400	11,036,275	18	1,026,195	14	4,584,529	19
15	16	E. I. du Pont de Nemours (Wilmington, Del.)	13,652,000	9,560,000	22	716,000	21	5,690,000	15
16	22	Phillips Petroleum (Bartlesville, Okla.)	13,376,563	9,844,382	20	1,069,614	13	4,937,355	17
17	18	Tenneco (Houston)	13,226,000	13,853,000	14	726,000	19	4,164,000	24
18	20	Sun (Radnor, Pa.)	12,945,000	10,955,000	19	723,000	20	4,311,000	23
19	14	U.S. Steel (Pittsburgh)	12,492,100	11,747,600	16	504,500	33	5,288,200	16
20	21	Occidental Petroleum (Los Angeles)	12,476,125	6,629,889	33	710,785	22	2,054,277	51
21	26	United Technologies (Hartford)	12,323,994	7,326,270	29	393,383	45	2,758,045	38
22	19	Western Electric (New York)[2]	12,032,100	8,047,500	25	693,200	23	4,449,300	21
23	32	Standard Oil (Ohio) (Cleveland)	11,023,196	12,080,050	15	1,811,224	7	4,561,547	20
24	23	Proctor & Gamble (Cincinnati)[3]	10,772,186	6,553,359	35	642,838	27	3,603,159	27
25	24	Dow Chemical (Midland, Mich.)	10,626,000	11,538,000	17	805,000	18	4,440,000	22
26	62	Getty Oil (Los Angeles)	10,150,411	8,266,676	24	871,866	17	4,143,912	25
27	25	Union Carbide (New York)	9,994,000	9,659,000	21	890,000	16	4,776,000	18
28	34	Union Oil of California (Los Angeles)	9,984,100	6,772,100	32	647,000	26	3,476,800	28
29	30	Eastman Kodak (Rochester, N.Y.)	9,734,303	8,753,991	23	1,153,579	12	6,027,806	14
30	29	Boeing (Seattle)	9,426,200	5,931,300	38	600,500	29	2,314,800	45
31	46	Dart & Kraft (Glenview, Ill.)[4]	9,411,500	4,650,300	53	383,100	46	2,620,500	40
32	17	Chrysler (Highland Park, Mich.)	9,225,300	6,617,800	34	(1,709,700)	492	(104,000)	499
33	33	Caterpillar Tractor (Peoria, Ill.)	8,597,800	6,098,200	37	564,800	31	3,432,000	30
34	37	Westinghouse Electric (Pittsburgh)	8,514,300	6,812,600	31	402,900	43	2,529,900	42
35	39	R.J. Reynolds Industries (Winston-Salem, N.C.)	8,449,000*	7,355,300	27	670,400	25	3,449,200	29
36	28	Goodyear Tire & Rubber (Akron, Ohio)	8,444,015	5,368,301	43	230,689**	81	2,302,500	46

Employees Number	Rank	Net Income as Percent of Stockholders' Sales %	Rank	Equity %	Rank	Earnings per Share 1980($)	1979($)	1970($)	Growth Rate 1970–80 %	Rank	Total Return to Investors 1980 %	Rank	1970–80 Average %	Rank	Indus-try Code
176,615†	9	5.5	194	22.2	48	12.99	9.74	2.96	15.94	147	56.05	82	14.59	131	29
212,800	6	5.5	192	25.0	25	15.40**	9.46	2.39	20.48	73	53.09	91	17.10	103	29
746,000†	1	—		—		(2.65)	10.04	2.09	—		(4.09)	419	2.10	383	40
66,745	50	5.2	217	21.1	61	9.79**	6.48	3.02	12.48	220	74.71	52	10.33	216	29
40,218	112	5.9	168	21.7	52	7.02	5.22	1.34	18.01	103	82.88	40	19.95	77	29
426,700†	2	—		—		(12.83)	9.75	3.82	—		(29.38)	473	(0.92)	425	40
58,900	61	5.3	207	14.6	237	7.21	6.78	2.65	10.53	274	32.49	173	9.86	222	29
341,279	5	13.6	14	21.6	55	6.10	5.16	1.78	13.11	201	10.78	314	3.84	359	44
56,401	68	7.3	104	20.4	68	6.54	5.12	1.14	19.09	85	107.61	16	24.23	37	29
402,000†	3	6.1	160	18.5	119	6.65	6.20	1.82	13.83	184	26.72	208	6.47	292	36
53,400	73	7.0	116	22.2	49	6.64	4.74	0.91	21.99	57	63.57	68	17.83	93	29
36,596	124	7.8	90	19.0	104	4.99	3.66	0.88	18.95	88	120.08	8	22.40	52	29
348,000	4	4.8	237	14.3	255	6.12	2.65	4.23	3.76	372	27.05	205	0.52	413	36
41,503	103	5.6	186	22.4	44	9.52	7.58	1.53	20.06	78	42.87	122	19.61	81	29
135,900†	13	5.2	209	12.6	310	4.83	6.42	2.25	7.94	323	10.83	312	4.12	354	28
32,400	141	8.0	81	21.7	53	7.01	5.77	0.79	24.40	45	26.14	210	18.88	88	29
106,000	21	5.5	193	17.4	145	5.95	5.30	2.09	11.03	260	39.55	141	14.19	140	29
48,806	86	5.6	187	16.8	166	5.92	5.89	1.17	17.60	110	44.47	119	14.61	130	29
149,172†	10	4.0	294	9.5	380	5.77	(3.41)	1.81	12.29	231	50.57	102	7.42	268	33
34,700	132	5.7	179	34.6	4	8.82	7.30	2.92	11.69	249	34.10	162	11.03	200	10
200,200	7	3.2	350	14.3	253	7.28	6.49	1.87	14.56	170	46.98	109	19.34	83	41
177,000†	8	5.8	177	15.6	207	N.A.	N.A.	N.A.	—		—		—		36
22,938	193	16.4	8	39.7	3	7.37	4.92	0.64	27.68	27	66.35	62	24.84	35	29
61,000	57	6.0	166	17.8	133	7.78	6.99	2.60	11.58	251	(2.38)	407	4.55	343	43
56,800	67	7.6	97	18.1	126	4.42	4.33	0.57‡	22.73	53	4.98	357	13.39	151	28
17,318	246	8.6	68	21.0	62	10.60	7.34	1.42**	22.26	56	27.15	204	20.09	74	10
116,105	17	8.9	61	18.6	111	13.36	8.47	2.60	17.78	106	27.03	206	8.08	254	28
17,995	238	6.5	140	18.6	113	3.73	2.88	0.80	16.64	130	102.68	22	21.79	57	29
129,500	15	11.9	23	19.1	101	7.15	6.20	2.50	11.08	258	51.28	98	2.07	384	38
106,300†	20	6.4	146	25.9	21	6.23	5.25	0.23	39.08	9	34.89	157	34.26	6	41
79,968†	39	4.1	292	14.6	236	7.03	6.71[5]	2.92[5]	9.18	305	(2.20)	404	5.35	316	20
92,596†	25	—		—		(26.00)	(17.18)	(0.16)	—		(27.79)	469	(11.69)	459	40
86,350†	33	6.6	135	16.5	174	6.53	5.69	1.69	14.47	175	11.71	305	10.55	211	45
145,513†	11	4.7	249	15.9	193	4.71	(0.87)‡	1.89	9.56	300	54.17	89	3.86	358	36
83,417	36	7.9	83	19.4	93	6.23	5.23	2.28	10.57	272	40.59	134	10.99	201	21
144,452†	12	2.7	375	10.0	369	3.18**	2.02	1.78	5.97	355	34.39	160	(0.80)	424	30

THE 100 LARGEST INDUSTRIALS (continued)

Rank 1980	Rank 1979	Company	Sales ($000)	Assets ($000)	Assets Rank	Net Income ($000)	Net Income Rank	Stockholders' Equity ($000)	Stockholders' Equity Rank
37	35	Beatrice Foods (Chicago)[6]	8,290,509	3,980,279	62	290,140	58	2,004,836	54
38	40	Xerox (Stamford, Conn.)	8,196,500	7,349,200	28	619,200	28	3,624,700	26
39	43	Marathon Oil (Findlay, Ohio)	8,179,751*	5,043,092	52	379,016	47	1,923,396	55
40	44	Ashland Oil (Russell, Ky.)[7]	8,118,369	3,357,614	76	205,129	89	916,634	158
41	36	RCA (New York)	8,011,300	7,147,600	30	315,300	52	1,862,200	59
42	31	LTV (Dallas)	8,009,958	4,029,669	60	127,893	149	818,946	173
43	41	Amerada Hess (New York)	7,868,963	5,895,444	39	540,242	32	2,357,257	44
44	47	Cities Service (Tulsa)	7,786,300	5,358,000	44	477,500	34	2,578,600	41
45	49	Philip Morris (New York)	7,328,300*	7,366,400	26	576,800	30	2,853,000	33
46	45	Rockwell International (Pittsburgh)[7]	6,906,500	4,430,900	56	280,200	62	1,740,200	65
47	38	Bethlehem Steel (Bethlehem, Pa.)	6,743,000	5,206,800	47	121,000	160	2,622,000	39
48	48	Monsanto (St. Louis)	6,573,600	5,796,400	41	148,800	126	2,802,200	37
49	27	International Harvester (Chicago)[8]	6,311,804	5,843,458	40	(397,328)	489	1,846,455	60
50	42	Esmark (Chicago)[8]	6,108,355	1,853,895	162	471,808	35	579,491	218
51	55	W. R. Grace (New York)	6,101,300	4,364,500	57	283,800	60	1,796,100	63
52	51	Minnesota Mining & Manufacturing (St. Paul)	6,079,540	5,045,672	51	678,029	24	3,294,639	31
53	54	McDonnell Douglas (St. Louis)	6,066,300	3,899,800	64	144,600	134	1,512,500	75
54	57	PepsiCo (Purchase, N.Y.)	5,975,220	3,417,538	72	273,990	65	1,428,923	84
55	50	General Foods (White Plains, N.Y.)[9]	5,959,587	2,978,485	87	255,821	70	1,480,304	79
56	59	Coca-Cola (Atlanta)	5,912,595	3,405,958	73	422,108	39	2,074,738	50
57	52	Gulf & Western Industries (New York)[10]	5,782,783	5,416,776	42	255,284	71	1,666,095	68
58	58	Armco (Middletown, Ohio)	5,678,000	3,805,400	67	265,300	68	2,053,200	52
59	69	Allied Chemical (Morristown, N.J.)	5,519,000	4,538,000	54	289,000	59	1,664,000	69
60	60	Deere (Moline, Ill.)[8]	5,469,825	5,202,424	48	228,271	82	2,141,066	48
61	82	Lockheed (Burbank, Calif.)	5,395,700	2,442,500	115	27,600	374	306,200	323
62	64	Consolidated Foods (Chicago)[3]	5,342,860	2,263,443	132	127,682	151	856,802	166
63	63	Aluminum Co. of America (Pittsburgh)	5,147,600	5,188,100	50	469,900	37	2,933,800	32
64	61	Colgate-Palmolive (New York)	5,130,464	2,578,134	110	173,225	107	1,274,013	103
65	72	Continental Group (Stamford, Conn.)	5,119,500	3,994,300	61	224,800	83	1,419,700	85
66	•	Coastal (Houston)	5,089,923	4,112,631	59	109,524	172	586,076	216
67	66	International Paper (New York)	5,042,900	5,197,400	49	314,000	53	2,817,300	36
68	56	Georgia-Pacific (Portland, Ore.)	5,016,000	4,512,000	55	244,000	76	1,909,000	56
69	92	Raytheon (Lexington, Mass.)[11]	5,002,088	2,928,535	90	282,257	61	1,303,596	98
70	68	TRW (Cleveland)	4,983,970	2,854,699	95	211,890	87	1,287,108	100
71	79	Honeywell (Minneapolis)	4,924,700	3,892,600	65	293,500	56	1,904,200	57
72	67	Ralston Purina (St. Louis)[7]	4,886,000	2,246,500	135	163,000	115	1,132,400	118
73	53	Firestone Tire & Rubber (Akron, Ohio)[8]	4,850,500	3,118,600	82	(105,900)**	486	1,343,000	90
74	78	Johnson & Johnson (New Brunswick, N.J.)	4,837,400	3,342,500	77	400,700	44	2,269,100	47
75	84	Union Pacific (New York)	4,831,676	6,195,147	36	404,546	42	2,831,833	35
76	70	American Can (Greenwich, Conn.)	4,812,200	2,822,000	97	85,700	205	1,048,400	125
77	80	Sperry (New York)[9]	4,785,425	4,262,186	58	277,092	64	2,033,746	53
78	65	Greyhound (Phoenix)	4,766,150	1,905,098	158	118,320	162	849,131	168
79	83	General Dynamics (St. Louis)	4,742,700	2,435,800	116	195,000	93	999,400	136
80	87	Farmland Industries (Kansas City, Mo.)[12]	4,725,071	2,094,339	144	N.A.[13]		530,667	228
81	77	Iowa Beef Processors (Dakota City, Neb.)[8]	4,639,454	509,492	368	53,164	274	290,480	334
82	73	Borden (New York)	4,595,795	2,643,294	103	147,863	128	1,234,935	106
83	71	Weyerhaeuser (Tacoma, Wash.)	4,535,814	5,238,692	46	277,987‡	63	2,836,754	34
84	74	Charter (Jacksonville, Fla.)	4,518,114	1,746,260	170	50,237	287	676,669	197
85	75	Signal Companies (La Jolla, Calif.)	4,285,300	3,100,600	83	167,700	112	1,312,600	96
86	89	American Brands (New York)	4,276,527*	3,970,883	63	405,489	41	1,809,530	61
87	88	Bendix (Southfield, Mich.)[7]	4,270,400	2,923,500	91	191,600	98	1,340,800	92
88	81	Litton Industries (Beverly Hills, Calif.)[10]	4,246,532	3,264,291	79	290,821	57	1,166,872	113
89	90	General Mills (Minneapolis)[14]	4,170,300	2,012,400	149	170,000	111	1,020,700	131
90	91	IC Industries (Chicago)	4,141,600	3,692,800	68	120,700	161	1,277,700	102
91	93	CPC International (Englewood Cliffs, NJ.)	4,120,300	2,328,300	126	197,400	91	1,107,200	121

Employees		Net Income as Percent of Stockholders'				Earnings per Share			Growth Rate 1970–80		Total Return to Investors				Indus-try Code
		Sales		Equity							1980		1970–80 Average		
Number	Rank	%	Rank	%	Rank	1980($)	1979($)	1970($)	%	Rank	%	Rank	%	Rank	
84,000	35	3.5	328	14.5	241	2.81	2.60	1.02	10.67	269	0.12	387	4.69	338	20
120,480	16	7.6	98	17.1	157	7.33	6.69	2.40	11.81	245	0.73	384	(1.46)	430	38
15,247	270	4.6	256	19.7	83	6.27	5.34	1.42	16.01	145	45.39	115	19.12	85	29
24,600	181	2.5	385	22.4	45	6.80	15.55	0.97‡	21.50	61	6.85	346	15.89	114	29
133,000	14	3.9	299	16.9	162	3.35	3.72	1.26	10.27	283	40.69	133	6.21	299	36
63,600	53	1.6	429	15.2	216	3.95	6.03	(17.09)‡	—		153.13	4	6.91	284	33
8,383†	390	6.9	123	22.9	41	6.44	6.07	1.29	17.44	113	82.04	41	10.65	210	29
18,900	225	6.1	155	18.5	116	5.73	4.18	1.37	15.38	159	77.07	47	17.85	91	29
72,000	45	7.9	88	20.2	72	4.63	4.08	0.84	18.61	93	24.34	219	15.69	118	21
108,199	19	4.1	293	16.1	187	3.77	3.67	1.00	14.19	177	91.74	31	23.56	43	41
89,200†	29	1.8	422	4.6	442	2.77	6.31	2.05	3.06	379	32.44	174	7.62	263	33
61,836	54	2.3	398	5.3	441	4.10	9.11	1.83‡	8.40	321	21.05	240	12.46	173	28
87,162	31	—		—		(12.91)	12.01	1.92	—		(28.12)	471	5.57	309	45
37,000	121	7.7	92	81.4	1	21.90	4.40	1.79	28.46	25	93.33	29	12.84	165	20
91,700	26	4.7	253	15.8	198	6.08	5.02	1.12‡	18.43	95	51.06	101	14.02	142	28
86,900	32	11.2	31	20.6	67	5.78	5.59	1.68	13.15	200	22.98	225	4.59	341	38
82,550	38	2.4	394	9.6	379	3.65	5.06	2.45	4.07	369	37.64	149	14.42	137	41
111,000	18	4.6	261	19.2	99	3.01	2.85	0.83	13.75	187	14.62	288	7.32	272	49
53,000	74	4.3	274	17.3	150	5.12	4.65	2.00‡	9.86	291	(3.65)	414	1.75	389	20
41,000	107	7.1	111	20.3	69	3.42	3.40	1.24	10.68	267	3.00	370	0.96	402	49
95,520	23	4.4	270	15.3	215	4.38	3.70	0.58	22.41	55	11.82	304	14.86	127	34
59,975	59	4.7	252	12.9	299	4.73	4.82	1.09	15.81	152	58.26	77	16.76	106	33
46,269	93	5.2	211	17.4	148	8.15	0.20	2.47**	12.68	215	13.29	295	13.21	159	10
61,000	56	4.2	283	10.7	361	3.72	5.12	0.78	16.91	121	27.42	201	20.80	64	45
74,600	43	0.5	458	9.0	391	1.53	3.56	(7.60)	—		(2.90)	411	13.88	143	41
88,600	30	2.4	393	14.9	227	4.12	3.60	2.14	6.77	343	(0.92)	395	0.09	417	20
45,600†	96	9.1	56	16.0	190	6.54	7.15	1.44‡	16.34	135	14.48	289	8.56	247	33
48,200†	87	3.4	340	13.6	279	2.12	1.39	0.92	8.71	315	9.31	333	3.03	375	43
58,300†	63	4.4	272	15.8	196	6.11	5.27	3.20	6.68	345	21.30	238	4.71	337	34
6,942	420	2.2	403	18.7	110	4.63	(0.05)	1.67	10.74	263	32.67	169	3.32	369	29
46,048	94	6.2	152	11.1	350	5.97	10.96	0.96‡	20.05	79	19.99	255	6.26	297	26
44,000	98	4.9	233	12.8	301	2.34	3.12	0.87	10.40	280	(0.66)	393	2.42	381	26
77,900	40	5.6	183	21.7	54	6.80	6.30	1.04‡	20.66	70	67.16	59	25.77	28	36
94,051	24	4.3	280	16.5	173	6.39	6.07	2.40	10.29	282	63.59	67	10.83	205	40
97,200	22	6.0	167	15.4	211	13.13	11.89	3.58	13.88	182	37.60	151	6.10	301	44
70,000	48	3.3	343	14.4	243	1.51	1.19	0.56	10.43	279	1.27	379	4.87	329	20
83,000	37	—		—		(1.84)**	1.96**	1.60	—		21.71	234	(2.32)	435	30
74,300	44	8.3	77	17.7	138	6.50	5.76	1.51	15.72	155	28.67	193	7.16	278	42
32,657†	140	8.4	74	14.3	252	4.22	4.01	0.89	16.84	122	121.87	7	24.74	36	29
51,000†	79	1.8	423	8.2	411	4.26	6.44	3.55	1.84	388	(6.60)	432	4.55	344	34
90,513	27	5.8	176	13.6	277	7.60	6.35	2.37	12.36	228	28.77	192	11.88	188	44
52,278†	78	2.5	388	13.9	263	2.67	2.80	1.40	6.67	346	4.60	359	6.09	303	20
84,400	34	4.1	289	19.5	91	3.58	3.43	(0.12)	—		43.10	121	27.73	20	41
10,100	354	—		—		N.A.	N.A.	N.A.	—		—		—		29
11,049	338	1.1	441	18.3	124	5.17	4.28	0.08	51.72	3	106.81	17	20.37	70	20
38,400†	114	3.2	347	12.0	324	4.79	4.31	1.83	10.10	288	15.73	280	5.02	322	20
45,714	95	6.1	156	9.8	375	2.12‡	4.02	0.94	8.47	319	11.57	307	4.29	348	26
11,093	337	1.1	443	7.4	419	1.59	14.83	0.30	18.15	99	(41.65)	478	23.74	41	29
49,500	84	3.9	303	12.8	302	2.89	3.52	(0.79)‡	—		18.99	261	25.71	29	40
52,456	77	9.5	47	22.4	43	14.02	12.00	4.03	13.28	197	22.87	227	12.74	168	21
74,600†	42	4.5	265	14.3	251	7.68	7.10	1.10‡	21.45	62	51.86	95	17.84	92	40
75,400	41	6.8	125	24.9	26	7.42	4.77	1.49	17.41	114	117.17	10	18.50	89	36
66,000	51	4.1	291	16.7	168	3.37	2.92	0.63‡	18.26	97	13.43	293	8.15	251	20
61,332	55	2.9	362	9.4	381	6.02	9.52	2.56	8.93	309	32.50	172	6.76	287	20
40,500	109	4.8	242	17.8	134	8.28	7.51	2.56	12.46	223	9.81	329	12.04	186	20

THE 100 LARGEST INDUSTRIALS *(concluded)*

Rank 1980	Rank 1979	Company	Sales ($000)	Assets ($000)	Assets Rank	Net Income ($000)	Net Income Rank	Stockholders' Equity ($000)	Stockholders' Equity Rank
92	104	Texas Instruments (Dallas)	4,074,700	2,413,700	117	212,200	86	1,164,500	114
93	98	Dresser Industries (Dallas)[8]	4,016,300	2,897,200	93	261,100	69	1,648,200	71
94	94	CBS (New York)	3,962,882	2,301,215	130	192,969	94	1,190,212	109
95	96	Owens-Illinois (Toledo)	3,905,700	3,066,000	85	149,400	125	1,316,000	94
96	99	American Home Products (New York)	3,798,524	2,370,262	123	445,889	38	1,472,774	80
97	97	United Brands (New York)[3]	3,762,580	1,264,015	212	31,056	354	563,744	221
98	85	Republic Steel (Cleveland)	3,760,042	3,016,832	86	50,983	284	1,507,816	76
99	86	Champion International (Stamford, Conn.)	3,752,718	3,339,518	78	147,068‡	130	1,753,290	64
100	76	National Steel (Pittsburgh)	3,706,658	3,446,674	71	83,759	210	1,444,092	82

The definitions and concepts underlying the figures in this directory are explained at the end of the table.
N.A. Not available.
* Does not include excise taxes; see the explanation of "sales" below.
** Reflects an extraordinary credit of at least 10 percent; see the explanations of "net income" and "earnings per share" below.
† Average for the year; see the reference to "employees" below.
‡ Reflects an extraordinary charge of at least 10 percent; see the explanations of "net income" and "earnings per share" below.
[1] Figures include Reliance Electric (1979 rank: 232), acquired by Exxon September 24, 1979.
[2] Company is wholly owned by American Telephone & Telegraph.
[3] Figures are for fiscal year ending June 30, 1980.
[4] Name changed from Kraft upon merger with Dart Industries (1979 rank: 146), September 25, 1980.
[5] Figure is for Kraft.
[6] Figures are for fiscal year ending February 29, 1980.
[7] Figures are for fiscal year ending September 30, 1980.
[8] Figures are for fiscal year ending October 31, 1980.

NOTES TO THE FORTUNE DIRECTORY

Sales include service and rental revenues but exclude dividends, interest, and other non-operating revenues. All companies on the list must have derived more than 50 percent of their sales from manufacturing and/or mining. Sales of subsidiaries are included when they are consolidated; sales from discontinued operations are included when these figures are published. All figures are for the year ending December 31, 1980, unless otherwise noted. Sales figures do not include excise taxes collected by the manufacturer, and so the figures for some corporations—most of which sell gasoline, liquor, or tobacco—may be lower than those published by the corporations themselves. When they are at least 5 percent lower for this reason, there is an asterisk (*) next to the sales figure.

Assets are those shown at the company's year-end.

Net Income is shown after taxes and after extraordinary credits or charges when any are shown on the income statement. A double asterisk (**) signifies an extraordinary credit reflecting at least 10 percent of the net income shown, a double dagger (‡) an extraordinary charge of at least 10 percent. Figures in parentheses indicate a loss.

Stockholders' Equity is the sum of capital stock, surplus, and retained earnings at the company's year-end. Redeemable preferred stock is excluded when its redemption is either mandatory or outside the control of the company, except in the case of cooperatives.

Employees The figure shown is a year-end total except when it is followed by a dagger (†), in which case it is an average for the year.

Earnings per Share For all companies, the figures shown are the "primary" earnings per share that appear on the company's income statement. These figures are based on a weighted average of the number of common shares and common-stock equivalents outstanding during the year. "Common-stock equivalents" generally include (a) convertible securities whose cash yield is less than two-thirds of the prime rate at the time the securities were issued and (b) options and warrants when the effect of their inclusion in the computation would reduce the "primary" earnings per share. Per-share earnings for 1979 and 1970 are adjusted for stock splits and stock dividends. They are not restated for mergers, acquisitions, or accounting changes made after 1970. A double asterisk (**) signifies an extraordinary credit reflecting at least 10 percent of the net income shown, a double dagger (‡) an extraordinary charge of at least 10 percent. Results are listed as not available (N.A.) where the companies are cooperatives, joint ventures, or wholly owned subsidiaries of other companies, or if the figures were not published in 1970. The growth rate is the average annual growth, compounded. No growth rate is given if the company had a loss in either 1970 or 1980.

Total Return to Investors includes both price appreciation and dividend yield, i.e., to an investor in the company's stock. The figures shown assume sales at the end of 1980 of stock

Employees		Net Income as Percent of Stockholders'				Earnings per Share			Growth Rate 1970–80		Total Return to Investors				Indus-try Code
		Sales		Equity							1980		1970–80 Average		
Number	Rank	%	Rank	%	Rank	1980($)	1979($)	1970($)	%	Rank	%	Rank	%	Rank	
89,875	28	5.2	214	18.2	125	9.22	7.58	1.36	21.09	66	39.48	142	13.04	161	36
52,800	76	6.5	137	15.8	195	3.35	2.94	0.75	16.14	142	107.98	15	23.09	44	45
35,630	125	4.9	232	16.2	182	6.92	7.21	2.20	12.14	232	(3.72)	415	9.37	233	48
58,891	62	3.8	306	11.4	341	5.09	4.56	1.56‡	12.55	219	32.84	168	3.30	370	32
49,829	83	11.7	25	30.3	8	2.84	2.51	0.86	12.69	214	9.46	332	5.17	320	42
50,400	80	0.8	449	5.5	438	2.54	1.72	(0.35)‡	—		56.14	81	0.76	408	20
40,746†	108	1.4	434	3.4	454	3.15	7.49	2.17	3.80	370	5.13	356	5.74	308	33
41,199	106	3.9	302	8.4	406	2.63‡	4.70	0.78‡	12.92	208	8.57	337	3.87	357	26
33,856	139	2.3	399	5.8	435	4.42	6.56	3.58	2.13	385	1.78	375	1.87	388	33

N.A. Not available.
• Indicates that a corporation was not among the 500 or the Second 500 in 1979.
* Does not include excise taxes; see the explanation of "sales" below.
** Reflects an extraordinary credit of at least 10 percent; see the explanations of "net income" and "earnings per share" below.
† Average for the year; see the reference to "employees" below.
‡ Reflects an extraordinary charge of at least 10 percent; see the explanations of "net income" and "earnings per share" below.
⁹ Figures are for fiscal year ending March 31, 1980.
¹⁰ Figures are for fiscal year ending July 31, 1980.
¹¹ Figures include Beech Aircraft (1979 rank: 396), merged into Raytheon February 8, 1980.
¹² Figures are for fiscal year ending August 31, 1980.
¹³ Cooperatives provide only "net margin" figures, which are not comparable with the net income figures in these listings.
¹⁴ Figures are for fiscal year ending May 31, 1980.

owned at the end of 1970 or 1979. It has been assumed that any proceeds from cash dividends, the sale of rights and warrant offerings, and stock received in spin-offs were reinvested at the end of the year in which they were received. Returns are adjusted for stock splits, stock dividends, recapitalizations, and corporate reorganizations as they occur; however, no effort has been made to reflect the cost of brokerage commissions or of taxes. Results are listed as not available (N.A.) where shares are not publicly traded or traded on only a limited basis. Where companies have more than one class of shares outstanding, only the more widely held and actively traded has been considered.

Total-return percentages shown are the returns received by the hypothetical investor described above. The ten-year figures are annual averages, compounded. Where corporations were substantially reorganized—e.g., because of mergers—the predecessor companies used in calculating total return are the same as those cited in the footnotes to the earnings-per-share figures.

Industry Code numbers used in the directory indicate which industry represents the greatest volume of industrial sales for each company. The numbers refer to the industry groups below, which are based on categories established by the U.S. Office of Management and Budget and issued by the Federal Statistical Policy and Standards Office. The median figures in the tables refer only to results of companies among the 500; no attempt has been made to

calculate medians in groups with less than four companies.

Code No.	Industry
10	Mining, crude-oil production
20	Food
21	Tobacco
22	Textiles, vinyl flooring
23	Apparel
25	Furniture
26	Paper, fiber, and wood products
27	Publishing, printing
28	Chemicals
29	Petroleum refining
30	Rubber, plastic products
31	Leather
32	Glass, concrete, abrasives, gypsum
33	Metal manufacturing
34	Metal products
36	Electronics, appliances
37	Shipbuilding, railroad and transportation equipment
38	Measuring, scientific, photographic equipment
40	Motor vehicles
41	Aerospace
42	Pharmaceuticals
43	Soaps, cosmetics
44	Office equipment (includes computers)
45	Industrial and farm equipment
46	Jewelry, silverware
47	Musical instruments, toys, sporting goods
48	Broadcasting, motion-picture production and distribution
49	Beverages

THE 100 LARGEST INDUSTRIAL CORPORATIONS OUTSIDE THE U.S. (ranked by sales)

Rank 1980	Rank 1979	Company	Country	Industry	Sales[1] ($000)	Assets[2] ($000)	Net Income[3] ($000)	Stockholders' Equity[4] ($000)	Employees
1	1	Royal Dutch/ Shell Group	Neth.-Britain	Petroleum	77,114,243	68,518,909	5,174,282	28,761,171	161,000
2	2	British Petroleum	Britain	Petroleum	48,035,941	42,378,471	3,337,121	14,154,825	118,200
3	4	ENI[5]	Italy	Petroleum	27,186,939[6]	20,091,996[6]	98,046[6]	2,927,556[6]	122,587[6]
4	5	Fiat	Italy	Motor vehicles	25,155,000	N.A.	N.A.	N.A.	342,654
5	6	Francaise des Pétroles	France	Petroleum	23,940,355[6]	16,165,949[6]	946,772[6]	4,340,606[6]	48,115[6]
6	3	Unilever	Britain-Neth.	Food products	23,607,516	13,238,166	658,820	5,076,386	300,000
7	10	Renault[5]	France	Motor vehicles	18,979,278	12,299,007	160,165	2,118,297	231,700
8	16	Petróleos de Venezuela[5]	Venezuela	Petroleum	18,818,931	19,336,851	3,450,921	13,425,948	36,275
9	19	Elf Aquitaine[5]	France	Petroleum	18,430,074	19,796,937	1,378,222	4,386,345	45,000
10	9	Philips' Gloeilam-penfabrieken	Netherlands	Electronics, appliances	18,402,818	18,440,613	165,210	6,044,700	372,600
11	8	Volkswagenwerk	Germany	Motor vehicles	18,339,046	12,645,613	170,964	2,951,972	257,930
12	11	Siemens[7]	Germany	Electronics, appliances	17,950,253	17,813,692	332,434	4,616,046	344,000
13	12	Daimler-Benz	Germany	Motor vehicles	17,108,100	8,856,846	605,149	2,570,678	183,392
14	7	Peugeot[6]	France	Motor vehicles and parts	16,846,434	11,638,427	(348,998)	2,667,827	245,000
15	13	Hoechst	Germany	Chemicals	16,480,551[6]	12,329,470[6]	251,605[6]	2,705,730[6]	186,850[6]
16	14	Bayer	Germany	Chemicals	15,880,596[6]	13,453,399[6]	356,342[6]	2,981,127[6]	181,639[6]
17	15	BASF	Germany	Chemicals	15,277,348[6]	9,263,801[6]	197,641[6]	3,476,343[6]	116,518[6]
18	18	Thyssen[7]	Germany	Steel and industrial products	15,235,998[6]	9,493,607[6]	61,611[6]	1,741,601[6]	151,709[6]
19	27	Petrobrás (Petróleo Brasileiro)[5]	Brazil	Petroleum	14,836,326	13,490,366	767,419	5,012,519	64,830
20	39	Pemex (Petróleos Mexicanos)[5]	Mexico	Petroleum	14,813,514	31,804,157	17,316	N.A.	128,294
21	20	Nestlé	Switzerland	Food products, beverages	14,615,187	10,126,423	407,785	4,702,093	152,653
22	17	Toyota Motor[9]	Japan	Motor vehicles	14,233,779[10]	7,842,615[10]	616,051[10]	4,504,592[10]	47,064[10]
23	21	Nissan Motor[11]	Japan	Motor vehicles	13,853,503	9,293,328	461,647	3,055,812	95,566
24	25	Imperial Chemical Industries	Britain	Chemicals	13,290,347	14,534,676	(46,510)	6,545,860	143,200
25	23	Nippon Steel[11]	Japan	Metal refining—steel	13,104,996	13,793,676	496,205	2,134,588	75,767
26	22	Hitachi[11]	Japan	Electronics, appliances	12,871,328	12,422,812	503,385	3,442,472	143,270
27	26	Matsushita Electric Industrial[12]	Japan	Electronics, appliances	12,684,404	11,599,230	541,923	5,112,591	107,057
28	24	Mitsubishi Heavy Industries[11]	Japan	Motor vehicles, industrial equipment	10,997,586	13,369,016	100,659	1,025,600	95,300
29	28	BAT Industries	Britain	Tobacco	10,987,175*	9,694,562	323,247	4,171,194	177,000
30	32	Générale d'Electricité	France	Electronics, appliances	10,847,129[6]	12,986,590[6]	96,407[6]	1,033,816[6]	179,600[6]
31	30	Saint-Gobain-Pont-à-Mousson	France	Building materials, metal products	10,303,979	9,333,499	215,310	1,979,459	163,504
32	38	Petrofina	Belgium	Petroleum	9,759,894	7,291,742	323,332	1,478,952	23,000
33	48	Esso	Germany	Petroleum	9,748,306[13]	2,745,507	236,689	1,039,600	4,567
34	37	Veba Oel	Germany	Petroleum, chemicals	9,645,994[6]	3,588,568[6]	35,975[6]	646,246[6]	24,962[6]
35	33	Montedison	Italy	Chemicals	9,103,770[6]	9,913,320[6]	(524,160)[6]	1,475,280[6]	105,532[6]
36	29	Ruhrkohle	Germany	Mining—coal	9,047,459[6]	6,553,615[6]	14,760[6]	310,260[6]	136,816[6]
37	35	Pechiney Ugine Kuhlmann	France	Metal refining—aluminum, steel	9,029,710	7,533,180	143,935	1,821,915	89,100
38	62	Idemitsu Kosan[11]	Japan	Petroleum	8,706,905[10]	7,361,874[10]	(13,736)[10]	51,826[10]	7,851[10]
39	40	Thomson-Brandt	France	Electronics, appliances	8,657,462	8,729,603	72,852	668,664	128,400
40	42	Canadian Pacific	Canada	Metal refining	8,539,483	10,915,442	498,757	2,949,506	121,549

Rank 1980	1979	Company	Country	Industry	Sales[1] ($000)	Assets[2] ($000)	Net Income[3] ($000)	Stock-holders' Equity[4] ($000)	Employ-ees
41	61	National Coal Board[11,5]	Britain	Mining	8,158,635	7,019,136	0	294,192	297,000
42	31	Toshiba[10]	Japan	Electronics, appliances	8,146,379	7,910,088	198,070	946,488	98,000
43	34	General Motors of Canada	Canada	Motor vehicles and parts	8,083,419	2,228,715	47,026	741,531	42,598
44	53	Michelin	France	Rubber products	7,731,084	8,408,703	65,813	1,993,606	128,000
45	41	Fried. Krupp	Germany	Metal refining—steel; mining	7,668,468	4,897,200	33,547	846,421	85,706
46	49	Schneider	France	Industrial equip.; metal refining—steel	7,599,648	14,499,436	(30,517)	314,391	117,000
47	51	DSM[5]	Netherlands	Chemicals	7,514,249[6]	4,511,106[6]	12,542[6]	1,037,218[6]	31,410[6]
48	56	Dunlop Pirelli Union	Britain-Italy	Rubber products	7,511,430	N.A.	N.A.	N.A.	151,000
49	69	Esso Petroleum	Britain	Petroleum	7,486,779[13]	7,131,165	486,731	1,186,377	10,246
50	44	Mannesmann	Germany	Industrial equipment; metal products	7,222,442	4,890,438	95,932	1,231,440	103,491
51	36	Rhône-Poulenc	France	Chemicals	7,155,049	6,527,292	(461,303)	1,305,107	95,389
52	59	Ciba-Geigy	Switzerland	Chemicals; pharmaceuticals	7,113,254	9,878,032	182,100	5,966,987	81,184
53	47	ESTEL	Netherlands	Metal refining—steel; metal products	7,046,069	5,759,674	(245,851)	902,147	77,500
54	72	Esso	France	Petroleum	7,028,623	2,490,389	71,292	444,484	4,848
55	63	Gutehoffnungshütte[9]	Germany	Industrial and transportation equipment	6,912,217	5,976,557	48,243	767,746	86,106
56	45	Ford Motor	Britain	Motor vehicles	6,799,820[13]	5,346,582	474,406	2,501,283	80,000
57	50	British Steel[11,5]	Britain	Metal refining—steel	6,772,688	7,415,280	(3,891,296)	1,717,200	166,400
58	46	AEG-Telefunken	Germany	Electronics, appliances	6,755,946[6]	4,335,112[6]	(163,847)[6]	432,305[6]	108,000[6]
59	52	BL[5]	Britain	Motor vehicles	6,690,754	5,674,114	(1,245,316)	1,547,116	143,324
60	73	General Electric Co.[11]	Britain	Industrial equipment, electronics	6,556,311	6,494,256	546,396	2,931,768	190,000
61	60	Robert Bosch	Germany	Motor-vehicle parts; electronics, appl.	6,505,872	4,228,431	114,588	1,224,143	120,020
62	67	Rio Tinto-Zinc	Britain	Mining—alum., lead, zinc, copper, iron	6,501,689	9,031,376	387,199	2,823,320	65,799
63	55	Akzo Group	Netherlands	Chemicals	6,272,300	4,470,129	(35,057)	1,054,055	83,100
64	68	Brown Boveri	Switzerland	Electrical equipment	6,005,726[6]	N.A.	N.A.	N.A.	105,300[6]
65	57	Nippon Kohan[11]	Japan	Metal refining—steel	5,930,483	9,741,196	114,219	811,796	37,752
66	98	Toa Nenryo Kogyo	Japan	Petroleum	5,841,797	3,841,580	162,253	751,343	3,824
67	92	Maruzen Oil[11]	Japan	Petroleum	5,815,731	4,412,104	(992)	97,504	4,689
68	70	Honda Motor[14]	Japan	Motor vehicles	5,703,204	3,546,191	122,986	894,576	33,405
69	65	Volvo	Sweden	Motor vehicles	5,628,743	5,275,339	9,104	648,077	63,893
70	76	Imperial Group[15]	Britain	Tobacco, food products, beverages	5,591,996*	5,665,381	211,310	2,656,567	127,300
71	66	Sumitomo Metal Industries[11]	Japan	Metal refining—steel	5,558,928	7,678,424	177,072	761,816	34,160
72	80	Hyundai Group	South Korea	Shipbldg., indus. equip., motor vehicles	5,540,543	4,415,363	97,164	847,360	125,600
73	54	Ford Motor of Canada	Canada	Motor vehicles	5,480,827[13]	1,812,054	(42,592)	661,950	33,726
74	105	Electrolux[16]	Sweden	Electronics; appliances	5,409,015[6]	4,068,906[6]	79,690[6]	625,670[6]	102,900[6]
75	119	Chinese Petroleum[5]	Taiwan	Petroleum	5,373,416[10]	3,475,029[10]	8,657[10]	1,292,990[10]	19,426[10]
76	112	ENPETROL[5]	Spain	Petroleum	5,275,030[6]	3,140,405[6]	17,233[6]	832,121[6]	8,399[6]
77	79	Alcan Aluminium	Canada	Metal refining—aluminum	5,215,000	5,470,000	542,000	2,463,000	66,900
78	64	Imperial Oil	Canada	Petroleum	5,202,607	5,227,289	583,294	3,172,037	16,029
79	94	Usinor	France	Metal refining—steel	5,149,864	7,515,456	(296,963)	175,833	40,000
80	88	Grand Metropolitan[7]	Britain	Beverages, food products	5,098,486	5,992,086	277,967	2,986,376	126,737
81	●	Adam Opel	Germany	Motor vehicles	5,081,645[13]	2,689,763	226,306	1,040,312	59,876
82	81	Metallgesellschaft[7]	Germany	Metal refining—nonferrous	5,081,174	2,457,709	22,189	353,698	27,220
83	71	Mitsubishi Electric[11]	Japan	Electronics, appliances	5,065,643	4,226,440	140,705	773,800	59,937
84	74	Kawasaki Steel[11]	Japan	Metal refining—steel	5,016,277[10]	6,826,337[10]	218,583[10]	833,810[10]	35,068[10]
85	77	Charbonnages de France[5]	France	Chemicals	4,959,182[6]	5,180,470[6]	(50,182)[6]	762,547[6]	77,600[6]
86	103	Schlumberger	Neth. Antilles	Measuring and scientific equipment	4,883,944	5,242,002	994,347	3,218,401	83,400
87	111	Degussa[7]	Germany	Metal products, chemicals	4,857,719	1,831,875	37,742	354,304	20,569

Rank 1980	Rank 1979	Company	Country	Industry	Sales[1] ($000)	Assets[2] ($000)	Net Income[3] ($000)	Stock-holders' Equity[4] ($000)	Employees
88	89	Salzgitter[7,5]	Germany	Metal refining—steel; shipbuilding	4,817,496	4,775,555	(48,668)	515,811	56,574
89	58	Ford-Werke	Germany	Motor vehicles	4,788,380[13]	2,081,288	(254,979)	535,339	49,767
90	84	YPF (Yacimientos Petroíferos)[5]	Argentina	Petroleum	4,784,103	9,737,875	113,460	4,850,971	33,602
91	83	Solvay	Belgium	Chemicals	4,741,913[6]	3,885,218[6]	59,458[6]	1,333,075[6]	49,057[6]
92	102	George Weston Holdings[11]	Britain	Food products	4,705,709	1,920,916	102,053	650,212	N.A.
93	75	Flick Group	Germany	Paper and wood products, chemicals	4,642,648	3,928,141	40,167	864,430	46,891
94	104	Indian Oil[11,5]	India	Petroleum	4,605,396[17]	2,054,906[17]	90,659[17]	532,972[17]	20,032[17]
95	91	Toyo, Kogyo[15]	Japan	Motor vehicles	4,572,614	3,265,016	82,772	591,533	28,297
96	93	Kuwait National Petroleum[5]	Kuwait	Petroleum	4,564,949	2,307,436	N.A.	622,934	3,452
97	●	Türkiye Petrolleri[5]	Turkey	Petroleum	4,515,629	2,718,956	114,977	148,581	9,723
98	86	VÖEST-Alpine[5]	Austria	Metal refining—steel	4,484,173	5,635,189	(65,026)	762,722	79,413
99	78	Kobe Steel[11]	Japan	Metal refining—steel	4,478,053[10]	5,225,833[10]	111,795[10]	581,605[10]	31,132[10]
100	82	Guest, Keen & Nettlefolds	Britain	Motor-vehicle parts	4,471,277	3,518,519	(209,064)	1,559,300	92,998

* Fortune estimate.
NA. Not available.
● Not on last year's list.
[1] All companies on the list have derived more than 50 percent of their sales from manufacturing and/or mining. Sales do not include excise taxes or customs duties levied according to either volume or value of sales, and so the figures for some companies—most of which sell gasoline, liquor, or tobacco—may be lower than those published by the companies themselves. Unless otherwise noted, figures exclude intracompany transactions and include consolidated subsidiaries more than 50 percent owned, either fully or on a prorated basis. Figures have been converted to dollars using an exchange rate that consists of the average rate in the official exchange market during each company's fiscal year (ending December 31, 1980, unless otherwise noted).
[2] Total shown at each company's year-end. Figures have been converted to dollars at the market rate prevailing at each company's year-end.
[3] After taxes, minority interest, and extraordinary items. Figures have been converted to dollars at the average market rate during each company's fiscal year. Figures in parentheses are losses.
[4] Total at each company's year-end. Figures have been converted to dollars at the market rate prevailing at each company's year-end. Minority interest is not included.
[5] Government owned.
[6] Also includes certain subsidiaries owned 50 percent or less, either fully or on a prorated basis.
[7] Figures are for fiscal year ending September 30, 1980.
[8] Name changed from Peugeot-Citroën on June 26, 1980.
[9] Figures are for fiscal year ending June 30, 1980.
[10] Parent only.
[11] Figures are for fiscal year ending March 31, 1980.
[12] Figures are for fiscal year ending November 20, 1980.
[13] Revenues include certain sales to foreign affiliates of the U.S. parent company.
[14] Figures are for fiscal year ending February 29, 1980.
[15] Figures are for fiscal year ending October 31, 1980.
[16] Figures include Gränges (1979 rank: 331), acquired January 1, 1980.
[17] Includes only wholly owned subsidiaries.

THE 25 LARGEST INDUSTRIAL COMPANIES IN THE WORLD

Rank 1980	Rank 1979	Company	Headquarters	Sales ($000)	Net Income ($000)
1	1	Exxon	New York	103,142,834	5,650,090
2	3	Royal Dutch/Shell Group	The Hague/London	77,114,243	5,174,282
3	4	Mobil	New York	59,510,000	3,272,000
4	2	General Motors	Detroit	57,728,500	(762,500)
5	7	Texaco	Harrison, N.Y.	51,195,830	2,642,542
6	6	British Petroleum	London	48,035,941	3,337,121
7	8	Standard Oil of California	San Francisco	40,479,000	2,401,000
8	5	Ford Motor	Dearborn, Mich.	37,085,000	(1,543,300)
9	13	ENI	Rome	27,186,939	98,046
10	9	Gulf Oil	Pittsburgh	26,483,000*	1,407,000
11	10	International Business Machines	Armonk, N.Y.	26,213,000	3,562,000
12	14	Standard Oil (Ind.)	Chicago	26,133,080	1,915,314
13	15	Fiat	Turin (Italy)	25,155,000	N.A.
14	11	General Electric	Fairfield, Conn.	24,959,000	1,514,000
15	16	Francaise des Pétroles	Paris	23,940,355	946,772
16	21	Atlantic Richfield	Los Angeles	23,744,302	1,651,423
17	12	Unilever	London/Rotterdam	23,607,516	658,820
18	26	Shell Oil	Houston	19,830,000	1,542,000
19	22	Renault	Paris	18,979,278	160,165
20	29	Petróleos de Venezuela	Caracas	18,818,931	3,450,921
21	18	International Telephone & Tel.	New York	18,529,655	894,326
22	32	Elf Aquitaine	Paris	18,430,074	1,378,222
23	20	Philips' Gloeilampenfabrieken	Eindhoven (Netherlands)	18,402,818	165,210
24	19	Volkswagenwerk	Wolfsburg (Germany)	18,339,046	170,964
25	36	Conoco	Stamford, Conn.	18,325,400	1,026,195

THE 25 LARGEST UTILITIES
(ranked by assets)

Rank 1980	Rank 1979	Company	Assets[1] ($000)	Operating Revenues[2] ($000)	Rank	Net Income[3] ($000)	Rank	Stockholders' Equity[4] ($000)	Rank
1	1	American Telephone & Telegraph (New York)	125,450,800	50,791,200	1	6,079,700	1	51,407,300	1
2	2	General Telephone & Electronics (Stamford, Conn.)	19,720,457	9,978,875	2	477,876	3	4,623,953	2
3	3	Southern Company (Atlanta)	11,466,555	3,763,483	6	344,395	6	2,834,736	7
4	4	Pacific Gas & Electric (San Francisco)	11,295,203	5,258,899	3	524,770	2	3,726,870	4
5	6	American Electric Power (Columbus)	10,951,984	3,756,464	7	348,377	5	3,095,346	5
6	5	Commonwealth Edison (Chicago)	10,177,142	3,324,043	12	382,003	4	4,025,015	3
7	8	Southern California Edison (Rosemead, Calif.)	7,733,898	3,661,117	8	317,536	8	2,529,577	9
8	7	Consolidated Edison (New York)	7,459,681	3,947,165	5	334,676	7	2,883,489	6
9	9	Middle South Utilities (New Orleans)	7,334,879	2,342,228	22	195,907	20	1,905,528	15
10	10	Public Service Electric & Gas (Newark)	6,724,860	2,994,054	16	261,717	11	2,646,928	8
11	12	Texas Utilities (Dallas)	6,552,972	2,174,553	24	297,844	10	2,090,520	12
12	11	Virginia Electric & Power (Richmond)	6,491,464	2,119,774	26	241,620	12	2,208,030	11
13	13	Duke Power (Charlotte)	6,328,174	1,682,822	32	311,091	9	1,969,140	14
14	14	Consumers Power (Jackson, Mich.)	6,276,596	2,303,983	23	223,798	14	1,586,495	17
15	16	Detroit Edison	5,741,686	1,812,514	29	188,566	21	1,842,420	16
16	15	Philadelphia Electric	5,702,549	2,123,394	25	227,131	13	2,380,416	10
17	18	Florida Power & Light (Miami)	5,492,053	2,347,278	21	198,318	19	1,524,285	18
18	17	General Public Utilities (Parsippany, N.J.)	5,042,972	1,831,741	28	20,591	49	1,414,223	23
19	21	Houston Industries	4,432,938	2,368,583	20	183,981	22	1,498,543	21
20	19	American Natural Resources (Detroit)	4,383,491	3,038,546	13	113,219	42	1,051,407	34
21	22	Pennsylvania Power & Light (Allentown, Pa.)	4,300,080	885,451	46	179,759	24	1,992,892	13
22	24	Carolina Power & Light (Raleigh)	4,241,607	1,075,604	42	161,388	28	1,519,386	19
23	23	Central & South West (Dallas)	4,219,589	1,731,327	31	206,077	17	1,366,314	24
24	20	United Telecommunications (Westwood, Kans.)	4,205,962	1,911,660	27	177,336	25	1,196,873	27
25	29	Ohio Edison (Akron)	3,979,965	1,080,869	40	135,150	33	1,332,482	25

• Not on last year's list.

[1] Assets shown as of December 31, 1980, unless otherwise noted. Only assets of consolidated subsidiaries are included.

[2] Gross receipts from operations during the 1980 fiscal year, including any non-utility revenues from manufacturing, transportation, etc., and revenues from discontinued operations when they are published.

[3] After extraordinary items. Figures in parentheses indicate net losses.

[4] Sum of capital stock, surplus, and retained earnings at the end of the fiscal year. Common and preferred stock of subsidiaries have been excluded. Redeemable preferred stock is excluded when its redemption is either mandatory or outside the control of the company.

[5] Year-end total, unless followed by a dagger (†), in which case average for the year.

Net Income as Percent of Equity		Employees[5]		Earnings per Share[6]			Growth Rate 1970–80[7]		Total Return to Investors[8] 1980[9]		1970–80 Average[9]	
%	Rank	Number	Rank	1980($)	1979($)	1970($)	%	Rank	%	Rank	%	Rank
11.8	27	1,044,041†	1	8.19	8.04	3.99	7.46	7	.43	37	6.84	13
10.3	39	200,534	2	2.94	4.20	2.11	3.37	24	6.09	26	6.12	14
12.1	23	27,940	4	2.23	1.51	1.94	1.40	35	20.07	8	1.97	39
14.1	13	27,582	5	3.60	3.55	2.47	3.84	22	0.26	42	3.03	32
11.3	32	26,659	6	2.41	2.29	2.30	0.47	41	6.87	23	4.04	26
9.5	46	16,400	10	2.97	2.51	2.95	0.07	43	3.61	32	1.28	41
12.6	18	14,157	13	3.50	4.56	2.71	2.59	32	15.93	12	5.73	17
11.6	30	23,156†	7	4.67	4.51	2.30	7.34	8	13.63	16	8.14	11
10.3	40	12,406	15	2.01	2.13	1.61	2.24	34	3.62	31	(0.32)	48
10.6	36	12,326	16	3.22	2.85	2.46	2.73	30	0.21	43	4.54	23
14.2	10	14,389	12	3.18	2.45	1.67	6.65	12	14.68	14	0.88	43
10.9	33	10,580	21	1.93	1.63	1.80	0.70	40	12.17	18	0.76	45
15.8	5	19,612	9	3.08	2.88	1.57	6.97	11	16.38	11	5.16	19
14.1	12	12,577†	14	3.08	3.24	2.95	0.43	42	0.58	39	2.53	37
10.2	41	10,789	20	1.75	1.90	1.88	(0.71)	45	0.80	38	3.02	33
9.5	45	9,721†	23	2.00	1.86	1.84	0.84	39	4.00	30	4.39	24
13.0	17	11,084	19	3.94	4.22	1.98	7.12	10	15.06	13	2.88	36
1.5	49	11,490	18	0.34	1.56	1.83	(15.49)	49	(42.00)	50	(5.94)	50
12.3	21	8,768	26	4.71	4.84	2.56	6.29	14	7.05	22	1.07	42
10.8	35	15,987	11	4.89	6.47	3.38	3.76	23	11.98	19	9.18	8
9.0	48	7,702	32	2.64	3.32	1.97	2.97	23	(0.13)	45	4.80	21
10.6	38	6,522	39	2.73	3.06	1.56	5.76	16	6.06	27	4.63	22
15.1	7	8,345	29	2.45	2.27	1.43	5.53	17	1.78	36	0.82	44
14.8	8	29,320	3	2.47	2.63	1.15	7.94	6	(4.76)	48	4.81	20
10.1	42	7,453	35	1.52	1.80	1.84	(1.89)	47	1.94	35	2.12	38

[6] Earnings per share have been computed as described in footnote 6, page 196.

[7] Average annual growth rate, compounded. No figure is given if the company had a loss in either 1970 or 1980.

[8] Total return has been computed as described in footnote 8, page 197.

[9] Percentages shown are the returns received by the hypothetical investor described in footnote 8, page 197. The ten-year figures are annual averages, compounded.

[10] Name changed from Northern Natural Gas on March 28, 1980.

[11] Name changed from People Gas on February 1, 1980.

[12] Figures are for fiscal year ending September 30, 1980.

THE 25 LARGEST COMMERCIAL BANKING COMPANIES
(ranked by assets)

Rank 1980	Rank 1979	Company	Assets[1] ($000)	Deposits ($000)	Deposits Rank	Loans[2] ($000)	Loans Rank	Employees[3] Number	Employees Rank
1	2	Citicorp (New York)	114,920,000	71,771,000	2	69,915,000	1	53,700	2
2	1	BankAmerica Corp. (San Francisco)	111,617,291	88,426,156	1	62,482,124	2	83,713	1
3	3	Chase Manhattan Corp. (New York)	76,189,567	56,846,002	3	46,506,335	3	33,450	3
4	4	Manufacturers Hanover Corp. (New York)	55,522,249	41,744,624	4	30,348,158	4	24,893	6
5	5	J. P. Morgan & Co. (New York)	51,990,646	35,593,807	5	25,972,414	6	11,325	14
6	7	Continental Illinois Corp. (Chicago)	42,089,408	27,313,667	7	27,120,625	5	12,257	10
7	6	Chemical New York Corp.	41,342,220	30,067,000	6	22,159,068	7	18,223	7
8	8	Bankers Trust New York Corp.	32,325,603	23,942,285	9	15,990,717	11	11,827	12
9	10	Western Bancorp. (Los Angeles)	32,110,327	24,863,703	8	17,707,309	9	30,085†	4
10	9	First Chicago Corp.	28,699,441	21,361,154	10	16,788,573	10	10,602	15
11	11	Security Pacific Corp. (Los Angeles)	27,794,208	21,168,617	11	18,147,918	8	25,069	5
12	12	Wells Fargo & Co. (San Francisco)	23,638,063	16,207,468	12	15,969,283	12	17,460	8
13	14	Crocker National Corp. (San Francisco)	19,062,665	14,908,644	13	12,402,443	13	16,700	9
14	13	Irving Bank Corp. (New York)	18,089,818	14,163,187	14	8,416,288	16	9,200	18
15	15	Marine Midland Banks (Buffalo)[10]	17,479,565	14,163,018	15	9,588,419	14	10,245†	17
16	17	Mellon National Corp. (Pittsburgh)	16,156,458	10,889,575	17	7,866,350	17	6,906†	21
17	16	First National Boston Corp.	15,948,497	10,815,011	18	8,563,278	15	11,500	13
18	18	Northwest Bancorp. (Minneapolis)	14,394,930	11,044,233	16	7,617,618	18	12,017†	11
19	20	First International Bancshares (Dallas)	13,780,872	10,076,250	19	6,999,729	20	5,845†	30
20	19	First Bank System (Minneapolis)	13,475,043	9,768,402	20	7,162,237	19	10,441	16
21	21	Republic of Texas Corp. (Dallas)	11,866,990	8,472,675	23	6,040,616	22	5,755	31
22	24	Texas Commerce Bancshares (Houston)	11,286,924	8,630,646	22	5,665,728	24	6,078	26
23	23	First City Bancorp. of Texas (Houston)	11,275,084	8,721,736	21	5,378,455	25	6,353	25
24	22	National Detroit Corp.	10,868,976	7,804,413	25	5,222,721	26	6,651	24
25	25	Bank of New York Co.	10,422,805	8,319,087	24	5,673,810	23	7,199	20

• Not on last year's list.
[1] As of December 31, 1980.
[2] Net of unearned discount and loan-loss reserve. Figure does not include direct lease financing.
[3] Year-end total unless followed by a dagger (†), in which case average for the year.
[4] After extraordinary items. Figures in parentheses indicate net losses. A double asterisk (**) signifies an extraordinary credit reflecting at least 10% of the net income shown; a double dagger (‡) signifies an extraordinary charge of at least 10%.
[5] Sum of capital stock, surplus, and retained earnings at the end of the fiscal year. Redeemable preferred stock is excluded when its redemption is either mandatory or outside the control of the company.
[6] For all companies, the figures are the "primary" earnings per share that appear in the company's income statement. These figures are based on a weighted average of the number of common shares and common-stock equivalents outstanding during the year. "Common-stock equivalents" generally include (a) convertible securities whose cash yield is less than two-thirds of the prime rate at the time the securities were issued and (b) options and warrants when the effect of their inclusion in the computation would reduce the "primary" earnings per share. Per-share earnings for 1979 and 1970 are adjusted for stock splits and stock dividends. They are not restated for mergers, acquisitions, or accounting changes made after 1970. A double asterisk (**) signifies an extraordinary credit reflecting at least 10% of the net income shown, a double dagger (‡) an extraordinary charge of at least 10%. Results are listed as not available (N.A.) where the companies are wholly owned subsidiaries of other companies, or if the figures were not published in 1970.

Net Income[4]		Stockholders' Equity[5]		Net Income as Percent of Equity		Earnings per Share[6]			Growth Rate 1970–80[7]		Total Return to Investors[8]			
											1980[9]		1970–80 Average[9]	
($000)	Rank	($000)	Rank	%	Rank	1980($)	1979($)	1970($)	%	Rank	%	Rank	%	Rank
499,000	2	3,891,000	2	12.8	32	4.02	4.34	1.28	12.12	15	7.96	30	7.16	25
643,443	1	3,908,407	1	16.5	7	4.38	4.10	1.19	13.92	5	14.61	24	10.37	9
354,178	3	2,407,715	3	14.7	18	10.15	8.81	3.68	10.68	20	31.86	10	5.40	32
228,528	5	1,708,585	5	13.4	26	6.87	6.42	2.77	9.51	24	13.31	26	5.04	35
341,687	4	2,180,399	4	15.7	11	8.33	7.07	2.37	13.39	9	17.67	22	8.36	15
225,941	6	1,524,942	6	14.8	17	5.75	4.99	1.69	13.03	11	13.45	25	10.50	8
173,451	10	1,307,215	8	13.3	28	11.05	8.53	5.06	8.12	29	25.66	15	3.07	39
213,800	8	1,009,640	11	21.2	2	8.65	4.65	2.72	12.27	13	62.62	2	6.86	27
225,064	7	1,401,328	7	16.1	9	5.70	5.38	1.59‡	13.62	7	20.46	19	9.20	13
63,008	24	1,204,519	9	5.2	47	1.59	2.83	1.25	2.44	42	8.54	29	5.24	34
181,304	9	1,170,326	10	15.5	12	6.55	5.94	2.24	11.33	19	29.16	13	9.54	11
121,864	11	913,573	12	13.3	27	5.33	5.45	1.78	11.59	16	13.00	28	8.23	16
95,735	18	729,668	18	13.1	29	5.66	8.94	3.27	5.64	37	35.43	8	7.56	20
85,339	21	568,773	24	15.0	15	9.70	7.77	3.59	10.45	21	47.34	4	9.22	12
62,728**	25	759,390	16	8.3	46	3.89**	3.18	3.40	1.36	43	(2.12)	41	(0.19)	44
112,452	14	901,173	13	12.5	33	4.19	4.92	2.28	6.27	35	21.23	17	7.27	23
102,146	16	729,965	17	14.0	22	8.22	6.84	3.47	9.01	25	31.56	11	7.26	24
113,495	13	796,605	14	14.2	20	4.39	4.13	1.49	11.41	18	18.88	20	8.91	14
117,966	12	687,910	19	17.1	6	5.66	4.79	1.41	14.91	3	33.62	9	14.48	3
111,986	15	782,035	15	14.3	19	7.42	6.80	2.79	10.28	22	6.31	33	6.69	28
86,878	20	583,956	21	14.9	16	4.81	4.08	1.33	13.72	6	28.87	14	10.07	10
101,493	17	576,088	22	17.6	3	3.48	2.85	0.68	17.74	1	51.36	3	18.72	1
89,047	19	575,371	23	15.5	13	6.61	5.34	1.78[11]	14.02	4	40.70	7	13.59	5
74,372	22	661,376	20	11.2	36	6.08	6.24	3.04	7.18	31	(10.18)	43	6.20	30
42,552‡	36	394,253	27	10.8	38	6.53‡	7.05	4.03	4.94	40	5.75	35	3.99	37

[7] Average annual growth rate, compounded.

[8] Total return includes both price appreciation and dividend yield, i.e., to an investor in the company's stock. The figures shown assume sales at the end of 1980 of stock owned at the end of 1970 or 1979. It has been assumed that any proceeds from cash dividends, the sale of rights and warrant offerings, and stock received in spin-offs were reinvested at the end of the year in which they were received. Returns are adjusted for stock splits, stock dividends, recapitalizations, and corporate reorganizations as they occur; however, no effort has been made to reflect the cost of brokerage commissions or of taxes. Results are listed as not available where shares are not publicly traded or traded on only a limited basis. Where corporations have more than one class of shares outstanding, only the more widely held and actively traded has been considered.

[9] Percentages are the returns received by the hypothetical investor described in footnote 8. The ten-year figures are annual averages, compounded. Where corporations were substantially reorganized—e.g., because of mergers—the predecessor companies used in calculating total return are the same as those cited in the footnotes to the earnings-per-share figures.

[10] Company is 51% owned by Hong Kong & Shanghai Banking Corp.

[11] Figure is for First National Bank of Houston.

[12] Company is wholly owned by Standard Chartered Bank Ltd.

[13] Figure is for Michigan National Bank (Lansing).

[14] Wholly owned by National Westminster Bank (No. 9 on the 1979 Commercial-Banking Companies Outside the U.S.).

THE 25 LARGEST COMMERCIAL BANKING COMPANIES OUTSIDE THE U.S.

Rank 1980	Rank 1979	Bank	Country	Assets[1] ($000)	Increase (Decrease) from Prior Year In U.S. Dollars %	Increase (Decrease) from Prior Year In Local Currencies %
1	2	Banque Nationale de Paris[7]	France	107,449,631	8.62	22.95
2	1	Caisse Nationale de Crédit Agricole[7]	France	105,906,369	0.80	14.10
3	4	Crédit Lyonnais[7]	France	98,147,449	7.69	21.89
4	5	Société Générale[7]	France	90,164,865	6.12	20.12
5	8	Barclays Bank	Britain	88,624,733	31.70	22.30
6	6	Dai-Ichi Kangyo Bank[9,10]	Japan	88,519,780	20.82	13.43
7	3	Deutsche Bank[8]	Germany	88,468,402	(3.89)	9.90
8	9	National Westminster Bank	Britain	82,585,341	28.60	19.42
9	12	Mitsubishi Bank[9,10]	Japan	76,433,197	24.26	16.66
10	10	Fuji Bank[9,10]	Japan	75,396,945	18.56	11.30
11	11	Sumitomo Bank[9,10]	Japan	73,459,526	18.66	11.40
12	14	Sanwa Bank[9,10]	Japan	70,268,863	17.17	10.01
13	7	Dresdner Bank[8]	Germany	62,595,548	(10.93)	1.84
14	26	Midland Bank	Britain	60,543,710	35.07	25.43
15	18	Industrial Bank of Japan[9,10]	Japan	60,475,895	17.52	10.33
16	13	Westdeutsche Landesbank Girozentrale[7]	Germany	57,898,325	(3.52)	10.31
17	16	Cie Financière de Suez[12]	France	57,279,713	7.33	21.49
18	19	Bank of Tokyo[8,13]	Japan	55,861,833	9.86	31.01
19	28	Royal Bank of Canada[14]	Canada	53,462,183	22.44	21.48
20	32	Mitsui Bank[9,10]	Japan	52,821,868	23.06	15.53
21	21	Cie Financière de Paris et des Pays-Bas[12]	France	52,282,105	8.27	22.56
22	20	Banco do Brasil[7]	Brazil	52,238,425	6.58	64.14
23	31	Tokai Bank[9,10]	Japan	50,998,711	18.53	11.28
24	15	Commerzbank[8]	Germany	50,685,657	(12.78)	(0.27)
25	24	Algemene Bank Nederland	Netherlands	50,576,613	10.88	25.34

● Not on last year's list.

[1] Asset figures have been converted into U.S. dollars using the market rate prevailing at each bank's fiscal year-end, which is December 31, 1980, unless otherwise noted. Figures for subsidiaries are included if they are more than 50 percent owned, unless otherwise noted. Daiwa Bank, Mitsubishi Trust & Banking, Sumitomo Trust & Banking, Mitsui Trust & Banking include holdings of major trusts in their assets.

[2] Deposit figures have been converted into U.S. dollars using the market rate as of each bank's fiscal year-end. Figures for all German banks include their own bonds; so do the figures for Norinchukin Bank, Industrial Bank of Japan, Bank of Tokyo, and Long-Term Credit Bank of Japan. Banco do Brasil includes funds for refinancing. Figures for Swiss banks include medium-term notes.

[3] Loan figures have been converted into U.S. dollars using the market rate prevailing at each bank's fiscal year-end. Figures include loans to banks and at call or available on short notice.

[4] Net income figures have been converted into U.S. dollars using the average rate in the official exchange market during the bank's fiscal year. Net income is after taxes and includes minority interest.

Deposits[2] ($000)	Rank	Loans[3] ($000)	Net Income[4] ($000)	Stockholders' Equity[5] ($000)	Offices[6]	Employees
105,936,955	1	76,422,834	203,535	1,420,195	2,424	57,054
85,615,316	4	89,471,505	368,142	6,140,488	10,025	65,000[11]
90,664,231	2	83,053,972	134,259	1,596,106	2,283	45,892
88,249,326	3	67,991,505	188,510	1,403,569	2,535	44,373
81,808,916	5	65,014,246	809,979	4,758,888	5,000	120,000
62,523,521	8	50,843,723	113,467	1,733,045	334	24,233
81,205,993	6	71,666,127	242,830	2,599,466	1,361	44,128
76,017,980	7	57,988,197	720,911	4,336,035	3,818	73,668[11]
53,901,110	14	40,761,313	116,560	1,730,949	233	17,159
55,741,323	10	41,684,395	104,383	1,789,720	244	18,826
54,286,198	13	39,948,007	99,825	1,780,894	265	18,390
51,711,809	15	40,102,434	88,988	1,512,531	263	18,520
58,510,727	9	50,535,231	107,909	1,688,625	1,154	31,402
54,721,478	11	40,707,604	392,780	3,221,805	3,626	77,900[11]
48,745,419	16	34,103,961	113,698	1,360,072	25	5,014
54,511,876	12	47,289,893	32,320	1,292,898	13	7,690
36,669,681	32	44,704,571	207,395	1,498,159	1,664	36,280
33,148,102	41	21,567,153	96,764	897,033	224	14,230
46,202,701	18	31,965,461	164,364	1,434,417	1,592	36,928
37,432,325	30	29,499,059	57,312	990,784	179	12,784
27,326,973	49	43,467,633	173,077	1,790,426	1,016	25,823
28,476,133	48	47,321,542	1,733,221	3,579,656	1,258	94,267
37,021,768	31	28,214,162	63,214	1,108,902	242	15,490
48,206,664	17	43,791,815	17,851	1,153,049	880	27,505
44,989,765	19	29,665,882	155,531	1,127,802	919	27,837

[5] Stockholders' equity figures have been converted into U.S. dollars using the market rate prevailing at each bank's fiscal year-end. Equity is the sum of capital stock, surplus, and retained earnings. Figures for all French banks are before appropriation of profits.
[6] Includes head office, branches, and agencies.
[7] Government owned.
[8] Excludes certain subsidiaries that are more than 50 percent owned.
[9] Figures are for fiscal year ending September 30, 1980.
[10] Parent company only.
[11] Average for the year.
[12] Includes certain subsidiaries owned 50 percent or less.
[13] Figures are for fiscal year ending March 31, 1980.
[14] Figures are for fiscal year ending October 31, 1980.

Source: Reprinted by permission from the 1981 *Fortune Directory,* © 1981, Time, Inc. All rights reserved.

THE 25 LARGEST DIVERSIFIED FINANCIAL COMPANIES
(ranked by assets)

Rank 1980	Rank 1979	Company	Assets[1] ($000)	Revenues[2] ($000)	Rank	Net Income[3] ($000)	Rank	Stockholders' Equity[4] ($000)	Rank
1	•	Federal National Mortgage Assn. (Washington, D.C.)	58,470,003	5,202,910	5	14,208	39	1,457,258	8
2	1	Aetna Life & Casualty (Hartford)	35,752,700	13,318,000	1	561,600	1	3,281,100	1
3	2	Travelers Corp. (Hartford)	21,637,986	8,790,092	2	362,739	3	2,643,125	2
4	3	American Express (New York)	19,709,000	5,504,000	3	376,000	2	2,162,000	3
5	5	Merrill Lynch & Co. (New York)	13,245,784	3,022,473	9	203,349	11	969,491	17
6	4	H. F. Ahmanson (Los Angeles)	13,109,603	1,317,119	22	54,322**	28	858,969	19
7	8	INA (Philadelphia)	10,604,000	5,255,000	4	292,738	4	1,841,585	5
8	7	Great Western Financial (Beverly Hills)	10,252,838	997,222	27	39,172	33	658,636	24
9	6	First Charter Financial (Beverly Hills)	9,676,378	955,093	29	39,206	32	798,152	22
10	9	Loews (New York)	9,125,112	4,535,098	6	206,099	10	1,194,589	12
11	10	Transamerica (San Francisco)	8,887,023	4,384,055	7	244,979	7	1,485,482	7
12	11	Lincoln National (Fort Wayne, Ind.)	8,470,373	2,692,911	11	175,697	12	1,311,817	10
13	12	Continental (New York)	8,215,970	3,419,046	8	269,192	6	2,122,756	4
14	14	Imperial Corp. of America (San Diego)	7,347,443	713,703	34	40,659	31	505,554	27
15	13	American General Corp. (Houston)[10]	7,293,328	2,291,716	12	229,906	8	1,076,156	14
16	16	American International Group (New York)	6,899,756	2,709,475	10	284,699	5	1,592,411	6
17	15	Beneficial (Wilmington)	6,030,000	1,323,000	20	94,000	18	1,084,000	13
18	21	First Boston (New York)	6,020,532	216,666	44	33,563	36	153,234	39
19	19	Avco Corp. (Greenwich, Conn.)[11]	5,843,526	2,149,906	14	118,550	17	998,685	16
20	18	Walter E. Heller International (Chicago)	5,728,288	747,945	33	43,011	30	340,843	29
21	24	Golden West Financial (Oakland, Calif.)	5,578,887	485,290	38	38,062	34	211,639	35
22	17	Household Finance (Prospect Heights, Ill.)	5,561,700	959,600	28	141,000	15	1,293,400	11
23	27	E. F. Hutton Group (New York)	4,706,635	1,125,271	25	82,630	23	259,208	33
24	23	Gibraltar Financial Corp. of California (Beverly Hills)	4,295,449	425,727	41	(7,934)‡	50	192,519	37
25	22	St. Paul Companies	4,252,380	1,868,314	16	123,625	16	1,042,950	15

• Not on last year's list.

N.A. Not available.

[1] Total assets shown as of December 31, 1980, unless otherwise noted. Only assets of consolidated subsidiaries are included. Holding companies that own commercial banks or life-insurance companies are listed here only when these subsidiaries represent less than 80% of the assets.

[2] Total income during the year, including any consolidated nonfinancial revenues from manufacturing, retailing, etc., and revenues from discontinued operations when published. All companies on the list must have derived more than 50% of their revenues from two or more kinds of financial business and be publicly held.

[3] After extraordinary items and realized capital gains and losses. Figures in parentheses indicate net loss. A double asterisk (**) signifies an extraordinary credit reflecting at least 10% of the net income shown; a double dagger (‡) signifies an extraordinary charge of at least 10%.

[4] Sum of capital stock, surplus, and retained earnings at the end of the fiscal year. Redeemable preferred stock is excluded when its redemption is either mandatory or outside the control of the company.

[5] Year-end total.

[6] Earnings per share have been computed as described in footnote 6, page 196.

Source: Reprinted by permission from the *1981 Fortune Directory;* © 1981 Time Inc. All rights reserved.

Net Income as Percent of Equity		Employees[5]		Earnings per Share[6]			Growth Rate 1970–80[7]		Total Return to Investors[8] 1980[9]		1970–80 Average[9]	
%	Rank	Number	Rank	1980($)	1979($)	1970($)	%	Rank	%	Rank	%	Rank
1.0	46	1,142	42	0.24	2.81	0.19	2.36	33	(19.41)	45	2.40	33
17.1	16	39,100	4	6.96	7.25	1.46	16.90	16	12.53	24	12.63	12
13.7	23	29,339	7	8.56	8.43	1.78	17.01	15	8.46	27	5.96	26
17.4	14	44,031	2	5.27	4.83	1.19	16.04	17	41.25	11	6.94	23
21.0	7	31,704	5	5.51	3.26	1.28	15.72	18	98.23	9	—	
6.3	38	4,300	32	2.34**	5.11	N.A.	—		(2.04)	36	—	
15.9	21	40,155	3	7.47	6.78	1.95	14.37	21	29.73	14	10.53	15
5.9	39	2,239	36	1.74	4.15	0.29	19.62	11	(11.35)	42	3.78	32
4.9	40	2,300	34	1.32	3.05	0.93	3.56	32	(7.40)	40	1.55	35
17.3	15	29,400	6	16.70	18.19	1.91	24.21	6	37.83	12	13.05	11
16.5	18	29,000	8	3.75	3.66	0.63	19.53	12	17.14	21	7.88	21
13.4	24	14,570	12	8.10	7.09	2.30	13.42	23	(2.06)	37	6.61	25
12.7	28	22,649	10	5.24	5.10	1.30	14.96	19	(1.12)	34	10.25	17
8.0	37	1,700	38	2.86	5.24	0.91	12.13	26	22.36	18	10.41	16
21.4	6	8,274	26	9.06	8.79	0.34	38.86	1	6.40	30	13.25	10
17.9	12	21,500	11	7.54	6.93	0.79	25.31	5	26.86	15	14.65	9
8.7	35	12,100	14	3.45	4.24	2.86	1.89	35	(10.34)	41	1.52	36
21.9	5	1,472	39	6.79	3.78	3.51	6.82	29	106.46	8	7.60	22
11.9	31	26,869	9	6.56	8.56	0.40	32.28	4	8.81	26	10.02	19
12.6	30	4,824	30	3.61	3.40	1.72**	7.70	28	(4.91)	38	2.26	34
18.0	11	1,128	43	1.80	1.74	0.25	21.82	10	35.84	13	15.21	6
10.9	34	78,000	1	2.88	3.33	1.98	3.82	31	(1.72)	35	0.25	38
31.9	2	10,075	18	6.16	2.90	N.A.	—		198.45	2	—	
—		1,300	41	(0.57)‡	2.12	0.35	—		(21.33)	48	5.61	29
11.9	32	11,219	16	5.90	7.77	1.65	13.59	22	0.00	33	6.66	24

[7] Average annual growth rate, compounded. No growth rate is give if the company had a loss in either 1970 or 1980.

[8] Total return has been computed as described in footnote 8, page 197.

[9] Percentages shown are the returns received by the hypothetical investor described in footnote 8, page 197. The ten-year figures are annual averages compounded. Where corporations were substantially reorganized—e.g., because of mergers—the predecessor companies used in calculating total return are the same as those cited in the footnotes to the earnings-per-share figures.

[10] Name changed from American General Insurance on June 30, 1980.

[11] Figures are for fiscal year ending November 30, 1980.

[12] Name changed from General Reinsurance on October 31, 1980.

[13] Figures are for fiscal year ending September 26, 1980.

[14] Figures are for fiscal year ending July 31, 1980.

[15] Figures are for fiscal year ending September 30, 1980.

[16] Figures are for fiscal year ending August 31, 1980.

THE 25 LARGEST
LIFE INSURANCE
COMPANIES
(ranked by assets)

Rank 1980	Rank 1979	Company	Assets[1] ($000)	Premium & Annuity Receipts[2] ($000)	Rank	Net Investment Income ($000)	Rank
1	1	Prudential (Newark)*	59,778,470	8,668,858	1	3,561,970	1
2	2	Metropolitan (New York)*	48,309,771	6,010,574	2	3,449,368	2
3	3	Equitable Life Assurance (New York)*	34,599,737	4,163,345	4	1,959,052	3
4	4	Aetna Life (Hartford)[7]	22,270,634	5,412,032	3	1,392,105	4
5	5	New York Life*	19,725,325	2,682,329	6	1,345,953	5
6	6	John Hancock Mutual (Boston)*	18,760,598	2,436,403	7	1,231,265	6
7	7	Connecticut General Life (Bloomfield)	13,776,921	1,861,488	8	956,218	7
8	8	Travelers (Hartford)[8]	13,351,227	3,955,025	5	934,764	8
9	9	Northwestern Mutual (Milwaukee)*	11,350,786	1,193,496	12	789,624	10
10	11	Teachers Insurance & Annuity (New York)	9,748,371	1,315,944	10	811,601	9
11	10	Massachusetts Mutual (Springfield)*	9,145,484	1,239,769	11	614,954	11
12	12	Mutual of New York*	8,005,708	891,919	18	559,314	13
13	13	Bankers Life (Des Moines)*	7,988,996	1,536,613	9	571,707	12
14	14	New England Mutual (Boston)*	6,823,015	991,410	17	465,489	14
15	15	Mutual Benefit (Newark)*	5,872,814	1,093,035	15	396,912	15
16	16	Connecticut Mutual (Hartford)*	5,384,922	683,008	21	353,202	16
17	17	Lincoln National Life (Fort Wayne)[9]	4,960,720	1,138,649	13	339,062	17
18	18	Penn Mutual (Philadelphia)*	3,866,281	419,127	31	254,832	18
19	21	State Farm Life (Bloomington, Ill.)	3,329,539	536,115	26	238,382	19
20	19	Continental Assurance (Chicago)[10]	3,259,254	1,034,807	16	171,094	24
21	20	Western & Southern (Cincinnati)*	3,062,024	315,904	37	211,185	21
22	23	Phoenix Mutual (Hartford)*	3,038,195	543,621	25	202,182	23
23	22	National Life & Accident (Nashville)	2,906,963	368,718	34	213,724	20
24	24	Pacific Mutual (Newport Beach, Calif.)*	2,903,753	889,612	19	202,480	22
25	25	Occidental of California (Los Angeles)[11]	2,674,866	1,097,020	14	159,434	27

Data for all companies are on the "statutory" accounting basis required by state insurance regulatory authorities.
* Indicates mutual company.
N.A. Not available.
[1] As of December 31, 1980.
[2] Includes premium income from life, accident, and health policies, annuities, and from contributions to deposit administration funds.
[3] After dividends to policyholders and federal income taxes, excluding capital gains and losses. Figures in parentheses indicate a loss.
[4] Face value of all life policies as of December 31, 1980.
[5] Change between December 31, 1979, and December 31, 1980.
[6] Includes home office, field force, and full-time agents.

Source: Reprinted with permission form the *1981 Fortune Directory;* © 1981 Time Inc. All rights reserved.

Net Gain from Operations[3]			Life Insurance in Force[4]		Increase in Life Insurance in Force[5]				Employees[6]	
($000)	Mutual	Stock	($000)	Rank	($000)	Rank	Percent of Increase	Rank	Number	Rank
444,269	2		406,571,823	1	39,288,247	1	10.7	29	62,453	1
479,092	1		349,192,320	2	25,603,444	2	7.9	38	48,000	2
33,307	11		197,338,258	3	13,846,881	4	7.5	39	26,160	4
185,597	—	1	144,214,809	4	16,595,961	3	13.0	18	17,399	7
82,341	5		122,764,294	6	10,871,835	5	9.7	30	19,623	6
127,841	3		133,703,479	5	8,109,034	9	6.5	43	20,294	5
171,120	—	2	80,402,921	8	6,828,078	10	9.3	33	9,642	12
168,555	—	3	104,402,349	7	8,749,788	8	9.1	34	40,887	3
116,475	4		61,308,461	10	9,641,074	6	18.7	8	6,673	19
68,756	—	7	7,587,077	43	1,391,106	34	22.5	6	1,738	44
65,066	6		50,934,797	13	6,408,083	11	14.4	15	9,678	11
45,353	8		37,968,654	15	4,031,877	17	11.9	26	7,898	14
18,531	17		35,051,210	17	3,900,307	18	12.5	20	5,730	22
53,833	7		31,672,479	19	3,477,497	21	12.3	21	6,864	17
41,753	9		40,241,181	14	5,542,931	14	16.0	13	4,494	24
22,085	16		26,223,401	22	2,835,450	25	12.1	24	4,828	23
81,291	—	5	59,931,472	11	8,797,640	7	17.2	9	8,039	13
23,302	15		18,061,591	28	1,399,370	33	8.4	36	3,874	26
76,202	—	6	50,955,938	12	5,670,099	13	12.5	19	15,869	8
16,331	—	21	27,791,432	21	5,966,017	12	27.3	4	N.A.	
40,829	10		14,415,905	34	267,831	46	1.9	47	7,676	16
23,542	14		29,059,755	20	2,938,092	24	11.2	27	2,987	33
87,451	—	4	16,639,025	30	233,317	47	1.4	48	7,685	15
(13,396)	25		18,581,590	27	2,268,635	28	13.9	17	3,406	30
52,296	—	10	67,965,680	9	5,137,761	15	8.2	37	6,015	21

[7] Wholly owned by Aetna Life & Casualty (No. 2 on the Diversified-Financial list).
[8] Wholly owned by Travelers Corp. (No. 3 on the Diversified-Financial list).
[9] Wholly owned by Lincoln National Corp. (No. 12 on the Diversified-Financial list).
[10] Company is 84% owned by Loews (No. 10 on the Diversified-Financial list).
[11] Wholly owned by Transamerica (No. 11 on the Diversified-Financial list).
[12] Wholly owned by American Brands (No. 86 on the FORTUNE 500).
[13] Wholly owned by Tenneco (No. 17 on the FORTUNE 500).
[14] Wholly owned by Alleghany Corp. (No. 33 on the Diversified-Financial list).
[15] Wholly owned by American General Corp. (No. 15 on the Diversified-Financial list).
[16] Wholly owned by Gulf & Western Industries (No. 57 on the FORTUNE 500).

Rank 1980	1981	Name of Firm	Total Capital	Equity Capital	Subordinated Debt	Excess Net Capital	Number of Employees	Number of Offices	Number of Registered Representatives
1.	1.	Merrill Lynch & Co.	$1,065,000,000	$965,000,000	$100,000,000	$342,315,000[1]	34,500	700	8,500
2.	2.	Shearson Loeb Rhoades	469,883,000	304,372,000[2]	165,511,000	269,466,000	10,100	266	3,500
3.	3.	The E. F. Hutton Group	448,037,000	259,208,000	188,829,000	129,686,000	10,075	275	3,958
5.	4.	Salomon Brothers	330,700,000[3]	253,793,000	76,907,000	125,245,000	2,437	10	630
4.	5.	Paine Webber	243,000,000	125,000,000	118,000,000	65,300,000	10,096	237	3,722
8.	6.	Bache Halsey Stuart Shields	233,788,000[4]	164,095,000	69,693,000	69,960,000	8,000	193	3,000
7.	7.	Goldman, Sachs & Co.	219,000,000[3]	200,000,000	19,000,000	218,500,000	2,217	15	657
6.	8.	Dean Witter Reynolds	216,338,000[5]	200,656,000	15,682,000	70,303,000	10,000	285	4,000
9.	9.	Stephens	167,250,416	167,250,416	0	39,226,507	137	1	85
10.	10.	The First Boston Corp.	153,200,000[6]	153,200,000	0	31,652,850[7]	1,472	13	494
12.	11.	Drexel Burnham Lambert	137,413,000	98,273,000	39,140,000	34,275,000	3,506	42	1,192
14.	12.	Lehman Brothers Kuhn Loeb	136,995,472	111,995,472	25,000,000	31,869,451	1,974	10	413
11.	13.	Morgan Stanley	135,000,000	93,000,000	42,000,000	40,000,000	1,803	8	239
13.	14.	Allen & Co.	125,360,169	125,360,169	0	58,481,492	N/A	1	4
17.	15.	A. G. Becker/Warburg Paribas Becker	119,089,000	94,970,000	24,119,000	36,337,000	2,600	17	160[8]
19.	16.	Bear, Stearns & Co.	112,000,000	90,000,000	22,000,000	50,191,795	2,420	11	700
15.	17.	Kidder, Peabody & Co.	108,700,000	94,000,000	14,700,000	29,000,000	3,800	64	1,050
16.	18.	Donaldson, Lufkin & Jenrette	105,500,000	68,000,000	37,500,000	34,200,000	2,260	10	149
20.	19.	Smith Barney, Harris Upham & Co.	94,676,000	57,739,000	36,937,000	35,471,000	4,410	91	1,320
18.	20.	Shelby Cullom Davis & Co.	92,056,980	92,056,980	0	41,827,041	N/A	3	4
21.	21.	L. F. Rothschild, Unterberg, Towbin	79,688,000[9]	60,533,000	19,155,000	27,072,000	1,292	9	478
22.	22.	Thomson McKinnon Securities	79,403,000	38,267,000	41,136,000	31,500,000	3,274	131	1,494
23.	23.	A. G. Edwards & Sons	73,367,504	73,367,504	0	41,527,000	2,693	175	1,325
24.	24.	Carl Marks & Co.	64,216,714	64,216,714	0	16,488,850	111	1	32
26.	25.	Spear, Leeds & Kellogg	60,352,369	41,549,619	18,802,750	14,973,526	559	7	56
25.	26.	Neuberger & Berman	55,978,134	55,978,134	0	23,875,488	328	1	40
28.	27.	Oppenheimer & Co.	50,625,000	28,243,000	22,382,000	15,433,000	1,340	7	350
27.	28.	Stern Brothers & Co.	47,700,000	47,700,000	0	26,800,000	69	4	20
30.	29.	John Nuveen & Co.	46,657,000	46,657,000	0	37,919,000	311	13	117
32.	30.	Alex. Brown & Sons	45,676,851	43,347,601	2,329,250	18,417,506	804	20	275
35.	31.	Moseley, Hallgarten, Estabrook & Weeden Holding Corp.	42,900,000	14,200,000	28,700,000	13,100,000	1,300	35	350
42	32.	Easton & Co.	38,853,000	37,483,000	1,370,000	20,615,000	56	3	5
34.	33.	Glickenhaus & Co.	38,502,000	38,202,000	300,000	26,751,000	41	2	17
33.	34.	Wertheim & Co.	37,940,000	30,390,000	7,550,000	5,800,000	397	4	94
—	35.	Cowen & Co.	35,302,265	28,457,265	6,845,000	19,877,073	751	13	350
37.	36.	Prescott, Ball & Turben	30,200,000	17,050,000	13,150,000	11,250,000	925	35	325
31.	37.	Dillon, Read & Co.	29,755,261	19,118,594	10,636,667	19,509,849	397	4	75
53.	38.	Rotan Mosle	28,062,969	28,062,969	0	10,210,681	832	16	225
—	39.	J. C. Bradford & Co.	27,231,934	27,231,934	0	8,890,000	620	41	280
40.	40.	Allen & Co. Inc.	26,611,970[5]	26,611,970	0	2,358,733	188	2	65
38.	41.	B. C. Ziegler and Co.	26,295,216	26,295,216	0	21,005,358	196	22	70
49.	42.	Gruntal & Co.	25,840,000	19,085,000	6,755,000	6,584,800	511	11	171
41.	43.	Piper, Jaffray & Hopwood	25,298,328	25,298,328	0	11,271,956	882	38	327
43.	44.	Dain Bosworth	24,909,000	22,159,000	2,750,000	8,989,000	916	40	363
47.	45.	Herzfeld & Stern	23,804,885	23,804,885	0	5,635,529	665	11	306
59.	46.	Advest	22,595,000	16,720,000	5,875,000	12,399,000	849	39	337
48.	47.	Batemen Eichler, Hill Richards	22,364,000	18,036,708	4,327,292	7,623,038	1,028	33	403
52.	48.	Wedbush, Noble, Cooke	21,259,755	19,297,000	1,962,755	12,818,327	416	20	150
56.	49.	Arnhold and S. Bleichroeder	20,830,000	17,830,000	3,000,000	10,065,007	120	1	14
50.	50.	M. A. Schapiro & Co.	19,762,777	19,762,777	0	9,045,647	28	1	6
54.	51.	Rauscher Pierce Refsnes	19,628,530	18,116,695	1,511,835	5,734,329	709	20	254
58.	52.	James Montgomery Scott	18,608,937	17,025,937	1,583,000	13,090,468	783	25	380

Rank 1980	Rank 1979	Firm	Total capital	Capital	Excess net capital	Net capital	(1)	(2)	(3)
54	51	Nomura Securities International	18,173,483	18,173,483	0	11,829,778	92	4	30
55	46	Lazard Freres & Co.	17,500,000	17,500,000	0	12,535,239	325	1	27
56	71	Robinson-Humphrey Co.	14,229,957	14,229,957	2,427,235	7,694,494	759	25	262
57	77	Eppler, Guerin & Turner	16,464,000	16,464,000	0	9,282,000	354	23	170
58	55	Mabon, Nugent & Co.	16,270,056	16,270,056	0	9,500,498	328	2	121
59	64	Foster & Marshall	16,220,000	16,220,000	0	6,155,000	785	47	304
60	60	Blunt Ellis & Loewi	16,099,874	16,099,874	0	5,158,204	693	49	300
61	70	Boettcher & Co.	15,476,347[10]	8,564,259	6,912,088	3,685,667	534	23	250
62	62	Ernst & Co.	15,382,712	14,582,712	800,000	5,337,460	156	3	38
63	61	Interstate Securities Corp.	15,337,053	10,187,053	5,150,000	6,106,778	505	47	154
64	78	Swiss American Securities	15,214,735	15,214,735	0	7,125,592	176	1	5
65	65	William Blair & Co.	14,376,258	14,376,258	0	5,919,631	254	4	131
66	85	Wheat First Securities	13,994,114	7,282,229	6,711,885	3,226,888	800	45	363
67	67	Tucker, Anthony & R. L. Day	13,854,514	10,675,514	3,179,000	5,030,699	836	28	392
68	79	Bacon, Whipple & Co.	13,160,025	13,160,025	0	3,312,793	190	3	75
69	69	Robert W. Baird & Co.	13,000,000	11,500,000	1,500,000	4,700,000	380	20	185
70	—	Hambrecht & Quist	12,800,473	12,800,473	0	5,470,894	90	1	20
71	75	Hickey & Co.	12,660,000	12,660,000	0	12,635,000	10		4
72	81	Underwood, Neuhaus & Co.	12,656,574	12,656,574	0	4,492,723	291	5	129
73	83	New Court Securities Corp.	12,541,312	12,541,312	0	4,143,251	78	1	6
74	74	Legg Mason Wood Walker	12,511,847	6,939,211	5,572,636	4,328,831	409	19	175
75	36	The Ohio Co.	11,961,824[11]	11,961,824	0	11,311,148	345	42	112
76	68	Daiwa Securities America	11,941,046	11,941,046	0	10,000,000	36	2	15
77	92	Van Kampen Filkin & Merritt	11,653,730	11,653,730	0	1,623,897	74	2	19
78	93	McDonald & Co.	11,597,106	10,597,106	1,000,000	5,742,460	330	19	88
79	76	Atlantic Capital Corp.	11,017,115	11,017,115	0	7,452,742	87	1	22
80	72	First Manhattan Co.	10,932,356	10,932,356	0	4,505,479	165	2	63
81	73	Folger Nolan Fleming Douglas	10,908,809	7,308,809	3,600,000	5,184,073	80	2	25
82	84	Sutro & Co.	10,771,701	8,583,201	2,188,500	2,998,000	534	15	175
83	—	Burns, Fry and Timmins	10,765,862	6,265,862	4,500,000	3,897,609	83	1	19
84	84	The Nikko Securities Co. International	10,324,849	10,324,849	0	4,093,300	41	3	15
85	—	EuroPartners Securities Corp.	10,081,839	10,081,839	0	8,774,478	53	1	13
86	86	Keefe, Bruyette & Woods	9,824,952	7,824,952	2,000,000	6,814,566	65	2	15
87	89	Fahnestock & Co.	9,820,589	9,095,589	725,000	2,565,929	604	24	186
88	88	B. C. Christopher & Co.	9,735,149	9,510,149	225,000	3,337,230	460	13	125
89	80	Mesirow & Co.	9,489,500	8,514,000	975,500	3,543,499	180	2	45
90	94	First of Michigan Corp.	9,099,095	9,099,095	0	4,152,246	335	20	187
91	90	J. J. B. Hilliard, W. L. Lyons	9,090,065	7,490,065	1,600,000	4,063,470	365	22	150
92	97	Butcher & Singer	9,054,000	6,028,000	3,026,000	2,449,000	653	28	215
93	91	Edward D. Jones & Co.	8,722,733	8,722,733	0	4,307,970	947	304	378
94	98	Ryan, Beck & Co.	8,587,000	8,587,000	0	5,281,000	80	1	34
95	87	Moore & Schley, Cameron & Co.	8,129,258	5,733,258	2,396,000	3,911,986	217	4	99
96	96	Reich & Co.	7,788,000	7,393,000	395,000	3,119,880	70	1	23
97	—	Yamaichi International (America)	7,500,000	7,500,000	0	4,215,000	47	2	18
98	—	F. Eberstadt & Co.	7,436,000	6,724,599	712,300	3,559,898	156	4	11
99	—	L. Cartwright & Co.	7,436,289	7,436,289	0	4,000,000	7	1	5
100	96	Cyrus J. Lawrence	7,318,389	5,568,389	1,750,000	3,330,218	167	1	65

[1] Excess net capital stated as of 9/26/80.
[2] Excess $30 million pursuant to profits participation agreement.
[3] All figures stated as of 9/30/80.
[4] Includes $150,000 redeemable preferred stock. All figures stated as of 10/31/80.
[5] All figures stated as of 11/30/80.
[6] Figures do not include holding company.
[7] Excess net capital stated as of 12/31/79.
[8] Producing personnel only.
[9] Includes $9,391,000 of freely withdrawable partners capital that is not used for regulatory capital purposes.
[10] All figures stated as of 9/26/80.
[11] All figures stated as of 12/26/80.

Source: Institutional Investor, April 1981.

The INC. 100 Fastest Growing Small Companies

Sales Growth 1976–80

1981	1980	Company	Percent Increase	Compound annual rate	Closing date	1980 Sales ($000)	1976 Sales ($000)
1	☐	Cobb Resources (Albuquerque)	366,567%	678%	6/30	$ 11,000	$ 3
2	☐	DSI (Nashville)	248,224	606	12/31	42,215	17
3	☐	Gulf Energy (Salt Lake City)	43,843	358	4/30	3,076	7
4	1	Tandem Computers (Cupertino, Calif.)	18,659	270	9/30	108,989	581
5	☐	Tandon (Chatsworth, Calif.)	12,475	235	9/26	22,761	181
6	☐	Electro-Biology (Fairfield, N.J.)	12,330	234	12/31	5,345	43
7	2	Cray Research (Mendota Heights, Minn.)	11,835	231	12/31	60,748	509
8	☐	Network Systems (Brooklyn Park, Minn.)	9,408	212	12/31	13,121	138
9	3	NBI (Boulder)	7,068	191	6/30	32,903	459
10	6	Cado Systems (Torrance, Calif.)	6,096	181	12/31	46,597	752
11	☐	Seal Fleet (Galveston)	5,036	168	12/31	11,402	222
12	☐	Nutri/System (Melrose Park, Pa.)	3,806	150	7/31	23,204	594
13	11	Printronix (Irvine, Calif.)	3,748	149	3/30	36,976	961
14	☐	Intelligent Systems (Norcross, Ga.)	3,684	148	3/31	14,492	383
15	☐	Creative Foods (Port Washington, N.Y.)	3,442	144	1/31	17,110	483
16	☐	Optel (Holbrook, Mass.)	3,317	142	12/31	120,876	3,538
17	☐	Saxon Oil (Dallas)	2,823	133	12/31	66,857[2]	2,287
18	☐	Bio-Medical Sciences (New York)	2,812	132	12/31	47,176[2]	1,620
19	4	Thousand Trails (Seattle)	2,799	132	12/31	33,950	1,171
20	10	RSI (Greenville, S.C.)	2,743	131	8/31	73,747	2,594
21	☐	Sterling Oil of Oklahoma (Tulsa)	2,681	130	12/31	14,600[1]	525
22	9	DPF (Hartsdale, N.Y.)	2,675	130	5/31	627,073	22,600
23	☐	Symbol Technologies (Hauppauge, N.Y.)	2,585	128	8/31	2,390	89
24	☐	Sterling Pipe & Supply (Oklahoma City)	2,579	127	10/31	48,644	1,816
25	☐	Silicon Systems (Tustin, Calif.)	2,325	122	9/30	10,500	433
26	☐	Dimis (Middleton, N.J.)	2,251	120	12/31	4,067	173
27	23	Air Florida System (Miami)	2,243	120	7/31	114,285	4,877
28	☐	Magnetic Head (Glen Head, N.Y.)	1,933	112	11/30	8,396	413
29	☐	Nike (Beaverton, Oreg.)	1,813	109	5/31	269,775	14,100
30	22	Tomlinson Oil (Wichita)	1,795	109	8/31	62,019	3,273
31	16	Wespercorp (Tustin, Calif.)	1,781	108	6/30	9,632	512
32	21	FSC (Pittsburgh)	1,719	107	12/31	159,861[2]	8,787
33	☐	Billings (Independence, Mo.)	1,643	104	12/31	10,007[1]	574
34	☐	Amarco Resources (Dallas)	1,518	101	6/30	7,604	470
35	26	Reeves Communications (New York)	1,512	100	6/30	44,408	2,754
36	☐	Tellabs (Lisle, Ill.)	1,499	100	12/31	43,680	2,732
37	☐	Pacer Technology & Resources (Campbell, Calif.)	1,483	99	12/31	4,100[1]	259
38	☐	Dysan (Santa Clara, Calif.)	1,424	98	10/31	62,871	4,125
39	☐	Polaris Resources (Denver)	1,395	97	12/31	9,000[1]	602
40	25	Triad Systems (Sunnyvale, Calif.)	1,363	96	9/30	56,513	3,864
41	100	Golden Oil (Denver)	1,362	96	6/30	3,568	244
42	☐	Chemold (Binghamton, N.Y.)	1,312	94	7/31	29,190	2,067
43	☐	Safecard Services (Ft. Lauderdale)	1,217	91	10/31	16,137	1,225
44	☐	Texas Energies (Amarillo)	1,217	91	4/30	1,528	116
45	☐	Transnet (Union, N.J.)	1,210	90	6/30	8,828	674
46	8	Floating Point Systems (Portland, Oreg.)	1,195	90	10/31	42,405	3,275
47	☐	Electromedics (Englewood, Colo.)	1,139	88	12/31	3,010	243
48	☐	Nuclear Pharmacy (Albuquerque)	1,137	88	5/31	12,275	992
49	☐	Sci Med Life Systems (Plymouth, Minn.)	1,107	86	2/29	3,029	251
50	20	Prime Computer (Natick, Mass.)	1,074	85	12/31	267,637	22,797

1980 Net income ($000)	1976 Net income ($000)	1980 Net income as % of sales	No of employees 1980	No of employees 1976	Acquisitions 1976-80	Date Inc.	Business description
$ 1,190	(40)	10.8	100	6	Yes	1969	Uranium, precious metals mining; oil & gas expl.
860	(121)	2.0	650	2	Yes	1967	Computer output microfilm and videotape services
140	(66)	4.6	84	12	Yes	1968	Oil, gas & coal development
10,687	(2,169)	9.8	1,630	71	No	1974	Mfr. multiple processor computers
1,507	20	6.6	578	20	No	1976	Mfr. flexible disk drives for minicomputers
(1,614)	(5)	—	145	8	No	1975	Medical services (electro-mag. treatment of fractures)
10,900	(1,551)	17.9	761	124	No	1972	Mfr. large-scale computers
1,884	(980)	14.4	204	37	No	1974	Mfr. data communications equipment
3,205	(860)	9.7	670	55	No	1973	Mfr. word processing systems
4,501	(107)	9.7	148	15	No	1973	Mfr. small business computers
1,805	(145)	8.2	200	2	Yes	1969	Owner-operator offshore supply vessels
3,751	44	16.2	425	45	Yes	1976	Owner/franchisor weight loss centers
3,137	(96)	8.5	850	60	No	1974	Mfr. computer line printers
487	(3)	3.4	185	20	No	1973	Mfr. display terminals & desktop computers
(103)	82	—	95[4]	10	No	1969	Operator 50 Burger King restaurants
1,442	(9,048)	1.2	840[4]	325	Yes	1969	Operator discount stores, drug wholesaler
5,750[2]	392	8.6	145	18	No	1968	Oil & gas exploration
2,572[3]	(5,159)	7.5[3]	625	296	Yes	1967	Mfr. women's sportswear & medical thermometers
4,536	(194)	13.4	790	75	Yes	1969	Develops/operates campground resorts
2,079	(695)	2.8	746	98	Yes	1972	Mfr. turf & heat transfer equip.; motels; bottler
300[1]	50	2.1	200	20	Yes	1948	Oil & gas production; mfr. mobile quarters; air service
7,400	2,234	1.2	14,000	150	Yes	1961	Equipment leasing; wholesale baking
(100)	(100)	—	68	5	No	1973	Mfr. laser scanners for bar coding
1,166	(183)	2.4	50	8	Yes	1976	Oil field equipment supplier
599	57	5.7	155	17	No	1972	Mfr. custom integrated circuits
480	(227)	11.8	41	7	No	1974	Designs/sells EDP systems for wholesalers
5,070	(748)	4.4	1,900	200	Yes	1955	Commercial airline
429	(110)	5.1	128	20	Yes	1968	Mfr. precision parts & protective coatings
12,505	600	4.6	2,600	400	No	1968	Mfr. athletic footwear
2,992	1,367	4.8	57	28	Yes	1957	Oil & gas exploration, production, refining
765	30	7.9	153	30	No	1975	Mfr. controllers for mini/micro computers
4,019[3]	(112)	3.4[3]	996	48	Yes	1969	Mfr. dry cleaning equip.; leasing; refinery
(608)[2]	(108)	—	218	38	Yes	1973	Mfr. hydrides & electrolyzers; hydrogen research
181	30	2.4	170	20	Yes	1972	Oil field services; oil & gas production
3,946	23	8.9	330	168	Yes	1969	Producer/distributor of movies for TV & cinema
6,608	194	15.1	571	48	No	1975	Mfr. telephone switching & signalling equipment
602[3]	17	18.7[3]	100	13	No	1975	Mfr. industrial adhesives
7,993	393	12.7	1,800	200	Yes	1972	Mfr. rotating magnetic media for computers
175[1]	2	1.9	50	15	Yes	1969	Oil & gas exploration; mining equipment supplier
5,031	201	8.9	1,000	80	No	1972	Mfr. microcomputer systems
872	(173)	24.4	7	2	No	1970	Oil & gas exploration
1,174	(1,193)	4.0	311	97	Yes	1949	Mfr. women's swimwear; refrigeration equip.
3,056	315	18.9	200	20	No	1969	Direct mail & marketing services
234	75	15.3	28	6	Yes	1966	Oil & gas exploration
971	(100)	11.0	29	6	Yes	1969	Marketing/leasing of computer terminals & equip.
3,765	479	8.9	850	82	No	1970	Mfr. array processors
230	(691)	7.6	106	5	No	1972	Mfr. medical temperature devices
(272)	(174)	—	250	100	Yes	1974	Dispenser of radio-pharmaceuticals
183	(135)	6.0	95	30	No	1972	Mfr. disposable & implantable medical products
31,222	2,429	11.7	4,011	520	No	1972	Mfr. computers

THE INC. 100 *(continued)*

Rank 1981	Rank 1980	Company	Sales Growth 1976–80 Percent increase	Sales Growth 1976–80 Compound annual rate	Closing date	1980 Sales ($000)	1976 Sales ($000)
51	5	Volunteer Capital (Brentwood, Tenn.)	1,051%	84%	12/31	$ 62,081	$ 5,394
52	☐	Nord Resources (Dayton)	1,050	84	12/31	12,471²	1,084
53	17	Econo-Therm Energy Systems (Minnetonka, Minn.)	1,041	84	2/28	24,585	2,154
54	29	Shopsmith (Vandalia, Ohio)	1,032	83	3/31	30,107	2,659
55	☐	Intermedics (Freeport, Tex.)	1,001	82	10/31	105,208	9,558
56	51	Petroleum Equipment Tools (Houston)	896	78	12/31	92,715	9,306
57	30	Commodore (Syracuse, Ind.)	896	78	6/30	179,954	18,066
58	28	Rolm (Santa Clara, Calif.)	886	77	6/29	200,729	20,357
59	33	Data Terminal Systems (Maynard, Mass.)	868	76	1/31	107,192	11,074
60	☐	Hurco Manufacturing (Indianapolis)	863	76	10/31	28,490	2,959
61	13	Acton (Acton, Mass.)	846	75	12/31	186,720	19,745
62	☐	Compact Video Systems (Burbank, CA)	808	74	4/30	34,002	3,744
63	☐	M.D.C. (Denver)	792	73	12/31	32,600	3,656
64	☐	Inter-Tel (Phoenix)	790	73	11/30	10,648	1,197
65	41	Quality Care (Rockville Centre, N.Y.)	770	72	11/30	30,738²	3,534
66	☐	Minnetonka (Chaska, Minn.)	767	72	12/31	73,214	8,446
67	☐	Petrominerals (Santa Ana, Calif.)	764	71	12/31	25,000¹	2,894
68	☐	Team (Houston)	747	71	5/31	24,197	2,856
69	☐	Staodynamics (Longmont, Colo.)	732	70	2/28	3,268	393
70	45	Data Access Systems (Blackwood, N.J.)	727	70	8/31	37,242	4,504
71	37	Chem-Nuclear Systems (Bellevue, Wash.)	720	69	7/31	46,390	5,655
72	☐	Nucorp Energy (San Diego)	717	69	12/31	93,951	11,493
73	32	Chuck Barris Productions (Hollywood)	714	69	5/31	38,514	4,730
74	☐	Health Extension Services (Syosset, N.Y.)	713	69	9/30	5,153	634
75	79	Interface Mechanisms (Lynnwood, Wash.)	690	68	3/31	10,164	1,287
76	☐	Swanton (New York)	688	68	1/31	9,327	1,183
77	☐	Newport Pharmaceuticals (Newport Beach, Calif.)	681	67	4/30	4,661	597
78	☐	CGA Computer Associates (Cranford, N.J.)	676	67	4/30	19,227	2,479
79	35	Rampart General (Santa Ana, Calif.)	676	67	3/31	27,589	3,553
80	☐	Mentor (Minneapolis)	673	67	3/31	2,946	381
81	☐	Ind'l. Solid State Controls (York, Pa.)	670	67	6/30	33,207	4,312
82	52	Auto-trol Technology (Denver)	640	65	12/31	51,600¹	6,971
83	55	Coradian (Latham, N.Y.)	637	65	12/31	35,919	4,875
84	☐	Key Pharmaceuticals (Miami)	630	64	12/31	23,726	3,252
85	☐	Seneca Oil (Oklahoma City)	617	64	9/30	8,591	1,198
86	☐	Dyco Petroleum (St. Louis Park, Minn.)	616	64	12/31	32,377	4,519
87	☐	Chomerics (Woburn, Mass.)	611	63	12/31	31,029	4,364
88	68	Paradyne (Largo, Fla.)	608	63	12/31	75,907	10,722
89	27	Telecom Equipment (Long Island City)	604	63	12/31	40,000¹	5,682
90	☐	Andersen 2000 (College Park, Ga.)	574	61	9/30	5,942	882
91	☐	Petro-Lewis (Denver)	572	61	6/30	111,087	16,531
92	☐	Kratos (La Jolla, Calif.)	568	61	12/31	55,507	8,313
93	63	Adac Laboratories (Sunnyvale, Calif.)	554	60	9/30	18,782	2,870
94	☐	Flight Transportation (Eden Prairie, Minn.)	551	60	6/30	8,039	1,234
95	92	Matrix (Northvale, N.J.)	550	60	8/31	19,571	3,009
96	☐	Presidio Oil (Denver)	542	59	6/30	4,919	766
97	☐	C3 (Reston, Va.)	528	58	3/31	13,984	2,228
98	☐	Kinder-Care Learning Centers (Montgomery, Ala.)	521	58	5/30	56,578	9,109
99	☐	Delhi International Oil (Dallas)	515	58	12/31	27,138	4,410
100	53	Wainoco Oil (Houston)	510	57	12/31	36,009	5,901

¹ Company estimate.
² INC. estimate.
³ 9-month figure.
⁴ Excludes part-time employees.

1980 Net Income ($000)	1976 Net Income ($000)	1980 Net Income as % of sales	No. of employees 1980	No. of employees 1976	Acquisitions 1976–1980	Date Inc.	Business description
$ (101)	370	—	5,310	566	Yes	1971	Fast-food franchisee & restaurant chain (Wendy's)
(184)³	(423)	—	210	348	Yes	1971	Mineral/ore mining & exploration
(257)	(61)	—	450	40	Yes	1961	Mfr. energy-related equip. for petrochemical industry
1,445	233	4.8	1,200	73	Yes	1972	Mfr. woodworking equipment
10,732	887	10.2	1,575	371	Yes	1973	Mfr. cardiac pacemakers, eye lenses, biomedical devices
13,822	1,445	14.9	1,196	398	Yes	1967	Rents oil & gas drilling equipment
(2,601)	(678)	—	2,400	400	Yes	1952	Mfr. mobile homes & recreation vehicles
17,340	1,264	8.6	4,225	475	Yes	1969	Mfr. computers & telephone switching systems
9,550	1,000	8.9	2,000	150	Yes	1970	Mfr. electronic terminals & cash registers
256	440	0.9	365	70	No	1968	Mfr. computerized machine tools
4,798	1,521	2.6	3,500	125	Yes	1960	Mfr. snack foods; owner/operator cable TV, radio
2,280	308	6.7	400	150	Yes	1971	Mfr./rental mobile video units & systems
2,183	139	6.7	130	49	No	1972	Real estate development, welding supplier
1,051	81	9.9	110	18	No	1969	Mfr. digital & electromech. telephone systems
64³	29	0.3³	2,100	241	Yes	1969	Home health care services, franchises
5,534	307	7.6	600	175	Yes	1964	Mfr. personal care products
4,993³	730	22.2³	200	10	Yes	1966	Oil & gas exploration
1,639	225	6.8	625	300	Yes	1973	Oilfield & energy conservation services
27	(52)	0.8	98	30	Yes	1975	Mfr. nerve stimulators
5,148	609	13.8	393	68	Yes	1969	Data terminal & peripheral equipment supplier
4,479	739	9.7	381	79	Yes	1969	Nuclear & chemical waste disposal services
8,845	(119)	9.4	1,200	147	Yes	1967	Oil & gas exploration; mfr. energy equip.
6,316	367	16.4	120	14	No	1968	TV programs & film production
235	(11)	4.6	2,000	8	No	1975	Home health care & related equipment rental
863	95	8.5	288	33	No	1969	Mfr. label printing & reading devices
952	(171)	10.2	70	9	Yes	1972	Coal & gas production; financial services
(333)	(381)	—	120	49	Yes	1971	Develop/mfr. antiviral pharmaceutical compounds
1,760	308	9.2	368	77	Yes	1968	Computer consulting services & software packages
(431)	(249)	—	180	28	No	1966	Mfr. fireplaces; real estate development
63	(44)	2.1	32	12	No	1969	Mfr. clinical devices; bio-medical engineering
1,866	78	5.6	649	200	Yes	1962	Mfr. programmable controllers
4,500¹	460	8.7	650	112	No	1962	Mfr. interactive graphic systems & digitizers
553	(2)	1.5	500	127	No	1959	Sells/services private telephone systems
3,177	373	13.4	400	100	Yes	1947	Mfr. ethical drugs
2,220	229	25.8	48	8	No	1936	Oil & gas exploration
8,503	1,530	26.3	150	39	Yes	1971	Mgmt. of public drilling programs for oil & gas
1,821	152	5.9	700	90	Yes	1961	Mfr. keyboards & shielding materials
8,247	516	10.9	1,736	229	No	1969	Mfr. data communications equipment
2,670¹	(466)	6.7	530	55	Yes	1969	Mfr. private telephone systems
536	173	9.0	27	16	No	1971	Mfr. pollution control equipment
22,259	1,030	20.0	1,500	300	Yes	1968	Oil & gas production
3,447	556	6.2	1,092	392	Yes	1964	Mfr. precision instruments
880	(497)	4.7	349	100	No	1970	Mfr. imaging computers for nuclear medicine
319	(7)	4.0	52	77	No	1968	Charter airline
1,858	23	9.5	260	54	Yes	1956	Mfr. diagnostic medical instruments
281	(13)	5.7	38	6	Yes	1976	Oil exploration & production
2,354	435	16.8	150	35	No	1971	Data processing systems design & services
3,449	510	6.1	7,200	1,300	Yes	1969	Day care services & learning centers
4,784	1,802	17.6	260	140	Yes	1958	Oil & gas exploration, contract drilling
7,051	1,542	19.6	250	48	No	1949	Oil & gas exploration, production

HOW THE INC. 100 ARE SELECTED

To be included in the INC. 100, each company must meet these criteria:

1. The company is an independent, publicly held corporation in a manufacturing, mining, or service industry. Utilities, banks, insurance companies, and other financial institutions are excluded.
2. The company's sales or revenues were less than $25 million in 1976.
3. The company shows a sales/revenues history of at least five years, with a demonstrated increase in its fiscal 1980 closing figure. Firms showing growth in the 1976–80 base period but a sales decline in the last year are excluded.

Sales and income figures were first gathered from 10-Ks, prospectuses, annual reports, and various data bases and directories. Additional information was collected from stock reports, trade magazines, and general business publications. By applying the three criteria above, as well as a five-year growth rate of at least 400%, the number of companies that potentially qualified for listing was pared from 8,600 to less than 500. Telephone interviews were conducted with corporate executives to verify the figures and an editorial team led by senior editor Bradford Ketchum, Jr., then selected the 1981 INC. 100.

INC. 100/INDEX

Trading	P/E Ratio	Company (Rank)	Trading	P/E Ratio	Company (Rank)	Trading	P/E Ratio	Company (Rank)
AMEX	12	Acton* (61)	OTC	23	Floating Point Systems* (46)	OTC	NA	Polaris Resources (39)
OTC	42	Adac Laboratories* (93)	OTC	41	Golden Oil** (41)	OTC	77	Presidio Oil (96)
OTC	33	Air Florida System* (27)	OTC	244	Gulf Energy (3)	NYSE	27	Prime Computer** (50)
OTC	42	Amarco Resources (34)	OTC	71	Health Extension Services (74)	OTC	21	Printronix* (13)
OTC	30	Andersen 2000 (90)	OTC	307	Hurco Manufacturing (60)	OTC	NA	Quality Care* (65)
OTC	17	Auto-trol Technology* (82)	OTC	14	Ind'l. Solid State Controls (81)	OTC	NA	RSI* (20)
OTC	loss	Billings (33)	OTC	62	Intelligent Systems (14)	OTC	loss	Rampart General** (79)
OTC	7	Bio-Medical Sciences (18)	OTC	24	Interface Mechanisms* (75)	OTC	27	Reeves Communications* (35)
OTC	22	CGA Computer Associates (78)	OTC	20	Intermedics (55)	NYSE	30	Rolm** (58)
OTC	27	C3 (97)	OTC	66	Inter-Tel (64)	OTC	15	SafeCard Services (43)
OTC	21	Cado Systems* (10)	AMEX	79	Key Pharmaceuticals (84)	OTC	24	Saxon Oil (17)
OTC	20	Chem-Nuclear Systems* (71)	OTC	26	Kinder-Care Learning Centers (98)	OTC	73	Sci Med Life Systems (49)
OTC	NA	Chemold (42)				OTC	12	Seal Fleet (11)
OTC	19	Chomerics (87)	OTC	12	Kratos (92)	OTC	32	Seneca Oil (85)
OTC	26	Chuck Barris Productions* (73)	OTC	12	M.D.C. (63)	OTC	8	Shopsmith* (54)
AMEX	loss	Cobb Resources (1)	AMEX	NA	Magnetic Head (28)	OTC	49	Silicon Systems (25)
OTC	16	Commodore* (57)	AMEX	31	Matrix* (95)	OTC	34	Staodynamics (69)
OTC	16	Compact Video Systems (62)	OTC	28	Mentor (80)	OTC	30	Sterling Oil of Oklahoma (21)
OTC	16	Coradian* (83)	OTC	16	Minnetonka (66)	OTC	16	Sterling Pipe & Supply (24)
NYSE	42	Cray Research** (7)	OTC	36	NBI* (9)	OTC	10	Swanton (76)
OTC	loss	Creative Foods (15)	OTC	49	Network Systems (8)	OTC	loss	Symbol Technologies (23)
NYSE	5	DPF* (22)	OTC	loss	Newport Pharmaceuticals (77)	OTC	51	Tandem Computers** (4)
OTC	18	DSI (2)	OTC	18	Nike (29)	OTC	51	Tandon (5)
AMEX	10	Data Access Systems* (70)	OTC	NA	Nord Resources (52)	OTC	15	Team (68)
NYSE	10	Data Terminal Systems* (59)	OTC	83	Nuclear Pharmacy (48)	OTC	41	Telecom Equipment** (89)
AMEX	143	Delhi International Oil (99)	OTC	25	Nucorp Energy (72)	OTC	18	Tellabs (36)
OTC	21	Dimis (26)	OTC	14	Nutri/System (12)	OTC	35	Texas Energies (44)
NYSE	28	Dyco Petroleum (86)	OTC	2	Optel (16)	OTC	7	Thousand Trails* (19)
OTC	49	Dysan (38)	OTC	95	Pacer Technology & Resources (37)	OTC	30	Tomlinson Oil** (30)
OTC	loss	Econo-Therm Energy Systems** (53)	AMEX	42	Paradyne* (88)	OTC	11	Transnet (45)
OTC	loss	Electro-Biology (6)	OTC	18	Petroleum Equipment Tools* (56)	OTC	29	Triad Systems* (40)
OTC	NA	Electromedics (47)				OTC	46	Volunteer Capital** (51)
OTC	2	FSC* (32)	AMEX	18	Petro-Lewis (91)	AMEX	32	Wainoco Oil** (100)
OTC	10	Flight Transportation (94)	OTC	NA	Petrominerals (67)	OTC	16	Wespercorp* (31)

*1980 INC. 100   **1979/1980 INC. 100   OTC - Over-the-counter   AMEX - American Stock Exchange   NYSE - New York Stock Exchange
P/E Ratio - Price as of February 27, 1981 divided by latest 12-month earnings.

Source: Reprinted with permission of INC., May 1981. Copyright © 1981 by INC. Publishing Company.

Stock Market

STOCK EXCHANGES

Common Stocks (shares of ownership in a corporation) are traded on several exchanges. The best known are the New York Stock Exchange and the American Stock Exchange, both located in Manhattan's financial district. Generally, the stocks of the largest companies are traded on the New York Stock Exchange, while somewhat smaller companies are traded on the American Exchange. There are also a number of regional exchanges such as the Midwest Exchange in Chicago and the Pacific Exchange in San Francisco. These exchanges trade stocks of local corporations as well as stocks listed on the New York and American Exchanges.

In addition, there is the Over-The-Counter Market (OTC) which, unlike the exchanges previously mentioned, does not have a specific location but consists of a network of brokers and dealers linked by telephone and private wires. Smaller or relatively new companies are traded on the OTC. Trading information for many (but far from all) stocks on the OTC market is collected and displayed on a computerized system, the National Association of Security Dealers Automatic Quote System (NASDAQ).

Large institutional traders (mutual and pension funds, insurance companies, etc.) often trade blocks of stocks directly with one another. This information is collected and displayed on the Instinet System.

MAJOR STOCK EXCHANGES

UNITED STATES

AMERICAN STOCK EXCHANGE, INC.
86 Trinity Place
New York, New York 10006

BOSTON STOCK EXCHANGE, INC.
53 State Street
Boston, Massachusetts 02109

THE CINCINNATI STOCK EXCHANGE, INC.
205 Dixie Terminal Building
Cincinnati, Ohio 45202

INTERMOUNTAIN STOCK EXCHANGE, INC.
39 Exchange Place
Salt Lake City, Utah 84111

MIDWEST STOCK EXCHANGE, INC.
120 South LaSalle Street
Chicago, Illinois 60603

NEW YORK STOCK EXCHANGE, INC.
11 Wall Street
New York, New York 10005

PACIFIC STOCK EXCHANGE, INC.
301 Pine Street
San Francisco, California 94104
and
618 South Spring Street
Los Angeles, California 90014

PHILADELPHIA STOCK EXCHANGE, INC.
17th Street & Stock Exchange Place
Philadelphia, Pennsylvania 19103

SPOKANE STOCK EXCHANGE, INC.
225 Peyton Building
Spokane, Washington 99201

CANADA

ALBERTA STOCK EXCHANGE
201 Sun Oil Building
500–4th Ave. S.W.
Calgary, Alberta T2P 2V6

MONTREAL STOCK EXCHANGE
The Stock Exchange Tower
800 Victoria Square
Montreal, Quebec H4Z 1A9

TORONTO STOCK EXCHANGE
234 Bay Street
Toronto, Ontario M5J 1R1

VANCOUVER STOCK EXCHANGE
536 Howe Street
Vancouver, B.C. V6C 2E1

WINNIPEG STOCK EXCHANGE
420, 167 Lombard Avenue
Winnipeg, Manitoba R3B OT

Investment Returns on Stocks, Bonds, and Bills

Roger G. Ibbotson *

Our look at history consists of examining the returns of five capital market sectors. We measure total returns (capital gains plus income) on common stocks, long-term corporate bonds, long-term government bonds, U.S. Treasury bills, and rates of inflation on consumer goods. Comparing the returns from the various sectors gives us insights into the returns available from taking risk and the relationships between capital market returns and inflation.

THE RISKS AND REWARDS

We display graphically the rewards and risks available from the U.S. capital markets over the past 55 years. Exhibit 1 shows the growth of

EXHIBIT 1: WEALTH INDEXES OF INVESTMENTS IN THE U.S. CAPITAL MARKETS, 1926–1980

(assumed initial investment of $1.00 at year-end 1925, includes reinvestment income)

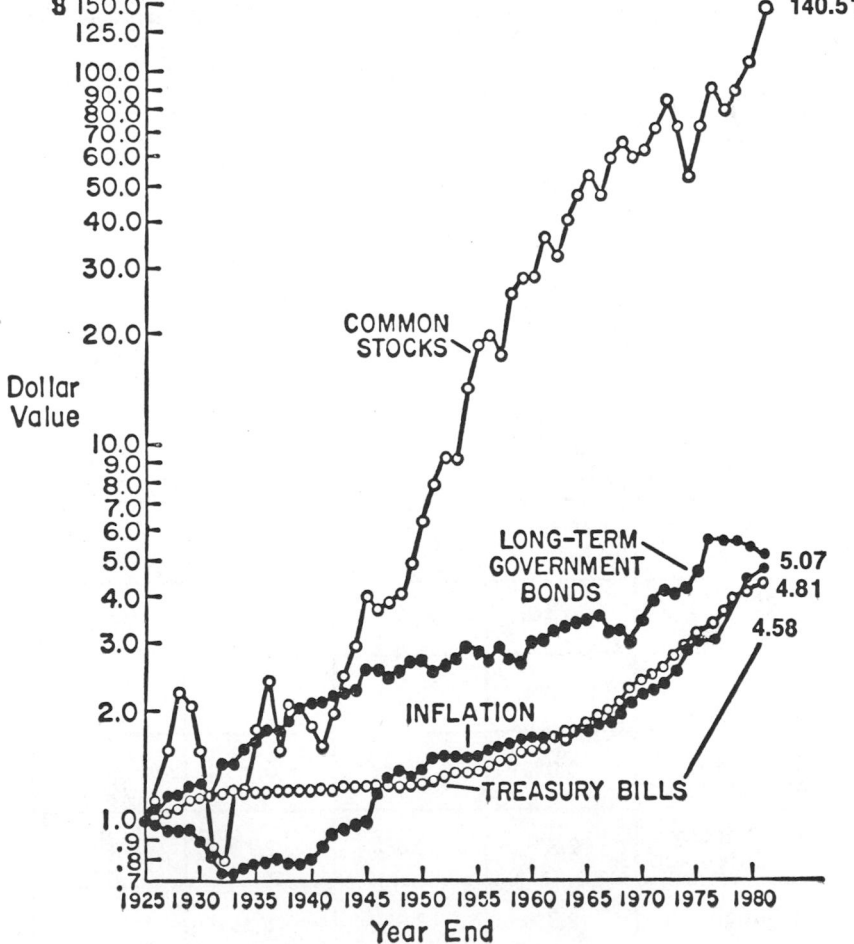

Source: Roger G. Ibbotson and Rex A. Sinquefield, *Stocks, Bonds, Bills, and Inflation: The Past and The Future* (1981 Edition), Financial Analysts Research Foundation (Charlottesville, Va.: 1981).

* Professor, Graduate School of Business, University of Chicago, Chicago, Illinois.

an investment in common stocks, long-term government bonds, and Treasury bills as well as the increase in the inflation index over the 55-year period. Each of the series is initiated at $1 at year-end 1925. The vertical scale is logarithmic so that equal distances represent equal percentage changes anywhere along the axis. The graph vividly portrays that common stocks were the big winner over the entire period. If $1 were invested in stocks at year-end 1925 and all dividends reinvested, the dollar investment would have grown to $140.51 by year-end 1980. This phenomenal growth was not without substantial risk, especially during the earlier portion of the period. In contrast, long-term government bonds (with a constant 20-year maturity) exhibited much less risk, but grew to only $5.07.

A virtually riskless strategy (for those with short-term time horizons) has been to buy U.S. Treasury bills. However, Treasury bills have had a marked tendency to track inflation, with the result that their real (inflation adjusted) return is near zero for the entire 1926–1980 period. Note that the tracking is only prevalent over the latter portion of the period. During periods of deflation (such as the late 1920s and early 1930s) the Treasury bill returns were near zero, but not negative, since no one intentionally buys securities with negative yields. Beginning in the early 1940s, the yields (returns) on Treasury bills were pegged by the government at low rates while high inflation was experienced. The government pegging ended with the U.S. Treasury-Federal Reserve Accord in March 1951.

We summarize the investment returns in Exhibit 2 by presenting the average annual returns over the 1926–1980 period. Common stocks returned a compounded (geometric mean) total return of 9.4 percent per year. The annual compound return from capital appreciation alone was 4.4 percent. After adjusting for inflation, annual compounded total returns were 6.2 percent per year.*

The average total return over any single year (arithmetic mean) for stocks was 11.7 percent, with positive returns recorded in more than two-thirds of the years (37 out of 55 years). The risk or degree of return fluctuation is measured by standard deviation as 22.0 percent. The frequency distribution (histogram) counts the number of years the returns fell in each 5 percent return increment. Note the wide variations in common stock returns relative to the other capital market sectors. Annual stock returns ranged from 54.0 percent in 1933 to −43.3 percent in 1931.

A simple example illustrates the difference between geometric and arithmetic means. Sup-

---

* Editor's note: Over the current decade the compounded growth rate for common stock with dividends reinvested after adjusting for inflation has been considerably less than the long-term value of 6.2 percent. Thus from the beginning of 1971 to the end of 1980 the compounded growth rate before adjusting for inflation has been 8.4 percent for common stock as compared to 4.2 percent for long-term corporate bonds and 6.8 percent for U.S. Treasury bills. All figures neglect taxes. The inflation rate during this period was 8.1 percent. After inflationary adjustments and income taxes, it is evident that all of these investments resulted in a net loss in terms of real income. Assuming a 40 percent tax rate and an 8 percent inflation rate, investments must earn 13.3 percent before taxes to break even.

EXHIBIT 2:   BASIC SERIES, INVESTMENT TOTAL ANNUAL RETURNS, 1926–1980

Series	Geometric Mean	Arithmetic Mean	Standard Deviation	Distribution
Common Stocks	9.4%	11.7%	22.0%	
Long-Term Corporate Bonds	3.7%	3.8%	5.6%	
Long-Term Government Bonds	3.0%	3.1%	5.7%	
U.S. Treasury Bills	2.8%	2.8%	2.7%	
Inflation	2.9%	3.0%	5.1%	

-50%   0%   +50%

Source: Ibbotson and Sinquefield, *Stocks, Bonds, Bills, and Inflation.*

EXHIBIT 3: BASIC SERIES, INDEXES OF YEAR-END CUMULATIVE WEALTH, 1925–1980

Year	Common Stocks		Long-Term Government Bonds		Long-Term Corporate Bonds	U.S. Treasury Bills	Consumer Price Index
	Total Returns	Capital Appreciation Only	Total Returns	Capital Appreciation Only	Total Returns	Total Returns	Rates of Inflation
1925	1.000	1.000	1.000	1.000	1.000	1.000	1.000
1926	1.116	1.057	1.078	1.039	1.074	1.033	0.985
1927	1.535	1.384	1.174	1.095	1.154	1.065	0.965
1928	2.204	1.908	1.175	1.061	1.186	1.099	0.955
1929	2.018	1.681	1.215	1.059	1.225	1.152	0.957
1930	1.516	1.202	1.272	1.072	1.323	1.179	0.899
1931	0.859	0.636	1.204	0.981	1.299	1.192	0.814
1932	0.789	0.540	1.407	1.108	1.439	1.204	0.730
1933	1.214	0.792	1.406	1.073	1.588	1.207	0.734
1934	1.197	0.745	1.547	1.146	1.808	1.209	0.749
1935	1.767	1.053	1.624	1.170	1.982	1.211	0.771
1936	2.367	1.346	1.746	1.225	2.116	1.213	0.780
1937	1.538	0.827	1.750	1.194	2.174	1.217	0.804
1938	2.016	1.035	1.847	1.228	2.307	1.217	0.782
1939	2.008	0.979	1.957	1.271	2.399	1.217	0.778
1940	1.812	0.829	2.076	1.319	2.480	1.217	0.786
1941	1.602	0.681	2.095	1.305	2.548	1.218	0.862
1942	1.927	0.766	2.162	1.315	2.614	1.221	0.942
1943	2.427	0.915	2.207	1.310	2.688	1.225	0.972
1944	2.906	1.041	2.270	1.314	2.815	1.229	0.993
1945	3.965	1.361	2.513	1.423	2.930	1.233	1.015
1946	3.645	1.199	2.511	1.392	2.980	1.238	1.199
1947	3.853	1.199	2.445	1.327	2.911	1.244	1.307
1948	4.065	1.191	2.528	1.340	3.031	1.254	1.343
1949	4.829	1.313	2.691	1.395	3.132	1.268	1.318
1950	6.360	1.600	2.692	1.366	3.198	1.283	1.395
1951	7.888	1.863	2.586	1.281	3.112	1.302	1.477
1952	9.336	2.082	2.616	1.262	3.221	1.324	1.490
1953	9.244	1.944	2.711	1.270	3.331	1.348	1.499
1954	14.108	2.820	2.906	1.325	3.511	1.360	1.492
1955	18.561	3.564	2.868	1.271	3.527	1.381	1.497
1956	19.778	3.658	2.708	1.164	3.287	1.415	1.540
1957	17.648	3.134	2.910	1.208	3.573	1.459	1.587
1958	25.298	4.327	2.733	1.097	3.494	1.482	1.615
1959	28.322	4.694	2.671	1.029	3.460	1.526	1.639
1960	28.455	4.554	3.039	1.124	3.774	1.566	1.663
1961	36.106	5.607	3.068	1.092	3.956	1.600	1.674
1962	32.955	4.945	3.280	1.122	4.270	1.643	1.695
1963	40.469	5.879	3.319	1.092	4.364	1.695	1.723
1964	47.139	6.642	3.436	1.084	4.572	1.754	1.743
1965	53.008	7.244	3.460	1.047	4.552	1.823	1.777
1966	47.674	6.295	3.586	1.036	4.560	1.910	1.836
1967	59.104	7.560	3.257	0.895	4.335	1.991	1.892
1968	65.642	8.139	3.248	0.846	4.446	2.094	1.981
1969	60.059	7.210	3.083	0.754	4.086	2.232	2.102
1970	62.465	7.222	3.457	0.791	4.837	2.378	2.218
1971	71.406	8.001	3.914	0.843	5.370	2.482	2.292
1972	84.956	9.252	4.136	0.840	5.760	2.577	2.371
1973	72.500	7.645	4.090	0.775	5.825	2.756	2.579
1974	53.311	5.373	4.268	0.748	5.647	2.976	2.894
1975	73.144	7.068	4.661	0.754	6.474	3.149	3.097
1976	90.584	8.422	5.441	0.815	7.681	3.309	3.246
1977	84.076	7.453	5.405	0.750	7.813	3.479	3.466
1978	89.592	7.532	5.342	0.682	7.807	3.728	3.778
1979	106.112	8.459	5.277	0.615	7.481	4.115	4.281
1980	140.513	10.639	5.069	0.530	7.285	4.578	4.812

Source: Ibbotson and Sinquefield, *Stocks, Bonds, Bills, and Inflation.*

pose $1 were invested in a common stock port-folio that experiences successive annual returns of +50 percent and −50 percent. At the end of the first year, the portfolio is worth $1.50. At the end of the second year, the portfolio is worth $0.75. The annual arithmetic mean is 0 percent, whereas the annual geometric mean (compounded return) is −13.4 percent. Natu-rally, it is the geometric mean that more di-rectly measures the change in wealth over more than one period. On the other hand, the arith-metic mean is a better representation of typical performance over any single annual period.

The other capital market sectors also had returns commensurate with their risks. Long-term corporate bonds outperformed the de-fault-free, long-term government bonds, which in turn outperformed the essentially riskless U.S. Treasury bills. Over the entire period the riskless U.S. Treasury bills had a return almost identical with the inflation rate. Thus, we again note that the real rate of interest (the inflation-adjusted riskless rate) has been on average very near 0 percent historically.

MEASUREMENT OF THE FIVE SERIES

The returns were computed by compound-ing monthly returns, with no adjustments made for transactions costs or taxes. We describe each of the five total return series which are listed annually in Exhibit 3.

COMMON STOCKS

The total return index is based upon Stan-dard & Poor's (S&P) Composite Index with divi-dends reinvested monthly. To the extent that the 500 stocks currently included in the S&P Composite Index (prior to March 1957, there were 90 stocks) are representative of all stocks in the United States, the market value weight-ing scheme allows the returns of the index to correspond to the aggregate stock market re-turns in the U.S. economy.

LONG-TERM CORPORATE BONDS

We measure the total returns of a corporate bond index with approximately 20 years to ma-turity. We use Salomon Brothers' High-Grade Long-Term Corporate Bond Index from its be-ginning in 1969 through 1980. For the period 1946–68 we backdate Salomon Brothers' index using Salomon Brothers' monthly yield data and similar methodology. For the period 1926–45 we compute returns using Standard & Poor's monthly high-grade corporate composite bond yield data, assuming a 4 percent coupon and a 20-year maturity.

LONG-TERM GOVERNMENT BONDS

To measure the total returns of long-term U.S. government bonds, we use the bond data obtained from the U.S. Government Bond File (constructed by Lawrence Fisher) at the Center for Research in Security Prices (CRSP) at the University of Chicago. We attempt to maintain a 20-year bond portfolio whose returns do not reflect the potential tax benefits, impaired ne-gotiability, or the special redemption or call privileges frequently characterizing govern-ment bond prices and yields.

U.S. TREASURY BILLS

For the U.S. Treasury bill index, we again use the data in the CRSP U.S. Government Bond File. We measure one-month holding pe-riod returns for the shortest-term bills not less than one month in maturity. Since U.S. Trea-sury bills were not initiated until 1929, we use short-term coupon bonds whenever bill quotes are unavailable.

CONSUMER PRICE INDEX

We utilize the Consumer Price Index (CPI) to measure inflation. The CPI is constructed by the U.S. Department of Labor, Bureau of Labor Statistics, Washington, D.C.

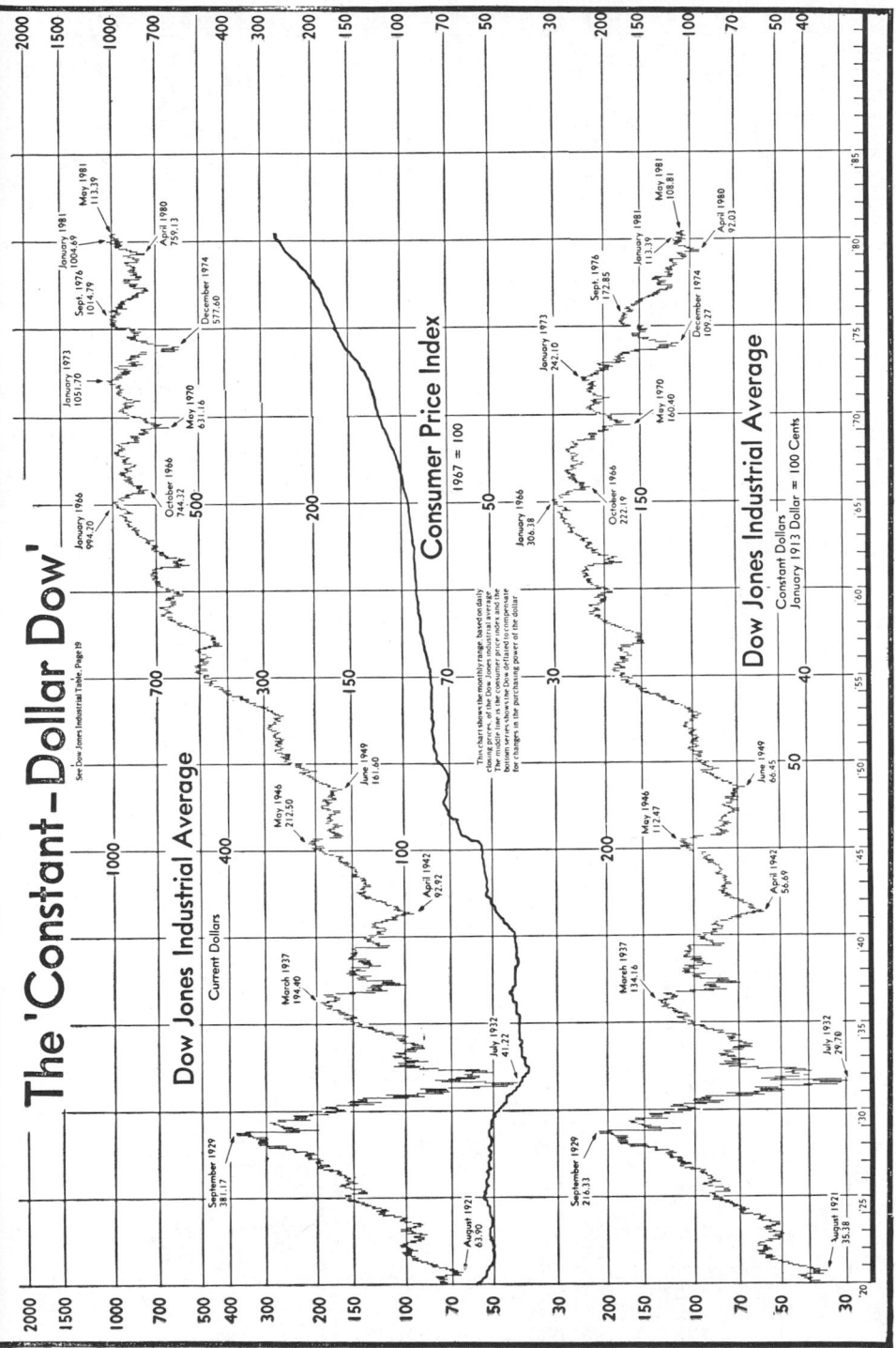

The 'Constant-Dollar Dow'

See Dow Jones Industrial Table, Page 19

Dow Jones Industrial Average
Current Dollars

September 1929
381.17

August 1921
63.90

July 1932
41.22

March 1937
194.40

April 1942
92.92

May 1946
212.50

June 1949
161.60

January 1966
994.20

October 1966
744.32

January 1973
1051.70

May 1970
631.16

December 1974
577.60

September 1976
1014.79

January 1981
1004.69

May 1981
1113.39

April 1980
759.13

Consumer Price Index
1967 = 100

This chart shows the monthly range, based on daily closing prices, of the Dow Jones industrial average. The middle line is the consumer price index and the bottom series shows the Dow deflated to compensate for changes in the purchasing power of the dollar

Dow Jones Industrial Average
Constant Dollars
January 1913 Dollar = 100 Cents

September 1929
216.33

August 1921
35.38

July 1932
29.70

March 1937
134.16

April 1942
56.69

May 1946
112.47

June 1949
66.45

January 1966
306.38

October 1966
222.19

January 1973
242.10

May 1970
160.40

December 1974
109.27

September 1976
172.85

January 1981
113.39

May 1981
108.81

April 1980
92.03

Source: *The Media General Financial Weekly*, Media General Financial Services, 301 E. Grace Street, Richmond, Va. 23261, June 29, 1981.

THE MAJOR MARKET AVERAGES

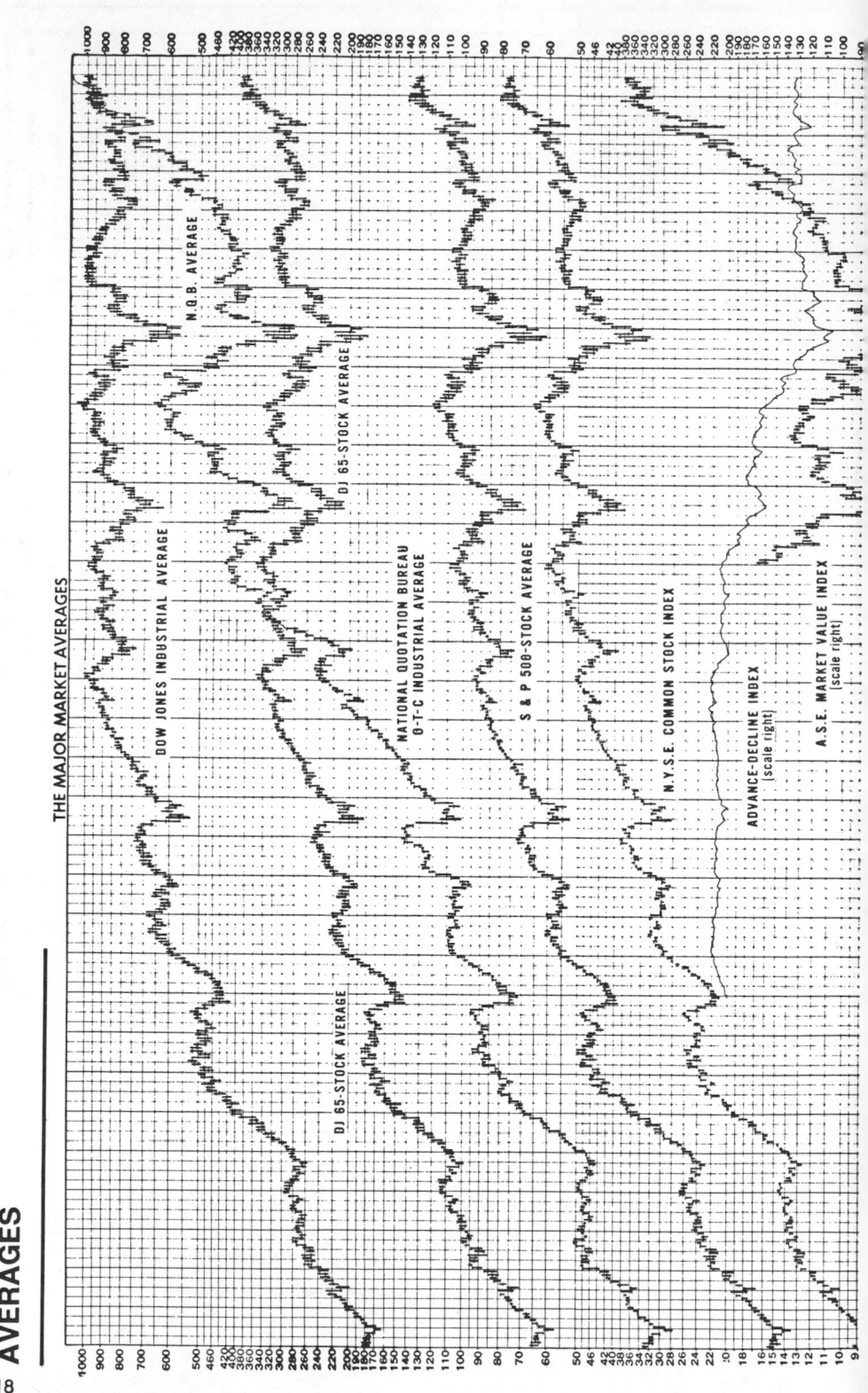

N.Q.B. AVERAGE

DJ 65-STOCK AVERAGE

DOW JONES INDUSTRIAL AVERAGE

NATIONAL QUOTATION BUREAU
O-T-C INDUSTRIAL AVERAGE

S & P 500-STOCK AVERAGE

N.Y.S.E. COMMON STOCK INDEX

DJ 65-STOCK AVERAGE

ADVANCE-DECLINE INDEX
(scale right)

A.S.E. MARKET VALUE INDEX
(scale right)

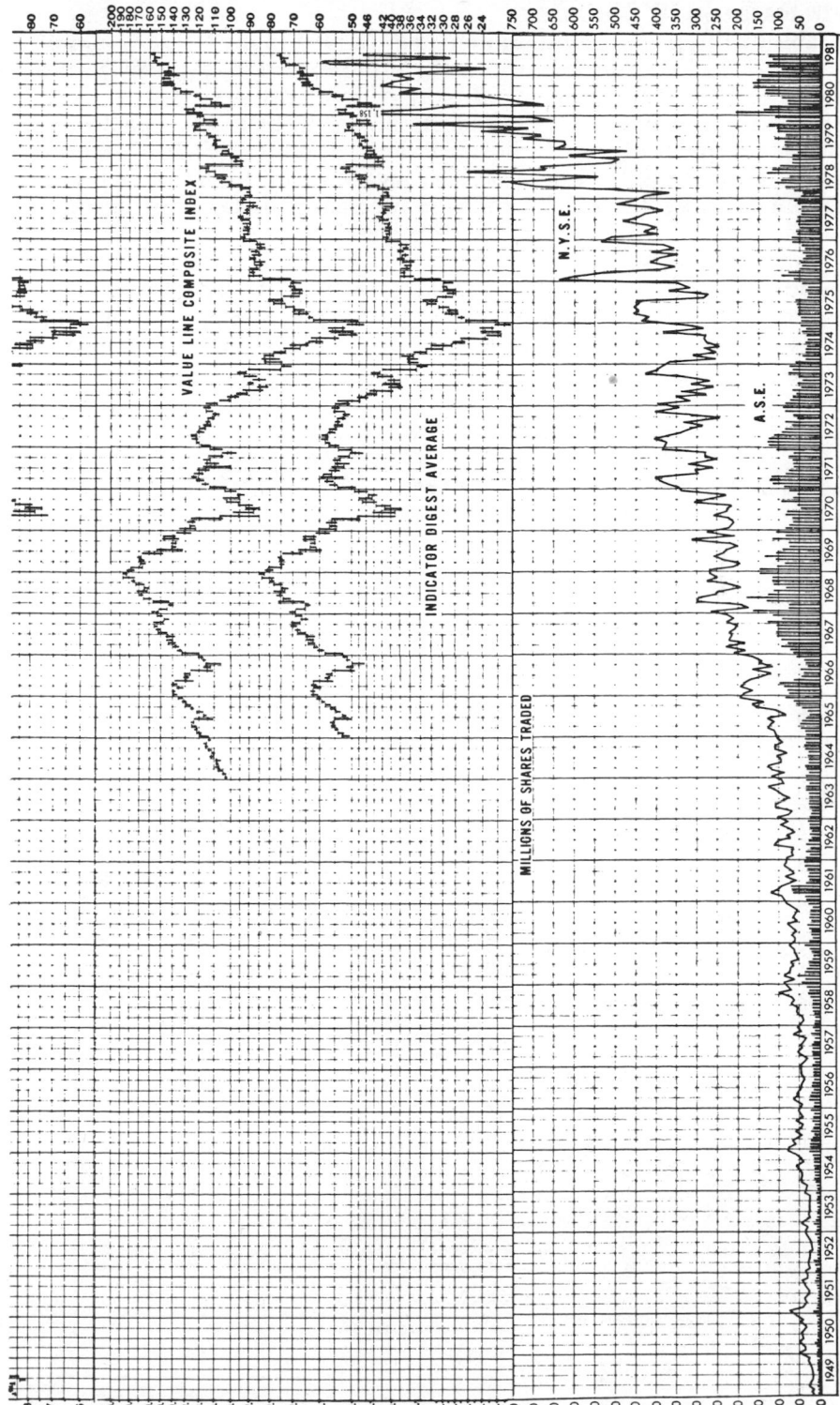

Source: 3-Trend CYCLI-Graphs. The charts are the courtesy of Securities Research Company, 208 Newbury Street, Boston, Mass. 02116, July quarterly edition, 1981.

Growth Rates in NYSE Index

The table on this page presents annual growth rates in the NYSE Common Stock Index from 1962-80. Growth rate is a term referring to the average rate of increase or decrease, compounded annually, between two periods.

To obtain the growth rate, for example, between 1974 and 1980, go down the vertical column under 1974 to the horizontal row opposite 1980, which shows a 13.7% rate. This means that stock prices, as measured by the NYSE Index, increased at a yearly rate of 13.7%, compounded annually, between the end of those years. With the strong rise in stock prices in the past three years, the growth rate of the NYSE Index has been substantial with 14%, 21% and 26% compounded annual increases from 1977, 1978 and 1979, respectively, to 1980.

The price appreciation on stocks is only a partial measure of the return on money invested in stock. For a complete return, it is necessary to add the dividends received each year

Compounded Growth Rates in NYSE Index•

	'62	'63	'64	'65	'66	'67	'68	'69	'70	'71	'72	'73	'74	'75	'76	'77	'78	'79	Index at Year End
'62																			33.81
'63	18.1																		39.92
'64	16.2	14.4																	45.65
'65	13.9	11.9	9.5																50.00
'66	6.6	3.1	-2.1	-12.6															43.72
'67	9.7	7.8	5.6	3.8	23.1														53.83
'68	9.7	8.1	6.6	5.6	16.1	9.4													58.90
'69	6.2	4.3	2.5	0.8	5.6	-2.2	-12.5												51.53
'70	5.1	3.3	1.6	0.1	3.5	-2.3	-7.7	-2.5											50.23
'71	5.9	4.4	3.1	2.0	5.2	1.2	-1.4	4.6	12.3										56.43
'72	6.7	5.5	4.4	3.7	6.7	3.7	2.3	7.8	13.3	14.3									64.48
'73	4.0	2.6	1.4	0.4	2.5	-0.6	-2.5	0.1	1.0	-4.2	-19.6								51.82
'74	0.6	-0.9	-2.3	-3.5	-2.4	-5.5	-7.8	-6.9	-7.9	-13.8	-25.1	-30.3							36.13
'75	2.7	1.5	0.4	-0.5	1.0	-1.5	-3.0	-1.3	-1.1	-4.1	-9.6	-4.1	31.9						47.64
'76	3.9	2.9	2.0	1.3	2.8	0.8	-0.2	1.7	2.4	0.5	-2.7	3.8	26.6	21.5					57.88
'77	3.0	2.0	1.1	0.4	1.7	-0.2	-1.3	0.2	0.6	-1.2	-4.0	0.3	13.3	5.0	-9.3				52.50
'78	2.9	2.0	1.2	0.5	1.7	•	-0.9	0.4	0.8	-0.7	-3.0	0.7	10.4	4.0	-3.8	2.1			53.62
'79	3.6	2.8	2.1	1.5	2.7	1.2	0.5	1.9	2.4	1.2	-0.6	3.0	11.4	6.8	2.3	8.6	15.5		61.95
'80	4.7	4.0	3.4	3.0	4.2	2.9	2.4	3.8	4.5	3.6	2.4	6.0	13.7	10.3	7.7	14.0	20.5	25.7	77.86

Header spanning '62 through '79: **Initial Year**

• Less than 0.05%

• Index figures taken at year end

Source: New York Stock Exchange *1981 Fact Book.*

STOCK MARKET AVERAGES
BY INDUSTRY GROUP

These definitions apply to the following charts.

Price scale: The price ranges are always read from the scale at the right-hand side of each chart. This scale is equal to 15 times the earnings scale at the left, so when the price range bars and the earnings line coincide, it shows the price is at 15 times earnings. When the price is above the earnings line, the ratio of price to earnings is greater than 15 times earnings; when below, it is less.

Monthly price ranges represented by the solid vertical bars show the highest and lowest point of each month's transactions. Cross-bars indicate the month's closing price.

Monthly ratio-cator: The plottings for this line are obtained by dividing the closing price of the stock by the closing price of the Dow Jones Industrial Average on the same day. The resulting percentage is multiplied by a factor of 4.5 to bring the line closer to the price bars and is read from the right-hand scale. The plotting indicates whether the stock has kept pace, outperformed, or lagged behind the general market as represented by the DJIA.

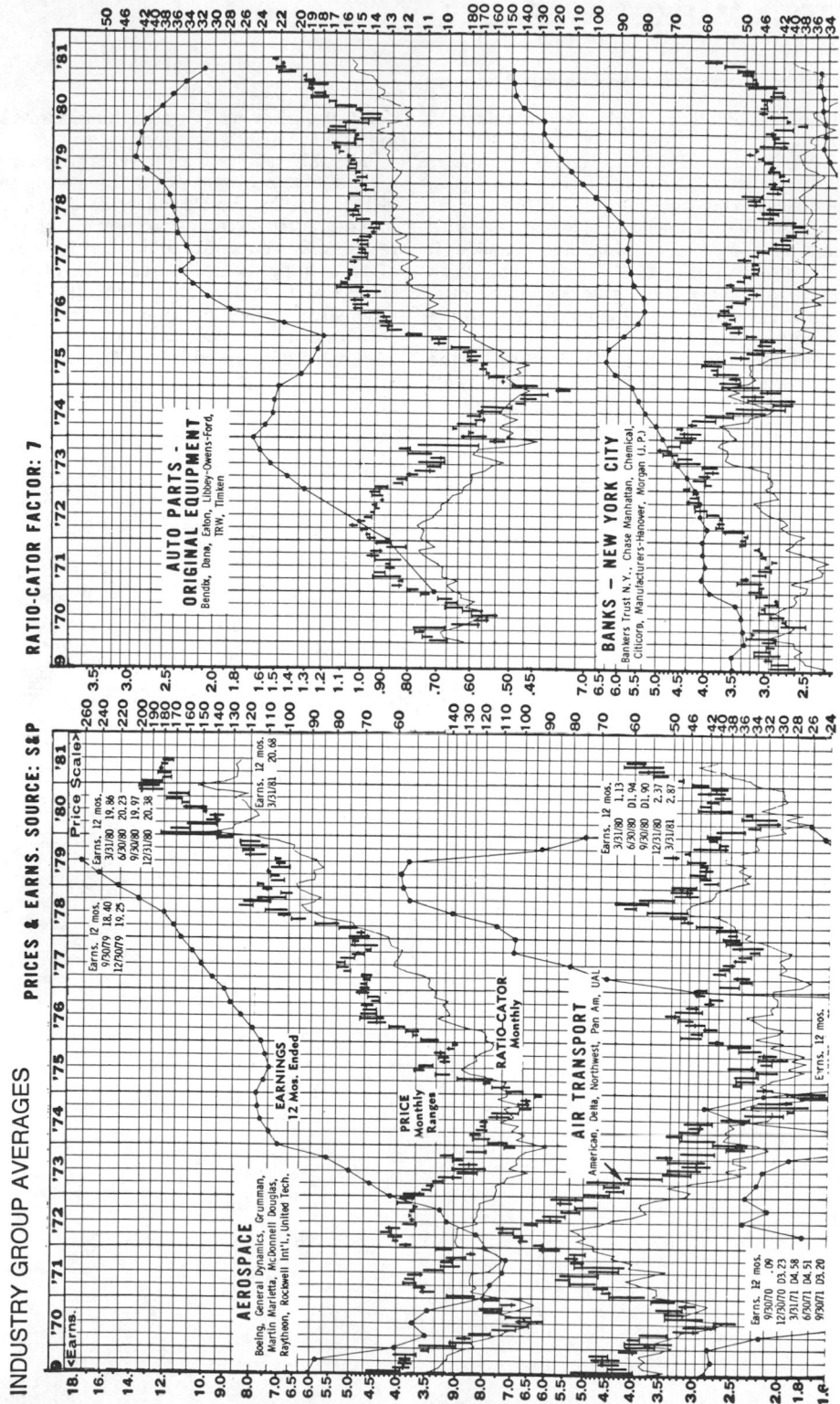

INDUSTRY GROUP AVERAGES   PRICES & EARNS. SOURCE: S&P

RATIO-CATOR FACTOR: 7

**AUTO PARTS -
ORIGINAL EQUIPMENT**
Bendix, Dana, Eaton, Libbey-Owens-Ford,
TRW, Timken

BANKS — NEW YORK CITY
Bankers Trust N.Y., Chase Manhattan, Chemical,
Citicorp, Manufacturers-Hanover, Morgan (J.P.)

Price Scale

Earns. 12 mos.
9/30/79   18.40
12/30/79 19.25

Earns. 12 mos.
3/31/80   19.86
6/30/80   20.23
9/30/80   19.97
12/31/80 20.38

Earns. 12 mos.
3/31/81   20.68

AEROSPACE
Boeing, General Dynamics, Grumman,
Martin Marietta, McDonnell Douglas,
Raytheon, Rockwell Int'l., United Tech.

EARNINGS
12 Mos. Ended

PRICE
Monthly
Ranges

RATIO-CATOR
Monthly

AIR TRANSPORT
American, Delta, Northwest, Pan Am, UAL

Earns. 12 mos.
3/31/80   1.13
6/30/80   D1.94
9/30/80   D1.90
12/31/80 2.37
3/31/81   2.87

Earns. 12 mos.
9/30/70   .09
12/30/70 D3.23
3/31/71   D4.58
6/30/71   D4.51
9/30/71   D3.20

Erns. 12 mos.

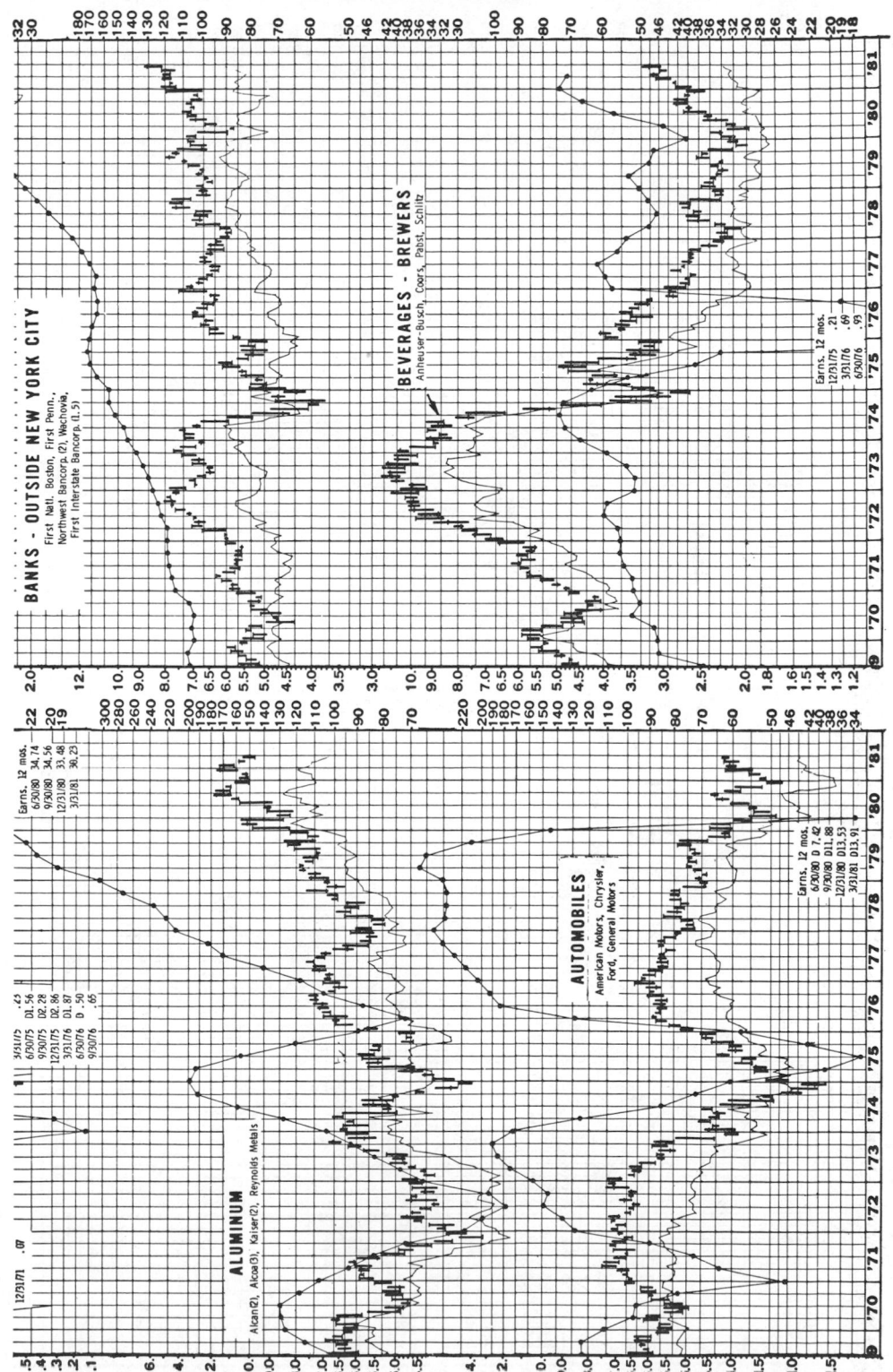

BANKS - OUTSIDE NEW YORK CITY

First Natl. Boston, First Penn.,
Northwest Bancorp (2), Wachovia,
First Interstate Bancorp (L.5)

BEVERAGES - BREWERS

Anheuser-Busch, Coors, Pabst, Schlitz

Earns. 12 mos.	
12/31/75	.21
3/31/76	.69
6/30/76	.93

ALUMINUM

Alcan (2), Alcoa (3), Kaiser (2), Reynolds Metals

Earns. 12 mos.	
6/30/80	34.74
9/30/80	34.56
12/31/80	33.48
3/31/81	30.23

3/31/72	.43
6/30/75	D1.56
9/30/75	D2.28
12/31/75	D2.86
3/31/76	D1.87
6/30/76	D .50
9/30/76	.65

12/31/71	.07

AUTOMOBILES

American Motors, Chrysler,
Ford, General Motors

Earns. 12 mos.	
6/30/80	D 7.42
9/30/80	D11.88
12/31/80	D13.53
3/31/81	D13.91

INDUSTRY GROUP AVERAGES *(continued)*

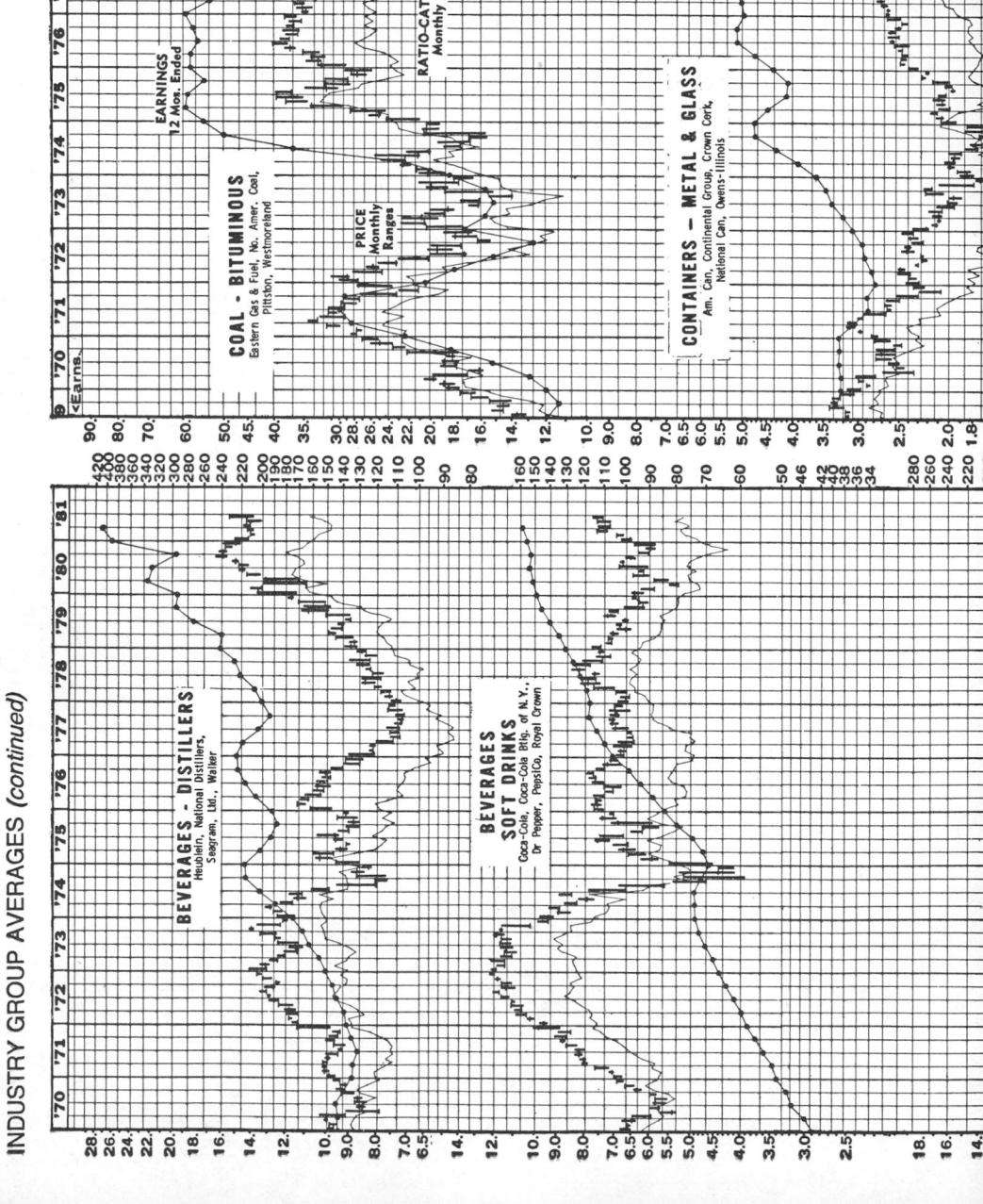

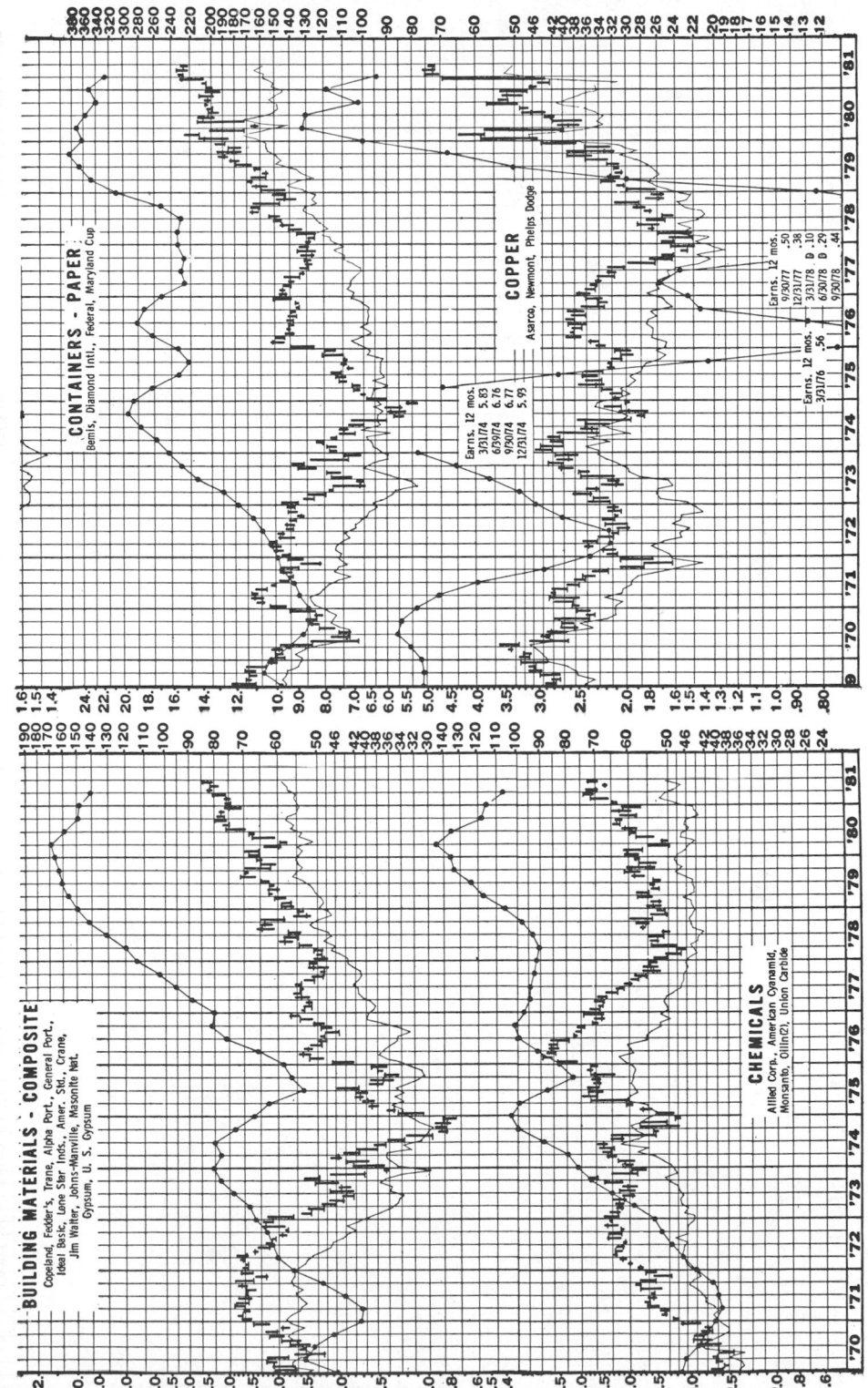

INDUSTRY GROUP AVERAGES *(continued)*

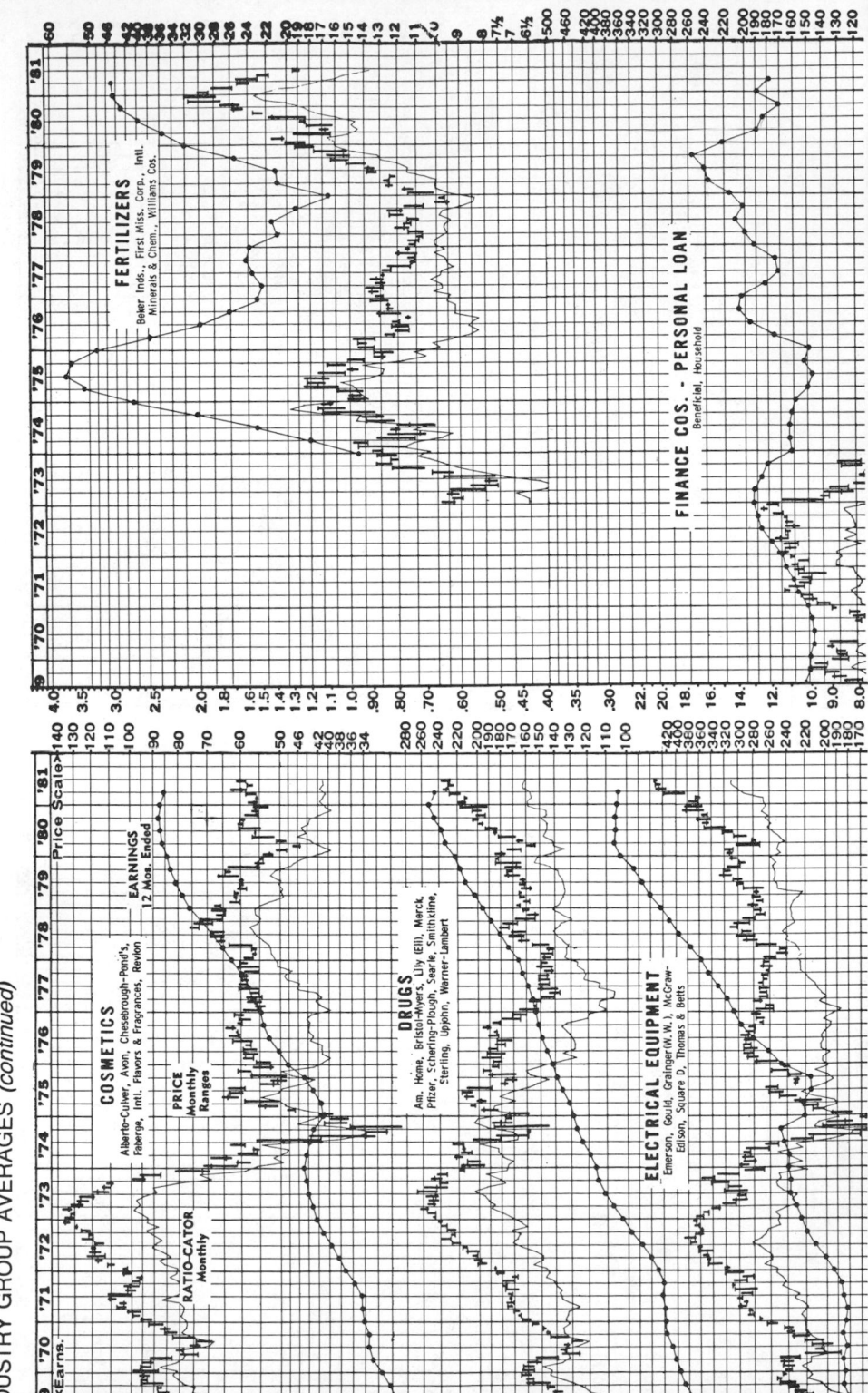

FERTILIZERS
Beker Inds., First Miss. Corp., Intl. Minerals & Chem., Williams Cos.

FINANCE COS. - PERSONAL LOAN
Beneficial, Household

COSMETICS
Alberto-Culver, Avon, Chesebrough-Pond's, Faberge, Intl. Flavors & Fragrances, Revlon

EARNINGS
12 Mos. Ended

PRICE
Monthly
Ranges

RATIO-CATOR
Monthly

DRUGS
Am. Home, Bristol-Myers, Lily (Eli), Merck, Pfizer, Schering-Plough, Searle, Smithkline, Sterling, Upjohn, Warner-Lambert

ELECTRICAL EQUIPMENT
Emerson, Gould, Grainger (W. W.), McGraw-Edison, Square D, Thomas & Betts

Price Scale>

<Earns.

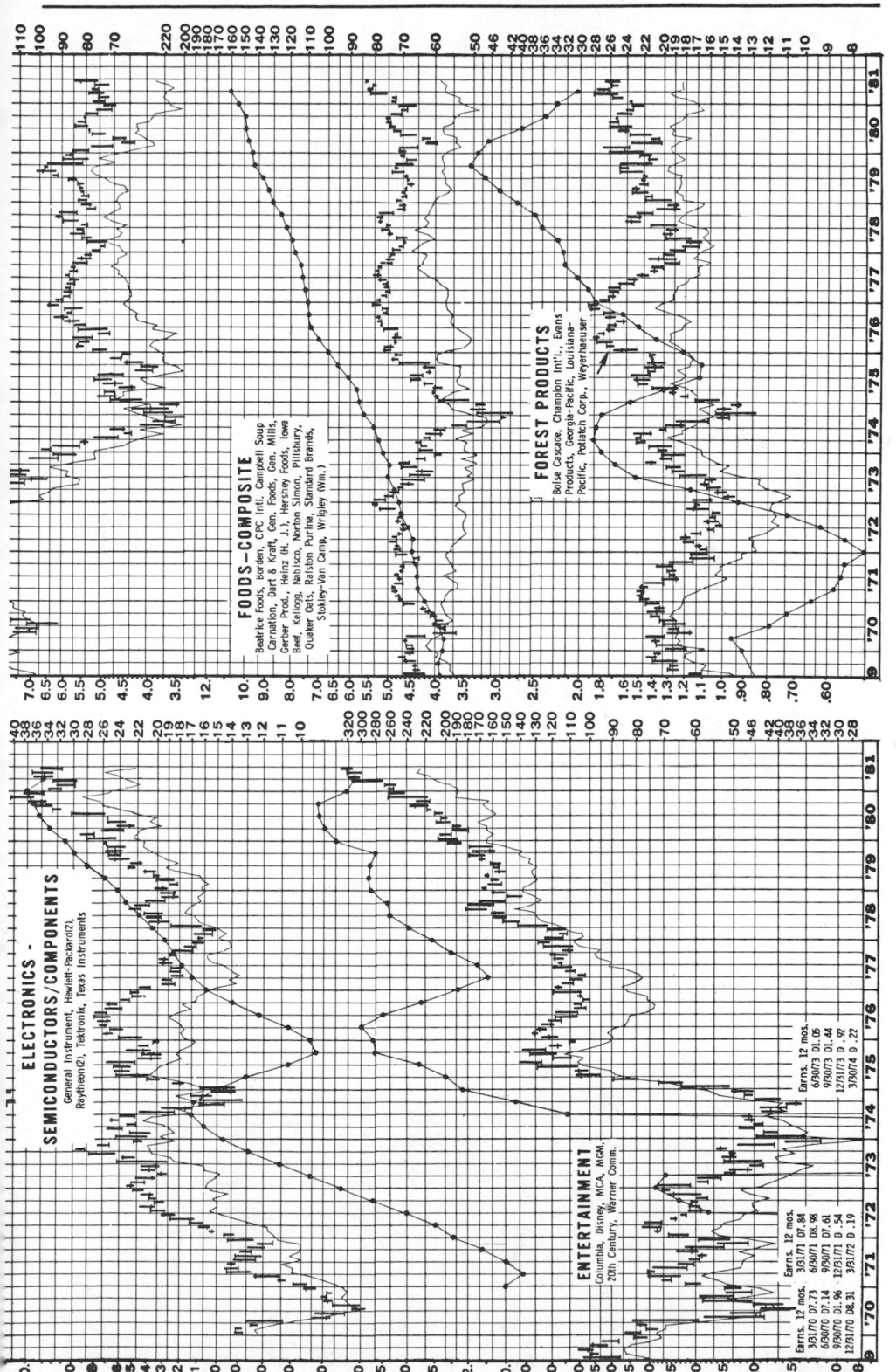

ELECTRONICS - SEMICONDUCTORS/COMPONENTS

General Instrument, Hewlett-Packard(2), Raytheon(2), Tektronix, Texas Instruments

FOODS—COMPOSITE

Beatrice Foods, Borden, CPC Intl, Campbell Soup Carnation, Dart & Kraft, Gen. Foods, Gen. Mills, Gerber Prod., Heinz (H. J.), Hershey Foods, Iowa Beef, Kellogg, Nabisco, Norton Simon, Pillsbury, Quaker Oats, Ralston Purina, Standard Brands, Stokely-Van Camp, Wrigley (Wm.)

FOREST PRODUCTS

Boise Cascade, Champion Int'l., Evans Products, Georgia-Pacific, Louisiana-Pacific, Potlatch Corp., Weyerhaeuser

ENTERTAINMENT

Columbia, Disney, MCA, MGM, 20th Century, Warner Comm.

Earns. 12 mos.	
3/31/70	DL.73
6/30/70	DL.14
9/30/70	DL.96
12/31/70	D8.31

Earns. 12 mos.	
3/31/71	D7.84
6/30/71	D8.98
9/30/71	D7.61
12/31/71	D .54
3/31/72	D .19

Earns. 12 mos.	
6/30/73	DL.05
9/30/73	DL.44
12/31/73	D .92
3/30/74	D .22

INDUSTRY GROUP AVERAGES *(continued)*

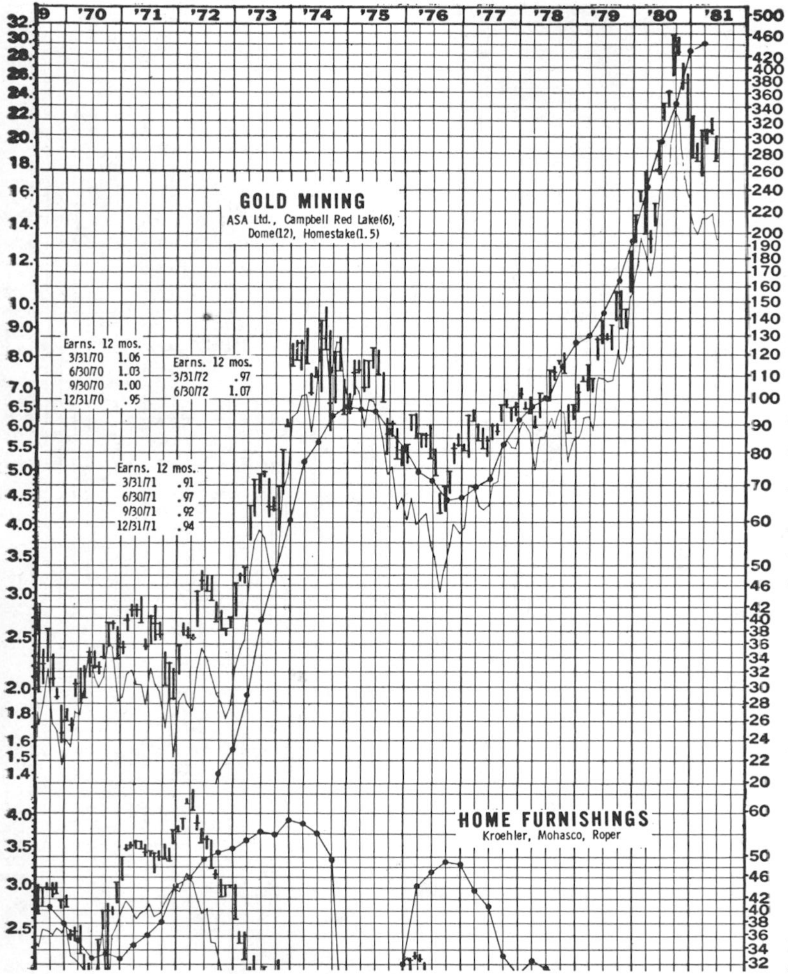

HOSPITAL MANAGEMENT
Am. Med. Intl., Hospital Corp. of Am.,
Humana Inc., Natl. Med. Enter.

HOSPITAL SUPPLIES
Abbott Labs.(2), Am. Hosp., Baxter Travenol,
Becton Dickinson, Johnson & Johnson(3)

PRICE
Monthly
Ranges

RATIO-CATOR
Monthly

EARNINGS
12 Mos. Ended

Price Scale>

<Earns.

GOLD MINING
ASA Ltd., Campbell Red Lake(6),
Dome(12), Homestake(1.5)

Earns. 12 mos.
3/31/70   1.06
6/30/70   1.03
9/30/70   1.00
12/31/70   .95

Earns. 12 mos.
3/31/71   .91
6/30/71   .97
9/30/71   .92
12/31/71   .94

Earns. 12 mos.
3/31/72   .97
6/30/72   1.07

HOME FURNISHINGS
Kroehler, Mohasco, Roper

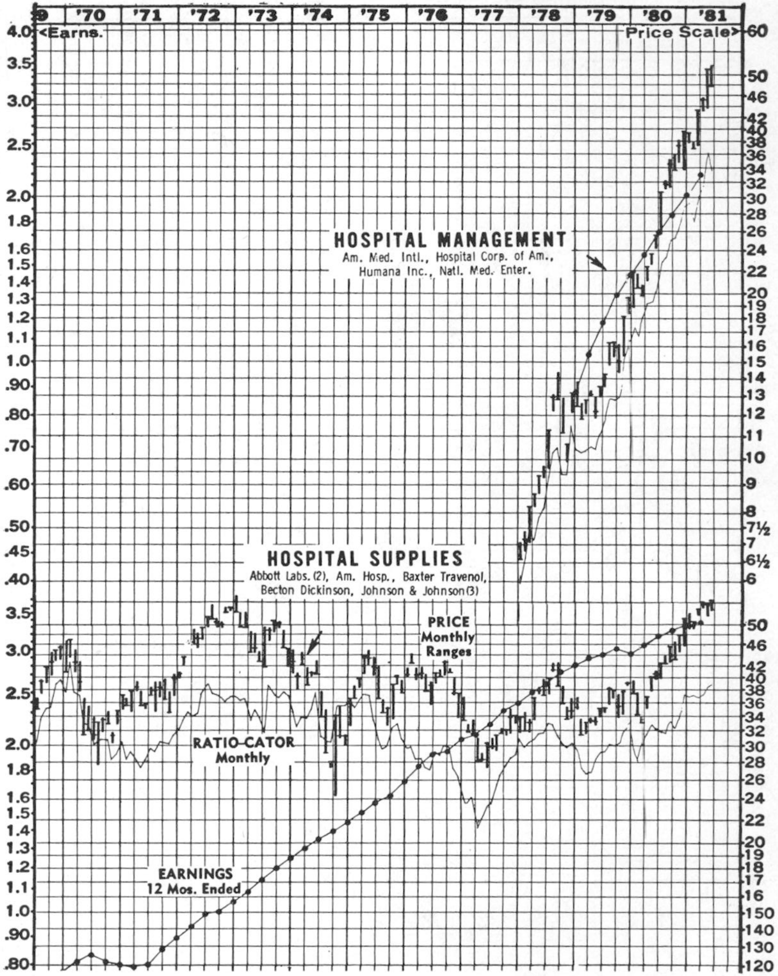

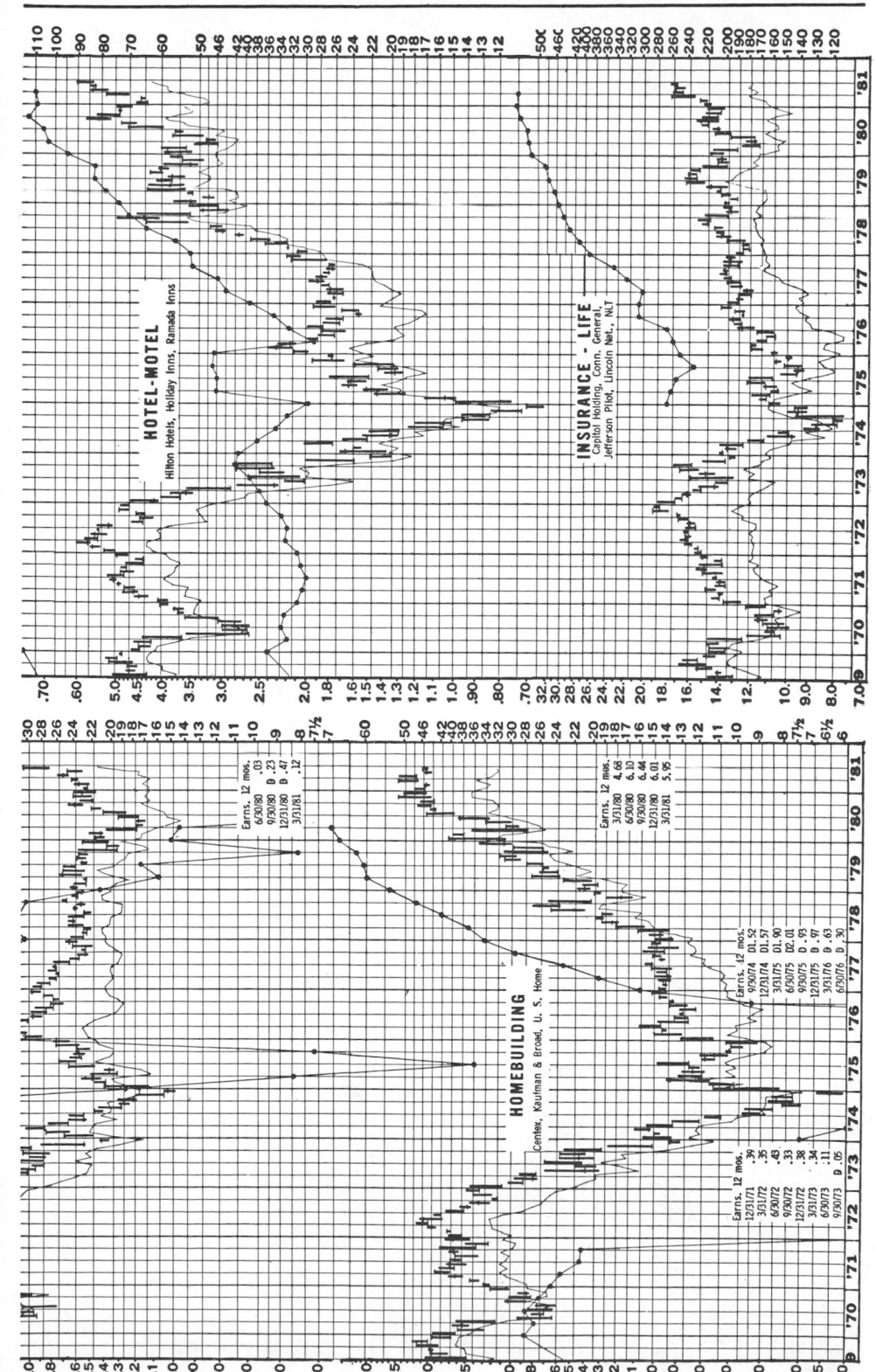

HOTEL-MOTEL
Hilton Hotels, Holiday Inns, Ramada Inns

INSURANCE - LIFE
Capitol Holding, Conn. General,
Jefferson Pilot, Lincoln Nat., NLT

HOMEBUILDING
Centex, Kaufman & Broad, U. S. Home

Earns, 12 mos.
6/30/80 .03
9/30/80 D .23
12/31/80 D .47
3/31/81 .12

Earns, 12 mos.
3/31/80 4.68
6/30/80 6.10
9/30/80 6.44
12/31/80 6.01
3/31/81 5.95

Earns, 12 mos.
9/30/74 D1.52
12/31/74 D1.57
3/31/75 D1.90
6/30/75 D2.01
9/30/75 D .93
12/31/75 D .97
3/31/76 D .63
6/30/76 D .30

Earns, 12 mos.
12/31/71 .39
3/31/72 .35
6/30/72 .43
9/30/72 .33
12/31/72 .38
3/31/73 .34
6/30/73 .11
9/30/73 D .05

INDUSTRY GROUP AVERAGES *(continued)*

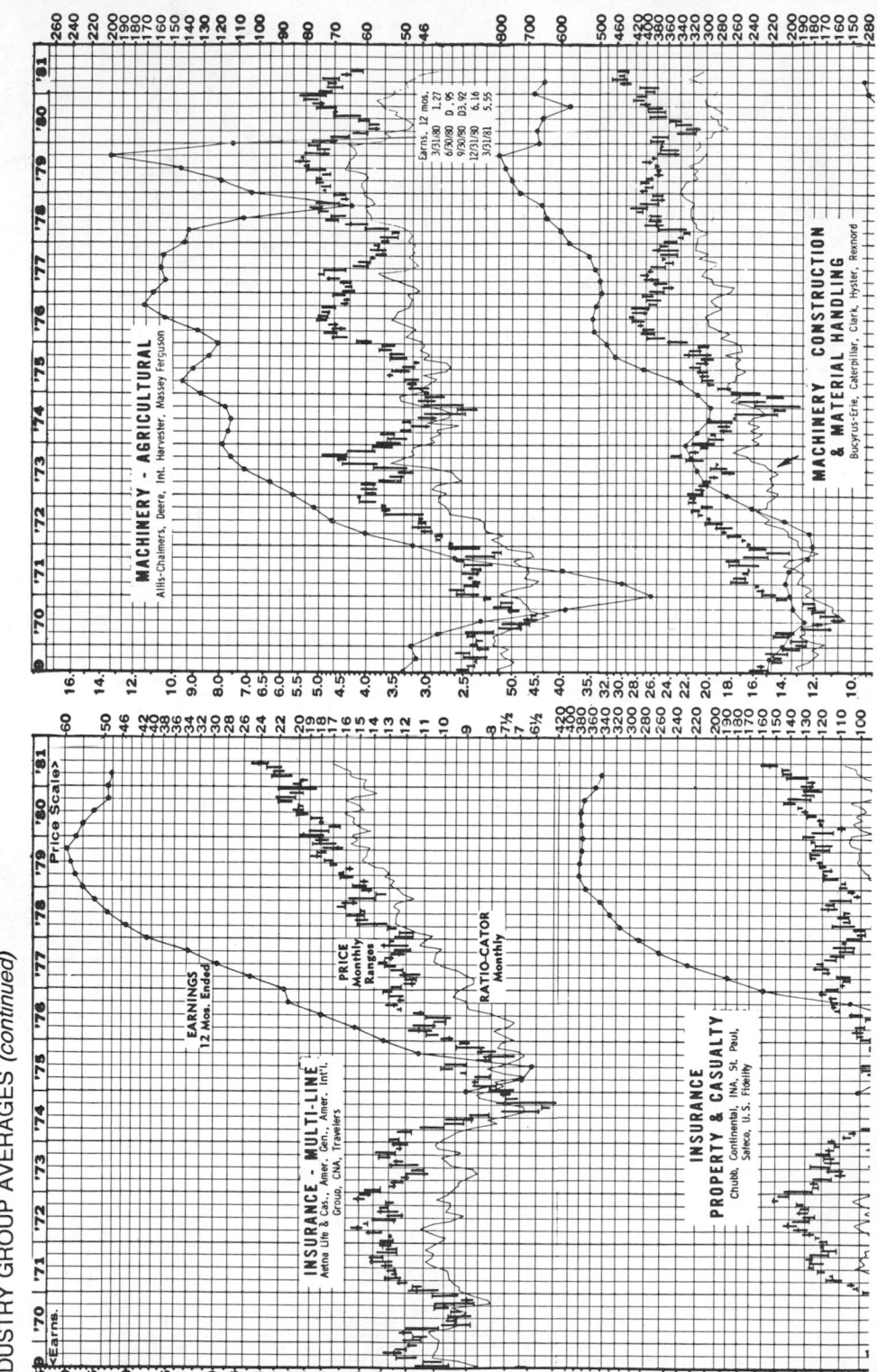

MACHINERY - AGRICULTURAL
Allis-Chalmers, Deere, Int. Harvester, Massey Ferguson

Earns. 12 mos.
3/31/80   1.27
6/30/80   D .95
9/30/80   D3.92
12/31/90   6.16
3/31/81   5.55

MACHINERY CONSTRUCTION & MATERIAL HANDLING
Bucyrus-Erie, Caterpillar, Clark, Hyster, Rexnord

EARNINGS
12 Mos. Ended

Price Scale▷

PRICE
Monthly
Ranges

RATIO-CATOR
Monthly

INSURANCE - MULTI-LINE
Aetna Life & Cas., Amer. Gen., Amer. Int'l.
Group, CNA, Travelers

◁Earns.

INSURANCE PROPERTY & CASUALTY
Chubb, Continental, INA, St. Paul,
Safeco, U.S. Fidelity

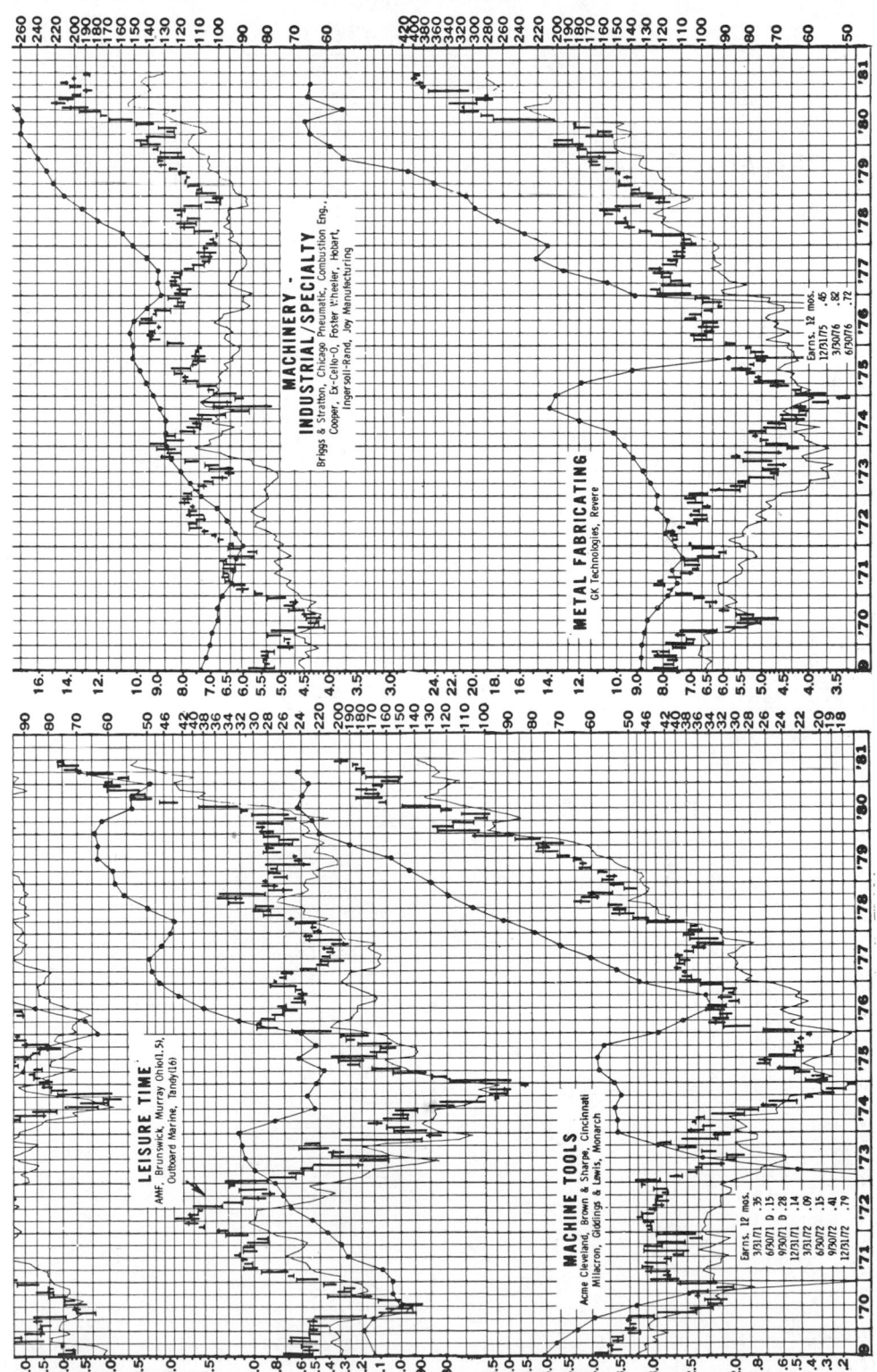

METAL FABRICATING
GK Technologies, Revere

Earns. 12 mos.
12/31/75   .45
3/9/76   .82
6/30/76   .72

LEISURE TIME
AMF, Brunswick, Murray Ohio(I.5),
Outboard Marine, Tandy(16)

MACHINE TOOLS
Acme Cleveland, Brown & Sharpe, Cincinnati
Milacron, Giddings & Lewis, Monarch

Earns. 12 mos.
3/31/71   D .35
6/30/71   D .15
9/30/71   D .28
12/31/71   .14
3/31/72   .09
6/30/72   .15
9/30/72   .41
12/31/72   .79

INDUSTRY GROUP AVERAGES *(continued)*

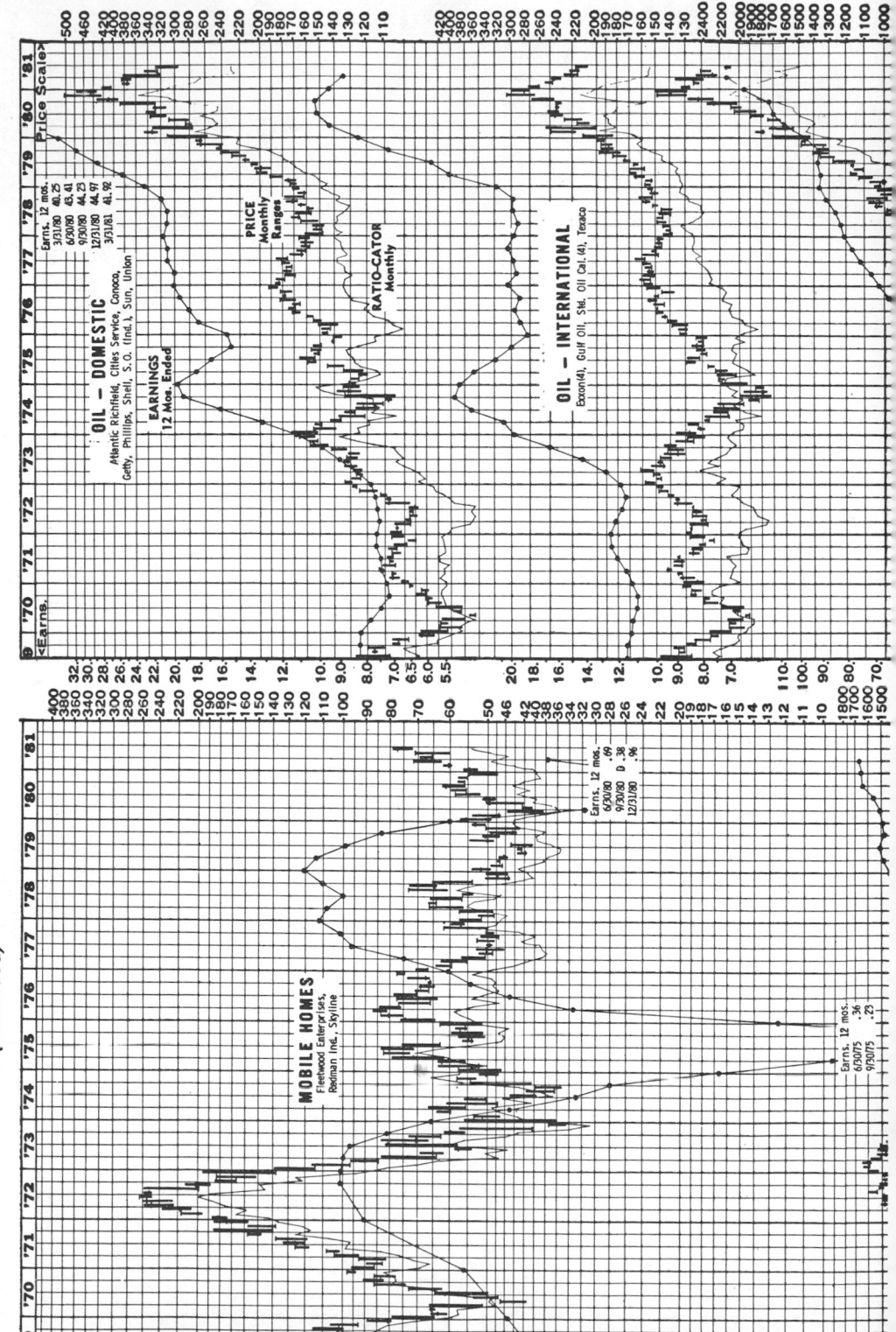

OIL — DOMESTIC
Atlantic Richfield, Cities Service, Conoco,
Getty, Phillips, Shell, S.O. (Ind.), Sun, Union

Earns. 12 mos.	
3/31/80	40.25
6/30/80	43.41
9/30/80	44.23
12/31/80	44.97
3/31/81	41.92

EARNINGS
12 Mos. Ended

PRICE
Monthly
Ranges

RATIO-CATOR
Monthly

Price Scale

OIL — INTERNATIONAL
Exxon(4), Gulf Oil, Std. Oil Cal.(4), Texaco

MOBILE HOMES
Fleetwood Enterprises,
Redman Ind., Skyline

Earns. 12 mos.	
6/30/80	D .69
9/30/80	D .38
12/31/80	.96

Earns. 12 mos.	
6/30/75	.36
9/30/75	.23

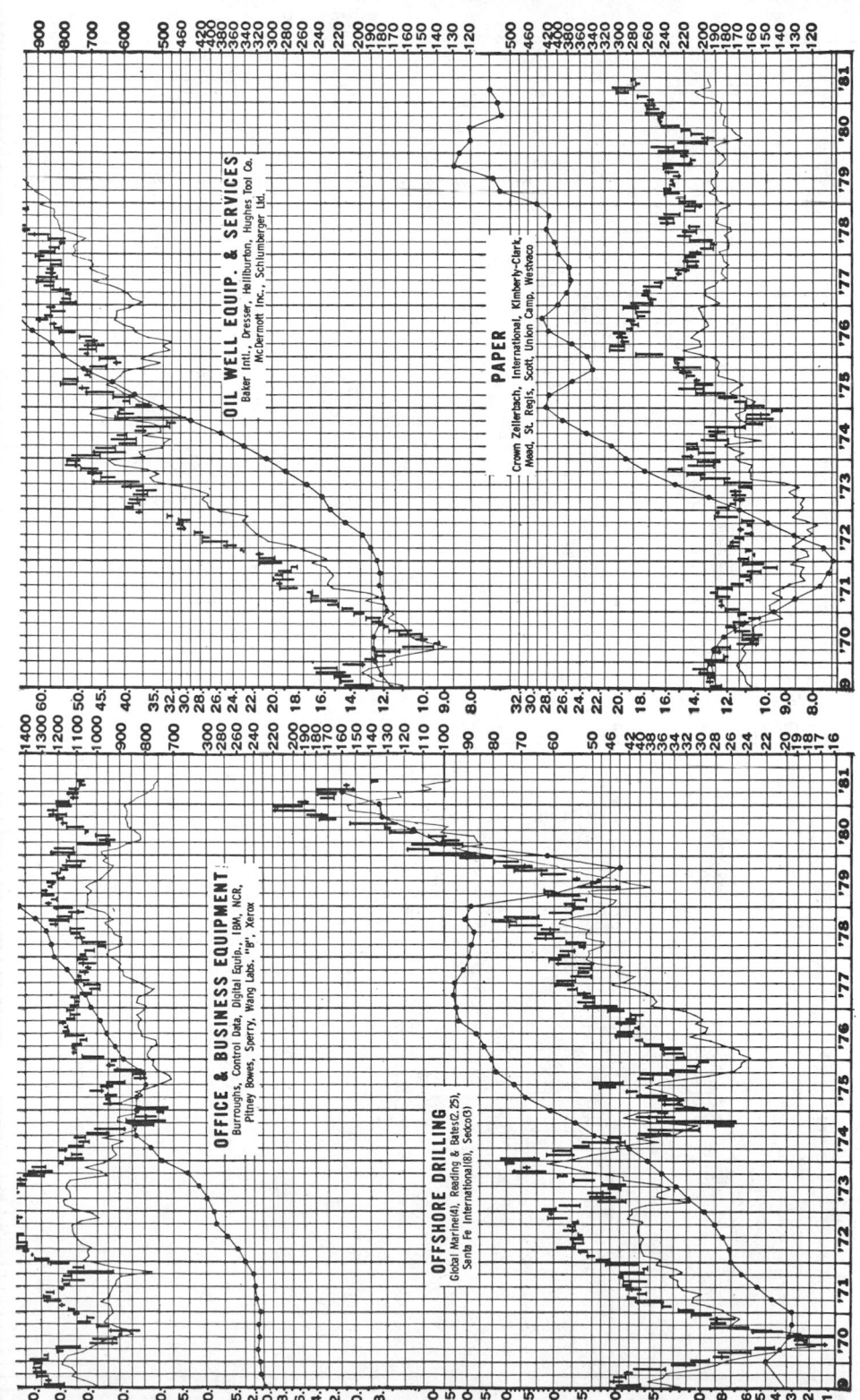

OIL WELL EQUIP. & SERVICES
Baker Intl., Dresser, Halliburton, Hughes Tool Co.
McDermott Inc., Schlumberger Ltd.

PAPER
Crown Zellerbach, International, Kimberly-Clark,
Mead, St. Regis, Scott, Union Camp, Westvaco

OFFICE & BUSINESS EQUIPMENT:
Burroughs, Control Data, Digital Equip., IBM, NCR,
Pitney Bowes, Sperry, Wang Labs, "B", Xerox

OFFSHORE DRILLING
Global Marine(4), Reading & Bates(2.25),
Santa Fe International(8), Sedco(3)

INDUSTRY GROUP AVERAGES *(continued)*

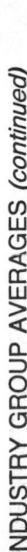

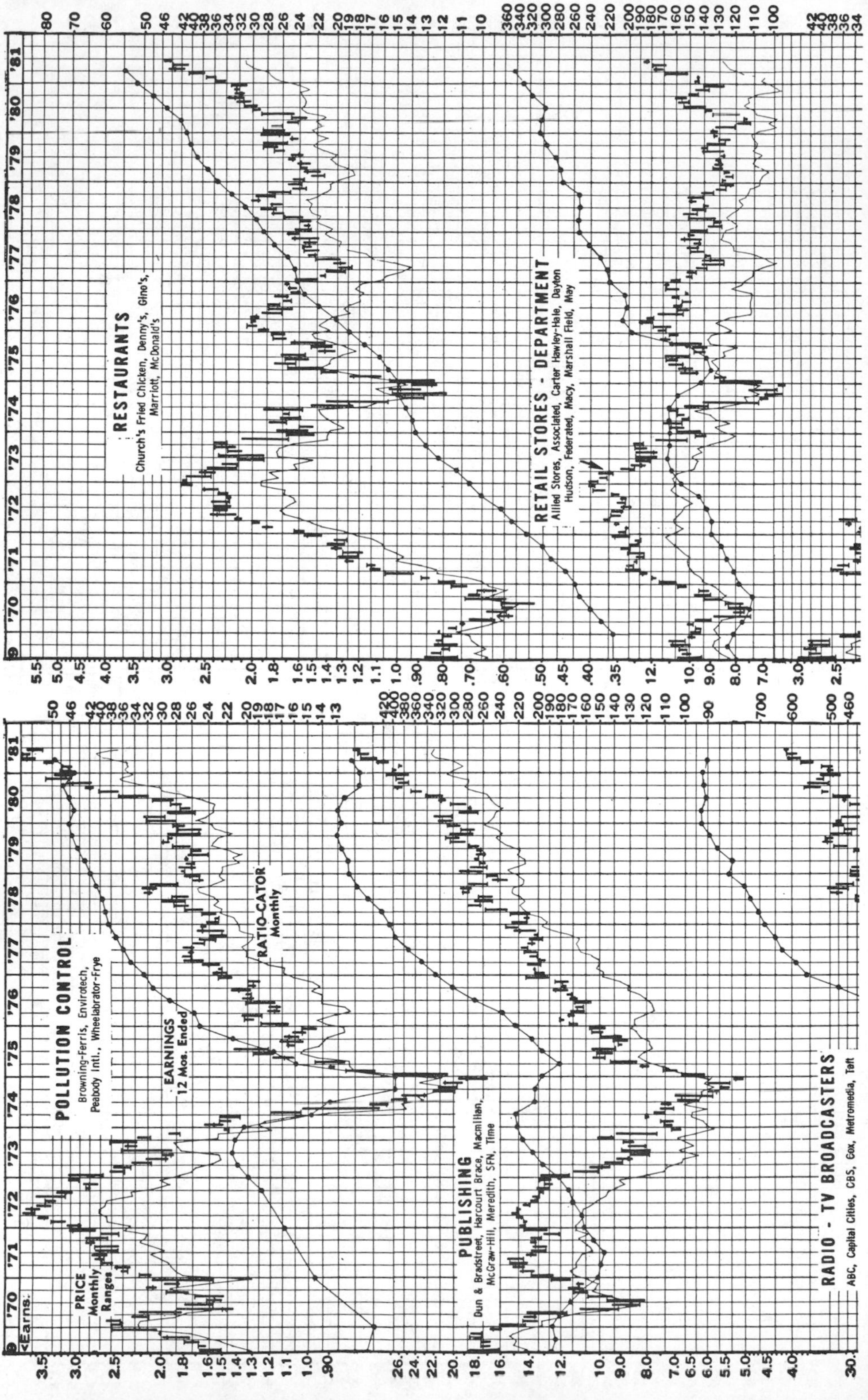
POLLUTION CONTROL
Browning-Ferris, Envirotech, Peabody Intl., Wheelabrator-Frye
PRICE Monthly Ranges
EARNINGS 12 Mos. Ended
RATIO-CATOR Monthly
<Earns.
PUBLISHING
Dun & Bradstreet, Harcourt Brace, Macmillan, McGraw-Hill, Meredith, SFN, Time
RADIO - TV BROADCASTERS
ABC, Capital Cities, CBS, Cox, Metromedia, Taft
RESTAURANTS
Church's Fried Chicken, Denny's, Gino's, Marriott, McDonald's
RETAIL STORES - DEPARTMENT
Allied Stores, Associated, Carter Hawley-Hale, Dayton Hudson, Federated, Macy, Marshall Field, May
'70
'71
'72
'73
'74
'75
'76
'77
'78
'79
'80
'81

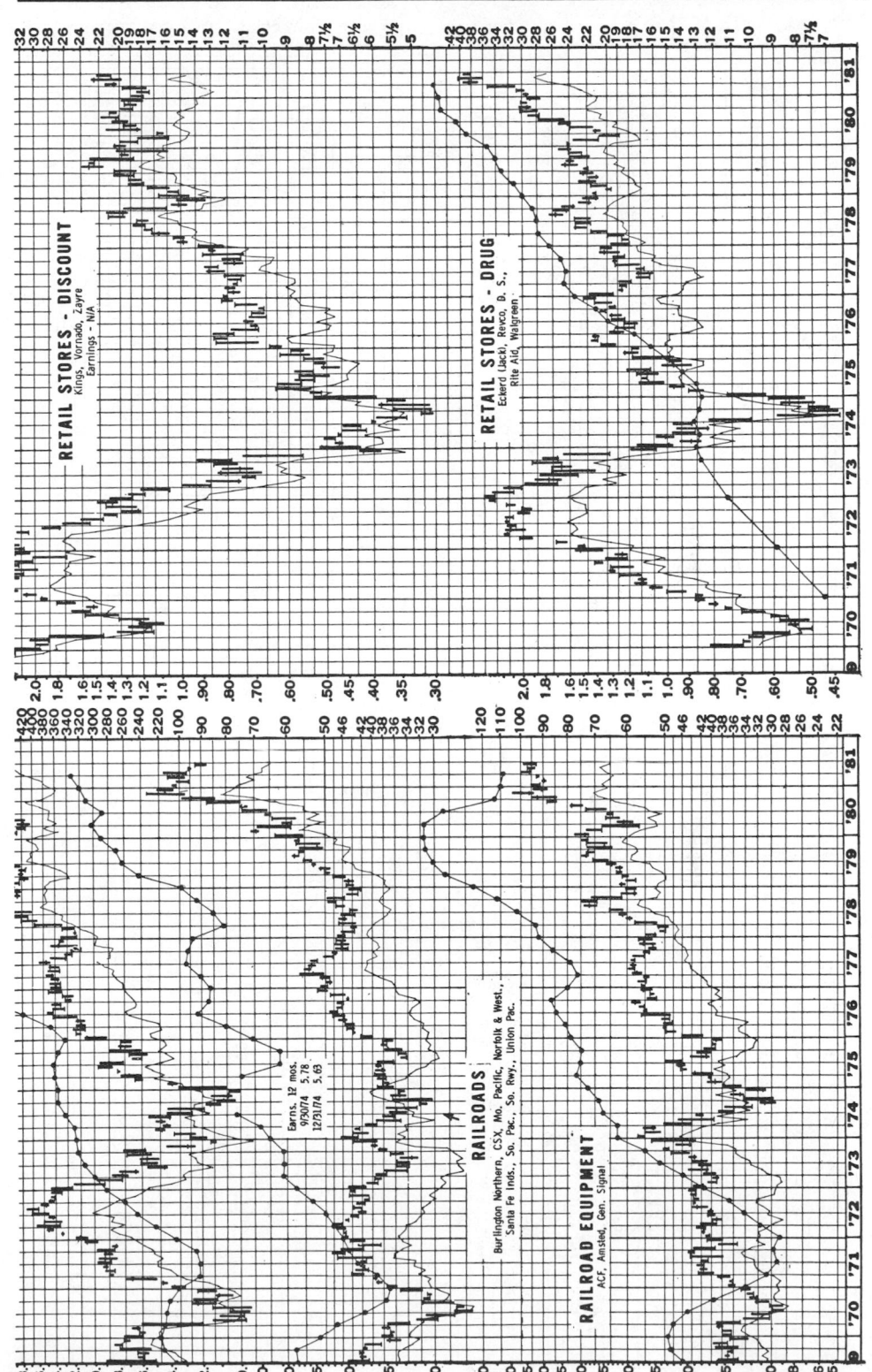

RETAIL STORES - DISCOUNT
Kings, Vornado, Zayre
Earnings - N/A

RETAIL STORES - DRUG
Eckerd (Jack), Revco, D. S.,
Rite Aid, Walgreen

RAILROADS
Burlington Northern, CSX, Mo. Pacific, Norfolk & West.,
Santa Fe Inds., So. Pac., So. Rwy., Union Pac.

Earns. 12 mos.
9/30/74   5.78
12/31/74 5.63

RAILROAD EQUIPMENT
ACF, Amsted, Gen. Signal

INDUSTRY GROUP AVERAGES *(continued)*

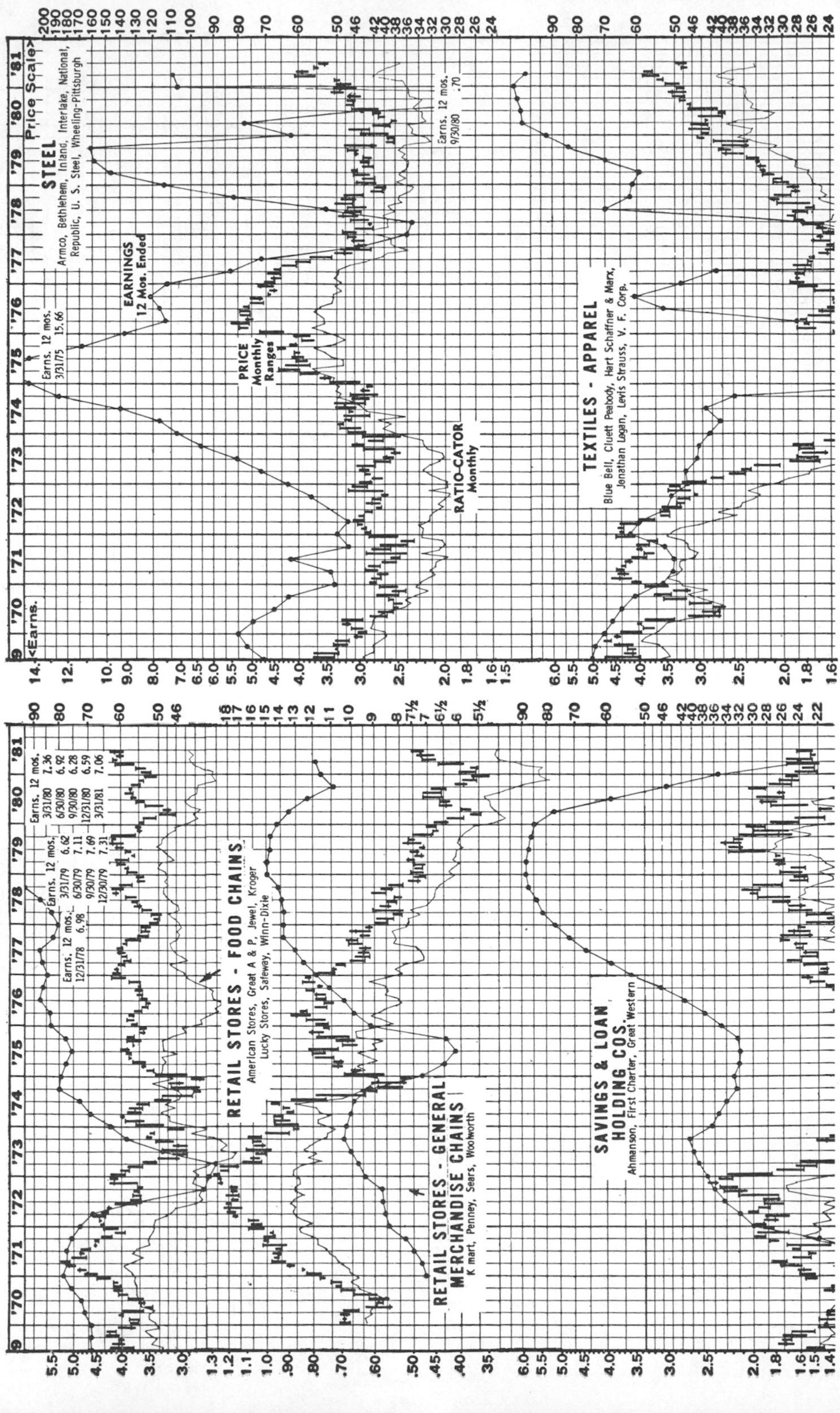

STEEL
Armco, Bethlehem, Inland, Interlake, National, Republic, U. S. Steel, Wheeling-Pittsburgh

EARNINGS
12 Mos. Ended

Earns. 12 mos.
3/31/75   15.66

Earns. 12 mos.
9/30/80   .70

PRICE
Monthly
Ranges

RATIO-CATOR
Monthly

TEXTILES - APPAREL
Blue Bell, Cluett Peabody, Hart Schaffner & Marx, Jonathan Logan, Levi Strauss, V. F. Corp.

RETAIL STORES - FOOD CHAINS
American Stores, Great A & P., Jewel, Kroger
Lucky Stores, Safeway, Winn-Dixie

Earns. 12 mos.
3/31/79   6.62
6/30/79   7.11
9/30/79   7.69
12/30/79 7.31

Earns. 12 mos.
3/31/80   7.36
6/30/80   6.92
9/30/80   6.28
12/31/80 6.59
3/31/81   7.06

Earns. 12 mos.
12/31/78 6.98

RETAIL STORES - GENERAL MERCHANDISE CHAINS
K mart, Penney, Sears, Woolworth

SAVINGS & LOAN HOLDING COS.
Ahmanson, First Charter, Great Western

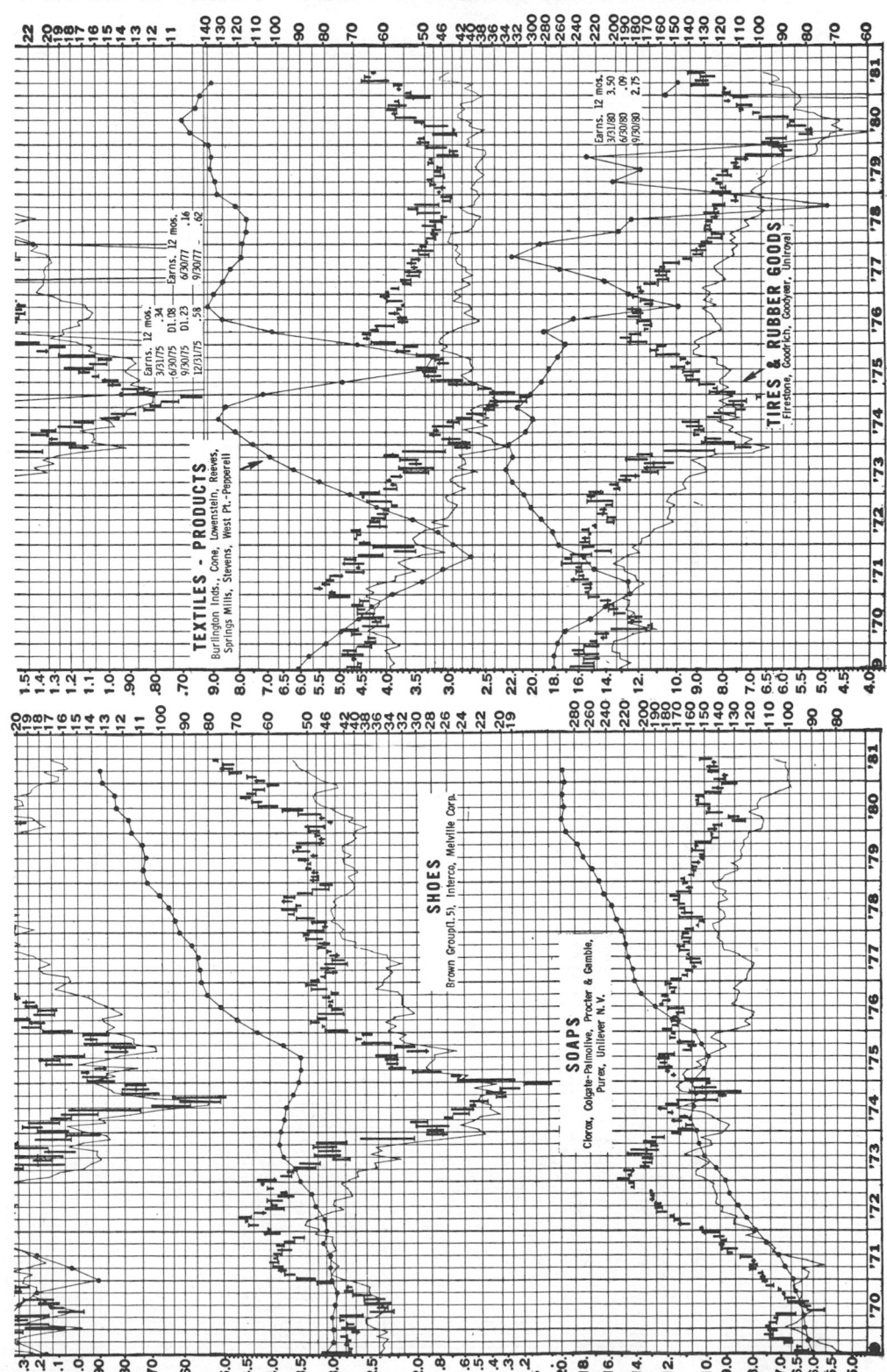

TEXTILES - PRODUCTS
Burlington Inds., Cone, Lowenstein, Reeves,
Springs Mills, Stevens, West Pt.-Pepperell

Earns. 12 mos.
3/31/75   .34
6/30/75   D1.08
9/30/75   D1.23
12/31/75   .58

Earns. 12 mos.
6/30/77   .16
9/30/77   .62

TIRES & RUBBER GOODS
Firestone, Goodrich, Goodyear, Uniroyal

Earns. 12 mos.
3/31/80   3.50
6/30/80   .09
9/30/80   2.75

SHOES
Brown Group, Int. St. Interco, Melville Corp.

SOAPS
Clorox, Colgate-Palmolive, Procter & Gamble,
Purex, Unilever N. V.

INDUSTRY GROUP AVERAGES *(concluded)*

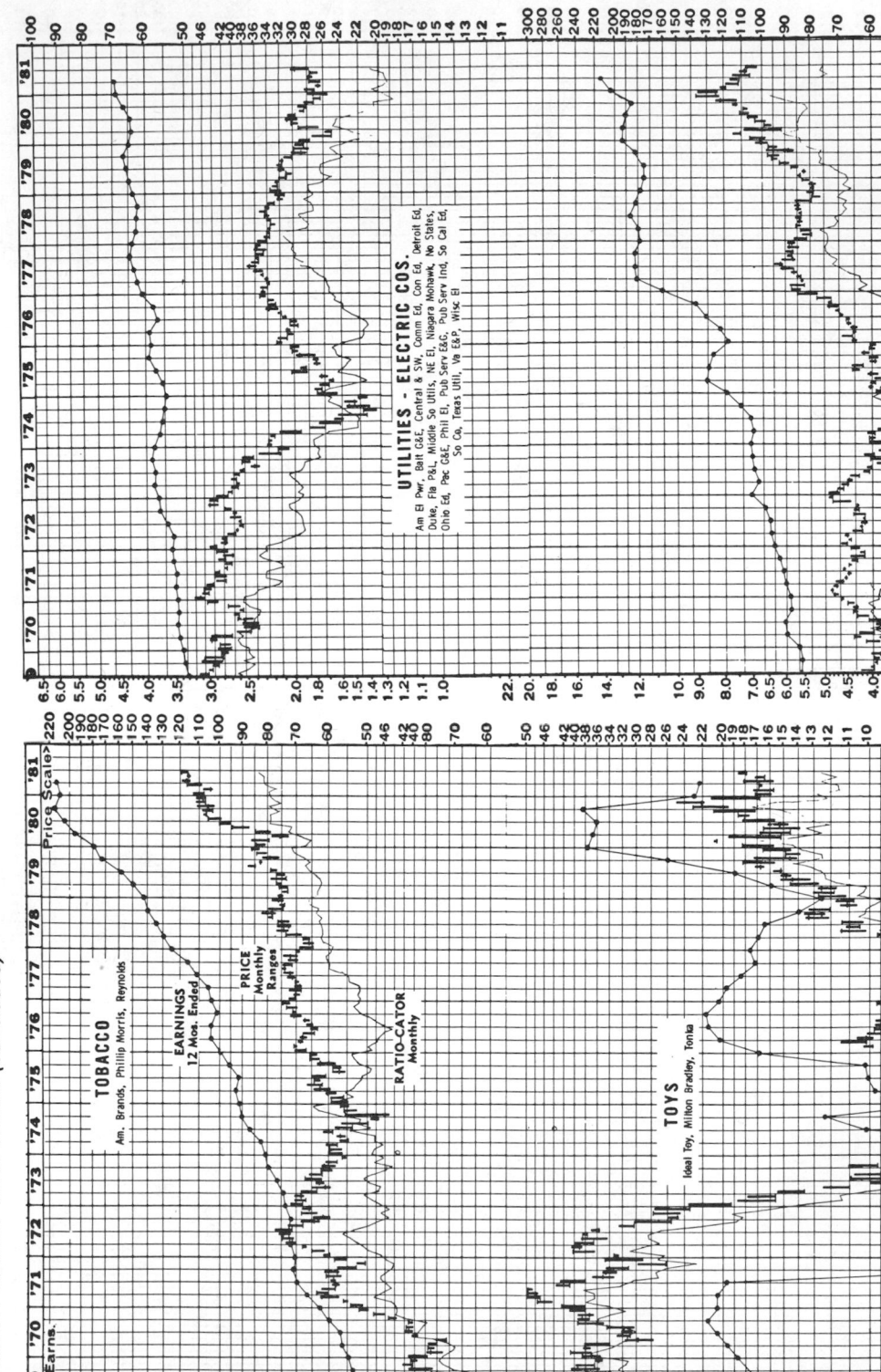

UTILITIES - ELECTRIC COS.

Am El Pwr, Balt G&E, Central & SW, Comm Ed, Con Ed, Detroit Ed, Duke, Fla P&L, Middle So Utils, NE El, Niagara Mohawk, No States, Ohio Ed, Pac G&E, Phil El, Pub Serv E&G, Pub Serv Ind, So Cal Ed, So Co, Texas Util, Va E&P, Wisc El

TOBACCO
Am. Brands, Phillip Morris, Reynolds

EARNINGS
12 Mos. Ended

PRICE
Monthly
Ranges

RATIO-CATOR
Monthly

TOYS
Ideal Toy, Milton Bradley, Tonka

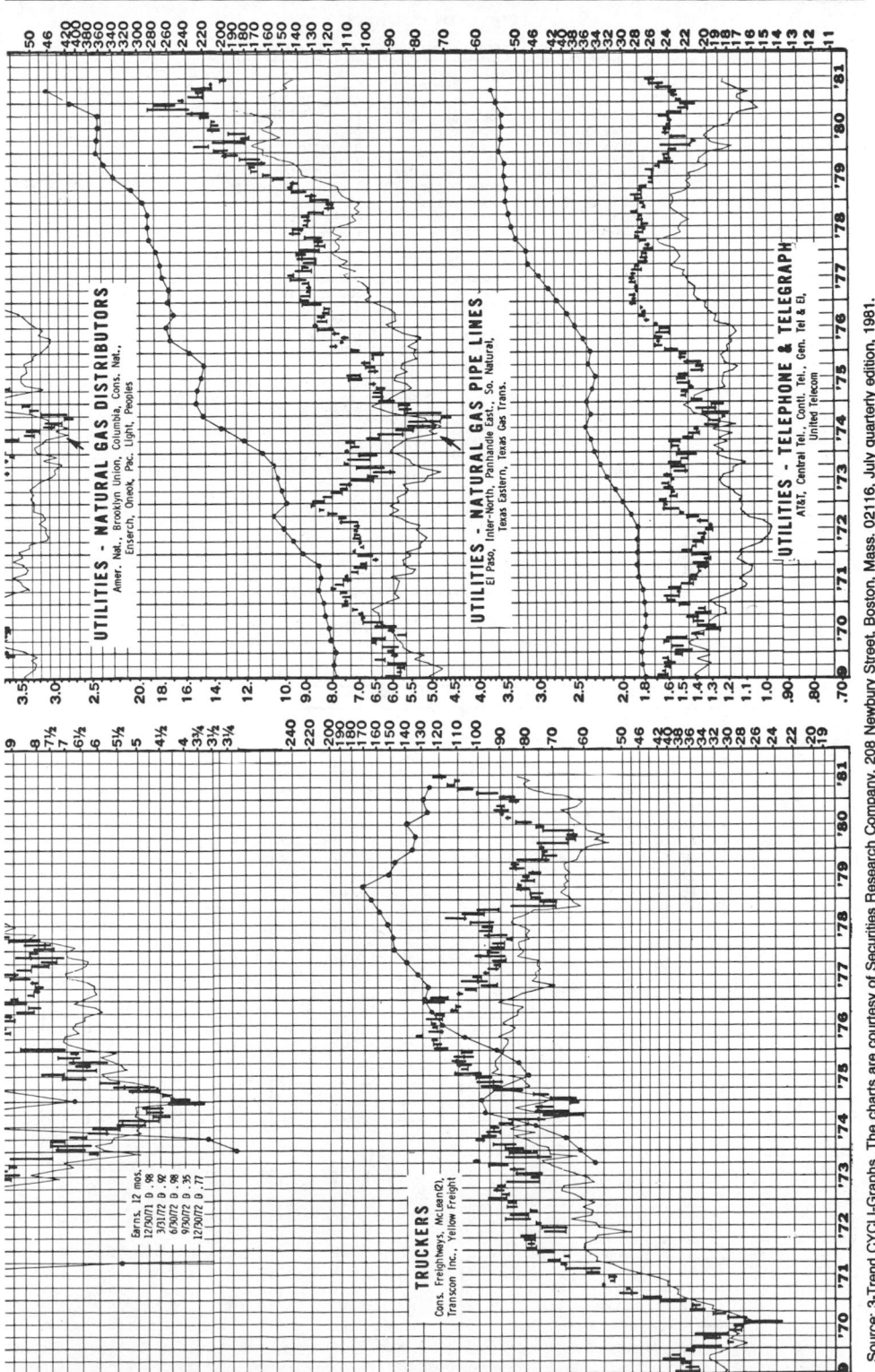

UTILITIES - NATURAL GAS DISTRIBUTORS
Amer. Nat., Brooklyn Union, Columbia, Cons. Nat.,
Enserch, Oneok, Pac. Light, Peoples

UTILITIES - NATURAL GAS PIPE LINES
El Paso, Inter-North, Panhandle East., So. Natural,
Texas Eastern, Texas Gas Trans.

UTILITIES - TELEPHONE & TELEGRAPH
AT&T, Central Tel., Contl. Tel., Gen. Tel & El,
United Telecom

TRUCKERS
Cons. Freightways, McLean(2),
Transcon Inc., Yellow Freight

Earns. 12 mos.
12/30/71 0 .98
3/31/72 0 .92
6/30/72 0 .98
9/30/72 0 .35
12/30/72 0 .77

Source: 3-Trend CYCLI-Graphs. The charts are courtesy of Securities Research Company, 208 Newbury Street, Boston, Mass. 02116, July quarterly edition, 1981.

COMPONENTS
DOW JONES STOCK AVERAGES

Industrials

Allied Corp.	General Foods	Owens-Illinois
Aluminum Co.	General Motors	Procter & Gamb
Amer Brands	Goodyear	Sears Roebuck
Amer Can	Inco	Std Oil of Calif
Amer Tel & Tel	IBM	Texaco
Bethlehem Steel	Inter Harvester	Union Carbide
Du Pont	Inter Paper	United Technologies
Eastman Kodak	Johns-Manville	US Steel
Exxon	Merck	Westinghouse El
General Electric	Minnesota M&M	Woolworth

Transportation

American Air	McLean Trucking	Southern Pacific
Burlington North	MoPac Corp	Southern Railway
CSX Corp	Norfolk & West'n	Transway Int'l
Canadian Pacific	Northwest Air	Trans World
Consolid Freight	Overnite Trans	UAL Inc
Delta Air Lines	Pan Am World Air	Union Pac Corp
Eastern Air Lines	Santa Fe Indust	

Utilities

Am Elec Power	Consol Nat Gas	Panhandle E Cp
Cleveland E Ill	Detroit Edison	Peoples Energy
Colum-Gas Sys	Houston Indust	Phila Elec
Comwlth Edison	Niag Mohawk P	Pub Serv E&G
Consol Edison	Pacific Gas & El	Sou Cal Edison

Source: *Barron's.*

FINANCIAL DATA ON DOW JONES INDUSTRIALS

	History				Earnings			P/E Ratio			Dvds	
	52-Week		5-Year		Last	%	5-Yr.		5-Year Avg		Indic	
	High	Low	High	Low	12Mos	Ch	Growth	Today	High	Low	Amt	Yield
	$	$	$	$	$	%	%	-	-	-	$	%
Dow Jones Ind	1024.05	908.45	1024.05	742.12	119.25	8.33	8	8.0	10.2	7.7	55.37	5.8
Allied Corp	61.75	46.88	61.75	27.63	8.80	27.17	16	6.1	8.9	6.0	2.40	4.5
Alum Co Am	38.19	26.75	38.19	19.25	4.78	-33.70	27	5.9	8.7	5.9	1.80	6.4
Am Brands	46.00	34.56	46.00	19.06	6.87	1.78	31	5.9	7.7	6.0	3.25	8.0
Am Can	45.25	27.00	45.25	27.00	3.92	-28.99	-5	9.4	7.6	6.0	2.90	7.9
Am Tel & Tel	69.25	45.00	65.63	45.00	8.30	2.98	7	6.8	8.8	7.3	5.40	9.6
Bethlehem Stl	32.00	22.75	48.00	18.25	2.11	-65.97	24	11.3	8.1	5.6	1.60	6.7
DuPont	56.00	36.00	56.00	31.13	5.14	-11.07	12	8.9	11.2	8.1	2.40	5.3
Eastman Kodak	85.38	61.50	120.75	41.13	7.78	23.89	17	9.6	17.1	10.7	3.50	4.7
Exxon	44.38	31.81	44.38	21.34	7.09	13.80	26	4.9	8.3	6.3	3.00	8.6
Gen. Electric	69.88	51.50	69.88	43.63	6.87	6.51	12	8.9	11.2	8.6	3.20	5.2
Gen Foods	35.00	27.88	37.00	23.50	4.71	-9.25	10	6.9	8.4	6.3	2.20	6.8
Gen Motors	58.88	40.38	78.88	39.50	.56	-15.15	-20	91.7	6.7	5.1	2.40	4.7
Goodyear Tire	20.25	15.00	28.38	10.75	3.19	98.14	9	6.1	9.4	6.5	1.30	6.7
Inco Ltd	27.25	17.75	37.00	13.38	1.56	-52.00	1	12.0	19.0	11.2	.72	3.8
Intl Bus Mach	72.75	54.63	80.50	50.38	6.24	16.64	10	9.0	15.2	11.7	3.44	6.1
Intl Harvester	35.00	14.25	45.50	14.25	-3.73	NE	-31	NE	5.6	3.7	.00	0
Intl Paper	51.50	38.63	79.75	30.50	7.15	40.75	5	6.7	11.1	7.5	2.40	5.0
Johns Manville	31.38	18.38	38.25	18.25	1.72	-49.85	-12	11.6	9.5	6.2	1.92	9.6
Merck & Co	103.00	73.13	103.00	47.38	5.68	6.97	13	16.2	18.0	13.3	2.60	2.8
Minn Mng Mfg	65.00	50.38	66.63	43.00	5.38	-5.28	16	10.1	15.0	11.2	3.00	5.5
Owens-Illinois	33.00	22.50	33.00	17.13	4.93	17.10	13	6.2	7.8	5.7	1.56	5.1
Proct & Gambl	82.75	63.00	100.13	62.75	7.94	3.12	11	9.1	15.2	12.0	3.80	5.2
Sears. Roebuck	20.88	14.38	39.63	14.38	2.03	-10.18	-4	9.0	12.0	9.2	1.36	7.5
Std Oil Cal	58.75	35.13	58.75	14.56	7.14	18.21	30	6.0	7.6	5.1	2.40	5.6
Texaco	54.38	33.13	54.38	22.13	8.55	12.80	32	4.2	7.9	5.9	2.80	7.7
Union Carbide	62.13	43.00	76.75	33.63	9.40	-4.86	11	6.0	7.7	5.5	3.40	6.0
US Steel Corp	35.25	21.00	59.38	16.25	6.57	NE	7	4.8	14.8	9.0	2.00	6.4
Unit Technols	65.75	47.13	65.75	23.19	6.92	14.19	15	7.3	9.8	6.6	2.40	4.7
Westinghouse	34.50	24.75	34.50	13.00	5.00	18.20	16	5.7	7.0	4.6	1.80	6.3
Woolworth FW	29.25	21.75	32.00	17.13	4.10	-35.23	12	5.4	6.9	4.8	1.80	8.1

Source: *The Media General Financial Weekly,* August 3, 1981, Media General Financial Services, 301 East Grace Street, Richmond, VA 23261.

DOW JONES INDUSTRIAL, TRANSPORTATION AND UTILITY AVERAGES

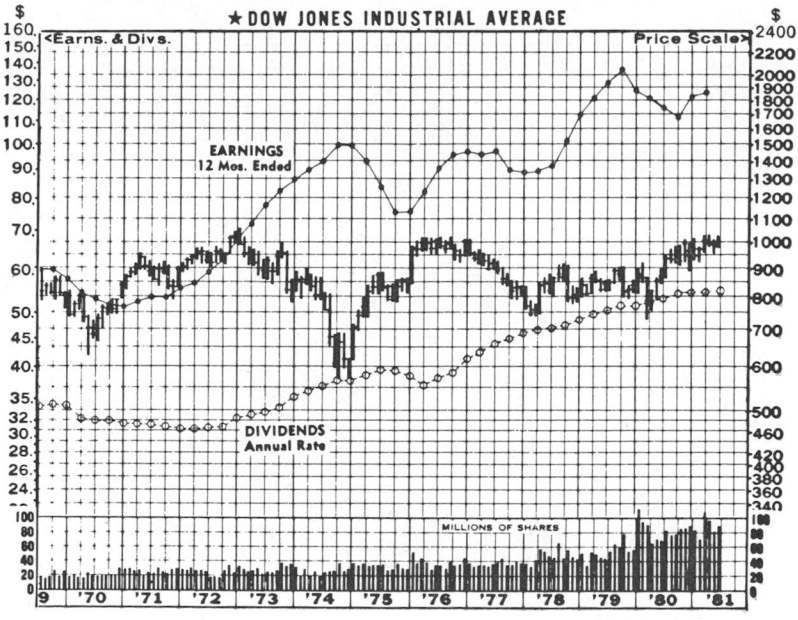

★ DOW JONES INDUSTRIAL AVERAGE

EARNINGS
12 Mos. Ended

DIVIDENDS
Annual Rate

MILLIONS OF SHARES

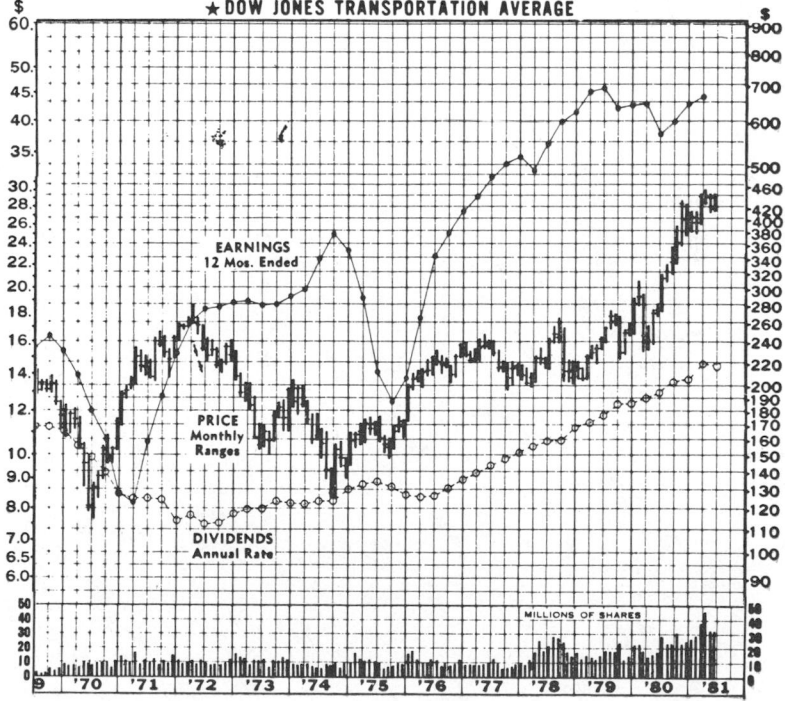

★ DOW JONES TRANSPORTATION AVERAGE

EARNINGS
12 Mos. Ended

PRICE
Monthly
Ranges

DIVIDENDS
Annual Rate

MILLIONS OF SHARES

DOW JONES INDUSTRIAL, TRANSPORTATION AND UTILITY AVERAGES *(continued)*

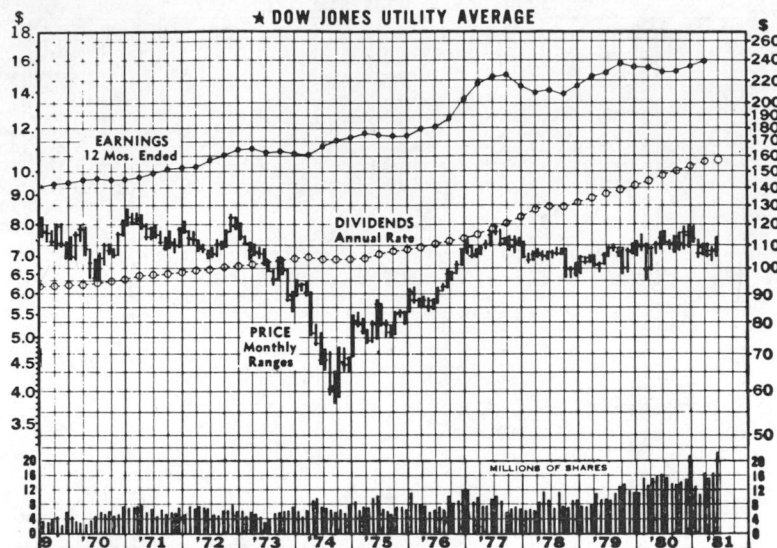

★ DOW JONES UTILITY AVERAGE

Source: 3-Trend CYCLI-Graphs. The charts are the courtesy of Securities Research Company, 208 Newbury Street, Boston, Mass. 02116, July quarterly edition, 1981.

NEW YORK STOCK EXCHANGE CASH DIVIDENDS AND YIELDS

Cash Dividends and Yields

	Common Stocks				Preferred Stocks			
Calen-dar Year	Number of Issues Listed at Year End	Number Paying Cash Dividends During Year	Estimated Aggregate Cash Payments (millions)	Median Yield[*]	Number of Issues Listed at Year End	Number Paying Cash Dividends During Year	Estimated Aggregate Cash Payments (millions)	Median Yield[*]
1929	842	554	$2,711	N/A	N/A	N/A	N/A	N/A
1930	848	576	2,667	N/A	N/A	N/A	N/A	N/A
1935	776	387	1,336	N/A	N/A	N/A	N/A	N/A
1940	829	577	2,099	6.1%	N/A	N/A	N/A	N/A
1945	881	746	2,275	3.6	388	341	$337	4.2%
1950	1,039	930	5,404	6.7	433	405	379	4.3
1951	1,054	961	5,467	6.5	441	406	380	4.6
1952	1,067	975	5,595	6.0	455	433	378	4.4
1953	1,069	964	5,874	6.3	461	443	383	4.7
1954	1,076	968	6,439	4.7	456	436	368	4.2
1955	1,076	982	7,488	4.6	432	412	336	4.2
1956	1,077	975	8,341	5.2	425	411	333	4.9
1957	1,098	991	8,807	6.1	424	409	335	4.9
1958	1,086	961	8,711	4.1	421	406	331	4.9
1959	1,092	953	9,337	3.8	415	403	337	5.1
1960	1,126	981	9,872	4.2	402	391	331	5.0
1961	1,145	981	10,430	3.3	396	381	341	4.8
1962	1,168	994	11,203	3.8	391	369	336	4.6
1963	1,194	1,032	12,096	3.6	378	359	342	4.6
1964	1,227	1,066	13,555	3.3	379	364	352	4.5
1965	1,254	1,111	15,302	3.2	373	358	388	4.7
1966	1,267	1,127	16,151	4.1	398	385	431	5.4
1967	1,255	1,116	16,866	3.2	445	432	596	5.8
1968	1,253	1,104	18,124	2.6	514	500	894	5.2
1969	1,290	1,121	19,404	3.6	499	487	1,142	6.8
1970	1,330	1,120	19,781	3.7	510	498	1,233	6.9
1971	1,399	1,132	20,256	3.2	528	499	1,360	6.7
1972	1,478	1,195	21,490	3.0	525	496	1,375	6.7
1973	1,536	1,276	23,627	5.0	522	497	1,487	8.0
1974	1,543	1,308	25,662	7.4	537	520	1,616	10.2
1975	1,531	1,273	26,901	5.0	580	552	1,682	9.3
1976	1,550	1,304	30,608	4.0	608	592	1,802	8.0
1977	1,549	1,360	36,270	4.5	628	619	1,954	8.4
1978	1,552	1,373	41,151	4.8	642	626	1,974	9.4
1979	1,536	1,359	46,937	5.0	656	644	2,225	10.9
1980	1,540	1,361	53,072	4.6	688	676	2,338	12.6

[*] Based on cash payments during the year and price at end of year for dividend-paying stocks only.
N/A—Not Available

Source: New York Stock Exchange *1981 Fact Book*.

VICKERS FAVORITE 50

Mar. 31 1976	Mar. 31 1980	Dec. 31 1980	Mar. 31 1981	Stocks	$ Value (Mil)	No. Funds Holding	No. of Shares Held	Net Chng. In Holdings	Net Chng. by Insiders	% Outst. Stk. Held by Funds
	Rank by $ Value									
1	1	1	1	International Business Machines	1,062.02	245	17,026,418	-306,766	-370,912	2.9
27	3	2	2	Schlumberger Ltd	755.79	129	7,437,014	-446,402	+120,201	3.9
2	2	3	3	Exxon Corp	609.43	174	8,880,581	-224,853	+8,931	2.1
3	10	11	4	American Tel & Tel	493.99	138	9,592,135	+2,328,857	+214	1.3
24	5	4	5	Atlantic Richfield	488.03	141	9,186,368	-98,312	-17,505	3.9
7	8	7	6	Philip Morris	465.75	95	9,109,966	-109,500	-2,484	7.3
-	11	5	7	Halliburton Co	446.14	110	5,870,315	-282,757	-376	5.0
5	12	9	8	Digital Equipment Corp	396.74	114	4,243,232	+322,668	+2,492	8.3
19	17	14	9	General Electric Co	391.46	116	5,842,646	+468,576	+761	2.6
-	13	6	10	Union Oil Company of California	359.04	84	9,118,427	-564,554	+2,286	5.3
4	29	19	11	Eastman Kodak	350.59	144	4,301,776	+405,837	-0-	2.7
43	14	10	12	Standard Oil Company (Indiana)	342.04	91	4,637,888	+24,284	+3,259	1.6
-	21	17	13	Smithkline Corp	301.11	53	3,793,559	-59,240	+4,908	5.7
20	9	16	14	Xerox Corp	299.89	126	5,295,988	+36,050	+500	6.3
9	37	25	15	Union Carbide Corp	297.94	90	4,854,496	+364,586	-1,715	7.2
-	45	29	16	Warner Communications Inc	285.59	53	5,980,927	+598,896	+1,505,554	10.0
-	4	21	17	Alcan Aluminium Ltd	275.60	99	7,398,676	-324,700	-0-	9.1
35	7	8	18	Mobil Corp	275.07	118	4,207,620	-446,800	-242	2.0
33	22	15	19	Conoco Inc	271.96	75	4,802,767	-44,950	+8,952	4.5
6	19	39	20	General Motors Corp	270.96	96	5,124,509	+964,885	+85,820	1.7
32	15	12	21	Phillips Petroleum Co	268.25	81	5,768,813	-145,800	+1,060	3.8
-	25	31	22	Dome Petroleum Ltd	267.15	62	3,597,945	+105,600	+30,740	7.3
18	30	38	23	E. I. duPont de Nemours	261.11	81	5,275,011	+676,421	+13,757	3.6
23	24	26	24	Minnesota Mining & Manufacturing	249.36	91	3,950,243	+220,795	-4,000	3.4
11	43	48	25	McDonald's Corp	241.11	79	3,842,410	+445,800	-215,550	9.6

				Company					
–	31	27	26	Hewlett Packard Co	235.21	56	2,542,772	+109,500	–35,710	4.2
16	16	13	27	Texaco Inc	234.62	106	6,277,530	–605,445	+7,339	2.3
–	40	40	28	Superior Oil Co	228.11	57	1,030,995	+90,455	+20	4.1
–	50	24	29	Honeywell Inc	216.54	49	2,062,285	–49,333	–2,933	9.1
–	36	44	30	Pfizer Inc	205.24	87	3,783,262	+579,500	–0–	5.2
–	35	–	31	Hospital Corp of America	204.73	54	5,199,444	–119,901	+10,358	11.4
38	30	–	32	Raytheon Co	198.77	59	1,897,570	+11,000	–1,833	4.6
26	22	–	33	Standard Oil Company of California	198.22	82	4,834,698	–85,278	+14,770	1.4
20	20	–	34	Gulf Oil Corp	195.93	75	5,519,160	–594,200	+3,184	2.8
–	36	–	35	Union Pacific Corp	192.74	58	2,604,644	+165,843	+80,591	2.7
–	–	–	36	**Johnson & Johnson	188.45	79	5,449,179	+548,400	–1,010	2.9
–	28	–	37	Dresser Industries Inc	186.75	55	3,791,840	–179,200	+12,778	4.9
–	41	–	38	Monsanto Co	184.90	66	2,559,204	–17,300	–30,507	7.1
23	18	–	39	Standard Oil Company of Ohio	180.21	79	3,432,477	–482,590	+46,114	1.4
–	42	–	40	Armco Inc	177.75	32	4,270,372	–380,750	–4,500	7.8
–	46	–	41	Texas Oil & Gas Corp	174.58	40	4,655,380	–49,140	+19,738	4.9
48	–	–	42	**Northwest Airlines Inc	171.05	57	5,725,661	+953,700	+400	26.5
–	–	–	43	*Tandy Corp	170.62	56	2,855,494	+101,096	–83,556	5.6
–	43	–	44	Royal Dutch Petroleum Co	165.31	47	4,145,742	+610,300	–0–	1.5
27	34	–	45	Merck & Co	163.44	73	1,931,384	–343,715	–326	2.6
15	–	47	46	Reynolds (R J) Industries Inc	161.00	57	3,618,013	–29,177	+5,466	3.5
–	–	–	47	**Matsushita Elec Industrial Co Ltd	157.74	17	3,004,601	+663,350	–0–	22.2
48	35	33	48	Tenneco Inc	156.33	82	3,282,481	–1,402,936	+3,021	2.8
–	28	49	49	NCR Corp	155.15	51	2,396,204	+217,170	+2,357	9.0
–	–	–	50	**PepsiCo Inc	152.75	64	4,611,247	+7,000	–10,875	5.1

*NEWCOMER

**RETURNEE

DISPLACED STOCKS: Amerada Hess Corp – Boeing Co – Houston Oil & Minerals – Natomas Company – Santa Fe International Corp

SUMMARY OF FAVORITE 50 BY INDUSTRY

Dollar Value of Stocks by Industry to Total Value of Favorite 50

	3/31/81	12/31/80	3/31/80	3/31/76
Oil & Natural Gas	39.0%	49.5%	41.0%	18.7%
Office Equipment	13.3	13.6	15.8	21.3
Chemicals & Drugs	11.1	8.5	9.5	17.9
Electric & Electronics	9.5	6.6	5.6	3.2
Leisure	6.1	4.3	5.0	7.4
Utilities	3.4	2.3	3.7	5.4
Miscellaneous	17.6	15.2	19.4	26.1
	100.0%	100.0%	100.0%	100.0%

Source: Vickers Guide to Investment Company Portfolios. Copyright © 1981 by Vickers Associates, Inc. Reproduction hereof permitted only on written permission from Vickers Associates, Inc., Huntington, N.Y., the Copyright owner.

SHARES SOLD ON REGISTERED EXCHANGES

Total Volume by Shares, 1980 (thousands)

Month	Total Shares	NYSE Shares	NYSE Percent of Total	ASE Shares	ASE Percent of Total	All Other Shares	All Other Percent of Total
Jan.	1,401,950	1,090,941	77.8%	178,074	12.7%	132,935	9.5%
Feb.	1,549,895	1,239,137	79.9	170,569	11.0	140,189	9.0
Mar.	1,146,792	904,380	78.9	132,927	11.6	109,485	9.5
Apr.	963,193	788,408	81.9	90,329	9.4	84,456	8.8
May	960,028	780,306	81.3	78,588	8.2	101,134	10.5
June	1,140,786	933,640	81.8	108,299	9.5	98,847	8.7
July	1,258,105	1,003,627	79.8	142,009	11.3	112,469	8.9
Aug.	1,433,202	1,122,269	78.3	168,080	11.7	142,853	10.0
Sept.	1,335,904	1,090,199	81.6	140,536	10.5	105,169	7.9
Oct.	1,501,010	1,216,081	81.0	141,072	9.4	143,857	9.6
Nov.	1,279,508	1,016,255	79.4	145,907	11.4	117,346	9.2
Dec.	1,515,313	1,204,629	79.5	162,450	10.7	148,234	9.8
Year'	15,485,686	12,389,871	80.0%	1,658,840	10.7%	1,436,974	9.3%

Total Volume by Value, 1980 (millions)

Month	Total Value	NYSE Value	NYSE Percent of Total	ASE Value	ASE Percent of Total	All Other Value	All Other Percent of Total
Jan.	$ 39,881	$ 33,942	85.1%	$ 2,437	6.1%	$ 3,502	8.8%
Feb.	45,731	37,721	82.5	3,577	7.8	4,433	9.7
Mar.	35,704	29,164	81.7	3,355	9.4	3,185	8.9
Apr.	26,248	22,320	85.0	1,636	6.2	2,292	8.7
May	28,029	23,402	83.5	1,705	6.1	2,922	10.4
June	33,490	27,996	83.6	2,268	6.8	3,226	9.6
July	38,611	31,949	82.7	3,362	8.7	3,300	8.5
Aug.	43,795	35,606	81.3	3,762	8.6	4,427	10.1
Sept.	41,216	35,308	85.7	2,664	6.5	3,244	7.9
Oct.	50,641	42,873	84.7	3,071	6.1	4,697	9.3
Nov.	43,157	36,015	83.5	3,420	7.9	3,722	8.6
Dec.	49,347	41,373	83.8	3,439	7.0	4,535	9.2
Year	$475,850	$397,670	83.6%	$34,696	7.3%	$43,485	9.1%

Source: New York Stock Exchange *1981 Fact Book.*

COMMON STOCK PRICES
AND YIELDS

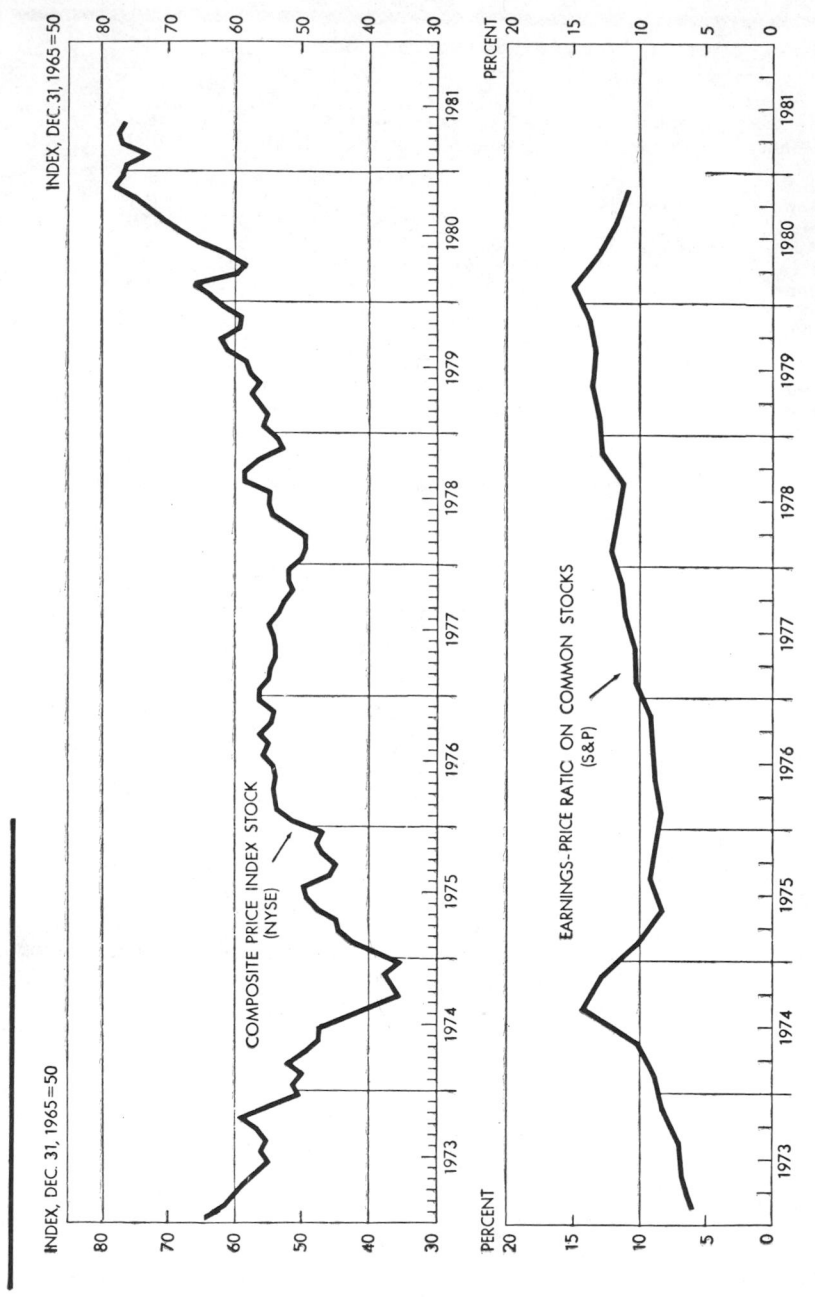

INDEX, DEC. 31, 1965=50

COMPOSITE PRICE INDEX STOCK
(NYSE)

EARNINGS-PRICE RATIO ON COMMON STOCKS
(S&P)

INDEX, DEC. 31, 1965=50

SOURCES: NEW YORK STOCK EXCHANGE AND STANDARD & POOR'S CORPORATION

COUNCIL OF ECONOMIC ADVISERS

Common Stock Prices and Yields

Period	Common stock prices [1]							Common stock yields (percent) [5]	
	New York Stock Exchange indexes (Dec. 31, 1965=50) [2]					Dow-Jones industrial average [3]	Standard & Poor's composite index (1941-43=10) [4]	Dividend-price ratio	Earnings-price ratio
	Composite	Industrial	Transportation	Utility	Finance				
1975	45.73	50.52	31.10	31.50	47.14	802.49	86.16	4.31	9.15
1976	54.46	60.44	39.57	36.97	52.94	974.92	102.01	3.77	8.90
1977	53.69	57.86	41.09	40.92	55.25	894.63	98.20	4.62	10.79
1978	53.70	58.23	43.50	39.22	56.65	820.23	96.02	5.28	12.03
1979	58.32	64.76	47.34	38.21	61.42	844.40	103.01	5.47	13.46
1980	68.10	78.70	60.61	37.35	64.25	891.41	118.78	5.26	12.66
1980: May	61.38	69.39	51.07	37.31	61.47	828.19	107.69	5.77	----
June	65.43	74.47	54.04	38.53	65.16	869.86	114.55	5.39	13.08
July	68.56	78.67	59.14	38.77	66.76	909.79	119.83	5.20	----
Aug	70.87	82.15	62.48	38.18	67.22	947.33	123.50	5.06	----
Sept	73.12	84.92	65.89	38.77	69.33	946.67	126.51	4.90	11.67
Oct	75.17	88.00	70.76	38.44	68.29	949.17	130.22	4.80	----
Nov	78.15	92.32	77.23	38.35	67.21	971.08	135.65	4.63	----
Dec	76.69	90.37	75.74	37.84	67.46	945.96	133.48	4.74	10.89
1981: Jan	76.24	89.23	74.43	38.53	70.04	962.13	132.97	4.80	----
Feb	73.52	85.74	72.76	37.59	68.48	945.50	128.40	5.00	----
Mar	76.46	89.39	77.09	37.82	72.82	987.18	133.19	4.88	----
Apr	77.60	90.57	80.63	38.34	74.59	1,004.86	134.43	4.86	----
May	76.28	88.78	76.78	38.27	74.65	979.52	131.73	4.98	----
Week ended:									
1981: May 23	76.49	88.86	77.22	38.60	75.47	978.19	131.94	4.97	----
30	77.27	89.75	78.46	38.80	76.86	990.78	133.15	4.92	----
June 6	76.28	88.46	76.64	38.29	77.66	991.14	131.38	5.08	----
13	77.06	89.07	77.47	38.94	80.12	999.53	132.75	5.03	----
20	76.99	88.46	76.19	39.91	81.77	1,002.64	132.60	4.98	----
27	77.02	88.73	76.84	39.75	80.08	997.97	132.67	5.02	----

[1] Average of daily closing prices.
[2] Includes all the stocks (more than 1,500) listed on the NYSE.
[3] Includes 30 stocks.   [4] Includes 500 stocks.
[5] Standard & Poor's series. Dividend-price ratios based on Wednesday closing prices. Earnings-price ratios based on prices at end of quarter.

NOTE.—All data relate to stocks listed on the New York Stock Exchange (NYSE).

Sources: New York Stock Exchange, Dow-Jones & Company, Inc., and Standard & Poor's Corporation.

Source: Economic Indicators, Council of Economic Advisers.

NEW SECURITY ISSUES of Corporations

Millions of dollars

Type of issue or issuer, or use	1978	1979	1981r	1980				1981		
				Sept.	Oct.r	Nov.	Dec.r	Jan.	Feb.	Mar.
1 All issues¹	47,230	51,533	73,688	5,025	5,819	3,936r	5,933	5,581r	4,157	6,667
2 Bonds	36,872	40,208	53,199	2,916	3,284	2,164r	3,044	3,386r	2,834	4,519
Type of offering										
3 Public	19,815	25,814	41,587	2,421	2,756r	1,405r	1,719	2,928	2,408r	4,022
4 Private placement	17,057	14,394	11,612	495	528	759r	1,325	458r	426	497
Industry group										
5 Manufacturing	9,572	9,678	15,409	553	623	132r	609	1,635	1,140	1,204
6 Commercial and miscellaneous	5,246	3,948	6,688	390	320	442r	509	231	356	212
7 Transportation	2,007	3,119	3,329	409	240	147r	165	353	45	172
8 Public utility	7,092	8,153	9,556	569	769	565	314	800	593	594
9 Communication	3,373	4,219	6,683	517	763	147r	653r	62r	272	958
10 Real estate and financial	9,586	11,094	11,534	477	569	732r	793	306	430	1,380
11 Stocks	10,358	11,325	20,490	2,109	2,535	1,772	2,889	2,195r	1,323	2,148
Type										
12 Preferred	2,832	3,574	3,632	392	543	256	241	364r	149	298
13 Common	7,526	7,751	16,858	1,717	1,992	1,516	2,648	1,831	1,174	1,850
Industry group										
14 Manufacturing	1,241	1,679	4,839	502	851	418	844	609r	204	735
15 Commercial and miscellaneous	1,816	2,623	5,245	569	400	509	908	603	589	816
16 Transportation	263	255	549	54	117	53	95	124	81	17
17 Public utility	5,140	5,171	6,230	633	526	227	669	562	260	414
18 Communication	264	303	567	6	67	113	65	14	31	......
19 Real estate and financial	1,631	12,931	3,059	345	574	452	308	284	159	167

1. Figures, which represent gross proceeds of issues maturing in more than one year, sold for cash in the United States, are principal amount or number of units multiplied by offering price. Excludes offerings of less than $100,000, secondary offerings, undefined or exempted issues as defined in the Securities Act of 1933, employee stock plans, investment companies other than closed-end, intra-corporate transactions, and sales to foreigners.

SOURCE. Securities and Exchange Commission.

Source: *Federal Reserve Bulletin*, Board of Governors of the Federal Reserve System.

How to Understand and Analyze Financial Statements*

Fred B. Renwick †

Analyzing financial statements in corporate annual reports can be easy, fun, and rewarding, if you know what to look for. This short essay explains in a nutshell what to look for and how to analyze financial statements.

Only four statements are important to understand and analyze, namely:

- The *balance sheet,* which states the financial condition of the corporation as of one particular date: the date posted at the top of the statement.
- The *income statement,* which shows the amount of earnings for the year currently ending, and conveys information regarding the efficiency and profitability of the business.
- The *statement of retained earnings,* which gives further information regarding one of the lines on the balance sheet, and also shows the division of net income for the year between dividend payout to stockholders and earnings retained and reinvested in the business.
- The *statement of sources and uses of funds,* which gives further information regarding total current assets and total current liabilities as stated on the balance sheet; and shows the net changes during the year in working capital.

Additionally, corporate annual reports usually contain supplementary information which expands upon items in the four basic statements, and includes: (1) a letter or report of independent accountants and auditors addressed to stockholders and directors of the company certifying and validating the figures in the four statements, (2) notes which report material information regarding line items in each statement, (3) segment information which summarizes selected information by industry and geographic segments, (4) restatement pursuant to Financial Accounting Standards Board (FASB) *Statement of Financial Accounting Standards No. 33* to account for effects of inflation and changing prices on items in the four primary statements, and (5) a long-term (5 or 10-year) summary of selected items from the four primary statements.

The following section explains each statement in detail, Section II explains how to analyze the statements, Section III explains notes and supplementary information.

---

* See also the definition of financial terms, p. 304.

† Fred B. Renwick is Professor of Finance at the Graduate School of Business Administration, New York University, New York, N.Y.

1. FOUR FINANCIAL STATEMENTS: WHAT TO LOOK FOR

BALANCE SHEETS

Exhibit 1 shows a balance sheet for Universal Manufacturing Corporation (UMC), a hypothetical company which produces and distributes goods and services in the health industry. Universal's single line of business is divided into two industry segments: human and animal health products, and environmental health products and services.

Observe the format of Universal's balance sheet, the *report form,* where total assets, $26 million, are itemized first and total financing (total liabilities and stockholders' equity), $26 million, are itemized below the asset section. Some corporations prefer to use the *account form,* where assets are listed on the left side of the form and liabilities and owners' equity sections are listed to the right of the asset section. UMC is using the *report form.*

The balance sheet shows the ownership of total corporate assets as of the date of the statement. For example, the following calculation implies that if UMC's tangible assets were liquidated as of the date posted at the top of the balance sheet, $17.8 million would be available for distribution among the preferred and common stockholders.

Total assets owned by UMC	$26,000,000
Less: Intangibles	200,000
Total tangible assets owned by UMC	$25,800,000
Amount required to pay total liabilities.......................	8,000,000
Amount remaining for the stockholders	$17,800,000

Further, the above example illustrates a critical point: the difference between *current market value* (the amount UMC's assets would really bring if sold) versus the *accounting book value* (the $17.8 million). Relationships exist between market and book values, but accounting statements (except for FASB *No. 33*) are factual reports of *book,* not *market,* values of corporate assets.

The following paragraphs explain each line entry on balance sheets.

Starting at the top of the balance sheet, after the name of the corporation, title, and date of the statement, total assets are itemized, with current assets (total, $13.6 million) always first. *Current assets* consist of:

1. *Cash,* $350,000, which is what you would expect, namely pocket-book currency and

251

coins in the treasurer's office, plus demand deposits at a commercial bank. Cash is synonymous with liquidity,

2. *Marketable securities,* $2.85 million, which usually are cash equivalents or highly liquid securities such as Treasury Bills of the federal government or negotiable certificates of deposit (CDs), or demand notes issued by large corporations,

3. *Accounts receivable,* $4.8 million, which consist of payments due from customers who purchased UMC's goods and services on credit and have not paid yet but are scheduled to pay within the next few months. Since a small fraction of customers might never pay (because of death, financial disaster, flood, or other catastrophe), an al-

lowance is made, $24,000, pursuant to good accounting practices for bad debts,

4. *Inventories,* $5.6 million, which consist of (*a*) finished goods in stock and ready for sale or shipment, (*b*) work and merchandise in process, and (*c*) supplies and raw materials inventories; and are priced on the balance sheet at the lower of cost or market on either a first-in-first-out (Fifo) or last-in-first-out (Lifo) basis. Pricing policy is usually stated in a note.

Total current assets, $13.6 million, are the sum of the four aforecited figures and usually are earmarked for use within the coming 12 months. In other words, *current* means within the next 12 months.

Fixed assets (property, plant and equipment)

EXHIBIT 1

UNIVERSAL MANUFACTURING CORPORATION
Balance Sheet
December 31, 1981

Assets	1981	1980
Current assets		
Cash	$ 350,000	$ 250,000
Marketable securities at cost		
(market value: 1981, $2,980,000; 1980, $1,900,000)	2,850,000	1,830,000
Accounts receivable		
Less: Allowance for bad debt: 1981, $24,000; 1980, $21,000	4,800,000	4,370,000
Inventories	5,600,000	4,950,000
Total current assets	$13,600,000	$11,400,000
Fixed assets (property, plant, and equipment)		
Land	$ 734,000	$ 661,000
Building	5,762,000	5,258,000
Machinery	11,435,000	10,011,000
Office equipment	614,000	561,000
	18,545,000	16,491,000
Less: Accumulated depreciation	6,435,000	5,671,000
Net fixed assets	12,110,000	10,820,000
Prepayments and deferred charges	90,000	61,600
Intangibles (goodwill, patent, trademarks)	200,000	200,000
Total assets	$26,000,000	$22,481,600

Liabilities	1981	1980
Current liabilities		
Accounts payable	$ 2,910,000	$ 2,300,000
Notes payable	1,420,000	730,000
Accrued expenses payable	430,000	350,000
Federal income taxes payable	1,240,000	1,320,000
Total current liabilities	$ 6,000,000	$ 4,700,000
Long-term liabilities		
First mortgage bonds, 8% interest, due 1995	$ 2,000,000	$ 2,000,000
Total liabilities	$ 8,000,000	$ 6,700,000

Stockholders' Equity		
Capital stock		
Preferred stock, 6% cumulative, $100 par value each;		
authorized, issued, and outstanding 13,600 shares	1,360,000	1,360,000
Common stock, 30 cents par value each; authorized, issued,		
and outstanding 760,000 shares	228,000	228,000
Capital surplus	1,112,000	1,112,000
Accumulated retained earnings	15,300,000	13,081,600
Total stockholders' equity	$18,000,000	$15,781,600
Total liabilities and stockholders' equity	$26,000,000	$22,481,600

are the permanent tangible capital owned by the business, and are listed *at cost* (original purchase price) next on the balance sheet; and consists of:

1. *Land,* $734,000, or ground upon which buildings or other assets such as forests, air or water rights, and the like are built,
2. *Building,* $5.762 million, which are structures such as offices, warehouses, and the like where business is conducted,
3. *Machinery,* $11.435 million, which are mechanical apparatus for increasing productivity and economic efficiency,
4. *Office equipment,* $614,000, which is what you would expect, namely desks, typewriters, copiers, and the like.

Accumulated depreciation, $6.435 million, is the total depreciation (deterioration of property, plant, and equipment due to physical wear and tear) accumulated to date for accounting purposes against UMC's assets. It is important to know about three concepts of depreciation, namely: (1) depreciation calculated for tax purposes which is figured pursuant to the Tax Code to benefit from allowable accelerated rates of depreciation, (2) accounting depreciation, which can be either straight-line or accelerated and is usually explained in a note, (3) economic depreciation, which comes from technological obsolescence and deterioration in ability to continue generating future income at current rates due to changes in demand and markets for the goods and services produced by UMC. The balance sheet states only number two, accounting depreciation.

Net fixed assets, $12,110,000, are the sum of the four above figures, minus accounting depreciation; and are used by the business to generate future (beyond the coming 12 months) income.

Prepayments and deferred charges, $90,000, state total amounts paid in advance for assets not yet obtained (such as paid-up premiums on a fire insurance policy covering the next five years, or rental paid on computers for the next three years); and for benefits to be received in future years for expenditures already made (such as for research and development, moving the business to a new location, or expenses incurred in bringing a new product to market).

Intangibles, $200,000, are assets such as goodwill, trademarks, franchises, patents, copyrights, and the like which have no physical existence; yet are valuable in producing business income.

Total assets, $26 million, are current, plus fixed, plus prepayments and deferred charges, plus intangibles; and state the size of the business and are the total property owned by the business.

Look next at the lower part of the balance sheet, which concerns the financing of the business. Financing must come from either borrowing (liabilities) or ownership equity.

Underneath the asset section of the balance sheet (or on the right side if the company uses the account form), total current liabilities, $6 million, always are itemized next, then long-term liabilities, $2 million, then finally stockholders' equity of $18 million.

Total current liabilities consist of bills due and payable by UMC within the next 12 months, all of which fall into one of four categories:

1. *Accounts payable,* $2.91 million, which are bills currently owed and due to creditors,
2. *Notes payable,* $1.42 million, which are current obligations owed to a bank or other short-term lender,
3. *Accrued expenses payable,* $430,000, include wages due employees, fees to attorneys, current pension or retirement obligations, and the like.
4. *Federal income taxes payable,* $1.24 million, is the current tax payable to the Internal Revenue Service, and is sufficiently important to merit a line of its own on the corporate balance sheet.

Long-term liabilities, $2 million for UMC, can include straight debt (like UMC's which pays 8 percent interest and matures in 1995), convertible bonds (bonds which pay interest like straight bonds but are convertible upon demand of the bond owner into a stated number of shares of common stock), or "other" long-term debt (like pollution control and industrial revenue bonds or sinking-fund debentures). UMC has only straight debt outstanding.

Total liabilities, $8 million, are the sum of current and long-term liabilities and constitute the total financing obtained from borrowings.

Stockholders' equity, $18 million consists of:

1. *Capital stock,* $1.588 million, which includes both preferred stock and common stock but no convertible preferred stock and no warrants or rights to purchase either bonds or common stock,
2. *Capital surplus,* $1.112 million, which is the amount paid in by shareholders over the par or legal value of 30 cents for each common share,
3. *Accumulated retained earnings,* $15.3 million, which are earnings not paid out in dividends but have been retained and reinvested in the business. Further information regarding accumulated retained earnings since inception of the business is set forth below in the *statement of retained earnings.*

Capital stock represents proprietary interest in the company, is represented by stock certificates authorized and issued by the company, and can belong to either of several classes, including:

1. *Preferred stock,* which has preference or takes priority over other shares regarding dividend payout (6 percent in UMC's case), and which can be cumulative, which means that if the company fails to pay dividends for whatever reason for any year, then the 6 percent of $100 or $6 per preferred share accumulates on the books and must be paid before common stockholders can receive future dividends. Total preferred stock authorized and issued by UMC is $100 per share times 13,600 shares or $1.36 million.
2. *Common stock,* which represents the remaining ownership of the company and is entitled to receive a dividend along with fluctuations in value of the stock. Par value is the legal stated value of each common share; so the par value (30 cents per share times 760,000 shares or $228,000) plus the additional amount or capital surplus ($1.112 million) together state the amount UMC received upon issuing 760,000 shares, namely $1.34 million divided by 760,000 or $1.76 per share.

The bottom line, *total liabilities and stockholders equity,* states the financing of the corporation, and shows where UMC obtained the $26 million to buy the total assets itemized at the top of the balance sheet.

We turn next to income statements.

INCOME STATEMENTS

Exhibit 2 shows UMC's income statement, where the important items to look for, after the name of the company, the title, and date of the statement at the heading, are:

1. *Net sales,* which is where most of the business revenue comes from for most businesses, except rental and leasing companies, $23,850,000.
2. *Net Operating Income* (NOI) or profit before interest and taxes, which states profit from business operations, without regard to financing, $5,878,000.
3. *Total Income* before interest and taxes, which states the return on total capital available to the business during the year, $6,220,000.
4. *Less:* provision for federal income tax, $2,240,000.
5. *Total Income,* after tax but before interest deduction, which states the after-tax profitability of the corporation and is widely used in computing cost of capital for a business enterprise, $3,980,000.
6. *Net income* (NI) or profit for the year, which

EXHIBIT 2

UNIVERSAL MANUFACTURING CORPORATION
Consolidated Income Statement
December 31, 1981 and 1980

	1981	1980
Net sales	$23,850,000	$19,810,000
Cost of sales and operating expenses		
Cost of goods sold	8,940,000	7,209,000
Depreciation	800,000	750,000
Selling and administrating expenses	8,232,000	6,814,000
Operating profit	$ 5,878,000	$ 5,037,000
Other income		
Dividends and interest	342,000	183,000
Total income	$ 6,220,000	$ 5,220,000
Less: Interest on bonds	160,000	160,000
Income before provision for federal income tax	$ 6,060,000	$ 5,060,000
Provision for federal income tax	2,240,000	1,980,000
Net profit for year	$ 3,820,000	$ 3,080,000
Common shares outstanding	760,000	760,000
Net earnings per share	$ 4.92	$ 3.95

Statement of Accumulated Retained Earnings

	1981	1980
Balance January 1	$13,081,600	$11,413,200
Net profit for year	3,820,000	3,080,000
Total	$16,901,600	$14,493,200
Less: Dividends paid on		
Preferred stock	81,600	81,600
Common stock	1,520,000	1,330,000
Balance December 31	$15,300,000	$13,081,600

states earnings after taxes and after all fixed charges. The net profit for the year is available for (a) dividend payout to preferred stockholders, (b) dividend payout to common stockholders, and (c) retention and re-investment in the business, $3,820,000.

7. *Net earnings per share* (EPS), which equals total earnings available for distribution to common stockholders ($3.82 million minus 6% dividend owed on 13,600 shares of $100 par value preferred stock, or $3,738,400), divided by 760,000 common shares outstanding, $4.92.

$$\$3,820,000 - 0.06(13,600)(\$100) =$$
$$\$3,738,400$$
$$\$3,738,400/760,000 =$$
$$\$4.92 \text{ per share}$$

Cost of sales and operating expenses falls into one of three categories:

1. *Cost of goods sold,* which states the amount of labor, material, and other expenses in producing the items sold, $8,940,000.
2. *Depreciation expense,* which states the amount of capital (producer's durables) consumed in producing the goods and services sold and which must be replaced or restored to its original capacity, $800,000.
3. *Selling and administrating expenses,* which includes office expenses, executives salaries, salespersons salaries, advertising and promotion expenses and the like, $8,232,000.

Operating profit, also called net operating income, $5.878 million, is the income from business operations, and is an important indicator of how efficiently the fixed assets were employed during the year.

Other income, $342,000, is from UMC's marketable securities of $1.83 million at cost as of one year ago.

Total income, $6.22 million, is the sum of operating profit from the business and income from other sources.

Interest on bonds, $160,000, (8 percent of 2 million) is itemized next on the income statement, followed by:

Income after interest, before tax	$6,060,000
Provision for federal income tax	2,240,000
Net profit for the year	3,820,000
Net earnings per share	$4.92

We turn next to statements of accumulated retained earnings.

STATEMENTS OF ACCUMULATED RETAINED EARNINGS

The bottom part of Exhibit 2 contains the accumulated retained earnings statement for UMC, and shows at the beginning of the balance, since the starting date of the business to January 1 of the current year, $13,081,600— to which is added the net profit for the year, $3,820,000, to get total accumulated retained earnings of $16,901,600.

Dividends paid to stockholders are itemized next:

Preferred stock dividend: 6 percent of $1,360,000	$ 81,600
Common stock dividend: $2.00 per share declared times 760,000 shares	1,520,000
Total dividends paid	$1,601,600

Balance, December 31 (15.3 million) equals the difference between the total available ($16,901,600) and total dividends paid. Retained earnings are an important source of finance of corporate capital assets.

We turn next to statements of sources and uses of funds.

STATEMENT OF SOURCE AND APPLICATION OF FUNDS

Exhibit 3 is a statement of source and application or use of funds for UMC. Ordinarily, *funds* imply cash; but in a broader sense, *funds* include cash equivalents and substitutes for cash, such as short-term credit, notes, and account payable and accrued liabilities to meet the short-term financing needs of the business. So *funds* in the broader sense imply net *working capital,* which is the difference between current assets and current liabilities.

Sources of funds in general include transactions which increase the amount of working capital, such as:

1. Net profit from operations.
2. Sale or consumption of noncurrent assets.
3. Long-term borrowing.
4. Issuing additional shares of capital stock.
5. Annual depreciation.

Uses of funds in general include transactions which decrease working capital, such as:

1. Declaring cash dividends.
2. Repaying long-term debt.
3. Buying noncurrent assets.
4. Repurchasing outstanding capital stock.

In the case of UMC and Exhibit 3, funds were provided by net income, $3.82 million, and current depreciation expense, $800,000. Some analysts worry that depreciation is not cash, depreciation is a bookkeeping entry. But the capital was consumed in the process of producing the goods and services sold; so the business pays the cash to itself to ultimately replace the consumed capital. Depreciation expense is a source of funds.

Total funds provided for UMC are $4,620,000.

EXHIBIT 3

UNIVERSAL MANUFACTURING CORPORATION
Statement of Source and Application of Funds
December 31, 1981

		1981
Funds were provided by		
Net income	$3,820,000	
Depreciation	800,000	
Total		$4,620,000
Funds were used for		
Dividends on preferred stock	$ 81,600	
Dividends on common stock	1,520,000	
Plant and equipment	1,720,300	
Sundry assets	398,100	
Total		$3,720,000
Increase in Working Capital		$ 900,000
Analysis of changes in working capital—1981		
Changes in current assets		
Cash	$ 100,000	
Marketable securities	1,020,000	
Accounts receivable	430,000	
Inventories	650,000	
Total		$2,200,000
Changes in current liabilities		
Accounts payable	$ 610,000	
Notes payable	690,000	
Accrued expenses payable	80,000	
Federal income tax payable	(80,000)	
Total		$1,300,000

Uses of funds are itemized next, where all uses fall into one of four categories:

Dividends on preferred stock	$ 81,600
Dividends on common stock	1,520,000
Plant and equipment	1,720,300
Sundry assets	398,100
Total uses or application of funds	$3,720,000

Increase in working capital, $900,000, is the difference between the total funds provided, $4.62 million, and the total funds used, $3.72 million.

An *analysis of changes in working capital* for the year is included in the statement of source and application of funds, and gives further information regarding the $900,000 increase in working capital, which is explained by analyzing changes in current assets together with changes in current liabilities.

Changes in current assets total $2.2 million, itemized as follows:

1. *Cash* increased from $250,000 to $350,000, giving a net change of $100,000,
2. *Marketable securities* increased from $1.83 million to $2.85 million, giving a net change of $1.02 million,
3. *Accounts receivable* increased from $4.37 million to $4.8 million, giving a net change of $430,000,
4. *Inventories* increased from $4.95 million to

$5.6 million, giving a net change of $650,000.

Changes in current liabilities total $1.3 million, itemized as follows:

1. *Accounts payable* increased from $2.3 million to $2.91 million, giving a net change of $610,000,
2. *Notes payable* increased from $730,000 to $1.42 million, giving a net change of $690,000,
3. *Accrued expenses payable* increased from $350,000 to $430,000, giving a net change of $80,000,
4. *Federal income taxes payable* decreased from $1.32 million to $1.24 million, giving a net change of ($80,000).

The difference between the changes in current assets ($2.2 million) and changes in current liabilities ($1.3 million) equals the $900,000 increase in working capital.

We turn next to understanding more regarding how to analyze financial statements.

II. ANALYZING FINANCIAL STATEMENTS

The analysis of all four statements consists primarily of calculating ratios; but other methods including the time trend of the ratio, information theory, and flow-of-funds analysis are sometimes used. We shall limit our analysis to using ratios.[1]

In general, financial analysts, investors, creditors, and others look for two kinds of information regarding business enterprises:

1. *Risk*, including financial, business, market, and country or political risks,
2. *Return*, including productivity, efficiency, and profitability of corporate capital investments.

A third factor, *growth rate*, is important too, primarily because high steady growth is usually worth more than low or no growth.

BALANCE SHEET RATIOS

Balance sheet ratios belong to one of the three following categories:

1. *Liquidity and turnover ratios*, which indicate the ability of the corporation to pay current liabilities,
2. *Capitalization*, also called *leverage*, or *debt ratios*, which is the amount of borrowing relative to other factors such as total capitalization, total assets, or total equity,
3. *Net asset ratios*, which indicate the amount of assets backing each class of outstanding securities.

Liquidity ratios are calculated to judge whether the corporation owns sufficient cash and cash-equivalents or substitutes to comfortably pay short-term obligations, and include:

1. *Current liquidity*, the ability to pay current liabilities from current assets:

Current ratio:

$$\frac{\text{Current assets}}{\text{Current liabilities}} = \frac{\$13,600,000}{\$\,6,000,000} = 2.3 \text{ to } 1$$

In total dollar amounts, the numerator in the current ratio, minus the denominator, states *net working capital*, where

Total current assets	$13,600,000
Less: Total current liabilities	6,000,000
Working capital	$ 7,600,000

2. *Quick asset* (sometimes called *acid test*) *ratio:*

$$\frac{\text{Quick assets}}{\text{Current liabilities}} = \frac{\$8,000,000}{\$6,000,000} = 1.33$$

Where quick assets are total current assets minus inventories, because inventories usually are

less liquid than either cash, marketable securities, or accounts receivable:

Total current assets	$13,600,000
Less: Inventories	5,600,000
Quick assets	$8,000,000
Less: Total current liabilities	6,000,000
Net quick assets	$2,000,000

3. The *cash plus marketable securities ratio* indicates the firm's ability to pay current liabilities without relying on either inventories or accounts receivable:

$$\frac{\text{Cash plus marketable securities}}{\text{Total current liabilities}} = \frac{\$3,200,000}{\$6,000,000} = 0.53$$

Liquidity and turnover of inventories ratios indicate how close inventories approximate true liquidity through total sales, and are the three following figures:

1. *Inventory as a percent of total current assets:*

$$\frac{\text{Inventory}}{\text{Total current assets}} = \frac{\$5,600,000}{\$13,600,000} = 41.18 \text{ percent}$$

2. *Cost of goods sold*, including depreciation and capital consumption, *to average inventory ratio:*

$$\frac{\text{Cost of goods sold plus depreciation}}{\text{Inventory}} = \frac{\$9,740,000}{\$5,600,000} = 1.74$$

3. *Inventory turnover ratio:*

$$\frac{\text{Net sales}}{\text{Inventory}} = \frac{\$23,850,000}{\$5,600,000} = 4.26 \text{ times}$$

Liquidity of receivables ratios indicate how close accounts receivable approximate true liquidity through total sales, and are the two following figures:

1. Average collection period ratio, which indicates the number of day's sales in accounts receivables:

$$\frac{\text{Receivables} \times \text{Days in year}}{\text{Annual sales}} =$$
$$\frac{\$4,800,000 \times 360}{\$23,850,000} = 72.45$$

2. Accounts receivable turnover ratio:

$$\frac{\text{Annual sales}}{\text{Accounts receivable}} = \frac{\$23,850,000}{\$4,800,000} = 4.97$$

Liquidity and turnover of tangible and fixed asset ratios indicate relationships between total sales and total assets, and are given by the following two figures:

---

[1] Comparison of these ratios with those typical of the industry is very helpful. Typical values are given on p. 112. More detailed tabulations are provided by Dun & Bradstreet and Robert Morris Associates.

1. Fixed asset turnover ratio:

$$\frac{\text{Sales}}{\text{Net fixed assets}} = \frac{\$23,850,000}{\$12,110,000} = 1.97$$

2. Total asset turnover ratio:

$$\frac{\text{Net sales}}{\text{Average total tangible assets}} = \frac{\$23,850,000}{\$25,800,000}$$
$$= 0.9244$$

Capitalization ratios include:

1. Debt ratio:

$$\frac{\text{Total liabilities}}{\text{Total assets}} = \frac{\$8,000,000}{\$26,000,000} = 30.77 \text{ percent}$$

2. Current liabilities as a percent of total liabilities:

$$\frac{\text{Current liabilities}}{\text{Total liabilities}} = \frac{\$6,000,000}{\$8,000,000} = 75 \text{ percent}$$

3. Debt-to-net-worth ratio:

$$\frac{\text{Total liabilities}}{\text{Net Worth}} = \frac{\$8,000,000}{\$18,000,000} = 0.4444$$

4. Long-term debt capitalization ratio:

$$\frac{\text{Long-term debt}}{\text{Total capitalization}} = \frac{\$2,000,000}{\$19,800,000}$$
$$= 10.10 \text{ percent}$$

5. Preferred stock ratio:

$$\frac{\text{Preferred stock}}{\text{Total capitalization}} = \frac{\$1,360,000}{\$19,800,000}$$
$$= 6.87 \text{ percent}$$

6. Common stock ratio:

$$\frac{\text{Common stock plus accumulated earnings}}{\text{Total capitalization}} = \frac{\$16,440,000}{\$19,800,000}$$
$$= 83.03 \text{ percent}$$

7. Summary:

Total assets	$26,000,000	
Less: Intangibles	$ 200,000	
Less: Total current liabilities	$ 6,000,000	
Total capitalization	$19,800,000	100.00%
Bonds (long-term debt)	2,000,000	10.10
Preferred stock	1,360,000	6.87
Common stock (including capital surplus and retained earnings)	16,440,000	83.03

8. Long-term debt as a percent of total liabilities:

$$\frac{\text{Long-term debt}}{\text{Total liabilities}} = \frac{\$2,000,000}{\$8,000,000} = 25.00 \text{ percent}$$

Net asset value ratios include:

1. Net asset value per $1,000 bond; $9,900 per bond.

$$\frac{\begin{array}{c}\text{Net tangible assets}\\\text{available to meet}\\\text{bondholders' claims}\\\hline\text{Number of \$1,000}\\\text{bonds outstanding}\end{array} = \frac{\$19,800,000}{2,000,000}}$$

where the numerator is calculated as follows:

Total assets	$26,000,000
Less: Intangibles	200,000
Total tangible assets	$25,800,000
Less: Current liabilities	6,000,000
Net tangible assets available to meet bondholders' claims	$19,800,000

2. Net asset value per share of preferred stock: $1,308.82

$$\frac{\begin{array}{c}\text{Net assets backing}\\\text{the preferred stock}\\\hline\text{Number of shares}\\\text{of preferred stock}\\\text{outstanding}\end{array} = \frac{\$17,800,000}{13,600}}$$

where the numerator is calculated as follows:

Total assets	$26,000,000
Less: Intangibles	200,000
Total tangible assets	$25,800,000
Less: Current liabilities	6,000,000
Less: Long-term liabilities	2,000,000
Net assets backing the preferred stock	$17,800,000

3. Net book value per share of common stock: $21.63

$$\frac{\begin{array}{c}\text{Net assets available}\\\text{for the common stock}\\\hline\text{Total number of}\\\text{shares outstanding}\end{array} = \frac{\$16,440,000}{760,000} = \$21.63}$$

where the numerator is calculated as follows:

Total assets	$26,000,000
Less: Intangibles	200,000
Total tangible assets	$25,800,000
Less: Current liabilities	6,000,000
Less: Long-term liabilities	2,000,000
Less preferred stock	1,360,000
Net assets available for the common stock	$16,440,000

Finally, estimate the youngest average plant age by dividing the current (1981) depreciation expense accrual ($800,000 from the Statement of Source and Application of Funds) into accumulated depreciation ($6,435,000 from the Balance Sheet) to get 8.04 years. Because some plants and pieces of equipment may have been fully written off over time, we can say that UMC's Fixed Assets, on average, are over 8 years old.

INCOME STATEMENT RATIOS

Income statement ratios belong to one of the two following categories:

1. *Coverage,* which analyzes financial risk by relating the financial charges of a corporation to its ability to service them.
2. *Productivity* or *capital efficiency ratios,* which relate income to total sales and to investment.

Coverage ratios include:

1. Interest coverage ratio: 38.875

$$\frac{\text{Net operating income before interest and taxes}}{\text{Interest charges on bonds}} = \frac{\$6,220,000}{\$160,000} = 38.875$$

2. Cash flow coverage ratio, which indicates the firm's ability to service debt, which is related to both interest and principal payments and is not met out of earnings per se, but out of cash: 19.5 times.

$$\frac{\text{Annual cash flow before interest and taxes}}{\text{Interest on bonds plus principal repayments}/(1-T)} = \frac{\$7,020,000}{\$360,000} = 19.5$$

where:

Net operating income before interest and taxes	$6,220,000
Plus annual depreciation expense	800,000
Annual cash flow before interest and taxes	$7,020,000
Face value 20-year 8% bonds due 1995	$2,000,000
Annual Repayment rate after taxes $2,000,000 divided by 20 years	100,000
Before tax annual bond repayment rate $100,000 divided by 1 minus the effective tax rate, say 50 %	$200,000
Plus: 8% interest on $2,000,000	160,000
Interest plus principal repayments	$360,000

Since interest payments are made before taxes, the adjustment is necessary to convert principal repayments which are made after taxes to before-tax equivalents.

3. Preferred dividend coverage ratio: 46.81

$$\frac{\text{Income available for paying preferred dividends}}{\text{Total dividends to preferred shareholders}} = \frac{\$3,820,000}{\$81,600} = 46.81$$

4. Earnings per common share: $4.92

$$\frac{\text{Earnings available for distribution to common shareholders}}{\text{Total number of common shares outstanding}} = \frac{\$3,738,400}{760,000} = \$4.92$$

where:

Net profit for the year	$3,820,000
Less: Dividend requirements on preferred stock	81,600
Earnings available for common stock	$3,738,400

5. Primary earnings for the year: $4.94

$$\frac{\text{Earnings for the year}}{\text{Common stock plus stock equivalents}} = \frac{\$3,820,000}{773,500} = \$4.94$$

Assuming the 13,600 preferred shares had been convertible and converted, on a share-for-share basis, into common stock.

13,600 + 760,000 = 773,600 common shares after conversion

6. Fully diluted earnings per share: $4.79

$$\frac{\text{Adjusted earnings}}{\text{Adjusted shares outstanding}} = \frac{\$3,900,000}{813,600}$$
$$= \$4.79$$

where:

Earnings for the year	$3,820,000
Plus: interest on convertible bonds	$ 160,000
Less: income tax applicable to interest deduction	80,000
Adjusted earnings for the year	$3,900,000
Common shares outstanding	760,000
Preferred convertible stock equivalent common shares	13,600
Twenty common shares per $1,000 convertible bond (2,000) outstanding	40,000
Adjusted shares outstanding	813,600

7. Summary:

Earnings per share	$4.92
Primary earnings	4.94
Fully diluted earnings	4.79

8. Price-earnings ratio: Approximately 15 times

$$\frac{\text{Market price of stock}}{\text{Earnings per share}} = \frac{\$72.25}{\$4.92} = 14.69$$

Productivity or capital efficiency ratios include:

1. Operating margin of profit: 24.65%.

$$\frac{\text{Operating profit}}{\text{Sales}} = \frac{\$5,878,000}{\$23,850,000} = 24.65\%$$

Previous year:

$$= \frac{\$5,037,000}{\$19,810,000} = 25.43\%$$

2. Operating cost ratio: 75.35%.

	Amount	Ratio
Net sales	$23,850,000	100.00%
Operating costs............	17,972,000	75.35
Operating profit............	$ 5,878,000	24.65%

3. Net profit ratio: 16.02%.

$$\frac{\text{Net profit for the year}}{\text{Net sales}} = \frac{\$3,820,000}{\$23,850,000} = 16.02\%$$

Previous year: 15.55%

$$= \frac{\$3,080,000}{\$19,810,000} = 15.55\%$$

RATIOS FROM STATEMENTS OF ACCUMULATED RETAINED EARNINGS

Retained earnings statements ratios belong to one of the two following categories:

1. Dividend payout ratio.
2. Earnings retention ratio.

The dividend payout ratio for UMC is: 40.66%.

$$\frac{\text{Dividends paid to common stockholders}}{\text{Income available for common stockholders}} = \frac{\$1,520,000}{\$3,738,400} = 40.66\%$$

where:

Net profit for the year	$3,820,000
Dividends on preferred stock	81,600
Earnings available for common	$3,738,400

The earnings retention ratio for UMC is: 59.34%.

$$\frac{\text{Earnings retained}}{\text{Earnings available for payout}} = \frac{\$2,218,400}{\$3,738,400} = 59.34\%$$

where:

Net profit for the year	$3,820,000
Less: Dividends paid on preferred stock	$ 81,600
Less: Dividends paid on common stock.....................	1,520,000
Earnings retained	$2,218,400

Summary:

Dividend payout ratio......	40.66%
Earnings retention ratio....	59.34
Earnings available	100.00%

Dividends per share: $2.00.

$$\frac{\text{Total dividends paid to common shareholders}}{\text{Number of common shares outstanding}} = \frac{\$1,520,000}{760,000} = \$2.00$$

Balance December 31, $15,300,000.

RATIOS FROM STATEMENTS OF SOURCE AND APPLICATION OF FUNDS

Since an analysis was stated directly on the statement of source and use of funds in Exhibit 3, that part of the analysis is completed; however we still need to calculate profitability ratios which belong to one of the two following categories:

1. Return on assets.
2. Return on equity.

Return on assets ratios include:
  Return on total assets: 27.67%.

$$\frac{\text{Total income}}{\text{Last year's total assets}} = \frac{\$6,220,000}{\$22,481,600}$$
$$= 27.67\%$$

After tax return on total assets: 17.70%.

$$\frac{\text{Total income after tax but before interest}}{\text{Last year's total assets}} = \frac{\$3,980,000}{\$22,481,600}$$
$$= 17.70\%$$

where:

Total income	$6,220,000
Less: Provision for total taxes	2,240,000
After tax total income	$3,980,000

Return on equity ratio: 25.92%.

$$\frac{\text{Income available for distribution to common stockholders}}{\text{Last year's total equity of common stockholders}} = \frac{\$3,738,400}{\$14,421,600} = 25.92\%$$

where:

Last year's total stockholder equity	$15,781,600
Less: Preferred stock value	1,360,000
Last year's common stock equity	$14,421,600

We turn next to further discussion of notes and supplemental information.

III. NOTES AND SUPPLEMENTAL INFORMATION

As explained in the introduction, financial statements in corporate annual reports usually are accompanied by:

- A *report of independent accountants and auditors* certifying the statements conform to generally accepted accounting principles and that generally accepted auditing standards and procedures were used.
- *Notes* which further explain details and

EXHIBIT 4
SEGMENT REPORTING AND FOREIGN OPERATIONS

| | Industry Segments | | | Geographic Segments | | | | |
| | | | | | Foreign | | | |
	Segment No. 1	Segment No. 2	Consolidated	Domestic	OECD	Other	Eliminations	Consolidated
1981								
Sales, unaffiliated customers	$20,044,000	$3,806,000	$23,850,000	$12,647,000	$ 9,029,000	$2,175,000		$23,850,000
Sales, intersegment				2,171,000	346,000	21,000	($2,539,000)	
Total sales	$20,044,000	$3,806,000	$23,850,000	$14,818,000	$ 9,375,000	$2,196,000	($2,539,000)	$23,850,000
Pretax operating income	5,435,000	443,000	5,878,000	3,690,000	1,820,000	211,000	157,000	5,878,000
Identifiable assets at December 31	21,700,000	4,300,000	26,000,000	16,549,000	10,168,000	2,353,000	(3,070,000)	26,000,000
Depreciation expense	666,000	134,000	800,000					
Capital spending	1,884,300	234,100	2,118,400					
1980								
Sales, unaffiliated customers	$16,629,000	$3,181,000	$19,810,000	$10,519,000	$ 7,511,000	$1,780,000		$19,810,000
Sales, intersegment				2,614,000	246,000	14,000	($2,878,000)	
Total sales	$16,629,000	$3,181,000	$19,810,000	$13,133,000	$ 7,757,000	$1,794,000	($2,878,000)	$19,810,000
Pretax operating income	4,627,000	410,000	5,037,000	3,512,000	1,449,000	126,000	(50,000	5,037,000
Identifiable assets at December 31	19,027,000	3,473,000	22,500,000	14,728,000	8,660,000	2,005,000	(2,893,000)	22,500,000
Depreciation expense	611,000	127,000	738,000					
Capital spending	1,751,000	190,000						
1979								
Sales, unaffiliated customers	$14,461,000	$2,779,000	$17,240,000	$ 9,504,000	$ 6,152,000	$1,584,000		$17,240,000
Sales, intersegment				2,677,000	155,000	3,000	($2,835,000)	
Total sales	$14,461,000	$2,779,000	$17,240,000	$12,181,000	$ 6,307,000	$1,587,000	($2,835,000)	$17,240,000
Pretax operating income	4,163,000	378,000	4,541,000	3,552,000	1,234,000	119,000	(364,000)	4,541,000
Identifiable assets at December 31	16,614,000	3,341,000	19,955,000	13,627,000	7,818,000	1,590,000	(3,179,000)	19,955,000
Depreciation expense	551,000	102,000	653,000					
Capital spending	1,969,000	238,000	2,207,000					

disclose relevant information regarding line items on all four statements.

- *Segment information,* which summarizes selected items by business, industry, and geographic segment.
- A *restatement* of almost everything in current (in contrast with the traditional historical original purchase) prices, and to account for the effects of inflation on items reported in the standard statements.
- *Long-term record* summarizing selected items over a five- or ten-year time span.

REPORT OF INDEPENDENT ACCOUNTANTS

A typical report of independent accountants is addressed to the stockholders and board of directors of the corporation and will read as follows:

"In our opinion, the accompanying consolidated financial statements, appearing on pages — through —, present fairly the financial position of Universal Manufacturing Corporation and its subsidiary companies at December 31, 1981 and 1980, and the results of their operations and changes in financial position for the years then ended, in conformity with generally accepted accounting principles consistently applied. Also, in our opinion, the five-year comparative consolidated summary of operations presents fairly the financial information included therein. Our examinations of these statements were made in accordance with generally accepted auditing standards and

EXHIBIT 5

UNIVERSAL MANUFACTURING CORPORATION
SCHEDULE OF INCOME FROM CONTINUING OPERATIONS
AND OTHER CHANGES IN SHAREHOLDERS' EQUITY
ADJUSTED FOR EFFECTS OF CHANGING PRICES
For the Year Ended December 31, 1981

| | | Adjusted for | |
	As Reported (historical cost)	General Inflation (constant 1981 $)	Specific (current) Costs
Income from continuing operations			
Net sales	$23,850,000		
Other income	342,000		
Total revenue from continuing operations	$24,192,000	$24,192,000	$24,192,000
Costs and other deductions			
Depreciation expenses	800,000	1,076,000	1,115,000
Other costs and expenses	17,172,000	17,699,000	17,273,000
Interest expense	160,000	160,000	160,000
Federal and foreign income taxes	2,240,000	2,240,000	2,240,000
Total costs and other deductions	$20,372,000	$21,175,000	$20,788,000
Net income from continuing operations	$ 3,820,000	$ 3,017,000	$ 3,404,000
Purchasing power gain on net monetary liabilities (Net amounts owed)		1,000	1,000
Increase in current cost of inventories and property, plant and equipment during 1981			1,911,000
Less: effect of increase in general price level during 1981			2,788,000
Excess of increase in specific prices over increase in the general price level			($ 877,000)
Net income	$ 3,820,000		
Adjusted net income		$ 3,018,000	
Net change in shareholders' equity from above	$ 3,820,000	$ 3,018,000	$ 2,528,000

Summarized Balance Sheet
Adjusted for Changing Prices
At December 31, 1981

| | | Adjusted for | |
	As reported	General Inflation (constant 1981 $)	Specific (current) Costs
Assets			
Inventories	$ 5,600,000	$ 6,175,000	$ 5,670,000
Property, plant and equipment	12,110,000	13,354,000	16,327,000
All other assets	8,290,000	9,141,000	7,506,000
Total assets	$26,000,000	$28,670,000	$29,503,000
Total liabilities	8,000,000	7,600,000	7,600,000
Shareholders' equity	$18,000,000	$21,070,000	$21,903,000

EXHIBIT 5 *(concluded)*

Supplementary financial data
Five-Year Comparison of Selected Data
Adjusted for Changing Prices

	Years Ended December 31				
	1977	1978	1979	1980	1981
Sales					
As reported	$14,020,000	$15,610,000	$17,240,000	$19,810,000	$23,850,000
1981 constant dollars	19,543,000	20,211,000	20,063,000	20,970,000	23,850,000
Net income					
As reported					$ 3,820,000
1981 constant dollars					3,017,000
Current costs					3,404,000
Earnings per share					
As reported					$4.92
1981 constant dollars					3.86
Current costs					4.37
Common stock dividends declared per share					
As reported	$1.40	$1.43	$1.55	$1.75	$2.00
1981 constant dollars	1.95	1.85	1.80	1.85	2.00
Net assets at year-end					
As reported					$18,000,000
1981 constant dollars					21,070,000
Current costs					21,903,000
Purchasing power gain on net monetary liabilities					1,000
Market price per common share at year-end					
Actual	$69.25	$68.13	$55.50	$67.63	$72.25
1981 constant dollars	90.50	84.95	64.80	72.45	68.50
Average consumer price index*	181.5	195.4	217.4	239.0	253.0

* Hypothetical, for illustrative purposes only.

accordingly included such tests of the accounting records and such other auditing procedures as we considered necessary in the circumstances."

The report will be signed with the name and address of the accounting firm and dated.

NOTES TO FINANCIAL STATEMENTS

Notes disclose additional information regarding entries in all four primary statements, and usually are considered an integral part of the statements, included in and covered by the auditor's certification. Some corporations include the next three items to be discussed, segment information, effects of inflation, and long-term comparative summary of operations, in the notes. If included in some place other than the notes, then look for whether the statement was excluded from the auditor's audit.

SEGMENT INFORMATION

Notes disclosing geographic area and industry segment information usually summarize selected items such as net sales, operating income, total assets, depreciation and amortization, and capital expenditures for industry segments (business segments or product groups) and foreign operations.

Exhibit 4 shows the segment information for UMC's two segments.

As you can see from Exhibit 4, industry segment number one, Human and Animal Health

Products, accounts for 84 percent ($20,044,000 divided by $23,850,000) of total sales, and 92 percent ($5,435,000 divided by $5,878,000) of UMC's operating income; all supported by 83.46 percent ($21,700,000 divided by $26,-000,000) of total assets. Eleven percent ($234,100 divided by $2,118,400) of total capital expenditures were made in industry segment number two, Environmental Health Products and Services for the treatment of water and air pollution.

Exhibit 4 also shows, based on the following ratios, that UMC's business is roughly 60 percent domestic United States; 40 percent nondomestic:

Net Sales:

$$\frac{\text{United States}}{\text{Total company}} = \frac{\$14,818,000}{\$23,850,000} = 62.13\%$$

Operating income:

$$\frac{\text{United States}}{\text{Total company}} = \frac{\$3,690,000}{\$5,037,000} = 62.78\%$$

Total assets:

$$\frac{\text{United States}}{\text{Total company}} = \frac{\$16,549,000}{\$26,000,000} = 63.65\%$$

SUPPLEMENTAL INFORMATION ON INFLATION ACCOUNTING

Pursuant to Financial Accounting Standards Board (FASB) *Statement of Financial Account-*

EXHIBIT 6

TEN-YEAR FINANCIAL SUMMARY
UNIVERSAL MANUFACTURING CORPORATION

	1981	1980	1979	1978	1977	1976	1975	1974	1973	1972
Net sales	$23,850,000	$19,810,000	$17,240,000	$15,610,000	$14,020,000	$12,604,000	$11,040,000	$9,426,000	$8,324,000	$7,611,000
Total income before tax	6,060,000	5,060,000	4,535,000	4,164,000	3,783,000	3,619,000	3,195,000	2,747,000	2,521,000	2,286,000
Net profit for the year	3,820,000	3,080,000	2,775,000	2,555,000	2,288,000	2,105,000	1,827,000	1,512,000	1,314,000	1,179,000
Earnings per share	4.92	3.95	3.56	3.28	2.94	2.71	2.36	1.95	1.70	1.53
Dividends per share	2.00	1.75	1.55	1.43	1.40	1.40	1.24	1.12	1.10	1.03
Net working capital	7,600,000	6,700,000	6,300,000	5,500,000	5,023,000	3,596,000	3,424,000	2,964,000	2,604,000	2,261,000
Total assets	26,000,000	22,481,600	19,934,000	17,594,000	15,390,000	12,433,000	9,890,000	8,348,000	7,365,000	6,643,000
Net plant and equipment	12,110,000	10,820,000	9,918,000	8,747,000	6,743,000	4,740,000	3,635,000	3,150,000	2,830,000	2,479,000
Long term debt	2,000,000	2,000,000	2,000,000	2,000,000	2,000,000	2,000,000	2,000,000	1,000,000	1,000,000	1,000,000
Preferred stock	1,360,000	1,360,000	1,360,000	1,360,000	1,360,000	1,360,000	1,360,000	1,360,000	1,360,000	1,360,000
Common stock and surplus	1,340,000	1,340,000	1,340,000	1,340,000	1,340,000	1,340,000	1,340,000	1,340,000	1,340,000	1,340,000
Book value per share	21.63									

ing Standards No. 33, public enterprises that have either (1) inventories and property, plant, and equipment (before deducting accumulated depreciation) amounting to more than $125 million or (2) total assets amounting to more than $1 billion (after deducting accumulated depreciation) are required to report supplementary information in addition to the primary financial statements. FASB *Standards No. 33* are:

For fiscal years ended on or after December 25, 1979, enterprises are required to report:

a. Income from continuing operations adjusted for the effects of general inflation.
b. The purchasing power gain or loss on net monetary items.

For fiscal years ended on or after December 25, 1979, enterprises are also required to report:

a. Income from continuing operations on a current cost basis.
b. The current cost amounts of inventory and property, plant, and equipment at the end of the fiscal year.
c. Increases or decreases in current cost amounts of inventory and property, plant, and equipment, net of inflation.

Enterprises are required to present a five-year summary of selected financial data, including information on income, sales and other operating revenues, net assets, dividends per common share, and market price

per share. In the computation of net assets, only inventory and property, plant, and equipment need be adjusted for the effects of changing prices.

UMC, because of its "small company" asset size, would be exempt from FASB *No. 33*'s reporting requirement. However, Exhibit 5 restates UMC's statement of income from continuing operations, restated for changing prices, for the year ending December 31, 1981; and UMC's five-year comparison of selected data adjusted for changing prices.

A final note on Notes: Feel free to speak with your friendly auditor, or sleuth on your own, regarding additional information which might remain undisclosed and could pertain to:

a. Liabilities arising out of company pension plans (e.g., ERISA).
b. Contractual obligations (e.g., the capitalized value of lease payments).
c. Legal judgments currently enforceable.
d. Contingent liabilities (e.g., pending lawsuits or possible income tax assessment).

TEN-YEAR FINANCIAL SUMMARY

Long-term performance of UMC is summarized and reported on the ten-year financial summary statement, Exhibit 6.

The long-term view is used for detecting trends and changes in trends in important factors such as net sales, total assets, net operating income, earnings per share, and dividends per share. On balance, the trends for UMC look pretty good: upward.

WHAT IS IN A 10K AND OTHER SEC REPORTS

PART I OF 10K

1. **Business.** Identifies principal products and services of the company, principal markets and methods of distribution and, if "material," competitive factors, backlog and expectation of fulfillment, availability of raw materials, importance of patents, licenses, and franchises, estimated cost of research, number of employees, and effects of compliance with ecological laws; if there is more than one line of business, for each of the last five fiscal years a statement of total sales and net income for each line which, during either of the last two fiscal years, accounted for 10 percent or more of total sales or pretax income.

2. **Summary of operations.** Summary of operations for each of the last five fiscal years and any additional years required to keep the summary from being misleading (per share earnings and dividends are included). Includes explanatory material describing reasons for changes in revenues, earnings, etc.

3. **Properties.** Location and character of principal plants, mines, and other important properties and if held in fee or leased.

4. **Parents and subsidiaries.** List or diagram of all parents and subsidiaries and for each named, the percentage of voting securities owned, or other basis of control.

5. **Legal proceedings.** Brief description of material legal proceedings pending; when civil rights statutes are involved, proceedings must be disclosed.

6. **Increases and decreases in outstanding securities.** Information for each security, including reacquired securities, new issues, securities issued in exchange for property, services or other securities, and new securities resulting from modification of outstanding securities.

7. **Approximate number of equity security holders.** Holders of record for each class of equity securities as of the end of the fiscal year.

8. **Executive officers of the registrant.** List of all executive officers, nature of family relationship between them, positions and offices held.

9. **Indemnification of directors and officers.** General effect under which any director or officer is insured or indemnified against any liability which he may incur in his capacity as such.

10. **Financial statements and exhibits filed.** Complete, audited annual financial information, and a list of exhibits filed.

PART II OF 10K

11. **Principal security holders and security holdings of management.** Identification of owners of 10 percent or more of any class of securities and of securities held by directors and officers according to amount and percent of each class.

12. **Directors of the registrant.** Name, office, term of office, and specific background data on each.

13. **Remuneration of directors and officers.** List of each director and three highest paid officers with aggregate annual remuneration exceeding $40,000—and total paid all officers and directors.

14. **Options granted to management to purchase securities.** Options granted to or exercised by directors and officers since the beginning of the fiscal year.

15. **Interest of management and others in certain transactions.** Material changes in significant transactions of such things as assets, pension, retirement, savings or other similar plans, or unusual loans.

SCHEDULES TO 10K

I. Marketable securities. Other security investments.
II. Amounts due from directors, officers, and principal holders of equity securities other than affiliates.
III. Investments in securities of affiliates.
IV. Indebtedness of affiliates (not current).
V. Property, plant, and equipment.
VI. Reserves for depreciation, depletion, and amortization of property, plant, and equipment.
VII. Intangible assets.
VIII. Reserves for depreciation and amortization of intangible assets.
IX. Bonds, mortgages, and similar debt.
X. Indebtedness to affiliates (not current).
XI. Guarantees of securities of other issuers.
XII. Reserves.
XIII. Capital shares.
XIV. Warrants or rights.
XV. Other securities.
XVI. Supplementary profit and loss information.
XVII. Income from dividends (equity in net profit and loss of affiliates).

OTHER REPORTS

12-K. The 12-K annual report is filed with the SEC by certain companies which are regu-

Source: *The National Investment Library*, 80 Wall Street, New York 10005.

lated by, and file reports with, the Federal Power Commission, Interstate Commerce Commission, and Federal Communications Commission. It is similar in content to the 10-K.

10-Q. This is the quarterly financial report filed by most companies, which, although unaudited, provides a continuing view of a company's financial position during the year. It must be filed within 45 days of the close of a fiscal quarter.

8-K. This is a report of unscheduled material events or corporate changes deemed of importance to shareholders or to the SEC—changes in control of the registrant; acquisition or disposition of assets; legal proceedings; changes in securities (i.e., collateral for registered securities); defaults upon senior securities; increase or decrease in the amount of securities outstanding; options to purchase securities; revaluation of assets; submission of matters to a vote of security holders; and any newly enacted requirements affecting the company's business.

Proxy statement. Provides official notification to stockholders of matters to be brought to a vote at shareholders meeting.

Registration statement. Discloses fully, all financial and relevant facts on a company, needed by investors to evaluate proposed sale of securities. Very detailed.

HOW TO READ THE NEW YORK STOCK EXCHANGE AND AMERICAN STOCK EXCHANGE QUOTATIONS

The composite quotations take into account prices paid for a stock on the New York or American Exchanges, plus those prices paid on regional exchanges, Over-the-Counter (OTC) and elsewhere, as shown in the example from the Wall Street Journal.

(1) High	(2) Low	(3) Stock	(4) Div.	(5) Yld %	(6) P-E Ratio A	(7) Sales 100s A	(8) High A	(9) low	(10) Close	(11) Net Chg.
	52 Weeks									
14¾	9⅛	AAR	.44	4.3	7	26	10½	10¼	10¼	¼
52¼	32¼	ACF	2.76	6.0	10	51	46	45½	46	
27	12⅞	AMF	1.24	5.1	12	1543	24¼	23¾	24⅛ +	¼
24¾	10⅞	AM Intl				51	13⅞	13¾	13¾	
11⅜	6⅜	APL				51	6⅜ d	6¼	6¼	⅛

The stock market quotations are explained below:

(1) The highest price per share paid in the past 52 weeks in terms of ⅛ of a dollar, i.e., 10⅛ means $10.125.

(2) The lowest price paid per share in the last 52 weeks.

(3) The name of the company in abbreviated form.

(4) The regular annual dividend paid. Special or extra dividends are specified by letters given in the footnotes in the Explanatory Notes shown below.

(5) The yield, that is, the annual dividend divided by the current price of the stock expressed in percent. For example, a stock that sells for $20.00 per share and pays a dividend of $2.00 per share has a yield of 10 percent (2/20).

(6) The P/E ratio is the current price of the stock divided by the company's last reported annual earnings per share. The P/E ratio is generally high for companies which are thought to have a relatively large and persistent earning's growth rate. The average P/E ratio for the Dow Jones stocks varied from 7.7 to 10.2 during the last five years.

(7) The number of shares sold on the day reported in 100s of shares.

(8) The highest price paid per share on the day reported.

(9) The lowest price paid per share on the day reported.

(10) The last price paid per share on the day reported.

(11) The change in the closing price from the previous day's closing price.

EXPLANATORY NOTES
(For New York and American Exchange listed issues)

Sales figures are unofficial.

The 52-Week High and Low columns show the highest and the lowest price of the stock in consolidated trading during the preceding 52 weeks plus the current week, but not the current trading day.

u—Indicates a new 52-week high. d—Indicates a new 52-week low.

s—Split or stock dividend of 25 percent or more in the past 52 weeks. The high-low range is adjusted from the old stock. Dividend begins with the date of split or stock dividend.

n—New issue in the past 52 weeks. The high-low range begins with the start of trading in the new issue and does not cover the entire 52-week period.

g—Dividend or earnings in Canadian money. Stock trades in U.S. dollars. No yield or PE shown unless stated in U.S. money.

Unless otherwise noted, rates of dividends in the foregoing table are annual disbursements based on the last quarterly or semi-annual declaration. Special or extra dividends or payments not designated as regular are identified in the following footnotes.

a—Also extra or extras. b—Annual rate plus stock dividend. c—Liquidating dividend. e—Declared or paid in preceding 12 months. i—Declared or paid after stock dividend or split up. j—Paid this year, dividend omitted, deferred or no action taken at last dividend meeting. k—Declared or paid this year, an accumulative issue with dividends in arrears. r—Declared or paid in preceding 12 months plus stock dividend. t—Paid in stock in preceding 12 months, estimated cash value on ex-dividend or ex-distribution date.

x—Ex-dividend or ex-rights. v—Ex-dividend and sales in full. z—Sales in full.

wd—When distributed. wi—When issued. ww—With warrants. xw—Without warrants.

vi—In bankruptcy or receivership or being reorganized under the Bankruptcy Act, or securities assumed by such companies.

HOW TO READ OVER-THE-COUNTER NASDAQ LISTINGS

(1) (2)	(3) Sales 100s	(4) Bid	(5) Asked	(6) Net Chg.
Stock & Div.				
CentVtPS 1.92	8	13⅝	13¾ +	⅛
Centrn Cp 2.56	4	23¼	23½	...
Centura Enrg	135	10½	10¾ −	½
CenturyBK .48	573	13	13⅛ −	⅛
CenturyOil Gs	49	7⅜	7⅝	...
Cetus Corptn	231	17⅛	17⅜ +	⅛
CFS Cont .40	18	13⅝	13⅞ +	⅛
CGA Assc Inc	155	10½	11 −	¼
Chalco Ind Inc	2	6	6½ −	¼

The over-the-counter quotations are explained below.

(1)   The company's name, usually abbreviated.

(2)   Annual regular dividend per share, unless accompanied by a notation which is explained in the OTC Explanatory Notes (below).

(3)   Number of shares sold that day in hundreds, i.e., 2 means 200 shares.

(4)   Bid price per share at closing time, i.e., the price at which broker-dealer will buy the stock from the investor. Prices do not include mark-up or commission.

(5)   Ask price per share at closing time, i.e., the price at which the broker-dealer will sell the stock.*

(6)   The change in the closing bid price from the previous day.

* Bid and ask prices are usually quoted in ⅛ (12.5 cents) of a dollar, i.e., 12⅛ means $12.125, 12½ means $12.50, etc. Very inexpensive stocks are quoted at ¹⁄₁₆ (6.25 cents) and ¹⁄₃₂ (3.125 cents) of a dollar.

OTC EXPLANATORY NOTES

z—Sales in full.

a—Annual rate plus cash extra. b—Paid so far in 1981, no regular rate. c—Payment of accumulated dividends. d—Paid in 1980. e—Cash plus stock paid in 1980. f—Cash plus stock paid in 1981. g—Annual rate plus stock dividend. h—Paid in 1981, latest dividend omitted. i—Percent paid in stock in 1980. j—Percent in stock paid in 1981, latest dividend omitted. k—Percent in stock paid in 1981. n—Asked price not applicable. p—Granted temporary exception from Nasdaq qualifications. q—In bankruptcy proceedings. ut—Units. wt—Warrants. x—Ex-dividend, ex-rights or ex-distribution. (z) No representative quote.

THE EX-DIVIDEND EXPLAINED

The ex-dividend status of a stock is indicated by an *x* in the newspaper quotation or *xd* on the ticker tape. This is an abbreviation for *without dividend*.

A stock that is purchased during the ex-dividend period will not pay a previously declared dividend to its new owner. The ex-dividend period spans four business days before the so-called record date—the date a dividend issuing corporation uses to tally its shareowners. An ex-dividend stock buyer is not entitled to a dividend because his name is not recorded with the dividend issuing corporation until after the record date.

The New York Stock Exchange requires that the buyer in every transaction be recorded with the issuing corporation on the fifth business day following a trade. A stock buyer, therefore, must purchase his shares at least five business days before the record date in order for the corporation to record his name in time for him to receive his dividend. A purchase one day later disqualifies a buyer from a dividend because the transfer of ownership cannot be completed by the record date. Therefore, on the fourth business day prior to the record date, a stock is sold ex-dividend.

In our example below, the corporation's Board has decided to pay a 50¢ dividend to shareholders of record on Monday, the 10th. A person buying shares up to the close of business on Monday, the 3rd, would be eligible for the dividend because normal settlement (5 business days) will be made on Monday the 10th. On Tuesday, the 4th, however, the stock would begin selling ex-dividend because a stock purchaser as of that date could not settle till after the record date.

On the ex-dividend date, the Exchange specialist will reduce all open buy orders and open sell stop orders by the amount of the dividend. This is done to more equitably reflect the stock's value since purchasers of stock on or after the ex-dividend date are ineligible for a dividend.

EX-DIVIDEND EXPLANATION

Any Month	Date	Calendar Day	Status
	3	Monday	With/Dividend
	4	Tuesday	Ex-Dividend (Without Dividend)
	5	Wednesday......	" "
	6	Thursday	" "
	7	Friday	" "
	8	Saturday	Not a trading day
	9	Sunday	Not a trading day
	10	Monday	Record Date/Business Day
	11	Tuesday	Business Day

Source: *Taking The Mystery Out of Ex-Dividend*, The New York Stock Exchange, Inc.

MARGIN ACCOUNTS EXPLAINED

Stocks may be purchased by paying the purchase price in full (plus commissions and taxes) or on a margin account. With the margin account, the investors put up part of the purchase price in cash or securities, and the broker lends the remainder. The margin investor must pay the usual commissions as well as interest on the broker's loan. The stocks purchased on margin are held by the broker as collateral on the loan. Dividends are applied to the margin account and help offset the interest payments.

Margin (M) is defined as the market value (V) of the securities less the broker's loan (L), divided by the market value of the securities. The ratio is expressed as a percentage:

$$M = \frac{V - L}{V} \times 100$$

Example: You buy 100 shares of a stock at $20 per share at a total cost (V) of $2,000. You put up $1,200 in cash and borrow (L) $800 from the broker. The margin at the time of purchase is

$$M = \frac{\$2,000 - \$800}{\$2,000} \times 100 = 60\%$$

The margin at the time of purchase is called *initial margin*. The smallest allowed value of initial margin (set by the Federal Reserve) is currently 50%. Thus, with the above stock, if you buy 100 shares at $20 per share on 50% initial margin, you put up $1,000 (.5 × $2,000), and the broker's loan is $1,000.

After the purchase there is a *maintenance margin* (set by the Exchange) below which the margin is not permitted to decrease. The main-

269

tenance margin on the New York Stock Exchange is 25%. Some brokers, however, require a higher maintenance margin of about 30%. Thus, if the 100 shares of stocks discussed above decrease in price from $20 to $13 per share, then the margin is

$$M = \left(\frac{\$1,300 - \$1,000}{\$1,300}\right) \times 100 = 23\%$$

The margin of 23% is now below the maintenance margin of 25% set by the Exchange. The securities are said to be *under margined*, and a call for additional cash (or securities) is issued by the broker in order to bring up the margin to 25%. If the investor does not meet the call for additional cash (margin call) within a specified time, the stocks in the margin account are immediately sold.

MARGIN REQUIREMENTS (percent of market value and effective date)

	Mar. 11, 1968	June 8, 1968	May 6, 1970	Dec. 6, 1971	Nov. 24, 1972	Jan. 3, 1974
Margin stocks	70	80	65	55	65	50
Convertible bonds	50	60	50	50	50	50
Short sales	70	80	65	55	65	50

Note: Regulations G, T, and U of the Federal Reserve Board of Governors, prescribed in accordance with the Securities Exchange Act of 1934, limit the amount of credit to purchase and carry margin stocks that may be extended on securities as collateral by prescribing a maximum loan value, which is a specified percentage of the market value of the collateral at the time the credit is extended. Margin requirements are the difference between the market value (100 percent) and the maximum loan value. The term "margin stocks" is defined in the corresponding regulation.

Source: *Federal Reserve Bulletin.*

SHORT SELLING EXPLAINED

Short selling provides an opportunity to profit from a decline in the price of a stock. If you believe that a stock is due for a substantial decline, you arrange to have your broker borrow the stock from another investor who owns the shares. The borrowed stock is then sold, and the cash proceeds are turned over to the stock lender. This cash is held as collateral against the borrowed shares. When (and if) the stock price declines, you purchase the stock at the market price and use it to replace the borrowed shares. The broker arranges the return of your cash collateral less the cost of the repurchased stock. Your profit per share is the price received on the sale of the stock less the purchase price.

There are certain cash outlays and costs associated with the short sale. Generally there is no charge for borrowing the stock, although occasionally stock lenders may charge a premium over the market price. You must deposit $2,000 or the required initial margin, whichever is the greater, at the time the stock is borrowed. Thus, if you borrow 100 shares of a stock priced at $50 per share and the margin required is 50%, you must put up $2,500 (.5 × $50 × 100) in cash or securities. The margin deposit is re-

turned when you close out the short sale. You pay commission when the stock is sold and when it is repurchased. In addition, you must pay the stock lender any dividends which are declared during the period you are short the stock. It is well to remember that if cash is used for the deposit, there is a loss of the interest which you would have obtained if the cash had been invested.

The dividend payments and interest loss can be reduced or eliminated if you short stocks which pay little or no dividends and use interest-bearing securities (such as T-bills or negotiable certificates of deposit) as the margin deposit.

An increase in the price of the stock can result in substantial losses since you may be forced to repurchase at a higher price than you sold. If there are many short sellers seeking to purchase the stock in order to close out their position, prices may be driven to very high levels.

The short sale cannot be executed while the stock price is declining on the exchange. According to the rules of the SEC, the stock must undergo an increase in price prior to the execution of a short sale.

HOW TO READ MUTUAL FUND QUOTATIONS

The following is an example of typical fund quotations as reported in the Wall Street Journal. The mutual fund quotations are explained in the adjacent column.

(1)	(2)	(3)	(4)
		Offer	NAV
	NAV	Price	Chg.
Able Assoc	24.33	N.L. +	.80
Acorn Fnd	28.28	N.L. +	.03
ADV Fund	15.38	N.L. +	.02
Afuture Fd	15.59	N.L. +	.10
AIM Funds			
Conv Yld	15.42	16.49 +	.09
Edsn Gld	14.59	15.60 +	.09
HiYld Sc	8.98	9.60 +	.02
Alpha Fnd	17.82	N.L. +	.01
Am Birthrt	12.29	13.43 −	.03
American Funds Group			
Am Bal	8.73	9.54	. . .
Amcap F	6.21	6.79 +	.01
Am Mutl	12.46	13.62 −	.01

(1) Name of fund in abbreviated form.
(2) NAV means "net asset value" per share of the stock. It is the price at which the fund will buy shares from investors.
The NAV is obtained from

$$NAV = \frac{M + C - L}{N}$$

M = market value of all stock in the fund's portfolio at the end of the trading day
C = fund's cash or cash equivalent position
L = fund's liabilities
N = number of shares issued by fund

(3) Offer price is the price per share at which the fund will sell shares to investors. With no load (NL, no sale's charge) funds, the offer price and the NAV are the same. With load funds, a sale's charge (load) is added to the NAV to arrive at the sale's price.
(4) The NAV change is the change in net asset value (at the close of the stock market) from that of the previous day.

THE TOP PERFORMING FUNDS FOR FIVE YEARS (% change in net asset value)

Fund (Invest. Objective)	Total Assets‡ (Mil.)	5 Yrs. 1976–80	10 Yrs. 1971–80	2 Yrs. 1973–74	Beta # (36 Mos.)	% Yield°
†20th Century Growth (AG)	$182	+597	+ 837	− 46	2.00	0.0
†44 Wall Street (AG)	194	+432	+ 482	− 75	2.28	0.0
†Hartwell Leverage (AG)	14	+427	+ 377	− 38	2.00	0.0
Security Ultra (AG)	48	+426	+ 484	− 57	1.96	0.4
▵ASA Ltd. (Au)	610	+420	+1,347	+208	0.40	11.0
†Evergreen Fund (AG)	83	+418	§	− 42	1.47	0.9
International Investors (Au)	352	+359	+1,073	+114	1.57	5.8
Value Line Spec. Sit. (AG)	155	+357	+ 170	− 62	1.83	0.6
†Constellation Growth (G)	55	+347	+ 321	− 38	2.00	0.0
Value Line Lev. Gr. (AG)	20	+347	§	− 64	1.34	1.9
†20th Century Select (AG)	18	+342	+ 456	− 33	1.56	0.7
†United Service (Au)	119	+330	+ 33	− 59	1.23	15.1
†Acorn Fund (AG)	115	+326	+ 354	− 43	1.27	3.2
†Weingarten Equity (AG)	53	+321	+ 382	− 47	1.70	0.5
†Hartwell Growth (AG)	8	+317	+ 231	− 51	1.53	0.0
Research Capital (Au)	70	+317	+ 268	− 24	1.20	8.1
Pace Fund (AG)	27	+316	+ 352	− 52	1.16	2.9
OTC Securities (G)	49	+315	+ 427	− 22	0.43	3.4
Keystone S-4 (AG)	613	+309	+ 183	− 67	1.72	1.2
†Lindner Fund (G)	11	+304	+ 504	− 40	NA	4.0
†Stn. Roe & Frn. Cap. Op. (G)	125	+302	+ 309	− 50	1.51	0.9
Sigma Venture (G)	18	+297	+ 317	− 65	1.27	1.2
†Dreyfus Number Nine (G)	115	+286	§	− 39	1.54	1.4
Mass. Cap. Dev	122	+286	+ 322	− 48	1.39	2.3
Oppenheimer Special (AG)	170	+283	§	§	NA	1.9
Medians	70	+326	− 354	− 49	1.52	1.3
S&P 500	—	+ 90	+ 123	− 37	1.00	4.8
Dow Industrials	—	+ 48	+ 85	− 33	—	5.7
Consumer Price Index	—	+ 52	+ 110	+ 18	—	—

* Per share, including all dividends and capital gains compounded annually.
‡ 12/31/80, except 1/30/81 for ASA Ltd.
# Source of open-end beta ratings: Computer Directions Advisors, Inc., 8750 Georgia Ave., Silver Spring, MD 20910. Data is based on the most recent 36 monthly returns through December.
° Based on latest 12-month dividend payout.
† No-Load.
▵ Publicly traded investment company. NA Not Available.
§ Fund not in operation for full period.
Key to Investment Objective Abbreviations: Au Gold oriented fund, AG Aggressive Growth, G Growth, GI Growth & Income, I Income.

THE TOP 25 PERFORMING FUNDS FOR THREE YEARS (1978–80)

	%		%
Strategic Investments	+431	†Weingarten Equity	+205
†United Services	+424	†Stn. Roe & Frn. Cap. Opp.	+203
International Investors	+383	†Hartwell Growth	+185
ᴬASA Ltd.	+376	Keystone S-4	+182
Franklin Res. Capital	+358	IDS Growth	+180
ᴬPrecious Metals	+329	†Evergreen Fund	+178
†Constellation Growth	+297	Mass Capital Develop.	+177
†20th Century Growth	+280	St. Paul Growth	+177
†Golconda Investors	+248	ᴬGeneral Am. Investors	+176
†Hartwell Leverage	+234	†20th Century Select	+171
Security Ultra	+229	Oppenheimer AIM	+171
American Gen. Enterprise	+214	Value Line Special Sit.	+166
†44 Wall Street	+209		

* Change in net asset value with all distributions.
† No-Load.
ᴬ Publicly traded investment fund.

Source: United Business Service Co., 212 Newbury Street, Boston, MA 02116. © United Business Service Co. 1981. All Rights Reserved.

MUTUAL FUNDS: TEN-YEAR SELECTED PERFORMANCE

QUARTER ENDED JUNE 30	1981 Net Asset Value per share	12 mos. Divs from Income	12 mos. Disb. fr. Cap. Gns(a)	1980 Net Asset Value per share	12 mos. Divs from Income	12 mos. Disb. fr. Cap. Gns(a)	1979 Net Asset Value per share	12 mos. Divs from Income	12 mos. Disb. fr. Cap. Gns(a)	1978 Net Asset Value per share	12 mos. Divs from Income	12 mos. Disb. fr. Cap. Gns(a)
Acorn Fund	27.48	.84	2.44	23.72	.60	2.34	21.80	.42	1.33	17.93	.31	....
Affiliated Fund	8.94	.55	.71	8.40	.48	.44	7.81	.42	.31	7.39	.37	.15
Afuture Fund	15.32	.41	3.09	14.29	....	....	13.77	.145	.102	11.15	.059	....
American Birthright Trust	11.92	....	....	12.46	....	....	11.01	....	....	9.81	....	....
American Gen. Venture	22.80	.66	2.49	19.11	.75	3.00	18.48	.41	2.53	16.87	.035	....
American Grth Fund (d)	7.75	.40	2.52	9.16	.15	.14	7.18	.27	....	6.19	.14	.14
American Industry Shrs	10.49	.41	....	9.43	.30	....	9.11	.41	....	8.93	.49	.13
American Investors Fund	13.21	.03	.77	10.21	.09	....	7.67	....	....	6.40	.08	....
American Inv. Inc. Fd.	11.03	1.36	.31	11.56	1.23	.55	12.00	1.05	.16	11.77	1.05	.12
American Mutual Fund	12.72	.60	.89	11.16	.54	.42	10.51	.51	.34	10.12	.49	.34
Anchor Growth Fund (b)	9.95	.44	....	8.03	.25	....	7.33	.18	....	6.77	.22	....
Axe-Houghton Fund B	8.75	.48	.10	8.23	.45	.12	8.05	.43	.08	7.73	.40	.08
Axe-Houghton Inco Fund	4.10	.41	....	4.51	.37	....	4.64	.36	....	4.70	.36	....
Axe-Houghton Stock Fund	9.60	.13	....	7.67	.28	....	6.34	.26	....	5.98	.06	....
D. L. Babson Income Trust	1.35	.16	....	1.66	.143	....	1.67	.132	....	1.69	.12	....
D. L. Babson Invest Trust	12.74	.41	....	11.25	.39	....	10.20	.30	....	9.40	.28	....
Beacon Hill Mutual	12.74	.07	....	10.27	.13	....	9.69	.12	....	9.40	.07	....
Boston Foundation Fund	10.09	.845	....	9.93	.71ᵉ	....	9.69	.60	....	9.21	.535	....
Broad Street Investing	12.82	.61	.95	11.47	.60	.80	11.12	.55	.59	10.74	.54	.60
Bullock Fund	16.64	.66	.61	14.72	.62	.45	13.55	.51	.35	12.48	.48	.28
Canadian Fund	9.47	.31	.81	9.53	.27	.78	8.88	.28	.38	7.31	.30	.29
Capital Shares	13.81	.15	....	10.38	.17	....	7.84	.12	....	6.94	.105	....
Century Shares Trust	12.55	.58	.70	11.44	.53	.96	12.12	.44	.79	11.21	.35	.60
Charter Fund	19.91	.61	3.32	18.39	.505	1.53	15.30	.281	3.836	16.31	.187	1.026
Chemical Fund	10.15	.30	.30	8.63	.27	.26	7.65	.235	.25	7.26	.21	.21
Colonial Fund	11.23	.59	....	10.32	.55	....	9.57	.52	....	8.99	.43	....
Colonial Growth Shares	8.17	.17	....	6.56	.16	....	5.23	.16	....	4.59	.12	....
Commerce Income Shares	9.30	.82	....	8.80	.645	....	8.26	.59	....	8.03	.52	.092
Composite Bond & Stock	9.35	.66	.40	9.06	.58	.19	8.95	.55	.15	8.51	.52	.10
Composite Fund	10.09	.38	.90	8.91	.31	6%S	8.26	.26	....	8.05	.22	....
Comstock Fund	12.00	.51	2.44	10.93	.43	....	8.62	.30	....	7.04	.22	....
Concord Fund	21.44	.57	....	17.78	.56	....	16.13	.48	....	13.84	.39	....
Decatur Income Fund	15.08	.95	1.02	14.22	.78	.17	12.68	.75	....	11.85	.72	....
Delaware Fund	16.81	.69	....	13.40	.58	....	11.79	.55	....	11.41	.515	....
DeVegh Mutual Fund	48.23	1.315	1.32	41.30	.45	....	34.40	1.17	....	30.31	1.034	....
Directors Capital Fund	2.48	....	....	2.26	....	....	3.00	....	....	3.94	....	....
Dividend Shares	2.95	.16	.15	2.80	.145	.14	2.82	.12	.13	2.72	.12	.12
Dodge & Cox Balanced Fund	23.41	1.50	1.01	23.16	1.35	.31	22.38	1.21	.20	20.85	1.15	.24
Dreyfus Fund	15.69	.61	1.97	14.11	.57	.745	12.78	.445	.725	12.18	.47	.51
Eaton & Howard Balanced	8.23	.52	.18	8.12	.458	.13	7.58	.472	.29	7.69	.463	.13
Eaton & Howard Income	4.31	.52	....	5.10	.535	....	5.63	.493	....	5.83	.478	....
Eaton & Howard Stock	11.23	.54	....	10.48	.43	....	9.24	.395	....	8.82	.382	....
Energy Fund	21.65	.86	1.96	21.13	.66	.70	16.40	.57	.63	14.38	.47	.51
Enterprise Fund	14.30	.14	....	9.92	.09	....	6.79	.095	....	5.70	.175	....
Evergreen Fund	36.85	.30	2.76	29.17	.689	2.294	23.47	.04	4.18	21.67	.251	1.188
Fairfield Fund	9.82	.055	....	6.62	.21	....	5.40	.16	....	5.01	.11	....
Fidelity Fund	19.32	.80	1.39	17.21	.77	.68	16.03	.73	.79	15.63	.69	.38
Fidelity Trend Fund	31.31	.76	....	25.89	.84	1.61	25.47	.515	....	22.84	.49	....
Financial Dynamics Fund	7.68	.47	.366	6.89	.42	....	5.97	.31	....	5.37	.153	....
Financial Industrial Fund	4.28	.304	.938	5.20	.254	.284	4.68	.222	.173	4.19	.186	.311
Financial Industrial Inco Fund	7.05	.56	.928	7.91	.51	.484	7.28	.50	.451	7.16	.41	.12
First Investors Discovery	11.10	.03	....	7.49	.16	....	7.84	.085	....	6.79	.03	....
First Invest. Fund For Inc.	6.81	.90	....	7.45	.90	....	8.19	.81	.07	8.27	.78	.33
First Investors Stock	7.17	.66	....	7.53	.773	....	8.08	.633	....	7.85	.57	....
44 Wall St Fund	23.87	....	.26	16.86	....	3.25	16.72	....	....	12.30	....	....

1977			1976			1975			1974			1973			1972			1971
Net Asset Value per share	12 mos. Divs from Income	12 mos. Disb. fr. Cap. Gns(a)	Net Asset Value per share	12 mos. Divs from Income	12 mos. Disb. fr. Cap. Gns(a)	Net Asset Value per share	12 mos. Divs from Income	12 mos. Disb. fr. Cap. Gns(a)	Net Asset Value per share	12 mos. Divs from Income	12 mos. Disb. fr. Cap. Gns(a)	Net Asset Value per share	12 mos. Divs from Income	12 mos. Disb. fr. Cap. Gns(a)	Net Asset Value per share	12 mos. Divs from Income	12 mos. Disb. fr. Cap. Gns(a)	Net Asset Value per share
16.17	.21	....	12.65	.20	....	10.04	.18	....	8.07	.12	.04	8.95	.15	1.12	14.86	.08	.26	12.90
8.22	.35	.22	8.33	.31	.12	7.22	.28	.03	5.79	.32	.17	6.21	.29	.20	6.92	.30	.24	7.42
9.39	.033	....	9.57	.018	....	8.25	.01	....	7.18	....	....	8.60	....	1.87	11.15	....	....	10.82
9.98	....	....	9.18	....	....	8.52	....	....	7.73	....	....	7.56	....	....	7.62	....	....	7.10
12.38	....	....	10.87	....	....	9.26	....	....	6.29	....	....	6.69	....	....	15.15	..	.87	12.25
5.61	.155	....	5.16	.18	....	4.67	.29	.53	4.82	.165	.12	5.92	.16	.085	6.22	.18	.63	6.72
10.52	.29	.20	11.56	.29	....	10.10	.30	....	8.98	.17	....	9.46	....	....				
5.92	.05	....	5.13	.06	....	5.06	.07	....	3.83	.05	....	4.53	....	....	6.01	.02	....	5.69
12.24	1.03	.31	11.08	.87	.36	10.00	....	....	....	....	....							
10.01	.48	.16	9.76	.46	....	8.35	.48	....	7.35	.37	.22	8.06	.36	.31	9.12	.36	.21	9.39
6.48	.14	.28	7.37	.14	....	6.79	.17	....	5.91	.19	....	7.42	.12	....	12.06	.10	....	11.79
8.17	.41	.05	7.55	.40	.04	6.74	.47	.04	6.33	.37	.23	6.96	.31	.22	8.00	.35	.20	8.03
5.05	.315	....	4.80	.22	....	4.45	.26	....	4.03	.24	.15	4.56	.20	.24	5.68	.24	.21	5.87
5.95	.08	....	6.31	.16	....	5.86	.22	....	5.16	.16	.14	5.68	.08	.07	6.37	.16	.11	6.07
1.80	.125	....	1.75	.128	....	1.74	.135	....	1.76	.14	....	1.90	.155	....	2.03	.095	..	2.00
9.27	.24	....	10.00	.25	....	10.22	.22	....	9.34	.20	....	10.66	.16	.09	10.90	.18	....	9.60
8.55	.06	....	8.63	.05	....	8.34	.16	....	7.28	.15	....	8.70	....	.21	12.30	....	.70	10.76
9.63	.475	....	9.25	.40	....	8.86	.42	....	7.94	.44	....	9.45	.45	.23	11.08	.39	.443	11.45
11.82	.53	.77	12.62	.49	.77	11.55	.48	.14	10.50	.45	.69	13.29	.42	1.20	15.21	.42	.83	14.76
13.02	.49	.26	13.17	.47	.21	12.03	.47	.21	10.30	.39	.61	12.45	.28	.30	15.75	.35	.51	15.27
7.69	.32	.30	8.88	.33	.28	9.00	.33	.26	9.53	.225	.38	10.68	.19	.40	10.92	.225	.35	9.79
6.30	.094	....	5.59	.084	....	4.95	.067	....	4.09	.12	....	5.30	.087	....	6.68	.133	....	6.55
11.79	.14	.30	10.10	.31	....	10.36	.30	.29	9.17	.285	.51	12.44	.275	.54	14.37	.285	.35	13.56
14.47	.125	....	11.93	.12	....	11.13	.138	....	9.08	.03	....	8.98	....	1.201	13.67	.133	....	9.04
7.13	.185	.21	8.36	.20	.198	8.71	.20	.15	8.46	.16	.455	10.42	.12	.52	10.80	.13	.50	9.42
9.42	.45	....	9.92	.45	....	9.48	.51	....	8.93	.44	....	9.64	.43	.25	11.11	.44	.15	11.09
4.66	.10	....	5.17	.097	....	5.17	.115	....	4.91	.06	.03	5.81	.04	.20	7.19	.10	....	6.59
8.93	.255	....	9.15	.14	....	8.41	.33	....	6.89	.355	.29	8.40	.143	.583	10.98	.14	....	9.87
9.09	.50	.09	8.72	.48	....	8.03	.48	....	7.26	.44	.20	8.22	.34	.30	8.87	.37	.38	9.36
7.48	.21	....	8.05	.26	....	7.93	.28	....	6.38	.28	....	7.11	.29	.30	9.28	.32	.40	10.14
6.11	.16	....	5.43	.10	....	4.55	.10	....	3.22	.08	....	3.12	.04	....	4.48	.10	....	4.41
13.14	.64	....	11.27	.16	....	8.84	.14	....	7.97	.11	....	8.94	....	....	11.45	.24	....	11.98
12.68	.63	....	11.63	.77	....	9.80	.65	....	8.36	.62	....	9.60	.60	.50	11.82	.60	.50	12.08
11.55	.435	....	11.17	.41	....	9.47	.40	....	7.83	.36	.11	9.21	.33	.78	13.21	.37	.73	13.40
31.08	.88	....	32.24	.79	....	31.29	1.018	....	25.75	.605	....	28.56	.71	....	34.87	.66	.75	34.73
4.32	.025	....	4.16	.054	....	3.83	.17	....	3.36	.187	.14	4.96	....	1.226	8.05	....	.564	6.87
3.06	.12	.12	3.30	.125	.10	3.06	.125	.11	2.88	.115	.14	3.62	.11	.15	3.89	.11	.14	3.77
22.33	1.06	....	21.96	.95	....	19.61	.95	....	17.65	.87	.19	20.62	.80	.62	23.17	.81	.16	22.36
12.15	.42	.48	11.98	.36	....	10.91	.33	....	8.76	.25	....	10.44	.265	....	12.87	.31	.02	12.63
8.39	.446	.15	8.78	.426	.09	8.36	.42	....	7.84	.415	.35	9.43	.409	.652	10.26	.431	.45	10.15
6.24	.463	....	5.78	.44	....	5.48	.439	....	5.29	.43	.112	6.07	.425	.15	6.56	.424	.052	6.26
9.16	.338	....	9.74	.292	....	9.68	.307	....	8.91	.303	.305	12.35	.31	.792	14.26	.347	.52	14.11
15.53	.46	.40	14.69	.46	....	12.84	.40	....	9.91	.28	.16	11.03	.25	.33	12.64	.32	.34	13.57
5.18	.10	....	5.54	.11	....	5.29	.17	....	4.53	.12	....	5.40	.07	....	7.20	.10	....	6.73
16.45	....	....	13.06	....	....	10.57	....	....	7.06	....	....	7.70	.045	1.267	12.50	....	....	
4.92	.09	....	4.94	.12	....	4.07	.06	....	3.22	.05	....	3.75	....	....	5.97	.06	....	5.36
16.33	.64	....	16.00	.59	....	14.55	.60	....	12.53	.53	.17	14.95	.51	.45	17.18	.54	.24	16.13
21.88	.40	....	22.96	.375	....	20.78	.36	....	18.55	.32	....	22.40	.28	....	27.88	.49	....	24.94
5.07	.085	....	4.52	.07	....	4.29	.076	....	3.28	.08	....	3.87	.02	....	4.78	.05	....	4.45
4.52	.159	....	4.38	.128	....	3.84	.158	.077	3.49	.07	.06	4.28	.086	.031	4.27	.10	....	3.90
7.41	.135	.617	7.21	.113	.354	6.38	.10	....	5.03	.10	....	5.53	.085	....	5.98	.08	....	5.91
5.24	.01	....	5.20	....	....	4.91	....	....	3.80	.05	....	5.05	....	....	8.97	....	....	9.57
8.97	.85	.57	8.39	.78	.04	7.27	.767	....	6.77	.738	....	8.29	.77	.06	9.84	.65	.02	7.79
8.54	.44	....	7.95	.22	..	7.10	.22	....	6.43	.23	....	7.55	.21	.39	9.93	.203	....	9.52
8.37	....	....	7.11	..	..	5.74	....	....	3.65	....	....	3.72	....	.626	8.36	....	....	6.57

MUTUAL FUNDS: TEN-YEAR SELECTED PERFORMANCE *(continued)*

QUARTER ENDED JUNE 30	1981 Net Asset Value per share	1981 12 mos. Divs from Income	1981 12 mos. Disb. fr. Cap. Gns(a)	1980 Net Asset Value per share	1980 12 mos. Divs from Income	1980 12 mos. Disb. fr. Cap. Gns(a)	1979 Net Asset Value per share	1979 12 mos. Divs from Income	1979 12 mos. Disb. fr. Cap. Gns(a)	1978 Net Asset Value per share	1978 12 mos. Divs from Income	1978 12 mos. Disb. fr. Cap. Gns(a)
Founders Growth	9.06	.28	.20	6.77	.23	....	5.38	.18	....	4.72	.10	....
Founders Income Fund	16.05	.87	.92	13.86	.76	....	12.90	.68	....	11.87	.61	....
Founders Mutual Fund	9.48	.431	.384	8.49	.406	.21	8.21	.371	.095	7.85	.351	.032
Founders Special Fund	22.58	.408	....	16.11	.432	....	12.46	.332	....	10.76	.197	....
Frank'n C. Fds. Dy Tech	14.01	.18	....	10.83	.27	....	9.07	.11	....	8.41	.23	....
Franklin Cust—Growth	8.08	.11	....	6.38	.10	....	6.33	.10	....	6.23	.08	....
Franklin Cust—Inc Shrs	6.36	.22	.115	2.22	.13	....	1.94	.15	.045	1.79	.14	.025
Franklin Cust—Util Shrs	4.35	.43	....	4.54	.38	....	4.68	.34	....	4.79	.31	....
Fundamental Investors (c)	8.78	.41	....	7.49	.36	....	7.03	.28	....	6.62	.27	....
General Securities	12.31	.54	1.38	12.07	.275	.215	11.05	.291	.069	9.88	.20	....
Growth Industry Shrs	18.42	.27	.58	14.08	.206	.54	11.99	.19	....	10.11	.18	....
Guardian Mutual Fund	32.42	1.25	4.95	32.07	1.15	2.68	29.53	1.10	1.67	27.62	1.05	1.20
Guardian Pk Ave. Fd.	14.90	.77	1.08	13.62	.81	1.57	13.31	.42	.68	12.71	.37	.46
Hamilton Fund H-DA	5.15	.21	....	4.52	.206	....	4.23	.184	....	4.06	.215	....
Hartwell Growth Fund	12.43	....	....	8.09	....	....	6.00	....	....	5.21	....	....
Hartwell Leverage Fd	29.26	....	....	17.52	....	....	11.34	....	....	10.09	....	....
Herold Fund	165.98	....	....	140.66	....	....	112.88	....	....	102.91	....	....
IDS Growth Fund	15.12	.21	.93	9.33	.152	.54	7.31	.119	.164	6.69	.076	.067
IDS New Dimension Fund	10.12	.18	.71	7.43	.186	....	5.83	.137	....	5.23	.081	....
IDS Progressive Fund	4.97	.12	....	3.90	.113	....	3.57	.115	....	3.41	.097	....
International Investors	9.60	.82	.29	11.15	.373	....	4.88	.187	....	3.23	.143	....
Investment Co. of America	9.28	.42	.66	8.34	.335	.20	7.90	.275	.09	7.38	.245	.14
Invest. Trust of Boston	11.10	.31	1.15	11.04	.32	.45	9.50	.37	.39	9.34	.31	.25
Investors Mutual	9.29	.664	....	9.07	.615	...	8.97	.555	....	8.70	.543	....
Investors Research	5.50	.10	.31	4.06	.09	.53	4.13	.06	.37	4.15	.08	....
Investors Selective	6.62	.87	....	8.03	.649	....	8.83	.771	....	8.91	.727	.052
Investors Stock Fund	20.89	1.06	1.49	20.05	1.03	....	19.00	.873	.16	17.61	.788	.15
Investors Variable Pay	10.16	.37	.18	8.24	.307	....	7.49	.235	....	6.74	.176	....
ISI Trust Fund	9.89	1.18	....	11.23	.92	.94	12.05	.83	....	10.81	.70	....
Istel Fund	33.09	1.40	3.00	32.36	1.12	....	26.32	.75	....	21.12	.48	....
Ivest Fund	13.32	.36	....	10.52	.34	....	9.76	.23	....	8.61	.16	....
JP Growth Fund	12.72	.60	.75	11.84	.55	....	10.84	.40	.34	10.19	.35	....
Johnston Cap. Appreciation	28.76	1.06	1.07	24.47	1.14	.27	22.33	.85	....	20.39	.57	.04
Kemper Growth Fund	11.25	.30	1.59	11.25	.30	1.59	10.51	.30	1.26	9.23	.24	.19
Kemper High Yield	8.64	1.26	....	9.94	1.215	...	11.28	1.18	....	11.59	.39	....
Keystone Series B-1	13.53	1.67	....	16.02	1.62	....	16.73	1.44	....	17.01	1.36	....
Keystone Series B-2	16.22	1.94	....	17.87	1.92	....	18.86	1.66	....	19.06	1.63	....
Keystone Serie B-4	7.18	.90	....	7.54	.80	....	8.11	.76	....	8.21	.72	....
Keystone Series K-1	7.62	.64	....	7.45	.61	....	7.43	.59	....	7.44	.54	....
Keystone Series K-2	6.76	.29	....	6.05	.27	....	5.40	.25	....	5.18	.18	....
Keystone Series S-1	17.66	1.20	1.30	18.63	.85	.85	18.39	.78	....	17.39	.65	.21
Keystone Series S-3	10.68	.37	.96	9.37	.53	.33	8.71	.34	.57	8.42	.07	....
Keystone Series S-4	6.67	.23	2.85	7.26	.13	....	5.57	.10	....	4.81	.07	....
Lexington Growth Fund	11.52	.33	2.93	11.29	.27	4.90	14.13	.06	.145	12.00	.09	....
Lexington Research Fund	17.30	.51	3.30	17.16	.93	1.55	15.35	.56	.34	14.51	.56	....
Life Insurance Investors	10.87	.41	.66	10.07	.94	....	11.22	.34	....	8.75	.23	.155
Lindner Fund	13.56	.26	1.45	10.09	.448	1.377	10.79	.26	.23	9.27	.125	.225
Loomis Sayles Cap Dev	18.78	.36	3.38	15.02	.36	1.65	13.68	.35	....	12.54	.27	....
Loomis Sayles Mutual	14.76	.97	....	14.30	.78	....	13.38	.68	....	12.95	.61	....
Lord Abbett Inco. Fd.	2.72	.30	....	2.95	.291	....	3.07	.238	.06	3.20	.24	.16
Magna Income Trust	7.19	.92	....	8.21	.91	....	9.01	.87	....	9.15	.77	....
Massachusetts Fund	12.57	.74	.24	12.18	.43	....	11.22	.61	....	10.57	.54	....
Mass. Investors Grth. Stk.	13.18	.30	1.08	11.03	.273	.381	9.39	.244	.283	8.78	.20	.264
Mass. Investors Trust	12.51	.56	.85	11.35	.535	.329	10.38	.473	.155	9.60	.43	.155
Mathers Fund	24.01	1.06	1.36	21.06	.76	1.04	17.15	.79	1.79	16.28	.41	.32

1977 NAV	1977 Divs Income	1977 Cap Gns(a)	1976 NAV	1976 Divs Income	1976 Cap Gns(a)	1975 NAV	1975 Divs Income	1975 Cap Gns(a)	1974 NAV	1974 Divs Income	1974 Cap Gns(a)	1973 NAV	1973 Divs Income	1973 Cap Gns(a)	1972 NAV	1972 Divs Income	1972 Cap Gns(a)	1971 NAV
4.54	.05	....	4.75	.09	.,..	4.90	.20	....	4.53	.23	..	5.23	.22	....	6.43	.06	....	5.47
12.48	.55	....	11.57	.55	..:	10.78	.73	...	9.76	.65	....	11.65	.65	....	12.76	.71	....	13.62
8.86	.322	.129	9.72	.275	.062	8.67	.289	.02	7.63	.205	....	8.70	.206	.104	9.44	.251	.021	8.83
9.57	.124	....	8.32	.242	....	8.99	.601	....	8.94	.434	....	10.90	....	.834	14.13	....	.246	11.68
6.93	.14	....	6.93	.12	....	6.66	.10	....	5.97	....	..	7.35	.07	....	11.50	.05	....	8.88
5.28	.10	.107	6.01	.11	.052	5.87	.075	.073	5.90	.05	.16	7.30	.02	.34	8.27	.04	....	6.68
1.76	.135	.022	1.69	.139	.015	1.73	.139	.051	1.66	.14	.05	1.94	.14	.06	2.16	.14	.06	2.12
4.90	.295	....	4.11	.295	....	4.04	.245	....	3.27	.235	....	5.25	.225	....	5.21	.22	....	6.13
6.82	.25	.21	7.29	.25	....	6.62	.28	....	5.90	.25	.25	7.38	.25	.49	9.33	.25	....	9.29
9.56	.21	....	9.18	.24	....	7.17	.24	....	5.54	.18	....	6.26	.12	....	8.63	.22	....	10.03
8.76	.13	....	9.18	.095	....	9.04	.108	....	8.06	.10	.085	9.58	.105	.93	12.49	.14	.20	11.03
28.93	1.08	1.65	28.40	1.14	.17	24.18	1.08	.10	20.09	.78	.55	22.01	.75	1.22	25.79	.79	1.34	26.36
11.85	.39	.62	10.78	.41	.07	9.00	.31	....	7.46	.265	.14	7.52	.265	.12	9.45	....	....	....
4.17	.155	....	4.47	.14	....	3.95	.14	....	3.43	.14	....	3.94	.15	....	4.59	.18	.065	4.75
3.91	....	....	3.93	.,,,	..	3.33	....	....	2.71	....	....	3.33	....	....	5.35	....	....	4.53
8.36	....	....	8.13	.,,.	....	6.23	....	....	4.43	....	....	4.69	....	....	8.20	....		7.40
97.44	....	....	93.91	..	....	90.33	1.43	....	76.80	.82	....	97.13	....	....	185.45	....		131.15
5.69	.044	....	5.48	.028	....	5.45	.021	....	4.71	....	....	6.01	.113	.115	7.22	....		....
4.75	.056	....	4.94	..	....	4.92	.061	....	4.25	.031	....	5.45	.015	...	7.52	....		5.28
3.13	.065	....	3.26	.074	....	3.14	.066	....	2.84	.047	....	4.11	.068	.717	6.06	....		4.58
2.42	.123	.01	2.88	.233	.023	5.96	.283	.023	5.77	.069	.023	4.38	.05	.02	2.77	.04	.013	1.87
7.08	.24	.115	7.14	.285	.035	6.38	.30	....	5.44	.21	.165	6.19	.195	.235	7.23	.195	.13	6.85
9.76	.34	.51	10.76	.28	.41	10.03	.44	.20	8.85	.42	.35	10.91	.34	.90	12.10	.32	.30	12.27
9.16	.495	....	8.99	.455	....	8.44	.438	....	7.77	.411	.053	9.52	.393	.23	10.42	.385	.168	10.06
3.59	.03	....	3.69	.09	....	3.73	.09	....	2.85	.04	....	3.26	....	.71	4.85	....	....	3.47
9.55	.699	.028	9.04	.688	....	8.61	.723	....	8.50	.679	....	9.49	.626	..--	9.58	.588	....	9.16
18.89	.638	....	19.58	.54	....	17.63	.558	....	15.56	.508	.08	19.03	.475	.29	21.20	.50	.155	19.73
6.49	....	....	6.65	.137	....	6.72	.124	....	6.13	.112	....	8.51	.119	....	9.20	.147	....	7.82
10.59	.58	.07	10.75	.84	.20	12.77	.94	2.14	14.21	.74	.085	13.34	.48	.238	12.80	.46	....	12.30
20.23	.77	....	21.39	.62	....	21.17	.78	....	17.74	.63	.68	19.90	.30	.65	23.13	.30	.61	22.72
7.92	.14	....	8.39	.09	....	8.02	.06	....	6.77	.15	.,,.	8.98	.11	.205	12.60	.147	....	11.02
10.56	.25	.34	11.17	.35	....	9.10	.40	....	7.82	.25	...,	8.26	.17	.08	12.10	.19	.12	11.74
19.90	.36	.44	21.35	.36	.32	21.23	.47	....	18.80	.49	.25	23.04	.33	.80	28.61	.14	.59	23.60
8.21	.15	....	7.44	.13	....	7.18	.13	....	6.04	.14	....	5.01	.12	....	5.76	.11	.30	7.87
	...,	...,		..	....	....	....	....		....	....		....	....		....	....	....
18.14	1.39	.....	17.35	1.40	....	16.90	1.73	....	17.51	1.44	....	18.95	1.37	....	19.09	1.34	....	18.64
20.04	1.63	....	18.84	1.63	....	17.25	1.70	....	17.73	1.57	....	20.07	1.60	....	20.78	1.57	....	19.61
8.55	.72	....	7.91	.75	....	7.33	.77	....	7.14	.73	....	8.25	.73	....	9.13	.71	....	8.42
7.85	.54	....	7.48	.52	....	6.74	.53	....	6.05	.48	....	7.06	.48	....	8.19	.48	...,	7.89
5.27	.13	....	5.55	.09	....	5.43	.10	....	4.49	.03	....	5.58	..,..		7.62	.04	....	5.74
17.72	.63	.34	19.45	.44	....	19.25	.42	.30	17.33	.27	.37	22.56	.21	....	22.42	.34	....	19.71
7.81	.17	.80	8.64	....	....	7.77	.18	....	5.83	.....		7.09	.09	.--..	9.61	.09	....	8.50
3.96	.06	....	3.72	.04	....	3.33	...	..	2.81	....		3.69	....	....	6.87	....		5.22
9.35	.05	....	7.78	.04	....	6.54	.07	....	4.80	.05	....	5.78	.04	.75	11.03	....	1.09	10.40
14.87	.54	....	15.09	.43	....	12.96	.40	....	11.24	.25	....	12.68	.14	.76	17.30	.17	.55	16.65
7.53	.19	.061	6.06	.17	.03	6.28	.15	.025	5.37	.125	.175	7.56	.115	.26	9.06	.10	.40	8.02
6.90	.10	....	5.42	.10	....	4.08	.11	....	4.00	.076	....	3.90	.072	1.148	5.30	.088	....	4.54
10.84	.18	....	10.77	.13	....	10.76	.15	.37	10.07	.14	.37	12.41	.08	....	13.86	.16	....	11.89
13.16	.42	.08	13.68	.43	....	13.15	.43	....	12.37	.46	....	14.39	.42	.42	15.30	.42	.35	14.74
3.60	.22	.10	3.31	.225	....	2.95	.18	....	2.62	.175	....	2.96	.17	.05	3.49	.16	.10	3.33
9.44	.70	....	8.65	.55	....	8.11	.60	....	7.61	.50	....	8.72	.47	...,	9.14	.52	....	8.79
10.75	.50	....	10.54	.49	....	9.88	.50	....	9.14	.43	.23	11.25	.42	.35	12.10	.40	.28	11.36
8.47	.15	.256	9.77	.148	.224	10.33	.19	....	9.51	.196	.17	12.72	.176	.723	14.87	.176	.347	13.23
10.40	.394	.217	11.37	.345	.168	10.32	.405	....	9.23	.393	.15	10.89	.379	.618	12.59	.416	1.71	14.32
13.96	.33	....	11.80	.24	....	10.23	.31	....	7.95	.25	....	10.50	.17	1.07	17.12	.32	....	13.75

MUTUAL FUNDS: TEN-YEAR SELECTED PERFORMANCE *(continued)*

QUARTER ENDED JUNE 30	1981 Net Asset Value per share	1981 12 mos. Divs from Income	1981 12 mos. Disb. fr. Cap. Gns(a)	1980 Net Asset Value per share	1980 12 mos. Divs from Income	1980 12 mos. Disb. fr. Cap. Gns(a)	1979 Net Asset Value per share	1979 12 mos. Divs from Income	1979 12 mos. Disb. fr. Cap. Gns(a)	1978 Net Asset Value per share	1978 12 mos. Divs from Income	1978 12 mos. Disb. fr. Cap. Gns(a)
MIF Fund	8.69	.55	.24	7.98	.44	....	7.90	.40	....	7.68	.39	....
MIF Growth Fund	5.73	.18	.09	4.83	.15	....	4.61	.11	....	4.26	.09	....
MONY Fund	12.06	.395	....	10.54	.395	....	9.61	.335	....	9.08	.225	....
Mutual Shares	44.69	2.17	4.63	41.11	1.08	3.92	38.66	.95	2.35	33.95	.60	1.35
National Investors	8.54	.19	.56	7.55	.17	.45	6.89	.16	.30	6.40	.14	.27
National Sec—Balanced	10.19	.64	....	9.77	.60	....	9.61	.56	....	9.24	.48	....
National Sec—Bond	3.23	.44	....	3.83	.425	....	4.22	.41	....	4.38	.39	....
National Sec—Dividend	5.49	.325	.16	4.81	.30	.12	4.38	.285	....	4.13	.27	....
National Sec—Growth	8.04	.185	....	6.40	.20	....	5.82	.185	....	5.62	.155	....
National Sec—Income	6.13	.47	.15	5.80	.425	.12	5.73	.39	....	5.57	.365	....
National Sec—Pfd.	6.23	.65	....	6.63	.63	....	7.17	.57	....	7.20	.51	....
National Sec—Stock	9.87	.48	.75	9.00	.43	.32	8.52	.39	.10	7.79	.37	.04
Nation-Wide Securities	9.60	.68	.22	9.59	.56	.14	9.55	.53	.16	9.21	.53	.16
Newton Growth Fund	21.31	.46	1.41	16.04	.495	....	13.94	.395	....	12.85	.275	....
Nicholas Fund	19.34	.522	.835	14.09	.389	....	11.96	.31	....	10.15	.185	....
Northeast Investors Trust	10.38	1.385	....	12.53	1.325	....	13.35	1.28	....	13.96	1.28	....
One William Street Fund	18.26	.745	2.125	16.93	.57	1.24	16.02	.48	.77	14.32	.325	.21
Oppenheimer Fund	10.13	.22	1.17	9.02	.19	....	6.83	.435	....	5.90	.23	....
O-T-C Securities Fund Inc.	26.44	.99	3.23	24.74	.50	.55	19.20	.43	1.08	16.08	.37	.42
Penn Square Mutual	8.91	.45	.53	7.86	.415	.41	7.63	.375	.35	7.49	.35	.31
Pennsylvania Mutual	5.89	.12	2.05	5.58	.16	.91	6.15	.075	....	5.46	.055	....
Philadelphia Fund	10.40	.375	.755	9.49	.33	.52	8.40	.23	.75	8.17	.179	.341
Pilgrim Fund	15.58	.60	2.18	14.89	.51	.33	12.86	.31	....	10.79	.15	....
Pine Street Fund	12.57	.595	.48	11.54	.675	.23	10.72	.59	.22	10.04	.502	.295
Pioneer Fund	20.59	.79	.63	18.07	.72	.615	16.20	.56	.48	14.33	.53	.475
Pioneer II Fund	13.64	.43	.50	10.68	.38	.60	10.14	.35	.75	9.71	.21	.265
Pligrowth Fund	16.69	.54	.09	14.48	.465	.055	11.91	.37	.06	11.05	.12	....
Plitrend Fund	15.01	.33	1.57	12.29	.34	2.01	13.09	.27	.74	10.48	.225	.10
T. Rowe Price Growth Stk	13.92	.497	.04	12.13	.419	....	11.35	.331	....	10.84	.277	....
Rowe Price New Era Fund	21.15	.71	1.45	18.78	.495	.337	13.63	.408	.36	10.74	.324	.246
Rowe Price New Horizons	17.65	.446	1.55	13.26	.232	.368	10.62	.157	....	9.70	.098	....
Provident Fund for Income	4.11	.31	....	3.82	.28	....	3.78	.07	....	3.76	.27	....
Puritan Fund	12.05	.81	.44	11.00	.72	.26	10.70	.675	.28	10.50	.665	.30
Putnam Fund	13.20	.96	.915	13.27	.87	.74	13.24	.69	.41	12.95	.66	.20
Putnam Growth Fund	11.81	.595	2.08	12.13	.545	.925	11.04	.525	.66	10.49	.42	.35
Putnam Income Fund	5.68	.678	....	6.74	.648	....	7.41	.76	....	7.69	.63	....
Putnam Investors Fund	9.78	.25	.69	8.01	.305	.515	7.60	.27	.42	7.25	.215	.68
Research Capital Fund	8.33	1.04	....	9.55	.47	....	4.41	.13	....	3.04	.14	....
Revere Fund	8.39	.195	....	7.07	.11	....	6.01	.10	....	5.20		....
SAFECO Equity Fund	12.08	.583	.75	10.54	.463	.473	10.05	.42	.661	9.74	.345	.239
St. Paul Cap Fund	14.72	.485	2.13	12.15	.275	....	9.24	.24	....	8.30	.24	....
St. Paul Grth Fund	15.19	.165	2.58	11.88	.12	1.51	10.14	.141	1.025	8.97	.14	....
Scudder Int'l Invests	18.22	.57	1.23	18.66	.493	1.356	16.19	.286	.496	14.93	.277	....
Scudder Special Fund	51.46	1.14	....	40.15	.72	....	33.75	.52	....	30.29	.45	....
Scudder Common Stock Fd	14.07	.50	....	13.38	.42	....	10.63	.37	....	9.97	.32	....
Scudder Income Fund	10.37	1.36	....	12.37	1.23	....	13.49	.107	....	13.61	1.04	.335
Security Equity Fund	7.28	.17	.18	5.95	.21	.05	4.92	.08	....	4.42	.14	....
Security Invest Fund	9.57	.60	.18	8.56	.56	.12	7.75	.50	.11	7.39	.48	.17
Selected Amer. Shares	7.49	.47	....	7.15	.375	....	7.01	.335	....	6.79	.285	....
Sentinel Bal Fund	7.44	.61	.20	7.75	.53	....	7.42	.50	.08	7.50	.47	.05
Sentinel Com Stk Fund	14.12	.90	.40	12.95	.78	.28	11.90	.69	.15	11.46	.635	.20
Sequoia Fund	26.58	1.02	1.74	22.58	.74	1.262	23.17	.38	.045	21.26	.34	.43
Sherman, Dean Fund	9.20	....	....	8.90	....	....	4.99	....	....	4.71	....	....
Sigma Capital Shares	8.68	.19	....	6.34	.19	....	5.48	....	....	5.01	.05	....
Sigma Investment Shares	13.27	.61	.21	11.35	.606	.151	10.48	.495	.145	9.98	.45	.201

1977 NAV	1977 Divs Inc	1977 Cap Gns(a)	1976 NAV	1976 Divs Inc	1976 Cap Gns(a)	1975 NAV	1975 Divs Inc	1975 Cap Gns(a)	1974 NAV	1974 Divs Inc	1974 Cap Gns(a)	1973 NAV	1973 Divs Inc	1973 Cap Gns(a)	1972 NAV	1972 Divs Inc	1972 Cap Gns(a)	1971 NAV
8.47	.33	.20	9.08	.33	....	7.66	.37	....	6.75	.35	.14	7.50	.33	.29	8.28	.33	.26	8.85
3.87	.08	....	3.99	.08	....	3.58	.12	....	3.31	.11	.18	4.10	.08	.25	5.92	.08	.21	5.77
9.24	.165	....	9.98	.148	....	9.67	.135	....	8.23	.065	....	10.09	.009	.351	13.47	.018	.252	11.91
30.41	.57	1.95	25.97	.50	1.05	20.52	.85	....	15.87	.30	....	14.50	.43	....	16.78	.39	....	16.24
6.36	.12	.24	6.84	.13	.14	6.65	.16	....	5.88	.12	.46	8.11	.10	.55	10.00	.10	.30	8.44
9.56	.44	....	9.24	.38	....	7.93	.49	....	7.16	.49	....	8.53	.47	....	10.40	.48	.22	10.85
4.64	.39	....	4.32	.39	....	4.09	.38	....	4.08	.38	....	4.77	.40	....	5.16	.38	....	4.94
4.16	.255	.04	3.82	.25	....	3.28	.24	....	2.99	.205	.07	3.55	.20	.12	4.14	.21	.12	4.27
5.63	.13	....	5.86	.13	....	5.64	.175	....	5.07	.195	....	6.38	.10	.45	9.94	.13	.35	9.44
5.61	.35	.04	5.13	.33	....	4.55	.325	....	4.16	.305	....	4.59	.30	.09	5.41	.29	.07	5.35
7.81	.41	....	6.87	.40	....	5.60	.43	....	5.28	.39	....	6.03	.40	....	7.28	.39	.07	7.28
8.28	.36	.12	7.99	.35	.10	6.86	.34	....	5.72	.32	.10	6.49	.32	.25	7.68	.32	.25	8.17
10.18	.51	.14	9.94	.50	.12	9.03	.50	.16	8.24	.47	.23	9.78	.49	.26	10.45	.49	.25	10.49
11.93	.185	....	11.48	.24	....	11.68	.35	....	10.75	.13	....	12.14	....	.988	21.44	.05	....	15.36
7.63	.07	....	6.69	.05	....	6.35	.05	....	4.95	.024	....	7.08	....	....	13.09	....	.22	8.31
14.94	1.28	....	14.15	1.245	....	13.51	1.19	....	13.21	1.15	....	15.37	1.15	....	15.80	1.14	....	15.04
14.04	.27	.315	14.77	.30	.23	14.77	.395	....	13.25	.38	.53	15.87	.305	1.035	17.51	.255	.53	16.17
6.20	.18	....	6.67	.111	....	6.25	.25	....	5.58	.145	....	6.91	.084	.542	9.24	.145	.095	8.61
12.79	.39	.51	11.09	.31	.43	10.07	.23	.35	9.42	.19	.18	9.71	.18	.32	12.05	.12	.23	10.67
8.19	.30	.37	8.36	.30	.28	7.19	.325	....	5.88	.255	.36	6.41	.24	.35	7.34	.25	.255	8.20
3.89	.124	....	3.24	....	....	2.56	....	....	1.64	....	....	2.10	....	....	4.53	....	....	4.88
7.43	.16	.31	7.43	.178	.077	6.91	.147	.038	4.97	.086	.55	6.06	.07	.415	7.98	.079	.311	7.80
9.05	.06	....	7.51	.085	....	7.03	.10	....	6.02	.06	....	7.74	.045	.035	11.02	.05	.54	10.05
10.91	.417	.32	10.72	.39	.315	10.30	.445	....	8.76	.445	.178	9.67	.35	.275	10.84	.295	.60	11.46
14.35	.48	.45	13.91	.43	.22	11.81	.41	.155	9.79	.385	.58	11.28	.37	.60	12.23	.365	.525	11.97
8.01	.135	.31	6.65	.095	.095	5.29	.085	.173	4.45	.085	.12	4.26	.08	.84	6.13	.075	.19	5.02
10.90	.295	.105	11.32	.345	.065	10.77	.385	.255	10.07	.27	.48	12.54	.19	.62	15.06	.175	.385	13.52
8.45	.225	.055	7.22	.21	.10	6.57	.178	.093	5.98	.25	.31	7.72	.16	....	8.72	.16	....	8.65
10.20	.226	....	11.27	.231	....	11.18	.229	....	10.10	.195	.23	12.77	.12	....	16.43	.125	.315	13.94
11.09	....	....	11.24	.279	....	11.50	.286	....	10.12	.184	.105	10.77	.105	.138	11.63	.16	....	10.37
7.35	.071	....	7.18	.074	....	7.62	.091	....	6.39	.055	.031	8.84	.042	.692	14.97	.037	.207	9.99
4.04	.245	....	3.68	.25	....	3.39	.26	.17	3.20	.25	.18	3.81	.25	.17	5.06	.22	.11	4.87
11.32	.615	.21	10.62	.585	.10	9.73	.565	.05	8.31	.56	.10	9.03	.53	.32	10.54	.61	.18	10.54
13.78	.60	.17	13.69	.535	....	12.56	.52	....	11.84	.51	.535	14.94	.51	.91	16.38	.49	.27	14.82
10.56	.28	.415	10.69	.25	....	10.04	.305	....	8.67	.30	.375	10.57	.20	.61	12.60	.16	....	10.80
8.16	.63	....	7.62	.61	....	7.26	.60	....	6.90	.54	....	8.02	.46	....	8.38	.46	....	8.16
7.69	.135	.215	8.01	.135	....	7.76	.21	....	7.27	.21	.655	9.62	.12	.77	10.72	.12	.16	8.49
2.44	.165	....	2.72	.26	....	5.75	.25	....	5.31	....	....	4.37	....	....	7.17	....	....	5.45
5.66	.03	....	5.21	.14	....	4.95	.145	....	5.10	.035	....	6.79	.11	.45	12.03	.64	.56	10.75
9.14	.299	.494	9.35	.302	.054	7.76	.324	.107	6.49	.36	.037	8.09	.28	.47	9.28	.27	.42	9.52
8.06	.23	....	8.46	.25	....	8.00	.40	....	7.35	.24	.445	9.35	.162	.628	11.15	.184	.303	10.14
7.49	.105	....	7.44	.134	....	6.73	.31	....	5.74	.17	....	6.83	.03	.435	9.37	.038	....	8.03
13.37	.148	....	13.11	.14	....	12.99	.21	....	12.12	.16	.25	17.02	.022	1.757	15.57	.173	1.21	14.11
24.30	.38	....	23.46	.46	....	22.09	.47	....	20.82	.48	....	27.57	.80	.95	38.67	.97	....	34.96
9.57	.30	....	9.61	.31	....	8.77	.30	....	7.96	.23	....	10.11	.22	.18	11.44	.23	.14	10.73
15.02	.78	....	15.06	.63	....	13.91	.59	....	12.77	.56	....	16.03	.54	.26	16.74	.59	.13	15.67
4.08	.06	....	3.91	.07	....	3.46	.07	.04	2.81	.05	....	3.11	.04	....	4.50	.02	....	3.86
7.69	.44	.17	6.83	.40	....	5.98	.50	....	5.27	.40	.20	6.53	.40	.35	8.03	.42	.33	8.19
7.13	.235	....	7.02	.18	....	6.63	.18	....	6.20	.305	.055	7.77	.26	.51	9.89	.18	.33	10.03
8.16	.46	.10	7.47	.45	.20	7.21	.49	....	6.73	.43	.34	7.86	.39	.34	8.55	.35	.52	8.88
12.54	.585	.33	12.13	.565	.30	11.10	.625	.12	9.51	.53	.39	10.95	.44	.38	12.12	.41	.62	13.04
16.55	.35	....	12.45	.30	....	10.12	.38	....	7.55	.29	.799	9.05	.25	.63	12.01	.15	....	11.11
3.78	....	....	3.12	....	....	3.42	....	....	2.43	....	....	2.19	....	....	3.31	.032	.014	3.37
4.53	.04	....	4.06	.14	....	3.59	.05	....	2.75	.03	.02	3.54	.02	.16	5.48	.02	.15	5.02
10.42	.392	.181	10.59	.327	.078	9.55	.379	....	8.12	.325	.28	10.10	.253	.702	12.21	.255	.595	11.64

MUTUAL FUNDS: TEN-YEAR SELECTED PERFORMANCE *(concluded)*

QUARTER ENDED JUNE 30	1981 Net Asset Value per share	1981 12 mos. Divs from Income	1981 12 mos. Disb. fr. Cap. Gns(a)	1980 Net Asset Value per share	1980 12 mos. Divs from Income	1980 12 mos. Disb. fr. Cap. Gns(a)	1979 Net Asset Value per share	1979 12 mos. Divs from Income	1979 12 mos. Disb. fr. Cap. Gns(a)	1978 Net Asset Value per share	1978 12 mos. Divs from Income	1978 12 mos. Disb. fr. Cap. Gns(a)
Sigma Trust Shares	9.19	.702	....	9.12	.685	....	9.10	.583	....	8.83	.539	....
Sigma Venture Shares	8.07	.09	....	5.48	.06	.26	4.66	....	....	4.42	.01	....
Sovereign Investors	15.04	.84	.10	13.73	.64	.10	12.08	.57	.10	11.42	.52	.10
Stein Roe & Farnham Bal	21.11	.76	.61	20.06	.87	....	18.67	.76	....	17.04	.68	....
Stein Roe & Far Cap Oppt Fd	21.29	.20	1.45	17.37	.25	.92	12.79	.25	....	9.78	.20	....
Stein Roe & Farnham Stk	19.43	.37	1.89	16.65	.46	.23	13.45	.41	....	12.02	.34	....
Strategic Invest Fd.	6.37	1.24	.72	10.08	.404	....	4.37	.297	....	2.79	.189	....
Stratton Growth Fd	23.65	....	....	18.95	.62	....	19.24	.52	....	17.79	.87	....
Surveyor Fund	17.05	.28	.32	13.72	.22	.21	10.72	....	....	9.58	.195	.18
Technology Fund	12.81	.32	.62	10.75	.37	.43	8.84	.26	.20	8.05	.22	.10
Templeton Growth Fund	7.89	.15	....	6.54	.12	.38	5.95	.08	.09	5.13	.043	.02
Templeton World Fund	19.45	.43	.07	15.92	.23	.20	13.83	.05	.06	11.63	....	....
Twentieth Cent Growth Inv	12.70	....	1.15	8.53	....	1.24	6.61	....	1.07	6.11	....	.456
Union Income Fund	11.27	1.03	.39	11.58	.99	.22	11.66	.90	.34	11.72	.86	.71
United Accumulative	8.97	.40	.35	7.87	.31	....	6.86	.29	....	6.42	.25	....
United Income Fund	9.70	.68	.22	9.14	.59	.28	9.33	.51	.28	9.41	.52	.28
United Science Fund	9.48	.32	.06	8.12	.20	....	6.78	.17	....	6.22	.14	....
United Services Fund	4.98	.90	....	6.84	.33	....	2.90	.094	....	1.87	.136	....
Value Line Fund	16.21	.31	2.10	13.06	.26	....	9.97	.17	....	8.92	.13	....
Value Line Income Fund	7.47	.37	.71	6.48	.345	.27	6.00	.315	...	5.31	.28	....
Value Line Leveraged Grth	18.41	.30	3.15	16.12	.40	3.26	16.11	.025	2.08	16.24	.045	....
Value Line Special Sit	12.59	.11	....	8.33	.07	....	6.55	.03	....	5.48	.04	....
Vance Sanders Investors	7.52	.48	.42	7.49	.375	.41	7.33	.34	.26	6.90	.33	....
Vance Sanders Common Stk	9.45	.21	.86	7.97	.21	.43	7.53	.16	.58	6.93	.14	.46
Vance Sanders Special Fd	13.60	.51	1.96	11.48	.40	1.82	11.06	.33	1.82	11.34	.17	....
Wall Street Fund	8.28	.25	.34	7.59	.24	....	6.91	.22	.02	6.19	.20	....
Wash Mutual Investors	7.76	.41	.48	6.64	.38	.32	6.72	.35	....	6.42	.34	.09
Weingarten Equity Fd.	29.04	.19	4.31	24.60	.15	3.15	18.53	.19	....	15.76	.09	....
Wellington Fund	10.34	.81	....	9.91	.66	....	9.31	.54	.25	8.87	.50	.25
Windsor Fund	12.02	.64	.79	10.17	.55	.85	10.47	.50	1.01	10.49	.45	.54
Wisconsin Fund	3.38	.46	....	4.14	.451	....	4.65	.418	....	4.80	.333	....

NOTES: (a) Capital gains distributions may include payments from other sources. (b) Paid 6% stock dividend in 1971; 8% record is used in determining in which period dividends and capital gains payments fall. To provide longer-term performance

Source: *Barron's,* August 10, 1981.

1977 NAV per share	1977 Divs	1977 Disb(a)	1976 NAV per share	1976 Divs	1976 Disb(a)	1975 NAV per share	1975 Divs	1975 Disb(a)	1974 NAV per share	1974 Divs	1974 Disb(a)	1973 NAV per share	1973 Divs	1973 Disb(a)	1972 NAV per share	1972 Divs	1972 Disb(a)	1971 NAV per share
8.86	.408	....	8.12	.486	....	7.08	.461	....	6.47	.459	.156	7.83	.40	.385	9.42	.365	.28	9.15
2.74	....	....	2.43	....	....	2.14	....	....	1.57	....	.04	2.05	....	.08	3.33	.28	.005	2.45
12.12	.49	.23	12.22	.48	.07	10.72	.46	.06	9.30	.42	.25	10.93	.38	.78	12.95	.40	.77	13.60
17.54	.51	....	18.40	.56	....	18.07	.58	....	15.68	.51	.89	20.71	.42	.99	23.95	.44	.56	20.72
9.03	.17	....	8.27	.17	....	8.03	.14	....	7.38	.11	.24	9.78	.05	.36	11.71	.06	.10	10.00
12.21	.30	....	13.10	.28	....	12.80	.30	....	10.82	.23	.70	14.61	.14	.75	17.33	.16	.42	14.70
2.05	.158	....	2.52	.23	....	....	....	....	....	....	....	....	....	....	....	....	....	....
16.95	.28	....	15.07	.25	....	13.05	.14	....	9.72	....	....	10.07	.0575	....	....	....	....	....
8.89	.165	.15	9.21	.15	.15	9.02	.18	.10	7.82	.21	....	9.45	.126	.10	14.39	.20	.46	13.91
7.55	.19	....	7.59	.19	....	6.55	.18	....	5.44	.15	....	5.93	.12	.36	7.92	.18	.30	7.87
4.12	.053	.237	3.36	.04	.037	2.80	.048	.01	2.48	.038	.05	2.84	.02	.265	2.44	.023	.05	1.74
4.39	....	....	3.76	....	....	2.87	....	....	2.14	....	....	2.12	....	....	3.57	....	....	2.09
12.98	.86	.72	12.57	.83	.29	11.41	.84	....	10.40	.55	.28	12.28	.43	1.12	15.17	.40	.37	13.35
6.36	.21	....	6.51	.18	....	6.23	.16	....	5.53	.13	.05	6.93	.16	.20	8.18	.13	.19	7.66
10.19	.50	.39	10.71	.40	.36	10.56	.42	.52	9.94	.40	.62	13.21	.37	.68	14.81	.36	.59	14.17
5.62	.10	....	6.21	.10	....	6.19	.13	....	5.45	.11	....	6.63	.14	.16	8.48	.16	.11	8.07
1.48	.117	....	1.80	.195	....	4.62	....	....	4.88	....	....	6.41	....	....	13.17	....	....	10.28
7.23	.12	....	6.93	.16	....	5.92	.135	....	4.55	.08	....	4.84	.08	....	6.77	.04	....	7.04
5.32	.28	....	4.85	.28	....	4.27	.28	....	3.60	.28	.02	4.32	.28	.07	4.99	.28	.05	5.26
10.36	....	....	8.24	....	....	6.95	....	....	4.48	....	....	5.91	.14	....	10.48	....	....	....
4.64	.02	....	3.98	.03	....	3.17	.025	....	2.39	....	....	2.93	....	....	5.56	....	....	5.81
7.41	.325	.13	7.03	.325	....	6.42	.325	....	5.70	.315	.30	6.97	.315	.50	8.18	.315	.28	8.40
6.45	.11	....	6.32	.13	....	6.20	.18	.21	5.78	.12	.67	7.02	.09	1.50	9.85	.125	.45	8.40
8.35	.08	....	7.15	.08	....	6.65	.14	....	5.50	.13	....	6.63	.055	.31	10.27	.047	1.31	9.40
6.38	.05	....	6.20	.10	....	5.91	.18	....	5.46	.10	.65	7.17	....	.90	9.68	.17	1.00	8.83
6.81	.32	.18	6.92	.305	.18	5.93	.305	.02	4.88	.275	.04	5.34	.245	.11	6.06	.245	.17	6.44
12.26	....	....	10.41	.05	....	10.73	....	....	8.18	....	....	10.28	....	1.38	15.13	....	....	11.59
9.85	.49	.25	10.10	.48	.25	9.51	.50	.25	8.92	.47	.25	10.81	.44	.25	11.78	.44	....	11.63
10.55	.38	.22	9.84	.34	....	7.93	.31	....	6.02	.32	.14	7.12	.19	.53	9.12	.30	.54	9.96
5.35	.28	.22	5.40	.16	....	5.05	.22	.10	4.68	.19	.04	5.38	.18	.26	6.69	.16	.435	6.69

in 1972. (c) Paid 5% stock dividend in 1971. (d) Paid 10% stock dividend in 1972. All figures are adjusted for split-ups. Stock of data, funds are not included in Quarterly Record until they have been offered publicly at least three years.

Closed-end Equity Funds

Closed-end investment companies are traded on either the New York Stock Exchange or the American Exchange. Unlike the open-end companies (mutual funds), the closed-end investment companies do not redeem their shares and only issue new shares.

> Adams Express[N]
> American General Convertible Securities[N]
> ASA Ltd.[N]
> Bancroft Convertible[A]
> Carriers & General[N]
> Castle Convertible[A]
> Central Securities[A]
> Chase Convertible[N]
> Energy & Utility Shares[A]
> General American Investors[N]
> Japan Fund[N]
> Lehman Corp.[N]
> Madison Fund[N]
> Niagara Share Corp.[N]
> Petroleum & Resources[N]
> Precious Metals[A]
> Tri-Continental Corp.[N]
> U.S. & Foreign Securities[N]

[N] Traded on the New York Stock Exchange.
[A] Traded on the American Stock Exchange.

Mutual Funds that Permit Switching

There are several no load (no sale's charge) companies that permit investors to conveniently transfer money out of equity (stock) funds and into money market funds (and vice versa) without any charge. These funds are listed below. In some instances fund switching can be done by telephone. Otherwise, written notification is required. Thus, investors who expect a market decline can move their money out of stocks and into money market funds, while investors who expect a rise in the market can do the reverse.

TELEPHONE SWITCHING PERMITTED

BABSON MONEY MARKET
2440 Pershing Road
Kansas City, MO 64108
(816) 471–5200
COMPOSITE CASH MANAGEMENT
Spokane and Eastern Building
Spokane WA 99201
(509) 624–4101
FIDELITY CASH RESERVE
82 Devonshire Street
Boston, MA 02109
(800) 225–6190

FINANCIAL DAILY INCOME SHARES
P.O. Box 2040
Denver, CO 80201
(800) 525–9831
LEXINGTON MONEY MARKET TRUST
P.O. Box 1515
Englewood Cliffs, NJ 07632
(201) 567–2375
T. ROWE PRICE PRIME RESERVE FUND
100 East Pratt Street
Baltimore, MD 21202
(800) 638–1527

WRITTEN NOTIFICATION REQUIRED

AMERICAN GENERAL RESERVE
2777 Allen Parkway
Houston, TX 77019
(800) 231–3638
COLUMBIA DAILY INCOME
621 S.W. Morrison Street
Portland, OR 97205
(800) 547–1037
DREYFUS LIQUID ASSETS
767 Fifth Avenue
New York, New York 10153
(212) 935–3000
JOHN HANCOCK CASH MANAGEMENT TRUST
John Hancock Place
Boston, MA 02117
(617) 421-4506
MUTUAL OF OMAHA MONEY MARKET ACCOUNT
3102 Farnam Street
Omaha, NB 68131
(402) 342–3328

Mutual Funds Investing in Gold Stocks*

> American Growth
> ASA Ltd[1]
> Golconda Investors Ltd[NL]
> International Investors
> Precious Metals Holdings[2]
> Research Capital
> Sherman Dean[NL]
> Strategic Investments
> United Services[NL]

[1] Traded on the New York Stock Exchange
[2] Traded on the American Stock Exchange
[NL] No Load Mutual Fund

* For addresses see page 283.

Largest Money Market Funds Invested in Government Securities*

Alliance Government Reserves
Capital Preservation Fund
Capital Preservation Fund II
Cardinal Government Securities Trust
First Variable Rate Fund for Government Income
Fund for Government Investors
Government Investors Trust
Merrill Lynch Government Fund
NRTA-AARP U. S. Government Money Market Trust
Shearson Government Agencies

* See below for addresses.

Mutual Funds Which Invest Abroad*

Canadian Fund
G. T. Pacific Fund†
Japan Fund (Closed-End, New York Stock Exchange)
Keystone International Fund
Merrill Lynch Pacific Fund
Putnam International Equities Fund
Scudder International Fund†
Templeton Growth Fund
Transatlantic Fund†
T. Rowe Price International Fund†

† No-Load.

* For addresses, see below.
  Japan Fund, 1 Rockefeller Plaza, New York, New York.

Off-Shore Mutual Funds

Off-Shore Mutual Funds are located in low tax havens such as the Bahamas, Bermuda, the Caymen Islands, the Netherlands, the Antilles, Luxemberg, Panama, Hong Kong, and the British Channel Islands. These governments do not levy capital gains taxes, and dividends are taxed at low rates. The names of investors are kept confidential. The funds are not regulated by the Securities and Exchange Commission and cannot transact business in the U.S. However, a U.S. citizen may purchase fund shares at the above-mentioned locations. Lack of SEC regulations often results in only vague disclosures of the fund's mode of operations. In recent years, however, several major firms such as the Dreyfus Corporation, Drexel Burnham Lambert, and Lazard Brothers Int'l. have set up off-shore funds. A partial list is given below:

Dreyfus Intercontinental (Nassau)
Fidelity World Fund (Bermuda)
Jardine Eastern Trust (Hong Kong)
Lazard Brothers International Capital Fund (Jersey, Channel Islands)
Pacific Fund (Bermuda)
Quantum Fund (Curacao)
Worldwide Special Fund (Curacao)

MUTUAL FUNDS BY INVESTMENT OBJECTIVES AND ADDRESSES[1]

Acorn Fund (AG)
120 South LaSalle Street
Chicago, Illinois 60603

ADV Fund (IG)
30 Wall Street
New York, New York 10005

Aetna Income Shares (I)
Aetna Variable Annuity Fund (G)
151 Farmington Avenue
Hartford, Connecticut 06156

Affiliated Fund (IG)
63 Wall Street
New York, New York 10005

Afuture Fund (AG)
Front & Lemon Streets
Media, Pennsylvania 19063

A.G.E. High Income Fund (I)
155 Bovet Road
San Mateo, California 94402

A.I.M. Whipple Fund (IG)
11400 Rockville Pike
Rockville, Maryland 20852

Alliance Bond Fund (I)
Alliance Capital Reserves (I)
Alliance Government Reserves (I)
140 Broadway
New York, New York 10005

Alpha Fund (AG)
Alpha Income Fund (I)
Alpha Tax-Exempt Bond Fund (MB)
2 Piedmont Center N E
Atlanta, Georgia 30305

AMCAP Fund (G)
333 South Hope Street
Los Angeles, California 90071

American Balanced Fund (IG)
Two Embarcadero Center
P.O. Box 7650
San Francisco, California 94120

[1] Abbreviations
AG—Aggressive Growth Fund
G—Growth Fund
I—Income Fund
IG—Income and Growth Fund
MB—Municipal Bond Fund
M—Money Market Fund

American Birthright Trust (G)
247 Royal Palm Way
Palm Beach, Florida 33480

American General Capital Bond Fund (IG)
American General Comstock Fund (AG)
American General Enterprise Fund (AG)
American General Harbor Fund (IG)
American General High Yield Investment Fund
  (I)
American General Municipal Bond Fund (MB)
American General Pace Fund (G)
American General Reserve Fund (I)
American General Venture Fund (AG)
2777 Allen Parkway
Houston, Texas 77019

American Growth Fund (G)
650 17th Street, Suite 800
Denver, Colorado 80202

American Industry Shares (IG)
P.O. Box 3942
St. Petersburg, Florida 33731

American Insurance & Industrial Fund (G)
4333 Edgewood Road
Cedar Rapids, Iowa 52406

American Investors Fund (AG)
American Investors Income Fund (I)
88 Field Point Road
P.O. Box 2500
Greenwich, Connecticut 06830

American Leaders Fund (G)
421 Seventh Avenue
Pittsburgh, Pennsylvania 15219

American Liquid Trust (M)
99 High Street
Boston, Massachusetts 02110

American Mutual Fund (IG)
333 South Hope Street
Los Angeles, California 90071

American National Bond Fund (I)
American National Growth Fund (AG)
American National Income Fund (IG)
Two Moody Plaza
Galveston, Texas 77550

Analytic Optioned Equity Fund (IG)
222 Martin Street
Irvine, California 92715

Anchor Growth Fund (G)
333 South Hope Street
Los Angeles, California 90071

Archer U.S. Government Guaranteed Securities
  Fund (I)
3100 Eastside
Houston, Texas 77098

Armstrong Associates (G)
2400 First International Building
Dallas, Texas 75270

Axe-Houghton Fund B (IG)
Axe-Houghton Income Fund (I)
Axe-Houghton Stock Fund (IG)
400 Benedict Avenue
Tarrytown, New York 10591

Babson (D.L.) Income Trust (IG)
Babson, David L. Investment Fund (G)
Babson Money Market Fund (M)
Babson Tax-Free Income Fund—Short Term
  (MB)
Babson Tax-Free Income Fund—Long Term
  (MB)
2440 Pershing Road
Kansas City, Missouri 64108

Bank Stock Fund (G)
333 North Tejon Street
Colorado Springs, Colorado 80903

Bascom Hill Investors (AG)
402 South Gammon Place
Madison, Wisconsin 53719

Beacon Income Fund (I)
First National Bank of Boston
Boston, Massachusetts 02104

Beacon Hill Mutual Fund (G)
75 Federal Street
Boston, Massachusetts 02110

BLC Growth Fund (G)
BLC Income Fund (I)
711 High Street
Des Moines, Iowa 50307

Bond Fund of America, Inc. (I)
333 South Hope Street
Los Angeles, California 90071

Bond Portfolio for Endowments (I)
P.O. Box 7650
Two Embarcadero Center
San Francisco, California 94120

Boston Foundation Fund, Inc. (IG)
421 Seventh Avenue
Pittsburgh, Pennsylvania 15219

Boston Mutual Fund (G)
120 Royall Street
Canton, Massachusetts 02021

Bridges Investment Fund (IG)
8401 West Dodge Road
Omaha, Nebraska 68114

Broad Street Investing Corporation (IG)
One Bankers Trust Plaza
New York, New York 10006

Brown Fund, Inc. (G)
155 Bovet Road
San Francisco, California 94402

Bullock Fund Ltd. (IG)
Bullock Tax Free Shares (MB)
One Wall Street
New York, New York 10005

Calvert Tax Free Reserves (M)
1700 Pennsylvania Avenue N.W.
Washington, D.C. 20006

Canadian Fund (G)
One Wall Street
New York, New York 10005

Capamerica Fund (IG)
11 Hanover Square
New York, New York 10005

Capital Preservation Fund (M)
Capital Preservation Fund II (M)
Capital Preservation Treasury Note Trust (M)
755 Page Mill Road
Palo Alto, California 94304
Capital Shares (G)
11 Hanover Square
New York, New York 10005
Cardinal Fund, The (G)
Cardinal Government Securities Trust (M)
155 East Broad Street
Columbus, Ohio 43215
Carnegie Government Securities (M)
429 Euclid Avenue
Cleveland, Ohio 44114
Cash Equivalent Fund (M)
120 South LaSalle Street
Chicago, Illinois 60603
Cash Management Trust of America (M)
P.O. Box 60822, Terminal Annex
Los Angeles, California 90060
Cash Reserve Management (M)
One Battery Park Plaza
New York, New York 10004
Centennial Capital Cash Management (M)
One New York Plaza
New York, New York 10004
Century Shares Trust (G)
111 Devonshire Street
Boston, Massachusetts 02109
CG Fund (G)
CG Income Fund (IG)
CG Money Market Fund (M)
CG Municipal Bond Fund (MB)
Connecticut General Equity Sales Co.
Hartford, Connecticut 06152
Chancellor High Yield Fund (I)
Chancellor High Yield Municipals (MB)
Chancellor New Decade Fund (G)
Chancellor Tax-Exempt Daily Income (M)
100 Gold Street
New York, New York 10038
Charter Fund (G)
Republic National Bank Tower
Dallas, Texas 75201
Chase Frontier Capital Fund of Boston (AG)
Chase Special Fund of Boston, The (AG)
535 Boylston Street
Boston, Massachusetts 02116
Cheapside Dollar Fund (AG)
One State Street
New York, New York 10015
Chemical Fund (G)
61 Broadway
New York, New York 10006
Colonial Fund (IG)
Colonial Growth Shares (G)
Colonial High Yield Securities (I)
Colonial Income Fund (I)

Colonial Option Income Fund (I)
Colonial Tax-Managed Trust (I)
75 Federal Street
Boston, Massachusetts 02110
Columbia Daily Income Company (M)
Columbia Growth Fund (AG)
621 S.W. Morrison Street
Portland, Oregon 97205
Commerce Income Shares (IG)
333 Clay Street, Suite 4300
Houston, Texas 77002
Common Stock Fund of State Bond & Mortgage Company (G)
100–106 North Minnesota Street
New Ulm, Minnesota 56073
Commonwealth Fund Plans A,B&C (IG)
One Winthrop Square
Boston, Massachusetts 02110
Composite Bond & Stock Fund (IG)
Composite Cash Management (M)
Composite Fund (IG)
Composite Income Fund (I)
Composite Tax-Exempt Bond Fund (MB)
402 Spokane & Eastern Building
Sea First Financial Center
Spokane, Washington 99201
Concord Fund (AG)
60 State Street, Room 930
Boston, Massachusetts 02109
Constellation Growth Fund, The (AG)
331 Madison Avenue
New York, New York 10017
Convertible Fund of Japan (I)
One Wall Street
New York, New York 10005
Convertible Yield Securities (IG)
11 Greenway Plaza, Suite 1919
Houston, Texas 77046
Copley Fund (AG)
109 Howl Street
Fall River, Massachusetts 02724
Corporate Leaders Trust B (IG)
580 Sylvan Avenue
Englewood Cliffs, New Jersey 07632
Country Capital Growth Fund (G)
Country Capital Income Fund (I)
Country Capital Tax-Exempt Bond Fund (I)
Country Capital Money Market Fund (M)
1701 Towanda Avenue
Bloomington, Illinois 61701
Current Interest (M)
3 Allen Center
Houston, Texas 77002
Daily Cash Accumulation Fund (M)
3600 South Yosemite Street
Denver, Colorado 80217
Daily Income Fund (M)
230 Park Avenue
New York, New York 10017

Decatur Income Fund (I)
Delaware Cash Reserve (M)
Delaware Fund (IG)
Delchester Bond Fund (I)
Delta Trend Fund (AG)
DMC Tax-Free Income Trust (MB)
7 Penn Center Plaza
Philadelphia, Pennsylvania 19103

de Vegh Mutual Fund, Inc. (G)
120 Broadway
New York, New York 10005

Directors Capital Fund (AG)
30 Broad Street
New York, New York 10004

Diversified Fund of State Bond and Mortgage
  Company (I)
100–106 North Minnesota Street
New Ulm, Minnesota 56073

Dividend Shares (IG)
One Wall Street
New York, New York 10005

Dodge & Cox Balanced Fund (IG)
Dodge & Cox Stock Fund (IG)
Crocker Plaza
One Post Street
San Francisco, California 94104

Dollar Reserves (M)
11 Hanover Square
New York, New York 10005

Drexel Burnham Fund (G)
60 Broad Street
New York, New York 10004

Dreyfus A Bonds Plus (I)
Dreyfus Fund (G)
Dreyfus Leverage Fund (AG)
Dreyfus Liquid Assets Fund (M)
Dreyfus Money Market Government Series (M)
Dreyfus Money Market—MM Series (M)
Dreyfus Number Nine (G)
Dreyfus Special Income Fund (IG)
Dreyfus Tax-Exempt Bond Fund (MB)
Dreyfus Third Century Fund (G)
767 Fifth Avenue
New York, New York 10153

Eagle Growth Shares (G)
110 Wall Street
New York, New York 10005

Eaton & Howard Balanced Fund (IG)
Eaton & Howard Cash Management Fund (M)
Eaton & Howard Growth Fund (G)
Eaton & Howard Income Fund (I)
Eaton & Howard Special Fund (AG)
Eaton & Howard Stock Fund (IG)
24 Federal Street
Boston, Massachusetts 02110

Eberstadt Energy Resources (G)
61 Broadway
New York, New York 10006

Edson Gould Fund (IG)
11 Greenway Plaza
Houston, Texas 77046

Elfun Tax Exempt Income Fund (MB)
112 Prospect Street
Stamford, Connecticut 06904

Energy Fund (G)
522 Fifth Avenue
New York, New York 10036

Equitable Money Market Account (M)
100 West 52nd Street
New York, New York 10019

Evergreen Fund (AG)
Evergreen Total Return Fund (IG)
550 Mamaroneck Avenue
Harrison, New York 10528

Explorer Fund (AG)
1250 Drummers Lane
Valley Forge, Pennsylvania 19482

Fairfield Fund (AG)
605 Third Avenue
New York, New York 10158

Farm Bureau Growth Fund (IG)
5400 University Avenue
West Des Moines, Iowa 50265

Federated High Income Securities (I)
Federated Master Trust (I)
Federated Option Income Fund (I)
Federated Tax-Free Income Fund (MB)
Federated Tax-Free Trust (I)
421 Seventh Avenue
Pittsburgh, Pennsylvania 15219

Fidelity Asset Investment Trust (G)
Fidelity Cash Reserve (M)
Fidelity Contrafund (AG)
Fidelity Corporate Bond Fund (I)
Fidelity Daily Income Trust (I)
Fidelity Destiny Fund (G)
Fidelity Equity Income Fund (IG)
Fidelity Fund (IG)
Fidelity Government Securities Fund (I)
Fidelity High Income Fund (I)
Fidelity High Yield Municipals Bond Fund
  (MB)
Fidelity Magellan Fund (IG)
Fidelity Money Market Trust—Domestic (M)
Fidelity Money Market Trust—U.S. Govern-
  ment (M)
Fidelity Municipal Bond Fund (MB)
Fidelity Puritan Fund (I)
Fidelity Select Portfolios (IG)
Fidelity Tax-Exempt Money Market Trust (M)
Fidelity Thrift Trust (I)
Fidelity Trend Fund (G)
82 Devonshire Street
Boston, Massachusetts 02109

Financial Bond Shares (I)
Financial Daily Income Shares (I)
Financial Dynamics Fund (AG)
Financial Industrial Fund (IG)
Financial Industrial Income Fund (IG)
P.O. Box 2040
Denver, Colorado 80201

Finomic Investments Fund (AG)
First International Plaza
1100 Louisiana
Houston, Texas 77002

First Investors Bond Appreciation Fund (I)
First Investors Cash Management Fund (M)
First Investors Discovery Fund (AG)
First Investors Fund (I)
First Investors Fund for Growth (AG)
First Investors Fund for Income (I)
First Investors Option Fund (I)
First Investors Tax-Exempt Fund (MB)
120 Wall Street
New York, New York 10005

First Variable Rate Fund for Government Income (M)
1700 Pennsylvania Avenue N.W.
Washington, D.C. 20006

Foster, Hickman & Zaenglein T/M Fund (AG)
183 East Main Street
Rochester, New York 14604

Founders Growth Fund (AG)
Founders Income Fund (IG)
Founders Mutual Fund (IG)
Founders Special Fund (AG)
First of Denver Plaza
Denver, Colorado 80202

Foursquare Fund (G)
24 Federal Street
Boston, Massachusetts 02110

44 Wall Street Fund, The (AG)
44 Wall Street Equity Fund (AG)
150 Broadway
New York, New York 10038

Franklin Dynatech Series (AG)
Franklin Growth Series (G)
Franklin Income Series (I)
Franklin Money Fund (M)
Franklin Money Fund II—U.S. Government (M)
Franklin Utilities Series (G)
155 Bovet Road
SanMateo, California 94402

Fund for Government Investors (M)
1735 K Street N.W.
Washington, D.C. 20006

Fund for U.S. Government Securities (I)
421 Seventh Avenue
Pittsburgh, Pennsylvania 15219

Fund of America (AG)
2777 Allen Parkway
Houston, Texas 77019

Fund of the Southwest (G)
P.O. Box 2994
Dallas, Texas 75221

Fundamental Investors Fund (IG)
333 South Hope Street
Los Angeles, California 90071

Gaming Sports & Growth Fund, Inc. (AG)
1700 Market Street
Philadelphia, Pennsylvania 19130

Gateway Option Income Fund (I)
1120 Carew Tower
Cincinnati, Ohio 45202

General Securities Fund (IG)
133 South Seventh Street
Minneapolis, Minnesota 55402

Golconda Investors Ltd. (G)
11 Hanover Square
New York, New York 10005

Goldfund, Inc. (AG)
80 Broad Street
New York, New York 10004

Government Investors Trust (M)
1800 North Kent Street
Arlington, Virginia 22209

GPM Fund (IG)
One Winthrop Square
Boston, Massachusetts 02110

Gradison Cash Reserves (M)
580 Building
Cincinnati, Ohio 45202

Growth Industry Shares (G)
135 South LaSalle Street
Chicago, Illinois 60603

G.T. Pacific Fund (G)
601 Montgomery Street
San Francisco, California 94111

Guardian Mutual Fund (IG)
522 Fifth Avenue
New York, New York 10036

Guardian Park Avenue Fund, The (G)
201 Park Avenue South
New York, New York 10003

Hamilton Growth Fund (AG)
Hamilton Income Fund (I)
Hamilton Series H-DA (IG)
P.O. Box 1500
Denver, Colorado 80201

Hartwell Growth Fund (AG)
Hartwell Leverage Fund (AG)
50 Rockefeller Plaza
New York, New York 10020

Herold Fund (AG)
35 Mason Street
Greenwich, Connecticut 06830

High Income Shares (I)
One Wall Street
New York, New York 10005

High Yield Securities (I)
11 Greenway Plaza
Houston, Texas 77046

Horace Mann Fund (IG)
One Horace Mann Plaza
Springfield, Illinois 62715

IDS Bond Fund (I)
IDS Cash Management Fund (M)
IDS Growth Fund (G)
IDS High Yield Tax-Exempt Fund (MB)
IDS New Dimensions Fund (AG)
IDS Progressive Fund (AG)

IDS Tax-Exempt Bond Fund (MB)
IDS Tax-Free Money Fund (M)
Roanoke Building
Minneapolis, Minnesota 55402
INA Cash Fund (M)
INA Tax Free Reserve Fund (MB)
Springer Building
3411 Silverside Road
Wilmington, Delaware 19810
Income Fund of America (IG)
Two Embarcadero Center
P.O. Box 7650
San Francisco, California 94120
Income Price & Index Fund (I)
One Boston Place
Boston, Massachusetts 02106
Industries Trend Fund (AG)
333 Clay Street
Houston, Texas 77002
Institutional Liquid Assets Government (M)
Institutional Liquid Assets-Prime
  Obligation (M)
8700 Sears Tower
Chicago, Illinois 60606
InterCapital High Yield Securities (I)
InterCapital Liquid Assets (M)
InterCapital Tax-Exempt Securities (MB)
5 World Trade Center
New York, New York 10048
International Investors (IG)
122 E. 42nd Street
New York, New York 10017
Investment Company of America (IG)
333 South Hope Street
Los Angeles, California 90071
Investment Quality Interest Fund (I)
333 Clay Street, Suite 4300
Houston, Texas 77002
Investment Trust of Boston (IG)
77 Franklin Street
Boston, Massachusetts 02110
Investors Mutual Fund (I)
Investors Selective Fund (I)
Investors Stock Fund (IG)
Investors Variable Payment (G)
1000 Roanoke Building
Minneapolis, Minnesota 55402
Investors Research Fund (G)
1900 State Street
Santa Barbara, California 93102
ISI Growth Fund (AG)
ISI Income Fund (I)
ISI Trust Fund (IG)
1608 Webster Street
Oakland, California 94623
Istel Fund (IG)
345 Park Avenue
New York, New York 10022
Ivest Fund (G)
P.O. Box 1100
Valley Forge, Pennsylvania 19482

Ivy Fund (G)
201 Devonshire Street
Boston, Massachusetts 02110
Janus Fund (AG)
789 Sherman Street
Denver, Colorado 80203
John Hancock Balanced Fund (IG)
John Hancock Bond Fund (I)
John Hancock Cash Management Trust (M)
John Hancock Growth Fund (G)
John Hancock Tax-Exempt Income Trust (MB)
Hancock Place
P.O. Box 111
Boston, Massachusetts 02117
Johnston Capital Appreciation Fund (G)
Johnston Cash Management Fund (M)
Johnston Income Fund (I)
One Boston Place
Boston, Massachusetts 02106
JP Growth Fund (G)
JP Income Fund (I)
P.O. Box 21008
Greensboro, North Carolina 27420
Kemper Cash Equivalent Fund (M)
Kemper Fund for Government Guaranteed Se-
  curities (I)
Kemper Growth Fund (G)
Kemper High Yield Fund (I)
Kemper Income & Capital Preservation (I)
Kemper Money Market Fund (M)
Kemper Municipal Bond Fund (MB)
Kemper Option Income Fund (I)
Kemper Summit Fund (AG)
Kemper Total Return (I)
120 South LaSalle Street
Chicago, Illinois 60603
Keystone B-1 (Investment Bond) (I)
Keystone B-2 (Medium Grade Bond) (I)
Keystone B-4 (Discount Bond) (I)
Keystone K-1 (Income Fund) (I)
Keystone K-2 (Growth Fund) (G)
Keystone S-1 (High Grade) (IG)
Keystone S-3 (Growth) (G)
Keystone S-4 (Lower Prices) (AG)
Keystone American Liquid Trust (M)
Keystone International Fund (G)
Keystone Money Market Options Fund (M)
Keystone Tax-Free Fund (MB)
99 High Street
Boston, Massachusetts 02104
Legg Mason Cash Reserve Trust (I)
421 Seventh Avenue
Pittsburgh, Pennsylvania 15219
Lehman Capital Fund (G)
55 Water Street
New York, New York 10041
Lexington GNMA Income Fund (I)
Lexington Growth Fund (AG)
Lexington Money Market Trust (M)
Lexington Research Fund (G)

Lexington Tax-Free Daily Income Fund (I)
580 Sylvan Avenue
Englewood Cliffs, New Jersey 07632

Liberty Fund (I)
522 Fifth Avenue
New York, New York 10036

Life Insurance Investors (G)
700 Harrison Street
Topeka, Kansas 66636

Lindner Fund (G)
Lindner Fund for Income (I)
200 South Bemiston
St. Louis, Missouri 63105

Liquid Capital Income Fund (I)
831 National City Bank Building
Cleveland, Ohio 44114

Loomis-Sayles Mutual Fund (I)
501 Boylston Street
Boston, Massachusetts 02117

Lord Abbett Bond-Debenture Fund (I)
Lord Abbett Cash Reserve Fund (M)
Lord Abbett Developing Growth Fund (AG)
Lord Abbett Income Fund (I)
63 Wall Street
New York, New York 10005

Lowry Fund (G)
419 Boylston Street
Boston, Massachusetts 02116

MagnaCap Fund (G)
Magna Income Trust (IG)
185 Cross Street
Fort Lee, New Jersey 07024

Mairs & Power Growth Fund (G)
Mairs & Power Income Fund (I)
First National Bank Building
St. Paul, Minnesota 55101

Manhattan Fund (G)
522 Fifth Avenue
New York, New York 10036

Massachusetts Capital Development Fund (G)
Massachusetts Cash Management Company (M)
Massachusetts Financial Bond Fund (I)
Massachusetts Financial Development Fund (IG)
Massachusetts Financial High Income Trust (I)
Massachusetts Financial International Trust-Bond Portfolio (I)
Massachusetts Income Development Fund (IG)
Massachusetts Investors Growth Stock Fund (G)
Massachusetts Investors Trust (IG)
200 Berkeley Street
Boston, Massachusetts 02116

Massachusetts Fund (IG)
Master Reserve Trust—Government (M)
Master Reserve Trust—Money Market (M)
99 High Street
Boston, Massachusetts 02104

Mathers Fund (AG)
125 S. Wacker Drive
Chicago, Illinois 60606

Medical Technology Fund, Inc. (G)
1107 Bethlehem Pike
Flourtown, Pennsylvania 19031

Merrill Lynch Basic Value Fund (IG)
Merrill Lynch Capital Fund (IG)
Merrill Lynch Corp. Bond Fund—High Income (I)
Merrill Lynch Corp. Bond Fund—High Quality (I)
Merrill Lynch Corp. Bond Fund—Intermediate (I)
Merrill Lynch Equi—Bond Fund (I)
Merrill Lynch Municipal Bond—High Yield Fund (MB)
Merrill Lynch Municipal Bond—Insured (MB)
Merrill Lynch Municipal Bond—Limited Maturity (MB)
Merrill Lynch Pacific Fund (G)
Merrill Lynch Ready Assets Trust (M)
Merrill Lynch Special Fund (G)
165 Broadway
New York, New York 10080

Merrill Lynch Government Fund (M)
Merrill Lynch Institutional Fund (M)
125 High Street
Boston, Massachusetts 02110

MFS Managed Municipal Bond Trust (MB)
200 Berkeley Street
Boston, Massachusetts 02116

MidAmerica Mutual Fund (G)
4333 Edgewood Road N.E.
Cedar Rapids, Iowa 52499

Midwest Income Trust Short Term Government Fund (M)
508 Dixie Terminal Building
Cincinnati, Ohio 45202

Money Market Management (M)
421 Seventh Avenue
Pittsburgh, Pennsylvania 15219

Money Market/Options Investments (IG)
99 High Street
Boston, Massachusetts 02104

Money Market Trust (M)
421 Seventh Avenue
Pittsburgh, Pennsylvania 15219

Money Shares (M)
One Wall Street
New York, New York 10005

MoneyMart Assets (M)
100 Gold Street
New York, New York 10038

Monthly Income Shares (I)
One Wall Street
New York, New York 10005

MONY Fund (G)
1740 Broadway
New York, New York 10019

Morgan Keegan Daily Cash Trust (M)
One Commerce Square
Memphis, Tennessee 38103

Morgan (W.L.) Growth Fund (G)
P.O. Box 1100
Valley Forge, Pennsylvania 19482

Municipal Fund for Temp. Investments (MB)
Concord Plaza
3411 Silverside Road
Wilmington, Delaware 19810

Mutual Benefit Fund (G)
520 Broad Street
Newark, New Jersey 07101

Mutual Investing Foundation—MIF/Nationwide Bond Fund (I)
Mutual Investing Foundation—MIF/Nationwide Money Market Fund (M)
Mutual Investing Foundation—MIF Fund (I)
Mutual Investing Foundation—MIF Growth (G)
One Nationwide Plaza
Columbus, Ohio 43216

Mutual of Omaha America Fund (I)
Mutual of Omaha Growth Fund (G)
Mutual of Omaha Income Fund (IG)
Mutual of Omaha Money Market Account (I)
Mutual of Omaha Tax-Free Income Fund (MB)
3102 Farnam Street
Omaha, Nebraska 68131

Mutual Shares Corporation (AG)
Mutual Qualified Income (I)
170 Broadway
New York, New York 10038

Naess & Thomas Special Fund (AG)
One State Street
New York, New York 10004

Nation-Wide Securities (I)
One Wall Street
New York, New York 10005

National Aviation & Technology Corp. (G)
50 Broad Street
New York, New York 10004

National Balanced Fund (IG)
National Bond Fund (I)
National Dividend Fund (I)
National Growth Fund (G)
National Income Fund (I)
National Liquid Reserves Fund (M)
National Preferred Fund (I)
National Stock Fund (IG)
National Tax Exempt Bonds (MB)
National Taxfree Money Fund (M)
605 Third Avenue
New York, New York 10016

National Industries Fund (IG)
2130 South Dahlia Street
Denver, Colorado 80222

National Investors Corp. (G)
One Bankers Trust Plaza
New York, New York 10006

NEL Cash Management Trust (M)
NEL Equity Fund (IG)
NEL Growth Fund (G)
NEL Income Fund (I)
NEL Retirement Equity Fund (G)
NEL Tax-Exempt Bond Fund (MB)
501 Boylston Street
Boston, Massachusetts 02117

Neuwirth Fund (AG)
120 Broadway
New York, New York 10005

New Perspective Fund (G)
333 South Hope Street
Los Angeles, California 90071

New York Venture Fund (AG)
231 Washington Avenue
Santa Fe, New Mexico 87501

Newton Growth Fund (G)
Newton Income Fund (I)
733 North Van Buren Street
Milwaukee, Wisconsin 53202

Nicholas Fund (AG)
312 East Wisconsin Avenue
Milwaukee, Wisconsin 53202

North Star Bond Fund (I)
North Star Regional Fund (G)
North Star Stock Fund (IG)
Dain Tower
Minneapolis, Minnesota 55402

Northeast Investors Growth (G)
Northeast Investors Trust (I)
50 Congress Street
Boston, Massachusetts 02109

Nova Fund
303 Wyman Street
Waltham, Massachusetts 02154

NRTA/AARP U.S. Government Money Market
Trust (M)
421 Seventh Avenue
Pittsburgh, Pennsylvania 15219

Nuveen Municipal Bond Fund (MB)
115 South LaSalle Street
Chicago, Illinois 60603

Old Dominion Investors Trust (IG)
P.O. Box 503
Suffolk, Virginia 23434

Omega Fund (AG)
77 Franklin Street
Boston, Massachusetts 02110

One Hundred and One Fund (IG)
One Hundred Fund (G)
899 Logan Street
Denver, Colorado 80203

One William Street Fund (IG)
55 Water Street
New York, New York 10041

Oppenheimer Aim Fund (AG)
Oppenheimer Directors Fund (G)
Oppenheimer Fund (AG)
Oppenheimer Income Fund of Boston (I)
Oppenheimer Money Market Fund (M)
Oppenheimer Option Income Fund (I)
Oppenheimer Special Fund (AG)

Oppenheimer Tax-Free Bond Fund (MB)

Oppenheimer Time Fund (AG)
Two Broadway
New York, New York 10004

Oppenheimer High Yield Fund (I)
3600 South Yosemite Street
Denver, Colorado 80237

Over-the-Counter Securities Fund (G)
Plymouth & Walnut Avenues
Oreland, Pennsylvania 19075

Pace Fund (AG)
2777 Allen Parkway
Houston, Texas 77019

Paine Webber CASHFUND (M)
815 Connecticut Avenue N.W.
Washington, D.C. 20006

Paramount Mutual Fund (G)
1888 Century Park East
Los Angeles, California 90067

Partners Fund, The (AG)
522 Fifth Avenue
New York, New York 10036

Pax World Fund (I)
224 State Street
Portsmouth, New Hampshire 03801

Penn Square Mutual Fund (G)
101 North Fifth Street
P.O. Box 1419
Reading, Pennsylvania 19603

Pennsylvania Mutual Fund (AG)
127 John Street
New York, New York 10038

Philadelphia Fund, Inc. (IG)
110 Wall Street
New York, New York 10005

Phoenix-Chase Balanced Fund (M)
Phoenix-Chase Growth Fund Series (AG)
Phoenix-Chase High Yield Fund Series (I)
Phoenix-Chase Money Market Series (M)
Phoenix Fund (I)
535 Boylston Street
Boston, Massachusetts 02110

Pilgrim Fund (G)
185 Cross Street
Fort Lee, New Jersey 07024

Pilot Fund (AG)
333 Clay Street
Houston, Texas 77002

Pine Street Fund (IG)
120 Broadway
New York, New York 10271

Pioneer Bond Fund (I)
Pioneer Fund (IG)
Pioneer II (IG)
60 State Street
Boston, Massachusetts 02109

Planned Investment Fund (G)
50 Congress Street
Boston, Massachusetts 02109

PLIGROWTH Fund (G)
PLIMONEY Fund (M)
PLITREND Fund (AG)
PLIYIELD Fund (I)
1 Independence Mall
Philadelphia, Pennsylvania 19106

Pro Fund (G)
Pro Income Fund (I)
1i07 Bethlehem Pike
Flourtown, Pennsylvania 19031

Progress Fund (G)
100–106 North Minnesota Street
New Ulm, Minnesota 56073

Provident Fund for Income (I)
2777 Allen Parkway
Houston, Texas 77019

Putnam Convertible Fund (IG)
Putnam Daily Dividend Trust (M)
Putnam (George) Fund of Boston (IG)
Putnam Growth Fund (G)
Putnam High Yield Trust (I)
Putnam Income Fund (I)
Putnam International Equities Fund (AG)
Putnam Investors Fund (G)
Putnam Option Income Fund (I)
Putnam Tax Exempt Income Fund (MB)
Putnam Vista Fund (AG)
Putnam Voyager Fund (AG)
1 Post Office Square
Boston, Massachusetts 02109

Qualified Dividend Portfolio I & II (I)
P.O. Box 1100
Valley Forge, Pennsylvania 19482

Quasar Associates (AG)
140 Broadway
New York, New York 10005

Quest for Value Fund (AG)
One New York Plaza
New York, New York 10004

Rainbow Fund (AG)
60 Broad Street
New York, New York 10004

Research Capital Fund (IG)
Research Equity Fund (AG)
155 Bovet Road
San Mateo, California 94402

Reserve Fund, The (IG)
810 Seventh Avenue
New York, New York 10019

Revere Fund (AG)
209 Lancaster Avenue
Reading, Pennsylvania 19611

SAFECO Equity Fund (IG)
SAFECO Growth Fund (G)
SAFECO Income Fund (I)
SAFECO Special Bond Fund (I)
SAFECO Plaza
Seattle, Washington 98185

St. Paul Capital Fund (IG)
St. Paul Growth Fund (G)

St. Paul Income Fund (I)
St. Paul Money Fund (M)
St. Paul Special Fund (G)
P.O. Box 43284
Minneapolis, Minnesota 55164

Salem Fund (G)
82 Devonshire Street
Boston, Massachusetts 02109

Schuster Fund (AG)
522 Fifth Avenue
New York, New York 10036

Scudder Cash Investment Trust (I)
Scudder Common Stock Fund (G)
Scudder Development Fund (AG)
Scudder Income Fund (I)
Scudder International Fund (G)
Scudder Managed Municipal Bond Fund (MB)
Scudder Special Fund (AG)
Scudder Tax-Free Money Fund (M)
175 Federal Street
Boston, Massachusetts 02110

Security Bond Fund (I)
Security Equity Fund (G)
Security Investment Fund (I)
Security Ultra Fund (AG)
700 Harrison Street
Topeka, Kansas 66636

Selected American Shares (IG)
Selected Money Market Fund (M)
Selected Special Shares (AG)
Selected Tax-Exempt Bond Fund (MB)
111 West Washington Street
Chicago, Illinois 60602

Sentinel Apex Fund (G)
Sentinel Balanced Fund (IG)
Sentinel Bond Fund (I)
Sentinel Common Stock Fund (IG)
Sentinel Growth Fund (G)
One Exchange Place
Jersey City, New Jersey 07302

Sentry Fund (G)
1800 North Point Drive
Stevens Point, Wisconsin 54481

Sequoia Fund (AG)
540 Madison Avenue
New York, New York 10022

Shareholders' Trust of Boston (IG)
535 Boylston Street
Boston, Massachusetts 02116

Shearson Appreciation Fund (G)
Shearson Income Fund (I)
Shearson New Directors Fund (IG)
Two World Trade Center
New York, New York 10048

Shearson Daily Dividend Fund (M)
Shearson Government & Agencies, Inc. (M)
14 Wall Street
New York, New York 10005

Sherman, Dean Fund (AG)
120 Broadway
New York, New York 10005

Short-Term Yield Securities (M)
11 Greenway Plaza
Houston, Texas 77046

Sierra Growth Fund (IG)
1880 Century Park East
Los Angeles, California 90067

Sigma Capital Shares (AG)
Sigma Government Securities Fund (M)
Sigma Income Shares (I)
Sigma Investment Shares (IG)
Sigma Money Market Fund (M)
Sigma Special Fund (G)
Sigma Tax-Free Bond Fund (MB)
Sigma Trust Shares (IG)
Sigma Venture Shares (G)
Greenville Center
3801 Kennett Pike
Wilmington, Delaware 19807

Smith, Barney Equity Fund (G)
Smith, Barney Income and Growth Fund (IG)
1345 Avenue of the Americas
New York, New York 10019

Sogen International Fund (G)
630 Fifth Avenue
New York, New York 10020

Southwestern Investors Fund (IG)
Southwestern Investors Income Fund (IG)
P.O. Box 2994
Dallas, Texas 75201

Sovereign Investors (IG)
1401 Walnut Street
Philadelphia, Pennsylvania 19102

State Farm Balanced Fund (I)
State Farm Growth Fund (G)
State Farm Interim Fund (I)
State Farm Municipal Bond (MB)
One State Farm Plaza
Bloomington, Illinois 61701

State Street Investment Corp. (IG)
225 Franklin Street
Boston, Massachusetts 02110

Steadman American Industry Fund (AG)
Steadman Associated Fund (IG)
Steadman Federal Securities Fund (M)
Steadman Investment Fund (IG)
Steadman Oceanographic, Technology &
    Growth (AG)
1100 17th Street N.W.
Washington, D.C. 20036

Stein, Roe & Farnham Balanced Fund (IG)
Stein, Roe & Farnham Capital Opportunity
    Fund (G)
Stein, Roe & Farnham Stock Fund (G)
SteinRoe Bond Fund (I)
SteinRoe Cash Reserves (M)
SteinRoe Special Fund (AG)
SteinRoe Tax-Exempt Bond Fund (MB)
SteinRoe Universe Fund (AG)
150 South Wacker Drive
Chicago, Illinois 60606

Stralem Fund (G)
One Post Office Square
Boston, Massachusetts 02109

Strategic Investments Fund (G)
10110 Crestover
Dallas, Texas 75220

Stratton Growth Fund (IG)
Axe Wood Building
Blue Bell, Pennsylvania 19422

Sun Growth Fund (IG)
One Sun Life Executive Park
Wellesley Hills, Massachusetts 02181

Surveyor Fund (G)
61 Broadway
New York, New York 10006

T. Rowe Price Growth Stock Fund (G)
T. Rowe Price International Fund (G)
T. Rowe Price New Era Fund (G)
T. Rowe Price New Horizons Fund (AG)
T. Rowe Price New Income Fund (I)
T. Rowe Price Prime Reserve Fund (M)
T. Rowe Price Tax-Free Income Fund (MB)
100 East Pratt Street
Baltimore, Maryland 21202

Tax-Exempt Bond Fund of America (MB)
333 South Hope Street
Los Angeles, California 90071

Tax Managed Fund for Utility Shares (G)
247 Royal Palm Way
Palm Beach, Florida 33480

Technology Fund (IG)
120 South LaSalle Street
Chicago, Illinois 60603

Templeton Growth Fund (G)
155 University Avenue
Toronto, Canada M5H 3B7

Templeton World Fund (G)
41 Beach Drive S.E.
St. Petersburg, Florida 33701

Temporary Investment Fund (M)
3411 Silverside Road
Wilmington, Delaware 19810

Transamerica Capital Fund (G)
Transamerica Cash Reserve (M)
Transamerica Investors Fund (IG)
P.O. Box 2438
Los Angeles, California 90051

Transatlantic Fund (G)
100 Wall Street
New York, New York 10005

Travelers Equities Fund (G)
One Tower Square
Hartford, Connecticut 06115

Triangle Income Fund (I)
421 Seventh Avenue
Pittsburgh, Pennsylvania 15219

Trust for Cash Reverves (M)
421 Seventh Avenue
Pittsburgh, Pennsylvania 15219

Trust for Short Term Federal Securities (Federal Funds) (M)
Trust for Short Term Treasury Securities (Treasury Funds) (M)
3510 Silverside Road
Wilmington, Delaware 19810

Trust for Short-Term U.S. Government Securities (M)

Trust for U.S. Treasury Obligations (M)
421 Seventh Avenue
Pittsburgh, Pennsylvania 15219

Trustee's Commingled Equity Fund (IG)
Drummers Lane
Valley Forge, Pennsylvania 19482

Tudor Fund (AG)
One New York Plaza
New York, New York 10004

Twentieth Century Growth Investors (AG)
Twentieth Century Select Investors (IG)
P.O. Box 200
Kansas City, Missouri 64141

Ultra Investors (AG)
P.O. Box 200
Kansas City, Missouri 64141

Unified Accumulation Fund (IG)
Unified Growth Fund (G)
Unified Income Fund (I)
Unified Mutual Shares (IG)
207 Guaranty Building
Indianapolis, Indiana 46204

Union Capital Fund (AG)
Union Cash Management Fund (M)
Union Income Fund (I)
One Bankers Trust Plaza
New York, New York 10006

United Accumulative Fund (G)
United Bond Fund (IG)
United Cash Management (M)
United Continental Growth Fund (G)
United Continental Income Fund (IG)
United Fiduciary Shares (IG)
United High Income Fund (I)
United Income Fund (I)
United Municipal Bond Fund (MB)
United Science & Energy Fund (G)
United Vanguard Fund (AG)
One Crown Center
P.O. Box 1343
Kansas City, Missouri 64141

United Service Fund (IG)
P.O. Box 2098
Universal City, Texas 78148

USAA Capital Growth Fund (G)
USAA Income Fund (I)
98 Fredericksburg Road
San Antonio, Texas 78288

Valley Forge Fund (G)
P.O. Box 262
Valley Forge, Pennsylvania 19481

Value Line Cash Fund (M)

Value Line Fund (G)
Value Line Income Fund (I)
Value Line Leveraged Growth Investors (AG)
Value Line Special Situations (AG)
711 Third Avenue
New York, New York 10017

Vance, Sanders Common Stock Fund (G)
Vance, Sanders Income Fund (I)
Vance, Sanders Investors Fund (IG)
Vance, Sanders Municipal Bond Fund (MB)
Vance, Sanders Special Fund (AG)
24 Federal Street
Boston, Massachusetts 02110

Vanguard Fixed Income Securities—GNMA (I)
Vanguard Fixed Income Securities—Investment Grade (I)
Vanguard Fixed Income Securities—High Yield (I)
Vanguard Index Trust (IG)
Vanguard Money Market Trust (M)
Vanguard Municipal Bond Funds (MB)
Vanguard Municipal Bond-Money Market (MB)
Vanguard Municipal Bond-Short Term Portfolio (M)
Drummers Lane
Valley Forge, Pennsylvania 19482

Variable Stock Fund (G)
1250 State Street
Springfield, Massachusetts 01133

Venture Income (+)Plus (I)
231 Washington Avenue, Suite 2
Santa Fe, New Mexico 87501

Wade Fund (G)
Suite 2224, 5100 Poplar Avenue
Memphis, Tennessee 38137

Wall Street Fund, The (IG)
One Wall Street
New York, New York 10005

Washington Mutual Investors Fund (IG)
Southern Building
Washington, D.C. 20005

Webster Cash Reserve Fund (M)
10 Hanover Square
New York, New York 10005

Weingarten Equity Fund (AG)
331 Madison Avenue
New York, New York 10017

Wellesley Income Fund (I)
Wellington Fund (IG)
Windsor Fund (G)
Drummers Lane
Valley Forge, Pennsylvania 19482

Wisconsin Income Fund (I)
312 East Wisconsin Avenue
Milwaukee, Wisconsin 53202

W. L. Morgan Fund (G)
Drummers Lane
Valley Forge, Pennsylvania 19482

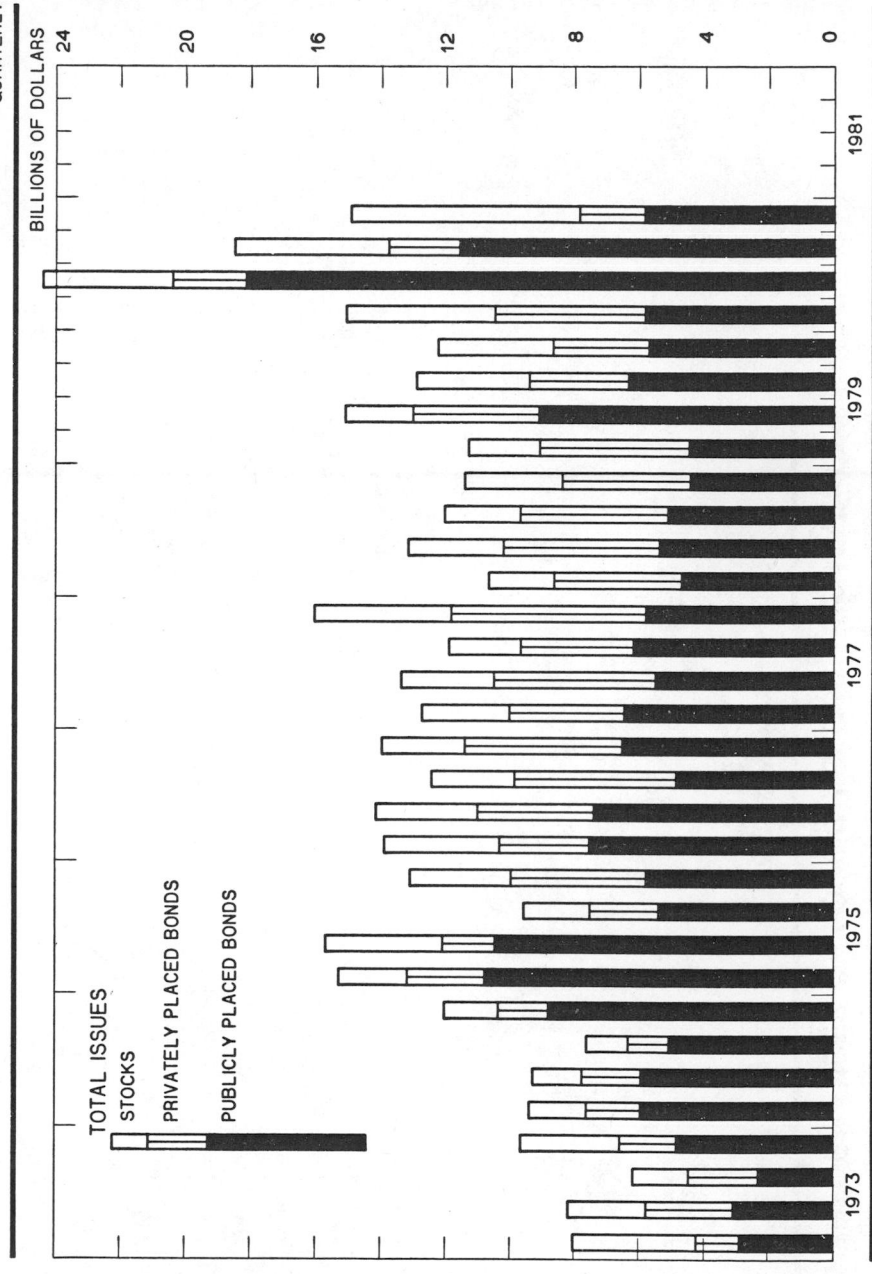

CORPORATE SECURITY ISSUES
GROSS PROCEEDS
QUARTERLY

BILLIONS OF DOLLARS

TOTAL ISSUES
STOCKS
PRIVATELY PLACED BONDS
PUBLICLY PLACED BONDS

Source: *Federal Reserve Chart Book*, Board of Governors of the Federal Reserve System.

PERFORMANCES OF FOREIGN SECURITIES MARKETS

STOCK MARKET INDEXES
Europe

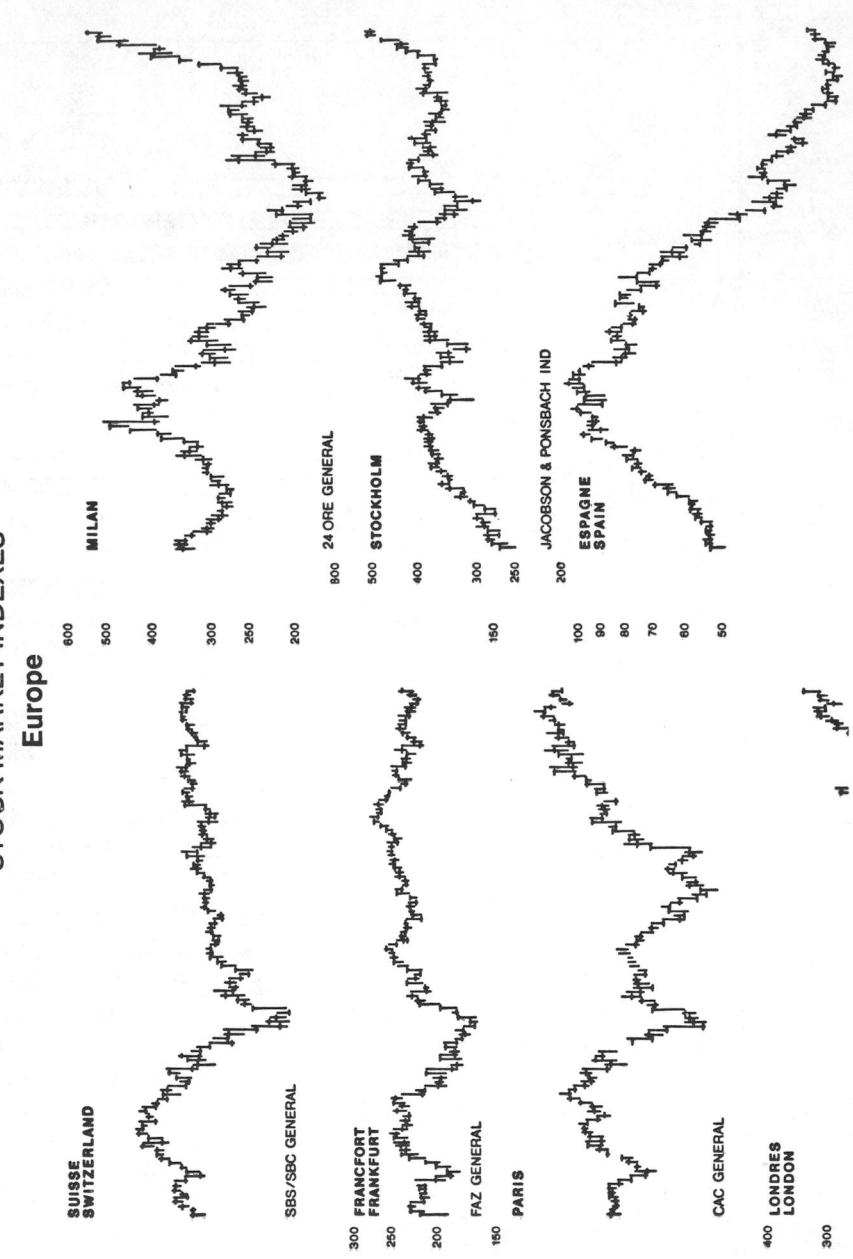

SUISSE
SWITZERLAND

SBS/SBC GENERAL

FRANCFORT
FRANKFURT

FAZ GENERAL

PARIS

CAC GENERAL

LONDRES
LONDON

MILAN

24 ORE GENERAL

STOCKHOLM

JACOBSON & PONSBACH IND

ESPAGNE
SPAIN

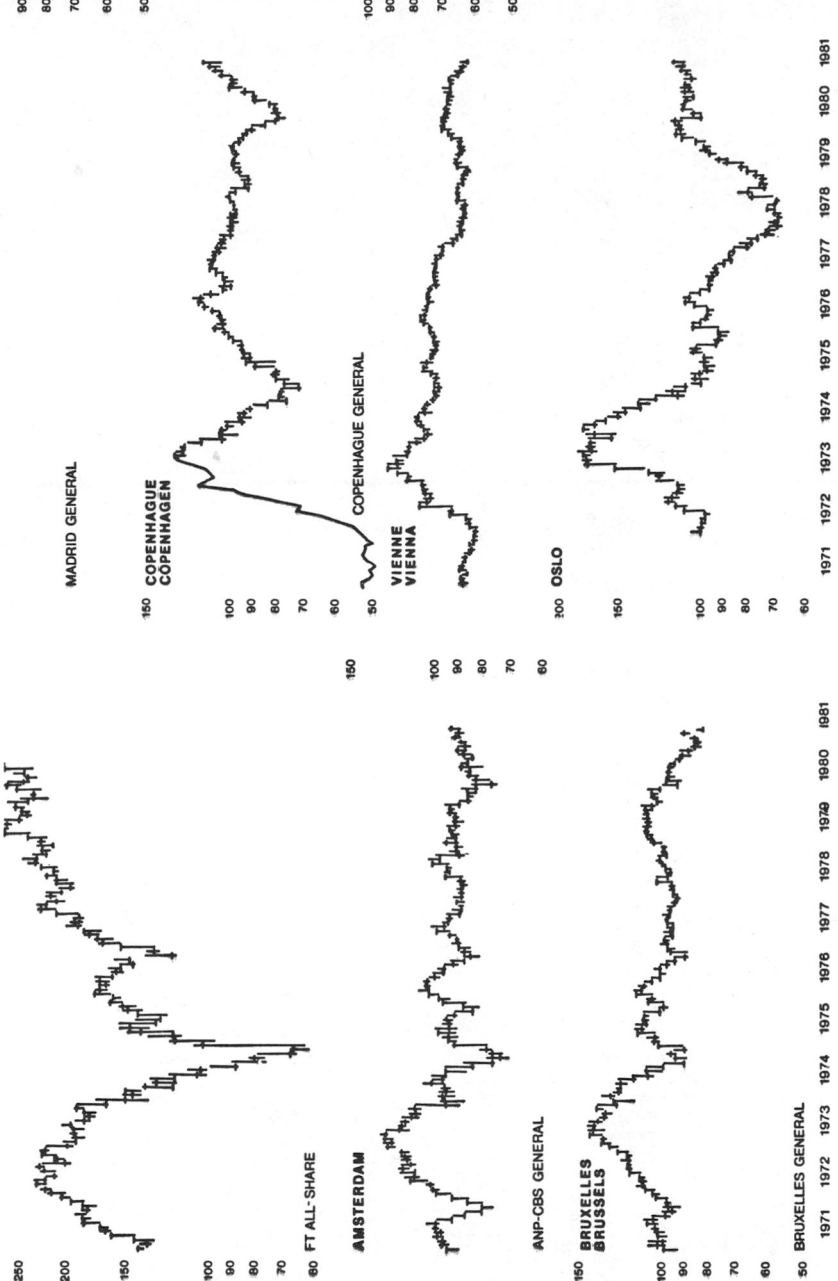

MADRID GENERAL

COPENHAGUE
COPENHAGEN

COPENHAGUE GENERAL

VIENNE
VIENNA

OSLO

FT ALL-SHARE

AMSTERDAM

ANP-CBS GENERAL

BRUXELLES
BRUSSELS

BRUXELLES GENERAL

1971 1972 1973 1974 1975 1976 1977 1978 1979 1980 1981

Source: *International Financial Markets*, Lombard, Odier & Cie; 717 Fifth Avenue, New York, NY 10022.

– Pacific

↙ North America

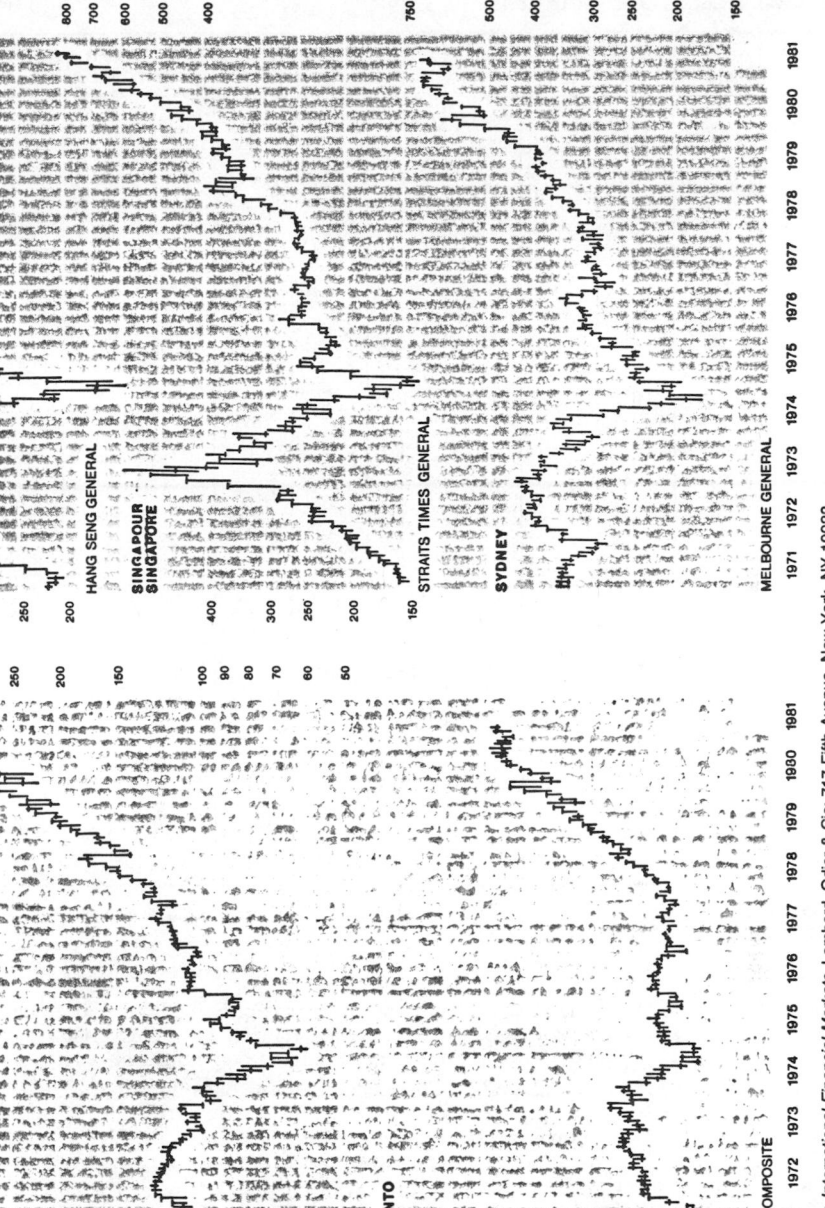

Source: *International Financial Markets*, Lombard, Odier & Cie; 717 Fifth Avenue, New York, NY 10022.

RETURN ON WORLD STOCK MARKETS

	Market Value	Return in each Currency %			Currency Valuation %			Return in U.S. Dollar %		
	Billion Dollar	3 m	1 y	5 y Ⓐ	3 m	1 y	5 y Ⓑ	3 m	1 y	5 y Ⓒ
New York	1 245.0	0.2	33.2	5.8	0.0	0.0	0.0	0.2	33.2	5.8
Tokyo	374.5	7.3	16.7	9.3	4.1	18.1	7.2	2.9	37.8	17.1
London	211.1	11.3	23.7	5.6	6.4	4.0	3.2	4.1	28.6	8.9
Toronto	123.0	2.8	29.8	17.2	0.8	0.9	-3.6	3.7	30.9	13.0
Frankfurt	66.9	0.5	2.4	-3.2	-6.5	-7.2	3.8	6.0	5.0	0.4
Sydney	59.2	-0.8	37.9	18.2	-1.2	7.9	-1.4	1.9	48.9	16.5
Paris	48.5	-1.5	6.2	7.2	-9.0	-9.4	-1.2	-10.4	3.8	5.9
Zurich	45.3	-0.4	7.0	0.6	-7.4	-3.8	5.6	-7.8	3.0	6.3
Hong kong	34.9	-7.1	74.9	24.6	-3.9	-4.1	-1.5	-10.6	67.7	22.7
Milan	35.8	43.1	166.7	25.1	-11.4	-14.3	-4.4	26.7	128.6	19.6
Amsterdam	26.9	9.9	14.6	-7.6	8.2	8.1	2.9	0.9	5.3	4.9
Singapore	30.3	24.6	82.6	26.3	0.4	8.9	3.5	24.1	98.8	30.6
Total	2301.4							0.9	32.3	9.1

Source: *Tokyo Stock Market Quarterly Review* 1981 Vol. 2. A publication of Daiwa Securities Co. Ltd. Available through: Daiwa Securities America, Inc. One Liberty Plaza, New York, NY 10006.

Market Value As of end of March, 1981.

Return in each currency Return derived solely based upon each market's Stock Price Index (dividends are not included) for the periods ending on the last trading date of the latest quarter. Five-years data are shown in the annual compound rate. Stock price indices referred to are; S & P500, Tokyo Stock Price Index, FT industrial, Toronto composite, Commerzbank general index. Sydney Stock Exchange all ordinaries, CAC industrial, Swiss Bank Corporation general index, Hang Seng Bank index, Banca Commerciale Italiana index, ANP-CBS industrial, and Straits Times industrial.

Currency valuation Rate of change of each currency's value in U.S. dollar terms (NY market) for the corresponding periods. Five-years data are shown in the annual compound rate.

Return in U.S. Dollar Return of each market in U.S. $ terms. Five-years data are shown in the annual compound rate.

FOREIGN STOCKS LISTED ON THE NEW YORK STOCK EXCHANGE

Company	Industry (Country)
Alcan Aluminium Limited	Aluminum (Canada)
ASA Limited	Investment company (Africa)
Bell Canada	Telecommunication services (Canada)
Benguet Corporation	Mining (Philippines)
British Petroleum Company Ltd.	Holding company—petroleum (Gt. Britain)
Campbell Red Lakes Mines Ltd.	Mining (Canada)
Canadian Pacific Enterprises Ltd.	Iron; steel; mines (Canada)
Canadian Pacific Limited	Natural resources; transportation (Canada)
Carling O'Keefe Limited	Breweries (Canada)
Dome Mines Limited	Mining (Canada)
Genstar Limited (2 issues)	Building (Canada)
Hiram Walker-Consumers Home Ltd.	Distilled spirits; gas; oil (Canada)
Honda Motor Co., Ltd.	Motorcycles; automobiles (Japan)
Hudson Bay Mining & Smelting Co., Ltd.	Mining (Canada)
Inco Ltd.	Mining (Canada)
KLM Royal Dutch Airlines	Airline (Netherlands)
Kubota, Ltd.	Agricultural machinery; pipe (Japan)
Kyoto Ceramic Co., Ltd.	Ceramic products (Japan)
MacMillan Bloedel Ltd.	Forest products (Canada)
Massey-Ferguson Ltd.	Agricul. mach., diesel eng. (Canada)
Matsushita Electric Industrial Co., Ltd.	Electronic products (Japan)
McIntyre Mines Ltd.	Mining (Canada)
Moore Corporation Ltd.	Business forms (Canada)
Norlin Corporation	Holding company—various (Panama)
Northern Telecom Ltd.	Telecommunication equipment (Canada)
Northgate Exploration Limited	Mining (Canada)
Pioneer Electronic Corporation	High fidelity stereo; audio (Japan)
Plessey Company Ltd.	Electronic equipment, systems (Gt. Britain)
Royal Dutch Petroleum Co.	Petroleum (Netherlands)
Schlumberger, N.V.	Petroleum (Netherlands Antilles)
Seagram Co. Ltd.	Distilleries (Canada)
"Shell" Transport and Trading Co., Ltd.	Petroleum (Gt. Britain)
Sony Corporation	Radios, recorders, televisions (Japan)
Tricentrol Limited	Oil and gas; car dealerships (Gt. Britain)
Unilever Limited	Foods, commodities (Gt. Britain)
Unilever, N.V.	Foods, commodities (Netherlands Antilles)
Westcoast Transmission Co., Ltd.	Natural gas distributor (Canada)

Source: New York Stock Exchange *1981 Fact Book*.

SECURITIES MARKETS: NOTABLE DATES

1792   Original brokers' agreement subscribed to by 24 brokers (May 17).

1817   Constitution and the name "New York Stock Exchange Board" adopted (March 8).

1830   Dullest day in history of exchange—31 shares traded (March 16).

1840s   Outdoor trading in unlisted securities begins at Wall and Hanover Streets, moves to Wall and Broad, then shifts south along Broad Street*

1863   Name changed to "New York Stock Exchange" (NYSE) (January 29).

1867   Stock tickers first introduced (November 15).

1868   Membership made salable (October 23).

1869   Gold speculation resulted in "Black Friday" (September 24).

1871   Continuous markets in stocks established.

1873   NYSE closed September 18–29.

Failure of Jay Cooke & Co. and others (September 18).

Trading hours set at 10 A.M. to 3 P.M.; Saturdays, 10 A.M. to noon (December 1).

1878   First telephones introduced in the exchange (November 13).

1881   Annunciator board installed for paging members (January 29).

1885   Unlisted Securities Department established (March 25).

1886   First million-share day—1,200,000 shares traded (December 15).

1908   E. S. Mendels forms New York Curb Agency in first departure from informal trading.*

1910   Unlisted Securities Department abolished (March 31).

1911   Trading rules established with formation of New York Curb Market Association.*

1914   Exchange closed from July 31 through December 11—World War I.

1915   Stock prices quoted in dollars as against percent of par value (October 13).

1919   Separate ticker system installed for bonds (January 2).

1920   Stock Clearing Corporation established (April 26).

1921   New York Curb Market association moves indoors at 86 Trinity Place; name shortened to New York Curb Market and ticker service initiated (June 21).*

1927   Start of ten-share unit of trading for inactive stocks (January 3).

1929   Stock market crash; 16,410,000 shares traded (October 29).

New York Curb Market modifies its name to New York Curb Exchange.*

1930   Faster ticker—500 characters per minute—installed (September 2).

1931   Exchange building expanded; Telephone Quotation Department formed to send stock quotes to member firm offices.*

1933   New York Stock Exchange closed for bank holiday, March 4–14.

1934   Enactment of Securities Exchange Act of 1934 (June 6).

1938   First salaried president elected—Wm. McC. Martin, Jr. (June 30).

1946   Listed stocks outnumber unlisted stocks for first time since the 1934 act imposed restrictions on unlisted trading.*

1952   Trading hours changed: weekdays, 10 A.M. to 3:30 P.M. Closed Saturdays (September 29).*

1953   Name of New York Curb Exchange changed to American Stock Exchange.*

1958   First member corporation—Woodcock, Hess & Co. (June 4).

Mary C. Roebling becomes first woman governor.*

1962   Committee system of administration replaced by expanded paid staff reporting to president. Specialist system strengthened, surveillance of trading increased, listing and delisting standards introduced, and board restructured to give greater representation to commission and out-of-town brokers.*

1964   New member classification—Registered Trader (August 3).

New ticker—900 characters per minute—put into service (December 1).†

Am-Quote computerized telephone-quotation service was completed as first step in major automation program.*

1965   Fully automated quotation service introduced (March 8).

Electronic Systems Center created (October 15).

First women, Phyllis S. Peterson and Julia Montgomery Walsh, elected to regular membership.*

1966   New NYSE Stock Price Index inaugurated (July 14).

AMEX Price Change Index System in-

---

* Refers to American Exchange (AMEX) (formerly Curb Exchange).

† Applies to both the New York Stock Exchange and the American Exchange. Other entries refer to the New York Stock Exchange.

Sources: New York Stock Exchange *Fact Book* and American Stock Exchange *Data Book*.

troduced; computer complex installed for ticker, surveillance, and compared-clearance operations.*

1967 First woman member admitted— Muriel F. Siebert (December 28).

1968 Ticker speed increased to maximum 900 characters per minute; transmission begun to six European countries. Trading floor modernized; line capacity for communications doubled. Visitors gallery expanded.*

1969 Central Certificate Service fully activated (February 26).

1970 Public ownership of member firms approved (March 26).

Securities Investor Protection Corporation Act signed (December 30).

1971 First negotiated commission rates effective (April 5).

First member organization listed— Merrill Lynch (July 27).

AMEX incorporates and marks 50th anniversary of move indoors; Listed Company Advisory Committee formed, composed of nine chief executives of AMEX-listed companies.*

1972 NYSE reorganization, based on Martin Report, approved (January 20).

Board of Directors, with ten public members, replaced Board of Governors (July 13).

Securities Industry Automation Corporation established with AMEX to consolidate facilities of both exchanges (July 17).*

First salaried chairman took office— James J. Needham (August 28).

Board of Governors reorganized to include ten public and ten industry representatives plus full-time salaried chairman as chief executive officer.*

1973 Depository Trust Company succeeded Central Certificate Service (May 11).

Chicago Board of Options Exchange opened with trading in 16 classes of call options (April 26).

AMEX formally adopts affirmative action employment plan; Market Value Indix System introduced to replace Price Change Index.*

1974 Trading hours extended to 4 P.M. (October 1).

Consolidated tape begun; 15 stocks reported (October 18).

1975 Fixed commission system abolished (April 30).

Full consolidated tape begun (June 16). AMEX trades call options.*

Trading begins in call options and odd lots of U.S. government instruments.*

1976 New data line installed, handling 36,000 characters per minute (January 19).

Specialists began handling odd lots in their stocks (May 24).

Varo, Inc.—first stock traded on both NYSE and AMEX (August 23).

Competition between specialists begun (October 11).

1977 Independent audit committee on listed companies' boards required (January 6).

Competitive Trader category for members approved (January 19).

Foreign broker/dealers permitted to obtain membership (February 3).

Full Automated Bond System in effect (July 27).

1978 First 60 million share day in history (63,493,000 shares) (April 17).

Intermarket Trading System (ITS) began.

Registered Competitive Market-Maker category for members approved (May 2).

First 65 million share day in history (66,370,000 shares (August 3).

Trading in Ginnie Maes inaugurated on the AMEX Commodities Exchange (ACE)* (September 12).

AMEX reached an index high of 176.87 (September 13).

1979 Trading began at pilot post on the exchange floor. First stage in a $12-million upgrading of exchange facilities (January 29).

Board of Directors of NYSE approved plan for the creation of the New York Futures Exchange, a wholly owned subsidiary of NYSE. Futures contracts in seven financial instruments will be traded on the NYSE (March 1).

New York Commodities Exchange and NYSE terminated merger talks (March 15).

81,619,000 shares were traded on the NYSE, making it the heaviest trade day in exchange history (October 10).

1980 American Stock Exchange reached an all-time daily stock volume record of 14,980,680 shares sold (January 15).*

NYSE volume of 67,752,000 shares traded was second largest volume on record to date (January 16).

NYSE Futures Exchange opened (August 7).

Option seat on the American Stock Exchange sold at an all-time high of $160,000 (December 24).*

NYSE index reached an all time high of 81.02 (November 28).

1981 First 90 million share day in the history of the Exchange, 92,881,000 (January 7).

The New York Stock Exchange subsidiary, the New York Futures Exchange, started trading futures in Domestic Bank Certificates of Deposit.

INVESTMENT AND FINANCIAL TERMS*†**

Abandonment value The amount that can be realized by liquidating a project before its economic life has ended.*

Accelerated depreciation Depreciation methods that write off the cost of an asset at a faster rate than the write-off under the straight-line method. The three principal methods of accelerated depreciation are: (1) sum-of-the-years'-digits, (2) double-declining balance, and (3) units-of-production.*

Accruals Continuing recurring short-term liabilities. Examples are accrued wages, accrued taxes, and accrued interest.*

Accrued interest Interest accrued on a bond since the last interest payment was made. The buyer of the bond pays the market price plus accrued interest. Exceptions include bonds that are in default and income bonds. (See: *Flat income bond.*)†

Ad valorem tax A tax based on the value (or assessed value) of property.**

Aging schedule A report showing how long accounts receivable have been outstanding. It gives the percent of receivables not past due and the percent past due by, for example, one month, two months, or other periods.*

Amortization Accounting for expenses or charges as applicable rather than as paid. Includes such practices as depreciation, depletion, write-off of intangibles, prepaid expenses, and deferred charges.†

Amortize To liquidate on an installment basis; an amortized loan is one in which the principal amount of the loan is repaid in installments during the life of the loan.*

Annual report The formal financial statement issued yearly by a corporation. The annual report shows assets, liabilities, earnings—how the company stood at the close of the business year, how it fared profit-wise during the year and other information of interest to shareowners.†

Annuity A series of payments of a fixed amount for a specified number of years.*

Sources: From *Managerial Finance*, 6th ed., by J. Fred Weston and Eugene F. Brigham. Copyright © 1978 by the Dryden Press, a division of Holt, Rinehart & Winston. Copyright © 1962, 1966, 1969, 1972, 1975 by Holt, Rinehart, & Winston. Reprinted by permission of Holt, Rinehart, & Winston.

The *Language of Investing Glossary* published by the New York Stock Exchange, Inc.

Tax-Exempt Securities & the Investor published by the Securities Industry Association.

* Entries from *Managerial Finance*, 6th edition, by J. Fred Weston and Eugene F. Brigham.

† Entries from *The Language of Investing Glossary.*

** Entries from *Tax-Exempt Securities & the Investor.*

Arbitrage The process of selling overvalued and buying undervalued assets so as to bring about an equilibrium where all assets are properly valued. One who engages in arbitrage is called an arbitrager.*

Arrearage Overdue payment; frequently omitted dividend on preferred stock.*

Assessed valuation The valuation placed on property for purposes of taxation.**

Assets Everything a corporation owns or due to it: Cash, investments, money due it, materials and inventories, which are called current assets; buildings and machinery, which are known as fixed assets; and patents and good will, called intangible assets. (See: *Liabilities.*)†

Assignment A relatively inexpensive way of liquidating a failing firm that does not involve going through the courts.*

Ask (See: *Bid and asked.*)†

Auction market The system of trading securities through brokers or agents on an exchange such as the New York Stock Exchange. Buyers compete with other buyers while sellers compete with other sellers for the most advantageous price. Most transactions are executed with public customers on both sides since the specialist buys or sells for his own account primarily to offset imbalances in public supply and demand. (See: *Dealers, Quotation, Specialist.*)†

Averages Various ways of measuring the trend of securities prices, one of the most popular of which is the Dow-Jones average of 30 industrial stocks listed on the New York Stock Exchange.

Formulas—some very elaborate—have been devised to compensate for stock splits and stock dividends and thus give continuity to the average.

In the case of the Dow-Jones industrial average, the prices of the 30 stocks are totaled and then divided by a divisor which is intended to compensate for past stock splits and stock dividends and which is changed from time to time. As a result point changes in the average have only the vaguest relationship to dollar price changes in stocks included in the average. Currently, the divisor is 1.465. (See: *NYSE common stock index, Point, Split.*)†

Balance sheet A condensed financial statement showing the nature and amount of a company's assets, liabilities and capital on a given date. In dollar amounts the balance sheet shows what the company owned, what it owed, and the ownership interest in the company of its stockholders. (See: *Assets, Earnings report.*)†

Balloon payment When a debt is not fully amortized, the final payment is larger than the preceding payments and is called a *balloon* payment.*

Bankruptcy A legal procedure for formally liquidating a business, carried out under the jurisdiction of courts of law.*

Basis book A book of mathematical tables used to convert yields to equivalent dollar prices.**

Basis price The price expressed in yield or percentage of return on the investment.**

Bear market A declining market. (See: *Bull market*.)†

Bearer bond A bond which does not have the owner's name registered on the books of the issuer and which is payable to the holder. (See: *Coupon bond, Registered bond*.)†

Bearer security A security that has no identification as to owner. It is presumed to be owned, therefore, by the bearer or the person who holds it. Bearer securities are freely and easily negotiable since ownership can be quickly transferred from seller to buyer.**

Beta coefficient Measures the extent to which the returns on a given stock move with "the stock market."*

Bid and asked Often referred to as a quotation or quote. The bid is the highest price anyone has declared that he wants to pay for a security at a given time, the asked is the lowest price anyone will take at the same time. (See *Quotation*.)†

Block A large holding or transaction of stock—popularly considered to be 10,000 shares or more.†

Blue chip A company known nationally for the quality and wide acceptance of its products or services, and for its ability to make money and pay dividends.†

Blue-sky laws A popular name for laws various states have enacted to protect the public against securities frauds. The term is believed to have originated when a judge ruled that a particular stock had about the same value as a patch of blue sky.†

Board room A room for registered representatives and customers in a broker's office where opening, high, low, and last prices of leading stocks used to be posted on a board throughout the market day. Today such price displays are normally electronically controlled although most board rooms have replaced the board with the ticker and/or individual quotation machines.†

Bond A long-term debt instrument.*

Bond funds Registered investment companies whose assets are invested in diversified portfolios of bonds.**

Book A notebook the specialist in a stock uses to keep a record of the buy and sell orders at specified prices, in sequence of receipt, which are left with him by other brokers. (See *Specialist*.)†

Book value the accounting value of an asset. The book value of a share of common stock is equal to the net worth (common stock plus retained earnings) of the corporation divided by the number of shares of stock outstanding.*

Break-even analysis An analytical technique for studying the relation between fixed cost, variable cost, and profits. A break-even *chart* graphically depicts the nature of break-even analysis. The break-even *point* represents the volume of sales at which total costs equal total revenues (that is, profits equal zero).*

Broker An agent, who handles the public's orders to buy and sell securities, commodities, or other property. For this service a commission is charged. (See: *Commission broker, dealer*.)†

Brokers' loans Money borrowed by brokers from banks or other brokers for a variety of uses. It may be used by specialists and to help finance inventories of stock they deal in; by brokerage firms to finance the underwriting of new issues of corporate and municipal securities; to help finance a firm's own investments; and to help finance the purchase of securities for customers who prefer to use the broker's credit when they buy securities. (See: *Margin*.)†

Bull market An advancing market. (See: *Bear market*.)†

Business risk The basic risk inherent in a firm's operations. Business risk plus financial risk resulting from the use of debt equals total corporate risk.*

Call (1) An option to buy (or "call") a share of stock at a specified price within a specified period. (2) The process of redeeming a bond or preferred stock issue before its normal maturity.*

Call premium The amount in excess of par value that a company must pay when it calls a security.*

Call price The price that must be paid when a security is called. The call price is equal to the par value plus the call premium.*

Call privilege A provision incorporated into a bond or a share of preferred stock that gives the issuer the right to redeem (call) the security at a specified price.*

Callable A bond issue, all or part of which may be redeemed by the issuing corporation under definite conditions before maturity. The term also applies to preferred shares which may be redeemed by the issuing corporation.†

Capital asset An asset with a life of more than one year that is not bought and sold in the ordinary course of business.*

Capital budgeting The process of planning expenditures on assets whose returns are expected to extend beyond one year.*

Capital gain or capital loss Profit or loss from the sale of a capital asset. A capital gain, under current federal income tax laws, may be either short-term (12 months or less) or long-term (more than 12 months). A short-term capital gain is taxed at the reporting individuals's full income tax rate. A long-term capital gain is subject to a lower tax. The capital gains provisions of the tax law are complicated. You should consult your tax advisor for specific information.†

Capital market line A graphical representation of the relationship between risk and the required rate of return on an efficient portfolio.*

Capital markets Financial transactions involving instruments with maturities greater than one year.*

Capital rationing A situation where a constraint is placed on the total size of the capital investment during a particular period.*

Capital stock All shares representing ownership of a business, including preferred and common. (See: *Common stock, Preferred stock*.)†

Capital structure The permanent long-term financing of the firm represented by long-term debt, preferred stock, and net worth (net worth consists of capital, capital surplus, and retained earnings). Capital structure is distinguished from *financial structure,* which includes short-term debt plus all reserve accounts.*

Capitalization Total amount of the various securities issued by a corporation. Capitalization may include bonds, debentures, preferred and common stock, and surplus. Bonds and debentures are usually carried on the books of the issuing company in terms of their par or face value. Preferred and common shares may be carried in terms of par or stated value. Stated value may be an arbitrary figure decided upon by the directors or may represent the amount received by the company from the sale of the securities at the time of issuance. (See: *Par*.)†

Capitalization rate A discount rate used to find the present value of a series of future cash receipts; sometimes called *discount rate.*

Carry-back; carry forward For income tax purposes, losses than can be carried backward or forward to reduce federal income taxes.*

Cash budget A schedule showing cash flows (receipts, disbursements, and net cash) for a firm over a specified period.*

Cash cycle The length of time between the purchase of raw materials and the collection of accounts receivable generated in the sale of the final product.*

Cash flow Reported net income of a corporation *plus* amounts charged off for depreciation, depletion, amortization, extraordinary charges to reserves, which are bookkeeping deductions and not paid out in actual dollars and cents. (See: *Amortization, Depletion, Depreciation*.)†

Cash sale A transaction on the floor of the Stock Exchange which calls for delivery of the securities the same day. In "regular way" trades, the seller is to deliver on the fifth business day except for bonds, which is the next day. (See: *Regular way delivery*.)†

Certainty equivalents The amount of cash (or rate of return) that someone would require *with certainty* to make him indifferent between this certain sum (or *rate of return*) and a particular uncertain, risky sum (or rate of return).*

Certificate The actual piece of paper which is evidence of ownership of stock in a corporation. Watermarked paper is finely engraved with delicate etchings to discourage forgery. Loss of a certificate may at the least cause a great deal of inconvenience—at the worst, financial loss.†

Characteristic line A linear least-squares regression line that shows the relationship between an individual security's return and returns on "the market." The slope of the characteristic line is the beta coefficient.*

Chattel mortgage A mortgage on personal property (not real estate). A mortgage on equipment would be a chattel mortgage.*

Closed-end investment company (See: *Investment company*.)

Coefficient of variation Standard deviation divided by the mean: CV.*

Collateral Assets that are used to secure a loan.*

Collateral trust bond A bond secured by collateral deposited with a trustee. The collateral is often the stocks or bonds of companies controlled by the issuing company but may be other securities.†

Commercial paper Unsecured, short-term promissory notes of large firms, usually issued in denominations of $1 million or more. The rate of interest on commercial paper is typically somewhat below the prime rate of interest.*

Commission The broker's basic fee for purchasing or selling securities or property as an agent.†

Commission broker An agent who executes the public's orders for the purchase or sale of securities or commodities.†

Commitment fee The fee paid to a lender for a formal line of credit.*

Common stock Securities which represent an ownership interest in a corporation. If the company has also issued preferred stock, both common and preferred have ownership rights. The preferred normally is limited to a fixed dividend but has prior claim on dividends and, in the event of liquidation, assets. Claims of both common and preferred stockholders are junior to claims of bondholders or other creditors of the company. Common stockholders assume the greater risk, but generally exercise the greater control and may gain the greater reward in the form of dividends and capital appreciation. The terms common stock and capital stock are often used interchangeably when the company has no preferred stock.†

Compensating balance A required minimum checking account balance that a firm must maintain with a commercial bank. The required balance is generally equal to 15 to 20 percent of the amount of loans outstanding. Compensating balances can raise the effective rate of interest on bank loans.*

Competitive trader A member of the Exchange who trades in stocks on the Floor for an account in which he has an interest. Also known as a Registered Trader.†

Composite cost of capital A weighted average of the component costs of debt, preferred stock, and common equity. Also called the *weighted-average cost of capital*, but it reflects the cost of each additional dollar raised, not the average cost of all capital the firm has raised throughout its history.*

Composition An informal method of reorganization that voluntarily reduces creditors' claims on the debtor firm.*

Compound interest An interest rate that is applicable when interest in succeeding periods is earned not only on the initial principal but also on the accumulated interest of prior periods. Compound interest is contrasted to *simple interest*, in which returns are not earned on interest received.*

Compounding The arithmetic process of determining the final value of a payment or series of payments when compound interest is applied.*

Conditional sales contract A method of financing new equipment by paying it off in installments over a one-to-five-year period. The seller retains title to the equipment until payment has been completed.*

Conglomerate A corporation that has diversified its operations, usually by acquiring enterprises in widely varied industries.†

Consolidated balance sheet A balance sheet showing the financial condition of a corporation and its subsidiaries. (See: *Balance sheet*.)†

Consolidated tape Under the Consolidated Tape Plan, the NYSE and AMEX ticker systems became the "Consolidated Tape," Network A and Network B respectively, on June 16, 1975. Network A reports transactions in NYSE listed securities that take place on the NYSE or any of the participating regional stock exchanges and other markets. Each transaction is identified according to its originating market. Similarly, transactions in AMEX-listed securities, and certain other securities listed on regional stock exchanges, are reported and identified on Network B.†

Consolidated tax return An income tax return that combines the income statement of several affiliated firms.*

Continuous compounding (discounting) As op-posed to discrete compounding, interest is added continuously rather than at discrete points in time.*

Conversion price The effective price paid for common stock when the stock is obtained by converting either convertible preferred stocks or convertible bonds. For example, if a $1,000 bond is convertible into 20 shares of stock, the conversion price is $50 ($1,000/20).*

Conversion ratio or conversion rate The number of shares of common stock that may be obtained by converting a convertible bond or share of convertible preferred stock.*

Convertibles Securities (generally bonds or preferred stocks) that are exchangeable at the option of the holder for common stock of the issuing firm.*

Correlation coefficient Measures the degree of relationship between two variables.*

Correspondent A securities firm, bank, or other financial organization which regularly performs services for another in a place or market to which the other does not have direct access. Securities firms may have correspondents in foreign countries or on exchanges of which they are not members. Correspondents are frequently linked by private wires. Member organizations of the N.Y.S.E. with offices in New York City may also act as correspondents for out-of-town member organizations which do not maintain New York City offices.†

Cost of capital The discount rate that should be used in the capital budgeting process.*

Coupon bond Bond with interest coupons attached. The coupons are clipped as they come due and are presented by the holder for payment of interest. (See: *Bearer bond, Registered bond*.)†

Coupon rate The stated rate of interest on a bond.*

Covariance The correlation between two variables multiplied by the standard deviation of each variable:

$$\text{Cov} = r_{xy}\sigma_x\sigma_y.*$$

Covenant Detailed clauses contained in loan agreements. Covenants are designed to protect the lender and include such items as limits on total indebtedness, restrictions on dividends, minimum current ratio, and similar provisions.*

Coverage A term usually connected with revenue bonds. It is a ratio of net revenues pledged to principal and interest payments to debt service requirements. It is one of the factors used in evaluating the quality of an issue.**

Covering Buying a security previously sold short. (See: *Short sale, Short covering*.)†

Cumulative dividends A protective feature on preferred stock that requires all past preferred dividends to be paid before any common dividends are paid.*

Cumulative preferred A stock having a provision that if one or more dividends are omitted, the omitted dividends must be paid before dividends may be paid on the company's common stock.†

Cumulative voting A method of voting for corporate directors which enables the shareholder to multiply the number of his shares by the number of directorships being voted on and cast the total for one director or a selected group of directors. A 10-share holder normally casts 10 votes for each of, say 12 nominees to the board of directors. He thus has 120 votes. Under the cumulative voting principle he may do that or he may cast 120 (10 × 12) votes for only one nominee, 60 for two, 40 for three, or any other distribution he chooses. Cumulative voting is required under the corporate laws of some states, is permitted in most others.†

Curb exchange Former name of the American Stock Exchange, second largest exchange in the country. The term comes from the market's origin on a street in downtown New York.†

Current assets Those assets of a company which are reasonably expected to be realized in cash, or sold, or consumed during the normal operating cycle of the business. These include cash, U.S. government bonds, receivables and money due usually within one year, and inventories.†

Current liabilities Money owed and payable by a company, usually within one year.†

Current return (See: *Yield.*)

Current yield A relation stated as a percent of the annual interest to the actual market price of the bond.**

Cut-off point In the capital budgeting process, the minimum rate of return on acceptable investment opportunities.*

Day order An order to buy or sell which, if not executed expires at the end of the trading day on which it was entered.†

Dealer An individual or firm in the securities business acting as a principal rather than as an agent. Typically, a dealer buys for his own account and sells to a customer from his own inventory. The dealer's profit or loss is the difference between the price he pays and the price he receives for the same security. The dealer's confirmation must disclose to his customer that he has acted as principal. The same individual or firm may function, at different times, either as broker or dealer. (See: *NASD, Specialist.*)†

Debenture A long-term debt instrument that is not secured by a mortgage on specific property.*

Debit balance In a customer's margin account that portion of purchase price of stock, bonds, or commodities covered by credit extended by the broker to the margin customer.†

Debt limit The statutory or constitutional maximum debt that a municipality can legally incur.**

Debt ratio Total debt divided by total assets.*

Debt service Refers to the payments required for interest and retirement of the principal amount of a debt.**

Decision tree A device for setting forth graphically the pattern of relationship between decisions and chance events.*

Default The failure to fulfill a contract. Generally, default refers to the failure to pay interest or principal on debt obligations.*

Degree of leverage The percentage increase in profits resulting from a given percentage increase in sales. The degree of leverage may be calculated for financial leverage, operating leverage, or both combined.*

Denomination The face amount or par value of a security which the issuer promises to pay on the maturity date. Most municipal bonds are issued with a minimum denomination of $5,000, although a few older issues are available in $1,000 denominations.**

Depletion accounting Natural resources, such as metals, oil and gas, and timber, which conceivably can be reduced to zero over the years, present a special problem in capital management. Depletion is an accounting practice consisting of charges against earnings based upon the amount of the asset taken out of the total reserves in the period for which accounting is made. A bookkeeping entry, it does not represent any cash outlay nor are any funds earmarked for the purpose.†

Depository trust company (DTC) A central securities certificate depository through which members effect security deliveries between each other via computerized bookkeeping entries thereby reducing the physical movement of stock certificates.†

Depreciation Normally, charges against earnings to write off the cost, less salvage value, of an asset over its estimated useful life. It is a bookkeeping entry and does not represent any cash outlay nor are any funds earmarked for the purpose.†

Devaluation The process of reducing the value of a country's currency stated in terms of other currencies; for example, the British pound might be devalued from $2.30 for one pound to $2.00 for one pound.*

Director Person elected by shareholders to establish company policies. The directors appoint the president, vice presidents, and all other operating officers. Directors decide, among other matters, if and when dividends shall be paid. (See: *Management, Proxy.*)†

Discount The amount by which a preferred stock or bond may sell below its par value. Also used as a verb to mean "takes into account" as the price of the stock has discounted the expected dividend cut. (See: *Premium*.)†

Discount rate The interest rate used in the discounting process; sometimes called *capitalization rate*.*

Discounted cash flow techniques Methods of ranking investment proposals. Included are (1) internal rate of return method, (2) net present value method, and (3) profitability index or benefit/cost ratio.*

Discounting The process of finding the present value of a series of future cash flows. Discounting is the reverse of compounding.*

Discounting of accounts receivable Short-term financing where accounts receivable are used to secure the loan. The lender does not *buy* the accounts receivable but simply uses them as collateral for the loan. Also called *assigning accounts receivable*.*

Discretionary account An account in which the customer gives the broker or someone else discretion, which may be complete or within specific limits, either to the purchases, or sale of securities or commodities including selection, timing, amount, and price to be paid or received.†

Diversification Spreading investments among different companies in different fields. Another type of diversification is also offered by the securities of many individual companies because of the wide range of their activities. (See: *Investment trust*.)†

Dividend The payment designed by the board of directors to be distributed pro rata among the shares outstanding. On preferred shares, it is generally a fixed amount. On common shares, the dividend varies with the fortunes of the company and the amount of cash on hand, and may be omitted if business is poor or the directors determine to withhold earnings to invest in plant and equipment. Sometimes a company will pay a dividend out of past earnings even if it is not currently operating at a profit.†

Dividend yield The ratio of the current dividend to the current price of a share of stock.*

Dollar cost averaging A system of buying securities at regular intervals with a fixed dollar amount. Under this system the investor buys by the dollars' worth rather than by the number of shares. If each investment is of the same number of dollars, payments buy more when the price is low and fewer when it rises. Thus temporary downswings in price benefit the investor if he continues periodic purchases in both good times and bad and the price at which the shares are sold is more than their average cost. (See: *Formula investing*.)†

Dollar bond A bond that is quoted and traded in dollars rather than in terms of yield.**

Double-barrelled bond A bond secured by the pledge of two or more sources of repayment, e.g., secured by taxes as well as revenues.**

Double exemption Refers to securities that are exempt from state as well as Federal income taxes.**

Double taxation Short for *double taxation of dividends*. The federal government taxes corporate profits once as corporate income; any part of the remaining profits distributed as dividends to stockholders may be taxed again as income to the recipient stockholder.†

Dow theory A theory of market analysis based upon the performance of the Dow-Jones industrial and transportation stock price averages. The theory says that the market is in a basic upward trend if one of these averages advances above a previous important high, accompanied or followed by a similar advance in the other. When the averages both dip below previous important lows, this is regarded as confirmation of a basic downward trend. The theory does not attempt to predict how long either trend will continue, although it is widely misinterpreted as a method of forecasting future action.†

Down tick (See: *Up tick*.)

Du Pont system A system of analysis designed to show the relationship between return on investment, asset turnover, and the profit margin.*

Earnings report A statement—also called an *income statement*—issued by a company showing its earnings or losses over a given period. The earnings report lists the income earned, expenses, and the net result. (See: *Balance sheet*.)†

EBIT Acronym for *earnings before interest and taxes*.*

Economical ordering quantity (EOQ) The optimum (least cost) quantity of merchandise which should be ordered.*

EPS Acronym for *earnings per share*.*

Equipment trust certificate A type of security, generally issued by a railroad, to pay for new equipment. Title to the equipment, such as a locomotive, is held by a trustee until the notes are paid off. An equipment trust certificate is usually secured by a first claim on the equipment.†

Equity The net worth of a business, consisting of capital stock, capital (or paid-in) surplus, earned surplus (or retained earnings), and occasionally, certain net worth reserves. *Common equity* is that part of the total net worth belonging to the common stockholders. *Total equity* would include preferred stockholders. The terms *common stock, net worth,* and *common equity* are frequently used interchangeably.†

Exchange acquisition A method of filling an order to buy a large block of stock on the floor of the exchange. Under certain circumstances, a member-broker can facilitate the purchase of a block by soliciting orders to sell. All orders to sell the security are lumped together and crossed with the buy order in the regular action market. The price to the buyer may be on a net basis or on a commission basis.†

Exchange distribution A method of selling large blocks of stock on the floor of the exchange. Under certain circumstances, a member-broker can facilitate the sale of a block of stock by soliciting and getting other member-brokers to solicit orders to buy. Individual buy orders are lumped together and crossed with the sell order in the regular auction market. A special commission is usually paid by the seller; ordinarily the buyer pays no commission.†

Exchange rate The rate at which one currency can be exchanged for another; for example, $2.30 can be exchanged for one British pound.*

Excise tax A tax on the manufacture, sale, or consumption of specified commodities.*

Exdividend A synonym for "without dividend." The buyer of a stock selling exdividend does not receive the recently declared dividend. Every dividend is payable on a fixed date to all shareholders recorded on the books of the company as of a previous date of record. For example, a dividend may be declared as payable to holders of record on the books of the company on a given Friday. Since five business days are allowed for delivery of stock in a "regular way" transaction on the New York Stock Exchange, the exchange would declare the stock "exdividend" as of the opening of the market on the preceding Monday. That means anyone who bought it on and after Monday would not be entitled to that dividend. When stocks go exdividend, the stock tables include the symbol "x" following the name. (See: *Cash sale, Net change, Transfer.*)†

Ex-dividend date The date on which the right to the current dividend no longer accompanies a stock. (for listed stock, the ex-dividend date is four working days prior to the date of record.)*

Exercise price The price that must be paid for a share of common stock when it is bought by exercising a warrant.*

Expected return The rate of return a firm expects to realize from an investment. The expected return is the mean value of the probability distribution of possible returns.*

Ex-rights The date on which stock purchase rights are no longer transferred to the purchaser of the stock.*

Extension An informal method of reorganization in which the creditors voluntarily postpone the date of required payment on past-due obligations.*

External funds Funds acquired through borrowing or by selling new common or preferred stock.

Extra The short form of *extra dividend.* A dividend in the form of stock or cash in addition to the regular or usual dividend the company has been paying.†

Face value The value of a bond that appears on the face of the bond, unless the value is otherwise specified by the issuing company. Face value is ordinarily the amount the issuing company promises to pay at maturity. Face value is not an indication of market value. Sometimes referred to as par value. (See: *Par.*)†

Factoring A method of financing accounts receivable under which a firm sells its accounts receivable (generally without recourse) to a financial institution (the *factor*).*

Field warehousing A method of financing inventories in which a "warehouse" is established at the place of business of the borrowing firm.*

Financial accounting standards board (FASB) A private (nongovernment) agency which functions as an accounting standards-setting body.*

Financial intermediation Financial transactions which bring savings surplus units together with savings deficit units so that savings can be redistributed into their most productive uses.*

Financial lease A lease that does not provide for maintenance services, is not cancellable, and is fully amortized over the life of the lease.*

Financial leverage The ratio of total debt to total assets. There are other measures of financial leverage, especially ones that relate cash inflows to required cash outflows.*

Financial markets Transactions in which the creation and transfer of financial assets and financial liabilities take place.*

Financial risk That portion of total corporate risk, over and above basic business risk, that results from using debt.*

Financial structure The entire right side of the balance sheet—the way in which a firm is financed.*

Fiscal year A corporation's accounting year. Due to the nature of their particular business, some companies do not use the calendar year for their bookkeeping. A typical example is the department store which finds December 31 too early a date to close its books after the Christmas rush. For that reason many stores wind up their accounting year January 31. Their fiscal year, therefore, runs from February 1 of one year through January 31 of the next. The fiscal year of other companies may run from July 1 through the following June 30. Most companies, though, operate on a calendar year basis.†

Fisher effect The increase in the nominal interest rates over real (purchasing power adjusted) interest rates reflecting anticipated inflation.*

Fixed charges Costs that do not vary with the level of output, especially fixed financial costs such as interest, lease payments, and sinking fund payments.*

Flat income bond This term means that the price at which a bond is traded includes consideration for all unpaid accruals of interest. Bonds which are in default of interest or principal are traded flat. Income bonds, which pay interest only to the extent earned are usually traded flat. All other bonds are usually dealt in "and interest," which means that the buyer pays to the seller the market price plus interest accrued since the last payment date.†

Float The amount of funds tied up in checks that have been written but are still in process and have not yet been collected.*

Floating exchange rates Exchange rates may be fixed by government policy *(pegged)* or allowed to *float* up or down in accordance with supply and demand. When market forces are allowed to function, exchange rates are said to be floating.*

Floor The huge trading area—about two-thirds the size of a football field—where stocks and bonds are bought and sold on the New York Stock Exchange.†

Floor broker A member of the Stock Exchange who executes orders on the floor of the exchange to buy or sell any listed securities. (See: *Commission broker, Two-dollar broker.*)†

Flotation cost The cost of issuing new stocks or bonds.*

Formula investing An investment technique. One formula calls for the shifting of funds from common shares to preferred shares or bonds as the market, on average, rises above a certain predetermined point—and the return of funds to common share investments as the market average declines. (See: *Dollar cost averaging.*)†

Free and open market A market in which supply and demand are freely expressed in terms of price. Contrasts with a controlled market in which supply, demand, and price may all be regulated.†

Fundamental research Analysis of industries and companies based on factors such as sales, assets, earnings, products or services, markets, and management. As applied to the economy, fundamental research includes consideration of gross national product, interest rates, unemployment, inventories, savings, and so on. (See: *Technical research.*)†

Funded debt Usually long-term, interest-bearing bonds or debentures of a company. Could include long-term bank loans. Does *not* include short-term loans, preferred, or common stock.†

Funding The process of replacing short-term debt with long-term securities (stocks or bonds).*

General mortgage bond A bond which is secured by a blanket mortgage on the company's property, but which may be outranked by one or more other mortgages.†

General obligation bond A bond secured by the pledge of the issuer's full faith, credit and taxing power.**

General purchasing power reporting A proposal by the FASB that the current values of nonmonetary items in financial statements be adjusted by a general price index.*

Gilt-edged High-grade bond issued by a company which has demonstrated its ability to earn a comfortable profit over a period of years and pay its bondholders their interest without interruption.†

Give up A term with many different meanings. For one, a member of the exchange on the floor may act for a second member by executing an order for him with a third member. The first member tells the third member that he is acting on behalf of the second member and "gives up" the second member's name rather than his own. For another, if you have an account with Doe & Company but you're in a town where Doe has no office, you go to another member firm, tell them you have an account with Doe & Company and would like to buy some stock. After verifying your account with Doe & Company, the firm may execute your order and tell the broker who sells the stock that the firm is acting on behalf of Doe & Company. They give up the name of Doe & Company to the selling broker. Or the firm may simply wire your order to Doe & Company who will execute it for you.†

Good delivery Certain basic qualifications must be met before a security sold on the exchange may be delivered. The security must be in proper form to comply with the contract of sale and to transfer title to the purchaser.†

Good 'til cancelled order (GTC) or open order An order to buy or sell which remains in effect until it is either executed or cancelled.†

Goodwill Intangible assets of a firm established by the excess of the price paid for the going concern over its book value.*

Government bonds Obligations of the U.S. government, regarded as the highest grade issues in existence.†

Growth stock Stock of a company with a record of growth in earnings at a relatively rapid rate.†

Guaranteed bond A bond which has interest or principal, or both, guaranteed by a company other than the issuer. Usually found in the railroad industry when large roads, leasing sections of trackage owned by small railroads, may guarantee the bonds of the smaller road.†

Guaranteed stock Usually preferred stock on which dividends are guaranteed by another company; under much the same circumstances as a bond is guaranteed.†

Hedge (See: *Arbitrage, Puts & Calls, Short sale.*)†

Holding company A corporation which owns the securities of another, in most cases with voting control.†

Hurdle rate In capital budgeting, the minimum acceptable rate of return on a project. If the expected rate of return is below the hurdle rate, the project is not accepted. The hurdle rate should be the marginal cost of capital.*

Hypothecation The pledging of securities as collateral—for example, to secure the debit balance in a margin account.†

Improper accumulation Earnings retained by a business for the purpose of enabling stockholders to avoid personal income taxes.*

Inactive stock An issue traded on an exchange or in the over-the-counter market in which there is a relatively low volume of transactions. Volume may be no more than a few hundred shares a week or even less. On the New York Stock Exchange many inactive stocks are traded in 10-share units rather than the customary 100. (See: *Round lot.*)†

In-and-out Purchase and sale of the same security within a short period—a day, a week, even a month. An in-and-out trader is generally more interested in day-to-day price fluctuations than dividends or long-term growth.†

Income bond Generally income bonds promise to repay principal but to pay interest only when earned. In some cases unpaid interest on an income bond may accumulate as a claim against the corporation when the bond becomes due. An income bond may also be issued in lieu of preferred stock.†

Incremental cash flow Net cash flow attributable to an investment project.*

Incremental cost of capital The average cost of the increment of capital raised during a given year.*

Indenture A written agreement under which bonds and debentures are issued, setting forth maturity date, interest rate, and other terms.†

Independent broker Members on the floor of the NYSE who execute orders for other brokers having more business at that time than they can handle themselves, or for firms who do not have their exchange member on the floor. Formerly known as *two-dollar brokers* from the time when these independent brokers received $2 per hundred shares for executing such or-

ders. Their fees are paid by the commission brokers. (See: *Commission broker.*)†

Index A statistical yardstick expressed in terms of percentages of a base year or years. For instance, the Federal Reserve Board's index of industrial production is based on 1967 as 100. An index is not an average. (See: *Averages, NYSE common stock index.*)†

Industrial revenue bond A security backed by private enterprises that have been financed by a municipal issue.**

Insolvency The inability to meet maturing debt obligations.*

Institutional Investor An organization whose primary purpose is to invest its own assets or those held in trust by it for others. Includes pension funds, investment companies, insurance companies, universities, and banks.†

Interest Payments a borrower pays a lender for the use of his money. A corporation pays interest on its bonds to its bondholders. (See: *Bond, dividend.*)†

Interest factor (IF) Numbers found in compound interest and annuity tables.*

Internal financing Funds made available for capital budgeting and working-capital expansion through the normal operations of the firm; internal financing is approximately equal to retained earnings plus depreciation.*

Internal rate of return (IRR) The rate of return on an asset investment. The internal rate of return is calculated by finding the discount rate that equates the present value of future cash flows to the cost of the investment.*

Intrinsic value That value which, in the mind of the analyst, is justified by the facts. It is often used to distinguish between the *true value* of an asset (the intrinsic value) and the asset's current market price.*

Investment The use of money for the purpose of making more money, to gain income or increase capital, or both. Safety of principal is an important consideration. (See: *Speculation.*)†

Investment banker Also known as an *underwriter.* He is the middleman between the corporation issuing new securities and the public. The usual practice is for one or more investment bankers to buy outright from a corporation a new issue of stocks or bonds. The group forms a syndicate to sell the securities to individuals and institutions. Investment bankers also distribute very large blocks of stocks or bonds—perhaps held by an estate. Thereafter the market in the security may be over-the-counter, on a regional stock exchange, the American Exchange, or the New York Stock Exchange. (See: *Over-the-counter, primary distribution, syndicate.*)†

Investment company A company or trust which uses its capital to invest in other companies. There are two principal types: the closed-end and the open-end, or mutual fund. Shares in closed-end investment companies, some of which are listed on the New York Stock Exchange, are readily transferable in the open market and are bought and sold like other shares. Capitalization of these companies remains the same unless action is taken to change, which is seldom. Open-end funds sell their own new shares to investors, stand ready to buy back their old shares, and are not listed. Open-end funds are so called because their capitalization is not fixed; they issue more shares as people want them.†

Investment counsel   One whose principal business consists of acting as investment adviser and a substantial part of his business consists of rendering investment supervisory services.†

Investment tax credit   Business firms can deduct as a credit against their income taxes a specified percentage of the dollar amount of new investments in each of certain categories of assets.*

Investors service bureau   A facility of the New York Stock Exchange which answers written inquiries from individual investors on all aspects of securities investing. Major areas of inquiries involve: finding local brokerage firms which take small orders or accounts, explaining investing methods and listed securities, clarifying exchange operations, providing instructions for tracing dubious securities.†

Issue   Any of a company's securities, or the act of distributing such securities.†

Issuer   A municipal unit that borrows money through the sale of bonds or notes.**

Legal list   A list of securities in which mutual savings banks, pensions funds, insurance companies, and other fiduciary institutions are permitted to invest.*

Legal opinion   An opinion concerning the legality of a bond issue usually written by a recognized law firm specializing in public borrowings.**

Leverage   The effect on the per-share earnings of the common stock of a company when large sums must be paid for bond interest or preferred stock dividends, or both, before the common stock is entitled to share in earnings. Leverage may be advantageous for the common stock when earnings are good but may work against the common when earnings decline. Example: Company A has 1,000,000 shares of common stock outstanding, no other securities. Earnings drop from $1,000,000 to $800,000 or from $1 to 80 cents a share, a decline of 20 percent. Company B also has 1,000,000 shares of common but must pay $500,000 annually in bond interest. If earnings amount to $1,000,000, there is $500,000 available for the common or 50 cents a share. But earnings drop to $800,000

so there is only $300,000 available for the common, or 30 cents a share—a drop of 40 percent. Or suppose earnings of the company with only common stock increased from $1,000,000 to $1,500,000—earnings per share would go from $1 to $1.50, or an increase of 50 percent. But if earnings of the company which had to pay $500,000 in bond interest increased that much—earnings per common share would jump from 50 cents to $1 a share, or 100 percent. When a company has common stock only, no leverage exists because all earnings are available for the common, although relatively large fixed charges payable for lease of substantial plant assets may have an effect similar to that of a bond issue.†

Leverage factor   The ratio of debt to total assets.*

Liabilities   All the claims against a corporation. Liabilities include accounts and wages and salaries payable, dividends declared payable, accrued taxes payable, fixed or long-term liabilities such as mortgage bonds, debentures, and bank loans. (See: *Assets, balance sheet.*)†

Lien   A lender's claim on assets that are pledged for a loan.*

Limit, limited order, or limited price order   An order to buy or sell a stated amount of a security at a specified price, or at a better price, if obtainable after the order is represented in the Trading Crowd.†

Limited tax bond   A bond secured by a pledge of a tax or group of taxes limited as to rate or amount.**

Line of credit   An arrangement whereby a financial institution (bank or insurance company) commits itself to lend up to a specified maximum amount of funds during a specified period. Sometimes the interest rate on the loan is specified, at other times, it is not. Sometimes a commitment fee is imposed for obtaining the line of credit.*

Liquidation   The process of converting securities or other property into cash. The dissolution of a company, with cash remaining after sale of its assets and payment of all indebtedness being distributed to the shareholders.†

Liquidity   Refers to a firm's cash position and its ability to meet maturing obligations.*

Listed stock   The stock of a company which is traded on a securities exchange, and for which a listing application and a registration statement, giving detailed information about the company and its operations, have been filed with the Securities and Exchange Commission, unless otherwise exempted, and the exchange itself. The various stock exchanges have different standards for listing. Some of the guides used by the New York Stock Exchange for an original listing are national interest in the company, a minimum of 1-million shares publicly held among not less than 2,000 round-lot stock-holders. The publicly held common shares should have a minimum aggregate market value of $16 million. The company should have net income in the latest year of over $2.5-million before federal income tax and $2-million in each of the preceding two years.†

Load The portion of the offering price of shares of open-end investment companies in excess of the value of the underlying assets which cover sales commissions and all other costs of distribution. The load is usually incurred only on purchase, there being, in most cases, no charge when the shares are sold (redeemed).†

Lock-box plan A procedure used to speed up collections and to reduce float.*

Locked in An investor is said to be locked in when he has a profit on a security he owns but does not sell because his profit would immediately become subject to the capital gains tax. (See: *Capital gain.*)†

Long Signifies ownership of securities: "I am long 100 U.S. Steel" means the speaker owns 100 shares. (See: *Short position, short sale.*)†

Management The board of directors, elected by the stockholders, and the officers of the corporation, appointed by the board of directors.†

Manipulation An illegal operation. Buying or selling a security for the purpose of creating a false or misleading appearance of active trading or for the purpose of raising or depressing the price to induce purchase or sale by others.†

Margin The amount paid by the customer when he uses his broker's credit to buy a security. Under Federal Reserve regulations, the initial margin required in past years has ranged from 50 percent of the purchase price all the way to 100 percent. (See: *Brokers' loans, Equity, Margin call.*)†

Margin call A demand upon a customer to put up money or securities with the broker. The call is made when a purchase is made; also if a customer's equity in a margin account declines below a minimum standard set by the exchange or by the firm. (See: *Margin.*)†

Margin—profit on sales The *profit margin* is the percentage of profit after tax to sales.*

Marginal cost The cost of an additional unit. The marginal cost of capital is the cost of an additional dollar of new funds.*

Marginal efficiency of capital A schedule showing the internal rate of return on investment opportunities.*

Marginal revenue The additional gross revenue produced by selling one additional unit of output.*

Marketability The measure of the ease with which a security can be sold in the secondary market.**

Market order An order to buy or sell a stated amount of a security at the most advantageous price obtainable. (See: *Good 'til cancelled order, Limit order, Stop order.*)†

Market price In the case of a security, market price is usually considered the last reported price at which the stock or bond sold.†

Matched and lost When two bids to buy the same stock are made on the trading floor simultaneously, and each bid is equal to or larger than the amount of stock offered, both bids are considered to be on an equal basis. So the two bidders flip a coin to decide who buys the stock. Also applies to offers to sell.†

Maturity The date on which a loan or a bond or debenture comes due and is to be paid off.†

Member corporation A securities brokerage firm, organized as a corporation, with at least one member of the New York Stock Exchange, Inc., who is an officer and a holder of voting stock in the corporation. (See: *Member firm.*)†

Member firm A securities brokerage firm organized as a partnership and having at least one general partner who is a member of the New York Stock Exchange, Inc. (See: *Member corporation.*)†

Member organization This term includes New York Stock Exchange Member Firm *and* Member Corporation. (See: *Member corporation, Member firm.*)†

Merger Any combination that forms one company from two or more previously existing companies.*

Money market Financial markets in which funds are borrowed or lent for short periods (i.e., less than one year). (The money market is distinguished from the capital market, which is the market for long-term funds.)*

Mortgage A pledge of designated property as security for a loan.*

Mortgage bond A bond secured by a mortgage on a property. The value of the property may or may not equal the value of the so-called mortgage bonds issued against it. (See: *Bond, Debenture.*)†

Municipal bond A bond issued by a state or a political subdivision, such as county, city, town, or village. The term also designates bonds issued by state agencies and authorities. In general, interest paid on municipal bonds is exempt from federal income taxes and state and local income taxes within the state of issue.†

Mutual fund (See: *Investment company.*)

NASD The National Association of Securities Dealers, Inc. An association of brokers and dealers in the over-the-counter securities business. The association has the power to expel members who have been declared guilty of unethical practices. NASD is dedicated to—among other objectives—"adopt, administer and enforce rules of fair practice and rules to prevent fraudulent and manipulative acts and practices, and in general to promote just and equitable principles of trade for the protection of investors."†

NASDAQ An automated information network which provides brokers and dealers with price quotations on securities traded over-the-counter. NASDAQ is an acronym for National Association of Securities Dealers Automated Quotations.†

Negotiable Refers to a security, title to which is transferable by delivery. (See: *Good delivery*.)†

Net asset value A term usually used in connection with investment companies, meaning net asset value per share. It is common practice for an investment company to compute its assets daily, or even twice daily, by totaling the market value of all securities owned. All liabilities are deducted, and the balance divided by the number of shares outstanding. The resulting figure is the net asset value per share. (See: *Assets, Investment company*.)†

Net change The change in the price of a security from the closing price on one day and the closing price on the following day on which the stock is traded. The net change is ordinarily the last figure on the stock price list. The mark + 1⅛ means up $1.125 a share from the last sale on the previous day the stock traded.†

Net debt Gross debt less sinking fund accumulations and all self-supporting debt.**

Net present value (NPV) method A method of ranking investment proposals. The NPV is equal to the present value of future returns, discounted at the marginal cost of capital, minus the present value of the cost of the investment.*

Net worth The capital and surplus of a firm—capital stock, capital surplus (paid-in capital), earned surplus (retained earnings), and, occasionally, certain reserves. For some purposes, preferred stock is included; generally, net worth refers only to the common stockholders' position.*

New housing authority bonds A bond issued by a local public housing authority to finance public housing. It is backed by Federal funds and the solemn pledge of the U.S. Government that payment will be made in full.**

New issue A stock or bond sold by a corporation for the first time. Proceeds may be issued to retire outstanding securities of the company, for new plant or equipment, or for additional working capital.†

New issue market Market for new issues of municipal bonds and notes.**

Nominal interest rate The contracted or stated interest rate, undeflated for price-level changes.*

Noncumulative A preferred stock on which unpaid dividends do not accrue. Omitted divi-

dends are, as a rule, gone forever. (See: *Cumulative preferred*.)†

Normal probability distribution A symmetrical, bell-shaped probability function.*

Notes Short-term unsecured promises to pay specified amounts of money. For municipal notes maturities generally range from six to twelve months.**

NYSE common stock index A composite index covering price movements of all common stocks listed on the "Big Board." It is based on the close of the market December 31, 1965 as 50.00 and is weighted according to the number of shares listed for each issue. The index is computed continuously and printed on the ticker tape each half hour. Point changes in the index are converted to dollars and cents so as to provide a meaningful measure of changes in the average price of listed stocks. The composite index is supplemented by separate indexes for four industry groups: industrials, transportation, utilities, and finances, (See: *Averages*.)†

Objective probability distributions Probability distributions determined by statistical procedures.*

Odd lot An amount of stock less than the established 100-share unit or 10-share unit of trading: from 1 to 99 shares for the great majority of issues, 1 to 9 for so-called inactive stocks. (See: *Round lot, Inactive stock*.)†

Off-board This term may refer to transactions over-the-counter in unlisted securities, or to a transaction involving listed shares which was not executed on a national securities exchange. (See: *Over-the-counter, Secondary distribution*.)†

Offer The price at which a person is ready to sell. Opposed to bid, the price at which one is ready to buy. (See: *Bid and asked*.)†

Official statement Document prepared by or for the issuer that gives in detail the security and financial information about the issue.**

Open order (See: *Good 'til cancelled order*.)

Open-end investment company (See: *Investment company*.)

Operating leverage The extent to which fixed costs are used in a firm's operation. Break-even analysis is used to measure the extent to which operating leverage is employed.*

Opportunity cost The rate of return on the best *alternative* investment that is available. It is the highest return that will *not* be earned if the funds are invested in a particular project. For example, the opportunity cost of *not* investing in bond A yielding 8 percent might be 7.99 percent, which could be earned on bond B.*

Option A right to buy (call) or sell (put) a fixed amount of a given stock at a specified price within a limited period of time. The purchaser hopes that the stock's price will go up (if he bought a call) or down (if he bought a put) by an amount sufficient to provide a profit greater than the cost of the contract and the commission and other fees required to exercise the contract. If the stock price holds steady or moves in the opposite direction, the price paid for the option is lost entirely. There are several other types of options available to the public but these are basically combinations of puts and calls. Individuals may write (sell) as well as purchase options and are thereby obliged to deliver or buy the stock at the specified price.

There are also listed call option markets on the Chicago Board Options Exchange, the American, Midwest, Pacific, and PBW Stock Exchanges. These differ from the over-the-counter market in that trading is limited to selected issues, expiration of contracts is standardized at four dates during the year, exercise prices are set at multiples of 5 below 50 and multiples of 10 above 50, and option prices are determined through a continuous competitive-auction market system.†

Orders good until a specified time A market or limited price order which is to be represented in the Trading Crowd until a specified time, after which such order or the portion thereof not executed is to be treated as cancelled.†

Ordinary income Income from the normal operations of a firm. Operating income specifically excludes income from the sale of capital assets.*

Organized security exchanges Formal organizations having tangible, physical locations. Organized exchanges conduct an auction market in designated ("listed") investment securities. For example, the New York Stock Exchange is an organized exchange.*

Overbought An opinion as to price levels. May refer to a security which has had a sharp rise or to the market as a whole after a period of vigorous buying, which it may be argued, has left prices "too high."†

Overdraft system A system where a depositor may write checks in excess of his balance, with his bank automatically extending a loan to cover the shortage.*

Overlapping debt That portion of the debt of other governmental units for which residents of a particular muncipality are responsible.**

Oversold An opinion—the reverse of overbought. A single security or a market which, it is believed, has declined to an unreasonable level.†

Over-the-counter A market for securities made up of securities dealers who may or may not be members of a securities exchange. Over-the-counter is mainly a market made over the telephone. Thousands of companies have insufficient shares outstanding, stockholders, or earnings to warrant application for listing on the

New York Stock Exchange, Inc. Securities of these companies are traded in the over-the-counter market between dealers who act either as principals or as brokers for customers. The over-the-counter market is the principal market for U.S. government and municipal bonds. (See: *NASD, NASDAQ, Off-board.*)†

Paper profit An unrealized profit on a security still held. Paper profits become realized profits only when the security is sold. (See: *Profit taking.*)†

Par In the case of a common share, par means a dollar amount assigned to the share by the company's charter. Par value may also be used to compute the dollar amount of the common shares on the balance sheet. Par value has little significance so far as market value of common stock is concerned. Many companies today issue no-par stock but give a stated per share value on the balance sheet. In the case of preferred shares and bonds, however, par is important. It often signifies the dollar value upon which dividends on preferred stocks, and interest on bonds, are figured. The issuer of a 6 percent bond promises to pay that percentage of the bond's par value annually. (See: *Capitalization, Transfer tax.*)†

Par value The nominal or face value of stock or bond.*

Participating preferred A preferred stock which is entitled to its stated dividend and, also, to additional dividends on a specified basis upon payment of dividends on the common stock.†

Passed dividend Omission of a regular or scheduled dividend.†

Payback period The length of time required for the net revenues of an investment to return the cost of the investment.*

Paying agent Place where principal and interest is payable. Usually a designated bank or the treasurer's office of the issuer.**

Payout ratio The percentage of earnings paid out in the form of dividends.*

Pegging A market stabilization action taken by the manager of an underwriting group during the offering of new securities. He does this by continually placing orders to buy at a specified price in the market.*

Penny stocks Low-priced issues often highly speculative, selling at less than $1 a share. Frequently used as a term of disparagement, although a few penny stocks have developed into investment-caliber issues.†

Percentage order A limited price order to buy (or sell) a stated amount of a specified stock after a fixed number of shares of such stock have traded.†

Perpetuity A stream of equal future payments expected to continue forever.*

Pledging of accounts receivable Short-term

borrowing from financial institutions where the loan is secured by accounts receivable. The lender may physically take the accounts receivable but typically has recourse to the borrower; also called *discounting of accounts receivable.**

Point In the case of shares of stock, a point means $1. If ABC shares rises 3 points, each share has risen $3. In the case of bonds a point means $10, since a bond is quoted as a percentage of $1,000. A bond which rises 3 points gains 3 percent of $1,000, or $30 in value. An advance from 87 to 90 would mean an advance in dollar value from $870 to $900 for each $1,000 bond. In the case of market averages, the word point means merely that and no more. If, for example, the Dow-Jones Industrial averages rises from 870.25 to 871.25, it has risen a point. A point in this average, however, is not equivalent to $1. (See: *Averages.*)†

Pooling of interest An accounting method for combining the financial statements of firms that merge. Under the pooling-of-interest procedure, the assets of the merged firms are simply added to form the balance sheet of the surviving corporation. This method is different from the "purchase" method, where goodwill is put on the balance sheet to reflect a premium (or discount) paid in excess of book value.*

Portfolio Holdings of securities by an individual or institution. A portfolio may contain bonds, preferred stocks, and common stocks of various types of enterprises.†

Portfolio effect The extent to which the variation in returns on a combination of assets (a "portfolio") is less than the sum of the variations of the individual assets.*

Portfolio theory Deals with the selection of optimal portfolios; that is, portfolios that provide the highest possible return for any specified degree of risk.*

Preemptive right A provision contained in the corporate charter and by laws that gives holders of common stock the right to purchase on a pro rata basis new issues of common stock (or securities convertible into common stock.)*

Preferred stock A class of stock with a claim on the company's earnings before payment may be made on the common stock and usually entitled to priority over common stock if the company liquidates. Usually entitled to dividends at a specified rate—when declared by the board of directors and before payment of a dividend on the common stock—depending upon the terms of the issue. (See: *Cumulative preferred, Participating preferred.*)†

Premium The amount by which a preferred stock, bond, or option may sell above its par value. In the case of a new issue of bonds or stocks, premium is the amount the market price rises over the original selling price. Also refers to a charge sometimes made when a stock is borrowed to make delivery on a short sale. May refer, also, to redemption price of a bond or preferred stock if it is higher than face value. (See: *Discount, Short sale.*)†

Present value (PV) The value today of a future payment, or stream of payments, discounted at the appropriate discount rate.*

Price-earnings ratio The price of a share of stock divided by earnings per share for a twelve-month period. For example, a stock selling for $50 a share and earning $5 a share is said to be selling at a price-earnings ratio of 10 to 1.†

Primary distribution Also called primary offering. The original sale of a company's securities. (See: *Investment banker, Secondary distribution.*)†

Primary market Market for new issues of securities.

Prime rate The lowest rate of interest commercial banks charge very large, strong corporations.*

Principal The person for whom a broker executes an order, or a dealer buying or selling for his own account. The term *principal* may also refer to a person's capital or to the face amount of a bond.†

Pro forma A projection. A *pro forma* financial statement is one that shows how the actual statement will look if certain specified assumptions are realized. *Pro forma* statements may be either furture or past projections. An example of a backward *pro forma* statement occurs when two firms are planning to merge and shows what their consolidated financial statements would have looked like if they had been merged in preceding years.*

Profit center A unit of a large, decentralized firm that has its own investments and for which a rate of return on investment can be calculated.*

Profit margin The ratio of profits after taxes to sales.*

Profitability index (PI) The present value of future returns divided by the present value of the investment outlay.*

Profit-taking Selling stock which has appreciated in value since purchase, in order to realize the profit which has been made possible. The term is often used to explain a downturn in the market following a period of rising prices. (See: *Paper profit.*)†

Progressive tax A tax that requires a higher percentage payment on higher incomes. The personal income tax in the United States, which is at a rate of 14 percent on the lowest increments of income to 70 percent on the highest increments, is progressive.*

Prospectus The official selling circular that must be given to purchasers of new securities registered with the Securities and Exchange

Commission so investors can evaluate those securities before or at the time of purchase. It highlights the much longer Registration Statement filed with the commission. It warns the issue has not been approved (or disapproved) by the commission and discloses such material information as the issuer's property and business, the nature of the security offered, use of proceeds, issuer's competition and prospects, management's experience, history, and remuneration, and certified financial statements. A preliminary version of the prospectus, used by brokers to obtain buying indications from investors, is called a *red herring*. This is because of a front-page notice (printed in red ink) that the preliminary prospectus is "subject to completion or amendment" and "shall not constitute an offer to sell . . ."†

Proxy A document giving one person the authority or power to act for another. Typically, the authority in question is the power to vote shares of common stock.*

Proxy statement Information required by SEC to be given stockholders as a prerequisite to solicitation of proxies for a security subject to the requirements of Securities Exchange Act.†

Prudent man rule An investment standard. In some states, the law requires that a fiduciary, such as a trustee, may invest the fund's money only in a list of securities designated by the state—the so-called legal list. In other states, the trustee may invest in a security if it is one which a prudent man of discretion and intelligence, who is seeking a reasonable income and preservation of capital, would buy.†

Pure (or primitive) security A security that pays off $1 if one particular state of the world occurs and pays off nothing if any other state of the world occurs.*

Put An option to sell a specific security at a specified price within a designated period.*

Puts and calls (See: *Option*.)

Quotation Often shortened to *quote*. The highest bid to buy and the lowest offer to sell a security in a given market at a given time. If you ask your broker for a "quote" on a stock, he may come back with something like "45¼ to 45½." This means that $45.25 is the highest price any buyer wanted to pay at the time the quote was given on the floor of the exchange and that $45.50 was the lowest price which any seller would take at the same time. (See: *Bid and asked*.)†

Rally A brisk rise following a decline in the general price level of the market, or in an individual stock.†

Rate of return The internal rate of return on an investment.*

Ratings Designations used by investors' services to give relative indications of quality.**

Record date The date on which you must be registered as a shareholder on the stock book of a company in order to receive a declared dividend or, among other things, to vote on company affairs. (See: *Ex dividend, Transfer*.)†

Recourse arrangement A term used in connection with accounts-receivable financing. If a firm sells its accounts receivable to a financial institution under a recourse agreement, then, if the accounts receivable cannot be collected, the selling firm must repurchase the account from the financial institution.*

Redemption price The price at which a bond may be redeemed before maturity, at the option of the issuing company. Redemption value also applies to the price the company must pay to call in certain types of preferred stock. (See: *Callable*.)†

Rediscount rate The rate of interest at which a bank may borrow from a Federal Reserve Bank.*

Refinancing Same as refunding. New securities are sold by a company and the money is used to retire existing securities. Object may be to save interest costs, extend the maturity of the loan, or both.*

Refunding Sale of new debt securities to replace an old debt issue.*

Registered bond A bond which is registered on the books of the issuing company in the name of the owner. It can be transferred only when endorsed by the registered owner. (See: *Bearer bond, Coupon bond*.)†

Registered representative Present name for the older term *customer's man*. In a New York Stock Exchange Member Organizations, a *registered representative* is an employee who has met the requirements of the exchange as to background and knowledge of the securities business. Also known as an *account executive* or *customer's broker*.†

Registrar Usually a trust company or bank charged with the responsibility of preventing the issuance of more stock than authorized by a company. (See: *Transfer*.)†

Registration Before a public offering may be made of new securities by a company, or of outstanding securities by controlling stockholders—through the mails or in interstate commerce—the securities must be registered under the Securities Act of 1933. The registration statement is filed with the SEC by the issuer. It must disclose pertinent information relating to the company's operations, securities, management, and purpose of the public offering. Securities of railroads under jurisdiction of the Interstate Commerce Commission, and certain other types of securities, are exempted. On security offerings involving less than $300,000, less information is required.

Before a security may be admitted to dealings on a national securities exchange, it must be registered under the Securities Exchange Act of 1934. The application for registration must be filed with the exchange and the SEC by the company issuing the securities. It must disclose pertinent information relating to the company's operations, securities, and management.†

Regression analysis A statistical procedure for predicting the value of one variable (dependent variable) on the basis of knowledge about one or more other variables (independent variables).*

Regular way delivery Unless otherwise specified, securities sold on the N.Y. Stock Exchange are to be delivered to the buying broker by the selling broker and payment made to the selling broker by the buying broker on the fifth business day after the transaction. Regular way delivery for bonds is the following business day. (See: *Transfer.*)†

Regulation T The federal regulation governing the amount of credit which may be advanced by brokers and dealers to customers for the purchase of securities. (See: *Margin.*)†

Regulation U The federal regulation governing the amount of credit which may be advanced by a bank to its customers for the purchase of listed stocks. (See: *Margin.*)†

Reinvestment rate The rate of return at which cash flows from an investment are reinvested. The reinvestment rate may or may not be constant from year to year.*

REIT Real Estate Investment Trust, an organization similar to an investment company in some respects but concentrating its holdings in real estate investments. The yield is generally liberal since REIT's are required to distribute as much as 90 percent of their income. (See: *Investment company.*)†

Reorganization When a financially troubled firm goes through reorganization, its assets are restated to reflect their current market value, and its financial structure is restated to reflect any changes on the asset side of the statement. Under a reorganizations the firm continues in existence; this is contrasted to bankruptcy, where the firm is liquidated and ceases to exist.*

Replacement-cost accounting A requirement under SEC release no. 190 (1976) that large companies disclose the replacement costs of inventory items and depreciable plant.*

Required rate of return The rate of return that stockholders expect to receive on common stock investments.*

Residual value The value of leased property at the end of the lease term.*

Retained earnings That portion of earnings not paid out in dividends. The figure that appears on the balance sheet is the sum of the retained earnings for each year throughout the company's history.*

Return (See: *Yield.*)

Revenue bond A bond payable from revenues derived from tolls, charges, or rents paid by users of the facility constructed from the proceeds of the bond issue.**

Rights When a company wants to raise more funds by issuing additional securities, it may give its stockholders the opportunity, ahead of others, to buy the new securities in proportion to the number of shares each owns. The piece of paper evidencing this privilege is called a right. Because the additional stock is usually offered to stockholders below the current market price, rights ordinarily have a market value of their own and are actively traded. In most cases they must be exercised within a relatively short period. Failure to exercise or sell rights may result in actual loss to the holder. (See: *Warrant.*)†

Rights offering A securities flotation offered to existing stockholders.*

Risk The probability that actual future returns will be below expected returns. It is measured by standard deviation or coefficient of variation of expected returns.*

Risk-adjusted discount rates The discount rate applicable for a particular risky (uncertain) stream of income: the riskless rate of interest plus a risk premium appropriate to the level of risk attached to the particular income stream.*

Risk premium The difference between the required rate of return on a particular risky asset and the rate of return on a riskless asset with the the same expected life.*

Risk-return trade-off function (See *Security market line.*)

Round lot A unit of trading or a multiple thereof. On the NYSE the unit of trading is generally 100 shares in stocks and $1,000 par value in the case of bonds. In some inactive stocks, the unit of trading is ten shares.†

Sale and leaseback An operation whereby a firm sells land, buildings, or equipment to a financial institution and simultaneously executes an agreement to lease the property back for a specified period under specific terms.*

Salvage value The value of a capital asset at the end of a specified period. It is the current market price of an asset being considered for replacement in a capital budgeting problem.*

Scale order An order to buy (or sell) a security which specifies the total amount to be bought (or sold) and the amount to be bought (or sold) at specified price variations.†

Seat A traditional figure-of-speech for a membership on an exchange. Price and admission requirements vary.†

SEC The Securities and Exchange Commission, established by Congress to help protect investors. The SEC administers the Securities Act of 1933, the Securities Exchange Act of 1934, the Securities Act Amendments of 1975, the Trust Indenture Act, the Investment Company Act, the Investment Advisers Act, and the Public Utility Holding Company Act.†

Secondary distribution Also known as a secondary offering. The redistribution of a block of stock, sometimes after it has been sold by the issuing company. The sale is handled off the NYSE by a securities firm or group of firms and the shares are usually offered at a fixed price which is related to the current market price of the stock. Usually the block is a large one, such as might be involved in the settlement of an estate. The security may be listed or unlisted. (See: *Exchange distribution, Investment banker, Primary distribution, Special offering, Syndicate.*)†

Secondary market Market for issues previously offered or sold.**

Securities and exchange commission (See *SEC.*)

Securities, junior Securities that have lower priority in claims on assets and income than other securities *(senior securities)*. For example, preferred stock is junior to debentures, but debentures are junior to mortgage bonds. Common stock is the most junior of all corporate securities.*

Securities, senior Securities having claims on income and assets that rank higher than certain other securities *(junior securities)*. For example, mortgage bonds are senior to debentures, but debentures are senior to common stock.*

Security market line A graphic representation of the relation between the required return on a security and the product of its risk times a normalized market measure of risk. Risk-return relationships for individual securities or investments.*

Self-supporting debt Debt incurred for a project or enterprise requiring no tax support other than the specific tax or revenue earmarked for that purpose.**

Seller's option A special transaction on the NYSE which gives the seller the right to deliver the stock or bond at any time within a specified period, ranging from not less than 6 business days to not more than 60 days. (See: *Delivery.*)†

Selling group A group of stock brokerage firms formed for the purpose of distributing a new issue of securities; part of the investment banking process.*

Sensitivity analysis Simulation analysis in which key variables are changed and the result-ing change in the rate of return is observed. Typically, the rate of return will be more sensitive to changes in some variables than it will in others.*

Serial bond An issue which matures in part at periodic stated intervals.†

Service lease A lease under which the lessor maintains and services the asset.*

Settlement Conclusion of a securities transaction in which a customer pays a debit balance he owes a broker or receives from the broker the proceeds from a sale. The term also applies to continuous daily netting out of transactions among brokerage houses, usually through centralized securities clearing corporations. (See: *Regular delivery, Cash sale, Depository trust company.*)†

Short covering Buying stock to return stock previously borrowed to make delivery on a short sale.†

Short position Stocks sold short and not covered as of a particular date. On the NYSE, a tabulation is issued once a month listing all issues on the exchange in which there was a short position of 5,000 or more shares and issues in which the short position had changed by 2,000 or more shares in the preceding month. *Short position* also means the total amount of stock an individual has sold short and has not covered, as of a particular date.†

Short sale A person who believes a stock will decline and sells it though he does not own any has made a short sale. For instance: You instruct your broker to sell short 100 shares of ABC. Your broker borrows the stock so he can deliver the 100 shares to the buyer. The money value of the shares borrowed is deposited by your broker with the lender. Sooner or later you must cover your short sale by buying the same amount of stock you borrowed for return to the lender. If you are able to buy ABC at a lower price than you sold it for, your profit is the difference between the two prices—not counting commissions and taxes. But if you have to pay more for the stock than the price you received, that is the amount of your loss. Stock exchange and federal regulations govern and limit the conditions under which a short sale may be made on a national securities exchange. Sometimes a person will sell short a stock he already owns in order to protect a paper profit. This is known as selling short against the box. (See: *Up tick.*)†

SIAC Securities Industry Automation Corporation, an independent organization established by the New York and American Stock Exchanges as a jointly owned subsidiary to provide automation, data processing, clearing, and communications services.†

Simulation A technique whereby probable future events are simulated on a computer. Estimated rates of return and risk indexes can be generated.*

Sinking fund A required annual payment designed to amortize a bond or a preferred stock issue. The sinking fund may be held in the form of cash or marketable securities, but more generally the money put into the sinking fund is used to retire each year some of the securities in question.*

SIPC Securities Investor Protection Corporation, which provides funds for use, if necessary, to protect customers' cash and securities which may be on deposit with a SIPC member firm in the event the firm fails and is liquidated under the provisions of the SIPC Act. SIPC is not a government agency. It is a nonprofit membership corporation created, however, by an act of Congress.†

Small business administration (SBA) A government agency organized to aid small firms with their financing and other problems.*

Special bid A method of filling an order to buy a large block of stock on the floor of the New York Stock Exchange. In a special bid, the bidder for the block of stock—a pension fund, for instance, will pay a special commission to the broker who represents him in making the purchase. The seller does not pay a commission. The special bid is made on the floor of the exchange at a fixed price which may not be below the last sale of the security or the current bid in the regular market, whichever is higher. Member firms may sell this stock for customers directly to the buyer's broker during trading hours.†

Special offering Opposite of special bid. A notice is printed on the ticker tape announcing the stock sale at a fixed price usually based on the last transaction in the regular auction market. If there are more buyers than stock, allotments are made. Only the seller pays the commission. (See: *Secondary distribution.*)†

Special tax bond A bond secured by a special tax, such as a gasoline tax.**

Specialist A member of the New York Stock Exchange, Inc., who has two functions: First, to maintain an orderly market, insofar as reasonably practicable, in the stocks in which he is registered as a specialist. In order to maintain an orderly market, the exchange expects the specialist to buy or sell for his own account, to a reasonable degree, when there is a temporary disparity between supply and demand. Second, the specialist acts as a broker's broker. When a commission broker on the exchange floor receives a limit order, say, to buy at $50 a stock then selling at $60—and he cannot wait at the post where the stock is traded to see if the price reaches the specified level. So he leaves the order with the specialist, who will try to execute it in the market if and when

the stock declines to the specified price. At all times the specialist must put his customers' interests above his own. There are about 400 specialists on the NYSE. (See: *Book, Limited order.*)†

Speculation The employment of funds by a speculator. Safety of principal is a secondary factor. (See: *Investment.*)†

Speculator One who is willing to assume a relatively large risk in the hope of gain. The speculator may buy and sell the same day or speculate in an enterprise which he does not expect to be profitable for years.†

Split The division of the outstanding shares of a corporation into a larger number of shares. A 3-for-1 split by a company with 1 million shares outstanding results in 3 million shares outstanding. Each holder of 100 shares before the 3-for-1 split would have 300 shares, although his proportionate equity in the company would remain the same; 100 parts of 1 million are the equivalent of 300 parts of 3 million. Ordinarily splits must be voted by directors and approved by shareholders. (See: *Stock dividends.*)†

Standard deviation A statistical term that measures the variability of a set of observations from the mean of the distribution (σ.)*

State-preference model A framework in which decisions are based on probabilities of payoffs under alternative states of the world.*

Stock ahead Sometimes an investor who has entered an order to buy or sell a stock at a certain price will see transactions at that price reported on the ticker tape while his own order has not been executed. The reason is that other buy and sell orders at the same price came in to the specialist ahead of his and had priority. (See: *Book, Specialist.*)†

Stock dividend A dividend paid in securities rather than cash. The dividend may be additional shares of the issuing company, or shares of another company (usually a subsidiary) held by the company. (See: *Ex-dividend, Split.*)†

Stock split An accounting action to increase the number of shares outstanding; for example, in a 3-for-1 split, shares outstanding would be tripled and each stockholder would be tripled and each stockholder would receive three new shares for each one formerly held. Stock splits involve no transfer from surplus to the capital account.*

Stockholder of record A stockholder whose name is registered on the books of the issuing corporation.†

Stop limit order A stop order which becomes a limit order after the specified stop price has been reached. (See: *Limit order, Stop order.*)†

Stop order An order to buy at a price above or sell at a price below the current market. Stop buy orders are generally used to limit loss or protect unrealized profits on a short sale. Stop sell orders are generally used to protect unrealized profits or limit loss on a holding. A stop order becomes a market order when the stock sells at or beyond the specified price and, thus, may not necessarily be executed at that price.†

Stopped stock A service performed—in most cases by the specialist—for an order given him by a commission broker. Let's say XYZ just sold at $50 a share. Broker A comes along with an order to buy 100 shares at the market. The lowest offer is $50.50. Broker A believes he can do better for his client than $50.50, perhaps might get the stock at $50.25. But he doesn't want to take a chance that he'll miss the market—that is, the next sale might be $50.50 and the following one even higher. So he asks the specialist if he will stop 100 at ½ ($50.50). The specialist agrees. The specialist guarantees Broker A he will get 100 shares at 50½ if the stock sells at that price. In the meantime, if the specialist or broker A succeeds in executing the order at $50.25, the stop is called off. (See: *Specialist*.)†

Street The New York financial community in the Wall Street area.†

Street name Securities held in the name of a broker instead of his customer's name are said to be carried in a *street name*. This occurs when the securities have been bought on margin or when the customer wishes the security to be held by the broker.†

Subdivision Any legal and authorized political entity under a state's jurisdiction (county, city, water district, school district, etc.).**

Subjective probability distributions Probability distributions determined through subjective procedures without the use of statistics.*

Subordinated debenture A bond having a claim on assets only after the senior debt has been paid off in the event of liquidation.*

Subscription price The price at which a security may be purchased in a rights offering.*

Switch order or contingent order An order for the purchase (sale) of one stock and the sale (purchase) of another stock at a stipulated price difference.†

Switching Selling one security and buying another.†

Syndicate A group of investment bankers who together underwrite and distribute a new issue of securities or a large block of an outstanding issue.†

Synergy A situation where "the whole is greater than the sum of its parts"; in a synergistic merger, the postmerger earnings exceed the sum of the separate companies' premerger earnings.*

Systematic risk That part of a security's risk that cannot be eliminated by diversification.*

Take-over The acquiring of one corporation by another—usually in a friendly merger but sometimes marked by a "proxy fight." In "unfriendly" take-over attempts, the potential buying company may offer a price well above current market values, new securities, and other inducements to stockholders. The management of the subject company might ask for a better price or fight the take-over or merger with another company. (See: *Proxy*.)†

Tangible assets Physical assets as opposed to intangible assets such as goodwill and the stated value of patents.*

Tax base The total resources available for taxation.**

Tax-exempt bond Another name for a municipal bond. The interest on a municipal bond is presently exempt from Federal income tax.**

Technical research Analysis of the market and stocks based on supply and demand. The technician studies price movements, volume, and trends and patterns which are revealed by charting these factors, and attempts to assess the possible effect of current market action on future supply and demand for securities and individual issues. (See: *Fundamental research*.)†

Tender offers A situation wherein one firm offers to buy the stock of another, going directly to the stockholders, frequently over the opposition of the management of the firm whose stock is being sought.*

Term issue An issue that has a single maturity.**

Term loan A loan generally obtained from a bank or an insurance company with a maturity greater than one year. Term loans are generally amortized.*

Thin market A market in which there are comparatively few bids to buy or offers to sell, or both. The phrase may apply to a single security or to the entire stock market. In a thin market, price fluctuations between transactions are usually larger than when the market is liquid. A thin market in a particular stock may reflect lack of interest in that issue or a limited supply of or demand for stock in the market. (See: *Bid and asked, Liquidity, Offer*.)†

Third market Trading of stock exchange listed securities in the over-the-counter market by non-exchange-member brokers and all types of investors.†

Ticker The instruments which display prices and volume of securities transactions worldwide within minutes after each trade.†

Time order An order which becomes a market or limited price order at a specified time.†

Tips Supposedly "inside" information on corporation affairs.†

Trade credit Interfirm debt arising through credit sales and recorded as an account receivable by the seller and as an account payable by the buyer.*

Trader One who buys and sells for his own account for short-term profit. (See *Investor, Speculator.*)†

Trading floor (See: *Floor.*)

Trading market The secondary market for outstanding securities.**

Trading post One of 23 trading locations on the floor of the New York Stock Exchange at which stocks assigned to that location are bought and sold. About 75 stocks are traded at each post.†

Transfer This term may refer to two different operations. One is the delivery of a stock certificate from the seller's broker to the buyer's broker and legal change of ownership, normally accomplished within a few days. The other is to record the change of ownership on the books of the corporation by the transfer agent. When the purchaser's name is recorded on the books of the company, dividends, notices of meetings, proxies, financial reports, and all pertinent literature sent by the issuer to its securities holders are mailed direct to the new owner. (See: *Registrar, Street name.*)†

Transfer agent A transfer agent keeps a record of the name of each registered shareowner, his or her address, the number of shares owned, and sees that certificates presented to his office for transfer are properly cancelled and new certificates issued in the name of the transferee. (See: *Registrar, Transfer.*)†

Treasury stock Common stock that has been repurchased by the issuing firm.* It may be held in the company's treasury indefinitely, reissued to the public, or retired. Treasury stock receives no dividends and has no vote while held by the company.†

Trust receipt An instrument acknowledging that the borrower holds certain goods in trust for the lender. Trust receipt financing is used in connection with the financing of inventories for automobile dealers, construction equipment dealers, appliance dealers, and other dealers in expensive durable goods.*

Trustee The representative of bondholders who acts in their interest and facilitates communication between them and the issuer. Typically these duties are handled by a department of a commercial bank.*

Turnover rate The volume of shares traded in a year as a percentage of total shares listed on an exchange, outstanding for an individual issue, or held in an institutional portfolio.

Underwriter (See: *Investment banker.*)

Underwriting (1) The entire process of issuing new corporate securities. (2) The insurance function of bearing the risk of adverse price fluctuations during the period in which a new

issue of stock or bonds is being distributed.*

Underwriting syndicate A syndicate of investment firms formed to spread the risk associated with the purchase and distribution of a new issue of securities. The larger the issue, the more firms typically are involved in the syndicate.*

Unlimited tax bond A bond secured by pledge of taxes that are not limited by rate or amount.**

Unlisted A security not listed on a stock exchange. (See: *Over-the-counter.*)†

Unlisted Securities Securities that are traded in the over-the-counter market period.*

Unlisted trading privileges On some exchanges a stock may be traded at the request of a member without any prior application by the company itself. The company has no agreement to conform with standards of the exchange. Today admission of a stock to unlisted trading privileges requires SEC approval of an application filed by the exchange. The information in the application must be made available by the exchange to the public. No unlisted stocks are traded on the New York Stock Exchange. (See: *Listed stock.*)†

Unsystematic risk That part of a security's risk associated with random events; unsystematic risk can be eliminated by proper diversification.*

Up tick A term used to designate a transaction made at a price higher than the preceding transaction. Also called a *plus-tick*. A stock may be sold short only on an up tick, or on a "zero-plus" tick. A *zero-plus* tick is a term used for a transaction at the same price as the preceding trade but higher than the preceding different price.

Conversely, a *down tick*, or *minus* tick, is a term used to designate a transaction made at a price lower than the preceding trade. A *zero minus* tick is a transaction made at the same price as the preceding sale but lower than the preceding different price.

A plus sign, or a minus sign, is displayed throughout the day next to the last price of each company's stock traded at each trading post on the floor of the New York Stock Exchange. (See: *Short sale.*)†

Utility theory A body of theory dealing with the relationships among money income, utility (or "happiness"), and the willingness to accept risk.*

Value additivity principle Neither fragmenting cash flows or recombining them will affect the resulting values of the cash flows.*

Volume The number of shares traded in a security or an entire market during a given period. Volume is usually considered on a daily basis and a daily average is computed for longer periods.†

Voting right The stockholder's right to vote his stock in the affairs of his company. Most common shares have one vote each. Preferred stock usually has the right to vote when preferred dividends are in default for a specified period. The right to vote may be delegated by the stockholder to another person. (See: *Cumulative voting, Proxy.*)†

Warrant A long-term option to buy a stated number of shares of common stock at a specified price. The specified price is generally called the *exercise price.**

Weighted cost of capital A weighted average of the component costs of debt, preferred stock, and common equity. Also called the *composite cost of capital.**

When issued A short form of "when, as, and if issued." The term indicates a conditional transaction in a security authorized for issuance but not as yet actually issued. All "when issued" transactions are on an "if" basis, to be settled if and when the actual security is issued and the exchange or National Association of Securities Dealers rules the transactions are to be settled.†

Wire house A member firm of an exchange maintaining a communications network linking either its own branch offices, offices of correspondent firms, or a combination of such offices.†

Working capital Refers to a firm's investment in short-term assets—cash, short-term securities, accounts receivable, and inventories. *Gross working capital* is defined as a firm's total current assets. *Net working capital* is defined as current assets minus current liabilities. If the term *working capital* is used without further qualification, it generally refers to gross working capital.*

Working control Theoretically, ownership of 51 percent of a company's voting stock is necessary to exercise control. In practice—and this is particularly true in the case of a large corporation—effective control sometimes can be exerted through ownership, individually or by a group acting in concert, of less than 50 percent.†

Yield Also known as return. The dividends or interest paid by a company expressed as a percentage of the current price. A stock with a current market value of $40 a share paying dividends at the rate of $2.00 is said to return 5 percent ($2 ÷ $40). The current return on a bond is figured the same way. A 3 percent $1,000 bond selling at $600 offers a current yield return of 5 percent ($30 ÷ $600). (See: *Dividend, Interest.*)†

Yield to maturity The yield of a bond to maturity takes into account the price discount from or premium over the face amount. It is greater than the current yield when the bond is selling at a discount and less than the current yield when the bond is selling at a premium.†

SECURITIES AND EXCHANGE COMMISSION

500 NORTH CAPITOL STREET, WASHINGTON, DC 20549
INFORMATION: 202-272-2650
FREEDOM OF INFORMATION ACT:
202-523-5530

FULL AND FAIR DISCLOSURE

The Securities Act of 1933 requires issuers of securities making public offerings of securities in interstate commerce or through the mails, directly or by others on their behalf, to file registration statements containing financial and other pertinent data about the issuer and the securities being offered. A similar requirement applies to such offerings on behalf of a controlling person of the issuer. Unless a registration statement is in effect with respect to such securities, it is unlawful to sell the securities in interstate commerce or through the mails. (There are certain limited exemptions, such as government securities, nonpublic offerings, and intrastate offerings, as well as offerings not exceeding $1,500,000 in amount, which comply with the commission's Regulation A.) The effectiveness of a registration statement may be refused or suspended after a public hearing, if the statement contains material misstatements or omissions, thus barring sale of the securities until it is appropriately amended. Registration of securities does not imply approval of the issue by the commission or that the commission has found the registration disclosures to be accurate. It does not insure investors against loss in their purchase but serves rather to provide information upon which investors may make an informed and realistic evaluation of the worth of the securities.

Persons responsible for filing false information with the commission subject themselves to the risk of fine or imprisonment or both; and persons connected with the public offering may be liable in damages to purchasers of the securities if the disclosures in the registration statement and prospectus are materially defective. Also, the above act contains antifraud provisions which apply generally to the sale of securities, whether or not registered (48 Stat. 74; 15 U.S.C. 77a et seq.).

REGULATION OF SECURITIES MARKETS AND PERSONS CONDUCTING A SECURITIES BUSINESS

The Securities Exchange Act of 1934 assigns to the commission broad regulatory responsibil-

Source: This material was abstracted from the United States Government Manual.

ities over the securities markets, the self-regulatory organizations within the securities industry, and persons conducting a business in securities. The commission is directed to facilitate the establishment of a national market system for securities and a national system for the clearance and settlement of securities transactions. Securities exchanges and certain clearing agencies are required to register with the commission, and associations of brokers or dealers are permitted to register with the commission. The Securities Exchange Act also provides for the establishment of the Municipal Securities Rulemaking Board to formulate rules for the municipal securities industry. The commission oversees the self-regulatory activities of the national securities exchanges and associations, registered clearing agencies, and the Municipal Securities Rulemaking Board. In addition, the commission regulates industry professionals, such as securities brokers and dealers, certain municipal securities professionals, and transfer agents.

The Securities Exchange Act authorizes national securities exchanges, national securities associations, clearing agencies, and the Municipal Securities Rulemaking Board to adopt rules that are designed, among other things to promote just and equitable principles of trade and to protect investors. The commission is required to approve or disapprove most proposed rules of these self-regulatory organizations and has the power to abrogate or amend existing rules of the national securities exchanges, national securities associations, and the Municipal Securities Rulemaking Board.

In addition, the commission has broad rulemaking authority over the activities of brokers, dealers, municipal securities dealers, securities information processors, and transfer agents. The commission may regulate such securities trading practices as short sales and stabilizing transactions. It may regulate the trading of options on national securities exchanges and the activities of members of exchanges who trade on the trading floors and may adopt rules governing broker-dealer sales practices in dealing with investors. The commission also is authorized to adopt rules concerning the financial responsibility of brokers and dealers and reports to be made by brokers and dealers. The Securities Exchange Act also empowers the Board of Governors of the Federal Reserve System to prescribe rules relating to the extension of credit by brokers and dealers for securities transactions. Such rules include the establishment of minimum margin requirements with respect to securities registered on national securities exchanges and certain securities traded over-the-counter (48 Stat. 881; U.S.C. 78a et seq.).

The Securities Exchange Act also requires the filing of registration applications and annual and other reports with national securities exchanges and the commission by companies whose securities are listed upon the exchanges, by companies that have assets of $1 million or more and 500 or more shareholders of record, and by companies that distributed securities pursuant to a registration statement declared effective by the commission under the Securities Act of 1933. Such applications and reports must contain financial and other data prescribed by the commission as necessary or appropriate for the protection of investors and to insure fair dealing. In addition, the solicitation of proxies, authorizations, or consents from holders of such registered securities must be made in accordance with rules and regulations prescribed by the commission. These rules provide for disclosures to securities holders of information relevant to the subject matter of the solicitation.

Disclosure of the holdings and transactions by officers, directors, and large (10 percent) holders of equity securities of companies is also required, and any and all persons who acquire more than 5 percent of certain equity securities are required to file detailed information with the commission and any exchange upon which such securities may be traded. Moreover, any person making a tender offer for certain classes of equity securities is required to file reports with the commission, if as a result of the tender offer such person would own more than 5 percent of the outstanding shares of the particular class of equity involved. The commission also is authorized to promulgate rules governing the repurchase by a corporate issuer of its own securities.

REGULATION OF MUTUAL FUNDS AND OTHER INVESTMENT COMPANIES

The Investment Company Act of 1940 provides for the registration with the commission of investment companies and subjects their activities to regulation to protect investors. The regulation covers sales and management fees, composition of boards of directors, and capital structure. Also, various transactions of investment companies, including transactions with affiliated interests, are prohibited unless the commission first determines that such transactions are fair. Under the act, the commission may institute court action to enjoin the consummation of mergers and other plans of reorganization of investment companies if such plans are unfair to security holders. It also may impose sanctions by administrative proceedings against investment company managements for violations of the act and other federal securities laws, and file court actions to enjoin acts and practices of management officials involving breaches of fiduciary duty involving personal misconduct and to disqualify such officials from office (54 Stat. 789; 15 U.S.C. 80a–1—80a–52).

REGULATION OF COMPANIES CONTROLLING ELECTRIC OR GAS UTILITIES

The Public Utility Holding Company Act of 1935 provides for regulation by the commission of the purchase and sale of securities and assets by companies in electric and gas utility holding company systems, their intra-system transactions and service and management arrangements. It limits holding companies to a single coordinated utility system and requires simplification of complex corporate and capital structures and elimination of unfair distribution of voting power among holders of system securities.

The issuance and sale of securities by holding companies and their subsidiaries, unless exempt (subject to conditions and terms which the commission is empowered to impose) as an issue expressly authorized by the state commission in the state in which the issuer is incorporated, must be found by the commission to meet statutory standards, namely: that the new security is reasonably adapted to the security structure and earning power of the issuer; that the proposed financing is necessary and appropriate to the economical and efficient operation of the company's business; that the consideration received, and fees, commissions, and other remuneration paid, are fair; and that the terms and conditions of the sale are not detrimental to investors, consumers, or the public.

The purchase and sale of utility properties and other assets may not be made in contravention of rules, regulations, or orders of the commission regarding the consideration to be received, maintenance of competitive conditions, fees and commissions, accounts, disclosure of interest, and similar matters. In passing upon proposals for reorganization, merger, or consolidation, the commission must be satisfied that the objectives of the act generally are complied with and that the terms of the proposal are fair and equitable to all classes of security holders affected (49 Stat. 803; 15 U.S.C. 79–92z–6).

REGULATION OF INVESTMENT COUNSELORS AND ADVISERS

The Investment Advisers Act of 1940 provides that persons who, for compensation, engage in the business of advising others with respect to their security transactions must register with the commission. The act prohibits certain types of fee arrangements, makes unlawful practices of investment advisers involving fraud or deceit, and requires, among other things, disclosure of any adverse interests the advisers may have in transactions executed for clients. The act authorizes the commission to issue rules proscribing acts and practices that may operate as a fraud or deceit upon investors (54 Stat. 847; 15 U.S.C. 80b–1—80b–21).

REHABILITATION OF FAILING CORPORATIONS

Chapter X of the Bankruptcy Act provides for commission participation as adviser to fed-

REGIONAL OFFICES (Securities and Exchange Commission)

Region	Address
1. New York, New Jersey	26 Federal Plaza, New York, NY 10007
2. Maine, Vermont, New Hampshire, Massachusetts, Connecticut, Rhode Island	150 Causeway Street, Boston, MA 02114
3. Tennessee, North Carolina, South Carolina, Mississippi, Alabama, Georgia, Florida, Louisiana (southeastern portion only)	1375 Peachtree Street NE, Atlanta, GA 30309
4. Minnesota, Wisconsin, Michigan, Iowa, Missouri, Illinois, Indiana, Ohio, Kentucky	219 S. Dearborn Street, Chicago, IL 60604
5. Kansas, Oklahoma, Texas, Arkansas, Louisiana (except southeastern portion)	411 W. 7th Street, Fort Worth, TX 76102
6. North Dakota, South Dakota, Colorado, Kansas, Utah, Wyoming, New Mexico	410 17th Street, Denver, CO 80202
7. California, Nevada, Arizona, Hawaii	10960 Wilshire Boulevard, Los Angeles, CA 90024
8. Washington, Oregon	915 Second Avenue, Seattle, WA 98174
9. Pennsylvania, West Virginia, Virginia, Maryland, Delaware	4015 Wilson Boulevard, Arlington, VA 22203

eral courts in proceedings for the reorganization of insolvent corporations. An important aspect of this activity is the advice rendered to the parties and the court with respect to the fairness and feasibility of proposed plans of reorganization (52 Stat. 883; 11 U.S.C. 501–676).

INDEPENDENT REPRESENTATION OF THE INTERESTS OF HOLDERS OF DEBT SECURITIES

The interests of purchasers of publicly offered debt securities issued pursuant to trust indentures are safeguarded under the provisions of the Trust Indenture Act of 1939. This act, among other things, requires the exclusion from such indentures of certain types of exculpatory clauses and the inclusion of certain protective provisions. The independence of the indenture trustee, who is a representative of the debt holder, is assured by proscribing certain relationships that might conflict with the proper exercise of his duties (53 Stat. 1149; 15 U.S.C. 77aaa–77bbbb).

ENFORCEMENT ACTIVITIES

The commission's enforcement activities are designed to secure compliance with the federal securities laws administered by the commission and the rules and regulations adopted thereunder. These activities include measures to compel obedience to the disclosure requirements of the registration and other provisions of the acts; to prevent fraud and deception in the purchase and sale of securities; to obtain court orders enjoining acts and practices that operate as a fraud upon investors or otherwise violate the laws; to revoke the registrations of brokers, dealers, and investment advisers who willfully engage in such acts and practices; to suspend or expel from national securities exchanges or the National Association of Securities Dealers, Inc., any member or officer who has violated any provision of the federal securities laws; and to prosecute persons who have engaged in fraudulent activities or other willful violations of those laws. In addition, attorneys or accountants who violate the securities laws face possible loss of their privilege to practice before the commission. To this end, private investigations are conducted into complaints or other evidences of securities violations. Evidence thus established of law violations in the purchase and sale of securities is used in appropriate administrative proceedings to revoke registration or in actions instituted in federal courts to restrain or enjoin such activities. Where the evidence tends to establish fraud or other willful violation of the securities laws, the facts are referred to the Attorney General for criminal prosecution of the offenders. The commission may assist in such prosecutions.

INVESTOR INFORMATION AND PROTECTION

Complaints and inquiries may be directed to the home office or to any regional office. Registration statements and other public documents filed with the commission are available for public inspection in the public reference room at the home office. Much of the information also is available in its New York, Chicago, and Los Angeles regional offices, and to a lesser extent in the other regional offices of the commission. Reproduction of the public material may be purchased from the commission at prescribed rates.

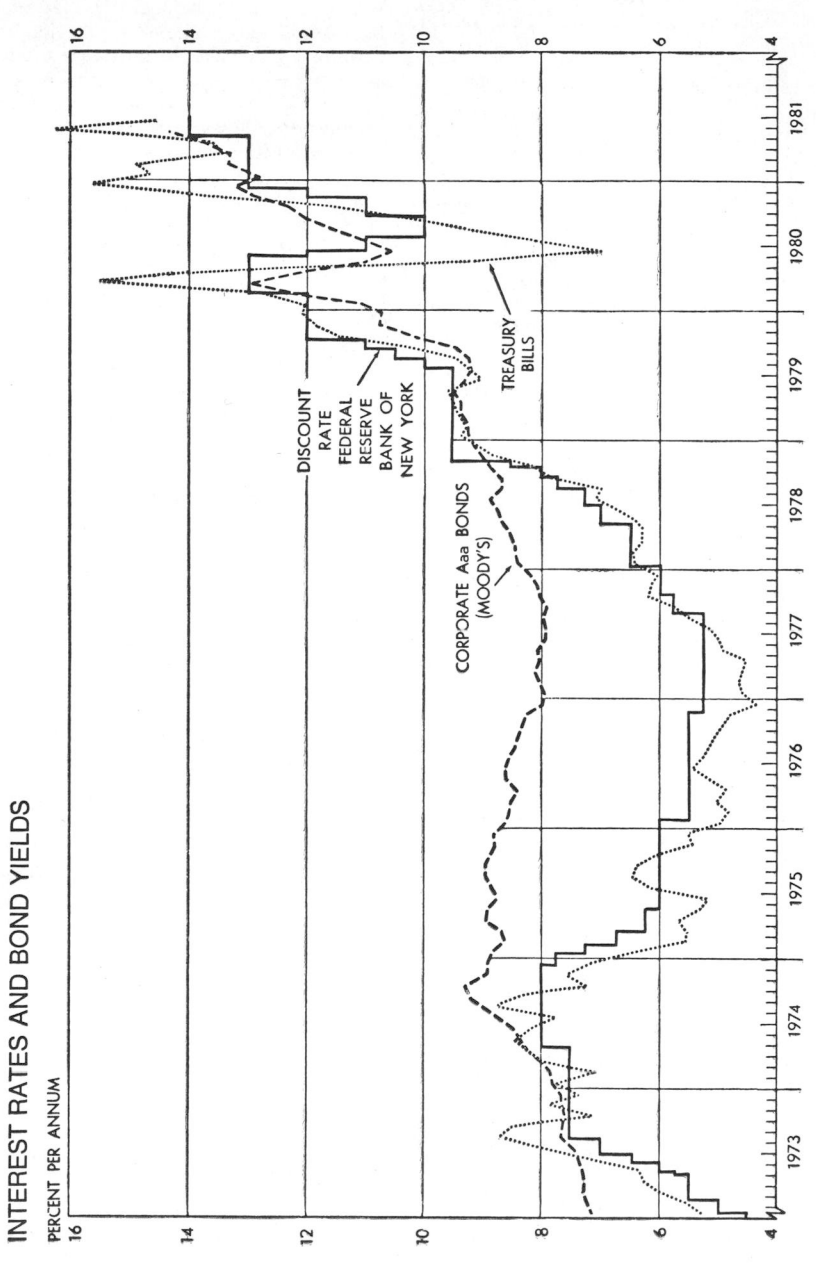

INTEREST RATES AND BOND YIELDS

PERCENT PER ANNUM

DISCOUNT RATE FEDERAL RESERVE BANK OF NEW YORK

TREASURY BILLS

CORPORATE Aaa BONDS (MOODY'S)

[Percent per annum]

Period	U.S. Treasury security yields			High-grade municipal bonds (Standard & Poor's) [3]	Corporate Aaa bonds (Moody's) [3]	Prime commercial paper, 4-6 months [4]	Discount rate (N.Y. F.R. Bank) [5]	Prime rate charged by banks [5]	New-home mortgage yields (FHLBB) [6]
	3-month bills [1]	Constant maturities [2]							
		3-year	10-year						
1975	5.838	7.49	7.99	6.89	8.83	6.33	6.25	7.86	9.01
1976	4.989	6.77	7.61	6.49	8.43	5.35	5.50	6.84	8.99
1977	5.265	6.69	7.42	5.56	8.02	5.60	5.46	6.83	9.01
1978	7.221	8.29	8.41	5.90	8.73	7.99	7.46	9.06	9.54
1979	10.041	9.71	9.44	6.39	9.63	[4]10.91	10.28	12.67	10.77
1980	11.506	11.55	11.46	8.51	11.94	12.29	11.77	15.27	12.65
1980: May	9.150	9.44	10.18	7.37	10.99	9.29	13-12	*18½-14	13.68
June	6.995	8.91	9.78	7.60	10.58	8.03	12-11	14-12	12.66
July	8.126	9.27	10.25	8.08	11.07	8.29	11-10	12-11	12.48
Aug	9.259	10.63	11.10	8.62	11.64	9.61	10-11	11-11½	12.25
Sept	10.321	11.57	11.51	8.95	12.02	11.04	10-11	11½-13	12.35
Oct	11.580	12.01	11.75	9.11	12.31	12.32	11-11	13½-14½	12.61
Nov	13.888	13.31	12.68	9.55	12.97	14.73	11-12	14½-17¾	13.04
Dec	15.661	13.65	12.84	10.09	13.21	16.49	12-13	17¾-21½	13.26
1981: Jan	14.724	13.01	12.57	9.65	12.81	15.10	13-13	21½-20	13.28
Feb	14.905	13.65	13.19	10.03	13.35	14.87	13-13	20-19	13.54
Mar	13.478	13.51	13.12	10.12	13.33	13.59	13-13	19-17½	14.02
Apr	13.635	14.09	13.68	10.55	13.88	14.17	13-13	17½-18	14.15
May	16.295	15.08	14.10	10.73	14.32	16.66	13-14	18-20½	14.15
June	14.557						14-	20½-	
Week ended:									
1981: May 23	16.034	15.05	13.92	10.63	14.18	16.70	14-14	19½-20½	
30	16.750	14.55	13.61	10.55	14.00	15.79	14-14	20½-20½	
June 6	15.456	14.42	13.53	10.52	13.84	15.72	14-14	20½-20	
13	14.982	14.16	13.34	10.50	13.73	15.12	14-14	20-20	
20	13.451	14.15	13.29	10.58	13.61	14.90	14-14	20-20	
27	14.337	14.39	13.61	10.65	13.77	15.12	14-14	20-20	

[1] Rate on new issues within period; bank-discount basis.

[2] Yields on the more actively traded issues adjusted to constant maturities by the Treasury Department.

[3] Weekly data are Wednesday figures.

[4] Beginning November 1, 1979, data are for 6 months paper.

[5] Average effective rate for year; opening and closing rate for month and week.

Source: Economic Indicators, Council of Economic Advisers.

[6] Effective rate (in the primary market) on conventional mortgages, reflecting fees and charges as well as contract rate and assumed, on the average, repayment at end of 10 years. Rates beginning January 1973 not strictly comparable with prior rates.

*On May 1, 1980 range of 18½-19 was in effect.

Sources: Department of the Treasury, Board of Governors of the Federal Reserve System, Federal Home Loan Bank Board, Moody's Investors Service, and Standard & Poor's Corporation.

SHORT-TERM INTEREST RATES
MONTHLY AVERAGES OF DAILY FIGURES

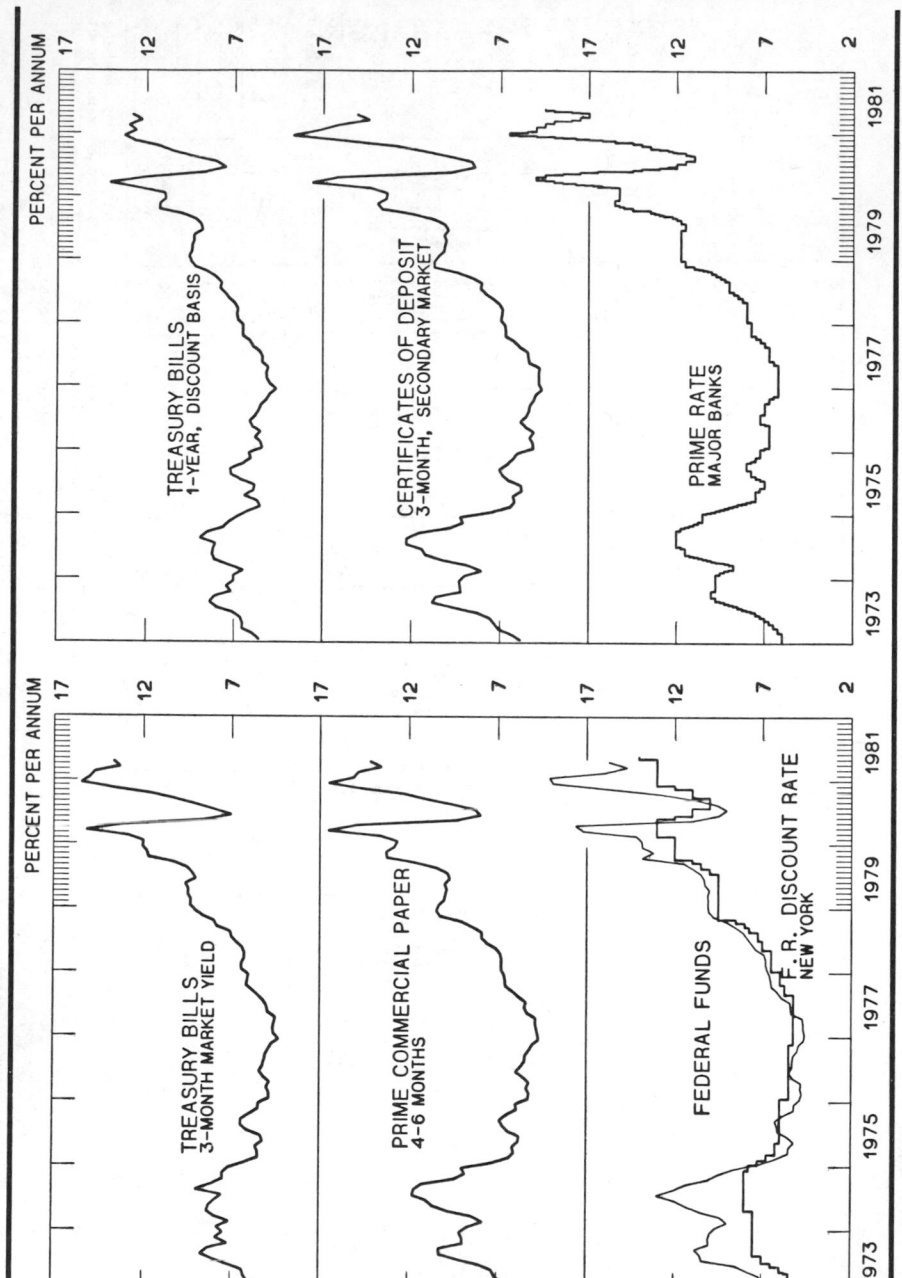

Source: *Federal Reserve Chart Book*, Board of Governors of the Federal Reserve System.

LONG-TERM INTEREST RATES

MONTHLY AVERAGES

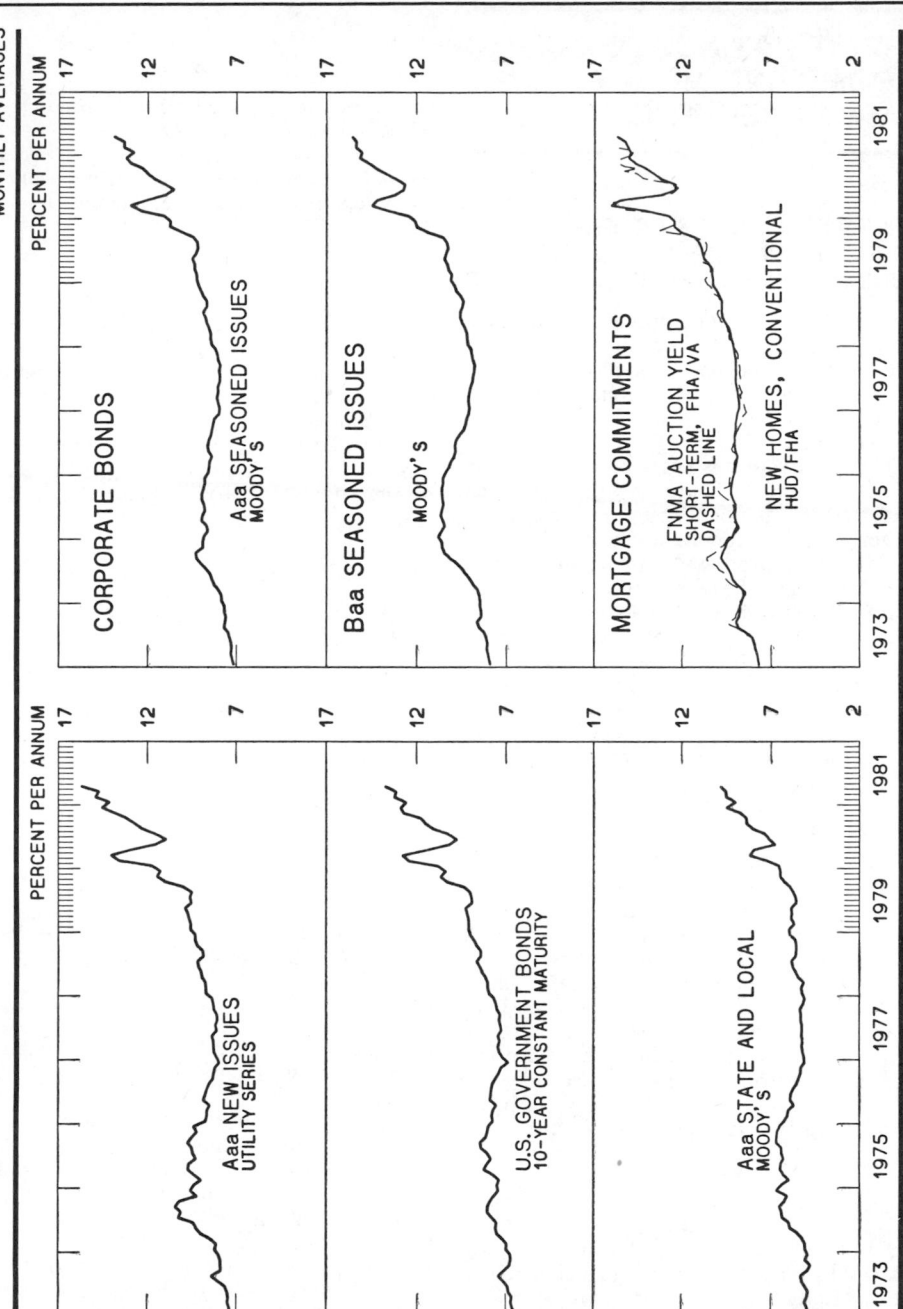

CORPORATE BONDS

Aaa SEASONED ISSUES
MOODY'S

Baa SEASONED ISSUES

MOODY'S

MORTGAGE COMMITMENTS

FNMA AUCTION YIELD
SHORT-TERM, FHA/VA
DASHED LINE

NEW HOMES, CONVENTIONAL
HUD/FHA

PERCENT PER ANNUM

Aaa NEW ISSUES
UTILITY SERIES

U.S. GOVERNMENT BONDS
10-YEAR CONSTANT MATURITY

Aaa STATE AND LOCAL
MOODY'S

Source: Federal Reserve Chart Book, Board of Governors of the Federal Reserve System.

CREDIT RATINGS OF FIXED INCOME AND MONEY MARKET SECURITIES

KEY TO STANDARD & POOR'S CORPORATION CORPORATE AND MUNICIPAL BOND RATING DEFINITIONS

A Standard & Poor's corporate or municipal bond rating is a current assessment of the creditworthiness of an obligor with respect to a specific debt obligation. This assessment may take into consideration obligors such as guarantors, insurers, or lessees.

The bond rating is not a recommendation to purchase, sell or hold a security, inasmuch as it does not comment as to market price or suitability for a particular investor.

The ratings are based on current information furnished by the issuer or obtained by Standard & Poor's from other sources it considers reliable. Standard & Poor's does not perform an audit in connection with any rating and may, on occasion, rely on unaudited financial information. The ratings may be changed, suspended or withdrawn as a result of changes in, or unavailability of, such information, or for other circumstances.

The ratings are based, in varying degrees, on the following considerations:

I. Likelihood of default—capacity and willingness of the obligor as to the timely payment of interest and repayment of principal in accordance with the terms of the obligation;

II. Nature of and provisions of the obligation;

III. Protection afforded by, and relative position of, the obligation in the event of bankruptcy, reorganization or other arrangement under the laws of bankruptcy and other laws affecting creditors' rights.

AAA

Bonds rated **AAA** have the highest rating assigned by Standard & Poor's to a debt obligation. Capacity to pay interest and repay principal is extremely strong.

AA

Bonds rated **AA** have a very strong capacity to pay interest and repay principal and differ from the highest rated issues only in small degree.

Source: From Standard & Poor's Debt Rating Division.

A

Bonds rated **A** have a strong capacity to pay interest and repay principal although they are somewhat more susceptible to the adverse effects of changes in circumstances and economic conditions than bonds in higher rated categories.

BBB

Bonds rated **BBB** are regarded as having an adequate capacity to pay interest and repay principal. Whereas they normally exhibit adequate protection parameters, adverse economic conditions or changing circumstances are more likely to lead to a weakened capacity to pay interest and repay principal for bonds in this category than for bonds in higher rated categories.

BB, B, CCC, CC

Bonds rated **BB, B, CCC,** and **CC** are regarded, on balance, as predominantly speculative with respect to capacity to pay interest and repay principal in accordance with the terms of the obligation. **BB** indicates the lowest degree of speculation and **CC** the highest degree of speculation. While such bonds will likely have some quality and protective characteristics, these are outweighed by large uncertainties or major risk exposures to adverse conditions.

C

The rating **C** is reserved for income bonds on which no interest is being paid.

D

Bonds rated **D** are in default, and payment of interest and/or repayment of principal is in arrears.

Plus (+) or minus (−)—The ratings from **AA** to **BB** may be modified by the addition of a plus or minus sign to show relative standing within the major rating categories.

Provisional ratings—The letter p indicates that the rating is provisional. A provisional rating assumes the successful completion of the project being financed by the bonds being rated and indicates that payment of debt service requirements is largely or entirely dependent upon the successful and timely completion of the project. This rating, however, while addressing credit quality subsequent to completion of the project, makes no comment on the likelihood of, or the risk of default upon failure of, such completion. The investor should exercise his own judgment with respect to such likelihood and risk.

NR

Indicates that no rating has been requested, that there is insufficient information on which to base a rating or that S&P does not rate a particular type of obligation as a matter of policy.

Debt Obligations of issuers outside the United States and its territories are rated on the same basis as domestic corporate and municipal issues. The ratings measure the creditworthiness of the obligor but do not take into account currency exchange and other uncertainties.

Bond Investment Quality Standards—Under present commerical bank regulations issued by the Comptroller of the Currency, bonds rated in the top four categories (**AAA, AA, A, BBB,** commonly known as "Investment Grade" ratings) are generally regarded as eligible for bank investment. In addition, the Legal Investment Laws of various states impose certain rating or other standards for obligations eligible for investment by savings banks, trust companies, insurance companies and fiduciaries generally.

KEY TO STANDARD & POOR'S PREFERRED STOCK RATING DEFINITIONS

A Standard & Poor's preferred stock rating is an assessment of the capacity and willingness of an issuer to pay preferred stock dividends and any applicable sinking fund obligations. A preferred stock rating differs from a bond rating inasmuch as it is assigned to an equity issue, which issue is intrinsically different from, and subordinated to, a debt issue. Therefore, to reflect this difference, the preferred stock rating symbol will normally not be higher than the bond rating symbol assigned to, or that would be assigned to, the senior debt of the same issuer.

The preferred stock ratings are based on the following considerations:

I. Likelihood of payment—capacity and willingness of the issuer to meet the timely payment of preferred stock dividends and any applicable sinking fund requirements in accordance with the terms of the obligation.
II. Nature of, and provisions of, the issue.
III. Relative position of the issue in the event of bankruptcy, reorganization, or other arrangements affecting creditors' rights.

AAA

This is the highest rating that may be assigned by Standard & Poor's to a preferred stock issue and indicates in extremely strong capacity to pay the preferred stock obligations.

AA

A preferred stock issue rated **AA** also qualifies as a high-quality fixed income security. The capacity to pay preferred stock obligations is very strong, although not as overwhelming as for issues rated **AAA.**

A

An issue rated **A** is backed by a sound capacity to pay the preferred stock obligations, although it is somewhat more susceptible to the adverse effects of changes in circumstances and economic conditions.

BBB

An issue rated **BBB** is regarded as backed by an adequate capacity to pay the preferred stock obligations. Whereas it normally exhibits adequate protection parameters, adverse economic conditions or changing circumstances are more likely to lead to a weakened capacity to make payments for a preferred stock in this category than for issues in the **A** category.

BB, B, CCC

Preferred stock rated **BB, B,** and **CCC** are regarded, on balance, as predominately speculative with respect to the issuer's capacity to pay preferred stock obligations. **BB** indicates the lowest degree of speculation and **CCC** the highest degree of speculation. While such issues will likely have some quality and protective characteristics, these are outweighed by large uncertainties or major risk exposures to adverse conditions.

CC

The rating **CC** is reserved for a preferred stock issue in arrears on dividends or sinking fund payments but that is currently paying.

C

A preferred stock rated **C** is a non-paying issue.

D

A preferred stock rated **D** is a non-paying issue with the issuer in default on debt instruments.

NR indicates that no rating has been requested, that there is insufficient information on which to base a rating, or that S&P does not rate a particular type of obligation as a matter of policy.

Plus (+) or Minus (−) To provide more detailed indications of preferred stock quality, the ratings from **AA** to **B** may be modified by the addition of a plus or minus sign to show relative standing within the major rating categories.

The preferred stock rating is not a recommendation to purchase or sell a security, inasmuch as market price is not considered in arriving at the rating. Preferred stock *ratings* are wholly unrelated to Standard & Poor's earnings and dividend *rankings* for common stocks.

The ratings are based on current information furnished to Standard & Poor's by the issuer, and obtained by Standard & Poor's from other sources it considers reliable. The ratings may be changed, suspended, or withdrawn as a result of changes in, or unavailability of, such information.

Standard & Poor's Corporation receives compensation for rating securities. Such compensation is based on the work done and is paid either by issuers of such securities or by the underwriters participating in the distribution thereof. The fees generally vary from $1,500 to $20,000 for corporate securities.

KEY TO STANDARD & POOR'S COMMERCIAL PAPER RATING DEFINITIONS

A Standard & Poor's Commercial Paper Rating is a current assessment of the likelihood of timely payment of debt having an original maturity of no more than 365 days.

Ratings are graded into four categories, ranging from A for the highest quality obligations to D for the lowest. The four categories are as follows:

A

Issues assigned this highest rating are regarded as having the greatest capacity for timely payment. Issues in this category are further refined with the designations 1, 2, and 3 to indicate the relative degree of safety.

A-1 This designation indicates that the degree of safety regarding timely payment is very strong.

A-2 Capacity for timely payment on issues with this designation is strong. However, the relative degree of safety is not as overwhelming as for issues designated A-1.

A-3 Issues carrying this designation have a satisfactory capacity for timely payment. They are, however, somewhat more vulnerable to the adverse effects of changes in circumstances than obligations carrying the higher designations.

B

Issues rated B are regarded as having only an adequate capacity for timely payment. However, such capacity may be damaged by changing conditions for short-term adversities.

C

This rating is assigned to short-term obligations with a doubtful capacity for payment.

D

This rating indicates that the issue is either a default or is expected to be in default upon maturity.

The Commercial Paper Rating is not a recommendation to purchase or sell a security. The rating applies only to the actual debt securities being rated and not to any other debt obligations of the same issuer. The ratings are based on current information furnished to Standard & Poor's by the issuer and obtained by Standard & Poor's from other sources it considers reliable. The ratings may be changed, suspended, or withdrawn as a result of changes in, or unavailability of, such information.

KEY TO MOODY'S MUNICIPAL RATINGS

Aaa

Bonds which are rated Aaa are judged to be of the best quality. They carry the smallest

---

General Note: Those bonds in the A and Baa groups which Moody's believes possess the strongest investment attributes are designated by the symbols A 1 and Baa 1. Other A and Baa bonds comprise the balance of their respective groups. These rankings (1) designate the bonds which offer the maximum in security within their quality group, (2) designate bonds which can be bought for possible upgrading in quality and (3) additionally afford the investor an opportunity to gauge more precisely the relative attractiveness of offerings in the market place.

Generally speaking, bonds in Moody's highest rating categories can be characterized as follows: Aaa obligations, their safety is so absolute that with the occasional exception of oversupply in a few specific instances, characteristically, their market value is affected solely by money market fluctuations; Aa bonds, their market value is virtually immune to all but money market influences, with the occasional exception of oversupply in a few specific instances; A-rated bonds may be influenced to some degree by economic performance during a sustained period of depressed business conditions but during periods of normalcy A-rated bonds frequently move in parallel with Aaa and Aa obligations, with the occasional exception of oversupply in a few specific instances; Baa-rated are more sensitive to changes in economic circumstances, and aside from occasional speculative factors applying to some bonds of this class, Baa issues will move in parallel with Aaa, Aa, and A obligations during periods of economic normalcy, except in instances of oversupply; Ba bonds are speculative, their market value may be affected by varying economic circumstances not necessarily geared to the business cycle; B-rated bonds are usually quite sensitive to day-to-day circumstances affecting the borrower's ability to service debt on schedule, especially during down trending economic cycle; Caa bonds reflect the market's concept of the probability and imminence of a workout; Ca bonds are speculative in high degree and usually indicate nominal workout value; and C-rated bonds appear to be hopelessly in default and usually have only a nominal speculative market value.

Unless otherwise noted, municipal ratings are for "general obligations" which are defined as validly issued and legally binding evidences of indebtedness secured by the full faith, credit and taxing powers of the issuer.

Source: Moody's Investors Service, Inc.

degree of investment risk and are generally referred to as "gilt edge." Interest payments are protected by a large or by an exceptionally stable margin and principal is secure. While the various protective elements are likely to change, such changes as can be visualized are most unlikely to impair the fundamentally strong position of such issues.

Aa

Bonds which are rated **Aa** are judged to be of high quality by all standards. Together with the **Aaa** group they comprise what are generally known as high grade bonds. They are rated lower than the best bonds because margins of protection may not be as large as in **Aaa** securities or fluctuation of protective elements may be of greater amplitude or there may be other elements present which make the long term risks appear somewhat larger than in **Aaa** securities.

A

Bonds which are rated **A** possess many favorable investment attributes and are to be considered as upper medium grade obligations. Factors giving security to principal and interest are considered adequate, but elements may be present which suggest a susceptibility to impairment sometime in the future. See general note on preceding page.

Baa

Bonds which are rated **Baa** are considered as medium grade obligations; i.e., they are neither highly protected nor poorly secured. Interest payments and principal security appear adequate for the present but certain protective elements may be lacking or may be characteristically unreliable over any great length of time. Such bonds lack outstanding investment characteristics and in fact have speculative characteristics as well. See general note on preceding page.

Ba

Bonds which are rated **Ba** are judged to have speculative elements; their future cannot be considered as well assured. Often the protection of interest and principal payments may be very moderate, and thereby not well safeguarded during both good and bad times over the future. Uncertainty of position characterizes bonds in this class.

B

Bonds which are rated **B** generally lack characteristics of the desirable investment. Assurance of interest and principal payments or of maintenance of other terms of the contract over any long period of time may be small.

Caa

Bonds which are rated **Caa** are of poor standing. Such issues may be in default or there may be present elements of danger with respect to principal or interest.

Ca

Bonds which are rated **Ca** represent obligations which are speculative in a high degree. Such issues are often in default or have other marked shortcomings.

C

Bonds which are rated **C** are the lowest rated class of bonds, and issues so rated can be regarded as having extremely poor prospects of ever attaining any real investment standing.

Con.(—)

Bonds for which the security depends upon the completion of some act or the fulfillment of some condition are rated conditionally. These are bonds secured by (a) earnings of projects under construction, (b) earnings of projects unseasoned in operation experience, (c) rentals which begin when facilities are completed, or (d) payments to which some other limiting condition attaches. Parenthetical rating denotes probable credit stature upon completion of construction or elimination of basis of condition.

KEY TO MOODY'S CORPORATE RATINGS

Aaa

Bonds which are rated **Aaa** are judged to be of the best quality. They carry the smallest degree of investment risk and are generally referred to as "gilt edge." Interest payments are protected by a large or by an exceptionally stable margin and principal is secure. While the various protective elements are likely to change, such changes as can be visualized are most unlikely to impair the fundamentally strong position of such issues.

Aa

Bonds which are rated **Aa** are judged to be of high quality by all standards. Together with the **Aaa** group they comprise what are generally known as high grade bonds. They are rated lower than the best bonds because margins of protection may not be as large as in **Aaa** securities or fluctuation of protective elements may be of greater amplitude or there may be other elements present which make the long term risks appear somewhat larger than in **Aaa** securities.

A

Bonds which are rated **A** possess many favorable investment attributes and are to be considered as upper medium grade obligations. Factors giving security to principal and interest are considered adequate but elements may be present which suggest a susceptibility to impairment sometime in the future.

Baa

Bonds which are rated **Baa** are considered as medium grade obligations, i.e., they are neither highly protected nor poorly secured. Interest payments and principal security appear adequate for the present but certain protective elements may be lacking or may be characterisically unreliable over any great length of time. Such bonds lack outstanding investment characteristics and in fact have speculative characteristics as well.

Ba

Bonds which are rated **Ba** are judged to have speculative elements; their future cannot be considered as well assured. Often the protection of interest and principal payments may be very moderate and thereby not well safeguarded during both good and bad times over the future. Uncertainty of position characterizes bonds in this class.

B

Bonds which are rated **B** generally lack characteristics of the desirable investment. Assurance of interest and principal payments or of maintenance of other terms of the contract over any long period of time may be small.

Caa

Bonds which are rated **Caa** are of poor standing. Such issues may be in default or there may be present elements of danger with respect to principal or interest.

Ca

Bonds which are rated **Ca** represent obligations which are speculative in a high degree. Such issues are often in default or have other marked shortcomings.

C

Bonds which are rated **C** are the lowest rated class of bonds and issues so rated can be regarded as having extremely poor prospects of ever attaining any real investment standing.

KEY TO MOODY'S COMMERCIAL PAPER RATINGS*

Moody's Commercial Paper ratings are opinions of the ability of issuers to repay punctually promissory obligations not having an original maturity in excess of nine months. Moody's makes no representation that such obligations are exempt from registration under the Securities Act of 1933, nor does it represent that any specific note is a valid obligation of a rated issuer or issued in conformity with any applicable law. Moody's employs the following three designations, all judged to be investment grade, to indicate the relative repayment capacity of rated issuers:

Prime-1	Highest Quality
Prime-2	Higher Quality
Prime-3	High Quality

If an issuer represents to Moody's that its Commercial Paper obligations are supported by the credit of another entity or entities, the name or names of such supporting entity or entities are listed within parenthesis beneath the name of the issuer. In assigning ratings to such issuers, Moody's evaluates the financial strength of the indicated affiliated corporations, commercial banks, insurance companies, foreign governments or other entities, but only as one factor in the total rating assessment. Moody's makes no representation and gives no opinion on the legal validity or enforceability of any support arrangement. You are cautioned to review with your counsel any questions regarding particular support arrangements.

KEY TO MOODY'S PREFERRED STOCK RATINGS

Moody's Rating Policy Review Board Extended its rating services to include quality designations on preferred stocks on October 1, 1973. The decision to rate preferred stocks, which Moody's had done prior to 1935, was prompted by evidence of investor interest. Moody's believes that its rating of preferred stocks is especially appropriate in view of the ever-increasing amount of these securities outstanding, and the fact that continuing inflation and its ramifications have resulted generally in the dilution of some of the protection afforded them as well as other fixed-income securities.

---

* The term "Commercial Paper" as used by Moody's means promissory obligations not having an original maturity in excess of nine months. Moody's makes no representation as to whether such Commercial Paper is by any other definition "Commercial Paper" or is exempt from registration under the Securities Act of 1933, as amended.

Source: Moody's Investors Service, Inc.

Because of the fundamental differences between preferred stocks and bonds, a variation of our familiar bond rating symbols is being used in the quality ranking of preferred stocks. The symbols, presented below, are designed to avoid comparison with bond quality in absolute terms. It should always be borne in mind that preferred stocks occupy a junior position to bonds within a particular capital structure.

Preferred stock rating symbols and their definitions are as follows:

aaa

An issue which is rated aaa is considered to be a top-quality preferred stock. This rating indicates good asset protection and the least risk of dividend impairment within the universe of preferred stocks.

aa

An issue which is rated aa is considered a high-grade preferred stock. This rating indicates that there is reasonable assurance that earnings and asset protection will remain relatively well maintained in the foreseeable future.

a

An issue which is rated a is considered to be an upper-medium grade preferred stock. While risks are judged to be somewhat greater than in the "aaa" and "aa" classifications, earnings and asset protection are, nevertheless, expected to be maintained at adequate levels.

baa

An issue which is rated baa is considered to be medium grade, neither highly protected nor poorly secured. Earnings and asset protection appear adequate at present but may be questionable over any great length of time.

ba

An issue which is rated ba is considered to have speculative elements and its future cannot be considered well assured. Earnings and asset protection may be very moderate and not well safeguarded during adverse periods. Uncertainty of position characterizes preferred stocks in this class.

b

An issue which is rated b generally lacks the characteristics of a desirable investment. Assurance of dividend payments and maintenance of other terms of the issue over any long period of time may be small.

caa

An issue which is rated caa is likely to be in arrears on dividend payments. This rating designation does not purport to indicate the future status of payments.

KEY TO CUMULATIVE INDEX OF SHORT-TERM LOAN RATINGS

Moody's ratings for state and municipal notes and other short-term loans are designated Moody's Investment Grade (MIG). This distinction is in recognition of the differences between short-term credit risk and long-term risk. Factors affecting the liquidity of the borrower are uppermost in importance in short-term borrowing, while various factors of the first importance in bond risk are of lesser importance in the short run. Symbols used are as follows:

MIG 1

Loans bearing this designation are of the best quality, enjoying strong protection from established cash flows of funds of their servicing or from established and broad-based access to the market for refinancing, or both.

MIG 2

Loans bearing this designation are of high quality, with margins of protection ample although not so large as in the preceding group.

MIG 3

Loans bearing this designation are of favorable quality, with all security elements accounted for but lacking the undeniable strength of the preceding grades. Market access for refinancing, in particular, is likely to be less well established.

MIG 4

Loans bearing this designation are of adequate quality, carrying specific risk but having protection commonly regarded as required of an investment security and not distinctly or predominantly speculative.

All state and municipal short-term loan or note ratings in effect are listed below. Issues are identified by date of issue, date of maturity or maturities, and description to distinguish each issue from other issues. The rating of any given issue carries no implications as to any other similar issue of the same obligor. Only issues listed below are rated. Ratings terminate at retirement of the note and may be withdrawn for failure to provide current information or for other reasons.

MAJOR MONEY MARKET AND FIXED INCOME SECURITIES

Type	Interest: When Paid	Marketability	Minimum Amount of Issue	Maturity
A. Interest Fully Taxable				
Corporate Bonds and Notes	S[1]	Very good to poor depending on quality	$1,000	1 to 50 years
Corporate Preferred Stock (Pays dividends as a fixed percentage of face value. Dividends not obligatory, but if declared must be paid before that of the common stock. Dividends fully taxable for individuals, but 85% exempt from federal tax for corporations)	Generally quarterly	Good to poor depending on quality	$100 or less	No maturity
Federal Home Loan Mortgage Corporate Bonds	S	Fair	$25,000	Up to 25 years
Federal Home Loan Mortgage Certificates	S	Fair	$100,000	Up to 3 years
Farmers' Home Administration Notes and Certificates	Annual	Fair	$25,000	1 to 25 years
Federal Housing Administration Debentures (Guaranteed by the U.S. Government)	S	Very good	$50	1 to 40 years
Federal National Mortgage Association Bonds	S	Fair	$25,000	2 to 25 years
Government National Mortgage Modified Pass through Certificates (interest plus some repayment of principal, guaranteed by U.S. Government)	Monthly	Good	$25,000	30 years; average life 12 years
Federal Home Loan Bank Bonds and Notes	S	Good	$10,000	1 to 20 years
Export-Import Bank Debentures and Certificates	S	Good	$5,000	3 to 7 years
International Bank for Reconstruction Development (World Bank), Inter-American Development Bank, Asia Development Bank	S	Fair to poor	$1,000	3 to 25 years
Foreign and Eurodollar Bonds and Notes	May be Annual or S	Poor	$1,000 (amounts vary in foreign currencies)	1 to 30 years
Bankers Acceptances (short-term debt obligations (resulting from international trade and guaranteed by a major bank)	Discounted[2] on a 360-day year basis	Fair	$5,000	1 to 270 days
Commercial Paper (short-term debt issued by a major corporation)	Discounted on a 360-day year basis	No secondary market	$100,000 (occasionally smaller)	1 to 270 days
Negotiable Certificates of Deposit (short-term debt issued by banks and which can be sold on the open market)	Interest paid on maturity; 360-day year basis	Fair	$100,000 (occasionally smaller)	30 days to 1 year
Non-negotiable Certificate of Deposit (savings certificates)	Interest paid on maturity; 360-day year basis	Non-negotiable	$500 $10,000	30 months 6 months
Repurchase Agreements (generally short term loans by large investors, secured by U.S. Government or other high quality issues)[3]	Interest paid on maturity; 360-day year basis	No secondary market	$100,000	1 to 30 days (sometimes more)

Type	Interest: When Paid	Marketability	Minimum Amount of Issue	Maturity
B. *Interest Exempt from State and Local Income Taxes*				
U.S. Treasury Bonds and Notes	S	Very good	$1,000	1 to 20 years
U.S. Treasury Bills	Discounted on a 360-day basis	Very good	$10,000	90 days to 1 year
U.S. Series EE Savings Bonds	Issued at discount, full interest, paid on maturity	No secondary market: available for resale	$50 minimum $15,000 maximum	11 years (can be redeemed before maturity at reduced yields
U.S. Series HH Savings Bonds	S	No secondary market	$500 $15,000 maximum	10 years
Federal Land Bank Bonds	S	Good	$1,000	1 to 10 years
Federal Financing Bank Notes and Bonds	S	Good	$1,000	1 to 20 years
Tennessee Valley Authority Notes and Bonds	S	Fair	$1,000	5 to 25 years
Banks for Cooperatives Bonds	Interest: 360-day year basis	Good	$5,000	180 days
Federal Intermediate Credit Bank Bonds	Interest: 360-day year basis	Good	$5,000.	270 days
Federal Home Loan Bank Notes and Bonds	Discounted: 360-day year basis	Good	$10,000.	30 to 360-day year basis (some more)
Farm Credit Bank Notes and Bonds	Interest: 360-day year basis	Good	$50,000.	270 days (some more)
C. *Interest Exempt from Federal Income Tax*				
State and Local Notes and Bonds (in-State issues, usually exempt from State and local income taxes)	S	Good to fair depending on rating	$5,000.	1 to 50 years
Housing Authority Bonds (in-State issues usually exempt from State and local income taxes)	S	Good to fair	$5,000.	1 to 40 years
Tax Exempt Saving Certificates[4]	Annual	No secondary market	$500	1 year

[1] S means semiannually.

[2] A discount means interest paid in advance, thus a 10% discounted security maturing at $10,000 would cost $9,000 to purchase.

[3] Recently some banks have issued repurchase agreements for smaller amounts of money, i.e., several thousands of dollars.

[4] The 1981 tax law provides for tax exemptions of $1,000 ($2,000 on a joint return) of interest received. Certificates are one year obligations paying interest at rates equal to 70% of the rate on the most recently issued 52 Treasury bills. The certificates are issued by banks and Credit Unions.

U.S. TREASURY BONDS, NOTES, AND BILLS: TERMS DEFINED*

U.S. Treasury bonds, notes and bills are interest paying securities representing a debt on the part of the U.S. Government. Treasury bonds have a maturity of over 5 years, while notes mature within 5 to 7 years. Bills are discussed below. Both Treasury bonds and notes are generally issued in minimum denominations of $1,000 and pay interest semiannually. The amount of semiannual interest paid is determined by the coupon rate specified on the bond and is calculated on a 365-day year basis. For a $1,000 face value* bond the interest is given by:

semiannual interest = $1/2$ ($1,000 × coupon rate)

Bonds may be priced higher (at a premium) or lower (at a discount) than the face value (par) depending on current interest rates. The *current yield* is the rate the investor receives based on the prices actually paid for a bond. The price is given by:

$$\text{current yield} = \frac{\$1,000 \times \text{coupon rate}}{\text{purchase price}}$$

Thus, a $1,000 face value bond with an 8% coupon rate purchased at $850 has a current yield by:

$$\text{current yield} = \frac{\$1,000 \times 8\%}{\$850} = 9.41\%$$

The *yield to maturity* (YTM) is the yield obtained on taking into account the years remaining to maturity, annual interest payments, and the capital gain (or loss) realized at maturity. It is obtained from special tables.

However, the yield to maturity (YTM) may be found approximately from the formula

$$\text{YTM} = \frac{I + A}{B}$$

I = annual interest rate

$$A = \frac{\$1,000 - M}{N}$$

$$B = \frac{\$1,000 + M}{2}$$

where M = current market price of the bond
N = years remaining to maturity

As an example, a bond ($1,000 face value) has a 10% coupon and is currently priced at $1,100 with 10 years remaining to maturity. What is the approximate YTM?

$I = \$1,000 \times .1 = \$100$ interest per year

$$A = \frac{\$1,000 - \$1,100}{10} = \$ - 10$$

$$B = \frac{\$1,000 + \$1,100}{2} = \$1,050$$

$$\text{YTM} = \frac{\$100 - \$10}{\$1,050} = .0857 = 8.57\%$$

U.S. Treasury bills (T-bills) are U.S. Government debt obligations which mature within one year. They are offered by the Federal Reserve Bank with maturities of 90 days (3 month bills) and 182 days (six month bills). Nine-month bills and one-year bills are also available. Treasury bills are sold in a minimum denomination of $10,000. Interest is paid by the discount method based on a 360-day year. With the discount method, interest is, in effect, paid at the time the bill is purchased. Thus a 91-day $10,000 bill (face value) with an 8% discount interest rate would provide the buyer with $202.22 ($10,000 × .08 × $91/360$) interest at the time of purchase. This amount is deducted from the face value of the bill at the time of purchase so the buyer actually pays a net amount of $9,797.78 ($10,000 − $202.22). When the bill matures, the buyer receives $10,000 on redemption.

Since T-bills pay interest at the time of purchase (discount basis) on a 360-day year basis, while bonds (and notes) pay interest semiannually on a 365-day year basis, the two rates cannot be compared directly. To compare the two rates, the discount rate must be converted to the so-called *bond equivalent yield*, given by

$$\text{bond equivalent yield} = \frac{365 \times \text{discount rate}}{360 - (\text{discount rate} \times \text{days to maturity})}$$

As an example, a newly issued 91-day note with a discount rate of 12% has a

$$\text{bond equivalent yield} = \frac{365 \times (.12)}{360 - (.12 \times 91)} = 12.55\%$$

Interest from U.S. Treasury bonds, notes, and bills are subject to federal income tax, but are exempt from state and local income taxes.

---

* The terms *current yield, yield to maturity,* etc. defined in this section are generally applicable to all fixed incomes.

* Face value is the amount of the bond or note payable upon maturity.

HOW TO READ U.S. GOVERNMENT BOND AND NOTE QUOTATIONS

TREASURY BONDS AND NOTES

(1) Rate	(2) Mat.	(3) Date	(4) Bid	(5) Asked	(6) Bid Chg.	(7) Yld.
6¾s,	1981	Jun n ...	99.3	99.7	+ .1	16.51
9⅛s,	1981	Jun n ...	99.12	99.16	+ .2	15.10
9⅜s,	1981	Jul n	98.21	98.25	+ .3	16.54
7s,	1981	Aug	97.26	98.10	+ .2	15.19
7⅝s,	1981	Aug n ...	97.30	98.2	+ .6	17.66
8⅜s,	1981	Aug n ...	98.2	98.6	+ .2	17.15
9⅝s,	1981	Aug n ...	98.5	98.9	+ .4	16.53
6¾s,	1981	Sep n ...	96.29	97.1	+ .5	16.10
10⅛s,	1981	Sep n ...	97.28	98	+ .4	16.28
12⅝s,	1981	Oct n ...	98.14	98.18	+ .4	16.18
7s,	1981	Nov n ...	96.4	96.8	+ .10	15.86
7¾s,	1981	Nov n ...	96.18	96.22	+ .13	15.55
12⅛s,	1981	Nov n ...	98.1	98.5	+ .3	16.14
7¼s,	1981	Dec n ...	95.12	95.16	+ .10	15.14

Source: Reprinted by permission of *The Wall Street Journal,* Dow Jones & Co., Inc., 1981. All rights reserved.

The above exhibit is an example of U.S. Government bond and note quotations as it appears in *The Wall Street Journal.*

(1) Indicates the coupon rate of interest which is designated by *s.* Rates are quoted to ⅛ of a percent. Thus 8⅜ means 8.375%. The semiannual interest payments are calculated, as described elsewhere, using this rate.

(2) Indicates the year of maturity.

(3) Indicates the month (of the above year) in which the bond or note matures. The letter *n* means the security is a note. Otherwise a bond is implied.

(4) The *bid price* per bond or note (the price at which the bond can be sold to the dealer), expressed as a percentage of the face value ($1,000) of the bond. Prices are quoted in terms of 1/32 of a percent. Thus 98.5 means 98 5/32. To find the dollar value of the price, convert 98 5/32 to a decimal (98 5/32 = .98156) and multiply by the face value of the bond to give $981.56 (.98156 × $1,000).

(5) The *ask price* per bond or note (the price at which the dealer will sell the bond). The dollar value is found as indicated above.

(6) The change in the bid price from the closing price of the previous day.

(7) The yield if the bond is held to maturity, based on the ask price.

Some U.S. Treasury bonds can be called back for redemption prior to maturity. These are shown with two dates (under item 2 for example)—*1993–98* indicating that the bonds mature in 1998, but may be called back and redeemed any time after 1993.

Some newspapers (such as *The New York Times*) use a slight modification of the above arrangement, though the various terms have the same meaning as defined above. Thus, a bond maturing in June of 1985 and bearing a 10⅜% coupon is indicated by *May '85 10⅜.*

HOW TO READ U.S. TREASURY BILL QUOTATIONS

(1) U.S. Treas. Mat. date	(2) Bills Bid	(3) Asked Discount	(4) Yield
-1981-			
6–18	17.62	17.44	17.69
6–25	17.15	17.03	17.33
7– 2	15.39	15.01	15.31
7– 9	15.18	15.04	15.39
7–16	15.02	14.78	15.17
7–23	14.83	14.67	15.10
7–30	14.72	14.42	14.88
8– 6	14.11	,3.89	14.36
8–13	13.94	13.72	14.22
8–20	13.94	.3.72	14.26
8–27	,3.92	13.70	14.28
9– 3	13.97	13.63	14.24
9–10	13.72	13.64	14.29
9–17	13.52	13.34	14.00
9–24	13.63	13.43	14.14
10– 1	13.74	13.54	14.30

Source: Reprinted by permission of *The Wall Street Journal,* Dow Jones & Co., Inc. 1981. All rights reserved.

The above exhibit is an example of Treasury bill quotations as it appears in *The Wall Street Journal.*

(1) The date of maturity, i.e., 6–18 means June 18, 1981.

(2) The bid price at market close quoted as a *discount* rate in percent. This bid price is the price at which the dealer will buy the bill. To convert the discount rate to a dollar price use the formula

dollar price = $10,000 − (discount rate × days to maturity × .2778)

In the above, the discount must be expressed in percent. For example, if the dealer bids 16.18% discount for a bill which will mature in 110 days, the dollar price is given by

dollar price = $10,000 − (16.18 × 110 × .2778) = $9,505.57 per bill

(3) The asked price at market close expressed as a discount rate in percent. The asked price is the price at which the dealer will sell a bill to a buyer. To convert to a dollar price use the above formula.

(4) The bond equivalent yield expressed in

percent. This is calculated (as explained elsewhere) from the asked price expressed as a discount rate. This rate is used to compare T-bill yields to that of bonds, notes and certificates of deposit.

Some newspapers (e.g., *The New York Times*) use a somewhat different arrangement, though the meaning of the terms is the same as defined above. Thus, a bill maturing on June 4, 1981, is indicated as such. Also included in some newspapers is the change in bid price expressed as a discount rate.

HOW TO READ CORPORATE BOND QUOTATIONS*

Corporate bonds are debt securities issued by private corporations. They generally have a face value (the amount due on maturity) of $1,000 and a specified interest rate (coupon rate) paid semiannually. Many corporate bonds have a *call* provision which permits the company to recall and redeem the bond after a specified date. Call privileges are usually exercised when interest rates fall sufficiently. Investors, therefore, cannot count on *locking in* high interest rates with corporate bonds. Bond quality designations used by Moody's and Standard & Poor's are given elsewhere in the Almanac (pp. 332–337).

The following is an example of price quotations for bonds traded on The New York Stock Exchange as they appear in *The Wall Street Journal.*

CORPORATION BONDS

VOLUME, $18,990,000

(1) Bonds		(2) Cur YID	(3) Vol	(4) High	(5) Low	(6) Close	(7) Net Chg.
AlaP	9s2000	14.	6	63	62	63	2
AlaP	8½s01	15.	10	57½	57½	57½	...
AlaP	8⅞s03	15.	25	60	59½	60	+ ½
AlaP	10⅞05	15.	3	72	72	72	− 2¼
AlaP	10½05	15.	12	70½	70½	70½	− 1
AlaP	12⅝10	16.	7	81¼	81⅛	81⅛	− 1⅝
AlaP	15¼10	16.	111	94⅝	93⅝	94	...
AlaP	14¾91	15.	31	97	96½	96½	...
AlaP	17⅜11	17.	99	104	103½	103¾	− ¼
Alexn	5½96	cv	34	61¾	61⅝	61¾	+ ¾
Allgl	10¾99	15.	2	70½	70½	70½	...
AllstF	8⅛87	11.	2	76⅜	76⅜	76⅜	+ 1⅞
AllstF	9⅝86	12.	10	83⅛	83	83	+ 1⅞

Source: Reprinted by permission of *The Wall Street Journal,* Dow Jones and Company, Inc. 1981.

(1) The name of the issue in abbreviated form, followed by the coupon rate of interest in percent (designated by the letter *s*), and the year in which the bond matures. The coupon rate is stated in terms of ⅛ of a percent; 9⅜ means 9.375%.

(2) This is the current yield which is calculated as stated elsewhere. (See U.S. Treasury Bonds, Notes, and Bills, p. 340.)

(3) This item is the number of bonds sold that day.

(4) This is the highest price quoted for the bond sold on that day, expressed as a percentage of face value ($1,000). To convert to dollars, express the price as a decimal and multiply by the face value of the bond. As an example:

$$58\tfrac{1}{2} = (.5850 \times \$1{,}000.) = \$585$$

(5) This is the lowest price quoted that day. It is converted into dollars as described above.

(6) This is the price at the close of the market that day.

(7) This is the change in the closing price from that of the previous day. To convert to dollars, express as a decimal and multiply by $1,000. Thus, −1⅞ means a decrease per bond of $18.75 (.01875 × $1,000) from that of the previous day.

* Yield terms are the same as those defined in the section on U.S. Treasury Bonds, Notes and Bills, p. 340.

TAX EXEMPT BONDS

Tax exempt (municipal) bonds are issued by state and local governments and are free from federal income tax on interest payments. The bonds are often issued in $5,000 denominations and pay interest semiannually. Capital gains are taxable. In addition, holders of out-of-state bonds may be subject to state and local income taxes of the state in which they reside. For example, a New York City resident holding Los Angeles municipal bonds would be subject to New York State and City income taxes on the interest.

The taxable equivalent yield of a tax exempt bond is obtained by means of the expression

$$\text{taxable equivalent yield} = \frac{\text{tax exempt yield}}{1 - (F + S + L)}$$

where

F is the federal tax bracket of the investor
S is the state tax bracket of the investor
L is the local tax bracket of the investor

Thus, an investor in the 50% federal bracket, 10% state bracket and 3% local bracket who holds a bond with a current yield of 6% which is exempt from all income taxes would enjoy a taxable equivalent yield (TEY) given by

$$\text{TEY} = \frac{6\%}{1 - (.5 + .1 + .03)} = 16.21\%$$

A taxable yield of 16.21% would be necessary to provide the same yield as the 6% current yield on the tax exempt security.

TAX EXEMPT VERSUS TAXABLE YIELDS

| tax bracket | To equal a tax-free yield of: a taxable investment has to earn: | | | | | | | | | | | |
	5½%	6%	6½%	7%	7½%	8%	8½%	9%	9½%	10%	10½%	11%
28%	7.64%	8.33%	9.03%	9.72%	10.42%	11.11%	11.81%	12.50%	13.19%	13.89%	14.58%	15.28%
30	7.86	8.57	9.29	10.00	10.71	11.43	12.14	12.86	13.57	14.29	15.00	15.71
31	7.97	8.70	9.42	10.14	10.87	11.59	12.32	13.04	13.77	14.49	15.22	15.94
32	8.09	8.82	9.56	10.29	11.03	11.76	12.50	13.24	13.97	14.71	15.44	16.18
34	8.33	9.09	9.85	10.61	11.36	12.12	12.88	13.64	14.39	15.15	15.91	16.67
36	8.59	9.38	10.16	10.94	11.72	12.50	13.28	14.06	14.84	15.63	16.41	17.19
37	8.73	9.52	10.32	11.11	11.90	12.70	13.49	14.29	15.08	15.87	16.67	17.47
39	9.02	9.84	10.66	11.48	12.30	13.11	13.93	14.75	15.57	16.39	17.21	18.03
42	9.48	10.34	11.21	12.07	12.93	13.79	14.66	15.52	16.38	17.24	18.10	18.97
43	9.65	10.53	11.40	12.28	13.16	14.04	14.91	15.79	16.67	17.54	18.42	19.30
44	9.82	10.71	11.61	12.50	13.39	14.29	15.18	16.07	16.96	17.86	18.75	19.64
46	10.19	11.11	12.03	12.96	13.89	14.81	15.74	16.67	17.59	18.52	19.44	20.37
49	10.78	11.76	12.75	13.73	14.71	15.69	16.67	17.65	18.63	19.61	20.59	21.57
54	11.96	13.04	14.13	15.22	16.30	17.39	18.48	19.57	20.65	21.74	22.83	23.91
55	12.22	13.33	14.44	15.56	16.67	17.78	18.89	20.00	21.11	22.22	23.33	24.44
59	13.41	14.63	15.85	17.07	18.29	19.51	20.73	21.95	23.17	24.39	25.61	26.83
63	14.86	16.22	17.57	18.92	20.27	21.62	22.97	24.32	25.68	27.03	28.38	29.73
64	15.28	16.67	18.06	19.44	20.83	22.22	23.61	25.00	26.39	27.78	29.17	30.56
68	17.19	18.75	20.31	21.88	23.44	25.00	26.56	28.13	29.69	31.25	32.81	34.38
70	18.33	20.00	21.67	23.33	25.00	26.67	28.33	30.00	31.67	33.33	35.00	36.67

TYPES OF TAX EXEMPT BONDS AND NOTES

General Obligation bonds, also known as GO's, are backed by a pledge of a city's or state's full faith and credit for the prompt repayment of both principal and interest. Most city, county and school district bonds are secured by a pledge of unlimited property taxes. Since general obligation bonds depend on tax resources, they are normally analyzed in terms of the size of the resources being taxed.

Revenue bonds are payable from the earnings of a revenue-producing enterprise such as a sewer, water, gas or electric system, airport, toll bridge, college dormitory, lease payments from property rented to industrial companies, and other income-producing facilities. Revenue bonds are analyzed in terms of their earnings.

Limited and Special Tax bonds are payable from the pledge of the proceeds derived by the issuer from a specific tax such as a property tax levied at a fixed rate, a special assessment, or a tax on gasoline.

Municipal notes are short term obligations maturing from 30 days to a year and are issued in anticipation of revenues coming from the sales of bonds (BANS), taxes (TANS), or other revenues (RANS).

Project notes, issued by local housing and urban renewal agencies, are backed by a U.S. Government guarantee and are also tax exempt.

HOW TO UNDERSTAND TAX EXEMPT BOND QUOTATIONS

Generally the prices of municipal bonds are quoted in terms of the yield to maturity (defined elsewhere) rather than in percentage of face value, as with other bonds. The yield to maturity can be converted to a dollar price if the years remaining to maturity and the rate of interest due are known. Certain tables used for this purpose are given in the *Basis Book* (published by the Financial Publishing Company, 82 Brookline Avenue, Boston, Massachusetts). The books list the dollar price (per $1,000 face value of the bond) corresponding to a given coupon rate, yield, and years to maturity.

Some municipal bonds, however, are quoted directly in terms of percentage of face value. Thus, a bid price (the price at which the dealer will buy the bonds from the investor) of 98⅝ for a $5,000 face value bond can be converted to a dollar price by first converting the bid to a decimal expression (.98625) and then multiplying by the face value of the bond. The result in this case is $4,931.25 (.98625 × $5,000). The same calculation applies to the ask price (the

price at which the dealer will sell the bond to the investor).

Prices of tax exempt bonds are not quoted in the daily press. They can be obtained by calling municipal bond dealers. Extensive quotations are given in some relatively expensive publications:

The Blue List
Standard & Poor's
25 Broadway
New York, New York 10004
(212–248–3377)

The Daily Bond Buyer
and
The Weekly Bond Buyer
The Bond Buyer
1 State Street
New York, New York 10004
(212–963–8200)

Bond Week (Formerly Money Manager)
Institutional Investor
488 Madison Avenue
New York, New York 10022

GOVERNMENT NATIONAL MORTGAGE ASSOCIATION (GNMA) MODIFIED PASS THROUGH CERTIFICATES

A GNMA Mortgage-Backed Security is a government-guaranteed security which is collateralized by a pool of federally-underwritten residential mortgages. The investor receives a monthly check for a proportionate share of the principal and interest on a pool of mortgages whether or not the payments have actually been collected from the borrowers.

The GNMA Mortgage-Backed Security offers the highest yield of any federally-guaranteed security. In addition, the GNMA security offers a very competitive return in comparison to private corporation debt issues. Moreover, the investor receives a monthly return on the GNMA guaranteed investment, rather than semi-annual payments as on most bonds. This monthly payment represents a cash flow available for reinvestment and has the effect of increasing the yield on GNMAs by 10 to 18 basis points (a basis point is 0.1%) when compared to the yield equivalent received on a bond investment with the same "coupon" rate but paying interest semi-annually.

On single-family securities (the most popular form) the maturity is typically 30 years. However, statistical studies have determined that the average life of a single-family security is approximately 12 years, due to prepayments of principal. Nevertheless, some of the mortgages in any pool are likely to remain outstanding for the full 30-year period.

The minimum size of original individual certificates is $25,000 with increments of $5,000 above that amount.

SELECTED BOND AND PREFERRED STOCK MUTUAL FUNDS (NO LOAD)

Alpha Income Fund
Babson (D L) Income Trust
Fidelity Corporate Bond Fund
Fund for U.S. Govt Securities
Lexington GNMA Income Fund
Liberty Fund
Mutual of Omaha American Fund
Northeast Investors Trust
T. Rowe Price New Income Fund
Steadman Associated Fund
Stein Roe Bond Fund

For addresses see page 283.

BOND AND PREFERRED STOCK FUNDS (CLOSED END)

These funds are traded on the New York Stock Exchange.

American General Capital Bond Fund
Drexel Bond-Debenture Trading Fund
Fort Dearborn Income Securities
Independence Square Income Securities
John Hancock Investors
Lincoln National Direct Placement Fund
MassMutual Corporate Investors
MassMutual Income Investors
Mutual of Omaha Interest Shares
St Paul Securities
Transamerica Income Shares
USLIFE Income Fund
Vestaur Securities

GENERAL PURPOSE MONEY FUNDS

Fund Name and Address	Phone Number	Minimum Initial Investment
American General Reserve Fund, Inc. P.O. Box 1411 Houston, TX 77001	(800) 421–5666 (213) 642–0865	$ 1,000
American Liquid Trust 99 High Street Boston, MA 02110	(800) 225–2618 (617) 338–3300	1,000
Boston Company Cash Management Fund One Boston Place Boston, MA 02117	(800) 343–6324 (617) 421–4506	2,500
Capital Preservation Fund, Inc. 755 Page Mill Road Palo Alto, CA 94304	(800) 227–8380 (Continental U.S.) (800) 982–6150 (CA)	1,000
Capital Preservation Fund II 755 Page Mill Road Palo Alto, CA 94304	(415) 858–2400 (800) 227–8380 (except CA) (800) 982–6150 (CA)	5,000
Cardinal Government Securities 155 East Broad St. Columbus, OH 43215	(614) 464–6811	2,500
Cash Management Trust of America P.O. Box 60829 Terminal Annex Los Angeles, CA 90060	(800) 421–8791 (213) 486–9562	5,000
Columbia Daily Income Co. 621 SW Morrison Street Portland, OR 97205	(800) 547–1037 (503) 222–3600	1,000
Delaware Cash Reserve, Inc. Seven Penn Center Plaza Philadelphia, PA 19103	(800) 523–4640 (215) 988–1200	1,000
Dreyfus Liquid Assets 600 Madison Avenue New York, NY 10022	(800) 223–5525 (212) 223–0303	2,500
Eaton & Howard Cash Management Fund Box 336 Boston, MA 02101	(800) 225–6265 (617) 482–8260	1,000

GENERAL PURPOSE MONEY FUNDS, *(continued)*

Fund Name and Address	Phone Number	Minimum Initial Investment
Equitable Money Market Account, Inc. 100 West 52nd Street New York, NY 10019	(800) 223–0970 (outside NY) (800) 442–8195 (NY) (212) 245–7333 (NYC) (212) 245–7333 (AL & HI collect)	2,500
Fidelity Cash Reserves 82 Devonshire Street Boston, MA 02109	(800) 225–6190 (617) 523–1919	1,000
Fidelity Daily Income Trust 82 Devonshire Street Boston, MA 02109	(800) 225–6190 (617) 523–1919	10,000
Financial Daily Income Shares, Inc. P.O. Box 2040 Denver, CO 80201	(800) 525–9831 (303) 779–1233	1,000
First Investors Cash Management Fund 120 Wall Street New York, NY 10005	(800) 221–3790 (212) 742–9620	1,000
First Variable Rate Fund for Government Income, Inc. 1700 Pennsylvania Avenue, #270 Washington, DC 20008	(800) 424–2444 (202) 328–4010	2,000
Franklin Money Fund 155 Bovet Road San Mateo, CA 94402	(800) 227–6781 (outside CA) (800) 632–2180 (CA) (415) 574–8800 (collect)	500
Fund for Government Investors, Inc. 1735 K Street, NW Washington, DC 20006	(202) 861–1800 (collect)	2,500
Government Investors Trust 1800 North Kent Street Arlington, VA 22209	(800) 336–3063	2,000
IDS Cash Management Fund, Inc. 1000 Roanoke Building Minneapolis, MN 55402	(800) 437–4332	2,500
John Hancock Cash Management Trust John Hancock Place P.O. Box 111 Boston, MA 02117	(617) 421–4506	1,000
Kemper Money Market Fund, Inc. 120 South LaSalle Street Chicago, IL 60603	(800) 621–1048 (312) 346–3223	,000
Lexington Money Market Trust Box 1515 580 Sylvan Avenue Englewood Cliffs, NJ 07632	(800) 526–4791	1,000
Lord Abbett Cash Reserve Fund, Inc. 63 Wall Street New York, NY 10005	(800) 221–9995 (212) 425–8720	1,000
Mass Cash Management Trust 200 Berkeley Street Boston, MA 02116	(617) 956–1200 (617) 423–3500 (collect)	1,000
Midwest Income Trust/Short-Term Government Fund 508 Dixie Terminal-5th Floor Cincinnati, OH 45202	(800) 543–0407 (513) 579–0414 (collect)	1,000
Money Market Management, Inc. 421 Seventh Avenue Pittsburgh, PA 15219	(800) 245–2423 (412) 288–1557	1,000
Mutual Investing Foundation-MIF/ Nationwide Money Market Fund One Nationwide Plaza Columbus, Ohio 43216	(800) 848–0920 (800) 282–1440 (in OH)	2,500
Mutual of Omaha Money Market Accounts 3102 Farnam Street Omaha, NB 68131	(800) 228–9011 (402) 342–3328	2,500
NEL Cash Management Trust 501 Boylston Street Boston, MA 02217	(800) 225–7670 (617) 267–6600	1,000

Fund Name and Address	Phone Number	Minimum Initial Investment
NRTA-AARP U.S. Government Money Market Trust 421 Seventh Avenue Pittsburgh, PA 15219	(800) 245–4770 (412) 392–6350	500
Putnam Daily Dividend Trust One Post Office Square Boston, MA 02109	(800) 225–1789 (617) 292–1470	1,000
The Reserve Fund, Inc. 810 Seventh Avenue New York, NY 10019	(800) 223–5547 (212) 977–9880	1,000
St. Paul Money Fund, Inc. Box 43284 St. Paul, MN 55164	(800) 328–1062 (800) 328–1064 (612) 738–4142 (in MN)	3,000
Scudder Cash Investment Trust 175 Federal Street Boston, MA 02110	(800) 343–2890 (617) 482–3990	1,000
STEINROE Cash Reserves, Inc. 150 South Wacker Drive Chicago, IL 60606	(800) 621–0320 (312) 368–7822	2,500
T. Rowe Price Prime Reserve Fund, Inc. 100 East Pratt Street Baltimore, MD 21202	(800) 638–5660 (301) 547–2308	1,000
Transamerica Cash Reserve, Inc. Box 2438 Los Angeles, CA 90051	(213) 742–4169 (213) 742–4141	5,000
Union Cash Management Fund, Inc. One Bankers Trust Plaza New York, NY 10006	(800) 221–2450 (212) 432–4000	1,000
United Cash Management, Inc. 1 Crown Center P.O. Box 1343 Kansas City, MO 64141	(800) 821–5664 (800) 892–5811 (in MO)	1,000
Value Line Cash Fund 711 Third Avenue New York, NY 10017	(800) 223–0818 (212) 687–3965 (in NY)	1,000
Vanguard Money Market Trust P.O. Box 1100 Valley Forge, PA 19482	(800) 523–7025 (800) 362–0530	3,000

Source: Excerpted from Donoghue's *Money Fund Directory*, published semiannually, Fall/Winter, Spring/Summer, $15 per edition. Box 540, Holliston, MA 01746.

TAX-EXEMPT MUTUAL FUNDS (NO LOAD)

Dreyfus Tax Exempt Bond Fund
Federated Tax-Free Income Fund
Fidelity High Yield Municipals
Fidelity Limited Term Municipal
Fidelity Municipal Bond Fund
Oppenheimer Tax-Free Bond Fund
T. Rowe Price Tax-Free Income Fund
Scudder Managed Municipal Bond Fund

For addresses see page 283.

TAX-EXEMPT MONEY MARKET FUNDS

Fidelity Tax-Exempt
Money Market Trust
82 Devonshire Street
Boston, MA 02109
(617) 726–0200
(800) 225–6190

Scudder Tax-Free Money Fund
175 Federal Street
Boston, MA 02110
(617) 482–3990
(800) 225–2470

Vanguard Municipal Bond
Fund—Short-Term
and
Vanguard Municipal Bond
Fund—Money Market
P.O. Box 1100
Valley Forge, PA 19482
(800) 362–7688 (in PA)
(800) 523–7910

HOW TO UNDERSTAND CONVERTIBLE SECURITIES

The term "Convertible Securities" refers to securities that can be exchanged for another type of security, usually the common stock of the company issuing the convertible.

The two basic types of convertible securities are debentures (commonly known as bonds) and preferred stock. These securities have intrinsic value. Bonds represent a debt of the issuing company. Preferred stock represents an ownership interest. Intrinsic value may be enhanced by the convertible feature.

There are other certificates or contracts which are sometimes considered to be convertible securities but which have no intrinsic value based on ownership interest or debt. Their value is derived solely from their ability to be converted into another type of security. To do so requires a payment in addition to the surrender of the security. These are rights, warrants and options. To many investors these securities may offer certain advantages. However, our emphasis here will be on convertible securities—bonds and preferred stock—which have broader application as investment vehicles.

CONVERTIBLE BONDS

Convertible debt securities are almost always issued in the form of debentures. That is, there is no specific collateral pledged by the issuing corporation in the indenture which states the terms under which the security is issued. Rather, the promise to pay interest on stated dates and the principal amount at maturity is backed by the full faith and credit of the corporation. However, even the most sophisticated investors and those in the securities industry commonly refer to this type of security as a convertible bond.

Convertible bonds have been extolled as the ultimate investment medium offering the desirable features of other securities without the normal risks. If this were so, it would not be for long. Demand for such a security would be so great that the price would be driven up to the point where the element of risk would be very evident. Convertible bonds like all other securities have both advantages and disadvantages and the informed investor can measure these against his own objectives.

Here are the three most important characteristics:

1. Convertible bonds pay interest—which, as a general rule yields more than the dividends on common stock of comparable quality and less than the interest on straight (non-convertible) bonds of equivalent quality and maturity.

   The issuing company's obligation to pay this interest comes before dividends on preferred and common stock.

2. Convertible bonds offer appreciable possibilities linked to the earnings and growth of the company. As the common stock rises in value to reflect this growth, the price of the convertible bond should also increase. Conversely, as the common stock declines in value, so should the convertible bond decline.

3. Convertible bonds enjoy some of the stability and relative safety associated with straight bonds and preferred stock. For each outstanding convertible bond, it is possible to estimate an investment value. This is the price below which the convertible bond is not expected to fall, if interest rates remain constant, even if the common stock price falls to such an extent as to render the convertible feature virtually valueless. Investment value is arrived at by estimating a price that would produce a yield comparable to straight bonds of equivalent quality. Investment value, it should be stressed, is only an estimate and subject to change from many influences such as fluctuating interest rates, economic and business conditions, ratings given by investment advisory services and the general well-being of the issuing company.

These characteristics can perhaps best be understood by examining how convertible bonds come into existence and how they behave in various circumstances.

XYZ COMPANY ISSUES CONVERTIBLE BONDS

Let's assume that the XYZ Company wants to raise more capital to expand its business. Interest rates are high and XYZ does not want to pay 8% or more to borrow money in the conventional bond market. XYZ is also reluctant at this time to issue additional common stock as a means of raising additional capital. This could be due to a number of reasons, one of which might be unwillingness to dilute the equity interest of its present stockholders. For example, if there are presently ten million shares outstanding and an additional million are issued, earnings per share will normally be reduced by ten percent at the moment of issue, and the market price of the common stock probably would fall proportionately unless it could support the higher price earnings ratio.

Source: Reprinted by permission of The New York Stock Exchange, Inc. from *Understanding Convertible Securities*. Further reprinting is prohibited without express written approval of The New York Stock Exchange, Inc.

(The dilution problem is not quite the same when additional stock is issued to acquire an interest in or control of another company. The acquired company will presumably have its own earnings to contribute to earnings per share.) The XYZ Company is also mindful of the fact that dividends on stock are paid after federal income taxes, whereas interest on debt securities, like bonds, is a deduction before taxes.

Accordingly, the management of the XYZ Company decides to issue convertible bonds. In conjunction with the underwriting firm, the interest is set at 5% and the bonds are priced at par—an even $1,000 per $1,000 face amount bond. Bond prices are commonly stated as a percentage of par which, in this case, would be 100. It is further stipulated that each $1,000 bond can be converted into 25 shares of XYZ common stock. At the time that the bonds are marketed, the common stocks is trading at $32 per share.

DEFINITION OF TERMS

In any discussion of convertible bonds, various terms, related to the above figures, are widely used. Before proceeding, these should be defined.

Market Price Price at which a convertible bond can be bought or sold at a given point in time. Market price is stated as a percentage of par, usually $1,000. 100 means $1,000, 90 means $900, 110 means $1,100, etc.

Conversion Ratio Number of shares of common stock obtainable through conversion of one bond. In the case of XYZ, conversion ratio is 25.

Conversion Price The reciprocal of conversion ratio or the price of the stock when the number of shares obtainable through conversion of one $1,000 bond equals exactly $1,000. Conversion price is $40 when conversion ratio is 25.

Conversion Value Current value of total shares into which a bond can be converted. Conversion value of XYZ $1,000 bond with conversion ratio of 25 shares is $800 when XYZ common stock is trading at $32 per share.

Conversion Premium Percentage difference between conversion value and market value of bond. When conversion value is $800 and market value is $1,000, conversion premium is 25% since difference between conversion and market values ($1,000 − $800 = $200) is 25% of conversion value ($800). This figure represents the judgment of investors, as expressed in the marketplace, with respect to the worth of the three characteristics of convertible securities discussed above. These were yield, appreciation potential and relative safety. With some issues, supply and demand is also a factor in the premium.

Investment Value Estimated price, usually set by investment advisory services, at which bond would be selling if it had no convertible feature. Investment value is arrived at by estimating the price at which the convertible bond would have to sell to provide a percentage yield comparable to percentage yield on a non-convertible bond of equivalent quality and maturity. Investment value, like market price, is normally stated as a percentage of $1,000. For the XYZ Bonds, investment value will be assumed to be 75 providing a current yield of 6.67%.

Premium Over Investment Value Percentage difference between estimated investment value and market price of bond. When market price is 100 and investment value is estimated at 75, the difference is 25 which is 33% of 75. Thus, the premium over investment value is 33%. This figure can be considered a measurement of the worth of the conversion privilege as well as an indication of the proportion of the price that is subject to the risks associated with common stock.

To summarize, the position of XYZ Convertible Bonds, and the related stock at the time the bonds are marketed, is as follows:

Market Price of Bond	100	(1,000)
Yield		5%
Conversion Ratio		25
Conversion Price	$40	$\left(\frac{\$1,000}{25}\right)$
Market Price of Stock		$32
Conversion Value	$800	(25 × 32)
Conversion Premium	25%	$\left(\frac{\$1,000 - \$800}{\$800}\right)$
Investment Value	75	($750)
Premium Over Investment Value	33%	$\left(\frac{\$1,000 - \$750}{\$750}\right)$

Obviously, no owners of the bonds would convert them into the common stock at this time, since they would be exchanging $1,000 for $800. However, it is not necessary to convert a convertible bond into stock in order to enjoy its advantages. Bonds are frequently sold many times before they are finally converted into stock and many investors have actively participated in the convertible bond market without ever exercising the conversion privilege. Let's now explore what could happen to the XYZ Convertible Bonds under various circumstances.

IF THE STOCK GOES UP

If the XYZ Company prospers and is considered to have appreciation potential, the price of the common stock should go up. By the same token, the price of the XYZ Convertible Bond should also rise. Let's assume the stock goes up by 25% to $40 per share. Normally, the bond will also go up but not necessarily at the same rate as the stock. There is a good reason for this. As the bond price increases, it acts more like a stock and less like a bond. Investment value is left further behind. The risk increases. Yield diminishes too. Accordingly, even though the appreciation potential of the stock may not have changed, the other factors (greater risk and lower yield) will tend to hold back the price of the bond. Therefore, a rise in the XYZ stock of 25% from $32 to $40 might be reflected in a rise in the bond of 20% from 100 to 120. The most significant figures are now as follows:

Market Price of Bond	$120	($1,200)
Current Yield	4.17%	$\left(\dfrac{\$50}{\$1,200}\right)$
Market Price of Stock		$40
Conversion Value	$1,000	(25 × $40)
Conversion Premium	20%	$\left(\dfrac{\$1,200-\$1,000}{\$1,000}\right)$
Premium Over Investment Value	60%	$\left(\dfrac{\$1,200-\$750}{\$750}\right)$

Conversion is still unrealistic. But bondholders who bought at the offering may want to take profits by selling their bonds to other investors who believe the stock will continue to go up but are not quite certain enough in their belief to buy the stock itself. Let's assume now that XYZ common stock goes up to $60 per share, an increase of 87½% since the bonds were issued. What is likely to happen to the XYZ bonds? The bond price may now rise to the level where virtually all of the bond-like characteristics are lost and, from the standpoint of risk, the bond is interchangeable with the stock. If we assume this is so, the bond's conversion value should be approximately the same as its market value and conversion premium will disappear. The picture would now look like this:

Market Price of Bond	$150	($1,500)
Current Yield	3.33%	$\left(\dfrac{\$50}{\$1,500}\right)$
Market Price of Stock		$60
Conversion Value	$1,500	(25 × $60)
Conversion Premium	0	$\left(\dfrac{\$1,500-\$1,500}{\$1,500}\right)$
Premium Over Investment Value	100%	$\left(\dfrac{\$1,500-\$750}{\$750}\right)$

Now the owner of the bond will think very seriously about converting. His decision may depend to some extent on the comparative yields of the bond and the stock. Interest on the bond is $50 per year. If the dividend on the stock is less than $2.00 per share, conversion would result in less income. If, on the other hand, the dividend is $2.40 (a yield of 4%) conversion would result in more current income.

In the meantime, while the stock has been rising from $32 to $60 per share, the company has presumably been using the money received from the sale of the convertible bonds to expand its business and improve its earnings. This should have put it in a better position to absorb the dilution that conversion into common stock entails.

When a convertible bond's conversion value and market price become the same, the stock and the bond should move up and down together within a limited range to maintain this relationship. It is virtually impossible for a convertible bond to sell with a negative conversion premium (below its conversion value) for any length of time. If this should happen, professional traders will quickly move in and employ a device known as arbitrage to make a small but rapid profit. They will buy the bonds and simultaneously sell the stock short. Converting the bonds enables them to replace the stock borrowed for the short sale. If, for example, XYZ convertibles are selling at $1,450 while the conversion value is $1,500, the trader can buy ten bonds for $14,500. By selling short 250 shares, he receives $15,000 for an immediate gross profit of $500. This activity will tend to drive the price of the bond back up to or above conversion value.

IF THE STOCK GOES DOWN

Let us now consider what might happen to the XYZ convertible bonds if the common stock took an opposite course and declined from the price of $32 per share which it was enjoying at the time that the convertible bonds were issued. As the price falls the convertible bond's price will also fall. However, the bond's downside potential is less than that of the stock, since the bond should not decline below its investment value which is the estimated value of the bond when we disregard the conversion feature. We have assumed this to be a price of 75 which is 25% below par. Therefore, while the stock is falling from $32 to an unknown level, the bond should only travel from 100 to 75. This factor serves as a brake on the bond and is the reason why convertible bonds are generally considered to be a more conservative investment than the stock of the same issuing company. In reality, conditions which would cause a stock to decline drastically would probably produce a re-adjustment in the investment value of the convertible bond. Investment value is also subject to adjustment when money rates change.

To see how the convertible bond might be affected by a decline in the common stock of the XYZ Company, let's assume that the market price of the stock sags from its original price of $32 all the way down to $16 per share. It has lost half its value. If we estimated correctly the investment value of the convertible bond, and if other factors are the same, it will be

Market Price of Bond $75   ($750)

Current Yield .... 6.67% $\left(\dfrac{\$50}{\$750}\right)$

Market Price of Stock $16
Conversion Value .... $400   (25 × $16)
Conversion
   Premium .... 87½% $\left(\dfrac{\$750 - \$400}{\$400}\right)$

Premium Over Investment
   Value 0

selling in the area of $750. Thus, a drop of 50% in the price of the stock produces a drop of 25% in the price of the bond. The table of values will now be as follows:

Thus, we have seen in this example that the price of a convertible bond is controlled primarily by the price of the stock into which it is convertible. However, when the stock goes up, the bond's rise should be held back somewhat as risk increases and yield decreases. Conversely, when the stock goes down, the bond's decline is cushioned as yield increases and investment value is approached. This is an oversimplification which disregards other influences but, hopefully, it provides a basic understanding of how convertible bonds behave. Prices, yields and ratios were chosen in order to illustrate the example and simplify the arithmetic. They are not intended to reflect actual market conditions at any time.

HEDGING

We have seen that convertible bonds offer an investor opportunities to participate in the stock market with somewhat less risk (and less profit potential) than is normally encountered with direct investment in common stocks. This opportunity can be pursued even further by employing hedges. Although extremely complex in practice, the basic principles of hedging are actually quite simple.

Typically, a hedge is established when an investor buys convertible bonds and, at the same time, sells short the stock into which the bond is convertible. If the stock goes up, there should be a profit in the bonds and a loss in the stock. If the stock goes down, there should

be a profit in the stock and a loss in the bonds. Obviously, there is no advantage in a hedge unless the profit exceeds the loss and expenses. There is no way to assure a profit but the skillful and judicious use of hedges can greatly reduce the risk of loss and enhance the possibility of profit. An essential feature is the ability to sell stock short without margin when the corresponding convertible security is held.

Convertible hedges are a highly sophisticated investment technique and should not be attempted without a complete understanding of all of their ramifications.

CALLABILITY AND OTHER LIMITATIONS

An important factor to consider with convertible bonds is the call feature. This is the right of the issuing company to redeem the bonds before maturity at a stated price slightly above par. Usually the original purchasers of a bond are given some protection against this privilege of the company through an initial period during which the bond is non-callable. If a bond has been on the market for four years and commands a price of 130, this price may be short lived if the bond can be called at 105 after five years. When a convertible bond issue listed on the New York Stock Exchange is called for redemption some notice is always given in a newspaper of general circulation to permit the holders to exercise their conversion privilege or sell the bond to someone else who may convert it. Holders of record of registered bonds are notified directly. If, for some reason, the bond is not converted before expiration date for conversion, which may be the same or a few days before the redemption date, it is then worth no more nor less than the call price. It is, therefore, most important for holders of convertible bonds to know what the call features are and to be sure that they will receive information about calls when and if they occur. Obviously, the best way to do this is to hold registered bonds.

Most convertible bonds are convertible into stock at a fixed rate during the entire life of the bond. However, this rate may change because of a stock split, stock dividend, merger or other circumstances. The conversion privilege may expire before the bond matures or it may not be effective until some time after the bond is issued. Sometimes the conversion rate declines at regular intervals. A bond that is convertible into 25 shares of common stock when first issued may become convertible into only 20 shares after five years, 15 shares after ten years, etc. Although the typical convertible bond is exchangeable for the common stock of the issuing company, this is also subject to variation. Conversion may be made into a combination of common and preferred stock. Or bonds of one company may be convertible into the stock of a parent company.

All of these possible limitations should be checked by investors when investigating convertible securities. A member firm of the New York Stock Exchange, Inc. can usually supply the essential information.

MARGIN AND COMMISSION

Two other features of convertible bonds have traditionally appealed to investors—margin requirements and commission rates. Although the current margin requirement for the purchase of common stock or convertible bonds is the same—50%, the convertible bond rate has usually been significantly less. In 1973, for instance, an investor with $6,500 available in cash could have bought $10,000 worth of common stock or $13,000 of convertible bonds. (Margin requirements are subject to change by the Federal Reserve Board).

The commission paid to a member firm broker for the purchase or sale of listed stocks is one of the lowest fees paid for the transfer of property of any kind. However, in most cases, the commission paid for the purchase or sale of bonds is even lower on a given dollar investment.

CONVERTIBLE PREFERRED STOCK

Convertible preferred stock possesses many of the basic characteristics of convertible bonds and will normally perform in approximately the same manner when subject to the same conditions and influences. However, there are also basic differences which should be pointed out.

Convertible preferred stock represents an equity interest and is, therefore, junior to all debt securities including convertible bonds and would not—all else being equal—have as high a degree of relative safety as convertible bonds. However, all else is rarely equal and the convertible preferred stock of Company A could have more relative safety than the convertible bonds of Company B. Convertible preferred stocks do not have maturity dates as do bonds but are usually subject to redemption.

Convertible preferreds, like common stock, require 50% margin currently, and are subject to the same commission structure.

FOREIGN SHORT TERM AND LONG TERM INTEREST RATES: SELECTED COUNTRIES

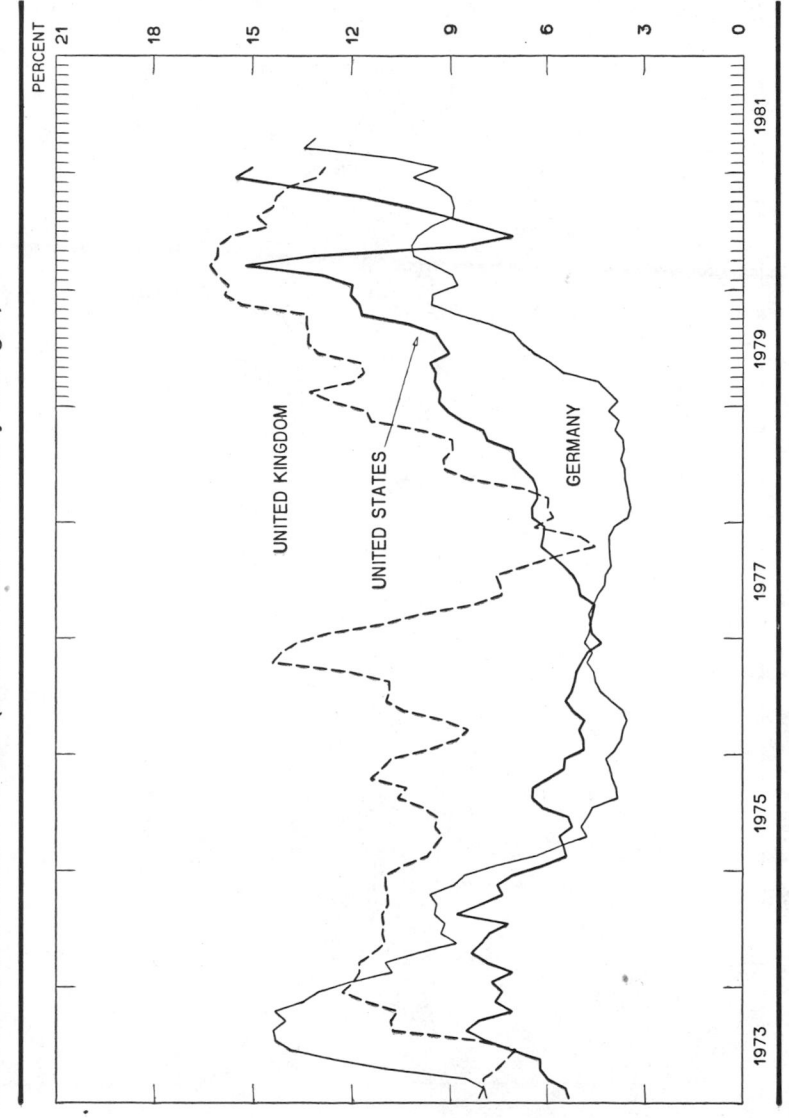

SHORT-TERM INTEREST RATES (selected countries monthly averages)

PERCENT

UNITED KINGDOM

UNITED STATES

GERMANY

Source: *Federal Reserve Chart Book,* Board of Governors of the Federal Reserve System.

LONG-TERM GOVERNMENT BOND YIELDS (selected countries monthly)

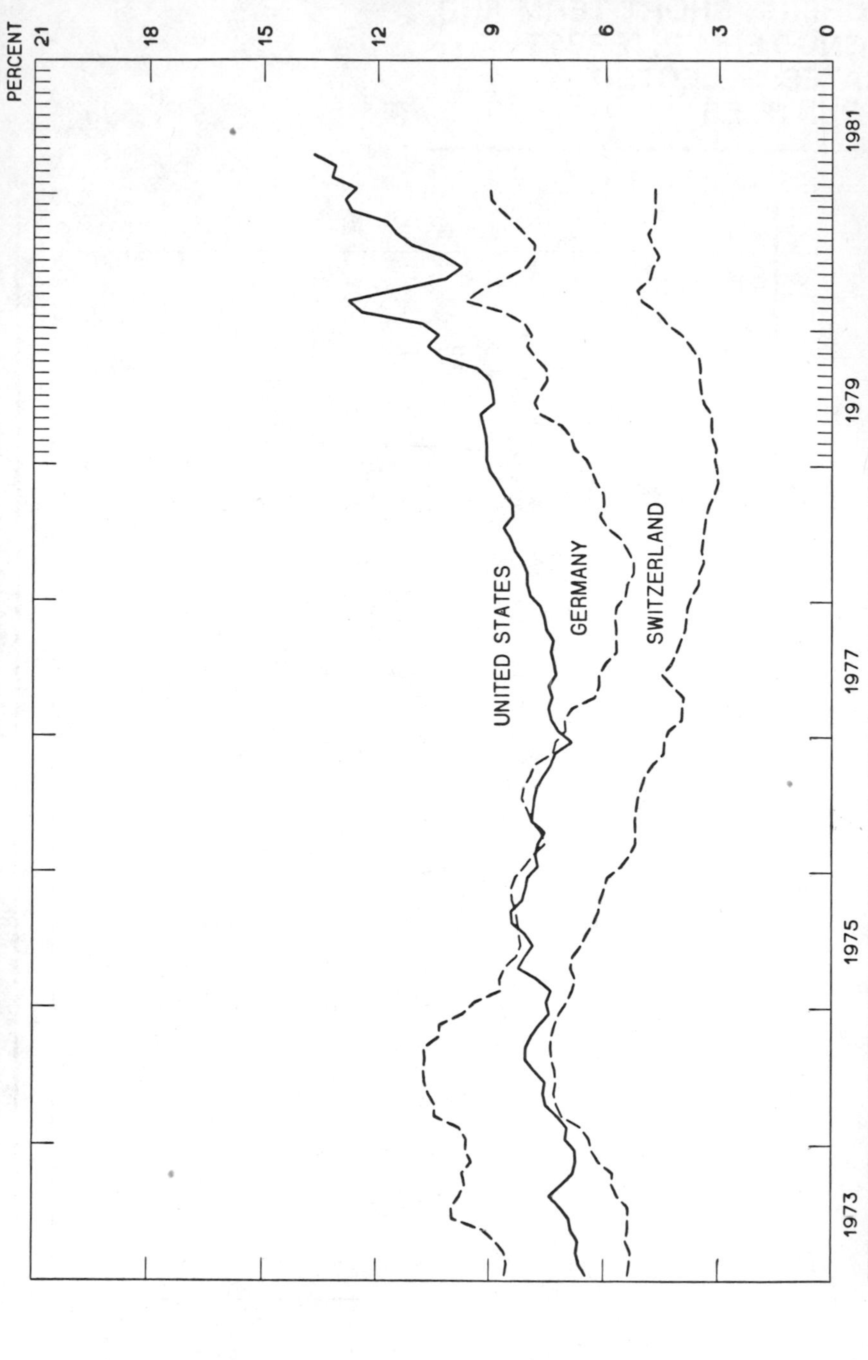

PERCENT

21 18 15 12 9 6 3 0

1981

1979

UNITED STATES

GERMANY

SWITZERLAND

1977

1975

1973

Source: *Federal Reserve Chart Book*, Board of Governors of the Federal Reserve System.

LONG-TERM GOVERNMENT BOND YIELDS (selected countries monthly)

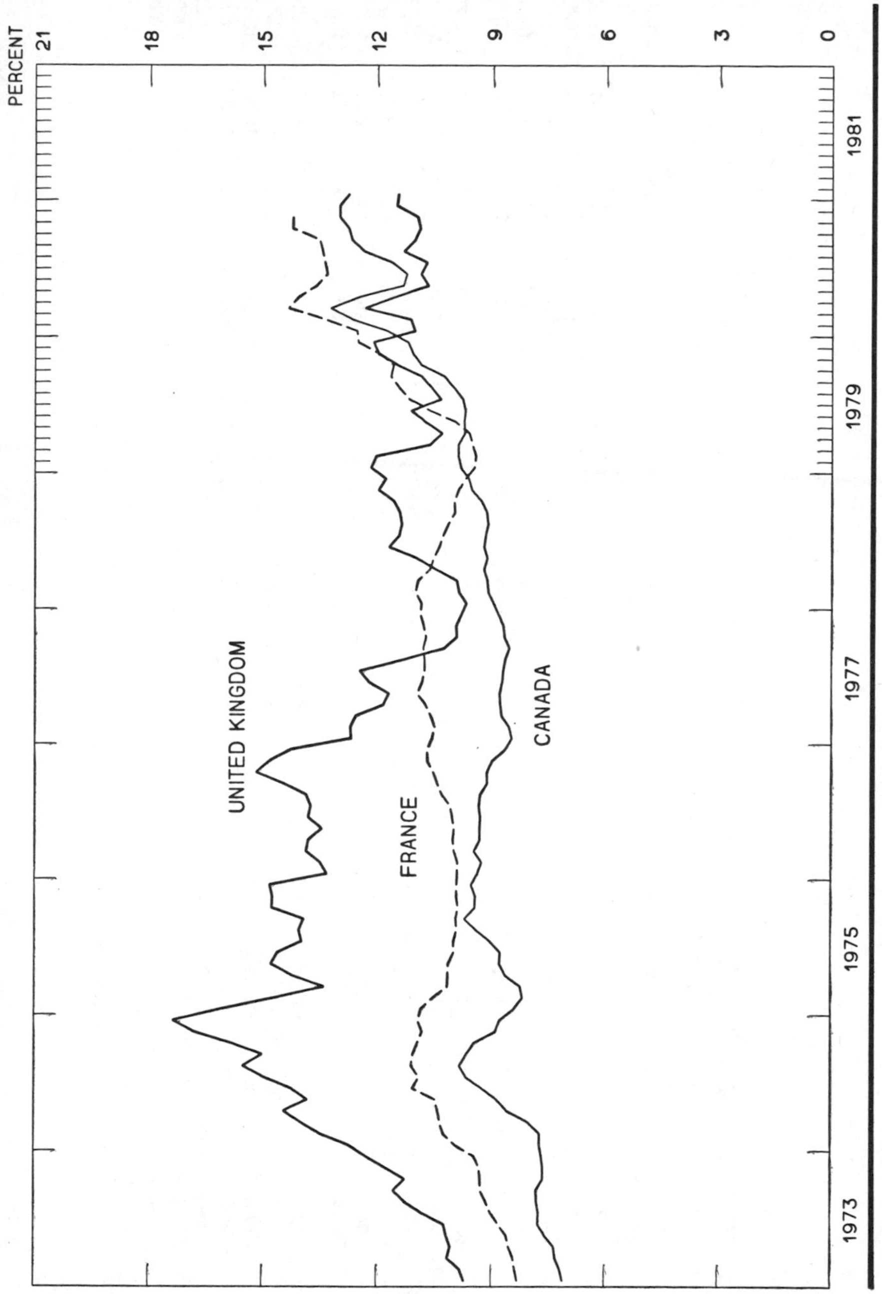

UNITED KINGDOM

FRANCE

CANADA

PERCENT

21

18

15

12

9

6

3

0

1973   1975   1977   1979   1981

Source: *Federal Reserve Chart Book*, Board of Governors of the Federal Reserve System.

FOREIGN TREASURY BILL RATES (bond-equivalent yields, at or near end of month)

	1977 Dec	1978 Dec	1979 Dec	1980 Oct	Nov	Dec	1981 Jan	Feb	Mar	Apr	May
United States	6.33	9.42	12.39	13.07	14.84	14.87	15.83	14.80	13.55	15.51	16.00
Canada	7.17	10.46	13.66	11.91	13.70	17.01	16.86	16.83	16.44	17.35	18.43
Japan	4.15	3.39	5.68	6.44	5.93	5.93	5.93	5.93	5.93	5.93	5.93
Australia	8.35	8.35	9.31	10.95	11.47	12.17	12.42	12.68	12.72	13.78	13.22
United Kingdom	6.42	12.01	16.45	14.44	13.38	13.45	13.02	11.93	11.87	11.57	11.78
Belgium	9.25	9.25	14.40	12.10	12.75	12.75	12.10	13.25	15.00	17.00	16.75
Ireland	6.74	11.83	16.37	12.72	12.78	12.84	12.83	12.84	12.70	13.85	14.65
Italy	12.81	12.81	15.62	16.87	16.87	16.87	16.87	16.87	19.18	19.84	21.18
Netherlands	6.00	9.50	12.75	8.85	8.75	8.00	8.75	8.75	9.25	9.75	11.75
Spain	n.a.	n.a.	n.a.	n.a.	n.a.	n.a.	n.a.	n.a.	n.a.	13.25	17.00
Sweden	9.21	5.84	9.74	12.90	12.90	12.87	16.85	16.85	15.73	15.73	15.77
Argentina	109.06	82.55	71.04	58.31	60.73	66.19	69.10	90.06	107.97	86.79	104.34
Brazil	38.08	41.21	27.84	50.18	66.34	76.84	78.24	73.58	70.46	71.33	71.88
Korea	16.88	17.01	19.53	19.50	16.35	16.35	18.98	18.98	18.98	18.98	18.16
Mexico	n.a.	12.75	17.89	24.73	25.81	27.73	28.87	28.76	28.55	28.27	n.a.
New Zealand	7.50	10.50	11.25	11.25	11.25	11.25	11.50	11.25	11.25	11.25	11.25
Philippines	10.04	12.08	12.63	12.70	12.75	12.74	12.65	12.65	12.69	12.76	12.76
Singapore	3.17	4.01	6.18	6.98	6.86	6.77	6.86	6.84	6.60	6.58	n.a.
South Africa	8.17	7.61	4.30	5.13	5.71	6.31	6.89	7.59	7.82	7.89	9.08

Source: Reprinted with permission from *World Financial Markets*, a publication of Morgan Guaranty Trust Company of New York.

FOREIGN MONEY-MARKET RATES (bond-equivalent yields on major short-term—mostly 3–4 month—money-market instruments, other than Treasury bills, at or near end of month)

	1977	1978	1979	1980			1981				
	Dec	Dec	Dec	Oct	Nov	Dec	Jan	Feb	Mar	Apr	May
United States	6.84	10.57	13.70	14.24	17.15	17.62	16.67	15.48	14.25	16.80	16.94
Canada	7.25	10.62	14.15	12.50	14.10	17.50	16.95	16.85	17.05	17.55	19.00
Japan	5.89	4.64	8.01	9.57	9.80	9.80	8.32	8.37	7.34	6.76	7.52
Australia	9.75	9.10	10.30	11.70	11.75	13.00	13.25	14.00	15.10	15.75	15.50
United Kingdom	6.50	12.50	17.00	16.62	14.50	14.75	13.19	12.50	12.50	12.37	12.44
Belgium	9.50	9.25	14.45	12.45	13.00	13.10	12.35	13.00	14.00	17.00	16.85
France	9.19	6.44	12.62	11.31	11.44	11.56	11.25	13.50	12.75	13.37	18.25
Germany	3.60	3.70	8.70	9.20	9.45	10.20	9.45	14.50	13.30	12.90	13.30
Ireland	6.75	13.00	18.12	13.37	13.75	13.62	13.87	14.78	14.00	15.37	15.94
Italy	11.75	11.37	17.12	17.75	17.37	17.37	17.37	17.50	19.75	19.75	20.00
Netherlands	6.25	10.50	13.00	9.25	10.00	9.37	9.50	11.25	10.37	11.25	12.25
Spain	12.06	22.80	13.20	15.30	16.00	17.40	17.40	15.00	13.20	13.79	16.28
Switzerland	2.02	0.50	6.12	5.62	6.12	7.50	6.00	8.50	9.37	10.00	10.50
Hong Kong	5.73	11.82	14.37	12.56	15.87	17.69	15.53	16.86	16.27	16.45	17.55
Korea	16.88	17.01	19.53	19.27	16.35	16.35	16.35	16.35	16.35	15.60	15.70
New Zealand	11.87	12.00	16.00	14.25	14.10	14.25	14.35	14.80	15.60	14.70	14.50
Philippines	11.96	11.48	10.41	11.96	13.15	15.01	15.98	16.86	16.63	16.67	17.50
Singapore	4.81	7.38	10.12	13.62	14.12	14.12	14.25	13.69	11.69	10.06	n.a.
South Africa	9.00	7.85	4.72	5.05	6.07	7.12	8.42	9.73	9.89	9.84	12.37

Source: Reprinted with permission from *World Financial Markets*, a publication of Morgan Guaranty Trust Company of New York.

FOREIGN GOVERNMENT BOND YIELDS (long-term issues, at or near end of month)

	1977	1978	1979	1980			1981				
	Dec	Dec	Dec	Oct	Nov	Dec	Jan	Feb	Mar	Apr	May
United States	7.97	9.00	10.20	12.33	12.25	11.46	12.76	13.16	13.21	14.13	13.52
Canada	8.77	9.68	11.32	13.22	13.01	12.69	12.96	13.38	13.48	15.07	14.96
Japan	6.40	6.40	8.63	8.84	9.26	9.04	8.84	8.89	8.67	8.84	9.23
Australia	9.50	8.90	10.45	12.40	12.60	13.00	13.10	13.10	13.10	13.10	13.10
United Kingdom	10.53	12.75	13.83	12.52	12.65	13.05	13.25	13.36	12.86	13.18	13.50
Belgium	8.76	8.80	11.13	12.46	12.61	13.04	13.19	13.44	13.57	13.52	13.85
France	11.07	9.94	12.59	14.27	14.24	14.31	14.58	15.05	14.98	14.95	17.25
Germany	5.52	6.65	7.91	8.55	8.59	9.19	9.07	10.38	9.97	10.12	10.68
Italy	10.82	10.89	11.28	12.53	12.42	12.12	12.44	12.88	14.46	14.53	14.27
Netherlands	8.11	8.48	9.29	10.20	10.46	10.48	10.43	10.96	11.38	11.29	11.89
Austria	9.00	7.91	8.20	9.90	10.11	9.62	9.80	10.06	10.33	10.18	n.a.
Denmark	16.83	17.27	18.28	19.24	19.40	19.62	18.56	18.90	19.12	19.23	19.48
Finland	10.25	9.19	9.58	10.48	10.43	10.42	10.92	10.92	10.96	10.97	10.96
Ireland	11.30	13.44	16.64	14.77	14.91	15.63	16.22	16.01	16.12	16.57	16.99
Norway	8.37	8.19	10.04	10.40	10.44	10.44	11.70	11.50	11.57	11.65	11.65
Spain	n.a.	n.a.	n.a.	n.a.	n.a.	n.a.	n.a.	n.a.	n.a.	13.00	12.75
Sweden	9.84	10.09	11.22	12.68	12.71	12.61	n.a.	n.a.	n.a.	n.a.	n.a.
Switzerland	3.75	3.03	4.20	4.69	4.67	4.63	4.79	5.20	5.40	5.79	5.85
Argentina	181.65	112.18	47.94	38.21	101.38	36.84	34.97	42.99	66.43	65.64	144.24
New Zealand	10.00	10.02	12.98	12.96	12.96	12.99	12.81	12.97	12.88	12.85	n.a.
Philippines	13.40	13.40	13.20	13.40	13.40	13.40	13.40	13.40	13.40	13.42	13.41
South Africa	10.75	9.85	9.44	11.10	11.75	11.80	12.67	12.77	12.77	12.80	13.03
Venezuela	7.24	7.24	7.29	7.40	7.43	7.39	7.44	7.40	7.30	10.00	10.00

Source: Reprinted with permission from *World Financial Markets*, a publication of Morgan Guaranty Trust Company of New York.

FOREIGN CORPORATE BOND YIELDS (long-term issues, at or near end of month)

	1977	1978	1979	1980			1981				
	Dec	Dec	Dec	Oct	Nov	Dec	Jan	Feb	Mar	Apr	May
United States	8.30	9.25	10.75	13.38	13.38	13.00	13.63	14.13	14.00	15.00	14.25
Canada	9.71	10.34	12.07	13.95	13.72	13.62	13.84	14.34	14.41	16.03	15.94
Japan	6.68	6.94	8.34	8.48	8.60	8.60	8.49	8.25	8.15	7.95	n.a.
Australia	11.00	10.25	11.65	13.75	14.00	14.25	14.25	14.10	14.25	14.50	15.00
United Kingdom	11.88	13.53	14.96	13.61	13.63	14.21	14.20	14.14	14.35	14.44	14.94
France	12.09	10.27	12.92	14.69	14.83	15.23	14.62	15.13	15.39	15.39	15.35
Germany	5.92	6.80	8.20	8.80	9.30	9.50	9.50	10.00	10.90	10.90	11.40
Italy	10.71	10.12	10.22	12.64	12.65	12.99	12.80	13.05	16.82	17.01	19.84
Netherlands	7.90	8.62	9.95	10.48	10.33	10.71	10.46	10.77	11.21	11.07	11.76
Norway	8.59	8.37	10.53	10.55	11.24	11.24	11.75	12.07	12.36	12.76	12.76
Spain	11.58	13.49	14.20	14.90	15.10	14.82	14.28	14.36	14.55	14.73	n.a.
Sweden	9.83	10.03	10.21	11.99	12.10	11.95	13.37	13.46	13.56	13.63	13.66
Switzerland	4.96	4.85	5.53	5.71	5.78	5.63	5.78	5.93	6.08	6.08	6.44
Korea	19.60	24.00	32.50	26.00	23.50	26.30	26.30	24.70	23.00	22.30	22.30
Mexico	17.56	20.37	21.99	26.12	27.55	28.03	28.33	30.90	30.20	30.97	28.92
Venezuela	10.39	12.43	14.55	13.55	14.78	16.15	16.65	16.20	16.00	16.25	16.30

Source: Reprinted with permission from *World Financial Markets*, a publication of Morgan Guaranty Trust Company, of New York.

COMPOSITION OF DOW JONES BOND AVERAGES

10 PUBLIC UTILITIES

Alabama Pwr 9¾s '04
Amer Tel & Tel 8.8s '05
Commonw'lth Edison 8¾s, 2005
Cons Ed 7.9s, 2001
Consumers Pwr 9¾s, '06
Detroit Edison 9s, '99
New York Tel 4½s, '91
Pac G&E 7¾ 2005
Philadelphia El 7⅜s, 2001
Pub Ser Ind 9.6s, 2005

10 INDUSTRIALS

BankAmerica 7⅞s, '03
Beth Steel 6⅞s, '99
Dow Chem 4.35s, '88
Exxon 6s, '97
Ford Mtr 8⅛s, '90
Gen Mtrs Accept 4½s, '85
Nat Cash Reg 4⅜s, '87
Pfizer 9¼s, 2000
Soc Mobil 4¼s, '93
Weyerhaeuser 5.20s, '91

BEST GRADE BONDS

Amer Tel & Tel 3⅞s, '90
Atchison Topeka & Santa Fe, 4s '95
Chesapeake & Ohio, 4½s, '92
Consumers Pwr 1st 5⅞s, '96
Exxon 6s, '97
Gen El 8½s, 2004
Illinois Bell Telephone, 8s, '04
Norfolk & Western, 4s, '96
Union Pacific, 2½s, '91
US Steel, 4½s, '86

INTERMEDIATE GRADE BONDS

Alabama Power 9¾s, 2004
Bethlehem Steel 6⅞s, '99
Detroit Edison 9s, '99
Ford Motor 8⅛s, '90
Louisville Nash 7⅜s, '93
Missouri Pac 4¼s, 2005
Pacific G&E 7¾s, 2005
Pfizer 9¼s, 2000
Philadelphia El 7⅜s, 2001
St. Louis San Fr 4s, '97

U.S. GOV'T. BOND AVG.

3¼s, 1978-83 June
3¼s, 1985 May
6⅛s, 1986 Nov.

DOW JONES MUNICIPAL BOND YIELD INDEX

Minneapolis	4s	Illinois	4s
Milwaukee	4½s	North Carolina	4½s
Buffalo	3.90s	New York City	4s
Pittsburgh	4½s	New York State	4s
Boston	4s	Seattle	4½s
St. Louis	4¼s	Los Angeles	4¼s
Houston	4.65s	California	4s
Kansas City	4s	New Orleans	4½s
Missouri	4s	Detroit	4½s
Chicago	4s	Cleveland	4s

Source: *Barron's*, 22 Cortlandt Street, New York, New York 10007.

FEDERAL RESERVE BANKS

Federal Reserve Bank of	
BOSTON	600 Atlantic Avenue, Boston, Massachusetts 02106—(617) 973-3462
NEW YORK	33 Liberty Street (Federal Reserve P.O. Station). New York, New York 10045—(212) 791-5823 (Telephone 24 hours a day, including Saturday & Sunday)
Buffalo Branch	160 Delaware Avenue (P.O. Box 961), Buffalo, New York 14240—(716) 849-5046
PHILADELPHIA	100 North Sixth Street (P.O. Box 90), Philadelphia, Pennsylvania 19105—(215) 574-6580
CLEVELAND	1455 East Sixth Street (P.O. Box 6387), Cleveland, Ohio 44101—(216) 241-2800
Cincinnati Branch	150 East Fourth Street (P.O. Box 999), Cincinnati, Ohio 45201—(513) 721-4787 ext 333
Pittsburgh Branch	717 Grant Street (P.O. Box 867), Pittsburgh, Pennsylvania 15230—(412) 261-7864
RICHMOND	701 East Byrd Street (P.O. Box 27622), Richmond, Virginia 23261—(804) 643-1250
Baltimore Branch	114-120 East Lexington Street (P.O. Box 1378), Baltimore, Maryland 21203—(301) 539-6552
Charlotte Branch	401 South Tryon Street (P.O. Box 300), Charlotte, North Carolina 28230—(704) 373-0200
ATLANTA	104 Marietta Street, N.W., (P.O. Box 1731) Atlanta, Georgia 30301—(404) 586-8657
Birmingham Branch	1801 Fifth Avenue, North (P.O. Box 10447), Birmingham, Alabama 35202—(205) 252-3141 ext. 215
Jacksonville Branch	515 Julia Street, Jacksonville, Florida 32231—(904) 632-4245
Miami Branch	9100 N.W. Thirty-sixth Street Extension, Miami, Florida 33178 (P.O. Box 520847, Miami, Florida 33152)—(305) 591-2065
Nashville Branch	301 Eighth Avenue, North, Nashville, Tennessee 37203—(615) 259-4006
New Orleans Branch	525 St. Charles Avenue (P.O. Box 61630), New Orleans, Louisiana 70161 (504) 586-1505 ext. 230, 240, 242

CHICAGO	230 South LaSalle Street (P.O. Box 834), Chicago, Illinois 60690—(312) 786–1110 (Telephone 24 hours a day, including Saturday & Sunday)
Detroit Branch	160 Fort Street, West (P.O. Box 1059), Detroit, Michigan 48231—(313) 961–6880 ext. 372, 373
ST. LOUIS	411 Locust Street (P.O. Box 442), St. Louis, Missouri 63166—(314) 444–8444
Little Rock Branch	325 West Capitol Avenue (P.O. Box 1261), Little Rock, Arkansas 72203—(501) 372–5451 ext. 270
Louisville Branch	410 South Fifth Street (P.O. Box 32710), Louisville, Kentucky 40232 (502) 587–7351 ext. 237, 301
Memphis Branch	200 North Main Street (P.O. Box 407), Memphis, Tennessee 38101—(800) 238–5293 ext. 225
MINNEAPOLIS	250 Marquette Avenue, Minneapolis, Minnesota 55480—(612) 340–2051
Helena Branch	400 North Park Avenue, Helena, Montana 59601—(406) 442–3860
KANSAS CITY	925 Grand Avenue (Federal Reserve Station), Kansas City, Missouri 64198—(816) 881–2783
Denver Branch	1020 16th Street (P.O. Box 5228, Terminal Annex), Denver, Colorado 80217 (303) 292–4020
Oklahoma City Branch	226 Northwest Third Street (P.O. Box 25129), Oklahoma City, Oklahoma 73125 (405) 235–1721 ext. 182
Omaha Branch	102 South Seventeenth Street, Omaha, Nebraska 68102—(402) 341–3610 ext. 242
DALLAS	400 South Akard Street (Station K), Dallas, Texas 75222—(214) 651–6177
El Paso Branch	301 East Main Street (P.O. Box 100), El Paso, Texas 79999—(915) 544–4730 ext. 57
Houston Branch	1701 San Jacinto Street (P.O. Box 2578), Houston, Texas 77001—(713) 659–4433 ext 19, 74, 75, 76
San Antonio Branch	126 East Nueva Street (P.O. Box 1471), San Antonio, Texas 78295—(512) 224–2141 ext 61, 66
SAN FRANCISCO	400 Sansome Street (P.O. Box 7702), San Francisco, California 94120—(415) 392–6639
Los Angeles Branch	409 West Olympic Boulevard (P.O. Box 2077, Terminal Annex), Los Angeles, California 90051 (213) 683–8563
Portland Branch	915 S.W. Stark Street (P.O. Box 3436), Portland, Oregon 97208—(503) 228–7584
Salt Lake City Branch	120 South State Street (P.O. Box 30780), Salt Lake City, Utah 84130—(801) 355–3131
Seattle Branch	1015 Second Avenue (P.O. Box 3567), Seattle, Washington 98124—(206) 442–1650
TREASURY	**General information concerning Treasury Securities and requests for forms:**
	Bureau of the Public Debt, Dept. F
	Washington, D.C. 20226
	Specific questions concerning Bills:
	Bureau of the Public Debt, Dept. X
	Washington, D.C. 20226
	Specific questions concerning registered Notes or Bonds:
	Bureau of the Public Debt, Dept A
	Washington, D.C. 20226
	Telephone: (202) 287–4113

Stock Options

WHAT ARE STOCK OPTIONS?

There are two types of stock options—call and put. A call option is the right to buy a specified number of shares of a stock at a given price before a specific date. A put option is the right to sell a specific number of shares of a stock at a given price before a specific date. Options, unlike a futures contract, are a right *not an obligation* to buy or sell stock. The price at which the stock may be bought or sold is referred to as the exercise (or striking) price. The date at which the option expires is the *expiration* date. The term "in-the-money" option refers to either a call option with an exercise price less than that of the market price of the stock, or a put option with an exercise price above the market price of the stock.

Expiration months are set at intervals of three months for the cycles: the January–April–July–October cycle, February–May–August–November cycle, and the March–June–September–December cycle. Options expire at 11:59 P.M. Eastern Standard Time on the Saturday immediately following the third Friday of the expiration month.

The exercise prices are set at 5 point (dollar) intervals for stocks trading below $50, 10 point intervals for stocks trading between $50 to $200, and 20 point intervals for securities trading above $200. Initial exercise prices are set above and below the price of the security. Thus, if a security is priced at 32½ on the New York Stock Exchange at the time new options are opened, the opening exercise prices would be set at 30 and 40. If the price of the security is close to a standard exercise price, three prices are set: at the standard price, as well as above and below the latter.

Standard option contracts are written for 100 shares of stock of the underlying security. The price at which the seller (writer) agrees to sell an option to the buyer is called the *premium*. The premium is quoted *per share* of the underlying stock so that the price per contract is 100 times the quote.

After the option is issued, the premium will fluctuate with the price of the stocks. With call options the premium will increase with an increase in the price of stock. With put options the premium will increase when the stock price declines. The reason should be clear from the following examples. Assume that in January a July call option is written at the exercise price of 50 ($50 per share) on the XYZ Corporation stock. We assume that the stock is selling at $51. The call option writer (seller) asks and receives a premium of $2 ($200 per option contract). After brokerage commission on the sale (say $25 per contract) the option writer nets a profit of $175 per contract. The call option buyer pays $200 for the contract plus the commission or $225. Assume that the stock increases to 60 per share. The option holder (buyer) can, in principle, purchase the stock at 50 (the Exercise price) and sell it at 60 netting a profit on transaction of $10 per share (neglecting commissions). Clearly the call option has acquired increased value which will be reflected in the premium (option price). Let us assume that the premium increases from 2 to 10 ($200 to $1,000 per contract). If the option holder now sells the option, he will make a profit (after commissions) of $750 on a $250 investment ($200 premium and $50 commission).

Alternatively, the option holder may elect to exercise the option and acquire the shares at 50 (the exercise price). The option writer must then deliver 100 shares of XYZ Corporation at $50 per share.

If the stock price drops below the exercise price and remains so until expiration of the option, the call option buyer can lose his entire investment. Sometimes the loss may be reduced if the option is sold before it matures. The holder then is said to have *closed out* his position.

Similar arguments apply to put options. In this case the option holder benefits if the price of the stock decreases below the exercise price. Assume that the above stock drops to 40. The put holder could, in principle, buy the stock at 40 and sell it at 50 (the exercise price) to the put writer. The put holder would make a profit of $10 per share (neglecting commissions). The put premium would reflect this situation and, as a result, increase.

Instead of selling the option and taking a profit, the put holder may elect to exercise the option and sell 100 shares to the put writer who must purchase these shares at the 50 exercise price.

If the market price of the stock is greater

than the exercise price when the put option expires, the holder will lose his investment.

Options are traded on the Chicago Board of Options Exchange, the American Stock Exchange, the Pacific Stock Exchange and the Philadelphia Stock Exchange.

HOW TO READ OPTION QUOTATIONS

Closing prices of all options. Sales unit usually is 100 shares. Security description includes exercise price. Stock close is New York or American exchange final price.

(1) Option & NY Close	(2) Strike Price	(3) Calls—Last			(4) Puts—Last		
		Aug	Nov	Feb	Aug	Nov	Feb
Slb							
94¾	100	2½	7	9½	5⅞	7¾	a
94¾	110	⅝	3⅜	5½	a	16	a
94¾	120	⅛	1⅛	b	a	a	b
94¾	130	¹⁄₁₆	b	b	a	b	b
Skylin	15	3⅜	4	a	a	⅝	a
17⅝	20	⅝	1¹¹⁄₁₆	2¼	a	a	a
Southn	10	a	2⅜	2⁷⁄₁₆	b	b	b

Source: Reprinted by permission of *The Wall Street Journal* © Dow Jones and Company, Inc., 1981. All rights reserved.

(1) The name of the company in abbreviated form. Below the company name is the New York or American Exchange closing price of the stock in terms of ⅛ of a dollar.
(2) The striking (exercise) price of the option.
(3) The expiration month of the call option, beneath which is the option's premium (price) per share of stock. Contracts are for 100 shares of stock so that, for example, the price of a contract quoted as 2⅛ ($2.125 per share) is $212.50. Options expire on the Saturday following the third Friday of the expiration month. The premium does not include commissions.
(4) The same as item 3, but for a put option. The letter *a* means the option was not traded that day, and *b* means the option is not offered.

OPTIONS TRADED, EXCHANGES WHERE TRADED AND TRADING CYCLE*

Underlying Stock/Symbol	Exchange[1]	Expiration Cycle[2]
Abbott Labs/ABT	PH*	2
Advanced Micro Devices/AMD	P*	1
Aetna Life/AET	A*	1
Air Products & Chemicals/APD	PH*	3
Allied Chemical/ACD	PH*	1
Allis Chalmers/AH	PH*	1
Aluminum Co. of America/AA	C*	1
Amax/AMX	A*	3
Amdahl Corp./AMH	C*	2
Amerada Hess/AHC	PH*	2
American Broadcasting/ABC	P*	2
American Cyanamid/ACY	A*	1
American Electric Power/AEP	C	2
American Express/AXP	C*,A*	1
American Home Products/AHP	A*	1
American Hospital Supply/ AHS	C	2
American Telephone & Telegraph/T	C*	1
AMF/AMF	A*	2
AMP/AMP	C	2
Anheuser-Busch/BUD	PH*	3
Apache/APA	C*	3
Archer-Daniels-Midland/ADM	PH*	3
ASA, Ltd./ASA	A*	2
Asarco/AR	A*	3
Ashland Oil/ASH	PH*	1
Atlantic Richfield/ARC	C*	1
Avco/AV	PH*	3
Avnet/AVT	A*	2
Avon/AVP	C*	1
Baker Intern'l./BKO	P*	3
Bally Mfg./BLY	C*,A*	2
BankAmerica/BAM	C	1
Bausch & Lomb/BOL	A*	1
Baxter Travenol Labs/BAX	C*	2
Beatrice Foods/BRY	A*	3
Becton, Dickinson/BDX	PH*	3
Bethlehem Steel/BS	C*	1
Black & Decker/BDK	C	2
Blue Bell/BBL	PH*	1
Boeing/BA	C*	2
Boise Cascade/BCC	C	2
Bristol-Myers/BMY	C*	3
Browning-Ferris Industries/BFI	A*	3
Brunswick/BC	C*	3
Bucyrus-Erie/BY	A*	3
Burlington Northern/BNI	C*	1
Burroughs/BGH	C,A*	1
Caesar's World/CAW	P	2
Caterpillar/CAT	A*	2
CBS/CBS	C	2
Cessna Aircraft/CEA	C*	2
Champion Intern'l./CHA	C*	3
Charter/CHR	PH*	3
Chase Manhattan/CMB	A*	3
Citicorp/FNC	C*	1
Cities Service/CS	PH*	3

Underlying Stock/Symbol	Exchange[1]	Expiration Cycle[2]	Underlying Stock/Symbol	Exchange[1]	Expiration Cycle[2]
City Investing/CNV	PH*	1	Homestake Mining/HM	C*	1
Coastal/CGP	C*,A*	3	Honeywell/HON	C*	2
Coca-Cola/KO	C*	2	Hospital Corp. of Amer./HSP	P	1
Colgate Palmolive/CL	C*	2	Household Finance/HFC	A*	1
Combustion Eng./CSP	P	3	Houston Natural Gas/HNG	P	1
Commonwealth Edison/CWE	C*	2	Hughes Tool/HT	C*	3
Communications Satellite/CQ	PH*	1	Hutton (E. F.) Group/EFH	A*	1
Computer Sciences/CSC	C*	3	INA/INA	C*	1
Computervision Corp./CVN	PH	**	Inexco Oil/INX	PH*	2
Conoco/CLL	PH*	1	Intern'l. Business Machines/ IBM	C*	1
Consolidated Edison/ED	A*	2	Intern'l. Flavors & Fragrances/		
Continental Telephone/CTC	A*	1	IFF	C	2
Control Data/CDA	C*	2	Intern'l. Harvester/HR	C*	1
Corning Glass/GLW	C*	3	Intern'l. Minerals & Chemical/		
Data General/DGN	P	3	IGL	C	1
Datapoint Corp./DPT	C*	2	Intern'l. Paper/IP	C*	1
Dean Witter Reynolds/DWR	PH	**	Intern'l. Telephone &		
Deere/DE	A*	3	Telegraph/ITT	C*	3
Delta Air Lines/DAL	C*	1	Johns-Manville/JM	C*	2
Diamond Shamrock/DIA	P*	1	Johnson & Johnson/JNJ	C*	1
Digital Equipment/DEC	C,A*	1	Joy Mfg./JOY	PH*	2
Disney/DIS	C,A*	1	Kaneb Services/KAB	A*	3
Dr. Pepper/DOC	A*	2	Kerr-McGee/KMG	C*	1
Dorchester Gas/DGS	P	2	K-Mart/KM	C*	3
Dow Chemical/DOW	C*	3	Lear Siegler/LSI	PH*	3
Dresser/DI	PH*	1	Levi Strauss/LVI	P*	1
Duke Power/DUK	PH*	1	Lilly (Eli)/LLY	A*	1
duPont/DD	C*,A*	1	Litton Industries/LIT	C*	3
Eastern Gas & Fuel Assoc./ EFU	PH*	1	Lockheed/LK	P*	3
Eastman Kodak/EK	C*	1	Louisiana Land & Explor./LLX	PH*	2
EG & G Inc./EGG	PH*	3	Louisiana Pacific/LPX	A*	2
El Paso/ELG	A*	2	LTV/LTV	A*	3
Esmark/ESM	C*	3	M/A Com Inc./MAI	A*	**
Evans Products/EVY	C*	3	MAPCO/MDA	P*	1
Exxon/XON	C*	1	Marathon Oil/MRO	A*	3
Federal Express/FDX	C*	1	Marriott/MHS	PH*	1
Fed. Nat'l. Mortgage Assoc./ FNM	C	1	Martin Marietta/ML	PH*	3
First Charter Financial/FCF	A*	1	McDermott (J. Ray)/MDE	PH*	2
Fluor/FLR	C*	1	McDonald's/MCD	C*	3
Ford Motor/F	C*	3	McDonnell Douglas/MD	P*	2
Foster Wheeler/FWC	P	1	Merck/MRK	C*	1
Freeport Minerals/FT	C*	3	Merrill Lynch/MER	C*,A*	1
Fuqua Industries/FQA	PH*	3	Mesa Petroleum/MSA	A*	1
GAF/GAF	PH*	1	MGIC Invest. Corp./MGI	C,A*	2
General Dynamics/GD	C*	2	MGM Grand Hotels/GRH	P	3
General Electric/GE	C*	3	Middle South Utilities/MSU	C*	3
General Foods/GF	C*	2	Minnesota Mining & Mfg./MMM	C*	1
General Instruments/GRL	PH*	3	Mobil/MOB	C*	2
General Motors/GM	C*	3	Mohawk Data Sciences/MDS	P	3
General Telephone & Electronics/GTE	A*	3	Monsanto/MTC	C*	1
Georgia Pacific/GP	PH*	1	Motorola/MOT	A*	1
Getty Oil/GET	PH*	3	NCR/NCR	C*	3
Gillette/GS	A*	3	Nat'l. Distillers/DR	A*	2
Global Marine Inc./GLM	A*	**	Nat'l. Medical Ent./NME	A*	2
Goodyear Tire/GT	A*	1	Nat'l. Semiconductor/NSM	C*,A*	2
Grace (W. R.)/GRA	A*	2	Natomas/NOM	A*	3
Great Western Financial/GWF	C	1	Newmont Mining/NEM	PH*	3
Greyhound/G	A*	1	NL Industries/NL	PH*	2
Gulf & Western/GW	C*	3	NLT Corp./NLT	A*	3
Gulf Oil/GO	A*	1	Northwest Airlines/NWA	C*	1
Halliburton/HAL	C*	1	Northwest Industries/NWT	C*	3
Harris Corp./HRS	C	2	Norton Simon/NSI	A*	2
Hercules/HPC	A*	3	Occidental Petroleum/OXY	C*	2
Heublein/HBL	P*	2	Owens-Corning Fiber/OCF	PH*	3
Hewlett-Packard/HWP	C*	2	Owens-Illinois/OI	C*	3
Hilton Hotels/HLT	P*	2	Penney (J. C.)/JCP	A*	2
Holiday Inns/HIA	C*	2	Pennzoil/PZL	C*	1
			PepsiCo Inc./PEP	C	1
			Perkin-Elmer/PKN	P*	3

Underlying Stock/Symbol	Exchange[1]	Expiration Cycle[2]
Pfizer/PFE	A*	3
Phelps Dodge/PD	A	1
Phibro Corp./PB	PH*	1
Philip Morris/MO	A*	3
Phillips Petroleum/P	A*	2
Pitney Bowes/PBI	A*	1
Pittston/PCO	PH*	2
Pogo Producing/PPP	P	1
Polaroid/PRD	C*,P*	1
PPG Industries/PPG	PH*	2
Prime Computer/PRM	A*	3
Procter & Gamble/PG	A*	1
Ralston Purina/RAL	C*	3
Raytheon/RTN	C*	2
RCA/RCA	C*	3
Reading & Bates/RB	P	2
Resorts Intern'l./RTA	P*	1
Revlon/REV	C*	3
Reynolds Metals/RLM	P*	2
Reynolds (R. J.)/RJR	C*	2
Rockwell Intern'l./ROK	C*	3
Ryder Systems/RDR	P	2
Safeway Stores/SA	C*	3
Sante Fe Industries/SFF	A*	3
Sante Fe Intern'l./SAF	P*	1
Schering-Plough/SGP	P*	2
Schlumberger Ltd./SLB	C*	2
Scott Paper/SPP	PH*	1
Searle (G. D.)/SRL	A*	2
Sears, Roebuck/S	C*	3
Signal Cos./SGN	P*	2
Skyline/SKY	C*	2
SmithKline/SKL	P*	3
Southern/SO	C*	2
Sperry/SY	C*	1
Squibb/SQB	C*	1
St. Joe Minerals/SJO	PH*	3
Standard Oil of Calif./SD	A*	3
Standard Oil of Ind./SN	C*	2
Standard Oil of Ohio/SOH	A*	3
Sterling Drug/STY	A*	2
Storage Technology/STK	C*	1
Sun/SUN	PH*	2
Superior Oil/SOC	C*	3
Syntex/SYN	C*	3
Tandy/TAN	C,A*	1
Tektronix/TEK	C*	3
Teledyne/TDY	C*,P*	1
Teleprompter/TP	A*	3
Tennaco/TGT	A*	2
Texaco/TX	A*	1
Texasgulf/TG	C	2
Texas Instruments/TXN	C*	1
Texas Oil & Gas/TXO	PH*	3
Tiger Intern'l./TGR	A*	2
Time/TL	PH*	3
Tosco/TOS	A*	2
Transamerica/TA	PH*	2
Travelers/TIC	P*	2
TRW/TRW	A*	1
UAL/UAL	C*	2
UNC Resources/UNC	C	2
Union Carbide/UK	A*	1
Union Oil (Calif.)/UCL	P*	1
Union Pacific/UNP	PH*	2
United States Steel/X	A*	1
United Technologies/UTX	C*	2
Upjohn/UPJ	C*	1
U.S. Air/U	P*	3
U.S. Home/UH	A*	3

Underlying Stock/Symbol	Exchange[1]	Expiration Cycle[2]
Valero Energy/VLO	A*	3
Virginia Electric & Power/VEL	PH*	1
Walter, Jim/JWC	C	2
Wang Labs B/WAN.B	P	1
Warner Communications/WCI	C*	2
Warner-Lambert/WLA	A*	1
Waste Management/WMX	PH	**
Wendy's Intern'l./WEN	P*	3
Western Union/WU	PH*	1
Westinghouse/WX	A*	1
Weyerhaeuser/WY	C*	1
Whittaker/WKR	A*	3
Williams Cos./WMB	C*	2
Woolworth (F. W.)/Z	PH*	2
Xerox/XRX	C*,P	1
Zapata/ZOS	P*	3
Zenith Radio/ZE	A*	2

[1] A-AMEX C-CBOE P-Pacific PH-Philadelphia
[2] 1   January/April/July/October
2   February/May/August/November
3   March/June/September/December
* All of the above have listed calls. Puts are indicated by an asterisk following the Exchange Symbol.
** not trading as of 7/15/81
TOTALS: A-81, C-120, P-38, PH-51.
List prepared as of July 15, 1981.
Source: *Stocks Underlying All Lists Options,* The Chicago Board Options Exchange.

CBOE CALL AND PUT OPTIONS INDEX

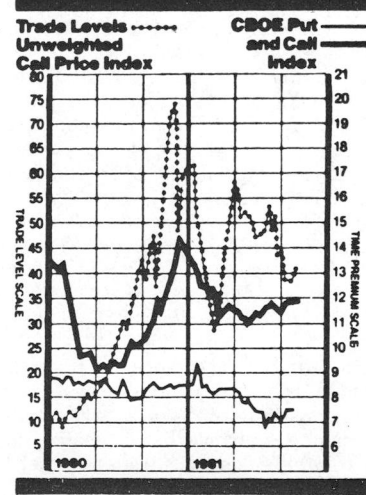

Source: Barron's, July 17, 1981.

The CBOE option indices are averages which express the current call or put premiums (adjusted to the estimated at-the-money* with six months to expiration values) as a percentage of the current market price of the underlying stock. The indices are useful for following the general trend of option premiums.

* The option is *at-the-money* when the stock is trading at the exercise price.

Commodities and Interest Rate Futures

UNDERSTANDING THE COMMODITIES MARKET

COMMODITY EXCHANGES

A Commodity Exchange is an organized market of buyers and sellers of various types of commodities. It is public to the extent that anyone can trade through member firms. It provides a trading place for commodities, regulates the trading practices of the members, gathers and transmits price information, inspects and governs commodities traded on the Exchange, supervises warehouses that store the commodity, and provides means for settling disputes between members. All transactions must be conducted in a pit on the Exchange floor within certain hours.

FUTURES CONTRACT

A futures contract is a contract between two parties where the buyer agrees to accept delivery at a specified price from the seller of a particular commodity, in a designated month in the future, if it is not liquidated before the contract reaches maturity. A futures contract is not an option; nothing in it is conditional. Each contract calls for a specified amount, and grade of product. For example: *A person buying a February Pork Belly contract at 52.40 in effect is making a legal obligation, now, to accept delivery of 38,000 pounds of frozen Pork Bellies, to be delivered during the month of February, for which the buyer will pay 52.40 per pound.*

The average trader does not take delivery of a futures contract, since he normally will close out his position before the futures contract matures. As a matter of fact, a survey conducted by a leading exchange has estimated that less than 3% of the contracts traded are settled by actual delivery.

THE HEDGER AND SPECULATOR

A hedger buys or sells a futures contract in order to reduce the risk of loss through price variation. A short hedger sells a futures contract to protect the possible decline in the actual commodity owned by him. A long hedger purchases a futures contract to protect the possible advance in the value of an actual commodity needed to be purchased in the future.

The speculator is an important factor in the volume of future trading today. He, in effect, voluntarily assumes the risk, which the hedger tries to avoid, with the expectations of making a profit. He is somewhat of an insurance underwriter. The largest number of traders on any commodity exchange is the speculator. In order for the hedger to participate, he must have continuous trading interests and activity in the market. This trading activity stems from the role of the speculator, because he involves himself in buying or selling of futures contracts with the idea of making a profit on the advance or decline of prices. The speculator tries to forecast prices in advance of delivery and is willing to buy or sell on this basis. A speculator involves himself in an inescapable risk.

CAN YOU BE A SPECULATOR?

Now, can you be a speculator? Before considering entering into the futures market as a speculator, there are several facts which you should understand about the market and also about yourself. In order to enter into the futures market, you must understand that you are dealing with a margin account. Margins are as low as 5 to 10% of the total value of the futures contract, so you are obtaining a greater leverage on your capital.

Fluctuations in price are rapid, volatile, and wide. It is possible to make a very large profit in a short period of time, but also, it is possible to take a substantial loss. In fact, surveys taken by the Agricultural Department have shown that up to 75% of the individuals speculating in commodity markets have lost money. This does not mean that some of their trades were not profitable, but after a period of time with a given sum of money they ended up being a loser.

Now taking you as an individual, let us see whether you have the characteristics to become a commodity trader. Number one and the most important is that you do not take money that you have set aside for your future, or money you need daily to support your family or yourself. Number two, and almost equally important, is that you must be willing to assume losses

Source: Commodity Educational Services, Division of Commodity Cassettes, Inc., P.O. Box 152, Wilmette, Illinois 60091.

and be willing to assume these losses with such a temperament that it is not going to affect your everyday life. Money used in the futures market should be money that has been set aside for strictly risk purposes, and if this money is not risk capital, your methods of trading could be seriously affected, because you cannot afford to be a loser.

Another very important factor is that you must not feel that you are going to take a thousand, two thousand, five or ten thousand dollars and place this with a brokerage firm and not follow the daily happenings of the market. Price fluctuations are fast, and as stated before, wide, so you must not only be in contact with your Account Executive daily, but know and study the technical facts that may be affecting the particular market in which you are speculating.

The individual who makes his first trade by buying a contract on Monday and selling this contract on the following Wednesday, making six hundred dollars on a $1,000 investment, in a period of two days, suddenly says to himself, *"Where has this market been all my life? Why am I working? Why not just concentrate on this market, if every two days or so I can make six hundred dollars?"* This is a fallacy, since this is an individual that is going to destroy himself and most likely his family. The next trade he will feel confident that because of his first profitable trade the market will always go his way even though he is now showing a loss in his position. He still feels that the market will turn around in his direction. If you become married to a particular commodity futures contract and constantly feel that the losses you are taking at the present time will reverse into profits, you are really fighting the market and in most cases fighting a losing battle. This could lead to disaster. There is a saying that you let your profits ride, but liquidate your losses fast.

In any way that you are uneasy with a position that you are holding, it is better to liquidate it. If, prior to the time of buying or selling a contract, you are not sure that this is the right step to take, do not take it. To protect yourself against this hazard you should pre-decide on every trade and exactly how much you intend to lose.

Another important point is not to involve yourself in too many markets. It is difficult to know all the technical facts and be able to follow numerous markets. In addition, if you are in a winning position, be conservative as to how you add additional contracts or pyramid your position. Being conservative will sometimes cause you to miss certain moves in certain markets and you may feel this to be wrong, but over a long period of time, this conservatism will be profitable to you.

If at this point you feel that you are ready, both financially and mentally to trade commodities, the next step is to begin the actual mechanics of trading a futures contract.

OPENING AN ACCOUNT

The first important factor is to decide which brokerage firm will afford you the best service. To accomplish this, you should do a little research by checking with the various exchanges about different brokerage firms. You should study their advertising, market letters, and other information. These should all be presented in a business-like manner and have no unwarranted claims, such as a guarantee of profit without indicating the possibility of loss.

The brokerage firm must be able to handle orders on all commodity exchanges. Do not pick just any Account Executive in a firm, but one you feel confident to help you make market decisions. Become acquainted with the Account Executive through phone or personal conversations. His knowledge of the factors entering into the market and the understanding of current market trends are important in your final choice.

After making a decision on the brokerage firm and the Account Executive that would be best for you, contact him and have him send you the literature concerning different contracts, and also, any additional information as to his organization. He will then send you the necessary signature cards required by the firm to open an account, and ask you for a deposit of margin money.

You will be trading in regulated commodities, and margin money will be deposited in a segregated fund at the brokerage firm's bank. A segregated account means that the money will only be used for margin and not for expenses of the brokerage firm.

Now you decide to enter into your first trade. Your Account Executive and you decide to enter into a December Live Cattle contract on the Chicago Mercantile Exchange. Your order will be executed as follows: Your Account Executive will place this order with his order desk who will then transmit the order to the floor of the Chicago Mercantile Exchange. There your order will be executed on the trading floor, in the pit. All technical details connected with the transaction will be handled by the brokerage firm.

Upon filling of your order, the filled order will be transmitted back to your Account Executive, who will then contact you, advising you that you have purchased one December Live Cattle contract at a given price. You will also receive a written confirmation on this transaction. You will now show an open position in December Live Cattle on the books of the brokerage firm.

MECHANICS OF A TRADE

Let us go back one step to explain in detail just how your order to buy one December Cattle was handled on the floor of the exchange.

All buying and selling in the pit is done by open out-cry, and every price change is reported on the exchange ticker system. Each firm has brokers in the different pits, a pit meaning a trading area for the purpose of buying and selling contracts.

When your order was received on the exchange floor, it was time stamped and then given to a runner. This is a person who takes the order from the desk on the exchange floor and gives it to one of the brokers in the December Cattle trading pit. He is then responsible to the brokerage firm to fill that order, if possible, at the stated price. After filling the order, he then has the runner return it to the desk where it is time stamped and transmitted back to the order desk at the brokerage house, and the filled order is reported to you.

MARGIN

Futures trading requires the trader to place margin with his brokerage firm. Initial margin is required and this amount varies with each commodity. The minimum margin is established by each commodity exchange. Additional funds are needed when the equity of your account falls below this level. This is known as a maintenance margin call.

All margin calls must be met immediately. Normally you will be given a reasonable amount of time to comply with this request. If you do not comply, the firm has the right to liquidate your trades or a sufficient number of trades to restore your account to margin requirements.

The brokerage firm has the right to raise margin requirements to the customer at any time. This is normally done if the price of the commodity is changing sharply or if it is the brokerage firm's opinion that due to the volatility of the market the margin requirement is not sufficient at that particular time.

Most commodity contracts have a minimum fluctuation and also a maximum fluctuation for any one particular day. For example, if you are trading frozen Pork Bellies on the Chicago Mercantile Exchange the fluctuation is considered in points. A point equals three dollars and eighty cents. This means that if you buy a contract at 52.40 and the next price tick is 52.45, you have made a paper profit of five points or nineteen dollars. The maximum fluctuation on a belly contract is 200 points, so your profit or loss cannot exceed in one day more than 200 points from the previous day's settlement. There are exceptions in some commodity contracts, where the spot month has no limit.

Let us assume that you had originally placed in the hands of your brokerage firm two thousand dollars margin money, and that you and your Account Executive decide to purchase a December Live Cattle contract whose initial margin is $1200 with maintenance of $900.00. After the purchase of the contract your account would show initial margin required $1200 dollars with excess funds of eight hundred dollars. At the end of each day the settlement price of December Cattle would be applied to your purchase price and your account would be adjusted to either an increase due to profit or decrease due to loss in your contract.

Further, assume that in a period of two or three days there is a decline in the price of the December Cattle contract and your account now shows a loss of three hundred dollars. Since maintenance margin is only nine hundred dollars on this contract, you will still show an excess of eight hundred dollars over and above maintenance margin. But, in the next four days suppose there is an additional loss of nine hundred dollars. Your account will now need one hundred dollars to maintain the maintenance margin and four hundred dollars additional in order to bring your account up to initial margin. Your Account Executive, or a man from the margin department of the brokerage firm will then contact you, stating that you must place additional money with the firm in order to maintain the December Cattle contract.

At this point, you must decide whether you should continue with the contract, feeling that it may be profitable in the next few days, and thus sending the brokerage firm the required four hundred dollars to maintain your position, or whether to assume your loss and sell the contract.

Let us assume that you decide to sell your December contract at this point and that the selling price causes a loss of four hundred dollars. Added to this loss would be the commission of forty dollars, so your total loss on the transaction would be four hundred forty dollars. A confirmation and purchase and sales statement will be sent to you, showing the original price paid for the contract, the price for which it was sold, the gross loss of four hundred dollars plus the commission of forty dollars making the total loss four hundred forty dollars, and your new ledger balance on deposit with the firm as fifteen hundred sixty dollars.

As shown in our example, commission was charged only when the contract was closed out. A single commission is charged for each round-turn transaction consisting of the creation and liquidation of a single contract.

CONTROLLED, DISCRETIONARY, AND MANAGED ACCOUNTS

There are two methods of trading your account. The first is the professional approach where you and your Account Executive decide on each trade with no discretion being given directly to your Account Executive. This method was illustrated in the discussion about margins. The second method is called a controlled discretionary or managed account. Under this method, you are giving your Account Executive authorization to trade your account at his discretion at any time and as many times that he considers that a trade should be made. The Chicago Mercantile Exchange, and the Board of Trade have rules governing this type of relationship. The following is an excerpt from the C.M.E. rule regarding controlled, discretionary and managed accounts.

REQUIREMENTS

No clearing member shall accept or carry an account over which any individual or organization, other than the person in whose name the account is carried, exercises trading authority or control, hereinafter referred to as controlled accounts, unless:

> The account is initiated with a minimum of $5000*, and maintained at a minimum equity of $3,750*, regardless of lesser applicable margin requirements. In determining equity the accounts or ledger balances and positions in all commodities traded at the clearing member shall be included. Whenever at the close of any business day the equity, calculated with all open positions figured to the settling price, in any such account is below the required minimum, the clearing member shall immediately notify the customer in person, by telephone or telegraph and by written confirmation of such notice mailed directly to the customer, not later than the close of the following business day. Such notice shall advise the customer that unless additional funds are promptly received to restore the customer's controlled account to no less than $5,000*, the clearing member shall liquidate all of the customer's open futures positions at the Exchange.
>
> In the event the call for additional equity is not met within a reasonable time, the customer's entire open position shall be liquidated. No period of time in excess of five business days shall be considered reasonable unless such longer period is approved in writing by an officer or partner of the clearing member upon good cause shown.

REVIEWING YOUR CONFIRMATIONS AND STATEMENTS

An important factor in trading is that you must be sure that no errors occur in your account. For every trade made you should receive a confirmation, and for every close-out a profit and loss statement known as a Purchase-and-Sale, showing the financial results of each transaction closed out in your account. In addition, a monthly statement showing your ledger bal-

ance, your open position, the net profit or loss in all contracts liquidated since the date of your last previous statement, and the net unrealized profit and loss on all open contracts figured to the market should be sent to you.

You should carefully review these statements. Upon receiving a confirmation of a trade you should immediately check its accuracy as far as type of commodity, month, trading price and quantity of contracts. If this does not agree with your original order, it should be immediately reported to the main office of your brokerage firm, and any differences should be explained and adjustments should be made.

If you do not receive a confirmation on a trade after it was orally reported to you by your Account Executive, be sure to contact him and the main office so that if an error was made it can be corrected immediately. You should receive written confirmation when you deposit money with your brokerage firm. If within a few days, you have not received this confirmation, report it immediately to the main office of your brokerage firm.

Never assume that an order has been filled until you receive an oral confirmation from your broker. A ticker or a board that you may be observing can be running several minutes behind and is not the determining factor as to whether your trade was executed or not. Until you receive this oral confirmation, never re-enter an order to buy or sell, against that position.

If you receive a confirmation in the mail showing a trade not belonging to you, immediately notify the main office of your brokerage firm and have them explain why this is on a confirmation with your account number. If it is an error, be sure that it is adjusted immediately and a written confirmation sent to you showing the adjustment of the error. If an error is made and it is profitable to you do not consider this any differently than if it was not profitable. Regardless of whether there is a profit or loss, all errors should be immediately reported to the brokerage firm.

Be sure that when you request funds to be mailed from your account that they are received within a few days from the time of your request. If not, contact the accounting department of the brokerage firm to see what is the cause of the delay.

Never make a check out to an individual. Always make your check out to the brokerage firm.

DAY TRADING

Day trading is where there is a buy and sell made during the trading hours on one particular day. Day trading is not considered to be a sound practice for the new speculator and inexperienced trader. Day trading is something that should be executed only by a sophisticated

---

* Minimums can be changed by each exchange, so consult your Account Executive for current regulations.

trader who is in frequent communication with the floor, and even then, on a limited basis.

ORDERS

In order to trade effectively in the commodity market there are several basic types of orders. The most common order is a market order. A market order is one which you authorize your Account Executive to buy or sell at the existing price. This is definitely not a predetermined price, but is executed at a bid or offer at that particular moment.

Example: Buy 5 Feb Pork Bellies at the market.

LIMITED OR PRICE ORDERS AND "OB" DESIGNATION

This type of order to buy or sell commodities at a fixed or "limited" price and the ordinary "market" order are the most common types of orders.

Example: Buy Three Jan Silver 463.10. This limit order instructs the floor broker to buy three contracts of January Silver futures at 463.10. Even with this simple order, however, one presumption is necessary—that the market price prevailing when the order enters the pit is 463.10 or higher. If the price is below 463.10, the broker could challenge on the basis that the client may have meant *"Buy Three Jan Silver 463.10 stop."* Therefore, while it is always assumed that a "limit: order means 'or better,' " if possible, it saves confusion and challenges if the "OB" designation is added to the limit price. This is particularly true on orders near the market, or on pre-opening orders with the limit price based on the previous close, because no one knows whether the opening will be higher or lower than the close, *i.e., Buy Three Jan Silver 463.10 OB.*

STOP ORDERS *(Orders having the effect of market orders)*

Buy Stop Buy stop orders must be written at a price higher than the price prevailing at the time of entry. If the prevailing price for December Wheat is 456 per bushel, a buy stop order must designate a price above 456.

Example: "Buy 20 Dec Wht 456½ Day Stop." The effect of this order is that if December Wheat touches 456½ the order to buy 20 December Wheat becomes a market order. From that point, 456½ on, all the above discussion regarding market orders applies.

Sell Stop Sell stop orders must be written at a price lower than the price prevailing at the time of entry in the trading pit. If the prevailing price of December Wheat is 456 per bushel, a sell stop order must designate a price below 456.

Example: "Sell 20 Dec Wht 455 Day Stop." If this order enters the trading pit with the above price of 456 prevailing, the order to sell 20 December Wheat becomes a market order. From that point 455 on, all the above discussion regarding market orders applies.

Buy stop orders have several specific uses. If you are short a December Wheat at 456, and wish to limit your loss to ½ cent per bushel, the above buy stop order at 456½ would serve this purpose. However, it is important to realize that such *"stop loss"* orders do not actually limit the loss to exactly ½ cent when *"elected"* or *"touched off"* because they become market orders and must be executed at whatever price the market conditions dictate.

Another use is when you are without a position and believe that, because of chart analysis or for other reasons, a buy of December Wheat at 456½ would signal the beginning of an important uptrend in Wheat prices. Thus, the same order to *"Buy 20 Dec Wheat 456½ Day Stop"* would serve this purpose.

Sell stop orders have the same uses in reverse. That is, if you are long 20 December Wheat at 456 and wish to limit this loss to 1 cent per bushel, the above sell stop order at 455 would serve this purpose, within the limitations of the market order possibilities. Similarly, if you are without a position and believe that a sale of December Wheat at 455 would signal a downtrend in wheat prices, and you wish to be short the market, you could use the order to *"Sell 20 December Wheat 455 Day Stop"* for this purpose.

STOP LIMIT ORDERS *(Variations of stop orders)*

Stop limit orders should be used by you when you wish to give the floor broker a limit beyond which he cannot go in executing the order which results when a stop price is *"elected."*

Example: "Buy 20 Dec Wheat 456½ Day Stop Limit." This instructs the broker that when the price of 456½ is reached and *"elects"* this stop order, instead of making it a market order, it becomes a limited order to be executed at 456½ *(or lower)*, but no higher than 456½. Another possibility:

Example: "Buy One February Pork Belly 58.10 Day Stop Limit 58.25 (or any other price above 58.10)." This instructs the broker that when the price of 58.10 *"elects"* the stop order instead of making it a market order, it becomes a limited order to buy at

58.25 *(or lower)*, but no higher as with any limit order.

Stop limit orders are particularly useful to you when you have no position and wish to enter a market via the stop order, but want to put some reasonable limit as to what you will pay. On the other hand, stop limit orders are not useful to you when you have an open position and wish to prevent a loss beyond a certain point. The reason is that by limiting the broker to a certain price after a *"stop loss"* order is elected, **you also run the risk that the market may exceed the limit too fast for the broker to execute.** This would leave you with your original position because the broker would have to wait for the return to the limit before executing. With a straight stop *(no limit)* order, the broker must execute *"at the market."*

Example: "Buy One February Pork Belly 58.10 Day Stop Limit 58.25." Suppose the market moves to 58.10 but then only 20 February Pork Bellies are offered at that price. Your broker bids for one at 58.10 but another broker in the pit catches the seller's eye first and buys 20 and your broker misses the sale. Your broker then bids 58.20 but the best offer is 58.30. He bids 58.25, but the offer at 58.30 remains unchanged. Then another broker bids for and buys February Pork Bellies at 58.30 and the market moves on up. Your broker is left with no execution to your order unless the market later declines to your limit making a fill possible.

If you did not have a position you might be disappointed, but you would be unhurt financially. However, if you had a position and were trying to limit your loss you would have defeated your purpose with the stop limit order, if you truly wanted *"out"* after the stop was elected.

Stop limit orders on the sell side have exactly the same uses, advantages and disadvantages as discussed above, but in reverse:

Example: "Sell 20 December Wheat 455 Day Stop Limit." This means that when the market declines to 455 per bushel, the broker may sell at 455 *(or higher)*, but no lower.

Another Example: "Sell One February Pork Belly 58.25 Stop Limit 58.10." This instructs the broker to sell a belly after the stop price of 58.25 is reached and *"elects"* the stop order, but no lower than 58.10.

M.I.T. ORDERS *(Market-if-touched)*

By adding MIT *(Market-If-Touched)* to a limit order, the limit order will have the effect of a market order when the limit price is reached or touched. This type of order is useful to you, when you have an open position and if a certain limit price is reached.

Example: "Sell One September Sugar 950 MIT." The floor broker is told that if and when the price of September Sugar rises to 9½¢ per pound, he is to sell one contract at the market. At this price of 9½¢ all prior discussion on market orders applies.

Under certain market conditions, not enough contracts are bid at 9½ cents to fill all offers to sell. Thus, you may see your straight limit price appear on the ticker, but your broker fails to make the sale.

But by adding MIT to the limit price, you will receive an execution, because the order becomes a market order, if the price is touched. However, the price will not necessarily be a good one in your eyes, since it became a market order when touched.

The same reasoning is true on the buy side of MIT orders but in reverse. Assume you are short one contract of September Sugar, with the prevailing price at 9½¢ per pound and you want to cover or liquidate your short at 9¢.

Example: "Buy One September Sugar 9¢ MIT." If and when the price of September sugar declines to 9¢ per pound, the floor broker must buy one contract at the market. Aside from the disadvantages of any market order, the MIT designation on the buy order prevents the disappointment which might arise if a straight limit buy at 9¢ were entered without the MIT added.

SPREAD ORDERS

As explained in the Glossary, a spread is a simultaneous long or short position in the same or related commodity. Thus a spread order would be to buy one month of a certain commodity and sell another month of the same commodity, or buy one month of one commodity and sell the same or another month of a related commodity.

Example: "Buy 5 July Beans Market and Sell 5 May Beans Market" or *"Buy 10 Kansas City Dec Wheat Market and Sell 10 Chicago May Wheat Market."*

Another Example: "Buy 5 May Corn Market and Sell 5 May Wheat Market."

In the example of the related commodity spread, normally the reason you would use such a spread, is that you expect to make a profit out of an expected tightness in the Corn Market, in the hope the corn contract will gain in value faster than wheat.

There may be a situation where you have a position either long or short in a commodity and want to change to a nearer or more distant option of the same commodity. For example you are long 5,000 bushels of May Soybeans on May 20 and want to avoid a delivery notice by moving your position forward into the July option. The basic spread order would be:

> "*Buy 5 July Beans Market and Sell 5 May Beans Market.*"

Sometimes you may prefer not to use market orders, in which case you use the difference spread.

> *Example:* "*Buy 5 July Beans and Sell 5 May Beans July 2¢ Over.*" Even though the prices of the two options are not specified, the broker is allowed to execute at any time he can

do so with July selling at 2¢ or less above May. Over or under designations are a necessity for clarity to the floor broker. Omitting either is like omitting the price.

All orders, except market orders, can be cancelled, prior to execution. Naturally, a market order is executed immediately upon reaching the pit, so its cancellation is almost impossible.

There are other variations of orders, but for you the new speculator, the types mentioned are sufficient for your trading.

The Commodities Glossary

Acreage allotment The portion of a farmer's total acreage that he can harvest and still qualify for government price supports, low interest crop loans and other programs. It currently applies to specialty crops—tobacco, peanuts and extra long staple cotton—for which complex federal marketing orders have been written to control production closely. Before the 1977 farm bill was passed, the same term also applied more loosely to the portion of a farmer's wheat or feed grain acreage for which government payments would be made. A farmer could harvest 100 acres of wheat, for instance, but he'd receive price support payments only for 70 acres if that was his allotment. The allotment in this sense is called "program acreage" in the new farm bill.

Arbitrage The simultaneous buying and selling of futures contracts to profit from what the trader perceives as a discrepancy in prices. Usually this is done in futures in the same commodity traded on different exchanges, such as cocoa in New York and cocoa in London or silver in New York and silver in Chicago. Some arbitrage occurs between cash markets and futures markets.

Asking price The price offered by one wishing to sell a physical commodity or a futures contract. Sometimes a futures market will close with an asking price when no buyers are around.

Backwardation An expression peculiar to New York markets. It means "nearby" contracts are trading at a higher price, or "premium," to the deferreds. See also *Inverted market.*

Basis A couple of meanings: (1) The difference between the price of the physical commodity (the cash price) and the futures price of that commodity. (2) A geographic reference point

for a cash price; for example, the price of a beef carcass is quoted "basis Midwest packing plants."

Bear A trader who thinks prices will decline. "Bearish" is often used to describe news or developments that have, or are expected to have, a downward influence on prices. A bear market is one in which the predominant price trend is down. Some think this term originated with an old axiom about "selling the skin before you've caught the bear."

Bid The price offered by one who wishes to purchase a physical commodity or a futures contract. Sometimes a futures market will close with a bid price when no sellers are around.

Broker An agent who buys and sells futures on behalf of a client for a fee. They work for brokerage firms, some of which have extensive research and analysis departments that occasionally issue trading advice. A few firms have so many customers who follow such advisories that recommendations to buy or sell can influence market prices materially.

Bull A trader who thinks prices will go up. "Bullish" describes developments that have, or are expected to have, an upward influence on prices. A bull market is one in which the predominant price trend is up. Some theorize this term originally related to a bull's habit of tossing its head upward.

Butterfly An unusual sort of spread involving three contract months rather than two. Often used to move profits or losses from one year to the next for tax purposes.

Cash The price at which dealings in the physical commodity take place. Used more sweepingly, it can mean simply the physical commodity itself (as in "cash corn" or "cash lumber"), or refer to a market. For example, the cash hog market is a terminal (or, collectively, all terminals) where live hogs are sold by farmers and bought by meat packers.

Source: The *Dow Jones Commodities Handbook*, edited by Dan Ruck, Dow Jones Books, Dow Jones Company, Inc. 1979.

Chart A graph of futures prices (and sometimes other statistical trading information) plotted in such a way that the charter believes gives insight into future price movements. Several futures markets regularly are influenced by buying or selling based on traders' price-chart indications.

Clearing house The part of all futures exchanges (usually a separate corporation with its own members, fees, etc.) which clears all trades made on the exchange during the day. It matches the buy transactions with the equal number of sell transactions to provide orderly control over who owns what and who owes what to whom. Although futures traders theoretically trade contracts among themselves, the clearing house technically is in the middle of each transaction—being the buyer to every seller and the seller to every buyer. That's how it keeps track of what is going on.

Close The end of the trading session. On some exchanges, the "close" lasts for several minutes to accommodate customers who have entered buy or sell orders to be consummated "at the close." On those exchanges, the closing price may be a range encompassing the highest and lowest prices of trades consummated at the close. Other exchanges officially use settlement prices as the closing prices.

Cold storage Refrigerated warehouses where perishable commodities are stored. In effect, the warehouses are secondary sources of commodities that aren't immediately available from the producers. The Agriculture Department periodically reports the quantities of various commodities stored in warehouses. Futures traders watch these reports to see if the supplies are building or dwindling abnormally fast, which indicates how closely supply and demand are balanced.

Commission The fee charged by a broker for making a trade on behalf of customers.

Contract In the case of futures, an agreement between two parties to make and in turn accept delivery of a specified quantity and quality of a commodity (or whatever is being traded) at a certain place (the delivery point) by a specified time (indicated by the month and year of the contract).

Country Refers to a place relatively close to a farmer where he can sell or deliver his crop or animals. For instance, a country elevator typically is located in a small town and accepts grain from farmers in the immediate vicinity. A country shipping point is a place where farmers in an area combine their marketings for shipment. A country price is the one these elevators, shipping points or whatever pay for the farmers' goods; it's based on the terminal-market prices, less transportation and handling costs.

Covering Buying futures contracts to offset those previously sold. "Short covering" often causes prices to rise even though the overall market trend may be down.

Crop report Estimates issued periodically by the Department of Agriculture on estimated size and condition of major U.S. crops. Similar reports are made on livestock.

Crush The process of reducing the raw, unusable soybean into its two major components, oil and meal. A "crush spread" is a futures spreading position in which a trader attempts to profit from what he believes to be discrepancies in the price relationships between soybeans and the two products. The "crush margin" is the gross profit that a processor makes from selling oil and meal minus the cost of buying the soybeans.

Deferred contracts In futures, those delivery months that are due to expire sometime beyond the next two or three months.

Delivery The tendering of the physical commodity to fulfill a short position in futures. This takes place only during the delivery month and normally takes the form of a warehouse receipt (from an exchange-accredited warehouse, elevator or whatever) that shows where the cash commodity is.

Delivery point The place(s) at which the cash commodity may be delivered to fulfill an expiring futures contract.

Discretionary accounts A futures trading account in which the customer puts up the money but the trading decisions are made at the discretion of the broker or some other person, or maybe a computer. Also known as "managed accounts."

Evening up Liquidating a futures position in advance of a significant crop report or some other scheduled development so as not to be caught on the wrong side of a surprise. In concentrated doses, evening up can cause a bull market to retreat somewhat and a bear market to rebound somewhat.

First notice day The first day of a delivery period when holders of short futures positions can give notice of their intention to deliver the cash commodity to holders of long positions. The number of contracts circulated on first notice day and how they are accepted or not accepted by the longs is often interpreted as an indication of future supply-demand expectations and thus often influence prices of all futures being traded, not just the delivery-month price. This effect also sometimes occurs on subsequent notice days. Rules concerning notices to deliver vary from contract to contract.

F.O.B. Free on Board, meaning that the commodity will be placed aboard the shipping vehicle at no cost to the purchaser, but thereafter the purchaser must bear all shipping costs.

Fundamentalist A trader who bases his buy-sell decisions on supply and demand trends or developments rather than on technical or chart considerations.

Futures Contracts traded on an exchange that call for a cash commodity to be delivered and received at a specified future time, at a specified place and at a specified price. Similar arrangements made directly between buyer and seller are called "forward contracts." They aren't traded on an exchange.

Hedge Using the futures market to reduce the risks of unforeseen price changes that are inherent in buying and selling cash commodities. For example, as an elevator operator buys cash grain from farmer, he can "hedge" his purchases by selling futures contracts; when he sells the cash commodity, he purchases an offsetting number of futures contracts to liquidate his position. If prices rise while he owns the cash grain, he sells the cash grain at a profit and closes out his futures at a loss, which almost always is no greater than his profit in the cash transaction. If prices fall while he owns the cash grain, he sells the cash grain at a loss but recoups all or almost all of the loss by buying back futures contracts at a price correspondingly lower than at which he first sold them. Some users of commodities assure themselves of supplies of their raw materials at a set price by buying futures, which is another form of hedging. When the time comes to acquire inventories, they can either take delivery on their futures contracts or, more likely, simply buy their supplies in the cash market. Futures-contract prices tend to match cash prices at the time the futures expire, so if cash prices have risen the users' higher costs are offset by profits on their futures contracts.

Hedger The Commodity Futures Trading Commission says a hedger in a general sense is someone who uses futures trading as a temporary, risk-reducing substitute for a cash transaction planned later in his main line of business. All other futures traders are classified as speculators. There are more legally specific definitions of hedging and hedgers in such markets as grains, soybeans, potatoes and cotton, where limits are placed on the number of contracts speculators may trade or own. The Commission has broadened these limits to allow hedging in closely related, rather than exactly matching, commodities. A sorghum producer, for instance, can use corn futures as a hedging tool where he couldn't before this rule-broadening. The more general distinction between hedgers and speculators may be important to potential traders. Some may want to use a market like interest rate futures to offset some expected heavy borrowing. The government hasn't set any speculative trading limits in those markets, but lenders or company directors are more apt to back a plan to trade futures for hedging purposes rather than speculation.

Inverted market A futures market where prices for deferred contracts are lower than those for nearby-delivery contracts because of great near-term demand for the cash commodity. Normally, prices of deferred contracts are higher, in part reflecting storage costs.

Last trading day The day when trading in an expiring contract ceases, and traders must either liquidate their positions or prepare to make or accept delivery of the cash commodity. After that, there is no more futures trading for that particular contract month and year.

Life of contract The period of time during which futures trading in a particular contract month and year may take place. This is usually less than a year, but sometimes up to 18 months.

Limit move The maximum that a futures price can rise or fall from the previous session's settlement price. This limit, set by each exchange, varies from commodity to commodity. Some exchanges have variable limits, whereby the limit is expanded automatically if the market moves by the limit for a certain number of consecutive trading sessions. When prices fail to move the expanded limit, or after a specified period of time, the limits revert to normal.

Liquidation Closing out a previous position by taking an opposite position in the same contract. Thus, a previous buyer liquidates by selling, and a previous seller liquidates by buying.

Long A trader who has bought futures, speculating the prices will rise. He is "long" until he liquidates by selling or fulfills his contracts by making delivery.

Margin The amount of "good faith" money that commodity traders must put in order to trade futures. The margins, set by each exchange, usually amount to 5% to 10% of the total value of the commodity contract. The "initial margin" is the amount of money that must be put up to establish a position in a futures market. Exchanges establish this margin, too, but brokerage firms often require even larger amounts to protect their own financial interests. "Maintenance margin" is the money that traders must put up to retain their position in the futures markets.

Margin call A request by a brokerage firm that a customer put up more money. That means the market price has gone against the customer's position and the brokerage firm wants the customer to cover his paper loss, which would become a real loss if the position were liquidated.

Nearby contracts The futures that expire the soonest. Those that expire later are called deferred contracts.

New crop The supply of a commodity that will be available after harvest. The term also is sometimes used in connection with pigs and hogs because the major farrowing periods in the spring and fall are referred to as "crops." There sometimes are substantial price differences between futures contracts related to new-crop supplies and those related to old-crop supplies.

Nominal price An artificial price—usually the midpoint between a bid and an asked price—that gives an indication of the market price level even though no actual transactions may have taken place at that price.

Old crop The supply from previous harvests.

Open The period each session when futures trading commences. Sometimes the open lasts several minutes to accommodate customers who have placed orders to buy or sell contracts "on the open." On these exchanges, opening prices often are reported by the exchange as a range, although these seldom are widely disseminated because of space restrictions in newspapers and periodicals; they are carried on tickers and display panels during that trading day, however.

Open interest Outstanding futures contracts that haven't been liquidated by purchase or sale of offsetting contracts, or by delivery or acceptance of the physical commodity.

Option The right to buy or sell a futures contract over a specified period of time at a set price. Commodity options trading tentatively has been approved by the Commodity Futures Trading Commission and may be authorized on U.S. exchanges in 1977.

Overbought A term used to express the opinion that prices have risen too high too fast and so will decline as traders liquidate their positions.

Oversold Like "overbought," except the opinion is that prices have fallen too far too fast and so probably will rebound.

Pit The areas on exchange floors where futures trading takes place. Pits usually have three or more levels and can accommodate a large number of traders. On several New York exchanges the trading areas are called rings and consist of open-center, circular tables around which traders sit or stand.

Position A trader's holdings, either long or short. A position limit is the maximum number of contracts a speculator can hold under law; it doesn't apply to bona-fide hedgers, although there really isn't any objective way of telling whether a person in position to hedge actually is hedging or is speculating instead.

Profit taking A trader holding a long position turns paper profits into real ones by selling his contracts. A trader holding a short position takes profits by buying back contracts.

Reaction A decline in prices following a substantial advance.

Recovery An increase in prices following a substantial decline.

Settlement price The single closing price, determined by each exchange's price committee of directors. It is used primarily by the exchange clearing house to determine the need for margin capital to be put up by brokerage-firm members to protect the net position of that firm's total accounts. It's also issued by some exchanges as the official closing price, and it is used to determine the price limits and net price changes on the following trading day. (See also: *Close.*)

Set-aside Acreage withdrawn from crop production for a season and used for soil conservation under a production-control program. Wheat farmers this year must set aside two acres of land for each 10 acres they plant to wheat in order to get any federal price support or disaster aid. The Agriculture Department has also said corn, sorghum and barley producers similarly may be required to set aside some of their acreage if it appears that surpluses will grow too much otherwise.

Short A trader who has sold futures, speculating that prices will decline. He is "short" until he liquidates by buying back contracts or fulfills his contracts by taking delivery.

Short squeeze A situation in which "short" futures traders are unable to buy the cash commodity to deliver against their positions and so are forced to buy offsetting futures at prices much higher than they'd ordinarily be willing to pay.

Speculation Buying or selling in hopes of making a profit. The word connotes a high degree of risk.

Spot The same as cash commodities. Literally, delivery "on the spot" rather than in the future.

Spreads and straddles Terms for the simultaneous buying of futures in one delivery month and selling of futures in another delivery month (or even the simultaneous buying of futures in one commodity and selling of futures in a different but related commodity). One purpose is to profit from perceived discrepancies in price relationships. Another purpose is to transfer current trading profits to some future time to avoid immediate tax liability.

Stop-loss order An open order given to a brokerage firm to liquidate a position when the market reaches a certain price so as to prevent losses from mounting or profits from eroding. Sometimes market price trends are accelerated when concentrations of stop-loss orders are touched off.

Support price A level below which the government tries to keep the agricultural-commodity prices that farmers receive from falling. They're set basically by Congress when farm legislation is passed and adjusted from time to time by the President or Agriculture Secretary. Subsidy payments, commodity purchases, production controls or commodity-secured loans are among the devices used to make up the difference when market prices dip below the support level. Futures and cash prices often tend to remain near the support level when there are large crop surpluses because lower prices keep commodities off the market and higher ones quickly draw willing sellers.

Switch A trading maneuver in which a trader liquidates his position in one futures delivery and takes the position in another delivery month in expectation that prices will change more rapidly in the second contract than in the first. Thus, a trader might switch out of a position in an October silver futures contract into a position in a December silver futures contract. Warning: Some people use the word "switch" when they mean "spread" or "straddle." Feel free to correct them.

Technical factors Futures prices often are affected by influences related to the market itself, rather than to supply-demand fundamentals of the commodity with which the market is concerned. For example, if a market moves up or down the limit several days in succession there frequently is a subsequent "technical reaction" caused in part by the liquidation of contracts held by traders on the wrong side of the price move.

Terminal Refers to an elevator or livestock market at key distribution points to which commodities are sent from a wide area.

Trading range The amount that futures prices can fluctuate during one trading session—essentially, the price "distance" between limit up and limit down. If, for instance, the soybean futures price can advance or fall by a maximum of 20 cents per bushel in one day, the trading range is double that, or 40 cents per bushel. In one market, cocoa, price movements are restricted to a daily range of six cents a pound.

Visible supply The amount of a commodity that can be accounted for and computed accurately, usually because it is being kept in major known storage places.

Warehouse or elevator receipt The negotiable slip of paper that a short can hand over to fulfill an expiring futures contract's delivery requirement. The receipt shows how much of the commodity is in storage.

DOW JONES FUTURES AND SPOT COMMODITY INDEXES

The method for arriving at the Dow Jones Futures and Spot Commodity Indexes differs from some others in the order in which the computations are made. Instead of first weighting each price, then adding them up and finally calculating the percentage or index, this method first turns each price into an index or percentage of its base-year price, then weights each individual index, and finally adds them up. Stated mathematically, the more usual method calculates the percentage relation of one average to another, while the Dow Jones Commodity Index method calculates the average of a set of percentage changes. These two methods do not result in exactly the same figures. However, they are equally valid when used consistently, and the indexes they produce are of the same general magnitude.

The Dow Jones Commodity Index method has two advantages. One is that it saves computation, because the factors or multipliers perform two computations at once. They calculate the individual percentages and weight them at one stroke. The other advantage is that if you have yesterday's index, you can apply the multipliers to today's individual price changes. Then all you do is add the resulting figures to yesterday's index, or subtract them from it, depending on whether they're up or down. That gives to-day's index. No need to recalculate the whole thing each day.

As for the weights, they were obtained by the usual mathematical methods. Basically, the weight of each commodity is the percentage of its commercial production value to the total commercial production value of all commodities in the index, in this case for the years 1927–31. In calculating the weights, consideration also was given to the relation between volume of trading in each commodity and its commercial production.

A further refinement was necessary because price changes of the various commodities are quoted in different units. Grain prices change in eighths of a cent, wool prices change in tenths of a cent, and all the other staples in the Dow Jones index move in hundredths of a cent. This adjustment merely required appropriate treatment in each case of the multiplier, so that it would give the right figure for any price change. In the case of grains it meant an adjustment of 20%, since one-tenth is that much smaller than one-eighth. In other cases a mere adjustment of decimal points was sufficient.

The twelve commodities, with the weight

Source: The *Dow Jones Commodities Handbook,* edited by Dan Ruck, Dow Jones Books, Dow Jones & Company, Inc.

of each and the multiplier applied to the price changes of each, are;

	Weight	Multiplier
Wheat	19.5	16
Corn	8	11
Oats	5	13
Rye	4	5
Wool Tops	5.5	4
Cotton	23	10
Cottonseed Oil	4.5	4
Coffee	7	3
Sugar	8.5	27
Cocoa	5	5
Rubber	6	3
Hides	4	3

These are the essentials for calculating the spot index. However, the futures index requires one more set of unusual steps. That's because several times a year an actual quoted "future" disappears. For instance, while early in the year it is possible to buy wheat to be delivered in December, when the month of December actually arrives that "delivery" expires and is no longer quoted.

The result is that futures prices are affected not only by market conditions but also by how close the delivery date looms. Interest charges and other such factors influence them. On July 1, the December delivery is just five months off, but a month later it is only four months away, and a five-month delivery should not, in a precise index, be compared with a four-month delivery.

This problem is overcome by the use of two futures quotations for each commodity. They are combined to produce on each market day the calculated price that would apply to a delivery exactly five months off.

On the first day of July, only the December delivery is used, since it is just five months away and thus no adjustment need be made. On the second day, the two quotations used are those for the same December delivery and the one for May of the following year. The quoted price for December is adjusted by one day's proportion of the difference between it and May's quoted price. Since there are 151 days between December and May (except in leap years) the figure for one day's proportion is 1/151 of the price difference between the two. The resulting fraction is added to December's price, or sub-

tracted from it, depending on whether May is quoted above or below December.

The following day 2/151 of the difference are added or subtracted, the third day 3/151 and so on until December 1, on which day only the May contract's price is used. On December 2, the combination used is May and July, and so on around the year.

To facilitate the work of calculating the futures index every hour of each business day and the spot index once a day, tables have been prepared—resembling somewhat tables of logarithms or bond yields—which give the figures arrived at by multiplying the various quotational units of each commodity by its factor or multiplier. For instance, the tables show the proper multiples for one-eighth, one-quarter, three-eighths, etc., when each is multiplied by each grain's factor or multiplier.

The commodity futures index is published once an hour and as of the close of commodity markets each day on the Dow Jones News Service, where also the spot index is published once daily. Both are published likewise in *The Wall Street Journal.*

DOW JONES COMMODITY INDEXES

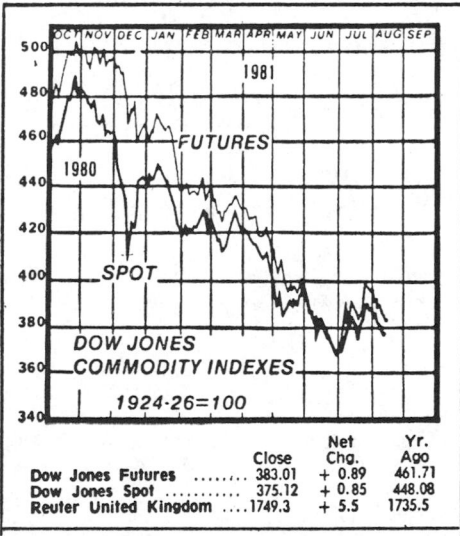

	Close	Net Chg.	Yr. Ago
Dow Jones Futures	383.01	+ 0.89	461.71
Dow Jones Spot	375.12	+ 0.85	448.08
Reuter United Kingdom	1749.3	+ 5.5	1735.5

TRADING FACTS AND FIGURES

All futures contracts on U.S. and foreign commodity exchanges are listed on the following pages. However, some of these contracts are not being traded at this time. The list does not include new contracts awaiting CFTC approval.

Details of all contracts are current, to the best of our knowledge, but any one of the areas listed is subject to change. The daily limit figure given is the normal limit that prices can move up or down from the previous day's close. A number of exchanges have variable limit policies which can alter these limits in a volatile market. In a fast-moving market, you should check with your broker about limit changes.

Commodity	Trading Months	Trading Hours (Local Time)	Contract Size	Minimum Price Fluctuation	Daily Limit
BOARD OF TRADE OF KANSAS CITY					
Wheat (hard red winter)	Mar/May/July Sept/Dec	9:30-1:15	5,000 bu.	¼¢/bu. = $12.50	25¢/bu. = $1,250
CHICAGO BOARD OF TRADE					
Iced Broilers	Mar/Apr/May June/July/Aug	9:15-1:20	30,000 lbs.	2.5/100¢/lb. = $7.50	2¢/lb. = $600
Commercial Paper (90-day)	Mar/June Sept/Dec	8:30-1:35	$1,000,000 face value at maturity	1 pt. = $25	50 pt. = $1,250
Commercial Paper (30-day)	Mar/June Sept/Dec	8:30-1:45	$3,000,000 face value at maturity	1 pt. = $25	50 pt. = $1,250
Corn	Mar/May/July Sept/Dec	9:30-1:15	5,000 bu.	¼¢/bu. = $12.50	10¢/bu. = $500
GNMA CD	Mar/June Sept/Dec	8:00-2:00	$100,000 principal	1/32 pt. = $31.25	64/32 pt. = $2,000
GNMA CDR	Mar/June Sept/Dec	8:00-2:00	$100,000 principal	1/32 pt. = $31.25	64/32 pt. = $2,000
Gold	Feb/Mar/Apr/May June/Aug/Oct/Dec	8:25-1:35	100 oz.	10¢/oz. = $10	$25/oz. = $2,500
Oats	Mar/May/July Sept/Dec	9:30-1:15	5,000 bu.	¼¢/bu. = $12.50	6¢/bu. = $300
Plywood	Jan/Mar/May July/Sept/Nov	9:00-1:00	76,032 sq. ft.	10¢/1000 sq. ft. = $7.60	$7/1000 sq. ft. = $532
Silver	Feb/Mar/Apr/May June/Aug/Oct/Dec	8:40-1:25	1,000 troy oz.	1/10¢/oz. = $5	Fluctuates

378

Commodity	Trading Months	Trading Hours (Local Time)	Contract Size	Minimum Price Fluctuation	Daily Limit
Soybeans	Jan/Mar/May/July Aug/Sept/Nov	9:30-1:15	5,000 bu.	¼¢/bu. = $12.50	30¢/bu. = $1,500
Soybean Meal	Jan/Mar/May/July Aug/Sept/Oct/Dec	9:30-1:15	100 tons	10¢/ton = $10	$10/ton = $1,000
Soybean Oil	Jan/Mar/May/July Aug/Sept/Oct/Dec	9:30-1:15	60,000 lbs.	1/100¢/lb. = $6	1¢/lb. = $600
U.S. Treasury Bonds	Mar/June Sept/Dec	8:00-2:00	$100,000 face value, coupon rate of 8%	1/32 pt. = $31.25	64/32 pt. = $2,000
U.S. Treasury Notes (4- to 6-yr.)	Mar/June Sept/Dec	8:00-2:00	Face value at maturity of $100,000	1/32 pt. = $31.25	64/32 pt. = $2,000
Wheat	Mar/May/July Sept/Dec	9:30-1:15	5,000 bu.	¼¢/bu. = $12.50	20¢/bu. = $1,000

CHICAGO MERCANTILE EXCHANGE

Commodity	Trading Months	Trading Hours (Local Time)	Contract Size	Minimum Price Fluctuation	Daily Limit
Broilers	Feb/Apr/June/July Aug/Oct/Dec	9:10-1:00	30,000 lbs.	2.5/100¢/lb. = $7.50	2¢/lb. = $600
Cattle, Feeder	Jan/Mar/Apr/May Aug/Sept/Oct/Nov	9:05-12:45	42,000 lbs.*	2.5/100¢/lb. = $10.50	1.5¢/lb. = $630
Cattle, Live	Jan/Feb/Apr/June Aug/Oct/Dec	9:05-12:45	40,000 lbs.	2.5/100¢/lb. = $10	1.5¢/lb. = $600
Eggs, Shell (fresh)	All months	9:20-1:00	22,500 doz.	5/100¢/doz. = $11.25	2¢/doz. = $450
Hogs, Live	Feb/Apr/June/July Aug/Oct/Dec	9:10-1:00	30,000 lbs.	2.5/100¢/lb. = $7.50	1.5¢/lb. = $450
Lumber (random-length)	Jan/Mar/May July/Sept/Nov	9:00-1:05	130,000 board feet	10¢/1,000 bd. ft. = $13	$5/1,000 bd. ft. = $650
Lumber (stud)	Jan/Mar/May July/Sept/Nov	9:00-1:05	100,000 board feet	10¢/1,000 bd. ft. = $10	$5/1,000 bd. ft. = $500
Pork Bellies	Feb/Mar/May July/Aug	9:10-1:00	38,000 lbs.	2.5/100¢/lb. = $9.50	2¢/lb. = $760
Potatoes (Russet Burbank)	Jan/Mar/May/Nov	9:00-1:00	80,000 lbs.	1¢/100 lbs. = $8	50¢/100 lbs. = $400

*Effective with Jan. 1982 contract, 44,000 lbs.

Commodity	Trading Months	Trading Hours (Local Time)	Contract Size	Minimum Price Fluctuation	Daily Limit

INTERNATIONAL MONETARY MARKET OF THE CHICAGO MERCANTILE EXCHANGE

Currencies

Commodity	Trading Months	Trading Hours (Local Time)	Contract Size	Minimum Price Fluctuation	Daily Limit
Deutsche-Mark	All months	7:30-1:20	125,000 DM	1/100¢/DM = $12.50	1¢/DM = $1,250
Canadian Dollar	All months	7:30-1:22	100,000 CD	1/100¢/CD = $10	¾¢/CD = $750
French Franc	All months	7:30-1:28	250,000 FF	5/1,000¢/FF = $12.50	½¢/FF = $1,250
Swiss Franc	All months	7:30-1:16	125,000 SF	1/100¢/SF = $12.50	1.5¢/SF = $1,875
Dutch Guilder	All months	7:30-1:30	125,000 DG	1/100¢/DG = $12.50	1¢/DG = $1,250
British Pound	All months	7:30-1:24	25,000 BP	5/100¢/BP = $12.50	5¢/BP = $1,250
Mexican Peso	All months	7:30-1:18	1,000,000 MP	1/1,000¢/MP = $10	1.5/100¢/MP = $1,500
Japanese Yen	All months	7:30-1:26	12,500,000 JY	1/10,000¢/JY = $12.50	1/100¢/JY = $1,250
Gold	All months	8:25-1:30	100 troy oz.	10¢/oz. = $10	$50/oz. = $5,000
U.S. Silver Coins	Mar/June/Sept Dec	8:50-1:25	$5,000 (5 bags @ $1,000 face value)	$2/bag = $10	$150/bag = $750
Treasury Bills (13-week)	Jan/Mar/Apr/June July/Sept/Oct/Dec	8:00-1:40	$1,000,000 face value	1 pt. = $25	60 pt. = $1,500
Treasury Bills (1-year)	Mar/June/Sept Dec	8:15-1:35	$250,000 face value	1 pt. = $25	60 pt. = $1,500
Treasury Notes (4-year)	Feb/May/Aug/Nov	8:20-1:55	$100,000 face value	1 pt. = $15.62½	48 pt. = $750

COFFEE, SUGAR & COCOA EXCHANGE, INC.

Commodity	Trading Months	Trading Hours (Local Time)	Contract Size	Minimum Price Fluctuation	Daily Limit
Cocoa	Mar/May/July Sept/Dec	9:30-3:00	10 metric tons	$1/metric ton = $10	$88/metric ton = $880
Coffee "C"	Mar/May/July Sept/Dec	9:45-2:30	37,500 lbs.	1/100¢/lb. = $3.75	4¢/lb. = $1,500

Commodity	Trading Months	Trading Hours (Local Time)	Contract Size	Minimum Price Fluctuation	Daily Limit
Coffee "B"	Mar/May/July Sept/Dec	9:45-2:30	32,500 lbs.	1/100¢/lb. = $3.25	4¢/lb. = $1,300
Sugar No. 11 (world)	Jan/Mar/May July/Sept/Oct	10:00-1:45	112,000 lbs.	1/100¢/lb. = $11.20	½¢/lb. = $560
Sugar No. 12 (domestic)	Jan/Mar/May July/Sept/Nov	10:00-1:45	112,000 lbs.	1/100¢/lb. = $11.20	½¢/lb. = $560

COMMODITY EXCHANGE (COMEX)

Commodity	Trading Months	Trading Hours (Local Time)	Contract Size	Minimum Price Fluctuation	Daily Limit
Copper	Jan/Mar/May July/Sept/Dec	9:50-2:00	25,000 lbs.	5/100¢/lb. = $12.50	5¢/lb. = $1,250
Gold	Feb/Apr/June Aug/Oct/Dec	9:25-2:30	100 troy oz. or 3 kilos	10¢/oz. = $10	$25/oz. = $2,500
Silver*	Jan/Mar/May July/Sept/Dec	9:40-2:15	5,000 troy oz.	10/100¢/oz. = $5	50¢/oz. = $2,500
Zinc	Jan/Mar/May July/Sept/Dec	9:15-2:15	60,000 lbs.	5/100¢/lb. = $30	3¢/lb. = $1,800
GNMA	Jan/Apr/July Oct	9:00-3:20	$100,000 principal	1/64 pt. = $15.62½	64/64/pt. = $1,000
U.S. Treasury Bills (90-day)	Feb/May/Aug Nov	9:05-3:30	$1,000,000 face value at maturity	1 pt. = $25	60 pts. = $1,500
U.S. Treasury Notes (2-year)	Mar/June Sept/Dec	9:00-3:00	$100,000 par value	1/64 pt. = $15,625	64/64 pt. = $1,000

*currently pending CFTC approval to be downsized to 1,000 oz.

MIDAMERICA COMMODITY EXCHANGE

Commodity	Trading Months	Trading Hours (Local Time)	Contract Size	Minimum Price Fluctuation	Daily Limit
Cattle, Live	Jan/Feb/Apr/June Aug/Oct/Dec	9:05-1:00	20,000 lbs.	2.5/100¢/lb. = $5	1.5¢/lb. = $300
Corn	Mar/May/July Sept/Dec	9:30-1:30	1,000 bu.	1/8¢/bu. = $1.25	10¢/bu. = $100
Gold	Mar/June/Sept Dec	8:25-1:40	33.2 fine troy oz.	2.5¢/oz. = $.83	$50/oz.
Hogs, Live	Feb/Apr/June July/Aug/Oct/Dec	9:15-1:05	15,000 lbs.	2.5/100¢/lb. = $3.75	1.5¢/lb. = $225
Oats*	Mar/May/July Sept/Dec	9:30-1:30	5,000 bu.	⅛¢/bu. = $6.25	6¢/bu. = $300
Silver Bullion	Feb/Apr/June Aug/Oct Dec/spot	8:40-1:40	1,000 troy oz.	5¢/oz. = 50¢	On sliding scale

Commodity	Trading Months	Trading Hours (Local Time)	Contract Size	Minimum Price Fluctuation	Daily Limit
Soybeans	Jan/Mar/May July/Aug/Sept	9:30-1:30	1,000 bu.	1/8¢/bu. = $1.25	30¢/bu. = $300
Wheat	Mar/May/July Sept/Dec	9:30-1:30	1,000 bu.	1/8¢/bu. = $1.25	20¢/bu. = $200

*Currently pending CFTC approval to be downsized to 1,000 bu.

MINNEAPOLIS GRAIN EXCHANGE

Commodity	Trading Months	Trading Hours (Local Time)	Contract Size	Minimum Price Fluctuation	Daily Limit
Spring Wheat	Mar/May/July Sept/Dec	9:30-1:15	5,000 bu.	1/8¢/bu. = $6.25	20¢/bu. = $1,000
Sunflower Seeds	Jan/Mar/May July/Nov	9:25-1:20	100,000 lbs.	1/100¢/lb. = $10	½¢/lb. = $500

NEW ORLEANS COMMODITY EXCHANGE

Commodity	Trading Months	Trading Hours (Local Time)	Contract Size	Minimum Price Fluctuation	Daily Limit
Milled Rice	Jan/Mar/May Sept/Nov	9:45-1:45	1,200 cwt. (120,000 lbs.)	$.005/cwt. = $10	$0.50/cwt. ($600)
Rough Rice	Jan/Mar/May July/Sept/Nov	9:45-1:45	2,000 cwt. (200,000 lbs.)	$.005/cwt. = $10	$0.30/cwt. ($600)

NEW YORK COTTON EXCHANGE

Commodity	Trading Months	Trading Hours (Local Time)	Contract Size	Minimum Price Fluctuation	Daily Limit
Cotton No. 2	Mar/May/July Sept/Dec	10:30-3:00	50,000 lbs.	1/100¢/lb. = $5	2¢/lb. = $1,000
Crude Oil	Mar/June/Sept/Dec	9:50-2:20	5,000 barrels	1/10¢/barrel = $5	25¢/barrel = $1,250
Orange Juice	Jan/Mar/May July/Sept/Nov	10:15-2:45	15,000 lbs.	5/100¢/lb. = $7.50	5¢/lb. = $750
Propane (liquified)	Jan/Mar/May July/Sept/Dec	9:45-2:35	100,000 gal.	1/100¢/gal. = $10	1¢/gal. = $1,000

NEW YORK FUTURES EXCHANGE

Commodity	Trading Months	Trading Hours (Local Time)	Contract Size	Minimum Price Fluctuation	Daily Limit
U.S. Treasury Bonds (20-year)	Feb/May/Aug/Nov	9:00-3:00	$100,000 face value	1/32 pt. = $31.25	96/32 (3 points) = $3,000
U.S. Treasury Bills (90-day)	Jan/Apr/July/Oct	9:00-3:00	$1,000,000	.01 (1 basis point) = 1/100 of 1% = $25	1.00 (100 basis points) = $2,500

Commodity	Trading Months	Trading Hours (Local Time)	Contract Size	Minimum Price Fluctuation	Daily Limit
British Pound	Feb/May/Aug/Nov plus 3 nearby months at all times	8:30-2:30	25,000 BP	.0005 (5 points) = $12.50	No limit.
Canadian Dollar	Feb/May/Aug/Nov plus 3 nearby months at all times	8:30-2:30	100,000 CD	.0001 (1 point) = $10	No limit
Swiss Franc	Feb/May/Aug/Nov plus 3 nearby months at all times	8:30-2:30	125,000 SF	.0001 (1 point) = $12.50	No limit
Deutsche Mark	Feb/May/Aug/Nov plus 3 nearby months at all times	8:30-2:30	125,000 DM	.0001 (1 point) = $12.50	No limit
Japanese Yen	Feb/May/Aug/Nov plus 3 nearby months at all times	8:30-2:30	12,500,000 JY	.000001 (1 point) = $12.50	No limit

NEW YORK MERCANTILE EXCHANGE

Commodity	Trading Months	Trading Hours (Local Time)	Contract Size	Minimum Price Fluctuation	Daily Limit
Imported Lean Beef	Jan/Mar/May Sept/July/Nov	10:15-1:45	36,000 lbs.	2/100¢/lb. = $7.20	1.5¢/lb. = $540
Palladium	All months	9:20-2:20	100 troy oz.	5¢/oz. = $5	$6/oz. = $600
Platinum	All months	9:30-2:30	50 troy oz.	10¢/oz. = $5	$20/oz. = $1,000
Potatoes	Mar/Apr/May Nov	10:00-2:00	50,000 lbs.	1¢/100 lbs. = $5	50¢/100 lbs. = $250
No. 2 Heating Oil	All months	10:30-2:45	42,000 gal.	1/100¢/gal. = $4.20	2¢/gal. = $840

THE WINNIPEG COMMODITY EXCHANGE

Commodity	Trading Months	Trading Hours (Local Time)	Contract Size	Minimum Price Fluctuation	Daily Limit
Barley	Mar/May/July Oct/Dec	9:30-1:15	100 metric tons	10¢/metric ton = $10	$5/metric ton = $500
Flaxseed	May/July/Oct Nov/Dec	9:30-1:15	100 metric tons	10¢/metric ton = $10	$5/metric ton = $500
Oats	Mar/May/July Oct/Dec	9:30-1:15	100 metric tons	10¢/metric ton = $10	$5/metric ton = $500
Rapeseed	Jan/Mar/June Sept/Nov	9:30-1:15	100 metric tons	10¢/metric ton = $10	$10/metric ton = $1,000
Rye	Mar/July/Oct Dec	9:30-1:15	100 metric tons	10¢/metric ton = $10	$5/metric ton = $1,000
Wheat	Mar/May/July Oct/Dec	9:30-1:15	100 metric tons	10¢/metric ton = $10	$5/metric ton = $500

Commodity	Trading Months	Trading Hours (Local Time)	Contract Size	Minimum Price Fluctuation	Daily Limit
Gold	Mar/June/Sept Dec	8:25-1:30	20 oz.	10¢/oz. = $2	$30/oz. = $600
Gold Options	Mar/June/Sept Dec	8:25-1:35	20 oz.	10¢/oz. = $2	$30/oz. = $600
Silver	Jan/Apr/July Oct	8:40-1:25	200 oz.	1¢/oz. = $2	50¢/oz. = $100
Treasury Bills (13-week)	Mar/June/Sept Dec	8:00-2:30	$200,000	One index point	Sixty index points
Long-Term Bonds	Mar/June/Sept Dec	8:00-2:30	$20,000	1/32 of $1 per $100 face value = $6.25 per contract	64/32 of $1 per $100 face value = $400 per contract

Source: Reproduced with permission of *Commodities Magazine, Inc.*, 219 Parkade, Cedar Falls, Iowa 50613.

COMMODITY FUTURES TRADING COMMISSION

Federal laws regulating commodity futures trading are enforced by the Commodity Futures Trading Commission.

NATIONAL OFFICE

Commodity Futures Trading Commission
2033 K Street, NW
Washington, DC 20581
   Telephone: 202–254–6970

REGIONAL OFFICES

Eastern Region
One World Trade Center, Suite 4747
New York, NY 10048
   Telephone: 212–466–2061

Central Region
233 So. Wacker Drive, 46th Floor
Chicago, IL 60606
   Telephone: 312–353–9499
510 Grain Exchange Building
Minneapolis, MN 55415
   Telephone: 612–725–2025

Southwestern Region
4901 Main Street, Room 208
Kansas City, MO 64112
   Telephone: 816–374–2994

Source: U.S. Government Manual.

Western Region
Two Embarcadero Center, Suite 975
San Francisco, CA 94111
   Telephone: 415–556–7503

The function of the Commodity Futures Trading Commission (CFTC) is to strengthen the regulation of futures trading, and to bring under regulation all agricultural and other commodities, including lumber and metals, which are traded on commodity exchanges. Major purposes of the trading regulation are to prevent price manipulation, market corners, and the dissemination of false and misleading commodity and market information affecting commodity prices. Other responsibilities are to protect market users against cheating, fraud, and abusive practices in commodity transactions and to safeguard the handling of traders' margin money and equities of establishing minimum financial requirements for futures commission merchants and by preventing the misuse of such funds by brokers.

The Commodity Futures Trading commission was established as an independent agency by the Commodity Futures Trading Commission Act of 1974 (88 Stat. 1389; 7 U.S.C. 4a).

As the successor to the Commodity Exchange Authority under the Department of Agriculture, this new Commission has been given several new authorities and responsibilities under the Commodity Exchange Act, which makes more effective regulation of the commodity futures markets possible. For example, the Commission regulates all commodity futures, whereas many commodities were not regulated under prior law. The act also requires the registration of additional persons involved in futures trading that had not been previously registered, such as commodity trading advisors, commodity pool operators, and persons associated with futures commission merchants. The CFTC also is empowered to regulate option and leverage transactions in commodities. The Commodity Exchange Act requires futures trading to be conducted on contract markets designated by the Commission. In order to obtain designation, a contract market must demonstrate that the market will not be contrary to the public interest. Once designation has been granted, a contract market must provide, among other things, settlement procedures for customers' claims and grievances. Further, the Commission is authorized to impose sanctions, such as fines and penalties, for violations under the act; to enjoin practices in violation of the act; and, finally, to litigate its own cases.

COMMODITIES EXCHANGES

CHICAGO BOARD OF TRADE (CBT)
141 West Jackson Boulevard
Chicago, Illinois 60604
312-435-3620

CHICAGO MERCANTILE EXCHANGE (CME) and INTERNATIONAL MONETARY MARKET (IMM)
444 West Jackson Boulevard
Chicago, Illinois 60606
312-648-1000

COFFEE, SUGAR & COCOA EXCHANGE (CSCE)
Four World Trade Center
New York, New York 10048
212-938-2800

COMMODITY EXCHANGE, INC. (CMX)
Four World Trade Center
New York, New York 10048
212-938-2900

KANSAS CITY BOARD OF TRADE (KCBT)
4800 Main Street, Suite 274
Kansas City, Missouri 64112
816-753-7363

MIDAMERICA COMMODITY EXCHANGE (MACE)
175 West Jackson Boulevard
Chicago, Illinois 60604
312-435-0606

MINNEAPOLIS GRAIN EXCHANGE (MGE)
150 Grain Exchange Building
Minneapolis, Minnesota 55415
612-338-6212

NEW YORK COTTON EXCHANGE & ASSOCIATES (NYCE)
Four World Trade Center
New York, New York 10048
212-938-2650
Citrus, Petroleum and Wool Associates

NEW YORK FUTURES EXCHANGE (NYFE)
20 Broad Street
New York, New York 10005
212-623-4949 & 800-221-7722

NEW YORK MERCANTILE EXCHANGE (NYME)
Four World Trade Center
New York, New York 10048
212-938-2222

NEW ORLEANS COMMODITY EXCHANGE (NOCE)
308 Board of Trade Place
New Orleans, Louisiana 70130
504-524-2184

COMMODITY CHARTS

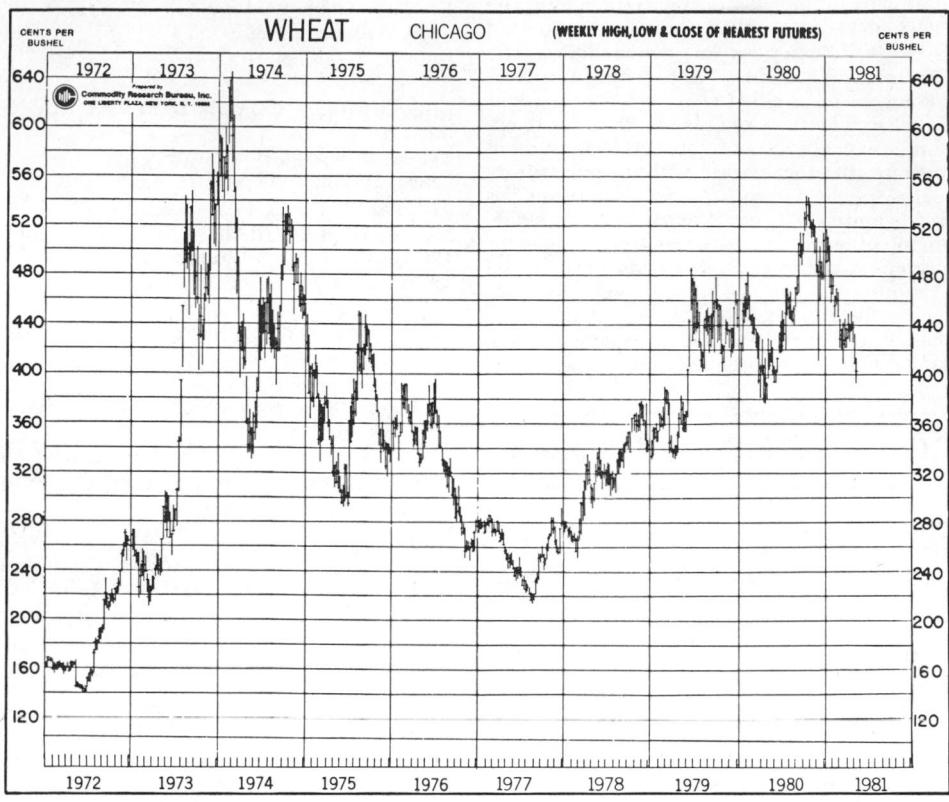

CENTS PER BUSHEL — WHEAT — CHICAGO — (WEEKLY HIGH, LOW & CLOSE OF NEAREST FUTURES) — CENTS PER BUSHEL

Source: Charts reproduced from *1981 Commodity Yearbook,*
a publication of Commodity Research Bureau, Inc., One Liberty
Plaza, New York, New York 10006.

386

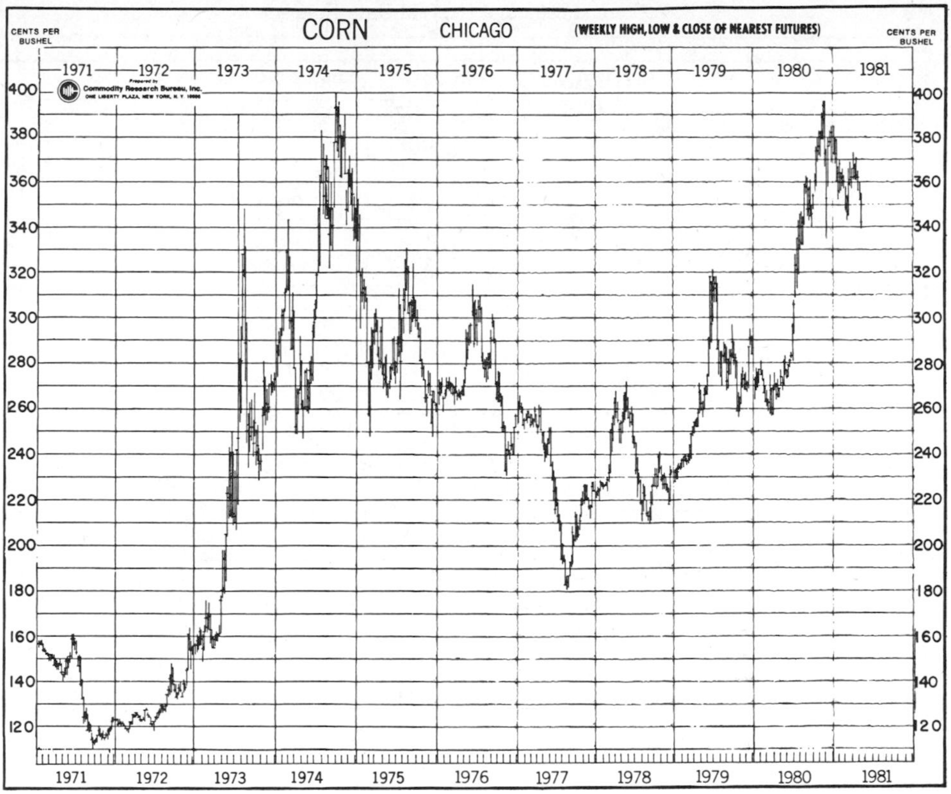

CENTS PER BUSHEL
CORN
CHICAGO
(WEEKLY HIGH, LOW & CLOSE OF NEAREST FUTURES)
CENTS PER BUSHEL
1971
1972
1973
1974
1975
1976
1977
1978
1979
1980
1981
Commodity Research Bureau, Inc.
400
380
360
340
320
300
280
260
240
220
200
180
160
140
120

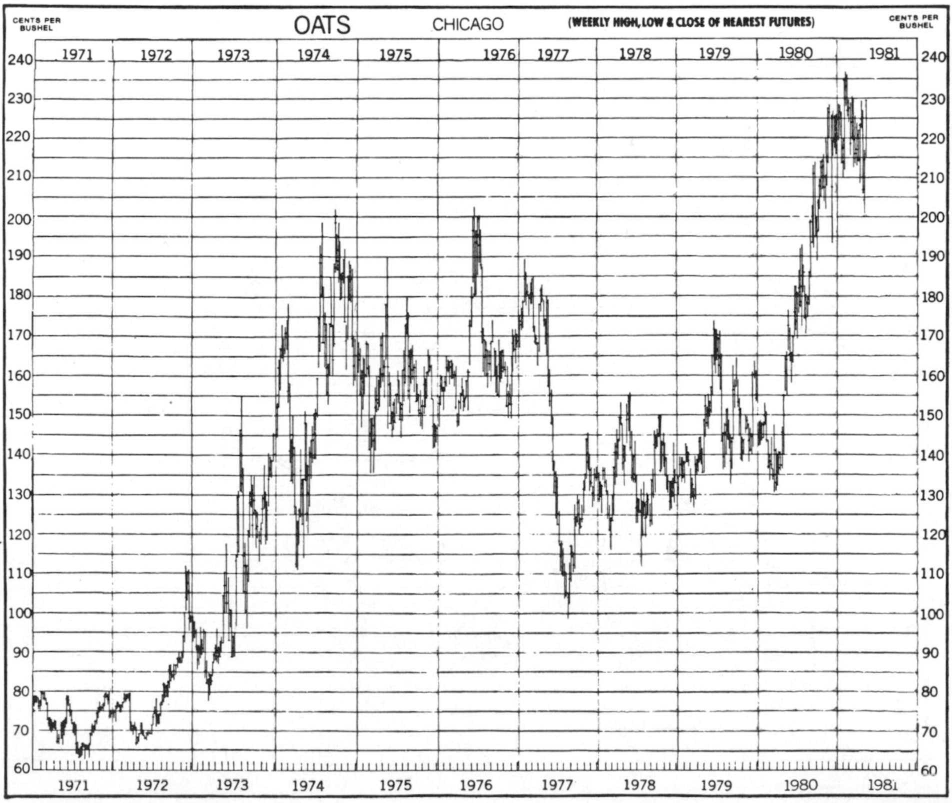

CENTS PER BUSHEL
OATS
CHICAGO
(WEEKLY HIGH, LOW & CLOSE OF NEAREST FUTURES)
CENTS PER BUSHEL
1971
1972
1973
1974
1975
1976
1977
1978
1979
1980
1981
240
230
220
210
200
190
180
170
160
150
140
130
120
110
100
90
80
70
60

SOYBEANS CHICAGO (WEEKLY HIGH, LOW & CLOSE OF NEAREST FUTURES)
CENTS PER BUSHEL
1972 1973 1974 1975 1976 1977 1978 1979 1980 1981
Prepared by Commodity Research Bureau, Inc. ONE LIBERTY PLAZA, NEW YORK, N.Y. 10006
1300 1200 1100 1000 900 800 700 600 500 400 300 200

CATTLE (LIVE) CHICAGO (WEEKLY HIGH, LOW & CLOSE OF NEAREST FUTURES)
CENTS PER POUND
1972 1973 1974 1975 1976 1977 1978 1979 1980 1981
Prepared by Commodity Research Bureau, Inc. ONE LIBERTY PLAZA, NEW YORK, N.Y. 10006
90 85 80 75 70 65 60 55 50 45 40 35 30

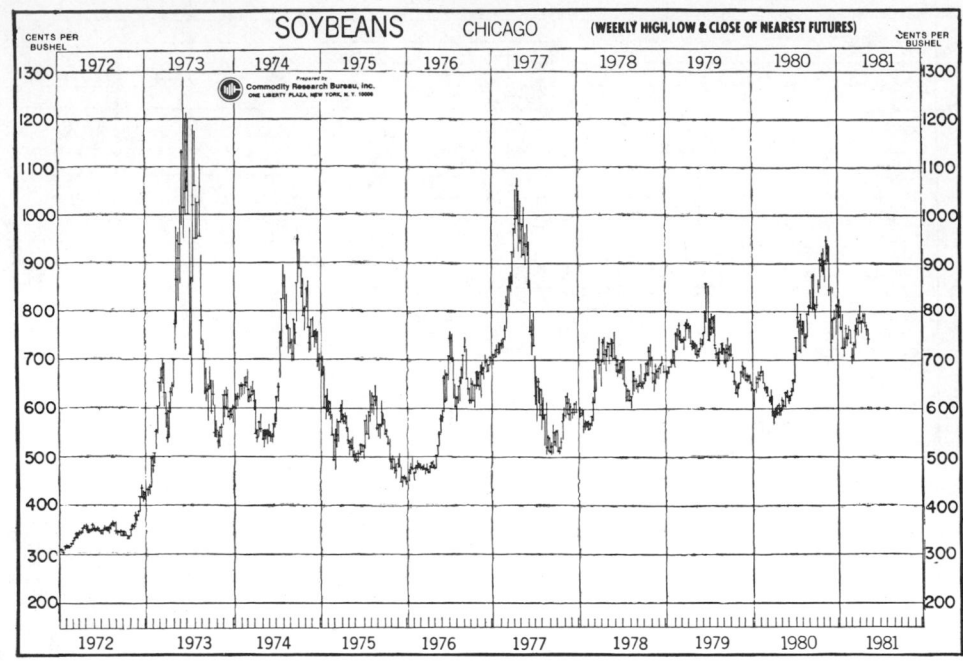

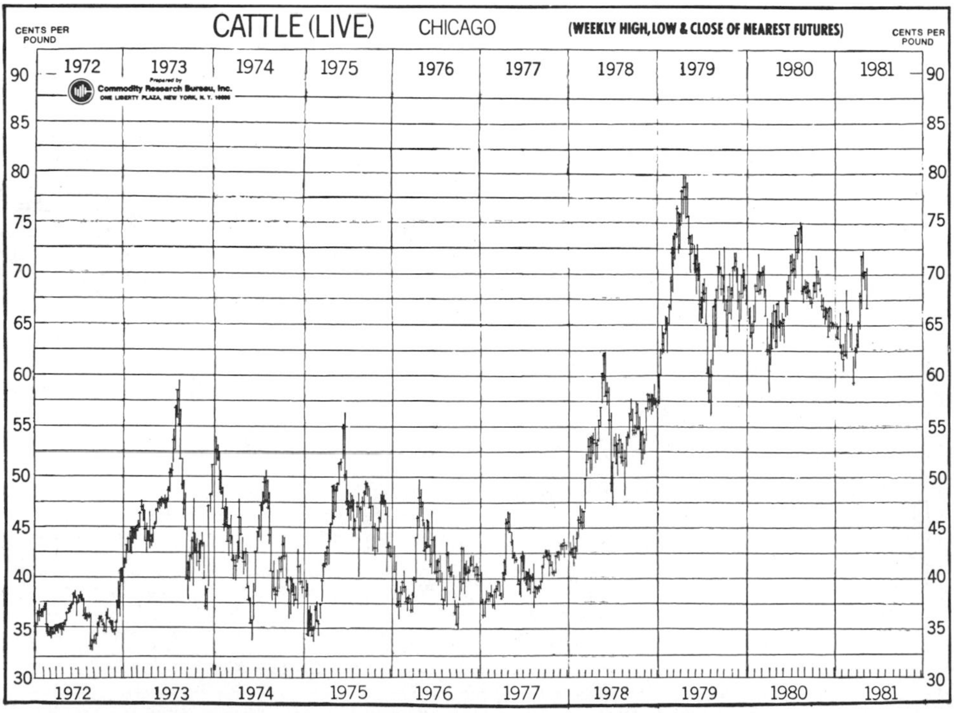

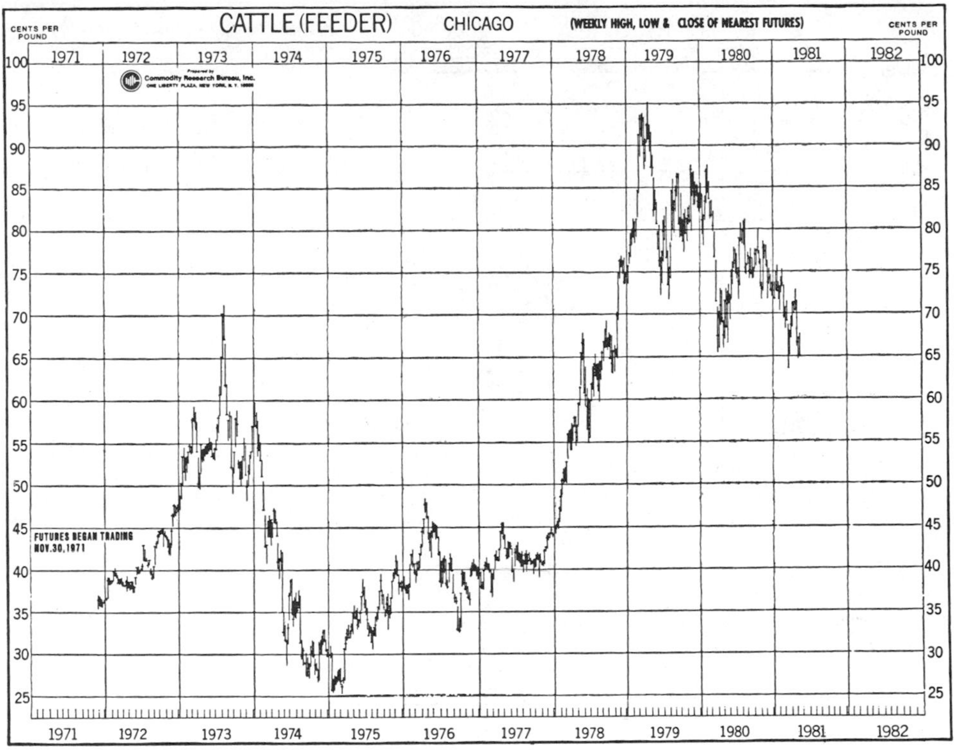

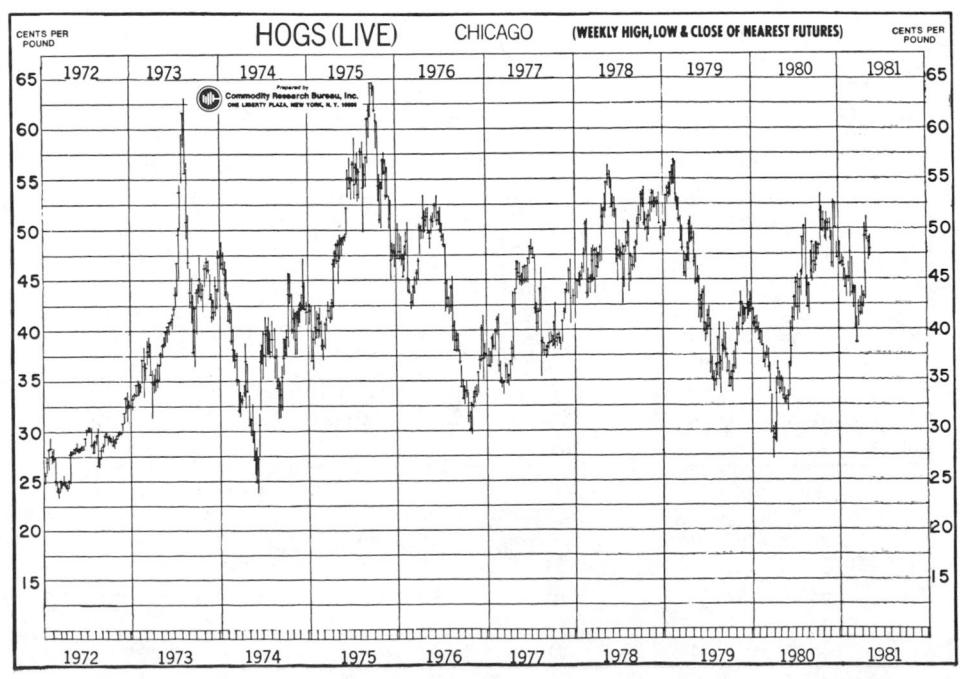

CATTLE (FEEDER)   CHICAGO   (WEEKLY HIGH, LOW & CLOSE OF NEAREST FUTURES)

CENTS PER POUND

Prepared by
Commodity Research Bureau, Inc.
ONE LIBERTY PLAZA, NEW YORK, N.Y. 10006

FUTURES BEGAN TRADING
NOV.30,1971

HOGS (LIVE)   CHICAGO   (WEEKLY HIGH, LOW & CLOSE OF NEAREST FUTURES)

CENTS PER POUND

Prepared by
Commodity Research Bureau, Inc.
ONE LIBERTY PLAZA, NEW YORK, N.Y. 10006

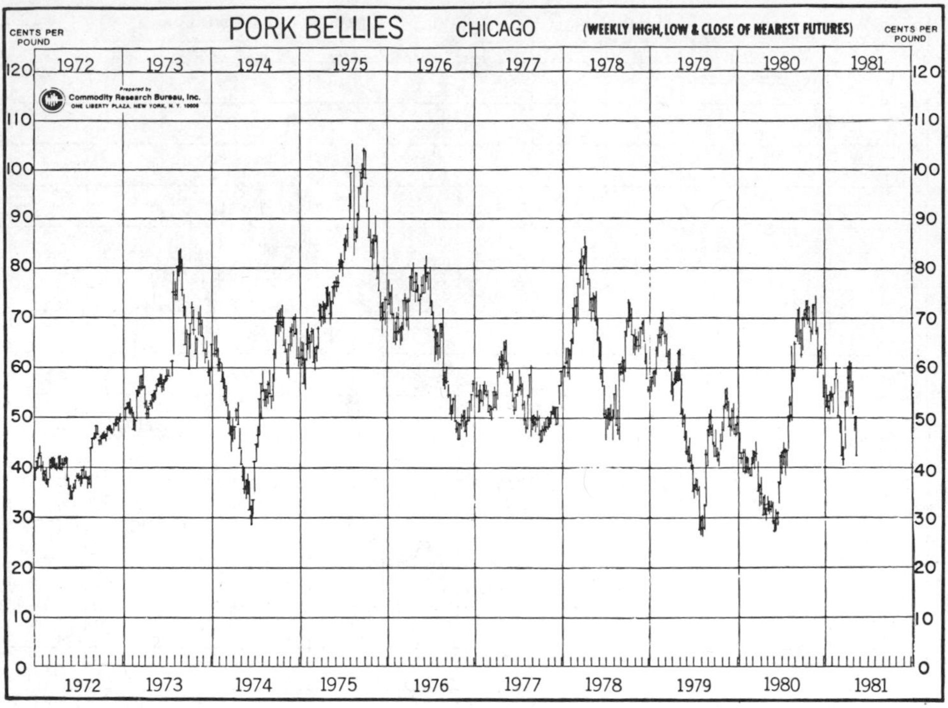

PORK BELLIES CHICAGO (WEEKLY HIGH, LOW & CLOSE OF NEAREST FUTURES)

CENTS PER POUND

Prepared by
Commodity Research Bureau, Inc.
ONE LIBERTY PLAZA, NEW YORK, N.Y. 10006

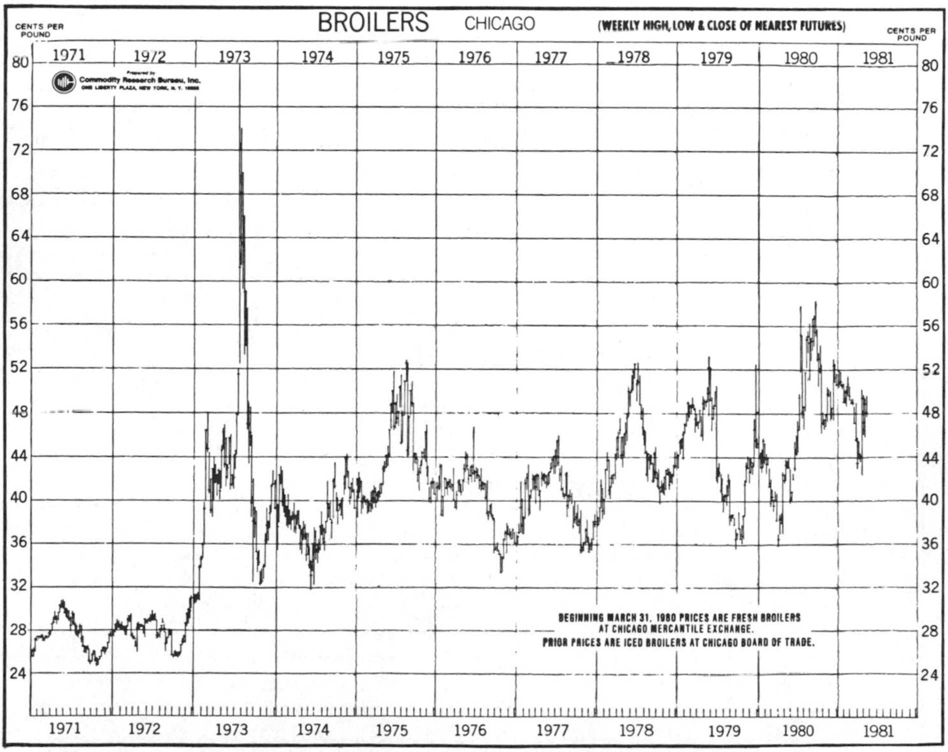

BROILERS CHICAGO (WEEKLY HIGH, LOW & CLOSE OF NEAREST FUTURES)

CENTS PER POUND

Prepared by
Commodity Research Bureau, Inc.
ONE LIBERTY PLAZA, NEW YORK, N.Y. 10006

BEGINNING MARCH 31, 1980 PRICES ARE FRESH BROILERS
AT CHICAGO MERCANTILE EXCHANGE.
PRIOR PRICES ARE ICED BROILERS AT CHICAGO BOARD OF TRADE.

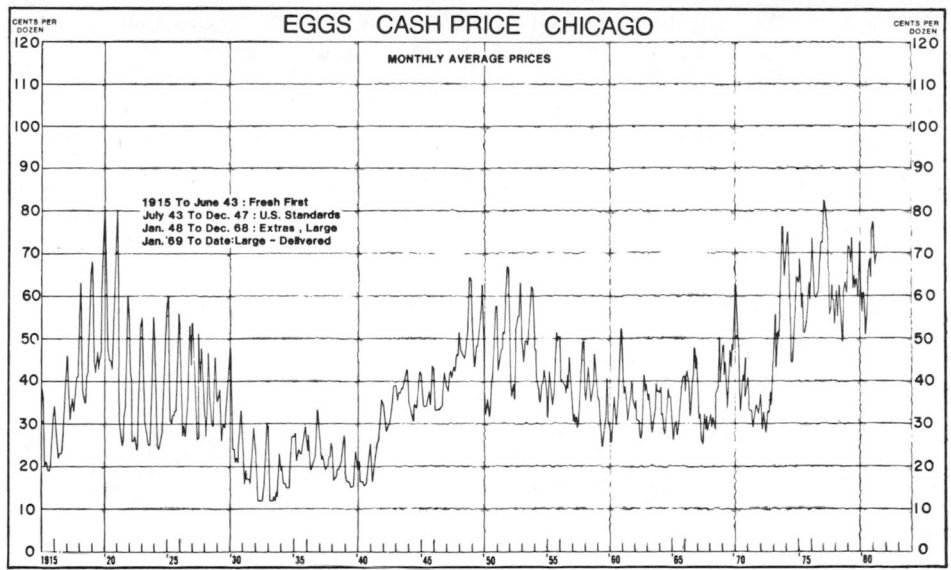

EGGS   CASH PRICE   CHICAGO

CENTS PER DOZEN

MONTHLY AVERAGE PRICES

1915 To June 43 : Fresh First
July 43 To Dec. 47 : U.S. Standards
Jan. 48 To Dec. 68 : Extras , Large
Jan. '69 To Date:Large - Delivered

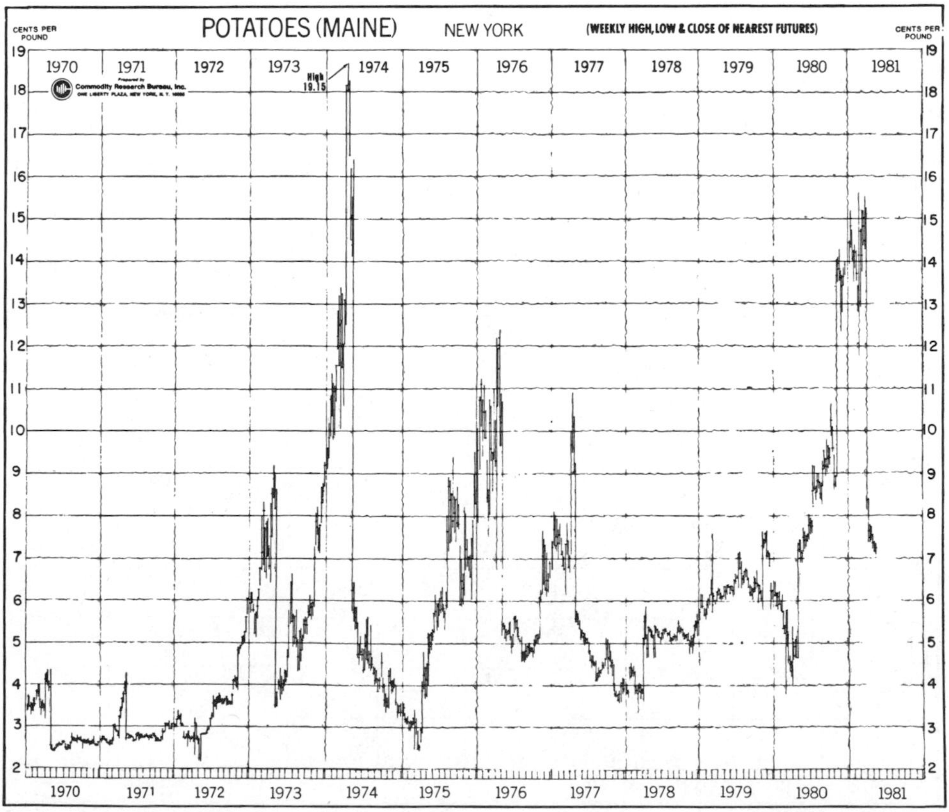

POTATOES (MAINE)   NEW YORK   (WEEKLY HIGH, LOW & CLOSE OF NEAREST FUTURES)

CENTS PER POUND

Prepared by
Commodity Research Bureau, Inc.
ONE LIBERTY PLAZA, NEW YORK, N. Y. 10006

High 19.15

1970   1971   1972   1973   1974   1975   1976   1977   1978   1979   1980   1981

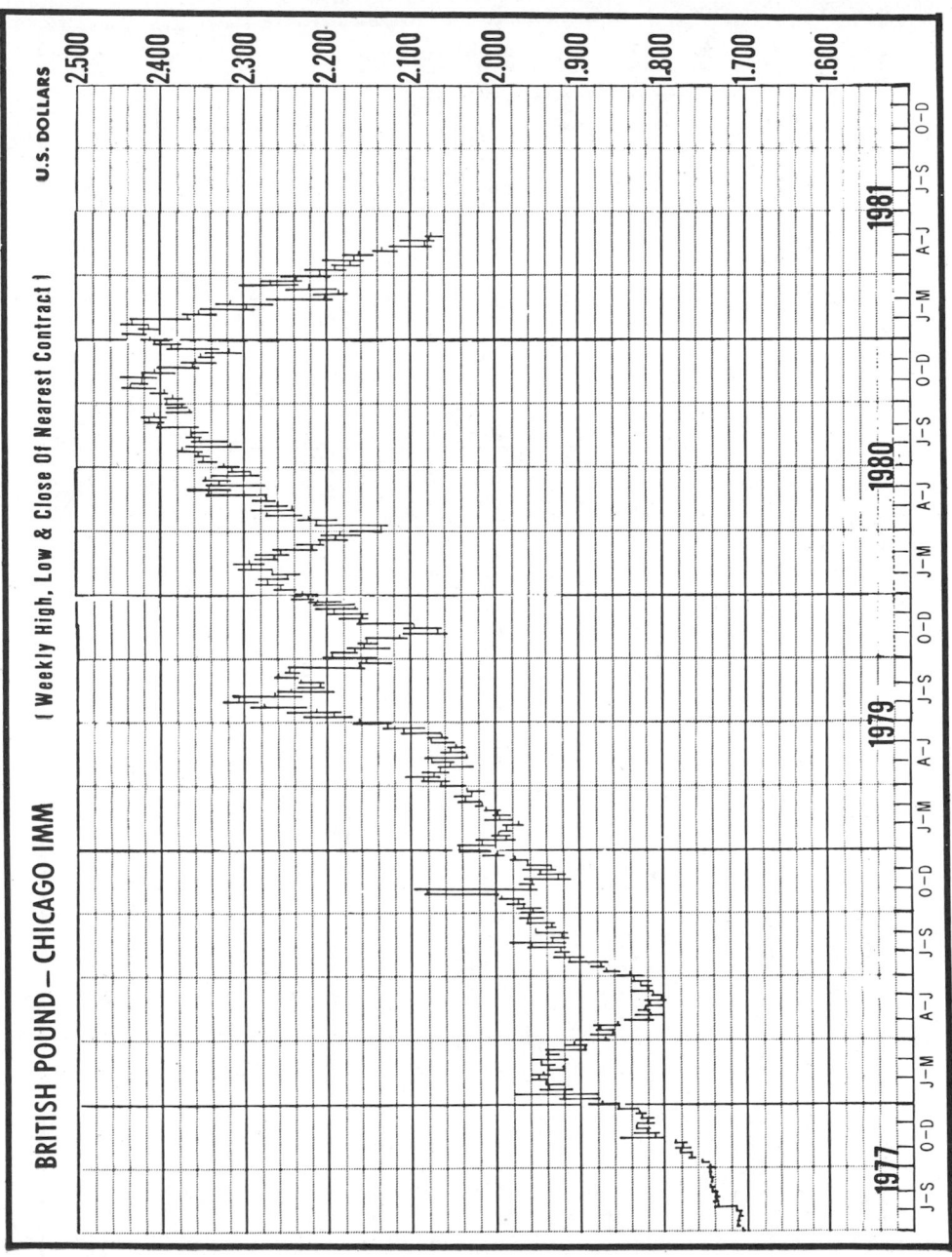

BRITISH POUND – CHICAGO IMM

(Weekly High, Low & Close Of Nearest Contract)

U.S. DOLLARS

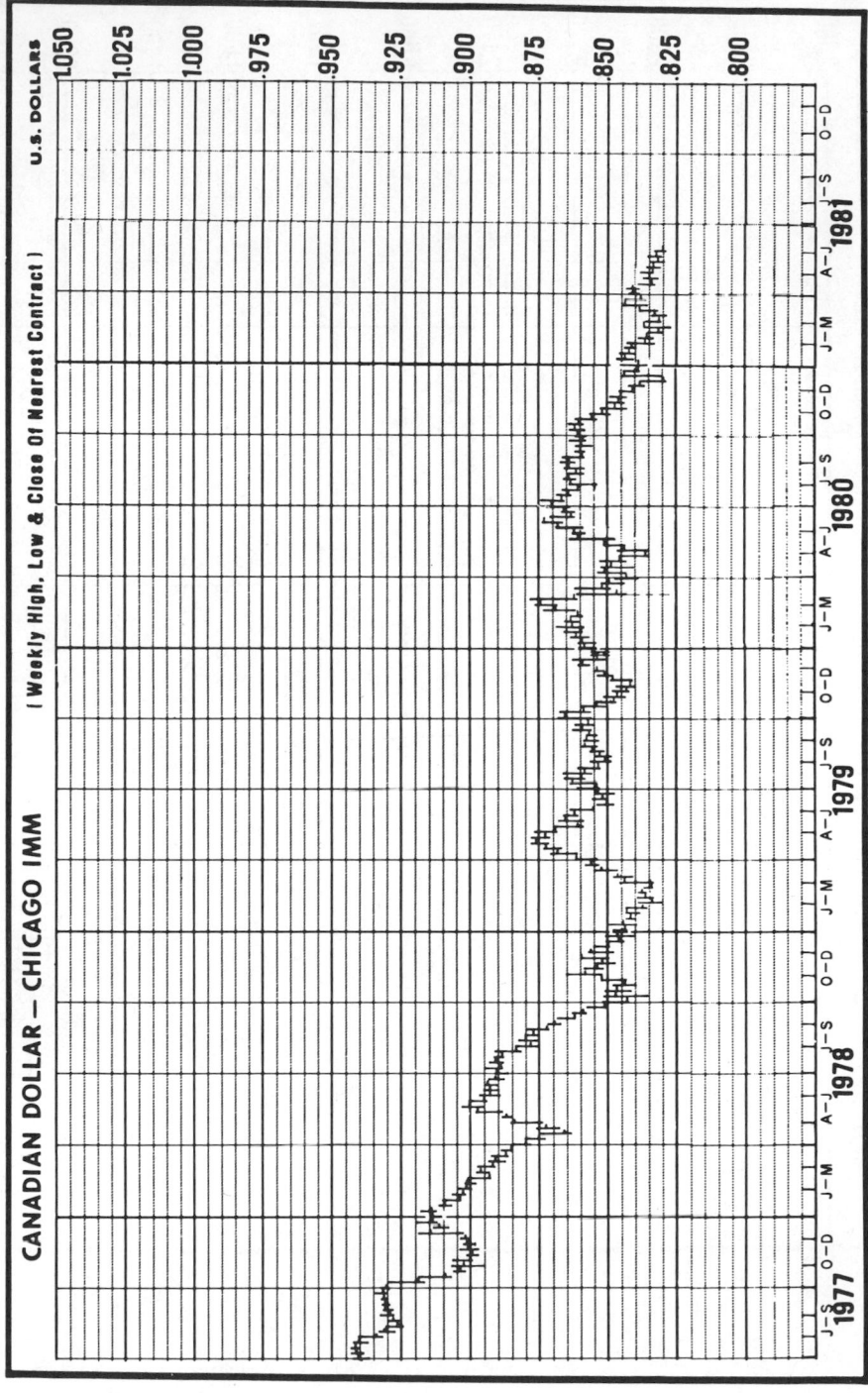

CANADIAN DOLLAR — CHICAGO IMM

(Weekly High, Low & Close Of Nearest Contract)

U.S. DOLLARS

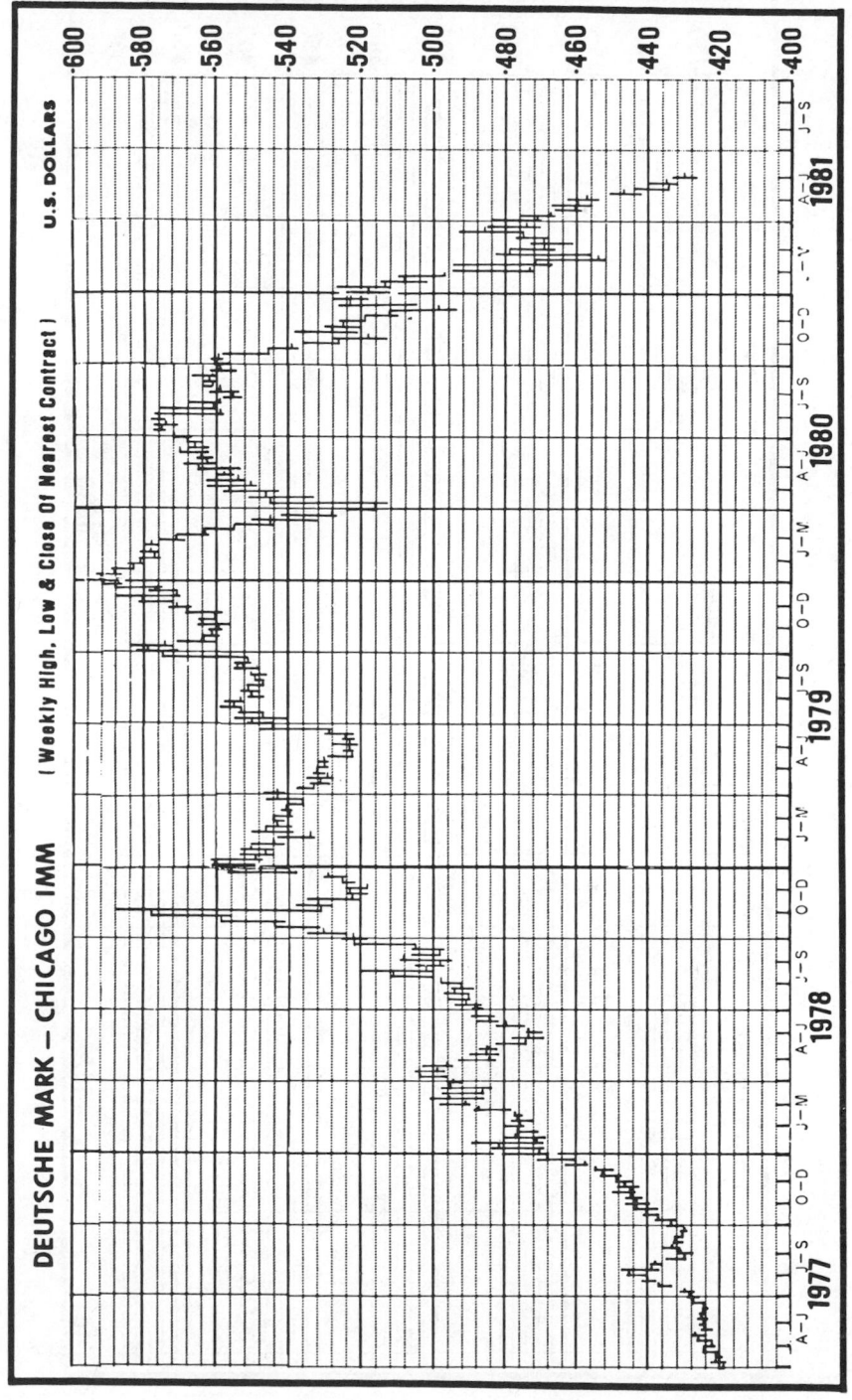

DEUTSCHE MARK — CHICAGO IMM

(Weekly High, Low & Close Of Nearest Contract)

U.S. DOLLARS

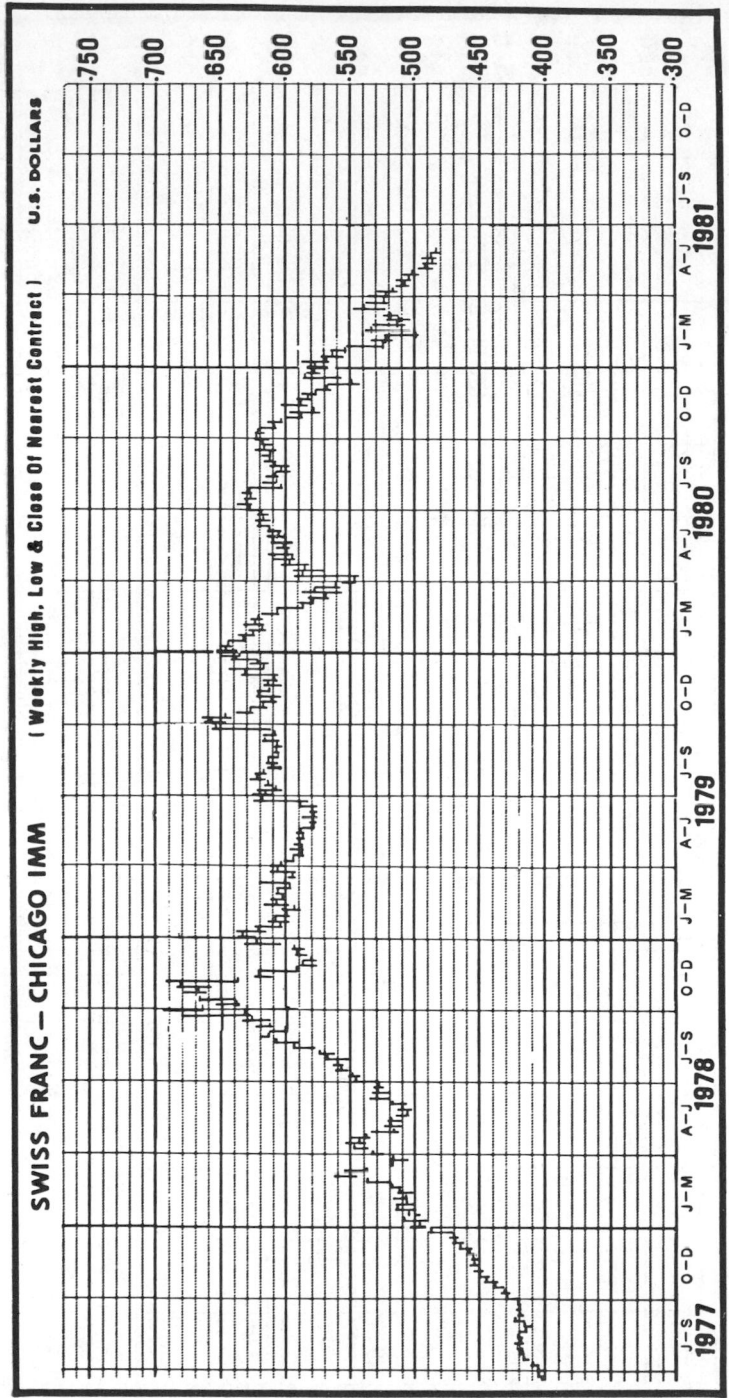

SWISS FRANC — CHICAGO IMM

(Weekly High, Low & Close Of Nearest Contract)

U.S. DOLLARS

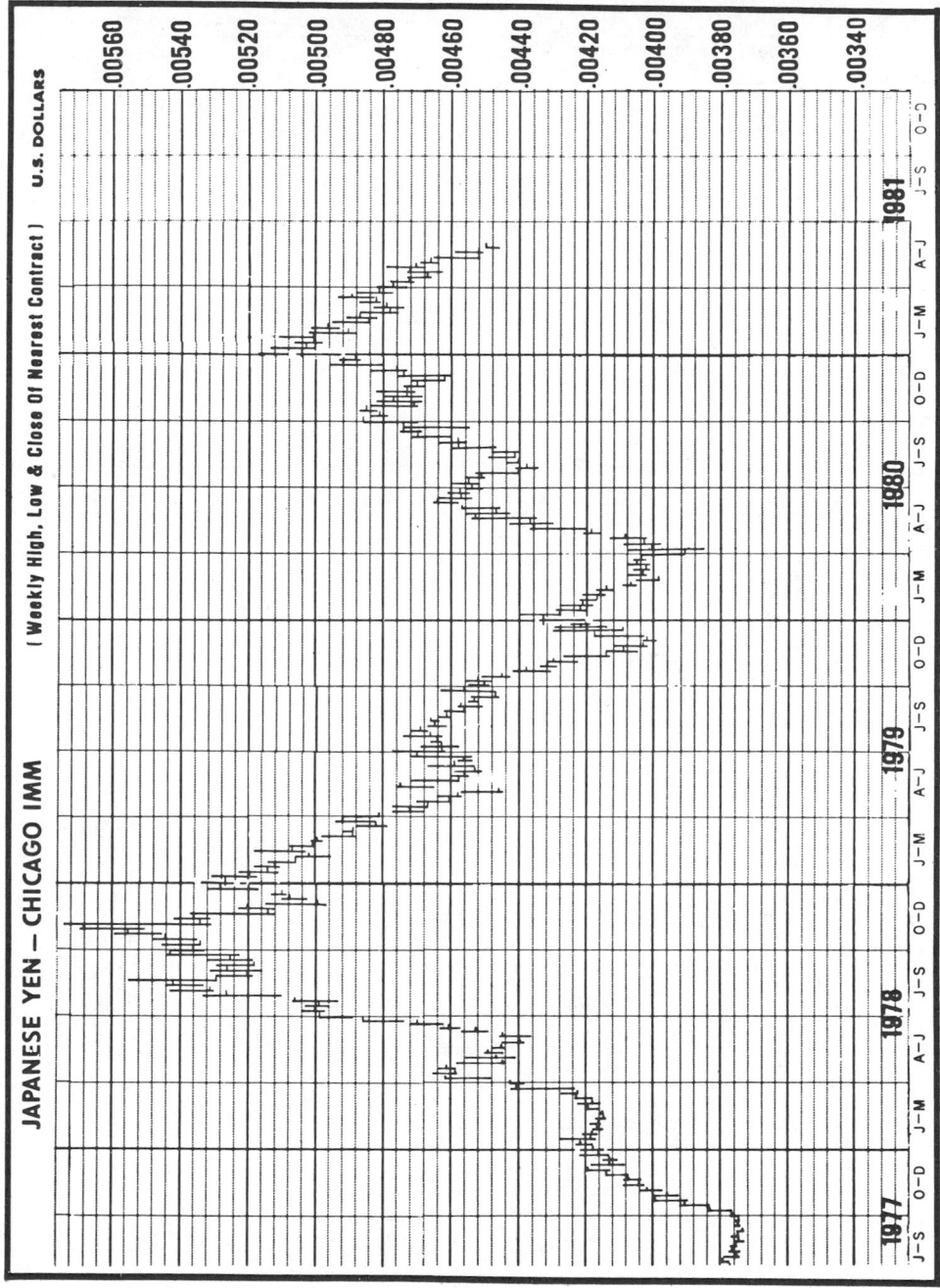

JAPANESE YEN – CHICAGO IMM

(Weekly High, Low & Close Of Nearest Contract)

U.S. DOLLARS

.00560 .00540 .00520 .00500 .00480 .00460 .00440 .00420 .00400 .00380 .00360 .00340

1977 1978 1979 1980 1981

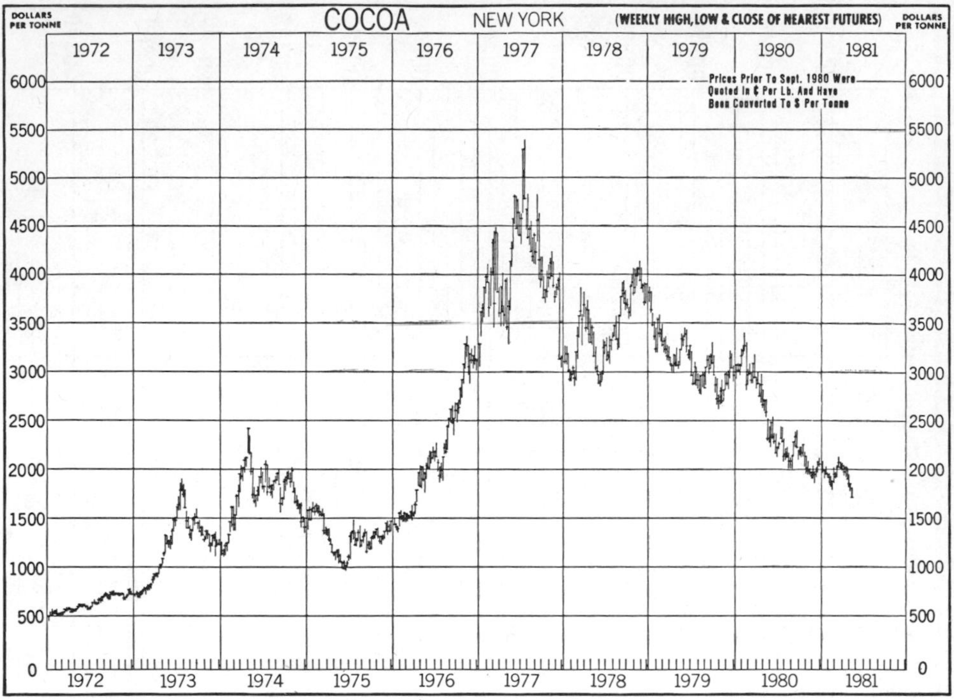

DOLLARS PER TONNE | COCOA   NEW YORK   (WEEKLY HIGH, LOW & CLOSE OF NEAREST FUTURES) | DOLLARS PER TONNE

Prices Prior To Sept. 1980 Were Quoted In ¢ Per Lb. And Have Been Converted To $ Per Tonne

ORANGE JUICE   NEW YORK   (WEEKLY HIGH, LOW & CLOSE OF NEAREST FUTURES)

CENTS PER POUND

Commodity Research Bureau, Inc.
ONE LIBERTY PLAZA, NEW YORK, N.Y. 10006

HIGH 220

COTTON "2" NEW YORK (WEEKLY HIGH, LOW & CLOSE OF NEAREST FUTURES)

CENTS PER POUND

Prepared by
Commodity Research Bureau, Inc.
ONE LIBERTY PLAZA, NEW YORK, N. Y. 10006

PLYWOOD CHICAGO (WEEKLY HIGH, LOW & CLOSE OF NEAREST FUTURES)

DOLLARS PER 1,000 SQ. FT.

Prepared by
Commodity Research Bureau, Inc.
ONE LIBERTY PLAZA, NEW YORK, N. Y. 10006

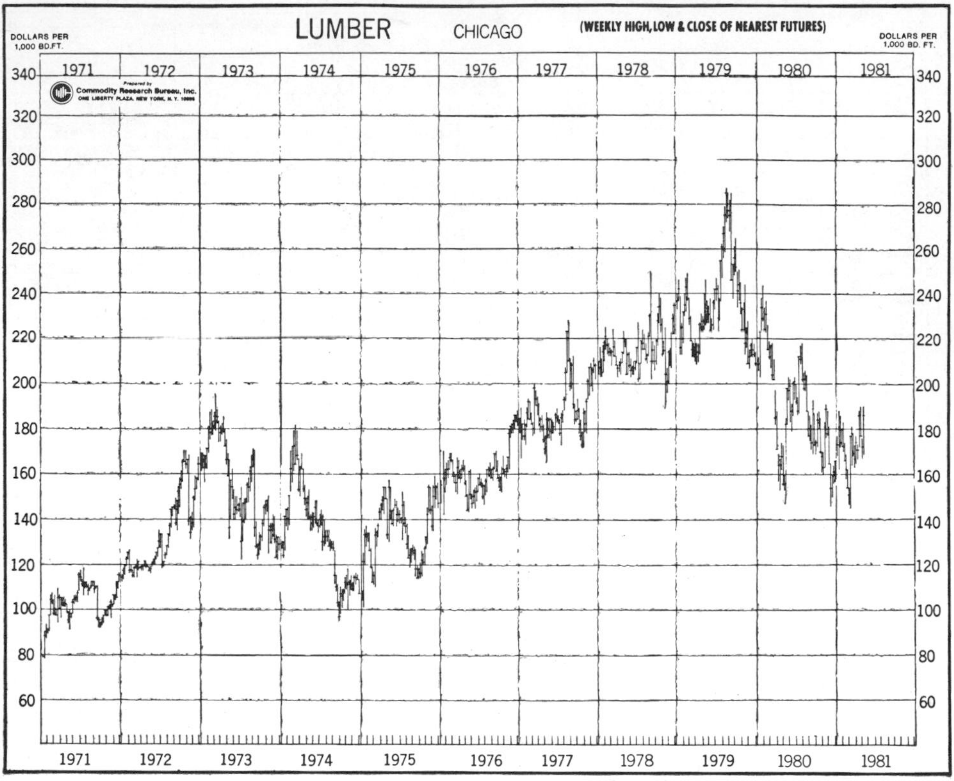

LUMBER   CHICAGO   (WEEKLY HIGH, LOW & CLOSE OF NEAREST FUTURES)

DOLLARS PER
1,000 BD.FT.

Prepared by
Commodity Research Bureau, Inc.
ONE LIBERTY PLAZA, NEW YORK, N.Y. 10006

GOLD   NEW YORK (COMEX)   (WEEKLY HIGH, LOW & CLOSE OF NEAREST FUTURES)

DOLLARS PER
OUNCE

Prepared by
Commodity Research Bureau, Inc.
ONE LIBERTY PLAZA, NEW YORK, N.Y. 10006

WINNIPEG QUOTED FROM
NOV. 16, 1972 TO JAN. 27, 1975

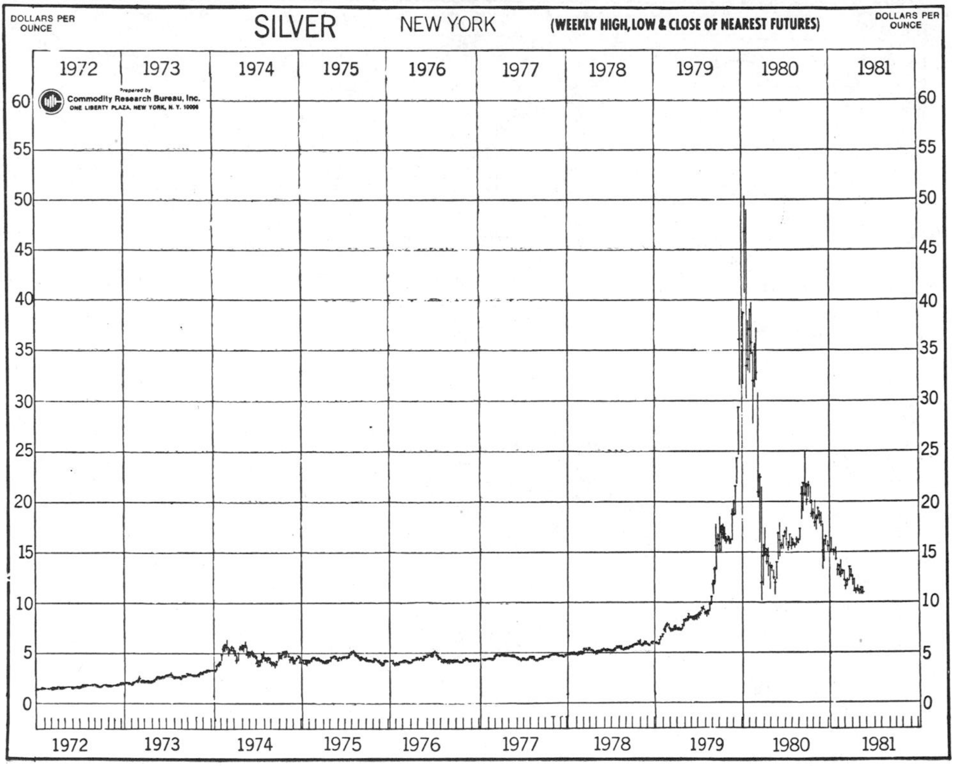
DOLLARS PER OUNCE
SILVER
NEW YORK
(WEEKLY HIGH, LOW & CLOSE OF NEAREST FUTURES)
DOLLARS PER OUNCE
1972 1973 1974 1975 1976 1977 1978 1979 1980 1981
Prepared by Commodity Research Bureau, Inc. ONE LIBERTY PLAZA, NEW YORK, N. Y. 10006
60 55 50 45 40 35 30 25 20 15 10 5 0
1972 1973 1974 1975 1976 1977 1978 1979 1980 1981

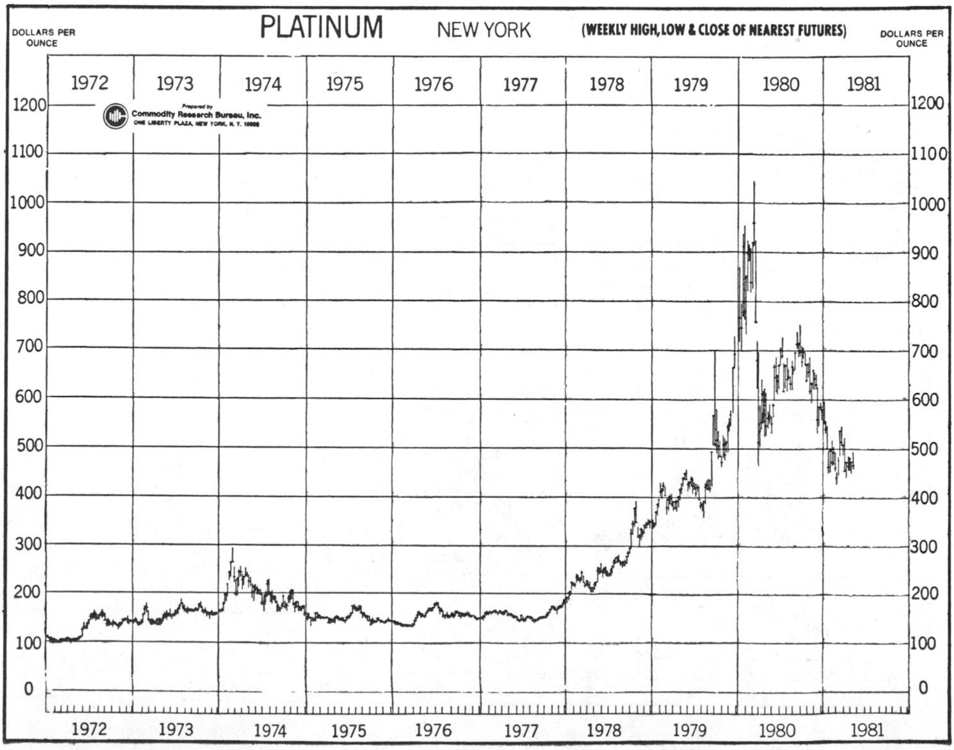
DOLLARS PER OUNCE
PLATINUM
NEW YORK
(WEEKLY HIGH, LOW & CLOSE OF NEAREST FUTURES)
DOLLARS PER OUNCE
1972 1973 1974 1975 1976 1977 1978 1979 1980 1981
Prepared by Commodity Research Bureau, Inc. ONE LIBERTY PLAZA, NEW YORK, N. Y. 10006
1200 1100 1000 900 800 700 600 500 400 300 200 100 0
1972 1973 1974 1975 1976 1977 1978 1979 1980 1981

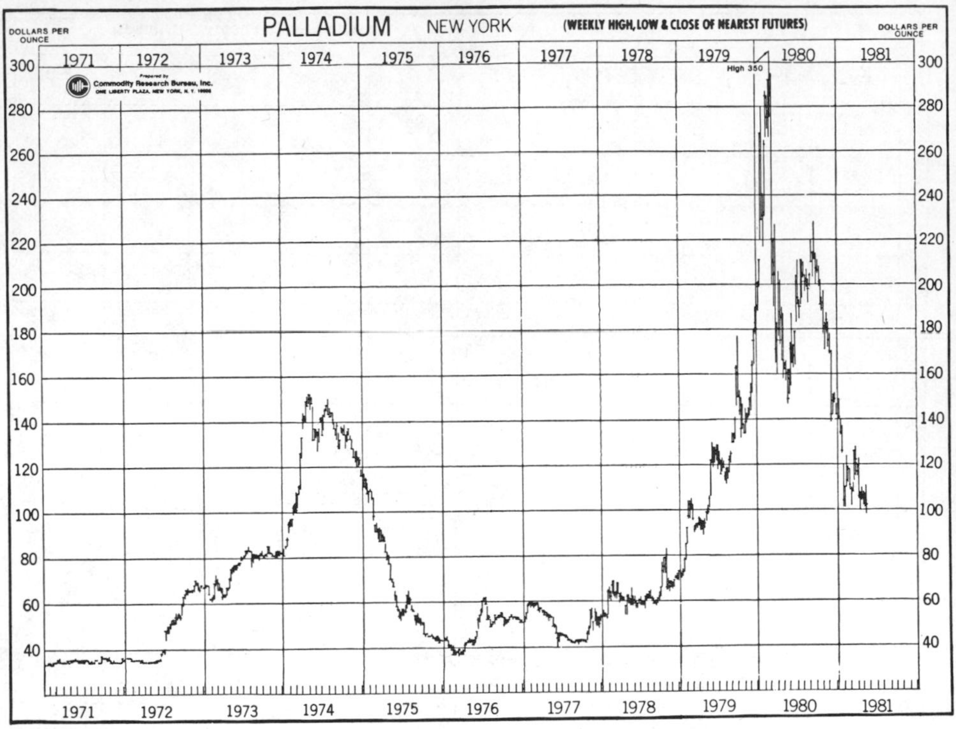

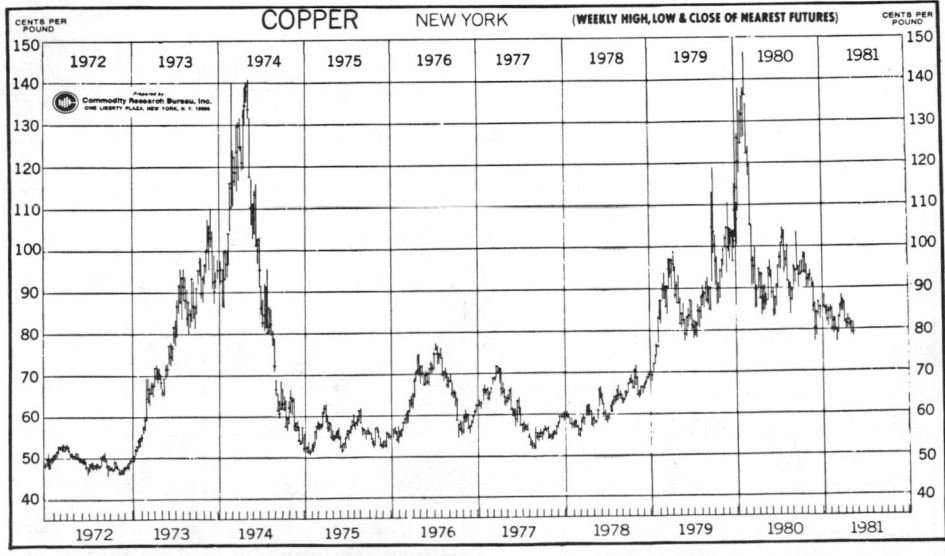

PALLADIUM NEW YORK (WEEKLY HIGH, LOW & CLOSE OF NEAREST FUTURES)

COPPER NEW YORK (WEEKLY HIGH, LOW & CLOSE OF NEAREST FUTURES)

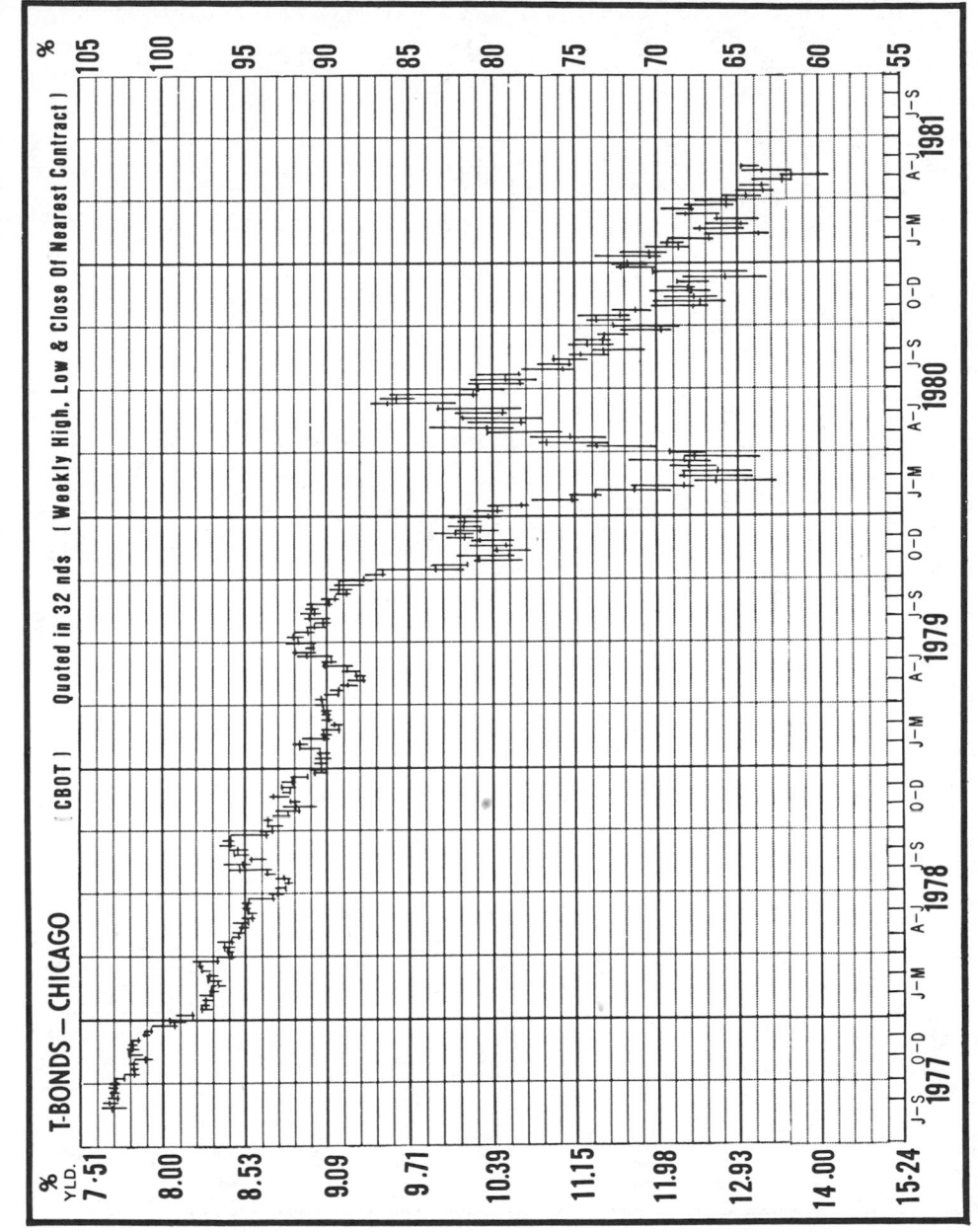

INTEREST RATES

T-BONDS – CHICAGO (CBOT) Quoted in 32 nds (Weekly High, Low & Close Of Nearest Contract)

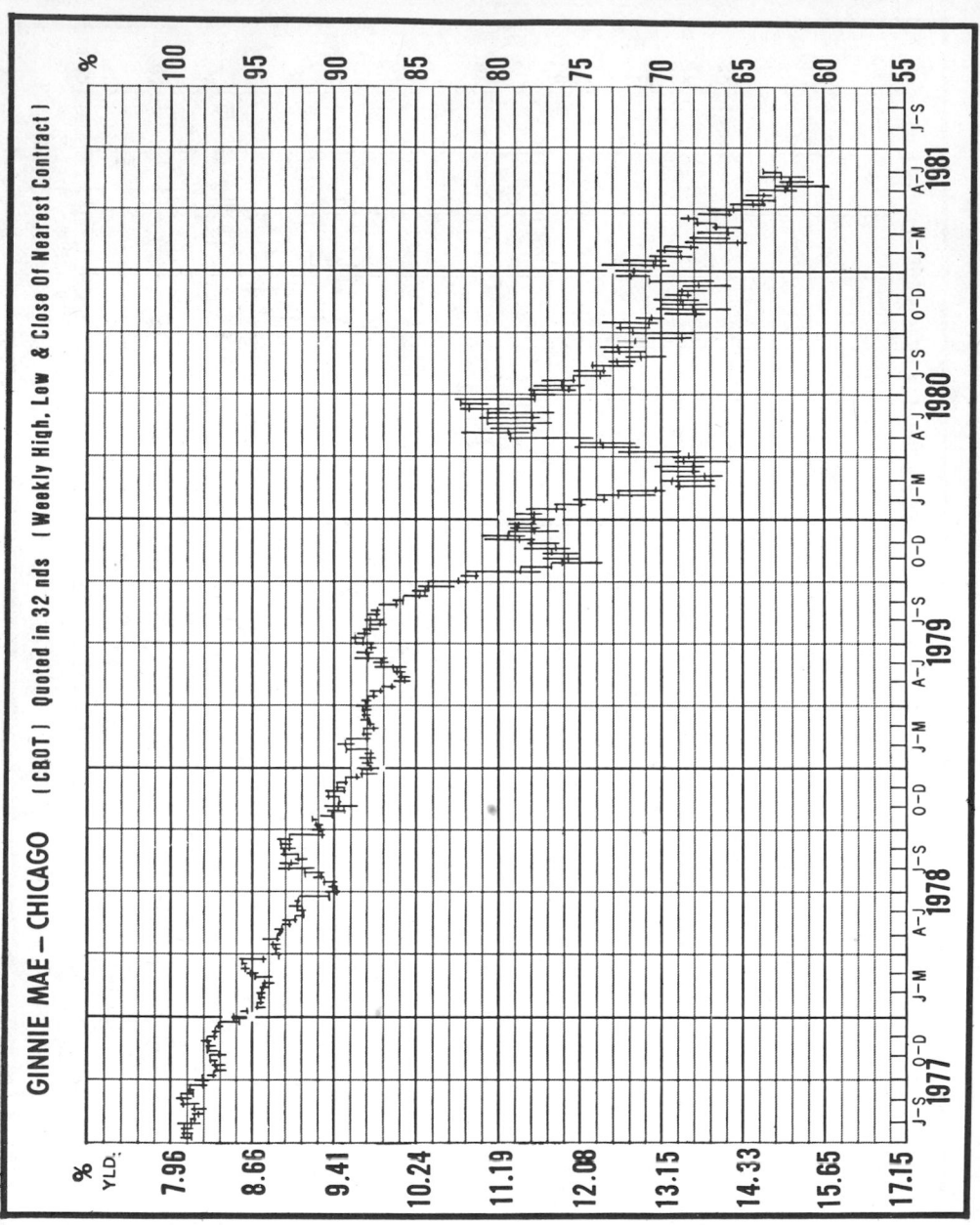

GINNIE MAE – CHICAGO (CBOT) Quoted in 32 nds (Weekly High, Low & Close Of Nearest Contract)

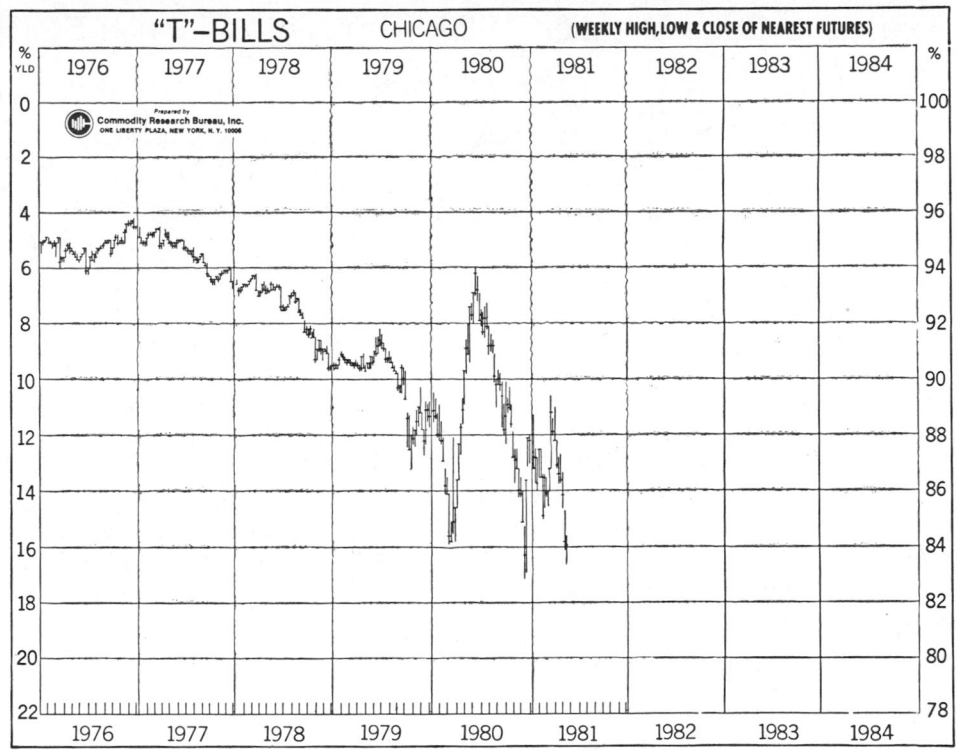

"T"-BILLS   CHICAGO   (WEEKLY HIGH, LOW & CLOSE OF NEAREST FUTURES)

Executive Compensation 1981: The Ninth Biennial Study

Edwin S: Mruk and James A Giardina
Arthur Young & Company
New York, New York

This article summarizes the results of the Ninth Biennial Study of Executive Compensation conducted by Edwin S. Mruk and James A. Giardina of Arthur Young & Company and sponsored by the Financial Executives Institute. The study includes data on over 12,450 Chief Executive Officers, Top Executives and Senior Financial Management in over 1,425 companies. Table I lists the executive positions included in the study.

TABLE 1
EXECUTIVE POSITIONS

Chief Executive Officer
Top Executives:

Chief Operating Officer
Top Financial Officer
Top Marketing Officer
Top Sales Executive
Top Manufacturing Executive
Top Human Resources Executive
Top Strategic Planning Executive
Top Legal Executive
Top International Executive
Controller
Treasurer

Senior Financial Executives:

Top Financial Relations Executive
Top General Accounting Executive
Top Tax Executive
Top Financial Analysis and Profit
  Planning Executive
Top Systems and Data Processing
  Executive
Top Budget Executive
Top Internal Audit Executive
Top Credit and Collection Executive
Corporate Risk Management Executive
Cash Management Executive

1980 was a tough financial year for U.S. corporations. Corporate profits of the Fortune 500 companies were up only 3.6%. (With inflation of 13.5% this amounts to a 10% decline in real terms.) Approximately 40% of the Fortune 500 companies had a decline in profits even before considering inflation. These results are reflected in the change in total cash compensation (base salary plus bonus) paid to senior executives in U.S. corporations in 1980. The average increase in cash compensation for the executives in our study on executive compensation was 14% in

1980. However, this amounts to a half percent increase in real terms before taxes. Because marginal federal income tax rates increase as income increases, the average increase in cash compensation in 1980 was a decline in real after-tax income.

This increase in executive compensation in 1980 is evidence of the difficulty in maintaining performance-based pay programs during a period of high inflation. Base salaries in both bonus- and nonbonus-paying companies increased at only approximately the same rate as inflation. This suggests that companies are setting salary increase merit budgets at close to the inflation rate. Reflecting both tougher corporate standards and less favorable corporate results, the increase in bonus payments declined from 23% in 1978 to 16% in 1980.

The increase in executive cash compensation might have been even lower than the inflation rate except for the fact that the demand for business executives during 1980 increased by 5%, compared to demand measured in 1979.[1] While "pay for performance" continues as the theme of many corporations, experience indicates that continued demand for executives, and high inflation have made it harder to administer pay for performance programs. In base salary programs, there is a strong feeling among many corporate managers that employees should be protected from inflation. With a fixed total salary increase budget, larger increases for poor or average performers in order to keep them whole with inflation means there is less for salary increases for above average or superior performers. While the average increase may be in line with corporate targets, the difference in increase in salary in percentage terms between the superior performer and the average performer may be nominal.

On the other hand bonus plans, if designed properly, provide a greater opportunity to adjust total cash compensation for corporate or individual performance than do the base salary programs. Reflecting this, bonus amounts increased only 16% in 1980 as compared with 23% in 1978.

There is, however, no magic formula in establishing bonus plan performance targets. There are several factors considered which include historical results, industry averages, and

---
[1] Source: AY/ERC Executive Demand Index.

expected economic conditions. In recent years, companies have moved away from performance targets which are relatively easy to achieve. These can lead to windfall bonus payments.

It is of course more difficult for Boards of Directors to establish realistic corporate performance targets in periods of rapidly changing economic conditions. High inflation obscures real financial results, making it even more difficult to communicate Board of Directors' expectations to Management. Determining performance standards for bonus purposes after the fact (i.e., after the close of the financial year) is not a realistic solution because such an approach does not give Management established performance targets toward which to work.

Most U.S. bonus plans use annual performance targets. This has been criticized in various circles as resulting in management of U.S. corporations taking a short-term view of performance. It has been argued that one of the reasons for the success of Japanese companies is that Japanese management takes the long-term view in terms of corporate performance. We will probably see a greater use of long-term programs, with payouts in either stock or cash, which are tied to meaningful performance targets. Such plans require that the Board of Directors establish long-term performance targets. This is even more difficult, however, than establishing annual performance targets. It requires an articulation of the long-term goals and objectives of the corporation. Essentially, the Board must articulate what the corporation should achieve over the next three years, five years, and ten years.

At present approximately 75% of U.S. corporations have bonus plans—at least for their Chief Executive Officers. Even industries such as utilities, which traditionally have not had such plans, are beginning to adopt them. Within the current economic environment, they are becoming increasingly important components of executive compensation programs.

CASH COMPENSATION TRENDS

As stated previously, total cash compensation (base plus bonus) for all 22 positions in the study increased by 14%. This rate of increase was above the 12% reported in this previous study. Average pay increases vary less by position in this year's study compared to the prior study (for positions that were in both studies). In the 1978 study, the average pay increase ranged from a low of 9% for the Top Internal Audit and Cash Management Executives to a high of 16% for the Chief Executive Officer. In this year's study, the average increase ranged from 11% for the Top Credit and Collection and Top Financial Relations Executives to 17% for the Top Manufacturing Executive.

In 1980, there seems to have been less differentiation in terms of granting increases to the various levels within companies compared to 1978. In 1980, both CEO and the top management group had average increases of 14%. The senior financial management group was only slightly lower at 13%. In the 1978 study, the CEO average increase was 16%, top management average increase was 13%, and the senior financial management group reported 11%. Companies seem to be managing cash compensation increases for each type of executive on a more similar basis than has existed in the past. One of the impacts of wage guidelines and standards in effect a few years ago was that they forced companies to differentiate between groups of employees in order to accommodate differences in demand and still stay within the overall guidelines.

The increase in compensation in nonbonus companies was much closer to that in bonus paying companies in 1980 compared to 1978. In 1978, the increase in total cash compensation in nonbonus companies was 9% compared to 14% in bonus companies. In 1980 executives in nonbonus companies received increases of 13%—very close to the 14% average increase in total cash compensation granted to executives in bonus companies. The reason is not simply that bonus increases have continued to moderate (32% in 1976, 23% in 1978 and 16% in 1980). Rather, base salaries in nonbonus companies increased nearly the same (14%) as did base salaries in bonus paying companies in 1980. In 1978, base salaries in bonus companies increased at 11% versus 9% in nonbonus companies. While total cash compensation is still higher in bonus paying companies than in nonbonus paying companies, the gap does not appear to be widening except possibly for the senior financial executive group.

CHIEF EXECUTIVE OFFICERS

This year's study includes data on over 1250 Chief Executive Officers in 24 industries.

Total cash compensation for the Chief Executive Officers for whom 1979 and 1980 data were reported rose 14% in 1980 compared to the 16% increase in 1978 reported in the last study. Approximately 74% of the CEOs received bonuses, almost the same as the 77% reported in 1978.

Base salaries in bonus paying companies continue to be greater than for nonbonus companies. On the average, the base salary of Chief Executives is 15% greater than that of their counterparts in nonbonus companies. There is, of course, an even greater difference in total cash compensation. However, the difference in salaries and total compensation between bonus and nonbonus companies may be stabilizing somewhat for Chief Executive Officers in that the increases in base salaries and total compensation were similar in 1980 for both groups.

In bonus companies, the trend of increasing bonus as a percentage of base salary which occurred in the early 1970s appears to have reversed itself slightly. The ratio of base to bonus increased from 40% to 49% between 1972 and 1976. Since 1976, the ratio has declined. It was 48% in 1978, 47% in 1979 and 43% in 1980. In 1980 bonus payments increased by only 9% (versus 26% in 1978) versus a 14% increase in base salaries. Companies appear to be adjusting base salaries in line with inflation, but making it tougher to earn bonus payments.

Chief Executives in manufacturing companies are still the highest paid. However, increases in this industry trailed both the nonmanufacturing and financial services industries.

TABLE 2
CHIEF EXECUTIVE OFFICER [Average percentage increase (decrease) in total compensation by industry]
(1979–1980)

	Bonus Companies	Nonbonus Companies
Manufacturing Group		
Durable Goods	21%	
Basic Materials	9%	14%
Electrical Machinery	10	18
Fabricated Metal Products	12	13
Instruments	21	14
Machinery	11	14
Primary Metals	11	14
Nondurable Goods		
Chemicals and Petroleum	15	13
Food Products	22	9
Paper Products	14	7
Publishing	12	11
Textiles and Apparel	7	13
Transportation Equipment	(1)	11
Nonmanufacturing Group		
Business Services	21	9
Construction and Contracting	19	24
Mining	22	22
Retail Sales	8	14
Transportation	29	5
Utilities	35	15
Wholesale Trade	6	15
Financial Services Group		
Banking (Commercial)	16	14
Banking (Thrift Institutions)	15	14
Financial Holding and Investment	8	19
Insurance	14	13
Real Estate	21	9

Source: *Executive Compensation 1981: The Ninth Biennial Study*, Arthur Young & Company.

CEO increases in total compensation were 12% in the manufacturing companies, 14% in financial services companies and 16% in nonmanufacturing companies. The data for individual industries is presented in Table 2.

Bonuses continue to be more prevalent in manufacturing companies than in either the nonmanufacturing or financial services industry groups. 86% of the manufacturing companies pay bonuses to CEOs compared to 63% in the nonmanufacturing companies and 65% in financial services companies.

Bonus payments as a percent of base salary are lowest (31%) in the financial services companies compared to manufacturing (48%) and nonmanufacturing (47%). However, bonus payments increased the least (5% on average) in manufacturing companies compared to the 13% in nonmanufacturing and financial services companies.

Companies in the construction and contracting industries reported paying the largest average bonus as a percentage of base salary—69%. This is a decline from the 74% in 1978 and 84% in 1976. The next highest ratios were in the real estate and publishing industries, each paying 61% of base salary. The commercial banking and insurance industries reported the lowest bonus to base salary ratios (25% in each).

TOP EXECUTIVE GROUP

This year's study was expanded to include eight positions in the top executive group in addition to the three executive positions (Top Financial Officer, Controller, and Treasurer) in previous studies. The eight additional positions are the Chief Operating Officer, Top Marketing Executive, Top Sales Executive, Top Manufacturing Executive, Top Human Resources Executive, Top Strategic Planning Executive, Top Legal Executive, and Top International Executive. In all, this year's study includes data on more than 6,700 top executives.

Compensation for these top executives increased 14%. There was little difference between increase in bonus (14%) and nonbonus (13%) and among industry groups. The highest average increases were granted to the Top Manufacturing Executives (17%), the Chief Operating Officers (15%) and Top Legal Executives (15%). The lowest increases were granted to the Top International Executives (12%) and the Treasurers (13%).

Approximately 75% of the top executives are included in bonus plans. A larger percentage of top executives in the manufacturing group (86%) receive bonuses than either the nonmanufacturing (68%) or financial services (59%). The greatest incidence of bonus payments was reported in the primary metals industry (95%). The lowest incidence was in the utilities industry (26%).

TABLE 3
TOP EXECUTIVES—MANUFACTURING GROUP (Compensation as a percentage of CEO's compensation)

Sales Volume	Chief Operating Officer	Top Financial Officer	Top Marketing Executive	Top Sales Executive	Top Manufacturing Executive	Top Human Resources Executive	Top Strategic Planning Executive	Top Legal Executive	Top International Executive	Controller	Treasurer
Under $10 Million	76%	63%	64%	51%	49%	36%	42%	66%	*	41%	43%
10–25	77	57	65	57	54	34	*	59	*	36	47
25–50	66	51	52	47	48	30	40	*	56%	30	33
50–100	76	49	49	52	47	33	37	40	45	29	28
100–200	72	47	41	37	42	29	36	42	42	29	33
200–500	77	45	41	37	40	29	36	36	37	27	28
500–1 Billion	70	44	36	29	44	30	27	32	41	27	25
1–2	73	46	33	26	33	26	26	35	34	24	23
over $2 Billion	72	44	32	28	35	28	28	35	41	24	24

Source: *Executive Compensation 1981: The Ninth Biennial Study*, Arthur Young & Company.

TABLE 4
CHIEF EXECUTIVE OFFICER (Comparison of average total compensation)

	Rank		Index (All CEOs = 1.00)	
	1980	1978	1980	1978
Chemicals and Petroleum	1	3	1.50	1.29
Primary Metals	2	5	1.40	1.11
Mining	3	8	1.35	1.09
Food Products	4	7	1.27	1.11
Financial Holding and Investment	5	2	1.22	1.38
Transportation Equipment	6	1	1.20	1.52
Paper Products	7	4	1.16	1.24
Publishing	8	18	1.11	.86
Basic Materials	9	9	1.09	1.07
Textiles and Apparel	10	17	1.08	.89
Transportation	11	12	1.02	.98
Electrical Machinery	12	10	1.01	1.01
Business Services	13	19	.99	.82
Machinery	14	11	.98	.98
Retail Sales	15	14	.98	.95
Fabricated Metal Products	16	16	.96	.91
Utilities	17	21	.95	.79
Instruments	18	13	.93	.96
Construction and Contracting	19	6	.83	1.11
Real Estate	20	22	.80	.70
Banking (Thrift Institutions)	21	23	.78	.66
Wholesale Trade	22	24	.78	.63
Banking (Commercial)	23	20	.75	.81
Insurance	24	15	.73	.94

Source: *Executive Compensation 1981: The Ninth Biennial Study*, Arthur Young & Company.

Bonuses as a percentage of base salary averaged 31% for this group of executives. Bonuses as a percentage of base salaries were highest in the construction industry (41%). The insurance industry reported the smallest bonuses—19% of base salaries.

The ratio of executive compensation to CEO compensation tends to be higher in smaller companies than in larger companies. This suggests that pay compression may be occurring in smaller companies. As expected, the Chief Operating Officer tends to be the second highest paid executive in a given industry and given sales size. The Top International Officer, however, tends to be the next highest paid executive in terms of compensation as a percentage of Chief Executive Officer compensation, followed by that for the top financial officer. Table 3 shows the pay relationships among the manufacturing companies in the study.

IMPACT OF INDUSTRY

In addition to the demand for executives, individual and corporate performance, and inflation, there are other factors which influence compensation for executives. Chief among these is the particular industry in which the executive works. Table 4 compares average compensation for Chief Executives in the 24 industries studied. In the table, industries are ranked in descending order, according to 1980 compensation. In addition, there is an index figure for each industry. The indices were calculated by dividing the average total CEO compensation in each industry by the average total compensation of all the Chief Executives in the study. Thus, indices above 1.0 show that the compensation in a particular industry is above average, while indices below 1.0 show that compensation in an industry falls below average.

The industry reporting the highest average total compensation to the CEO was chemicals and petroleum—50% above the average. In 1978, this industry ranked third, paying only 29% above average. The transportation equipment industry, which ranked first in 1978, dropped to sixth place this year—its index declining substantially from 1.52 to 1.20. The commercial banking and insurance industries reported the lowest average total compensation for CEOs, 25% and 27% below average CEO compensation, respectively.

Taxes and Tax Sheltered Investments

TAX SHELTERED INVESTMENTS*

TAX SHELTER HIGHLIGHTS

Worthwhile *tax sheltered investments* offer both investment merit and tax benefits.

Tax shelter means turning dollars otherwise paid to Uncle Sam into assets or income, through: (1) *tax deferral,* (2) conversion of ordinary income into long-term capital gains, and (3) conversion and deferral—the conversion of this year's ordinary income into future years' long-term capital gains.

Limited partnerships are the best *tax-sheltered investment* for most investors because of limited liability and flow-through of tax losses.

As a tax shelter investor, you should have: (1) substantial net worth and assets, (2) sufficient current assets and liquidity, and (3) an understanding of tax-shelter risk.

The three major investment goals of tax shelter—*tax savings, tax-sheltered cash flow,* and *capital gains—cannot all be maximized simultaneously.*

Most tax shelters will involve *public programs* organized as *limited partnerships* in: newly constructed real estate, existing income producing real estate, net leased real estate, oil and gas drilling, equipment leasing, or agriculture.

Certain investors find specialized tax shelters/Keogh Plans, individual retirement accounts, annuities, corporate pension and profit-sharing plans, or municipal bonds well suited to their needs.

Selecting a tax shelter requires analysis of your own qualifications and characteristics, your investment goals and desired results.

Always consult your tax advisor before finalizing any tax-shelter investment decision.

INTRODUCTION

A tax shelter is any investment made more attractive by the timing of the profit or the way it is taxed. Before we go further, please do not

Source: *Tax Shelters,* Bache-Halsey Stuart Shields Incorporated.

* See Summary of 1981 Tax Law for updates, pp. 425–456.

worry that tax shelters are somehow illegal or immoral; they are not. And do not confuse *tax shelter* with *loophole.* Tax shelters are not loopholes at all.

Tax-sheltered investments are based on specific provisions of the tax laws enacted by Congress to encourage investment capital to flow directly into the basic areas of our economy such as housing, petroleum, manufacturing, and agriculture. In one sense *tax shelter* means investing in vital industries in a way that permits you—rather than the companies you invest with—to keep the tax benefits . . . while retaining your opportunities for significant profits.

If you have a substantial net worth and your combined federal and state income taxes place you in at least the 50 percent tax bracket, you ought to consider some of the established ways to reduce the amount you have to pay the government on April 15.

A tax shelter should have two components. First and foremost, it has to be an investment with potential economic benefits. Any tax shelter that does not offer promise of being a worthwhile economic investment should be ignored. Without profit possibilities, chances are you would do just as well at tax time giving money to a favorite charity. In addition there has to be favorable tax treatment permitting you—and other properly qualified, high tax bracket investors—to reduce or defer your overall taxes.

VIEWPOINT

THE TAX SHELTER INDUSTRIES

The majority of investment-quality tax shelters are found in four areas:

Real estate.
Oil and gas.
Equipment leasing.
Agriculture.

In addition, there are several specialized tax-shelter areas which may interest you: Keogh Plans, annuities, pension and profit sharing plans, individual retirement accounts, and municipal bonds.

TAX SHELTER CONCEPTS

The idea behind tax shelters lies in turning dollars otherwise paid to Uncle Sam into income or into assets which may be sold for a profit. This process involves three concepts:

1. *Deferral:* Postponing payment of taxes from the current taxable year until a later year when you are in a lower tax bracket or have more cash.

2. *Conversion:* Obtaining current tax *deductions* against ordinary income while turning future revenues into income taxable at more favorable *capital gains* rates or lower rates derived from favorable tax features such as *depletion* or *depreciation.*

3. *Leverage:* Obtaining current deductions in excess of cash investment through the use of loans, either *nonrecourse loans* which increase *deductions* without increasing your investment or personal liability, or *recourse loans* for which you are personally liable. Nonrecourse loans currently apply only to real estate tax shelters. Since enactment of the Tax Reform Act of 1976 and the Revenue Act of 1978, recourse loans must be used for all tax shelters other than real estate if you are to have deductions in excess of 100 percent of your investment.

If you have unusually high income for one year, but do not expect to be at the same level in subsequent years, you may select a tax shelter emphasizing deferral. On the other hand, if your income continually puts you in a high tax bracket, you may want a shelter which will generate deductions for several years. In both cases the use of leverage may help you increase your tax benefits.

TAX SHELTER ORGANIZATIONS

Probably the most frequent question asked about tax shelters is: "Just what is a tax shelter?"

The answer: A tax shelter is a security, but not a stock, bond, or commodity. What you receive when you invest in a tax shelter is an interest in a *limited partnership, joint venture,* or, in rare instances, a *Subchapter S corporation.*

LIMITED PARTNERSHIP TAX SHELTERS

To fully understand a limited partnership, you need to study its five basic features: partnership, general partner, limited partners, limited liability, and flow-through of tax benefits. In addition, you should understand the difference between a "public" program and a "private" program.

THE PARTNERSHIP CONCEPT

A limited partnership is an undertaking between an individual and/or a company (called the *general partner*) that has investment expertise in a tax-shelter industry and a group of investors (called *limited partners*) seeking specific tax benefits, risks, and rewards. The general partner provides investment expertise; investors supply the money, or most of it. Tax benefits normally accrue to investors; profits are shared according to a stated formula designed to compensate company and investors for their respective contributions.

THE GENERAL PARTNER'S ROLE

Principal activities of the general partner include: assembling investors' capital, making investments, keeping partnership books, reporting results, and distributing any partnership profits.

"Making investments" involves purchasing direct interests in oil wells, real estate, leasable equipment, or various forms of agriculture on behalf of the limited partnership.

THE LIMITED PARTNER'S ROLE

Your function involves providing a share of the capital to finance initial selection and operation of partnership projects. You receive periodic progress reports and your share of partnership cash distributions. To preserve the tax status of the limited partnership, you and other limited partners must not take any active role in partnership management.

LIMITED LIABILITY

Your personal liability as a limited partner is legally limited to what you have actually invested or committed to invest plus your share of any undistributed profits. If something goes wrong (a major fire or an earthquake for example), the partnership's creditors can not attach your personal assets except to the extent of any recourse loans for which you have agreed to become personally liable.

FLOW-THROUGH OF TAX BENEFITS

The partnership itself pays no taxes; benefits pass directly to the partners. You include your share of partnership profits and losses (usually losses in the early years) on your own tax return. Later, if your partnership begins generating taxable profits, those profits are added to your other income.

PUBLIC AND PRIVATE PROGRAMS

Often, the general partner's role of "assembling investor's capital" means a formal offering registered with the SEC. Typically, these public programs involve a minimum $5,000 *subscription* with additional investment amounts available in *units* as small as $1,000. Assessments, if any, are limited to a stated amount or percentage of the original subscription. Public programs can be *blind pools,* an approach which gives the sponsor flexibility in selecting a diversified group of projects designed to meet partnership goals.

The substantial investor with much more income to shelter than the $5,000 minimum subscription required of most public programs may find a private program more suitable. Private offerings of tax shelters generally involve a large *subscription* with *units* of $50,000 or more. *Assessments* are more common than in public programs. The *offering amount* is typically less than $1 million; many are *specified property programs* involving one or a very few projects.

INVESTMENT GOALS

Before considering a *tax-sheltered partnership* you should determine whether your own financial and tax position justifies such an investment.

Before getting into tax shelters, you should conduct a "personal audit" to determine whether you have the prerequisites to become a tax-shelter investor and, more importantly, whether you can really benefit.

PREREQUISITES

As a tax-shelter investor, it's vital that you have: (1) substantial net worth and income, (2) sufficient current assets to avoid impairing other investment goals, and (3) an understanding of the risks and the lack of liquidity.

NET WORTH AND INCOME

The definition of *substantial* net worth and income varies from person to person and from tax shelter to tax shelter; however, there are some guidelines. Many states require that prospective tax-shelter investors meet "suitability requirements." For example, state regulators usually require that oil and gas investors have minimum net worth of $200,000 or net worth of $50,000 and some income taxed at a 50 percent rate. Tax shelters with lesser risk, for example, equipment leasing, have correspondingly lower suitability requirements.

CURRENT ASSETS

Another way to analyze whether you are "suitable" is to evaluate your current assets—possible sources of tax-shelter investment cash. Your investment should not come out of funds earmarked for college education or retirement. And you should not forego other investments. Tax-shelter funds should come out of current income, borrowings which you will repay out of current income, or current capital gains. Remember, your objective is sheltering current taxable income.

UNDERSTANDING RISK AND LIQUIDITY

The reasons for concern about current assets, income, and net worth relate to two characteristics of all tax shelters: investment risk and lack of liquidity.

It is difficult to quantify investment risk, but in every tax-sheltered investment there is underlying danger that oil wells will be dry, that apartments will not rent, that even companies with Triple A credit cannot meet lease payments, or that tax laws will change. Even if you have sufficient income, net worth, and available cash, you should understand that you may be faced with disappointing performance. "Investment risk" implies a range of returns—some great years, some less than great, some bad. With some tax shelters, you must be prepared to continue reinvesting for enough years to average your investment performance.

An understanding of *liquidity* is also required. Whatever shelter you choose, it may be at least six months before you begin receiving any cash distributions and up to two years before you can sell out and receive the *cash liquidating value* of your chosen partnership. Do not count on being able to sell a partnership interest like a stock or a bond on a moment's notice, even in an emergency.

If you meet the suitability requirements . . . if you have capital available from proper sources . . . if you are prepared to invest in your chosen tax-shelter industry long enough to smooth out the effect of investment risk . . . if you can live with the idea that it may be two years or longer before you get your money out . . . then you can probably benefit from a long-term tax-shelter investment program.

POSSIBLE BENEFITS

Once you have determined that tax shelters are suitable for your portfolio, you will have to decide what combination of the benefits offered by tax shelters fits your own investment goals:

(1) tax savings,
(2) tax-sheltered cash flow, or
(3) capital gains.

TAX SAVINGS

Reducing current taxes is the principal goal of most tax-shelter investors. Limited partnerships are usually structured to maximize tax *deductions* in the first year. The objective is to have *tax losses,* that is, a tax shelter that generates more deductions than income the first year or first few years. When combined with other income on your tax return, your share of partnership deductions offsets an equal amount of your taxable income from other sources on April 15. If you are in a 50 percent federal tax bracket,

TAX DEDUCTIONS FROM SHELTER IN FIRST YEAR AS A PERCENTAGE OF THE INVESTMENT

	50% Deductible	100% Deductible	150% Deductible	Nothing Deductible
Taxable income*	$75,000	$75,000	$75,000	$75,000
Deductions from shelters	(5,000)	(10,000)	(15,000)	—
Revised taxable income	$70,000	$65,000	$60,000	$75,000
Tax due	$24,700	$22,200	$19,700	$27,200
Tax savings	$ 2,500	$ 5,000	$ 7,500	$ —
Net investment cost ($10,000 minus tax savings)	$ 7,500	$ 5,000	$ 2,500	$ —

* Personal service income after exemptions and itemized deductions.

for example, each dollar of your share of net partnership deductions generates *tax savings* of up to 50 cents.

Let us illustrate the effect of various degrees of deductibility in tax shelters. Assume you are in a 50 percent federal tax bracket, file a joint return, have $75,000 of taxable income and invest $10,000: (see table above)

The 50 percent deduction on a $10,000 investment, for example, saves $2,500 in taxes, so the net cost is only $7,500 even though you have $10,000 invested. The 100 percent and 150 percent deductible shelters produce tax savings of $5,000 and $7,500 respectively.

Try to resist the urge to conclude that the 150 percent deductible tax shelter is "best" because it saves the most taxes. It may be the best if reducing current taxes is your only goal. But remember, deductions in excess of your investment are achieved only through borrowing which utilizes either *nonrecourse loans* (in real estate) or *recourse loans* (all other tax shelters). You cannot deduct more than your share of partnership expenses; without borrowing, your partnership cannot expend more than you invest. Also remember, borrowing has to be repaid; this will involve additional risk especially if recourse loans are used. The funds used to make those repayments may increase your tax bill in later years and reduce your potential economic benefits.

TAX SHELTERED CASH FLOW

Any income received from a tax-shelter partnership may be partially or wholly offset by on-going deductions for depreciation, depletion, interest, and operating costs. Depreciation and depletion are particularly important because they are *noncash charges;* your taxable income is reduced by the deductions, but no cash is actually paid to anyone—it is only a bookkeeping transaction. Let us look at how one dollar of tax-sheltered income from a hypothetical tax-sheltered investment might yield *tax-sheltered cash flow:*

JOINT RETURN—50% TAX BRACKET

	Cash Flow	Tax Flow
Tax shelter gross income	$ 1.00	$ 1.00
Operating expenses	(0.46)	(0.46)
Operating income	$ 0.54	$ 0.54
Deductions:		
Depreciation (noncash)	—	(0.34)
Interest payments	(0.30)	(0.30)
Principal payments	(0.06)	—
Cash flow received	$ 0.18	
Taxable income (loss)		$(0.10)

In this example, you receive 18 cents in cash out of each dollar of gross income generated by your tax-sheltered investment. In addition, deductions reduce your taxable income from the same dollar to minus 10 cents which offsets 10 cents in taxable income from other sources and reduces your tax bill by 5 cents. Because deductions offset the tax liability, you receive 18 cents of tax-sheltered cash flow.

Some tax shelters yield fully tax-sheltered cash flow plus additional tax losses, as in the example above. Other shelters produce some deductions but not enough to absorb all the tax liability, thus partially sheltering your cash flow received. Still other shelters generate: (1) fully taxable cash flow, (2) tax losses but no cash flow, or (3) taxable income but no cash flow received, as in some high *leverage* situations requiring large loan repayments.

Because of the necessity to repay borrowed funds, leverage will reduce the possibility of receiving cash flow. Thus, a tax shelter offering maximum first year deductions through leverage will not generally satisfy a need for tax-sheltered cash flow in later years.

CAPITAL GAINS

If your partnership sells any assets, or if you sell your interest in a partnership, you have to pay a tax on your share of any profits.

If the assets sold are *capital assets,* the sale

may qualify for taxation at long-term *capital gains* rates rather than ordinary income tax rates. Since long-term capital gains are taxed at a maximum rate of 28 percent against a 70 percent maximum rate for other types of income, capital gains may provide a significant degree of tax shelter.

Any investment plan seeking maximum tax savings in the first few years, or maximum tax-sheltered cash flow in later years, may limit capital gains possibilities. Here is why: In certain instances when *accelerated depreciation* or *intangible drilling costs* have been claimed as *deductions*, a portion of those deductions are subject to *recapture* as ordinary income in the year of the sale. This feature may limit capital gains, particularly if leverage has been employed.

In summary, you will not find a tax shelter that offers maximum tax savings, maximum tax-sheltered cash flow and maximum capital-gains opportunities. You will have to decide which tax-shelter investment goals are best for your situation. For example, if you have a very high annual income continuing for several years, some combination of tax savings and capital gains may be your goal. On the other hand, if you are nearing retirement, you may want to forego maximum tax savings in favor of tax-sheltered cash flow to augment your retirement fund; alternatively, you may decide to seek ways to defer your current taxes and pay them at your lower, post-retirement tax rate.

Whichever approach you take, the possible benefits from your chosen tax shelter may be lessened by certain aspects of the Tax Reform Act of 1976 and the Revenue Act of 1978. To insure that really substantial investors do not utilize tax shelters to avoid all taxes, Congress has enacted certain changes affecting the *minimum tax* on *tax-preference items* and the *maximum tax*, and has added a new alternative minimum tax.

Under the *minimum tax*, you pay additional income tax equal to 15 percent of your total *tax-preference items* (except that there is no minimum tax due on the first $10,000 of tax preferences or one half of your regular income tax, whichever is greater). There are seven tax-preference items; for purposes of the regular 15 percent minimum tax, three relate to tax shelters: *(a) accelerated depreciation of real property and leased personal property, (b) depletion,* and *(c) intangible drilling costs.* (See the definition of *tax-preference items* in the Glossary for details.)

Maximum tax relates to personal service income, that is, what is commonly called *earned income,* wages, salaries, professional fees, and certain payments for pensions, annuities, and deferred compensation. It is subject to a maximum tax of 50 percent; however, the amount of income eligible for the maximum tax is offset by the amount of the year's tax-preference

items. The amount offset is taxable as unearned income at rates up to 70 percent. Under the Revenue Act of 1978, the nontaxed portion of long-term capital gains no longer offsets the personal service income eligible for maximum tax.

However, the Revenue Act of 1978 enacted the "alternative minimum tax" to replace the exemption of capital gains and adjusted itemized deduction tax preferences from the regular 15 percent minimum tax. This tax, which is imposed only if it exceeds the noncorporate taxpayer's regular tax (including the regular minimum tax), is computed by adding to regular taxable income the amount of the capital gains and adjusted itemized deduction preferences. This amount is subject to various rates, the maximum being 25 percent in excess of $80,000.

These three concepts are complex, but in general, the larger your taxable income and the more you invest in tax shelters, the more likely you will be affected.

THE MAJOR TAX SHELTERS

Many tax-shelter recommendations are concentrated in the areas of real estate, oil and gas, equipment leasing, and agriculture. This group offers: (1) a wide range of benefits satisfying virtually any tax-shelter investment goal; (2) a broad spectrum of risk/reward relationships; (3) a variety of offerings from which to select; and, (4) well established principles of taxation.

REAL ESTATE

Real estate is undoubtedly the most popular tax shelter. Because of its similarity to home ownership, it is easily understood.

The obvious distinction between a home and investment real estate is that tenants occupy investment buildings and make periodic lease or rental payments to cover costs of operations, maintenance, and debt retirement as well as profit. The not-so-obvious difference relates to taxation. Owners of investment real estate are allowed deductions for taxes, operating and maintenance expenses, interest on mortgage money, and depreciation on buildings (but not land). Homeowners are allowed deductions for taxes and interest paid on mortgages, thus making home ownership probably the most widely used tax shelter. However, homeowners are denied the other deductions.

TYPES OF PROGRAMS

Real estate is an umbrella term describing a variety of investments. Real estate limited partnerships involve raw land, office buildings, apartments, industrial parks, shopping centers, and mobile home parks, to name a few.

Generally real estate partnerships cluster in

four areas: newly-constructed real estate, existing income-producing real estate, net leased real estate, and government-assisted housing.

Some real estate partnerships are *specified property programs;* others are *blind pool programs* involving properties selected after partnership operations begin.

Newly Constructed Real Estate. These programs construct new buildings or purchase new "first user" buildings. Typically, newly constructed real estate programs involve maximum *leverage* and employ *accelerated depreciation.* Because of more favorable *double-declining-balance* depreciation (at 200 percent of the straight-line depreciation rate), these programs usually concentrate on new apartment construction. Sometimes commercial properties (office buildings and shopping centers), which are limited to 150 percent declining-balance depreciation, are included for diversification.

High *leverage* from *nonrecourse loans* and accelerated depreciation mean tax losses of up to 50 percent of the amount invested the first year and in excess of 100 percent over the first five-ten years of the partnership.

New buildings (which might not rent easily) financed with high leverage imply high risk. Because of leverage, tax losses may continue for several years. Unusually attractive capital gains possibilities may be reduced by *recapture* of a portion of accelerated depreciation, particularly in the early years.

Interest and Taxes During Construction. The Tax Reform Act of 1976 enacted special rules regarding the deductibility of interest and taxes related to real property during construction periods. When fully operative, these rules will require that such interest and taxes be capitalized and amortized over a ten-year period, thereby reducing the deductions otherwise available from real estate ventures. There are transitional rules which apply this treatment to nonresidential real estate, residential real estate, and government-subsidized housing where the construction period begins after 1975, 1977, and 1981, respectively.

Existing Income-Producing Real Estate. These partnerships usually invest in existing commercial properties and apartments. Because of slower depreciation methods (125 percent declining-balance on apartments, straight-line on commercial) and lower leverage, most existing property programs offer lower tax losses in early years (10 percent to 20 percent the first year) and significant opportunities for tax-sheltered cash flow, hence the name *income-producing real estate.* Lower leverage on existing (hence more predictable) rental properties implies lesser risk. Established properties offer capital gains opportunities with fewer recapture problems because of lower accelerated depreciation.

Net-Leased Real Estate. These partnerships purchase office buildings, hotels, shopping centers, factory buildings, warehouses, and miniwarehouses, and so on, on a leveraged basis. Properties are leased to major corporations on a long term, "triple-net-lease" basis: the corporate tenant is responsible for a specified lease payment plus all taxes, insurance, maintenance, and other expenses during the life of the lease.

Tax losses the first year are minimal (remember, tenants pay operating costs; the partnership's only deductions are interest and straight-line depreciation). The real benefit in a net-lease program is the opportunity for a relatively low-risk investment yielding cash flow partially tax sheltered by depreciation (usually about 50 percent of the cash received over the life of the partnership is tax sheltered).

Government-Assisted Housing. These investments depend upon funding from various state and federal housing-finance programs; therefore, they are not always available. All involve construction or rehabilitation of properties for low-income, middle-income or elderly tenants. Accelerated depreciation plus extreme leverage (made possible by government loan guarantees and/or rent subsidies) create excellent tax loss possibilities, up to 200 percent first year. Leverage and provisions of some federal laws may limit tax-sheltered cash flow; however, there will be a continuing stream of tax losses for several years. Recapture provisions severely reduce possibilities for early capital gains.

REAL ESTATE PARTNERSHIP OPERATIONS

All real estate limited partnerships function similarly—only the properties purchased and the tax treatment vary. Typically the general partner is a real estate developer, property management company, or real estate broker. The general partner subtracts a *management fee* and *organization and offering expenses.* Then he applies partnership *proceeds* to a group of properties which meet stated partnership objectives. First-year tax losses are derived from partnership and property operating expenses, depreciation, interest deductions, and so on.

After partnership properties are in operation, rental income is designated for property management, maintenance, and repayment of loans. (In partnerships involving net leases, the tenants pay all expenses except loan repayment.) Any excess is divided among the general and limited partners according to an established formula. Some general partners also receive compensation from brokerage commissions or property management fees.

OIL AND GAS

Oil and gas accumulate in pore spaces of underground rock formations. A given *reser-*

voir, as these accumulations are called, may be small or may contain millions of barrels of oil or billions of cubic feet of natural gas.

Because of the technology required, and because of "dry holes," the search for oil and gas is expensive. Industry statistics indicate that only about 1 exploratory well in 10 finds a new field and only 1 out of 40 or 50 is a significant commercial success. Because of high costs and risks, oil and gas companies are often forced to look outside for cash to finance drilling. Individual investors supply much of this drilling capital through tax-shelter limited partnerships.

Oil and gas investment represents perhaps the best all-around tax shelter. It offers opportunities for high first-year tax losses, partially tax-sheltered cash flow, and capital gains. Oil and gas is also the riskiest tax shelter because of "dry holes." However, diversifying partnership proceeds among numerous wells spreads the risk.

TYPES OF PROGRAMS

Limited partnerships that drill for oil and gas may be *blind pool programs* or *specified property programs.* Blind pools are most popular. Drilling programs are further classified according to risk. A few drill only exploratory or "wildcat wells." The majority seek to diversify risk by combining wildcats with 10 percent to 75 percent *development wells*—the wells which must be drilled over the extent of the reservoir before it can produce its maximum yield. Development drilling is considerably less risky. Roughly eight out of ten are completed as producers according to industry statistics; however, remember that a successful well may not be a profitable well. Development well sites result from someone's wildcat discovery. As you might suspect, they are expensive, limiting potential profitability of a balanced drilling partnership while lessening the risk.

General and administrative expenses, offering expenses, and *intangible drilling costs* combine to offer first-year tax losses of 70 percent to 90 percent of the amount invested. In one type of drilling program, the general partner pays all nondeductible costs, making 100 percent of your investment deductible.

Once successful wells are on stream, depletion partially shelters oil and gas gross income. You can deduct up to 22 percent of your share of this gross oil and gas income limited to the lesser of 65 percent of the partner's taxable income before the depletion allowance or 50 percent of the taxable income from each property in the partnership before the depletion allowance . . . as long as the wells produce. This percentage will decrease from 22 percent to 15 percent between 1980 and 1984.

Capital gains opportunities, reduced by *recapture* of a portion of *intangible drilling costs,* arise if the general partner exchanges partnership interests for common stock and you sell your stock profitably, or he offers a *cash liquidating value* which you accept.

DRILLING PROGRAM OPERATIONS

Drilling-partnership general partners are normally oil and gas producers seeking investors' capital to finance operations. After deducting the *front-end load,* the general partner typically drills as many wells as possible with available *proceeds.* While selecting wells which meet partnership objectives, he usually seeks diversification of risk, depth, and geological area. During drilling, progress reports are distributed frequently. After drilling is complete, any income is apportioned between the general partner and the investors (quarterly in most cases), according to an established formula.

EQUIPMENT LEASING

For industrial corporations, equipment leasing spreads large cash outlays over several years. In some instances, a lease may be classified as "off-the-balance-sheet" financing that does not hurt the corporation's borrowing capacity.

Virtually any industrial equipment can be leased: airplanes, computers, trucks, drilling rigs, entire factories, and railroad cars are examples.

Equipment-leasing partnerships all require: (1) investors to provide equity capital, (2) sponsors to supervise partnership operations, (3) lenders (banks or insurance companies) to provide loans, (4) users, and (5) leasable equipment.

Equipment leasing offers a lesser-risk approach to tax shelter. However, do not conclude that equipment leasing is riskless. The risk of user failure is always present; even companies with top credit ratings sometimes cannot meet obligations. Another risk is obsolescence. Tax laws require that a lease must have a shorter term than the equipment's useful life if certain tax benefits are to be retained. Thus, investors bear the risk of re-leasing or selling—even if technology has rendered the equipment obsolete. Also, upon successful sale, *recapture* of certain deductions may offset gains significantly.

TYPES OF PROGRAMS

The common type of equipment-leasing partnership offers deferral opportunities. Early-year tax losses result from *leverage* and *accelerated depreciation* (double-declining balance on new equipment or 150 percent declining balance on used equipment). Also, some equipment, a computer for example, has a very short useful life. *Useful life* is a tax concept related to depreciation. It may not coincide with the actual time equipment is used. For example, owners of railroad cars may elect to depreciate their equipment over a 12-year useful life even though the equipment may actually operate for several decades.

Accelerated depreciation and short useful life mean very high deductions in early years converting to taxable income when depreciation is exhausted—thereby deferring taxable income. Continuous reinvestment over several years creates an on-going deferral of taxable income.

LEASING-PARTNERSHIP OPERATIONS

The general partner typically deducts a management fee and offering expenses. Equipment is purchased using partnership proceeds and loans. The general partner typically receives a small portion of the lease payments plus a share of any equipment-sale proceeds; he may earn additional compensation by providing equipment maintenance for users. In equipment-leasing partnerships, the general partner is usually a company that specializes in equipment leasing.

AGRICULTURE

Agricultural tax shelters include cattle feeding, cattle and other livestock breeding, crops, and timber. With the exception of cattle feeding and breeding, none are widely available as *public programs*.

CATTLE FEEDING

Young *feeder cattle* are purchased with partnership *proceeds*. These cattle become collateral for recourse loans to purchase more cattle and grain for the feeding period. Interest and feed costs push total first-year deductions to 50 percent to 100 percent. When *finished cattle* are sold after four to six months, bank loans are repaid and the general partner's share is deducted. Any balance is ordinary income to the limited partners.

Because the holding period for cattle is 24 months, there are no capital gains. Disease and price fluctuations are major risks. Risks, however, can be partially offset, but not eliminated, with hedging and insurance.

BREEDING PROGRAMS

In addition to cattle, *breeding* refers to fur-bearing animals, other farm animals, and fish or shellfish. Although the "livestock" varies, program operations are similar. An initial "herd" is purchased. First-year tax losses can equal up to 50 percent to 90 percent; feed costs and depreciation are the principal deductions. Depreciation and investment-tax credit is available on the initial herd but not on offspring.

Sale of offspring generates income. Except for fish and shellfish programs, most females and superior males are retained to increase herd size and quality. Capital gains are available on livestock held more than 12 months (24 months for horses and cattle). Disease and price fluctuations are major risks. *Recapture* may reduce profitability.

CROPS

The list of potential crop partnerships covers virtually anything grown in an orchard, field, grove, or vineyard; fruits, nuts, grains, vegetables, and so on. Wine grapes, nuts, and citrus are the most popular program types.

Labor costs, interest, and operating expenses are deductible. By using leverage, first-year tax losses may approach 50 percent to 90 percent. Crop sales generate ordinary income. Depreciation may offer partially tax-sheltered cash flow. Risks depend on weather, price fluctuations, and whether new or mature properties are involved. Capital gains, subject to recapture restrictions, are primary investment objectives when the land on which the crops are grown is finally sold.

SUMMARY

Most investors satisfy their tax-shelter investment objectives through public or private programs organized as limited partnerships in newly-constructed real estate, existing income-producing real estate, net-leased real estate, government-assisted housing, oil and gas drilling, equipment leasing, or agriculture.

Each major tax shelter offers a specific package of possible tax and investment benefits. In addition, each shelter investment involves risk. Although some are riskier than others, there is always the danger that your rate of return from a given investment will be less than you anticipated or, in some instances, that you may suffer total loss. Always keep risk in mind as you consult your tax advisor about possible benefits.

SPECIALIZED TAX SHELTERS

In addition to the real estate, oil and gas, equipment leasing, and agriculture tax shelters, there are a number of personal and corporate investment vehicles which may apply to your financial situation; Keogh Plans, annuities, pension and profit sharing plans, individual retirement accounts, and municipal bonds. None of these tax shelters utilizes the limited partnership format.

KEOGH PLANS

If you are self-employed, depending on your income level, a defined-contribution Keogh

Plan can help you set aside between $750 and $7,500 each year, tax-free, for your retirement. A defined-benefit Keogh Plan, when permissible in certain cases, may result in higher allowable contributions. Contributions to a Keogh Plan may be invested in a variety of investments: stocks, bonds, mutual funds, and so on; all growth and income accumulate tax free. After retirement, you pay tax on the money as you withdraw it from the plan.

ANNUITIES

An annuity is simply a contractual agreement between you and an insurance company that provides you with a very safe tax-advantaged accumulation vehicle. You pay no federal or state income tax on the earnings while they accumulate. You never have to worry about market fluctuations since both your principal and interest are 100 percent guaranteed by a major insurance company. Interest is credited daily, compounded automatically at competitive secure-dollar investment rates. You can withdraw money at any time and under specified conditions, without a penalty.

At retirement, you can choose an option that will provide you with income for a specified period of years . . . for life . . . beneficiary payments upon death . . . or income for your life and your spouse's life. The monthly payments you receive are partially tax sheltered because they represent, to a degree, return of your initial deposit. In addition, the interest portion of each monthly payment is taxable at your lower, post-retirement tax rate.

PENSION AND PROFIT-SHARING PLANS

Since enactment of the Employee Retirement Income Security Act of 1974 (ERISA), professionals (doctors, lawyers, accountants, architects, etc.) who incorporate can set up profit-sharing plans: generally up to 15 percent of the annual compensation paid each participant (limited to a maximum of $32,700 in 1979 and adjusted in later years by a cost-of-living adjustment factor) may be paid out free of corporate income tax. Pension-plan contributions, also free of corporate income tax, are limited based on an actuarial funding-formula compensation. Incorporated professionals may also establish pension plan contributions which are tax deductible. As in Keogh Plans, all growth and income accumulate tax free.

INDIVIDUAL RETIREMENT ACCOUNTS

ERISA also established a retirement plan for employed individuals. Any employee who is not participating in a qualified pension plan can establish his own *Individual Retirement Account*. Up to $1,500 or 15 percent of annual compensation (whichever is smaller) may be invested in

an IRA each year. A married employee with a nonworking spouse can establish a joint IRA; contributions are limited to the lesser of $1,750 or 15 percent of compensation. If both spouses work, each can establish an IRA; the $1,500/ 15 percent limitation applies to each. All interest and appreciation in an IRA accumulate tax free. No withdrawals are permitted before age 59½; withdrawals must begin by age 70½. Withdrawals are taxed as ordinary income as received (at the lower post-retirement tax rate).

MUNICIPAL BONDS

Debt securities of state, cities, and special purpose "authorities" (turnpikes, sewer and water districts, etc.) pay interest that is free of federal and some state taxes. There are no tax losses, but 100 percent of the income is tax free, fully tax-sheltered cash flow. Municipal bonds may be purchased directly or by investing in one of several municipal-bond trusts or municipal-bond mutual funds which pool the funds of several investors and purchase diversified portfolios of bonds.

INVESTING IN TAX SHELTERS

SELECTING THE PROGRAM

Analyzing any program requires in-depth knowledge of partnership law, taxation, the industry, and the general partner's management and operations.

Some tenets that should guide you include:

Diversification. Pooling capital of several investors and spreading risk among several projects is a key benefit of limited partnerships.

Program Size. Too small a program may offer only limited diversification, or it may be excessively burdened by *front-end load.* Too large a program may force the sponsor into unwise decisions if he is under pressure to complete partnership projects before year-end.

Management. Decisions are based on integrity, past performance, experience in the operating area, financial stability, limited partnership experience, experience with comparable-size programs, and quality of investor communications.

Sharing Arrangement. The general partner's compensation should encourage superior performance. Compensation should be derived from operating profits, not front-end fees.

Tax Features. Well-accepted taxation principles avoid unnecessary "tax-risk." Programs promising excessive deductions or unreasonable expectation of investment returns are avoided.

Liquidity. Any liquidity is better than none; however, all tax shelters are, at best, illiquid. Emphasis is placed on the general partner's financial ability to provide liquidity at the appropriate time.

INVESTMENT APPLICATIONS

An integral part of selecting the "right" industry and "right" program is what you hope to accomplish by making the investment. Applications of tax-sheltered investments include: (1) saving taxes by sheltering high-level, recurring income, (2) reducing tax effects of major capital gains, (3) building retirement income, (4) increasing charitable contributions, (5) employing sophisticated estate-planning tactics, and (6) enhancing corporate tax planning.

RECURRING INCOME

The most familiar use of tax shelters is related to softening the burden of taxes on high-level, recurring income. If you are a high-salaried corporate executive, doctor, or lawyer, for example, you pretty well know that, short of some unpredictable economic or personal calamity, you will earn at least X dollars each year for the next Y years. You can use this knowledge and apply tax shelters to help offset your annual tax liability.

Let us assume that each year for the next ten years, you will file a joint return with $75,000 taxable income (after exemptions and itemized deductions). Also, assume you will make a 100 percent deductible, $10,000 annual tax-shelter investment and you are in the 50 percent federal tax bracket.

Over a ten-year period, you will invest $100,000, but because of tax savings you will be out of pocket only $50,000. You will have accomplished four things: (1) reduced your annual tax bill by $5,000, (2) invested $100,000 at an out-of-pocket cost of only $50,000, (3) purchased assets which can yield an investment return with dollars that normally go to pay taxes, and (4) spread your risk.

CAPITAL GAINS

Let us suppose that in one year you have, in addition to your $60,000 recurring taxable income, a $200,000 capital gain. A good rule of thumb is to consider investing 40 percent

of a large capital gain in a tax shelter, in this case $80,000.

This technique: (1) puts $80,000 to work for a net cost of 56 cents on the dollar, (2) reduces your tax bill 52 percent, and (3) still leaves you at least $120,000 cash remaining for your capital gain—a very powerful tax and investment planning tool.

Note: The alternative minimum tax is used in the computation of the With Tax Shelter example.

RETIREMENT PLANNING

If you are a few years from retirement, tax shelters—particularly those with a deferral feature—can help you take advantage of needed tax savings up to your retirement date. After retirement your tax shelter may yield ordinary income which will be taxed at your lowest post-retirement tax rate.

CHARITY CONTRIBUTIONS

You invest in a tax-shelter limited partnership and hold it until the cash liquidating value or other fair market value is determined. Tax laws permit a deduction up to the fair market value of an asset contributed to a qualified charitable organization. Using this technique, you have the opportunity—assuming a successful tax-shelter investment—to take two deductions on the same dollars: first when you invest, then when you contribute. Your charity receives an income-producing asset free of any administrative responsibilities. Note, however, that charity giving is a very sensitive tax area requiring advance consultation with both your tax advisor and your charity.

ESTATE PLANNING

The same invest-hold-contribute technique used for charity giving can be used to transfer tax-shelter assets out of your estate to your children. This technique: (1) decreases your taxable estate and ultimately, reduces inheritance

JOINT RETURN—50 PERCENT TAX BRACKET

	With Tax Shelter	Without Tax Shelter
Taxable Income*	$260,000	$260,000
Sixty percent capital gains deduction	(120,000)	(120,000)
Net taxable income	$140,000	$140,000
One hundred percent deductible tax shelter†	(80,000)	—
Revised taxable income	$ 60,000	$140,000
Tax due (including tax preference)	$ 32,000	$ 67,000
Tax savings	$ 35,100	
Net investment cost	$ 44,900	

* Personal service net income $60,000; capital gains $200,000.
† Assumes $40,000 of tax preference items.

taxes; also, it (2) reduces overall family tax liability by shifting your high-bracket taxable income into your children's lower tax bracket. Like charity contributions, estate planning requires careful study by your tax advisor.

CORPORATE TAX PLANNING

Corporations—particularly closely-held entities—can employ tax shelters a number of creative ways, including: (1) sheltering recurring income; (2) utilizing tax benefits, then contributing the investment to employee-pension and profit-sharing plans; (3) avoiding the penalty tax on accumulated earnings; and (4) providing executive compensation through tax-shelter investment-loan plans.

INVESTMENT RETURNS

Because of risk, it is impossible to say what rate of return you may receive from a given tax-shelter program; losses or less-than-anticipated returns are always possible. However, with tax savings (which reduce your initial out-of-pocket investment costs), proper diversification, a proven management team, and, when feasible, a three- to five-year program of recurring investments, risks are significantly reduced.

As soon as possible, your general partner will begin distributing your share of any partnership profits—usually within six months to two years of the date you invest (longer when a highly leveraged partnership repays bank debt). After distributions begin, you will probably continue receiving them on a fairly regular basis; quarterly is the most common distribution pattern.

GLOSSARY

Note: Terms in *italics* are defined elsewhere in the glossary.

Accelerated depreciation Any method of *depreciation* which permits *deduction* of a greater percentage of the cost of an asset in early years of the asset's useful life with smaller deductions in later years. Two methods are widely used: (1) the "sum-of-the-years-digits" method and (2) the more popular "declining-balance" method. Under the declining balance, annual deductions are calculated as a percentage of the *straight-line depreciation* rate, that is, 200 percent declining balance (also called "double-declining balance") available for new residential construction; 150 percent declining balance, available for new commercial construction; 125 percent declining balance for existing improved real estate. Note that accelerated depreciation is usually a *tax preference item*.

Assessment Additional amounts of money which a *limited partner* in a *tax-sheltered part-*

nership may be required to furnish beyond his original *subscription*. A given program, depending on the terms, may be either "assessable" or "nonassessable." An assessable program may have limited or unlimited assessments. Assessments may be optional or mandatory.

"At-risk" limitations This limitation is designed to prevent noncorporate taxpayers from deducting losses in excess of their economic investment in the activity involved. These rules now apply to all activities except real estate and certain companies leasing equipment. In addition, where your amount of investment deemed to be "at risk" is reduced below zero (by distributions or change of status of liabilities from recourse to nonrecourse), income recognition may be required of deductions previously taken.

Blind pool program A *tax-sheltered partnership* which, at the time sale of *subscriptions* begins, does not have the *proceeds* of the offering allocated to specific projects or properties. (Contrast with *Specified property program*.)

Capital asset Any asset (property, equipment, livestock, etc.) which is: (1) used in a trade or business (except inventories or items held for sale to customers), (2) held for production of income, or (3) given the effect of a capital asset by a tax law provision. With certain exceptions, capital assets—including interests in *tax-shelter partnerships*—are subject to *capital-gains* treatment on any profit (or loss) arising from sale or exchange.

Capital gains Usually gain (or loss) from sale or exchange of any property is included in income and taxed at ordinary income tax rates. However, if the gain is from the sale or exchange of a *capital asset* owned for more than 12 months, the tax is calculated at the lower long-term capital-gains rate, generally no more than 28 percent. Almost all types of *tax-sheltered investments* except cattle feeding and equipment leasing offer some capital-gains opportunities. Certain types of real estate, and oil and gas offer the most potential. It has been said that capital gains offer the major source of tax relief. Note however that capital-gains benefits may be reduced by *recapture*. Note also that 60 percent of long-term capital gains may be taxed under the alternative minimum tax.

Cash liquidating value The amount, generally based on an evaluation of a qualified independent appraiser, which will be paid by the *general partner* for an interest in a *tax-sheltered partnership* upon exercise by a *limited partner* of his right to receive such value. Programs that offer cash liquidation can be described as offering "liquidity," as opposed to illiquid programs which do not have cash liquidating features.

Conversion Obtaining current tax *deductions* against ordinary income while turning future revenues into income taxable at more favorable *capital-gains* rates or lower rates derived from favorable tax features such as *depletion* or *depreciation.*

Deductions In this context, the interest, taxes, *depreciation, depletion,* and other expenses incurred in the trade or business of a *tax-sheltered partnership* which are passed on to the *limited partners* thereby reducing their taxable income and, ultimately, their tax liability. The "ordinary and necessary" expenses of any business are allowable as deductions; (1) *tax-sheltered intangible drilling costs* associated with oil and gas, (2) depreciation and interest costs associated with real estate, equipment leasing, and certain agricultural tax shelters, particularly when *leverage* is employed, and (3) the feed and maintenance costs associated with cattle feeding. Ideally, a *tax-sheltered partnership* will generate deductions in excess of income for the first year or first few years, thereby permitting program *limited partners* to recover part or all of their investments out of *tax losses.*

Deferral In this context, a form of tax shelter that results from an investment timed so that *deductions* take place during the investor's high-income years and taxable income is realized after retirement, in some other period of reduced income, or at a time when the tax will be more convenient to pay. Equipment leasing and certain types of real estate offer the best deferral opportunities.

Depletion A form of *deduction* that applies to "wasting-asset" interest. The purpose is to encourage exploration for new deposits by permitting recovery of exploration and development costs out of tax savings. The annual depletion deduction for any mineral property is the greater of "cost depletion" (based on the ratio of annual production to remaining reserves) and "percentage depletion" (a fixed annual percent). The major advantage of percentage depletion is that benefits are available each year a property produces income and do not cease when the cost of the property has been recovered. Oil and gas, timber, and minerals all offer some depletion. Percentage depletion on oil and gas is 22 percent of gross income from each property, limited to the lesser of 65 percent of the individual's taxable income or 50 percent of the taxable income from the property. However, beginning in 1981, this percentage decreases down to 15 percent ratably from 1981–84. Percentage depletion on other minerals ranges from 22 percent for sulfur down to 5 percent for clay and shale. Note that percentage depletion is a *tax preference item.*

Depreciation A form of *deduction* to permit recovery of the cost (less any salvage value) of an asset in the form of tax savings. This cost recovery is spread over the asset's "useful life" as an annual deduction from taxable income. Depreciation is most attractive in real estate,

equipment leasing, and some types of cattle breeding, especially if *leverage* is employed. Tax laws permit choosing a constant annual depreciation amount over useful life (called straight-line depreciation) or, in some cases, one of several *accelerated-depreciation* methods.

Double-declining balance See: *Accelerated depreciation.*

Front-end load A slang term for the total of *organizational and offering expenses* plus *management fees:* that is, the total deductions from the *offering amount* to arrive at the *proceeds* of a *tax-sheltered partnership.* (See also: *Management fees.*)

General partner In this context, the manager or sponsor of a *tax-sheltered investment* which has been organized as a *limited partnership.* (See *Limited partnership* for details.)

Intangible drilling costs A tax *deduction* for certain expenditures incurred in drilling and completing oil and gas wells. "Intangibles" are the items which have no salvage value (commonly nonmaterial costs such as labor, chemicals, drill-site preparation, etc.). Intangibles frequently account for 50 percent to 80 percent of the cost of drilling and completing a given well. Note that intangible drilling costs on producing wells in excess of oil and gas net income is a *tax preference item.*

Joint venture A form of business organization. In this context, a *tax-sheltered investment* in which the manager and the investors share jointly in the ownership, management authority, and liability. (Contrast with *Limited partnership.*)

Leverage In this context, a method of increasing a tax shelter through borrowing (see *nonrecourse loans* and *recourse loans*) as a part of a *tax-sheltered investment.* The investor (in certain circumstances) is permitted *deductions* for interest, *management fees, depreciation,* and so on, on the amount he invests plus his pro-rata share of the amount the partnership borrows on a nonrecourse basis or any amounts for which he is personally liable on a recourse basis. Any properly-structured loans, therefore, serve to increase total deductions from income for tax purposes. Real estate offers excellent leverage possibilities, as do cattle breeding and equipment leasing.

Limited partner In this context, the purchaser of a *subscription* in a *tax-sheltered investment* which has been organized as a *limited partnership;* that is, an investor.

Limited partnership A form of business organization in which some partners exchange their right to participate in management for a limitation on their liability for partnership losses. Commonly, *limited partners* have liability only to the extent of their investment in the business plus their share of any undistributed profits. To establish limited liability, there must be at least one *general partner* who is fully liable for all claims against the business. Limited partnerships are a popular organizational form for *tax-sheltered investments* because of the ease with which tax benefits flow through the partnership to the individual partners. (Contrast with *Joint venture.*)

Liquidity See: *Cash liquidating value.*

Management fee An amount paid to the *general partner* of a *tax-sheltered partnership* to cover *organization and offering expenses* and/ or to repay costs of operating and administrating the partnership, commonly expressed as a percentage of the total *offering amount.* Prior to the Tax Reform Act of 1976, the management fee was claimed as a *deduction* by many limited partnerships. Under present law, only the general partner's reimbursements to cover costs of operating and administrating the partnership are considered fully deductible. (See also: *Front-end load.*)

Maximum tax Individuals are taxed at a maximum rate of 50 percent on that portion of their taxable income attributable to personal-service income. However, the amount of income eligible for the maximum rate is offset by the amount of the year's *tax preference items.* The amount offset is taxable as unearned income at rates of up to 70 percent.

Minimum subscription The smallest dollar amount which an investor must initially commit in order to become a *limited partner* in a *tax-sheltered partnership,* usually one or more *units.* In a *public program* the minimum subscription is generally almost always $5,000. (See also: *Subscription.*)

Minimum tax Fifteen percent of total tax preference items which exceed the greater of $10,000 or one half the taxpayer's regular federal income tax liability. (See also: *Tax preference items.*)

Alternative minimum tax A tax on regular taxable income plus the long-term capital-gain preference (60 percent untaxed portion) plus adjusted itemized deductions in excess of 60 percent of adjusted gross income. The resulting "alternative minimum taxable income," after a specific exemption of $20,000, is subject to the following rates of tax: 10 percent on the first $40,000; 20 percent on the next $40,000 and 25 percent of any excess. This tax replaces the regular tax (including the 15 percent minimum tax) if it exceeds that tax.

Noncash charges *Deductions* for *depreciation and depletion* which are not actually paid to anyone, yet are subtracted from taxable income before calculating tax due. *Tax-sheltered partnerships* such as real estate and equipment leasing which employ *leverage* may be able to pyramid noncash charges to the point that limited partners receive *tax-sheltered cash flow* in the early years against which there is limited or no tax liability.

Nonrecourse loan In this context, any borrowing by a *tax-sheltered partnership,* structured in such a way that lenders can look only to specific assets pledged for repayment and not to the individual assets of the various partners. However, in the event of a foreclosure, if partnership cash and assets are not sufficient to repay the loan balance, the limited partners may be left with a substantial tax bill because of "forgiveness of debt." Real estate is the only tax-shelter area where nonrecourse financing is permitted. (Contrast with *recourse loan;* see also: *Leverage.*)

Offering amount The total dollar amount sought by a *general partner* from prospective *limited partners in a particular tax-sheltered partnership.*

Organization and offering expenses Those expenses incurred in connection with preparing a *tax-sheltered partnership* for registration with federal and/or state securities agencies and subsequently selling subscriptions to *limited partners.* Organizational and offering expenses typically include legal fees, printing costs, registration fees, sales commissions, and selling costs. (See also: *Management fee; Front-end load.*)

Private program A *tax-sheltered partnership* which is offered and sold pursuant to the private-offering exemption available under the Securities Act of 1933 and/or some registration exemption allowed under the securities laws of one or more states; that is, a program which is not registered with the Securities and Exchange Commission. (Contrast with *Public program.*)

Proceeds The dollar amount remaining for the general partner to conduct partnership operations after deduction of *organization and operating expenses* or other items of *front-end load* from the total amount committed.

Public program

A *tax-sheltered partnership* which is registered with the Securities and Exchange Commission (SEC) and distributed in a public offering by broker dealers and/or employees of the *general partner.* The principal differences between a public program and a *private program* relate to: (1) the number of *investors,* which may be several hundred in a public program, but which is limited, with certain exceptions, to 35 in a private program; (2) *minimum subscription: $5,000 in a public program, $50,000 or more in a private program; and (3) the fact that "private" investors are subject to stricter suitability standards.*

Recapture Upon profitable sale of certain assets, *capital gains* may be severely restricted when previously claimed *deductions* for *depreciation, farming losses, intangible drilling* *costs,* or *investment credit* are taken back into ordinary income (i.e., "recaptured"). Since ordinary income tax rates can run as high as 70 percent—versus 28 percent for capital gains— recapture can severely reduce or eliminate capital-gains benefits. The amount of recapture depends on the type of asset, holding period, type of depreciation (straight-line or accelerated), as well as dollar amount of gain versus the amount of "recaptured" deductions.

Recourse loan In this context, any borrowing by a *tax-shelter* investor for which he is personally liable. (Contrast with *Nonrecourse loan.*)

Specified property program A *tax-sheltered partnership* which, at the time sale of *subscriptions* begins, has the proceeds of the offering allocated to definite projects or properties which are described in detail in the prospectus or offering circular. (Contrast with *Blind pool program.*)

Straight-line depreciation See: *Depreciation.*

Subchapter S corporation A form of corporation with a limited number of qualified stockholders who elect to utilize a specific tax law provision which permits them to be taxed so the corporation pays no taxes and each stockholder reports his share of the corporate income (or loss) on his own tax return. (Also called a "tax option corporation.")

Subscription The total dollar amount for which a *limited partner* in a *tax-sheltered partnership* initially commits. Legally it represents the amount he is obligated to pay, exclusive of any *assessment* amount which he has the option to reject. (See also: *Unit.*)

Tax loss A situation that occurs when the *deductions* generated by a *tax-sheltered partnership* exceed program revenues. Thus, the *limited partner's* taxable income is lower, resulting in a tax saving. Ideally, a *tax-sheltered partnership* will generate enough tax losses the first year or first few years to permit the limited partners to recover their investment from "tax savings." However, *recapture* may ultimately limit these benefits.

Tax preference items Items of tax preference subject to the 15 percent *minimum tax* include: *accelerated depreciation* in excess of *straight-line depreciation* on real property and leased personal property, appreciation on certain stock options, excess intangible drilling costs on productive wells, and excess percentage depletion.

Tax savings See: *Tax losses.*

Tax-sheltered cash flow The situation that arises when *noncash charges* and other *deductions* exceed gross income from a tax-shelter partnership so that the program has cash to distribute to *limited partners* even though the cash they may receive involves no current tax liability or is taxed at a lower rate. Real estate and equipment-leasing programs employing *accelerated depreciation* and *leverage* are the best sources of tax-sheltered cash flow.

Tax-sheltered investment An investment that has an expectation of economic profit, made even more attractive because of the timing of the profit or the way it is taxed, generally having some or all of the following characteristics:

1. *Deferral* of taxes,
2. *Conversion of deductions* to possible future *capital gains,*
3. *Leverage.*

The flow-through of tax benefits is a material factor whether the entity is organized as a *limited partnership, joint venture,* or *Subchapter S corporation* and whether it is offered to investors as a *private program* or a *public program.* Common forms of tax-sheltered investments include: real estate, oil and gas, equipment leasing, and agriculture.

Tax-sheltered partnership A *tax-sheltered investment* organized as a *limited partnership.* Commonly, a tax-sheltered program is created to mutually benefit a *general partner* and a group of *limited partners.* It may be organized as a *public program* or a *private program.*

Unit The smallest dollar amount into which *subscriptions* in a *tax-shelter partnership* may be divided, usually $1,000 or $5,000. For example, a $1 million *public program* might consist of 200 units of $5,000 each. Alternately, it might consist of 1,000 units of $1,000 each. Each type would normally have a *minimum subscription* of $5,000.

This account has been prepared for informational purposes only and is not an offer to sell or the solicitation of an offer to buy any tax-sheltered investment or any other security.

The material contained in this description of tax-sheltered investments is based upon the provisions of the Internal Revenue Code of 1954, as presently amended, the existing applicable regulations, and current administrative rulings and practice. However, it is emphasized that no assurance can be given that legislative or administrative changes will not be forthcoming which would modify this description. Any such changes may or may not be retroactive with respect to transactions entered into prior to the effective date of such changes.

Investment in tax shelters may give rise to liability for state income, property, or inheritance taxes which are not discussed herein and may create the necessity for ancillary probate proceedings. Due to the complex tax and other legal considerations surrounding an investment in a tax shelter, each prospective investor is urged to consult with his own counsel before obligating himself to purchase an interest in a tax shelter.

FUNDS THAT SELL WRAPAROUND ANNUITIES

Wraparound annuities are annuities which invest in money market mutual funds. The original intent was to provide an annuity which confers tax deferment of the accumulated interest returns from the money market funds until the interest is withdrawn. On withdrawal, presumably at retirement, the accumulated interest would be taxed at a lower rate since the taxpayer at retirement would generally have a lower taxable income. *However, in late September the IRS ruled against such plans,* requiring that investors pay income taxes yearly on earnings from annuities. The ruling was made retroactive to include earnings accumulated since December 31, 1980. Companies offering such annuities are requesting a review of the IRS ruling.

FUNDS THAT SELL WRAPAROUND ANNUITIES

	sales charge	minimum investment Initial	minimum investment subsequent	annual administration fee	annual insurance fee	early withdrawal fees, restrictions	eligible funds*
Dreyfus Rainbow Annuity 767 Fifth Ave. New York, N.Y. 10053 800 223-0982 212 489-4900 (N.Y., collect)	none	$1,500	$500	$35	1%	none	2
Federated Flexible Plan 421 Seventh Ave. Pittsburgh, Pa. 15219 800 245-5051 412 288-1561 (Pa., collect)	none	$1,000	$25	$30	1.4%	5% of amount withdrawn when that amount exceeds 6% of purchase payment; no fees after eighth year	6
Fidelity Income Plus 82 Devonshire St. Boston, Mass. 02109 800 225-6190 617 523-1919 (Mass., collect)	none	$5,000	$500	$18	0.8%	$10 each withdrawal	6
INA/Putnam Galaxy Variable Annuity Putnam Fund Distributors, Inc. 265 Franklin St. Boston, Mass. 02110 800 225-2482 617 423-4960 (Mass., collect)	none	$3,000	—	$25	0.95%	none for amounts up to 10% per year of original purchase payment; excess subject to 6% first year, reducing by 1% each year, no charge after six years	5
Kemper AdVantage Kemper Investors Life Insurance Co. 120 S. LaSalle St. Chicago, Ill. 60603 800 621-1148 312 346-3223 (Ill., collect)	none	$2,500	$500	$25	1%	none for amounts up to 10% of account; excess over 10% subject to 6%, reducing by 1% a year; no charge after six years	7
Keystone 100 Keystone Massachusetts, Inc. 99 High St. Boston, Mass. 02110 800 343-2826 617 338-3400 (Mass., collect)	none	$5,000	$300	$30	1%	5% of purchase payment first year, reducing by 1% a year thereafter on amounts exceeding 7% of purchase payment; no fees after fifth year	9

MFS/Nationwide Spectrum Annuity Massachusetts Financial Service 200 Berkeley St. Boston, Mass. 02116 617 423-3500 (collect)	none	$1,500	$10	$30	1.3%	5% of purchase payment during first year; next seven years up to 5% of account may be withdrawn each year on a cumulative basis with no charge; no charge after eight years	9
Oppenheimer/Bankers Security Variable Annuity Two Broadway New York, N.Y. 10004 800 221-9839 212 668-5100 (N.Y., collect)	6% to 8.5% depending on purchase plan	$2,000	$50 a month or $200 a year on installment purchase plans	included in sales charge	1%	none	6
Shearson/Hartford Tax Deferred Variable Annuity c/o Shearson Loeb Rhoades, Inc. 14 Wall St. New York, N.Y. 10005 212 577-5822	none	$3,000	—	$35 first year, $25 thereafter	1%	6% of purchase payment in first year, reducing by 1% a year thereafter on amounts exceeding 10% of original investment; no fees after sixth year	4

* *Subject to some restrictions, so total may not be available to all investors.*

Source: Reprinted with permission from *Changing Times Magazine*, © 1981, Kiplinger Washington Editors, Inc., July 1981.

SUMMARY OF THE 1981
TAX LAW

A. Individual Income Tax Reductions

1. Individual income tax rate reductions

Under present law, individual income tax rates begin at 14 percent on taxable income above $3,400 on a joint return and $2,400 on a single return. The rates range up to 70 percent on taxable incomes, in excess of $215,400 on a joint return, and $108,300 on a single return.

The highest marginal rate is 70 percent on taxable income in excess of $215,400 on a joint return and $108,300 on a single return. However, the top rate on personal service income is limited to 50 percent (the maximum tax). This rate applies above $60,000 on a joint return and $41,500 on a single return.

A deduction from gross income is allowed for 60 percent of any net capital gain for the year. The remaining 40 percent of any net capital gain is taxed at the ordinary rates up to 70 percent. Thus, the top effective tax rate on capital gains is 28 percent (70 percent rate times the 40 percent included in taxable income).

The Act provides for cumulative across-the-board reductions in individual income tax rates of 23 percent by 1984 on the following schedule:

1981	1¼ percent
1982	10 percent
1983	19 percent
1984	23 percent

Withholding changes take place on October 1, 1981, July 1, 1982, and July 1, 1983. The Act makes several other withholding changes to give the Secretary the authority to issue regulations to permit workers to adjust their withholding to more closely match their tax liability.

The Act reduces the top marginal rate from 70 percent to 50 percent (and, thus, the maximum effective rate on capital gains from 28 percent to 20 percent) in 1982 and repeals the maximum tax in 1982.

A special alternative tax for 1981 provides that a maximum 20-percent rate on net capital gains applies to sales or exchanges occurring after June 9, 1981. Thus, this provision does not apply to taxable receipts after June 9, 1981, of proceeds of sales or exchanges which occurred prior to that date. However, proceeds received in taxable years after 1981 will be taxed at the rate in effect for that year.

2. Deduction for two-earner married couples

Under present law, married taxpayers generally are treated as a single taxpaying unit. If married taxpayers elect to file separate rather than joint returns, they usually pay a higher tax. The differing rate schedules for single and married taxpayers give rise to a marriage penalty when two single wage earners with relatively equal incomes marry.

The Act allows couples filing a joint return a deduction in computing adjusted gross income equal to a percentage of the lower earning spouse's qualified earned income (up to $30,000 of income). In 1982,

Source: Excerpted from the Summary of H.R. 4242 of the Economic Recovery Tax Act of 1981, prepared by the staff of the Joint Committee on Taxation, August 5, 1981.

the percentage will be 5 percent (up to a $1,500 maximum deduction) and in 1983 and subsequent years the percentage will be 10 percent (up to a $3,000 maximum deduction).

3. Indexing

Under present law, the individual income tax is based on various fixed amounts including the amounts that define the tax brackets, the zero bracket amount, and the personal exemption. These amounts are set by statute and are not adjusted for inflation.

Under the Act, the income tax brackets, zero bracket amount, and personal exemption are adjusted for inflation (as measured by the Consumer Price Index), starting in 1985. The first adjustment, for 1985, will be based on the increase in the CPI between fiscal year 1983 and fiscal year 1984.

4. Child and dependent care credit

Present law provides a tax credit equal to 20 percent of expenditures, for the care of children and other dependents, which are incurred in connection with the taxpayer's employment. The maximum amount of expenditures that may be taken into account is $2,000 (one dependent) or $4,000 (two or more dependents). Thus, the maximum credit is $400 or $800. In general, expenses incurred for services outside the household are not creditable unless incurred for the care of a dependent under the age of 15.

The Act increases the child and dependent care credit to 30 percent of employment-related expenses for taxpayers with adjusted gross income of $10,000 or less. For each $2,000 (or fraction thereof) above $10,000, the percentage of creditable expenses is reduced by one percent (but not below 20 percent). Taxpayers with adjusted gross income in excess of $28,000 will be entitled to a credit of 20 percent of employment-related expenses.

The Act also increases the amounts of employment-related expenses that may be taken into account to $2,400 (one dependent) and $4,800 (two or more dependents). Furthermore, the Act provides that qualified, employer-provided child care will not be included in an employee's gross income.

The provisions are effective for taxable years beginning after December 31, 1981.

5. Charitable contribution deduction for nonitemizers

Under present law, individual taxpayers may claim deductions for charitable contributions only if they itemize deductions.

The Act provides that all taxpayers may deduct charitable contributions, whether or not they itemize deductions. The deduction for nonitemizers will be phased in over a five-year period, with a cap on the amount of contributions that qualify for deduction in the first three years, as follows:

Year	Percentage	Cap
1982	25	$100
1983	25	100
1984	25	300
1985	50	
1986	100	
1987	Provision expires	

The contributions' cap is not doubled for married taxpayers filing jointly. Thus, in 1982, for example, the maximum deduction for a nonitemizer who files a joint return, or who is single, will be $25. The maximum deduction for a married taxpayer filing separately in 1982 will be $12.50.

6. Gain on sale of residence

a. Rollover of gain time on sale of residence

Present law provides for the nonrecognition, or rollover, of gain on the sale of a taxpayer's principal residence if a new principal residence is purchased and used by the taxpayer within a period beginning 18 months before, and ending 18 months after the sale.

The Act extends the 18-month replacement period of present law to 2 years. This change is effective for sales and exchanges of principal residences after July 20, 1981, and for such sales and exchanges with respect to which the 18-month rollover period has not expired on July 20, 1981.

b. Exclusion of gain on sale of residence

Present law allows individuals who have attained the age of 55 to elect a one-time exclusion of up to $100,000 of gain on the sale of their principal residence. Generally, the individual must have owned and used the property as a principal residence for three years or more out of the five-year period preceding the sale.

The Act increases from $100,000 to $125,000 the amount of gain excludable from gross income on the sale or exchange of a principal residence by an individual who has attained the age of 55.

The provision is effective for sales and exchanges of a principal residence after July 20, 1981.

7. Foreign earned income

Present law allows a variety of deductions and exclusions for U.S. citizens and residents living abroad, including deductions for excess cost of living, housing, education expenses, and home leave. Also, an exclusion is provided for the value of food and lodging in a camp in a hardship area.

The Act replaces the existing provisions for income earned abroad with an exclusion for the first $95,000 of such income and an exclusion for excess housing costs. The maximum foreign earned income exclusion will be $75,000 in 1982 and will be phased up to $95,000 by 1986 in $5,000 per year increments. The combination of housing and earned income may not exceed earned income of the taxpayer for the year.

The provision is elective, and once an election is made it is binding. An exclusion for camps whether or not in hardship areas is provided.

The provisions are effective with respect to taxable years beginning in 1982.

B. Capital Cost Recovery Provisions

1. General concept

Prior law was designed to allocate depreciation deductions over the period the asset is used in business so that deductions for the cost of an asset were matched with the income produced by the asset.

Under the Act, the prior law Asset Depreciation Range (ADR) system is terminated for recovery property placed in service after December 31, 1980 and replaced with the Accelerated Cost Recovery

System (ACRS). Under ACRS, the cost of an asset is recovered over a pre-determined period generally shorter than the useful life of the asset or the period the asset is used to produce income.

2. Eligible property

Assets used in a trade or business or for the production of income are depreciable if they are subject to wear and tear, decay or decline from natural causes or obsolescence. Assets that do not decline in value on a predictable basis or that do not have a determinable useful life, such as land, goodwill, and stock, are not depreciable.

Under the Act, most tangible depreciable property (real and personal) is covered under the accelerated cost recovery system (ACRS). However, ACRS does not apply to (1) property not depreciated in terms of years (except certain railroad property), and (2) property amortized (e.g., leasehold improvements and certain rehabilitation expenditures.)

3. Useful lives and methods

a. Personal property useful lives and methods

Under prior law, a principal method used to determine useful lives for personal property was the Asset Depreciation Range (ADR) system. For assets not eligible for ADR and for taxpayers who did not elect ADR, useful lives were determined according to the facts and circumstances pertaining to each asset or by agreement between the taxpayer and the IRS.

The Act provides that the cost of eligible personal property (and certain real property) is recovered over 3, 5, 10, or 15 years. The classification of property by recovery period is as follows:

3 years_____Autos, light-duty trucks, R&D equipment, racehorses over 2 years old and other horses over 12 years old and personal property with an ADR midpoint life of 4 years or less.

5 years_____Most other equipment except long-lived public utility property. Also includes single purpose agricultural structures and petroleum storage facilities, which are designated as section 1245 property under the Act.

10 years_____Public utility property with an ADR midpoint life greater than 18 but not greater than 25 years; burners and boilers using coal as a primary fuel if used in a public utility powerplant and if replacing or converting oil- or gas-fired burners or boilers; railroad tank cars; mobile homes; and real property with an ADR midpoint life of 12.5 years or less (e.g. theme park structures).

15 years_____Public utility property with an ADR midpoint life exceeding 25 years (except certain burners and boilers using coal as a primary fuel).

Under a flexibility provision (described below), taxpayers may elect to use the regular recovery period or one of two longer recovery periods as set forth below:

3-year property_____	3, 5 and 12 years
5-year property_____	5, 12 and 25 years
10-year property_____	10, 25 and 35 years
15-year property_____	15, 35 and 45 years

Under prior law, taxpayers could use the straight-line method, a declining balance method at a rate up to 200-percent of the straight-line rate, or the sum of the years-digits method with respect to new personal property. For used personal property, taxpayers could use either the straight-line method or a declining balance method at a rate up to 150-percent of the straight-line rate

Under the Act, taxpayers have the option to use the straight-line method over the regular or optional longer recovery period or a prescribed accelerated method over the regular recovery period. The prescribed accelerated method for property placed in service in the following years is based on depreciation methods as set forth below, using a half-year convention and no salvage value limitation:

Year property placed in service:	Prescribed method
1981–1984	150 percent declining balance, changing to straight-line
1985	175 percent declining balance, changing to SYD
After 1985	200 percent declining balance, changing to SYD.

b. Real property

Prior to the Act, IRS guideline lives ranged from 40 to 60 years for real property, but actual lives claimed under a facts and circumstances approach could be shorter. Non-residential property could be depreciated using a 150-percent declining balance method (if new) or the straight-line method. New residential property could be depreciated using straight-line, the 200-percent declining balance method, or the sum of the years-digits method. Used residential could use up to the 125-percent declining balance method (if 20 years useful life remaining) or straight-line. Taxpayers could use different lives for each separate component of a building, such as plumbing, wiring, etc. (component depreciation) or use a single life for the building and all components (composite depreciation).

Under the Act, real property is assigned a 15-year recovery period, but taxpayers may elect a 35- or 45-year extended recovery period. Composite depreciation is required. For real property other than low-income housing, the property can be depreciated using the 175-percent declining balance method, changing to the straight-line method to maximize acceleration. Low-income housing can be depreciated under the 200-percent declining balance method changing to straight-line. As an option, taxpayers may elect to use the straight-line method over 15, 35, or 45 years.

4. Election to expense certain depreciable business assets

Under prior law, a deduction was provided for "bonus" first-year depreciation up to 20-percent of up to $10,000 of eligible property ($20,000 for individuals filing a joint return) (sec. 179).

The Act repeals the "bonus" depreciation provision (sec. 179) and replaces it with an election to expense the cost of new or used personal property used in a trade or business. The maximum annual amount a person can expense is $5,000 for 1982 and 1983, $7,500 for 1984 and 1985, and $10,000 for years after 1985. No investment credit is allowed for expensed property.

5. Recapture of depreciation

Under prior law, gain on the disposition of personal property was treated as ordinary income rather than capital gain to the extent of prior depreciation taken (sec. 1245). Gain on the disposition of real property was treated as ordinary income rather than capital gain only to the extent prior depreciation taken exceeds what would have been allowable if straight-line depreciation had been used (sec. 1250). In the case of installment sales of personal and real property, the recognition of any gain realized could be deferred (sec. 453).

Under the Act, the treatment of personal property is unchanged, except that the recognition of gain cannot be deferred by installment sales treatment to the extent a deduction was taken for the property under the special expensing election. The treatment of residential real property is unchanged. The treatment of nonresidential real property is unchanged if the straight-line depreciation method is used. However, for nonresidential real property depreciated under an accelerated method, gain is treated as ordinary income to the extent of all prior depreciation taken.

6. Flexibility

Under prior law, taxpayers had several options that permit a degree of flexibility in computing depreciation deductions and net operating losses. Taxpayers have an option to use a useful life 20 percent shorter or longer than ADR midpoint life. There was an option to use straight-line or accelerated methods, where allowed. In determining the date of additions to and retirements from a depreciation account, taxpayers had an option to use an averaging convention for personal property. In general, net operating losses, and operating losses of certain insurance companies, could be carried back 3 years and forward 7 years.

Under the Act, taxpayers have an option to use one of two recovery periods that are longer than the recovery period prescribed for each class of property. In addition, taxpayers have an option to use an accelerated or straight-line method over the regular recovery period. Under the Act, the carryover period for operating losses is extended to 15 years. Net operating losses of a financial institution are carried back 10 years and forward 5 years as under prior law. The carryover period for Cuban expropriation losses remains at 20 years.

7. Earnings and profits

Distributions by a corporation to its shareholders are taxable as dividends only to the extent the distribution is out of current or accumulated earnings and profits. Earnings and profits for U.S. corporations were computed, under prior law, using straight-line depreciation over the useful life of the property. The 20-percent ADR useful life variance could be used to determine the useful life for this purpose. Under the Act, earnings and profits for U.S. corporations are based on straight-line depreciation over extended recovery periods as set forth below:

Property	Extended recovery period
3-year property	5 years
5-year property	12 years
10-year property	25 years
15-year property	35 years

If, to compute the recovery deduction under section 168, a taxpayer uses a recovery period longer than the applicable extended recovery period described above, the taxpayer must use such longer period in lieu of the regular extended period to compute earnings and profits.

8. Depreciation of assets held outside the United States

Property used outside the United States for more than half the taxable year generally is considered a foreign asset. The investment tax credit generally is not allowed for such property (sec. 48(a)(2)). However, railroad rolling stock owned by a domestic railroad and used within and without the United States is not considered a foreign asset, even if it is used outside the United States for more than half the taxable year.

Under prior law, foreign assets were depreciated using useful lives based on facts and circumstances or the guideline lives under the ADR system, but the 20-percent useful life variance under ADR could not be used. Accelerated methods of depreciation generally could be used with respect to such property.

The Act provides that foreign personal property is depreciated using the 200-percent declining balance method, changing to the straight-line method, over the ADR midpoint life in effect for the property on January 1, 1981, or 12 years if no ADR midpoint life is in effect at such time. Taxpayers have the option to use the straight-line method over the regular recovery period (ADR midpoint life or 12 years, whichever is applicable) or an optional recovery period. Foreign real property can be depreciated over 35 years using the 150-percent declining balance method, changing to the straight-line method, or the straight-line method over 35 or 45 years.

The Act also provides that railroad rolling stock used within and without the United States is not treated as a foreign asset, whether it is owned by a domestic railroad or other U.S. person. However, this provision does not apply to rolling stock not owned by a domestic railroad if it is leased to a foreign person for periods aggregating more than 12 months out of any 24-month period.

9. Add-on minimum tax and maximum tax

A 15-percent minimum tax is imposed on a portion of a taxpayer's items of tax preference. Accelerated depreciation on leased personal property is an item of tax preference for taxpayers other than corporations (but including subchapter S corporations and personal holding companies). Under prior law, accelerated depreciation on real property is an item of tax preference for all taxpayers. Under prior law, the amount of the preference item was the excess of depreciation taken over what would have been allowable using the straight-line method over the property's useful life (ADR midpoint life for property depreciated under the ADR system).

Under the Act, accelerated depreciation is an item of tax preference for only individuals, subchapter S corporation, and personal holding companies.[1] The amount of the tax preference item for accelerated depreciation is the excess of the depreciation taken over the amount

---

[1] The elimination of the tax preference item for accelerated depreciation of real property for corporations other than subchapter S corporations and personal holding companies is a technical error and was not intended.

that would have been allowable using the straight-line method over prescribed periods as set forth below:

Property	Prescribed period
3-year property	5 years
5-year property	8 years
10-year property	15 years
15-year real property	15 years
15-year personal property	22 years

10. Regular investment credit

a. Eligibility for the credit

The regular investment credit applies to tangible personal property and other tangible property used in connection with manufacturing, production and certain other activities not including distribution. Petroleum storage facilities were ineligible under prior law unless used in connection with production. Property used predominately outside the United States is not eligible. Although there is an exception from the foreign use rule permitting the credit for railroad rolling stock of a domestic railroad that was used within and without the United States, railroad rolling stock of other persons used within and without the United States was not eligible under prior law.

The Act adds to eligible property facilities used for storage of petroleum and its primary products, even if used in connection with distribution and not production.

The Act retains the prior law "within and without" foreign use exception for rolling stock of a domestic railroad and adds to that exception rolling stock of other U.S. persons. However, rolling stock owned by a U.S. person other than a domestic railroad and used within and without the U.S. is not eligible if it is leased for periods aggregating more than 12 months in any 24-month period to a foreign person.

b. Amount of credit

Under prior law, the amount of regular credit was determined as follows:

Estimated useful life (years):	Credit (%)
Less than 3	0
3–4	$3\frac{1}{3}$
5–6	$6\frac{2}{3}$
7 or more	10

Under the Act, the regular credit amount is as follows:

Recovery period (years):	Credit (%)
3	6
5, 10 and 15	10

c. Used property limitation

Under prior law, only $100,000 of used property was eligible for the investment credit.

The Act raises the limitation to $125,000 for 1981 through 1984 and to $150,000 in 1985.

d. Recapture of credit

Under prior law, the credit was recomputed on early disposition of property as if the actual useful life had been used to determine the amount of credit.

Under the Act, the credit is recomputed on early disposition by allowing a 2-percent credit for each full year the property is held. Thus, no recapture is required for eligible 5-year, 10-year, or 15-year property actually held for at least 5 years, or for eligible 3-year property held at least 3 years.

e. Carryover of credit

Under prior law, unused investment credit could be carried back 3 years and forward 7 years. The Act extends the carryover period to 15 years.

11. Normalization rules for public utility property

Under prior law, a public utility could use an accelerated depreciation method only if it also used a normalization method of accounting, unless the company used flow-through accounting for accelerated depreciation in 1969. A public utility that had to normalize accelerated depreciation could use the ADR system only if it normalized certain differences between the ADR useful life and the ratemaking useful life of eligible property. Similarly, a utility that had to normalize accelerated depreciation also had to normalize the investment tax credit. In addition, some utilities not required to normalize accelerated depreciation were required to normalize all or part of the investment credit.

Under the Act, except as provided in relevant transition rules, normalization of accelerated depreciation, useful lives, and the investment credit is mandatory for all public utilities with respect to property depreciated under ACRS. Under transition rules, taxpayers are considered to satisfy the new normalization requirements for depreciation or the investment credit under a rate order that complies with the prior law requirements if (1) the rate order was put into effect before the date of enactment of the Act and (2) a superseding rate order determining cost of service is put into effect complying with the new applicable normalization requirement before January 1, 1983.

12. Investment credit at-risk limitation

Under prior law, there was no at-risk limitation on the allowance of investment credits.

Under the Act, the allowance of investment credits is subject to an at-risk limitation. The limitation applies to business activities, the losses from which are subject to limitation under the at-risk rules of section 465, engaged in by individuals, subchapter S corporations, and certain closely held corporations. The investment credit is not allowed with respect to amounts invested in qualifying property to the extent the invested amounts are not at risk, within the meaning of section 465 (b) (without regard to subsection (b) (5)).

The Act contains an exception for certain qualified lenders and direct or guaranteed Federal, State or local government loans, if the taxpayer has a minimum 20-percent at-risk investment in the property. Qualified lenders include banks, savings and loan institutions, credit unions, insurance companies, pension trusts and unrelated third parties engaged in the business of loaning money. For this exception, the lender must be unrelated to the borrower, the promoter, and the seller. In addition, the borrower must be unrelated to the seller.

The Act also contains a safe harbor rule for certain loans related to certain energy property. This special safe harbor rule applies only to solar or wind energy property, recycling equipment, qualified hydroelectric generating property, biomass property, equipment for converting alternative substances into alcohol fuels, geothermal equipment, and to ocean thermal energy equipment. The special safe harbor rule also applies to energy property which comprises a system for using the same energy source for the sequential generation of electrical power, mechanical shaft power, or both, in combination with steam, heat, or other forms of useful energy.

Amounts borrowed with respect to these types of property would be considered, under certain circumstances, at risk, even though such amounts are not otherwise considered at risk under the Act. In order to qualify under the safe harbor, the taxpayer must have a minimum 25-percent at risk investment in the property. In addition, any nonrecourse financing for the property (other than financing by a qualified lender that is considered at risk) must be a level payment loan. A level payment loan is a loan repaid in substantially equal installments which include both principal and interest. If the taxpayer does not make adequate repayments of loan principal, some of the credit allowed will be recaptured, and additional interest added to the increase in tax, determined as if the increase in tax were for the taxable year in which the property was placed in service.

13. Qualified progress expenditures

Under prior law, the investment credit was available for qualified progress expenditures made for property with a 2-year normal construction period and at least a 7-year useful life.

The Act repeals the 7-year useful life requirement. Thus, the amount of credit allowed with respect to progress expenditures will be determined in accordance with the recovery period the taxpayer expects the property to have when the property is placed in service.

14. Leasing

Under prior IRS guidelines, a transaction was characterized as a lease if—(1) the lessor's minimum at-risk investment in the property throughout the lease term was 20 percent of cost; (2) the lessor had a positive cash flow and a profit from the lease independent of tax benefits; (3) the lessee did not have a right to purchase the property at less than fair market value; (4) the lessee did not have an investment in the lease and does not lend any of the purchase costs to the owner, and use of the property at the end of the lease term by a person other than the lessee must be commercially feasible to the lessor.

The Act creates a safe harbor that guarantees that a transaction will be characterized as a lease for purposes of allowing investment credits and cost recovery allowances to the nominal lessor. To come within the safe harbor, both the lessor and the lessee must elect affirmatively to treat the lessor as the owner of the property. The lessor must be a corporation, a partnership of corporations, or a grantor trust, the grantor and beneficiaries of which are all corporations. At all times during the term of the lease and at the time that the property is in service, the lessor must have a minimum "at risk" investment of not less than 10 percent of the adjusted basis of the property. In addition, the term of the lease (including all extensions) cannot exceed the greater of (1) 90 percent of the useful life of the property under section 167 or (2) 150 percent of the present class life (ADR midpoint as of January 1, 1981).

Only property that is new section 38 property (or certain mass commuting vehicles) may come within the safe harbor rules. The leased property must be leased within 3 months after its acquisition or, in the case of a sale-leaseback transaction, it must be purchased by the lessor within 3 months of the lessee's acquisition for a purchase price that does not exceed the adjusted basis of the property in the hands of the lessee at the time of the lessor's purchase.

If a transaction meets the requirements above, the parties will be treated as lessor and lessee without regard to (1) whether the lessor or lessee must take into account tax benefits to derive a profit or cash flow from the transaction (2) the fact that the lessee retains title and the burdens, benefits, and incidents of ownership, (3) whether a person other than the lessee may use the property at the end of the lease, (4) the fact the property may be purchased at the end of the lease at a fixed or determinable price that is more or less than its fair market value at that time, (5) the fact the lessee has provided financing or has guaranteed financing (other than for the lessor's minimum 10 percent investment), and (6) the fact an obligation of any person is subject to a contingency or offset agreement.

15. Effective dates and phase-in provisions

In general, the capital cost recovery provisions apply to property placed in service after December 31, 1980. Although there is no phase-in period, the most accelerated method of depreciation for personal property is not available until 1986. In general, the rules for extension of the carryover period for operating losses apply for operating losses in taxable years ending after December 31, 1975. A special rule applies for losses of a former REIT. The effective dates for extension of the carryover periods for various credits are as follows:

(1) Investment credit and WIN credits—Unused credit years ending after December 31, 1973.

(2) New employee credit—Unused credit years ending after December 31, 1976.

(3) Alcohol fuel credits—Unused credit years ending after September 30, 1980.

The at risk rule for the investment credit applies to property placed in service on or after February 19, 1981, except for property acquired by the taxpayer pursuant to a binding contract entered into on or before February 18, 1981. A technical amendment to section 46(e) relating to investment credit for non-corporate lessors applies to leases entered into after June 25, 1981. The rules relating to railroad rolling stock apply for taxable years beginning after December 31, 1980.

Special rules are provided to prevent the taxpayer from bringing its property used during 1980 (pre-1981 property) within the system by certain post-1980 transactions (i.e., "churning" transactions). Similar rules are provided to prevent the taxpayer from taking advantage of the increased recovery percentages available after 1984 for its property used before 1985 (pre-1985 property). Under these anti-churning rules ACRS will not apply to personal property in use during 1980 unless the property is transferred after 1980 in a transaction in which the owner and user (if different) change. Also ACRS does not apply to personal property leased back to a person that owned or used the property during 1980 or to a person related to that person.

For the anti-churning rules, a corporation is not a related person to the taxpayer if either (1) the person is a distributing corporation in a transaction described in section 334(b)(2)(B) and 80 percent of the stock is acquired by purchase after December 31, 1980, by the taxpayer or (2) if the person is a distributing corporation in a complete or partial liquidation to which section 331 applies and 80 percent of the stock of that corporation is acquired by purchase by one or more taxpayers or by persons related to the taxpayer after December 31, 1980.

C. Rehabilitation Expenditures

1. Tax credit for rehabilitation expenditures

Under prior law, the 10-percent investment tax credit (and additional energy credit) was available for expenditures to rehabilitate a building that is at least 20 years old. The credit allowed did not reduce the basis of the property for purposes of depreciation. In lieu of the investment credit, the taxpayer could elect with respect to rehabilitation of a certified historic structure to amortize the expenditures over a 60-month period. (sec. 191.)

Under the Act, the 10-percent regular investment credit (and the additional energy credit) for rehabilitation expenditures and the 60-month amortization provision for certified historic rehabilitation expenditures are replaced by a 3-tier investment credit. The credit is 15 percent for structures at least 30 years old, 20 percent for structures at least 40 years old, and 25 percent for certified historic structures. No credit is allowed for rehabilitation of a building (other than a certified historic structure) less than 30 years old.

The 15- and 20-percent credits are limited, as under prior law, to nonresidential buildings. However, the 25-percent credit for certified historic rehabilitation is available for both nonresidential and residential buildings. These credits are available only if the taxpayer elects to use the straight-line method of cost recovery with respect to rehabilitation expenditures. In addition, there must be a substantial rehabilitation of the building to qualify for the credit.

For rehabilitation credits other than the credit for certified historic rehabilitations, the basis of the property must be reduced by the amount of the credit allowed. If subsequently there is a recapture of the credit, the resulting increase in tax (or adjustment in carrybacks and carryovers) will increase the basis of the building immediately before the recapture event.

No credit is available for a certified historic structure if approval of the rehabilitation is not obtained from the Secretary of Interior. The Act treats a noncertified building in an historic district as a certified historic structure for this purpose unless the taxpayer obtains a certification from the Secretary of Interior that it is not of historic significance to the district. This changes the prior law rule under which a building in an historic district was not a certified historic structure unless the Secretary of the Interior took action to designate the property as being of historic significance to the district.

Under the Act, the prior law rule denying investment credit for property leased to tax-exempt organizations (sec. 48(a)(4)) or governmental units (sec. 48(a)(5)) does not apply to the portion of the basis of the building attributable to qualified rehabilitation expenditures. This corrects a clerical error in the enrollment of the Miscellaneous Revenue Act of 1980. Due to the error, this provision was omitted from the Act.

The Act applies to expenditures made after December 31, 1981. Rehabilitation expenditures which are paid or incurred both prior to January 1, 1982, and after that date, can qualify for the prior law credit of 10 percent for buildings over 20 years old, or for the credits under the Act after December 31, 1981, for other qualifying buildings. Thus, some expenditures may be subject to two different credit rates as a rehabilitation is completed. For a certified historic structure, the taxpayer may use either the prior law 10-percent credit or 60-month amortization for pre-1982 expenditures, but generally is allowed only the 25-percent credit for post-1981 expenditures. However, if a rehabilitation begins before January 1, 1982, on a certified historic structure that does not qualify for the new credits because of the substantial rehabilitation requirement, 60-month amortization or the 10-percent credit will continue to apply to both post-1981 and pre-1982 expenditures. The rule permitting a rehabilitation credit for property leased to tax-exempts applies to uses after July 29, 1980.

2. Demolition of historic structures

Under prior law, buildings constructed or reconstructed at the site of a demolished or substantially altered certified historic structure had to be depreciated using the straight-line method over its useful life (sec. 167(n)). Demolition costs had to be capitalized as part of the basis of land and, thus, could not be deducted as a loss or depreciated.

The Act retains the loss deduction prohibition of present law, but repeals the straight-line depreciation requirement. The provision applies to expenditures made after December 31, 1981.

D. Incentives for Research and Experimentation

1. Tax credit for research and experimentation

Under present law, a taxpayer may elect to deduct currently the amount of research or experimental expenditures incurred in connection with the taxpayer's trade or business, or may elect to amortize certain research costs over a period of 60 months or more (sec. 174). These rules apply to the costs of research conducted by the taxpayer and, in general, to expenses paid for research conducted on behalf of the taxpayer by a research firm, university, etc. Treasury regulations define qualifying expenditures to mean "research and development costs in the experimental or laboratory sense," and provide illustrations of qualifying and nonqualifying expenditures.

The Act provides a 25-percent tax credit for certain research and experimental expenditures paid in carrying on a trade or business of the taxpayer, but only to the extent that current-year expenditures exceed the average amount of research expenditures in a base period (generally, the preceding three taxable years). Subject to certain exclusions, the Act adopts the definition of research used for purposes of the special income tax deduction rules under section 174.

Under the Act, research expenditures qualifying for the new incremental credit consist of (1) "in-house" expenditures for research wages and supplies, plus certain lease or other charges for research use of computers, laboratory equipment, etc.; (2) 65 percent of amounts paid (e.g., to a research firm or university) for contract research; and (3) 65 percent of corporate grants for basic research to be performed by universities or certain scientific research organizations (or of grants to certain funds organized to make basic research grants to universities).

The credit under the Act applies to research expenditures made after June 30, 1981, and before 1986.

2. Charitable contributions of newly manufactured equipment to universities for research

Under present law, the amount of charitable deduction for a contribution of inventory or other ordinary-income property generally is limited to the amount of the taxpayer's basis in the property. An exception is provided for corporate contributions of certain property for use in the care of the needy, the ill, or infants; in such case, 50 percent of any appreciation plus the basis (but not more than twice the basis) may be deducted.

The Act allows a deduction equal to the taxpayer's basis plus 50 percent of any appreciation (but not to exceed twice the basis) for qualified corporate contributions, by the manufacturer, of new scientific equipment or apparatus to a college or university for research or experimentation, including research training, in the United States in the physical or biological sciences. This provision applies to qualified charitable contributions made after the date of enactment of the Act.

3. Allocation of research expenditures to domestic income

Taxpayers must allocate and apportion research and experimentation expenditures between their domestic and foreign source income. To the extent that such expenditures are allocated to foreign source income, the taxpayers foreign tax credit limitation is reduced, which may reduce utilization of foreign tax credits. Other results also flow from the allocation.

The Act provides that for two years, taxpayers must allocate or apportion all research and experimental expenditures paid or incurred in activities conducted in the United States to U.S. source income. The Treasury is required to study the impact of its allocation regulations on domestic research and development and on the foreign tax credit.

The provision is effective for the first two taxable years of a taxpayer beginning after the date of enactment of the Act.

E. Small Business Provisions

1. Accumulated earnings credit

Under present law, an accumulated earnings tax is imposed on earnings accumulated in a corporation to avoid income tax on the corporation's shareholders. In computing the tax base, a credit (of not less than $150,000) is allowed for earnings retained for the reasonable needs of the business.

The Act increases the minimum accumulated earnings credit to $250,000 except for service corporations in health, law, engineering, architecture, accounting, actuarial science, performing arts and consulting. The provision is effective for taxable years beginning after December 31, 1981.

2. Subchapter S corporations

Under present law, a subchapter S corporation may not have more than 15 shareholders and, generally, trust may not be shareholders.

The Act increases the number of permitted shareholders to 25 and allows "section 678" trusts to be shareholders. In addition, under the

Act the sole income beneficiary of a trust which distributes all its income currently can elect to be treated as the owner, under section 678, of the stock of any subchapter S corporation held by the trust, and the trust will be eligible as a shareholder of that subchapter S corporation. The income beneficiary must be a U.S. citizen or resident, and must be a beneficiary for his life unless the corpus of the trust is to be distributed to the income beneficiary upon termination of the trust. The election under this section may be made retroactive for up to 60 days.

The provision is effective for taxable years beginning after December 31, 1981.

3. LIFO inventory and small business accounting

Taxpayers with inventories must use accrual accounting rather than cash accounting. LIFO is a method of accrual accounting that, during periods of inflation results in the highest cost goods being deducted from income, thus, producing low taxable income. Dollar-value LIFO is an advantageous method of computing LIFO inventories but because of its inherent complexity it is considered by some, especially small businessmen, as unworkable.

Under the Act, businesses with average gross receipts of less than $2 million for the 3 years (ending with the taxable year) may elect one inventory pool for purposes of dollar-value LIFO inventory accounting. Also, taxpayers electing LIFO will have 3 years (beginning with the year of the election to LIFO) to take back into income inventory writedowns taken in years prior to the year of the LIFO election. The Secretary shall also prescribe regulations providing for the simplification of LIFO inventory accounting through the use of published government indexes.

Also under the Act, the Secretary of the Treasury is directed to conduct a full and complete study of methods of tax accounting for inventory (including but not limited to the LIFO method and the cash receipts and disbursements method) with a view toward the development of simplified methods. The Secretary is also directed to submit to the Committee on Ways and Means of the House of Representatives and to the Committee on Finance of the Senate a report on this study, together with such recommendations as he deems appropriate, by December 31, 1982.

F. Windfall Profit Tax and Other Energy Provisions

1. Royalty owners credit and exemption

Qualified royalty owners were allowed a credit (or refund) of up to $1,000 against the windfall profit tax imposed on their royalty oil during calendar year 1980.

The Act makes the royalty owner credit available for calendar year 1981 and increases it from $1,000 to $2,500.

For 1982 and subsequent years, the Act provides a limited exemption from the windfall profit tax for specified amounts of royalty production. For 1982 through 1984, the exemption is 2 barrels a day; starting in 1985 the exemption is 3 barrels a day.

2. Producer exemption

Independent producers are eligible for reduced windfall profit tax rates on up to 1,000 barrels a day of tier 1 and tier 2 oil. The reduced rate applicable to an independent producer's tier 2 oil (including stripper oil) is 30 percent rather than 60 percent.

The Act exempts from the windfall profit tax, starting in 1983, stripper oil production of independent producers. The Act also provides that stripper oil cannot qualify for this exemption if it is produced from a stripper well property which has been transferred on or after July 23, 1981, by a producer other than an independent producer.

3. Reduced tax rate on newly discovered oil

Under present law, newly discovered oil is taxed at a 30-percent rate on the difference between its removal price and a severance tax adjustment plus a base price of $16.55 adjusted for grade, quality, location and inflation plus 2 percent.

The Act reduces the tax rate on newly discovered oil from 30 to 15 percent, over 5 years, in accordance with the following schedule:

Year	Rate (%)
1982	27. 5
1983	25. 0
1984	22. 5
1985	20. 0
1986 and thereafter	15. 0

4. Exemption for qualified charities

Under present law, oil production attributable to certain qualifying charitable interests is exempt from the windfall profit tax. A charitable organization for the residential placement, care, or treatment of delinquent, dependent, orphaned, neglected, or handicapped children is not within this exemption.

The Act extends the existing windfall profit tax exemption for qualified charities to oil production attributable to economic interests held by charitable organizations. described in Code section 170(c)(2), which are organized and operated primarily for the residential placement, care, or treatment of delinquent, dependent, orphaned, neglected, or handicapped children.

5. Production credit for certain gases

Present law allows a credit for the production of specified alternative fuels, including several types of natural gas which are eligible for incentive prices under the Natural Gas Policy Act of 1978 (NGPA). The credit phases out as the price of uncontrolled domestic oil rises from $23.50 to $29.50 a barrel, adjusted for inflation. Because of the phase out based on the price of oil, the credit generally was not available during 1980.

Section 107(d) of the NGPA provides that gas production is not eligible for an incentive price if any special tax provision applies and if the producer does not file a price election with the Federal Energy Regulatory Commission within 30 days of enactment of the special tax provision.

The Act provides that no production credit is available unless the taxpayer elects it on the appropriate tax return. This has the effect of allowing the producer to elect the incentive price under the NGPA after the 30-day period has elapsed.

The Act does not change any provision of the NGPA or deal with the FERC's administration of that Act. It is intended, however, that the amendment be administered by Treasury and, to the extent appropriate, by FERC so as to prevent any producer from obtaining the benefits of the production credit and the incentive price.

G. Corporate Rate Reductions and Other Business Provisions

1. Corporate rate reduction

The corporate income tax has been imposed on taxable income under the following schedule:

Taxable income:	*Rate (%)*
Less than $25,000	17
25,000–50,000	20
50,000–75,000	30
75,000–100,000	40
Over $100,000	46

The Act reduces the tax rate on taxable income below $50,000 in two steps.

Taxable income:	*Rate (%)*
In 1982—	
Less than $25,000	16
$25,000–$50,000	19
1983 and later years—	
Less than $ 25,000	15
25,000–$50,000	18

2. Incentive stock options

Under present law, the taxation of stock options granted by an employer to an employee as compensation is governed by section 83. The value of the option constitutes ordinary income to the employee when granted only if the option itself has a readily ascertainable fair market value at that time. If the option does not have a readily ascertainable value when granted, it does not constitute ordinary income at that time. Instead, when the option is exercised, the difference between the value of the stock at exercise and the option price constitutes ordinary income to the employee. Ordinary income on grant or on exercise of a stock option is treated as personal service income and, hence, generally is taxed at a maximum rate of 50 percent.

An employer who grants a stock option generally is allowed a business expense deduction equal to the amount includible in the employee's income in its corresponding taxable year (sec. 83(h)).

The Act provides for "incentive stock options," under which there will be no tax consequences when an incentive stock option is granted or when the option is exercised, and the employee will be taxed at capital gains rates when and if he sells the stock received on exercise of the option. Similarly, no business expense deduction will be allowed to the employer with respect to an incentive stock option.

The term "incentive stock option" means an option granted to an individual, for any reason connected with his or her employment, by the employer corporation or by a parent or subsidiary corporation of the employer corporation, to purchase stock of any of such corporations.

To receive incentive stock option treatment, the Act provides that the employee must not dispose of the stock within two years after the option is granted, and must hold the stock itself for at least one year. If all requirements other than these holding period rules are met, the tax will be imposed on sale of the stock, but gain will be treated as ordinary income rather than capital gain, and the employer will be alowed a deduction at that time.

In addition, for the entire time from the date of granting the option until three months (12 months if disabled) before the date of exercise, the option, a parent or subsidiary of that corporation, or a successor corporation. This requirement and the holding period requirements are waived in the case of the death of the employee.

For an option to qualify as an "incentive stock option," the following conditions must be met:

1. The option must be granted under a plan specifying the number of shares of stock to be issued and the employees or class of employees to receive the options. This plan must be approved by the stockholders of the corporation within 12 months before or after the plan is adopted.

2. The option must be granted within ten years of the date the plan is adopted or the date the plan is approved by the stockholders, whichever is earlier.

3. The option must by its terms be exercisable only within 10 years of the date it is granted.

4. The option price must equal or exceed the fair market value of the stock at the time the option is granted. This requirement will be deemed satisfied if there has been a good faith attempt to value the stock accurately, even if the option price is less than the stock value.

5. The option by its terms must be nontransferable other than at death and must be exercisable during the employee's lifetime only by the employee.

6. The employee must not, immediately before the option is granted, own stock representing more than 10 percent of the voting power or value of all classes of stock of the employer corporation or its parent or subsidiary. However, the stock ownership limitation will be waived if the option price is at least 110 percent of the fair market value (at the time the option is granted) of the stock subject to the option and the option by its terms is not exercisable more than five years from the date it is granted.

7. The option by its terms is not to be exercisable while there is outstanding any incentive stock option which was granted to the employee at an earlier time. For this purpose, an option which has not been exercised in full is outstanding for the period which under its initial terms it could have been exercised. Thus, the cancellation of an earlier option will not enable a subsequent option to be exercised any sooner. Also, for this purpose an option is considered to retain its original date of grant even if the terms of the option or the plan are later amended to qualify the option as an incentive stock option.

8. In the case of options granted after 1980, the terms of the plan must limit the amount of aggregate fair market value of the stock (determined at the time of the grant of the option) for which any employee may be granted incentive stock options in any calendar year to not more than $100,000 plus the carryover amount. The carryover amount from any year after 1980 is one-half of the amount by which $100,000 exceeds the value (at time of grant) of the stock for which incentive stock options were granted in such prior year. Amounts may be carried over 3 years. Options granted in any year use up the $100,000 current year limitation first and then the carryover from the earliest year.

The Act provides that stock acquired on exercise of the option may be paid for with stock of the corporation granting the option. The different between the option price and the fair market value of the stock at the exercise of the option will not be an item of tax preference.

Additional cash or other property may be transferred to the employee at the time the option is exercised, so long as such property is subject to inclusion in income under the provisions of section 83.

An option will not be disqualified because of the inclusion of any condition not inconsistent with the qualification requirements.

The Act will apply to options granted after January 1, 1976, and exercised after December 31, 1980, or outstanding on such later date.

However, in the case of options (including qualified options) granted before January 1, 1981, an option is an incentive stock option only if the employer elects such treatment for an option. The aggregate value (determined at time of grant) of stock for which any employee may be granted incentive stock options prior to 1981 shall not exceed $50,000 per calendar year and $200,000 in the aggregate.

In the case of an option granted after January 1, 1976, and outstanding on the date of enactment, the option terms (or the terms of the plan under which the option was granted may be changed, or shareholder approval obtained, to conform to the incentive stock option rules, within one year of the date of enactment, without the change giving rise to a new option requiring the setting of an option price based on a later valuation date.

All such changes relate back to the time of granting the original option. For example, if the option price of a ten-year option granted in 1978 is increased during the one year after date of enactment to 100 percent (110 percent, if applicable) of the fair market value of the stock on the date the option was granted in 1978, the price requirement will be met. Likewise, if the term of an option held by a 10-percent shareholder is shortened to five years from the date the option was granted, the 10-percent stock ownership limitation will not apply.

3. Extension and modification of targeted jobs tax credit

Under present law, the targeted jobs tax credit, which applies to eligible trade or business wages paid before January 1, 1982, is available on an elective basis for hiring individuals from one or more of seven target groups. In general, the credit is equal to 50 percent of the first $6,000 of first-year wages and 25 percent of the first $6,000 of second-year wages. Qualified first-year wages are limited to 30 percent of FUTA wages (the first $6,000 per calendar year) for all employees.

In the case of trade or business employment, taxpayers are allowed a WIN tax credit equal to 50 percent of qualified first-year wages and 25 percent of qualified second-year wages paid to WIN registrants and AFDC recipients. For employment other than in a trade or business, the credit is 35 percent of qualified first-year wages.

The Act extends and modifies the targeted jobs credit as follows:

Extension and eligible wages.—The Act provides that the full credit is available for targeted employees who begin work before January 1, 1983. The provision limiting qualified first-year wages to 30 percent of FUTA wages is repealed.

Targeted groups.—AFDC recipients and WIN registrants are added as a targeted group, and the WIN credit is terminated. Eligible cooperative education students are limited to those who are economically disadvantaged, effective for wages paid after December 31, 1981. The age limitation for Vietnam veterans (under age 35) is eliminated, and employees laid off from public service employment funded by CETA are made eligible for the credit.

Changes in certification requirements.—Certifications issued or requested after the individual begins work are invalid, and certifications based on false information provided by the employee are revoked prospectively. These requirements generally apply to all individuals, regardless of the date they begin work for their employer. However, for an individual, other than a cooperative education student, who began work earlier than 45 days before the date of enactment, the certification has to have been requested or received before July 23, 1981. For an individual who begins work for the employer during the 90-day period beginning with the date 45 days before the date of enactment or for a cooperative education student who begins work before the end of this period, the certification must be requested or received before the last day of this 90-day period.

In addition, certifications that individuals are members of economically disadvantaged families are valid for a period of 45 days; certification and marketing are to be performed by State employment security agencies; and the credit is not allowed for rehires.

Hiring of relatives.—The credit is denied for hiring relatives of the employer.

Authorization for administrative expenses.—For fiscal year 1982, $30 million of appropriations is authorized for program administration, of which $5 million is to be used for a quality control program.

4. Motor carrier operating rights

Taxpayers are not allowed a loss deduction for the diminution in the value of a license or permit if the license or permit continues to have value as a right to carry on a business.

Under the Act, an ordinary deduction is allowed ratably over a 60-month period for the adjusted bases of motor carrier operating authorities held by the taxpayer on July 1, 1980. The Act provides a special stock acquisition rule for cases in which a corporation acquired the stock of another corporation that directly or indirectly held an operating authority. The provision applies to taxable years ending after June 30, 1980.

5. Bad debt deduction of commercial banks

Under present law, commercial banks compute their bad debt deductions under either the experience method or the percentage of outstanding loans method (sec. 585). Under the Tax Reform Act of 1969, the percentage of outstanding loans method is phased out over an 18-year period. Under the phase-out of the method, bad debt deductions generally are permitted to the extent necessary to increase the bad debt reserve to the following percentages of eligible outstanding loans: 1969 to 1975, 1.8 percent; 1976–1981, 1.2 percent; and 1982–1987, 0.6 percent. After 1987, the bad debt deduction of commercial banks is to be computed under the experience method.

The Act provides that the applicable percentage under the percentage of eligible loans method is to be 1.0 percent for taxable years beginning in 1982. For years after 1982, and before 1988, the applicable percentage will continue to be 0.6 percent.

6. Reorganizations involving financially troubled thrift institutions

Under present law, a tax-free merger or other reorganization is permitted only if shareholders of the acquired corporation acquire stock in the acquiring corporation in the transaction. This restriction is a nonstatutory requirement generally described as the "continuity of interest" requirement. Net operating losses of the acquired corporation in a reorganization are restricted where the shareholders of the acquired corporation are not shareholders of the surviving corporation (sec. 382(b)). Distributions by a domestic building and loan association from its bad debt reserve are recaptured as ordinary income (sec. 593(a)). Contributions to a corporation are excluded from income (sec. 118) but, when made by a nonshareholder, require a reduction in the basis of the corporation's property (sec. 362(c)).

The Act amends the reorganization provisions to permit, in the case of a mutual savings bank, a domestic building and loan association, or a cooperative bank (i.e., a thrift institution to which sec. 593 applies), a transaction to qualify as a reorganization even though the shareholders of the transferor do not receive stock or securities in the acquiring corporation. The amendment applies only to thrift institutions and only after certification by the Federal Home Loan Bank Board, the Federal Savings and Loan Insurance Corporation, or, where neither has supervisory authority, an equivalent State authority that one of the grounds in section 1464(d)(6)(A), (i), (ii), or (iii) of 12 U.S.C. exists with respect to the transferor or, without action by the appropriate agency, will exist in the near future. The amendment requires that substantially all the assets of the transferor be acquired by the transferee and that substantially all of the liabilities of the transferor, including deposits, before the transfer become liabilities of the transferee.

The Act provides that in applying section 382(b) to operating loss carryovers to the surviving corporation after a reorganization of a thrift institution which has been certified by the appropriate agency as described above, deposits in the acquired corporation which become deposits in the transferee are treated as stock of both corporations. Deposits in the transferee are also treated as stock for this purpose.

The Act provides that distributions out of excess bad debt reserves in redemption of the principal amount of an interest of the Federal Savings and Loan Insurance Corporation in the distributing domestic building and loan association received in exchange for financial assistance is not subject to recapture under section 593(e).

The Act excludes from income of a building and loan association all money or property contributed to the association by the Federal Savings and Loan Insurance Corporation under its financial assistance program without any reduction in the basis of property.

7. Tax treatment of mutual savings banks that convert to stock associations

Under present law, building and loan associations, cooperative banks, and nonstock mutual savings banks compute their bad debt deduction under a special set of rules (sec. 593). Under one of these rules, called the percent of taxable income method, these institutions are allowed a bad debt deduction equal to 40 percent of the institution's taxable income (computed without regard to the bad debt deduction). However, in order to qualify for the full amount of this deduction, at least 82 percent of its assets in the case of a building and loan association or cooperative bank, or 72 percent of its assets in the case of a mutual savings bank, must be invested in certain assets (hereafter called "qualified assets").

Present law also provides rules which recapture excess bad debt deductions of building and loan associations when there are dividends in excess of post-1951 earnings and profits or when there are liquidations or redemptions of stock (sec. 593(e)). Finally, present law permits mutual savings banks to compute the tax on their life insurance business as if the life insurance business was in a separate corporation subject to the special rules applicable to life insurance companies (sec. 594).

The Act makes two changes which are designed to facilitate the conversion of mutual savings banks into stock associations. First, the Act provides that a stock association which is subject to the same regulation as a mutual savings bank is to be treated as a mutual savings bank and, thus, is eligible to compute its bad debt deduction under section 593. However, consistent with the treatment of building and loan associations which may be organized as stock associations, such stock associations would compute their bad debt deduction under the percentage of eligible loan method under the same rules applicable to building and loan associations (i.e., 82 percent of their assets would have to be invested in qualified assets in order to receive the full 40-percent deduction). Similarly, the Act requires recapture of excess bad debt deductions by such stock associations in the same manner as building and loan associations (sec. 593(e)).

Second, the Act extends the special rule under which mutual savings banks can compute their tax on life insurance business as if it were a separate corporation to stock associations which are regulated as mutual savings banks. The Act also clarifies that amounts paid to depositors of such stock associations are deductible to the same extent as mutual savings banks (sec. 591).

H. Savings Incentives Provisions

1. Partial dividend and interest exclusion

Under present law, individuals may exclude from income up to $200 ($400 on a joint return) of dividends and interest earned from domestic sources in 1981 and 1982. After 1982, only the $100 per taxpayer dividend exclusion of prior law will be available.

The Act repeals present law after 1981 and reinstates the $100 dividend exclusion of prior law for 1982 and subsequent years; however, the $100 per taxpayer limitation for the reinstated dividend exclusion is replaced by a limitation of $100 per separate return and $200 per joint return.

Effective in 1985, the Act provides for a 15-percent net interest exclusion on up to $3,000 of net interest ($6,000 on a joint return). For taxpayers who itemize deductions, interest is eligible for the percentage exclusion only to the extent it exceeds the taxpayer's qualified interest expense. Qualified interest expense is interest allowed other than interest paid on a home mortgage or in connection with a trade or business.

2. Tax-exempt savings certificates

Individuals may exclude $200 ($400 on a joint return) of interest and dividends from income in 1981 and 1982 under present law.

The Act provides tax exemption for an aggregate of $1,000 ($2,000 on a joint return) for interest received on a qualified savings certificate. Certificates are 1-year obligations and may be issued between October 1, 1981, and December 31, 1982, by qualified depository institutions (banks, thrift institutions, and credit unions). The certificates must pay interest at rates equal to 70 percent of the rate on the most recently issued 52 weeks Treasury bill. Seventy-five percent of the proceeds must be used for residential financing and agricultural loans, except for credit unions which are limited in the amount of savings certificates they may issue. Residential financing includes 2, 3, and 4 family residences and loans on stock of a cooperative housing corporation.

Interest (other than a qualified savings certificate) will not be eligible for exclusion after 1982, and the dividend exclusion will be limited to $100 ($200 on a joint return). (See, however, the description of the net interest exclusion under No. H.1. above.)

3. Individual retirement accounts

In the case of an individual who is not an active participant in an employer-sponsored plan, the annual contribution limit is raised from the lesser of $1,500 or 15 percent of compensation to the lesser of $2,000 or 100 percent of compensation. The limit for a spousal IRA is increased from $1,750 to $2,250, and the present-law requirement that contributions under a spousal IRA be equally divided between the spouses is deleted.

In the case of an employee who is an active participant is a plan, a deduction is allowed of up to $2,000 for contributions to an IRA or for voluntary contributions to the plan. The voluntary contributions and earnings thereon under a plan are subject to IRA-type rules, except that (1) distributions starting at age 70½ are not mandated and (2) rollovers may be made to an IRA with regard to the present law rule limiting rollovers to one per year.

Under the Act, benefits under a qualified plan (including deductible employee contributions and earnings thereon) are taxed only when paid to the employee or a beneficiary and are not taxed if merely made available. As under present law, if benefits are paid with respect to an employee to a creditor of the employee, a child of the employee, etc., the benefits paid would be treated as if paid to the employee.

Under present law, individuals generally may self-direct IRA investments or investments under an account in a qualified plan. Under the Act amounts invested in collectibles (antiques, art, gems, stamps, etc.) under an IRA or a self-directed account in a qualified plan are treated as distributions for income tax purposes.

Under the Act, the proceeds of a redeemed U.S. retirement bond which is distributed under a qualified bond purchase plan may be rolled over, tax-free, to an IRA. U.S. retirement bonds purchased for an employee may be redeemed only after the employee attains age 59½, dies or becomes disabled. Also, the Act clarifies the treatment of IRA retirement bonds acquired in a taxfree rollover.

In addition, the Act provides that a divorced spouse is allowed a deduction for contributions to a spousal IRA established by the individual's former spouse at least 5 years before the divorce if the former spouse contributed to the IRA under the spousal IRA rules for at least three of the five years preceding the divorce. If these requirements are met, the limit on the divorced spouse's IRA contributions for a year is not less than the lesser of (1) $1,125, or (2) the sum of the divorced spouse's compensation and alimony includible in gross income.

4. Self-employed retirement savings (Keogh plans)

The deduction limit for employer contributions to a defined contribution Keogh plan, to a defined contribution plan maintained by a subchapter S corporation, or to a simplified employee pension (SEP) is increased from $7,500 to $15,000. The 15-percent limit on contributions is not changed. To provide a similar increase in the level of benefits permitted under a defined benefit Keogh or subchapter S corporation plan, the compensation taken into account in determining permitted annual benefit accruals is increased from $50,000 to $100,000.

The Act also increases the amount of compensation which may be taken into account to determine contributions to a Keogh plan, to a subchapter S plan, or to a SEP. Under the Act, the includible compensation limit is increased from $100,000 to $200,000. However, if annual compensation in excess of $100,000 is taken into account, the rate of employer contributions for a plan participant who is a common-law employee cannot be less than the equivalent of 7½ percent of that participant's compensation.

The Act also extends to all partners the present-law rule under which a loan from a Keogh plan to an owner-employee or his use of an interest in the plan as security for a loan is treated as a distribution.

In addition, the Act permits (1) the penalty-free correction of an excess contribution to a Keogh plan if the excess is withdrawn before the return filing due date and (2) early withdrawals from a terminated Keogh plan by an owner-employee without regard to the 5-year ban on Keogh plan contributions for the owner-employee.

5. Employee stock ownership plans (ESOPs)

Present law provides an investment tax credit for contributions to employee stock ownership plans (ESOP).

The Act terminates, after 1982, the present law investment-based tax credit for ESOP contributions and replaces it with a payroll-based tax credit. The payroll-based credit is allowed for wages paid in calendar years 1983 through 1987. For calendar years 1983 and 1984, the credit is limited to 0.5 percent of compensation paid to employees under the plan, and to 0.75 percent of such compensation for 1985, 1986, and 1987.

For profit-sharing plans, the present law rule requiring a flow through of voting rights is deleted, effective January 1, 1980. This requirement continues to apply to other defined contribution plans.

6. Dividend reinvestment plans

Under present law, stock dividends received as part of a pro rata distribution to all shareholders are taxable when the dividend is disposed of or sold. Stock distributions that are not on a pro rata basis are taxable at fair market value when the shares are initially received. Distributions are taxable at fair market value when received if the shareholder has the option to receive cash or stock.

The Act provides that shareholders in a domestic public utility corporation who choose to receive a dividend in the form of a common stock dividend, instead of cash or other property, may exclude up to $750 ($1,500 on a joint return) from income.

These shares will have a zero basis, and the full amount will be taxed as a capital gain if sold after a year. If sold within a year, the stock will be taxed as ordinary income. Only individual shareholders are eligible for dividend reinvestment.

The stock must be common stock newly issued for this purpose and valued between 95 and 105 percent of the stock's value immediately before the distribution date. Penalties will be applied to a corporation which purchases its stock for distribution under this plan.

I. Estate and Gift Tax Provisions

1. Increase in unified credit and reduction in rates

Under present law, estate and gift taxes are unified so that a single progressive rate schedule is applied to cumulative gifts and bequests. Estate and gift tax rates range from 18 percent for the first $10,000 in taxable transfers to 70 percent on taxable transfers in excess of $5 million. Generally, the estate or gift tax liability is determined by first computing the gross estate or gift tax and then subtracting the unified credit to determine the amount of estate of gift tax. The amount of the present unified credit is $47,000. With a unified credit of $47,000, there is no estate or gift tax owed on transfers up to $175,625.

The Act increases the unified credit as follows:

Year of death	Amount of credit	Equivalent amount
1982	$62,800	$225,000
1983	79,300	275,000
1984	96,300	325,000
1985	121,800	400,000
1986	155,800	500,000
1987 and thereafter	192,800	600,000

The Act also reduces the maximum estate and gift tax rate by 5 percentage points a year over a four-year period from 70 percent to 50 percent, beginning in 1982.

2. Marital deduction

The Act eliminates the present quantitative limits on both the gift and estate tax martial deductions so that one spouse can transfer an unlimited amount of property tax-free to the other spouse. In addition, transfers of community property and transfers of certain terminable interests will qualify for the marital deduction. With regard to property held in joint tenancy by spouses with right of survivorship, only one-half of the property will be included in the estate of the first spouse to die. A transition rule will continue present law for marital deduction clauses in wills executed before 30 days after the date of enactment and not subsequently amended to specifically indicate an intent to adopt an unlimited marital deduction.

3. Changes to current use valuation provision

The Act expands the current use valuation provision in several ways:

(1) The present $500,000 limit by which the fair market value of farms, and other business real property can be reduced for estate tax purposes is increased over three years to $750,000, as follows:

1981	$600,000
1982	700,000
1983 and thereafter	750,000.

(2) The required trade or business use during pre-death periods can be that of a member of the decedent's family as well as that of the decedent. This change is retroactive to January 1, 1977.

(3) The material participation requirement for retired and disabled decedents is measured before the beginning of the disability or retirement.

(4) "Active management" by a surviving spouse of a decedent whose estate was eligible for current use valuation with respect to property is treated as material participation in determining whether the spouse's estate qualifies for the provision.

(5) Replacement property acquired in a like-kind exchange within five years before death is not automatically ineligible for current use valuation.

(6) Replacement property acquired following an involuntary conversion occurring within five years before death is not automatically ineligible for current use valuation.

(7) The election to specially value property can be made on a late return as long as the return is the first return filed. As under present law, the election is irrevocable.

(8) Net share rentals can be used in the formula valuation method for farm real property when no cash rentals are available.

(9) Property transferred to a discretionary trust is eligible for current use valuation, provided all trust beneficiaries are qualified heirs. The change is retroactive to January 1, 1977.

(10) The definition of family member is expanded to include lineal descendants of the surviving spouse who are not descendants of the decedent.

(11) Family membership is redefined to include lineal descendants of an individual's parents rather than his grandparents.

(12) Property purchased from a decedent's estate by a qualified heir can be specially valued in certain circumstances. This change is retroactive to January 1, 1977.

(13) The recapture period is reduced to 10 years (from 15 years).

(14) A 2-year grace period immediately after the decedent's death is provided during which failure by a qualified heir to commence the qualified use does not trigger recapture. The change is retroactive to January 1, 1977.

(15) Active management by surviving spouses, minor and disabled heirs, and full-time students is treated as material participation.

(16) Like-kind exchanges of specially valued real property do not automatically result in imposition of a recapture tax. This change applies to exchanges occurring after December 31, 1981.

(17) The requirement of an election to avoid imposition of the recapture tax in the case of an involuntary conversion of specially valued property is repealed. This change applies to conversions occurring after December 31, 1981.

(18) If a recapture tax is imposed, an election can be made to step-up (to fair market value as of the decedent's death) the heir's income tax basis in specially valued property. The heir is required to pay interest on the amount of the recapture tax.

(19) Standing timber can be specially valued as an interest in the underlying real property. A recapture tax is imposed when such timber is severed or disposed of within 10 years of death.

4. Gifts made within 3 years of death

In general, the Act provides that section 2035(a) (which generally requires that gifts made by a decedent within 3 years of death be included in the decedent's gross estate at their value as of the date of death or alternate valuation date) does not apply to decedents dying after December 31, 1981. However, present law continues to apply to certain types of property covered by sections 2036, 2037, 2038, 2041, and 2042. In addition, all gifts made within 3 years of death are included for purposes of qualifying for current use valuation, deferred payment of estate tax, qualified redemptions of stock to pay estate tax, and estate tax liens.

5. Installment payment of estate tax attributable to closely held business

The Act combines the more liberal provisions of present law sections 6166 and 6166A, relating to the deferred payment of estate taxes attributable to interests in closely held businesses, into one provision. The new provision permits deferred payment if interests in closely held businesses exceed 35 percent of the adjusted gross estate. Conforming changes are made to section 303, which permits redemption of stock in a closely held business to pay estate taxes, funeral expenses, and administration expenses. The Act also provides that any remaining unpaid estate tax balance will not be accelerated upon the death of the decedent's heir or a subsequent transferee, provided the interests in closely held businesses passes to a member of the heir's family.

6. Disclaimers

The Act provides that a timely transfer of property to the person who would have received it had an effective disclaimer been made under the applicable local law is considered an effective disclaimer for purposes of Federal estate and gift taxes where the other Federal requirements of qualified disclaimers are met.

7. Basis of property received within 1 year of death

The Act provides that the basis of appreciated property acquired by gift within one year of death is not adjusted to its fair market value at date of the decedent's death (as is done under present law) if it is returned to the donor (or donor's spouse).

8. Certain charitable contributions

The Act provides that a charitable estate and gift tax deduction will be allowed for a transfer of a copyrightable work of art to a qualified charitable organization, whether or not the copyright itself is simultaneously transferred to the charitable organization.

9. Certain bequests, etc., to minor children

The provision of present law which allows deduction from a parent's gross estate of $5,000 for each year that an orphaned child is below age 21 is repealed.

10. Annual gift tax exclusion

Under the Act, the annual gift tax exclusion is increased from $3,000 to $10,000 per donee ($20,000 in the case of a married couple who elect to split gifts). In addition, an unlimited gift tax exclusion is provided for amounts paid directly to the service provider for the benefit of the donee for medical expenses and school tuition. A transition rule allows present law to continue to apply to existing trusts, which contain provisions referring to the maximum annual exclusion amount.

11. Annual filing of gift tax returns

Under the Act, gift tax returns are required to be filed only on an annual basis, rather than quarterly as is required in some cases under present law.

12. Generation-skipping transfer tax

The Tax Reform Act of 1976 imposed a tax on generation-skipping transfers. A transitional rule exempts from the tax generation-skipping trusts created by wills or revocable trusts in existence on June 11, 1976, if (1) such wills and trusts were not amended after that date to create or increase the amount of a generation-skipping transfer, and (2) the testator or trust grantor dies before January 1, 1982. Under the Act, the January 1, 1982, date contained in the present transitional rule is extended one additional year to January 1, 1983.

13. Effective dates

Except as indicated otherwise in the discussion of specific provisions, the changes to the estate tax are effective for estates of decedents dying after December 31, 1981, and the changes to the gift tax are effective for gifts made after December 31, 1981.

J. Tax Straddles

1. Gains or losses on straddles

In Revenue Ruling 77–185, the Internal Revenue Service denied deductions for losses on certain partial dispositions of straddles on the grounds that the transactions were incomplete, tax-motivated and not reflective of true economic position. The theory of this ruling is currently in litigation.

The Act marks all commodity futures contracts to market at year end and treats them as if 60 percent of the capital gains and losses on them were long-term and 40 percent were short-term. Net losses under the mark-to-market rule may be carried back three years against mark-to-market gains. Taxpayers may elect to mark their futures to market for the entire 1981 year as if 1982 rates were in effect. Tax due on gains rolled forward from prior years into 1981 may be paid in five annual installments with interest. The first installment payment is due with the taxpayer's 1981 taxes.

In the case of straddles involving property other than futures which are marked-to-market, the Act allows straddle losses only to the extent such losses exceed the unrealized gains on offsetting positions. Disallowed losses are deferred. The wash sale and short sale principles of present law are extended to straddles by regulation. The loss deferral rule applies to actively-traded personal property but not to such property as real estate, stock and short-term stock options. Hedging transactions are excepted from this provision. The provision applies to property acquired and positions established by the taxpayer after June 23, 1981.

2. Interest and carrying charges

Present law allows a current deduction for interest and carrying charges for purchasing or carrying commodity investments. The Act requires that such charges be added to the basis of the commodity if it is part of a straddle. Hedging transactions are excepted from the capitalization rule.

This rule applies to property acquired and positions established by the taxpayer after June 23, 1981.

3. Hedging exception

The Act excepts hedging transactions from the mark-to-market, loss deferral and capitalization rule. Syndicates are not entitled to the hedging exemption.

4. Characterization of Treasury bills

Under present law, gain and loss on certain governmental obligations (including Treasury bills) issued at discount and payable at a fixed maturity date less than one year from issue date are treated as ordinary income and loss. The Act treats such obligations as capital assets and the discount on these obligations as ordinary income.

5. Dealer identification of securities held for investment

Present law requires dealers to identify securities held as investments within 30 days of the date of acquisition. The Act requires identification of securities by the close of business on the date of acquisition. Securities acquired after the date of enactment and before January 1, 1982, must be identified by the close of business on the first day after the date of acquisition. Floor specialists are allowed seven business days to designate stock for which they are registered specialists.

6. Sale or exchange of capital assets

Under present law, for gain or loss to be capital gain or loss, it must result from the sale or exchange of a capital asset. The Act provides that taxable dispositions of capital assets which are commodity-related property are treated as sales or exchanges. This change applies to property acquired after June 23, 1981.

Investing in Gold and Diamonds

INVESTING IN GOLD

Gold has been one of the more widely promoted investment vehicles over the last several years. Prices have moved from about $140 per ounce in early 1977 to over $800 in early 1980. However, by mid-1981 prices declined to $460 an ounce. Because of such large fluctuations, the metal has stimulated a great deal of speculative interest among many investors.

Investment in gold can be made in a variety of ways:

Gold bullion (bars and wafers) This can be purchased through many stock brokers, bullion currency dealers, and some investment (mutual fund) companies. The purity of gold is indicated by the fineness. Pure gold has a fineness of 1.000 and corresponds to 24 karats.* Each bar is stamped with the fineness as determined by an assay, the refiner's number, a bar identification number and the weight. A bar fineness of .995 or better is acceptable.

Individuals who accept delivery of gold bars and who subsequently wish to resell must have the bar reassayed prior to sale because of the possibility of adulteration with cheaper metals. Because of the latter possibility, individuals should always buy from reputable dealers, and the bar should bear the stamp of well-recognized refiners or assayers. Individuals taking physical possession of the metal also have sales taxes, storage, and insurance costs.

The purchaser may arrange to have the dealer (or agent) retain physical possession of the bullion. In this case, evidence of ownership is provided by a *gold deposit certificate* (receipt) issued by the dealer. Since gold certificates are generally nonnegotiable or assignable, there is no loss if it is stolen. The gold deposit certificate method of buying bullion eliminates sales taxes, storage risks (though the dealer will charge a modest storage fee) and the need for assay on resale. It is probably the most convenient way of purchasing gold.

Gold bullion coins Bullion coins are issued in large number by several governments which guarantee their gold content. They have no numismatic value. The best known gold bullion coins are the South African Krugerand, Canadian Maple Leaf, Austrian 100 Corona and the Gold Mexican 50 peso. The first two coins have a pure gold content of one ounce. The Austrian Corona has a gold content of .9802 ounce and the Mexican peso 1.2057 ounces. The premium (cost above the gold value) varies from dealer to dealer. For those who do not want to take physical possession, deposit certificates are available for the coins.

Gold stocks The stocks of a number of Canadian and U.S. gold mining companies are traded on the New York (N), American (A) and Over-The-Counter (O) exchanges. Of course, with stocks, the investor is not just buying into gold, but also into the many special problems associated with running a company—production costs, quality of the ore, lifetime of the deposit, etc. However, many gold stocks pay dividends, whereas other gold investments do not pay any return during the holding period.

Some listed stocks are given below:

Agrico-Eagle Mines (O)
Campbell Red Lake Mines (N)
Dome Mines (N)
Giant Yellow Knife Mines (N)
Homestake Mining Company (N)

A publicly-held New York Stock Exchange closed-end gold fund is ASA Limited. Several mutual funds which invest in gold are given in the mutual fund section of the Almanac (page 282).

South African gold mines are traded on the Over-The-Counter Market by means of ADR (American Depository Receipt). ADR is a claim on foreign stocks (South African gold shares, in this case) held by the foreign branches of large U.S. banks. Holders of ADRs are entitled to dividends which, in the case of South African gold shares, may be substantial. The ADRs of these companies are listed in *The Wall Street Journal* under the Foreign Securities section, which follows the OTC quotations.

Some major South African gold mining companies are:

Blyvooruitzicht
Buffelsfontein
East Driefontein

---

* This "karats" is not to be confused with the "carats" that apply to diamonds.

Kloof
President Brand
President Steyn
Randfontein
West Dreifontein
Western Deep Levels
Western Holdings

Options on gold stocks Put and call options are available on Homestake Mining (Chicago Options Exchange) and on ASA Limited (American Options Exchange). These options may be used for leveraged speculation or for hedging existing gold holdings. Holders of call options gain if the gold shares increase, while holders of put options benefit if prices decline.

Options on gold bullion Put and call options on gold bullion are available from Mocatta Metals Corporation with offices in Chicago and New York, Dowdex Corporation of Chicago, Comark Metals Options and Monex of California, both of the latter with offices in Newport Beach, California, and Valeurs White Weld with options through First Boston Inc.

Typically, options are written on 100 ounces of gold, with maturities ranging from 3 to 9 months, though a number of other variations are available depending on the dealer. Some dealers do not always guarantee repurchase of options before maturity, hence it is wise to check this matter out prior to purchase.

Since options are paid in full, they are not subject to margin calls or forced liquidation as is the case with futures contracts. At this time, quotations on bullion options are not available in the daily press.

Gold futures contract Gold futures contracts are obligations to buy or sell 100 ounces of gold on or before a specified date at a specified price. Futures contracts must be exercised if held to maturity, while options contracts need not be exercised if held to maturity. Futures contracts are purchased on margin, and hence, are subject to margin call and possible forced liquidation. They are widely quoted in the financial press, and the market is highly organized.

As with options, futures contracts may be used for leveraged speculation or for hedging. Speculators will buy contracts if they anticipate a price increase or sell contracts in anticipation of a price decrease.

Gold futures are traded on the N.Y. Commodity Exchange, the International Monetary Market of the Chicago Mercantile Exchange, and other markets.

INVESTING IN DIAMONDS

Diamonds have appreciated on the average of about 12.6% over the ten-year period 1969–1979 (compared to a consumer price index of 6.1% during the same period of time). There have been periods (the recession of 1973–1974 and in 1981) when the price of investment quality diamonds slipped as much as 40%. A major factor stabilizing the market is DeBeers, a South African diamond company which handles as much as 80% of the world's diamonds. While the appreciation of diamonds has been impressive, potential buyers should be aware that prices are not quoted in the daily newspapers; therefore, selling the stones at a profit may be difficult. *The PreciouStones Newsletter* (P.O. Box 4649, Thousand Oaks, CA 91359, Telephone (213) 889–4367) is one of the few reliable sources of prices. Buyers should only deal with reputable firms, and the stones should be certified by an independent laboratory such as the Gemological Institute of America, International Gemological Institute and the European Gemological Laboratories. They maintain offices in New York and Los Angeles.

Diamonds are ranked in terms of the 4 C's—carat (one carat equals 1/142 ounces weight), color, clarity, and cut.

Carat For investment purposes the diamond should be more than .5 carat. However, diamonds of more than 2 carats may be difficult to sell.

Color There are six main categories, each with subdivisions:

D,E,F,—Colorless
G,H,I,J—Near colorless
K,L,M—Faint yellow
N,O,P,Q,R—Very light yellow
S,T,U,V,W,X,Y,Z—Light yellow
Fancy yellow stone

Color should be in the range from D to H. However, Fancy Yellow Stones often command very high prices because of their scarcity.

Clarity Although bubbles, lines, and specks (inclusions) are natural to diamonds, they may interfere with the passage of light through the diamond. With a 10X magnification, a professional appraiser can grade the diamond according to the ten clarity grades:

FL—Flawless
IF—Internally flawless
VVS-1, VVS-2—Very, very slight inclusions

VS-1, VS-2—Very slight inclusions
SI-1, SI-2—Slight inclusions
I-1, I-2, I-3—Imperfect

Investment grade stones should be in the range FL to VS-2.

Cut There are several types of cuts—oval, marquise, pear shaped, round brilliant and emerald. Round brilliant stones are preferred for invest-ment purposes. Proportions are important, and the preferred values are:

Depth % (total depth divided by girdle diameter): 57% to 63%.

Table (table diameter divided by girdle diameter): 57% to 66%.

Girdle thickness should be neither very thick nor very thin.

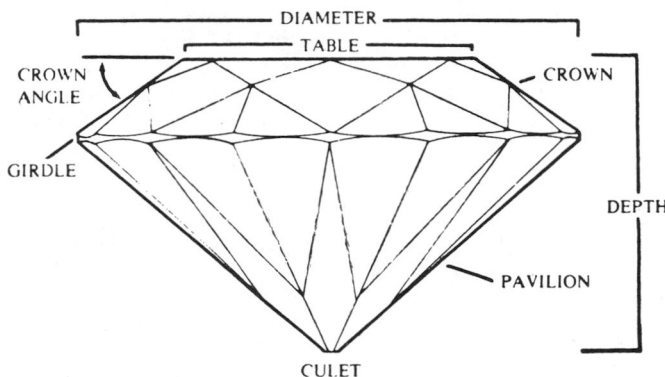

THE ROUND BRILLIANT DIAMOND

Investing in Real Estate

MEDIAN SALES PRICE OF EXISTING SINGLE-FAMILY HOMES IN THE UNITED STATES
FOR THE MONTH OF MAY 1975–1981

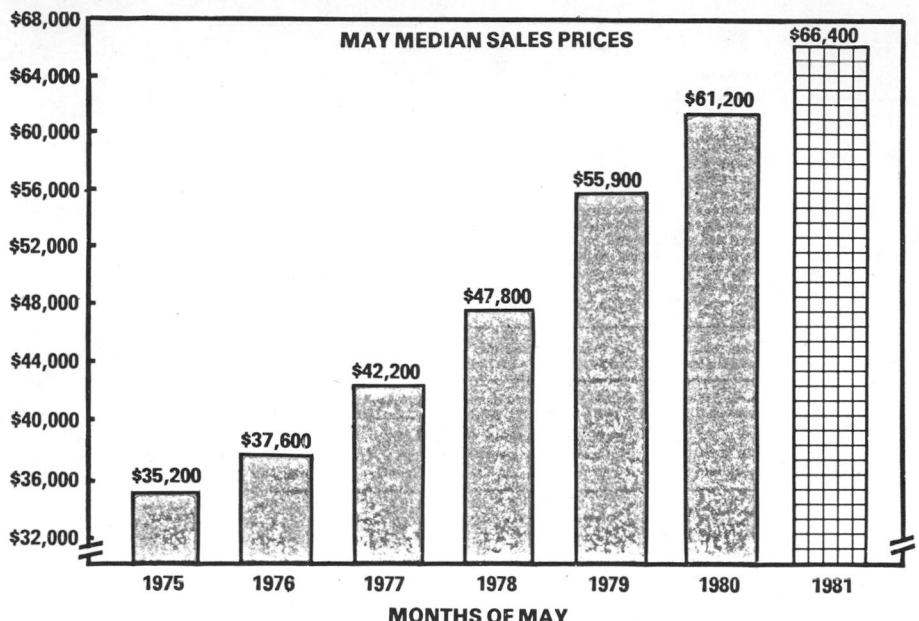

Source: National Association of Realtors, Economics & Research Division, 777 14th Street, N.W., Washington, D.C. 20005.

SALES PRICE OF EXISTING SINGLE-FAMILY HOMES FOR THE UNITED STATES AND EACH REGION (Not Seasonally Adjusted)

Year	United States Median	United States Average (Mean)	Northeast Median	Northeast Average (Mean)	North Central Median	North Central Average (Mean)	South Median	South Average (Mean)	West Median	West Average (Mean)
1968	$20,100	$22,300	$21,400	$24,200	$18,200	$19,900	$19,000	$22,000	$22,900	$25,200
1969	21,800	23,700	23,700	26,600	19,000	21,100	20,300	23,500	23,900	26,700
1970	23,000	25,700	25,200	28,400	20,100	22,600	22,200	25,300	24,300	27,400
1971	24,800	28,000	27,100	30,600	22,100	24,300	24,300	27,800	26,500	29,700
1972	26,700	30,100	29,800	33,600	23,900	25,700	26,400	30,100	28,400	32,300
1973	28,900	32,900	32,800	36,800	25,300	28,100	29,000	33,200	31,000	35,400
1974	32,000	35,800	35,800	39,700	27,700	30,600	32,300	36,200	34,800	39,000
1975	35,300	39,000	39,300	43,600	30,100	33,100	34,800	38,800	39,600	44,100
1976	38,100	42,200	41,800	45,900	32,900	35,900	36,500	40,900	46,100	50,300
1977	42,900	47,900	44,400	49,100	36,700	40,200	39,800	45,000	57,300	63,200
1978	48,700	55,500	47,900	55,200	42,200	45,700	45,100	51,300	66,700	75,500
1979	55,700	64,200	53,600	63,300	47,800	51,600	51,300	59,000	77,400	89,400
1980	62,200	72,800	60,800	71,700	51,900	56,300	58,300	67,700	89,300	104,700
1980										
Jan	$57,900	$68,200	$54,700	$65,300	$48,500	$52,600	$53,900	$62,700	$85,200	$100,500
Feb	59,000	69,400	55,400	66,600	49,900	53,500	54,600	63,100	88,800	103,300
Mar	59,500	69,400	58,400	68,500	50,500	54,200	54,700	63,300	86,200	100,100
Apr	60,400	70,600	60,300	70,300	51,200	55,300	57,100	66,300	83,800	98,300
May	61,200	71,200	58,000	67,800	51,400	55,900	57,900	66,600	87,000	102,600
Jun	63,400	74,100	61,000	71,900	52,700	56,700	59,900	69,300	91,800	107,600
Jul	64,100	75,700	61,700	72,900	53,300	58,000	60,200	69,200	96,300	113,100
Aug	64,900	76,200	65,200	76,600	53,700	58,000	61,400	71,200	93,600	108,400
Sep	64,200	75,500	64,600	76,400	53,400	57,600	60,600	71,000	91,600	106,700
Oct	62,700	73,400	60,000	71,000	52,400	56,800	59,200	68,900	90,200	105,300
Nov	64,300	74,900	63,600	74,100	53,600	58,100	60,700	70,400	90,500	105,300
Dec	63,000	74,000	62,400	74,800	51,500	56,700	59,300	69,200	89,300	104,500
1981										
Jan	$64,500	$76,100	$62,400	$74,400	$53,700	$58,100	$60,600	$72,300	$93,000	$108,100
Feb	64,100	75,700	58,500	69,800	53,100	57,400	61,500	71,900	96,000	111,400
Mar	64,400	76,200	61,900	73,900	52,100	56,300	61,200	71,800	96,800	112,300
Apr r	65,300	77,300	62,700	73,700	53,600	58,300	62,700	73,300	97,100	112,200
May p	66,400	78,600	62,100	75,200	56,600	61,300	63,200	73,900	95,900	112,200

r Revised
p Preliminary

Source: National Association of Realtors, Economics and Research Division, 777 14th Street, N.W., Washington, D.C. 20005.

MEDIAN SALES PRICE OF EXISTING SINGLE-FAMILY HOMES FOR THE UNITED STATES BY NUMBER OF BEDROOMS

Number of Bedrooms	May 1977	May 1978	May 1979	May 1980	May$_p$ 1981
2 Bedrooms or less	$30,800	$35,000	$41,400	$45,500	$49,900
3 Bedrooms	$40,600	$46,700	$54,500	$59,900	$65,200
4 Bedrooms or more	$59,700	$66,300	$78,300	$87,800	$94,500
All Homes	$42,200	$47,800	$55,900	$61,200	$66,400

p Preliminary

Source: National Association of Realtors, Economics and Research Division, 777 14th Street, N.W., Washington, D.C., 20005.

MEDIAN AND AVERAGE SALES PRICE OF NEW HOMES BY REGION (In dollars. Includes value of improved lot)

Month and year	Median sales price					Average sales price				
	United States	North-east	North Central	South	West	United States	North-east	North Central	South	West
1979	62,900	65,500	63,900	57,300	69,600	71,800	71,500	73,000	63,800	82,000
1980	64,500	69,300	63,300	59,700	72,300	76,300	79,300	74,300	69,200	89,300
1980 - April	62,800	69,800	55,400	59,300	74,600	74,100	86,000	72,800	65,500	88,400
November	67,100	67,700	65,600	64,300	71,300	82,200	82,400	79,000	76,700	94,200
December	67,200	71,400	63,900	62,300	81,800	81,500	82,900	72,700	73,400	103,100
1981 - January[r]	67,900	71,900	63,600	65,000	71,500	80,200	85,500	89,700	72,000	90,300
February[r]	65,900	67,400	69,200	59,800	77,400	79,600	79,100	87,200	69,800	94,800
March[r]	67,300	76,300	70,800	62,400	76,400	80,800	90,500	83,000	73,100	94,700
APRIL[p]	69,300	91,100	73,300	60,800	74,500	84,000	94,700	90,700	76,100	91,400
Relative standard error of monthly estimates (percents).........	3	8	8	5	3	(NA)	(NA)	(NA)	(NA)	(NA)

[p]Preliminary   [r]Revised   (NA) Not available   (X) Not applicable

[1]Ratio of houses for sale to houses sold. Seasonally adjusted ratio derived from unadjusted ratio.
[2]Relative standard errors shown are averages for the period September 1980 through February 1981.

Source: National Association of Realtors, Economics and Research Division, 777 14th Street, N.W., Washington, D.C., 20005.

FARM REAL ESTATE VALUES: AVERAGE VALUE PER ACRE OF LAND AND BUILDINGS, BY STATE, GROUPED BY FARM PRODUCTION REGION, MARCH 1, 1950, 60, 70, 75, AND FEB. 1, 1977–81[1]

State	1950	1960	1970	1975	1977	1978	1979	1980	1981[2]
					Dollars				
Northeast									
Maine	54	84	161	341	420	475	536	580	614
New Hampshire	73	104	239	564	705	802	912	986	1,045
Vermont	56	81	224	462	543	600	663	716	758
Massachusetts	190	314	565	961	1,156	1,289	1,440	1,554	1,647
Rhode Island	232	379	734	1,500	1,843	2,080	2,349	2,536	2,687
Connecticut	248	446	921	1,525	1,809	2,009	2,231	2,409	2,553
New York	92	145	273	510	592	607	669	709	752
New Jersey	293	528	1,092	1,807	2,211	2,384	2,705	2,919	2,977
Pennsylvania	107	188	373	734	992	1,112	1,273	1,401	1,443
Delaware	114	243	499	971	1,250	1,351	1,500	1,755	1,931
Maryland	125	290	640	1,060	1,363	1,594	1,827	2,284	2,604
Lake States									
Michigan	99	194	326	553	776	874	975	1,113	1,268
Wisconsin	89	133	232	434	600	721	857	986	1,114
Minnesota	84	155	226	429	671	761	902	1,064	1,235
Corn Belt									
Ohio	136	248	399	706	1,110	1,243	1,484	1,676	1,727
Indiana	137	264	406	720	1,192	1,361	1,589	1,826	1,973
Illinois	174	316	490	846	1,457	1,626	1,857	2,004	2,125
Iowa	161	257	392	719	1,256	1,326	1,548	1,812	1,939
Missouri	64	115	224	396	546	636	726	878	939
Northern Plains									
North Dakota	29	53	94	195	275	301	348	400	424
South Dakota	31	51	84	145	194	227	257	292	310
Nebraska	58	89	154	282	425	419	525	598	658
Kansas	66	101	159	296	402	421	500	569	587

Appalachian									
Virginia	82	140	286	558	701	774	931	1,015	1,087
West Virginia	59	75	136	300	442	478	592	651	697
North Carolina	99	186	333	590	762	835	1,051	1,135	1,237
Kentucky	81	137	253	427	619	714	862	956	995
Tennessee	77	132	268	467	618	735	863	957	1,024
Southeast									
South Carolina	69	137	261	467	613	675	774	835	885
Georgia	43	99	234	474	577	679	779	872	915
Florida	57	217	355	685	859	977	1,143	1,350	1,513
Alabama	49	91	200	364	479	530	637	790	932
Delta States									
Mississippi	55	107	234	379	462	568	682	826	1,049
Arkansas	60	113	260	419	550	619	769	922	1,061
Louisiana	82	173	321	512	668	822	1,002	1,293	1,526
Southern Plains									
Oklahoma	51	86	173	302	395	451	513	605	666
Texas	46	85	148	243	299	336	384	445	490
Mountain									
Montana	17	35	60	112	156	174	196	229	238
Idaho	70	112	177	339	454	514	588	672	719
Wyoming	13	22	41	80	109	119	140	150	160
Colorado	32	54	95	188	253	268	322	377	411
New Mexico	15	24	42	78	107	122	143	160	171
Arizona	15	48	70	111	147	170	202	226	242
Utah	43	60	92	188	288	337	399	447	478
Nevada	19	31	53	85	119	154	192	215	230
Pacific									
Washington	85	133	224	330	533	598	691	726	857
Oregon	60	88	150	250	344	417	506	556	606
California	154	360	479	653	754	903	1,178	1,412	1,723
48 States	65	117	196	340	475	533	628	720	790

¹Figures for 1977-80 are revisions of previously published estimates. Revisions are based on 1978 Census of Agriculture data.

Source: *Farm Real Estate Developments*, Economics and Statistics Service, U.S. Department of Agriculture.

CONVENTIONAL LOANS ON NEW HOMES

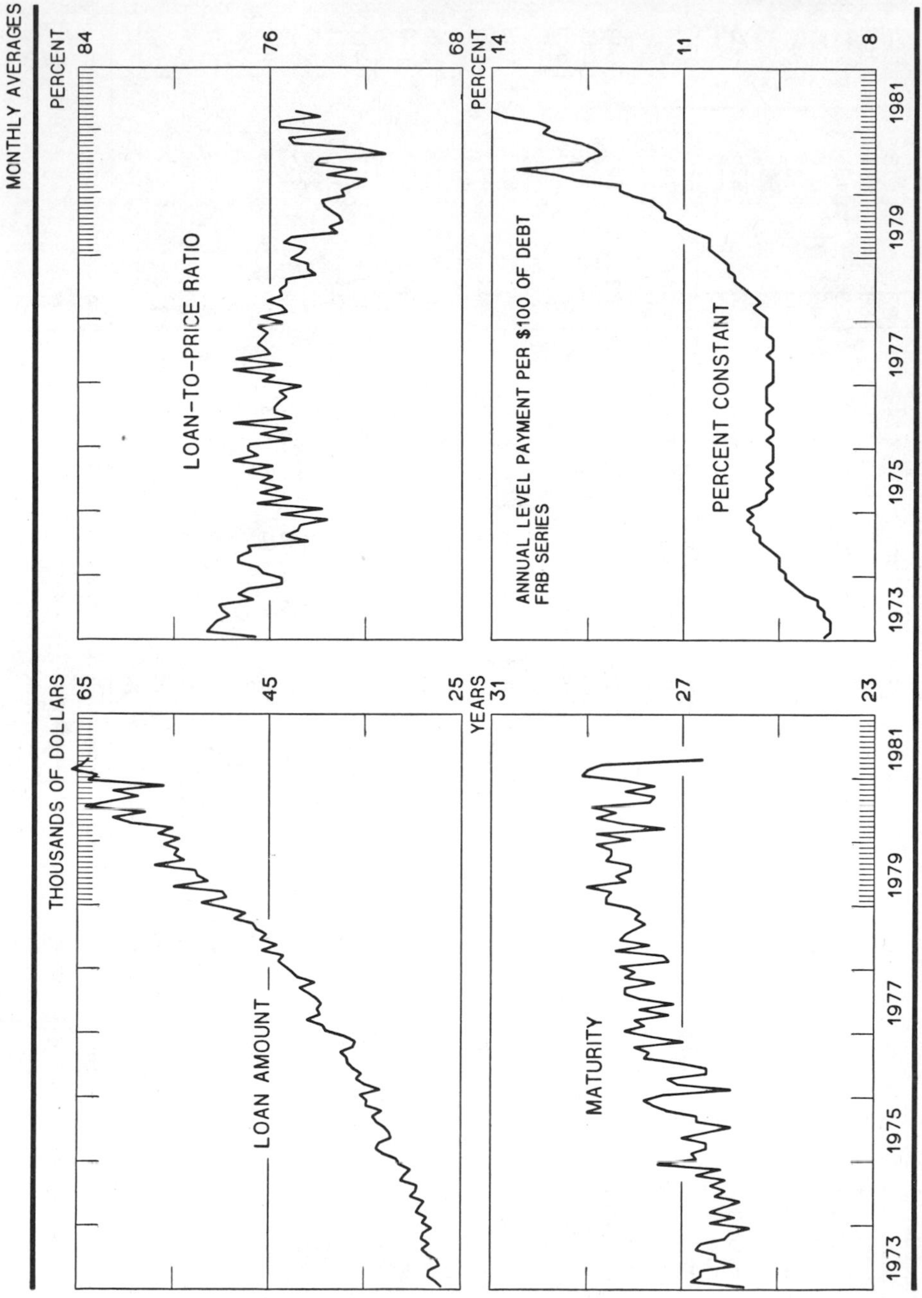

MONTHLY AVERAGES

PERCENT

84

76

68

LOAN-TO-PRICE RATIO

PERCENT

14

11

8

ANNUAL LEVEL PAYMENT PER $100 OF DEBT
FRB SERIES

PERCENT CONSTANT

1973 1975 1977 1979 1981

THOUSANDS OF DOLLARS

65

45

25

LOAN AMOUNT

YEARS

31

27

23

MATURITY

1973 1975 1977 1979 1981

Source: *Federal Reserve Chart Book*, Board of Governors of the Federal Reserve System.

REAL ESTATE INVESTMENT TRUSTS

WHAT IS A REAL ESTATE INVESTMENT TRUST?

In their most basic form, real estate investment trusts (REITs) are financial intermediaries that specialize in real estate investment by channeling funds from financial markets to the real estate sector of the economy. They do this by selling shares and debt instruments to the public and by borrowing from banks and other financial institutions to obtain funds for investment in income-producing properties and mortgages.

A major distinguishing feature between REITs and other real estate-oriented businesses is the conduit tax treatment of their earnings. Basically, as long as a REIT concentrates most of its investments in real estate-related assets and passes through most of its earnings to shareholders, a REIT is not taxed at the trust (corporate) level.

This conduit tax treatment is essentially the same as that permitted the mutual funds which invest in common stock, bonds and money market instruments. The purpose of this tax concession is to give the general investing public access to a professionally-managed portfolio of quality real estate investments, an opportunity that would otherwise be available only to wealthier individuals and institutions.

THE REIT INDUSTRY TODAY

While REITs are highly diverse in terms of size, investment strategy, earnings and geographic location, there are a number of common threads that bind them together as an industry. For one, since REITs must have at least 75% of their assets in real estate-related investments, the industry effectively participates in only one sector of the economy. However, within this sector, REITS are permitted wide latitude in their choice of investments.

In terms of broad distinctions between trusts, REITs may choose to hold their assets in the form of mortgages, in ownership interests in income-producing property, or in some combination of the two. But within each of these broad categories, there are still a wide variety of diverse investment strategies to choose from. For example, a mortgage-oriented trust may specialize in short-term construction and devel-

opment loans, in long-term first mortgages, in second, junior and wrap-around loans, in some form of interim financing, or in a combination of any of the above. Furthermore, it may have a geographic preference for its lending.

If its preference is property ownership, in which case it is referred to as an "equity" REIT, a trust might concentrate its investments in a single property type such as office buildings, shopping centers, apartments, hotels or warehouses. Within this equity category, the trust may prefer alternative forms of ownership such as land purchase-leasebacks or joint ventures.

Although the industry exhibits wide diversity in investment preferences, the twenty year history of REITs is characterized by a number of general trends in asset concentration. Beginning in 1961, when Congress passed the legislation necessary to establish the industry, the early REITs were primarily owners of income producing real estate. Through most of the 1960's, this property orientation was the main characteristic of the industry. At the end of 1968, slightly more than half of the industry's assets were in owned properties. But this was beginning to change.

In the mid-1960s, the successful performance of a couple of trusts that specialized in short-term mortgage lending convinced investors and entrepreneurs that there were attractive profit opportunities for REITs in mortgage lending. These opportunities were expanded in the late 1960's and early 1970's when the construction market began a five year expansion that created a tremendous demand for mortgage money to finance the building boom. New mortgage-oriented REITs were formed while many existing ones shifted their investment strategies to lending. By 1973, after a quadrupling of industry assets, owned properties constituted only 16% of the industry's assets while mortgages accounted for most of the rest.

The collapse of the real estate market beginning in 1974 resulted in substantial losses to many mortgage lenders and several REITs were pushed to the brink of insolvency as a result of massive loan defaults. As a consequence of this experience, as well as the growing perception of the unique value of property ownership in an inflationary environment, the REIT industry gradually shifted its emphasis back to ownership of income properties. By early 1980, 58% of industry assets were in owned properties, while total mortgage holdings had fallen to less than 40%.

Even though the industry's investment preferences have shifted back to ownership, there still remain a number of trusts that have continued to specialize in mortgage lending and have been very successful at it. Of significance, one newly-formed REIT whose investments are concentrated in second mortgages raised $100 million in equity capital in 1979 and 1980.

Source: National Association of Real Estate Investment Trusts, 1101 Seventeenth Street, N.W., Washington, D.C., 20036.

The shift to ownership coincided with a period of marked improvement in the commercial real estate market. Having learned their lessons from the period of speculative overbuilding in the early 1970's, virtually all participants in the real estate market, from the developers to the lenders, became cautious and careful in their approach to new investments, insisting on a number of checks and high standards of management that would lead to more successful development. Partly as a result of this changed attitude, new construction advanced at only modest rates during the latter part of the decade, and by the end of 1979 and the beginning of 1980, construction had yet to reach the peak levels of activity recorded in the years 1971 to 1973.

Because this moderation allowed the demand for commercial space to grow faster than its supply, occupancy rates for all types of income producing projects increased with each passing year. With the increase in occupancy rates and the growing shortage of space came substantially higher rents and, hence, higher asset valuations and better earnings for the owners of these properties. As an indication of the strength of the present market, non-residential construction is expected to fall only 5% during 1980. This is in sharp contrast to the much greater declines that are being experienced by single-family construction and the production of other durable goods such as autos.

With their assets now concentrated in this sector of the market, REIT earnings have risen steadily since 1976. Total industry dividend distributions in 1979 were 40% greater than those of 1976, and preliminary data for 1980 suggests that the upward trend will continue. More impressive is the fact that these earnings gains have taken place over a period during which the industry's assets declined by about $5 billion, or nearly one-third of their 1976 total.

As the economy goes through the present period of stress and decline, the REIT industry finds itself in better financial condition than it has been in a decade. For one, the bulk of its assets are in income producing properties which are, to a large extent, fully leased. Barring a catastrophic recession, the near-term earnings of these projects are relatively secure. Second, the REIT balance sheet is the strongest it has been since the early 1970's. Short-term borrowing plus commercial paper comprise the lowest percentage of assets since 1971, while cash and cash equivalents are at their highest percentage of assets since 1970. In short, the REIT industry enters this downturn with the strongest balance sheet in nearly a decade.

Also of significance is that today's REIT loans to developers are of a much higher quality than those of the early 1970's. The REITs that are still active in construction lending are the successful survivors of the last recession. They are the lenders who had few problems then and who have since reinforced their careful approach to lending in light of earlier experience. Moreover, since the demand for commercial real estate is still strong because of the limited supply of space, projects now underway should have little or no problems in leasing up and securing long-term financing.

These improvements in both REIT performance and real estate markets in general have not gone unnoticed by stock market investors. Since the middle of 1976, NAREIT's share price index of 160 REITs increased by 89%. At one point during 1979, the index had risen a remarkable 38% over a seven month period. Part of these gains, unfortunately, were wiped out by the severe monetary policies adopted by the Federal Reserve System in Autumn of 1979 and Spring of 1980 as investors feared a repeat of the events of the mid-1970s. But following the restoration of stability, the index once again resumed its upward progress.

Although REIT share prices have been rising steadily over the past several years, the corresponding increases in dividends over the same period have kept their yields at attractive levels. Since the middle of 1978, the shares of all qualified REITs have collectively yielded more than 8% annually and, at times, about a third of these trusts have offered investors yields in excess of 10%.

SUMMARY BALANCE SHEET AND INCOME STATEMENT DATA FOR REITS[1]

Rankings			Report	millions		% Long-term	% Other	% Prop.
TA	MV	Company	Date	Assets	R.E. Investment	First Mtgs.	Mtgs.	Owned
83	73	ALAMAND	1/80	$ 38.5	$ 40.7	18%	21%	61%
75	55	AMER CENT (ACT/N)	* 6/80	$ 44.4	$ 48.0	18%	21%	61%
55	28	AMER EQ (AEQTS)	* 6/80	$ 56.3	$ 50.7	0%	27%	73%
119	150	AMER FIDELITY	12/79	$ 25.0	$ 24.0	0%	12%	88%
129	139	AMER FLETCH (AFMIS)	4/80	$ 20.5	$ 24.1	0%	52%	48%
203	NA	AMER REAL EST INV	4/77	$ 1.9	$ 1.9	0%	0%	100%
92	91	AMER REALTY (ARB)	3/80	$ 34.9	$ 34.1	2%	16%	82%
208	NA	ANACONDA REIT	9/73	$ 1.7	NA	NA	NA	NA
135	86	ANRET INC (ARET)	2/80	$ 17.3	$ 21.0	18%	53%	30%
113	133	API TRUST (APITS)	* 3/80	$ 27.6	$ 25.9	14%	51%	35%
107	152	ASSOCIATED MTG	* 6/80	$ 29.1	$ 37.7	13%	30%	57%
210	155	B F REALTY INV	8/79	$ 1.1	$ 1.1	0%	0%	100%
17	10	BANKAMER (BRLTS)	4/80	$170.6	$170.2	14%	41%	45%
191	NA	BAPTIST MTG TRUST	12/77	$ 3.4	$ 3.3	73%	27%	0%
20	50	BAY FINAN (BAY/N)	2/80	$153.8	$154.6	3%	25%	72%
98	77	BAYSWATER (BRITS)	4/80	$ 32.3	$ 25.3	0%	67%	33%
216	NA	BELLE REIT	2/78	$ 0.4	$ 0.2	0%	0%	100%
140	96	BRADLEY REAL EST	* 5/80	$ 16.2	$ 15.5	5%	3%	92%
39	NA	BROOKS HARVEY	7/78	$ 69.4	$ 62.2	0%	25%	75%
161	149	BRT RLTY (BRT/A)	5/80	$ 10.5	$ 13.5	24%	43%	33%
64	127	BT MTG INV (BTM/N)	3/80	$ 50.0	$ 59.1	3%	50%	47%
41	100	BUILDS INV (BULDS)	* 3/80	$ 65.4	$ 63.6	9%	9%	82%
73	35	C I MORTGAGE (CI)	* 4/80	$ 44.8	$ 47.7	0%	30%	70%
198	NA	CAL-AMERICAN	12/78	$ 2.2	$ 2.0	0%	0%	100%
180	NA	CALIF REAL EST TR	9/79	$ 5.9	$ 5.2	0%	0%	100%
123	NA	CALIF REIT	12/79	$ 22.4	$ 17.3	0%	8%	92%
79	76	CAMERON BRN (CB/N)	* 6/80	$ 43.0	$ 44.2	6%	25%	69%
217	NA	CAPITOL INV TR	12/78	$ 0.3	$ 0.2	0%	0%	100%
152	90	CENTR MTG (CMRTS)	* 6/80	$ 12.3	$ 12.6	6%	61%	33%
151	NA	CENTURY REALTY	12/79	$ 12.5	$ 9.7	0%	4%	96%
166	NA	CHICAGO DOCK	4/77	$ 9.7	NA	NA	NA	NA
61	NA	CHURCH LOANS	* 3/80	$ 51.4	$ 46.0	95%	5%	0%
174	131	CIT GROWTH (CITGS)	4/80	$ 7.5	$ 5.9	2%	58%	41%
170	122	CITINATIONAL DEV	* 3/80	$ 8.5	$ 8.7	0%	14%	86%
40	156	CITIZENS MTG (CZM)	* 3/80	$ 67.7	$ 63.1	22%	20%	58%
38	43	CLEVETRUST (CTRIS)	3/80	$ 70.6	$ 74.8	7%	14%	78%
34	92	CMT INV (CMTIS)	3/80	$ 77.5	$ 61.8	2%	47%	50%
125	NA	COMMONWEALTH EQTY	* 3/80	$ 21.2	$ 19.0	12%	0%	88%
132	67	COMM RLTY (CRTYZ)	* 5/80	$ 19.8	$ 18.4	0%	0%	100%
93	57	COMPASS INV (CMPS)	3/80	$ 34.6	$ 34.5	1%	32%	67%
6	1	CONN GENL (CGM/N)	* 6/80	$332.3	$320.2	39%	8%	53%
91	27	CONS CP INC (CCITS)	* 3/80	$ 35.1	$ 21.8	0%	100%	0%
21	12	CONS CP RTY (CCPLS)	* 5/80	$133.1	$124.6	0%	17%	83%
1	82	CONT MTG (CMI)	4/79	$497.1	$480.3	10%	43%	46%
163	NA	CORONDOLET	12/75	$ 10.2	$ 10.0	0%	0%	100%
185	NA	CRODDY MORTGAGE	* 3/80	$ 4.1	$ 4.0	0%	72%	28%
197	NA	CUMBERLAND EQ	12/76	$ 2.3	$ 2.6	0%	0%	100%
118	62	DEL-VAL FINANCIAL	* 6/80	$ 25.8	$ 27.3	39%	56%	5%
63	30	DENVER REI (DENVS)	* 6/80	$ 51.0	$ 49.9	0%	7%	93%
190	NA	DERAND REIT	* 1/80	$ 3.5	$ 3.5	0%	0%	100%
23	37	DIVERS MTG (DMG/N)	3/80	$113.4	$135.2	9%	56%	35%
105	97	DOMINION MG (DMRT)	2/80	$ 29.4	$ 29.0	5%	25%	70%
116	63	EASTOV CRP (EASTS)	* 6/80	$ 26.5	$ 17.6	1%	51%	48%
4	6	EQUIT LIFE (EQ/N)	4/80	$379.0	$373.6	32%	53%	16%
77	36	FED'L RLTY (FRT/A)	* 6/80	$ 43.7	$ 42.0	0%	0%	100%
198	NA	FEDERAL UNION	6/78	$ 2.2	$ 2.1	0%	100%	0%
86	103	FGI INV (FGI/A)	* 5/80	$ 37.3	$ 35.6	12%	1%	87%
185	NA	FINANCIAL FLA	6/75	$ 4.1	$ 3.7	0%	100%	0%
96	58	FLA GULF (FGLFS)	4/80	$ 32.8	$ 31.0	0%	0%	100%
115	106	FLATLEY (FLTLU)	3/80	$ 26.6	$ 25.0	0%	5%	95%

| Rankings | | | Report | millions | | % Long-term | % Other | % Prop. |
TA	MV	Company	Date	Assets	R.E. Investment	First Mtgs.	Mtgs.	Owned
179	NA	FLATO REALTY	6/79	$ 6.0	$ 5.6	0%	0%	100%
206	NA	FOUNDERS REIT	2/78	$ 1.8	$ 1.0	0%	0%	100%
89	41	FRANKLIN RL (FR/A)	3/80	$ 35.7	$ 29.1	0%	19%	81%
57	78	FRASER MTG (FRASS)	* 5/80	$ 54.1	$ 47.7	28%	69%	3%
114	65	FST CAROL (FCARS)	* 6/80	$ 27.0	$ 26.7	12%	43%	44%
97	54	FST CONT (FCRES)	5/80	$ 32.6	$ 31.6	0%	94%	6%
87	126	FST DENVER (FDENS)	3/80	$ 36.1	$ 40.9	20%	44%	36%
19	53	FST MTG IN (FMTGS)	4/80	$162.4	$168.8	24%	37%	40%
47	108	FST NEWP (FNRIS)	4/80	$ 61.6	$ 73.2	27%	21%	52%
45	128	FST PENN (FPM/N)	4/80	$ 62.0	$ 73.4	1%	23%	76%
168	117	FST REIT OF NJ	* 4/80	$ 9.3	$ 8.3	0%	0%	100%
9	3	FST UNION (FUR/N)	* 6/80	$239.1	$229.8	0%	5%	95%
99	NA	FST WSTN INCOME	* 3/80	$ 32.2	$ 25.8	0%	0%	100%
42	49	FST WIS (FWMTS)	3/80	$ 64.2	$ 67.9	2%	5%	92%
208	NA	GALL, R A REALTY	12/79	$ 1.7	$ 1.3	0%	23%	77%
3	2	GEN'L GRTH (GGP/N)	3/80	$445.8	$346.7	0%	0%	100%
51	NA	GENL RE SH (GREL)	* 6/80	$ 58.4	$ 57.5	3%	13%	84%
177	141	GLOBAL DEVEL	* 3/80	$ 6.3	$ 4.6	0%	0%	100%
65	109	GMR PROPS (GMR/N)	* 5/80	$ 48.7	$ 58.1	43%	19%	38%
80	56	GOULD INV (GTR/A)	9/79	$ 42.9	$ 40.4	0%	14%	86%
15	33	GREAT AM MGMT&INV	4/80	$200.2	$219.0	0%	29%	71%
184	NA	GREAT LAKES REIT	12/76	$ 4.6	$ 4.5	0%	0%	100%
213	NA	GREAT WESTERN	2/80	$ 0.5	$ 0.5	0%	100%	0%
143	NA	GREATER WSTN REIT	10/76	$ 14.9	$ 14.2	0%	0%	100%
105	68	GREIT RLY (GRT/A)	* 4/80	$ 29.4	$ 25.6	0%	16%	84%
30	79	GROWTH RLY (GRW/N)	3/80	$ 84.8	$ 86.5	0%	39%	61%
12	145	GUARDIAN MTG INV	11/79	$218.0	$170.4	43%	8%	50%
68	94	HAMILTON (HAMTS)	3/80	$ 47.7	$ 56.3	14%	66%	20%
120	116	HANOVER SQ(HSQ/A)	5/80	$ 23.6	$ 23.9	45%	38%	16%
81	71	HEALTH CARE (HCFDS)	* 6/80	$ 42.4	$ 40.8	0%	20%	80%
85	111	HEITMAN (HTM/A)	3/80	$ 37.5	$ 45.1	27%	42%	31%
213	NA	HELIX REIT	12/77	$ 0.5	$ 0.4	0%	0%	100%
180	81	HIBBARD SPENCER	3/80	$ 5.9	$ 4.5	0%	0%	100%
51	125	HOMAC-BARNES (HOMC)	* 6/80	$ 58.4	$ 57.5	3%	13%	84%
48	60	HOSPITAL (HMG/A)	3/80	$ 60.4	$ 56.2	21%	8%	70%
33	21	HOTEL INV (HOT/A)	* 5/80	$ 80.6	$ 78.4	42%	4%	55%
26	11	HUBBARD RE (HRE/N)	4/80	$105.4	$ 95.5	0%	2%	98%
50	14	ICM REALTY (ICM/A)	5/80	$ 58.8	$ 63.6	0%	33%	67%
169	120	IND-FLA	3/80	$ 8.8	$ 7.8	0%	3%	97%
133	70	INDEPENDENCE MTG	3/80	$ 19.0	$ 16.9	0%	2%	98%
111	124	INDIANA FIN (IFII)	3/80	$ 28.1	$ 28.5	36%	36%	28%
70	95	INST INV (INV/N)	4/80	$ 46.0	$ 47.3	1%	12%	86%
117	52	INT INC PROP (IIPI)	* 6/80	$ 26.4	$ 25.3	0%	0%	100%
146	NA	INV REAL EST	4/79	$ 14.4	$ 14.0	40%	0%	60%
155	NA	INV REIT 1	12/74	$ 11.8	$ 16.2	1%	52%	47%
141	NA	INV REIT 2	12/74	$ 15.0	$ 15.1	0%	29%	71%
46	34	INT PROP (INTPR/A)	2/80	$ 61.9	$ 50.9	2%	28%	71%
139	83	JMB REALTY (JMBRU)	* 5/80	$ 16.5	$ 16.4	0%	48%	52%
25	4	KENILWORTH (KRT/N)	* 5/80	$110.0	$ 83.5	5%	4%	91%
159	146	KENTUCKY P (KYPTS)	5/80	$ 10.8	$ 11.7	4%	7%	89%
203	NA	LASALLE ST REIT	1/78	$ 1.9	$ 1.8	32%	0%	68%
144	137	LINCOLN	3/80	$ 14.6	$ 14.0	13%	42%	45%
5	8	LOMAS NET (LOM/N)	3/80	$351.6	$340.3	4%	85%	11%
54	51	M & T MTG (MTMI)	5/80	$ 56.7	$ 56.6	13%	87%	0%
172	129	MADISON REIF	*12/79	$ 8.3	$ 8.0	0%	44%	56%
154	123	MD REALTY (MDRTS)	5/80	$ 12.1	$ 12.9	19%	27%	54%
16	13	MASSMUT'L (MML/N)	4/80	$177.6	$175.3	83%	11%	5%
188	NA	MCCORMICK MTG	* 6/80	$ 3.7	$ 3.7	5%	70%	24%
112	NA	MCKEE INCOME RLTY	* 6/80	$ 27.7	$ 25.8	0%	0%	100%
193	NA	MEDINA COUNTY PROP	*12/79	$ 2.7	$ 2.7	0%	0%	100%

Rankings			Report	millions		% Long-term	% Other	% Prop.
TA	MV	Company	Date	Assets	R.E. Investment	First Mtgs.	Mtgs.	Owned
217	NA	MET ATLANTA	7/70	$ 0.3	$ 0.3	0%	0%	0%
147	121	METROPLEX RLTY	* 3/80	$ 13.8	$ 16.1	14%	17%	70%
203	NA	MID-ATLANTIC REIT	* 2/80	$ 1.9	-$ 2.0	0%	57%	43%
164	107	MIDLAND (MMT/N)	3/80	$ 10.1	$ 11.8	30%	25%	45%
212	NA	MIDWESTERN RET	* 6/80	$ 0.6	$ 0.4	0%	0%	100%
130	80	MILLER, H S (HSMTS)	5/80	$ 20.3	$ 20.1	7%	12%	80%
121	87	MISSION (MIT/A)	* 5/80	$ 23.2	$ 23.9	6%	21%	73%
192	NA	MISSOURI INDUSTRIA	3/78	$ 3.1	$ 3.0	0%	3%	97%
173	153	MONETARY R (MRTRS)	3/80	$ 7.7	$ 8.0	0%	13%	87%
178	151	MONMOUTH REIT	* 3/80	$ 6.2	$ 6.2	0%	71%	29%
14	7	MONY MTG (MYM/N)	* 5/80	$207.9	$201.8	45%	42%	13%
194	NA	MTG BANCTRUST	6/80	$ 2.6	$ 2.2	0%	100%	0%
65	32	MTG GROWTH (MTG/A)	5/80	$ 48.7	$ 41.0	0%	27%	73%
109	113	MTG I WASH (MINVS)	* 3/80	$ 28.3	$ 28.3	19%	13%	68%
44	26	MTG TR AMER (MT/N)	* 5/80	$ 62.3	$ 66.4	17%	56%	28%
156	143	MURRAY MTG (MMTGS)	* 6/80	$ 11.6	$ 11.3	0%	83%	17%
128	105	MUTUAL REIT	12/79	$ 20.7	$ 19.3	0%	21%	79%
22	44	NAMI (NAM/N)	3/80	$125.8	$125.2	11%	7%	83%
95	59	NAT'NWIDE (NRELS)	3/80	$ 32.9	$ 27.9	43%	9%	49%
144	NA	NATIONAL MTG FUND	2/80	$ 14.6	$ 16.0	3%	20%	77%
137	NA	NATIONAL REAL EST	9/79	$ 16.7	$ 15.2	0%	47%	53%
104	29	NEW PLAN (NPR/A)	1/80	$ 29.5	$ 20.4	3%	7%	90%
196	NA	NEWPORT	7/77	$ 2.4	$ 2.2	0%	36%	64%
11	17	NWSTN MT'L (NML/N)	* 6/80	$232.2	$230.0	57%	24%	19%
101	144	NOVA REIT	3/80	$ 31.4	$32.7	38%	14%	48%
130	119	OLD DOMIN (ODRES)	* 6/80	$ 20.3	$ 20.0	0%	1%	99%
188	NA	OLD KENTUCKY REIT	12/79	$ 3.7	$ 3.5	3%	69%	29%
167	110	PACIF-STHN (PSMTS)	* 6/80	$ 9.6	$ 8.3	51%	36%	13%
124	NA	PACIFIC REIT	* 6/80	$ 21.5	$ 20.9	0%	0%	100%
69	48	PACTRUST (PTR/A)	2/80	$ 46.4	$ 45.2	0%	22%	78%
7	NA	PAN-AMER PR	4/80	$326.8	$314.9	0%	4%	96%
103	99	PARKWAY CO	3/80	$ 29.5	$ 29.6	0%	28%	72%
31	25	PENN REIT (PEI/A)	2/80	$ 81.7	$ 71.8	0%	5%	95%
206	154	PHILADELPHIA MTG	* 3/80	$ 1.8	$ 0.7	0%	0%	100%
156	134	PIEDMONT	3/80	$ 11.6	$ 10.7	0%	0%	100%
162	NA	PITTS RLTY INV	11/79	$ 10.4	$ 10.4	0%	5%	95%
84	93	PITTS W VA (PW/A)	* 3/80	$ 37.6	$ 37.5	0%	0%	100%
148	142	PLAZA RLTY (PRISS)	* 3/80	$ 13.7	$ 15.0	0%	25%	75%
18	18	PNB MTG (PNI/N)	* 6/80	$169.4	$159.6	38%	55%	6%
88	40	PR TR AMER (PTRAS)	3/80	$ 35.8	$ 32.7	0%	27%	73%
201	NA	PRODUCE EX REALTY	12/79	$ 2.0	$ 1.2	0%	0%	100%
70	19	PROP CAP (PCL/A)	4/80	$ 46.0	$ 45.4	0%	34%	66%
24	31	RAMPAC (RPC)	5/80	$111.4	$109.4	31%	26%	43%
183	NA	REAL EST FUND INV	3/80	$ 5.7	$ 5.5	2%	0%	98%
175	85	R E INV PR (REIPS)	3/80	$ 7.4	$ 6.6	0%	0%	100%
195	NA	REALAMERICA INV	12/79	$ 2.5	$ 2.0	35%	0%	65%
102	NA	REALTY GROWTH INV	4/80	$ 30.5	$ 26.9	0%	51%	49%
72	20	REIT AMER (REI/A)	5/80	$ 45.9	$ 40.7	0%	0%	100%
158	74	REIT OF CALIF	6/80	$ 11.1	$ 7.2	4%	4%	92%
213	NA	REIT OF LA	2/72	$ 0.5	NA	NA	NA	NA
110	114	REPUBLIC (RMI/N)	3/80	$ 28.2	$32.3	2%	21%	76%
121	157	RIVERSIDE (RIVES)	* 3/80	$ 23.2	$ 22.9	0%	93%	7%
127	135	RIVIERE REALTY TR	* 3/80	$ 20.8	$ 20.4	0%	9%	91%
56	69	RLTY INC (RIT/A)	* 4/80	$ 54.4	$ 51.5	54%	19%	27%
37	61	RLTY REF'D (RRF/N)	4/80	$ 72.7	$ 69.5	0%	100%	0%
165	147	RYAN MTG (RYNMS)	6/80	$ 10.0	$ 10.4	0%	55%	45%
67	24	SAN FRAN (SFI/A)	* 6/80	$47.8	$ 48.4	0%	12%	88%
29	5	SANTA ANITA	3/80	$ 90.3	$ 43.5	0%	21%	79%
10	16	SAUL BF (BFS/N)	* 6/80	$235.7	$223.5	1%	1%	99%
28	38	SECUR CAP (SCC/A)	* 6/80	$ 93.4	$ 97.5	15%	60%	25%

Rankings			Report	millions		% Long-term	% Other	% Prop.
TA	MV	Company	Date	Assets	R.E. Investment	First Mtgs.	Mtgs.	Owned
137	NA	SECURITY FIRST	12/79	$ 16.7	$ 16.0	0%	0%	100%
187	NA	SELECT INCOME PROP	12/79	$ 3.9	$ 3.6	0%	0%	100%
53	84	SOUTH ATL (SAT/N)	* 4/80	$ 57.5	$ 61.6	4%	5%	91%
27	66	SOUTHMARK (SM/N)	3/80	$102.3	$112.8	12%	10%	77%
150	132	SOUTHWEST MTG	3/80	$ 13.4	$ 13.2	0%	17%	83%
182	138	STADIUM RLTY	1/80	$ 5.8	$ 5.5	0%	0%	100%
59	64	STATE MUT (SMU/N)	4/80	$ 53.5	$ 54.4	28%	25%	47%
126	104	TERRYDALE (TRYLS)	* 6/80	$ 20.9	$ 20.4	0%	0%	100%
90	72	TIERCO (TIER)	3/80	$ 35.2	$ 27.1	1%	14%	85%
135	118	TOWERMARC	* 5/80	$ 17.3	$ 16.6	14%	28%	58%
171	NA	TRANSCO REALTY	* 3/80	$ 8.4	$ 3.2	0%	25%	75%
35	136	TRECO (TRECS)	3/80	$ 75.4	$ 80.7	3%	12%	84%
60	89	TRI-SOUTH (TSI/N)	3/80	$ 52.9	$ 67.4	19%	20%	61%
8	140	TRITON GROUP	2/80	$276.3	$225.3	14%	28%	58%
159	98	U S EQUITY	* 4/80	$10.8	$ 9.5	0%	9%	91%
93	46	U S MUTUAL (USMRS)	4/80	$ 34.6	$ 36.5	89%	10%	0%
32	22	U S REALTY (UTY/N)	3/80	$ 81.4	$ 80.4	3%	15%	82%
73	112	UMET TRUST (UAT/N)	5/80	$ 44.8	$ 53.2	25%	17%	58%
200	NA	UNITED MTG TRUST	9/79	$ 2.1	$ 1.9	42%	16%	42%
36	23	UNITED RLY (URT/A)	* 5/80	$ 73.2	$ 74.7	23%	36%	41%
49	39	UNIVERSITY (URETS)	3/80	$ 59.9	$ 53.3	0%	11%	89%
62	45	USP REIT (USPTS)	3/80	$ 51.3	$ 47.6	7%	0%	93%
100	42	VA REIT (VARE)	* 6/80	$ 31.9	$ 31.1	1%	5%	94%
141	101	VYQUEST	5/80	$ 15.0	$ 18.5	23%	11%	66%
58	47	WACHOVIA (WRI/N)	5/80	$ 53.7	$ 65.4	34%	29%	37%
149	115	WALTER RLY (WALJS)	4/80	$ 13.5	$ 14.9	0%	23%	77%
211	NA	WALTHAM REALTY	6/76	$ 0.9	$ 0.9	0%	0%	100%
108	148	WASHINGTON CORP	3/80	$ 28.9	$ 37.3	34%	17%	49%
77	15	WASH REIT (WRE/A)	* 3/80	$ 43.7	$ 40.9	0%	0%	100%
13	9	WELLS FARG (WFM/N)	3/80	$210.5	$210.7	0%	65%	35%
43	NA	WESPAC INVESTORS	2/80	$ 64.1	$ 55.9	0%	0%	100%
153	88	WESTERN INV REAL	* 3/80	$ 12.2	$ 12.1	0%	0%	100%
201	NA	WESTLAND INV FUND	4/79	$ 2.0	$ 1.6	0%	88%	13%
134	130	WESTN MTG (WMTGS)	* 5/80	$ 17.9	$ 17.7	7%	35%	58%
82	75	WESTPORT CO (WSPTS)	4/80	$ 41.3	$ 51.4	13%	21%	66%
76	102	WISC REIT (WREIS)	3/80	$ 44.2	$ 47.9	6%	34%	59%

NA—Not available.
TA—Ranking of total assets.
MV—Ranking of market value of trust's shares.
Report Date—Month and year of report used as source for this table.
R.E. Invest.—Total mortgage and property ownership investments after accumulated depreciation and before allowance for loss reserves.
% Long-term First Mtgs.—Percentage of R.E. Invest. identified as long-term first mortgages.
% Other Mtgs.—Percentage R.E. Invest. identified as being mortgages other than long-term first mortgages.
% Prop. Owned—Percentage of R.E. Invest. identified as the ownership of property. Includes purchased and foreclosed property, land purchase-leasebacks, partnerships, and joint venture interests at the dollar amount reported on the balance sheet.
[1] The symbol of the REIT and the Exchange on which it is traded appear in the parenthesis after the name of the REIT. **N** stands for the New York Stock Exchange and **A** for the American Exchange. All other REITS are traded Over-the-Counter.

Source: National Association of Real Estate Trusts, 1101 Seventeenth Street, N.W., Washington, D.C. 20036.

Glossary of REIT Terms

This glossary of terminology used in conjunction with discussions of real estate investment trusts has been prepared by the Research Department of the National Association of Real Estate Investment Trusts. Credit should be given to Realty Income Trust, a NAREIT member, which produced a glossary of terms upon which NAREIT drew heavily.

Acceleration clause A condition in a loan contract or mortgage note which permits the lender to demand immediate repayment of the entire balance if the contract is breached or conditions for repayment occur, such as sale or demolition.

Accrued interest or rent An amount of interest or rent which has been earned but which may not have been received in the same period as earned. On many short-term first mortgages, accrued interest is not received in cash until permanent financing is obtained.

Acquisition loan See C&D loan.

Advisor A REIT's investment advisor (usually pursuant to a renewable one-year contract) provides analysis of proposed investments, servicing of the portfolio, and other advisory services. Fee limits for advisory services are prescribed by many state securities regulators. Also spelled "adviser."

Amortization The process of retiring debt or recovering a capital investment through scheduled, systematic repayments of principal; that portion of fixed mortgage payment applied to reduction of the principal amount owed.

Anchor Tenant An important tenant, usually with an excellent credit rating (also known as a triple-A tenant), which takes a large amount of space in a shopping center or office building and is usually one of the first tenants to commit to lease. The anchor tenant usually is given lower rent because of the desirability of having that tenant at the property, both because of its credit rating and its ability to generate traffic.

Appraisal An opinion by an expert of the value of a property as of a specified date, supported by the presentation and analysis of relevant data. The appraisal may be arrived at by any or all of three methods: the cost approach (cost to reproduce), the market approach (comparison with other similar properties), or the income approach (capitalization of actual or projected income figures).

Assessed value The value of a property which is assigned to it by a taxing authority for purposes of assessing property taxes; often assessed value bears a fixed relationship by local statute to market value.

Asset swaps See swap program.

Assets Anything of value owned by the company. Assets are either financial, as cash or bonds; or physical, as real or personal property. For REIT tax purposes, more than 75% of the trust's assets must be property owned or securities backed by real estate.

Assumption of mortgage When the responsibility for repaying existing indebtedness secured by property is "assumed" by the second purchaser. In most jurisdictions, this relieves the first owner of the original obligations, at least to the extent that can be satisfied by sale of this asset after foreclosure.

Attribution More than 50% of a REIT's shares cannot be held by fewer than six people (otherwise it becomes a personal holding company for tax purposes). When someone has indirect control over someone else's shares (such as a trustee over shares held for the benefit of another) then "control" for personal holding company purposes may be "attributed." This complicated legal topic of "attribution" arises, however, only when the REIT's shares are held by a few.

Audit An examination of the financial status and operations of an enterprise, based mostly on the books of account, and undertaken to assure conformity to generally accepted accounting principles and to secure information for, or to check the accuracy of, the enterprise's balance sheet, income statement, and/or cash flow statement.

Balloon mortgage A mortgage loan which provides for periodic payments, which may include both interest and principal, but which leaves the loan less than fully ammortized at maturity, requiring a final large payment which is the "balloon." Usually the term does not apply to an "interest only" loan whose full principal is due upon maturity or upon call during its life.

Bankrupt When liabilities exceed assets, Federal laws enable the entity to dissolve in an orderly fashion (Chapter VII), or permit a court officer to restructure the company into a survivor "going business" (Chapter X), or permit existing management to do the same under court supervision (Chapter XI), or to do so despite the preferred position of secured creditors if real property is the only asset of the business (Chapter XII).

Beneficial owner The person who ultimately benefits from ownership of shares or other securities—in contrast to "nominees" (often pseudonyms for control of investment professionals so as to facilitate security transactions without having to track down beneficial owners to participate in each step of the procedures).

Source: National Association of Real Estate Trusts, 1101 Seventeenth Street, N.W., Washington, D.C. 20036.

Blue sky laws State laws regulating conditions of sale of securities of companies, (particularly those just starting out of the "clear blue sky") for the protection of the investing public. National stock exchange rules usually supercede state laws pursuant to a "blue chip" exemption contained in such state laws. The federal securities laws dovetail with state laws and pertain to publicly held companies, primarily as to accounting and disclosure practices.

Bond A debt certificate which (a) represents a loan to a trust, (b) bears interest, and (c) matures on a stated future date. Short term bonds (generally with a maturity of five years or less from the date of issuance) are often called notes. See debentures.

Book value per share Shareholder equity as adjusted to tangible net worth (assets minus liabilities plus paid-in capital) per share outstanding.

Borrower A person or entity who received something of value, ordinarily money, and is obligated to pay it back, as the debtor to the creditor, usually pursuant to a note or "IOU" containing terms and conditions.

Broker A person who is paid to act as an intermediary in connection with a transaction, in contrast to a dealer or principal who buys or sells for his own account. In the REIT world, the term "broker" usually refers to a real estate salesman, although the term is also used for "stockbrokers" too.

Building lien An encumbrance upon the property by the contractor or subcontractors. Also known as a "mechanic's" or "materialman's" lien.

Building permit Written permission by the local municipality (usually through the building inspector or other agent) allowing construction work on a piece of property in accordance with plans which were submitted and conforming to local building codes and regulations.

Business trust An unincorporated business in which assets are given to trustees for management to hold or to sell, as investments. The business trust form was first fully developed in Massachusetts, under common law, and the term "Massachusetts business trust" is sometimes used to describe entities formed in other states. It is a form of business through a trustee or trustees who hold legal title to the property of the business. Capital contributions are made to the trustees by the beneficaries whose equitable title and interest in the property of the trust are evidenced by trust certificates, usually called shares of beneficial interest. The earnings of the trust are paid to them, as dividends are paid to stockholders. The beneficiaries generally enjoy limited liability, as the control and management of the trust rests solely with the trustees, but the trust form or organization can be distinguished from a corporation. Early REIT tax laws relied on this distinction to define eligible real estate operations.

Capital gain The amount by which the net proceeds from resale of a capital item exceed the adjusted cost (or "book value") of the asset. If a capital asset is held for more than twelve months before disposition it is taxed on a more favorable basis than a gain after a shorter period of time.

Capitalization rate The rate of return utilized to value a given cash flow, the sum of a Discount Rate and a Capital Recapture Rate. It is applied to any income stream with a finite term over which the invested principal is to be returned to the investor or lender.

Cash flow The revenue remaining after all cash expenses are paid, i.e., non-cash charges such as depreciation are not included in the calculation.

Cash flow per share. Cash flow divided by the common shares outstanding. Shareholders must make this computation themselves since the SEC has prohibited companies from stating this calculation.

Net cash flow. Generally determined by net income plus depreciation less principal payments on long-term mortgages.

Cash on cash return The "cash flow" from a property expressed as a percentage of the cash "equity" invested in a property.

Chapter X See bankrupt.

Collateral An item of value, such as real estate or securities, which a borrower pledges as security. A mortgage gives the creditor the right to seize the real estate collateral after non-performance of the debtor.

Commitment A promise to make an investment at some time in the future if certain specified conditions are met. A REIT may charge a fee to the borrower at the time of making the commitment. A REIT's level of commitments minus expected repayments can be regarded as an indication of future funding requirements.

"Take-out" commitment is one provided by the anticipated long-term lender, usually with complicated terms and conditions that must be met before the "take out" becomes effective.

"Gap" commitment is an anticipated short-term loan to cover part of the final "take-out" that the long-term lender refuses to advance until certain conditions are met (like 90% rent-up of an apartment after construction is completed). The amount above the "floor" or basic part of the loan is the "gap," and the gap commitment is issued to enable the construction lender to make a construction loan commitment for the full amount of the takeout loan instead of only for the "floor" amount.

"Standby" commitment is one that the lender and borrower doubt will be used. It exists as reassurance to a short-term construction lender that if, after completion of a building, the borrower cannot find adequate long-term "take-out" financing, the construction lender will be repaid.

Compensating balances Money which is sometimes required by banks to be held in checking accounts by borrowers, as part of their loan agreement.

Condominium A form of fee ownership of whole units or separate portions of multi-unit buildings which facilitates the formal filing, recording and financing of a divided interest in real property. The condominium concept may be used for apartments, offices and other professional uses. See cooperatives.

Conduit tax treatment So long as most (if not all) earnings are passed along by an entity, then federal taxation is avoided at the entity's level. REITs, mutual funds, and certain kinds of holding companies are elibible for "conduit tax treatment" under certain conditions.

Constant The agreed-upon periodic (usually monthly) payment to pay the face interest rate, with any residual amount going to amortize the loan.

Construction and development loan (C&D) A short-term loan for the purpose of constructing a building, shopping center, or other improvement upon real estate, or developing a site in preparation for construction. A C&D loan is normally disbursed in increments (called *draws* or *draw-downs*) as building proceeds, rather than in a single disbursement, and is conditioned upon compliance with a variety of factors. It is usually repaid with the proceeds of the permanent loan. A land loan or purchase and development loan is sometimes made for the purpose of acquiring unimproved vacant land, usually as a future building site and for financing improvements to such land (street, sewers, etc.) as a prerequisite to construction of a building upon the site.

Contingent Interest Interest on a loan that is payable only if certain conditions occur, in contrast to interest that becomes an accrued liability (whether or not paid) at a specific time.

Cooperative A form of ownership whereby a structure is owned by a corporation or trust with each individual owner holding stock in the corporation representative of the value of his apartment. Title to the apartment is evidenced by a proprietary lease which often does not qualify as adequate collateral for some lenders.

Cost-to-carry The concept specified by the accounting profession to be used by REITs in computing anticipated interest cost on debt needed to "carry" non-earning or partially-earning assets until they're restored to earning status or sold.

Current Liabilities Money owed and due to be paid within one year.

Dealer Someone who buys property with the purpose of selling it at a profit rather than holding it as an investment. A dealer's profits are taxed at the ordinary income rate rather than the capital gains rate regardless of how long the property is held for resale (in contrast to the investor who sells a property after a year and pays at the capital gains rate). A REIT is not permitted to be a dealer unless it is willing to pay a 100% tax on gains from such sales in the year in which it is deemed to be a dealer; sales of foreclosed property do not fall within this definition. See principal.

Debenture An obligation which is secured only by the general credit of the issuing trust, as opposed to being secured by a direct lien on its assets, real estate or otherwise. A debenture is a form of a bond.

Declaration of Trust Similar to articles of incorporation for a corporation, this document contains rules for operation of the trust, selection of its governing trustees, etc., and is the keystone of a REIT.

Deed A legal instrument which conveys title from one to another. It must be (a) made between competent parties (b) have legally sound subject matter (c) correctly state what is being conveyed (d) contain good and valuable consideration (e) be properly executed by the parties involved and (f) be delivered to be valid.

Deed in lieu of foreclosure The device by which title to property is conveyed from the mortgagor (borrower) to the mortgagee (lender) as an alternative to foreclosure. While this procedure can transfer effective control more quickly, many lenders eschew it because undiscovered prior liens (from a workman who was never paid but hadn't gotten around to filing his valid, but late, claim for example) remain enforceable in contrast to the more formal foreclosure procedures which wipe out prior claims after due notice.

Deferred maintenance the amount of repairs that should have been made to keep a property in good running condition, but which have been put off. The term contemplates the desirability of immediate expenditures, although it does not necessarily denote inadequate maintenance in the past.

Deficiency dividend The process of paying an "extra" dividend after the close of the fiscal year so as to comply with REIT tax requirements to pay out more than 90% of income. See dividend.

Depreciation The loss in value of a capital asset, due to wear and tear which cannot be compensated for by ordinary repairs, or an allowance made to allow for the fact that the asset may become obsolete before it wears out. The purpose of a depreciation charge is to write off the original cost of an asset by equitably distributing charges against its operation over its useful life, matching "cost" to the period in which it was used to generate earnings. Depreciation is an optional noncash expense recognizable for tax purposes. If the REIT pays out more than its taxable earnings, then it is distributing a "return of capital" or—as is commonly stated in the industry—"paying out depreciation."

Development loans See Construction and development loan.

Dilution The situation which results when an increase occurs in a company's outstanding securities without a corresponding increase in the company's assets and/or income.

Discount rate An interest rate used to convert a future stream of payments into a single present value. See capitalization rate.

Dividend or distribution The distribution of cash or stock to shareholders of a company which is made periodically as a means of distributing all or a portion of net income or cash flow. Technically, a dividend can be paid only from net taxable income, so many REITs distribute cash and later characterize their distributions as capital gains or a tax-free return of capital if net taxable income is less than the cash paid out.

Dividend or distribution yield The annual dividend or distribution rate for a security expressed as a percent of its market price. For most REITs, the "annualized" rate is the previous quarter's distribution times four, regardless of how the distribution is characterized.

Draw A request from a borrower to obtain partial payment from the lender pursuant to a loan commitment. The lender reassures himself that the borrower has completed the required steps (such as putting in the concrete properly) before advancing money. Often, the borrower submits bills from subcontractors, which are then "paid" by the lender after inspecting the subcontractor's work. In such cases, the check is usually made out to the subcontractor but must be signed by the borrower, too, so that the lender ends up only with one borrower. See construction and development loan.

Effective Borrowing Costs The cost of borrowing after adjustment for compensating balances or fees in lieu of compensating balances, and selling expenses in the case of publicly sold debt.

Encumbrance A legal right or interest in real estate which diminishes its value. Encumbrances can take a number of forms, such as easements, zoning restrictions, mortgages, etc.

Entrepreneur An individual who is responsible for a commercial or real estate activity who takes a certain risk of loss in a transaction for the right to enjoy any profit which may result.

Equity The interest of the shareholders in a company as measured by their paid-in capital and undistributed income. The term is also used to describe (i) the difference between the current market value of a property and the liens or mortgages which encumber it or (ii) the cash which makes up the difference between the mortgage(s) and the construction or sale price.

Equity leveraging The process by which shares are sold at a premium above book value (in anticipation of greater earnings).

Equity participation Usually, the right of an investor to participate to some extent in the increased value of a project by receiving a percentage of the increased income from the project. If a REIT were to participate in a percentage of the net income of a venture (such as the shopping center's owner/lessor), then it could be deemed to be a partner in an active business. Thus, most REIT leases spell out the "equity participation" as a percentage of gross receipts or sales (which is a more stable measure of sales activity, anyway, and one readily identifiable from the lessor's federal income tax statement).

Escrow A deposit of "good faith" money which is entrusted to a third party (often a bank) until fulfillment of certain conditions and agreements, when the escrow may be released or applied as payment for the purchase of property or for services rendered.

Estoppel certificate An instrument used when a mortgage or lease is assigned to another. The certificate sets forth the exact remaining balance of the lease or mortgage as of a certain date and verifies any promises to tenants that may have been made by the first owner for which the second owner may be held accountable.

Exculpatory clause A clause which relieves one of liability for injuries or damages to another. Exculpatory clauses are placed in REIT documents with the intention of eliminating personal liability of its trustees, shareholders and officers.

Expenses The costs which are charges against current operations or earnings of a building, company or other reporting entity. They may have been "paid out" in cash, or accrued to be paid later, or charged as a bookkeeping procedure to reflect the "using up" of assets (as in depreciation) utilized in the production of income during the period of current operations.

Face value The value which is shown on the face of an instrument such as a bond, debenture or stock certificate. The "face rate" of a debt instrument is often known as its "coupon rate."

Fair market value See Market value.

Fee or fee simple Title to a property which is absolute, good and marketable; ownership without condition.

Fiduciary A relationship of trust and confidence between a person charged with the duty of acting for the benefit of another and the person to whom such duty is owed, as in the case of guardian and ward, trustee and beneficiary, executor and heir.

First mortgage That mortgage which has a prior claim over all other liens against real estate. In some jurisdictions, real estate taxes, mechanics liens, court costs, and other involuntary liens may take priority over such a contractual lien: title companies "clear" properties so as to reassure first mortgage lenders (and owners) of their uncontested position and to guarantee them of that position under certain conditions.

Fiscal year The 12-month period selected as a basis for computing and accounting for a business. A fiscal year need not coincide with the calendar year, except for all REITs initially qualifying for special tax treatment after 1976.

Fixed assets Assets, such as land, buildings and machinery, which cannot be quickly converted into cash. For REITs, most "fixed assets" are real property although some (like furniture in an apartment lobby) may be personal property.

Fixed charges Those interest charges, insurance costs, taxes and other expenses which remain relatively constant regardless of revenue. See net lease.

Floating rate A variable interest rate charged for the use of borrowed money. It is determined by charging a specific percentage above a fluctuating base rate, usually the prime rate as announced by a major commercial bank.

Floor loan A portion or portions of a mortgage loan commitment which is less than the full amount of the commitment and which may be funded upon conditions less stringent than those required for funding the full amount, or the "ceiling" of the loan. For example, the floor loan, equal to perhaps 80% of the full amount of the loan, may be funded upon completion of construction without any occupancy requirements, but substantial occupancy of the building may be required for funding the full amount of the loan, which is referred to as the "ceiling." See commitment, gap.

Foreclosure The legal process of enforcing payment of a debt by taking the properties which secure the debt, once the terms of the obligation are not followed. Upon foreclosure, the entire debt might not be fully discharged by transfer and disposition of the property (as determined by the courts). If so, a "deficiency judgment" may be obtained, at which point the lender is like any other creditor in attempting to get the debtor to pay the deficiency. Collection of the deficiency judgment in major real estate transactions is rare, but it becomes a major factor in negotiations if the borrower decides to return to the real estate business in the future.

Fully diluted earnings The hypothetical earnings per share of a company, computed after giving effect to the number of shares which would be outstanding if all convertible debt and warrants were exercised, and also to any reduction in interest payments resulting from such exercise.

Gap commitment See commitment, gap. Also see floor loan.

General lien A lien against the property of an individual or other entity generally, rather than against specific items of realty or personal property.

Ground lease See sale-leaseback.

Holding company A corporation that owns or controls the operations of various other companies. Many REITs were sponsored by bank or insurance holding companies whose subsidiary companies advise and manage REITs, pursuant to contracts with the REIT's trustees.

Independent contractor A firm hired to actively manage property investments. A tax-qualified REIT must hire an independent contractor to manage and operate its property, so as to distinguish itself as an investor rather than an active manager.

Income property Developed real estate, such as office buildings, shopping centers, apartments, hotels and motels, warehouses and some kinds of agricultural or industrial property, which produce a flow of income—in contrast to non-income generating real estate like raw land which would be bought and held for a speculative profit upon resale or development.

Indenture The legal document prepared in connection with, for example, a bond issue, setting forth the terms of the issue, its specific security, remedies in case of default, etc. It may also be called the "deed of trust."

Indentured trustee A trustee, generally the trust department of a major bank, which represents the interest of bondholders under a publicly offered issue.

Insider A person close to a trust who has intimate knowledge of financial developments before they become public knowledge.

Interest rate The percentage rate which an individual pays for the use of borrowed money for a given period of time.

Intermediate-term loan A loan for a term of three to ten years which is usually not fully amortized at maturity. Often, developers will seek interim loans by which to pay off construction financing, in anticipation of obtaining long-term financing at a later date on more favorable terms, either because long-term rates decline generally or because the project can show an established, stable earnings history.

Interim loan A type of loan which is to be repaid out of the proceeds of another loan. Ordinarily, not self-liquidating (amortized), the lender evaluates the risk of obtaining refinancing as much as the period risk. See C&D loans.

Investment advisor See advisor.

Joint venture The entity which is created when two or more persons or corporate entities join together to carry out a specific business transaction of real estate development. A joint venture is usually of limited duration and usually for a specific property; it can be treated as a partnership for tax purposes. The parties have reciprocal and paralleling rights and obligations.

Junior mortgage loan Any mortgage loan in which the lien and the right of repayment is subordinate to that of another mortgage loan or loans. A "second mortgage" is a junior mortgage. "Third, fourth," etc. mortgages are always deemed to be secondary.

Land loan See Construction and development loan.

Land-purchase leaseback See sale-leaseback.

Late charge The charge which is levied against a borrower for a payment which was not made in a timely manner.

Lease A contract between the owner of property (lessor) and a tenant (lessee) setting forth the terms, conditions and consideration for the use of the property for a specified period of time at a specified rental. See sale-leaseback and net lease.

Leasehold improvements The cost of improvements or betterments to property leased for a period of years, often paid for by the tenant. Such improvements ordinarily become the property of the lessor (owner) on expiration of the lease; consequently their cost is normally amortized over the life of the lease if the lessor pays for them.

Leverage The process of borrowing upon one's capital base with the expectation of generating a profit above the cost of borrowing.

Liability management The aspect of the management of a company concerned with the planning and procurement of funds for investment through the sale of equity, public debt and bank borrowings. In the REIT industry, the phrase contrasts to "asset management" or the real estate side of the business.

Line of credit Usually, an agreement between a commercial bank and a borrower under which the bank agrees to provide unsecured credit to the borrower upon certain terms and conditions. Normally, the borrower may draw on all or any part of the credit from time to time.

Limited partnership A partnership which limits certain of the partners' (the limited partners) liability to the amount of their investment. At least one partner (the "general partner") is fully liable for the obligations of the partnership and its operations, usually with the limited partners participating as investors only.

Loan loss reserve A reserve set up to offset asset values in anticipation of losses that are reasonably expected. Initially, REITs had insufficient operating experience to anticipate losses in any one class of investments or for a portfolio as a whole, so tax authorities would not permit substantial contributions toward a reserve as an allowable period expense. When difficulties arose, the conversion of short-term loans to longer-term property holdings required some form of recognition of likely losses in the financial statements. A novel procedure for REITs was devised by requiring, for book purposes, computation of additions to the reserve based in part on the probable cost of sustaining the troubled assets over the longer period of time necessary to "cure" the problem. Also known as "allowance for losses."

Loan run-off The rate at which an existing mortgage portfolio will reduce (or "run-off") to zero if no new loans are added to the portfolio.

Loan swaps See asset swaps.

Long-term mortgage Any financing, whether in the form of a first or junior mortgage, the term of which is ten years or more. It is generally fully amortized.

Loss carry forwards The net operating loss (NOL) incurred in prior years, which may be applied for tax purposes against future earnings, thereby reducing taxable income. For REITs (which must pay out most of their taxable income), NOLs can be carried forward eight years; for non-REIT-taxed companies, NOL can be carried forward for only seven years.

Market value The highest price in terms of money which a property will bring in a competitive and open market under all conditions requisite to a fair sale—the buyer and the seller each acting prudently, knowledgeably, and at arm's length. See appraisal.

Moratorium A period in which payments of debts or other performance of a legal obligation is suspended temporarily, usually because of unforeseen circumstances which make timely payment or performance difficult or impossible. This forebearance can be whole or partial.

Mortgage A publicly recorded lien by which the property is pledged as security for the payment of a debt valid even beyond death ("mort" is death in French). In some states a mortgage is an actual conveyance of the property to the creditor until the terms of the mortgage are satisfied. While there is always a "note" secured by a mortgage document, both the note and mortgage instrument are commonly called "the mortgage." For types, see: first, junior, short-term, long-term, wrap-around and construction and development mortgage definitions.

Mortgage banker A non-depository lender who makes loans secured by real estate and then usually packages and sells those loans in large groups to institutional investors, pursuant to a "long-term commitment" he has negotiated with the life insurance company or other institutional investor. Mortgage bankers frequently arrange to service these mortgages for the out-of-town institutions, collecting regular payments, keeping the lender up to date on the progress of the loan, escrowing payments for taxes and insurance premiums, and, if necessary, administering foreclosure proceedings. Many REITs were sponsored by mortgage bankers.

Mortgage constant The total annual payments of principal and interest (annual debt service) on a mortgage with level-payment amortization schedule, expressed as a percentage of the initial principal amount of the loan.

Mortgagee in possession A lender or one who holds a mortgage who has taken possession of a property in order to protect an interest in the property. Usually, this is done with commercial properties as to which rents, management fees and other disbursements continue even if the mortgage is in default. The possession must be taken with the consent of the mortgagor (or a court, in cases of foreclosure) and the mortgagee must be careful to do only those things to the property that the mortgagor (or court) will agree to accept, should it resume its role as a credit-worthy owner.

Net Income The dollar amount that remains after all expenses, including taxes, are deducted from gross income. For regular companies, it is also called after-tax profit, the "bottom line" figure of how a company has performed with its investors' money. For REITs, it is net taxable income which, if fully distributed, is not taxed.

Net lease A lease, sometimes called a net-net (insurance and taxes) or even a net-net-net lease (insurance, taxes, and maintenance) in which the tenant pays all costs, including insurance, taxes, repairs, upkeep and other expenses, and the rental payments are "net" of all these expenses. See lease and fixed charges.

Net worth The remaining asset value of a property company or other entity after deduction of all liabilities against it.

Non-accrual loans See non-earning investments.

Non-earning investments The category of loans or investments which are not earning the originally anticipated rate of return. Some may be characterized as "partially earning." When interest is recorded as earned rather than as received (accrued interest), "non-accrual investments" are those which management expects not to receive interest as originally contemplated. In the vernacular, nonearning investments are "problem loans" or "troubled properties."

Non-qualified REIT A REIT that was formerly qualified, or conducts its affairs as if it is qualified, but that has elected for the tax year in question to be treated like a normal business corporation for tax purposes. Thus, some restraints (primarily against active management and holding property for sale) are lifted, while REIT conduit tax treatment is lost.

Occupancy rate The amount of space or number of apartments or offices or hotel rooms which are rented as compared with the total amount or number available. The rate is usually expressed as a percentage.

Operating expenses Expenses arising out of or relating to business activity such as interest expense, professional fees, salaries, etc.

Operating income Income received directly from business activity in the normal course, as contrasted with capital gains income, or other extraordinary income.

Option A right to buy or lease property at a certain specified price for specified terms. Consideration is typically given for the option, which is exercisable over a limited time span. If the option is not exercised, the consideration is forfeited. A loan to a developer secured by his option to obtain real estate is considered a "qualified" REIT asset.

Origination The process by which a loan is created, including the search for (or receipt of) the initial plans, the analysis and structuring of the proposed financing, and the review and acceptance procedures by which the commitment to make the investment is finally issued.

Overage income Rental income above a guaranteed minimum depending on a particular level of profit or retail sales volume by the tenant, payable under the terms of a lease.

Participations A lender often "participates out" or sells a portion of his loan to another lender while retaining a portion and managing the investment. REITs buy real estate secured participations as well as originating them.

Par Value The face value assigned to a security when it is issued. The stated par value of a security generally has nothing to do with its market or book value.

Passivity The state of owning investments but not actively managing them (as a property management firm does for the investor) or engaging in trading the securities (like a broker or dealer). This "passivity" test is implicit behind several of the REIT tax requirements.

Pension funds Money which is accumulated in trust to fund pensions for companies or unions and which is frequently invested in part in real estate. A co-mingled real estate pension fund account is managed, usually under contract to a financial institution, much like a REIT except that its shares are not publicly traded but instead sold to other pension funds.

Permanent financing See long-term loan.

Point An amount which represents 1% of the maximum principal amount of an investment. Used in connection with a discount from, or a share of, a principal amount deducted at the time funds are advanced, it represents additional compensation to the lender.

Portfolio The investments of a company, including investments in mortgages and/or ownership of real property. REIT portfolios usually consist of equity in property, short-term mortgages, long-term mortgages and/or subordinated land sale-lease-backs.

Portfolio turnover The average length of time from the funding of investments until they are paid off or sold.

Preferred shares Stocks which have prior claim on distributions (and/or assets in the event of dissolution) up to a certain definite amount before the shares of beneficial interest are entitled to anything. As a form of ownership, preferred shares stand behind senior subordinated and secured debtholders in dissolution, as well as other creditors.

Prepayment penalty The penalty which is imposed on the borrower for payment of the mortgage before it is due. Often a mortgage contains a clause specifying that there is to be no prepayment penalty, or limits the prepayment penalty to only the first few years of the mortgage term.

Price earning ratio A ratio which consists of the market price divided by current annualized earnings per share. Such a computation is now found in most daily stock listings. For REITs, annualization of quarterly earnings is computed by multiplying the most recent distribution by four, regardless of the distribution's later characterization as a dividend, return-of-capital, or capital gains.

Prime lending rate The rate at which commercial banks will lend money from time to time to their most credit-worthy customers, used as a base for most loans to financial intermediaries such as REITs.

Principal The buyer or seller in a real estate transaction as distinguished from an agent.

Principal The sum of money loaned. The amount of money to be repaid on a loan excluding interest charges.

Prior lien A lien or mortgage ranking ahead of some other lien. A prior lien need not itself be a first mortgage.

Pro forma Projected or hypothetical as opposed to actual as related, for example, to a balance sheet or income statement.

Problem investments See nonearning investments.

Prospectus A document describing an investment opportunity; the detailed description of new securities which must be supplied to prospective interstate purchasers under the Securities Act of 1933.

Provision for loan losses Periodic allocation of funds to loan loss reserves in recognition of a decline in the value of a loan or loans in a trust's portfolio due to a default on the part of the borrowers.

Proxy An authorization given by a registered security holder to vote stock at the annual meeting or at a special meeting of security holders.

Purchase and leaseback See sale-leaseback.

Pyramiding In stock market transactions, this term refers to the practice of borrowing against unrealized "paper" profits in securities to make additional purchases. In corporate finance, it refers to the practice of creating a speculative capital structure by a series of holding companies, whereby a relatively small amount of voting stock in the parent company controls a large corporate system. In real estate, it refers to the practice of financing 100% or more of the value of the property.

Qualified assets Assets which meet tax requirements for special REIT tax treatment, i.e. real property. In any tax year, 75% of a REIT's assets must be invested in real property, either through ownership or by securities secured by real estate. A "partially qualified" asset is one that qualifies under the 90% test of being a passive investment in a security, but not under the 75% real estate test.

Qualified income That portion of income which is classified as interest, rents, or other gain from real property, as spelled out in the REIT tax laws.

Raw land Land which has not been developed or improved.

RCA See revolving credit agreement.

Real estate investment trust (REIT, pronounced "reet") A trust established for the benefit of a group of investors which is managed by one or more trustees who hold title to the assets for the trust and control its acquisitions and investments, at least 75% of which are real estate related. A major advantage of a REIT is that no federal income tax need be paid by the trust if certain qualifications are met. Congress enacted these special tax provisions to encourage an assembly method, which is essentially designed to provide for investment in real estate what the mutual provided for investment in securities. The REIT provides the small investor with a means of combining his funds with those of others, and protects him from the double taxation that would be levied against an ordinary corporation or trust.

Revolving credit agreement (or "revolver") A formal credit agreement between a group of banks and a REIT, the terms of which are reviewed periodically when it is "rolled over" or "revolved" or refinanced by a similar agreement. For many trusts, "revolvers" have replaced informal lines of credit extended by individual banks to REITs, thereby providing a uniform (and usually restrictive) approach by all creditors, reassuring each bank that others in the RCA would not be paid off preferentially.

Registration statement The forms filed by a company with the Securities and Exchange Commission in connection with an offering of new securities or the listing of outstanding securities on a national exchange.

Reserves for loss See loan loss reserve.

Return of capital A distribution to shareholders in excess of the trust's earnings and profits, usually consisting of either depreciation or repayment of principal from properties or mortgages held by the trust. Each shareholder receiving such a distribution is required to reduce the tax basis of his shares by the amount of such distribution. For financial accounting purposes, what constitutes a return of capital may differ from that determined under Federal income tax requirements.

Return on equity A figure which consists of net income for the period divided by equity and which is normally expressed as a percentage.

Right of first refusal The right or option granted by a seller to a buyer, to have the first opportunity of acquiring a property.

Rights offering The privilege extended to a shareholder of subscribing to additional stock of the same or another class or to bonds, usually at a price below the market and in an amount proportional to the number of shares already held. Rights must be exercised within a time limit and often may be sold if the holder does not wish to purchase additional shares.

Sale-leaseback A common real estate transaction whereby the investor buys property from and simultaneously leases it back to, the seller. This enables the previous owner (often a developer) to "cash out" on an older property while retaining control.

Land sale-leaseback—this procedure, made common by several REITs that specialize in the transaction, affects only the land under income—producing improvements (such as shopping centers, etc.)—leaving the depreciable improvements in the hands of those who might benefit from the tax consequences. Since the improvements were probably financed with the proceeds of a first mortgage which remains in effect, the rights of the new investor are made

second, or junior, to those of the first mortgage holder. Hence the common phrase "subordinated land sale-leaseback." In return for accepting a less secure position, the new investor usually obtains an "overage" clause whereby additional rent is paid anytime gross income of the shopping center (or whatever) exceeds a pre-determined floor.

Seasoned issues Securities of large, established companies which have been known to the investment public for a period of years, covering good times and bad.

Second mortgages See junior mortgage loan.

Secured debt For REITs, senior mortgage debt secured by specific properties. In case of default on "nonrecourse" debt, the lender may assume property ownership but may not pursue other assets of the lender.

Senior mortgage A mortgage which has first priority.

Senior unsecured debt Funds borrowed under open lines without security. Most bank lines to REITs were unsecured.

Shares of beneficial interest Tradable shares in a REIT. Analogous to common stock in a corporation.

Shareholders' equity Primarily money invested by shareholders through purchase of shares, plus the accumulation of that portion of net income that has been reinvested in the business since the commencement of operations.

Short-term mortgage A loan upon real estate for a term of three years or less, bearing interest payable periodically, with principal usually payable in full at maturity.

Sinking fund An arrangement under which a portion of a bond or preferred stock issue is retired periodically, in advance of its fixed maturity. The company may either purchase a stipulated quantity of the issue itself, or supply funds to a trustee or agent for that purpose. Retirement may be made by call at a fixed price, or by inviting tenders, or by purchase in the open market.

Sponsor The entity which initiated the formation of a REIT and usually acts (often via a subsidiary) as investment advisor to the trust thereafter. The sponsor puts the reputation of its institution on the line for the REIT and usually arranges lines of credit, provides support services and, occasionally, compensating balances.

Spread Difference between percentage return on an investment and cost of funds to support the investment.

Standby commitment See commitment, standby.

Standing loan Usually not amortized, the loan is secured by completed property that has not yet been refinanced with a "permanent" long-term mortgage.

Subordinated debt Debt which is junior to secured and unsecured senior debt, it may be convertible into shares of beneficial interest for REITs. Senior subordinated debt is senior to other subordinated debt.

Subordinated ground lease See sale-leaseback.

Swap Program A procedure for reducing debt (by a troubled REIT) by trading an asset to the creditor in return for cancellation of part of a loan to the REIT. Often a cash premium payment is made in addition to reduction of the debt. The premium may then be distributed to the other creditors pro rata. The amount of the cash premium, or the ratio of cash-to-debt reduction to be applied against the value of the asset, is sometimes determined by a sealed-bid "auction" process as set forth in the "revolving credit agreement" between the creditors and the REIT. See RCA.

Syndicate A group of investors who transact business for a limited period of time and sometimes with a single purpose. It is a short-term partnership.

Take-out commitment See commitment.

Tax shelter The various aspects of an investment which offer relief from income taxes or opportunities to claim deductions from taxable income. Although tax shelters are an important facet of real estate investment, they do not have a direct influence on REIT investment choices because qualified trusts are exempt from income taxes.

Usury The charging of interest rates for the use of money higher than what's allowed by local law.

Warrants Stock purchase warrants or options give the holder rights to purchase shares of stock, generally running for a longer period of time than ordinary subscription rights given shareholders. Warrants are often attached to other securities, but they may be issued separately or detached after issuance.

Working capital Determined by subtracting current liabilities from current assets. It represents the amount available to carry on the day-to-day operation of the business.

Work-out When a borrower has problems, the process undertaken by the lender to help the borrower "work out" of the problems becomes known itself as a "work out." The presumption during a "work out" is that the borrower will eventually resume a more normal debtor's position once problems are solved within (presumably) a reasonably short time.

Wrap-around mortgage A type of junior mortgage used to refinance properties on which there is an existing first mortgage loan. The face amount of the wrap-around loan is equivalent to the unpaid balance on the existing mortgage plus cash advanced to the property owner upon funding. Such loans carry a higher interest rate than the existing mortgage. The wrap-around lender assumes the obligation to maintain payments of principal and interest on the existing mortgage so as to enhance his right to make claim from his secondary position.

Yield In the stock market, the rate of annual distribution or dividend expressed as a percentage of price. Current yield is found by dividing the market price into the distribution rate in dollars. In real estate, the term refers to the effective annual amount of income which is being accrued on an investment expressed as a percentage of its value.

How to Do Business With the Government

SMALL BUSINESS ADMINISTRATION

1411 L Street NW
Washington, DC 20416
Telephone: 202–653–6356

The federal government is required by law to help and protect small business enterprise. In fiscal year 1979, the government contracted with small businesses for $19.6 billion out of $82.4 billion worth of supplies and services, or 23.8 percent of its procurement dollars.

The Small Business Administration (SBA) was established in 1953 to help small businesses to obtain financing and to provide loans, within budget limitations, when private funding is not available. SBA reviews federal agency procurement requests for requirements that can be set aside for small businesses. It encourages agencies to break out certain sections from large contracts for small business firms. When a government contracting officer doubts the technical or financial capabilities of a small business, he must refer the matter to SBA. If, after studying the specific case, SBA is satisfied that the firm could perform, SBA awards a certificate of competency by which the contracting officer must abide.

MILITARY PROCUREMENT PROGRAMS

There are four basic methods of procurement for the armed forces:

Departmental programs.
Consolidated purchasing programs (interdepartmental).
Procurement by other government agencies (principally GSA).
Local sources of supply.

Specific information about these programs can be found in *Selling to the Military;* this publication is available from the Superintendent of Documents, U.S. Government Printing Office, Washington, DC 20402.

Source: "Doing Business with the Federal Government," U.S. General Services Administration, Washington, D.C.

The following is an outline of military procurement.

DEPARTMENT OF DEFENSE

The Department of Defense (DOD) integrates policies and procedures and provides unified direction for the three military services (army, air force, and navy) and for the Defense Logistics Agency (DLA), formerly Defense Supply Agency (DSA). This policy control provides maximum national security through coordinated operations of DOD components.

The Assistant Secretary of Defense generally does not effect procurements. Individual military departments and defense agencies let contracts to supply their respective needs or the combined needs of DOD activities when the department or agency is designated as an executive agent.

The Under Secretary of Defense for Research and Engineering, in addition to other duties, is responsible for the development and acquisition of weapon systems, including procurement policy and production planning.

The Assistant Secretary of Defense, (manpower, reserve affairs, and logistics) formulates policy and procedures for military supply and related fields. This action shapes the development of procurement systems and logistical relationships among military organizations. The assistant secretary's office also coordinates the procurement actions of major DOD activities.

The Defense Acquisition Regulations (DAR) formerly designated as the Armed Services Procurement Regulations (ASPR) contain military procurement policies and procedures authorized by Title 10 of the United States Code. Each military department and the DLA implement the ASPR in their own manuals and publications.

· All military departments and the DLA have small business specialists at major procurement activities. These specialists are available to furnish detailed information on how to do business with DOD agencies.

DEPARTMENT OF THE ARMY

The U.S. Army Materiel Development and Readiness Command (DARCOM) is responsible for the materiel functions of the Army, including research and development, product improvement, human factors engineering, testing and evaluation, procurement and production, new equipment training, scientific and technical intelligence production, international logistics programs, storage, distribution, transportation, maintenance, demilitarization, and disposal.

DARCOM consists of a nationwide network of 66 military installations and 250 separate units. It commands subordinate commands, installations and activities as assigned, develops managerial and related logistics management services, and provides worldwide technical and professional guidance and assistance.

DARCOM headquarters is in Alexandria, Va.

DEPARTMENT OF THE NAVY

The Naval Material Command, Arlington, Virginia, has chief responsibility for navy procurement. The Military Sealift Command, the Commandant of the Marine Corps, and the Office of Naval Research also conduct major procurement programs.

The Naval Material Command, Department of the Navy, Crystal Plaza, Arlington, Virginia (mail to Washington, DC 20360), has subordinate commands for air, electronics, sea, and supply systems as well as for facilities engineering. It makes limited procurements for the Marine Corps.

The Military Sealift Command contracts for ocean shipping, including ship chartering and ocean towage, and contracts for repair of ocean-going ships.

The Office of Naval Research contracts for studies in electronics, materials, chemistry, physics, earth and ocean sciences, and biological and psychological sciences. It also coordinates the research programs of the navy's technical commands.

The Bureau of Naval Personnel, Department of the Navy, Columbia Pike and Arlington Ridge Road, Arlington, Virginia (mail to Washington, DC 20370) is responsible for personnel research programs, special studies, and recruiting and training services. Naval Material Command supply activities handle procurement for the Bureau of Naval Personnel.

Major navy purchasing offices are listed in the Department of Defense publication *Selling to the Military.*

DEPARTMENT OF THE AIR FORCE

The Air Force Logistics Command buys all supplies and services for weapons support and other operational systems.

The Air Force Systems Command procures all air force systems and makes initial purchase of related support equipment. This command is also responsible for all research and development.

In general, all other air force commands purchase supplies and services needed to operate air force bases. In addition, the Military Airlift Command procures services to provide airlift and air taxi service; the Air Training Command procures services for flight training; the Air Force Communications Service operates and maintains ground communication services. Both major command and air base contracting activities are listed in *Selling to the United States Air Force,* available from the Office of Small and Disadvantaged Business Utilization, HQ USAF, Washington, DC 20330.

THE DEFENSE LOGISTICS AGENCY

The Defense Logistics Agency (DLA), which was formerly the Defense Supply Agency, manages approximately 2 million general supply items for the military services. Some typical items DLA buys are food, clothing, textiles, medical and dental equipment, industrial and chemical equipment, electrical equipment and electronics, food preparation equipment, construction equipment, automotive equipment and fuel, and petroleum products and services.

The six DLA supply centers that buy and manage specific commodities are listed below.

Defense Construction Supply Center
3990 East Broad Street
Columbus, OH 43215
(614) 236–3541

Defense Electronics Supply Center
1507 Wilmington Pike
Dayton, OH 45444
(513) 296–5231

Defense Fuel Supply Center
Cameron Station, Building 8
5010 Duke Street
Alexandria, VA 22314
(202) 274–7428

Defense General Supply Center
Bellwood, Petersburg Pike
Richmond, VA 23297
(804) 275–3617 or 275–3287

Defense Industrial Supply Center
700 Robbins Avenue
Philadelphia, PA 19111
(215) 697–2747

Defense Personnel Support Center
2800 South 20th Street
Philadelphia, PA 19101
(215) 271–2321

Interested suppliers should contact the small and disadvantaged business specialist of the appropriate supply center to obtain Standard Form 129, Bidder's Mailing List Application Form, and the appropriate commodity list. These forms should be completed and returned to the supply center so the company can be placed on the appropriate bidder's mailing list.

Management and administration of most defense contracts are consolidated under DLA through the Defense Contract Administration Services (DCAS) regional offices. Firms interested in subcontracting should contact the small and disadvantaged business specialist at the nearest DCAS regional office listed below.

Defense Contract Administration
Services Region
805 Walker Street
Marietta, GA 30060
(404) 424–6000, Ext. 231

Defense Contract Administration
Services Region
666 Summer Street
Boston, MA 02210
(617) 542–6000, Ext. 886

Defense Contract Administration
Services Region
O'Hare International Airport
P.O. Box 66475
Chicago, IL 60666
(312) 694–6390

Defense Contract Administration
Services Region
Federal Office Building
Room 1821
1240 E. Ninth Street
Cleveland, OH 44199
(216) 522–5122 or 522–5150

Defense Contract Administration
Services Region
500 South Ervay Street
Dallas, TX 75201
(214) 670–9205

Defense Contract Administration
Services Region
11099 South La Cienega Blvd.
Los Angeles, CA 90045
(213) 643–0620 or 643–0621

Defense Contract Administration
Services Region
60 Hudson Street
New York, NY 10013
(212) 264–9090 or 264–9091

Defense Contract Administration
Services Region
2800 South 20th Street
P.O. Box 7478
Philadelphia, PA 19101
(215) 271–4006

Defense Contract Administration
Services Region
1136 Washington Avenue
St. Louis, MO 63101
(314) 263–6617

DLA, through the Defense Property Disposal Service (DPDS), has worldwide responsibility for disposal of military surplus personal property. DPDS maintains a centralized bidder's mailing list at Battle Creek, Michigan. To be placed on this list, individuals and firms should write to Defense Property Disposal Service, P.O. Box 1370, Battle Creek, MI 49016.

Additional information concerning DLA procurement is contained in the booklets *How to Do Business With DLA, An Introduction to DLA,* and *An Identification of Commodities Purchased by the DLA.* Copies of these publications are available from the Public Affairs Office or the Office of the Small Business and Economic Utilization Advisor, DLA, Cameron Station, 5010 Duke Street, Alexandria, VA 22314, (202) 274–6471.

GENERAL SERVICES ADMINISTRATION PROCUREMENT PROGRAMS

A large volume of goods and services utilized by civilian agencies and military departments is contracted for by the General Services Administration (GSA). GSA has six major subdivisions. They are the Automated Data and Telecommunications Service (ADTS), the Public Buildings Service (PBS), the Federal Supply Service (FSS), the Transportation and Public Utilities Service (TPUS), the Federal Property Resources Service (FPRS), and the National Archives and Records Service (NARS). All make procurements in their respective areas of responsibility.

Business representatives interested in selling products and services to the Government should contact the nearest GSA Business Service Center (see page 500).

AUTOMATED DATA AND TELECOMMUNICATIONS SERVICE

The Automated Data and Telecommunications Service (ADTS) has introduced several new procedures aimed at fostering greater competition for Federal contracts for automated data processing services and equipment.

First, individual Federal agencies now have authority for competitive purchases up to $300,000. Second, tentative selection of a supplier from a Federal schedule is now announced in the *Commerce Business Daily,* so other firms can compete. And third, simpler procedures for validating the performance characteristics of equipment have been introduced.

ADTS has also increased its competitive procurement of local Government telephone systems and for its intercity telephone network rather than leasing exclusively from the regulated communications utilities.

ADP/communications schedules. Each year ADTS negotiates ADP/communications schedules for most types of commercially available

ADP/communications equipment. These fixed-price, indefinite-quantity schedules are used by Federal agencies for the rental, purchase, and maintenance of equipment. Where authorized by regulation, schedule contracts allow the continuation of rental and maintenance and the addition of peripherals and features for existing equipment, thereby eliminating time and money that would be used in procurement by separate contract.

The ADP schedules cover computer systems and on-line peripherals, proprietary software, and accessorial ADP equipment used primarily off-line or in a stand-alone mode. Examples of accessorial ADP equipment are analog instrumentation records, tape cleaners/certifiers, key-to-key preparation equipment, terminals, modems, multiplexers, disk packs, and computer output microfilm equipment. The communications schedules cover radio, telephone, telemetry, and recording/reproducing video equipment as well as recording and instrumentation tapes.

ADP equipment requirements contracts. ADTS awards requirements contracts for a variety of ADP equipment. These contracts cover such items as disk drives, terminals, and punch card machines. A Federal agency must use the contracts when the equipment available will meet the agency's needs. The contracts simplify the user agency's procurement procedures and provide savings over commercial rates.

Teleprocessing Services Program. The Teleprocessing Services Program (TSP) enables Federal agencies to obtain a full range of commercial remote computing services, including off-the-shelf specialized application software, at better-than-commercial rates.

Under this program, ADTS awards annual fixed-price, indefinite-quantity schedule contracts that are mandatory sources for Federal agencies. ADTS also negotiates basic agreements with vendors for agencies that need customized services to support specific requirements.

Service contracts. ADTS awards ADP service contracts for use by Federal agencies nationwide in obtaining systems analysis and programming, data entry, key punch, and computer-output microfilm.

Telecommunications. In its operation of the Federal Telecommunications System, ADTS contracts for transmission facilities with common carriers and makes competitive procurements where possible. It also leases and purchases terminals for teletype, data, and facsimile transmission. Installation and maintenance services are also arranged.

PUBLIC BUILDINGS SERVICE

Design contracts. Within the Public Buildings Service (PBS), the Office of Construction

Management, through its design and construction divisions in the GSA regional offices, contracts with architect-engineers for such projects as office buildings, courthouses, and research centers. These contracts are normally negotiated. Design contracts for air-conditioning systems, elevators, repairs, and alterations are also negotiated.

It is GSA's policy to acquire design services from the most highly qualified architect-engineer firms. This policy is implemented by announcing publicly, in the *Commerce Business Daily*, requirements for design services. Firms are selected, according to previously published criteria, on demonstrated competence and qualification for the type of professional service required.

Negotiations are conducted following an evaluation of Standard Form 254, Architect-Engineer and Related Services Questionnaire, and photos of completed projects previously filed with the GSA regional and central offices. Generally, only architect-engineers in the geographic area of the project are considered. An exception may be made for projects of national significance.

The architect is responsible for furnishing complete design services. Subcontracts with consulting engineers are subject of GSA approval. If a project is basically of an engineering nature, the prime contract is negotiated with an engineering firm.

Topographic surveys, soil tests, and soil analyses are generally subcontracted by the architect-engineer. They are reimbursable items exclusive of the design fee.

The GSA regional offices commission murals and sculptures to be placed in public buildings. Artists are selected in cooperation with the National Endowment for the Arts (NEA). NEA-appointed panels, consisting of local civic and art-oriented representatives and the project architect, recommend artists to GSA. These recommendations provide the basis for the GSA selection process.

Construction contracts. Contracts for construction or alteration are awarded to the lowest responsive and responsible bidder on the basis of competitive bids.

When competitive bids are solicited, a notice is placed in local newspapers, various trade journals, technical publications serving the construction industry, and *Commerce Business Daily*.

Each of GSA's PBS regional offices maintains mailing lists of interested prospective bidders. Firms may apply by contacting the nearest Business Service Center.

Leasing of real property. GSA leases space in urban centers in the 50 states of the United States, Puerto Rico, and the Virgin Islands for federal agencies. However, there are certain exceptions. The Departments of Agriculture,

Commerce, and Defense may lease their own building space after GSA clearance. GSA does not lease space for post offices or in foreign countries.

Leases normally are obtained by negotiation. Occasionally, invitations for sealed bids are issued.

Maintenance and repair of government-owned buildings. PBS operates buildings under the control of GSA. To perform this function, it purchases such items as tools, hardware, paints and janitorial supplies (including uniforms), shop and cafeteria equipment as are necessary. Purchases from non-Government sources are usually contracted for by authorized buildings managers, who may spend up to $2,500 per purchase for equipment, supplies, and materials. The Office of Contracts procures guard, janitorial, window-cleaning, and utility services; cafeteria operation; garbage removal; and dry-cleaning.

Businesses interested in selling supplies or performing services of the types mentioned above should contact the nearest GSA Business Service Center.

Appraisal. GSA employs its own staff, independent appraisal companies, and individuals to report the estimated fair market value or the estimated fair annual rental of properties. A period of 30 to 90 days is usually required for appraisals, although the actual time is dependent upon the size and complexity of the properties. Appraisers are selected from the GSA Register of Available Real Estate Appraisers.

Interested appraisers should write to the nearest GSA Business Service Center and request GSA Form 1195, Application for Placement on GSA Register of Available Real Estate Appraisers.

Broker services. Real estate brokers are employed in a manner similar to that used in private commerce. Under GSA procedures, brokers are also required to locate buyers and provide for wide public notice. Brokers are selected from those qualified who have informed GSA of their interest in performing brokerage services.

Surveying. Surveying and related cadastral services are obtained from civil engineers, surveyors, and land-development firms. Since this need is limited, GSA has not established a listing. Regional offices usually employ local surveyors under a selective professional services contract. Surveyors should inform the appropriate GSA Business Service Center of their interest.

Bid bonds. Bid bonds are required for construction contracts in excess of $25,000. Standard Form 24, Bid Bond, a certified cashier's or bank check, or a money order can be accepted. Successful bidders must provide a performance bond for the total amount of the bid and a payment bond for half that amount.

To obtain these bonds, contact a surety or bonding company. The Small Business Administration can be of help.

Maintenance contracts do not require bid bonds.

FEDERAL SUPPLY SERVICE

The Federal Supply Service (FSS) is responsible for supplying thousands of common-use items such as office supplies and equipment, furniture, and books; hardware, refrigerators, air conditioners, and water coolers; and laboratory, medical, photographic, and audio-video recording equipment and supplies.

The various programs under which procurements are made are described in the following sections.

Stock program. Under this program, approximately 20,000 common-use items are stored in supply distribution facilities located for timely and cost-favorable service to customer agencies.

Agencies submit their requisitions to the GSA regional office serving their area. Orders are then directed to the appropriate supply distribution facility to be shipped from stock, unless the order is large enough to make direct delivery from the supplier more advantageous. Examples of items available under this program are paint, tools, and office supplies.

Federal supply schedules. Where economical to do so, an item may be purchased under the federal supply schedules program. This program provides federal agencies with sources for products and services such as furniture, electric lamps, appliances, photographic and duplicating equipment and supplies, athletic equipment, laboratory equipment and supplies, and audio and video recording equipment and supplies.

Schedules are indefinite quantity contracts usually established for a term of one year. They permit agencies to place orders directly with suppliers. Payment is made directly to the contractor by the ordering agency.

Solicitations for bids under the federal supply schedule program are advertised in *Commerce Business Daily*. Under certain conditions, contracts are negotiated in lieu of formal advertising procedures.

Consolidated purchase contracts. Items sometimes are not suitable for inclusion in either the stock or federal supply schedule programs. Agency requirements for such items are consolidated by GSA, and special definite quantity contracts are executed. Direct delivery is made from the contractor to the agency involved. These contracts are usually formally advertised but may be negotiated in certain circumstances.

Direct order purchasing. Upon request, GSA makes special procurements for agencies that:

Lack technical personnel or expertise.
Believe GSA can buy more advantageously because of its knowledge of the market.
Have special requirements, such as the Agency for International Development.

If the quantity of an order for a Federal supply schedule item exceeds the maximum order limitation, a special purchase may be made. Other special conditions and exceptions may necessitate direct-order purchasing.

TRANSPORTATION AND PUBLIC UTILITIES SERVICE

The most recently formed service in GSA, the Transportation and Public Utilities Service (TPUS), procures goods and services ranging from fuel-efficient cars and trucks through discount motel accommodations for Federal travelers.

Vehicles, accessories, and services. TPUS, through a central purchasing program, buys vehicles for Federal use and develops the standards and specifications by which they are selected, rents passenger vehicles and trucks, and purchases or sets the standards for buying automotive parts, accessories, services and fuel (such as gasohol). In 1980 it bought 15,000 fuel-efficient vehicles.

Locally, through the managers of its 100 motor pools in the 50 States and Puerto Rico, TPUS buys automotive maintenance and repair, parts, accessories, and fuel.

Information on TPUS automotive purchases can be obtained from the nearest Business Service Center. However, since the TPUS motor pools are only a fifth of the total Federal fleet, other agencies should be contacted directly for information on vehicle and related procurements.

Travel services. TPUS negotiates and contracts for special discount air and rail fares for Federal passengers on high-traffic routes through a central purchasing program. It also sets policies on the procurement of travel and travel services by all Executive agencies, the purchase of rail, truck, ocean, and air freight, and the settlement of travel and freight loss and damage claims.

Public utilities. Electric, gas, water, steam, and sewage services are procured by TPUS for individual Executive agencies or on an area basis for government-run buildings. Individual purchases are for $10,000 and up and may be for a term up to 10 years.

FEDERAL PROPERTY RESOURCES SERVICE

The General Services Administration attempts as much as possible to repair and reha-

bilitate personal property, such as furniture or office machines, for further Federal use. This is one of the jobs of its Federal Property Resources Service (FPRS).

FPRS awards contracts for maintenance, repair, and/or rehabilitation of office machines, metal and wood furniture (including electrostatic spray painting of metal furniture), carpets and drapes, motor vehicles, pneumatic tires, household appliances, fire extinguishers, and many other items.

Contracts are also awarded for recycling activities, such as recovery of silver from used photographic solutions and scrap film and collection of wastepaper from remilling.

Federal agencies may contract for their own repair and maintenance services only if an FPRS contract is not available.

The majority of the contracts are set aside for small and minority businesses, workshops for the blind and severely handicapped, and Federal Prison Industries, Inc.

For further information, contact one of the GSA Business Service Centers.

NATIONAL ARCHIVES AND RECORDS SERVICE

The National Archives and Records Service (NARS) Trust Fund makes special procurements related to its mission. These are primarily in the audiovisual field and include photographic supplies and related equipment, microfilm services, and processing of various types of film.

For further information on NARS procurements, contact the Administrative Services Division, Procurement and Property (NASP), Room B-21, National Archives and Records Service, Washington, DC 20408.

OTHER CIVILIAN AGENCY PROCUREMENT

Agencies publicize proposed procurements by means of news releases, paid advertising, *Commerce Business Daily*, and by mailing notices of requirements to known suppliers.

Most agencies, however, still rely on firms to demonstrate an interest by submitting Standard Form 129, Bidder's Mailing List Application. In this way, a prospective supplier will be placed only on the mailing list of the agency to which the application is submitted and only for the items listed.

Firms should not send company catalogs with requests to be placed on the mailing lists for all the items shown.

Before placing a firm on its bidder's mailing list, an agency will often require additional information such as:

Production capability.
Description of items normally produced.
Number of employees.
Plant and transportation facilities.
Government contract experience.
Financial status.
Scope of the firm's operations.

Procurement by civilian agencies is generally decentralized so that regional and field offices may purchase their own supplies.

GSA procures common-use supplies. Requests to supply such items to other civilian agencies are usually referred to GSA.

The supply activities of those agencies that make substantial open-market purchases are described in the balance of this chapter.

DEPARTMENT OF AGRICULTURE

The purchasing activities and requirements of the U.S. Department of Agriculture (USDA) are varied; a wide range of supplies, services, and construction is purchased by over 200 local offices throughout the United States.

The department's Office of Operations and Finance exercises general responsibility for all phases of the department's procurement, supply, and property management functions and for the acquisition, management, utilization, and disposition of department-owned and leased real estate.

The department has prepared its own pamphlet, *Selling to the United States Department of Agriculture*, which outlines the department's procurement process, lists agencies and their procurement needs, and includes a directory of agency purchasing offices and their locations. This pamphlet, as well as information about the procurement requirements of the USDA agencies or subdepartments, is available without charge from the U.S. Department of Agriculture, Office of Operations (PGAMS), Room 131-W, Administration Building, Washington, DC 20250.

Four USDA agencies account for about 90 percent of the dollar value of USDA purchases, including the goods and services described below.

Science and Education Administration (SEA). SEA buys special laboratory, scientific, and testing equipment; light trucks and laboratory-type trailers; farm equipment and supplies; refrigerating and dehumidifying equipment, and laboratory, scientific, and testing equipment, furniture, and supplies.

Its construction requirements include animal pens, insectaries, and greenhouses; storage sheds and laboratory buildings (including prefabricated types); windmills and wells; dock and harbor repairs; soil moisture tanks; fences; and roads, driveways, and parking areas.

SEA procurement is decentralized and on a regional level. For additional information,

contact the Science and Education Administration (SEA), U.S. Department of Agriculture, General Services Division, 6505 Belcrest Road, Hyattsville, MD 20782. (301) 436–7690.

Animal and Plant Health Inspection Service (APHIS). APHIS buys laboratory supplies, vehicles, farm equipment, aircraft, office supplies and equipment, radio transmitting and receiving equipment, insecticides, data processing, and service and construction contracts.

For additional information about APHIS procurement, contact either of the following two offices.

Administrative Services Division
  Purchasing and Contracting Branch
6505 Belcrest Rd.
Hyattsville, MD 20782
(301) 436–8665

Field Servicing Office
  Administrative Operations Branch
123 East Grant St.
Minneapolis, MN 55403
(612) 725–2233

Forest Service (FS). FS buys petroleum products; building and construction supplies; transportation equipment, including motor vehicles, aircraft, parachutes, and boats; engineering, laboratory test, scientific, photographic and radio equipment; refrigerators; heavy equipment including tractors, graders, compressors, concrete mixers, truck tractors, trailers, and cranes; explosives; chemicals and insecticides; seeds and fertilizers; hardware supplies, including hand tools, machine tools, barbed wire, and paints; and firefighting tools, lookout towers and binoculars.

Its public works projects include the construction of roads, bridges, and buildings. Forestry work projects include insect control, tree planting, range vegetation, and brush disposal.

FS procurement is decentralized and handled by regional and national forest staffs. For additional information, contact the Director of Administrative Services, Forest Service, U.S. Department of Agriculture, 1621 North Kent Street, Arlington, VA 22209; (703) 235–8165.

Soil Conservation Service (SCS). SCS buys architect, engineering, and construction services (including core drilling); laboratory, photographic, radio, and soil sampling equipment; laboratory and office furniture and supplies, data processing equipment, office machines, and supplies; vehicles and other transportation equipment; and drafting and engineering equipment and supplies. It also purchases farm equipment and supplies such as feed, insecticides, and fertilizers.

Construction requirements include small dams, reservoirs, channels, debris basins, and other water use and control structures. The agency also rents construction equipment.

SCS procurement is decentralized and on

the state level. For additional information, contact the Soil Conservation Service, U.S. Department of Agriculture, Administrative Services Division, Procurement Management Branch, Washington, DC 20250. (202) 477–3123.

DEPARTMENT OF COMMERCE

This Department provides centralized procurement for a variety of supplies, equipment, and services for supporting nearly all the organizational elements of the department. Inquiries relative to these procurements, obtaining Bidder's Mailing List Application forms, procurement policies, or assistance and guidance should be directed to the Office of Administrative Services and Procurement, U.S. Department of Commerce, Washington, DC 20230.

Inquiries regarding business opportunities for minority business enterprises should be addressed to Market Development, Office of Minority Business Enterprise, Washington, DC 20230.

Certain specialized procurement needs of major purchasing activities located outside the Washington, D.C., area may be directed to the following offices and addresses.

NATIONAL BUREAU OF STANDARDS (NBS)

Supply Division, Procurement Section
U.S. Department of Commerce
Building No. 301, Room B118
Gaithersburg, MD 20234

Contracting Officer
U.S. Department of Commerce
325 Broadway
Boulder, CO 80302

BUREAU OF THE CENSUS (CB)

Property and Supply Branch
U.S. Department of Commerce
Federal Office Building 4
Room 1205
Suitland, MD 20233

NATIONAL OCEANIC AND ATMOSPHERIC ADMINISTRATION (NOAA)

Eastern Region
National Weather Service (NWS)
585 Stewart Avenue
Garden City, NY 11530

Southern Region
National Weather Service (NWS)
819 Taylor Street
Fort Worth, TX 76102

Central Region
National Weather Service (NWS)
601 East 12th Street
Kansas City, MO 64106

Western Region
National Weather Service (NWS)
Box 11188, Federal Building
125 South State Street
Salt Lake City, UT 84111

Alaska Region
National Weather Service (NWS)
632 6th Avenue
Anchorage, AK 99501

Pacific Region
National Weather Service (NWS)
Bethel-Pauahi Building
1149 Bethel Street
Honolulu, HI 96813

Atlantic Marine Center
National Ocean Survey (NOS)
439 West York Street
Norfolk, VA 23510

Southeast Region
National Marine Fisheries Service (NMFS)
Federal Office Building
Sixth Floor
114 First Avenue, South
St. Petersburg, FL 33701

Northwest Region
National Marine Fisheries Service (NMFS)
Federal Building
14 Elm Street
Gloucester, MA 01930

National Climatic Center
Environmental Data Service (EDS)
Federal Building
Room 301-D
Asheville, NC 28801

Northwest Administrative Services Office (NASO)
Lake Union Building
1700 West Lake Avenue
Seattle, WA 98109

DEPARTMENT OF EDUCATION

The Department of Education (ED) procures articles and services for staff and operation of programs of education from elementary school through post graduate and vocational, including education of the handicapped and of minorities. Procurement responsibility is divided between two offices in Washington, DC.

ED requirements, aside from educational research and improvement, are procured by the Grants and Procurement Management Division, Office of Management, Rm. 5680, ROB 3, 400 Maryland Ave., SW., Washington, DC 20202.

Educational research and improvement requirements are procured by the Contracts and Grants Management Division, Office of Educational Research and Improvement, Rm. 808, Brown Building, 1200 19th St., NW., Washington, DC 20036.

DEPARTMENT OF ENERGY

The Department of Energy (DOE) was established in 1977 to develop and execute a national energy program. To supplement its in-house efforts, it acquires research and development by contracts and interagency agreements and assists both private and public institutions through grants and agreements.

Research, development, and demonstration business opportunities exist in the DOE Washington headquarters and in numerous field organizations. The Department also uses Government-owned, contractor-operated facilities, where significant subcontracting opportunities are available.

The DOE publication, *Doing Business With the Department of Energy,* lists major DOE purchasing offices and their responsibilities. For copies, write to the Department of Energy Technical Information Center, P.O. Box 62, Oak Ridge, TN 37830.

DEPARTMENT OF HEALTH AND HUMAN SERVICES

The Department of Health and Human Services (DHHS) buys goods and services for programs involving health, social security, and general welfare. The greatest dollar volume goes to the Public Health Service.

General information about contracts and grants and about the special administrative articles and services purchased for headquarters offices can be obtained by writing or calling the Division of Contract and Grant Operations, Office of the Secretary, 200 Independence Ave., SW., Rm. 443H, Washington, DC 20201, (202) 755–6166.

Inquiries regarding small, disadvantaged, and women-owned businesses may be directed to the Office of Small and Disadvantaged Business Utilization, 200 Independence Ave., SW., Rm. 624E, Washington, DC 20201.

Address inquiries about architectural/engineering and construction services to the Office of Facilities Engineering, 330 Independence Ave., SW., Washington, DC 20201, (202) 245–7426.

The Department's pamphlet, *How To Do Business With DHHS,* contains both general and detailed information about DHHS procurement requirements and includes a directory of purchasing offices. This pamphlet is available free from the Division of Contract and Grant Operations and the Office of Small and Disadvantaged Business Utilization at the above addresses or from any DHHS regional office.

Since procurement responsibility is decentralized, businesses should also direct inquiries to the constituent agencies of DHHS or to the regional office nearest them.

Regional offices are located in Atlanta, Ga.; Boston, Mass.; Chicago, Ill.; Dallas, Texas; Denver, Colo.; Kansas City, Mo.; New York, N.Y.; Philadelphia, Pa.; San Francisco, Calif.; and Seattle, Wash. For addresses and telephone numbers, consult local telephone directories under Department of Health and Human Services.

A listing of DHHS constituent agencies follows.

Social Security Administration
Division of Contracts and Grants Management
6301 Security Blvd.
Baltimore, MD 21235
(301) 594–3340

Health Care Financing Administration
Division of Procurement Services
Area BI, Gwynn Oak Building
Baltimore, MD 21207
(301) 594–3340
Small Business Office
6401 Security Blvd.
Baltimore, MD 21235
(301) 594–1502

Office of Human Development Services
Contracts Branch
Room 1271A
330 Independence Avenue SW
Washington, DC 20201
(202) 245–0016

Office of Equal Opportunity and Civil Rights
200 Independence Avenue SW
Room 336E
Washington, DC 20201
(202) 245–2890

Public Health Service
General Inquiries may be directed to one of the following addresses.

Division of Grants and Contracts
5600 Fishers Lane
Rm 18A19
Rockville, MD 20857
(301) 443–6630
Small Business Office
6500 Fishers Lane
Rockville, MD 20857
(301) 443–4547

Specific inquiries may be directed to the following Public Health components.

Alcohol Drug Abuse and Mental Health Administration
Contracts Office
5600 Fishers Lane
Mr.13C 12
Rockville, Md. 20857
(301) 443–3420
Small and Disadvantaged
Business Utilization
5600 Fishers Lane
Rm. 12–105
Rockville, MD 20857
(301) 443–4795

Center for Disease Control
Procurement and Grants Office
255 East Paces Rd., NE.
Atlanta, GA 30305
(404) 262-6545

Food and Drug Administration
Division of Contracts and Grants Management
5600 Fishers Lane
Rm. 1207
Rockville, MD 20857
(301) 443-2525

Health Resources Administration
Contract Operations Branch
Rm. 9-22, Center Building
3700 East-West Highway
Hyattsville, MD 20782
(301) 436-7192

Health Services Administration
Office of Contracts and Grants
5600 Fishers Lane
Rm. 13A-03
Rockville, MD 20857
(301) 443-1433

National Institutes of Health
Division of Contracts and Grants
Rm. 1B05, Bldg. 31
9000 Rockville Pike
Bethesda, MD 20014
(301) 496-4637

DEPARTMENT OF HOUSING AND URBAN DEVELOPMENT

The Department of Housing and Urban Development (HUD) administers programs concerning housing needs and the improvement and development of the nation's communities.

The headquarters office procures water and space heaters, ranges and refrigerators, lawn mowers, paint, screen wire, water closet seats, ash and garbage cans, hot-air furnace filters, window shades and cloth, and furniture. Inquiries should be directed to the Office of Procurement and Contracts, U.S. Department of Housing and Urban Development, 451 7th Street, SW., Washington, DC 20410.

Supplies and services for the rehabilitation, repair, management, maintenance, sale, or demolition of secretary-acquired properties are contracted for by the area and insuring offices of HUD if requirements are up to $10,000. Persons interested in being placed on HUD regional source lists should contact the appropriate regional office. These bidder source lists are not maintained at the national level. A list of regional and area insuring offices may be obtained by requesting HUD Form 788, Field Office Jurisdiction, from the Publications Services Center, U.S. Department of Housing and Urban Development, 451 7th Street, SW., Washington, DC 20410.

DEPARTMENT OF THE INTERIOR

Most purchases are made by individual bureaus. Central office procurements are arranged by the Division of Property and Records, U.S. Department of the Interior, Washington, DC 20240.

National Park Service. The National Park Service contracts for physical improvements and concessions. A list of offices that issue bid invitations is available from the Division of Contracting and Property Management. Write to the National Park Service, U.S. Department of the Interior, Washington, DC 20240.

Bureau of Mines. Many of the Bureau purchases are related to laboratory needs and helium production. They are made at field research centers, laboratories, area and district offices, and helium plants.

Suppliers should file Standard Form 129, Bidder's Mailing List Application, at a field office. For a list of offices that issue bid invitations, write to the Chief, Branch of Procurement, Bureau of Mines, U.S. Department of the Interior, Washington, DC 20241 (202) 634-4704.

Fish and Wildlife Service. The service buys small boats, outboard motors, construction and farming equipment, two-way radio transmitters and receivers, and fish foods.

Business representatives should send inquiries to the Procurement Officer, Fish and Wildlife Service, U.S. Department of the Interior, Washington, DC 20240, or to any one of its six regional offices. (202) 343-4825.

Bureau of Indian Affairs. The Bureau purchases supplies and equipment for agriculture, building maintenance, and construction—especially roads and irrigation. It also buys subsistence items and school supplies.

Inquiries and requests for inclusion on mailing lists should be sent to the nearest office. They are listed in the Small Business Administration's *U.S. Government Purchasing and Sales Directory*, which can be purchased from the Superintendent of Documents, U.S. Government Printing Office, Washington, DC 20402.

Geological Survey. Purchases include scientific equipment (both commercial and noncommercial) and ADP services and equipment. The Survey also enters into research and development contracts and a variety of service contracts. It administers certain Federal grants and cooperative agreements. As much as possible, awards are made to economically and socially disadvantaged firms.

Inquiries or requests to be placed on mailing lists should be addressed to U.S. Geological Survey, Branch of Procurement and Contracts, Policy and Procedures Section, 12201 Sunrise Valley Dr., Reston, VA 22092.

Bureau of Land Management. Purchases include firefighting equipment, range-grass seed, and tree thinning and planting services. The

Bureau also contracts for cultural resource studies; construction of fences, roads, and earthfill dams; and oceanographic environmental studies.

Acquisitions are made by the Washington office, the Denver Service Center, and field offices. For information contact the Bureau of Land Management at the Branch of Contract Operations (WO-851), Washington, DC 20240, or the Denver Service Center, Branch of Procurement (D-551), Denver, CO 80225.

Office of Surface Mining. Purchases include office supplies and equipment, special photographic supplies and equipment, two-way radio mobile communication equipment, and automotive fleet maintenance.

This office also contracts for such services as applied research, ecological investigation, environmental monitoring, geotechnical research, laboratory testing services, engineering support (exploratory drilling, testing, reclamation site specifications development), reclamation construction (dredging, contouring, backfilling, revegetation, mine sealing), training programs, and computer software and systems design.

Inquiries may be directed to the Chief, Branch of Procurement, Office of Surface Mining, 1951 Constitution Ave., NW., Washington, DC 20240; (202) 343-4685.

Water and Power Resources Service. Because the Service develops and manages water and related land resources in the 17 contiguous western States, construction accounts for about 70 percent of its total business. On construction projects, contractors furnish all equipment and materials necessary, except for special design components like pumps, turbines and generators for hydroplants, and large transformers. These are bought separately.

Contracts for construction and architect-engineering services are handled by seven regional offices. Research, development, and automated data processing contracting is done primarily by the Engineering and Research Center in Denver, Colo. Both the Center and the regional offices procure supplies and services for their in-house needs.

Inquiries and requests to be placed on the Bidder's Mailing Lists should be made to the Business Utilization and Development Specialist, Water and Power Resources Service, at one of the offices listed below.

Engineering and Research Center
Denver Federal Center
Bldg. 67
Denver, CO 80225
(303) 234-6637

Pacific Northwest Region
P.O. Box 043
Boise, ID 83724
(208) 384-1391

Mid-Pacific Region
2800 Cottage Way
Sacramento, CA 95825
(916) 484-4852

Lower Colorado Region
P.O. Box 427
Boulder City, NV 89005
(702) 293-8522

Upper Colorado Region
P.O. Box 11568
Salt Lake City, UT 84111
(801) 524-5542

Southwest Region
Suite 201, Commerce Bldg.
714 Tyler
Amarillo, TX 79101
(806) 376-9432

Upper Missouri Region
P.O. Box 2553
Billings, MT 59103
(406) 245-6543

Lower Missouri Region
Denver Federal Center
Bldg. 20
Denver, CO 80225
(303) 234-3885

DEPARTMENT OF JUSTICE

The various bureaus and services under this department are responsible for their own procurement, with the department itself only buying to meet the needs of headquarters offices. Requirements of the various bureaus include paper and paper products, fingerprint supplies, arms and ammunition, handcuffs and leg irons, medical supplies and equipment, and miscellaneous office supplies and equipment.

Bureau of Prisons. Prisons procure a range of general commodities since many of them are, in effect, self-contained cities. Purchases are made by the individual prisons from local sources of supply or from national supply houses.

Inquiries or applications for inclusions on mailing lists should be directed to specific penal institutions. Personal contacts by company representatives are recommended. They should be arranged sufficiently in advance to permit appropriate technicians and interested officials to be present, particularly for demonstrations of new or improved products.

Businesses making general inquiry about doing business with the federal prison system should write to the Bureau of the Prisons, U.S. Department of Justice, Washington, DC 20537.

Federal Prison Industries, Inc. This corporation purchases the raw materials required in the various prison workshops. Most procurements are by negotiated contract. Materials purchased include steel for steel furniture construction, wool and cotton for textile production, textiles for the production of clothing, leather for shoe production, bristles for making brushes, lumber for making furniture, and broom corn for brooms.

Federal prison products are for sale to government agencies only—usually through the facilities of the General Services Administration. Inquiries and requests to be put on mailing lists for solicitations of raw materials should be directed to the Purchasing Division, Federal Prison Industries, Inc., U.S. Department of Justice, Washington, DC 20537.

Drug Enforcement Administration (DEA). The procurement interests of this administration center on communications equipment, laboratory equipment, guns, ammunition, and automatic data processing and development contracts directly applicable to law enforcement activities.

Inquiries with regard to DEA procurement should be made to the Drug Enforcement Administration, Administrative Services Division, U.S. Department of Justice, Washington, DC 20537.

Federal Bureau of Investigation (FBI). The major commodities purchased by this bureau are radio and electronic equipment, special laboratory equipment, guns and ammunition, and other types of law-enforcement supplies.

Inquiries with regard to FBI procurement, or visits of business representatives who are interested in selling their products, should be made to the Procurement and Administrative Services Section, Federal Bureau of Investigation, U.S. Department of Justice, Washington, DC 20535.

United States Marshals Service. Purchases by the United States Marshals Service include weapons, ammunition, communications equipment, and related services. It also leases special-purpose real estate.

Businesses desiring information on agency requirements should write to the Administrative Services Division, United States Marshals Service, U.S. Department of Justice, Washington, DC 20530.

DEPARTMENT OF LABOR

Among procurements by the Department of Labor (DOL) are health and safety equipment, including protective clothing and mine safety equipment; ADP hardware and software; and audiovisual equipment and services. Service requirements include architecture, engineering, and construction; research, evaluation, and training; auditing and statistical services; and publications, arts, and graphics.

One office from which to obtain general information is the Office of Procurement, Rm. S-1521, 200 Constitution Ave., NW., Washington, DC 20210; (202) 523-9631.

A second office to contact is the Office of Printing Management, Rm. S-1516, 200 Constitution Ave., NW., Washington, DC 20210; (202) 523-6411.

Inquiries regarding business opportunities for small, minority, and women-owned firms should be addressed to the Director, Small and Disadvantaged Business Utilization, Rm. S-1325, 200 Constitution Ave., NW., Washington, DC 20210; (202) 523-9148.

Employment and Training Administration. To inquire about purchases of statistical services, research, evaluation, and training, write or call one of the three offices below.

Office of Administrative Services
Rm. 8400, 601 D St., NW.
Washington, DC 20213
(202) 376-6300

Office of Policy, Evaluation and Research
Central Procurement Staff
Rm. 9002, 601 D St., NW.
Washington, DC 20213
(202) 376-6620

Office of National Programs
Division of Contracting Services
Rm. 6320, 601 D St., NW.
Washington, DC 20213
(202) 376-7465

Mine Safety and Health Administration. Inquiries about sales of health or safety services or equipment should be directed to the Division of Management Services, Rm. 731, 4015 Wilson Blvd., Arlington, VA 22203; (703) 235-8500.

DEPARTMENT OF THE TREASURY

The Department of the Treasury purchases supplies and services primarily through the procurement offices at its 12 bureau headquarters. Purchases are also made at many field-office locations. However, these are generally limited to housekeeping or off-the-shelf items.

For a detailed listing of all the Department's procurement offices throughout the United States, as well as complete information on procurement policies and practices, consult the publication *Selling to the Department of the Treasury.* This booklet may be purchased from the Superintendent of Documents, U.S. Government Printing Office, Washington, DC 20402.

The Bureaus of Government Financial Operations, Mint, Engraving and Printing, Customs Service, and Internal Revenue Service have the larger procurement activities of the treasury. They issue the majority of the department bid/proposal solicitations.

To determine whether a treasury procurement office has interest in your product or service, send a copy of Standard Form 129, Bidder's Mailing List Application, to the appropriate procurement office listed below.

Those bureaus listed in darker type procure at the field office level.

Chief, Procurement Division (Operations)
Office of the Secretary of the Treasury
Washington, DC 20220

Director, Division of Facilities Management
Bureau of Government Financial Operations
Treasury Annex
Washington, DC 20226

Chief, Procurement Branch
Bureau of Alcohol, Tobacco and Firearms
12th Street and Pennsylvania Avenue
Washington, DC 20226

Procurement Officer
Office of the Comptroller of the Currency
Fifth Floor, East Building
L'Enfant Plaza
Washington, DC 20219

Procurement Officer
Federal Law Enforcement Training Center
Brunswick, GA 31520

Chief, Contracts and Procurement Branch
Logistics Management Division
U.S. Customs Service
Washington, DC 20229

Superintendent, Materials Management Division
Bureau of Engraving and Printing
U.S. Department of the Treasury
Engraving and Printing Annex
Washington, DC 20228

Chief, Contract and Procurement Section
Internal Revenue Service
U.S. Department of the Treasury
Washington, DC 20224

Chief, Procurement Division
Bureau of the Mint
U.S. Department of the Treasury
Washington, DC 20220

Chief, Procurement Section
Bureau of the Public Debt
U.S. Department of the Treasury
Engraving and Printing Annex
Washington, DC 20226

Chief, Office of Facilities and Procurement
United States Savings Bond Division
U.S. Department of the Treasury
Washington, DC 20226

Procurement Officer
United States Secret Service
U.S. Department of the Treasury
Washington, DC 20005

DEPARTMENT OF TRANSPORTATION

Procurement is decentralized throughout the Department of Transportation (DOT) as each of the operating administrations has in-house procurement capabilities. Specific information concerning each administration's requirements is contained in DOT Pamphlet 4200.1, *Contracting with the United States Department of Transportation*, which is available upon request from the Procurement Operations Division, M-43, U.S. Department of Transportation, 400 7th Street, SW., Washington, DC 20590.

The Office of the Secretary of Transportation contracts for studies and services relating to transportation management, research, and operations. Information concerning contracting opportunities may be obtained from the Department of Transportation, M-43, 400 7th Street, SW., Washington, DC 20590.

Federal Aviation Administration. The Federal Aviation Administration (FAA) makes procurements nationwide for aircraft and for equipment for communications, air navigation, and air traffic control, which may include computer hardware, supporting software, and software service. Purchases are made at headquarters for research and development and for major electronics systems. Further information may be obtained from any FAA regional office or the Procurement Management and Services Branch, Contracts Division, Federal Aviation Administration, U.S. Department of Transportation, Washington, DC 20591.

Federal Highway Administration. The Federal Highway Administration procures supplies, materials, equipment, and services, including research and development, construction, and professional and technical services.

To be notified of contract opportunities, submit Standard Form 129, Bidder's Mailing List Application, to the Procurement Branch, Federal Highway Administration, U.S. Department of Transportation, 400 7th Street, NW., Washington, DC 20590.

U.S. Coast Guard. U.S. Coast Guard district offices and other units procure ship repairs and ship replacement parts, aircraft repairs and aircraft replacement parts, buoys and appendages, and materials and construction to support Coast Guard operating units.

The Washington, D.C., office procures vessels, aircraft, electronics equipment and supplies for new vessels, and research services. The contracts of the Department of the Navy and other military services are used when practical. Inquiries should be directed to the Commandant (G-FCP), U.S. Coast Guard, U.S. Department of Transportation, 2100 2nd Street, SW, Washington, DC 20593.

Urban Mass Transportation Administration. The Urban Mass Transportation Administration (UMTA) contracts for research, development, and demonstration projects related to mass transportation. Information may be obtained from UMTA, Office of Procurement and Third Party Review, U.S. Department of Transportation, Washington, DC 20590.

Saint Lawrence Seaway Development Corporation. The Saint Lawrence Seaway Development Corporation procures navigational lock-operating equipment and related maintenance parts and heavy construction equipment and spare parts. Information may be obtained from the Administrative Services Officer, Saint Lawrence Seaway Development Corporation, U.S. Department of Transportation, P.O. Box 520, Massena, NY 13662.

Federal Railroad Administration. The Federal Railroad Administration (FRA)—which oversees the northeast corridor program to improve service between Washington, D.C., and Boston, Mass., is responsible for the Alaska Railroad, and manages the DOT Transportation Test Center at Pueblo, Colo.—contracts for research in such subjects as aerodynamics, vehicle propulsion, vehicle control, communications, and vehicle safety. FRA also purchases studies and demonstrations relating to the safety, environment, and efficiency of our national rail system. Information on FRA procurement can be obtained from the Federal Railroad Administration, 400 7th St., SW., Washington, DC 20590.

National Highway Traffic Safety Administration. The National Highway Traffic Safety Administration (NHTSA) procures research, development, test and evaluation services which promote highway and vehicle safety. Information on all NHTSA procurements may be obtained from National Highway Traffic Safety Administration, Office of Contracts and Procurement, 400 7th St., SW., Washington, D.C. 20590.

Research and Special Program Administration. The Research and Special Program Administration procures studies and services to plan, develop, initiate and manage programs in all fields of transportation research and development. Information may be obtained from the Procurement Division (DPA-14), Research and Special Program Administration, Washington, DC 20590 or the Transportation Systems Center, Acquisition Division, Kendall Square, Cambridge, MA 02142.

Maritime Administration. The Maritime Administration's primary contracting needs are in areas of ship design and construction, development of advance ship operations, port and intermodal development, and marine technology. For procurement information contact the Maritime Administration, Office of Administration and Contracts, 400 7th St., SW., Washington, DC 20590.

ENVIRONMENTAL PROTECTION AGENCY

The purchasing activities and requirements of the Environmental Protection Agency (EPA) are diversified because of the many types of programs for which the Agency is responsible.

First and foremost, EPA is a regulatory agency with responsibilities for establishing and enforcing environmental standards concerning air and water pollution, solid waste management, pesticides, radiation, noise, and toxic substances. Some of the data gathering and analysis required to develop effective standards and guidelines are obtained under contracts with experts or companies specializing in technical services. Most of the automated data processing equipment required is procured by negotiated contracts; these contracts may also cover software and support services.

EPA also requires construction, alteration, and repair of buildings, structures, and other real property. Construction is normally procured by means of formal advertising, and EPA has established an architect-engineer selection board.

For more detailed information on EPA procurements, write to one of the three major contracting offices listed below for the booklet *Contracting with EPA—A Guide for Prospective Contractors.*

Headquarters Contract Operations (PM-214)
U.S. Environmental Protection Agency
Washington, DC 20460

Contracts Management Division
U.S. Environmental Protection Agency
Cincinnati, OH 45268

Contracts Management Division
U.S. Environmental Protection Agency
Research Triangle Park, NC 27711

NATIONAL AERONAUTICS AND SPACE ADMINISTRATION

National Aeronautics and Space Administration (NASA) operations—essentially of a research and development nature—are performed at spaceflight centers, research centers, and other installations throughout the country. Each installation has a specifically prescribed mission and procures the material and services needed to carry it out.

NASA awards contracts to universities and nonprofit research organizations as well as private industry. Detailed information on business opportunities may be obtained from the Small Business Specialist, NASA, at any of the following addresses.

Headquarters Contracts Division
Washington, DC 20546

Ames Research Center
Moffett Field, CA 94035

Dryden Flight Research Center
P.O. Box 273
Edwards, CA 93523

Goddard Space Flight Center
Greenbelt, MD 20771

Jet Propulsion Laboratory
4800 Oak Grove Drive
Pasadena, CA 91103

Johnson Space Center
Houston, TX 77058

Kennedy Space Center
Kennedy Space Center, FL 32899

Langley Research Center
Langley Station
Hampton, VA 23365

Lewis Research Center
21000 Brookpark Rd.
Cleveland, OH 44135

Marshall Space Flight Center
Huntsville, AL 35812

National Space Technology
Laboratories
Bay St. Louis, MS 39520

Wallops Flight Center
Wallops Island, VA 23337

TENNESSEE VALLEY AUTHORITY

Purchases by the Tennessee Valley Authority (TVA) are primarily for construction and operation of electric power plants and transmission systems, construction of dams and locks, and development and experimental production of fertilizers. Items required include electrical generating equipment such as turbo-generators, steam-generating units, nuclear plant equipment, hydraulic turbines and generators, transformers, boilers, piping systems, and switchgear. Coal, coke, and nuclear fuel are bought. Electrical and electronic supplies, equipment, and spare parts, and communications equipment are stocked. Supplies procured include structural and milled steel, phosphate rock and chemicals, and items for medical, laboratory, and photographic purposes.

TVA has a centralized Division of Purchasing. Requests for information or for mailing list applications should be addressed to the Chief of the branch responsible for the equipment or supplies of interest at the Division of Purchasing, Tennessee Valley Authority, Chattanooga, TN 37401.

The Nuclear Procurement Branch buys nuclear fuel, turbogenerators, and nuclear steam-supply systems. The Equipment Procurement Branch is responsible for all other (nonnuclear) equipment. The Materials Procurement Branch buys construction and structural and building materials, architect-engineer services, and general supplies. The Fuels Procurement Branch buys coal and coke; and transportation services are bought by the Traffic Branch. The Open Market Procurement Branch buys equipment and materials for which the aggregate amount of the requisition is $10,000 or less.

UNITED STATES POSTAL SERVICE

The Postal Service purchases both goods and services. Goods include mail-processing and mail-handling equipment; transport and delivery equipment; customer service equipment; office furniture, machines, equipment, and supplies; and custodial, protective, building, and vehicle maintenance equipment. Services bought are building protection and maintenance and vehicle maintenance and repair.

Procurements in excess of $10,000 are published in *Commerce Business Daily,* including those for facilities, architect-engineering services, and specific research and development programs and projects.

The *Postal Contracting Manual, Publication 41,* outlines uniform policies and procedures for the procurement of mail transportation, facilities, equipment, supplies, and services. It is available at current rates, under stock number 039–000–81003–4, from the Superintendent of Documents, U.S. Government Printing Office, Washington, DC 20402.

The Eastern Area Supply Center, U.S. Postal Service, Contract Branch, VA Depot, Sommerville, NJ 08877, purchases open market items such as wood bulletin boards, carrier satchel straps, conveyors, corrugated boxes, custodial supplies, envelopes, workroom and lobby furniture, gloves, hardware products, marginal punched forms, materials handling equipment, paper products, metal signs, and other postal supplies.

The Western Area Supply Center, U.S. Postal Service, Contract Branch, Topeka, KS 66624, purchases spare parts for electrical, electronic, vehicle, and mechanical equipment and assemblies and bulk conveyors.

To be placed on the appropriate bidder's mailing list for supplies, services, and equipment, other than for construction and transportation of mail services, file PS Form 7429, *Bidder's Mailing List Application,* and Form 7429-A, *Commodity and Geographic Location Check-Off,* with the Data Automation Division, Bidder's Mailing Lists, Western Area Supply Center, U.S. Postal Service, Topeka, KS 66619.

For information on construction and leasing and to be placed on the appropriate bidder's list, contact the General Manager, Facilities Procurement Division, Real Estate and Buildings Department, U.S. Postal Service, 475 L'Enfant Plaza West, SW., Washington, DC 20260, or the Regional Director, Real Estate and Buildings Department, in the appropriate region listed below.

To obtain information on transporting mail, write to the Director, Office of Transportation Services, Mail Processing Department, U.S. Postal Service, 475 L'Enfant Plaza West, SW., Washington, DC 20260.

Further details concerning Postal Service

procurement programs are contained in *Selling to the Postal Service, Publication 151,* available free from the Office of Contracts, Documents Processing Branch, Procurement and Supply Department, U.S. Postal Service, 475 L'Enfant Plaza, SW., Washington, DC 20260, or from any regional office.

Each Postal Service regional office has a number of procurement services offices in its geographic area which purchase supplies, utilities, fuel, vehicle rental, vehicle maintenance and services, building repairs and services (such as cleaning, window cleaning, trash removal, snow removal, and elevator maintenance), and other minor construction requirements. Information on procurements by the regional offices may be obtained by contacting the Contracts and Supply Management Branch, Procurement Division, U.S. Postal Service, at the following addresses:

Northeast Region
New York, NY 10098

Central Region
433 West Buren St.
Chicago, IL 60699

Eastern Region
1845 Walnut St.
Philadelphia, PA 19101

Western Region
850 Cherry Ave.
San Bruno, CA 94099

Southern Region
1407 Union Ave.
Memphis, TN 38166

VETERANS ADMINISTRATION

The Veterans Administration (VA) has a central purchasing facility, the Marketing Center, P.O. Box 76, Hines, IL 60141; (312) 687-6782. It purchases medical, dental, and surgical supplies; drugs and chemicals (reagent and medicinal); nonperishable foods; prosthetic and orthopedic aids; medical, radiological, and laundry equipment; and uniforms and flags.

Some items are procured locally by individual VA medical centers. They include perishable foodstuffs, maintenance supplies, off-the-shelf drug items, medical supplies, services (extermination, laundry, repairs to buildings, maintenance and repair of medical and scientific equipment), and books.

The Office of Supply Services awards management consultant contracts. Notices of contract opportunities appear in three information bulletins: IB 13-4, *Could You Use a Multibillion Dollar Customer?;* IB 13-5, *Let's Do Business,* and IB 13-9, *Doing Business With the Veterans Administration.* They are available from the Office of Supply Services (93), Veterans Adminis-

tration, 810 Vermont Ave., NW., Washington, DC 20420; (202) 389-3515.

The Office of Construction awards contracts to private firms for building design, construction, and technology research. New facilities are built and old ones are improved to provide quality medical care for veterans. This office is also responsible for the design and construction activities of the National Cemetery System. Contracts are the lump-sum type. The Washington, D.C., office negotiates for all professional services (design work) and makes all construction contract awards.

Both buildings and cemetery projects are advertised in *Commerce Business Daily.* Awards are made on the basis of competitive firms located in the geographic area of the bidding. Where possible, they are made to firms located in the geographic area of the project. Architects, engineers, and contractors should apply to the Assistant Administrator for Construction, Veterans Administration, 810 Vermont Avenue, NW, Washington, DC 20420.

GOVERNMENT SALES OF SURPLUS PROPERTY

PERSONAL PROPERTY

The General Services Administration and the Department of Defense are the principal agencies that sell surplus personal property. A few civilian agencies—including the Tennessee Valley Authority, the U.S. Postal Service, and the Maritime Administration—conduct their own sales.

Among the many thousands of items sold are motor vehicles and aircraft, medical equipment and supplies, plumbing and heating equipment, paper products, office machines and supplies and equipment, and industrial equipment. Goods may be used or unused, in good condition, requiring repair, or have value only as scrap.

As items become available for sale, public notice is given. "Invitations for Bids" are distributed to those who have expressed an interest in the types of property offered. Quantities are such that businesses of all sizes, as well as individuals, may participate without preference or priority. Sales are open to the public.

Sales generally are on a competitive basis. Bids must be responsive to the bid invitation and acceptable to the government. Prices and other factors are considered.

Mailing lists and catalogs. Each GSA regional office maintains its own mailing lists for sales of property located in the geographic area it serves. For general information about sales conducted by GSA ask for the pamphlet *Federal Surplus Personal Property Sales Programs,* available free from the GSA Business Service Center that serves the area where your business is located. To be placed on the mailing list write or call the same center (see page 500).

The Department of Defense maintains a centralized mailing list for sales of goods in the United States. This list is maintained by the Defense Surplus Bidder's Control Office. Requests for inclusion on mailing lists should be mailed to DoD Surplus Sales, P.O. Box 1370, Battle Creek, MI 49016. Surplus property sales catalogs describe the property, indicate dates and times for inspection, and provide other details.

Public notice of sales. Public notice of sales may be provided through newspaper, radio, or television announcements; by stories or advertisements; in trade journals and periodicals; through notices placed in public buildings; and through announcement in the *Commerce Business Daily,* which contains a listing of the larger current sales of personal property.

Sale Methods. Any of the following may be used.

Sealed bids—Bids must be signed and returned to the office specified. If a deposit is required, it must be included. On the sale date, bids are opened publicly and awards made.

Public auction—Notice is given in newspapers or other media, and catalogs are provided. Traditional commercial auction methods are followed.

Spot bid—Generally, buyers place their bids in a box at the site, or submit them during the conduct of the sale. Awards are made on an item by item basis as the sale progresses. On some sales, provisions are made for those who cannot attend the sale to submit bids.

General conditions of sale. Sales brochures and announcements contain the instructions for bidding, payment, and property removal. Close attention should be paid to those instructions.

Deposits, usually 20 percent, are often required with sealed bids. They are promptly refunded to unsuccessful bidders.

Bidders should inspect the property carefully before placing bids. Property is offered "as is, where is."

REAL PROPERTY

Surplus real property is first available to state and local governments and certain nonprofit health and educational institutions. If it is not acquired by them, competitive bids are sought.

GSA has the principal responsibility for surplus real property sales. However, special categories of land and improvements may be offered for sale by other agencies. The Veterans Administration sells houses that have been acquired through foreclosure on "GI bill" mort-gages. The Department of Housing and Urban Development disposes of homes and other properties acquired because of defaults under mortgage insurance programs. Each agency is normally responsible for the sale of buildings and improvements on land in its custody.

GSA sells nearly every type of real estate found on the commercial market. In many cases, buyers may use the properties immediately.

Publicizing real property sales. When government real property is for sale, the GSA regional office prepares a notice describing the property and how it will be sold. The notice is mailed to those who have shown an interest in buying similar property. A computerized mailing list is maintained in Denver, Colo., and bidders' applications are available at each of GSA's Business Service Centers.

Announcements are made in newspapers, magazines, trade journals, the *Commerce Business Daily,* and on radio and television. Specialists in the regional offices provide advice on current and future property sales.

Sale methods. The following are the two most common methods. Both are competitive and public.

Sealed bids—In response to an invitation, bids are submitted along with a deposit to the issuing regional office. On a specified date, bids are opened and read publicly. If the high bid is acceptable, an award is made—usually within 60 days. Deposits are returned promptly to all unsuccessful bidders.

Public auction—Bidders must submit a predetermined and publicly announced deposit of earnest money. Award is made to the highest bidder whose offer is acceptable to the government.

Auction sales are usually conducted on the property site.

Advice to buyers of real property. Give close attention to the instructions provided in the sales brochures and announcements.

Carefully inspect the property being offered for sale before bidding. It will be sold "as is, where is." Lack of information will not constitute grounds for adjustment of bids.

Be prepared to submit a deposit with your bid in the form and amount specified by the government. When credit terms are desired, make certain that the financial information necessary for credit is available. GSA generally follows commercial practices in extending credit.

STRATEGIC AND CRITICAL MATERIALS

The Strategic and Critical Materials Stock Piling Act provides for the acquisition and retention of certain materials in order to prevent a dependence upon foreign nations in times of national emergency. The Federal Emergency Management Agency (FEMA) is responsible for determining the quantity, quality and type of materials to be stockpiled. GSA is responsible for the acquisition, storage, upgrading, rotating, and disposition of the commodities identified.

Disposals are made when materials in inventory are found to be in excess of national security needs and—usually—are approved by Congress. The Office of Stockpile Transactions in GSA's Federal Property Resources Service (FPRS) conducts disposals on a nonexclusive, nondiscriminatory basis by means of sealed bids, auctions, negotiations, or other sales methods.

Every reasonable effort is made to carry out a long-term acquisition and disposal plan as formally announced. This allows industry to make developmental, research, and investment plans in anticipation of these disposals. However, market conditions and the impact of actions on the economy must be taken into account.

The proceeds from disposals are returned to the Stockpile Transaction Fund for use in authorized acquisitions.

For information on types and quantities of materials presently being acquired for or disposed of from the stockpile, contact the appropriate GSA Business Service Center or the Office of Stockpile Transactions, Federal Property Resources Service, General Services Administration, Crystal Square #5, Room 902, Washington, DC 20406.

Specific items to be acquired will be announced as authorizations are approved. Usual materials available for disposal are metals, minerals and ores, and agricultural products. Examples include mercury, tin, tungsten ores and concentrates, industrial diamonds, and vegetable tannin extracts.

BUSINESS SERVICES DIRECTORY

Director or Manager	Mailing Address and Telephone	Area of Service
Regional Director of Business Affairs	Business Service Center General Services Administration John W. McCormack Post Office and Courthouse Boston, MA 02109 (617) 223–2868	Connecticut, Maine, Massachusetts, New Hampshire, Rhode Island, and Vermont
Regional Director of Business Affairs	Business Service Center General Services Administration 26 Federal Plaza New York, NY 10007 (212) 264–1234	New Jersey, New York, Puerto Rico, and Virgin Islands
Regional Director of Business Affairs	Business Service Center General Services Administration 7th and D Streets, SW., Rm. 1050 Washington, DC 20407 (202) 472–1804	District of Columbia, nearby Maryland, Virginia
Manager	Business Service Center General Services Administration 9th and Market Streets Room 5142 Philadelphia, PA 19107 (215) 597–9613	Delaware, Pennsylvania, West Virginia, Maryland, Virginia
Regional Director of Business Affairs	Business Service Center General Services Administration Richard B. Russell Federal Building and Court House 75 Spring Street Atlanta, GA 30303 (404) 221–5103/3032	Alabama, Florida, Georgia, Kentucky, Mississippi, North Carolina, South Carolina, and Tennessee
Regional Director of Business Affairs	Business Service Center General Services Administration 230 South Dearborn Street Chicago, IL 60604 (312) 353–5383	Illinois, Indiana, Ohio, Michigan, Minnesota, and Wisconsin

Director or Manager	Mailing Address and Telephone	Area of Service
Regional Director of Business Affairs	Business Service Center General Services Administration 1500 East Bannister Road Kansas City, MO 64131 (816) 926–7203	Iowa, Kansas, Missouri, and Nebraska
Regional Director of Business Affairs	Business Service Center General Services Administration 819 Taylor Street Fort Worth, TX 76102 (817) 334–3284	Arkansas, Louisiana, New Mexico, Oklahoma, and Texas
Manager	Gulf Coast Business Service Center General Services Administration Federal Office Building and Courthouse 515 Rusk Street Houston, TX 77002 (713) 226–5787	Gulf Coast from Brownsville, Texas, to New Orleans, Louisiana
Regional Director of Business Affairs	Business Service Center General Services Administration Building 41, Denver Federal Center Denver, CO 80225 (303) 234–2216	Colorado, Montana, North Dakota, South Dakota, Utah, and Wyoming
Regional Director of Business Affairs	Business Service Center General Services Administration 525 Market Street San Francisco, CA 94105 (415) 556–0877	California (northern), Hawaii, and Nevada (except Clark County)
Manager	Business Service Center General Services Administration 525 Market Street San Francisco, CA 94105 (415) 556–2122	
Manager	Business Service Center General Services Administration 300 North Los Angeles Street Los Angeles, CA 90012 (213) 688–3210	Arizona, Los Angeles, California (southern), and Nevada (Clark County only)
Regional Director of Business Affairs	Business Service Center General Services Administration 440 Federal Building 915 Second Avenue Seattle, WA 98174 (206) 442–5556	Alaska, Idaho, Oregon, and Washington

GSA SMALL BUSINESS INFORMATION OFFICES

Alabama
Birmingham
(205) 254–1755
Huntsville
(205) 895–5326
Mobile
(205) 690–2361
Montgomery
(205) 832–7310

Arizona
Phoenix
(602) 261–3294
Tucson
(602) 792–6301

Arkansas
Little Rock
(501) 378–5285
Ft. Smith
(501) 782–1934

California
Fresno
(209) 487–5069
Sacramento
(916) 440–3171
San Diego
(714) 293–6640

Colorado
Colorado Springs
(303) 635–8911

Connecticut
Hartford
(203) 244–3540

Florida
Jacksonville
(904) 791–2791
Miami
(305) 350–5751
Tampa
(813) 228–2351

Georgia
Savannah
(912) 232–4321
Thomasville
(912) 226–2716

Hawaii
Honolulu
(808) 546–7516

Idaho
Boise
(208) 384–1242

Illinois
Springfield
(217) 525–4270

Indiana
Indianapolis
(317) 269–6234

Iowa
Des Moines
(515) 284–4114

Kansas
Topeka
(913) 295–2518
Wichita
(316) 267–6311

Kentucky
Covington
(513) 684–1393
Louisville
(502) 582–6436

Louisiana
Lafayette
(318) 234–7346
New Orleans
(504) 589–6677
Shreveport
(318) 226–5006

Maine
Augusta
(207) 622–6171

Maryland
Baltimore
(301) 962–2211

Massachusetts
Andover
(617) 475–0371
Dorchester
(617) 223–2633
Waltham
(617) 894–2400
Worcester
(617) 791–2251

Michigan
Detroit
(313) 226–4910

Minnesota
Twin Cities
(612) 725–4015

Mississippi
Jackson
(601) 969–4449
Tupelo
(601) 842–4311

Missouri
St. Louis
(314) 268–3151

Montana
Billings
(406) 657–6279
Helena
(406) 449–5285
Missoula
(406) 329–3117

Nebraska
Omaha
(402) 221–4702

Nevada
Las Vegas
(702) 385–6444
Reno
(702) 784–5302

New Hampshire
Manchester
(603) 669–7011

New Jersey
Edison
(201) 549–4441
Newark
(201) 645–2416
Trenton
(609) 989–2082

New Mexico
Albuquerque
(505) 766–2101
Santa Fe
(505) 988–6361

New York
Albany
(518) 472–5770
Binghamton
(607) 773–2743
Brooklyn (NYC)
(212) 330–7474
Buffalo
(716) 846–4582
Jamaica (NYC)
(212) 995–8575
Plattsburg
(518) 563–0931
Rochester
(716) 263–6288
Scotia
(518) 370–3408
Syracuse
(315) 473–3378

North Carolina
Asheville
(704) 258–2850
Raleigh
(919) 755–4680

North Dakota
Bismarck
(701) 255–4011
Fargo
(701) 237–5771

Ohio
Cincinnati
(513) 684–2306
Cleveland
(216) 522–4220
Columbus
(614) 469–6824

Oklahoma
Muskogee
(918) 687–2283
Oklahoma City
(405) 231–4791
Tulsa
(918) 581–7755

Oregon
Eugene
(503) 687–6640

Pennsylvania
Erie
(814) 452–2903
Pittsburgh
(412) 644–3483

Puerto Rico
Hato Rey
(809) 753–4370

Rhode Island
Providence
(401) 528–4472

South Carolina
Charleston
(803) 724–4233
Columbia
(803) 765–5581

South Dakota
Aberdeen
(605) 225–0250
Pierre
(605) 224–5842

Tennessee
Memphis
(901) 521–3675
Nashville
(615) 251–5221
Oak Ridge
(615) 576–0583

Texas
Beaumont
(713) 838–0271
Dallas
(214) 767–0023
El Paso
(915) 543–7714
Laredo
(512) 723–6642
Lubbock
(806) 762–7401
San Antonio
(512) 229–6040

Utah
Ogden
(801) 626–3541

Vermont
Burlington
(802) 862–6501

Virginia
Richmond
(804) 782–2101
Roanoke
(703) 982–6174

Washington
Bellingham
(206) 676–8440

Richland
(509) 942–7252
Spokane
(509) 456–4663

West Virginia
Parkersburg
(304) 422–8551

Wisconsin
Milwaukee
(414) 291–3035

Wyoming
Casper/Mills
(307) 265–5550
Cheyenne
(307) 778–2220

GOVERNMENT DATA CENTER

The Federal Procurement Data System provides Government-wide information on procurement actions with data on a fiscal year quarter generally available from the Center approximately 75 days after the end of the quarter.

The system tracks acquisition spending by the U.S. Government agencies which totaled approximately $110 billion in fiscal year 1980. Approximately 920,000 procurement actions are in the current master file.

The system contains 27 data elements, the basic ones being the reporting agency providing the data; the report date of the period covered; the contract number; the modification number of the procurement action; the purchasing or contracting office; date of the award; the principal place of performance; the dollars obligated on the transaction; and the principal product or service.

Additional details provided under the system include:

Subject to statutory requirements: Walsh-Healy Act, Service Contract Act, Davis-Bacon Act, etc.

Type of procurement action: letter contract, definitive contract, order under contract, modification, GSA Supply Schedule, etc.

Method of Contracting: Formal Advertisement or Negotiated, competitive or noncompetitive; negotiation authority—section of statute that applies; type of contract or modification-firm-fixed price, cost-plus-fixed-fee, time and materials, etc.

Also, socio-economic data such as small and large business, minority, educational, nonprofit, women-owned, labor surplus areas, etc.

The name and address of the contractor, as well as all subsidiaries and divisions of a company that have Government contracts, can also be identified.

Estimated completion date: year and month.

Foreign trade data, including the number of offerors offering foreign end products, and the percent difference if a Buy American factor is used.

The Center prepares and distributes a number of publications each quarter. A copy of the latest issue of each publication is available at no charge. The Center also maintains a mailing list for each publication and, if requested, the publication(s) can be provided as they are produced.

The Center has the capability of responding to special requests for specific or tailored detailed data. These requests also must be in writing, and there will be a charge for direct costs incurred for professional search, programmer effort, and computer search.

Any requests for data or information should be in writing to the FPDC: Director, Federal Procurement Data Center, 4040 N. Fairfax Drive, Arlington, Virginia 22203. For assistance or questions: (703) 235–1326.

Business Information Directory

GENERAL INFORMATION SOURCES

Government publications referred to below may be obtained from the Government Printing Office (GPO), Washington, DC, 20402, unless otherwise indicated.

GENERAL SOURCES

The *United States Government Manual* is an annual publication. It describes the organization, purposes, and programs of most government agencies and lists top personnel. Available from the GPO.

Washington Information Directory is an annual publication listing, by topic, organizations and publications which provide information on a wide range of subjects. It also lists congressional committee assignments, regional federal offices, embassies, and state and local officials. Published by the Congressional Quarterly, Inc., 1414 22nd Street NW, Washington, DC 20037.

Statistical Abstracts of the United States, published annually, is the standard summary on the social, political, and economic statistics of the United States. It includes data from both government and private sources. Appendix II gives a comprehensive list of sources. (GPO)

Professional and trade organizations and publications are a major source of contacts and information. Key directories to these sources are listed below.

Encyclopedia of Associations, published by Gale Research Co., Book Tower, Detroit, MI 48226.

The World Guide to Trade Associations gives a comprehensive national and international listing of associations. Published by R. R. Bowker Co., 1180 Avenue of the Americas, New York, NY 10036.

Ulrich's International Periodical Directory covers both domestic and foreign periodicals. Published by R. R. Bowker Co., 1180 Avenue of the Americas, New York, NY 10036.

Standard Periodical Directory covers U.S. and Canadian periodicals. Published by Oxbridge Communications, Inc., 183 Madison Avenue, New York, NY 10016.

Ayer's Directory of Newspapers and Periodicals provides titles of trade newspapers and periodicals. Published by Ayer Press, W. Washington Square, Philadelphia, PA 19106.

Standard Rate and Data Service provides information on periodical circulation and advertising rates. Published by Standard Rates and Data Service, Inc., 5201 Old Orchard Road, Skokie, IL 60076.

Listings of trade directories are given in the following guides:

Guide to American Directories, published by B. Klein Publications, Inc., P.O. Box 8503, Coral Springs, FL 33065.

Directory of Directories, published by Gate Research Co., Book Tower, Detroit, MI 48226.

Encyclopedia of Business Information, a comprehensive single-volume source, is updated periodically. Available from Gale Research Co., Book Tower, Detroit, MI 48226. *Researcher's Guide to Washington Experts,* Washington Researchers, 918 16th Street NW, Washington, D.C. 20006.

BUSINESS AND ECONOMICS INFORMATION

Business and economic information is provided by the following key references.

Survey of Current Business is a major publication which is supplemented on a weekly basis with *Current Statistics.* The publication contains articles as well as comprehensive statistics on all aspects of the economy, including data on the GNP, employment, wages, prices, finance, foreign trade, and production by industrial sector. (GPO)

Business Conditions Digest is a monthly with an extensive collection of charts and tables on the national income and products, leading coincident and lagging cyclical indicators, foreign trade, prices, wages, analytical ratios, and international production and stock prices. (GPO)

Economic Indicators is a monthly summary-type publication prepared by the Council of Economic Advisers. It contains charts and tables on natural output, income, spending, employment, unemployment, wages, industrial production, construction, prices, money, credit, federal finance, and international statistics. (GPO)

Federal Reserve Bulletin is a monthly issued by the Federal Reserve System, containing articles and very extensive tabulated data on all aspects of the monetary situation, credit, mortgage markets, interest rates, and stock and bond yields. A monthly *Chart Book* is available which contains charts of financial and monetary data. Both are available from the Division of Administrative Services, Board of Governors, Federal Reserve System, Washington, DC 20551.

Monthly Labor Review. This monthly publication provides articles and statistics on employment, productivity, wages, earnings, prices, wage settlements, and work stoppages. (GPO)

U.S. Industrial Outlook is an annual providing evaluations and projections of all major industrial and commercial segments of the domestic economy. (GPO)

Quarterly Financial Report of Manufacturing Corporations is issued by the Securities and Exchange Commission and the Federal Trade Commission. It covers corporate financial statistics including sales, profits, assets, and financial ratios, classified by industry group and size. (GPO)

Current Industrial Reports are a series of over 100 monthly, quarterly, semiannual, and annual reports on major products manufactured in the United States. For subscription, contact the Bureau of the Census, U.S. Department of Commerce, Washington, DC 20233. (GPO)

Annual Survey of Manufacturers. General statistics of manufacturing activity for industry groups, individual industries, states, and geographical regions are provided. (GPO)

County Business Patterns is an annual publication on employment and payrolls, which include a separate paperbound report for each state. (GPO)

Foreign Trade is a Bureau of the Census publication giving monthly reports on U.S. foreign trade. (GPO)

Population: Current Report is a series of monthly and annual reports covering population changes and socioeconomic characteristics of the population. (GPO)

Retail Sales: Current Business Report is a weekly report which provides retail statistics. (GPO)

Wholesale Trade, Sales and Inventories: Current Business Report provides a monthly report on wholesale trade. (GPO)

Directory of Marketing Research Houses and Services is an annual available from the American Marketing Association, 420 Lexington Avenue, New York, NY 10022.

CORPORATE INFORMATION

The major sources of information on publicly held corporations (as well as government and municipal issues) are: *Moody's Investor Services, Inc.*, owned by Dun & Bradstreet, 99 Church Street, New York, NY 10007, and *Standard & Poor's Corp.*, owned by McGraw-Hill, 345 Hudson Street, New York, NY 10014.

Standard & Poor's *Corporate Records* and Moody's *Manuals* are large multivolume works published annually and kept up to date with daily (for Standard & Poor's) or semiweekly (for Moody's) reports. The services provide extensive coverage of industrials, public utilities, transportation, banks, and financial companies. Also included are municipal and government issues.

In addition, the above corporations provide computerized data services and magnetic tapes. Compustat tapes, containing major corporate financial data, are available from Investor's Management Services, Inc., Denver, CO, a subsidiary of Standard & Poor's. Time-sharing access to Compustat and other financial data bases is available through Interactive Data Corporation, Waltham, MA (617) 890–1234.

The 10-K and other corporate reports are filed with the Securities and Exchange Commission and are available at local SEC offices, investor relations departments of publicly traded companies, as well as various private services, such as Disclosure Inc., Reliance Group, 120 Broadway, New York, NY 10005, which provides a complete microfiche service.

How to Find Information About Companies, Washington Researchers, 918 16th Street, NW, Washington, DC 20006.

Major trade directories include the *Thomas Register of American Manufacturers* (published by Thomas Publishing Company, 1 Pennsylvania Plaza, New York, NY) and Dun & Bradstreet's *Reference Book of Manufacturers.*

Thomas Register includes in one volume an alphabetical listing of manufacturers, giving address, phone number, product, subsidiaries, plant location, and an indication of assets.

Dun & Bradstreet's *Reference Book* covers similar information, including sales and credit. Dun & Bradstreet also publishes directories on transportation and apparel trades, the *Million Dollar Directory* (a listing of firms with a net worth of $1 million or more), and a *Middle Market Directory* (a listing of firms with a net worth of $500,000 to $1 million).

FEDERAL GOVERNMENT DEVELOPMENTS

Commerce Business Daily. This daily provides information on contract awards and subcontract opportunities, Defense Department awards, and surplus sales. (GPO)

Federal Register. This daily provides information on federal agency regulations and other legal documents (GPO).

CQ Weekly Report. This major service follows every important piece of legislation through both houses of Congress and reports on the political and lobbying pressures being applied. Available from the Congressional Quarterly Service, 1414 22nd Street, Washington, DC 20037.

Daily Report for Executives. A daily series of reports giving Washington developments that affect all aspects of business operations. Available from the Bureau of National Affairs,

Inc., 1231 25th Street NW, Washington, DC 20037.

Two major services, the *Bureau of National Affairs, Inc.* (address above) and the *Commerce Clearing House, Inc.* (4025 West Peterson Avenue, Chicago, IL 60646), publish a large number of valuable weekly loose-leaf reports covering developments in all aspects of law, government regulations, and taxation.

INDEX PUBLICATIONS

Indexes of a wide variety of articles appearing in periodicals, trade presses, and financial services dealing with corporations, industry, and finance are given in the following:

Business Periodicals Index published by H. W. Wilson Co., 950 University Avenue, Bronx, NY.

Funk and Scott Index of Corporations and Industries, published by Predicast, Inc., 11001 Cedar Street, Cleveland, OH 44141.

Major newspaper indexes are:

New York Times Index published by the New York Times Company, 229 W. 43rd Street, New York, NY 10036 (semimonthly, cumulates annually).

Wall Street Journal Index published by Dow Jones & Co. Inc., 22 Cortland Street, New York, NY 10007 (monthly).

HOW TO FOLLOW ECONOMIC INDICATORS

In the current turbulence of the economy, fluctuations in economic conditions are increasingly significant. Researchers investigating markets and economic developments should monitor the nation's economic indicators closely. The indicators are surveys performed by the government, illustrating the country's economic health. The following list describes several of the indicators and tells how to follow them.

Consumer Price Index—This covers changes in the cost of goods to consumers. Press releases reporting on it are issued monthly by the Department of Labor's Bureau of Labor Statistics. To be put on a mailing list to receive the reports, write:

Bureau of Labor Statistics
441 G St. NW, Room 1539
Washington, DC 20212

To receive data from the index within 24 hours of release, subscribe to the Consumer Price Index Mailgram service.

Source: *The Information Reports,* Washington Researchers, 918 16th Street NW, Washington, DC 20006.

National Technical Information Service
5285 Port Royal Road
Springfield, VA 22161
703-487-4650

Producer Price Index—Formerly called the *Wholesale Price Index,* this measures changes in prices received in primary markets by producers. It is calculated monthly. To regularly receive free releases, write the Bureau of Labor Statistics at the address above.

Composite Index of Leading Economic Indicators—The Commerce Department's Bureau of Economic Analysis compiles this each month from 12 major economic indicators. It is published in *Business Conditions Digest,* which can be purchased for $55 per year from:

Superintendent of Documents
Government Printing Office
Washington, DC 20402
202-783-3238

To receive the numbers only, contact:

Bureau of Economic Analysis
Department of Commerce
Washington, DC 20230
202-523-0589

Personal Consumption Expenditure Deflator—This is the Commerce Department's version of the Consumer Price Index. It is prepared monthly by the Bureau of Economic Analysis, and it tends to appear more optimistic than the Consumer Price Index. Its findings are released in a regular Personal Income and Outlays news release. The bureau will supply single copies of this free upon request, and will put those associated with the media (the bureau isn't too rigid in its definition of "media") on the mailing list. Contact the Bureau of Economic Analysis at the address above, or at this telephone number: 202-523-0777.

The data also are available in the *Survey of Current Business,* a monthly journal of research. Contact the Government Printing Office at the address and telephone number listed above.

State and Metropolitan Area Unemployment—The index measures changes in the unemployment situation. A free release is available monthly from the Bureau of Labor Statistics.

Unemployment Insurance Claims Weekly Report—A weekly release, the report gives the number of persons receiving unemployment insurance benefits. Obtain the release free from:

Division of Information
Employment and Training Administration
Department of Labor
601 D St. NW
Washington, DC 20213
202-376-6172

Employment Cost Index—A quarterly study, this measures wage and salary rates and changes. A free release can be obtained by writing the Bureau of Labor Statistics.

Employment Situation—Also from the Bureau of Labor Statistics, this monthly study surveys households to determine total employment. Releases are free.

Money Supply—The Federal Reserve Board issues a free release on the nation's money supply each week. Ask for report H-6 from:

Publications Services
Federal Reserve Board
Washington, DC 20551
202-452-3244

Consumer Credit—A free report on consumer credit is issued monthly by the Federal Reserve Board. Write or call the office above and request report G-19.

Value of New Construction Put in Place—The Census Bureau charts the dollar amount of new construction in this monthly report (published in what is called the C-30 series). The price is $13 annually. The information, however, is first available in press releases on the first working date of each month at 1:30 P.M. for the press and 2 P.M. for the general public. Contact:

Bureau of the Census
Construction Statistics Division
Construction Progress Branch
Washington, DC 20233
301-763-5717

Monthly Retail Trade Report—The Census Bureau compiles this index of retail sales and accounts receivable. The figures are published in *Current Business Reports*, which can be purchased from the Government Printing Office.

The annual subscription includes monthly reports, advance monthly reports, and an annual report. Ask for the publication by title and say it is part of the BR Series.

Survey of U.S. Export and Import Merchandise Trade—This gives the value of exports and imports, and also lists oil and petroleum products. Reports can be purchased from:

Subscriber Services Section
Bureau of the Census
Washington, DC 20233
301-763-5140

Only written requests are accepted by the Bureau of Labor Statistics, and they should include the name of the index. The bureau will place interested persons on mailing lists to receive releases regularly. But, because of staff limitations, sometimes it takes several months to be placed on the lists.

USEFUL CONTACTS FOR BUSINESS INFORMATION

Association addresses of any organization may be obtained by writing the Director of Information Central, American Society of Association Executives, 1571 "Eye" Street NW, Washington, DC 20005, or calling 202-626-2723.

Congressional action information can be obtained from several sources. The Bill Status Office will provide information on whether legislation has been introduced, who sponsored it, and its current status. For House action, call 202-225-1772; for Senate action, call 202-224-7106.

Cloakrooms of both houses will provide details on what is happening on the floor of the chamber. House cloakrooms: Democrat 202-225-7330; Republican 202-225-7350. Senate cloakrooms: Democrat 202-224-4691; Republican 202-224-6191.

Corporate reports filed with the SEC can be ordered from the National Investment Library, 32 Union Square, New York, NY 10005; or call 212-254-1700.

Reliance group, 120 Broadway, New York, NY 10005.

The Commerce Department's ombudsman operates throughout the entire government complex to assist both business and consumers. Services include dissemination of information and reports such as *Outlook*. Write Office of Business Liaison, U.S. Department of Commerce, Washington, DC 20230, or call 202-377-3176.

European Community country information is available free from the European Community Information Service, 2100 M Street NW, Washington, DC 20037; or call 202-862-9500.

Economic data and indicators provided on a weekly, monthly, or quarterly basis may be obtained as released. Telephone numbers of the offices publishing and producing the information are given in the table on page 508.

Department and Information	Telephone Number
Agriculture Department	Area Code: 202
To order publications	447–2791
Agricultural prices	447–3570
Bureau of Economic Analysis	
Business Conditions Digest	523–0535
Gross national product (preliminary)	523–0824
Personal income	523–0813
Merchandise trade balance, balance of payments basis	523–0668
Bureau of Labor Statistics	
To order publications	523–1221
Consumer price index	272–5160
Employment situation	523–1944
Producer price index	523–1239
Census Bureau	
To order publications	449–1600
Population and Housing Subjects	
Age and Sex:	
States (age only)	763–5072
United States	763–5184
Aliens	763–5184
Annexation Population Counts	763–7955
Apportionment	763–7955
Births and Birth Expectations; Fertility Statistics	763–5303
Census Tracts:	
Boundary Information	763–7290
Census Data	763–5002
	763–5020
Citizenship:	
Foreign Born Persons, Country of Birth; Foreign Stock Persons	763–7571
Commuting:	
Means of Transportation; Place of Work	763–3850
Congressional Districts:	
Census Data	763–5002
	763–5020
Definitions, Component Areas, Address Locations	763–5437
Population Estimates	763–5072
Consumer Expenditure Survey	763–2380
Consumer Purchases and Ownership of Durables	763–5032
Crime Surveys:	
Data Analysis and Publication	763–1765
Victimization, General Information	763–1735
Current Population Survey	763–2773
(See detailed listing on page 2 for Population Estimates)	
Decennial Census:	
Content and Tabulations	763–1840
Count Complaints	763–3814
General	763–2748
Minority Statistics Program	763–5987
Special Tabulations:	
Population Data	763–7962
Housing Data	763–2873
Housing:	
Annual Housing Survey	763–2881
Components of Inventory Change Survey	763–1096
Contract Block Program	763–2873
Housing Information, Decennial Census	763–2873
Housing Vacancy Data	763–2880
Market Absorption	763–2866
Quarterly Household Survey	763–2802
Residential Finance	763–2866
Income Statistics:	
Current Surveys	763–5060
Decennial Statistics	763–5060
Household	763–5060
Revenue Sharing	763–5060

Department and Information	Telephone Number
Incorporated/Unincorporated Places	763-7955
Industry and Occupation Statistics	
(See also Economic Fields)	763-5144
Institutional Population	763-7950
International Population	763-2870
Language, Current; Mother Tongue	763-5050
Longitudinal Surveys	763-2764
Marital Status; Living Arrangements	763-7950
Metropolitan Areas (see SMSA's)	
Migration	763-3850
Neighborhood Statistics	763-1818
Outlying Areas (Puerto Rico, etc.)	763-5184
Population:	
General Information; Published Data from Censuses, Surveys, Estimates, and Projections	763-5020 (TDY) 763-5002
Population Estimates Methodology:	
Congressional Districts; SMSA's	763-5072
Counties; Federal-State Cooperative Program for Local Population Estimates	763-7722
Estimates Research	763-7883
Local Areas; Revenue Sharing	763-7964
States	763-5072
United States (National)	763-5184
Population Projections Methodology:	
National	763-5300
State	763-5300
Economic Subjects	
Agriculture:	
Crop Statistics	763-1939
Farm Economics	763-5819
General Information	763-5170
Livestock Statistics	763-1081
Puerto Rico, Guam, etc.	763-5914
Construction Statistics:	
Census/Industries Surveys	763-5435
Special Trades; Contractors; General Contractor Built	763-7547
Construction Authorized by Building Permits (C40 Series) and Residential Demolitions (C45 Series)	763-7244
Current Programs	763-7165
Expenditures on Residential Additions, Alterations, Maintenance and Repairs, and Replacements (C50 Series)	763-5717
New Residential Construction:	
Housing Starts (C20 Series)	763-7842
Housing Completions (C22 Series)	763-7843
In Selected SMSA's (C21 Series)	763-7842
Sales of New One-Family Homes (C25 Series)	763-5731
Price Index for New One Family Homes (C27 Series)	763-7314
Characteristics of New Housing (C25 Annual Report)	763-5732
Value of New Construction Put in Place (C30 Series)	763-5717
County Business Patterns	763-7642
Employment/Unemployment Statistics	763-2825
Energy Related Statistics	763-7184
Enterprise Statistics	763-7086
Foreign Trade Information	763-5140
Governments:	
Criminal Justice Statistics	763-2842
Eastern States Government Sector	763-5017/-2890
Employment	763-5086
Finance	763-5847
Governmental Organization and Special Projects	763-5308
Revenue Sharing (See also Demographic Fields)	763-5272
Taxation	763-2844
Western States Government Sector	763-5344
Industry and Commodities Classification	763-5449

Department and Information	Telephone Number
	Area Code: 202
Manufactures:	
Census/Annual Survey of Manufactures	763–7666
Durables	763–7304
Nondurables	763–2510
Subject Reports (Concentration, Production	
Index, Water, etc.)	763–1503
Current Programs	763–7800
Durables	763–2518
Environmental Surveys	763–5616
Fuels/Electric Energy Consumed by Manufactures	763–5938
Nondurables	763–5911
Origin of Exports	763–7666
Shipments, Inventories, and Orders	763–2502
Mineral Industries	763–5938
Minority Businesses	763–5182
Puerto Rico:	
Censuses of Retail Trade, Wholesale Trade, and	
Selected Service Industries	763–5282
Retail Trade:	
Annual Retail Trade Report; Advance Monthly	
Retail Sales; Monthly Retail Inventories Survey	763–7660
Census	763–7038
Monthly Retail Trade Report: Accounts	
Receivable; and Monthly Department Store Sales	763–7660
Selected Service Industries:	
Census	763–7039
Current Services Reports	763–7077
Transportation:	
Commodity Transportation Survey; Truck	
Inventory and Use; Domestic Movement	
of Foreign Trade Data	763–5430
Wholesale Trade:	
Census	763–5281
Current Wholesale Sales and Inventories:	
Green Coffee Survey; Canned Food Survey	763–7007
Federal Reserve	
To order publications	452–3244
Money stock measures	452–3591
Consumer credit	452–2410
Industrial production and related data	452–3153
Capacity utilization in manufacturing	452–2933
Joint Economic Committee	224–3081
To obtain latest economic information	
(employment, housing starts, price	
Indices, retail sales, industrial production)	

Economic news and highlights of the day are provided by phone from the Department of Commerce; call 202–393–1847.

The Energy Information Center will provide free information on energy and related matters. Write National Energy Information Center, Forrestal Building, 1000 Independence Avenue SW, Washington, DC 20585.

Industry information statistics and details on specific industries can be obtained from the Bureau of Industrial Economics Department of Commerce, Washington, DC 20230; or call 202–377–4356.

Technical and scientific information is provided by the National Technical Information Service of the Department of Commerce, 8001 Forbes Place, Springfield, VA 22161, which handles requests about government-sponsored research of all kinds. For $125 it will research a subject. If a search has been done, a copy will be provided for $30. Call 703–557–4642. For rush orders, call 703–557–4650.

The reference section of the Library of Congress, Science and Technology Division, 10 First Street SE, Washington, DC 20540, provides answers to specific questions; call 202–287–5580. The National Referral Center provides names, addresses, and descriptions of information resources; call 202–287–5670.

Population information on all aspects of national and world population is provided by the Population Reference Bureau, Inc., 1337 Connecticut Avenue NW, Washington, DC 20036; or call 202–785–4664.

Smithsonian Institution Science Information Exchange provides, at a fee to cover costs, information both on individuals currently working in specific fields and on sources of research support; it also covers general research trends. Write 1730 M Street NW, Washington, DC 20036; or call 202–634–3933.

The **Washington Information Research Service** provides reports and guidance to information on a fee basis. Write Washington Researchers, 918 16th Street NW, Washington, DC 20006, or call 202–828–4800.

Foreign trade information as well as general business data are provided by the World Trade Information Center, One World Trade Center, New York, NY 10048, which maintains extensive data banks. The charge for a preliminary search is $25 an hour. Call 212–466–3063.

Federal Information Centers (FICS) located in key cities throughout the country are a joint venture of the U.S. General Services Administration and the U.S. Civil Services. Each center is a focal point for obtaining information about the federal government and often about state and local governments. A member of the center's staff can either provide information or direct inquiries to an expert who can. Some centers have specialists who speak foreign languages. The coordinator of the FICS is located at 18th and F Streets, NW, Washington, DC 20405; call 202–566–1937. The Federal Information Centers and their telephone numbers are listed below.

Alabama
Birmingham: 322–8591. Toll-free tieline to Atlanta, GA.
Mobile: 438–1421. Toll-free tieline to New Orleans, LA.

Alaska
Anchorage: (907) 271–3650. Federal Building and U.S. Courthouse, 701 C Street 99513.

Arizona
Phoenix: (602) 261–3313. Federal Building, 230 N. First Avenue 85025.
Tucson: 622–1511. Toll-free tieline to Phoenix, AZ.

Arkansas
Little Rock: 378–6177. Toll-free tieline to Memphis, TN.

California
Los Angeles: (213) 688–3800. Federal Building, 300 N. Los Angeles Street 90012.
Sacramento: (916) 440–3344. Federal Building, U.S. Courthouse, 650 Capitol Mall 95814.
San Diego: (714) 293–6030. 880 Front Street 92188.
San Francisco: (415) 556–6600. Federal Building, U.S. Courthouse, 450 Golden Gate Avenue 94102.
San Jose: 275–7422. Toll-free tieline to San Francisco, CA.
Santa Ana: 836–2386. Toll-free tieline to Los Angeles, CA.

Colorado
Colorado Springs: 471–9491. Toll-free tieline to Denver, CO.
Denver: (303) 837–3602. Federal Building, 1961 Stout Street 80204.
Pueblo: 544–9523. Toll-free tieline to Denver, CO.

Connecticut
Hartford: 527–2617. Toll-free tieline to New York, NY.
New Haven: 624–4720. Toll-free tieline to New York, NY.

District of Columbia
Washington: (202) 755–8660. Seventh and D Streets SW, Room 5716, 20407.

Florida
Fort Lauderdale: 522–8531. Toll-free tie line to Miami, FL.
Jacksonville: 354–4756. Toll-free tieline to St. Petersburg, FL.
Miami: (305) 350–4155. Federal Building, 51 Southwest First Avenue 33130.
Orlando: 422–1800. Toll-free tieline to St. Petersburg, FL.
St. Petersburg: (813) 893–3495. William C. Cramer Federal Building, 144 First Avenue S. 33701.
Tampa: 229–7911. Toll-free tieline to St. Petersburg, FL.
West Palm Beach: 833–7566. Toll-free tieline to Miami, FL.
Northern Florida (Sarasota, Manatee, Polk, Osceola, Orange, Seminole, and Volusia counties and north): (800) 282–8556. Toll-free line to St. Petersburg, FL.
Southern Florida (Charlotte, De Soto, Hardee, Highlands, Okeechobee, Indian River, and Brevard counties and south): (800) 432–6668. Toll-free line to Miami, FL.

Georgia
Atlanta: (404) 526–6891. Federal Building, 75 Spring Street NE 30303.

Hawaii
Honolulu: (808) 546–8620. Federal Building, 300 Ala Moàna Boulevard, P.O. Box 50091, 96850.

Illinois
Chicago: (312) 353–4242. Everett McKinley Dirksen Building, 219 S. Dearborn Street 60604.

Indiana
Gary/Hammond: 883–4110. Toll-free tieline to Indianapolis, IN.
Indianapolis: (317) 269–7373. Federal Building, 575 North Pennsylvania 46204.

Iowa
Des Moines: (515) 284–4448. Federal Building, 210 Walnut Street 50309.
Other Iowa locations: (800) 532–1556. Toll-free line to Des Moines, IA.

Kansas
Topeka: (913) 295–2866. Federal Building and U.S. Courthouse, 444 S.E. Quincy 66683.
Other Kansas locations: (800) 432–2934. Toll-free line to Topeka, KS.

Kentucky
Louisville: (502) 582–6261. Federal Building, 600 Federal Place 40202.

Louisiana
New Orleans: (504) 589–6696. Federal Building, Room 1210, 701 Loyola Avenue 70113.

Maryland
Baltimore: (301) 962–4980. Federal Building, 31 Hopkins Plaza 21201.

Massachusetts
Boston: (617) 223–7121. J. F. K. Federal Building, Cambridge Street, Lobby, 1st Floor 02203.

Michigan
Detroit: (313) 226–7016. McNamara Federal Building, 477 Michigan Avenue 48226.
Grand Rapids: 451–2628. Toll-free tieline to Detroit, MI.

Minnesota
Minneapolis: (612) 725–2073. Federal Building and U.S. Courthouse, 110 S. Fourth Street 55401.

Missouri
Kansas City: (816) 374–2466. Federal Building, 601 East Twelfth Street 64106.
St. Louis: (314) 425–4106. Federal Building, 1520 Market Street 63103.
Other Missouri locations within area code 314: (800) 392–7711. Toll-free line to St. Louis, MO.
Other Missouri locations within area codes 816 and 417: (800) 892–5808. Toll-free line to Kansas City, MO.

Nebraska
Omaha: (402) 221–3353. Federal Building, U.S. Post Office, and Courthouse, 215 N. 17th Street 68102.
Other Nebraska locations: (800) 642–8383. Toll-free line to Omaha, NB.

New Jersey
Newark: (201) 645–3600. Federal Building, 970 Broad Street 07102.
Paterson/Passaic: 523–0717. Toll-free tieline to Newark, NJ.
Trenton: 396–4400. Toll-free tieline to Newark, NJ.

New Mexico
Albuquerque: (505) 766–3091. Federal Building and U.S. Courthouse, 500 Gold Avenue SW 87101.
Santa Fe: 983–7743. Toll-free tieline to Albuquerque, NM.

New York
Albany: 463–4421. Toll-free tieline to New York, NY.
Buffalo: (716) 846–4010. Federal Building, 111 West Huron Street 14202.
New York: (212) 264–4464. Lobby, Federal Building, 26 Federal Plaza 10278.
Rochester: 546–5075. Toll-free tieline to Buffalo, NY.
Syracuse: 476–8545. Toll-free tieline to Buffalo, NY.

North Carolina
Charlotte: 376–3600. Toll-free tieline to Atlanta, GA.

Ohio
Akron: 375–5638. Toll-free tieline to Cleveland, OH.
Cincinnati: (513) 684–2801. Federal Building, 550 Main Street 45202.
Cleveland: (216) 522–4040. Federal Building, 1240 E. Ninth Street 44199.
Columbus: 221–1014. Toll-free tieline to Cincinnati, OH.
Dayton: 223–7377. Toll-free tieline to Cincinnati, OH.
Toledo: 241–3223. Toll-free tieline to Cleveland, OH.

Oklahoma
Oklahoma City: (405) 231–4868. U.S. Post Office and Courthouse, 201 N.W. 3rd Street 73102.
Tulsa: 584–4193. Toll-free tieline to Oklahoma City, OK.

Oregon
Portland: (503) 221–2222. Federal Building, 1220 S.W. Third Avenue 97204.

Pennsylvania
Allentown/Bethlehem: 821–7785. Toll-free tieline to Philadelphia, PA.
Philadelphia: (215) 597–7042. Federal Building, 600 Arch Street 19106.
Pittsburgh: (412) 644–3456. Federal Building, 1000 Liberty Avenue 15222.
Scranton: 346–7081. Toll-free tieline to Philadelphia, PA.

Rhode Island
Providence: 331–5565. Toll-free tieline to Boston, MA.

Tennessee
Chattanooga: 265–8231. Toll-free tieline to Memphis, TN.
Memphis: (901) 534–3285. Clifford Davis Federal Building, 167 N. Main Street 38103.
Nashville: 242–5056. Toll-free tieline to Memphis, TN.

Texas
Austin: 472–5494. Toll-free tieline to Houston, TX.
Dallas: 767–8585. Toll-free tieline to Fort Worth, TX.

Fort Worth: (817) 334–3624. Fritz Garland Lanham Federal Building, 819 Taylor Street 76102.

Houston: (713) 226–5711. Federal Building, U.S. Courthouse, 515 Rusk Avenue 77002.

San Antonio: 224–4471. Toll-free tieline to Houston, TX.

Utah
Ogden: 399–1347. Toll-free tieline to Salt Lake City, UT.

Salt Lake City: (801) 524–5353. Federal Building, Lobby, 125 S. State Street 84138.

Virginia
Newport News: 244–0480. Toll-free tieline to Norfolk, VA.

Norfolk: (804) 441–3101. Federal Building, 200 Granby Mall, Room 120 23510.

Richmond: 643–4928. Toll-free tieline to Norfolk, VA.

Roanoke: 982–8591. Toll-free tieline to Norfolk, VA.

Washington
Seattle: (206) 442–0570. Federal Building, 915 Second Avenue 98174.

Tacoma: 383–5230. Toll-free tieline to Seattle, WA.

Wisconsin
Milwaukee: 271–2273. Toll-free tieline to Chicago, IL.

INFORMATION SOURCES IN THE U.S. DEPARTMENT OF COMMERCE (by subject)

Subject	Source	Telephone Number
Aeronautical charting	NOAA	(301) 443–8708
Agriculture Census	CEN	(301) 568–1200
Air-quality research	NOAA	(303) 499–1000
Appliance labeling	NBS	(301) 921–3181
Applied technology	NBS	(301) 921–3181
Arab Boycott	ITA	(202) 377–2253
Atmospheric remote sensing	NOAA	(303) 499–1000
Atmospheric research	NOAA	(303) 499–1000
Atomic, nuclear, isotopic research	NBS	(301) 921–3181
Automation technology	NBS	(301) 921–3181
Broadcast news	SEC	(202) 377–5610
Building technology	NBS	(301) 921–3181
Business Censuses	CEN	(301) 568–1200
Business Conditions Digest	BEA	(202) 523–0777
Business Conditions Report	BIE	(202) 377–4356
Business development loans	EDA	(202) 377–5113
Capacity Utilization, Manufacturing	BEA	(202) 523–0777
Capital equipment	BIE	(202) 377–4356
Censuses	CEN	(301) 568–1200
Climate monitoring	NOAA	(301) 443–8243
Coal gasification	NBS	(301) 921–3181
Coastal Zone Management	NOAA	(202) 634–4239
Commerce Business Daily	ITA	(202) 377–3094
Commerce Publications Update	SEC	(202) 377–2135
Commerce Technical Advisory Board (CTAB)	S&T	(202) 377–5065
Commodity statistics	BIE	(202) 377–4356
Computer Science & Technology	NBS	(301) 921–3181
Construction & forest products	BIE	(202) 377–4356
Construction Review	BIE	(202) 377–4356
Consumer goods	BIE	(202) 377–4356
Consumer products safety	NBS	(301) 921–3181
Corporate Profits	BEA	(202) 523–0777
Decennial (1980 Census)	CEN	(301) 568–1200
Disaster research	NBS	(301) 921–3181
East-West Trade	ITA	(202) 377–2253
Economic Affairs	OCE	(202) 377–2235
Economic Censuses	CEN	(301) 568–1200
Economic development programs	EDA	(202) 377–5113

INFORMATION SOURCES IN THE U.S. DEPARTMENT OF COMMERCE *(continued)*

Subject	Source	Telephone Number
Education statistics	CEN	(301) 568–1200
Employment & unemployment surveys	CEN	(301) 568–1200
Energy (conservation)	NBS	(301) 921–3181
Energy (inventions)	NBS	(301) 921–3181
Environment (pollution)	NBS	(301) 921–3181
Environment affairs	S&T	(202) 377–4335
Environment data services	NOAA	(302) 634–7305
Environmental research	NOAA	(303) 499–1000
Environmental satellites	NOAA	(301) 443–8243
Export Development	ITA	(202) 377–2253
Export information	ITA	(202) 377–2253
Export licenses	ITA	(202) 377–2253
Export Awards	ITA	(202) 377–2253
Expositions (international)	SEC	(202) 377–4987
Failure analysis	NBS	(301) 921–3181
Federal Economic Indicators	OCE	(202) 377–2235
Federal Receipts Expenditures	BEA	(202) 523–0744
Field Operations	ITA	(202) 377–2253
Fire protection (see also research & education)	NBS	(301) 921–3181
Fisheries	NOAA	(202) 634–7281
Flash floods	NOAA	(301) 427–7622
Foreign investment statistics	BEA	(202) 523–0777
Foreign trade analysis	ITA	(202) 377–3259
Foreign trade statistics	CEN	(301) 568–1200
Freedom of Information	SEC	(202) 377–5659
Frequency Allocations (Federal Use)	NTIA	(202) 377–1832
Geodetic surveys	NOAA	(301) 443–8708
Government finances (state & local)	CEN	(301) 568–1200
Grants to local government	EDA	(202) 377–5113
Great Lakes research	NOAA	(303) 499–1000
Gross National Product	BEA	(202) 523–0777
Health	NBS	(301) 921–3181
Housing & Construction Statistics	CEN	(301) 568–1200
Hurricane research	NOAA	(303) 499–1000
Hurricane warning	NOAA	(301) 427–7622
Hydrology, Office of	NOAA	(301) 427–7622
Import programs	ITA	(202) 377–2253
Income, family	CEN	(301) 568–1200
Industrial Economics, Bureau of	BIE	(202) 377–4356
Industry surveys	CEN	(301) 568–1200
Information Policy	NTIA	(202) 377–1832
Input-Output analysis	BEA	(202) 523–0683
Interdepartment Radio Advisory Committee (IRAC)	NTIA	(202) 377–1832
International finance, investment & marketing	ITA	(202) 377–3259
International investment statistics	BEA	(202) 523–0777
International transactions	BEA	(202) 523–0620
Investment services	ITA	(202) 377–2253
Laser information	NBS	(301) 921–3181
Law enforcement standards	NBS	(301) 921–3181
Leading Economic Indicators	BEA	(202) 523–0777
Manufacturing industry (by commodity)	BIE	(202) 377–4356
Marine ecosystem studies	NOAA	(303) 499–1000
Marine Mammals	NOAA	(202) 634–7281
Marine technology	NOAA	(301) 443–8243
Maritime technology	MARAD	(202) 377–2746
Materials research	NBS	(301) 921–8181
Merchandise Trade	BEA	(202) 523–0668
Meteorological center	NOAA	(301) 427–7622
Metric	NBS	(301) 921–3181
Minority business development programs	MBDA	(202) 377–1936
National Marine Fisheries	NOAA	(202) 634–7281
Nautical charts	NOAA	(301) 443–8708
News releases & speeches (see also PIO's)	SEC	(202) 377–4901
Non-ferrus metals	BIE	(202) 377–4356
Occupation and industry statistics	CEN	(301) 568–1200
Overseas business opportunities	ITA	(202) 377–2253
Patent & Trademarks	PTO	(703) 557–3428

INFORMATION SOURCES IN THE U.S. DEPARTMENT OF COMMERCE *(continued)*

Subject	Source	Telephone Number
Patents, government-owned, foreign filing	NTIS	(703) 557–4735
Personal Income & Outlays	BEA	(202) 523–0777
Plant & Equipment Expenditures	BEA	(202) 523–0777
Pollution Abatement and Control Expenditures	BEA	(202) 523–0777
Population information	CEN	(301) 568–1200
Product standards	S&T	(202) 377–3221
Productivity, Technology & Innovation	OPTI	(202) 377–3653
Public works projects	EDA	(202) 377–5113
Publications, requests	SEC	(202) 377–4233
Publications, sales & distribution	SEC	(202) 377–5494
Radiation measurements	NBS	(301) 921–3181
Regional Economic Statistics	BEA	(202) 523–0966
Regional Planning Commissions	SEC	(202) 377–4901
Research (economic)	OCE	(202) 377–2235
Research (Maritime)	MARAD	(202) 377–2746
Retail, Wholesale, & Service Trade Statistics	CEN	(301) 568–1200
Satellites	NOAA	(301) 443–8243
Sea Grants	NOAA	(301) 443–8243
Secretarial statements	SEC	(202) 377–4901
Service industries (statistics)	BIE	(202) 377–4356
Ship operations and shipbuilding	MARAD	(202) 377–2746
Solar forecasts	NOAA	(303) 499–1000
Solar standards, research	NBS	(301) 921–3181
Space environment research	NOAA	(303) 499–1000
Spectrum Management	NTIA	(202) 377–1832
Standard Industrial Classification (SIC)	BIE	(202) 377–4356
Standard reference materials	NBS	(301) 921–3181
Statistical Reporter	OFSPS	(202) 673–7965
Stratospheric research	NOAA	(303) 499–1000
Survey of Current Business	BEA	(202) 523–0777
Technical Document Sales (all Govt. agencies)	NTIS	(703) 557–4600
Technical Help to Exporters	NTIS	(703) 557–4733
Technology transfer to developing countries	NTIS	(202) 724–3370
Telecommunications Applications	NTIA	(202) 377–1832
Telecommunications Policy (int'l & domestic)	NTIA	(202) 377–1832
Telecommunications Research	NTIA	(202) 377–1832
Telecommunications Technology	NTIA	(202) 377–1832
Textiles	ITA	(202) 377–3259
Time and frequency (standards)	NBS	(303) 323–3198
Tornado & severe storms research	NOAA	(303) 499–1000
Tornado warning	NOAA	(301) 427–7622
Tourism, international and domestic	USTS	(202) 377–4987
Trade adjustment assistance	EDA	(202) 377–5113
Trade fairs, trade centers and missions	ITA	(202) 377–2253
Trademarks	PAT	(703) 557–3428
Trade negotiations	ITA	(202) 377–3259
Trade Zone Board	ITA	(202) 377–2253
Transportation equipment	BIE	(202) 377–4356
Travel to and in USA	USTS	(202) 377–4610
U.S. Industrial Outlook	BIE	(202) 377–4356
Weather Modification (cloud seeding)	NOAA	(303) 499–1000
Weather Service	NOAA	(301) 427–7622
Weights and Measures	NBS	(301) 921–3181

ABBREVIATIONS

BEA	Bureau of Economic Analysis	NTIA	National Telecommunications and Information Administration
CEN	Bureau of the Census		
EDA	Economic Development Administration	NTIS	National Technical Information Service
ITA	Industry and Trade Administration	OCE	Office of Chief Economist
MARAD	Maritime Administration	OFSPS	Office of Federal Stat. Policy and Standards
MBDA	Minority Business Development Administration		
		PTO	Patent and Trademark Office
NBS	National Bureau of Standards	SEC	Office of the Secretary
NOAA	National Oceanic and Atmospheric Administration	S&T	Office of the Assistant Secretary for Science and Technology

ADDRESSES OF U.S. DEPARTMENT OF COMMERCE INFORMATION SOURCES

Office of Assistant Secretary for Science and Technology
Main Commerce Building
14th and Constitution Avenues
Washington, DC 20230
Telephone: 202-377-3653

Office of the Chief Economist
Main Commerce Building
14th and Constitution Avenues
Washington, DC 20230
Telephone: 202-377-2235

Bureau of the Census
Federal Office Building No. 3
Suitland, MD 20023
Telephone: 301-568-1200

Bureau of Economic Analysis
Tower Building
1401 K Street NW
Mailing Address:
U.S. Department of Commerce
14th and Constitution Avenues
Washington, DC 20230
Telephone: 202-523-0777

Bureau of Industrial Economics
Main Commerce Building
14th and Constitution Avenues
Washington, DC 20230
Telephone: 202-377-4356

Industry and Trade Administration
Main Commerce Building
14th and Constitution Avenues
Washington, DC 20230
Telephone: 202-377-3808

Economic Development Administration
Main Commerce Building
14th and Constitution Avenues
Washington, DC 20230
Telephone: 202-377-5113

Maritime Administration
Main Commerce Building
14th and Constitution Avenues
Washington, DC 20230
Telephone: 202-377-2746

Minority Business Development Administration
Main Commerce Building
14th and Constitution Avenues
Washington, DC 20230
Telephone: 202-377-1936

National Bureau of Standards
Administration Building
National Bureau of Standards
Washington, DC 20234
Telephone: 301-921-3112

National Oceanic and Atmospheric Administration
11400 Rockville Pike
Rock-Wall Building
Rockville, MD 20852
Telephone: 202-377-4190

National Technical Information Service
Pennsylvania Building
425 13th Street NW
Washington, DC 20004
Telephone: 202-724-3382

National Telecommunications and Information Administration
1800 G Street NW
Washington, DC 20504
Telephone: 202-377-1832

Patent and Trademark Office
Crystal Plaza Building 3
2021 Jefferson Davis Highway
Arlington, VA 20231
Telephone: 703-557-3428

United States Travel Service
Main Commerce Building
14th and Constitution Avenues
Washington, DC 20230
Telephone: 202-377-4987

COMMERCE DEPARTMENT DATA BASE RESEARCH SERVICES

Fourteen field offices of the U.S. Department of Commerce offer computerized literature searches on most any business topic. The field offices have access to Lockheed's DIALOG system as well as data generated by the Commerce Department. The offices charge out-of-pocket expenses plus a $15 overhead fee. The offices that provide this service are located in Alabama, Arizona, California, Georgia, Illinois, Massachusetts, Michigan, Minnesota, Missouri, New York, North Carolina, Ohio, Texas and Washington.

STATE INFORMATION GUIDE

Regional Directories

Central Atlantic States Manufacturing Directory, T. K. Sanderson Organization, 200 E. 25 Street, Baltimore, MD 21218

Commercial Classified Directory and Buyers Guide 1977, Commercial Classified Publishers, Inc., 225 Broadway, New York, NY 10007

Daltons' Greater Philadelphia Industrial Directory, Dalton Corp., 2925 N. Broad Street, Philadelphia, PA 19132

Directory of Central Atlantic States Manufacturers, Manufacturers' News, Inc., 3 E. Huron Street, Chicago, IL 60611; George D. Hall Company, 20 Kilby Street, Boston, MA 02109

Source: *The Information Report,* Washington Researchers, 918 16th Street, NW, Washington, DC 20006.

Directory of New England Manufacturers, The, George D. Hall Company, 20 Kilby Street, Boston, MA 02109

Eastern Manufacturers' and Industrial Directory, Bell Directory Publishers, Inc., 2112 Broadway, New York, NY 10023

Midwest Manufacturers' and Industrial Directory, Industrial Directory Publishers, 1002 Park Avenue Building, Detroit, MI 48226

New England Apparel Directory, Register Publication, Inc., 99 Chauncey Street, Boston, MA 02111

New England Industrial Service Directory, George D. Hall Company, 20 Kilby Street, Boston, MA 02109

New England Manufacturers Directory, Manufacturers' News, Inc., 3 E. Huron Street, Chicago, IL 60611

State Sales Guides, Dun & Bradstreet, Inc., 99 Church Street, New York, NY 10007

Survey of Industries in Texarkana (Arkansas-Texas), Texarkana Chamber of Commerce, Box 1468, Texarkana, AK 75501

Alabama

STATE CAPITOL, MONTGOMERY, AL 36130
(205) 832–3511

INFORMATION OFFICES

Commerce/Economic Development
Alabama Development Office
State Capitol
Montgomery, AL 36130
Taxation
Department of Revenue
Administrative Building
Montgomery, AL 36130
State Chamber of Commerce
Alabama Chamber of Commerce
468 S. Perry Street
P.O. Box 76
Montgomery, AL 36101
Small Business Administration
908 S. 20th Street†
Birmingham, AL 35205

PUBLICATIONS

Economic Abstract of Alabama, (irregular publication), University of Alabama, Center for Business and Economic Research, University, AL 35486

Estimates of Population of Alabama Counties and Metropolitan Areas, (annual), Superin-

tendent of Documents, U.S. Government Printing Office, Washington, DC 20402

Alabama Business (income statistics, annual), Center for Business and Economic Research, P.O. Box AK, University, AL 35486

Alabama Labor Market (employment statistics, monthly), Department of Industrial Relations, Montgomery, AL 36130

INDUSTRIAL AND BUSINESS DIRECTORIES

Alabama Directory of Mining and Manufacturing, Alabama Development Office, State Capitol, Montgomery, AL 36130

Alabama Industrial Directory, Manufacturers' News, Inc., 3 E. Huron Street, Chicago, IL 60611; State Industrial Directories Corp., 2 Penn Plaza, New York, NY 10001

Alabama International Trade Directory, Alabama State Chamber of Commerce, P.O. Box 76, Montgomery, AL 36101

Birmingham Industrial Directory, Birmingham Chamber of Commerce, 1914 6th Avenue, Birmingham, AL 35203

Alaska

STATE CAPITOL, JUNEAU, AK 99811
(907) 465–2111

INFORMATION OFFICES

Commerce/Economic Development
Department of Commerce & Economic Development
Pouch D
Juneau, AK 99811
Taxation
Department of Revenue
Pouch S
Juneau, AK 99811
State Chamber of Commerce
Alaska State Chamber of Commerce
310 2nd Street
Juneau, AK 99801
Small Business Administration
Anchorage, Alaska†
1016 W. 6th Avenue
Anchorage, AK 99501
Fairbanks, Alaska
101 12th Avenue
Fairbanks, AK 99701

PUBLICATIONS

Alaska Economy, Department of Commerce and Development, Division of Economic Enterprise, Juneau, AK 99801

Alaska Statistical Review, Department of Eco-

---

* Refers throughout this section to the Small Business Administration regional office.

† Refers throughout this section to the Small Business Administration district office.

nomic Development, Division of Economic Enterprise, Juneau, AK 99801

Alaska Population by Area (population statistics, annual), Department of Labor, Research and Analysis, Box 1149, Juneau, AK 99811

Alaska Review of Business and Economic Conditions Series (income statistics, five times a year), Institute of Social, Economic and Government Research, University of Alaska, Fairbanks, AK 99701

Alaska Economic Trends (employment statistics, monthly), Department of Labor, Research and Analysis, Box 1149, Juneau, AK 99811

Alaska's Manpower Outlook—1970s Regional Population and Employment Estimates 1961–1980 (employment statistics, annual), Employment Security Division, Department of Labor, Juneau, AK 99801

INDUSTRIAL AND BUSINESS DIRECTORIES

Alaska Directory of Commercial Establishments, Manufacturers' News, Inc., 3 E. Huron Street, Chicago, IL 60611; State Industrial Directories Corp., 2 Penn Plaza, New York, NY 10001

Alaska Petroleum and Industrial Directory, 409 W. Northern Lights Boulevard, Anchorage, AK 99603

Arizona

STATE CAPITOL, PHOENIX, AZ 85007
(602) 255–4900

INFORMATION OFFICES

Commerce/Economic Development
Office of Economic Planning and Development
1700 W. Washington Avenue
Phoenix, AZ 85007
Taxation
Department of Revenue
State Capitol
Phoenix, AZ 85007
State Chamber of Commerce
Arizona State Chamber of Commerce
3216 N. Third Street
Phoenix, AZ 85012
Small Business Administration
3030 N. Central Avenue†
Phoenix, AZ 85012

301 W. Congress Street
Tucson, AZ 85715

PUBLICATIONS

Arizona Statistical Review, Valley National Bank, Economic Research Department, P.O. Box 71, Phoenix, AZ 85001

Statistical Abstract of Arizona, University of Arizona, Division of Economic Business Research, College of Business and Public Administration, Tucson, AZ 85724

Arizona Basic Economic and Manpower Data (annual), Arizona Department of Economic Security, P.O. Box 6123, Phoenix, AZ 85005

Arizona Review (income statistics, monthly), Division of Economic and Business Research, University of Arizona, Tucson, AZ 85724

Arizona Newsletter (income statistics, monthly), Arizona Department of Economic Security, Research Institute Statistics Bureau, P.O. Box 6123, Phoenix, AZ 85005

Phoenix Area Manpower Newsletter (income statistics, monthly), Arizona Department of Economic Security, Research Institute Statistics Bureau, P.O. Box 6123, Phoenix, AZ 85005

Tucson Area Manpower Newsletter (income statistics, monthly), Arizona Department of Economic Security, Research Institute Statistics Bureau, P.O. Box 6123, Phoenix, AZ 85005

Arizona Indicator (income statistics, monthly), Arizona Department of Economic Security, Research Institute Statistics Bureau, P.O. Box 6123, Phoenix, AZ 85005

Manpower Newsletter (employment statistics, monthly), Unemployment Compensations Division, Employment Security Commission, Phoenix, AZ 85005

INDUSTRIAL AND BUSINESS DIRECTORIES

Arizona Directory of Industries, Manufacturers' News, 3 E. Huron Street, Chicago, IL 60611

Arizona Directory of Manufacturers, Manufacturers' News, Inc., 3 E. Huron Street, Chicago, IL 60611; State Industrial Directories Corp., 2 Penn Plaza, New York, NY 10001

Arizona Exports and Imports, Office of Economic Planning and Development, 1700 W. Washington Avenue, Phoenix, AZ 85007

Arizona USA International Trade Directory, Arizona State Department of Economic Planning and Development, 1700 W. Washington Avenue, Phoenix, AZ 85007

Directory of Arizona Manufacturers, Phoenix Chamber of Commerce, Phoenix, AZ 85001

Arkansas

STATE CAPITOL, LITTLE ROCK, AR 72201
(501) 371–3000

INFORMATION OFFICES

Commerce/Economic Development
Department of Commerce
1501 N. University Avenue
Little Rock, AR 72207
Department of Economic Development
One State Capitol Mall
Little Rock, AR 72201
Taxation
Division of Revenue Services
Department of Finance and Administration
7th and Wolfe Streets
Little Rock, AR 72201
State Chamber of Commerce
Arkansas State Chamber of Commerce
911 Wallace Building
Little Rock, AR 72201
Small Business Administration
320 W. Capitol Avenue†
Little Rock, AR 72201

PUBLICATIONS

Arkansas Business Economic Review (population statistics, quarterly), Bureau of Business and Economic Research, University of Arkansas, Fayetteville, AR 72701
Annual Estimates of Total Personal and Per Capita Income (annual), Industrial Research and Extension Center, University of Arkansas, P.O. Box 3017, Little Rock, AR 72203
Arkansas Current Employment Development (monthly), Employment Security Division, Department of Labor, Little Rock, AR 72203
Employment and Payroll (quarterly), Employment Security Division, Department of Labor, Little Rock, AR 72203

INDUSTRIAL AND BUSINESS DIRECTORIES

Arkansas Almanac, Arkansas Almanac, Inc., Little Rock, AR 72114
Arkansas Directory of Industries, Manufacturers' News, 3 E. Huron Street, Chicago, IL 60611
Directory of Arkansas Manufacturers, Arkansas Department of Economic Development, One State Capitol Mall, Little Rock, AR 72201; State Industrial Directories Corp., 2 Penn Plaza, New York, NY 10001

California

STATE CAPITOL, SACRAMENTO, CA 95814
(916) 332–9900

INFORMATION OFFICES

Commerce/Economic Development
Economic and Business Development
1120 N Street
Sacramento, CA 95814
Taxation
Franchise Tax Board
920 23d Street
Sacramento, CA 95814
Board of Equalization
1020 N Street
Sacramento, CA 95814
State Chamber of Commerce
California Chamber of Commerce
455 Capitol Mall
P.O. Box 1736
Sacramento, CA 95808
Small Business Administration
450 Golden Gate Avenue*
San Francisco, CA 94102
211 Main Street†
San Francisco, CA 94105
1229 N Street
Fresno, CA 93712
350 S. Figueroa Street†
Los Angeles, CA 90071
880 Front Street†
San Diego, CA 92188
2800 Cottage Way
Sacramento, CA 95825

PUBLICATIONS

California Statistical Abstract, Department of Finance, Budget Division, Sacramento, CA 95814
California's Population (annual), Population Research Unit, Department of Finance, Sacramento CA 95814
The UCLA Forecast for the Nation and California (income statistics, annual), UCLA Business Forecasting Project, Graduate School of Management, UCLA, Los Angeles, CA 90024
California Economic Indicators (income statistics, quarterly), California Department of Finance, 1025 P Street, Sacramento, CA 95814
California Employment and Payroll (quarterly), Employment Development Department, 800 Capitol Mall, Sacramento, CA 95814
California Labor Market Bulletin Statistical Supplement (employment statistics, monthly) Employment Development Department, 800 Capital Mall, Sacramento, CA 95814
Taxable Sales in California (sales statistics, quarterly), State Board of Equalization, P.O. Box 1799, Sacramento, CA 95814
California-The Future, Office of Business and Industrial Development, P.O. Box 1499, Sacramento, CA 95805

INDUSTRIAL AND BUSINESS DIRECTORIES

California Handbook, Center for California Public Affairs, 226 W. Foothill Boulevard, Claremont, CA 91711

California International Business Directory, Center for International Business, 333 S. Flower Street, Los Angeles, CA 90071

California Manufacturers Register, Time-Mirror Press, 1115 S. Boyle Avenue, Los Angeles, CA 90023; Manufacturers' News, Inc., 3 E. Huron Street, Chicago, IL 60611; State Industrial Directories Corp., 2 Penn Plaza, New York, NY 10001

Los Angeles Area Chamber of Commerce Southern California Business Directory and Buyers Guide, Los Angeles Chamber of Commerce, 404 S. Bixel Street, Los Angeles, CA 95113

San Francisco Manufacturers Directory, San Francisco Chamber of Commerce, 333 Pine Street, San Francisco, CA 94577

Colorado

STATE CAPITOL, DENVER, CO 80203
(303) 839–5000

INFORMATION OFFICES

Commerce/Economic Development
Division of Commerce and Development
Department of Local Affairs
Centennial Building
1313 Sherman Street
Denver, CO 80203
Taxation
Administrative Division
Department of Revenue
1375 Sherman Street
Denver, CO 80203
State Chamber of Commerce
Colorado Association of Commerce and Industry
1390 Logan Street
Denver, CO 80203
Small Business Administration
1405 Curtis Street*
Denver, CO 80202
721 19th Street†
Denver, CO 80202

PUBLICATIONS

Economic Growth at a Glance (population statistics, annual), Denver Chamber of Commerce, 1301 Walton Street, Denver, CO 80202

Annual Report—Colorado Department of Revenue (income statistics, annual), Colorado De-

partment of Revenue, 1375 Sherman Street, Denver, CO 80203

Colorado's Current Monthly Estimate of Nonfarm Employment (monthly), Colorado Division of Employment, 251 East 12th Avenue, Denver, CO 80203

Colorado Manpower Review (employment statistics, monthly), Colorado Division of Employment, 251 East 12th Avenue, Denver, CO 80203

Sales Tax Statistical Summary (annual), Department of Revenue, Denver, CO 80203

INDUSTRIAL AND BUSINESS DIRECTORIES

Colorado Industrial Capability Register, Public Affairs Department, Colorado Interstate Gas Co., P.O. Box 1087, Colorado Springs, CO 80901

Directory of Colorado Manufacturers, Business Research Division, University of Colorado, Boulder, CO 80309; State Industrial Directories Corp. 2 Penn Plaza, New York, NY 10001

Connecticut

STATE CAPITOL, HARTFORD, CT 06115
(203) 566–2211

INFORMATION OFFICES

Commerce/Economic Development
Department of Economic Development
210 Washington Street
Hartford, CT 06106
Taxation
Department of Revenue Statistics
92 Farmington Avenue
Hartford, CT 06115
State Chamber of Commerce
Connecticut Business and Industry Association
60 Washington Street
Hartford, CT 06106
Small Business Administration
1 Financial Plaza†
Hartford, CT 06103

PUBLICATIONS

Connecticut Market Data, Connecticut Department of Economic Development, Hartford, CT 06106

Weekly Health Bulletin (population statistics, annual), Public Health, Education Section, State Department of Health, State Office Building, Hartford, CT 06115

Connecticut Area Trends in Employment and Unemployment (income statistics, annual),

Research and Information, Connecticut Labor Department, Hartford, CT 06115

Labor Situation (employment statistics, monthly), Employment Security Division, Department of Labor, Wethersfield, CT 06109

Sales and Use Tax Information (sales statistics, quarterly), State Tax Department, 92 Farmington Avenue, Hartford, CT 06115

INDUSTRIAL AND BUSINESS DIRECTORIES

Classified Business Directory—State of Connecticut, Connecticut Directory Co., Inc., 322 Main Street, Stamford, CT 06901

Connecticut Classified Business Directory, Connecticut Directory Co., Inc., 322 Main Street, Stamford, CT 06901

Connecticut State Industrial Directory, Manufacturers' News, 3 E. Huron Street, Chicago, IL 60611; State Industrial Directories Corp., 2 Penn Plaza, New York, NY 10001

Directory of Connecticut Manufacturing Establishments, Connecticut Department of Labor, 200 Folly Brook Boulevard, Wethersfield, CT 06109

Delaware

LEGISLATIVE HALL, DOVER, DE 19901
(302) 736–4000

INFORMATION OFFICES

Commerce/Economic Development
Department of Community Affairs and Economic Development
Division of Economic Development and Minority Business Enterprise
630 State College Road
Dover, DE 19901
Taxation
Department of Finance
Division of Revenue
601 Delaware Avenue
Wilmington, DE 19899
State Chamber of Commerce
Delaware State Chamber of Commerce, Inc.
1102 West Street
Wilmington, DE 19801
Small Business Administration
844 King Street
Wilmington, DE 19801

PUBLICATIONS

Comparison of Corporate Taxes in Delaware, New York, Pennsylvania and Maryland, Division of Economic Development, P.O. Box 1401, Dover, DE 19901

Dimensions on Delaware, Office of Management, Budget and Planning, Townsend Building, Dover, DE 19901

Estimates of the Population of Delaware Counties (population statistics, annual), Superintendent of Documents, U.S. Government Printing Office, Washington, DC 20402

Delaware Economic Indicators (income statistics, quarterly), Office of Management, Budget and Planning, Townsend Building, Dover, DE 19901

Employment, Hours and Earnings (employment statistics, monthly), University Plaza office, Chapman Road and Route 273, Newark, DE 19702

INDUSTRIAL AND BUSINESS DIRECTORIES

Delaware Directory of Commerce and Industry, Delaware State Chamber of Commerce, 1102 West Street, Wilmington, DE 19801

Delaware State Industrial Directory, State Industrial Directories Corp., 2 Penn Plaza, New York, NY 10001

Florida

STATE CAPITOL, TALLAHASSEE, FL 32301
(904) 488–1234

INFORMATION OFFICES

Commerce/Economic Development
Department of Commerce
Collins Building
Tallahassee, FL 32301
Division of Economic Development
Department of Commerce
Collins Building
Tallahassee, FL 32301
Taxation
Department of Revenue
Carlton Building
Tallahassee, FL 32301
State Chamber of Commerce
Florida State Chamber of Commerce
P.O. Box 5497
Tallahassee, FL 32301
Small Business Administration
2222 Ponce de Leon Boulevard†
Coral Gables, FL 33134
700 Twiggs Street
Tampa, FL 33602
400 W. Bay Street†
Jacksonville, FL 32202
701 Clematis Street
West Palm Beach, FL 33402

PUBLICATIONS

Florida Statistical Abstract (population, income statistics, annual), University of Florida, Bureau of Economic and Business Research, 221 Matherly Hall, Gainesville, FL 32611

Economic Report of the Governor (quarterly income statistics, annual), Office of the Governor, Office of Planning and Budgeting, The Capitol, Tallahassee, FL 32301

Florida Employment Statistics (monthly), Department of Labor and Employment Security, Division of Employment Security, Caldwell Building, Tallahassee, FL 32301

Annual Report of the Comptroller (sales statistics, annual), Department of Banking and Finance, Office of Comptroller, The Capitol, Tallahassee, FL 32301

Population Studies (quarterly), University of Florida, Bureau of Economic and Business Research, 221 Matherly Hall, Gainesville, FL 32611

INDUSTRIAL AND BUSINESS DIRECTORIES

Directory of Florida Industries, Manufacturers' News, Inc., 3 E. Huron Street, Chicago, IL 60611; Florida State Chamber of Commerce, P.O. Box 5497, Tallahassee, FL 32301; State Industrial Directories Corp., 2 Penn Plaza, New York, NY 10001

Florida Industries Guide, McHenry Publishing Co., Inc., Box 935, Orlando, FL 32802

Georgia

STATE CAPITOL, ATLANTA, GA 30334
(404) 656-2000

INFORMATION OFFICES

Commerce/Economic Development
Department of Industry and Trade
1400 N. Omni Boulevard
Atlanta, GA 30303
Taxation
Department of Revenue
270 Washington Street, SW
Atlanta, GA 30334
State Chamber of Commerce
Georgia Chamber of Commerce
1200 Commerce Building
Atlanta, GA 30303
Small Business Administration
1720 Peachtree Street NW†
Atlanta, GA 30309

1375 Peachtree Street, NE
Atlanta, GA 30309

PUBLICATIONS

Georgia Statistical Abstract, University of Georgia, Division of Research, College of Business Administration, Athens, GA 30602

Georgia Vital Statistics (population statistics, annual), Management and Analysis Unit, Department of Human Resources, 47 Trinity Avenue, SW, Atlanta, GA 30334

Georgia Statistical Abstract (income statistics, annual), Division of Research, College of Business Administration, University of Georgia, Athens, GA 30602

Employment and Earnings (employment statistics, annual), Employment Security Agency, Department of Labor, Atlanta, GA 30303

Employment and Wages Insured by the Georgia Employment Security Law (quarterly), Employment Security Agency, Department of Labor, Atlanta, GA 30303

INDUSTRIAL AND BUSINESS DIRECTORIES

Directory of Associations in Georgia, 1974–1975, Basic Data Research, Industrial Development Division, Engineering Experiment Station, Atlanta, GA 30332

Georgia Manufacturing Directory, Georgia Department of Industry and Trade, P.O. Box 1776, Atlanta, GA 30332

Georgia World Trade Directory, Georgia Chamber of Commerce, 1200 Commerce Building, Atlanta, GA 30303

Industrial Sites in Georgia, Georgia Power, Box 4545R, Atlanta, GA 30302

Hawaii

STATE CAPITOL BUILDING, HONOLULU, HI 96813
(808) 548-2211

INFORMATION OFFICES

Commerce/Economic Development
Department of Planning and Economic Development
250 S. King Street
Honolulu, HI 96813
Taxation
Department of Taxation
425 Queen Street
Honolulu, HI 96813
State Chamber of Commerce
Chamber of Commerce of Hawaii
735 Bishop Street
Dillingham Building
Honolulu, HI 96813

Small Business Administration
300 Ala Moana†
Honolulu, HI 96850

PUBLICATIONS

State of Hawaii Data Book, A Statistical Abstract (income statistics, annual), State of Hawaii Department of Planning and Economic Development, P.O. Box 2359, Honolulu, HI 96804

Labor—Area News (employment statistics, monthly), Department of Labor, Industrial Relations, Honolulu, HI 96813

Employment and Payrolls in Hawaii (annual), Department of Labor, Industrial Relations, Honolulu, HI 96813

INDUSTRIAL AND BUSINESS DIRECTORIES

Directory of Manufacturers, State of Hawaii, Chamber of Commerce of Hawaii, Dillingham Building, 735 Bishop Street, Honolulu, HI 96813

Hawaii Business Directory, Hawaii Business Directory, Inc., Box 2057, Honolulu, HI 96805

Hawaii Directory of Manufacturers, Manufacturers' News, Inc., 3 E. Huron Street, Chicago, IL 60611; State Industrial Directories Corp., 2 Penn Plaza, New York, NY 10001

Idaho

STATE CAPITOL, BOISE, ID 83720
(208) 334-2470

INFORMATION OFFICES

Commerce/Economic Development
Division of Economic and Community Affairs
Capitol Building
Boise, ID 83720
Taxation
Department of Revenue and Taxation
Capitol Building
Boise, ID 83720
State Chamber of Commerce
Idaho Association of Commerce and Industry
805 Idaho Street
Boise, ID 83720
Small Business Administration
1005 Main Street†
Boise, ID 83701

PUBLICATIONS

Estimates of the Population of Idaho Counties (population statistics, annual), Superinten-

dent of Documents, U.S. Government Printing Office, Washington, DC 20402

Annual Wages in Idaho (employment statistics, annual), Department of Employment, State of Idaho, P.O. Box 7189, Boise, ID 83707

Distribution by Industry of Covered Workers in Idaho (employment statistics, annual), Department of Employment, State of Idaho, P.O. Box 7189, Boise, ID 83707

Distribution by Industry of Wages Paid for Covered Employment in Idaho (annual); Department of Employment, State of Idaho, P.O. Box 7189, Boise, ID 83707

Idaho Manpower Review (employment statistics, monthly), Department of Employment, State of Idaho, P.O. Box 7189, Boise, ID 83707

Monthly Employment by Industry and County (quarterly), Department of Employment, State of Idaho, P.O. Box 7189, Boise, ID 83707

Centerpoint; Focus on Business and Economics (quarterly), Center for Business and Research, University of Idaho, Moscow, ID 83843

INDUSTRIAL AND BUSINESS DIRECTORIES

Manufacturing Directory of Idaho, Center for Business and Research, University of Idaho, Moscow, ID 83843

Idaho Prospectus, Bureau of Tourism and Industrial Development, Capitol Building, Boise, ID 83720

Illinois

STATE HOUSE, SPRINGFIELD, IL 62706
(217) 782-2000

INFORMATION OFFICES

Commerce/Economic Development
Department of Commerce and Community Affairs
222 S. College Street
Springfield, IL 62706
Taxation
Department of Revenue
1515 S. 9th Street
Springfield, IL 62708
State Chamber of Commerce
Illinois State Chamber of Commerce
20 N. Wacker Drive
Chicago, IL 60606
Small Business Administration
219 S. Dearborn Street*†
Chicago, IL 60604

1 North Old State Capitol Plaza
Springfield, IL 62701

PUBLICATIONS

Vital Statistics of Illinois (population statistics, annual), Illinois Department of Health, 535 W. Jefferson Street, Springfield, IL 62706

Employment and Annual Payrolls of Firms (annual), Illinois Bureau of Employment Security, Department of Labor, Chicago, IL 60605

Illinois Employment Report (monthly), Illinois Bureau of Employment Security, Department of Labor, Chicago, IL 62605

Illinois Economic Data Book, Department of Commerce and Community Affairs, 222 S. College Street, Springfield, IL 62706

Report of Department of Revenue (sales statistics, annual), Department of Revenue, Springfield, IL 62706

Monthly Economic Data Sheets (monthly), Department of Commerce and Community Affairs, 222 S. College Street, Springfield, IL 62706

INDUSTRIAL AND BUSINESS DIRECTORIES

Chicago Buyers' Guide, Chicago Association of Commerce and Industry, 130 S. Michigan Avenue, Chicago, IL 60603

Chicago Cook County and Illinois Industrial Directory, National Publishing Corp., 3150 Des Plaines Avenue, Des Plaines, IL 60018

Chicago Geographic Edition, Manufacturers' News, Inc., 3 E. Huron Street, Chicago, IL 60611; State Industrial Directories Corp., 2 Penn Plaza, New York, NY 10001

Illinois Industrial Directory, Illinois Industrial Directories National Publishing Corp., 3150 Des Plaines Avenue, Des Plaines, IL 60018

Illinois Manufacturers Directory, Manufacturers' News, Inc., 3 E. Huron Street, Chicago, IL 60611; State Industrial Directories Corp., 2 Penn Plaza, New York, NY 10001

Illinois Services Directory, Manufacturers' News, Inc., 3 E. Huron Street, Chicago, IL 60611

International Buyers' Directory to Illinois Products, Department of Business and Economic Development, 222 S. College Street, Springfield, IL 62706

Indiana

STATE HOUSE, INDIANAPOLIS, IN 46204
(317) 633-4740

INFORMATION OFFICES

Commerce/Economic Development
Department of Commerce
440 N. Meridian Street
Indianapolis, IN 46204

Taxation
Department of Revenue
State Office Building
Indianapolis, IN 46204
State Board of Tax Commissioners
201 State Office Building
Indianapolis, IN 46204
State Chamber of Commerce
Indiana State Chamber of Commerce, Inc.
201–212 Board of Trade Building
Indianapolis, IN 46204
Small Business Administration
575 N. Pennsylvania Street†
Indianapolis, IN 46204

PUBLICATIONS

Statistical Abstract of Indiana Counties, Indiana State Chamber of Commerce, Indianapolis, IN 46200

Estimates of Population of the Indiana Counties (population statistics, annual), Superintendent of Documents, Government Printing Office, Washington, DC 20402

Indiana Business Review (income statistics, annual), Division of Research, School of Business, Indiana University, Bloomington, IN 47401

Data Supplement to the Indiana Business Review (quarterly), Division of Research, School of Business, Indiana University, Bloomington, IN 47401

Covered Employment and Payrolls (employment statistics, quarterly), Employment Security Division, Research and Statistics Section, Indianapolis, IN 46204

Indiana Labor Market Information (employment statistics, quarterly), Employment Security Division, Research and Statistics Section, Indianapolis, IN 46204

Indiana Fact Book, Indiana State Planning Service Agency, Harrison Office Building, Indianapolis, IN 46204

INDUSTRIAL AND BUSINESS DIRECTORIES

Indiana Industrial Directory, Manufacturers' News, Inc., 3 E. Huron Street, Chicago, IL 60611; Indiana State Chamber of Commerce, 201–212 Board of Trade Building, Indianapolis, IN 46204; State Industrial Directories Corp., 2 Penn Plaza, New York, NY 10001

Iowa

STATE CAPITOL, DES MOINES, IA 50319
(515) 281-5011

State Information Guide

Commerce/Economic Development
Development Commission
250 Jewett Building
914 Grand Avenue
Des Moines, IA 50309
Taxation
Department of Revenue
Lucas Building
East 21st and Walnut Streets
Des Moines, IA 50319
Small Business Administration
210 Walnut Street†
Des Moines, IA 50309

PUBLICATIONS

Statistical Profile of Iowa, Iowa Development Commission, Research Division, Des Moines, IA 50319
Iowa Detailed Report of Vital Statistics (population statistics, annual), Records and Statistics Division, Iowa State Department of Health, Lucas State Office Building, Des Moines, IA 50319
The Construction of Personal Income Estimates for Counties: A Study in Economic Statistics (income statistics), Bureau of Business and Economic Research, College of Business Administration, The University of Iowa, Iowa City, IA 52242
Iowa Employment and Earnings (employment statistics, monthly), Iowa Employment Security Commission, Des Moines, IA 50310
Report of Iowa Employment Security Commission (annual), Iowa Employment Security Commission, Des Moines, IA 50319
Retail Sales and Use Tax Annual Report (sales statistics, quarterly), Research and Statistics Division, Iowa Department of Revenue, Lucas State Office Building, Des Moines, IA 50319

INDUSTRIAL AND BUSINESS DIRECTORIES

Directory of Iowa Manufacturers, Iowa Development Commission, 250 Jewett Building, 914 Grand Avenue, Des Moines, IA 50319

Kansas

STATE HOUSE, TOPEKA, KS 66612
(913) 296–0111

INFORMATION OFFICES

Commerce/Economic Development
Department of Economic Development
503 Kansas Avenue
Topeka, KS 66603

Taxation
Department of Revenue
State Office Building
Topeka, KS 66612
State Chamber of Commerce
Kansas Association of Commerce and Industry
500 First National Tower
1 Townsite Plaza
Topeka, KS 66603
Small Business Administration
110 E. Waterman Street†
Wichita, KS 67202

PUBLICATIONS

Kansas Statistical Abstract, University of Kansas, Center for Public Affairs, 601 Blake Hall, Lawrence, KS 66045
Kansas Data for Site Selection, Kansas Department of Economic Development, 503 Kansas Avenue, Topeka, KS 66603
Fifty Interesting Facts About Kansas, Kansas Association of Commerce and Industry, 500 First National Tower, Topeka, KS 66603
Annual Economic Report of the Governor (income statistics, annual), Division of the Budget, State Capitol Building, Topeka, KS 66612
Annual Manpower Planning Report (employment statistics, annual), Research and Analysis Section, Department of Human Resources, 401 Topeka Boulevard, Topeka, KS 66603
Area Manpower Reviews (employment statistics, biennial), Research and Analysis Section, Department of Human Resources, 401 Topeka Boulevard, Topeka, KS 66603
Kansas Facts, Kansas Department of Economic Development, 503 Kansas Avenue, Topeka, KS 66603

INDUSTRIAL AND BUSINESS DIRECTORIES

Directory of Kansas Manufacturers and Products, Kansas Department of Economic Development, 503 Kansas Avenue, Topeka, KS 66603; State Industrial Directories Corp., 2 Penn Plaza, New York, NY 10001
Directory of Manufacturers, Wichita, Kansas, Wichita Area Chamber of Commerce, 350 West Douglas, Wichita, KS 67202

Kentucky

STATE CAPITOL, FRANKFORT, KY 40601
(502) 564–3130

INFORMATION OFFICES

Commerce/Economic Development
Department of Commerce
Capitol Plaza Tower
Frankfort, KY 40601
Taxation
Department of Revenue
Capitol Annex
Frankfort, KY 40601
State Chamber of Commerce
Kentucky Chamber of Commerce
Versailles Road
Frankfort, KY 40601
Small Business Administration
600 Federal Place†
Louisville, KY 40202

PUBLICATIONS

Deskbook of Kentucky Economic Statistics, Department of Commerce, Frankfort, KY 40601
Kentucky Vital Statistics (population statistics, annual), Kentucky Vital Statistics, Kentucky Department for Human Resources, 275 E. Main Street, Frankfort, KY 40601
Kentucky Employment Statistics (monthly), Department for Human Resources, Frankfort, KY 40601
Number of Workers in Manufacturing Industries and Total Wages Covered by Kentucky Unemployment Insurance Law Classified by Industry and County (quarterly), Department for Human Resources, Frankfort, KY 40601
Department of Revenue Annual Report (sales statistics, annual), Department of Revenue, Frankfort, KY 40601

INDUSTRIAL AND BUSINESS DIRECTORIES

Exporters Directory, Kentucky Department of Commerce, Capitol Plaza Tower, Frankfort, KY 40601
Kentucky Directory of Manufacturers, Department of Commerce, Capitol Plaza Tower, Frankfort, KY 40601; and from Manufacturers' News, 3 E. Huron Street, Chicago, IL 60611; State Industrial Directories Corp., 2 Penn Plaza, New York, NY 10001

Louisiana

STATE CAPITOL, BATON ROUGE, LA 70804
(504) 389–6601

INFORMATION OFFICES

Commerce/Economic Development
Department of Commerce and Industry
State Land and Natural Resources Building
Baton Rouge, LA 70804

Taxation
Department of Revenue
Capitol Annex
Baton Rouge, LA 70804
State Chamber of Commerce
Louisiana Association of Business and Industry
P.O. Box 3988
Baton Rouge, LA 70821
Small Business Administration
1001 Howard Avenue†
New Orleans, LA 70113

500 Fannin Street
Shreveport, LA 71101

PUBLICATIONS

Statistical Abstract of Louisiana, University of New Orleans, Division of Business and Economic Research, New Orleans, LA 70122
Vital Statistics of Louisiana (population statistics, annual), Louisiana Health and Human Resources Administration, Division of Health, Public Health Statistics, P.O. Box 60630, New Orleans, LA 70160
The Louisiana Economy (income statistics, annual), Research Division, College of Administration and Business, Louisiana Tech University, Ruston, LA 71272
Employment and Total Wages Paid by Employees Subject to the Louisiana Employment Security Law (employment statistics, quarterly), Department of Employment Security, Baton Rouge, LA 70804
Louisiana Labor Market (monthly), Department of Employment Security, Baton Rouge, LA 70804

INDUSTRIAL AND BUSINESS DIRECTORIES

Louisiana Directory of Manufacturers, Department of Commerce and Industry, State Land and Natural Resources Building, Baton Rouge, LA 70804; and from Manufacturers' News, Inc., 3 E. Huron Street, Chicago, IL 60611; State Industrial Directories Corp., 2 Penn Plaza, New York, NY 10001
Louisiana International Trade Directory, International House, New Orleans, LA 70150

Maine

STATE HOUSE, AUGUSTA, ME 04333
(207) 289–1110

INFORMATION OFFICES

Commerce/Economic Development
State Development Office
State House
Augusta, ME 04333

Private Development Associations
  Maine Development Foundation
  1 Memorial Circle
  Augusta, ME 04330
  Maine Capital Corporation
  1 Memorial Circle
  Augusta, ME 04330
Taxation
  Bureau of Taxation
  Department of Finance and Administration
  State Office Building
  Augusta, ME 04333
State Chamber of Commerce
  Maine State Chamber of Commerce
  477 Congress Street
  Portland, ME 04111
Small Business Administration
  40 Western Avenue†
  Augusta, ME 04430

PUBLICATIONS

Maine Economic Data Book, Department of Commerce and Industry, Augusta, ME 04330
Maine Vital Statistics (population statistics, annual), Department of Health and Welfare, Augusta, ME 04330
Employment, Wages Contribution Under Employment Security Program (employment statistics, annual), Employment Security Commission in the State Department of Manpower Affairs, Union Street, Augusta, ME 04330
Maine Manpower (employment statistics, monthly), Employment Security Commission in the State Department of Manpower Affairs, Union Street, Augusta, ME 04330
Sales and Use Tax Assessments (sales statistics, monthly), Bureau of Taxation, Sales Tax Division, State Office Building, Augusta, ME 04330
Facts About Industrial Maine, Maine State Development Office, Augusta, ME 04330

INDUSTRIAL AND BUSINESS DIRECTORIES

Doing Business in Maine, State Development Office, Augusta, ME 04333
Maine Marketing Directory, State Development Office, Augusta, ME 04333
Maine Register, Tower Publishing Company, 163 Middle Street, Portland, ME 04111
Portland Directory, Tower Publishing Company, 163 Middle Street, Portland, ME 04111

Maryland

STATE HOUSE, ANNAPOLIS, MD 21404
(301) 269-3091

INFORMATION OFFICES

Commerce/Economic Development
  Department of Economic and Community Development
  1748 Forest Drive
  Annapolis, MD 21401
Taxation
  Comptroller of the Treasury
  State Treasury Building
  Calvert Street
  Annapolis, MD 21404
State Chamber of Commerce
  Maryland State Chamber of Commerce
  60 West Street
  Annapolis, MD 21401
Small Business Administration
  8600 LaSalle Road†
  Towson, MD 21204

PUBLICATIONS

Maryland Statistical Abstract, Department of Economic and Community Development, 2525 Riva Road, Annapolis, MD 21401
Maryland Population Estimates and Projections (population statistics, annual), State Department of Health and Hygiene, 201 W. Preston Street, Baltimore, MD 21201
Labor Market Information Review (employment statistics, quarterly) Maryland Department of Human Resources, Office of Program and Planning Evaluation, 1100 Eutau Street, Baltimore, MD 21201

INDUSTRIAL AND BUSINESS DIRECTORIES

Directory of Maryland Exporters-Importers, Maryland Department of Economics and Community Development, 2525 Riva Road, Annapolis, MD 21401
Directory of Maryland Manufacturers, Maryland Department of Economic and Community Development, 2525 Riva Road, Annapolis, MD 21401
Maryland State Industrial Directory, State Industrial Directories Corp., 2 Penn Plaza, New York, NY 10001

Massachusetts

STATE HOUSE, BOSTON, MA 02133
(617) 727-2121

INFORMATION OFFICES

Commerce/Economic Development
  Executive Office of Economic Affairs
  State House, Room 212
  Boston, MA 02133

Department of Commerce and Development
Leverett Saltonstall Building
100 Cambridge Street
Boston, MA 02202
Taxation
Department of Revenue
Leverett Saltonstall Building
100 Cambridge Street
Boston, MA 02202
Small Business Administration
60 Batterymarch Street†
Boston, MA 02110

150 Causeway Street†
Boston, MA 02114

302 High Street
Holyoke, MA 01050

PUBLICATIONS

Business Incentives, Department of Commerce and Development, Boston, MA 02202
Annual Report of Vital Statistics of the Commonwealth of Massachusetts (population statistics, annual), Office of Health Statistics, Lemuel Shattuck Hospital, 170 Morton Street, Jamaica Plain, MA 02130
City and Town Monographs (income statistics, annual), Massachusetts Department of Commerce and Development, 100 Cambridge Street, Boston, MA 02202

INDUSTRIAL AND BUSINESS DIRECTORIES

Directory of Directors in the City of Boston and Vicinity, Bankers Service Co., 14 Beacon Street, Boston, MA 02108
Directory of Massachusetts Manufacturers, George D. Hall Company, 20 Kilby Street, Boston, MA 02109
Massachusetts Directory of Manufacturers, Manufacturers' News, Inc., 3 E. Huron Street, Chicago, IL 60611
Massachusetts State Industrial Directory, State Industrial Directories Corp., 2 Penn Plaza, New York, NY 10001

Michigan

STATE CAPITOL, LANSING, MI 48913
(517) 373–1837

INFORMATION OFFICES

Commerce/Economic Development
Department of Commerce
525 W. Ottawa Street
P.O. Box 30225
Lansing, MI 48909

Taxation
Bureau of Collection
Department of Treasury
Treasury Building
Lansing, MI 48922
State Chamber of Commerce
Michigan State Chamber of Commerce
501 S. Capitol Avenue
Lansing, MI 48933
Small Business Administration
477 Michigan Avenue†
Detroit, MI 48226

540 W. Kaye Avenue
Marquette, MI 49885

PUBLICATIONS

Michigan Statistical Abstract, Michigan State University, Graduate School of Business Administration, Division of Research, East Lansing, MI 48823
County Population Data (population statistics, annual), Department of Management and Budget, Information Systems Division, Lewis Cass Building, Lansing, MI 48909
Michigan Statistical Abstract (income statistics, biennial), Bureau of Business and Economic Research, Michigan State University, East Lansing, MI 48824
Annual Report of Michigan Employment Security (employment statistics, monthly), Employment Security Commission, Detroit, MI 48202
Michigan Manpower Review (employment statistics, monthly), Employment Security Commission, Detroit, MI 48202
County Economic Profiles (statistics on income, population, manufacturing, selected services and retail trade), Office of Economic Development, P.O. Box 30225, Lansing, MI 48909
Annual Report of Michigan Department of Treasury Annual Report (sales statistics, annual), Michigan Department of Treasury, Lansing, MI 48922
Research and Statistical Bulletin (sales statistics, monthly), Michigan Department of Treasury, Lansing, MI 48922
Quarterly Report of the Michigan Department of Treasury, Lansing, MI 48922

INDUSTRIAL AND BUSINESS DIRECTORIES

Directory of Michigan Manufacturers, Manufacturers' News, Inc., 3 E. Huron Street, Chicago, IL 60611; Manufacturers Publishing Co., 8543 Puritan Avenue, Detroit, MI 48238
Harris Michigan Manufacturers Industrial Directory, Harris Publishing Company, 33140 Aurora Road, Cleveland, OH 44139
Michigan State Industrial Directory, State Industrial Directories Corp., 2 Penn Plaza, New York, NY 10001

Minnesota

STATE CAPITOL, ST. PAUL, MN 55155
(612) 296–6013

INFORMATION OFFICES

Commerce/Economic Development
  Department of Commerce
  Metro Square Building
  St. Paul, MN 55101
  Department of Economic Development
  480 Cedar Street
  St. Paul, MN 55101
  Division of Small Business and Finance
    Agency
  480 Cedar Street
  St. Paul, MN 55101
Taxation
  Department of Revenue
  Centennial Office Building
  St. Paul, MN 55145
State Chamber of Commerce
  Minnesota Association of Commerce and Industry
  Hanover Building
  480 Cedar Street
  St. Paul, MN 55101
Small Business Administration
  12 S. 6th Street†
  Minneapolis, MN 55402

PUBLICATIONS

Minnesota Vital Statistics (population statistics, annual), Section of Health Statistics, Department of Health, 717 Delaware Street, SE, Minneapolis, MN 55440
Employment Trends, A Manpower Analysis (employment statistics, monthly), Minnesota Department of Economic Security, Communications and Publication, 390 N. Robert Street, St. Paul, MN 55101
Minnesota Statistical Profile, Minnesota Department of Economic Development, 480 Cedar Street, St. Paul, MN 55101

INDUSTRIAL AND BUSINESS DIRECTORIES

Minnesota Directory of Manufacturers, Manufacturers' News, Inc., 3 E. Huron Street, Chicago, IL 60611; Documents Section, State of Minnesota, 140 Centennial Building, St. Paul, MN 55155; State Industrial Directories Corp., 2 Penn Plaza, New York, NY 10001

Mississippi

NEW CAPITOL, JACKSON, MS 39205
(601) 354–7011

INFORMATION OFFICES

Commerce/Economic Development
  Mississippi Department of Economic Development
  P.O. Box 849
  Jackson, MS 39205
  Department of Agriculture and Commerce
  1604 Sillers Building
  Jackson, MS 39205
Taxation
  Tax Commission
  102 Woolfolk Building
  Jackson, MS 39201
State Chamber of Commerce
  P.O. Box 1849
  Standard Life Building
  Jackson, MS 39205
Small Business Administration
  111 Fred Haise Boulevard
  Biloxi, MS 39530
  100 W. Capitol Street†
  Jackson, MS 39201

PUBLICATIONS

Mississippi Statistical Abstract, State University, College of Business and Industry, Division of Research, Mississippi State, MS 39762
Annual Bulletin of Vital Statistics (population statistics, annual), State Board of Health, Statistical Services Unit, P.O. Box 1700, Jackson, MS 39205
Mississippi Business Reveiw (income statistics, annual), Division of Business Research, College of Business and Industry, Mississippi State University, P.O. Box 5288, State College, MS 39762
Mississippi Covered Employment and Wages (employment statistics, monthly), Mississippi Employment Security Commission, P.O. Box 1699, Jackson, MS 39205
Monthly Employment and Quarterly Wages of Workers Covered by the Mississippi Employment Law (annual), Mississippi Employment Security Commission, P.O. Box 1699, Jackson, MS 39205
Quarterly Bulletin on Employment and Wages of Workers Covered by the Mississippi Employment Security Law (quarterly), Mississippi Employment Security Commission, Jackson, MS 39205
Annual Service Bulletin (sales statistics, annual), State Tax Commission, P.O. Box 960, Jackson, MS 39205

Mississippi Industrial Development Brochure, Mississippi Department of Economic Development, P.O. Box 849, Jackson, MS 39205

INDUSTRIAL AND BUSINESS DIRECTORIES

Mississippi International Trade Directory, Mississippi Marketing Council, Box 849, Sillers State Office Building, Jackson, MS 39205

Mississippi Manufacturers' Directory, Manufacturers' News, Inc., 3 E. Huron Street, Chicago, IL 60611; Public Information Office, Mississippi Research and Development Center, Jackson, MS 39205; State Industrial Directories Corp., 2 Penn Plaza, New York, NY 10001

Missouri

STATE CAPITOL, JEFFERSON CITY, MO 65101
(314) 751-2151

INFORMATION OFFICES

Commerce/Economic Development
Department of Consumer Affairs, Regulation and Licensing
1014 Madison Street
Post Office Box 118
Jefferson City, MO 65102
Taxation
Department of Revenue
Division of Taxation
Jefferson State Office Building
Post Office Box 629
Jefferson City, MO 65105
State Chamber of Commerce
Missouri Chamber of Commerce
428 East Capitol Avenue
Post Office Box 149
Jefferson City, MO 65102
Small Business Administration
911 Walnut Street
Kansas City, MO 64106
1150 Grand Avenue†
Kansas City, Missouri 64106
Mercantile Tower†
1 Mercantile Center
St. Louis, Missouri 63101

PUBLICATIONS

Data for Missouri Counties, University of Missouri, Extension Division Publications, 206 Whitten Hall, Columbia, MO 65211 (Available, 1982)

Missouri Vital Statistics (population statistics, annual), Missouri Center for Health Statistics, Broadway State Office Building, Post Office Box 570, Jefferson City, MO 65102

Missouri State and Area Labor Trends (employment statistics, monthly), Missouri Division of Employment Security, Post Office Box 59, Jefferson City, MO 65104

Manual Combined Financial Report of the Department of Revenue and the State Treasurer (annual), Department of Revenue, Division of Taxation and Collection, Post Office Box 629, Jefferson City, MO 65105

Report of Collections (monthly), Department Cashier, Department of Revenue, Division of Taxation and Collection, Post Office Box 629, Jefferson City, MO 65105

INDUSTRIAL AND BUSINESS DIRECTORY

Contacts Influential: Commerce and Industrial Directory (for Kansas City Area), Contacts Influential, Inc., 6347 Brookside Boulevard, Suite 204, Kansas City, MO 64113

Montana

STATE CAPITOL, HELENA, MT 59601
(406) 449-3111

INFORMATION OFFICES

Commerce/Economic Development
Governor's Office of Commerce and Small Business Development
State Capitol Building
Helena, MT 59601
Department of Community Affairs
Research and Information Division
1424 9th Avenue
Helena, MT 59601
State Chamber of Commerce
Montana Chamber of Commerce
P.O. Box 1730
Helena, MT 59601
Small Business Administration
301 South Park†
Helena, MT 59601

PUBLICATIONS

Montana Data Book, Department of Community Affairs, Division of Research and Information, Helena, MT 59601

Unpublished estimates on population, Department of Labor and Industry, Employment Security Division, Helena, MT 59601

Montana Personal Income Series (income statistics, annual), Department of Community Affairs, Division of Research and Information, Helena, MT 59601

Montana Labor Market Supplements (employment statistics, annual), Department of Labor and Industry, Employment Security Division,

Research and Analysis Section, Helena, MT 59601

Montana County Profiles (county reports, regional summaries, periodically updated), Department of Community Affairs, Division of Research and Information, Helena, MT 59601

INDUSTRIAL AND BUSINESS DIRECTORIES

Montana Directory of Manufacturers, Research and Information Systems Division, Department of Community Affairs, State Capitol, Helena, MT 59601

Nebraska

STATE CAPITOL, LINCOLN, NB 68509
(402) 471-3111

INFORMATION OFFICES

Commerce/Economic Development
Department of Economic Development
301 Centennial Mall South
Lincoln, NB 68509
Taxation
Department of Revenue
301 Centennial Mall South
Lincoln, NB 68509
State Chamber of Commerce
Nebraska Association of Commerce and Industry
P.O. Box 81556
Lincoln, NB 68501
Small Business Administration
19th and Farnam Streets†
Empire State Building
Omaha, NB 68102

PUBLICATIONS

Nebraska Statistical Handbook, Nebraska Department of Economic Development, Division of Research, Box 94666, Lincoln, NB 68509

Nebraskans' Book, Nebraska Department of Economic Development, Division of Research, P.O. Box 94666, Lincoln, NB 68508

Business in Nebraska (income statistics, annual), Bureau of Business Research, University of Nebraska, Lincoln, NB 68588

Nebraska Work Force Trends (employment statistics, monthly), Department of Labor, Division of Employment, Lincoln, NB 68501

INDUSTRIAL AND BUSINESS DIRECTORIES

Directory of Nebraska Manufacturers and Their Products, Manufacturers' News, Inc., 3 E. Huron Street, Chicago, IL 60611

Directory of Nebraska Manufacturers, State Department of Economic Development, Lincoln, NB 68509

Manufacturers and Wholesalers Directory, Lincoln Chamber of Commerce, 200 Lincoln Building, Lincoln, NB 68508

Nevada

LEGISLATIVE BUILDING, CARSON CITY, NV 89710
(702) 885-5627

INFORMATION OFFICES

Commerce/Economic Development
Department of Commerce
321 Nye Building
Carson City, NV 89710
Department of Economic Development
Capitol Complex
Carson City, NV 89710
Taxation
Tax Commission
1340 S. Curry Street
Carson City, NV 89710
State Chamber of Commerce
Nevada Chamber of Commerce Association
P.O. Box 2806
Reno, NV 89505
Small Business Administration
301 E. Stewart†
Las Vegas, NV 89101
50 S. Virginia Street
Reno, NV 89505

PUBLICATIONS

Nevada Community Profiles, Department of Economic Development, Carson City, NV 89710

Nevada Manpower Report (employment statistics, monthly), Employment Security Department, Carson City, NV 89710

Nevada Employment and Payroll (annual), Employment Security Department, Carson City, NV 89710

County Data Files (irregular update), Department of Economic Development, Carson City, NV 89710

INDUSTRIAL AND BUSINESS DIRECTORIES

Nevada Industrial Directory, Department of Economic Development, Capitol Complex, Carson City, NV 89710

Nevada Directory of Business, Manufacturers' News, Inc., 3 E. Huron Street, Chicago, IL 60611

New Hampshire

STATE HOUSE, CONCORD, NH 03301
(603) 271-1110

INFORMATION OFFICES

Commerce/Economic Development
Department of Resources and Economic Development
Division of Economic Development
6 Loudon Road
Concord, NH 03301
Taxation
Board of Taxation
61 S. Spring Street
Concord, NH 03301
State Chamber of Commerce
Business and Industry Association of New Hampshire
23 School Street
Concord, NH 03301
Small Business Administration
55 Pleasant Street†
Concord, NH 03301

PUBLICATIONS

Resident Population Figures (population statistics, annual), Office of State Planning, Concord, NH 03301
Employment and Unemployment in New Hampshire (monthly), Department of Employment Security, Concord, NH 03301
Employment and Wage by County (quarterly), Department of Employment Security, Concord, NH 03301
Economic Conditions in New Hampshire (employment statistics, quarterly), Department of Employment Security, Concord, NH 03301

INDUSTRIAL AND BUSINESS DIRECTORIES

Made in New Hampshire, New Hampshire Office of Industrial Development, Department of Resources, Concord, NH 03301
New Hampshire Register, Tower Publishing Company, 163 Middle Street, Portland, ME 04111

New Jersey

STATE HOUSE, TRENTON, NJ 08625
(609) 292-2121

INFORMATION OFFICES

Commerce/Economic Development
Department of Labor and Industry
John Fitch Plaza
Trenton, NJ 08625
Division of Travel and Tourism
P.O. Box 400
Trenton, NJ 08625
Economic Development Authority
P.O. Box 1446
Trenton, NJ 08625
Taxation
Division of Taxation
West State and Willow Streets
Trenton, NJ 08625
State Chamber of Commerce
New Jersey State Chamber of Commerce
5 Commerce Street
Newark, NJ 07102
Small Business Administration
970 Broad Street†
Newark, NJ 07102

1800 E. Davis Street
Camden, NJ 08104

PUBLICATIONS

Facts and Facets of New Jersey, Division of Economic Development, P.O. Box 2766, Trenton, New Jersey 08625
New Jersey Population Estimates (population statistics, annual), Division of Planning and Research, Office of Demographic and Economic Analysis, P.O. CN-388, Trenton, New Jersey 08625
County Profiles, Division of Economic Development, P.O. Box 2766, Trenton, New Jersey 08625
Covered Employment Trends in New Jersey (employment statistics, annual), Division of Planning and Research, P.O. Box CN-383, Trenton, New Jersey 08625
New Jersey Covered Employment Trends by Geographic Areas of the State, Division of Planning and Research, Office of Labor Statistics, P.O. Box CN-383, Trenton, New Jersey 08625
New Jersey Employment and the Economy, Division of Planning and Research, P.O. Box CN-056, Trenton, New Jersey 08625
New Jersey Economic Indicators, Division of Planning and Research, P.O. Box CN-056, Trenton, New Jersey 08625
Industrial Development Network, Division of Economic Development, P.O. Box 2766, Trenton, New Jersey 08625

INDUSTRIAL AND BUSINESS DIRECTORIES

New Jersey State Industrial Directory, Manufacturers' News, Inc., 3 E. Huron Street, Chicago, IL 60611; State Industrial Directories Corp., 2 Penn Plaza, New York, NY 10001

New Mexico

STATE CAPITOL, SANTE FE, NM 87503
(505) 827–4011

INFORMATION OFFICES

Commerce/Economic Development
Economic Development Division
Bataan Memorial Building
Sante Fe, NM 87503
Taxation
Bureau of Revenue
Manuel Lujan Sr. Building
Santa Fe, NM 87501
State Chamber of Commerce
Association of Commerce and Industry of New Mexico
117 Quincy NE
Albuquerque, NM 87108
Small Business Administration
5000 Marble Avenue NE†
Albuquerque, NM 87110

PUBLICATIONS

New Mexico Statistical Abstract, University of New Mexico, Bureau of Business Research, Albuquerque, NM 87131
New Mexico Blue Book (population statistics, biennial), Office of the Secretary of State, 400 Legislative Executive Building, Santa Fe, NM 87503
Income and Employment in New Mexico, Selected Years (New Mexico Studies in Business and Economics, No. 22—income statistics, biennial), Bureau of Business and Economic Research, University of New Mexico, Albuquerque, NM 87131
New Mexico Socio and Economic Statistics (income statistics, published irregularly), New Mexico State Planning Office, Executive Legislative Building, Santa Fe, NM 87503
New Mexico Manpower Review (employment statistics, monthly), Research and Statistics Section, Employment Security Commission of New Mexico, P.O. Box 1928, Albuquerque, NM 87103
The State of New Mexico Bureau of Revenue Receipts and Disbursements Monthly Statement (sales statistics, monthly), Bureau of Revenue, Santa Fe, NM 87503

INDUSTRIAL AND BUSINESS DIRECTORIES

Directory of New Mexico Manufacturing and Mining, Manufacturers' News, Inc., 3 E. Hu-

ron Street, Chicago, IL 60611; New Mexico Commerce and Industry Department, Bataan Memorial Building, Santa Fe, NM 87503; State Industrial Directories Corp., 2 Penn Plaza, New York, NY 10001

New York

STATE CAPITOL, ALBANY, NY 12224
(518) 474–8390

INFORMATION OFFICES

Commerce/Economic Development
Department of Commerce
99 Washington Avenue
Albany, NY 12245

Division of Industrial and Corporate Development
99 Washington Avenue
Albany, NY 12245

Office of Development Planning
Executive Chamber
Albany, NY 12224
Taxation
State Tax Commission
Department of Taxation and Finance
State Campus Building #9
Albany, NY 12227
State Chamber of Commerce
New York State Business Council
150 State Street
Albany, NY 12207
Small Business Administration
26 Federal Plaza†*
New York, NY 10007

111 W. Huron Street
Buffalo, NY 14202

100 S. Clinton Street†
Syracuse, NY 13202

180 State Street
Elmira, NY 14901

99 Washington Avenue
Albany, NY 12210

425 Broad Hollow Road
Melville, NY 11747

100 State Street
Rochester, NY 14014

PUBLICATIONS

New York Statistical Yearbook, Division of Budget, Albany, NY 12207
Vital Statistics of New York State (population statistics, annual), Office of Biostatistics, State Department of Health, Albany, NY 12208
Personal Income in Areas and Counties of New York State (income statistics, annual), *Quarterly Summary of Business Statistics* (variety

of economic time series); *Business Trends in NY State* (analysis of economic trends, monthly); *Best Business Advantages; Report to Business; Your Business.* New York State Department of Commerce, 99 Washington Avenue, Albany, NY 12245

New York Employment Review (employment statistics, monthly), Division of Research and Statistics, 370 7th Avenue, New York, NY 10001

INDUSTRIAL AND BUSINESS DIRECTORIES

New York and Surrounding Territory Classified Business Directory, New York Directory Co., Inc., 1440 Broadway, New York, NY 10018

New York Classified Business Directory, New York Directory Co., Inc., 1440 Broadway, New York, NY 10018

New York State Industrial Directory, State Industrial Directories Corp., 2 Penn Plaza, New York, NY 10001; Manufacturers' News, Inc., 3 E. Huron Street, Chicago, IL 60611

Directory of Minority Business Enterprise, Minority Business Development Bureau, New York State Department of Commerce, 230 Park Avenue, New York, NY 10169

North Carolina

STATE LEGISLATIVE BUILDING, RALEIGH, NC 27602
(919) 733–1110

INFORMATION OFFICES

Commerce/Economic Development
Department of Commerce
430 N. Salisbury Street
Raleigh, NC 27611
Taxation
Department of Revenue
2 S. Salisbury Street
Raleigh, NC 22760
State Chamber of Commerce
North Carolina Citizen's Association
P.O. Box 2508
Raleigh, NC 27602
Small Business Administration
230 S. Tryon Street†
Charlotte, NC 28202

215 S. Evans Street
Greenville, NC 27834

PUBLICATIONS

North Carolina State Statistical Abstract, Department of Administration, Office of the State Budget and Association for Coordinating Interagency Statistics, Raleigh, NC 27601

Vital Statistics (population statistics, annual), North Carolina State Board of Health, Division of Administration Service, Public Health Statistical Section, Raleigh, NC 27611

Statistics of Taxation (income statistics, biennial), Tax Research Division, North Carolina Department of Revenue, Raleigh, NC 27640

North Carolina Insured Employment and Wage Payments (employment statistics, quarterly), Bureau of Employment Security Research, Employment Security Commission, P.O. Box 25903, Raleigh, NC 27611

North Carolina Insured Employment and Wage Payments (annual), Bureau of Employment Security Research, Employment Security Commission, P.O. Box 25903, Raleigh, NC 27611

Labor Force Estimates by County Area and State (annual), Bureau of Employment Security Research, Employment Security Commission, P.O. Box 25903, Raleigh, NC 27611

Statistics of Taxation (sales statistics, biennial), Division of Tax Research, North Carolina Department of Revenue, Revenue Building, Raleigh, NC 27640

INDUSTRIAL AND BUSINESS DIRECTORIES

Directory of North Carolina Manufacturing Firms, North Carolina Department of Commerce, Raleigh, NC 27611; State Industrial Directories Corp., 2 Penn Plaza, New York, NY 10001; Manufacturers' News, Inc., 3 E. Huron Street, Chicago, IL 60611

North Dakota

STATE CAPITOL, BISMARCK, ND 58505
(701) 224–2000

INFORMATION OFFICES

Commerce/Economic Development
Department of Business and Industrial Development
513 E. Bismarck Avenue
Bismarck, ND 58505
Taxation
Tax Department
State Capitol
Bismarck, ND 58505
State Chamber of Commerce
Greater North Dakota Association—State Chamber of Commerce
P.O. Box 2467
Fargo, ND 58102
Small Business Administration
657 2d Avenue N.†
Fargo, ND 58108

PUBLICATIONS

North Dakota Growth Indicators, Business and Industrial Development Department, Bismarck, ND 58505

Population estimates are available annually from Business and Industrial Development Department, 513 E. Bismarck Avenue, Bismarck, ND 58505

Area Report of Employment and Total Wages by County and Industry (employment statistics, quarterly), Employment Security Bureau, Bismarck, ND 58505

Prairie Employer Review (employment statistics, monthly), Job Service North Dakota, P.O. Box 1537, Bismarck, ND 58505

INDUSTRIAL AND BUSINESS DIRECTORIES

North Dakota Business Directory, Box 736, W. Fargo, ND 58078

North Dakota Manufacturers Directory, North Dakota Business and Industrial Development, 513 E. Bismarck Avenue, Bismarck, ND 58505; Manufacturers' News, Inc., 3 E. Huron Street, Chicago, IL 60611; State Industrial Directories Corp., 2 Penn Plaza, New York, NY 10001

Strictly Business, Frontier Directory Co., Inc., 222 W. Bowen Avenue, Bismarck, ND 58501

Ohio

STATE HOUSE, COLUMBUS, OH 43215
(614) 466-2000

INFORMATION OFFICES

Commerce/Economic Development
Ohio Department of Economic and Community Development
30 E. Broad Street
Columbus, OH 43216

Taxation
Department of Taxation
30 E. Broad Street
Columbus, OH 43215

State Chamber of Commerce
Ohio Chamber of Commerce
Huntington Bank Building
17 South High Street
Columbus, OH 43215

Small Business Administration
550 Main Street
Cincinnati, OH 45202

1240 E. 9th Street†
Cleveland, OH 44199

85 Marconi Boulevard†
Columbus, OH 43215

PUBLICATIONS

Profit in Ohio, Department of Economic and Community Development, Office of Industrial Development, Columbus, OH 43216

Population Estimates for Ohio (population statistics, annual), Department of Economics and Community Development, Human Resources Development Division, Bureau of Research and Analysis, 30 E. Broad Street, Columbus, OH 43216

Bulletin of Business Research (income statistics, monthly), Center for Business and Economic Research, The Ohio State University, 1775 College Road, Columbus, OH 43210

Ohio Labor Market Information (employment statistics, monthly), Ohio Bureau of Employment Services, 1455 Front Street, Columbus, OH 43216

Ohio Labor Market Information (employment statistics, quarterly), Ohio Bureau of Employment Service, 1455 Front Street, Columbus, OH 43216

Annual Report of Ohio Department of Taxation (sales statistics, annual), Department of Taxation, Columbus, OH 43215

INDUSTRIAL AND BUSINESS DIRECTORIES

Akron, Ohio Membership Directory and Buyers Guide, Akron Area Chamber of Commerce, Windsor Publications, 20229 Erwin Street, Woodland Hills, CA 91364

Directory of Manufacturers in the Toledo Area, Toledo Area Chamber of Commerce, 218 Huron Street, Toledo, OH 43604

Directory of Ohio Manufacturers, Harris Publishing Co., 33140 Aurora Road, Cleveland, OH 44139; Manufacturers' News, Inc., 3 E. Huron Street, Chicago, IL 60611

Manufacturers Directory, Columbus Area Chamber of Commerce, 50 W. Broad Street, Columbus, OH 43215

Ohio and International Trade, Division of International Trade, Department of Economic and Community Development, 30 E. Broad Street, Columbus, OH 43216

Oklahoma

STATE CAPITOL, OKLAHOMA CITY, OK 73105
(405) 521-2011

INFORMATION OFFICES

Commerce/Economic Development
Department of Industrial Development
4024 N. Lincoln
Oklahoma City, OK 73152

Department of Economic and Community Affairs
5500 N. Western Avenue
Oklahoma City, OK 73118
Taxation
Tax Commission
M. C. Connors Building
Oklahoma City, OK 73105
State Chamber of Commerce
Oklahoma State Chamber of Commerce
4020 North Lincoln
Oklahoma City, OK 73105
Small Business Administration
200 N.W. 5th Street†
Oklahoma City, OK 73102

333 W. Fourth Street
Tulsa, OK 74103

PUBLICATIONS

Statistical Abstract of Oklahoma, University of Oklahoma, Center for Economic and Management Research, Norman, OK 73019

Oklahoma Population Estimates (population statistics, annual), Research and Planning Division, Oklahoma Employment Security Commission, Will Rogers Memorial Office Building, Oklahoma City, OK 73105

Oklahoma Business Bulletin (income statistics, monthly), Center for Economic and Management Research, Norman, OK 73019

Oklahoma Labor Market (employment statistics, monthly), Employment Security Commission, Oklahoma City, OK 73105

Oklahoma Labor Newsletter (employment statistics, monthly), Employment Security Commission, Oklahoma City, OK 73105

Oklahoma Sales Tax Statistical Report (sales statistics, annual), Oklahoma Tax Commission, Oklahoma City, OK 73105

INDUSTRIAL AND BUSINESS DIRECTORIES

Oklahoma Directory of Manufacturers and Products, Industrial Development Department, P.O. Box 53424, Oklahoma City, OK 73152

Tulsa Area Manufacturers Directory, Metro Tulsa Chambers of Commerce, 616 S. Boston Avenue, Tulsa, OK 74119

Oregon

STATE CAPITOL, SALEM, OR 97310
(503) 378-3131

INFORMATION OFFICES

Commerce/Economic Development
Department of Commerce
Labor and Industries Building
Salem, OR 97310

Department of Economic Development
155 Cottage Street, N.E.
Salem, OR 97310
Taxation
Department of Revenue
204 State Office Building
Salem, OR 97310
Small Business Administration
1220 SW Third Avenue
Portland, OR 97204

PUBLICATIONS

Oregon Blue Book (population statistics, annual), State Capitol Building, Room 136, Salem, OR 97310

Oregon Covered Employment and Payrolls by Industry and County (employment statistics, quarterly), Department of Employment, Salem, OR 97310

Oregon's Labor Market (monthly), Departυ ent of Employment, Salem, OR 97310

INDUSTRIAL AND BUSINESS DIRECTORIES

International Trade Directory of Oregon and Southern Washington, Chamber of Commerce, 824 SW 5th Avenue, Portland, OR 97204

Oregon Manufacturers Directory, Department of Economic Development, 155 Cottage Street, N.E., Salem, OR 97310; State Industrial Directories Corp., 2 Penn Plaza, New York, NY 10001; Manufacturers' News, Inc., 3 E. Huron Street, Chicago, IL 60611

Pennsylvania

MAIN CAPITOL BUILDING, HARRISBURG, PA 17120
(717) 787-2121

INFORMATION OFFICES

Department of Commerce
Department of Commerce
419 S. Office Building
Harrisburg, PA 17120

Bureau of Economic Development
Department of Commerce
425 S. Office Building
Harrisburg, PA 17120

Bureau of Economic Assistance
Department of Commerce
412 S. Office Building
Harrisburg, PA 17120

Small Business Action Center
Department of Commerce
400 S. Office Building
Harrisburg, PA 17120

Taxation
Department of Revenue
Strawberry Square
Harrisburg, PA 17120

State Chamber of Commerce
Pennsylvania Chamber of Commerce
222 N. Third Street
Harrisburg, PA 17101

Small Business Administration
231 St. Asaphs Road†*
1 Bala Cynwyd Plaza
Bala Cynwyd, PA 19004

100 Chestnut Street
Harrisburg, PA 17101

1000 Liberty Avenue†
Pittsburgh, PA 15222

Penn Place
20 Pennsylvania Avenue
Wilkes-Barre, PA 18702

PUBLICATIONS

Pennsylvania Statistical Abstract, Department of General Services, Bureau of Management Services, State Book Store, P.O. Box 1365, Harrisburg, PA 17125

A Business Guide to Pennsylvania, Department of Commerce, Bureau of Economic Development, Harrisburg, PA 17120

Investors Handbook (annual), Department of Commerce, Bureau of Statistics, Research and Planning, Harrisburg, PA 17120

Industrial Census Series (annual), Department of Commerce, Bureau of Statistics, Research and Planning, Harrisburg, PA 17120, including *Statistics for Manufacturing Industries, Statistics by Industry and Size of Establishment,* and *County Industry Reports.*

Pennsylvania Economic Chartbook (quarterly), Department of Commerce, Bureau of Statistics, Research and Planning, Harrisburg, PA 17120

Estimates of the Total and Household Population for Counties by Age, Sex and Race (annual), Governor's Office of Budget and Administration, Bureau of Management Services, Harrisburg, PA 17105.

Employment and Wages of Workers Covered by the Pennsylvania Unemployment Compensation Law by County and Industry (employment statistics, annual), Department of Labor and Industry, Bureau of Employment Security, Harrisburg, PA 17121

Pennsylvania Employment and Earnings (monthly), Department of Labor and Industry, Bureau of Employment Security, Harrisburg, PA 17121

Statistical Data Sheet (employment statistics, quarterly), Department of Labor and Industry, Bureau of Employment Security, Harrisburg, PA 17121

INDUSTRIAL AND BUSINESS DIRECTORIES

Directory of Pennsylvania Manufacturing Exporters, Department of Commerce, Bureau of Statistics, Research and Planning, Harrisburg, PA 17120

Industrial Directory of the Commonwealth of Pennsylvania, Department of General Services, Bureau of Management Services, State Book Store, Box 1365, Harrisburg, PA 17125

Rhode Island

STATE HOUSE, PROVIDENCE, RI 02903
(401) 277-2000

INFORMATION OFFICES

Commerce/Economic Development
Department of Economic Development
7 Jackson Walkway
Providence, RI 02903

Taxation
Division of Taxation
Department of Administration
CIC Complex
Providence, RI 02908

State Chamber of Commerce
Rhode Island Chamber of Commerce
206 Smith Street
Providence, RI 02908

Small Business Administration
40 Fountain Street†
Providence, RI 02903

PUBLICATIONS

Rhode Island Basic Economic Statistics, Department of Economic Development, 7 Jackson Walkway, Providence, RI 02903

Employment Bulletin (employment statistics, monthly), Division of Statistics and Census, Department of Labor, Providence, RI 02903

Sales Tax Collection by City or Town and County (sales statistics, monthly), Rhode Island Office of Admission Processing and Methods, State House, Providence, RI 02901

Sales Tax Collection by Kind of Business (monthly), Rhode Island Office of Admission

Processing and Methods, State House, Providence, RI 02901

INDUSTRIAL AND BUSINESS DIRECTORIES

Rhode Island Directory of Manufacturers and List of Nonmanufacturing Establishments, Department of Economic Development, 7 Jackson Walkway, Providence, RI 02903

Rhode Island State Industrial Directory, State Industrial Directories Corp., 2 Penn Plaza, New York, NY 10001

South Carolina

STATE HOUSE, COLUMBIA, SC 29211
(803) 758–0221

INFORMATION OFFICES

Commerce/Economic Development
South Carolina State Development Board
1301 Gervais Street
Columbia, SC 29201
Taxation
Tax Commission
John C. Calhoun Office Building
Columbia, SC 29201
State Chamber of Commerce
South Carolina Chamber of Commerce
1002 Calhoun Street
Columbia, SC 29201
Small Business Administration
1801 Assembly Street†
Columbia, SC 29201

PUBLICATIONS

South Carolina Statistical Abstract, Budget and Control Board, Division of Research and Statistical Services, Columbia, SC 29201

Annual Report of the State Board of Health (population statistics, annual), Division of Vital Statistics, State Board of Health, State Office Building, Columbia, SC 29201

Average Monthly Coverage Employment and Total Payroll (employment statistics, annual), Employment Security Commission, Columbia, SC 29202

The South Carolina Labor Market (employment statistics, monthly), Employment Security Commission, Columbia, SC 29202

Report to the Governor and General Assembly (sales statistics, annual), South Carolina Tax Commission, Columbia, SC 29201

Economic Report for South Carolina, Budget and Control Board, Division of Research and Statistical Services, Columbia, SC 29201

INDUSTRIAL AND BUSINESS DIRECTORIES

Industrial Directory of South Carolina, South Carolina State Development Board, 1301 Gervais Street, Columbia, SC 29201

South Carolina International Trade Directory, South Carolina State Development Board, 1301 Gervais Street, Columbia, SC 29201

South Dakota

STATE CAPITOL, PIERRE, SD 57501
(605) 224–3011

INFORMATION OFFICES

Commerce/Economic Development
Department of Commerce and Consumer Affairs
State Capitol
Pierre, SD 57501
Department of Economic and Tourism Development
State Office Building #2
Pierre, SD 57501
Division of Industrial Development
S. Cliff Street
Sioux Falls, SD 57103
Taxation
Department of Revenue
Capitol Lake Plaza
Pierre, SD 57501
State Chamber of Commerce
Greater South Dakota Association
P.O. Box 190
Pierre, SD 57501
Small Business Administration
8th and Main Avenue†
Sioux Falls, SD 57102
515 9th Street
Rapid City, SD 57701

PUBLICATIONS

South Dakota Economic and Business Abstract, University of South Dakota, Business Research Bureau, Vermillion, SD 57069

Annual estimates of population statistics are available from the Department of Manpower Affairs, Employment Security Division, 607 N. Fourth Street, Pierre, SD 57501

Annual Report of Employment Security Department of South Dakota (employment statistics, annual), South Dakota Department of Manpower Affairs, Employment Security Division, 607 N. 4th Street, Aberdeen, SD 57401

Labor Bulletin: An Analysis of Current Labor Statistics in South Dakota (monthly), South

Dakota Department of Manpower Affairs, Employment Security Division, 607 N. 4th Street, Aberdeen, SD 57401

South Dakota Facts, University of South Dakota, Business Research Bureau, Vermillion, SD 57069

INDUSTRIAL AND BUSINESS DIRECTORIES

Directory of South Dakota Industries, Manufacturers' News, Inc., 3 E. Huron Street, Chicago, IL 60611

South Dakota Manufacturers and Processors Directory, South Dakota Industrial Development Division, 620 S. Cliff Street, Sioux Falls, SD 57104; State Industrial Directories Corp., 2 Penn Plaza, New York, NY 10001

Tennessee

State Capitol, Nashville, TN 37219
(615) 741–3011

INFORMATION OFFICES

Commerce/Economic Development
Department of Economic and Community Development
1007 Andrew Jackson Building
Nashville, TN 37219
Taxation
Department of Revenue
927 Andrew Jackson Building
Nashville, TN 37219
State Chamber of Commerce
State Chamber Division of the Tennessee Taxpayers Association
1070 Capitol Hill Building
Nashville, TN 37219
Small Business Administration
502 S. Gay Street
Knoxville, TN 37902
404 James Robertson Parkway†
Nashville, TN 37219
167 N. Main Street
Memphis, TN 38103

PUBLICATIONS

Tennessee Statistical Abstract, University of Tennessee, Center for Business and Economic Research, Knoxville, TN 37916

Tennessee Survey of Business (population statistics, annual), Center for Business and Economic Research, University of Tennessee, Knoxville, TN 37916

Population statistics are available from Statistical Service, State Department of Public

Health, Cordell Hull Office Building, Nashville, TN 37219

Mid-South Quarterly Business Review (income statistics, quarterly), Bureau of Business and Economic Research, College of Business Administration, Memphis State University, Memphis, TN 38111

Basic Employment Security Data—State of Tennessee with County Data (employment statistics, annual), Department of Employment Security, Nashville, TN 37219

The Labor Market Report (employment statistics, monthly), Department of Employment Security, Nashville, TN 37219

Comparative Statement of Collected Revenue (sales statistics, monthly), Department of Revenue, Nashville, TN 37242

Sales and Use Tax (sales statistics, monthly), Department of Revenue, Nashville, TN 37242

Tennessee Pocket Data Book, University of Tennessee, Center for Business and Economic Research, Knoxville, TN 37916

INDUSTRIAL AND BUSINESS DIRECTORIES

Directory of Tennessee Industries, Manufacturers' News, Inc., 3 E. Huron Street, Chicago, IL 60611; State Industrial Directories Corp., 2 Penn Plaza, New York, NY 10001

Tennessee Directory of Manufacturers, Industrial Development Division, Andrew Jackson Building, Nashville, TN 37219

Texas

State Capitol, Austin, TX 78701
(512) 475–2323

INFORMATION OFFICES

Commerce/Economic Development
Industrial Commission
410 East 5th Street
Austin, TX 78711
Taxation
Comptroller of Public Accounts
104 LBJ State Office Building
Austin, TX 78711
State Chamber of Commerce
Texas State Chamber of Commerce
77001 N. Lamar
Suite 302
Austin, TX 78752
Tourist Development Agencies
P.O. Box 12008
Austin, TX 78711

Lower Rio Grand Valley Chamber of Commerce
P.O. Box 975
Weslaco, TX 75896

South Texas Chamber of Commerce
6222 NW IH 19
San Antonio, TX 78201

East Texas Chamber of Commerce
P.O. Box 1592
Longview, TX 75601

West Texas Chamber of Commerce
P.O. Box 1516
Abilene, TX 79604

Small Business Administration
1720 Regal Row*
Dallas, TX 75235

1100 Commerce Street†
Dallas, TX 75202

4100 Rio Bravo
El Paso, TX 79902

500 Dallas Street†
Houston, TX 77002

222 E. Van Buren Street†
Lower Rio Grand Valley
Harlingen, TX 78550

3105 Leopard Street†
Corpus Christi, TX 78408

1205 Texas Avenue†
Lubbock, TX 79401

727 E. Durango†
San Antonio, TX 78206

PUBLICATIONS

Texas Almanac, Dallas Morning News, Dallas, TX 75201

Population Estimates for Texas (annual), Population Research Center, University of Texas, Austin, TX 78712

Annual population estimates are available from the Division of Vital Statistics, State Department of Health, Austin, TX 78756

Employment, Establishments and Wages Covered by the Texas Unemployment Compensation Act (quarterly), Texas Employment Commission, Austin, TX 78701

A Brief Guide to Business Regulations and Services in Texas. Texas Industrial Commission, P.O. Box 12728, Austin, TX 78711

Texas Facts: The Book on Profitable Plant Locations, Texas Industrial Commission, 714 Sam Houston Office Building, Austin, TX 78711

Texas Labor Market Employment Trends and Outlook (monthly), Texas Employment Commission, Austin, TX 78701

Texas Industrial Update (monthly), Texas Industrial Commission, P.O. Box 12728, Austin, TX 78711

INDUSTRIAL AND BUSINESS DIRECTORIES

Dallas Business Guide, Dallas Chamber of Commerce, Fidelity Tower, Dallas, TX 75201

Directory of Texas Manufacturers, Bureau of Business Research, University of Texas, Austin, TX 78712; State Industrial Directories Corp., 2 Penn Plaza, New York, NY 10001

Fort Worth Directory of Manufacturers, Fort Worth Area Chamber of Commerce, 700 Throckmorton Street, Fort Worth, TX 76102

Texas Exporter-Importer Directory, Gulf International Trades, Box 52717, Houston, TX 77052

Texas Manufacturers Directory, Manufacturers' News, Inc., 3 E. Huron Street, Chicago, IL 60611

Utah

STATE CAPITOL, SALT LAKE CITY, UT 84114
(801) 533-4000

INFORMATION OFFICES

Commerce/Economic Development
Trade Commission
Department of Business Regulation
330 E. 4th South Street
Salt Lake City, UT 84111

Department of Community and Economic Development
Division of Economic and Industrial Development
#2 Arrow Press Square, Suite 200
165 South West Temple
Salt Lake City, UT 84101

Taxation
Tax Commission
200 State Office Building
Salt Lake City, UT 84134

Small Business Administration
125 S. State Street
Salt Lake City, UT 84138

PUBLICATIONS

Statistical Abstract, University of Utah, Bureau of Economic and Business Research, Salt Lake City, UT 84112

Utah Economic and Business Review (population statistics, annual), Utah Population Work Committee, Utah Committee on Industrial and Unemployment Planning, 174 Social Hall Avenue, Salt Lake City, UT 84111

Personal Income in Utah and Utah's Counties (income statistics, three to four years), Bureau of Economic and Business Research, University of Utah, Salt Lake City, UT 84112

Utah Department of Employment Security Annual Report (employment statistics, annual), Department of Employment Security, Salt Lake City, UT 84147

Employment News Letter (monthly), Department of Employment Security, Salt Lake City, UT 84147

Statistical Review of Government in Utah, Utah Foundation, 32 First South Street, Salt Lake City, UT 84111

Utah Shines, Division of Economic and Industrial Development, #2 Arrow Press Square, 165 South West Temple, Salt Lake City, UT 84101

INDUSTRIAL AND BUSINESS DIRECTORIES

Directory of Utah Manufacturers, Manufacturers' News, Inc., 3 E. Huron Street, Chicago, IL 60611; Department of Employment Security, 1234 S. Main Street, Salt Lake City, UT 84147

Vermont

STATE HOUSE, MONTPELIER, VT 05602
(802) 828–1110

INFORMATION OFFICES

Commerce/Economic Development
Agency of Development and Community Affairs
Department of Economic Development
109 State Street
Montpelier, VT 05602
Taxation
Department of Texas
Agency of Administration
109 State Street
Montpelier, VT 05602
State Chamber of Commerce
Vermont State Chamber of Commerce
P.O. Box 37
Montpelier, VT 05602
Small Business Administration
87 State Street†
Montpelier, VT 05602

PUBLICATIONS

Vermont Facts and Figures, Department of Budget and Management, Montpelier, VT 05602

The Vermont Labor Market (employment statistics, monthly), Department of Employment Security, Montpelier, VT 05602

INDUSTRIAL AND BUSINESS DIRECTORIES

Vermont Directory of Manufacturers, Vermont Agency of Development and Community Affairs, Montpelier, VT 05602

Vermont State Industrial Directory, Manufacturers' News, Inc., 3 E. Huron Street, Chicago, IL 60611; State Industrial Directories Corp., 2 Penn Plaza, New York, NY 10001

Vermont Yearbook, The National Survey, Chester, VT 05143

Virginia

STATE CAPITOL, RICHMOND, VA 23219
(804) 786–0000

INFORMATION OFFICES

Commerce/Economic Development
Division of Industrial Development
1010 State Office Building
Richmond, VA 23219
Department of Conservation and Economic Development
1100 State Office Building
Richmond, VA 23219
Taxation
Department of Taxation
2200 W. Broad Street
Richmond, VA 23219
State Chamber of Commerce
Virginia State Chamber of Commerce
611 E. Franklin Street
Richmond, VA 23219
Small Business Administration
400 N. 8th Street†
Richmond, VA 23240

PUBLICATIONS

Estimates of Population, Virginia Counties and Cities (annual), Tayloe Murphy Institute, Graduate School of Business Administration, University of Virginia, Charlottesville, VA 22903

Personal Income Estimates for Virginia (annual), Tayloe Murphy Institute, Graduate School of Business Administration, University of Virginia, Box 3430, Charlottesville, VA 22903

Personal Income Estimates for Virginia SMSAs and Non-SMSAs Counties (annual), Tayloe Murphy Institute, Graduate School of Business Administration, University of Virginia, Box 3430, Charlottesville, VA 22903

Personal Income Estimates for Virginia Counties and Cities (annual), Tayloe Murphy Institute, Graduate School of Business Administration, University of Virginia, Box 3430, Charlottesville, VA 22903

Covered Employment and Wages (employment statistics, quarterly), Manpower Research Division, Virginia Employment Commission, Richmond, VA 23214

Trends in Employment, Hours and Earnings in Virginia (monthly), Manpower Research Division, Virginia Employment Commission, Richmond, VA 23214

INDUSTRIAL AND BUSINESS DIRECTORIES

Industrial Directory of Virginia, Chamber of Commerce, 611 E. Franklin Street, Richmond, VA 23219

Virginia Industrial Directory, Manufacturers' News, Inc., 3 E. Huron Street, Chicago, IL 60611; State Industrial Directories Corp., 2 Penn Plaza, New York, NY 10001

Washington

LEGISLATIVE BUILDING, OLYMPIA, WA 98501 (206) 753–5000

INFORMATION OFFICES

Commerce/Economic Development
Department of Commerce and Economic Development
101 General Administration Building
Olympia, WA 98504
Taxation
Department of Revenue
General Administration Building
Olympia, WA 98504
State Chamber of Commerce
Association of Washington Business
1414 S. Cherry Street
Olympia, WA 98501
Small Business Administration
710 2d Avenue*
Seattle, WA 98104
915 2d Avenue†
Seattle, WA 98174
W. 920 Riverside Avenue
Spokane, WA 99210

PUBLICATIONS

The Research Council's Handbook, Washington State Research Council, Olympia, WA 98504

Vital Statistics Summary (population statistics, annual), Bureau of Vital Statistics, Health Service Division, 214 General Administration Building, Olympia, WA 98504

Estimates of Personal Income for SMSAs and Non-SMSAs Counties—State of Washington (income statistics, annual), Office of Program and Fiscal Management, Population Studies Division, House Office Building, Olympia, WA 98504

Employment and Payrolls in Washington State by County and Industry (employment statistics, quarterly), Employment Security Department, Olympia, WA 98504

The Washington Labor Market (monthly), Employment Security Department, Olympia, WA 98504

Annual Report of the Tax Commission (sales statistics, annual), Washington State Department of Revenue, General Administration Building, Olympia, WA 98504

State of Washington Pocket Data Book, Washington State Office of Program Planning and Fiscal Management, Olympia, WA 98504

INDUSTRIAL AND BUSINESS DIRECTORIES

Washington Manufacturers Register, Times Mirror Press, 1115 S. Boyle, Los Angeles, CA 90023

Washington State International Trade Directory, Washington State Department of Commerce and Economic Development, Olympia, WA 98504

Washington State Manufacturers Directory, Manufacturers' News, Inc., 3 E. Huron Street, Chicago, IL 60611

West Virginia

STATE CAPITOL, CHARLESTON, WV 25305 (304) 348–3456

INFORMATION OFFICES

Commerce/Economic Development
Governor's Office of Economic and Community Development
State Office Building R-150
Charleston, WV 25305
Taxation
Tax Department
West Wing
State Capitol
Charleston, WV 25305
State Chamber of Commerce
P.O. Box 2789
1101 Kanawha Valley Building
Charleston, WV 25301
Small Business Administration
Charleston National Plaza
Charleston, WV 25301
109 N. 3d Street†
Clarksburg, WV 26301

PUBLICATIONS

The Statistical Handbook, West Virginia Research League, Inc., Charleston, WV 25414 Annual population estimates are available from the Division of Resource Management, Agricultural Economics Committee, West Virginia University, Morgantown, WV 26505

West Virginia Work Force Annual Average (employment statistics, annual), Research and Statistics Division, 112 California Avenue, Charleston, WV 25305

Employment Wages Covered by West Virginia Unemployment Compensation Law (annual), Research and Statistics Division, 112 California Avenue, Charleston, WV 25305

West Virginia Statistical Handbook, West Virginia University, Bureau of Business Research, Morgantown, WV 26505

West Virginia Economic Profile, Governor's Office of Economic and Community Development, State Office Building #6, Charleston, WV 25305

INDUSTRIAL AND BUSINESS DIRECTORIES

West Virginia Manufacturing Directory, Governor's Office of Economic and Community Development, State Office Building #6, Charleston, WV 25305; State Industrial Directories Corp., 2 Penn Plaza, New York, NY 10001

Wisconsin

STATE CAPITOL, MADISON, WI 53702
(608) 266-2211

INFORMATION OFFICES

Commerce/Economic Development
  Department of Business Development
  123 W. Washington Avenue
  Madison, WI 53702
Taxation
  Department of Revenue
  201 E. Washington Avenue
  Madison, WI 53703
State Chamber of Commerce
  Wisconsin Association of Manufacturers and Commerce
  111 E. Wisconsin Avenue
  Milwaukee, WI 53202
Small Business Administration
  212 E. Washington Avenue†
  Madison, WI 53703

  500 S. Barstow Street
  Eau Claire, WI 54701

  517 E. Wisconsin Avenue
  Milwaukee, WI 53202

PUBLICATIONS

Wisconsin Statistical Abstract, Department of Administration, Information Systems Unit, 101 S. Webster, Madison, WI 53702

Wisconsin Blue Book (population statistics, biennial), Legislative Reference Bureau, 201 N. State Capitol Street, Madison, WI 53702

Wisconsin Statistical Abstract (income statistics, biennial), Information Systems Unit, Wisconsin Department of Administration, 101 S. Webster, Madison, WI 53702

Wisconsin Work Force (employment statistics, monthly), Bureau of Research and Statistics Administration, Madison, WI 53702

New Industries and Plant Expansions (annual summary), *Available Industrial Buildings* (annual), *Available Industrial Sites* (annual), Wisconsin Department of Business Development, 123 W. Washington Avenue, Madison, WI 53702

INDUSTRIAL AND BUSINESS DIRECTORIES

Classified Directory of Wisconsin Manufacturers, Wisconsin Association of Manufacturers and Commerce, 111 E. Wisconsin Avenue, Milwaukee, WI 53202; State Industrial Directories Corp., 2 Penn Plaza, New York, NY 10001

Wisconsin Manufacturers Directory, Manufacturers' News, Inc., 3 E. Huron Street, Chicago, IL 60611

Wisconsin Local Development Organizations (annual), Wisconsin Department of Business Development, 123 W. Washington Avenue, Madison, WI 53702

Wyoming

STATE CAPITOL, CHEYENNE, WY 82002
(307) 777-7011

INFORMATION OFFICES

Commerce/Economic Development
  Department of Economic Planning and Development
  Barrett Building
  Cheyenne, WY 82002
Taxation
  Department of Revenue and Taxation
  2200 Carey Avenue
  Cheyenne, WY 82002
Small Business Administration
  100 E. B Street†
  Casper, WY 82602

PUBLICATIONS

Wyoming Data Book, University of Wyoming, Division of Business and Economic Research, Laramie, WY 82070

Report of Employment and Wages E.S.—202 (income statistics, quarterly), Employment Security Commission, State Capitol Building, P.O. Box 2760, Casper, WY 82601

Employment and Total Payrolls by Industry Selected from Employer Quarterly Reports (employment statistics, quarterly), Employment Security Commission, P.O. Box 2760, Casper, WY 82601

Wyoming Labor Force Trends (monthly), Employment Security Commission, P.O. Box 2760, Casper, WY 82601

Biennial Report of the State Board of Equalization of the State of Wyoming (sales statistics, annual), Wyoming Board of Equalization, Department of Revenue, Supreme Court Building, Cheyenne, WY 82002

INDUSTRIAL AND BUSINESS DIRECTORIES

Wyoming Directory of Manufacturing and Mining, Manufacturers' News, Inc., 3 E. Huron Street, Chicago, IL 60611; Department of Economic Planning and Development, 720 W. 18th Street, Cheyenne, WY 82002; State Industrial Directories Corp. 2 Penn Plaza, New York, NY 10001

Puerto Rico

CAPITOL, SAN JUAN, PR 00901
(809) 723–6040

INFORMATION OFFICES

Commerce/Economic Development
Department of Commerce
Box S 4275
San Juan, PR 00905

Economic Development Administration
Box 2350
San Juan, PR 00936
Taxation
Income Tax Bureau
Department of Treasury
San Juan, PR 00905

Industrial Development Company
GPO Box 2350
San Juan, Puerto Rico 00936

Office of Industrial Tax Exemption
Fomento Building, 8th Floor
Hato Rey, Puerto Rico 00918

Government Development Bank
Box 42001
Minillas Station
Santurce, Puerto Rico 00940
Chamber of Commerce
Camara De Comercie de Puerto Rico
P.O. Box 3789
San Juan, PR 00904
Small Business Administration
Chardon and Bolivia Streets
Hato Rey, PR 00919

PUBLICATIONS

Statistical Yearbook, Bureau of Statistics, Planning Board, Santurce, PR 00940

INDUSTRIAL AND BUSINESS DIRECTORIES

Puerto Rico Official Industrial and Trade Directory, Witcom Group, Inc., P.O. Box 2310, San Juan, PR 00902

The Businessman's Guide to Puerto Rico, Puerto Rico Almanacs, Inc., P.O. Box 9582, Santurce, Puerto Rico 00908

INTERNATIONAL INFORMATION SOURCES

U.S. GOVERNMENT AGENCIES

Business people seeking information about foreign commercial opportunities or sources of business contacts have available a number of government and private services that are described in this and subsequent sections. The extensive nature of these services is not always fully appreciated by members of the business community. Some of the most helpful services are provided by the Industry and Trade Administration (ITA) of the Department of Commerce, described below. This agency is particularly helpful in establishing initial contacts and in evaluating foreign markets.

Business people traveling abroad will find the following services of help in initiating contacts:

1. U.S. Export Development Offices, U.S. Department of Commerce.
2. Commercial offices at U.S. embassies or consulates.

Foreign credit information sources are provided at the end of this section.

DEPARTMENT OF COMMERCE

Address: Constitution and 14th Street NW, Washington, DC 20230. Information phone: 202-377-4901.

The central information source within the Department of Commerce is the **Industry and Trade Administration** (ITA), which promotes the growth of U.S. industry and commerce, both foreign and domestic. The ITA consists of the following:

International Economic Policy and Research (IEPR) assists the department in research, analysis, and formulation of international economic programs.

The **Export Development** area (ED) helps U.S. business to sell its goods in international markets by providing commercial, economic, and marketing information. ED conducts export development activities including the management of trade fairs and export development facilities overseas (locations listed below). In addition, ED organizes trade missions for groups of business people interested in specific markets. Businesses interested in attracting foreign capital or in seeking foreign investment opportunities can also get help from ED.

World Traders Data Reports: ED provides very helpful reports on foreign firms in its *World Traders Data Reports* (WTDRS). Each report contains detailed commercial information on individual firms, including financial and credit references. The complete name and address of the foreign firm must be submitted when ordering WTDRS. To order, write Trade Facilitation and Services Division, Room 1033 WTDR, Washington, DC 20230.

Foreign Traders Index: Information on more than 140,000 foreign importing organizations in 130 countries is stored in ITA's *Foreign Traders Index* (FTI), a computerized file. New information on listed firms and information on newly identified firms are constantly added to the index. The information in the file is collected and supplied to Commerce by the U.S. Foreign Service—Department of State.

Most of the lists or services described here are products of the *Foreign Traders Index*. Some, however, are prepared from special source material.

Export Mailing List Service: U.S. firms wishing to make export contacts may obtain lists of foreign organizations selected by electronic data processing techniques from the *Foreign Traders Index*. Selection of firms in one or more countries or geographic areas may be made according to the products or product groups handled by the foreign organizations.

The information is available either on pressure-sensitive mailing labels or in standard printout format.

Data Tape Service: U.S. firms with computer facilities may purchase magnetic tapes containing information on all firms in selected countries or in all countries covered in the *Foreign Traders Index*. This service makes it possible for users to retrieve various segments of data from the *Foreign Traders Index* through their own computer facilities.

The Agent/Distributor Service: ITA's *Agent/Distributor Service* (A/DS) helps U.S. firms find agents or distributors for their products in almost every country of the world. U.S. commercial officers overseas will identify up to six foreign firms that have expressed interest in a specific U.S. proposal.

Application forms (ITA-424P) may be obtained from any Commerce Department district office. Trade specialists at district offices will help a U.S. firm prepare an application. They will offer guidance and determine whether there are factors to discourage a business relationship.

Trade List Service: The names and addresses of foreign distributors, agents, purchasers, and other firms, classified by products they handle and services they offer, are made available to U.S. firms through printed *Trade Lists* (TL). Some of the lists are produced from information in the *Foreign Traders Index*. Others are prepared from data compiled in connection with ITA's export promotion programs and from other sources.

Trade Opportunities Program: Up-to-the-minute direct sales leads and representation opportunities from overseas are now available to interested U.S. companies through a computerized mail service, the *Trade Opportunities Program* (TOP). A U.S. businessman, as a subscriber to TOP, specifies the products and the countries for which he wants trade opportunities, and that information is fed into the TOP computer.

Foreign Market Reports: Reports on commodities, industries, and economic conditions prepared by U.S. foreign service officers, and in-depth foreign market surveys prepared by private research organizations on a contract basis for ITA or by ITA's market research officers and U.S. foreign service officers are available for a nominal fee. Monthly indices list the reports and surveys in three sections—a numerical listing of documents, a country section, and the Standard Industrial Classification (SIC), and/or a general subject matter section.

Business Counseling Service: Counseling services are provided by the U.S. Departments of Commerce and State in Washington, DC, and by the Commerce district offices located in major commercial and industrial centers throughout the United States and Puerto Rico.

The Business Counseling Section of ITA's Office of Export Development in Washington offers guidance, in-depth counseling, and scheduling of appointments with appropriate Commerce officials as well as with officials in other agencies. This service is designed to give the businessperson a maximum amount of information in a minimum of time.

An important part of this program is an Export Information Reference Room where businesspeople can review a wide range of major foreign projects under consideration by international financial institutions—World Bank Group, Inter-American Development Bank, Asian Development Bank, and the United Nations Development Programme.

For further information on all of the above services, contact the nearest Department of Commerce District Office.

Trade Administration of ITA administers controls on exports that may be limited for national security, foreign policy, or short-supply reasons. This office also administers the antiforeign boycott program, U.S. foreign-trade zones program, and duty-free importation for scientific or educational reasons. The bureau indicates quotas for duty-free import of watches and watch parts from the Virgin Islands, Guam, and American Samoa.

The Office of Business Liaison is a focal point for handling inquiries for business information as well as suggestions and complaints. Call 202-377-3176.

The Office of East-West Trade Development (OEWTD) coordinates programs and provides information with regard to commercial relations with the socialist nations. The OEWTD also manages export administration and issues export licenses, where required, for shipment to the Soviet bloc and China.

Information on specific countries may be obtained by calling the country marketing manager of ITA listed by region under Regional Marketing Managers, page 549. Assistance or information about marketing in these countries may be obtained by dialing these key people directly.

DISTRICT OFFICES OF THE U.S.
DEPARTMENT OF COMMERCE

Alabama
Suite 200-201
908 So. 20th Street
Birmingham, AL 35205
Telephone: 205-254-1331
Alaska
701 C Street
P.O. Box 32
Anchorage, AK 99513
Telephone: 907-271-5041
Arizona
Suite 2950, Valley Bank Center
201 N. Central Avenue
Phoenix, AZ 85073
Telephone: 602-261-3285
Arkansas
320 W. Capitol Avenue
Suite 635

Little Rock, AR 77201
Telephone: 501-378-5794
P.O. Box 2525
ASU State University
Jonesboro, AR 72467*
Telephone: 501-792-4760
California
11777 San Vicente Boulevard
Los Angeles, CA 90049
Telephone: 213-824-7591
110 W. C Street
San Diego, CA 92101*
Telephone: 714-293-5395
Federal Building
Box 36013
450 Golden Gate Avenue
San Francisco, CA 94102*
Telephone: 415-556-5868
Colorado
Room 165, New Customhouse
19th and Stout Streets
Denver, CO 80202
Telephone: 303-837-3246
Connecticut
Room 610-B, Federal Office Building
450 Main Street
Hartford, CT 06103
Telephone: 203-244-3530
Florida
Room 821
City National Bank Building
25 W. Flagler Street
Miami, FL 33130
Telephone: 305-350-5267
128 N. Osceola Avenue
Clearwater, FL 33515*
Telephone: 813-461-0011
815 S. Main Street
Suite 100
Jacksonville, FL 32207*
Telephone: 904-791-2796
Collins Building, Room G-20
Tallahassee, FL 32304*
Telephone: 904-488-6469
Georgia
Suite 600
1365 Peachtree Street NE
Atlanta, GA 30309
Telephone: 404-881-7000
222 U.S. Courthouse
P.O. Box 9746
125-29 Bull Street
Savannah, GA 31412
Telephone: 912-232-4321
Hawaii
4106 Federal Building
P.O. Box 50026
300 Ala Moana Boulevard
Honolulu, HI 96850
Telephone: 808-546-8694

---

* Denotes trade specialist.

Illinois
1406 Mid Continental Plaza Building
55 E. Monroe Street
Chicago, IL 60603
Telephone: 312–353–4450

Indiana
357 U.S. Courthouse and Federal Office
Building
46 E. Ohio Street
Indianapolis, IN 46204
Telephone: 317–269–6214

Iowa
817 Federal Building
210 Walnut Street
Des Moines, IA 50309
Telephone: 515–284–4222

Kentucky
U.S. Post Office and Court House Building
Room 636
Louisville, KY 40202
Telephone: 502–582–5066

Louisiana
432 International Trade Mart
No. 2 Canal Street
New Orleans, LA 70130
Telephone: 504–589–6546

Maine
Memorial Circle
40 Casco Bank Building
Augusta, ME 04333
Telephone: 207–623–2239

Maryland
415 U.S. Customhouse
Gay and Lombard Streets
Baltimore, MD 21202
Telephone: 301–962–3560

Massachusetts
441 Stuart Street
Boston, MA 02116
Telephone: 617–223–2312

Michigan
445 Federal Building
231 W. Lafayette
Detroit, MI 48226
Telephone: 313–226–3650

350 Ottawa Street NW
Grand Rapids, MI 49503*
Telephone: 616–456–2433

Minnesota
218 Federal Building
110 S. Fourth Street
Minneapolis, MN 55401
Telephone: 612–725–2133

Mississippi
Suite 550
200 E. Pascagoula
Jackson, MS 39201
Telephone: 601–969–4388

Missouri
120 S. Central Avenue
St. Louis, MO 63105
Telephone: 314–425–3302–4

Room 1840
601 E. 12th Street
Kansas City, MO 64106*
Telephone: 816–374–3142

Nebraska
Capitol Plaza, Suite 703A
1815 Capitol Avenue
Omaha, NB 68102
Telephone: 402–221–3665

Nevada
777 W. 2nd Street
Reno, NV 89503
Telephone: 702–784–5203

New Jersey
Gateway Building
Market Street and Penn Plaza
Newark, NJ 07102
Telephone: 201–645–6214

New Mexico
505 Marquette Avenue NW
Suite 1015
Albuquerque, NM 87102
Telephone: 505–766–2386

New York
1312 Federal Building
111 W. Huron Street
Buffalo, NY 14202
Telephone: 716–846–4191

Federal Office Building
26 Federal Plaza
Foley Square
New York, NY 10007*
Telephone: 212–264–0634

North Carolina
203 Federal Building
West Market Street
P.O. Box 1950
Greensboro, NC 27402
Telephone: 919–378–5345

Ohio
10504 Federal Office Building
550 Main Street
Cincinnati, OH 45202
Telephone: 513–684–2944

666 Euclid Avenue
Cleveland, OH 44114*
Telephone: 216–522–4750

Oklahoma
4020 Lincoln Boulevard
Oklahoma City, OK 73105*
Telephone: 405–231–5302

Oregon
1220 S.W. 3d Avenue
Portland, OR 97204
Telephone: 503–221–3001

Pennsylvania
9448 Federal Building
600 Arch Street
Philadelphia, PA 19106
Telephone: 215–597–2850

2002 Federal Building
1000 Liberty Avenue
Pittsburgh, PA 15222*
Telephone: 412–644–2850
Puerto Rico
Federal Building
San Juan, PR 00918
Telephone: 809–753–4555, ext. 555
Rhode Island
7 Jackson Walkway
Providence, RI 02903*
Telephone: 401–277–2505, ext. 22
South Carolina
Strom Thurmond Federal Building
1835 Assembly Street
Columbia, SC 29201
Telephone: 803–765–5345

505 Federal Building
334 Meeting Street
Charleston, SC 29403*
Telephone: 803–677–4361

P.O. Box 10048
Greenville, NC 29603*
Telephone: 803–235–5919
Tennessee
147 Jefferson Avenue
Room 710
Memphis, TN 38103
Telephone: 901–521–3213

Andrew Jackson Office Building
Room 1020
Nashville, TN 37219*
Telephone: 615–251–5161
Texas
1100 Commerce Street
Dallas, TX 75242
Telephone: 214–767–0542

2625 Federal Building, Courthouse
515 Rusk Street
Houston, TX 77002*
Telephone: 713–226–4231
Utah
1201 Federal Building
125 S. State Street
Salt Lake City, UT 84138
Telephone: 801–524–5116
Virginia
8010 Federal Building
400 N. 8th Street
Richmond, VA 23240
Telephone: 804–782–2246

8550 Arlington Boulevard
Fairfax, VA 22031*
Telephone: 703–560–6460
Washington
Lake Union Building
1700 Westlake Avenue North
Seattle, WA 98109
Telephone: 206–442–5615
West Virginia
3000 New Federal Building
500 Quarrier Street

Charleston, WV 25301
Telephone: 304–343–6181, ext. 375
Wisconsin
Federal Building/U.S. Courthouse
517 E. Wisconsin Avenue
Milwaukee, WI 53202
Telephone: 414–291–3473
Wyoming
6022 O'Mahoney Federal Center
2120 Capitol Avenue
Cheyenne, WY 82001
Telephone: 307–778–2220, ext. 2151

PUBLICATIONS, DEPARTMENT OF COMMERCE

The following publications on international commerce are available from the Government Printing Office, Washington, DC 20402.

Foreign Trade Report FT 410: U.S. Exports Commodity by Country is one of the best sources for locating export markets. These monthly publications provide a statistical record of the shipments of all merchandise from the United States to foreign countries.

Market Share Reports. These annual reports provide a five-year record of U.S. participation in foreign markets for manufactured products. Both country and product series are available.

International Economic Indicators and Competitive Trends is a quarterly report providing basic international data.

Overseas Business Reports (OBR). These reports provide a great deal of basic background data for businessmen who are evaluating export markets. Each OBR discusses separate topics for a single country. About 80 reports per year are issued.

Global Market Surveys are in-depth reports covering 15 to 20 of the best foreign markets for a single industry or a group of related industries.

Foreign Economic Trends is an in-depth series of country-by-country reports prepared annually or semiannually by the U.S. Foreign Service of the Department of State that covers individually almost every country in the world. It gives the latest data on GNP, foreign trade, and wages and prices.

Special Reports. ITA publishes special reports detailing economic data, marketing, and trade opportunities.

Index to Business International Publications is an index to materials appearing in *Overseas Business Reports, Global Market Surveys, Foreign Economic Trends,* and *Special Reports.*

Country Market Surveys are in-depth reports covering the most promising U.S. export opportunities.

A Guide to Financing Exports. A summary of sources of credit and credit information for exports. Reviews services offered by Export-Import Bank.

International Marketing News Memo. This includes information bulletins received directly from the U.S. Foreign Service—reports prepared by U.S. businessmen or Department of Commerce officers. Reports cover a wide variety of industries, products, and countries.

Business America (formerly *Commerce Today*). This biweekly is the Commerce Department's principal periodical for domestic and international business news.

Commerce Business Daily is a daily record containing synopses of U.S. government procurement limitations, subcontracting leads, contract awards, sales of surplus property, and foreign business opportunities.

Commerce News. Published weekly, this publication lists books, pamphlets, and reports by the Department of Commerce.

The Overseas Export Promotion Calendar lists U.S. trade-promotion events held abroad. These include exhibitions, missions, and seminars featuring U.S. products and services. The calendar is indexed by product, gives the location and date of each event, and also identifies U.S. Export Development Offices (i.e., International Marketing Centers) promoting sales of U.S. goods and services. Subscription information may be obtained by calling ITA's Office of Export Promotion at 202-377-5783.

MARKETING DIRECTORY, DEPARTMENT OF COMMERCE

Current information relating to political, commercial, and economic developments in foreign countries and trade agreements is provided by a large staff of country specialists in the Department of Commerce.

If you are in the United States, a convenient way of obtaining information or contacting personnel is to call the Regional Marketing Managers (see below). You can also obtain information by writing to the U.S. Export Development Offices listed under that title, p. 550.

If you are traveling abroad, contact the local U.S. Commercial Attaché or the U.S. Export Development Offices overseas. In-country phone numbers are given on page 550.

REGIONAL MARKETING MANAGERS

Dial 202-377 plus the given extension.

United Kingdom/Canada 4504
  United Kingdom   Malta
  Canada   Ireland
France/Benelux 4504
  France   Luxembourg
  Belgium   The Netherlands
Germany/Nordic 3187
  Germany   Denmark
  Austria   Norway
  Finland   Iceland
  Sweden

Southern Europe 3944
  Italy   Spain
  Turkey   Portugal
  Greece   Yugoslavia
  Cyprus   Switzerland
Andean/Caribbean 4673
  Bahamas   Guyana
  Barbados   Haiti
  Belize   Jamaica
  Bermuda   Leeward Islands
  Bolivia   Netherlands Antilles
  Chile   Peru
  Colombia   Surinam
  Dominican Republic Trinidad/Tobago
  Ecuador   Venezuela
  French Guiana   Windward Islands
  French West Indies
Mexico/Central America 2314
  Costa Rica   Mexico
  El Salvador   Nicaragua
  Guatemala   Panama
  Honduras
Brazil/River Plate 5427
  Argentina   Paraguay
  Brazil   Uruguay
Arab states 5767
  Bahrain   Saudi Arabia
  Iraq   People's Democratic
  Jordan   Republic, Yemen
  Kuwait   Syria
  Lebanon   United Arab Emirates
  Oman   Yemen Arab Republic
  Qatar
Arab countries of North Africa 3752
  Algeria   Tunisia
  Libya   Egypt
  Morocco
Non-Arab countries of the Middle East 3752
  Iran   Israel
Asia/India/Pakistan 2522
  Singapore   Sri Lanka
  Malaysia   Burma
  Indonesia   Nepal
  Philippines   Bhutan
  Thailand   Maldives
  India   Cambodia
  Pakistan   Viet Nam
  Bangladesh   Laos
  Afghanistan   Brunei
East Asia/Taiwan/Australia/New Zealand ... 3646
  Australia   Papua New Guinea
  New Zealand   Fiji
  Taiwan   Pacific Islands
Japan/Korea/Hong Kong 2896
Africa 4927
  Angola   Ghana
  Benin   Guinea
  Botswana   Guinea-Bissau
  Burundi   Ivory Coast
  Cameroon   Kenya
  Cape Verde Islands Lesotho
  Central African   Liberia
    Empire   Madagascar
  Chad   Malawi
  Comoros   Mali
  Congo (Brazzaville) Mauritania
  Djibouti   Mauritius
  Equatorial Guinea Mozambique
  Ethiopia   Niger
  Gabon   Nigeria
  Gambia   Rhodesia

Rwanda	Swaziland
Sao Tome and Principe	Tanzania
Senegal	Togo
Seychelles	Uganda
Sierra Leone	Upper Volta
Somalia	Zaire
South Africa	Zambia
Sudan	

East-West Trade 2543
U.S.S.R Affairs 4505
Peoples' Republic of China Affairs 3583
Rumanian and Hungarian Affairs 2645
German Democratic Republic Affairs 2645
Czechoslovakian and Bulgarian Affairs 2645
Poland 2645

U.S. EXPORT DEVELOPMENT OFFICES*

Milan
U.S. Export Development Office
c/o American Consulate General
APO New York 09689
Phone 469–6451

Sydney
U.S. Export Development Office
c/o American Consulate General
APO San Francisco 96209
Phone 929–0977

Singapore
U.S. Export Development Office
c/o American Embassy
30 Hill Street
FPO San Francisco 96699
Phone 373–1000

Tokyo
U.S. Export Development Office
c/o American Embassy
APO San Francisco 96503
Phone 987–244

Bonn
U.S. Export Development Office
c/o American Embassy, Bonn
APO New York 09080
Phone 330–045

London
U.S. Export Development Office
c/o American Embassy
FPO New York 09510
Phone 499–9000

Paris
U.S. Export Development Office
c/o American Embassy
APO New York 09777
Phone 624–3313

San Paulo
U.S. Export Development Office
c/o American Consulate General
APO Miami 34030
Phone 455–778

---

* The phone numbers listed in this section are "in-country" numbers and are the most current available. Since phone numbers do change, it is best to check with U.S. Embassy to confirm them.

COMMERCIAL OFFICES OVERSEAS, DEPARTMENT OF COMMERCE*

Athens
Regional Trade Development Office
91 Vasilissi Sophia Boulevard (at the Embassy)
Athens, Greece
Phone 712–951

Moscow
U.S. Commercial Office
15 Chaykovskovo
Moscow, USSR
Phone 252–0011

Nagoya
American Commercial Information Office
Aichiken Sangyo Boeki Kaikan,
Nishikan, 4–7
Marunouchi 2-chome, Naka-ku
Nagoya, Japan
Phone 231–7791

Osaka
U.S. American Merchandise Display
Sankei Kaikan Building
4–9, Umeda 2-chome
Osaka, Japan
Phone 341–2754

Vienna
U.S. East-West Trade Development Support Office
Vienna I, Friedrich Schmidt Platz 2
Austria
Phone 31–55–11

Warsaw
U.S. Trade Development Center
Ulica Wiejska, 20
Warsaw, Poland
Phone 21–45–15

U.S. DEPARTMENT OF STATE

Address: New State Building, 2201 C Street, NW, Washington, DC 20520.
Information: 202–632–9884.

PUBLICATIONS

Background Notes of the Countries of the World gives profiles of foreign countries.

Key Officers of Foreign Service Posts lists the addresses and phone numbers of all American embassies and consulates and their key personnel.

Department of State Bulletin is a weekly publication devoted to the latest developments in international politics and trade agreements.

THE LIBRARY OF CONGRESS

The Library of Congress's international divisions provide overseas free research assistance on social, economic, political, and marketing topics. Call:

African and Middle East
   Division 202–287–7937
Asian Division 202–287–5420
European Division 202–287–5413
Hispanic Division 202–287–5397

Write: Library of Congress, 10 First St. S.E., Washington, D.C. 20540.

UNITED STATES INTERNATIONAL TRADE COMMISSION

Address: 701 E Street NW, Washington, DC 20436. Information phone: 202–523–0161.

Formerly the U.S. Tariff Commission, the name was changed to the U.S. International Trade Commission in 1974.

The commission is given broad powers of investigation relating to the customs laws of the United States and foreign countries, the volume of importation in comparison with domestic production and consumption, the conditions, causes, and effects relating to competition of foreign industries with those of the United States and all other factors affecting competition between articles of the United States and imported articles.*

Businesspersons who believe they have been injured by unfair trade methods from abroad may file a complaint with this commission.

Summaries of trade and tariff information may be obtained directly from the commission.

The following agencies are important in arranging trade financing and credit insurance:

EXPORT-IMPORT BANK

Address: 811 Vermont Avenue NW, Washington, DC 20471. Phone: 202–566–8990.

FOREIGN CREDIT INSURANCE ASSOCIATION (FCIA)

Address: One World Trade Center, New York, NY 10048. Phone: 212–432–6200.
Ombudsman: 212–432–6216.

The Export-Import Bank, established in 1934, is an independent agency of the U.S. government with the basic mission of encouraging U.S. exports. The policies of the bank recognize that credit terms are as important to foreign buyers as price and quality, and that U.S. exporters should be provided with financing that is competitive with that offered by foreign competitors. The bank cooperates with and supplements private capital sources. Loans to exporters are generally for specific purposes and most offer reasonable assurance of repayment.

A number of programs are offered by the

Eximbank, including direct credit to foreign buyers, credit guarantees of commercial banks, loans to exporters, export credit insurance, and discount loans.

Credit insurance protection for exporters is provided by FCIA, an association of commercial insurance companies formed by the Eximbank and the insurance industry in 1961. Policies issued by FCIA insure repayment if the foreign buyer should default. The exporter may use FCIA insurance as collateral for obtaining a commercial loan.

The Eximbank will make a preliminary commitment concerning the amount it will guarantee or lend, a feature of particular value to U.S. importers submitting proposals in response to a foreign bid. The bank is also helpful in providing credit information on foreign buyers.

Marketing assistance for exporters is also available and can be obtained by calling Eximbank's hotline at 800–424–5201.

PUBLICATION

Eximbank: How It Works (free on writing to the Export-Import Bank).
Marketing Assistance for Exporters.

OVERSEAS PRIVATE INVESTMENT CORPORATION (OPIC)

Address: 1129 20th Street NW, Washington, DC. Information phone: 202–632–1804.

OPIC, established in 1971, is an independent agency of the U.S. government with the mission of reducing or eliminating private investment risks in the developing countries. OPIC insures U.S. investors against political risks of expropriation, inconvertibility of local currency holdings, and damage from war, revolution, or insurrection. The agency offers lenders protection by guaranteeing payment of principal, interest, and loans.

The corporation offers investment information and counseling to business and participates in the cost of locating and developing projects.

FINANCING EXPORTS

Many sources of financial assistance are available to exporters. First, of course, is your own working capital or bank line of credit. Use of your own facilities may, however, restrict your total cash availability even if you were to establish a separate export line of credit with your bank.

Commercial Banks. More than 250 U.S. banks have qualified international banking departments with specialists familiar with particular foreign countries and experts in different

---

* Source: *Government Organization Manual.*

Source: Excerpted from *A Basic Guide to Exporting,* U.S. Department of Commerce.

types of commodities and transactions. These banks, located in all major U.S. cities, maintain correspondent relationships with smaller banks throughout the United States. This banking network enables any exporter to find assistance (for himself or his overseas customer) for his export financing needs. The larger banks also maintain correspondent relationships with banks in most foreign countries or operate their own overseas branches, providing a direct channel to overseas customers.

Factoring Houses. Exporters should also be aware of factoring houses that deal in accounts receivable of American exporters. Although possibly charging higher fees, they will purchase your receivables, often without recourse, assuring you of prompt payment for your export sale.

Export Management Companies. Export management companies not only will act as your export representative, but some of these professional export houses also will carry the financing for the export sale, again assuring you of immediate payment and removing from your company any foreign credit risk. For names of export management companies in your area, you may contact your local Department of Commerce district office.

Eximbank. The U.S. Government also participates in the financing of America's exports. The Export-Import Bank of the United States (Eximbank) offers direct loans for large projects and equipment sales that usually require longer term financing. It cooperates with commercial banks in the United States and abroad in providing a number of financial arrangements to help U.S. exporters offer credit to their overseas buyers. It provides export credit guarantees to commercial banks that finance export sales; and, through the Foreign Credit Insurance Association (FCIA), provides insurance to American exporters which enables them to extend credit terms to their overseas buyers. In all cases, the Bank must find a "reasonable assurance of repayment" as a precondition of participating in the transaction.

Eximbank regulations and conditions of assistance are, of course, subject to change. For more information, consult your commercial bank, or write directly to the Export-Import Bank of the United States, 811 Vermont Avenue, NW., Washington, D.C. 20571. Telex 89-461.

Foreign Credit Insurance Association. The FCIA administers the U.S. export credit insurance program on behalf of its member insurance companies and the Government-owned Eximbank. The private insurers cover the normal commercial credit risks, mainly the insolvency of or the prolonged payment default by the overseas buyer. Eximbank assumes all liability for the political risks including, in addition to exchange transfer delay, such hazards as war, revolution, or similar hostilities; unforeseen withdrawal or nonrenewal of a license to export or import; requisition, expropriation, confiscation, or intervention in the business of the buyer by a governmental authority; transport or insurance charges caused by interruption or diversion of shipment; and certain other government acts which may prevent or unduly delay payment and which are beyond the control of the seller or the buyer.

One of FCIA's major forms of coverage is the master policy, designed to provide under one policy substantially automatic coverage for all of an exporter's sales to overseas buyers both short- and medium-term, on credit terms ranging up to 5 years. The policy may provide political risks coverage only, or comprehensive risks coverage.

For information on other types of policies offered by FCIA, exporters should consult with FCIA at One World Trade Center, 9th Floor, New York, N.Y. 10048.

INTERNATIONAL ORGANIZATIONS

UNITED NATIONS (UN)

Address: New York, NY 10017. Information phone: 212-754-1234.

The UN and its affiliated organizations publish a large number of reports and statistical tables covering all member nations. Publications may be obtained by writing: Sales Section, United Nations Publications, New York, NY 10017. A periodic check list of UN publications is available on request.

PUBLICATIONS

Journal of Development Planning.
Guidelines for Contracting for Industrial Projects in Developing Countries.
World Economic Survey.
Annual Bulletin of Exports of Chemical Products.
Annual Bulletin of Coal Statistics for Europe.
Statistics of World Trade in Steel.
Annual Bulletin of Gas Statistics for Europe.
Annual Bulletin of Electric Energy Statistics for Europe.
Economic Bulletin for Europe.
Economic Bulletin for Asia and the Pacific.
Quarterly Bulletin of Statistics for Asia and the Pacific.
Statistical Yearbook for Asia and the Pacific.
Demographic Yearbook.
Yearbook of International Trade Statistics Vol. I: Trade by Country; Vol. II: Trade by Commodity.
Monthly Bulletin of Statistics provides monthly statistics on 70 subjects from more than 200 countries and territories together with spe-

cial tables illustrating important economic developments. Quarterly data for significant world and regional aggregates are also prepared regularly for the bulletin.

Statistical Yearbook is a comprehensive compilation of international statistics relating to: population and manpower; agricultural, mineral, and manufacturing production; construction; energy; trade; transport; communications; consumption; balance of payments; wages and prices; national accounts; finance; development assistance; health; housing; education; science and technology; and culture.

Population and Vital Statistics Reports (quarterly).
Yearbook of National Accounts Statistics.
Yearbook of International Trade Statistics.
Yearbook of Construction Statistics.
Commodity Trade Statistics (quarterly).
World Trade Annual.
The Growth of World Industry: Vol. I General Industrial Statistics; Vol. II Commodities Production Data.

INTERNATIONAL MONETARY FUND (IMF)

Address: 19th and H Streets NW, Washington, DC 20431. Phone: 202–477–7000.

The IMF was organized in 1945 with the purpose of promoting international monetary cooperation and consultation. The fund also seeks to facilitate the expansion of international trade and currency exchange stability. The fund issues Special Drawing Rights (SDR), a form of reserve currency used by central banks for settling balance of payment obligations.

PUBLICATIONS

The IMF issues a broad range of publications (some in conjunction with the World Bank Group) of interest to the business community.

Foreign Trade Statistics. Series A. This monthly bulletin provides a breakdown of overall trade by main commodity categories and available indices of foreign trade unit values and volumes. *Series B. Trade by Commodities. Analytical Abstracts* (quarterly). *Series C. Trade by Commodities. Market Summaries* (yearly). *Provisional Oil Statistics* (quarterly).

The Annual Report of the Executive Directors reviews the funds' activities, policies, organization, and administration and surveys the world economy, with special emphasis on international liquidity, payments problems, exchange rates, and world trade.

Annual Report on Exchange Restrictions reviews developments in exchange controls and restrictions and other measures that may have direct implications for the balance of payments of member countries.

International Financial Statistics (monthly) reports for most countries of the world current data needed for analyzing problems of international payments and inflation and deflation, i.e., data on exchange rates, international liquidity, money and banking, international trade, prices, production, government finance, interest rates, and other items. Information is presented in country tables for each country and in tables with area and world aggregates. Charts on each country page show recent changes in important series.

Balance of Payments Yearbook presents statistics in a standard form, expressed in a common unit of account, for countries that report information to the fund on their balance of payments transactions. In the tables that are designated as "standard presentations," these transactions are classified in terms of objective criteria; in the tables designated as "analytic presentations," they are regrouped to facilitate further analysis and certain cumulative balances are drawn.

Direction of Trade is published jointly by the International Monetary Fund and the International Bank for Reconstruction and Development. The monthly issues provide the latest available information on each country's direction of trade, with comparative data for the corresponding period of the preceding year.

The *IMF Survey* is a topical report of the fund's activities (including all press releases, texts of communiques and major statements, SDR valuations, and exchange rates) presented in the broader context of developments in national economics and international finance.

ORGANIZATION FOR ECONOMIC COOPERATION AND DEVELOPMENT (OECD)

Address: 2 Rue Andre Pascal, Paris, France. 1750 Pennsylvania Avenue NW, Washington, DC 20026. Phone: 202–724–1857.

The OECD, established in 1961, is an outgrowth of the Organization for European Economic Cooperation, set up under the Marshall Plan in 1948. It consists of 24 developed countries: Canada, United States, Japan, Australia, New Zealand, Austria, Belgium, Denmark, England, Finland, France, West Germany, Greece, Iceland, Italy, Luxembourg, Netherlands, Norway, Portugal, Spain, Sweden, Turkey, Switzerland, and Yugoslavia. Together, the OECD countries account for 20 percent of world population, 60 percent of world industrial production, and 73 percent of world trade.

PUBLICATIONS

OECD Observer is intended for people who are interested in and concerned with economic and social planning in the broadest sense and who want to have relevant information in the most succinct form possible. It presents in readable fashion the entire range of OECD's work—in economic affairs, trade, manpower, social affairs, science and education, the environment, financial affairs, and development assistance. (Published bimonthly.)

The *OECD Economic Outlook* is a twice yearly, detailed survey of economic trends and prospects for the immediate future.

OECD Financial Statistics supplies complete, up-to-date, authoritative information on financial markets in 16 European countries, the United States, Canada, and Japan. (Published yearly with bimonthly supplements.)

OECD Economic Surveys is an annual analysis of the economic policy of each OECD country as seen by the others.

Main Economic Indicators, a monthly publication, is an essential source of statistics for the student of the international business cycle.

GENERAL AGREEMENT ON TRADE AND TARIFFS (GATT)

Address: Centre William Rappard, 154 Rue de Lausanne, Geneva, Switzerland.

GATT is a multilateral trade treaty (entered into force in 1948) among 83 countries providing for the reduction of tariffs and other trade barriers, standardization of trade procedures, and the resolution of trade disputes. GATT publishes *Compilations of Basic Information on Export Markets; Guide to Sources of Foreign Trade Information; Analytical Bibliography: A Compendium of Sources: International Trade Statistics;* and *World Directory of Industry and Trade Associations.*

COMMERCIAL ORGANIZATIONS

DUN & BRADSTREET

Address: 99 Church Street, New York, NY. Phone: 212–285–7000.

Dun & Bradstreet provides a number of valuable services and publications in the area of international business, i.e., international credit reports on companies, international marketing guides and services, and directories of foreign firms. Dun & Bradstreet publishes the comprehensive annual, *Exporters Encyclopedia,* with monthly supplements. It details the rules and regulations in over 220 world markets and is arranged alphabetically by country and market area. *Principal International Businesses* is a useful marketing publication providing addresses, lines of business, sales figures, and other information on nearly 50,000 foreign firms.

INTERNATIONAL REPORTS

Address: 200 Park Avenue South, New York, NY 10003.

International Reports publishes reports on sources of worldwide export credit insurance, foreign investment guarantees, and export financing under the title of *Insurance in International Finance.*

It also publishes the monthly *International Commercial Finance Service,* containing extensive information and data on financing and interest rates, surveys of credit ratings, and foreign payment records of individual countries.

BUSINESS INTERNATIONAL

Address: One Dag Hammarskjold Plaza, New York, NY 10017. Phone: 212–750–6300.

Business International publishes a series of weekly reports: *Business International* (a global view of business); *Business Europe; Business Latin America; Business Asia; Eastern Europe Report; Business China* (People's Republic); *Business International Money Report; Investing, Licensing, Trading Report;* and *Financing Foreign Operations.* It publishes a multivolume series, *Doing Business with Eastern Europe.*

COMMERCE CLEARING HOUSE

Address: 4025 West Peterson Avenue, Chicago, IL 60646. Phone 312–583–8500.

Commerce Clearing House publishes a number of widely used looseleaf series updated on a weekly or monthly basis. In the international field these include: *Euromarket News; Doing Business in Europe; Balance of Payment Reports; Common Market Reports;* and *Income Taxes World Wide.* It also publishes a number of detailed tax and legal guides for specific countries, i.e., Canada, Mexico, Australia, England, and Germany.

OTHER PUBLICATIONS

Europa Year Book is an annual two-volume work covering a wide range of commercial, economic, and political statistics and information about every country in the world. Volume I deals with international organizations and the countries of Europe, while Volume II covers Africa, the Americas, Asia, and Australia. It is published by Europe Publications, Ltd., 18 Bedford Square, London, England.

Jane's Major Companies of Europe is an annual providing extensive information about all major European companies. It is available from Jane's Yearbooks, 8 Shepherdess, London N1 7LW, England.

SOURCES OF INTERNATIONAL CREDIT INFORMATION

Export Information Division, Domestic and International Business Administration, U.S. Department of Commerce, Washington, DC.

Dun & Bradstreet (address given above).

FCIB-NACM Corp., 475 Park Avenue South, New York, NY 10015.
Major Commercial Banks

INTERNATIONAL BUSINESS INFORMATION DIRECTORY

This Directory lists helpful addresses in the United States for those doing business with countries where business practices may present certain problems.

JAPAN

Exporters and importers generally find it essential to use the services of the Japanese trading companies, which offer a wide range of services including negotiation of overseas deals, transportation, storage, finance, and marketing. The largest trading companies are listed below. The small exporter will often do better using smaller trading companies that specialize in one or two types of products. Exporters seeking an appropriate trading company should contact the local office of the Japan Trade Center:

Bank of America Tower
555 S. Flower Street
Los Angeles, CA 90071

1737 Post Street
San Francisco, CA 94115

230 N. Michigan Avenue
Chicago, IL 60601

1221 Avenue of the Americas
New York, NY 10020

One World Trade Center
2100 Stemmons Freeway
Dallas, TX 75258

1221 McKinney
One Houston Center
Houston, TX 77002

P.O. Box 3356
Marina Station
Mayaguez, PR 00708

MAJOR TRADING COMPANIES (U.S. OFFICES)

Mitsubishi
277 Park Avenue
New York, NY 10017

Bank of America Tower
555 S. Flower Street
Los Angeles, CA 90071

601 California Street
San Francisco, CA 94108

Mitsui & Co. (USA), Inc.
200 Park Avenue
New York, NY 10017

611 W. Sixth Street
Los Angeles, CA 90017

Marubeni Corporation
200 Park Avenue
New York, NY 10017

One Wilshire Building
624 S. Grand Avenue
Los Angeles, CA 90017

C. Itoh & Co. (America), Inc.
270 Park Avenue
New York, NY 10017

555 S. Flower Street
Los Angeles, CA 90017

Sumitomo Shoji America, Inc.
345 Park Avenue
New York, NY 10022

606 S. Olive Street
Los Angeles, CA 90014

Nissho-Iwai American Corp.
1211 Avenue of the Americas
New York, NY 10036

One Wilshire Building
624 S. Grand Avenue
Los Angeles, CA 90017

Toyomenka (America), Inc.
One World Trade Center
New York, NY 10048

445 South Figueroa Street
Los Angeles, CA 90017

Kanematsu-Gosho (USA), Inc.
One World Trade Center
New York, NY 10048

350 California Street
San Francisco, CA 94104

Itoman USA Inc.
1211 Avenue of the Americas
New York, NY 10036

Nichimen Co., Inc.
1185 Avenue of the Americas
New York, NY 10036

Occidental Center
1150 S. Olive Street
Los Angeles, CA 90015

Chori New York, Inc.
350 Fifth Avenue
New York, NY 10001

HELP FOR TRADING PROBLEMS IN JAPAN*

Help is available for firms, groups, and trade associations which have trouble gaining access to the Japanese market. The Joint U.S. Japan Trade Facilitation Committee staff will intervene with Japanese authorities on behalf of the U.S. companies or groups when Japanese regulations present trade problems.

*Source: *The Information Report*, Washington Researchers, 918 16th Street NW, Washington, DC 20006.

For more information and aid, contact:

Trade Facilitation Committee
Industry and Trade Administration
Department of Commerce
14th & Constitution Ave. NW, Room 3053
Washington, DC 20230
202-377-5722

THE PEOPLE'S REPUBLIC OF CHINA

For information or advice on contacting the Chinese on commercial matters, call or write to:

U.S. Department of Commerce
Industry and Trade Administration
Office of East-West Country Affairs
PRC Affairs Division—Room 4044
Washington, DC 20230
Telephone: 202-377-3583/4681

Commercial Office
Embassy of the People's Republic of China
2300 Connecticut Avenue, N.W.
Washington, DC 20008

THE NATIONAL COUNCIL FOR U.S.-CHINA TRADE

Address: 1050 17th Street NW, Suite 350, Washington, DC 20036. Phone: 202-828-8300.

The Council, a nonprofit, private organization maintaining close liaison with the U.S. government, serves as a forum for the discussion of trade policy and issues. It also serves as a focal point for business contact and the dissemination of information on marketing in the PRC. The council maintains a business counseling service; it also publishes the *China Business Review* bimonthly. The council facilitates the reciprocal arrangements of trade missions and trade exhibitions in the United States and China.

USSR AND EASTERN EUROPE*

USSR

USSR Affairs Division, Office of East-West Country Affairs (202-377-4655). This division collects, analyzes, and disseminates current information on economic, commercial, and other developments in the USSR and estimates their impact on the U.S. business community. The division develops policy guidance in our commercial relationship with the Soviet Union and provides staff support to and representation on the Joint Commercial Commission. It also maintains close contact with the U.S. Commercial Office in Moscow and with USSR commercial

officials in the United States in order to initiate and pursue official representations on behalf of the American business community.

Office of East-West Trade Development. This office's Trade Promotion Division (202-377-4161) plans, organizes, and conducts the export promotion program of the Office of East-West Trade in the USSR, including participation in Soviet international trade fairs, staging seminar/exhibits in the Commercial Office, and participating in catalog shows. The Trade Development Assistance Division (202-377-2835) arranges contacts between businesspeople and appropriate Soviet officials, provides specialized guidance on contract negotiations and other commercial techniques, advises on obtaining necessary U.S. government clearances, and disseminates information about trade opportunities.

Office of East-West Policy and Planning (202-377-2456). This office identifies trade policy issues, conducts broad studies, reviews present and proposed legislation, and collects and disseminates detailed East-West trade statistics.

The Department of Commerce, Office of East-West Trade, USSR Affairs Division, and Trade Development Assistance Division, Washington, DC 20230. These two divisions together can provide businesspeople with foreign trade and economic data, five-year and annual plan targets, and advice on which organizations and personalities to contact in the USSR. The bureau should be a firm's first stop or call when it decides to do business with the USSR.

The U.S. Commercial Office (USCO), Moscow. The USCO should be a firm's first stop when visiting the USSR.

It may also be to the company's advantage to touch base with the following USSR commercial organizations in the United States to try to obtain some indication of Soviet interest and to identify contacts in the Soviet Union:

The Trade Representation of the USSR in the U.S.A., 2001 Connecticut Avenue NW, Washington, DC 20008, telephone 202-232-5988.

The Amtorg Trading Corporation, 750 Third Avenue, New York, NY, telephone 212-682-7404.

The staffs of both Amtorg and the Trade Representation include representatives of individual foreign trade organizations (FTOs).

The KAMA Purchasing Commission (KPC), General Motors Building, 767 Fifth Avenue, 6th floor, New York, NY 10022, telephone 212-593-2600. KPC was established in 1973 and serves as a direct channel to FTOs involved in procuring equipment and implementing contracts for five major projects currently underway in the USSR: the Kama River truck plant, the Cheboksary industrial tractor factory, the fertilizer complex at Tol'yatti, the International Trade Center in Moscow, and exploratory work in the

---

* Source: Excerpted from Department of Commerce Overseas Reports, "Trading with the USSR."

Yakutsk natural gas fields. The KPC's staff has the authority to make purchasing decisions and to negotiate contracts; it is, therefore, an important contact point for preliminary discussions and after-sale follow-up for firms wishing to participate in the above projects.

The USSR Consulate General, 2790 Green Street, San Francisco, CA 94123, telephone 415–922–6642, may have information conveniently available for companies on the West Coast.

Insurance Coverage

Insurance coverage for U.S.-USSR. trade is available from a number of U.S. insurance companies on a case-by-case basis in the areas of export insurance, transportation insurance, and insurance on fixed locations. No political or commercial credit risk coverage is currently available for the USSR from the Foreign Credit Insurance Association (FCIA) or the Export-Import Bank because of the 1974 Trade Act provisions. Many of the private U.S. companies, however, have established working and contractual relationships with the USSR State Insurance Company (Ingosstrakh) and with the wholly owned Soviet insurance companies, Black Sea and Baltic Company, Ltd., in London, Schwarzmeer und Ostee A.G. in Hamburg, and Garant A.G. in Vienna.

Private American insurers which write policies on some or all of the areas of standard property, casualty transportation, marine and war risk insurance, and more specialized insurance for Soviet-American cooperative projects in the USSR or a third country are:*

AFIA Reinsurance Insurance
North American Control Office
110 William Street
New York, NY 10038
Telephone: 212–732–9070

Members of the American Institute of
  Marine Underwriters
14 Wall Street
New York, NY 10005
Telephone 212–233–0550

American International Underwriters Corporation
70 Pine Street
New York, NY 10005
Telephone: 212–770–7000

Chubb and Son, Inc.
International Department
100 William Street
New York, NY 10038
Telephone: 212–285–2850

Insurance Company of North America
International Insurance Section
2 INA Plaza
1600 Arch Street
Philadelphia, PA 19101
Telephone: 215–440–4100

EASTERN EUROPE

Commercial transactions with Bulgaria, Czechoslovakia, East Germany, Hungary, Poland, and Romania are similar to those with the USSR. Contracts are negotiated with the appropriate Foreign Trade Organization. For detailed information about trade shows, missions, export licenses, and FTOs, contact the Office of East-West Trade, Department of Commerce in Washington, or the Commerce Department Offices at the district level. Another key source of information is the U.S. East-West Trade Development Office in Vienna.

BULGARIA

Bulgarian Embassy
2100 16th Street NW
Washington, DC 20009

Bulgarian Commercial Counselor
50 E. 42nd Street
New York, NY 10017

CZECHOSLOVAKIA

Czechoslovakian Embassy
3900 Linnean Avenue NW
Washington, DC 20008

Office of the Czechoslovakian Commercial
  Counselor
292 Madison Avenue
New York, NY 10016

EAST GERMANY
(German Democratic Republic)

Embassy of the German Democratic Republic
1717 Massachusetts Avenue NW
Washington, DC 20036

Permanent Mission of German Democratic
  Republic to the United Nations
58 Park Avenue
New York, NY 10016

U.S. banks with offices in Berlin
Citibank, New York NY

HUNGARY

Embassy of Hungary to the United States
2437 15th Street NW
Washington, DC 20009

Office of the Commercial Counselor of the Embassy of Hungary
2401 Calvert Street
Washington, DC 20008

---

* This listing is not to be considered an endorsement by the Department of Commerce, the U.S. government or the *Business and Investment Almanac.*

Trade Representation of the Hungarian
People's Republic
150 E. 58th Street
New York, NY 10022

POLAND

Economic Counselor's Office
Embassy of the Polish People's Republic
2540 16th Street NW
Washington, DC 20008

Polish Consulate General
233 Madison Avenue
New York, NY 10016

Polish Commercial Counselor's Office
1 Daghammarskjold Plaza
New York, NY 10017

Office of Polish Commercial Consul
333 E. Ontario Street
Chicago, IL 60611

Polish Chamber of Foreign Trade
44 Montgomery Street
San Francisco, CA 94104

U.S. banks with offices in Warsaw
First National Bank, Chicago

ROMANIA

Romanian Embassy
1607 23rd Street NW
Washington, DC 20008

Romanian Office of the Economic Counselor
573–577 Madison Avenue
New York, NY 10016

Romanian Foreign Trade Promotion Office
100 W. Monroe Street
Chicago, IL 60603

Romanian Foreign Trade Promotion Office
22 Battery Street
San Francisco, CA 94111

U.S. banks with offices in Bucharest

NEAR EAST AND NORTH AFRICA*

The Commerce Action Group for the Near
East (CAGNE) within the International Trade
Administration serves as the focal point for the
U.S. Department of Commerce response to the
dramatically changed economic situation and
significant business opportunities in the Near
East and North Africa. The group assembles,
analyzes, and disseminates to the U.S. business
community information on economic conditions and new opportunities in the area, provides counseling for and makes representations
on behalf of U.S. exporters, and plans and orga-

---

* Source: *A Business Guide to the Near East & North Africa,*
Industry and Trade Association, U.S. Department of
Commerce.

nizes promotional programs to assist U.S. firms
to take advantage of the market boom. CAGNE
also coordinates Department of Commerce participation in joint commission activities.

To take advantage of these programs call
202–377–5767 (Arab Near East); 202–377–5737
(North Africa); 202–377–3752 (Iran, Israel,
Egypt). For information concerning major projects, call 202–377–4441. The mailing address
is Commerce Action Group for the Near East,
International Trade Administration, Room
3203, Washington, DC 20230.

ALGERIA

Embassy of Algeria
2118 Kalorama Road NW
Washington, DC 20008
Telephone: 202–234–7246

SONATRACH, Inc.
(Algerian State Enterprise for Oil, Gas,
Petrochemicals, Plastics, Fertilizers)
816 Connecticut Avenue NW
Washington, DC 20006
Telephone: 202–638–7180

BAHRAIN

Embassy of Bahrain
2600 Virginia Avenue NW
Washington, DC 20037
Telephone: 202–965–4930

ARAB REPUBLIC OF EGYPT

Embassy of the Arab Republic of Egypt
2310 Decatur Place NW
Washington, DC 20008
Telephone: 202–232–5400

Commercial and Economic Office
2715 Connecticut Avenue NW
Washington, DC 20008
Telephone: 202–234–1414

Consulate of the Arab Republic of Egypt
1110 Second Avenue
2nd Floor
New York, NY 10022
Telephone: 212–759–7120

Consulate of the Arab Republic of Egypt
3001 Pacific Avenue
San Francisco, CA 94115
Telephone: 415–346–9700

IRAQ

Iraqi Interests Section
Indian Embassy
1801 P Street NW
Washington, DC 20008
Telephone: 202–483–7500

ISRAEL

Embassy of Israel
1621 22nd Street NW
Washington, DC 20008
Telephone: 202–483–4100

Israel Supply Mission
Empire State Building
350 Fifth Avenue
New York, NY 10001
Phone: (212) 560–0680

Israel Consulates General
  Atlanta, Boston, Chicago, Houston, Los
  Angeles, New York City, Philadelphia, and
  San Francisco

Investment Authority and Branches:
350 Fifth Avenue
New York, NY 10001
Telephone: 212–560–0610

174 N. Michigan Avenue
Chicago, IL 60601
Telephone: 312–332–2160

Israel Trade Center
350 Fifth Avenue
New York, NY 10001
Telephone: 212–560–0680

6380 Wilshire Boulevard
Los Angeles, CA 90048
Telephone: 213–658–7924

805 Peachtree Street, NE
Atlanta, GA 30308
Telephone: 404–875–6947

JORDAN (HASHEMITE KINGDOM OF)

Embassy of Jordan
2319 Wyoming Avenue, NW
Washington, DC 20008
Telephone: 202–265–1606

Consulate General
866 U.N. Plaza
New York, NY 10017
Telephone: 212–752–0135

Consulates are also located in Houston, Texas;
  Chicago, Illinois; Scottsdale, Arizona; and
  Palm Beach, Florida.

STATE OF KUWAIT

Embassy of Kuwait
2940 Tilden Street NW
Washington, DC 20008
Telephone: 202–966–0702

LEBANON

Embassy of Lebanon
2560 28th Street NW
Washington, DC 20008
Telephone: 202–332–0300

Consulate General
9 E. 76th Street
New York, NY 10021
Telephone: 212–744–7905

Consulate General
1300 Lafayette East, Suite 407
Detroit, Michigan 48207
Telephone: 313–963–0233

LIBYA

Embassy of the Socialist People's Libyan Arab
  Jamakiriya
1118 22nd Street NW
Washington, DC 20037
Telephone: 202–452–1290

MOROCCO

Embassy of Morocco
1601 21st Street NW
Washington, DC 20009
Telephone: 202–462–7979/82

Consulate General
  (includes Moroccan National Tourist
  Office)
597 Fifth Avenue
New York, NY 10017
Telephone: 212–421–5771

OMAN

Embassy of the Sultanate of Oman
2342 Massachusetts Avenue NW
Washington, DC 20008
Telephone: 202–387–1980

Combined Consulate and Permanent Mission
  to the United Nations
605 Third Avenue
Room 3304
New York, NY 10016
Telephone: 202–682–0447

QATAR

Embassy of Qatar
600 New Hampshire Avenue NW
Washington, DC 20037
Telephone: 202–338–0111

SAUDI ARABIA

Saudi Arabian Embassy
1520 18th Street NW
Washington, DC 20036
Telephone: 202–483–2100

Consulate General
866 United Nations Plaza
New York, NY 10017
Telephone: 212–752–2740

Consulate
5433 West Heimer, Suite 825
Houston, Texas 77056
Phone: (713) 961–3351

SYRIAN ARAB REPUBLIC

Embassy of the Syrian Arab Republic
2215 Wyoming Avenue NW
Washington, DC 20008
Telephone: 202–232–6313

TUNISIA

Embassy of Tunisia
2408 Massachusetts Avenue NW
Washington, DC 20008
Telephone: 202–234–6644

Tunisian Investment Promotion Agency
Tunisian National Tourist Office
630 Fifth Avenue, Suite 863
New York, NY 10020
Telephone: 212–582–3760

UNITED ARAB EMIRATES

Embassy of the United Arab Emirates
Suite 740
600 New Hampshire Avenue, N.W.
Washington, DC 20037
Telephone: 202–338–6500

YEMEN ARAB REPUBLIC

Embassy of the Yemen Arab Republic
600 New Hampshire Avenue, NW
Suite 860
Washington, DC 20037
Telephone: 202–965–4760

Consulate of the Yemen Arab Republic
211 East 43rd Street
Room 2402
New York, NY 10017
Telephone: 212–986–0990

FAST—MATCH

A quick, easy way to match your international business requirements to the appropriate Government programs or services designed to satisfy those needs

IF YOU ARE SEEKING INFORMATION REGARDING ➡

USE ⬇

	Potential Markets	Market Research *	Direct Sales Leads	Agents/Distributors	Licenses	Credit Analysis	Financial Assistance	Risk Insurance	Tax Incentives
Foreign Trade Statistics (FT-410)	•								
Global Market Surveys	•	•							
Foreign Market Reports	•	•							
Market Share Reports	•	•							
Foreign Economic Trends	•	•							
Business America	•	•	•	•	•				
Commercial Exhibitions	**	**	•	•	•				
Overseas Business Reports (OBR)		•							
Overseas Private Investment Corp.		•					•	•	
Commerce Business Daily			•						
New Product Information Service			•	•	•				
Trade Opportunity Program (TOP)			•	•	•				
Industry Trade Lists			•	•	•				
Special Trade Lists			•	•	•				
Export Mailing List Service (EMLS)			•	•	•				
Agent/Distributor Service (ADS)				•					
World Traders Data Reports (WTDR)						•			
Export—Import Bank							•	•	
Foreign Credit Insurance Assoc. (FCIA)								•	
Domestic Int'l. Sales Corp. (DISC)							•		•

* Foreign Trade Outlook Market Profiles; Industry Trends; Distribution and Sales Channels; Transportation Facilities; Local Business Practices and Customs; Investment Criteria; Import Procedures and Trade Regulations; and Industrial Property Rights.

** Research material developed regarding a planned exhibition and released to support promotional activities.

Cost of services may be obtained from Commerce District Offices.

Source: Industry and Trade Administration, U.S. Department of Commerce.

Index